CANADIAN
INCOME TAXATION
PLANNING AND DECISION MAKING
2012–2013 edition

Bill Buckwold, CA
University of Victoria

Joan Kitunen, FCA
University of Toronto

McGraw-Hill Ryerson

Connect. Learn. Succeed.

CANADIAN INCOME TAXATION
Planning and Decision Making
2012–2013 Edition

Copyright © 2013, 2012, 2011, 2010, 2009, 2008, 2007, 2004, 2003, 2001, 2000, 1994, 1993, 1990 by McGraw-Hill Ryerson Limited, a Subsidiary of The McGraw-Hill Companies. All rights reserved. No part of this publication may be reproduced or transmitted in any form or by any means, or stored in a data base or retrieval system, without the prior written permission of McGraw-Hill Ryerson Limited, or in the case of photocopying or other reprographic copying, a licence from The Canadian Copyright Licensing Agency (Access Copyright). For an Access Copyright licence, visit www.accesscopyright.ca or call toll free to 1-800-893-5777.

The Internet addresses listed in the text were accurate at the time of publication. The inclusion of a website does not indicate an endorsement by the authors or McGraw-Hill Ryerson, and McGraw-Hill Ryerson does not guarantee the accuracy of information presented at these sites.

ISBN-13: 978-0-07-087660-6
ISBN-10: 0-07-087660-6

1 2 3 4 5 6 7 8 9 0 QDB 1 9 8 7 6 5 4 3 2

Printed and bound in the United States of America

Care has been taken to trace ownership of copyright material contained in this text; however, the publisher will welcome any information that enables it to rectify any reference or credit for subsequent editions.

Editorial Director: *Rhondda McNabb*
Sponsoring Editor: *Keara Emmett*
Executive Marketing Manager: *Joy Armitage Taylor*
Developmental Editor: *Chris Cullen*
Supervising Editor: *Cathy Biribauer*
Senior Editorial Associate: *Christine Lomas*
Copy Editor: *Evan Turner/Row House Publishing Services*
Production Coordinator: *Michelle Saddler*
Cover and Inside Design: *Valid Design & Layout/Dave Murphy*
Cover Photo: © *Shaun Lowe/istockphoto.com*
Composition: *Aptara® Inc.*
Printer: *Quad/Graphics*

Library and Archives Canada Cataloguing in Publication Data

Buckwold, W. J.
    Canadian income taxation: planning and decision making / Bill Buckwold, Joan Kitunen.—2012–2013 ed.

Includes index.
ISBN 978-0-07-087660-6

    1. Business enterprises—Taxation—Canada—Textbooks.
2. Income tax—Canada—Textbooks.   3. Tax planning—Canada—Textbooks.
I. Kitunen, Joan   II. Title.

HD2753.C3B64 2012   343.7105'268   C2012-902212-8

Dedication

If Patrick Henry thought taxation without representation was bad, he should see it with representation.
—HANDY NEWS

Author Biographies

Bill Buckwold has extensive experience in academic and professional tax education. A chartered accountant and graduate of the University of Western Ontario's School of Business Administration, with cross-studies at the Faculty of Law, he currently is a member of the Faculty of Business at the University of Victoria. He has lectured extensively across Canada for various provincial Institutes of Chartered Accountants, the Canadian Society of Management Accountants, the Banff School of Advanced Management, and the Bar Admission program of the Law Society of Manitoba. Before joining the academic community on a full-time basis, he was self-employed, providing tax consulting services to accounting and legal firms. From 1983 to 1986, Professor Buckwold served as a governor of the Canadian Tax Foundation. He has received numerous awards, including the University of Manitoba's prestigious Olive Beatrice Stanton Award for Excellence in Teaching and the Board of Advisors Distinguished Educator Award at the University of Victoria's Faculty of Business. Professor Buckwold has served as a member of the Council of the Institute of Chartered Accountants of Manitoba and as a member of the Professional Development Committee of the Canadian Institute of Chartered Accountants.

Joan A. Kitunen is a Fellow of the Institute of Chartered Accountants of Ontario (FCA) and is a member of the Accounting Faculty at the Rotman School of Management and UTM at the University of Toronto. She designs, coordinates, and teaches taxation courses offered in the MBA, MMPA (Master of Management and Professional Accounting), and in the Accounting Specialist program in the B COM. She has been the recipient of numerous teaching awards, including the Roger Martin Award for Teaching Excellence. In 2011, she was named a Rotman Teaching Fellow. Kitunen is the Co-Director of the ICAO/Rotman Centre for Innovation in Accounting Education, Coordinator of the taxation segment of the Institute of Chartered Accountants of Ontario School of Accountancy, and a member of Canadian Institute of Chartered Accountants Tax Education Task Force. Kitunen was a Tax Partner at Deloitte, one of Canada's leading professional services firms, before joining the faculty at the University of Toronto.

Contributors

We would like to thank and acknowledge the contributors of the support material available with the text.

Deborah L. Jarvie, *University of Lethbridge*
Prepared Test Bank

Nathalie Johnstone, *University of Saskatchewan*
Prepared Microsoft® PowerPoint® Presentations

Dan Jakubowicz, *Retired Partner, KPMG National Tax*
Prepared Student Quizzes for the Online Learning Centre

Summary of Contents

Contents

Preface

Introduction

The 2012–2013 Edition of *Canadian Income Taxation: Planning and Decision Making* and the revisions to recent editions clearly places this text as a key player in professional accounting education without compromising its student friendly format. Joan Kitunen from the University of Toronto's Rotman School of Management joined as co-author several years ago because, as she states, "I have great success using this text partnered with the *Income Tax Act*. It works extremely well in professional accounting tax courses at the undergraduate level. The students find the text to be very student friendly (readable). The decision-making approach to explaining the tax law gives the students a deeper understanding of the rules and enhances their ability to apply the rules in non-directed simulations. The students come to class better prepared to discuss the assigned problems and cases, which in turn means that we can discuss the tax issues in greater depth. The integrated nature of the problems and cases makes them excellent preparation for students planning to write the *professional accounting examinations*."

Taxation is more exciting and interesting, and less complex, than it is reputed to be. This 2012–2013 Edition of *Canadian Income Taxation: Planning and Decision Making* is written in a manner consistent with this view. The textbook develops the fundamental principles of the Canadian income tax laws and examines their effect on business decision making and financial planning.

Experience has shown that the most efficient and productive method of studying income taxation and its financial implications involves combining three distinctive learning resources. These are diagrammed below:

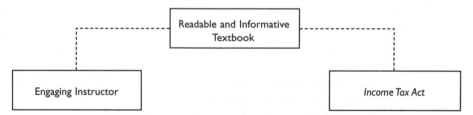

In this three-point process, a clear and readable text allows the student to better understand where they are going and why they are going there. This fundamental understanding permits the instructor to be more productive in class and improve the study of the complex *Income Tax Act*.

> The three-point process builds a solid base for continual learning and avoids or significantly diminishes the memorization syndrome that so often plagues the study of income taxation.

What's New in the 2012–2013 Edition

The changes to this edition continue to broaden the subject base and provide current updates, ensuring that the text adheres to the competency maps of the professional accounting bodies. The primary changes are listed below:

- The level of detail of several topics has been expanded or added. These include employee benefits (Chapter 4), accounts receivable, ceasing to carry on business (Chapter 5), replacement property, cost of a website (Chapter 6), royalties (Chapter 7), attribution, retiring allowances, pooled registered pension plans (Chapter 9), capital gain deduction (Chapter 10), and the capital dividend account (Chapter 13).
- Each text includes access to a *current version* of *ProFile*, Intuit's highly regarded professional *tax preparation software*. Students can apply their tax knowledge and develop valuable workplace computer skills with *ProFile's* Personal (T1), Corporate (T2), and Trust (T3) tax software programs.
- The *2012 federal budget* has been fully incorporated including the revision of capital cost allowance rates and classes, personal and corporate tax rates, and personal tax credits.
- Demonstration calculations throughout the text have been revised to reflect the *changing corporate and personal tax rates* to continue providing realistic samples of the current and expected tax environment.
- The 2012 version of *Tax Facts and Figures* published by PricewaterhouseCoopers is featured on the Online Learning Centre. The publication provides a wealth of relevant information about personal and corporate taxation.
- Thirteen new key concepts have been added as requested by users.
- An *expanded test bank* of questions is available to instructors for tests and examinations. The test bank includes multiple-choice and short-answer questions, as well as short problems, multiple-chapter comprehensive problems, and new mini-case questions.
- The *Microsoft® PowerPoint® Presentations* available for instructors have been updated with *ITA references* where applicable.

The text went into production shortly after the 2012 federal budget was tabled in the House of Commons. The reader should be aware that certain changes to the budget proposals may occur before the final legislation is developed. All relevant examples, demonstration problems, and the Solutions Manual have been revised to reflect the previously mentioned changes and ensure that the text is current. Some of the changes announced in recent federal budgets are to be phased in over several years. Where appropriate, examples in this edition have jumped forward to reflect the ultimate change in the legislation.

Audience

This text is applicable to a range of academic programs. Business schools, professional accounting programs, law schools, community colleges, and executive training programs all offer tax courses with different objectives. When used in conjunction with the *Income Tax Act*, the text is extremely effective in tax courses offered to accounting majors and students preparing professional accounting programs. When used as a stand-alone text, it supports tax courses for general management students, finance majors, and executive programs. This book will educate in the fundamental principles of Canadian income tax laws as well as their effect on business decision making and financial planning.

Approach

While the book follows a traditional sequence of topics, it departs from other texts in both its comprehensive approach to the learning process and in its accessible style. Each chapter emphasizes the fundamental principles of the topic and their relationship to the overall framework of the Canadian tax system. Any revisions to the tax laws will not render the reader's knowledge obsolete; rather, it will require only minor adjustments.

A major component in learning taxation involves the development of a **decision-making approach** that emphasizes **problem recognition**. To this end, each chapter in the text relates the basic principles to business and investment decision situations. Through numerous situational examples, together with a number of case study analyses, the reader can develop and enhance decision-making skills. These skills will permit the student to approach business decision making in terms of alternative actions and alternative tax consequences and at the same time integrate the results with relevant non-tax considerations.

Written in a student friendly style and refraining, as much as possible, from the use of technical jargon and descriptions of the *Income Tax Act*, the text allows the student to begin each chapter with a clear understanding of the objectives. The student will find the chapter easy and enjoyable to read and will finish reading with a sound understanding of the fundamental issues. By adhering to the fundamental framework, complex issues are presented in a clear and concise manner and tied to their practical applications.

Content Overview

Part One: A Planning and Decision-Making Approach to Taxation (Chapters 1, 2) develops the concept of a decision-making approach to taxation. It also outlines the fundamentals of tax planning by stating the techniques and skills required to apply tax knowledge.

Part Two: An Overview of Income Determination and Tax for the Two Primary Entities (Chapters 3–11) provides an overview of the fundamentals of income determination for the two primary taxable entities: individuals and corporations. These chapters develop the basic principles of the tax system and discuss their impact on cash flow and on business decisions.

Part Three: The Corporate Structure (Chapters 12–14) considers the corporate entity, which is the primary business structure.

Part Four: Other Forms of Business Organization (Chapters 15–17) develops the fundamental principles and implications of other business structures, such as joint ventures, partnerships, limited partnerships, and trusts.

Part Five: Selected Topics (Chapters 18–21) deals with a number of specific business-decision problems; it also integrates and further applies the fundamentals developed in the first four parts of the text.

Pedagogy Overview

- Throughout the 2012–2013 Edition, **review questions, key concept questions, problems, and cases** have been used to develop the student's fundamental knowledge of the Canadian income tax system and to nurture the skills they require to effectively consider tax implications in business decision making and financial planning. These learning tools range from easy to difficult and, depending on course objectives, may be used as assignment material or for class discussion.

- **Review questions and key concept questions** follow the flow of the text and test the reader's understanding of the main tax principles developed in each chapter.

- **Problems** demonstrate specific applications and also show, in a directed manner, the impact of taxation on business decision making.

- **Cases** require the student to identify particular problems, determine how tax factors may affect those problems, consider alternative courses of action, and make a decision.

The text's questions, problems, and cases are designed such that the student will be able to:

- develop a basic understanding of tax;
- identify situations in which taxation has application to business decision making;
- structure alternative courses of action, and recognize that each course of action may result in additional problems which must be solved;

- determine the tax impact of decisions on investment returns, earnings per share, risk, and share values; and
- anticipate the effect of current decisions on possible future events.

Other learning tools featured in this text:

- **Tax Planning Checklists**
- **Chapter Summaries and Conclusions**
- **Demonstration Questions**

Student Supplements

Online Learning Centre (www.mcgrawhill.ca/olc/buckwold)

This text-specific web-site provides vital support for learning and teaching. Please see the inside front cover for more information.

Tax Preparation Software

Through the generous co-operation of Intuit Canada, we are able to provide you with access to ProFile, Intuit's highly regarded professional tax preparation software. Using this software, students can apply their tax knowledge and develop valuable workplace skills. Access includes:

- Intuit Canada's T1 ProFile software for preparing personal tax returns
- Intuit Canada's T2 ProFile software for preparing corporate tax returns
- Intuit Canada's T3 ProFile software for preparing trusts returns

Please see the inside back cover for more information.

Instructor Supplements

Available for download on the Instructor's area of the OLC are

- Microsoft® PowerPoint® Presentations
- Solutions Manual—Complete *Income Tax Act* references included
- Test Bank—Includes multiple-choice and short-answer questions and problems, as well as new mini-case questions
- Sample Course Syllabus matching the professional association competencies

Acknowledgments

We are grateful to the Institute of Chartered Accountants of Ontario, the Canadian Institute of Chartered Accountants, and the Certified General Accountants Association of Canada for granting permission to adapt a number of their national and provincial exam questions for the text. Specific permissions from these bodies are listed after the acknowledgments.

Whatever merit this book may have must be attributed to those people who have most influenced us in the taxation field. Bill Buckwold acknowledges the following: Professor Brian Arnold, of Goodman, Phillips, and Vineberg, Toronto, whose challenging instructional approach sparked his interest in the dynamics of taxation; Joe Hershfield, of the Tax Court of Canada, Ottawa, whose inquisitive and analytical mind stimulated long hours of debate on tax policy, interpretation, and planning; and Cy Fien, of Fillmore and Riley, Winnipeg, whose interpretive skills set a standard of excellence that he admires and seeks to attain. Joan Kitunen expresses special appreciation to Bob Beam, Professor Emeritus, University of Waterloo, who introduced her to taxation, shared his enthusiasm for Canadian tax law, and provided guidance throughout her career.

The task of completing this manuscript was made easier by those who worked closely with us on the project. Rhondda McNabb, Editorial Director, Keara Emmett, Sponsoring Editor, Chris Cullen, Developmental Editor, and Christine Lomas, Senior Editorial Associate at McGraw-Hill Ryerson provided advice and encouragement. Their efforts and professionalism are the reasons for the changes in the 2012–2013 Edition. Cathy Biribauer, Supervising Editor, has made the transition from manuscript to finished product the smoothest part of this project. Special thanks go to Evan Turner for her careful proofreading of the text. We also acknowledge Mathew Kudelka, copy editor of past editions, who transformed complex sentences and paragraphs into flowing, understandable text. His wizardry with words is amazing. More than anyone else, he assisted in making this a highly readable text. Wayne Bridgeman provided his usual proficient technical check of the text's calculations.

We also acknowledge the excellent staff and partners of PricewaterhouseCoopers who developed the online Tax News Network (**www.ca.taxnews.com**). Their research, tax planning ideas, and timely exposure of tax law changes have been invaluable to us.

A special thanks must also go out to the reviewers whose thoughts and comments have guided this work through this edition. Reviewers for the 2012–2013 Edition were:

Francois Brouard, Carleton University
Ling Chu, Wilfrid Laurier University
George Cummins, Memorial University of Newfoundland
Brent Groen, Trinity Western University
Sandy Hilton, University of British Columbia/Okanagan College
David Hiscock, University of Guelph
Don Jones, University of Windsor
Susan Lade, Wilfrid Laurier University
Amin Mawani, York University
Michel Paquet, Southern Alberta Institute of Technology
Tara Ramsaran, Concordia University
Brad Sacho, Kwantlen Polytechnic University
Don Smith, Georgian College
Christine Tworo, Cambrian College
Julie Wong, Dawson College

We would also like to thank the many reviewers of past editions. While too numerous to mention them all, we would like to include here our thanks to reviewers of recent years.

Reviewers for 2011–2012 Edition were:

Jane Chong, Kwantlen Polytechnic University
George Cummins, Memorial University of Newfoundland
Larry Goldsman, McGill University,
David Sale, Kwantlen Polytechnic University

Reviewers for the 2010–2011 Edition were:

Noreen Irvine, University of Calgary
Ling Chu, Wilfrid Laurier University
Michael Malkoun, St. Clair College
Denise Cook, Durham College
Terry Walsh, Algonquin College

Reviewers for the 2009–2010 Edition were:

Francois Brouard, Carleton University
Michelle Causton, Canadore College
George Cummins, Memorial University of Newfoundland
Edward Gough, Centennial College
Andrew Hilton, University of British Columbia, Okanagan
Donald Jones, University of Windsor

Reviewers for the 2008–2009 Edition were:

Ann Bigelow, University of Western Ontario
Nathalie Johnstone, University of Saskatchewan
Michael Konopaski, Trent University
Brad Sacho, Kwantlen Polytechnic University

Of course, a large part of the burden associated with the preparation of this text has been shared by our families. Their lives have been uprooted by our constant focus on this project. In spite of this, they have been ever supportive and have made many sacrifices. We are extremely grateful.

And finally, we are most proud to acknowledge the thousands of students who, over the years, have been both critical and appreciative. From them we have received our greatest reward.

BILL BUCKWOLD
JOAN KITUNEN

Permissions

Institute of Chartered Accountants of Ontario:

Text Reference			ICAO Reference*
Chapter	Key Concept Question	Problem	
3	7		CA Reciprocity Examination (2001), paper 2, question 4, part 1
3	9		CA Reciprocity Examination (2001), paper 2, question 4, part 2
3	13		CA Reciprocity Examination (2001), paper 2, question 4, part 3
3		Case 2	ICAO School of Accountancy (2003), pre-assignment problem 12
11		7	CA Reciprocity Examination (2003), paper 2, question 3
11		8	CA Reciprocity Examination (1999), paper 2, question 2
11		9	CA Reciprocity Examination (2005), paper 2, question 2
12		3	CA Reciprocity Examination (2001), paper 2, question 2
12		5	CA Reciprocity Examination (2003), paper 2, question 5, part 2
12		8	ICAO School of Accountancy— practice exam one, question 3
13		3	CA Reciprocity Examination (1999), paper 2, question 3, part VI
13		6	CA Reciprocity Examination (2000), paper 2, question 3
13		13	CA Reciprocity Examination (2004), paper 2, question 2
13		14	ICAO School of Accountancy (1999), pre-assignment problem 2
13		15	CA Reciprocity Examination (1999), paper 2, question 3, part II
19		3	CA Reciprocity Examination (2003), paper 2, question 5, part 1
19		5	CA Reciprocity Examination (2003), paper 2, question 5, part 3

*(Adapted and) reprinted with the permission of the Institute of Chartered Accountants of Ontario, copyright ICAO.

Canadian Institute of Chartered Accountants:

Text Reference	CICA Reference*
Chapter 8—Problem Three, R.M. Inc.	Uniform Final Examination (1991)
Chapter 14—Case two, Realco	Uniform Final Examination (1989)
Chapter 19—Case two, Mattjon Limited	Uniform Final Examination (1990)

*Reprinted (or adapted) with permission from the *Uniform Evaluation Report*, (1989, 1990, 1991), The Canadian Institute of Chartered Accountants, Toronto, Canada. Any changes to the original material are the sole responsibility of the authors and have not been reviewed or endorsed by the CICA.

Certified General Accountants Association of Canada:

	Text Reference		CGA Reference*	
Chapter	Demonstration Question	Problem	Examination	Question #
4		7	September 1994	1
4		8	March 1994	3
4		9	September 1997	3
4		10	September 1998	3
4		12	Practice Exam 1992	
4	1		March 1995	2
4	2		September 1996	3
5	1		September 1997	2
5		5	Practice Exam 1992	
5		7	June 1995	1
5		8	March 2010	2
5		9	June 1995	2
5		10	June 1994	3
6	1		March 1996	2
6	2		March 1993	2
6		5	Practice Exam 1992	
6		9	June 1992	3
6		11	March 1999	3
7	1		June 1995	4
7		7	June 1993	2
7		8	June 1998	3
7		9	March 1998	2
8	1		September 1994	4
8		7	March 1994	1
8		8	March 1996	1
9		7	June 1992	4
10		2	March 1992	2
10		3	June 1992	1
10		6	June 1996	4
10		7	September 1999	4
11		2	Practice Exam 1992	
11		6	Practice Exam 1992	
13	1		June 1996	3
13		8	June 1997	2
17		1	June 1999	3

*Extracts from *Taxation 1 Examinations* (dates specified above), published by the Certified General Accountants Association of Canada (© CGA-Canada, 1992–1999), reprinted by permission.

Extract from (Taxation 1 [TX1]) published by the Certified General Accountants Association of Canada, © CGA-Canada, (1992-1999), reproduced with permission. Because of Tax Act updates and/or changes to the CICA Handbook, the contents of these examinations may be out of date; therefore the accuracy of the contents is the sole responsibility of the user.

PART

A Planning and Decision-Making Approach to Taxation

Management's job is to see the company not as it is... but as it can become.

JOHN W. TEETS

CHAPTER 1

Taxation—Its Role in Decision Making

Taxation has an important effect on business and investment decision making. Decisions on the form of business organization, expansion, the raising of capital, wage and salary settlements, and business acquisitions and divestitures are significantly influenced by alternative tax treatments. Personal financial planning and investment decisions are similarly influenced. While the structure of the tax system is highly technical, its application to decision making is not.

This chapter briefly discusses the role of taxation in the financial decision process, examines the issue of tax complexity and its significance to business and investment issues, and provides an overview of the basic income tax structure.

I. Taxation and the Financial Decision Process

Business enterprises and individuals are subject to many forms of taxation by municipal, provincial, and federal authorities. The most significant form of taxation affecting return on investment is income tax—at both the federal and provincial level. This form of taxation, by its nature, taxes more heavily those enterprises that are more successful at maximizing profits. Ultimately, an investor's return on investment is measured by the cash flow returned after the payment of all related taxes. Obviously, decisions that reduce or postpone the payment of tax will make it easier to maximize total earnings—and ultimately increase the overall wealth.

Managing an enterprise involves making many important decisions at different levels of management. Decisions about marketing, production, finance, labour relations, policy strategy, and expansion are all made with the common goal of maximizing long-term wealth by cash-flow enhancement. The same applies when a person acquires or disposes of an investment. Cash flow exists only on an after-tax basis; therefore, every decision necessarily has a tax impact, whether or not the ultimate result of that decision is successful.

Normally, the decision-making process involves identifying alternative courses of action and analyzing the short-range and long-range costs and benefits for each alternative. The quantitative portion of a cost/benefit analysis consists of determining the amount and timing of cash outflows and inflows. The amount of tax payable and the timing of the payment may vary significantly between alternatives. Two important principles must be adhered to when applying taxation to financial decision making. First, tax should be considered a *controllable cost.* Second, *cash flow* exists only on an *after-tax* basis. These two principles are examined below.

A. Taxation—A Controllable Cost

The tax cost to a business enterprise must be regarded as a *cost of doing business* similar to other relevant costs. Decision makers continually attempt to understand and control costs that are affected by decisions within their spheres of responsibility. An intimate knowledge of product costs, occupancy costs, selling costs, and other costs is fundamental to the success of any business organization. Similarly, investors attempt to control financing and other direct investment costs. Tax costs must also be looked at as controllable. As such, components of the tax cost should be analyzed in order to determine which actions or activities have a greater or lesser impact on the resulting tax cost.

Consider the following marketing-expansion situation, which is typical:

Situation:

> A wholesale enterprise that has, to date, marketed its product line exclusively within its home province is considering an expansion into a neighbouring province. Three strategy options are being considered as a means to gain initial market penetration.
>
> 1. The new territory could be serviced with a *direct sales* approach by home-based sales personnel, who would travel regularly to the neighbouring province.

2. A small *branch sales office* could be established in the neighbouring province and staffed by local personnel familiar with the territory.

3. A *separate corporation* could be established in the new market province to house a small sales office staffed by local personnel.

Analysis:

Provincial income tax rates vary considerably among provinces. The neighbouring province may have a higher or a lower rate of tax on profits subject to its jurisdiction. Each of the above-mentioned options affects, in a different way, the amount of income to be allocated and taxed in each province. If the provincial rates of tax vary, then the resulting after-tax cash flow will vary, and this variance must be included in the related cost/benefit cash-flow analysis.

Under the direct sales option, all income earned in the new province is taxed in the home province. However, if a branch sales office is established, a portion of the organization's total profits is allocated to the new province by an arbitrary formula based on the ratio of sales and wages paid in the new province to the sales and wages paid by the total entity. As a result, the profits (or losses) allocated under the branch-sales option may have no relationship whatsoever to the actual operating results in the new territory. If a separate corporation is utilized, the actual profits (or losses) in the new province will be attributed to that jurisdiction.

Each of the above options is subject to different tax costs, as well as to different selling, administrative, and overhead costs. The added cost of maintaining a small branch office, for example, may be partly or fully offset by a reduction of provincial income taxes because the formula for allocation (based on sales and wages—not on profits) has captured profits that were realized in one jurisdiction and allocated them to another jurisdiction.

In addition to the provincial tax cost, each option has other, broader federal and provincial tax implications. For example, if the new territory suffers losses for several years before the full potential of the territory is realized, then the direct-sales or the branch-sales office approach permits an enterprise to use the losses incurred in the new province to reduce immediately the profits of home-based operations. This offset reduces annual tax and enhances annual cash flow, which assists in funding the loss requirements. If a separate corporation were utilized instead, such losses would be locked into the new corporation and could not be utilized until the new territory became profitable or the separate corporation was formally amalgamated with its parent corporation.

Clearly, each alternative has a different impact on the amount of tax and the timing of the payment of tax. Even though the decision is primarily a marketing one, it has a direct effect on the long-term tax cost of the firm and thus on its profits and value. Thus, tax costs are relevant when alternative marketing strategies are being considered.

The above situation demonstrates that tax is an important consideration in the decision-making process and, to an important degree, is controllable. It is important to recognize that this is true at all levels of management, in all functional areas of business, and in a broad range of problems, from union negotiations to business acquisitions and divestitures.

B. Cash Flow after Tax

All cash flow, whether it relates to revenue, expense, asset acquisition or divestiture, or debt or equity restructuring, should be considered *after tax*. Cash flow before tax has no relevance whatsoever to the value of an enterprise or investment, or when it comes to analyzing the alternative courses of action that affect value. Most financial decisions are quantitatively analyzed by examining the timing of cash inflows and outflows; to the extent that the net present value of future cash flows is positive, the action is considered to be favourable. If the decision involves choosing among several alternative courses of action, the net present value of each option is compared and ranked. Such analysis cannot be of value unless the real tax impact is included. It is necessary for each decision maker to think "after tax" for every decision at the time the decision is being made. In addition, it is necessary to seek out alternative courses of action that will minimize the tax impact, in the same way that one would seek out alternative production or procurement methods to minimize the cost of products manufactured or acquired for resale. Consider the following:

- The cost of an 8% wage increase to an employer in a 25% tax bracket is really 6% after tax, and the value of the raise to an employee in a 45% tax bracket is 4.4% after tax. The real cost to one party is different from the real benefit to the other (see Chapter 4).
- The cost of a 6% interest-bearing debt instrument is 4.5% to a business subject to 25% tax rates; the value to an investor in a 45% tax bracket who receives the interest is 3.3%. On the other hand, a 5% dividend on the equity capital of a *public* corporation, which is *not* deductible to the business, has a real cost of 5% after tax, and its net value to an individual investor subject to a 45% tax rate is 3.6%, after applying the dividend tax credit (see Chapter 10). The cost of debt (as opposed to equity) to the business, or its value to the investor, has meaning to the parties involved only when it is viewed on an after-tax basis (see Chapter 21).
- The after-tax cash returns as a result of expansion through the acquisition of new ventures will vary considerably depending on the method of acquisition. Acquiring the assets (land, equipment, inventory, goodwill, and so on) and assuming the liabilities of the target entity, instead of acquiring the shares of the corporation that houses those assets and liabilities, will dramatically alter the amount and timing of taxable income and therefore the after-tax cash flows on profits realized after acquisition (see Chapter 18).
- The value of a business is usually based on its potential for after-tax profits. Therefore, the value of a "for sale" subsidiary may vary considerably, since it depends on a given potential buyer's particular tax structure compared with that of the present owner. It is just as important to target potential buyers when selling a business as it is to target potential vendors when acquiring a business (see Chapter 18).
- The after-tax returns and funds available for reinvestment may vary considerably for a company attempting to expand sales volume by penetrating markets in out-of-province or foreign jurisdictions. Much depends on the strategy involved, as described earlier in this chapter (see also Chapter 20).

Failure to take an after-tax approach at the time a decision is being considered may impose a permanently inefficient tax structure or result in decisions that appear favourable on a pre-tax basis but are, on an after-tax basis, unfavourable or marginally favourable.

II. The Fundamental Income Tax Structure and its Complexity

A major roadblock to entrenching taxation in the formal decision process is the perception that Canadian tax laws are extremely complex. Because of this perception, tax issues are often completely delegated to professional advisors. While outside advisors have strong technical knowledge, they are often not in tune with the decision-making process of the particular organization. The result is that fundamental aspects of taxation are often ignored at the time decisions are being made.

While complexity certainly exists in Canada's tax system, the issue does not have to be an impediment to good decision making. It is true that the *Income Tax Act* is written and presented in a complex manner; however, its fundamental structure and concepts are *not* complex and certainly are not beyond the comprehension of responsible managers and informed individuals. Approximately two-thirds of the *Income Tax Act* deals with special areas and exceptions and with items that do not regularly affect business decisions. The remaining one-third has a logical flow and a close-knit structure that includes a limited number of variables that have an impact on the business decision process. The major variables include the following;

Q3

- **Taxpayers** There are only three entities subject to tax in Canada.

- **Types of income** Each of the taxpayer entities can earn five types of income, of which four have general application to business activity.

- **Business and investment structures** There are six basic forms of organization in which a business or investing activity can take place. Of the six, only three are directly subject to tax.

- **Tax jurisdictions** A Canadian business or investor is normally subject to two taxation authorities, unless it extends its operations to international markets.

The key variables that are relevant to the decision process are summarized in Exhibit 1-1.

Exhibit 1-1:

Fundamental Tax Variables in the Financial Decision Process

Primary types of income	Entities subject to taxation on income	Alternative forms of business and investing structures used by taxable entities	Tax jurisdictions
Business	Individuals	Proprietorship	Provincial
Property	Corporations	Corporation	Federal
Employment	Trusts	Partnership	Foreign
Capital gains		Limited partnership	
		Joint venture	
		Income trusts	

The basic tax rules relating to each of the four areas in Exhibit 1-1 are neither complex nor lengthy. Each variable encompasses a handful of general concepts that, once understood, are sufficient to enable managers to recognize which items affect normal business decisions. More important, however, is the *interaction* among these major variables: taxpayer, type of income, and form of organization. When the variables are changed in each of the major categories, alternative tax structures are created that can then be applied to the decision process. For example, consider the variables in the following three situations:

1. Two investor *corporations* (the taxpayers) jointly entering into a new venture that will earn *business income* (type of income) could utilize a *partnership*, a *joint venture*, or a *separate corporation* (business structure). Each alternative structure may affect the amount and timing of tax on operating results.

2. A *corporation* that earns *business income* and requires new capital could expand either its equity base or its debt structure. Equity capital is serviced by dividend distributions, which are not deductible by the payer and constitute *property income* taxed in a certain way to the investor. Debt capital is serviced by interest payments, which are deductible by the payer and constitute *property income* to the recipient. Regardless of whether debt or equity is used, the investor providing the capital may be an *individual* or a *corporation* and, therefore, taxed differently on the receipt of dividends or interest. Identifying the variables permits a global analysis to be made that identifies costs and benefits to both the corporation and its supplier of capital, thereby permitting an informed decision.

3. A *corporation* earning *business income* can compensate employees in different ways. Simply understanding that the payment of compensation by the corporation reduces its *business income* for tax purposes, but at the same time increases the employee's *employment income*, can assist in ascertaining the true costs and benefits of compensation packages for all levels of staff. Employment income is subject

to a completely different set of general rules from business income. In addition, corporate tax rates differ from individual tax rates. Identifying these variables and their different applications lets managers examine alternatives for compensating executives as well as union and non-union staff, with a view to reducing the after-tax costs of employee benefits while increasing the after-tax income to the employees.

Although the details of our tax system are presented in a maze of complex legal jargon, this cannot be used by the decision makers as an excuse for ignoring the importance of tax on decision making. In the tax process, there is a role for the decision maker as well as for the professional tax advisor. Decision makers need only acquire a basic knowledge of the tax structure and its key variables in order to fulfill their role and can obtain this knowledge and understanding without having to learn how to interpret specific tax laws. Decision makers continually work under the umbrella of many legal statutes, and the tax statute is no different: its fundamentals can be readily understood and applied.

III. Conclusion

Visit the Canadian Income Taxation Web site at **www.mcgrawhill.ca/ olc/buckwold** to view any updated tax information.

The thrust of a decision-making approach to taxation is *not* to place tax planning in a vacuum but rather to include, in a formal way, taxation as a major variable to be considered in decisions made regarding all financial matters. Obviously, decisions are not made solely for tax purposes, but if the tax consequences are excluded as a contributing variable, the full impact of decisions will not be understood, and wealth will not be maximized. Including taxation as a part of the formal decision-making process leads to improved cash flows and the long-term maximization of the value of an enterprise or an investment portfolio.

The next chapter reviews the basic concepts of tax planning. The remaining chapters of this text are devoted, first, to developing a broad understanding of the fundamental principles of each of the variables outlined in Exhibit 1-1 and, second, to applying those principles to decisions that confront business managers and individual financial investors.

Review Questions

1. If income tax is imposed after profits have been determined, why is taxation relevant to business decision making?

2. Most business decisions involve the evaluation of alternative courses of action. For example, a marketing manager may be responsible for choosing a strategy for establishing sales in new geographical territories. Briefly explain how the tax factor can be an integral part of this decision.

3. What are the fundamental variables of the income tax system that decision makers should be familiar with so that they can apply tax issues to their areas of responsibility?

4. What is an "after-tax" approach to decision making?

Fundamentals of Tax Planning

The previous chapter discussed how to integrate taxation into the financial decision process. Improving cash flow by means of tax planning involves taking actions that result in a reduction, elimination, or change in the timing of tax. A knowledge of the fundamentals of the income tax system is essential if one is to understand the tax planning process, and the bulk of this text will be devoted to those fundamentals. However, it is important first to introduce some of the basic tax planning techniques that are used throughout the text. This will provide a foundation upon which tax planning skills can be developed.

This chapter explains what tax planning is and how to go about it. Specifically, this chapter covers the following areas:

1. The meaning of tax planning and how it is distinguished from tax avoidance and tax evasion.

2. The basic types of tax planning and the skills required to implement them.

3. The formal limitations to tax planning.

I. What Is Tax Planning?

A. Tax Planning Defined

Tax planning is the legitimate arranging of one's financial activities in a manner that reduces or defers the related tax cost. The difficulty with this definition lies in the term "legitimate." Certainly, if the tax authorities do not attempt to prevent certain transactions, then those transactions can be considered legitimate. A number of years ago, the Canada Revenue Agency (CRA) described legitimate tax planning as

> cases in which a taxpayer, in seeking a beneficial result, has merely selected a certain course of action that is either clearly provided for or not specifically prohibited in law and has implemented that decision in a real way.[1]

The *Income Tax Act* includes what is called the general anti-avoidance rule (GAAR), which attempts to indicate what is not legitimate tax planning. (This rule is discussed later in the chapter.) Concurrent with this change, the CRA has removed the preceding quote from its official publication. Even so, its principle forms part of the new anti-avoidance rule.

An example of a legitimate tax planning activity is presented in the following situation:

Situation:

A Canadian-controlled private corporation will earn a profit of $150,000 in 20X1. Included in the calculation of that profit is a deduction of $20,000 as a reserve for the anticipated non-collection of certain accounts receivable (bad debts). The corporation has recently signed a new contract and anticipates that profits for the following year (20X2) will be $550,000. The following tax rules are assumed to be applicable:

1. A taxpayer is given the choice of deducting or not deducting a reserve for bad debts in any particular year (see Chapter 5).

2. The corporation pays tax at the rate of 15% on the first $500,000 of annual business income and 25% on income above that amount (bracket and rates assumed).

Analysis:

Because the reserve deduction is optional, the corporation can choose not to deduct it in 20X1. Not claiming the deduction in 20X1 does not mean that it is lost because the taxpayer has the option of deducting the reserve in 20X2 or a subsequent year (see Chapter 5).

Based on the income levels for each year, all of the 20X1 income will be taxed at 15%, whereas part of the 20X2 income will be taxed at 25%. If the $20,000 deduction is not

---

1   IC 73-10R2. Revised IC 73-10R3 (archived) excludes this quote.

deduct 2001 or 2002?

> claimed in 20X1, the profits for 20X1 will increase to $170,000 from $150,000, causing a tax increase of $3,000 (15% of $20,000). However, when the amount is deducted in 20X2, the expected profit in that year will decline to $530,000 from $550,000, creating a tax saving of $5,000 (25% of $20,000). Therefore, the decision to pay more tax in 20X1 results in an overall tax reduction of $2,000 ($5,000 − $3,000 = $2,000).[2]

The above tax planning action is clearly provided for in the *Income Tax Act* and constitutes a legitimate tax planning activity.

To better appreciate what tax planning involves, it is useful to understand the terms "tax evasion" and "tax avoidance."

B. Tax Evasion

The CRA's definition of tax evasion is very clear: it is the commission or omission of an act with the intent to deceive. This includes knowingly failing to report revenue, claiming the deduction of a false expense, or both. It also includes knowingly omitting material facts from tax records.[3] (See Chapter 3, Part IV, Section D for civil and criminal penalties for tax evasion.)

Tax evasion is so removed from the concept of tax planning that distinguishing between the two is not difficult.

C. Tax Avoidance

Between tax planning and tax evasion lies a grey area referred to as tax avoidance. Generally, tax avoidance involves transactions which, while legal in themselves, are planned and carried out mainly to avoid, reduce, or defer tax payable under the law. In some cases, the transactions do not reflect the real facts of the situation and may be regarded as an abuse of the system. What constitutes such an abuse is debatable. Consider the following example.

Losses accumulated within a corporation become restricted as to their use when control of the corporation is transferred to a new party. The purpose of this restriction is to prevent the new owners from using these losses to reduce their otherwise taxable income. However, such restrictions do not occur within a related group of corporations— for example, between two corporations owned by the same shareholders.

Now, assume that two corporations are owned by the same shareholders and that one has unused losses, while the other has taxable profits. If these two entities carried out a series of legal steps to shift income to the loss corporation, would that constitute an abusive avoidance transaction? Likely not, because the spirit of the *Income Tax Act* and its various provisions pertaining to losses are designed to permit flexibility for loss utilization within a group of commonly owned corporations. Therefore, this series of transactions to avoid tax would not be challenged.

However, if the two corporations described above were not initially related, a different result might occur. For example, if steps were taken to cause the two unrelated corporations to become related for the sole purpose of circumventing the loss restriction rules, then the transaction might well be considered abusive.

The distinction between the two situations is important. In the first, the steps were carried out between two *already related* corporations to take advantage of the rules and did not run counter to the spirit of the system; in the second, the steps taken were designed to alter the facts by causing two unrelated corporations to be related to circumvent the intended rules and went *against* the spirit of the system.

When the CRA perceives tax avoidance transactions to be abusive, it will attempt to deny the resulting benefits. The general means at its disposal are reviewed in Part IV of this chapter.

---

2   The analysis has ignored the time value of money, which is discussed later in the chapter.
3   IC 73-10R3 (archived).

Often, it is difficult to distinguish between legitimate tax planning and abusive tax avoidance. When the line is unclear, the tax planner must choose between passing up the opportunity and embracing it. The latter course means risking an adverse ruling by the CRA.

Unless otherwise indicated, the suggestions offered in this text are legitimate tax planning techniques.

II. Types of Tax Planning

The objective of tax planning is to reduce or defer (or both) the tax cost of financial transactions. There are many specific tax planning opportunities; all of them fall into one of three categories.[4]

1. Shifting income from one time period to another.

2. Transferring income to another entity or alternative taxpayer.

3. Converting the nature of income from one type to another.

A. Shifting Income from One Time Period to Another

In most cases, there is a very definite time frame for recognizing income for tax purposes, and so there is little opportunity to choose between discretionary alternatives. However, a taxpayer can sometimes choose to recognize income or claim a deduction from income in a different time period. Even when this opportunity exists, however, it does not inevitably follow that wealth will be enhanced if those discretionary choices are exercised.

Future tax rates may be greater than, less than, or the same as current tax rates. If current tax rates are lower than the expected future rates, the absolute tax cost can be reduced by recognizing income now rather than later. However, this reduction in tax cost incurs another cost—the cost of financing the payment of tax in advance of when it would otherwise occur. As long as the tax saving is greater than the related financing cost, a wealth enhancement will result for the taxpayer. This can be demonstrated by reconsidering the situation described on pages 8–9.

Situation:

Summary of previous facts:

- The assumed corporate tax rate is 15% on the first $500,000 of annual business income and 25% on the remainder.

- The 20X1 income of the corporation is $150,000 after a deduction of $20,000 is claimed as a reserve for doubtful accounts receivable.

- The 20X2 income is projected to be $550,000, and so some of that income will be subject to a 25% tax rate.

- The $20,000 reserve can be delayed until 20X2 at the taxpayer's discretion.

Also, the company is using its available cash resources to take advantage of early payment discounts on purchases of merchandise. Specifically, these invoice costs can be reduced by 2% by paying the supplier within 10 days instead of the normal 30 days.

Analysis:

If the corporation chooses to delay the deduction of $20,000 until 20X2, the 20X1 profits increase, and the 20X2 profits decrease. Shifting income from 20X2 back to 20X1 in this way takes advantage of the lower tax rate. As stated previously, the overall tax cost is reduced by $2,000, as follows:

---

4   *Taxes and Business Strategy—A Planning Approach,* Scholes and Wolfson, Prentice-Hall, 1992, pp. 15–18.

Increase in 20X1 tax (15% × $20,000)	$3,000
Decrease in 20X2 tax (25% × $20,000)	($5,000)
Tax reduction	$2,000

However, to achieve this, $3,000 of tax must be paid one year in advance. This reduces the cash available for securing purchase discounts over the next year. The value of the purchase discount is 2% for prepaying invoices by 20 days. As there are eighteen 20-day periods in a year, the opportunity savings cost is 36% (2% × 18 periods). This means that the cost of prepaying tax one year in advance is $1,080 (36% × $3,000). This, of course, is before tax. The additional purchasing costs would be deductible in 20X2 and would save tax at the rate of 25%. The net cost is therefore $810 ($1,080 − 25% of $1,080).

After costs associated with reduced cash flows are taken into account, the net advantage of shifting income in this situation is seen to be $1,190 ($2,000 − $810).

Clearly, in the above situation, the corporation would be wise to shift income from 20X2 to 20X1. When making this judgment, it was necessary to determine

(a) future tax rates, or income levels that will cause those tax rates, or both;
(b) the discretionary opportunities within the tax system; and
(c) the time value of money.

Of the above variables, only (b) can be determined with a reasonable degree of certainty. Tax information on discretionary items can be obtained, though this may require some effort. The other two variables are more difficult to determine in that both involve predicting future activities.

The above situation and analysis required that profits and cash flows be predicted over several years. Specifically, the planner had to realize that paying out $3,000 in 20X1 would reduce cash flows for a one-year period, thereby increasing the cost of inventory owing to a weakened ability to claim prepayment discounts. However, the actual cash cost of failing to obtain a discount is the after-tax cost, which can be reduced if the corporation still has borrowing capacity. In this case, the $3,000 could be financed with increased debt without disturbing the purchase discount opportunities.

In this situation, the magnitude of the tax saving is obvious. Even so, the tax planner must consider the impact, if any, of not having $3,000 of cash available for business use. In some cases, especially when a business is subject to the risk of sudden market fluctuations or is clearly in financial difficulty, the benefits of keeping cash available as added insurance must be considered, whatever the numbers say. In other words, the realities of the specific business must prevail, and common sense may sometimes override the quantitative results.

As a general rule, if future tax rates will likely be the same as or lower than the current tax rate, one should seek to delay income recognition. When tax rates are expected to rise, the decision to delay the recognition of income must be made in the context of the potential use of those funds in the shorter term.

In some cases, the shifting of income from one period to another may simply involve choosing a *type* of investment. Consider the following situation:

Situation: A taxpayer has $100,000 to invest for three years. Two investments are available:

1. A corporate bond paying annual interest of 10%.

2. Secure corporate shares that have no annual dividend but have an anticipated growth rate of 10% per year.

Annual after-tax cash flow can be reinvested in securities earning 6%. The taxpayer has a tax rate of 45%.

Analysis:

The interest income on the bond investment is subject to tax annually (see Chapter 7) at the rate of 45%. The after-tax annual return is therefore 5.5% (10% − [45% of 10%] = 5.5%). Similarly, the interest income on the reinvestment securities has an annual after-tax return of 3.3% (6% − [45% of 6%] = 3.3%). Based on this, the bond investment provides the following value at the end of three years:

Initial investment	$100,000
End of year 1:	
Bond interest received (5.5% of $100,000)	5,500
End of year 2:	
Reinvestment interest (3.3% of $5,500)	182
Bond interest received (as above)	5,500
	11,182
End of year 3:	
Reinvestment interest (3.3% of $11,182)	369
Bond interest (as above)	5,500
	17,051
Total value of bond investment	$117,051

The share investment is taxed differently. Its annual growth of 10% will not be recognized for tax purposes until the shares are sold at the end of year 3. In addition, the growth will likely be considered a capital gain (see Chapter 8), and, as a result, only one-half of the gain will be taxable. The share investment provides the following value after three years:

Initial investment	$100,000
End of year 1:	
Growth—10% of $100,000	10,000
	110,000
End of year 2:	
Growth—10% of $110,000	11,000
	121,000
End of year 3:	
Growth—10% of $121,000	12,100
	133,100
Tax at end of year 3:	
45% (½) ($133,100 − $100,000)	(7,448)
Total value of share investment	$125,652

The return on the share investment is greater by $8,601 ($125,652 − $117,051). Much of this is because only one-half of the return on the shares is taxable. The advantage to be gained by shifting the income for tax purposes from years 1, 2, and 3 (bond) to year 3 (shares) can be isolated as $1,153, as follows:

Total advantage (above)	$8,601
Tax preference (non-taxable portion):	
45% (½) ($133,100 − $100,000)	(7,448)
	$1,153

This analysis shows that delaying the recognition of income for tax purposes permits the annual returns to accrue and compound without annual tax cost. The longer the delay, the greater is the advantage.

This section has demonstrated two simple examples of the benefits that can be gained by shifting income from one time period to another. (Many other examples will be offered throughout this text.) Also demonstrated here has been the importance of considering the time value of money and of anticipating financial scenarios related to a particular issue.

B. Transferring Income to Another Entity

Only individuals can enjoy the benefits of accumulating wealth. However, they can do so by using several different entities, all of which ultimately lead back to themselves or to members of their families. For example, an individual may own all or part of one or more corporations (see Chapters 11, 12, and 13), which, in turn, may hold several types of investments or operate businesses. Also, the individual or his or her corporation may participate in partnerships or joint ventures with other individuals or their corporations (see Chapters 15 and 16). As well, individuals may direct their income into various types of trusts (see Chapter 17). A trust can be created during one's lifetime or upon death. Some trusts—registered pension plans, registered retirement savings plans, and so on—may not be taxable. Finally, in certain circumstances, it may be possible to arrange for income to be earned by other members of a family.

The tax treatment often varies with the entity chosen. There may be many non-tax reasons for choosing a particular structure to carry out certain financial activities, but the tax factor is always an important one—sometimes the only one. Shifting income to another entity may reduce or significantly delay the amount of tax otherwise payable.

Consider the following simple example of shifting income from one entity to another:

Situation: An individual operates an unincorporated service business that generates annual pre-tax profits of $100,000. She requires approximately $39,000 to meet her personal financial obligations. The *assumed* personal tax rates (federal plus provincial) are as follows:

On the first $42,000	24%
On the next $43,000	32%
On the next $47,000	40%
On income over $132,000	45%

Any cash generated in excess of personal needs and income taxes is generally used to expand the business operations.

Corporate tax rates for a Canadian-controlled private corporation are *assumed* to be 15% on the first $500,000 of annual business profits and 25% on the excess.

Analysis: Under the existing structure, the individual has annual excess cash of $31,100 available for business expansion, as follows:

Business profits		$100,000
Tax: 24% of $42,000	$10,100	
32% of $43,000	13,800	
40% of $15,000	6,000	(29,900)
$100,000		70,100
Personal expenditures		(39,000)
		$ 31,100

As an alternative, she could create a separate corporation to operate the service business. She would be a shareholder and also would be employed by the corporation and earning a salary. In order to provide for her personal financial needs, the corporation would have to pay her an annual salary of $52,500 (after-tax amount—$39,000).

Salary		$52,500
Less tax:		
24% of $42,000	$10,100	
32% of $10,500	3,400	(13,500)
Personal requirements		$39,000

Consequently, the corporation would be able to retain after-tax profits of $40,400 for business expansion, as follows:

Business profits	$100,000
Salary to shareholder	(52,500)
Corporate business profit	47,500
Tax (15% of $47,500)	(7,100)
Available for expansion	$ 40,400
Cash-flow enhancement ($40,400 − $31,100)	$ 9,300

In the above situation, shifting income to the corporation results in a new tax base that permits a lower tax rate on a certain amount of annual income. Note, however, that a tax reduction is not achieved on the full $100,000 of business income. This is because the corporation had to shift income back to the individual in order to provide her with cash for personal needs. In other words, a tax reduction was achieved only to the extent that the profits could be retained in the corporation and only as long as the corporate profits were below $500,000 (the level at which the tax rate increases to about 25%).[5]

In order to fully appreciate the implications of the above tax planning activity, certain other factors must be considered—for example, the tax implications if the following should occur:

- The shareholder requires further cash distributions from the corporation.
- The corporation earns profits in excess of $500,000 that will incur a higher rate of tax.
- Losses are incurred by the corporation.
- The business fails to survive.
- The business is sold by the corporation.
- The shares of the corporation are sold.
- The shareholder dies or leaves the country.

This is another reminder that tax planning must involve anticipating possible future events. When income is shifted from one entity to another, the cash-flow map is altered. However, the map always eventually leads one back to the original source. Usually, any change in plans will affect the treatment of a number of future events that were not originally targeted for change. In some cases, transferring income from one entity to another may have beneficial results in one area but negative results if certain future events should occur. Potential events must therefore be considered.

C. Converting Income from One Type to Another

The third general type of tax planning activity involves the conversion of one type of income into another. As was stated in Chapter 1, the income tax system recognizes five general types of income, of which four have substantial application—employment income, business income, property (investment) income, and capital gains. The amount

---

5   As will be shown in Chapter 13, this tax saving is not permanent because additional tax may be payable when the amount is eventually distributed to the shareholder or the shares are sold.

of taxable income to be claimed and the timing of that claim for tax purposes can depend greatly on the type of income being claimed. This means that the amount of tax and the timing of its payment can be altered by adjusting a financial transaction so that it generates one type of income instead of another.

It is not always simple to convert one type of income to another. For example, one cannot simply choose to call business income a capital gain. In most cases, converting income also involves shifting that income from one entity to another, as was discussed previously. Consider the following situation:

Situation: Individual A is the sole shareholder of Opco, a Canadian-controlled private corporation. Opco operates a successful wholesale business. The shares of Opco were recently valued at $410,000. These shares were acquired by A several years ago for $10,000. A intends to sell all of the shares of Opco. In 20X1, after the share valuation but just before the share sale, A arranged for Opco to pay a dividend of $40,000 to himself in order to remove excess cash from the corporation.

Two years earlier, A had incurred a loss of $500,000 on the sale of shares of another corporation. That loss could not be used at the time for tax purposes, and so A has been carrying it forward.

The assumed marginal tax rate (federal plus provincial) for Individual A in 20X1 is 45% on all income other than Opco dividends. Dividends from Opco are subject to an assumed tax rate of 33%.

Analysis: First of all, note that A has already taken the tax planning step of shifting income from himself to another entity by operating the business from within a corporation. It should also be explained that the loss on the previous share sale was a capital loss, which means it can be offset only against a capital gain and not against other sources of income (see Chapter 3). Unused capital losses can be carried forward indefinitely until a capital gain is realized (see Chapter 10). Also, only one-half of a capital gain is included in taxable income (see Chapter 8).

In the above situation, the corporation paid a dividend of $40,000 *after* its shares were valued at $410,000. Consequently, the value of the company and therefore of its shares declined by $40,000, and so the sale price of the shares must be reduced to $370,000 ($410,000 − $40,000). A has realized his full share value of $410,000 as follows:

Dividend	$ 40,000
Share price	370,000
	$410,000

His tax cost on the above is $13,200, as follows:

Dividend (33% × $40,000)		$13,200
Capital gain:		
Price of shares	$370,000	
Cost	(10,000)	
Capital gain	$360,000	
Taxable portion (½)	$180,000	
Loss carry-over	(180,000)	
Taxable income	–0–	
Tax on capital gain		–0–
Total tax cost		$13,200

Note that the tax treatment of the capital gain is more to A's advantage than the tax treatment of the dividend. This is because he has a loss carry-over of $250,000 (½ × $500,000) from a previous year that can only be used against new capital gains.

If A had not declared himself a dividend, the share value would have remained at $410,000, and the total tax would have been zero, as shown below.

The decision to pay or not to pay a dividend belonged to A. By choosing not to pay the dividend, he would have converted dividend income (property income) into a capital gain that, in this case, had a preferred tax treatment.

Dividend		–0–
Capital gain:		
Price of shares	$410,000	
Cost	(10,000)	
Capital gain	$400,000	
Taxable portion (½)	$200,000	
Loss carry-over	(200,000)	
Taxable income	–0–	
Tax on capital gain		–0–
Total tax cost		–0–

It is important to appreciate that tax planning does not consist of a definitive list of rules. In the above situation, an advantage would have been achieved by converting property income (dividends) into a capital gain, but this does not mean that it is always better to convert dividends into a capital gain.

Because tax planning does not consist of a definitive list of rules, one must test alternative courses of action, with a view to achieving specific financial goals. In the situation being discussed, A sought to receive the value from his corporation and had two fundamental choices—distribute dividends or sell shares.

It is also worthwhile to approach tax planning decisions in the context of expenditures. Advantages may be gained when the cost for acquiring a good or service is converted from one type of expenditure to another, just as it is when income is converted from one type to another. Consider the following situation:

Situation: Corporation X requires more land to provide parking facilities for its staff at one of its branch locations. Two options are available: it can purchase land for $100,000 or lease it for $10,000 per year. The corporation's long-range restructuring plans call for the closing of the branch after five years. Real estate studies indicate that land values will likely continue to increase at 4% annually.

Corporation X has limited borrowing capacity, and so if it uses current funds, it will have to forgo certain business opportunities. Typically, the corporation's investments provide a minimum pre-tax return of 20%. The corporation's tax rate is 25%.

Analysis: Whether the land is purchased or leased, Corporation X will obtain the right to use the property to fulfill its objective of providing more parking facilities. If the land is purchased, the expenditure will be classified as a capital item and will not be deductible for tax purposes from the company's business income. Instead, when the land is sold, the cost will be deducted from the selling price to determine the amount of the capital gain or loss at that time. One-half of that gain or loss will be applicable for tax purposes.

The real cost of purchasing the land is thus the initial cash outflow of $100,000 less the cash proceeds (net of tax) from the sale of the land at the end of five years. Because the cash received from the sale occurs at year 5, its value must be discounted at an appropriate discount rate, which, in this case, may be 20% pre-tax or 15% after tax (20% – [25% of 20%] = 15%). The cash flows from this alternative are as follows:

Beginning of year 1:	
Cash outflow (purchase)	$100,000
End of year 5:	
Value of land sold ($100,000 + [4% × 5 years])	$121,665
Tax on gain (25%)(½)($121,665 − $100,000)	(2,708)
Net cash inflow	$118,957

The net cost of the land acquisition is $40,857, as follows:

Purchase price	$100,000
Recovered from future sale:	
Present value—$118,957 discounted at 15% for 5 years	(59,143)
	$ 40,857

In comparison, if the land is leased, the annual rent cost of $10,000 is deductible from business income for tax purposes as a current expenditure rather than a capital expenditure.

Effectively, the expenditure for land has been converted from one type to another. Because the rent is deductible, tax savings of 25% will occur annually, resulting in a cash cost of only $7,500 for the lease ($10,000 − 25% of $10,000 = $7,500). The actual cost of this alternative is the present value of five payments of $7,500.

Present value—$7,500 annually for 5 years, discounted at 15%	$25,141

In the above situation, converting the land costs from a capital item to an expense item results in an overall cost reduction of $15,716 ($40,857 − $25,141).

This example can also be used to demonstrate that the tax planning process can involve considerable uncertainty. In the above example, the following factors require significant speculation:

- The rate of growth of the value of the land.
- The appropriate discount rate.
- The anticipated tax rate at the end of year 5.
- Whether the planned branch closure will occur after five years and, if not, how the lease option will be affected.

Each of these items is important but uncertain. For example, if the corporation still has borrowing capacity and can borrow funds at 10% interest, the appropriate discount rate can be reduced to 7.5% after tax (10% − 25% of 10% = 7.5%), in which case the outcome of the analysis can be completely reversed, and, all else being equal, purchase would be the least costly alternative.

III. Skills Required for Tax Planning

This chapter has emphasized three basic types of tax planning. In order to implement tax planning activities, it is necessary to develop certain skills. Certainly one of these is an ability to understand the fundamentals of the Canadian income tax system and how they relate to domestic and international transactions. But there are others, which are summarized below.

- **Anticipation**   All financial investments have a beginning, an activity period, and an end. From the outset, one must try to envision the complete cycle, even if the time frame is long. For example, when investing in a corporation, one must envision the returns that the investment will yield as well as its disposal at some future time.

- **Flexibility**   Any objective can be achieved in a number of different ways. It is therefore highly worthwhile to seek out alternative methods of achieving particular goals. For example, an asset used in the operation of a business can be leased or purchased. As another example, consider a situation in which three separate entities plan to pool their resources to operate a new business venture. The new venture can be organized as a partnership of three partners or as a corporation having three shareholders. Once the alternatives have been identified, the future activities can be predicted, and the tax and financial implications can be examined and compared.

- **Speculation**   One must be able to anticipate the tax effects, if any, should events turn out different from the expected—for example, if losses should occur for a period of time or if the activity should fail completely.

- **Applying the eighth wonder of the world**   It has been said that the eighth wonder of the world is compound interest.[6] Achieving a good return on investment is important, but the ability to reinvest that return is essential for wealth accumulation. Obviously, the amount that is available for reinvestment is affected by the tax cost. For example, if a taxpayer invests $6,000 every year for 30 years ($6,000 × 30 = $180,000) and obtains an annual return of 16% on the invested amount, the accumulated value is $3,691,000. However, if that same taxpayer is subject to a 45% tax rate, the annual return will be only 8.8%, and the invested amounts will accumulate to only $857,000 after 30 years. Note the enormous difference: even though the return has dropped by 45%, wealth accumulation over the 30-year period has declined over fourfold.

  Respect for the time value of money is central to tax planning. Most people are familiar with the saying that "a dollar received today is worth more than a dollar received in the future." Even so, few people appreciate the magnitude of this value until the simple calculation of compound interest is made.

- **Perspective**   Another skill needed for tax planning is the ability to put the tax factor in perspective. Taxation is only one of many considerations in financial decision making. Whenever a tax-driven course of action is being considered, common sense and general business judgment must prevail. The participants in the activity must understand the transactions and accept them for business as well as tax reasons.

- **Global approach**   Yet another skill that has not been previously referred to is the ability to view transactions in a global context. Financial transactions always involve more than one party. For example, the sale of a business involves a buyer and a seller. Each attempts to carry out tax planning activities to improve its own position. A buyer that can take steps to assist the seller in achieving its tax planning goals may gain an advantage in price or other specific terms. For this to happen, the buyer must take a global approach and attempt to understand the tax implications for the seller. This concept is applicable in many types of transactions. An employer should consider the tax position of its employees, a corporation should consider the tax position of its bondholders and shareholders, and so on.

  How difficult is it to develop all these skills? On the surface, very. But in fact, there is a common factor that binds them together, and keeping it in mind will make the

---

6   Professor E. Vogt, Professor of Actuarial Mathematics, University of Manitoba.

task achievable. This common factor, which is the essence of financial decisions, is *cash flow*. Cash flow involves three factors:

- the amount of money coming in;
- the amount of money going out; and
- timing.

By considering these factors, tax planners can develop or greatly improve their decision-making skills.

IV. Restrictions to Tax Planning

Earlier in this chapter, it was indicated that the benefits from certain tax avoidance activities may be denied. Consequently, tax planning is divided between acceptable and unacceptable activities.

The *Income Tax Act* specifically prohibits a number of activities. These prohibitions are referred to as anti-avoidance rules. In addition, the act has a general rule that attempts to state in general terms what is considered to be unacceptable activity. This section cannot examine all of these rules in depth. Instead, it provides a brief overview to suggest the general flavour of the types of restrictions that exist. Many of these restrictions will become even clearer as you proceed through the text.

A. Specific Anti-Avoidance Rules

It should be noted at the outset that there are two general types of financial transactions. There are those in which the parties have a close relationship, such as a parent and child or two corporations owned by members of the same family. These taxpayers, who are specifically defined in the *Income Tax Act*, are said to be not at arm's-length. And there are those transactions in which the parties are completely independent of each other. These taxpayers are at arm's-length.[7]

The tax authorities are more concerned with transactions between taxpayers who are closely associated (not at arm's-length) because these often are not motivated by normal market forces. In contrast, transactions between arm's-length or opposing parties usually reflect economic realities, and so the structure of such transactions is usually consistent with their substance. Outlined below are several examples of provisions that have been designed to limit certain tax avoidance activities.

- When a person transfers property to a party who is not at arm's-length, the transaction price normally cannot be less than the fair market value of the property transferred.[8] This prevents taxpayers from avoiding taxable gains by simply altering the transaction price.

- When a Canadian taxpayer sells property or services to a non–arm's-length foreign entity for an amount that is less than what would have been reasonable if it were sold on the open market, the reasonable price is imposed for tax purposes. A similar treatment applies to expenses between such parties.[9] This rule prevents a Canadian entity from avoiding tax by shifting Canadian taxable income to its foreign parent corporation.

- A taxpayer who directs an anticipated taxable receipt to be paid directly to another person must still include that amount in his or her income.[10] This rule prevents a person from shifting taxable amounts to other parties. For example, one cannot avoid tax by directing that one's salary be paid to a creditor.

---

7 ITA 251, 252; IT-419R2.
8 ITA 69(1)(b).
9 ITA 247(2).
10 ITA 56(2); IT-335R2.

- A taxpayer cannot transfer a right to income to a related party.[11] For example, an individual who has earned consulting income cannot simply transfer the right to that income to his or her own corporation. For a corporation to earn that income, it must be under contract to do so.

- When property is transferred to a spouse, the future income from that property is included in the income of the original owner for tax purposes.[12] Similar rules apply for the transfer of property to children who are less than 18 years old (see Chapter 9). This rule prevents taxpayers from shifting income to family members who may be subject to lower tax rates.

- The ability to recognize certain losses may be restricted or delayed when an entity undergoes restructuring. These anti-avoidance rules, referred to as "stop loss rules," are reviewed in some detail in subsequent chapters.

The above list is far from complete. It does, however, suggest which types of transactions are unacceptable.

B. The General Anti-Avoidance Rule—GAAR

The Canadian tax authorities have enacted a broadly based general anti-avoidance rule (GAAR) to supplement the more specific rules.[13] GAAR stipulates that when a person is involved in an "avoidance transaction," tax will be adjusted to deny the benefit that would have resulted from the transaction or from the series of transactions. This rule raises two questions: (1) what is an avoidance transaction, and (2) what is the nature of the benefit referred to in the rule?

A *tax benefit* is a reduction, avoidance, or deferral of tax or an increase in the refund of tax. Obviously, all tax planning activities attempt to achieve one or more of these, and so the key to understanding the anti-avoidance rule lies in establishing whether a transaction is an *avoidance transaction*.

A transaction is not an avoidance transaction simply because it results in the achieving of a tax benefit. In order for a transaction not to be considered an avoidance transaction, its primary objective must be other than to obtain a tax benefit; in the words of the Canada Revenue Agency (CRA), "a transaction will not be an avoidance transaction if the taxpayer establishes that it is undertaken primarily for bona fide business, investment or family purposes."[14] In effect, this establishes a business purpose or economic reality test to distinguish between acceptable and unacceptable planning activities.

It would appear that the business purpose test described above eliminates the principle that an individual can organize his or her affairs in such a manner as to pay the least amount of tax required by law.[15] However, the anti-avoidance rule maintains this basic principle by tempering the business purpose test with what it refers to as the "misuse or abuse" criterion. Effectively, this states that even when an avoidance transaction occurs, the anti-avoidance rule will not be applied if it may reasonably be considered that the transaction would not result in a misuse or abuse of the provisions of the *Income Tax Act* as a whole. *Therefore, for a tax plan to be rejected, it must fail the business purpose test and, in addition, must be extreme to the extent that it is not within the "spirit" of the tax system as a whole.* "It is relatively straightforward to set the GAAR scheme. It is much more difficult to apply it."[16]

All of this is very subjective and places a responsibility on taxpayers to develop their own degree of certainty by adequately investigating the circumstances in which a misuse or abuse may occur.

---

11 ITA 56(4); IT-440R2.
12 ITA 74.1, (2), (3); IT-510, -511R.
13 ITA 245.
14 IC 88-2.
15 *Stubart Investments Ltd. v. The Queen*, 84 DTC 6305 (SCC).
16 Copthorne Holdings (2011 SCC 63).

Draft legislation, introduced on August 27, 2010 and still pending, provides rules for an information reporting requirement for the disclosure to the CRA, in a timely manner, of certain aggressive tax avoidance transactions. A taxpayer, who benefits from such a transaction, as well as any adviser or promoter who is entitled to a fee in respect of the transaction, would be required to report the avoidance transaction. This draft legislation is not currently law and is not intended to replace the GAAR.[17]

V. Summary and Conclusion

Tax planning is the conscious effort of directing one's financial activities in such a manner as to eliminate, reduce, or defer the incidence of tax on those activities. It is important to recognize that the tax system provides a certain degree of flexibility in determining income and organizational structures. This means that taxpayers can, within certain limits, take planned steps to convert one type of income to another, shift income from one time period to another, and transfer income to a different entity for tax purposes.

In many cases, these actions are consistent with prudent business activities, as may be the case when, for example, a proprietorship is transferred into a corporation. In other situations, the activities are undertaken mainly for tax reasons, in which case potential tax advantages may be denied if the activities are considered to be a misuse or abuse of the income tax system.

Businesspeople must recognize that the ability to plan their taxes is not based solely on the acquiring of a certain amount of tax knowledge; any such knowledge must be combined with certain general skills if decisions are to be effective and creative. Those skills and the factor common to all of them—cash flow—were discussed in this chapter. Generally, good tax planning involves applying the business basics.

As the reader proceeds through this text and acquires knowledge of the fundamentals of the tax system, he or she should try to relate the principles of this chapter to the particular item being reviewed. At the end of most chapters, a checklist of tax planning items is provided.

Visit the Canadian Income Taxation Web site at **www.mcgrawhill.ca/ olc/buckwold** to view any updated tax information.

Review Questions

1. "Tax planning and tax avoidance mean the same thing." Is this statement true? Explain.

2. What distinguishes tax evasion from tax avoidance and tax planning?

3. Does the Canada Revenue Agency deal with all tax avoidance activities in the same way? Explain.

4. The purpose of tax planning is to reduce or defer the tax costs associated with financial transactions. What are the general types of tax planning activities? Briefly explain how each of them may reduce or defer the tax cost.

5. "It is always better to pay tax later rather than sooner." Is this statement true? Explain.

6. When corporate tax rates are 15% and tax rates for individuals are 40%, is it always better for the individual to transfer his or her business to a corporation?

7. "As long as all of the income tax rules are known, a tax plan can be developed with certainty." Is this statement true? Explain.

---

17 Draft ITA 237.3.

8. What basic skills are required to develop a good tax plan?

9. An entrepreneur is developing a new business venture and is planning to raise equity capital from individual investors. Her advisor indicates that the venture could be structured as a corporation (i.e., shares are issued to the investors) or as a limited partnership (i.e., partnership units are sold). Both structures provide limited liability for the investors. Should the entrepreneur consider the tax positions of the individual investors? Explain. Without dealing with specific tax rules, what general tax factors should an investor consider before making an investment?

10. What is a tax avoidance transaction?

11. "If a transaction (or a series of transactions) that results in a tax benefit was not undertaken primarily for bona fide business, investment, or family purposes, the general anti-avoidance rule will apply and eliminate the tax benefit." Is this statement true? Explain.

Key Concept Questions

QUESTION ONE

The *Income Tax Act* contains a general anti-avoidance rule (GAAR) in section 245. Consider each of the following situations and determine whether the GAAR will likely apply. *Income tax reference: ITA 245(2); IC 88-2.*

1. Chris transferred her consulting business to a corporation primarily to obtain the benefit of the low corporate tax rate.

2. Paul owns 100% of the shares of P Ltd. Paul provides services to P Ltd. In the current year he received no remuneration for his services because the payment of a salary to Paul would increase the amount of the loss that P Ltd. will incur in the year.

3. A Canadian-controlled private corporation pays its shareholder/manager a bonus that will reduce the corporation's income to the amount eligible for the low tax rate. The bonus is not in excess of a reasonable amount.

4. A profitable Canadian corporation has a wholly owned Canadian subsidiary that is sustaining losses and needs additional capital to carry on its business. The subsidiary could borrow the funds from its bank but could not obtain any tax saving in the current year by deducting the interest expense due to its loss situation. Therefore, the parent corporation borrows the funds from its bank and subscribes for additional common shares of the subsidiary. The parent corporation reduces its taxable income by deducting the interest expense. The subsidiary uses the funds to earn income from its business.

QUESTION TWO

John has owned all of the shares of Corporation A and Corporation B since their inception. In the current year, John had Corporation A transfer, on a tax-deferred basis, property used in its business to Corporation B. The reason for the transfer is to enable Corporation B to apply the income earned on the transferred assets against its non-capital losses. *Income tax reference: ITA 245(2); IC 88-2.*

Will the GAAR in ITA 245(2) apply to disallow the tax benefit?

PART 2

An Overview of Income Determination and Tax for the Two Primary Entities

You're acting like a thing from a different tax bracket.

FROM *BUFFY THE VAMPIRE SLAYER*

CHAPTER 3

Liability for Tax, Income Determination, and Administration of the Income Tax System

The Canadian income tax system has a two-part structure: one part states which parties are subject to tax and the other how to determine the income to which the tax is applied. It is essential to understand this because every financial activity involves a particular type of transaction by certain parties, and activities or parties that are not within the scope and parameters of the fundamental structure are not subject to Canadian income taxation. This chapter briefly outlines the sources of Canadian tax law and explains which entities fall within its scope and how those entities determine their income for tax purposes. This chapter also briefly reviews the more important items relating to the administration of the Canadian income tax system. In addition, the chapter explains how the income tax relates to the goods and services tax/harmonized sales tax.

I. Sources of Canadian Tax Law

There are three separate sources that govern income tax law in Canada:

- statute law
- common law
- international tax conventions

A. Statute Law

The Canadian federal income tax system is developed in the legal statute known as the *Income Tax Act.* The statute is lengthy, and its form is complex as the result of its authors' efforts to be precise and equitable. Notwithstanding the complex presentation, all taxpayers are responsible for assessing their liability for tax on various types of income earned.

In addition, all provincial jurisdictions impose a tax on income, and each province has enacted its own separate provincial income tax act. However, every province, with the exception of Quebec, has adopted the federal *Income Tax Act*, with minor variations, as the basis for its own particular provincial statute.

B. Common Law

Disputes regarding the application and interpretation of various sections of the *Income Tax Act* and related provincial statutes are often settled within the Canadian court system. While many cases settled before the courts deal with a narrow set of facts, over the years, sufficient jurisprudence has been developed in many areas that it is now the primary source of definitions and interpretations. For example, the *Income Tax Act* does not provide a definition of business income and capital gains, but substantial jurisprudence has developed general guidelines for distinguishing between the two. Common law is, therefore, an integral source of tax law.

C. International Tax Conventions

Canadian taxpayers often invest, carry on business, or are employed in foreign jurisdictions that also impose income tax. In addition, foreign entities engage in similar activities in Canada. As a result, Canada has entered into reciprocal tax treaties with many foreign countries in order to

(a) rationalize and define the jurisdictional authority on transactions of an international nature; and

(b) avoid the incidence of double taxation resulting from applicable provisions of tax legislation in two or more jurisdictions.

In many cases, provisions of international treaties are in conflict with the *Income Tax Act*. When this occurs, the international treaty takes precedence.

Federal tax law is the responsibility of the Department of Finance. However, assessing and collecting tax is the job of the CRA. In order to assess tax, the CRA must interpret the law, and its interpretations may sometimes conflict with the intentions of the designers. The CRA's interpretations of complex or controversial sections of the

Income Tax Act are made public through two primary publications—Interpretation Bulletins and Information Circulars.

It is important to recognize that the interpretations published by the CRA are not law and can be disputed through the court system. However, they do reflect current assessment policy and should always be an important factor when tax planning activities are being considered.

Except on rare occasions, the body of this text will not make reference to specific provisions found in the above sources of tax law; rather, it will explain the structure of the tax system in layperson's terms to provide a broad understanding of its general principles for the purposes outlined in Chapter 1. However, to provide a trail for further study and review, appropriate references to the *Income Tax Act* (ITA) and other sources of tax law are provided in footnotes.

II. Liability for Tax

Federal and provincial income taxes are imposed on only three basic types of entities:[1]

A. The Entities

- individuals
- corporations
- trusts

Trusts have limited application to business and investment structures; therefore, this text will direct most of its discussion to the two primary entities—individuals and corporations. A subsequent chapter is devoted to various types of trusts (see Chapter 17).

There are other forms of business organizations, such as proprietorships, partnerships, joint ventures, and limited partnerships (reviewed in Chapters 15 and 16). None of these entities is directly taxable; rather, they are organizational structures whose profits (or losses) are allocated to the participating owners for tax purposes. The participating owners of the non-taxable structures mentioned above are either individuals or corporations, and therefore all income, regardless of the organizational structure that is used to earn it, is eventually subject to tax.

A corporation is considered to be an artificial person having the same legal rights and responsibilities as an individual. Its affairs are formally separate from the affairs of its owner or owners—the shareholder(s). A building owned by a corporation is not the property of the corporation's shareholder, even though the shareholder may control its use and disposition. Similarly, for tax purposes, corporate profits earned or losses incurred belong to the corporation. At some point, individual shareholders will realize the profits of the corporation by receiving dividends and/or by disposing of their shares, if and when they rise in value.

While the individual and the corporation are separate taxable entities, there is only one ultimate recipient of profit and cash flow—the *individual*. This means that the separate taxation of the two primary entities is only temporary and that ultimately the two will be integrated.

Exhibit 3-1 shows two simple organizational structures. Structure A consists of an *individual* operating a business as a proprietorship. The proprietorship itself is not a taxable entity, and all income earned by it is taxed directly in the hands of the individual. Structure B, on the other hand, consists of an *individual* as a shareholder of a *corporation* that operates a business; this structure involves both primary taxpayers. The corporation, as a taxpayer, is subject to tax on its business income. If and when the individual shareholders receive the remaining after-tax profits as dividends or sell their shares in the

---

1   ITA 2(1), 104(1), 248(1).

corporation, they are subject to further tax treatment. Both structures are created for the same purpose—to permit an owner to carry on a business—but the amount of tax as well as the point in time at which that tax is paid may vary considerably.

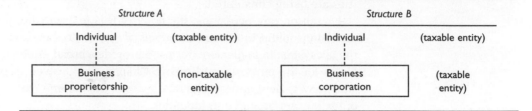

Exhibit 3-1:

Simple Structures of the Two Primary Taxpayers

Structure A		Structure B	
Individual	(taxable entity)	Individual	(taxable entity)
Business proprietorship	(non-taxable entity)	Business corporation	(taxable entity)

In summary, the Canadian income tax system taxes two primary entities—the individual and the corporation. While, at times, decisions with respect to each can be made in isolation, they generally must be considered as integrated in order for taxpayers to appreciate the impact on cash-flow decision making.

B. Resident Individuals and Corporations

Both individuals and corporations are subject to the full thrust of Canadian tax laws if they are considered to be *resident* in Canada.[2] As will be outlined in Part III of this chapter, Canadian residents, whether individuals or corporations, are subject to tax on their *world income*, the scope of which is very broad.[3] Non-resident entities may also be subject to tax in Canada, but in such cases, the scope of that income is limited to particular types of income earned only in Canada. This means that residency is an important factor in determining how an entity is taxed in Canada, especially with regard to investments and business expansion abroad. Each of the two primary taxpayers is subject to its own particular definition of residency; the term is often a point of confusion.

1. Individuals

The concept of "residency," although it is key to the process of determining an individual's obligation to pay tax, is left virtually undefined in the *Income Tax Act*. Past court decisions provide a common-law definition, though even that in itself is not specific.

A perspective can be gained by first considering what the definition of residency does *not* include. Residency does not refer to one's domicile; that is, one is not considered a resident of Canada simply by virtue of being present at a particular address. Also, residency does not mean citizenship; individuals who are not citizens can be resident, while individuals who are citizens can be non-resident. The United States uses citizenship as the primary basis for taxing individuals, but Canada does not.

To be a resident of Canada, an individual must maintain a "continuing state of relationship" with the country.[4] While the fact that one is present in the country indicates a state of relationship, it is only one of the factors that must be considered. Even when an individual is present in the country for only a short period annually, other factors may provide a set of circumstances that show a continuing relationship. It is, therefore, a question of fact whether one is resident or not, and each case is judged on its own special circumstances.

The courts have concluded that a number of factors must be collectively considered when determining residency.[5] The factors include

(a) the amount of time spent in Canada on a regular basis;
(b) the motives for being present or absent;

---

2   ITA 2(1).
3   ITA 3.
4   ITA 250(3); IT-221R3.
5   *Thomson v. MNR*, 2 DTC 812 (1946).

(c) the maintenance of a dwelling place in Canada while away, and its accessibility;

(d) the origin and background of the individual;

(e) the general mode and routine of the individual's life; and

(f) the existence of social and financial connections with Canada.

For example, consider an individual who resides and works in another country but who maintains a dwelling place in Canada, which, although rented out, is accessible on short notice; maintains formal social ties with clubs and other associations; holds Canadian investments; and visits Canada for short periods regularly. That person may be considered a resident of Canada because a continuing state of relationship exists. As a result, all world income of that individual would be taxable in Canada.

Individuals who do not exhibit a continuing state of relationship but do spend time sojourning in Canada are automatically deemed to be Canadian residents if their presence exceeds 182 days in the year.[6]

Residency is determined on a year-to-year basis. Once the criteria are met, one is considered a resident throughout the entire year. The only exceptions to this occur when an individual, at some time during the year, severs all previous ties with the country; or when a non-resident establishes new ties with the country. In such cases, the individual is considered a resident for the relevant portion of the year and accordingly is taxed on world income for that portion.[7]

2. Corporations

Determining a corporation's resident status is significantly less complicated than determining an individual's. Basically, all corporations *incorporated* in Canada are considered residents of Canada and consequently are subject to tax on world income.[8] Therefore, any corporation incorporated under the federal or a provincial jurisdiction is a Canadian resident, regardless of where the controlling shareholders reside—they may be in Canada or in any foreign jurisdiction.

It is also possible for a foreign corporation to be considered a Canadian resident. Under Canadian common law, a company incorporated in a foreign jurisdiction may be resident in Canada if it can be established that the "central management and control" over the major policy affairs of the entity's business is exercised from within Canada.[9] This common-law test is seldom applied, however, due to the obvious difficulties of enforcement and the negative effects it would have on international trade with respect to Canadians carrying on business abroad. Rather, it seems to be used to combat tax avoidance schemes and usually does not affect normal international business or investment structures.

3. Dual Jurisdictions

That an individual or corporation has achieved Canadian-resident status—making that entity's world income taxable in Canada—does not preclude other foreign jurisdictions from claiming the right to tax the same activity and income generated within their boundaries. In such cases, the process is rationalized by the application of both the International Tax Treaty and Canada's *Income Tax Act*. The International Tax Treaty determines the rights of the foreign jurisdiction to tax the particular income; the *Income Tax Act* offers, in most cases, a reduction of Canadian tax by the amount paid to the foreign jurisdiction on the same income.

For example, consider the situation of a Canadian corporation that carries on business in Canada but also operates a major branch operation in the United States. As the

---

6 ITA 250(1).

7 ITA 114; IT-193R; *Schujahn v. MNR*, 62 DTC 1225.

8 ITA 250(4). This rule applies to companies incorporated after April 26, 1965. Companies incorporated prior to that date should consult paragraph 250(4)(c) of the *Income Tax Act*.

9 *De Beers Consolidated Mines Ltd. v. Howe* (1906), AC 455.

corporation is a resident of Canada, the foreign-branch income is part of its world income and is therefore taxable in Canada. The branch is also subject to taxation in the United States. The Canada–U.S. tax treaty permits the United States to tax the branch profits at its applicable rates and according to its rules of income determination. While Canada also includes the branch income in its tax calculation, the resulting Canadian tax can be reduced by the amount of tax paid in the United States. Although double taxation is avoided when income is taxed simultaneously by Canada and a foreign country, the result is that the rate of tax paid on foreign income by the Canadian entity will always equal the tax rate imposed by the country with the higher tax rate (see Chapter 20).

C. Non-Resident Individuals and Corporations

As mentioned previously, non-residents of Canada (both individuals and corporations) are not subject to tax in Canada on their world income but are, at times, taxable on specific activities that occur within this country. A review of this topic may at first appear to be of little value to a Canadian reader; however, Canada treats the activities of foreign entities in much the same way that other countries treat the activities of Canadian entities. This review will help the reader understand how taxation affects a Canadian entity's international business activities.

International business transactions can be placed in two broad categories:

1. Transactions that are started and are completed in the foreign host country.

2. Transactions that originate in one country but are concluded in a second country.

For example, the payment of a dividend by a Canadian resident corporation to a foreign shareholder would fall within the second category, since the payment originates in Canada but the transaction is not completed until the dividend is received by the non-resident. Similarly, the purchase of a product by a Canadian resident directly from a foreign supplier is also of the second category. On the other hand, the selling of merchandise in Canada by a foreign enterprise via the establishment of a branch warehouse and sales office would come under the first category, as each sale would originate and conclude within the Canadian branch. Income in the first category can generally be determined on a net basis, being the revenues minus the expenses incurred to earn the revenues, whereas transactions that originate in one country and conclude in the other, such as the payment of dividends, relate only to the revenue component of net income. Both types of activity are taxed in Canada on a selective basis.

1. Tax on Net Income

Non-residents are taxed in Canada on the net income (revenues minus expenses permitted for tax purposes) arising when the non-resident

(a) carries on business in Canada;

(b) disposes of certain Canadian property (taxable Canadian property); or

(c) is employed in Canada.[10]

Note that in order for a foreign entity (individual or corporation) to be taxed in Canada on business activities, that entity must carry on business in Canada. While the term "carrying on business in Canada" has broad scope within the *Income Tax Act*, most international tax treaties between Canada and other countries indicate that it applies only when the business is being carried on through a "permanent establishment" in Canada.[11] A permanent establishment is regarded as either a fixed place of business or an agency relationship where a resident party has authority to regularly contract on behalf of the non-resident entity. Therefore, the method by which a foreign entity does business in

---

10 ITA 2(3), 115; IT-176R2, IT-420R3.
11 ITA 253, also see Chapter 20: rules regarding a deemed permanent establishment.

Canada (it might involve direct sales to customers, sales to independent contractors who resell to customers, the establishing of a warehouse and/or a branch sales office, or the creation of a separate corporate entity) has a significant impact on how that entity is taxed in Canada and, in turn, on the amount and timing of income taxes.

As noted above, non-residents of Canada are subject to income tax on gains arising from dispositions of *taxable Canadian property* except where exempted by tax treaty.[12] The common items are:

- real estate in Canada;
- capital property used in carrying on business in Canada;
- shares of private corporations resident in Canada that derive their value, principally from real estate located in Canada; and
- investments in partnerships and trusts where the value of the investment is generally attributable to taxable Canadian property.

2. Tax on Canadian Source Income

The tax on an amount that originates in Canada but is paid directly to a non-resident is referred to as a "withholding tax" because the payer must withhold a portion of the obligated payment and remit it directly to the Canadian tax authorities. Normally, this type of tax is calculated at a flat rate and is based on the gross amount paid, without consideration of any related expenses that may have been incurred by the recipient.

The rate of withholding tax has been set at 25% by the *Income Tax Act*.[13] Most negotiated international tax treaties, however, have reduced the rate to 5%, 10%, or 15% on most types of revenues. Listed below are the *major* types of payments that may be subject to Canadian withholding tax when paid to non-residents:[14]

- dividends
- rents
- royalties
- pension benefits
- registered retirement savings plan (RRSP) and registered retirement income fund (RRIF) payments
- certain management and administration fees
- interest (only if paid to a non–arm's-length related party)[15]

The above list is not complete, and there are major exceptions within each category. Note that the direct sale of goods and services across international boundaries between independent parties is not subject to this form of taxation. *Also note that interest paid to arm's-length parties is not subject to withholding tax.*[16]

D. Decision Making and the Residence Issue

The issue of who is liable for tax in Canada has a significant impact on decisions Canadians make about investing abroad or expanding a business enterprise into international markets. The knowledge that the two primary entities are subject to tax on world income only if they are resident in Canada provides an insight into which international transactions are taxable in Canada. In addition, knowledge of the Canadian framework for taxing non-residents carrying on business in Canada can be reversed and applied to Canadian activities in foreign jurisdictions, thereby permitting a general appreciation of the foreign taxes that affect such activities.

---

12 ITA 248(1).
13 ITA 212.
14 IC 76-12R5 provides agreed withholding tax rates with treaty countries.
15 ITA 212(1) (b). The Canada/US tax treaty has no withholding tax on interest paid between one country to the other.
16 Effective January 1, 2008.

Always, the intention is to create an organizational structure that will meet the desired business objectives with a minimum of cash requirements and permit the maximum repatriation of generated funds for reinvestment. While international tax issues are complex and extensive (see Chapter 20), the areas reviewed to this point provide a sufficient base to appreciate the relationship between cash flow and organizational structure. Consider Exhibit 3-2, which outlines three simple alternative structures for accomplishing the same basic objective—to expand Canadian business operations into a foreign market. By applying Canada's residence rules and using the framework of Canadian taxation of non-residents as a guide to Canadian expansion, the following analysis on cash flow can be made.

Exhibit 3-2:

*Basic Structures for
Foreign Expansion*

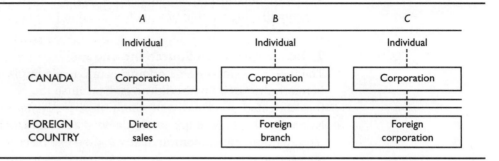

Structure A

Under this structure, penetration into the foreign market is achieved by direct sales from the Canadian business entity to the foreign customer. Payments for all sales are made directly to Canada.

Operations in the foreign country are not carried on from a permanent establishment; therefore, they are not subject to tax by the foreign jurisdiction. Both the individual and the Canadian corporation are resident in Canada and subject to tax on world income. As they are separate entities, the profits of the corporation, if and when they are distributed to the individual shareholder, are included in the individual's taxable income as dividends.

Therefore, under structure A, foreign profits are taxed in Canada at Canadian corporate tax rates and are then available for reinvestment in Canada and the foreign country or for distribution to shareholders.

Structure B

In structure B, foreign operations are conducted out of a branch location that houses inventory for selling and personnel for administration. Payments for all foreign sales are made to the branch location.

The branch operation constitutes a permanent establishment, and the profits (if any) attributable to it are subject to tax in the foreign country. (In addition, some foreign jurisdictions annually impose a low, flat-rate tax on after-tax branch profits accumulated.) Within Canada, the Canadian corporation is considered a Canadian resident and is taxed on its world income. The branch operation is considered a separate entity by the foreign jurisdiction but is not a separate taxable entity for Canadian purposes, since it is not one of the two primary entities. As a result, any profits it makes constitute part of the corporation's *world income*. Branch profits are, therefore, simultaneously taxable in Canada, at Canadian corporate tax rates, and in the foreign country. However, Canadian corporate taxes can be reduced by the amount of tax that was paid in the foreign jurisdiction. Also, in this structure, any *losses* incurred by the foreign branch can be offset against Canadian income to reduce tax, which would enhance corporate cash flow and assist in funding the branch operations.

In summary, the branch alternative directs cash flow from the customer to the branch and then to the Canadian corporation, with branch profits being taxed annually at either the Canadian or the foreign corporate tax rate, whichever is greater.

Structure C

Under this alternative, the foreign operations are based formally in a foreign corporation as a subsidiary of the Canadian corporation.

As a foreign corporation is one of the two primary entities, a determination must be made as to its residence status. It was pointed out earlier that to be a resident of Canada by statute law, a corporation must be incorporated in Canada. The foreign corporation, even though its shareholders are based in Canada, is not resident and accordingly is not taxed on world income in Canada. This means that profits earned by the foreign entity are taxable only in the foreign country at the foreign rates of corporate tax, which are likely to differ from Canadian rates. As well, any losses incurred by the foreign operation belong exclusively to the foreign corporation and cannot be offset against profits in Canada.

If and when after-tax profits of the foreign entity are distributed to the Canadian shareholder (also a corporation), they flow as dividends and are subject to a source-withholding tax by the foreign jurisdiction.

With this structure, funds flow from the foreign customer to the foreign corporation and are subject to tax at foreign corporate rates. The after-tax profits in the foreign corporation can be used for investment in the foreign country or distributed to the Canadian corporate shareholder. If funds are distributed to Canada as dividends, the amount—net of foreign withholding tax—is then available for reinvestment by the Canadian corporation or for distribution, with further tax, to the individual Canadian shareholders.

The above alternatives illustrate the substantial tax differences that can occur as business structures are changed. More importantly, they demonstrate a framework for utilizing basic tax principles in the decision process. Cash flows along many different paths and at various speeds before it finally comes to rest with the ultimate investor. When applying the tax factor to business and investment decisions, the key is to *identify the point* along that path at which the cash flow and the power to reinvest are going to be reduced. Cash flow must therefore be charted and anticipated, and always in terms of the basic entities. While business structures can be extensive and complicated, cash flow is taxed only as it enters one of the two primary entities—the individual and the corporation—each of which is separately taxed.

In order to complete the process of charting cash flow, it is also necessary to appreciate the fundamentals of two additional variables as they apply to each of the two primary entities:

(a) the types of income that are taxable; and

(b) the rates of tax.

III. Determination of Income

Each of the primary entities is required to pay a rate of tax on its *taxable income* in each taxation year.

"Income," by itself, is a broad term, and its definition varies with the point of view of the person defining it. The economist's concept of income is different from a professional accountant's concept of income, and both are different from the dictionary definition. Some parties would restrict the definition such that it includes only wealth enhancement in terms of money or money's worth, and only as the result of labour or enterprise; others would include such items as inheritance and windfalls (lottery winnings, gifts, and the like). "Income for tax purposes," while embracing parts of both definitions, does not subscribe wholly to either; rather, it stands by itself as a separate concept. In order to understand the consequences of financial decisions, it is necessary for one to cast off other views of income determination and develop an appreciation of the concept of *income for tax purposes.*

This concept has no concise definition. (In fact, the *Income Tax Act* does not specifically provide a single definition of income.) Instead, it more closely resembles a framework, which includes the following:

1. Each entity subject to tax determines its taxable income on the basis of a taxation year.

2. Income for each entity includes and is restricted to the world income generated from five general categories. Each category of income is determined in accordance with its own brief set of fundamental principles.

3. The net incomes (revenues minus expenses) for each of the five categories are aggregated in accordance with a strict formula, the sum of which is referred to as net income for tax purposes.

4. The sum of the five categories of income is then reduced by a limited number of specific items. Such items differ for the two primary entities. This total is referred to as *taxable income* and is the base to which the rate of tax is applied.

The taxable income for a taxation year of an entity subject to tax in Canada can be expressed in the following simple formula.

$$TI = \text{Net income} - \text{Special reductions}$$

A. The Taxation Year

Taxable income is determined and assessed on the basis of an entity's taxation year. The term "taxation year" is defined differently for the two primary entities.[17]

• **Corporations**   The taxation year of a corporate entity is regarded as its fiscal period, being any time period not exceeding 53 weeks (one year) for which the entity accounts for its financial affairs.[18] This means that corporate taxpayers can choose the annual period for which tax will be assessed. It is accepted practice for corporations to account to their shareholders on an annual basis, and this same fiscal period is normally used for tax purposes. Once a corporation chooses a fiscal period, it must continue with the same period in the future unless concurrence is given by the CRA. Such concurrence is normally not withheld if the primary purpose of the change is business related as opposed to tax related.[19]

A fiscal period, and therefore a taxation year, may be less than 12 months in the year in which a corporation comes into existence or ceases to exist or in which a change in year end is granted. For example, a corporation that is created on June 1 may choose an October 31 fiscal year end, in which case the first taxation year would include only the five months from June 1 to October 31.

There is an exception to the above rules. **Professional corporations** (a corporation that carries on the professional practice of an accountant, dentist, lawyer, medical doctor, veterinarian or chiropractor) are required to have a fiscal period that coincides with the calendar year.[20]

• **Individuals**   The taxation year for an individual taxpayer is simply the calendar year, and therefore includes the 12-month period ending on December 31 of every year.[21]

---

17 ITA 249.
18 ITA 249.1.
19 IT-179R.
20 ITA 249.1(1)(b).
21 ITA 249(1).

The choice of a 12-month period for both individuals and corporations to determine taxable income is arbitrary and does not necessarily coincide with the timing of revenues earned and expenses incurred. Transactions often straddle more than one taxation year. For example, a taxpayer with a taxation year ending on December 31 may

(a) earn salary in one year but receive payment in the next;
(b) invest in a bond bearing 6% interest on September 1 but not receive the interest payment until August 31 of the next year; and/or
(c) buy shares of a public company in year 1 for $10,000 and sell them for $15,000 in year 6.

Certainly, the income over the life of the above transactions is recognizable; even so, the arbitrary imposition of a 12-month taxation year is a common source of confusion and may require a departure from economic reality when the tax input and its effect on return on investment are being considered. The effect is most dramatic when the income process involves long-term depreciable assets. Consider the simple situation of a business entity purchasing a truck to earn revenue over several years. If the truck cost $10,000 in year 1 and earned revenues of $5,000 annually for six years before being scrapped, the profit over the six years (ignoring operating and maintenance costs) can be determined exactly, as shown below.

Revenues (6 y × $5,000)	$30,000
Expense (cost of truck)	10,000
Profit	$20,000

However, the arbitrary use of a taxation year requires profits to be determined annually. In the above example, this presents no problem for the revenues ($5,000 annually), but it does present a problem when it comes to determining annual expenses. A logical solution would be to estimate the useful life of the asset at the time of its purchase and allocate the total cost over that period. Since it is difficult to estimate accurately the useful life of long-term assets, this procedure would certainly result in some degree of error. Whether an error is made or not, the final profit will be $20,000 over the six years. The tax system removes the need for estimating the useful life of assets by providing a uniform allocation rate for certain types of assets (see Chapter 6). This uniform procedure may allocate the cost of depreciable property over a period of time in a way that does not correspond to either the owner's estimate of useful life or the asset's active life span. As a result, profits for tax purposes, which over the life of the asset will total the proper amount, will, in many cases, differ every year from economic reality.

The impact of different taxation years on cash flow must also be examined in terms of the business structure. For example, consider the structure outlined in Exhibit 3-3, which concerns an individual who owns 100% of a corporation that carries on an active business. The taxation year of the individual is December 31 and the taxation year of the

Exhibit 3-3:

Taxation Years and Business Structure

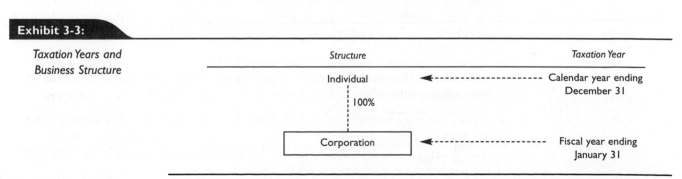

corporation is chosen as January 31. There are two entities and both earn income independently. For example, the corporate profits from February 1, 20X1 to January 31, 20X2 may be distributed to the shareholder as a dividend on January 31, 20X2, the last day of the fiscal year. Note that $^{11}/_{12}$ of the corporate business profits were earned in 20X1. However, they are distributed to the shareholder on January 31, 20X2. The shareholder includes the entire dividend in the 20X2 taxation year. So, the distribution to the shareholder of corporate profits earned in 20X1 is not taxed until 20X2. Of course, a corporation may declare a dividend at any time but, as will be shown in later chapters, there may be an advantage to paying a dividend on or before the corporate year end.

The concept of taxation years, although a simple one in terms of tax interpretation, can have an impact on the cash-flow process. The choice of year end for various entities within a business structure must be considered. As well, the timing of cash-flow activities between entities must be examined in relation to the taxation years in existence at the time.

B. Types of Income

Within the framework of income determination, an entity's world income is derived from five basic sources:[22]

- employment income
- business income
- property income
- capital gains and losses
- other specific sources

Income for each category is determined by applying those basic principles that are special to the particular category. The basic principles determine the extent to which items are included in income, the extent to which deductions from that income are permitted, and the point in time at which the transaction is recognizable for tax purposes. For example, if a transaction giving rise to income falls within the category of "employment income," the application of the basic principles for that category will determine to what extent (if any), and when, the item is to be included.

The basic principles are different for each category, and in some cases, these differences are substantial. It is important to note that income determination varies as a function of how the income is earned—whether the entity is an individual or a corporation is normally *not* a factor. The commonly held view is that the corporate taxpayer is entitled to greater deductions than the individual taxpayer. This is untrue: an individual who earns business income determines that income according to exactly the same principles used by a corporation earning business income. It is also important to recognize that both of the primary entities can earn more than one type of income and, therefore, can be subject to several formats of income determination; for example, an individual could derive income from all five categories in one taxation year and would have to apply different principles to each one.

The first step toward understanding how a specific transaction or an ongoing activity will be taxed is to relate that transaction or activity to one of the five income categories mentioned earlier. The importance of this process is twofold.

1. If the item falls within a particular category, then the process of determining the amount and timing of its income is directed by the basic principles that apply only to that category.

2. If the item does not fall within one of the five categories, it is not subject to tax within the Canadian system. For example, such items as lottery winnings, inheritances, and the receipt of gifts do not fall within the definition of any of the categories and as such are not taxable.

---

22 ITA 3.

The five types of income will be defined and developed in detail in later chapters. A brief, general definition for each income category is given below. These definitions are not complete and are provided at this point solely to help the reader gain an appreciation of the formula for total income determination, which is developed in a later section of this chapter.

- **Income from employment** Income from employment[23] is derived when an entity engages the general services of an individual in return for a salary, wage, and/or other fringe benefits. An individual who independently contracts specific services on a fee-for-service basis and who is not under the general direction and control of an employer, is not receiving employment income.

- **Income from business** Income from business[24] includes many things. Generally, it includes all enterprise carried out with the intention to profit. It is not necessary that the activity be ongoing or that it provide the physical appearance of a formal business. The once-in-a-lifetime purchase of land for the purpose of trading it at a profit is a business activity and is treated in the same manner as the affairs of a large land-trading company. Similarly, a person who is not in the painting business but who paints a neighbour's fence in return for a quoted fee has derived income from business.

- **Income from property** Income from property[25] can generally be regarded as the return that is earned on invested capital. It includes items that are normally thought of as investment income, such as interest, dividends, rents, and royalties. It **does not** include the gain that may be realized on the sale of the investment itself but, rather, is restricted to the regular return generated from its ownership. Income from property is often referred to as "passive" income because the earning process requires little effort or labour by the recipient.

- **Capital gains** Capital gains[26] refer to the profit realized on the sale of assets that were acquired for the purpose of generating monetary returns or personal enjoyment over a long period of time. It is not the nature of the asset itself that causes the profit on sale to be considered a capital gain; rather, the use of the asset is the important factor. For example, the tractor used by a farmer to generate farm revenue is a capital asset, and a gain on its sale in excess of the original cost would be considered a capital gain. The same treatment may be applied to profits from the sale of land that was originally acquired and used as part of an apartment complex generating annual returns in the form of rent. On the other hand, the profit on the sale of a tractor by an implement dealer would be regarded as business income and not as a capital gain because the dealer acquired the property in order to profit from its resale. Similarly, the profit realized on the sale of land that was acquired with the intention of trading it at a profit would not be a capital gain.

- **Other income and deductions** While the title of this category appears to capture all activities that fall outside the previous categories, its scope, in fact, is extremely limited. The term "other income and deductions" cannot be generally defined, except to state that it *includes* and is *limited* to the few specific items referred to in sections 56 to 66 of the *Income Tax Act. Other income* includes such items as superannuation and pension receipts (including Old Age Security and Canada Pension Plan benefits), Employment Insurance benefits, alimony payments, receipts from RRSPs, and deferred profit-sharing plans. *Other deductions* includes RRSP contributions, alimony payments, child care expenses, and moving expenses.

---

23 ITA 5–8.
24 ITA 9–37.
25 ITA 9–37.
26 ITA 38–55.

C. Net Income for Tax Purposes— The Aggregating Formula

The second step in determining a taxpayer's income subject to tax is to arrive at net income for tax purposes by aggregating the five types of income eligible for inclusion. While this process is not complex, it requires a strict adherence to a basic accumulating formula.[27] The formula is often referred to as the "statutory scheme," as it is the foundation upon which the entire income tax system is based. In effect, the formula is the *definition of net income for tax purposes* because it establishes the scope of taxable activities and presents the overall method of computation. Its importance cannot be overemphasized, as it is the broom that sweeps away much of the tax system's complexity.

The formula, which is outlined in Exhibit 3-4, consists of four segments, each of which is reviewed below. It is important to recognize that *the same formula is used by both individuals and corporations*, that is, the determination of net income for tax purposes is identical for all taxable entities.

Exhibit 3-4:

The Statutory Scheme: A Formula for Determining Net Income for Tax Purposes

A	*Determine* the aggregate of:	
	Employment income	+
	Business income	+
	Property income	+
	Other items of income	+
	Subtotal 1 (must be positive or zero)	+ or 0
B	*Increase* subtotal 1 by the amount by which:	
	Taxable capital gains* +	
	exceed	
	Allowable capital losses −	+ or 0
	Subtotal 2 (must be positive or zero)	+ or 0
C	*Reduce* (but do not exceed) subtotal 2 by:	
	Other items of deduction −	
	Subtotal 3 (must be positive or zero)	+ or 0
D	*Reduce* (but do not exceed) subtotal 3 by:	
	Employment losses −	
	Business losses −	
	Property losses −	
	Allowable business investment losses −	− or 0
	Total—net income for tax purposes	
	(must be positive or zero)	+ or 0

* A small portion of the formula relating to capital gains (losses) on listed personal property has been omitted. The area has limited application and is discussed briefly in Chapter 8. **The entire formula is reviewed in more detail in Chapter 9 and also in Chapter 10.**

Segment A[28]

This segment adds together four sources: employment income, business income, property income, and other income. The remaining category, capital gains, is dealt with separately in segment B.

The reference to each of the income items does not allude to the gross income but, rather, to the *net income* from each source. Therefore, the business income added into segment A is the gross revenue less the expenses incurred to earn that revenue. Similarly, "employment income" refers to employment income after permitted expenses have been deducted for tax purposes.

Keep in mind that each category of income may have more than one source within it.[29] For example, an entity may operate more than one business, in which

---

27 ITA 3.
28 ITA 3(a).
29 ITA 4.

case the revenues less the expenses must be computed separately for each business. Similarly, an individual may be employed at two jobs, in which case the income less the deductions must be computed separately for each. Segment A includes only those specific sources of income that, net of deductions, result in *positive net income*. Any source that results in a net loss is included later in the formula, at segment D. Consider the situation where an entity operates two businesses. Business #1 has a net profit of $60,000, while business #2 incurs a net loss of $40,000. Even though the entity's combined income from both businesses is $20,000, segment A includes only the net income from business #1—that is, $60,000.

Because only those sources of income that show a positive net income are included in segment A, the subtotal of all items in that segment must be positive or at least zero.

Segment B[30]

This segment deals exclusively with capital property and includes both taxable capital gains and allowable capital losses. Because the term "exceeds" must be adhered to, this segment applies only when total capital gains for a particular year are greater than the total capital losses for that year. As a result, the calculation in segment B cannot be negative and must show a positive or zero amount. Consider the following two examples:

	Situation 1	Situation 2
Taxable capital gains:		
Property A	$10,000	$10,000
Property B	15,000	15,000
Allowable capital losses:		
Property C	(11,000)	(35,000)
Net gains (losses)	$14,000	($10,000)

In situation 1, the capital gains exceed the capital losses by $14,000 and, therefore, the formula under segment B increases net income for tax purposes by $14,000. However, in situation 2, the capital losses are greater than the gains by $10,000. Because *the gains do not exceed the losses*, segment B results in a zero amount, and net income for tax purposes remains unchanged.

Implicit in this segment of the formula is that capital losses incurred by a taxpayer can be offset in the year only to the amount that capital gains were realized in the year, and **cannot** be used to offset any of the other sources of income included in segment A. Unused capital losses as exemplified in situation 2 are available for use in certain other years if other capital gains are realized; however, it is possible that a taxpayer's capital losses may remain unused indefinitely (see Chapters 10 and 11).

The reader may already be aware that only one-half of the actual capital gains and losses are applicable for tax purposes (see Chapter 8). The reference to "taxable" capital gains and "allowable" capital losses in the formula reflects this.

Segment C[31]

This segment simply deducts from all other sources of income a limited number of items referred to as "Other items of deduction." These include RRSP contributions, moving expenses, and the like. The fact that these specific items are located at this point of the formula (that is, after the five sources of income have been included) indicates that they can be offset against any form of income.

---

30 ITA 3(b).
31 ITA 3(c).

Note that the formula in Exhibit 3-4 does not permit these deductions to exceed the total of income included to that point. If the deductions in segment C are in excess of all other sources of income, such excess is lost and, except in limited circumstances, cannot be used in any other taxation year.

Segment D[32]

This segment further reduces net income for tax purposes. Losses incurred from employment, business, and property and allowable business investment losses, are stated here. It was indicated previously that these items are specifically excluded from other segments. The fact that they are located as the last item within the formula is significant because it means that such losses can be offset against all other forms of income previously included. They therefore are of greater value in the tax process than are capital losses, which are restricted by segment B.

The term "allowable business investment loss" is introduced for the first time in segment D and requires a word of explanation.[33] An allowable business investment loss refers to a loss on the sale of shares of a small business corporation *or* a loss on a loan to a small business corporation (see Chapter 8). Such a loss, though a capital loss, is given a special category outside segment B. Its inclusion in segment D means that such a loss can be offset against all other sources of income. (This is not the case with segment B capital losses.) The result is that the risk of investing in this type of capital property is relatively lower, as potential tax savings on a loss are more readily usable.

The losses in segment D can only reduce income for the year to zero. However, the unused amount (if any) is available for use in a limited number of other taxation years (see Chapters 10 and 11).

The process of aggregating income by strict application of the four-step formula provides many answers to questions concerning how an entity's various income activities interact with each other. In turn, these answers can provide assistance in assessing risk factors in financial decision making. Almost every investment carries with it some risk of failure. The real loss on any activity is the actual cash loss incurred less the tax savings (if any) that are generated when the loss is deducted against other sources of income. A business loss of $100,000 that can be offset against other taxable income may reduce tax by $45,000 (assuming a 45% tax rate). In such a case, the investor's real risk exposure when considering such a venture is really $55,000, not $100,000.

Consider the following questions, which are often asked:

1. Can a business loss incurred by an individual be offset against that individual's employment income? *Answer*: Yes. Net income for tax purposes is determined by including employment income in segment A and then deducting a business loss in segment D.

2. Can a corporation deduct its business loss against a capital gain realized on the sale of its subsidiary's shares? *Answer*: Yes. Taxable capital gains are included in income first in segment B. The business loss is deducted in segment D.

3. Can an entity's capital loss on the sale of shares be offset against its business income? *Answer*: No. Capital losses are included in the formula only as a deduction against capital gains in segment B.

4. Can interest expense incurred by an individual on loans acquired for investment purposes be offset against pension income? *Answer*: Yes. Pension income, being "other income," is included in segment A. The interest expense in excess of investment returns, being a loss from property, is deducted later, in segment D.

---

32 ITA 3(d).
33 ITA 38(c).

It is apparent that because of the requirement that the formula be used when determining income for tax purposes, the amount of tax and the timing of its payment are both affected by the *type* of income earned as well as by the amount earned. Consider the following two situations, each of which indicates the same total actual income but a considerably different income for tax purposes:

	Situation 1	Situation 2
Business income (loss)	$(200,000)	$200,000
Capital gains (loss)	200,000	(200,000)
Actual net income	NIL	NIL
Income for tax purposes	NIL	$200,000

In each situation, the actual cash profit of the entity was zero. In situation 1, the zero profit was generated by a business loss of $200,000 and a capital gain of $200,000. The formula permits business losses to be offset against all sources of income, and therefore, income for tax purposes was zero. However, in situation 2, the zero profit was generated by business profits of $200,000 and a capital loss of $200,000. Since the formula restricts the use of the capital loss because there is no capital gain, income for tax purposes was $200,000, and the entity in situation 2 may have incurred taxes of $90,000 (assuming a tax rate of 45%) even though no cash profits were realized in the year. The activities and total results were the same for both entities—that is, both carried on a business and also invested in capital properties; however, their after-tax cash flows and therefore their ability to compete in the marketplace turned out to be greatly different. Such results can be anticipated by constant reference to the formula for net income determination. This kind of advance knowledge may permit steps to be taken to avoid unfavourable outcomes; it may also provide additional insight when it comes to analyzing the downside cash-flow risk associated with alternative investment opportunities.

The formula can also be applied to business structures in order to determine the tax consequences of income flows between the entities within the structure. Each taxable entity (the individual and the corporation) determines its income separately, and each does so according to the formula. Exhibit 3-5 outlines two simple business structures. In both cases, the owner contributed $100,000 of capital to fund an enterprise and, after incurring operating losses of $100,000, terminated the venture. Under structure A, the owner operated the business as a proprietorship. Since a proprietorship is not one of the two taxable entities, its income—or loss, in this case—was simply allocated directly to the individual owner. The formula, therefore, applied only to the individual, and the business loss of $100,000 could be immediately offset against any other income earned by the individual, with a resulting reduction in taxes.

Exhibit 3-5:

The Net Income Formula and Business Structures

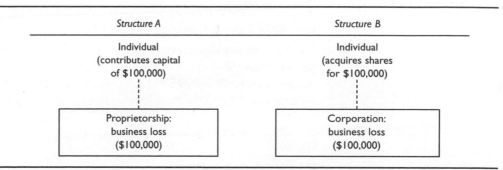

Under structure B, the business was operated in a corporation that had been capitalized by the individual, who contributed $100,000 for share capital. In this case, both entities were taxable and determined their income separately. The business loss of $100,000 belonged only to the corporation and could not be offset against any other income earned by the individual shareholder. The individual also suffered a loss due to the decline in value of the corporation's shares. This loss of $100,000 was realized only when the shares were disposed of and included in the formula as a capital loss. Also, only one-half of the loss ($50,000) is allowable to be offset against taxable capital gains or against other income sources if it qualifies as an allowable business investment loss.

In this example, the formula and the concept of taxable entities interacted to significantly alter the tax impact on both structures, even though the unsuccessful ventures were identical.

It can be seen that the formula for determining income for tax purposes has a formidable impact on the tax process. Its simple format, when applied, provides direct answers to many specific questions as well as a general overview of a broad range of tax issues. Despite its importance, a person who examines the individual or the corporate tax return will find absolutely no hint that such a formula exists. It is hard to understand why the formula is not the primary focus of tax returns; the fact that it is not is likely a major contributing factor to the lack of understanding of the tax process on the part of many taxpayers.

D. Taxable Income

The final step in arriving at the base amount of income to which a rate of tax is applied is to reduce net income for tax purposes (as established by the formula) by a limited number of specified reductions.[34] This final reduced amount is referred to as "taxable income." The items that reduce net income for tax purposes to taxable income are different for the two primary taxpayers, which means that the framework of income determination that has so far applied to both individuals and corporations begins to branch at this point. The number of income reduction items in this area is not significant; only a few have a major impact on business and investment decisions. An *abbreviated* list of the taxable-income reductions for individuals and corporations is given below.

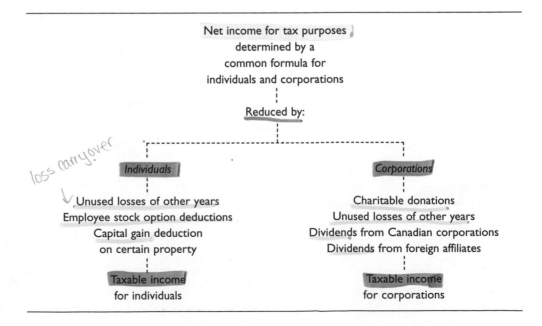

Net income for tax purposes
determined by a
common formula for
individuals and corporations

Reduced by:

Individuals	Corporations
Unused losses of other years	Charitable donations
Employee stock option deductions	Unused losses of other years
Capital gain deduction	Dividends from Canadian corporations
on certain property	Dividends from foreign affiliates

Taxable income for individuals

Taxable income for corporations

loss carryover

---

34 ITA, Part I, Division C, 110–116.

Detailed explanations of the items shown and their relationship to the decision-making process are deferred until later chapters (see Chapters 10 and 11). They are identified at this point only to show the limited scope of this part of the income-determination process. In later chapters, special attention will be given to the utilization of losses and the flow of intercorporate dividend distributions, both of which are significant variables in the management of cash flows.

IV. Administration of the Income Tax System

The design and ongoing development of income tax law is the responsibility of the Department of Finance. However, the monumental task of administering the law and ensuring that taxpayers comply with it is the responsibility of the Canada Revenue Agency (CRA). The *Income Tax Act* includes many provisions that deal with the following administrative issues:

- Who must file tax returns and when they must be filed.
- Procedures for assessing returns that have been filed.
- Deadlines for income tax payments.
- Penalties for failing to meet the compliance provisions.
- Taxpayers' rights, and procedures for appealing disputed assessments.

This section briefly reviews the most important provisions relating to each of these areas.

A. Filing of Returns

Every taxpayer, whether an individual, a corporation, or a trust, must file an income tax return. However, the filing deadline is different for each of these entities.

1. Corporations

A corporation must file an annual income tax return within six months of its taxation year end, even if it has no income or has no financial activity.[35]

2. Individuals

Every taxpayer who is an individual must file an income tax return by April 30 for the most recent calendar year.[36] This date is extended to June 15 if the individual or his or her spouse carries on a business.[37] However, unlike a corporation, an individual is usually not required to file a return in a year in which no tax is payable.[38] Even so, taxpayers should be aware that a penalty may be imposed if no return was filed as a result of an incorrect determination that no tax was payable. For this reason, every individual is well advised to file a return every year.

Tax returns of a deceased taxpayer that were not due at the date of death, are due the later of six months from the date of death and the normal filing deadline (April 30 or June 15).[39] This due date also applies for the tax return of the surviving spouse. The deceased's legal representative is responsible for filing the tax return.[40] It should be noted that certain portions of a deceased person's income may be filed in separate tax returns (see Chapter 10).[41]

---

35 ITA 150(1)(a).
36 ITA 150(1)(d)(i).
37 ITA 150(1)(d)(ii).
38 ITA 150(1.1).
39 ITA 150(1)(b).
40 ITA 150(1)(d)(iii).
41 ITA 70(2), 104(23)(d), IT-326R3, -212R3.

3. Trusts and Estates

Every trust must file an income tax return within 90 days of its taxation year.[42] The taxation year of a trust created by an individual during his or her lifetime (*inter vivos* trust) is the calendar year. A trust created upon an individual's death (testamentary trust) can choose a fiscal period as its taxation year.[43]

4. Tax Returns Filed Electronically

Where a tax return is filed electronically it is not considered filed until the CRA acknowledges receipt of the tax return.[44] If someone other than the taxpayer files the tax return electronically, Form T183 or T183CORP "Information return for electronic filing of an income tax return" must be completed and signed. The taxpayer and the tax return filer must each keep a copy of the form.[45]

Summary of Income Tax Return Filing Requirements

Entity	Latest Filing Date
Corporation ----------------------➤	6 months after the taxation year
Individual -------------------------➤	April 30 or June 15 if the taxpayer or spouse carries on a business in the year
Deceased Individual -----------------➤	Normal filing deadline (April 30 or June 15) or 6 months from the date of death, whichever is later
Trusts -----------------------------➤	90 days after the taxation year

B. Assessment

After receiving an income tax return, the CRA is required to assess it "with all due dispatch."[46] Usually, this means within two to four months of the date the return was filed, which is only enough time for the CRA to scrutinize the calculations. However, CRA has the right to reassess returns at a later time. This right is subject to the following limitations:

1. A filed return can be reassessed *at any time* if the taxpayer has made any misrepresentation that is attributable to neglect, carelessness, or wilful default or has committed any fraud in filing the return or supplying information.[47]

2. In all other circumstances, individuals, trusts, and Canadian-controlled private corporations can be reassessed within three years of the date the original assessment was mailed.[48] For public corporations, the time limit is extended to four years. It should be noted that any taxpayer has the right to waive these time limits.

3. At the individual's request, the CRA is permitted to reassess tax returns for up to 10 years back to allow a deduction or credit the individual neglected to claim.[49] This provision does not apply to corporations.

When a taxpayer files a return that shows no taxable income, the CRA issues a statement that no tax is payable. However, this statement does not constitute an assessment. Often, there was no taxable income because there was a loss for the year in question. The taxpayer may be able to apply that loss against an earlier or later

---

42 ITA 150(1)(c).
43 ITA 108(1), 249.1(1)(b)(i–i.1).
44 ITA 150.1(3).
45 ITA 150.1(4).
46 ITA 152(1).
47 ITA 152(4); IC 75-7R3.
48 ITA 152(3.1)
49 ITA 152(4.2).

year's income, and so it is in the taxpayer's interest to establish that the loss has been accepted by the CRA and that its availability is certain. A taxpayer can request that the CRA make a determination of the non-capital loss, net capital loss, restricted farm loss, or limited-partnership loss for the particular year.[50] Once determined, it is binding on the parties as if it were an assessment.

C. Payment of Tax

Usually, all taxpayers must pay tax at various times throughout and after the taxation year. Those times are different for individuals and corporations.

1. Individuals

Individuals must pay tax on certain types of income at the time such income is received; with other types of income, payments must be made on an instalment basis.

The most important type of income for most individuals is employment income. For this type of income, the employer is required to withhold the appropriate amount of tax and remit it to the CRA on the employee's behalf.[51] Tax must also be withheld on a number of other types of income, such as retiring allowances, Employment Insurance benefits, pension benefits, and payments from a registered retirement savings plan (RRSP).

Income that is not subject to withholding taxes at source may be subject to quarterly tax instalments. This is required whenever the individual's tax owing (federal and provincial combined, after deducting taxes withheld at source) exceeds $3,000 for both the current year and either of the past two taxation years.[52] These instalments are due on the 15th day of March, June, September, and December. The amount of tax payable for each instalment is calculated using one of the methods given below:

(a) one-quarter of the estimated tax payable that is not withheld at source;

(b) one-quarter of the previous year's tax liability that was not withheld at source; or

(c) for the March and June instalments, one-quarter of second preceding year's tax liability that was not withheld at source; and for the September and December instalments, one-half of the preceding year's tax liability that was not withheld at source, in excess of the March and June instalment payments.

The CRA provides each taxpayer with a calculation of his or her required instalments; this calculation is based on method (c) above. It is up to each individual to estimate the current year's tax if he or she wants to pay a lower instalment. Instalments need not be made when the federal and provincial tax for the current year or for each of the two previous years is less than $3,000.[53] Also, special rules exist for taxpayers whose chief source of income is farming or fishing.[54]

The balance of tax is due April 30th of the following year. The only exception is for deceased taxpayers. The balance of tax, not due at the date of death, is due the later of six months after the date of death and April 30th.[55]

An instalment calculation for an individual carrying on a business is demonstrated below:

Situation: Angela's only source of income is from a business she carries on in a province in Canada. The total Canadian tax (federal and provincial) on her income was $20,000 in year 1 and $32,000 in year 2. She estimates her tax liability for year 3 to be $36,000.

---

50 ITA 152(1.1); IT-512.
51 ITA 153(1).
52 ITA 156(1), 156.1(1) and (2).
53 ITA 156.1(2).
54 ITA 155.
55 ITA 156.1(4), "balance-due day" in ITA 248(1).

Analysis:

Since Angela expects her tax liability for year 3 will exceed $3,000 and her tax liability for year 2 and year 1 exceeded $3,000 (only one of the two prior years is required), she is required to pay quarterly tax instalments in year 3. The instalments are due the 15th day of March, June, September, and December. The amount payable for each instalment is calculated under one of the following three methods:

(a) $9,000; $1/4 \times$ estimated tax payable for year 3 ($1/4 \times$ $36,000)

(b) $8,000; $1/4 \times$ tax payable for year 2 ($1/4 \times$ $32,000)

(c) $5,000 for the March and June instalments; $1/4 \times$ tax payable for year 1 ($1/4 \times$ $20,000); and $11,000 for the September and December instalments; $1/2$ ($32,000 − $10,000)

Since method (c) results in Angela paying the least amount of tax in the March and June instalments, this is the method she will choose. The balance of tax owing for year 3 is due April 30, year 4, although her tax return is not due until June 15, year 4.

2. Corporations

Corporations usually do not earn income that is subject to withholding tax. Consequently, instalment payments are the primary method of remitting corporate tax. A corporation must make 12 instalments per year beginning at the end of the first month of the taxation year. Instalments are *not* required if either the current year's estimated tax or the previous year's actual tax is less than $3,000.[56] Unless the current year's taxes will be lower than in the previous year, the monthly instalment is equal to one-twelfth of the previous year's tax liability. Often, the previous year's tax liability is not known when the first and second instalments are due. In such cases, the first two instalments can be based on the total tax paid in the second previous year, and the remaining 10 instalments are adjusted after the tax liability of the previous year is known.[57]

Eligible Canadian-controlled private corporations are allowed to make quarterly instalments on the last day of each quarter. The amount of tax payable for each instalment is calculated using one of the three methods described below:

(a) one-quarter of the corporation's estimated income tax payable for the taxation year;
(b) one-quarter of the corporation's income tax payable for the preceding taxation year;
(c) for the first quarterly (March) instalment, one-quarter of the corporation's income tax payable for the second preceding taxation year and, for the remaining (June, September, and December) quarterly instalments, one-third of the amount, if any, by which the corporation's income tax payable for the preceding taxation year exceeds the first quarterly instalment determined above.[58]

To be eligible to use the quarterly method rather than the monthly method, the Canadian-controlled private corporation must have had a perfect compliance history, claimed the small business deduction for the current or previous taxation year, and (with associated corporations) have taxable income of $500,000 or less and taxable capital employed in Canada of $10,000,000 or less.[59]

If more tax is owing after all of the required instalments have been made, the amount must, for most corporations, be paid within two months of the taxation year end.[60] This period is extended to three months if the corporation is a Canadian-controlled private corporation whose taxable income in the previous year did not exceed the $500,000 annual business limit and if, during the year or the previous year, a small business deduction was claimed.

---

56 ITA 157(2.1).
57 ITA 157(1).
58 ITA 157(1.1)
59 ITA 157(1.2)
60 ITA 157(1)(b), "balance-due day" in ITA 248(1).

A corporate tax instalment calculation is demonstrated in the following situation:

Situation: X Corp is a private corporation earning investment income. For its year ended December 31, year 1 and December 31, year 2, X Corp's tax liability was $24,000 and $30,000, respectively. The tax liability for year 3 is expected to be $36,000.

Analysis: Since the tax liability for year 3 is expected to exceed $3,000 and the tax liability for year 2 exceeded $3,000, X Corp is required to pay monthly tax instalments in year 3. The instalments are due the end of each month. The amount payable for each instalment is calculated under one of the following three methods:

(a) $3,000; $1/12 \times$ estimated tax payable for year 3 ($1/12 \times$ $36,000)

(b) $2,500; $1/12 \times$ tax payable for year 2 ($1/12 \times$ $30,000)

(c) $2,000 for the January and February instalments; $1/12 \times$ tax payable for year 1 ($1/12 \times$ $24,000); and $2,600 for the March through December instalments; $1/10 \times$ ($30,000 − $4,000)

Method (c) will probably be selected by X Corp because it permits lower payments in the earlier months. Typically taxpayers will choose the method that allows the greatest payment deferral and the lowest amount of total instalments. The balance of tax owing for year 3 is due the last day of February, year 4, although the tax return is not due until June 30, year 4.

For both individuals and corporations, the CRA charges interest on any tax that is due and payable but not paid. Interest is also charged on late or deficient tax instalments. The rate of interest is the rate prescribed by the regulations and is adjusted quarterly.[61] The interest charged by the CRA is compounded daily, and so the effective annual rate is higher than the published prescribed rate. The prescribed rate is 4% higher for overdue taxes than for taxable benefits. Such interest costs are not deductible for tax purposes.[62] Worth noting is that the CRA will *pay* interest on overpayments of tax. Interest is paid by the CRA on corporate overpayments at the same prescribed rate as is used to calculate taxable benefits. Interest is paid at 2% higher on non-corporate taxpayers' overpayments. Interest on overpayments is usually calculated from 30 days after April 30th of the following year for individuals and 120 days following the end of the taxation year for corporations.[63] However, for individuals, the refund interest calculation will not start until 30 days after the tax return is filed. The same 30-day rule applies for corporations only if the tax return is filed late.[64] No interest is paid on excess tax instalments.

Summary of Deadline Dates for Payment of Taxes

Entity	Date Balance Due
Corporation ---------------------->	2 months after the taxation year end
Canadian-Controlled Private Corporation --------------->	3 months after the taxation year *if* the corporation's previous year taxable income did not exceed $500,000 and it has claimed the small business deduction in the current or previous taxation year
Individual ----------------------->	April 30 even if the individual can defer the filing date to June 15
Trusts ---------------------------->	90 days after the taxation year

---

61 ITA 161(1), (2); Regulation 4301. For the second quarter of 2011 the prescribed rate on unpaid taxes was 5%.
62 ITA 18(1)(t).
63 For corporations, the rate of interest is equal to the average yield of the three-month government of Canada Treasury Bills sold in the first month of the preceding quarter.
64 ITA 164(3); Regulation 4301.

D. Penalties and Offences

To ensure compliance, the *Income Tax Act* imposes a number of penalties. These penalties are over and above any interest costs on late payments of tax. Some of the more relevant penalties are outlined below.

- **Failure to file an annual return**   5% of the tax unpaid for the year, plus 1% for each full month after the due date, to a maximum of 12 months.[65] This makes the maximum penalty 17% of the unpaid tax at the filing due date.

- **Repeated failures to file an annual return**   10% on a second or further late filing. This relates to returns applicable to the three years after a 5% penalty has been assessed. This 10% penalty is increased by 2% for each month after the due date, for a maximum of 20 months.[66]

- **Failure to report an item of income**   10% of the unreported income *if* the failure to report occurs more than once in a three-year period.[67]

- **Knowingly making a false statement or omission**   50% of the tax owing on the excluded or understated amount.[68]

- **Late or insufficient instalments**   50% of the amount by which the interest assessed on the late or deficient instalments exceeds the greater of $1,000 and 25% of the interest that would be assessed if no instalment was made. The penalty will not apply to small amounts of late or deficient instalments due to the $1,000 threshold.[69]

- **Misrepresentation of a tax matter by a third party**   There are two separate civil penalties for third parties such as tax preparers, advisors, tax shelter promoters, and valuators who cause or assist others to misrepresent their tax owing.[70] Promoters and other third-party representatives are penalized when they make false statements involving schemes that are against the law. Tax preparers can be penalized when they knowingly make false statements on their clients' returns, such as including false deductions or not including all of their clients' income. The penalties are:

- **Tax planner's penalty** ranges from $1,000 up to the fee charged for the planning.
- **Tax return preparer's penalty** ranges from $1,000 up to 50% of the tax avoided. The penalty is capped at $100,000 plus the preparer's fee for the engagement.

   The penalty for participating in a misrepresentation in the preparation of a tax return applies where the preparer knows, or would reasonably be expected to know, but for circumstances amounting to *culpable conduct*, that a statement is false. Culpable conduct is defined in the *Income Tax Act* as conduct, whether an act or a failure to act, that is tantamount to intentional conduct, or shows an indifference as to whether the Act is complied with, or shows a wilful, reckless, or wanton disregard of the law.

   The CRA in IC 01-1 "Third-Party Civil Penalties" provides many examples of the application of the penalty provision and clarifies that advisors and tax return preparers are entitled to rely in good faith on information provided to them by a client that is not obviously incorrect, misleading, or contradictory to other information.

   The total of penalties and interest can be a significant amount. It should be noted that the CRA has the authority to waive or cancel the interest and penalties if the non-compliance resulted from circumstances beyond the taxpayer's control, such as a major illness.

---

65 ITA 162(1).
66 ITA 162(2).
67 ITA 163(1).
68 ITA 163(2).
69 ITA 163.1.
70 ITA 163.2; IC 01-1.

Regarding some of the above activities, a taxpayer may be liable to a fine and/or imprisonment. For example, a taxpayer who fails to file a return as and when required may, upon conviction, be subject to a fine of between $1,000 and $25,000 or to a fine and imprisonment for a term not exceeding 12 months.[71] In addition, a person who has participated in making a false statement or who has destroyed documents to evade the payment of tax, is liable to a fine of between 50% and 200% of the tax that he or she sought to evade or to a fine and imprisonment for a term not exceeding two years.[72]

E. Objection and Appeal

Taxpayers who receive an assessment with which they do not agree have the right to appeal. Such appeals are subject to certain formalities and must conform to certain time limits.

The first step is to request a formal review of the items in dispute. At this review, the taxpayer makes a representation to the CRA. The CRA then confirms or alters the assessment.

To obtain this review, *individuals must file a formal notice of objection within one year of the required tax return filing date of the year in question or within 90 days of the day the notice of assessment was mailed, whichever is later.* All *other taxpayers* must file the objection *within 90 days of the date the assessment was mailed.*[73]

A taxpayer who is not satisfied with the result of this first appeal may make a second appeal, this to the Tax Court of Canada, within 90 days of the day the CRA confirmed its assessment or made its reassessment.[74] A taxpayer who is still not satisfied can then appeal (within time limits) to the Federal Court of Canada and perhaps to the Supreme Court of Canada.

Where a notice of assessment or reassessment is received showing a balance of tax owing, the tax is payable *forthwith*.[75] Where a notice of objection is filed, the CRA is precluded from taking collection action. However, non-deductible interest on the balance will continue to be calculated, compounded daily at the high prescribed rate, so payment of the amount in dispute is usually a good idea. If the taxpayer succeeds, any refund will be paid with taxable interest calculated at a prescribed rate which is 2% lower for individuals and 4% lower for corporations.

V. Income Tax and the GST/HST

In addition to the income tax, Canada has a national goods and services tax (GST). A detailed description of this tax is given in Appendix A at the end of the text. Below is a brief summary of the key elements of the tax and its relation to the income tax.

Except for a few exempt items, the GST is imposed at the rate of 5% on the value of all goods or services sold by registered businesses. The tax is charged to businesses as well as to individual consumers. However, most business entities are entitled to a full rebate of the tax on all goods and services purchased, provided that those goods and services were acquired for business purposes. As a result, the tax applies primarily to individuals as the ultimate consumers. Businesses are generally responsible for collecting and remitting the GST to the government. Businesses that are required to have a GST registration are called registrants. In effect, the GST is a

---

71 ITA 238.
72 ITA 239.
73 ITA 165(1).
74 ITA 169.
75 ITA 158.

sales tax on consumer goods and services. This is demonstrated in the following situation and analysis:

Situation: A wholesale business purchased inventory from a manufacturer for an invoice cost of $1,000. It then sold that inventory to a retail business for $1,500. The retail business increased the price to $2,500 and sold it to a consumer.

Analysis: Both the wholesaler and the retailer will pay GST on their purchases and charge GST on their sales. However, for each business, the net cost will be zero, as follows:

	Product sale price (cost)	GST rate	GST collected (paid/remitted)
The wholesaler:			
Sale price to retailer	$1,500	5%	$ 75
Cost from manufacturer	(1,000)	5%	(50)
Gain	$ 500		25
Remitted to CRA			25
GST cost			–0–
The retailer:			
Sale price to consumer	$2,500	5%	$125
Cost from wholesaler	(1,500)	5%	(75)
Gain	$1,000		50
Remitted to CRA			50
GST cost			–0–

The above demonstrates that although wholesalers and retailers are involved in the GST process (collecting, paying, and remitting tax), they merely act as a conduit, passing the tax on to the ultimate consumer. Note that the wholesaler in this case collected $75 of GST (5% of $1,500) but remitted only $25 to the government. That is because the wholesaler was entitled to claim a GST refund of $50 (5% of $1,000). If costs happen to exceed sales, no tax is remitted, and a business is entitled to a GST refund.

Also, note that in this case, the net amount of tax collected and remitted by the wholesaler ($25) was equal to 5% of the value added to the goods that were sold (5% of $500). The same was true for the retailer.

As was pointed out previously, the 5% GST applies to most goods and services. The tax does not apply to items that are classified as either *zero-rated* or *exempt*.

When a vendor business sells goods or services that are zero-rated, the GST is not collected; however, that business can claim credits for any GST paid on costs associated with those items. Zero-rated goods and services include but are not limited to the following:

- prescription drugs
- basic groceries
- agricultural products
- medical devices
- fishery products
- exported items

Vendors that sell goods and services that are classified as exempt also do not collect GST on those items. However, these vendors cannot claim a credit for any GST paid in relation to those exempt items.

Exempt goods and services (as opposed to zero-rated ones) include the following:

- used housing
- education services
- financial services (domestic)
- health care services
- legal aid services

The above brief outline indicates that, as a general rule, the GST does not create any revenues or expenses for a business entity and has no effect on its income. Consequently, the GST does not have a major impact on income tax. There are, of course, some exceptions to this. For example, businesses that have annual revenues under $30,000 are not required to be GST registrants (though they can elect to do so). Businesses that are not registrants do not collect the GST on their revenues, but neither are they entitled to claim a credit (or refund) for the GST paid on goods and services acquired. In such circumstances, the GST becomes a real cost, and the GST paid on inventory purchases forms part of the inventory cost for income tax purposes and so on. Similarly, many individuals who are not GST registrants earn investment income and incur related costs. When the GST is paid on those costs, it becomes part of those items for income tax purposes.

GST registrants must file a regular GST return. The return is a simple form with requirements to state the total GST collected during the period and deduct the total GST paid. The filing dates vary based on the size of the registered business. A business with $1,500,000 of sales or less files annually (but can file quarterly or monthly if it chooses). Filing quarterly is required if sales are between $1,500,000 and $6,000,000 (monthly filing is optional). Any business with sales over $6,000,000 must file monthly. Also, businesses with sales in excess of $1,500,000 annually must file the monthly returns electronically. Keeping track of the exact amounts of GST collected and paid can be a burden for small businesses. For this reason, businesses with taxable sales of $200,000 or less can use a simplified "quick method" to calculate the amount of tax owing or refund due (the $200,000 is increased to $400,000 for report periods beginning after 2012). The method allows the business to apply a simple formula to the annual revenues and expenses. Certain businesses cannot use this method and the formulas vary depending on the type of business.

There are several other areas where the GST and the income tax system are closely linked. These are referred to throughout the text in the appropriate chapters.

The GST and provincial sales tax harmonization. Most provinces impose a sales tax on certain goods and services. Currently five provinces have chosen to harmonize their provincial sales tax regimes with the federal GST. When this occurs the tax is referred to as the Harmonized Sales Tax or HST. The HST applies in the same manner and to the same base of taxable goods and services as the GST, substantially. In fact, the federal CRA administers the HST on behalf of the participating provinces. Ontario, New Brunswick, and Newfoundland and Labrador participate with an HST of 13% (5% GST plus 8% PST). Nova Scotia uses a rate of 15% and British Columbia 12% until April 1, 2013.[76] Registrants in an HST province can file a single HST return, which reduces the administration costs of managing two separate and unique systems. Prince Edward Island plans to move to HST with a rate of 14%, effective April 1, 2013.[77]

VI. Tax Planning Checklist

This chapter has introduced a number of topics in a very general way. They can be condensed to this short list of tax planning items.

1. When starting a new business or investment venture, consider alternative forms of organization. The structures considered should include the taxable entities

---

76 B.C. returns to 5% GST and 7% PST an April 1, 2013.
77 PEI 2012 Budget.

(individuals, corporations, and trusts) as well as the non-taxable entities (partnerships, limited partnerships, and joint ventures).

2. From time to time, review existing organizational structures and consider making alterations in the context of the changing business environment.

3. When creating an organization, choose the fiscal period carefully in order to optimize timing for the recognition of income or losses.

4. An individual who intends to leave Canada permanently or for an extended period is strongly advised to anticipate the impact of the residence rules—in particular, to identify the relevant dates when his or her status will change. That person should also consider completing certain transactions before or after that date.

5. If capital property has declined in value and a potential capital loss exists, consider when the property should be sold in order to ensure that the capital loss can be offset against any capital gains.

Note that the first two items deal with a transfer of income from one entity to another. The last three deal with shifting income or losses from one time period to another.

VII. Summary and Conclusion

This chapter has covered an extensive number of topics and has discussed all major areas of the Canadian income tax system, except the one involving the actual rate of applicable tax. The following summary will be useful in drawing together the topics covered.

Residents of Canada

1. Taxpayers who are resident in Canada are subject to tax on their world income within each taxation year.

2. There are only three categories of taxpayers—individuals, corporations, and trusts—even though other forms of business organization exist.

3. An individual is considered to be a resident of Canada if he or she maintains a "continuing relationship" with the country. A corporation is resident if it is incorporated in Canada.

4. The taxation year normally includes 12 months. For the individual, it is the calendar year; for the corporation, it is the fiscal year chosen by the corporation.

5. World taxable income is limited to five basic sources: employment income, business income, property income, other income, and capital gains. The aggregate of these five sources of income is the taxpayer's net income for tax purposes.

6. Net income for tax purposes is determined in accordance with a four-step formula that applies identically to both primary taxpayers—the individual and the corporation. The formula establishes that losses incurred from business, employment, and property and allowable business investment losses can be offset against any of the five types of income earned by the entity. However, capital losses can be offset only against other capital gains.

7. Taxable income is established by reducing net income for tax purposes by a limited number of items. Certain of these items apply only to individuals, others only to corporations.

Non-Residents of Canada

Non-resident individuals and corporations are subject to tax in Canada under two circumstances.

1. If the non-resident carries on business in Canada, is temporarily employed in Canada, or disposes of certain Canadian property, the income from only those

particular sources is taxed, in a manner similar to the one faced by Canadian individuals and corporations.

2. Certain income that is paid from a Canadian source is subject to a flat-rate tax, which is withheld by the Canadian payer. Income subject to this tax includes dividends, rents, royalties, interest paid to non–arm's-length parties, and certain management fees paid to non-residents.

The above summary and the preceding comments constitute the full framework of the Canadian income tax system, which is predicated on four basic concepts:

- residency
- individuals and corporations—two separate taxable entities
- taxation year
- net income for tax purposes

Visit the Canadian Income Taxation Web site at **www.mcgrawhill.ca/ olc/buckwold** to view any updated tax information.

An appreciation of these basic concepts by itself provides a significant insight into the tax structure. More importantly, as demonstrated in the brief examples within the chapter, the concepts are tools that can be applied to enhance financial decision making by including the tax impact. In particular, the concepts permit the decision maker to locate the points along the cash-flow path at which the tax factor is relevant. The result is informed decision making leading to the enhancement of cash flow and therefore improved return on investment.

The remainder of Part Two is devoted to expanding the general understanding of the framework developed in Chapter 3. A major portion of this (Chapters 4 through 9) defines and discusses the five types of income included in the formula for determining net income.

Demonstration Questions

QUESTION ONE

John Murphy and his family have lived in Winnipeg for 20 years. John owns 100% of the shares of Teulon Ltd., which operates a successful small manufacturing business. 20X0 is shaping up to be a big year for Murphy and his family, as both the business and the family will undergo the following major changes:

1. Teulon plans to expand its operations internationally. To accomplish this, the company will purchase the shares of a Belgian corporation that is manufacturing products similar to those produced by Teulon. The Belgian corporation will generate good profits; it is anticipated that an annual dividend will be paid to Teulon Ltd.

   In addition, Teulon will begin expanding into the United States, by entering into a 50/50 partnership with an American corporation. The partnership will develop a sales and distribution depot in California to market Teulon's products throughout the United States and Central America.

2. Murphy plans to sell 50% of his shares in Teulon to three senior managers. They will purchase the shares with a small cash payment and will pay the balance to Murphy over the next 10 years, with 8% interest.

3. Murphy has indicated that after he sells 50% of the shares of Teulon, he and his family will move to California on a permanent basis. The move will take place on September 30, 20X0. In the United States, Murphy will work part-time for the new American partnership but will also pursue some other business ventures on his own. He will receive regular payments from Canada on the amount owing from the sale of shares. He also hopes to receive dividends on his remaining shares of Teulon.

Required:
Describe briefly how each of the above activities will be affected by Canadian tax laws.

Solution:

Teulon Ltd. is a *resident* of Canada for tax purposes because it is incorporated in Canada. It is subject to tax on its world income. The Belgian corporation is *not* resident in Canada (not incorporated in Canada) and therefore its profits are not taxed in Canada. Dividends received by Teulon from the Belgian corporation are part of Teulon's *world income* and will be included in net income for tax purposes as *income from property*.

The California partnership constitutes a permanent establishment in the United States, and its profits are subject to tax in that country. The partnership is not a separate taxable entity. Therefore, Teulon's share of its profits must be included in Teulon's world income for Canadian tax purposes. Canadian tax will be reduced by taxes paid in the United States.

Murphy is resident in Canada until he leaves to live in the United States. Therefore, he is taxed in Canada on his world income up to the date of departure. Any gain or loss on the sale of Teulon shares is included as part of this world income as a *capital gain or loss*. After his departure, Murphy will be a non-resident for tax purposes. Dividends paid to Murphy after departure are subject to a withholding tax in Canada. The interest payments are not subject to a withholding tax because John is not related to the persons paying the interest.

QUESTION TWO

Barbara Tomchuk operates a full-time law practice in southern Manitoba. In addition, she owns a 25% interest in a retail store operating as a partnership and has several other sources of income. Her financial information for the taxation year 20X1 is summarized below.

Net income from law practice	$75,000
Taxable capital gains on shares of public corporations	5,000
Withdrawal from a Registered Retirement Savings Plan —*other income*	2,000
Interest income—*(property)*	1,000
Allowable capital loss from the sale of shares of a small business corporation	18,000
Allowable child care expenses	3,000
Allowable capital loss on the sale of bonds	7,000
Share of loss from partnership business — *Business loss*	22,000
Net rental income from a property in the United States — *Property*	13,000
Salary from teaching a college course	4,000
Contribution to a Registered Retirement Savings Plan	8,000

Required:

Calculate Tomchuk's net income for tax purposes for the 20X1 taxation year.

Solution:

(a) Employment income—salary		$ 4,000
Business income—law practice		75,000
Property income:		
Interest	$ 1,000	
Net rental income—United States	13,000	14,000
Other income—withdrawal from RRSP		2,000
		95,000
(b) Taxable capital gains—public corporation shares	5,000	
Allowable capital loss—bonds	(7,000)	–0–
		95,000
(c) Other deductions:		
Child care expenses	3,000	
Contribution to an RRSP	8,000	(11,000)
		84,000
(d) Losses:		
Business loss—partnership	22,000	
Allowable business investment loss—shares of a small business corporation	18,000	(40,000)
Net income for tax purposes		$44,000

QUESTION THREE

In 20X1, George earned employment income of $70,000, interest income from investments of $7,000, and a taxable capital gain of $12,000. In the same year, his wife, Carolyn, earned employment income of $50,000 and $9,000 from her small consulting business that was organized as a proprietorship.

Required:

What are the due dates for George and Carolyn to file their 20X1 income tax returns? At what dates must the final balance of taxes owing for 20X1 be paid?

Solution:

The normal deadline for an individual to file an income tax return would be April 30, 20X2. However, in this situation, because Carolyn has carried on a business in 20X1, both she and her husband, George, are entitled to extend their due date to June 15, 20X2. Note that George is granted the extension even though he has not carried on a business. Presumably, the reason for this is that each spouse must be aware of each other's income in order to best claim certain tax credits (discussed in Chapter 10). However, although the deadline for filing the tax returns is extended to June 15, 20X2, the deadline for paying the taxes due remains at April 30, 20X2 for each of them. Therefore, to avoid excessive interest charges on late payments, it is necessary for each spouse to estimate the taxes due and remit that amount by April 30. Of course, they can choose to file the returns on April 30, 20X2 to make certain that no further interest will be charged on the balance due.

QUESTION FOUR

TPP Inc. is a Canadian-controlled private corporation earning active business income. For its year ended May 31, 20X1, TPP reported taxable income of $280,000 and claimed the small deduction to obtain a lower rate of tax. The company filed a 20X1 tax return on February 1, 20X2 and paid the balance of tax owing at that time, which amounted to $42,000. This represents the entire tax payable for the year as no instalments had been made, nor were they required based on previous year's incomes. In June 20X2, TPP received a Notice of Assessment (notice dated June 15, 20X2) from the Canada Revenue Agency (CRA) indicating that income for the corporation for the year ending May 31, 20X1 had been assessed at $20,000 higher than reported and additional tax of $3,000 was due immediately. In addition, TPP was charged a penalty for failing to file a tax return on time plus interest on the taxes unpaid.

Required:

1. At what date was TPP required to file its tax return?

2. At what date was the balance of tax due to be paid?

3. Calculate the penalty that CRA would have charged in the assessment notice.

4. Explain how any interest charged would be calculated.

5. If TPP disagrees with the assessment, explain the formal procedure required to object to all or some of the items in the assessment.

Solution:

1. All corporations must file a tax return within six (6) months of their taxation year end. Therefore, TPP was required to file its return by November 30, 20X1.

2. Generally, corporations must pay the balance of tax owing within two (2) months from the corporation's taxation year end. However, TPP is a Canadian-controlled private corporation that claimed the small business deduction in the current or previous taxation year and did not earn sufficient income to pay tax at the higher corporate rate. Therefore, it is entitled to pay the balance of its tax owing within three (3) months from its taxation year end being August 31, 20X1 in this case.

3. The penalty for failing to file a return is 5% of the unpaid tax plus an additional 1% for each *full month* after the due date to a maximum of 12 months. For TPP, the return was

late for two (2) full months after November 30, 20X1, so the penalty is 7% (5% + 2%) of the unpaid taxes of $45,000 ($42,000 + $3,000) or $3,150.

4. The interest will be calculated at a prescribed rate on a daily basis from the due date of August 31, 20X1 to the date of assessment (June 15, 20X2). The interest expense is not deductible for tax purposes.

5. To object to the assessment, TPP must file, in writing, a Notice of Objection within 90 days from the date of the Notice of Assessment. In this case, the deadline is September 13, 20X2, which is 90 days from June 15, 20X2 (the date on the assessment notice). One should note that the deadline for an individual is slightly different—it is 90 days from the Notice of Assessment date or one year from the filing deadline of the taxation year (April 30 or June 15), whichever is later.

Review Questions

1. Which of the following entities are subject to income tax?
   (a) proprietorship
   (b) individual
   (c) joint venture
   (d) trust
   (e) limited partnership
   (f) corporation
   (g) partnership

2. Describe how the income earned by any of the non-taxable entities listed above is included in the Canadian tax system.

3. How and when does income earned by a corporation affect the tax position of an individual who is a shareholder?

4. In describing who is liable for tax in Canada, the *Income Tax Act* simply states, "An income tax shall be paid, as required by this Act, on the taxable income for each taxation year of every person resident in Canada at any time in the year." Accepting that "person" includes both an individual and a corporation, briefly discuss the meaning and ramifications of this statement.

5. In what circumstances are non-residents subject to Canadian income tax?

6. Can a Canadian resident be subject to tax in Canada as well as in a foreign country on the same earned income? If yes, explain how. Also, what mechanism is available to minimize double taxation?

7. Explain the difference between *net income for tax purposes* and *taxable income* for the taxable entities.

8. Explain what is meant by the statutory scheme, and describe the scheme's relevance to the Canadian income tax system.

9. For tax purposes, would you prefer that a financial loss be a capital loss or a business loss? Explain.

10. Explain the difference between *income from property and a gain on the sale of capital property*.

11. One often hears that "corporations are entitled to more deductions for tax purposes than individuals." Based on your reading of Chapter 3, is this statement true? Explain.

12. If an individual earns a living as a lawyer, what possible categories of income, for tax purposes, may he or she generate? Describe the circumstances for each possible classification.

13. What types of income for tax purposes may result when a profit is achieved on the sale of property (e.g., land)?

14. Individual A, a Canadian resident, owns and operates a profitable small farm in North Dakota, U.S.A. He also has a large amount of money earning interest in an American bank. Individual B, also a Canadian resident, owns 100% of the shares of an American corporation that operates a profitable small farm in North Dakota. The corporation also has a large amount of money earning interest in an American bank.

    Describe and compare the tax positions of these two individuals who conduct the same activities but use different organizational structures.

15. Jane Q owned an apple orchard for 20 years. During that time, she had cultivated a unique brand of apple that was popular with health food fans. Toward the end of the 20X0 growing season, Q became seriously ill and put the orchard up for sale. Q's neighbour agreed to purchase the entire orchard for $250,000. It upset Q to have to sell at that time of year because that year's crop was of high quality and in three weeks would have been ripe for picking.

    What types of property might have been included in the total purchase price of $250,000? For tax purposes, what types of income might have been generated from the sale of the orchard? Explain your answer.

Key Concept Questions

QUESTION ONE

Determine the Canadian residency status for the current year for each of the following taxpayers. *Income tax reference: ITA 250(1), (4); IT-221R3.*

a) Paula was born and lived her life to date in Canada. On November 1st of the current year she left Canada permanently.

b) Al spent the current year in Belgium on temporary work assignment. His family and friends are looking forward to his return to Canada in June of next year.

c) Kimberley lives in Ireland. In the current year she was in Canada throughout the months of February through May and again throughout the months August through October caring for her sick friend.

d) 102864 Limited was incorporated in Canada five years ago. The corporation has always carried on business exclusively in Bermuda since incorporation.

e) Navy Ltd. was incorporated in the United States. In the current year Navy Ltd. carried on business in Canada as well as in the United States.

QUESTION TWO

Bill is *not* a resident of Canada. For the current year Bill has worldwide income of $120,000, including $15,000 of employment income earned in Canada and $2,000 of interest received on Canada savings bonds. The remainder of his income was from sources outside of Canada. *Income tax reference: ITA 2(3).*

What amount of income must be reported on Bill's Canadian personal income tax return for the current year?

QUESTION THREE

A Ltd. is resident in Canada for tax purposes. In the current year A Ltd. earned interest income of $4,000 in Canada, $6,000 in England, and $8,000 in Bermuda. *Income tax reference: ITA 2(1), 3(a).*

What amount of interest income must be reported on A Ltd.'s Canadian corporate income tax return for the current year?

QUESTION FOUR

The Canadian income tax system includes five specific categories of income. Identify the income category to which each of the following pertains:

1. Interest earned on a bond investment. *property*
2. Pension income. *other*
3. Consulting fees. *business*
4. Profit on the sale of shares of a public corporation. The shares were acquired as a long-term investment. *capital gain*
5. Wages from employment services. *employment*
6. Share of profits from a partnership that operates a restaurant. *business*
7. Dividends from the shares of a corporation that carries on a retail business. *property*
8. Tips from customers of an employer's business. *employment*
9. Rents from tenants of a commercial building. *property*
10. Fees for providing piano lessons to several students. *business*
11. Profit on the sale of land that was used by the owner for farming. *capital gains*
12. Profit on the sale of a summer cottage that was used by the owner for personal enjoyment. *capital gains*
13. Profit on the sale of land that was purchased for resale. *business* *(inventory)*

QUESTION FIVE

	Taxpayer A	Taxpayer B	Taxpayer C
Employment income			$30,000
Business income (loss)		$(20,000)	
Property income (loss)	$ (1,000)		
Pension income	40,000		
Capital gain (loss)		50,000	(6,000)

Calculate net income for tax purposes for each of the three taxpayers. *Income tax reference: ITA 3.*

QUESTION SIX

Maureen, a resident of Canada, has the following sources of income and losses for tax purposes for the current year.

• Employment income	$60,000
• Business X profit	3,000
• Business Y loss	7,000
• Interest income	2,000
• Taxable capital gain on sale of land	18,000
• Allowable capital loss on sale of securities	20,000
• Allowable business investment loss	5,000

Calculate Maureen's net income for tax purposes for the current year in accordance with section 3 of the *Income Tax Act*.

QUESTION SEVEN

What is the filing due date for each of the following income tax returns? *Income tax reference: ITA 150(1)(a), (b), (d).*

a) A corporation for its year ending November 30, 20X6.

b) An individual for the year 20X6. The individual carried on business in 20X6.

c) An unmarried individual living alone for the year 20X6. The individual did not carry on a business.

d) An individual for the year 20X6. The individual died on February 21, 20X7.

QUESTION EIGHT

For each of the following individuals, determine when their income tax return for the current year is due and when any balance of tax owing is due. *Income tax reference: ITA 150(1), 156.1(4), 248(1) balance-due day.*

a) Bob is a bachelor. He has two sources of income, employment income and interest income.

b) Mary is a self-employed lawyer. Her law practice has a December 31 year end.

c) Ron's only source of income is employment income. Ron is married to Mary. See (b) above.

d) Zeta is married to Leo. Their only source of income is pension income. Zeta died on November 20th of the current year.

e) Sarah died on March 12th of the current year without having filed her tax return for the prior year.

QUESTION NINE

When is the balance of tax due for each of the following entities? *Income tax reference: ITA 156.1(4), 157(1)(b).*

a) A public corporation, resident in Canada.

b) A Canadian-controlled private corporation, with taxable income less than $400,000, and claiming the small business deduction.

c) An individual who carried on business in the year.

d) An individual where no business is carried on by the individual or the spouse.

QUESTION TEN

For each of the following corporations, determine when the income tax return for the current year is due and when any balance of tax owing is due. *Income tax reference: ITA 150(1), 157(1)(b), 248(1) balance-due day.*

A Ltd. is a public corporation with a May 30 year end.

B Ltd. is a private corporation with an October 31 year end. All of B's income is taxed at the high corporate rate.

C Ltd. is a Canadian-controlled private corporation with an October 31 year end. Last year all of C's income was subject to the low rate of tax from claiming the small business deduction.

D Ltd. is a Canadian-controlled private corporation with a May 30 year end. Last year D had taxable income of $550,000. D claimed the small business deduction this year as well as last year.

QUESTION ELEVEN

A taxpayer's tax liability was $1,000 for 20X1, $12,000 for 20X2, and is expected to be $36,000 for 20X3. *Income tax reference: ITA 156(1), 156.1(1), (2), 157(1), (2.1), 157(1.1), (1.2).*

Is the taxpayer required to make tax instalments for 20X3 and if so, what are the amounts and the due dates for each instalment?

QUESTION TWELVE

The mailing date on the notice of reassessment for the taxpayer's 20X2 tax return was July 10, 20X7. The mailing date on the original notice of assessment for the taxpayer's 20X2 tax return was June 20, 20X3. *Income tax reference: ITA 152(3.1), 165(1).*

a) Does the CRA have the right to reassess the 20X2 tax return on July 10, 20X7?

b) If the taxpayer wishes to dispute the reassessment, by what date must the notice of objection be filed?

QUESTION THIRTEEN

Tooblue Ltd., a Canadian-controlled private corporation, filed its tax return for its year ended December 31, 20X6 on June 30, 20X7. The Notice of Assessment was received August 31, 20X7. The mailing date on the Notice of Assessment was August 28, 20X7.

1. Assuming there were no misrepresentations and that a waiver was not filed, how long does the CRA have to issue a reassessment for Tooblue Ltd.'s 20X6 taxation year? *Income tax reference: ITA 152(3.1).*

2. If Tooblue Ltd. wishes to object to the original Notice of Assessment for the 20X6 taxation year, by what date must the Notice of Objection be filed? *Income tax reference: ITA 165(1).*

QUESTION FOURTEEN

Successful Ltd. is a Canadian company with a December 31 year end. The federal income tax return for last year was filed with the CRA on September 30th of this year. The balance of tax owing, $10,000, was paid at the bank on September 30th as well. *Income tax reference: ITA 162(1).*

Calculate the late-filing penalty for Successful Ltd.

QUESTION FIFTEEN

Dee Ltd. is a Canadian company carrying on a clothing wholesale business. For the first quarter of the current year, its financial results were as follows:

Revenue:	Sales within Canada	$200,000
	Exports	30,000
Expenses:	Inventory purchased	50,000
	Salaries & wages	40,000
	Rent	10,000

1. Assuming Dee Ltd. is a GST registrant, calculate the GST to be remitted to the CRA for the first quarter of the year.

2. Assuming Dee Ltd. is an HST registrant, calculate the HST to be remitted to the CRA for the first quarter of the year. Assume an HST rate of 13%.

Problems

PROBLEM ONE

John Day and Carol Knight conduct similar financial activities. Each is employed and has a portfolio of investments, and during the current year, each started a separate small business. Their financial results for the year ended December 31, 20X1, are identical, as follows:

Employment income	$40,000
Interest income from investment portfolio	15,000
Loss from new small business operation	(20,000)

The only difference between Day and Knight is that Day operated his business as a proprietorship, whereas Knight operated her business from a wholly owned corporation.

Required:

1. Assuming that individual tax rates are 40%, compare the tax liability of Day with that of Knight for 20X1.

2. How and when may Knight utilize her business loss to reduce her tax liability?

3. What impact may the difference in tax treatment have on Day's and Knight's wealth accumulation and on their long-term returns on investment?

PROBLEM TWO

To what extent, if any, are the following individuals or corporations liable for tax in Canada?

1. An individual who lives and works in Canada received an inheritance from an uncle in France. The inheritance consists of shares, bonds, and French real estate. During the year, the investments generated interest, dividends, and rents, which were retained in France and reinvested.

2. A large corporation based in Alabama operates a branch in Winnipeg that employs Canadian staff, holds a supply of inventory, and sells to the Canadian market.

3. An American citizen who normally resides in New York and has extensive American income, for health reasons takes an extended vacation of six-and-a-half months in Banff, Alberta in the current calendar year.

4. A Manitoba corporation is controlled and managed by its British parent corporation.

5. A Canadian individual, who is a student at the University of Saskatchewan, earns income during the summer by operating a street-vending unit in Boulder, Colorado.

6. An individual has been employed in Canada by a large Canadian corporation. He accepts a transfer to manage, on a permanent basis, the corporation's operations in Denver, Colorado. He leaves Canada with his family on March 31, 20X0.

7. An individual who resides in England receives annual dividend income from an investment in a Canadian corporation.

PROBLEM THREE

Read the Tax Court of Canada case *Min Shan Shih v the Queen* (2000), DTC 2072 and explain in your own words the reason for the decision in the case.

PROBLEM FOUR

Indicate the category of income under the *Income Tax Act* into which each of the following items falls:

1. Annual stipend received by an individual for serving as a director of a public corporation.

2. Receipt of alimony (spousal support) payments.

3. Receipts from an employer's registered pension plan.

4. Dividends received from a foreign corporation.

5. Proceeds from the sale of land acquired for resale.

6. Loss from a loan to a small business corporation.

7. Moving expenses.

8. Gain from the sale of shares of a public corporation.

9. Fees received for providing legal services.

10. Alimony (spousal support) paid.

11. Gain on the sale of an automobile purchased for resale.

12. Bonus from an employer.

PROBLEM FIVE

A taxpayer has the following financial results for a particular year:

Business profit—A Enterprise	$10,000
Business loss—B Enterprise	3,000
Other sources of income—pension	12,000
Property income—interest	5,000
Allowable capital losses on sale of land	20,000
Allowable business investment loss	2,000
Taxable capital gains on sale of securities	15,000
Other deductions—alimony payments (spousal support)	3,000
Employment income	30,000

Required:
Determine the taxpayer's net income for tax purposes in accordance with the statutory scheme formula.

PROBLEM SIX

Meadows Enterprises Ltd. is a Canadian corporation located in Regina. The company operates a retail business that has shown consistent profits for several years. Cash generated from those profits has been used to acquire investments. The company prefers two types of investments: real estate and shares in other corporations. Unfortunately, in 20X1 the investments resulted in some losses.

A summary of the corporation's 20X1 financial results is given below.

Retail sales		$1,240,000
Cost of sales		868,000
Gross profit		372,000
Retail administrative expenses		191,000
Income from operations		181,000
Other income (losses)		
Net loss from real estate rentals	$ (22,000)	
Net loss on the sale of shares of other corporations	(170,000)	(192,000)
Net loss for the year		$ (11,000)

The real estate investments include several small commercial buildings that are rented to retail tenants. In 20X1, one of those tenants ceased operations, and a replacement tenant could not be found until the current year. That is the main reason for the $22,000 loss in real estate rentals.

The net loss of $170,000 on shares of other corporations arose from two sale transactions in 20X1, which are summarized below.

	Sale 1	Sale 2
Selling price	$72,000	$ 10,000
Original cost of shares	65,000	187,000
Gain (loss)	$ 7,000	$(177,000)

Both investments, which were in public corporations, had been owned for several years.

An accountant has just completed Meadows 20X1 tax return and has informed the president that Meadows owes $23,850 in income taxes for 20X1. The president is upset by this and exclaims, "That's impossible! Our company lost $11,000 last year, so it can't owe $23,850 in income taxes! I know that the corporate tax rate for my company is 15%, and 15% of nothing is nothing."

Required:
Briefly explain why the company owes $23,850 in income tax for 20X1. Show your calculations.

Cases

CASE ONE   Bendana Corporation

Bendana Corporation is a Canadian company that specializes in the construction of sports facilities. Although its head office is in Edmonton, final approval of all major construction projects is given by the executive officers of Bendana's parent company, Holdings Limited.

Holdings Limited is incorporated in the United Kingdom, and all of its shares are owned by British residents. Holdings owns 100% of Bendana's shares.

The president of Bendana has called for a meeting next week to discuss the company's expansion to the United States. The executives are considering two basic options for the American organization. One is to open an administrative office in Chicago. The office would bid on all American contracts and service those contracts by hiring American staff and leasing all equipment from American companies. Alternatively, Bendana has an opportunity to acquire the shares of a small construction company that already has an experienced staff and good basic equipment. The president is hopeful that the meeting will settle the issue so that a plan of action can be set in motion.

Whichever option is chosen, Carl Peters, a senior vice-president, will move to Chicago to head the American operation. Peters intends to leave Edmonton in October 20X0 and rent an apartment in Chicago. His wife and two children will follow in late December when the school break begins. A third child, Carla, will remain in Edmonton to complete her remaining two years at university. Carla will reside at their house near the university until she graduates, at which time the house will be put up for sale. The house is owned by Mrs. Peters. Carla intends to have two boarders staying at the house, who will pay rent monthly to Mrs. Peters.

Peters holds 10% of the shares of a Canadian private corporation. The majority shareholder of that corporation is his brother Jason. The company pays regular quarterly dividends. Peters has agreed to sell the shares to Jason early in 20X1. The sale will result in a small profit for Peter. Jason will pay 40% of the purchase price in cash and the balance over two years, with interest at 7%.

Bendana has recently been awarded a contract to build a soccer stadium in Regina. The company has asked the British parent company to send its soccer field expert to Regina to consult on the project. Feiffer Thompson will arrive in Regina on November 1, 20X0, and remain there until August 20X1, by which time the project will be substantially finished. She will be paid a salary by Bendana while she is in Canada. Feiffer's husband will remain in the United Kingdom to manage her large investment portfolio, which was left to her by her late father, the Earl of Feiffdom.

Sally Watkins, Bendana's financial expert, works out of the company's Toronto office. Watkins left last month for the Sudan, where she will arrange the financing for a large project of the Sudanese government. Basically, Watkins is on loan to that government. She is excited about taking a break from her normal duties and pleased to hear that the Sudan does not levy any income tax. She has kept her apartment in Toronto, as she plans to be away only until November 20X1. While she is away, her sister will occupy her apartment.

Required:

Describe briefly how each of the above activities will be affected by Canadian tax laws.

CASE TWO   Greg and GK Ltd.

Greg is the sole shareholder of GK Ltd., a Canadian-controlled private corporation carrying on an active business, with a December 31 fiscal year end. Greg met with you on January 6, 20X6 (the current year) about a number of issues.

On August 1, 20X5, Greg received a demand to file a tax return for the 20X3 taxation year. Greg did not file a tax return for 20X3, because salary from GK Ltd. was his only income for the year. The payroll clerk at GK Ltd. was careful to ensure that the correct amount of tax was withheld from Greg's pay and remitted to the CRA monthly. Thus, Greg is looking for confirmation that he is not required to file a tax return for 20X3.

In 20X4, Greg won $500,000 in a lottery which he invested wisely. Because of the investment income, he prepared a tax return for 20X4. He personally delivered the tax return, together with a cheque in the amount of $9,200 for the balance of tax owing, to the CRA on September 30, 20X5. According to Greg's calculations, he will owe $12,000 in tax on his investment income earned in 20X5, so he plans to file his 20X5 tax return on time. He did not make any tax instalments in 20X5, as he did not receive an instalment notice from the CRA. Greg wonders whether he should make instalments for 20X6. He estimates that the tax on his 20X6 investment income will be $16,000.

GK Ltd.'s total federal tax liability was $18,000 in each of 20X3 and 20X4. It increased to $26,200 for 20X5. GK Ltd. made monthly federal tax instalments of $1,500 on the last day of each month in 20X5. Greg wants to ensure that the corporate tax return for 20X5 is filed on time and that all taxes owing are paid by the due date so as to avoid paying interest.

GK Ltd. received a notice of reassessment for the 20X1 taxation year, dated December 6, 20X5, stating that the corporation was assessed additional tax for the 20X1 year in the amount of $42,000. Greg is convinced that the reassessment is in error. Greg has the original notice of assessment for 20X1, dated February 21, 20X3, which indicated that the return was assessed as filed.

Greg is married and has three children. His wife is a self-employed computer consultant.

Required:

Prepare a memo to Greg providing advice on the issues. Assume the prescribed rates of interest under Reg. 4301 for computing taxable benefits are 3% for the first, third, and fourth quarters, and 2% for the second quarter of 20X5.

Income from Employment

Income from employment is the largest single source of Canadian income tax revenue and applies to the largest number of taxpayers. From a business perspective, employee compensation constitutes a significant portion—in many cases, the largest portion—of any enterprise's overall annual expenses. The taxation of income earned from employment is, therefore, a concern to the employer as well as to the employee.

A review of the management and taxation issues surrounding employee compensation is made at the end of this chapter. The major part of this chapter develops a general framework for determining income from employment activities—in other words, it expands on the general formula for calculating net income for tax purposes as outlined in Chapter 3. Specifically, this chapter covers the following areas relating to employment income:

1. The scope of employment activities and the general rules for income determination.

2. The tax treatment of salaries, wages, employee benefits, and allowances.

3. The scope and limitations of deductions permitted in arriving at net income from employment.

4. A sample calculation of employment income.

5. Planning employee compensation.

I. Scope and Structure of Employment Income

A. Definition of "Employed"

An individual's income from providing service can be regarded as income from employment only if that individual is considered to be *employed* by another party. The definition of *employed* is not specifically established within the *Income Tax Act* and therefore rests on common-law decisions. Normally, people are considered employed when they agree to provide their services, at the full direction and control of the employer, in return for a specific salary or wage. Implicit in this relationship is the employer's right to decide when, where, how, and what work is to be done. In the vast majority of cases, this relationship can be readily identified.

In some cases, an individual may provide services to another party as an independent contractor. When service is provided in this manner, the individual is not subject to the same direction and control described above and is paid in the form of a fee for the specifically contracted activities. In such cases, the individual is considered to be self-employed, rather than employed, and earning business income, rather than employment income. This distinction is important, as the rules for determining income for tax purposes differ considerably when an individual is giving service as an employee, rather than as an independent businessperson.

When it is not clear whether a person is employed or self-employed as an independent contractor, the courts consider four test factors that are used as guidelines.[1]

• **Control test**   Who determines what is done, where, when, and how? A principal tells a self-employed agent what to do; an employer has the right not only to tell an employee what to do but also how to do it.[2]

• **Ownership of tools test**   A self-employed contractor normally supplies the tools required to do a job; an employer normally provides the tools to an employee.

---

1   671122 Ontario Ltd. v. Sagaz Industries Canada Inc. (2001) 2 S.C.R. 983.
2   Wolf v. The Queen, 2002 FCA96.

- **Chance of profit or loss test** A self-employed contractor normally has a chance to earn a profit on a job and also bears the risk of realizing a loss on the job. Usually, an employer assumes all the risk of profit or loss on a particular job, and the employee normally earns a wage or salary no matter what happens on the job.

- **Integration test** How integral to the business is the worker? A worker who is part of the business, or whose work is an integral part of the business, is probably an employee. If, however, the worker is an accessory to the business, he or she is probably a self-employed contractor. Evidence of the worker receiving the economic rights, privileges, and benefits normally enjoyed by employees would be facts supporting employment status. Benefits normally enjoyed by employees include paid vacation and statutory holidays and access to existing employee benefit plans. Evidence of the worker having other clients (or the ability to have other clients) would support self-employed status.[3]

In many cases, these tests will provide conflicting indicators. When that occurs, all four tests are considered and weighed against each other. In addition, the courts have recently given importance to what is referred to as "the common understanding of the relationship," even if the evidence cannot be deemed conclusive.[4] This highlights the importance of a written contract that clearly sets out the intentions of the parties involved.

It is important to recognize that it is not the *nature* of the service that determines whether or not one is employed; instead, it is the *relationship* that exists between the individual providing the service and the entity receiving the service.

When attempting to establish whether a service is supplied by an employee or an independent contractor, consider which party (the payer or the person providing the service) is responsible for or decides on the following:[5]

- Planning the work to be done.
- Time frame for completion of the work.
- How the work is to be done.
- Hours of work.
- Location of the work.
- Assignment of specific tasks.
- Standards of quality.
- Training.
- Providing and maintaining tools and equipment and their related costs.
- Liability insurance.
- Performance of work.
- Guarantee of quality.
- Costs of worker's benefits, such as vacation pay, health insurance, life insurance premiums, and so on.

If the payer is responsible for or decided on most of the above items, an employer–employee relationship may exist.

B. Employment Income— Fundamental Rules and Basic Formula

Compensation for employment services can take several forms. In addition, some employees are required to incur non-reimbursable expenses as part of the earning process. Four fundamental rules exist that set the general framework of employment income. These rules determine what items are included in employment income, when such items are included for tax purposes, and what items may be deducted against that income. These four fundamental rules are stated below.

---

3 Dynamic Industries v. The Queen, 2005 FCA211.
4 Royal Winnipeg Ballet v. MNR, 2006 DTC 6323 (F.C.A.).
5 CRA RC4110(E) 1219.

1. All remuneration from an office or employment, including salary, wages, commissions, and gratuities, is included as employment income at the point in time that it is *received* by the employee—not necessarily when it is earned.[6]

2. Subject to specific exceptions, *all benefits* received or enjoyed by employees by virtue of their employment are taxable as employment income.[7]

3. Subject to specific exceptions, all amounts received as an *allowance* for personal living expenses or for any other purpose are included in employment income for tax purposes.[8]

4. Except for a specific, limited list of items, *no deductions* are permitted in arriving at net income from employment.[9]

Essentially, the four rules indicate that an employee must include all forms of remuneration in income, must do so on a cash basis (that is, when received), and is not permitted to deduct expenses incurred. However, as the last three rules indicate, there are a limited number of exceptions, which are the focus of tax planning for compensation programs.

The formula for arriving at net income from employment for tax purposes can be expressed simply as

$$\text{Employment income} = (A + B + C) - D$$

Where:

A = the salary, wages, commissions, gratuities, and other forms of remuneration received
B = the sum of the benefits received or enjoyed
C = the sum of the allowances received
D = deductions that are specifically permitted as exceptions to the general rule

The aggregate of this formula is the net income from employment (income minus deductions), which is included in the overall formula for determining a taxpayer's total net income (see Chapter 3).

Each of the fundamental rules of employment income is reviewed below, together with its major exceptions.

II. Cash Basis

A. Scope

The first fundamental rule for determining employment income concerns the inclusion of the formal compensation arrangements, such as salary, wages, commissions, gratuities, bonuses[10] (including bonuses for past performance and signing bonuses),[11] honoraria, and director's fees.[12] This rule is very broad and requires that all items of remuneration earned as a result of a position as an employee or an officer be included. It further requires that an employee include amounts in income for tax purposes in the year they are *received*, which is not necessarily the year they are *earned*. For example, a salary received in January for work carried out in December of the previous calendar year is included in income for tax purposes in the calendar year of receipt.

B. Salary Deferrals

Any gap between the time that employment income is earned and the time that it is received can influence both the rate of tax payable and the pre-tax value of the remuneration. Consider the situation where an employer awards an employee a $10,000

---

6   ITA 5(1).
7   ITA 6(1)(a).
8   ITA 6(1)(b).
9   ITA 8(2).
10 ITA 5(1).
11 ITA 6(3); IT-196R2.
12 ITA 6(1)(c); IT-377R (archived).

bonus for work carried out in 20X1 but does not make the payment until six months later, on June 30, 20X2. Because the employer must withhold and remit tax for the employee when the bonus is paid, that tax payment is also deferred to June 30, 20X2. Whether this deferral is to the advantage of the employee depends on

(a) the rate of tax applicable to the employee in 20X2 compared with 20X1; and
(b) whether or not interest is to be paid on the deferred payment.

Both the time value of money and the rate of tax must be considered if one is to properly assess the benefit (if any) of deferring employee remuneration. For example, if the above bonus were paid at the end of 20X1 and taxed at a rate of 45% and if the balance were then invested at 10% for six months to June 30, 20X2, it would accumulate to $5,651, calculated as follows:

Bonus—end of 20X1	$10,000
Less tax @ 45%	(4,500)
Amount invested	5,500
Add interest @ 10% on $5,500 for six months	
minus tax on the interest	151
Value at June 30, 20X2	$ 5,651

On the other hand, if payment of the bonus were delayed to June 30, 20X2 and taxed at a rate of 45% and if the employer then paid 10% interest on the deferred amount, the individual would have $5,775 at June 30, 20X2, calculated as follows:

Interest @ 10% on $10,000 for six months	$500
Bonus received on June 30, 20X2	10,000
	10,500
Tax @ 45% on the bonus and interest	(4,725)
Value at June 30, 20X2	$ 5,775

In the above example, delaying the payment enhanced the value of the bonus because interest was earned on the pre-tax value of the bonus, rather than on its after-tax value. The outcome of the deferred bonus would be different if the individual's 20X2 tax rate were higher or lower than the 20X1 tax rate. It should be noted that it is not common for an employer to pay interest on a deferred bonus. If no interest is paid, a remuneration delay may be beneficial to the employee only if the future tax rate will decline.

The deferral of remuneration has advantages to the employer as well. The employer's income, which is reviewed in Chapter 5, is calculated on an accrual basis, rather than on a cash basis. This means that the employer can deduct employment expenses when they are incurred, rather than when they are paid. In the previous example, a bonus payment applicable to 20X1, though deferred to June 30, 20X2, would still be deductible as an expense against the employer's 20X1 income. This would enhance the employer's cash flow by reducing its 20X1 income taxes.

Significant abuses of salary deferral programs have led to the development of two anti-avoidance rules that limit the extent to which employers and employees can defer employment benefits. If an employer wishes to deduct deferred compensation on an accrual basis, that compensation must be paid (and therefore included in the employee's income) within 180 days of the fiscal year end in which the expense was incurred. If the payment is delayed beyond 180 days from year end, the employer must delay the deduction of the remuneration until the year in which it is paid.[13] This, of course, makes the employer less interested in using deferred payments. In addition, when an employer and an employee enter into an arrangement, the main purpose of which is to defer the receipt of remuneration that would otherwise have been paid, the employee is deemed to have received it in the year that it was earned.[14]

III. Employee Benefits

Employers often provide indirect forms of compensation to their employees, as well as direct ones. Such indirect forms of compensation are commonly referred to as "fringe benefits"; they include such items as employee pension plans, insurance programs, stock options, and automobile benefits. For employees, the tax treatment of such programs varies considerably: some fringe benefits are taxable in the year in which they are received or enjoyed; others are taxable at some future time or are not taxable at all. Most forms of compensation are, however, deductible for the employer. Because the tax treatment varies for these indirect compensation programs, it is essential that compensation decisions be made that maximize the after-tax cash flow to the employee and minimize the after-tax cost to the employer (see Part VIII of this chapter).

A. Taxable Benefits

The second general rule for determining income from employment states that the value of all benefits of any kind whatsoever (subject to specific exceptions), if received or enjoyed in respect of, in the course of, or by virtue of an office or employment, must be included in the taxpayer's income.[15] This means that such benefits as the personal use of an employer's car, the receipt of a substantial gift for a birthday or anniversary, the winning of a prize such as a paid vacation for special efforts, and the free use of an employer's vacation home are all benefits received by virtue of one's employment and therefore taxable. Even when certain benefits are provided by parties other than the employer—for example, when supplier A of employer B provides prizes for B's employees if A's product is used or sold in certain quantities—a taxable benefit from employment exists. The scope of the general rule is extremely broad. A reasonable starting point is to assume that all benefits are taxable unless a search of the limited list of specific exceptions discloses that the benefit is not taxable.

The CRA's Interpretation Bulletin IT-470R as well as T-4130, *Employer's Guide—Taxable Benefits* review the topic of employee fringe benefits. The following typical benefits are taxable and are discussed in the bulletin:

- Board and lodging provided to employees free or at a reduced price, except at a remote location (IT-91R4).
- Rent-free and low-rent housing.
- Personal use of the employer's motor vehicle (discussed below).
- Gifts from the employer to the employee that are in cash or near cash, including wedding and Christmas gifts. However, *non-cash gifts and non-cash awards* with a total value to the employee not exceeding $500 can be excluded from the employee's income annually.[16] In addition, a further tax-free amount is available for non-cash long service/anniversary awards that do not exceed $500 provided the award is for a minimum of five years of service and such an award has

---

13 ITA 78(4); IT-109R2.
14 ITA 6(11), 248(1).
15 ITA 6(1)(a).
16 Income Tax Technical News #40, CRA.

not been issued within the previous five years. This long service/anniversary award policy is separate from the policy on other non-cash gifts and awards described above. Both gift and award policies apply only when made to arm's-length employees, and a gift has to be for a special occasion such as a religious holiday, a birthday, a wedding, or the birth of a child. An award has to be for an employment-related accomplishment such as long or outstanding service, employees' suggestions, or meeting or exceeding safety standards. An award given to an employee for performance-related reasons is considered a "reward" and is a taxable benefit.[17] Items that are of "an immaterial or nominal value" (for example—coffee, tea, T-shirts with logo, mugs, plaques, and trophies) are not taxable. If the total value of non-cash gifts and non-cash awards exceeds $500, the excess will be taxable to the employee. The same is true for a long service/anniversary award.

- Group term life insurance policies.
- Holiday trips and other prizes and *incentive* awards, including benefits for trips not associated with business and the use of vacation properties.
- Travelling expenses of an employee's spouse if no business reason for spouse's presence.
- Premiums under provincial hospitalization and medical care insurance plans.
- Reimbursement from the employer for the cost of tools required to perform duties of employment.
- Interest-free and low-interest loans (discussed below) (IT-421R2).
- Financial counselling and income tax return preparation, except as it relates to the re-employment or retirement of the employee.
- Reimbursement for day care costs for children, except when the employer provides on-site facilities.
- Fitness, gym or health club memberships, even if part of an employee wellness program to increase job performance (IT-148R3).
- Reimbursement by the employer for two specific types of expenses incurred to move to a new work location (discussed below).
- Public transit passes provided to employees.

The above list is not complete but does provide a sense of how the general rule on employee benefits applies.

The amount of the benefit that must be included in the income of the employee is usually determined as either the cost to the employer of supplying the benefit or the fair market value of the benefit, whichever is lower. If, for example, an employer in the jewellery business gives a retiring employee a gold bracelet that retails for $700 but has cost the employer $400 on a wholesale basis, the value of the taxable benefit is $400. On the other hand, when an employer owns a vacation home that is available to employees, it is the fair rental value of the property that is relevant, not the cost associated with owning the property. In some circumstances, the benefit is determined in accordance with a rigid pre-set formula. Special benefit calculations apply to the use of employer automobiles, loans from employers, the reimbursement of specific relocation expenses, and stock-option benefits. These four unusual items are reviewed here.

Automobiles

It is not uncommon, especially at the management level, for an employer to provide an employee with an automobile for business and personal use. To the extent that an automobile is for personal use, a taxable benefit results.[18]

---

17 CRA Publication T4130—Employer's Guide Taxable Benefits and Allowances.
18 IT-63R5.

There are two components to the benefit. First, the employer—either by purchase or by lease agreement—has paid for the vehicle and in doing so has relieved the employee of the need to acquire a personal car. This benefit can be referred to as the *capital* portion (the technical term is *standby charge*).[19] Second, the employer may pay for costs associated with operating the vehicle—insurance, repairs, fuel, maintenance, and so on. The benefit to the employee from this activity is referred to as the *operating* portion.

The taxable benefits from the operating portion and the capital portion are calculated separately. The operating benefit is based on the actual personal use as opposed to business use; the standby charge is based primarily on the *availability* for use.

The operating benefit is determined by multiplying a prescribed rate by the number of personal kilometres driven by the employee for personal use in the year.[20] The prescribed rate changes from time to time. In 2012, the prescribed rate was 26¢.[21] This rate applies whatever the actual expenses incurred by the employer to operate the vehicle. The total value of the operating benefit for personal use is as follows:

$$\text{Operating benefit} = \text{Prescribed rate [26¢ in 2012]} \times \text{\# of personal km driven}$$

For purposes of the prior calculation, driving between home and the employer's place of business is considered personal use. In certain circumstances, the operating benefit can be calculated using an alternative method by which the benefit is *deemed* to be one-half of the amount of the standby charge for the capital benefit (see below).[22] The taxpayer can choose, on a yearly basis, the method that results in the lowest taxable benefit. This alternative is available only if the automobile is used primarily in the performance of employment duties (i.e., more than 50% of the total use).

In cases where the employee is not provided with a company car but the employer pays some or all of the employee's car operating expenses (example—provides the employee with a company gas card), the operating benefit is the actual operating costs paid by the employer prorated for the employee's personal usage.[23]

The capital benefit, referred to as the *standby charge*, is normally based on the time period that the automobile was available to the employee for personal use, rather than on the number of kilometres driven. It makes a difference here whether the employer owns or leases the automobile. The basic calculations are as follows:

If the *employer owns* the automobile:

$$\text{Standby charge} = \text{Original cost of the automobile} \times 2\% \times \text{\# of months available}$$

If the *employer leases* the automobile:

$$\text{Standby charge} = \text{Monthly lease cost} \times \tfrac{2}{3} \times \text{\# of months available}$$

The original cost of the car *includes* any GST/HST and provincial sales tax that is applicable. Note that the original cost of the car, and not the unamortized cost of the car, is used each year for calculating the standby charge.

The value of the standby charge is substantial and, in some cases, unfair. For example, over a four-year period, 96% (2% × 48 months) of the cost of the car to the

---

19 ITA 6(1)(e), 6(2).
20 ITA 6(1)(k).
21 Regulation 7305.1. The rate is 23¢ for persons employed principally in selling or leasing automobiles.
22 ITA 6(1)(k); IT-63R5.
23 ITA 6(1)(I).

employer may be included in the employee's personal income, even if the car is used only half the time for personal activity.

The following is provided for demonstration:

Situation: An employer provides a car costing $25,000 to an employee. The car is to be used for business travel and for personal use throughout the year. During the year, the employer expends $5,000 for operating costs relating to insurance, gas, maintenance, and repairs. During the year, the employee drives the car 30,000 km, of which 16,000 km is for personal use and 14,000 km is for business use.

Analysis: The taxable benefit for the year is $10,160, as calculated below.

Operating benefit:*	
16,000 km × 26¢ =	$ 4,160
Standby charge:	
$25,000 × 2% × 12 months	$ 6,000
Total taxable benefit for the year	$10,160

* The option of treating the operating benefit as 50% of the standby charge is not available because business use was not greater than 50%.

It is obvious that the benefit relating to the capital portion is considerable. The employer will, over a period of years, deduct the full cost of the car as an expense; however, the employee will take the same amount into income over four years, even though 47% of the car's use was for business purposes.

With respect to the standby charge, the after-tax cost to both the employer and the employee is determined in the following calculations (which assume the employer's tax rate is 35%, the employee's tax rate is 45%, and the car has no value after four years).

Employer:	
Purchase price of car	$25,000
Less tax saving on write-off of car over a number of years (35%)	(8,750)
Net cost to employer	$16,250
Employee:	
Cost of car	NIL
Tax cost of employee benefit over four years (6,000 × 4) × 45%	10,800
Net cost to employee	$10,800

In some cases, the standby charge can be reduced to reflect a low amount of personal use. The reduction occurs only when the distance travelled is *primarily* for employment duties. The CRA considers "primarily" to mean more than 50%.[24] Even when this is the case, the benefit is fractionalized, as the number of personal kilometres divided by an arbitrary amount of approximately 20,000 km (1,667 km per month).

If automobile is driven primarily for employment:

$$\text{Reduced standby charge} = \frac{\text{personal kms driven}}{1,667 \text{ kms per month}} \times \text{Standby charge}$$

For example, consider the situation of an employee who drives 30,000 km in a year. Of this amount, 18,000 km (60%) is for business and 12,000 km (40%) is for personal use.

---

24 ITA 6(2); IT-63R5.

If the employer's car has a cost of $25,000, the normal standby charge will be $6,000 ($25,000 × 2% × 12 m). However, because the 50% test has been met, the standby charge is reduced to $3,600 ($6,000 × [12,000 km / 20,000 km]). It is important to recognize that if the number of business kilometres had been 14,000 instead of 18,000, the standby charge would have remained the usual $6,000 because the 50% test had not been met.

As a final point, it is important to recognize that there is a fundamental difference in the way that the benefit is calculated for an *owned* vehicle as opposed to a *leased* vehicle. When the employer owns the car, its full cost is used to calculate the benefit (cost of car—$25,000; benefit—24% of $25,000). However, when the employer leases the car, the benefit is arbitrarily equal to two-thirds of the lease cost. Presumably, this reduction reflects the fact that the lease cost includes some financing costs. Employers should attempt to determine which method (own or lease) reduces their costs and balance that with the best alternative for the employee.

Employee Loans

Low-cost or non–interest-bearing loans provided by employers are attractive to employees, as most individuals have a need for borrowed funds to finance investments and personal asset acquisitions. The benefit the employee receives from the reduced rate of interest is, of course, taxable.[25] In order to simplify the process in a market of changing and variable interest rates, a prescribed formula is used to determine the value of the benefit to the employee.[26]

Every three months, on a regular basis, the CRA determines a prescribed interest rate that reflects existing financial conditions.[27] The taxable benefit to an employee on a loan made from an employer is the difference between the prescribed rate at the time and the actual interest paid.

This form of compensation can be of significant value to the employee. Consider the following circumstances:

Situation:	An employee has a large, outstanding house mortgage bearing 6% interest. Her employer offers her a $30,000 loan bearing interest at 1%. The prescribed interest rate designated at the time by the CRA is 4%. The employee is in the 40% tax bracket.
Analysis:	The taxable benefit and tax cost of the loan are $900 and $360 respectively, calculated as follows:

Prescribed interest ($30,000 @ 4%)	$1,200
Actual interest paid* ($30,000 @ 1%)	300
Benefit for tax purposes	$ 900
Tax cost to employee ($900 @ 40%)	$ 360

The actual cost of the $30,000 loan to the employee is 2.2%, determined as follows:

Actual interest on loan ($30,000 @ 1%)	$ 300
Tax on taxable benefit	360
Total cost of financing	$ 660
Effective rate on financing = $660/$30,000 = 2.2%	

*Must be paid by January 30th of the following year at the latest. ITA 80.4(1)(c).

---

25 ITA 6(9).
26 ITA 80.4.
27 Regulation 4301. For the first and second quarters of 2012, the prescribed rate was 1% for employee loans.

Usually, the prescribed interest rate will change every quarter of the year for purposes of calculating the benefit. However, in situations like the one just shown, an exception applies: when a *loan is used to acquire a house* or to *repay an existing house loan*, the benefit can be determined using the prescribed interest rate that was in force at the time the loan was made. If the prescribed rate declines, the lower rate can be used. However, if it *increases*, the rate in force at the time the loan was made will remain, for a maximum of five years.[28] When there is an interest benefit from an employer house loan created from a work relocation, all, or a portion of, the benefit may be deducted from net income for tax purposes in arriving at taxable income. The deduction is available only when the employee moves 40 kilometres closer to the new work location. This *home relocation loan deduction* is equal to the lesser of the interest benefit described above or CRA's prescribed interest rate multiplied by $25,000. See Chapter 10, Exhibit 10-1 for the deduction's position in the overall taxable income calculation.

It is important to recognize that in the above situation, the benefit derived from the low-interest loan was equivalent to a salary increase or cash bonus of $1,900. This assumes that the $30,000 loan was used by the employee to reduce an existing house mortgage that bore interest at 6%. See the following calculations:

Value of loan:	
Current interest on mortgage ($30,000 @ 6%)	$1,800
Cost of alternative financing from employer	
(as previously determined)	660
Net savings to employee	$1,140
Value of salary:	
Income from salary	$1,900
Less tax @ 40%	(760)
Net after-tax value of salary	$1,140

The saving of $1,140 in loan costs is therefore equivalent to a pre-tax cash salary of $1,900 for this particular employee.

An employee sometimes uses the funds borrowed from the employer to invest in shares, bonds, or the like that will generate financial returns. In such cases, any taxable benefit (prescribed interest less actual interest) is treated as interest paid by the employee.[29] This means that the employee can deduct the deemed interest when determining investment income for tax purposes. For example, assume that the $30,000 loan in the previous example was used to purchase shares. The employee would include $900 as a taxable benefit, as previously calculated. However, when calculating investment income, the $900 benefit would be deemed an interest expense and would be deducted from investment income earned in that year. This would apply only when the interest on the loan was otherwise deductible (see Chapter 7).[30]

Sometimes, an employer will forgive a loan to an employee. When this occurs, the debt forgiven is a taxable benefit.[31]

It is important that the employee as well as the employer appreciate the real value of certain types of employee benefits in order that realistic compensation decisions can be made (see Part VIII of this chapter).

---

[28] ITA 80.4(4), (6); IT-421R2.
[29] ITA 80.5.
[30] ITA 20(1)(c).
[31] ITA 6(1)(a), 6(15).

Relocation Expenses

Employers sometimes reimburse employees for all or part of their costs to permanently relocate to a new work location. Generally, the reimbursement of moving costs is *not* a taxable benefit (as discussed in this chapter under the heading "Tax-exempt benefits"). However, the reimbursement of two specific types of relocation expenses is taxable to the employee. The first type deals with the reimbursement of costs to finance the use of a residence—for example, a reimbursement of interest costs on a mortgage. Here, the full amount of the reimbursement is taxable.[32] The second type deals with the reimbursement of a loss suffered by the employee from the decrease in value or impairment of proceeds of disposition of the employee's residence. The first $15,000 of this type of benefit is *not* taxable to the employee, but *one-half* of any amount above $15,000 is taxable.[33] For example, a $40,000 reimbursement by an employer to an employee for a loss suffered on the sale of a residence caused by a relocation creates a taxable benefit of $12,500 (½ × [$40,000 − $15,000]). To qualify for this treatment the loss must be an "eligible housing loss," which normally means that the loss occurs when an employee moves at least 40 kilometres closer to the new work location.

Stock Options

Benefits arise under stock-option programs when an employee is given the opportunity to acquire shares in the employer corporation at a price lower than the fair market value of the shares at the time of the purchase. Stock options are a unique form of compensation, as they do not require the payment of cash by the employer. In fact, the employee contributes cash to the company treasury, thereby strengthening the employer's resources (although also diluting the existing shareholders' percentage of ownership because new corporate shares must be issued).

Theoretically, under a stock-option plan, employees receive a benefit at the time they purchase the shares because they have acquired an asset (the shares) that has a market value in excess of the price paid. They can make further gains by continuing to hold the shares for value enhancement. The initial benefit received by acquiring the shares at lower than current value and the gain or loss from subsequent value changes are treated differently for tax purposes. The taxable value of a gain made on a stock option is determined in accordance with specific rules.[34] These rules cover three categories of stock-option plans.[35]

1. Stock options of *public companies* with a designated *option price below fair market value* at the date the option is granted by the employer.

2. Stock options of *public companies* with a designated *option price equal to or greater than the fair market value* at the date the option is granted by the employer.

3. Stock options of *Canadian-controlled private companies*.

• **First category**   When a public corporation offers an employee an option to acquire shares at a specific price that is below those shares' present fair market value, the employee will have tax consequences both at the time the shares are acquired and later on when the shares are sold. Consider the following situation: An employee of a public company is given an option to acquire 1,000 shares from the company's treasury at a price of $20 per share. At the date that the option contract was offered to the employee, the share value was $22 per share. The contract requires that the employee

---

32 ITA 6(1)(a), 6(23).
33 ITA 6(1)(a), 6(19), (20), (21).
34 ITA 7; IT-113R4.
35 A fourth category applies to employees of mutual fund trusts who receive options to purchase mutual fund trust units.

exercise the option within five years. Stock prices over the next five years increase continuously, as shown in the table below.

Date option is offered	$22
Year 1	23
Year 2	26
Year 3	28
Year 4	31
Year 5	33

The employee exercises the option in year 3 and purchases 1,000 shares at $20 per share ($20,000). Although not required to do so, the employee decides to sell all the shares at the end of year 5 for $33 per share ($33,000).

The tax treatment of option benefits from shares of public corporations requires that a taxable benefit be included as *employment income* at the time the option is exercised and the employee purchases the shares. The taxable employment benefit is the difference between the fair market value of shares at the purchase date and the agreed option price. To the extent that the shares change in value after the purchase date, the value change is considered to be a capital gain or loss (when the shares are sold), of which only one-half is included in income.

In the above situation the tax treatment is as follows:

Year 3 (date of purchase of shares):	
Value of shares (1,000 @ $28)	$28,000
Option purchase price (1,000 @ $20)	20,000
Employment income	$ 8,000
Year 5 (date of sale of shares):	
Selling price (1,000 @ $33)	$33,000
Value at share purchase date (1,000 @ $28)	28,000
Capital gain	$ 5,000
Taxable capital gain ($\frac{1}{2}$)	$ 2,500

All of this burdens the employee with a decision concerning when to exercise the stock option. In the previous example, if the option had been exercised immediately at the offer date, the employment income would have amounted to only $2,000 ($22,000 – $20,000), and the subsequent increase in value to year 5 would have been a capital gain that was one-half taxable. This would have reduced significantly the tax cost of the investment but speeded up the requirement for a cash outlay to purchase the shares; as a result, the cost of money would have to have been considered a negative factor. As an alternative, the decision to exercise the option could have been delayed until year 5, when the share value reached $33, in which case the employment benefit would have amounted to $13,000 ($33,000 – $20,000). This amount would have been fully taxable, with none of the gain considered a capital gain. Such a delay increases the tax cost but reduces the cost of money, as there is no need for an outlay of cash to acquire the shares until just before they are sold.

• **Second category**　When a public company offers an employee a stock option without the opportunity of an immediate benefit (that is, when the option price is the same as or greater than the fair market value of the shares at the date the option is offered), the tax treatment is improved over the first category. If the shares do not have special dividend or redemption rights, one-half of the employment income calculated when the shares are purchased is deducted as a *stock option deduction* in determining *taxable* *income.*[36] This leaves one-half of the benefit taxable, similar to the way capital gains are treated. To illustrate: if, in the previous example, the option price granted had been $22 per share (that being the shares' value on the offering date), the tax consequences would have been as follows:

Year 3 (date of purchase of shares):	
Value of shares (1,000 @ $28)	$28,000
Option purchase price (1,000 @ $22)	22,000
Employment income	$ 6,000
Stock option deduction:	
When calculating *taxable income* − ½ ($6,000)	$ (3,000)
Year 5 (date of sale of shares):	
Capital gain:	
Selling price (1,000 @ $33)	$33,000
Value at share purchase date (1,000 @ $28)	28,000
Capital gain	$ 5,000
Taxable capital gain (½)	$ 2,500

Note that the stock option deduction in the above example is deducted in arriving at *taxable income*, rather than net income for tax purposes (see Chapter 3, page 40, and Chapter 10). Thus, the full employment income is included in the aggregating formula for net income for tax purposes.

• **Third category** This category relates only to options granted to employees of Canadian-controlled private corporations. The *employment benefit,* rather than being taxable at time of purchase, is *not taxable until the shares are sold.*[37] Also, provided that the employee holds such shares for two years after acquisition, one-half of the employment income benefit is deducted as a *stock option deduction* in determining *taxable income.*[38] If the shares are not held for two years, then the stock option deduction is available based on the same requirements as those in the second category described above (that is, when the option price is the same as or greater than the fair market value of the shares at the date the option is offered). Using the same facts as given in the first category, except that a Canadian-controlled private corporation is the employer, the tax consequences to the employee are as follows:

Year 5 (date of sale of shares):	
Employment income:	
Value of shares at date shares acquired in year 3 (1,000 @ $28)	$28,000
Option purchase price (1,000 @ $20)	20,000
Employment income	$ 8,000
Capital gain:	
Selling price (1,000 @ $33)	$33,000
Value at option purchase date	28,000
Capital gain	$ 5,000
Taxable capital gain	$ 2,500*
Stock option deduction:	
In arriving at *taxable income*	$ (4,000)

*May be eligible for the capital gain deduction if the shares are qualified small business corporation shares (see Chapter 11).

---

36 ITA 110(1)(d).
37 ITA 7(1.1).
38 ITA 110(1)(d) and (d.1).

The special treatment given to shares of this category is designed to stimulate employee participation in private corporations. However, in spite of the beneficial tax treatment, Canadian-controlled private corporations rarely grant stock options, for the following reasons:

1. The market value of shares is not readily available and is often difficult to determine.

2. Minority shares of private corporations have a low marketability, and buyers, other than the major shareholders, are difficult to find. For this reason, the share values are often significantly discounted unless buy/sell agreements are contracted with all shareholders.

3. Controlling shareholders of private corporations normally want to retain full control and flexibility of corporate activity and do not wish to be accountable to minority shareholders for their actions.

B. Non-Taxable and Tax-Deferred Benefits

As pointed out previously, the general rule that all benefits received or enjoyed by an employee are taxable has a limited number of exceptions. The *Income Tax Act* specifically allows certain tangible benefits from employment to be excluded from taxable income. Some of the benefits are taxable at a later time, which means their exclusion is actually a deferral. Other benefits are permanently excluded from taxable income. It is important to note that in addition to the excluded benefits described in the *Income Tax Act*,[39] the CRA, by administrative policy, arbitrarily excludes certain other benefits. These items are discussed at the end of this section.

The following specific benefits (described in the *Income Tax Act*) are excluded from income on a deferred or permanent basis:[40]

1. Employer contributions for an employee to a registered pension plan (RPP).

2. Employer contributions on behalf of an employee to a deferred profit-sharing plan (DPSP).

3. Employer contributions for an employee to a pooled registered pension plan (PRPP).[41]

4. The payment of insurance premiums for group sickness or accident plans that protect the income of employees who are unable to work due to illness or injury.

5. The payment of premiums for private health service plans that provide extended medical coverage beyond public plans. (This applies only to private health plans and not to premiums for public health insurance plans.)

6. The payment by an employer, on an employee's behalf, of premiums for supplementary unemployment insurance plans, including both private and public plans that protect employees in the event of a loss of job.

7. Counselling services relating to the mental or physical health or to the re-employment or retirement of the employee.

8. When an employer provides scholarships, bursaries, and free tuition for post-secondary education to family members of employees to assist them to further their education, it is scholarship income to the family member *and not employment income* to the employee.[42]

---

39 ITA 6(1)(a).
40 ITA 6(1)(a)(i) to (iv).
41 Proposed by Department of Finance on December 14, 2011, ITA 6(1)(a)(i).
42 ITA 6(1)(a)(vi).

Regarding the insurance benefits mentioned above, note that the tax-free benefit relates to the payment of the premium and not to the payments that may be made from the insurance plans when a claim is made. Claims paid out of a private health service plan on an employee's behalf are not taxable. However, when the employer has paid premiums for a sickness or accident insurance plan or an income maintenance insurance plan, claims paid to the employee are considered taxable.[43] The amount taxable is equal to the total payments from the plan in the year *less* the sum of all premiums paid in the current year *and* past years by the *employee*.

The first three benefits listed—RPP, PRPP, and DPSP contributions—are tax deferrals; the remaining five are permanently excluded from taxable income. All eight are extremely valuable to employees.

• **Tax-deferred benefits**   The registered pension plan and the proposed pooled registered pension plan are valuable forms of employee compensation. While several types of plans are used, all involve a contribution by an employer to a trustee on behalf of specific employees. The trustee holds the contributions and invests the funds; at some time in the future, both the contributions and the accumulated investment returns are used to acquire a pension for the employee. The funds are taxable to the employee only when they are withdrawn as a pension; they are not taxable while they remain in the plan earning investment income. The two benefits of this arrangement are as follows:

1. An employee is permitted to save and invest a portion of his or her income that has not been subject to tax. Obviously, this creates a larger investment base than if the employee were to receive the benefit as a cash bonus, pay tax, and then invest the after-tax remainder. Investment income earned on money saved is therefore enhanced, since the return is based on pre-tax income as opposed to after-tax income.

2. The annual return on investments accumulated within the plan is also not taxable while the funds remain within the plan. This means that all annual returns that are reinvested also compound on a pre-tax basis rather than on a substantially reduced after-tax basis. A 10% return is compounded at 10% within the plan; if the income had been subject to tax before being reinvested, it would have been compounded at only 5.5% (assumed tax rate of 45%).

The calculations below demonstrate the value of such a tax deferral. The example compares an annual benefit of $3,500 paid to an employee as a cash bonus for 30 years and invested at a 10% return with the same $3,500 paid annually to an RPP and invested within the plan for the same number of years at the same rate of return. The example assumes that the employee is in a marginal tax bracket of 45%.[44]

RPP—$3,500 annual benefit:

$$\$3,500 \times 30 \text{ y @ } 10\% = \underline{\$633,000}$$

Cash bonus—$3,500 annual benefit:

	Bonus	Investment return
Pre-tax bonus	$3,500	10%
Tax @ 45%	(1,575)	4.5%
Available for investment	$1,925	5.5%

$$\$1,925 \times 30 \text{ y @ } 5.5\% = \underline{\$147,000}$$

---

43 ITA 6(1)(f).

44 The compounding calculation assumes that the annual deposit is made at the beginning of each year. This is so throughout the text, unless otherwise indicated.

The compounding of $3,500 at 10% on a pre-tax basis in the RPP provides an investment value that is four times greater than that achieved on an after-tax basis. While the $633,000 in this example is fully taxable when withdrawn as a pension, its after-tax value still far exceeds the value of the cash bonus arrangement.

In a deferred profit-sharing plan, an employer arranges to share, annually, a certain percentage of the business profits with specified employees by contributing to a trustee who holds and invests the funds on the employee's behalf. As with an RPP and PRPP, a DPSP must be registered with the CRA, and contributions are subject to an annual limit. The tax treatment of a DPSP, from the employee's perspective, is identical to that given to RPPs; the benefits, when compared with those of other forms of taxable compensation, are substantial.

- **Tax-exempt benefits**   The three insurance and counselling benefits that are fully tax exempt have a lesser dollar value individually than the tax-deferred benefits; nevertheless, in total, they are a valuable means of compensation for the employee.

Most individuals are in need of income protection insurance and supplemental health insurance. When such programs are not provided by an employer, individuals have to pay premiums from their after-tax disposable income. For example, an individual in a 40% tax bracket who purchased $1,500 of the above insurance premiums would have to earn a salary of $2,500 ($2,500 less tax @ 40% = $1,500) in order to fund the purchase. It is important that the employee and the employer recognize the value of tax-free benefits provided as compensation. When an employer provides the above insurance programs as part of the employee's compensation package, the tax-free benefits can be assigned a pre-tax value. Using the above example, when the employer provides an employee with $1,500 of tax-free insurance benefits, it is equivalent to giving that employee a salary increase of $2,500.

From the employer's perspective, the cost of providing $1,500 in insurance benefits is dramatically lower than it would be to provide $2,500 in salary, even though the employee receives the same value under both alternatives. This substantial saving to the employer can be kept by the employer for business expansion or be given back to the employees, in whole or in part, by expanding other forms of compensation (see Part VIII of this chapter).

While the *Income Tax Act* appears to define clearly which benefits are tax exempt, the CRA has, for administrative purposes, chosen to arbitrarily consider certain benefits to be non-taxable. For example, in certain circumstances, benefits derived from subsidized meals, merchandise discounts, and moving expenses are considered to be non-taxable. A complete list of tax-free benefits and the circumstances in which they apply is given in the CRA's IT-470R and T-4130, *Employer's Guide—Taxable Benefits*, which should be consulted when compensation programs are being designed. Some of these benefits are listed below.

- Discounts on merchandise, except to the extent that the price is reduced below the employer's cost.
- Subsidized meals, provided that the employee pays a reasonable charge.
- Cell phones, if primarily for business purposes. Personal use within a reasonably priced basic plan with a fixed cost for a flat package of minutes normally is non-taxable.
- Child care, if provided at the workplace, managed directly by the employer, provided to all employees at minimal or no cost, and available only to employees.
- Clothing paid for or supplied by an employer, if it is a uniform required for employees, or protective clothing.
- Computers provided by an employer, if provided to enhance employees' quality of life and computer literacy, or if the employee requires the computer to carry out employment duties.

- In-house recreational facilities available to employees.
- Club dues, when it is clearly to the employer's advantage for the employee to be a member of the club (see IT-148R3).
- Reimbursement of moving expenses for relocating employees to a new work location, except for the two specific items discussed on page 74.
- Employer's contributions under a provincial hospitalization and medicare plan, when these are required by law to be made (i.e., the employer's contribution—if the employer also pays the employee's share of the premium, that amount is a taxable benefit).
- Transportation passes for bus, rail, and airline employees, unless travelling on a space-confirmed basis. Free or discounted passes for family members are taxable benefits.
- Internet service at home if primarily to benefit the employer.
- Non-cash gifts and awards that do not exceed $500 (see Part III for detail).
- Non-cash long service/anniversary awards not exceeding $500 (see Part III for detail).
- Tuition reimbursement or training expenses where the course is taken primarily to benefit the employer.
- Frequent-flyer points and other loyalty points earned on an employee's personal credit card, used for business travel reimbursed by the employer, as long as the points are not converted to cash or being used as alternative remuneration. Note that points accumulated, which are under the control of the employer (for example when an employer credit card is used), will result in a taxable benefit if the employer allows the points to be used by the employee for personal use.[45]

IV. Allowances

A. Definition

The third general rule for determining income from employment states that all allowances of any kind whatever, including personal and living allowances, are taxable, subject to specific exceptions.[46] The term *allowance* refers to a fixed, specified amount that is paid to an employee on a regular basis, over and above a normal salary, to cover certain expenses incurred by the employee.[47] The unique aspect of an allowance is that the employee does not have to account for the allowance or provide details of how the money has been spent. The receipt of $300 a month for clothing or for travel, regardless of whether the employee has expended such an amount, is an allowance.

An allowance is not a reimbursement. A reimbursement is the repayment of a specific expenditure incurred by an employee on the employer's behalf. For example, if an employee travels on behalf of an employer and submits an account of travel expenses incurred, the repayment of the specific amount is a reimbursement, which is *not* taxable to the employee.

B. Exceptions
not taxable

Nine specific allowances are excepted from the general rule and considered not taxable. Only three of the exceptions have broad application; the remaining six, which include allowances for ministers and volunteer firefighters, apply only in limited situations. The three broader exceptions relate to travel expenses and are reviewed briefly below.

• Overtime meals and allowances   Often employers provide a meal allowance to employees who are required to work overtime. Reasonable overtime meal allowances are not taxable if: "the employee works two or more hours of overtime right after the

---

45 CRA Income Tax Technical News 40 (June, 2009).
46 ITA 6(1)(b).
47 CRA Income Tax Technical News 40 (June, 2009).

scheduled hours of work; and the overtime is infrequent and occasional in nature (less than three times a week)."[48] Otherwise, the allowance is a taxable benefit. A meal value of up to $17 will generally be considered reasonable.[49]

• **Employees selling property or negotiating contracts**   Employees engaged in the selling of property (salespeople) or in negotiating contracts for an employer are entitled to a non-taxable allowance for travel expenses, provided that the allowance is reasonable.[50] Travel expenses include transportation (by car, plane, and so on), meals, lodging, and other incidental costs. The allowance *must* be reasonable; if it is unreasonably high or low in relation to the actual costs incurred, the allowance is taxable. The most common use of this exception is to provide a car allowance to salespeople who regularly use their car in the performance of their duties. For a car allowance to be tax-free it must be reasonable *and* based on the number of kilometres used to conduct employment duties. This tax-free allowance is not always beneficial, as its receipt usually eliminates the right to claim expenses that would otherwise be permitted (see the section on salespeople's expenses later in this chapter). An allowance, if less than the expenses incurred, may be considered unreasonably low and thus be included in taxable income, in which case expenses can be deducted.

• **Employees other than salespeople**   Employees who are not salespeople are also entitled to receive a tax-free allowance for travel expenses. However, for these expenses to be tax-free, they must meet certain criteria that are more extensive than those for salespeople. In addition, the criteria that apply to travel allowances relating to the use of an automobile are different from those for other travel allowances. A non-salesperson's travel allowance that does *not* relate to the use of an automobile is considered tax-free only if[51]

(a) the allowance is a reasonable amount; and
(b) the employee travels outside the municipality or metropolitan area in which the employer is located. However, if travel is within the municipality or metropolitan area the allowance can be non-taxable when "its principal objective is to ensure that the employee's duties are undertaken in a more effective manner during the course of the work shift and where the allowance paid was not indicative of an alternative form of remuneration."[52]

Automobile allowances paid to employees who are not salespeople are considered tax-free if[53]

(a) the allowance is for the purpose of travelling in the performance of their duties as employees; and
(b) the allowance is reasonable and is based solely on the number of kilometres used to conduct employment duties.[54]

The criteria for the automobile allowance are different from the criteria for other travel expenses in that the former are not restricted to travel outside the municipality or metropolitan area of the employer. In addition, the question of reasonableness

---

48 CRA Income Tax Technical News 40 (June, 2009).
49 T-4130 *Employer's Guide—Taxable Benefits*, CRA.
50 ITA 6(1)(b)(v).
51 ITA 6(1)(b)(vii).
52 CRA, *Income Tax Technical News*, June 11, 2009; T-4130 *Employer's Guide—Taxable Benefits*.
53 ITA 6(1)(b)(vii.1).
54 ITA 6(1)(b)(x).

is more tightly defined in that it relates to the number of kilometres driven. The CRA does not issue statements on what is "reasonable." However, a reasonable allowance would include those costs that would normally be deductible, such as fuel, maintenance, insurance, capital cost allowance (amortization/depreciation), and so on.

As with salespeople's allowances, if the allowance is considered tax-free, the employee cannot claim certain expenses that are specifically permitted; and the benefit of a tax-free allowance is eliminated if the actual expenses are greater than the allowance. Keep in mind that an allowance can also be considered unreasonable if it is *too low*. In other words, an allowance that is less than the actual reasonable expenses may be considered unreasonably low and included in taxable income. If this happens, the higher actual costs can be used as a deduction.

V. Deductions from Employment Income

The fourth and last general rule for determining net income from employment states that no deductions are permitted except those specifically provided for in the *Income Tax Act*.[55] Since the list of permitted deductions is not extensive, determining employment deductions is a simple procedure that involves merely scrutinizing that list. If an item in question is not on the list, it is not deductible when calculating employment income.

The major items that can be deducted as employment deductions are as follows:

1. Expenses incurred by employees who earn remuneration in the form of commissions from selling or negotiating contracts for an employer.[56]

2. Travelling expenses, including motor vehicle expenses, in certain circumstances.[57]

3. Professional membership dues required to maintain professional status in a profession recognized by statute.[58]

4. The cost of supplies consumed directly in the performance of employment duties, provided that the employee is required by the employment contract to be responsible for payment of such items.[59]

5. Annual dues paid to a trade union.[60]

6. Contributions to an employer's registered pension plan.[61]

7. Office rent or workspace-in-the-home expenses in certain circumstances.

8. Legal expenses paid in the year to collect or establish a right to salary or wages owed to the employee by the employer or former employer.[62]

The above list of deductible items is not complete; however, all of the items omitted have an extremely narrow application. Some of the major deductions require further explanation, as certain criteria must be met before they can be applied. They are discussed below.

---

55 ITA 8(2).
56 ITA 8(1)(f).
57 ITA 8(1)(h), (h.1).
58 ITA 8(1)(i).
59 ITA 8(1)(i).
60 ITA 8(1)(i).
61 ITA 8(1)(m).
62 ITA 8(1)(b).

A. Travel Expenses

An employee can deduct travel expenses incurred in the course of work-related duties provided that the following circumstances exist:[63]

- The employee is ordinarily required to carry on the duties of employment away from the employer's place of business or in different places.
- Under the employment contract, the employee is required to pay the travel costs incurred in the performance of duties.
- The employee has not received a non-taxable allowance designed to cover such costs.

Travel expenses include the costs of all forms of transportation (including automobile costs), meals, lodging, and all other expenses created by the travel activity.

It is sometimes difficult to determine the exact cost of the travel activity when the employee uses his or her own car. The costs include gas, oil, general repairs, insurance, financing costs (interest), and amortization (depreciation) of the automobile from its use.[64] All of these items are accepted for tax purposes and must be determined as they apply to the travel activity. An accepted method for determining travel costs is to total the full costs for the year and prorate the total on the basis of the number of kilometres driven for employment purposes as opposed to personal use. The rate of amortization (depreciation—referred to as *capital cost allowance* for tax purposes) is arbitrarily determined as 30% annually on the undepreciated cost (see Chapter 6). The calculation of capital cost allowance on an automobile is more complicated in a taxation year when a new automobile is purchased and/or a previous one is sold. Special rules apply to these transactions (reviewed in Chapter 6—automobiles costing less than $30,000 are subject to capital cost allowance under class 10; those costing more fall under class 10.1 and are reviewed under the heading "Special Treatment of Passenger Vehicles").

Certain of the above travel expenses are subject to an arbitrary reasonableness test which limits the amount that can be deducted against employment income.[65] The imposed limits are subject to regular changes. Currently, the maximum cost of an automobile available for capital cost allowance is $30,000 plus federal and provincial sales tax. If an automobile is leased, the maximum lease deduction is $800 plus federal and provincial sales tax per month. The deduction for interest paid on a loan to finance the acquisition of an automobile is limited to an average of $300 per month. And the deduction for meals incurred during travel is limited to 50% of the actual costs incurred. (Specifically, the *Income Tax Act* restricts the amount of the deduction for any "food and beverages consumed or entertainment enjoyed" to 50% of amounts *actually paid*. If the actual costs are unreasonably high, the deduction is limited to 50% of what is reasonable. This applies to all taxpayers and to all types of income. See Chapter 9.)[66]

There is no requirement that the travel costs be incurred away from the metropolitan area of the employer; consequently, costs incurred within the employer's city or town are acceptable for deduction. An exception is meals—an employee must be travelling away from the metropolitan area of the employer for at least 12 hours for this cost to be deductible.[67]

Employees must fulfill all of the three criteria mentioned earlier to be eligible to deduct travel costs. In addition, to the extent the employee is reimbursed, the expenses deducted must be reduced accordingly.

---

63 ITA 8(1)(h), (h.1); IT-522R.
64 ITA 8(1)(j).
65 ITA 67.2, 67.3.
66 ITA 67.1.
67 ITA 8(4).

Situation: An employee is required to use her own automobile for employment duties. She acquired a new car at the beginning of the year for $40,000 (including GST and PST of 8%) and during the year incurred the following expenses:

Gasoline	$2,200
Repairs and maintenance	400
Insurance and registration	800
Meals while away from the office	
($200 relates to out-of-town travel)	420
Parking during employment duties	300
Interest on loan to acquire car	3,900

During the year, the employee drove 26,000 km, of which 14,000 were for employment duties and the remaining 12,000 were personal.

Analysis: First of all, note that some of these expenses related to both personal and employment activities (e.g., gasoline). Others related only to employment activities (e.g., parking). Also, meal costs were entirely personal, as the employee had to eat whether she was working or not. Remember, however, that meal costs while travelling out of town can be deducted, provided that the time away is greater than 12 hours.

The cost of an automobile can be deducted in the form of capital cost allowance (see Chapter 6). The designated capital cost allowance rate for automobiles is 30%, except in the first year when it is only 15%. In this case, the rate of 15% applied only to the maximum permitted cost of $33,900 ($30,000 + taxes), even though the actual cost was $40,000.

Combined personal and employment expenses were as follows:

Gasoline	$ 2,200
Repairs and maintenance	400
Insurance and registration	800
Interest on loan (actual $3,900—limited to $300 × 12 months)	3,600
Capital cost allowance (15% of $33,900)	5,085
	$12,085
Employment portion:	
$\dfrac{\text{Employment km—14,000}}{\text{Total km—26,000}} \times \$12,085 =$	$ 6,507
Total employment expenses:	
Allocated above	$ 6,507
Parking	300
Out-of-town meals (50% × $200)	100
Total expenses	$ 6,907

B. Cost of Supplies Consumed

When the contract of employment requires that the employee pay for supplies used in carrying out the duties of employment, the costs of supplies are normally deductible only to the extent that they are fully consumed when used.[68] The consumption requirement eliminates the employee's ability to deduct a broad range of items. For example, items such as small tools or books purchased by teachers are not deductible even when employees must purchase such items under the employment contract, because they are not consumed by use in a short period of time. Supplies consumed would include such items as postage and stationery. The deductions under this category are extremely limited.[69]

---

68 ITA 8(1)(i); IT-352R2.
69 ITA 8(1)(s).

Tradesperson's tools deduction—Employed tradespersons can deduct the cost of eligible tools (excludes communication devices and computers) in excess of $1,000 (indexed—$1,095 in 2012) to a maximum of $500.[70] The term "tradesperson" applies to any person engaged in an occupation that demands a certain level of skill. The deduction applies to items such as a hairstylist's hair dryers, curling irons, and scissors.

C. Salespeople's Expenses

Employees who act in a selling capacity or who negotiate contracts for employers fall into a special category, one which permits a broad range of deductions, provided that any remuneration includes either some amount of commissions or some other similar amount that is a function of sales volume.[71] In addition, such salespeople must be required to pay their own expenses under the contract of employment; ordinarily, they must also be carrying on their duties of employment away from the employer's place of business; as well, they must not be receiving a tax-free travel allowance.

Effectively, salespeople can deduct *all* amounts expended in the year for the purpose of earning employment income, up to the total amount of commissions or other similar payments. The following, however, constitute exceptions to this:

1. Payments for the use of a yacht, camp, lodge, or golf course.

2. Membership fees or dues in a club, when the main purpose of that club is to provide dining, recreational, or sporting facilities to its members.

3. Expenditures of a capital nature that have a long-term benefit, such as a computer, desk, or filing cabinet. (However, capital cost allowance on an automobile can be deducted.)[72]

Note that the expenses incurred cannot exceed the amount of the commissions—in other words, a loss from commission activity cannot occur for tax purposes. To the extent that permitted expenses exceed commissions in any year, the excess is lost and cannot be used in other years. It should be pointed out that the capital cost allowance on an automobile, along with any related financing costs, is not subject to the commission limitation and can be deducted over and above commissions earned in a year.

The expenses that can be deducted by salespeople are wide ranging and include, but are not restricted to, such items as advertising, promotion, telephone, parking, automobile, supplies, accounting costs, fees paid to assistants, the costs of maintaining an exclusive office in a home, and travel expenses. However, such expenses are deductible only if they are incurred solely in an attempt to earn the employment income. They are not deductible if they are for personal use. In addition, the arbitrary reasonableness test limits the amounts that can be deducted for automobiles (cost—$30,000 plus taxes; lease cost—$800 plus taxes per month; interest—$300 per month) and meals and entertainment (50%), as described in part A above. Consider the following:

Situation: An employee receives a salary of $40,000 and commissions of $4,000 in a taxation year. He is required to use his automobile to earn commissions and receives a travel allowance of $3,000 for this purpose. At the end of the previous year, the automobile had an undepreciated capital cost for tax purposes of $18,000. The automobile was driven 24,000 km during the year, of which 16,000 km were for employment purposes. The following additional costs were incurred to earn commissions during the year:

---

70 ITA 8(1)(s).
71 ITA 8(1)(f); IT-522R.
72 ITA 8(1)(j).

Advertising	$ 1,200
Parking	400
Entertainment—meals for customers	900
Golf club membership for entertaining customers	1,000
Purchase of new home computer	2,000
Automobile operating costs	4,000
Interest on automobile loan (12 months)	3,800
	$13,300

Analysis:
First, it is necessary to establish whether the automobile allowance of $3,000 is taxable. It is tax-free if it is considered to be a reasonable allowance.[73] If the allowance is tax-free, no deductions can be claimed for any of the above commission expenses.[74] Here, it is apparent that the automobile expenses (operating costs, capital cost allowance, and interest on the loan) far exceed the allowance of $3,000. It can be concluded that the allowance is unreasonably low and therefore is taxable.

The computer is a capital expenditure and cannot be deducted from employment income.[75] Capital cost allowance on the computer cannot be deducted (it could be if the individual was self-employed carrying on a business). However, if the computer is leased, the annual lease costs are deductible. The golf club membership is specifically disallowed as a deduction, even if it was used to earn commission income.

The remaining expenses (except the automobile capital cost allowance and related interest on the loan) are deductible, but only to the extent of the commission income earned in the year. Capital cost allowance on the automobile and interest on the related loan are deductible (within limits) but are not restricted to the amount of commission income.[76]

Employment income:		
Salary		$40,000
Travel allowance		3,000
Commissions		4,000
		47,000
Salesperson expenses:		
Advertising	$1,200	
Parking	400	
Entertainment—meals—50% × $900	450	
Automobile operating costs		
16,000 km/24,000 km × $4,000	2,667	
	$4,717	
Limited to commission income		(4,000)
Other automobile costs:		
Capital cost allowance—30% × $18,000	$5,400	
Interest on loan—limited to $300 per month		
$300 × 12 m	3,600	
	$9,000	
Employment portion—16,000 km/24,000 km × $9,000		(6,000)
Employment income		$37,000

---

73 ITA 6(1)(b)(v).
74 ITA 8(1)(f).
75 ITA 8(1)(f).
76 ITA 8(1)(j).

D. Work Space in Home

In some circumstances, certain salespeople and other employees must carry out their duties from a home office. The home in question may be owned or rented. The associated costs are permitted as a deduction from their commission income, provided that certain criteria are met.[77]

A home-office deduction is permitted if that office is the "place where the individual principally performs the duties of employment." The CRA has interpreted this to mean more than 50% of the time.

If the above criterion is not met, a deduction may still be permitted if the space is used *exclusively* to earn employment income *and is used on a regular and continuous basis* for meeting customers or clients of the employer.

Both of the above tests may be difficult to meet. When they *are* met, the costs for salespeople are normally the prorated portion of the home's property taxes, insurance, maintenance, and utilities (or the rent cost when the home is not owned). Employees who are not salespeople can deduct only the maintenance and utility costs (not the insurance and property taxes). Such costs cannot be greater than the employment income earned in the year. When they are greater, the excess can be carried forward to the next year. An employee cannot deduct interest on a house mortgage as part of office costs at any time.[78] A self-employed person *can* do so.[79]

E. Registered Pension Plan Contributions

It was indicated previously that employers often contribute amounts to a registered pension plan on behalf of an employee and that such contributions, although a benefit, are not taxable until funds are withdrawn from the pension plan. Most RPPs permit or require the employee to contribute an annual amount to the plan; as a result, the pension's value is determined by combining employer and employee contributions. Within specified limits, the contribution made by an employee is deductible in arriving at net income from employment.[80]

The specified limits for employee contributions to an RPP are complex and are integrated with other retirement plans such as deferred profit-sharing plans and personal registered retirement savings plans (see Chapter 9). The maximum amount that can be contributed by the employer and the employee combined with all of the above-mentioned plans is 18% of the employee's compensation. For *money purchase RPPs*, the contribution limit is further limited by a dollar amount of $23,820 in 2012,[81] from which point it will be indexed to increases in the average industrial wage. In most cases, the required contribution specified by the employer's pension plan will fall within the designated limits and is fully deductible by the employee.

The value of investing in tax-deferred pension plans was discussed in Part III of this chapter and will be reviewed more extensively in Chapter 9.

VI. Employment Income and the GST/PST/HST

The *Income Tax Act* rarely refers specifically to the goods and services tax (GST). One of the few times it does so is in the section relating to employment income. There are two important areas where a relationship between the GST and employment income is obvious.

Taxable Employee Benefits

The first relates to taxable employee benefits. When an employer provides an employee with tangible taxable benefits, the employee has, in effect, received a salary and then used it to acquire a particular service or good. Had the employee acquired that item directly, he or she would have paid a GST of 5% (unless it was

---

77 ITA 8(13); IT-352R.
78 ITA 8(1)(f).
79 ITA 20(1)(c).
80 ITA 8(1)(m), 147.2(4).
81 ITA 147.1(1).

an exempt item, such as insurance). This means that the employer must include the value of the GST when calculating the amount of a benefit for an employee.[82] Similarly, the value of any provincial sales tax (PST) or harmonized sales tax (HST) is included in the value of the benefit.

Employee GST/HST Rebate

A second GST implication arises when an employee incurs expenses as part of a contract of employment. For example, salespeople who incur promotion, travel, and other expenses must pay the GST on those items. However, employees are not GST registrants and so are not usually eligible for a rebate or credit. Because of this, as a special rule, any employee who has expenses that are deductible for tax purposes can claim a GST rebate on those expenses. For example, an employee who has expenses of $1,050 ($1,000 + $50 GST) can apply for a refund of $50. (To calculate the rebate, the deductible employment expenses on which GST was paid are multiplied by $5/105$.) Because the full $1,050 would have been deducted for income tax purposes, the refund of $50 is taxable to the employee when it is received.[83] An employee has up to four years to claim the refund. Similarly, in provinces where the HST applies, an HST rebate can be claimed on employee expenses that are deductible for tax purposes. The employee's HST rebate, in this case, would be $130 in a province with a 13% HST rate ($1,000 + $130 HST) $\times$ $13/113$.

See Appendix A at the end of the text for a more in-depth review of the GST/HST.

VII. Sample Calculation of Employment Income

Summary of Facts

Ms. X is employed by a Canadian public corporation as a middle-level manager. Information relating to her financial affairs for a particular year is outlined below.

1. Ms. X received a salary of $40,000 during the year. In addition, she was awarded a bonus of $5,000 for her special efforts during the current year. The payment is to be made in two instalments during the following year.

2. Two years earlier, the employer had granted Ms. X an option to acquire 500 shares of the public corporation at $30 per share. At the time the option was granted, the shares were trading at $32 each. During the early part of the current year, Ms. X exercised the option and acquired 500 shares, which at that time had a value of $35 per share. In December of the current year, after their value rose unexpectedly, she sold them at $41 a share.

3. The company had a generous benefit program and, during the year, provided Ms. X with the following:[84]
   - A contribution to the company pension plan of $3,300.
   - A group term life insurance premium of $500 for $50,000 of life insurance for the beneficiaries of her estate.
   - A membership valued at $1,000 in a private squash club, to which many of the employer's customers belonged.
   - A company car for personal use throughout the year. (The car cost the company $40,000, including tax; during the year, the company paid $5,000 of operating expenses. The car was driven a total of 20,000 km, of which 11,000 were for personal use.)
   - A gift costing $600 (including tax) in honour of Ms. X's 20th wedding anniversary. She also received a watch costing $400 (including tax) as an award for 10 years of service with the employer.

---

82 ITA 6(7).
83 ITA 6(8).
84 It is assumed that the values of the benefits include the appropriate amount of tax, if applicable.

4. During the year, Ms. X made the following payments, some of which were deducted directly from her monthly salary by the employer and paid on her behalf:

Employment Insurance	$ 720
Canada Pension Plan	1,807
Donations to registered charities	200
Income tax	8,000
Contribution to the company RPP	3,000
Interest to the employer of 3% on a $10,000 loan (the CRA's prescribed interest rate was 5%)	300

5. The contract of employment required that Ms. X acquire, at her own expense, a small laptop computer to be used while travelling and at home. During the year, she purchased a laptop computer for $2,000; she also purchased and used $75 worth of special computer paper.

6. From time to time, Ms. X travelled out of town on behalf of the employer. For this reason, the company provided her with a monthly travel allowance of $500, which she was not required to account for. During the year, she spent $2,000 on airline tickets, $500 on meals, and $1,000 on lodging. This year's travel expenses were similar to amounts spent in previous years.

7. Over several weekends during the year, Ms. X completed a consulting project for her brother-in-law's business, for which she received $3,000.

Employment Income

The net income from employment for Ms. X amounts to $55,435 during the year, determined as shown in the following table:

A. Remuneration received:		
Salary		$40,000
B. Benefits received or enjoyed:		
Stock option:		
Value at date of acquisition ($35 × 500)	$17,500	
Cost of acquisition ($30 × 500)	15,000	2,500
Group term life insurance		500
Automobile for personal use:		
Operating costs:		
11,000 km × 26¢		2,860
Capital value, referred to as a "standby charge":		
$40,000 × 24% (2% × 12m)†		9,600
Anniversary gift (value exceeds $500) ($600 − $500)		100
Company loan:		
Prescribed interest ($10,000 @ 5%)	$ 500	
Interest paid ($10,000 @ 3%)	(300)	200
C. Allowances received:		
Travel allowance ($500 × 12 m)		
(see explanation below)		6,000
Total remuneration, benefits, and allowances		61,760
D. Deductions permitted:§		
Contribution to company pension plan	$ 3,000	
Computer supplies consumed	75	
Travel costs (including 50% of meal costs)		
—$2,000 + 50% ($500) + $1,000	3,250	− 6,325
Net income from employment		$55,435

† The automobile was not used "primarily" for business use, and the standby charge reduction cannot apply.
§ The GST or HST included in the computer supplies and travel costs will be refunded upon application. The GST or HST rebate is taxable in the year received.

Explanation of Items Omitted

Several items in the summary of facts are omitted from the determination of income. Their exclusion is explained below.

- **Bonus**   The bonus of $5,000, although earned in the current year, is not received until the following year. As employment income is on a cash basis, it will be included in income in the following year when received.

- **Gain on sale of employer shares**   This is a capital transaction resulting in a capital gain of $3,000, calculated as follows:

Selling price ($41 × 500)	$20,500
Value at date of acquisition ($35 × 500)	17,500
Capital gain	$ 3,000

The taxable capital gain of $1,500 (½ of $3,000) would be included in income within the capital gains area. While this may affect the individual's net income for tax purposes, it is not part of employment income.

- **RPP benefit**   The employer's contribution of $3,300 to the registered pension plan, although a benefit, is excluded because it is one of the specific primary exceptions to the benefit rule.

- **Membership fee**   The payment of a club membership fee is clearly a benefit; however, it is currently a matter of administrative practice that the payment of club dues for employees is not a taxable benefit, provided that membership at the club is useful to the employer's income-earning process. In any event, the employer is not permitted to deduct club membership fees for dining, recreational, or sporting activities.

- **Donations**   These are not specifically permitted as an employment deduction, and therefore, the general rule that no deductions are allowed is in force. Donations, however, qualify for a tax credit, thereby reducing federal and provincial taxes payable (see Chapter 10).

- **Travel allowance**   The travel allowance is included as a taxable benefit because it does not meet the criteria to qualify as an exception to the general rule that all allowances are taxable. As the travel allowance appears to be in excess of a reasonable amount ($6,000 compared with normal travel expenses of $3,500), it remains taxable. Because the allowance is taxable, the actual expenses incurred by the employee can be deducted from employment income. If the allowance had qualified as tax-free, the actual travel costs could not have been deducted.

- **Computer**   While it is a requirement of the contract of employment that the employee acquire a laptop computer to be used in the performance of duties, the cost of $2,000 does not qualify as a specific deduction permitted because it does not constitute supplies *consumed* and is thus a capital expenditure. This means that only the $75 spent on computer paper during the year qualifies as a deduction.

- **Gift**   The gift (watch) valued at $400 is exempt because it is an award for long service of not less than five years and is below the threshold of $500.

- **Consulting fee**   The consulting fee of $3,000 earned for independent activities does not imply an employer–employee relationship and, as such, does not constitute employment income. It does, however, qualify as business income and is included in the individual's income within the business income category, which is subject to a separate set of general rules.

handwritten margin note: reduced = personal km / 1667 × mostly r standby r standby charge

- **Canada Pension Plan and Employment Insurance premiums**   These amounts are not deductible, in accordance with the general rule that no deductions are permitted except those specified. However, both items qualify for a tax credit that reduces federal and provincial taxes payable (see Chapter 10).

- **Alternative calculation for operating benefit on automobile**   The alternative calculation (i.e., 50% of the standby charge) cannot be used because the business use of the automobile is not greater than 50%.

VIII. Efficient Management of Employee Compensation

One of the more significant costs associated with conducting a business is employee compensation. Employers face various types of decisions when paying employees. They must decide if they will pay more or less than other employers, which employees within the organization will be paid differently, whether the compensation will provide short-term or long-term incentives, and which methods of compensation will be used. While managers approach compensation as a major expense that must be minimized, they also recognize that providing a flexible compensation program which meets the various needs of employees will enhance long-term profitability. A strong compensation package is a positive influence on employee attitudes—it attracts the best employees, enhances efficiency, reduces staff turnover, and improves union relations.

A major influence on compensation decisions is the tax treatment associated with the various methods of compensation. This segment will discuss the tax treatment of the most common methods of employee compensation and examine the impact of those methods on costs (to the employer) and value (to the employee).

A. Basic Objectives and General Tax Principles

A fundamental objective of the compensation program of any business is to provide maximum satisfaction to the employees at the least possible cost. From the employer's perspective, the real cost of compensation is measured in after-tax terms. Similarly, the employees judge the value of compensation they receive in terms of available after-tax disposable income for acquiring the necessities of life and creating savings. Too often, compensation programs are negotiated only in pre-tax terms; the result of this is greater after-tax costs for the employer and reduced after-tax disposable income for the employee.

The general tax principles relating to employment income received by employees were developed earlier in this chapter. Chapter 5 examines the tax treatment of compensation expenses incurred by the employer. These chapters explain that an employee's employment income is calculated in a different way from that of the employer's business income. In general terms, compensation expenses are fully deductible from the employer's business income when they are incurred, whereas the related employment income, in the form of wages or benefits, is fully taxable to the employee when received. However, not all forms of compensation follow these basic principles. Certain types of benefits are not taxable to the employee; others are taxable on a deferred basis, even though they remain deductible by the employer.

The employer can offer non-taxable or tax-deferred compensation items to create increased after-tax value. This increased value can be transferred entirely to the employee, retained by the employer, or shared by both parties (see Section B on the next page). In order to make the fullest use of available tax preferences, the decision maker must take into account the employee's tax position. This involves acquiring a thorough knowledge of how employment income is taxed.

The employer can achieve further cost savings from economies of scale. For example, when an employer purchases group life insurance for its employees, the normal premium rate can be substantially reduced. As with tax savings, the savings from economies of scale can be fully passed on to employees, kept by the employer as a cost advantage, or shared by both parties.

It is also important to recognize that different forms of compensation may have different values to different employees within the organization. For example, a tax-free benefit, such as family health insurance, may be more attractive to an employee with a family than to a single employee, who may prefer some other type of benefit, such as the payment of club dues in a sporting facility. It is therefore important that a range of compensation forms be made available so that employees can choose those which best suit their particular needs.

The various forms of compensation are usually categorized in terms of their desired influence on employee behaviour; however, they can also be categorized in terms of the nature of payment. The compensation categories by nature of payment are as follows:

- direct
- indirect
- deferred

Direct compensation consists primarily of salaries, hourly wages, commissions, bonuses, and other base-pay methods. Direct compensation is fully deductible by the employer and fully taxable when received by the employee. This form of compensation does not require further analysis because of its obvious impact on both parties. When a 10% wage increase is awarded by an employer who pays tax at the rate of 25%, the actual after-tax cost to that employer is 7.5% (10% − 25% tax = 7.5%). However, as employees are subject to a progressive tax rate, the after-tax value of that 10% wage increase will vary among employees. A 10% raise in pay to an employee in a 45% tax bracket amounts to 5.5% after tax, whereas an employee in a 24% tax bracket will receive 7.6% after tax. This information is valuable because it helps employers identify which employees within the organization would prefer forms of compensation that offer reduced tax costs.

The tax consequences of indirect and deferred compensation are now reviewed.

B. Indirect Compensation

Indirect forms of compensation provide employees with specific benefits and/or perquisites. In most cases, indirect compensation is fully deductible by the employer. However, the tax to the employee varies—some benefits are fully taxable, others are tax-free.

1. Taxable Indirect Compensation

As discussed earlier in this chapter, the *Income Tax Act* states that with certain exceptions, all benefits employees receive or enjoy, if incurred by virtue of their employment, are taxable. Below are some of the common types of indirect compensation that are fully taxable to the employee:

- Personal use of employer's automobile.
- Holiday trips, other prizes, and incentive awards.
- Travel expenses of an employee's spouse.
- Interest-free and low-interest loans from the employer.
- Premiums under provincial hospitalization and medical care insurance plans. (Plans obtained from the private sector are not taxable.)
- Gifts. (Certain gifts below $500 are not taxable.)
- Board and lodging, except at remote locations.
- Life insurance.
- Employee counselling services, such as financial planning and tax services.

Considering that the above types of indirect compensation are fully taxable to the employee, this question arises: What value is gained by the employer and by the employee from such types of compensation? Overall cash savings can result if two conditions are present:

1. The employee needs the particular benefit and would acquire it in any case from after-tax disposable income if it were not provided by the employer.

2. The employer can acquire the particular benefit at a lower cost than can the employee because of its greater purchasing power and financial strength.

As indicated previously, the cash flow gained can be transferred to the employee, kept by the company as a cost saving, or shared between the two. Consider the following situation:

Situation: An employee who is in a 45% marginal tax bracket needs to acquire additional life insurance of $100,000. The annual premium cost to the employee is $1,000. The employer, by establishing a group life insurance program for a large number of employees, could provide the additional insurance at a substantially reduced premium cost of $600 per annum. The employer is contemplating a raise in pay for the employee in the form of a $2,000 increase in annual gross salary.

Analysis: If the employer provides a $2,000 salary increase, the employee will first pay tax on the salary and then use the after-tax proceeds to acquire life insurance at a cost of $1,000. The result is shown below.

Salary received	$2,000
Tax @ 45%	(900)
After-tax salary	1,100
Life insurance cost	(1,000)
Net cash to employee	$ 100

Assuming that the employer is subject to a 25% tax rate, the after-tax cost of awarding a $2,000 salary increase is $1,500 ($2,000 − 25% tax saving = $1,500).

As an alternative to a $2,000 salary increase, the employer could offer a salary increase of $673 and, in addition, provide $100,000 of life insurance at a cost to the company of only $600 (for a total pre-tax cost of $1,273). The after-tax positions of the parties involved would be as follows:

Employee:		
Salary received		$ 673
Less tax:		
Salary	673	
Insurance benefit	600	
	$1,273	
Tax (45% of $1,273)		(573)
Net cash to employee		$ 100
Employer:		
Salary paid		$ 673
Insurance premium paid		600
		1,273
Tax saving @ 25%		(318)
After-tax cost		$ 955

These two positions are summarized in the following table. Under both alternatives, the employee receives $100,000 of additional life insurance in addition to $100 of disposable income; in effect, that employee has achieved an overall remuneration increase equivalent to $2,000 in pre-tax terms. However, the employer, by using the benefit form of remuneration, has reduced its annual after-tax cost from $1,500 to $955. When applied to a number of employees, this approach can result in significant cost reductions in employee compensation.

	Salary only	Salary plus benefit
Employee (net cash received)	$ 100	$100
Employer (after-tax cash cost)	1,500	955

In the above example, the cost savings achieved by providing equivalent benefits were retained fully by the employer. As an alternative, the employer could pass the entire cost savings on to the employee. For example, the employer could provide the employee with a salary increase of $1,400 and also pay the $600 life insurance premium for a total cost of $2,000. This cost, on an after-tax basis, would amount to $1,500 ($2,000 − tax savings of 25% = $1,500), which is identical to the cost of a $2,000 salary increase. However, the employee would achieve much higher after-tax remuneration, as shown below.

Cash salary received		$1,400
Less tax:		
Salary	1,400	
Benefit	600	
	$2,000	
Tax (45% of $2,000)		(900)
Net cash to employee		$ 500

Note that the employee would receive after-tax cash of $500 and still have $100,000 of life insurance. In order to achieve this position without the enjoyment of the employer's benefit program, the employee would have needed to receive a salary increase of $2,727, as shown below.

Salary	$2,727
Tax @ 45%	(1,227)
After-tax salary	$1,500
Life insurance cost	(1,000)
Net cash to employee	$ 500

In summary, for an after-tax cost of $1,500 to the employer (which in pre-tax terms is $2,000), the employee can receive a remuneration increase equivalent to $2,727. This constitutes a raise in pay higher than was originally contemplated.

As a third alternative, the cost savings from the benefit program could be shared by the employer and the employee in some ratio. For example, the employer could pay an increased salary of $1,000 and, as well, provide $100,000 of insurance at a cost of $600, for a total pre-tax cost of $1,600 and an after-tax cost of $1,200 ($1,600 − tax savings of 25% = $1,200). The employee would receive net cash after tax of $280 in addition to the value of the life insurance. In this case, the employer's cost would be reduced from $1,500, and the employee's cash position would be improved from $100.

The three alternatives analyzed were all compared with a straight salary increase of $2,000 for a particular employee. The results are summarized below.

	Salary only	Salary and Benefit		
		Cost saving retained by employer	Cost saving shifted to employee	Cost saving shared
Cost to employer	$1,500	$ 955	$1,500	$1,200
Benefit to employee:				
Cash	$ 100	$ 100	$ 500	$ 280
Insurance value	1,000	1,000	1,000	1,000
	$1,100	$1,100	$1,500	$1,280
Salary equivalent	$2,000	$2,000	$2,727	$2,327

Clearly, the use of fully taxable employee benefits as an alternative form of compensation can result in significantly increased cash flow for the employer, the employee, or both.

It is very important that the employer examine compensation costs in after-tax terms. In addition, the value of alternative forms of compensation must be communicated to employees in terms of salary equivalents. For example, it is important that the employee (in the above summary) realize that a salary increase of $1,000 plus a $100,000 life insurance policy is equivalent to a pre-tax salary increase of $2,327 in that both provide the same benefits and disposable income. Many employers fail to communicate this information to their employees, with the result that salary and wage negotiations become more difficult.

2. Non-Taxable Indirect Compensation

Although, as a general rule, benefits provided by the employer are fully taxable to the employee, the *Income Tax Act*, by exception, permits certain benefits to be received tax-free.[85] In addition, by administrative policy, the CRA considers certain other types of benefits also to be non-taxable.[86] Listed here again are some of the common benefits that qualify for special treatment:

- Group sickness or accident insurance plans.
- Private health services plans.
- Supplementary unemployment benefit plans.
- Counselling services relating to the mental or physical health of the employee.
- Membership fees for a social or athletic club, if the membership is principally for the employer's advantage. (Note that the employer cannot deduct the cost of such fees under any circumstances—Chapter 5.)
- Moving expenses for transferring employees to a new location. When an employer compensates an employee for a decrease in value or impairment of the employee's residence, 50% of the compensation in excess of $15,000 is a taxable benefit.
- Discounts on merchandise.
- Scholarships, bursaries, and free tuition provided to family members of the employee.[87]

---

85 ITA 6(1)(a).
86 IT-470R.
87 ITA 6(1)(a)(vi).

While the above benefits are not taxable to the employee, all of them, with the exception of club memberships, are fully deductible by the employer as compensation expenses against business income. These types of benefits can create additional cash flow in two ways:

1. Eliminating tax on the amount of benefits received by the employee.

2. Reducing costs resulting from economies of scale when services are purchased for a large number of employees.

Consider the following situation:

Situation: An employer is prepared to pay an extra $2,000 to an employee who is subject to a 32% tax rate. The employee needs additional family health insurance and disability insurance. The employer, who pays tax at the rate of 25%, can purchase these types of insurance under a group plan at a 20% discount.

Analysis: The employer can provide the additional remuneration as a salary increase or in the form of a benefit package to the employee. The cost of each alternative to the employer is $2,000 before tax and $1,500 after tax ($2,000 − 25% tax savings = $1,500). However, each alternative has a dramatically different value to the employee. A $2,000 salary will provide the employee with the following:

Salary	$2,000
Tax @ 32%	(640)
After-tax value	$1,360

On the other hand, providing the employee with $2,000 of benefits that are not taxable to that employee is equivalent to providing after-tax benefits of $2,500, calculated as follows:

Cost of benefits provided	$2,000
Add discount obtained by employer	500
Retail value of benefits	2,500
Personal tax	–0–
After-tax value to employee	$2,500

In other words, a benefit package with an after-tax value of $2,500 for the employee is equivalent to a salary increase of $3,676 ($3,676 − tax of 32% = $2,500). In this particular case, an employer who provides $2,000 of the desired tax-free benefits incurs an after-tax cost of $1,500, while rewarding the employee with the equivalent of a gross salary increase of $3,676.

This analysis indicates that it is highly worthwhile to provide employees with tax-free benefits that can be purchased at a discount. Again, this increase in after-tax value can be shared between the employer and the employee, thereby reducing the employer's remuneration costs and increasing the employee's after-tax disposable income.

Always remember that the value to employees of tax-free benefits will vary from group to group according to income levels and the corresponding rates of personal tax. All tax-free benefits create some amount of value; together, they form a vital part of compensation programs. It is important to stress to employees again and again the value of tax-free benefits in terms of pre-tax salary equivalents. Otherwise, it is difficult to maximize the cost efficiency of such programs. Communicating the value of employee benefits should start when wage settlements are being negotiated and should continue thereafter. A simple annual statement to each employee pointing out the pre-tax value of all of the components of remuneration can have a positive impact on employee relations and on future wage negotiations.

C. Deferred Compensation

The highly progressive tax rates imposed on individuals constitute a strong inducement to utilize compensation methods that provide tax-free benefits. There are few such forms of compensation, however. A next-best alternative is to compensate employees on a deferred basis; that is, by delaying the payment until some future time. From the employee's perspective this may present two advantages:

1. Taxing income later, rather than sooner, may result in lower tax rates under the progressive system, especially if payments are delayed until retirement.

2. If the delayed payments are invested on the employee's behalf, investment returns will be achieved on pre-tax income, rather than on after-tax income.

Deferred compensation programs are established on the assumption that employees will attempt to save some portion of their annual income for retirement. As the annual personal living expenses of each employee vary, so does the general attractiveness of the different deferred compensation programs. When analyzing the benefits to employees of deferred compensation, one must compare the wealth accumulation and investment returns from a deferred program with what would be achieved if employees attempted to save and invest a portion of their normal after-tax salary.

A number of deferred compensation programs are available. Not all are subject to the same tax treatment. There are three categories of deferred plans: registered plans, non-registered plans, and stock-based plans. Each of these categories is discussed briefly below.

1. Registered Plans

The *Income Tax Act* sanctions three specific registered deferred compensation plans that provide preferential tax treatment. As already indicated, these are the registered pension plan (RPP), the proposed pooled registered pension plan (PRPP), and the deferred profit-sharing plan (DPSP). All of these plans permit the employer to deduct, for tax purposes, a limited amount of contributions on behalf of specified employees. In neither case is the value of the benefit to the employee taxed until the funds are removed from the plan. This removal usually occurs at retirement. In addition, investment returns on accumulated contributions are not taxable until they are distributed to the employee.

Because contributions to registered plans are deductible by the employer, the after-tax cost of such contributions is the same as the after-tax cost of compensation in the form of normal salaries. However, receiving the compensation as a registered plan, rather than as salary, makes a vast difference to the employee. As explained earlier in the chapter, an employee who receives $3,500 annually for 30 years in the form of an RPP or DPSP and who earns compound interest on it at 10% accumulates $633,000. In comparison, an employee in the 45% tax bracket who receives salary of $3,500 annually for 30 years and invests the after-tax amount ($3,500 − 45% tax = $1,925) to earn interest at 10% (5.5% after tax) accumulates only $147,000.

While the difference between these two plans is significant, one must recognize that the $633,000 accumulated under the deferred option is fully taxable when paid to the employee, whereas the $147,000 accumulated under the salary option is not subject to further taxation. It is difficult to estimate the future tax liability on the deferred option because it depends on the manner in which the funds are paid to the employee (lump-sum or a monthly pension payment) and on the future applicable tax rate. However, even when the worst-case scenario is assumed—which is, that the employee will withdraw the deferred amount in a lump sum that is taxable at a high rate of 45%—the deferred option still amounts to $348,000 ($633,000 – 45% tax = $348,000).

The value of deferred compensation can be expressed as a pre-tax salary equivalent, using this worst-case scenario. The following calculation shows that a deferred compensation amount of $3,500 annually is equivalent to an annual taxable salary of $8,278:

Salary received	$ 8,278
Tax @ 45%	(3,725)
Net after-tax salary	$ 4,553
Compound value of investing $4,553 annually for 30 y at 5.5% after tax (10% – 45% tax = 5.5%)	$348,000

This means that an employer (with a 33% tax rate) who provides $3,500 annually to a registered deferred compensation program at an after-tax cost of $2,345 ($3,500 – 33% tax saving = $2,345) is, in effect, providing the employee with a salary equivalent of $8,278. Of course, the pre-tax salary equivalent will vary with the tax bracket of the given employee. However, deferring tax on the benefit and on the investment returns accumulated will always result in a significant value spread between the benefit cost and its salary equivalent.

2. Non-Registered Plans

The *Income Tax Act* makes reference to the following non-registered deferred compensation plans:[88]

- Employee profit-sharing plans.[89]
- Employee trusts.[90]
- Salary deferral arrangements.[91]
- Retirement compensation arrangements.[92]

While these plans exist to provide a formal deferral of compensation, they are seldom used because there is no tax relief for the amounts deferred. For example, under an employee profit-sharing plan and an employee trust, the employer contributes amounts on behalf of the employees to an intermediary or trustee, who invests the funds for the employees' benefit. The payments to the plan are deductible from the employer's income but must also be included, along with any investment returns, in the employees' income in the year in which they are received by the plan.

In effect, the rules applicable to non-registered deferral plans are anti-avoidance provisions designed to prevent the deferral of tax on employee compensation.

3. Stock-Based Plans

To provide employees with long-term incentives and rewards, corporate employers can develop compensation plans that give the employee an opportunity to purchase shares, which will grow in value as corporate profits increase. There are several such

---

88 IT-502.
89 ITA 6(1)(d), 144(1), (3), (5).
90 ITA 6(1)(h), 6(1)(a)(ii), 248(1).
91 ITA 6(1)(i), 6(11), (12), (14), 20(1)(oo), 56(1)(w), 248(1).
92 ITA 6(1)(a)(ii), 56(1)(x), 248(1).

plans available. Some are described briefly below, together with their general tax treatment.

• Stock Options

Stock-option plans provide the employee with the right to purchase shares from the corporate treasury at a specified price for a specified period of time. In many cases, the option price offered is less than the shares' value at the time. The tax treatment to the employee from stock-option benefits was described in detail earlier in this chapter. In general terms, the employee is taxed on the benefit received at the time the option is exercised and the shares are purchased.[93] For example, an employee may be granted an option to purchase treasury stock at $10 per share any time over the next five years. Because the option price is fixed but the shares' value may grow, the employee can receive a growth in value without actually purchasing the shares. However, when the shares are purchased, the employee will incur a taxable benefit equal to the difference between the shares' value and the option price. After exercising the option, the employee can retain the shares or sell them on the open market.

From the employer's perspective, this form of incentive is attractive because it does not involve a cash payment, although it does result in dilution of ownership. In addition, stock-option plans are an incentive to employees to enhance the long-term profitability of the business. Stock-based compensation expense is not deductible for the employer.[94]

• Stock Purchase Plans

Employees working for a public company can purchase shares in their employer's corporation on the open market at any time. However, they are usually constrained by a lack of funds to do so. A stock-purchase plan permits employees to purchase a specific number of shares from the corporate treasury at fair market values using funds loaned to them by the employer.[95] Because the funds loaned to the employees come back to the company in exchange for the shares, there is no cash cost to the employer.

From an employee's perspective, stock purchase plans provide an investment opportunity without a financial burden. In many cases, the corporation issues the employee preferred shares that are convertible into common shares; such shares have little downside risk but do have an opportunity for growth. As the employee does not purchase the shares at a discount, no taxable benefit occurs. When the shares are sold, the employee will incur a capital gain if the shares have increased in value.

• Stock Bonus Plans

Under a stock bonus arrangement, an employer simply issues shares to an employee in lieu of a cash bonus. Usually, the number of shares issued is a function of the profitability of the business, and awards are given to employees based on their particular contributions.

The full value of all shares received as a stock bonus is taxable to the employee as employment income in the year the shares are issued.[96] Therefore, while the stock bonus results in no cash cost to the employer, it results in a tax cost to the employee.

• Phantom Stock Plans

A phantom stock plan does not actually provide employees with shares; rather, it is an elaborate deferred bonus agreement. It is called a "phantom stock plan" because the

---

93 ITA 7.
94 ITA 7(3)(b).
95 ITA 15(2), IT-119R4 (paragraph 19).
96 ITA 5; treated in the same manner as a cash bonus.

amount of the bonus is tied directly to changes in the value of the corporation's shares. For example, an employer may award points to an employee, having tied the value of those points to the value of the common shares traded on a stock exchange. Although the points are awarded, the employee does not cash them in until the end of a specified vesting period. Points may be forfeited if the employee is dismissed for cause. Once the vesting period is over, the employee will receive a cash bonus that is taxable at that time. The employer will receive a tax deduction in the year the bonus is paid.

A phantom stock plan is beneficial to the employer because it preserves cash flow until the end of the vesting period. It is also beneficial to the employees in that the company shares its profits with them on a tax-deferred basis. A phantom stock plan requires careful planning to avoid being classified as a salary deferral arrangement; the latter, as described previously, would result in the employee being taxed on the benefit when it is earned, rather than when it is received.

Each of these four stock-based plans was reviewed only briefly; it should be clear, however, that each provides long-term incentive rewards, which, in turn, can enhance the cash flow of the employer while enhancing the employee's wealth.

IX. Tax Planning Checklist

1. Employees should try to maximize their use of employer-provided benefit programs, even when the benefit is taxable, because often the employer can acquire the particular service or good at a lower cost.

2. In lieu of salaries, employers should consider offering a shopping list of benefits from which employees can choose. This way, employees receive only those benefits that are relevant to their personal situation.

3. Salary deferrals may be beneficial when the employer pays interest on the deferred amount. However, employees should consider whether the deferral to a future taxation year will alter the rate of tax that would otherwise be applicable.

4. When provided with an automobile for extensive personal use over several years, an employee should eventually consider purchasing the vehicle from the employer at its depreciated value. The taxable benefit (standby charge) is based each year on the original cost of the car, even when its value is declining. At some point, the employee may find it worthwhile to purchase the car, rather than incur the tax cost based on the original cost.

5. An employee who wants to take advantage of the reduced standby charge for low personal use of an employer's automobile (i.e., less than 50%) must maintain a careful record of kilometres travelled.

6. An employer who is prepared to fund an employee's personal automobile costs should investigate whether the automobile should be owned or leased and by which party.

7. When an employee uses his or her own car for the employer's business, a decision should be made as to the method of employer funding (i.e., allowance or regular reimbursement). In the case of an allowance, the employer should consider including that allowance in the employee's income as unreasonable so that he or she can deduct the higher actual travel costs.

8. When an employee uses an employer's automobile less than 50% of the time for personal use, and when the employer pays the operating costs (alternative calculation—50% of standby charge), the employee must tell the employer

before year end whether he or she wants to use the alternative calculation for the benefit derived.

9. The taxable benefit calculation on low-interest employer home purchase loans is fixed on loans up to a five-year term. When interest rates decline, it may be worth renegotiating the loan to guarantee the lower rate for a new five-year period.

10. Employees who have been granted stock options should consider when such options should be exercised. If the share price is rising, an early purchase reduces the amount of employment income and enhances the amount of the capital gain, of which only one-half is taxable. This benefit must be weighed against the cost of funding the purchase sooner.

11. A commissioned salesperson cannot deduct expenses in excess of commissions earned, and the excess is not available for carry-over to another year. When it would improve the salesperson's tax position, consideration should be given to delaying expenses to the next taxation year.

12. Salespeople cannot deduct capital expenditures except for capital cost allowance on automobiles and airplanes. Therefore, capital equipment required for work, such as cellular phones, computers, and so on, should be leased, rather than purchased. The lease cost is then deductible.

X. Summary and Conclusion

The determination of employment income is governed by a narrow set of rules. These rules require that remuneration—including benefits and allowances—received under a term of employment be taxable. Knowledge of the exceptions to the general rules is vital if one is to understand completely how employment income is taxed. As stated in this chapter, the exceptions are not significant in number, but their value to the employee is significant.

Similarly, deductions from employment income are limited to a very short list of items, which simplifies the process of income determination. One often hears the complaint that employees are at a disadvantage because they are permitted so few deductions. It must be recognized that in most cases, employees do not incur many direct expenses for the purpose of earning their employment income. Those that do appear to be adequately covered by the special deductions that *are* permitted. The deductions attempt to recognize the major types of expenses that employees must incur to earn their income; with the exception of the shortcomings of the deduction for supplies consumed, they appear to accomplish this.

Employment income is usually earned from employers who are carrying on a business. Employers determine their income for tax purposes according to the principles of business income (see Chapter 5), which are different from the principles of employment income. It is essential that while studying the remaining chapters in Part Two of the text, readers compare the general principles for each category; doing so will enable them to understand the full scope of various financial transactions. Employees and employers, while governed by different rules, interact in a way that binds them together in a common decision process. Employers cannot adequately develop compensation packages without understanding their impact on the employees.

This chapter has also examined how the tax system affects decisions relating to employee compensation. Employers and employees are separate taxable entities and determine their taxable income by different principles; however, they also interact in ways that bind them together in a common decision process. Employers who are sensitive to the tax status of their employees can develop compensation programs that maximize the after-tax income of those employees and, at the same time, minimize the company's after-tax cost.

There are a number of compensation methods available besides the basic ones, which are salaries, commissions, and bonuses. Employers can compensate employees indirectly by providing benefits that those employees would otherwise have to acquire on their own from after-tax salaries. Although some of these benefits are taxable to the employee, the amount taxable may be less than the value to the employee. For example, when employers can purchase benefits for less than retail cost, the employee is taxed only on the discounted cost. Certain other benefits are not taxable to the employee. The savings the employer gains by obtaining benefits at a lower cost and by the reduction of income taxes can be passed on to the employees or shared between the employer and the employees.

As well, employers can help maximize their employees' long-term wealth accumulation. By utilizing tax-deferred compensation methods, such as RPPs, DPSPs, and stock-based investment plans, employers can substantially increase their employees' savings as well as the returns on those savings.

Whenever possible, the employer should offer a range of compensation alternatives so that it meets the needs of the greatest possible number of employees. At first glance, this may seem more costly to the employer; however, in the long run, providing benefits that have greater after-tax value to the employee will result in a more cost-efficient compensation program. In this regard, it is important to explain to the employees the value, in terms of cash equivalents, of each alternative form of compensation. Flexible and creative compensation programs can improve productivity and, in so doing, make the business more competitive.

Visit the Canadian Income Taxation Web site at **www.mcgrawhill.ca/ olc/buckwold** to view any updated tax information.

Demonstration Questions

QUESTION ONE

Carl Collins celebrated his 65th birthday in 20X4. A car accident forced him to quit his job and retire on June 30, 20X4. He received $120,000 from an insurance company for potential loss of earnings. At his retirement party, his employer presented him with an original work of art costing $2,500 in honour of his long service (20 years). He also received a cheque for $40,000 in recognition of his 20 years of valued service. Information relating to his employment activities is presented below.

1. Collins retired on June 30, 20X4. Up to that date, he received a salary of $48,000. Collins negotiated contracts for his employer and was also paid ¼ of 1% of the value of contracts negotiated. As of June 30, 20X4, this amounted to $22,000 and was paid in two instalments of $11,000 each on September 30, 20X4, and January 15, 20X5.

2. To carry out his employment duties, Collins used a company car that was also available for his personal use. He returned the car to the employer on June 30, 20X4. He drove the car 20,000 km for business and 4,000 km for personal use in 20X4.

    The employer's lease cost for the car to June 30, 20X4, was $4,494. In addition, the employer paid operating costs of $3,800. Collins paid the employer $200 as a partial reimbursement for the personal use of the automobile.

3. On June 30, 20X4, Collins paid the employer $20,400. This covered the full principal repayment of an employee loan of $20,000 plus interest of $400 from January 1, 20X4, to June 30, 20X4. The CRA's prescribed interest rate for the period was 6%. Collins had used half of the borrowed funds to repair his home and the other half to help buy an investment in shares of public corporations.

4. As a condition of employment, Collins had worked from an office in his home. A desk was available to him at his employer's place of business, which he used one afternoon a week. He spent the remaining time in his home office or visiting customers. The home office occupied 80 square metres of his 800 square-metre home. His home expenses for the entire year were as follows:

Mortgage interest	$ 4,200
Utilities	2,200
Property taxes	2,600
Insurance	800
Minor repairs and maintenance	1,200
	$11,000

5. After the car accident, Collins received $4,200 ($700 × 6 weeks) from the employer's sickness, accident, and income maintenance insurance plan. In addition, the employer's private medical insurance plan paid hospital expenses of $3,000.

6. Besides Collins's salary, the employer paid the premiums for private medical insurance ($380) and group sickness, accident, and income maintenance insurance ($500). The following amounts were withheld from Collins's salary and remitted to the appropriate parties:

Income tax	$14,000
Registered pension plan	4,000
Share of premiums for group sickness, accident, and income maintenance plan	500
Canada Pension Plan and Employment Insurance	3,147

The group sickness, accident, and income maintenance plan originated in 20X0. By the end of 20X3, Collins had paid $2,000 in premiums, which was matched by the employer.

7. In January 20X4, Collins purchased a computer for $2,000 on time payments. He incurred interest costs of $240. Until his retirement, he used the computer for employment activities 60% of the time. He also obtained a fax machine on a two-year lease arrangement. In 20X4, lease payments were $240. He used the fax entirely for employment until his retirement. The following additional costs were incurred for employment:

Advertising	$300
Entertainment: Meals for clients	400
Collins's meals when travelling out of town on occasional 10-hour round trips	200

Required:
Determine Collins's net income from employment for the 20X4 taxation year. Comment on any items that have been excluded from the calculation.

Solution:

Employment income:		
Salary		$48,000
Commissions received in 20X4		11,000
Retirement gift—painting ($2,500 − $500 threshold)		2,000
Automobile:		
Standby charge (see comment below)		
⅔ × $4,494 = $2,996 × 4,000 km ÷		
(1,667 km × 6 months)	1,198	
Operating benefit—lesser of:		
4,000 km × 26¢ = $1,040		
50% × $1,198 = $599	599	
	1,797	
Less reimbursement	(200)	1,597

Employee loan—interest benefit:		
Prescribed interest—6% × $20,000 × 6 m/12 m	600	
Less interest paid	(400)	200
Payments from income maintenance insurance	4,200	
Less premiums paid by Collins ($2,000 + $500)	(2,500)	1,700
		64,497
Employment expenses:		
Home office ($2,200 utilities + $1,200 maintenance) × 80/800 × ½ year		(170)
Registered pension plan		(4,000)
Sales expenses:		
Home office ($2,600 property tax +		
$800 insurance) × 80/800 × ½ year	$(170)	
Fax lease payments—$240 × ½ year	(120)	
Advertising	(300)	
Entertainment meals—50% × $400	(200)	
Total sales expenses	$790	
Limited to commission income ($11,000)		(790)
Income from employment		$59,537

- **Standby Charge**   The standby charge (above) was reduced from its normal calculation because the number of kilometres driven for employment purposes was greater than 50% of the total kilometres driven (20,000 ÷ 24,000 = 83%). Therefore, the normal standby charge was reduced by the number of personal kilometres driven divided by the arbitrary amount of 1,667 km for each month the automobile was available.

  The following amounts were excluded from the calculation of employment income:

- **Home office**   Collins is entitled to deduct his home office expenses since his home office is the place where Collins principally performs the duties of his employment. This is one of two *either/or* criteria used to establish qualification.

  Employees who meet this test are entitled to deduct utilities and minor repairs and maintenance. These home office expenses are considered to be *supplies consumed* for tax purposes. Property taxes and insurance on a home office are only deductible as sales expenses and are subject to the sales expense limitation (commission income).

  Mortgage interest is not deductible in computing employment income.

- **Deferred commissions**   Of the total commissions of $22,000, only $11,000 was received in 20X4. The remaining amount of $11,000 was received in 20X5 and will be included in that year's employment income.

- **Insurance for loss of earnings**   The $120,000 of insurance proceeds is not employment income. Also, it does not qualify as "other sources" of income and therefore is not taxable.

- **Retiring allowance**   The retirement payment of $40,000 is a retiring allowance and is not classified as employment income. Instead, it is considered to be other income and is included in a separate part of the aggregating formula for net income for tax purposes.[97]

- **Hospital insurance**   The $3,000 of hospital expenses paid by the employer's insurance plan is not a taxable benefit, unlike the insurance for the lost salary under the sickness, accident, and income maintenance insurance plan.

- **Insurance premiums**   The private medical insurance premium and the group sickness, accident, and income maintenance insurance premium are specifically allowed as non-taxable benefits.

---

97 ITA 56(1)(a)(ii).

- **Computer** The computer cost is a capital item and cannot be deducted as selling expenses. Similarly, the interest of $240 on the computer loan is on account of capital.

- **Canada Pension Plan and Employment Insurance** The contributions by Collins to the Canada Pension and Employment Insurance plans are not deductible from employment income, as they are not specifically mentioned in section 8 of the *Income Tax Act*, which lists the permitted deductions. The amounts can be used to claim a tax credit when calculating tax (see Chapter 10).

- **Out-of-town meals** The cost of meals while travelling out of town is deductible only if the employee was away for more than 12 hours in the day. Here, Collins was away for only 10 hours.

- **Interest benefit** Note that the employee loan was used by Collins partially to make an investment in shares of public companies. Therefore, one-half of the interest cost paid plus one-half of the low-interest benefit on the loan can be deducted when arriving at income from property.

QUESTION TWO

Francine Leduc is a senior employee with OM Inc., a public corporation. Information relating to her employment with OM for 20X5 is summarized below.

1. In 20X5 Leduc received a salary of $110,000. From this, deductions of $33,000 for income tax, $3,147 for Canada Pension Plan and Employment Insurance, $6,000 for contributions to a registered pension plan, and $1,200 for charitable donations were made and remitted to the appropriate parties. On November 30, 20X5, Leduc was awarded a $30,000 bonus, receiving $3,000 at the time and the balance payable on June 30, 20X6.

2. OM provides three of its senior executives with an allowance to attend conventions of their choice. In 20X5, Leduc received $2,000 for this allowance and was not required to account for the costs. Leduc attended one convention and incurred travel costs of $2,200.

3. Leduc's employment contract requires that she use her own car on company business. In 20X5, OM paid Leduc a car allowance of $5,600, being 35¢ for each of 16,000 km driven for employment purposes. Leduc drove her car a total of 24,000 km in 20X5 and incurred the following costs:

Parking—visiting customers	$ 600
Insurance	1,150
Repairs and maintenance	1,400
Fuel	1,800
Interest on car loan	4,200

The undepreciated capital cost of her car at the end of 20X4 was $20,400.

4. On December 20, 20X5, Leduc asked for and received from OM a $6,000 advance against her January 20X6 salary. The funds were needed for a family vacation. OM reduced Leduc's January 20X6 salary for the advance.

5. In June 20X5, OM announced two new employee compensation plans. One plan allowed each employee to purchase 1,000 shares of OM Inc. at $14 per share. At the time of the announcement, OM's shares were trading at $15 per share. Leduc purchased her 1,000 shares at $14 per share in August 20X5. At that time, the shares were trading at $18 per share. On December 31, 20X5, Leduc sold all the OM shares at $16 per share.

OM also introduced a holiday cruise award for executives who achieved employer goals for sales volume. Leduc qualified for the award, and in 20X5, she and her spouse enjoyed the five-day cruise. The cost of the cruise was $3,000 ($1,500 each) including tax.

Required:
Determine Leduc's net income from employment for the 20X5 taxation year.

Solution:

Employment income			
Salary			$110,000
Bonus—portion received			3,000
Convention allowance—see below			2,000
Car allowance—considered to be unreasonably low			5,600
Salary advance			6,000
Stock option benefit—$1,000 × ($18 − $14)			4,000
Holiday cruise award—Leduc $1,500 + $1,500 for spouse			3,000
			133,600
Deduct			
Registered pension plan		$6,000	
Parking		600	
Auto:			
Insurance	$1,150		
Repairs	1,400		
Fuel	1,800		
Interest ($300 × 12 months—limit)	3,600		
Capital cost allowance $20,400 × 30%	6,120		
	$14,070		
16,000/24,000 km × 14,070		9,380	(15,980)
Employment income			$117,620

Several other items require further explanation. The *convention allowance* is taxable under the general rule that all allowances are taxable. There is no exception for a convention allowance, unlike a travel allowance, which can be tax-free if it is a reasonable amount. Also, even though the convention allowance is taxable, the actual convention expenses incurred by Leduc cannot be deducted from employment income because section 8 of the *Income Tax Act* does not list convention expenses as a deductible item. The treatment of travel allowances and travel expenses is unique.

When Leduc exercised the *stock option*, the related employment income was established as the difference between the market value of the shares at that time ($18) and the cost of the shares ($14). For reasons indicated in this chapter, the cost of the shares for capital gain or capital loss purposes was established at $18. Thus, when Leduc sold the shares for $16 per share on the last day of the year, she incurred a capital loss of $2,000 (1,000 × [$16 − $18]). One-half of this is allowable, though it can be deducted only against other capital gains.

The *holiday cruise award* is a performance-related award and, as such, does not qualify for the tax-free treatment given to long service/anniversary awards of up to $500 in value. Performance-related awards (for achieving an employment-related economic objective, e.g., sales targets) are always taxable.

Charitable donations are not deductible from employment income. Instead, they qualify as a tax credit when calculating tax (see Chapter 10).

QUESTION THREE

In 20X3, Bonita received a salary of $62,000 and earned commission income of $9,000. Of the $9,000 earned from commissions, only $7,500 was received in 20X3 with the remaining $1,500 received in January 20X4. She also received a car allowance of $0.19 per employment km for a total of $3,040 for the year. Bonita is required to pay her own expenses relating to her sales duties. She has paid the following expenses in 20X3, all of which are considered reasonable:

Automobile operating costs (gas, repairs, insurance)	$7,200
Interest on a loan to purchase a car	1,200
Advertising and promotion items	2,000
Entertainment meals and drinks	1,000
Parking	400
Cost of new home computer (30% employment use)	1,100
Home office costs:	
Utilities – heat, water, electricity	4,800
Mortgage interest	6000
Property taxes	3000
Insurance	800

Bonita purchased a new car two years ago for $28,000. At December 31, 20X2, the car had an undepreciated capital cost of $19,000. In 20X3, she drove the car 24,000 km of which 16,000 were for employment purposes.

Bonita used her home office exclusively for her employment and routinely met there with clients. Normally she worked one day a week from the home office and the other days at her employer's place of business or out of the office visiting customers. Her home office occupies 5% of the space in her home.

Required:

Determine Bonita's net income from employment for the 20X3 taxation year. If Bonita was not a salesperson and did not earn commissions but rather received a salary only, how would the calculation of expenses change? Explain.

Solution:

Before calculating net income from employment several of the items are discussed.

- **Commissions** Employment income is included on a cash basis—when received. Therefore, the $1,500 of commissions earned in 20X3 but not received until 20X4 are not included in the calculation.

- **Car allowance** It is first necessary to establish if the allowance of $3,040 is taxable. An automobile allowance is not taxable if it is reasonable. If the allowance is reasonable and not taxable, then all sales expenses and auto expenses are not deductible. The car allowance is calculated based on the employment km travelled. Therefore, it is possible for the car allowance to be a reasonable allowance. The deductible automobile expenses calculated below (operating costs, capital cost allowance, interest, and parking) show that the actual expenses are much higher than the allowance. This establishes that the allowance is not reasonable because it is much too low. So, the allowance of $3,040 is taxable and the sales expenses and auto expenses can be deducted.

- **Sales expenses** Bonita qualifies for a deduction of sales expenses because she is required to pay her own expenses, is normally required to work away from her employer's business, and is paid in part by commissions and did not receive a tax-free allowance for travelling expenses. The total of the deductions under paragraph 8(1)(f) of the *Income Tax Act* are limited to the selling commissions earned in the year. However, if an item can be deducted under a different section of the *Income Tax Act,* the item will not be subject to the commission income limit. Interest on the car loan, capital cost allowance, and the utilities portion of the home office expenses can be deducted under different paragraphs of the *Income Tax Act* and are not restricted to commission income.

- **Home office** The home office qualifies for a deduction because it can be argued that it is used exclusively and continuously for employment duties and is used on a regular basis in the ordinary course of performing employment duties. This is one of two *either/or* criteria used to establish qualification. As a salesperson, Bonita can deduct insurance and property taxes in addition to utility costs and repairs. However, she cannot deduct mortgage interest. If she were self-employed the mortgage interest would also be deductible.

- **Computer** The cost of the computer cannot be deducted by claiming capital cost allowance because it is not specifically mentioned in the employment sections. A self-employed person could deduct capital cost allowance on the computer.

With the above in mind the net income from employment is calculated as follows:

Salary		$62,000
Commissions received		7,500
Car allowance		3,040
		72,540
Deduct sales expenses (8(1)(f):		
Auto operating costs		
$7,200 × 16,000 km/24,000 km	4,800	
Parking	400	
Advertising and promotion	2,000	
Entertainment meals and drink—50% × 1,000	500	
Home office [5% × ($3,000 property tax +		
$800 insurance)]	190	
	$7,890	
Deduction limited to commission income of $7,500		(7,500)
Deduct other expenses:		
Interest on car loan—$1,200 × 16,000 km/24,000 km		(800)
CCA on auto—30% × $19,000 × 16,000 km/24,000 km		(3,800)
Home office		
5% ($4,800 utilities)		(240)
Net income from employment		$60,200

Bonita has the option of deducting car expenses of $5,200 ($4,800 operating costs + $400 parking) plus other travel expenses (0 in this case), without any limit, under a different section of the *Income Tax Act.* If she does so, she cannot deduct any sales expenses under paragraph (8)(1)(f). This would not be to her advantage in this case since her deductible sales expenses ($7,500) exceed $5,200.

If Bonita did not receive commission income, but only a salary, she would not be entitled to deduct expenses relating to sales. However, she would be entitled to deduct motor vehicle expenses if she was required to use her vehicle for employment purposes, was required to pay for her own expenses, and was not in receipt of a tax-free motor vehicle allowance. Therefore, the deductions allowed for her car expenses would include the operating costs ($4,800), parking ($400), interest on car loan ($800), and the CCA on the auto ($3,800). The advertising and entertainment expenses would not be allowed. Bonita would also be allowed to deduct certain home office expenses. If she does not receive commissions the expenses allowed for the home office include *only the utility costs*. The expenses relating to property taxes, insurance, and interest are not permitted.

QUESTION FOUR

ABC Inc. decided to acquire an automobile for a recently hired salesperson. ABC received a quote from an auto dealer for both a purchase and a lease of the auto. The salesperson will be permitted to use the car for personal use as well as for employment. In deciding between the lease and a purchase option, ABC felt it would be useful to determine the tax implications to the employee for each alternative.

A purchase of the auto would cost $31,500 including the HST. A lease of the same vehicle would cost $420 per month for 48 months including the HST.[98] Annual operating costs are estimated to be $6,000 under either option. It is estimated that the auto will be driven 20,000 km annually of which between 9,000 km and 11,000 km would be for employment purposes.

The employee will use the auto for personal use throughout the entire year. It is anticipated that a new auto will be acquired every four years.

Required:
Calculate the annual taxable benefit to the employee from the personal use of the auto for each acquisition alternative.

Solution:
The tax implication for each option is significantly different. Before the calculations are made it is necessary to determine if the auto will be used *primarily for employment purposes*. CRA has indicated that "primarily" means more than 50%. The range of employment use in this case is between 9000 km (45%; 9,000/20,000 = 45%) and 11,000 km (55%; 11,000/20,000). The calculations below demonstrate each of these amounts.

The auto will be available to the employee for personal use throughout the entire year—12 months. Therefore, benefit from the capital value of the auto—the standby charge— is applicable for 12 months.

Auto is **NOT** used primarily for employment—*employment 9,000 km—45%*:

The standby charge is based on the full benefit without regard to the proportion of personal use. So, the benefit will be the same for an employee who uses the auto for personal use for 11,000 km or 15,000 km.

Purchase option—Cost $31,500 including HST.

Standby charge—$31,500 (original cost) × 2% × 12 months =	$7,560
Operating benefit—11,000 km (personal use) × 26¢ =	2,860
Total taxable benefit	**$10,420**

Lease option—Cost $420 monthly × 12 m = $5,040 including HST.

Standby charge—$5,040 × ²/₃ =	$3,360
Operating benefit—11,000 km (personal use) × 26¢ =	2,860
Total taxable benefit	**$6,220**

---

*Auto **IS** used primarily for employment—employment: 11,000 km—55%:*

When the auto is used primarily for employment purposes the proportion of personal use will be relevant. So using the auto for 5,000 km or 9,000 km for personal use will give a

---

98 Actual quote obtained in February, 2011.

different result. The normal standby charge can be reduced to an amount equal to the proportion of personal km to 20,004 annual km or 1,667 km per month. In addition, when the auto is used primarily for employment purposes the employee has the option to accept an operating benefit of 26 cents per km or an amount equal to 50% of the standby charge. The employee must inform the employer in writing before the end of the taxation year to use the latter method. It should be noted that in some circumstances the latter method may result in a higher taxable benefit, so an estimate must be made before choosing.

Purchase option—Cost $31,500 including HST.

$$\text{Standby charge—above} = \$7,560 \times \frac{9,000 \text{ km (personal)}}{1,667 \text{ km} \times 12 \text{ months}} = \qquad \$3,402$$

Operating benefit—lesser of:		
Fixed rate—9,000 km × 26¢ =	$2,340	
or		
50% of $3,402 (standby charge)	$1,701	1,701
Total benefit		$5,103

Lease option—Cost $420 monthly × 12 m = $5,040 including HST.

$$\text{Standby charge—above} = \$3,360 \times \frac{9,000 \text{ km (personal)}}{1,667 \text{ km} \times 12 \text{ months}} = \qquad \$1,512$$

Operating benefit—Lesser of:		
Fixed rate—9,000 km × 26¢ =	$2,340	
or		
50% of $1,512 (standby charge)	$ 756	756
Total benefit		$2,268

It is clear that, in this particular situation, the lease option is best for the employee regardless whether or not the auto is used primarily for employment purposes.

QUESTION FIVE

Carmen is employed by a public corporation as a senior vice-president. In January, 20X4 she was transferred from the Vancouver regional office to the company's head office in Toronto. The employer's generous compensation program rewarded Carmen with the following:

- $70,000 for the loss incurred on the sale of her Vancouver condo.

- A housing loan of $75,000 to assist with the purchase of a new home in Toronto. The loan has a low interest rate of 2% per annum. In January 20X4, CRA's prescribed interest rate was 5% and it increased to 6% on July 1, 20X4.

- The third-party mortgage on her new home in Toronto had an interest rate that was 1% higher than her mortgage on her Vancouver condo, which had three years remaining on its term. For this extra cost she received a lump sum compensation of $15,000.

- $18,000 as a reimbursement for part of her moving costs to Toronto.

In March 20X4, Carmen exercised a stock option and purchased 2,000 shares of her employer's corporation for $40 per share. At the time, the stock had a market value of $60. In January 20X5, she sold the 2,000 shares for $90 per share. Carmen was granted the right to acquire shares in 20X2 at a time when the stock was valued at $44 per share.

Required:
Describe how each of the above items will affect Carmen's *net income from employment* for 20X4. Would your answer change if the stock value had been $40 per share at the time when the option right was granted in 20X2? Explain.

Solution:

The first $15,000 of the $70,000 compensation for the loss on the condo sale is not taxable. One-half of the remainder is taxable and added to net income from employment. So, the taxable amount is $27,500 ($70,000 − $15,000 = $55,000 × ½ = $27,500).

The housing loan will create a taxable employment benefit equal to the difference between CRA's prescribed rate of 5% × the $75,000 loan, prorated for the number of days in 20X4 that the loan exists. The employment benefit is reduced by the 2% interest paid by Carmen, provided the 2% is paid by January 30 of 20X5 at the latest. It does not matter that the prescribed interest rate has increased to 6% during the year as the prescribed rate of 5% is guaranteed for 5 years from the date of the loan since the loan was used to purchase a home. However, if the prescribed rate declines below 5% that lower rate can be used. Effectively, on an annual basis, the housing loan will create a taxable employment benefit of $2,250 ($75,000 × (5% − 2%)). In arriving at taxable income *after* the overall net income for tax purposes has been determined, Carmen is entitled to a home relocation deduction. This deduction is equal to the lesser of the benefit, in this case $2,250, or the prescribed interest rate multiplied by the arbitrary amount of $25,000, which is $1,250 (5% × $25,000). So, Carmen's overall taxable income can be reduced by $1,250.

The $15,000 to cover the higher mortgage interest rate is fully taxable and is added to income from employment.

The reimbursement of $18,000 for moving expenses is not a taxable benefit. However, the amount that Carmen can deduct for moving expenses (discussed in Chapter 9) must be reduced by the amount of the reimbursement.

In March 20X4, when Carmen purchased 2,000 shares in her employer's corporation, she is deemed to have earned employment income of the difference between the market value of the stock purchased and her cost at the time. In this case the employment income is $40,000 (2,000 shares × ($60 market value − $40 cost)). In 20X5, when she sells the stock, she will have a taxable capital gain of one-half the difference between the selling price and the stock's market value when purchased. This amounts to $30,000 (½ (2,000 × $90 selling price − $60 value at purchase date)). It should noted that a different result would occur if, at the time the option right was granted, the market value of the stock was $40 (the same value as the option price). If this were so, Carmen would still have a benefit of $40,000 (above) added to her employment income BUT she would be entitled to claim a stock option deduction and, thereby, reduce her taxable income after determining net income for tax purposes by one-half of the employment income, which is $20,000 (1/2 × $40,000).

Review Questions

1. Explain this statement: "It is not the nature of the service that determines whether or not one is employed but, rather, the relationship which exists between the individual providing the service and the entity receiving the service."

2. Distinguish between
   (a) individual A (a student), who spent the summer painting three houses. The contract for one house provided for a fixed fee; the contracts for the other two provided for a fee per hour and materials costs; and
   (b) individual B, who worked for a painting company and received a wage of $10 per hour for painting three houses.

3. "Income from employment for tax purposes includes the gross earnings from employment less expenses incurred to earn that income." Is this statement true? Briefly outline the fundamental rules for establishing income from employment.

4. An individual begins employment on December 16, 20X0. The employer pays salaries monthly on the 15th day of each month. The individual receives her first salary payment of $3,000 on January 15, 20X1. How much, if any, of the $3,000 is taxable in 20X0? How much in 20X1? Explain.

5. An employer follows the policy of awarding bonuses to employees for their exceptional efforts. Bonuses are awarded on the last day of each calendar year but are not paid until two years later. Does this policy benefit the employer and the employee? Explain.

6. In addition to salaries, wages, and commissions, an employer may provide a wide range of benefits to employees. Describe the general tax treatment to the employee of benefits received from an employer, and explain how the value of these benefits is determined for tax purposes. If an employee is permitted to operate an employer's automobile for personal use, does the treatment of this benefit conform to the general treatment of benefits? Explain.

7. From the employee's perspective, what benefits, if any, receive preferential tax treatment? Explain briefly and compare the tax treatment these different benefits receive.

8. Distinguish between an allowance and a reimbursement.

9. What effect does the receipt of an allowance have on an employee's ability to deduct expenses incurred to earn employment income?

10. With respect to deductions from employment income, compare the general tax treatment of an employee who is a salesperson and earns commissions with that of an employee who earns a fixed salary.

11. Can employees who earn commission income and are required to pay their own expenses to generate that income incur losses from employment for tax purposes? Explain.

12. When an employee is entitled to deduct particular expenses incurred to earn employment income, what restrictions, if any, are placed on the amount of expenses that can be deducted?

13. Why is it important for an employer to be familiar with the marginal tax rates that apply to its employees?

14. A number of indirect compensation benefits are considered to be taxable benefits to the employee. What advantage can the employer and/or the employee gain by including such benefits as part of a compensation package?

15. When an employer provides a taxable benefit to an employee at a cost that is lower than the normal retail price, what amount is included in the employee's income for tax purposes?

16. Certain indirect forms of compensation are deductible by the employer but not taxable to the employee. Does this special tax treatment provide a benefit to the employee or to the employer? Explain.

17. How should the employer describe the value of benefits provided in a compensation package to an employee?

18. What is deferred compensation? How can it be of value to the employee?

19. An employer contributes $2,000 annually to a deferred profit-sharing plan on behalf of an employee for 10 years. The plan invests the funds and earns an annual return of 12%. What is the pre-tax annual salary equivalent of such a benefit for an employee who is subject to a marginal tax rate of 40%?

20. Explain what benefits the employer and the employee can achieve by establishing
    (a) a stock option plan;
    (b) a stock purchase plan; and
    (c) a stock bonus plan.

Key Concept Questions

QUESTION ONE

Carol received salary of $60,000 during the current year. In addition she earned commission income of $25,000 of which she received $15,000 in the current year. She received the remaining $10,000 in the first quarter of the following year. *Income tax reference: ITA 5(1).*

Determine Carol's employment income for the current year.

QUESTION TWO

Mike's employer has a generous benefit program. During the current year his employer provided him with the following benefits:

*   A contribution to the company RPP of $6,000.

*   Group term life insurance coverage of $100,000. The premium for the coverage was $400.

*   Group sickness or accident insurance coverage. The premium paid was $550.

*   A private health services plan that provided Mike with dental, vision, prescription drugs, and private-hospital room coverage. The premium was $800.

*   Mental health counselling for Mike's daughter. The psychologist's fee was $1,500.

*   Fitness club membership for Mike's personal enjoyment. The membership dues were $900.

*   Public transit pass for city bus. The annual cost was $800.

Determine the amount to be included in Mike's employment income for tax purposes. *Income tax reference: ITA 6(1)(a), 6(4).*

QUESTION THREE

Jennifer's employer provided her with the following gifts and awards in 20X9:

Golf shirt with the employer logo (cost amount)	$15
Birthday gift—monetary restaurant gift certificate	75
Reward for meeting sales performance—holiday weekend	400
10-year anniversary award (golf club); previous award was on her 5th anniversary with the employer	275
Wedding gift (cutlery)	300
Innovation and excellence award (tickets to a concert)	250
Holiday season gift (artwork)	150

Required:
Briefly describe the tax consequences to Jennifer from the above gifts and awards.[99]

QUESTION FOUR

On September 1 of the current year, Teresa will have worked for A Ltd. for three years and will be entitled to a company car as of that date. For A Ltd. to purchase the car that Teresa wants, they will have to pay $48,000, including tax. If the car is leased, the monthly lease cost will be $950, including tax. In either case, A Ltd. will pay all of the operating costs for the car which are expected to be $2,500 annually. Teresa anticipates that she will drive the car 2,000 km per month of which 200 km will be for employment purposes. *Income tax reference: ITA 6(1)(e), (k), 6(2).*

A. Determine the amount to be included in Teresa's employment income for the current year (i) if A Ltd. purchases the car, and (ii) if A Ltd. leases the car.

---

99 Adapted from example in the CRA *Income Tax Technical News*, June 11, 2009.

B. If in the following year, Teresa drives the car 12,000 km for employment purposes and 8,000 km for personal use, determine the amount to be included in her income for tax purposes, assuming the car is purchased by A Ltd.

QUESTION FIVE

On March 1 of the current year, Len received a $100,000 loan from his employer. The loan bears interest at 1% per year. The interest is payable monthly. The principal is repayable at the end of five years. Len used $90,000 of the loan toward the purchase of his home. The $10,000 that was left over, he used to purchase investments. The prescribed interest rates for the current year were 4% for the first quarter and 5% for the remainder of the year. *Income tax reference: ITA 6(9), 80.4(1), (4), (6), 80.5, 20(1)(c), 110(1)(j).*

A. Determine the amount to be included in Len's employment income for tax purposes for the current year. Assume Len purchased the home because of an *eligible relocation*.

B. Calculate the home relocation deduction.

QUESTION SIX

In Year 1, Kayla, an employee of a public company, was granted an option to acquire 100 shares from the company's treasury at a price of $12 per share. At the date that the option was granted, the shares were trading on the stock market at $22 per share. In Year 2, Kayla exercised the option and acquired 100 shares. At that time the shares were trading at $40 per share. In Year 6, Kayla sold the shares for $66 per share. *Income tax reference: ITA 7(1).*

Discuss the income tax consequences of Kayla's transactions (show calculations).

QUESTION SEVEN

How would Kayla's tax consequences change in Question Six (above) if her employer was a Canadian-controlled private corporation? *Income tax reference: ITA 7(1.1), 110(1)(d.1).*

QUESTION EIGHT

In Year 1, a public company granted an employee resident in Canada an option to purchase 1,000 common shares of the employer company for $10 per share. The fair market value of the shares at the date the option was granted was $8 per share. No other stock options were granted to this employee during Year 1. In Year 2, when the shares were worth $16 per share the employee exercised the option and purchased all 1,000 shares. In Year 5, the employee sold the 1,000 shares for $38 per share. The shares do not have any special dividend rights or restrictions. *Income tax reference: ITA 7(1), 110(1)(d).*

Discuss the income tax consequences to the employee from these transactions (show calculations).

QUESTION NINE

Richard earned a salary of $40,000 plus commissions of $6,000 in the current year as a salesperson employed by B Ltd. He incurred the following expenses to earn his income:

Car expenses	$ 2,500
Transportation (other than car) & accommodation	5,000
Client entertainment meals	600
Advertising and promotion	2,000
	$10,100

Determine the maximum deduction that Richard is entitled to claim in computing his employment income for the current year. *Income tax reference: ITA 8(1)(f), (h), (h.1), 67.1.*

QUESTION TEN

Julie is required to use her own automobile and pay for all her travelling expenses in carrying out her duties of employment. She purchased a new car on January 2nd of the current year for $45,000 (plus tax) and incurred the following expenses during the year:

• Gasoline	$2,100
• Repairs and maintenance	400
• Parking (employment related)	100
• Licence and insurance	2,300
• Interest on loan to acquire car (12 months)	4,100

Julie drove her car 20,000 km in the current year of which 8,000 km were driven in carrying out her duties of employment. *Income tax reference: ITA 8(1)(h.1), (j), 13(7)(g), 67.2.*

Calculate the maximum tax deduction available to Julie for her car for the current year. (The CCA rate for automobiles is 30%, except in the first year when it is only 15%.)

QUESTION ELEVEN

Howard is employed as a computer programmer and is required by his employment contract to maintain an office in his home. There is only one telephone line in Howard's home. He estimates that 40% of the usage of his telephone is employment related (all local calls). He purchased a new computer for his office on September 1 of the current year. He estimates that he uses the computer 90% for employment purposes. Howard works in his home office four days each week and attends meetings at his employer's place of business on the fifth day. The office occupies 10% of the square footage of his home. He incurred the following costs in the current year:

• Mortgage interest (10%)	$1,200
• Property taxes (10%)	340
• House insurance (10%)	120
• Utilities (10%)	420
• Maintenance (10%)	200
• Telephone (40%)	210
• New computer (100% of cost)	1,300

What is the maximum amount that Howard can claim in the current year for the costs he has incurred in respect of his home office? *Income tax reference: ITA 8(1)(i), 8(13).*

QUESTION TWELVE

Paul is employed as a real estate salesman, selling multimillion dollar homes. He drives a Mercedes S350, which he leases for $1,380 plus 13% tax per month, to carry out his duties of employment. The lease term is 48 months, commencing January 1, 20X1. The manufacturer's list price for the Mercedes is $92,500. Paul is required by his employment contract to provide his own car and he does not receive a car allowance or a reimbursement. *Income tax reference: ITA 67.3; Reg. 7307.*

Determine the maximum car lease payments deductible for tax purposes by Paul for 20X1, assuming that 60% of the kilometres driven by Paul in 20X1 were for employment purposes.

Problems

PROBLEM ONE

Bill Watkins is a chartered accountant. He carried on a professional business as a tax consultant for 12 years. By the end of 20X0, the practice had grown very large. Watkins was overworked and under pressure to hire additional staff or take a partner. Watkins was interested in education and several years earlier had contracted with a publisher to write a book on taxation for university students. Because of the pressures of his practice, this project made little progress.

To optimize his work life, Watkins decided to close his professional practice and enter into an arrangement with Anthony and Anthony, a national firm of chartered accountants. According to the agreement, he would work a minimum of 600 hours per year for the firm; he would also be free to pursue his writing and other interests. He would provide the 600 hours mainly during the winter months and would not be expected at the office every day of the week.

Anthony and Anthony made a formal announcement in the newspaper that Watkins was now associated with their firm and provided him with business cards stating both his name and the firm's. The firm did not give him a specific title, though most of its employees had one, whatever their level. The firm did provide him with an office (of the same size as was given to partners) and a secretary at no cost to him.

As a tax consultant, Watkins met with the clients of the firm and corresponded with them under the firm's letterhead. Jobs were assigned to him by any partner who required his services. Usually, he charged any time spent on a client directly to the particular partner's account; that partner, in turn, billed the client and collected the fees.

Anthony and Anthony charged clients for Watkins's time at $150 per hour. The agreement stated that he was to be paid $100 for each hour charged to a client whether the client paid the fee or not. At the end of each month, Watkins prepared an invoice requesting that the firm pay $100 for each hour charged that month.

Throughout the year, Watkins paid for his own parking and for his own subscriptions to several tax services, the latter being necessary for him to carry out his duties.

Whenever the firm held a social function, Watkins was invited. In 20X1, he gave three speeches to various business groups and was always introduced as "Bill Watkins, a tax consultant with Anthony and Anthony."

In 20X1, Watkins worked 820 hours for the firm. He spent the balance of his working time writing his book and giving tax seminars to various professional groups.

Required:

Was Watkins employed or self-employed in 20X1? Give reasons to support your conclusions and reasons to support the opposing view.

PROBLEM TWO

Jennifer Ratushny is a middle-level manager at a New Brunswick–based advertising agency. Her contract of employment requires her employer to provide her with an automobile for personal use. Two years ago, the employer purchased for her an automobile that cost $23,000. All costs to operate the vehicle are paid by Ratushny. She is not required to use the vehicle for any of her employment duties.

The employment contract also stipulates that Ratushny may, if she chooses, purchase the vehicle from the employer at any time for a price equal to the depreciated value of the car. The automobile's depreciated value is now $14,000.

Ratushny is thinking of purchasing the car from her employer. Her bank is willing to loan her the money for it at 8%. The car is in good condition. If she makes the acquisition, she intends to use the car for at least three more years. A friend of hers, who is in the automobile business, has informed her that, subject to any mechanical problems, the car should have a resale value of $8,000 three years from now.

Ratushny earns a high salary; her marginal income tax rate is 45%.

Required:

Should Ratushny purchase the car at this time, or should she continue to use it as an employer-owned vehicle?

PROBLEM THREE

Charles and Cathy are employed by different companies. They earn the same amount of income and share a similar lifestyle. However, each receives a different type of remuneration.

Charles earns a total of $50,000, which is paid in the form of a monthly salary. His annual personal expenses (excluding income tax) are shown in table A, below.

Cathy also earns $50,000 annually. Her remuneration is as shown in table B. Her personal expenses (excluding income tax) are shown in table C.

Both Charles and Cathy pay income tax at a rate of 40%. Both invest any savings in an effort to build up a substantial investment portfolio.

Required:

1. For the current year, compare Cathy's after-tax cash flow with that of Charles, and determine the amount each has available to add to an investment portfolio.

2. What amount of salary would Charles have to receive in order to have the same amount of cash available as Cathy for his investment portfolio?

A. Life insurance ($100,000)		$ 1,000
Lease payments on automobile		6,000
Interest on house mortgage (10% on $70,000)		7,000
Family private medical insurance		1,000
Golf club dues		2,000
Automobile operating expenses		3,000
Other personal living expenses		9,000
		$29,000

B. Salary		$39,000
Private medical insurance		1,000
Group term life insurance ($100,000)		1,000
Lease payments on company automobile used personally by Cathy		6,000
Low-interest (5%) loan of $20,000:		
Prescribed interest rate (10%)	$ 2,000	
Actual interest charged (5%)	(1,000)	1,000
Paid golf club dues (benefits employer)		2,000
		$50,000

C. Interest on house mortgage:		
10% of $50,000		$ 5,000
Interest on employee loan used to acquire house:		
5% of $20,000		1,000
Automobile operating costs		3,000
Other personal living expenses		9,000
		$18,000

PROBLEM FOUR

Pasqual Melo is employed by a public corporation. On January 1, 20X0, she was given an option to purchase 1,000 shares of the public corporation for $8 per share (the option extended for two years).

On December 15, 20X0, she exercised her option and bought 1,000 shares at $8 per share (total = $8,000).

On June 15, 20X3, she sold the 1,000 shares.

The value of the shares at the particular dates was as follows:

Date option granted	$8.50
Date option exercised	10
Date shares sold	14

Required:

1. Determine the amount and type of income received by Melo and when that income was taxable.

2. How would your answer change if the value of the shares at the date the option was granted was $8 rather than $8.50?

3. How would your answer change if the employer were a Canadian-controlled private corporation?

PROBLEM FIVE

Carol Posh is a senior advertising executive with a large Winnipeg company. With winter fast approaching, Posh is seriously considering an offer of employment from Westcoast Promotions Inc. (WPI), a large public company in Vancouver. Although housing costs are high in Vancouver, the climate and opportunities for career advancement would be better.

Posh has received a letter outlining a proposed remuneration package. The package is attractive but she is uncertain of the tax consequences. She has asked you to advise her.

WPI recognizes the problem of housing costs and begins its letter with an offer to loan Posh $150,000, interest-free, to help finance a new house. In addition, WPI will reimburse her for 75% of her moving costs.

In addition to an annual salary of $120,000, WPI has offered the following benefits:

1. Posh will be appointed a director of the company's American subsidiary in California; this will require her to travel to Los Angeles three times a year for board meetings. Posh will be paid a director's fee of $5,000 directly from the American company. Company policy permits spouses to take these trips as well. When a director takes his or her spouse, all travel expenses are paid for by the company.

2. A luxury automobile will be provided for her personal use, even though she will never require the car for business. The company will pay all of the operating costs—approximately $3,200 per year—as well as the monthly lease cost of $850. Posh will drive the car approximately 20,000 kilometres per year.

3. WPI will include Posh in its group term life insurance program and pay the premium, which provides coverage for $75,000. It will also pay the premiums for a private health plan, a dental plan, and a drug plan.

4. The company has a deferred profit-sharing plan, for which Posh will qualify. The maximum contribution will be made to this plan only when the company's profit for the year is greater than 12% of the stated balance sheet equity.

5. Posh will be eligible for an annual bonus of up to $40,000, with the actual amount to be based on her productivity. The bonus will be awarded on November 30 of each

year (the company's year end) but will not be paid until May 31 of the following year. Of the above-mentioned bonus, 25% will be retained in an employee benefit plan for five years. The investment income earned by the plan will be distributed to Posh each year.

6. WPI will provide Posh with a monthly allowance of $800 to cover any expenses she may incur. In addition, she will be reimbursed for travel costs to attend the annual advertising convention in Paris.

7. All WPI employees are entitled to participate in a stock-option plan. The available shares are non-voting but do participate fully in profits. The option price is $12 per share; this price is guaranteed for three years and will then increase to $14 per share. Currently, the shares are trading at $12 per share; they are expected to rise significantly within two years.

8. Posh will be provided with club memberships in the "better" social clubs in the area for relaxation purposes. This will help her be more productive in her work.

Required:
Prepare a brief report for Posh.

PROBLEM SIX

Paul Fenson is employed as a shipping supervisor. In the evenings and on weekends, he holds a second job as a real estate salesperson for a national real estate firm. His financial information for 20X0 is as follows:

1. His salary from his day job is $30,000 per annum. However, the employer deducts a number of items from his salary, so his net take-home pay is only $19,228. The following amounts were deducted in 20X0:

Income tax	$3,900
Union dues	600
Canada Pension Plan	1,312
Employment Insurance premiums	560
Registered pension plan contribution	3,000
Reimbursement for personal use of employer's car	600
Charitable donations remitted to United Way	800
	$10,772

The employer paid the following amounts on behalf of Fenson:

Canada Pension Plan	$1,312
Employment Insurance premiums	790
Registered pension plan	3,000
Premiums for a mandatory provincial health insurance plan	600
Group term life insurance premiums ($50,000 coverage)	1,200
	$6,902

Fenson used the employer's summer camp for a one-month holiday and paid the employer $200 rent. When not being used by employees, the summer camp is rented for the normal amount of $600 per month.

Although Fenson owned his own automobile, he was provided with a company car. The car cost the company $35,000. During the year, he drove a total of 24,000 km, of which 16,800 were for personal use. The employer also paid all of the operating costs, which amounted to $3,000.

During the year, Fenson attended a shipping conference in Toronto. His wife travelled with him at the company's expense ($1,000).

The employer permitted staff to purchase merchandise from its retail outlet at the company's cost. During the year, Fenson purchased for $800 merchandise with a retail value of $1,200.

2. As a real estate salesperson, Fenson earned a base salary of $8,000 and received commissions of $7,000. In relation to his real estate work, he incurred the following expenses:

Dues to a local real estate association	$ 400
Fee for a three-day seminar on how to be an effective salesperson	800
Advertising—calendars and pens	1,700
Automobile operating costs	4,000
Promotion (meals and drinks for clients)	2,800
Personal meals (during in-town business)	400
Purchase of a cellular telephone	2,000

Fenson used his own automobile for his real estate activities. The car has an undepreciated capital cost for tax purposes of $10,000. During the year, he drove a total of 30,000 km, of which 27,000 was related to selling real estate. His employer provided him with a monthly car allowance of $200 ($2,400 per year).

Required:

Determine Fenson's net income from employment for the particular year.

PROBLEM SEVEN

Riley Fontaine has requested that you review the calculation of his 20X1 net income for tax purposes. He has provided you with the following information:

1. His salary consists of the following:

Basic salary	$92,000
Bonus	6,000
	$98,000

The bonus of $6,000 was awarded to him on December 31, 20X1, and was paid on January 15, 20X2.

2. His employer deducted the following items from his salary and remitted them to the appropriate party on his behalf:

Canada Pension Plan	$2,307
Employment Insurance premiums	840
Registered pension plan	4,400
Income tax	26,000
Charitable donations (United Way)	3,500

3. Fontaine is employed by Remco, a Canadian public corporation. Two years ago, Remco granted Fontaine an option to purchase 1,000 of its common shares at $16 per share. At the time the option was granted, Remco's shares were trading at the same value of $16 per share. On January 31, 20X1, Fontaine purchased 1,000 shares of Remco (trading value at purchase date—$22 per share). On November 30, 20X1, he sold all of the shares at $24.

4. Remco requires that Fontaine work out of his home from time to time. Remco has supplied him with a computer and modem for this purpose; however, Fontaine must pay for his own supplies. His house is 2,000 square feet and his workstation is a room of about 200 square feet. He also uses the room as a den and guest room. Utility costs for his home for 20X1 amounted to $1,200.

5. Fontaine travels out of town from time to time to his employer's manufacturing plant. Remco reimburses him for all travel costs, except meal costs. The plant is only 90 km from the head office, and he always returns home the same day after working a normal eight-hour day.

6. Fontaine has calculated his net income for tax purposes as follows:

Employment income		
Salary and bonus		$98,000
Deductions		
Registered pension plan		4,400
Employment expenses:		
Meal costs while out of town: $300 × 50%		150
Office at home:		
Minor repairs		340
Utilities (200/2,000 × $1,200)		120
Office supplies and stationery		410
Computer software (word processor)		220
		92,360
Capital gains (Remco shares)		
Selling price (1,000 × $24)	$24,000	
Cost (1,000 × $16)	16,000	
Gain	8,000	
Taxable (¹/₂ of $8,000)		4,000
Net income		$96,360

Required:

Advise Fontaine whether his calculation of 20X1 net income for tax purposes is correct. If it is not, recalculate a revised 20X1 net income for tax purposes, and briefly explain the changes you made.

PROBLEM EIGHT

On January 2, 20X3, Sheldon Bass, a professional engineer, moved from Calgary to Edmonton to commence employment with Acco Ltd., a large public corporation. Because of his new employment contract, Bass requires assistance in determining his employment income for tax purposes. He has provided the following financial information:

1. Bass's salary in 20X3 was $95,000. From this, Acco deducted the appropriate income tax, Employment Insurance premiums of $840, Canada Pension Plan contributions of $2,307, registered pension plan payments of $6,000, and charitable donations of $1,200.

2. Acco provides its executives with a bonus plan. Bass's 20X3 bonus was $20,000, of which $5,000 was received in December 20X3 and the balance in March 20X4.

3. In November 20X3, Bass asked his employer to loan him $12,000 so that he could acquire an investment. Acco advised him that it was company policy not to make loans to employees. However, they gave him the $12,000, stipulating that it was an advance against his 20X4 salary, which would be reduced accordingly.

4. In 20X3, Bass was provided with a company car, which he drove 14,000 km for employment duties and 8,000 km for personal use. The car was leased at $500 per month. The total operating costs of $7,000 were paid by Acco. The car was available for personal use throughout the year.

5. Bass's moving expenses to transport his belongings to Edmonton were $3,000. Acco paid this cost directly to a moving company on Bass's behalf.

6. Bass travels extensively for Acco. In December 20X3, he and his spouse used some of the travel points he had accumulated from this travel to attend his father's funeral in Toronto. As a result, he saved the normal airfare of $400 per ticket.

7. Acco paid the following additional amounts for Bass:

Allowance ($300 per month) for acquiring executive apparel	$3,600
Investment counsellor fees as part of Acco's counselling program	600
Golf club dues (Bass rarely uses the club to conduct business)	1,500

8. In 20X3 Bass paid for the following:

Dues to the engineers' association	$ 800
Laptop computer and printer	2,200
Computer supplies (paper, etc.)	100

Acco had asked each senior executive to acquire a laptop computer at his or her own expense for work during travel.

9. In 20X3, Bass sold 1,000 shares of Kolex Ltd. (his former employer) at $10 per share. Kolex is a Canadian-controlled private corporation. The shares were purchased under a stock-option plan in 20X0 at $3 per share. Appraised value at that time was $5 per share.

Required:
Determine Bass's net income from employment for the 20X3 taxation year.

PROBLEM NINE

Barry Yuen is district sales manager for a Vancouver-based distribution company. He has requested that you help him establish his employment income for tax purposes for the 20X3 taxation year. He has provided the following information:

1. Yuen's base salary in 20X3 was $78,000. As sales manager, he is entitled to a small commission on the sales made by staff under his supervision. He received $7,200 in such commissions in 20X3, which included $1,000 of commissions earned in late 20X2. The December 20X3 commissions had been computed as $1,800 and were received in January 20X4. The employer deducted the following from his salary in 20X3:

Canada Pension Plan contributions	$2,307
Employment Insurance premiums	840
Private medical plan premiums	300

2. In addition to the above, the employer paid the following to Yuen or on his behalf:

Travel allowance	$2,400
Group term life insurance premiums for $50,000 coverage	600
Premiums for a private medical insurance plan	300

3. Yuen's wife died in late 20X2, leaving him to support three children. In 20X3, he hired a person at a cost of $9,000 to provide baby-sitting services for the two youngest children. Following his wife's death, Yuen suffered from depression. As a result, his employer paid the cost of $3,000 for counselling services and also provided him with airline tickets costing $2,300 so that he and the children could attend a relaxation resort.

4. Yuen uses his own vehicle for employment duties. The vehicle (class 10.1) had an undepreciated capital cost of $14,000 at the end of 20X2. Yuen paid $4,000 in 20X3 to operate the car and used it 70% of the time for employment duties.

5. Yuen incurred the following additional costs relating to his employment:

Promotion (meals)	$ 800
Purchase of a cellular phone	1,200
Lease costs for laptop computer	700
Golf club dues	1,000
Hotel costs—out-of-town travel	4,300

6. When not travelling, Yuen works from an office at his employer's place of business. Increasingly, he has been taking home work to do in the evenings and on weekends. He intends to set aside a specific room in his house that he will use only for this purpose. His house costs include property taxes, insurance, utilities, and mortgage interest. He will also purchase a work desk and chair.

Required:

1. For the 20X3 taxation year, determine Yuen's net income from employment for tax purposes.

2. Briefly explain the tax treatment of the intended home-office expenses.

PROBLEM TEN

Charles Ebo was terminated from his employment with QR Ltd. in July 20X6. In November 20X6, he began work as a commission salesperson for AP Ltd., a Canadian public corporation.

Ebo has asked you to help him prepare his 20X6 tax return. Information regarding his employment is outlined below.

1. Ebo's employment with QR was terminated on July 31, 20X6. His salary to that date was $56,000. Besides income tax, QR had deducted the following amounts from his salary:

Registered pension plan	$4,000
CPP and EI contributions	3,147
Group sickness and accident insurance plan premium	500
Reimbursement for personal use of employer auto	800

QR also contributed $4,000 to an RPP and $500 to a group sickness and accident insurance plan on Ebo's behalf.

Ebo took a medical stress leave from January 10 to March 15, 20X6. His salary was not paid during the leave. However, he received $4,500 for loss of earnings from the group sickness and accident insurance plan. In previous years, Ebo had paid a total of $3,000 in premiums to the plan.

2. On July 31, 20X6, Ebo returned the company car to QR, which had been available for his personal use. The car had an original cost of $35,000 and a book value of $24,000. Ebo had driven the car 20,000 km in 20X6, of which 8,000 km was for employment purposes. QR paid the operating expenses of $2,900.

3. In December 20X6, Ebo sold 4,000 shares of AP Ltd. at $10 per share. He had acquired them in November 20X6 under a stock-option plan at $6. At the time of acquisition, the shares were valued at $8 per share. When the option was granted, the shares were valued at $6 per share.

4. When his employment was terminated, Ebo paid a lawyer $800 to settle compensation issues. As a result, he received additional holiday pay of $1,000 and a retiring allowance of $6,000 for his 10 years of service.

5. Ebo collected employment insurance of $5,400 before starting his employment with AP on November 1, 20X6. Besides a base salary of $1,000 per month, Ebo receives commissions on sales.

Ebo's commission is 4% of sales. His first sales were made in late December 20X6 and totalled $150,000. The related commission was received on January 15, 20X7. On December 1, 20X6, AP paid Ebo $1,500 as an advance against commissions.

AP certified that Ebo was required to pay his own car and other expenses. On November 1, 20X6, he leased a car at $960 per month (including tax). Operating expenses for November and December were $900 in total. The car was used 70% of the time for employment purposes.

Ebo incurred the following additional expenses:

Entertainment—meals and beverages	$600
Promotion—gift calendars for customers	200
Purchase of a cellular phone	500

Required:

Determine Ebo's net income from employment for the 20X6 taxation year.

PROBLEM ELEVEN

After a recent staff evaluation, Susan Pearson's employer offered her the following alternative remuneration proposals:

1. A salary increase of $2,500 per annum, from $40,000 to $42,500.

2. A contribution of $2,000 per year to the company's deferred profit-sharing plan.

Pearson's living expenses are modest, and if she accepts the salary increase she intends to invest the additional cash flow in secure 10% bonds. Coincidentally, the company's deferred profit-sharing plan also achieves an average investment return of 10%.

Pearson plans to retire in 30 years, and her intention is to use the remuneration increase to help fund her retirement. Currently, she pays tax at a marginal rate of 40%.

Required:

Assuming that investment returns and tax rates remain stable at 10% and 40%, respectively, which alternative should Pearson prefer? You may also assume that if she accepts the deferred profit-sharing plan, it will be paid to her in a lump sum at the end of 30 years.

PROBLEM TWELVE

Carla Ram is a professional engineer. In 20X1, she sold her consulting business in Hamilton, Ontario, and moved to Vancouver, British Columbia, where she was employed by an equipment-manufacturing business. The following financial information is provided for the 20X1 taxation year:

1. Ram began her employment on February 1, 20X1, and during the year, received a salary of $90,000, from which the employer deducted income tax of $30,000 and CPP and EI of $3,147. In addition to her salary, Ram earned a commission of 1% of sales obtained by salespeople under her supervision. At December 31, 20X1, these sales amounted to $1,000,000, for which she had received $6,000 by year end, with the balance received in January 20X2. Ram also received an annual clothing allowance of $1,500 to maintain a professional dress standard. During the year, she spent $1,800 on clothing for work.

2. Ram's employer does not have a company pension plan; instead, the employer contributed $13,000 directly to her RRSP in 20X1.

3. In December 20X1, Ram received a payroll advance of $3,000 against her January 20X2 salary to help fund a family holiday.

4. Ram is required to use her automobile for employment purposes and to pay certain other employment expenses. In 20X1, she incurred the following costs:

Meals and drinks for customer entertainment	$1,600
Golf club dues used to entertain customers	1,100
Travel—airfares and hotel lodging	3,000
Purchase of a cell phone	800
Cell phone bill—pay-as-you-go-plan (employment related)	1,200
Automobile expenses:	
Operating costs	3,800
Parking	100
Interest on car loan	2,200
Purchase of new automobile in Ontario	37,000

The automobile was used 60% of the time for business.

5. In 20X1, Ram took advantage of her employer's counselling services. She received personal financial planning advice valued at $400, and her 14-year-old son received mental health counselling valued at $800.

6. Ram purchased a new home in Vancouver in 20X1 and incurred qualified moving expenses of $18,000 to transport her family and household effects to Vancouver. Her new employer reimbursed her for $10,000 of these costs and also paid her $20,000 for the loss incurred on the sale of her former residence.

7. In early 20X2, Ram intends to borrow $20,000 from her employer for the purpose of acquiring shares in the employer's corporation. A low interest rate of 2% per annum will be payable on the loan.

Required:

1. Determine Ram's *minimum net income from employment* for the 20X1 taxation year.

2. Briefly describe the tax implications from the intended employee loan to Ram.

Cases

CASE ONE

John Markowski is a senior mechanic in the logging industry. Because of the specialized nature of his work, he is highly paid. His current employer pays him a basic salary with no special benefits.

Recently, Markowski received an offer of employment from a corporation in the same line of business. The salary offered is lower than what he currently receives but a number of benefits are included in the remuneration package.

Markowski is confused by the offer. He does not like the idea of a reduced salary but realizes that the benefits have some value. He also realizes that what is really important is the level of disposable income that he has for himself and his family.

Markowski has provided you with the pertinent information (see Exhibits 1 and 2) and has asked you to help him make a decision.

Required:

1. Determine what Markowski's net income from employment for tax purposes will be if he remains with his current employer (Exhibit 1).

2. Determine what Markowski's net income from employment for tax purposes will be if he accepts the offer from the competitor (Exhibit 2).

3. Assuming that Markowski pays tax at a rate of 40%, determine the amount by which his personal disposable income will increase (or decrease) if he accepts the new offer.

Exhibit 1:

Information Regarding Current Employment and Certain Other Expenditures

1. Markowski's gross salary next year will be $70,000. From this, the employer will deduct the required income tax, Canada Pension Plan contributions of $2,307, and Employment Insurance premiums of $840.

2. It is part of Markowski's ordinary duties to work on equipment at locations other than the main repair depot. On average, he is called out of town two or three days each month. On such trips, he must always stay overnight in a hotel. His contract of employment requires that he pay his own automobile expenses. The company reimburses him for his hotel costs (lodging but not meals). No reimbursement is made for the vehicle.

3. Markowski leases his own car at $500 per month. He incurred the following additional travel costs in the current year:

Insurance	$ 800
Repairs and maintenance	600
Gasoline	2,200
Meals (out of town)	200

During the year, Markowski drove a total of 22,000 kilometres, of which 4,000 were for his employer. Markowski anticipates that travel costs in the future will be about the same as they were this year.

4. Markowski is required to purchase and maintain his own small tools. Every year, he spends approximately $500 on new tools and to replace lost or stolen tools. He also purchases his own work coveralls and pays for their cleaning, which amounts to another $300 per year.

5. Markowski will take possession of his new home in three months, and he is currently shopping for a mortgage. He expects to obtain a $90,000 mortgage with interest at 8% for a term of five years.

6. Markowski maintains the following insurance policies:

	Premium cost
Term life insurance of $300,000	$1,200
Private medical insurance	600
House fire insurance	1,000

7. Markowski is a golfer and belongs to a private club. His annual membership dues are $1,200.

Exhibit 2:

Information Regarding Offer of Employment with Competitor

1. The proposed salary is $60,000 per year. From that amount, the employer will deduct the required income tax, Canada Pension Plan contributions of $2,307, and Employment Insurance premiums of $840.

2. The employer will lease an automobile identical to the one currently used by Markowski. However, the employer's lease cost will be only $450 per month because of a fleet discount. In addition, the employer will pay the annual insurance cost of $800, the repair and maintenance costs, which are estimated to be $600 annually, and the gasoline costs of $2,200.

   Markowski will be entitled to operate the car for personal use. The number of business kilometres and personal kilometres driven will be the same as they are now. The employer will pay for all out-of-town meals when an overnight stay is required. The cost of meals is expected to be $200 per year.

3. The employer maintains a good supply of small tools, and mechanics are not required to purchase or use their own. In addition, the employer maintains a complete wardrobe of work coveralls, and so Markowski will not have to purchase or launder his own.

4. As a senior mechanic, Markowski will be entitled to a low-interest loan (3%) from the employer of up to five years' duration. Such loans can be renewed at the end of term. The maximum loan amount is $10,000. Assume the prescribed interest rate set by the CRA is currently 7%.

5. The employer maintains a group term life insurance program and a private medical insurance program. At no cost to Markowski, the employer will provide $300,000 of group term life insurance as well as medical coverage equal to what he currently has. The premium costs to the employer will be as follows:

Life insurance	$900
Medical insurance	500

   These amounts are lower than Markowski's current costs because group discounts are available to the employer.

6. The employer has agreed to pay Markowski's annual golf club dues of $1,200. As Markowski does not entertain and deal with customers, the employer derives no benefit from Markowski's membership in the club.

CASE TWO

SAPASCO INDUSTRIES LTD.

Sapasco Industries Ltd. is a Canadian-controlled private corporation that manufactures a small line of plastic containers. The company has been in existence for only nine years but has grown rapidly. Last year, sales reached $8,000,000, and a record high profit of $750,000 was achieved.

The company now employs 41 staff in addition to the president, who is the sole shareholder. The current annual payroll, exclusive of the income of the shareholder/president, is $1,730,000 and consists of salaries, bonuses, and compulsory benefits, such as Canada Pension Plan and Employment Insurance contributions. The company is concerned about its increasing payroll costs, especially since recent wage increases in their industry have averaged 10%. The company's year end is approaching, and Sapasco must soon decide on salary adjustments for its existing staff.

Not long ago, Sapasco was approached by an insurance company, which suggested that it start up an employee benefit plan, which would include a deferred profit-sharing plan and three basic insurance plans. The insurance company indicated that if the insurance plans were accepted as a group, it could reduce the annual premiums by 20% of the normal retail rate. Also, it could invest the deferred profit-sharing plan funds to yield an average return 1% higher than that earned by individuals who invest separately in RRSPs.

The president of Sapasco has asked Carol Asaki, the personnel manager, to review the insurance company's proposal. The president tells her, "I have always felt that excessive benefit programs create more administrative headaches than they are worth. But I'm willing to look at them further in view of the large wage settlements we may be facing. Let me know the value of the proposal to us as well as to the employees."

To prepare her report to the president, Asaki gathers together certain information, which is summarized in Exhibit I. In addition, she pulls the personnel file on one of the company's employees. The information in this file is summarized in Exhibit II.

Required:
On behalf of Asaki, prepare a draft report for the president.

Exhibit I

SAPASCO INDUSTRIES LTD.
Selected Financial Information

PAYROLL SUMMARY

# of employees	Salary range	Payroll
2	$100,000 and over	$ 240,000
4	$60,000 – $100,000	320,000
9	$40,000 – $60,000	450,000
14	$25,000 – $40,000	460,000
12	$18,000 – $25,000	260,000
41		$1,730,000

Tax rates

Sapasco Industries Ltd.	25%
Employees (by income range):	
$0 – $42,000	26%
$42,000 – $85,000	34%
$85,000 – $132,000	40%
$132,000 and over	45%

Proposed benefit plan

DPSP:

Contributions will range from $0 to $3,500 and should average $2,000 annually per employee. Currently, DPSP funds can be invested to yield 12% annually.

Insurance plans

	Average premium per employee
Group term life insurance:	
Basic ($25,000 coverage)	$100
Additional ($75,000 coverage)	300
	$400
Group health and dental plan	$500
Group accident and sickness plan (disability)	$600

Exhibit II

SAPASCO INDUSTRIES LTD.
Summary of Personnel File

Jason Steiman

Age: 33
Family status: Married, three children
Current salary: $50,000
Amounts withheld from salary

- Canada Pension Plan
- Employment Insurance
- Monthly contributions made directly to employee's bank for the purchase of his private RRSP ($200 per month).

CHAPTER 5

Income from Business

Income from business encompasses a wide range of financial activity. Businesses vary considerably in size and nature, but they all formulate income for tax purposes in accordance with a common set of principles. The student entrepreneur who paints houses or maintains lawns to finance a university education is subject to the same formula for income determination on those activities as that used by a large Canadian public corporation. The *Income Tax Act* does not attempt to make provision for each type of business activity or transaction. Instead, it contains a set of fundamental rules that are applied to every business transaction, regardless of its size or nature but that also make specific provisions for certain exceptional situations. In most cases, determinations as to whether an item must be included in income, or is permitted as a deduction, can be made by applying the general principles.

This chapter defines *business income* and develops the broad principles that form the foundation of such income. Specifically, this chapter covers the following major areas:

1. The meaning of the term *business income* and the general scope of the definition.

2. The general rules for determining income from business, and the relationship of those rules to generally accepted accounting concepts.

3. The format for determining the exceptions to the general rules, and a summary of the most commonly used exceptions.

4. A sample calculation of business income utilizing the general rules developed.

I. Business Income Defined

Business income can be earned by all three of the taxable entities within the Canadian tax system—individuals, corporations, and trusts—and each entity determines that income in an identical manner. In order to earn business income or incur a business loss, the taxpayer must, of course, be involved in an undertaking that constitutes a "business."

The term *business* is broadly defined in the *Income Tax Act* to include "a profession, calling, trade, manufacture, or undertaking of any kind whatsoever and an adventure or concern in the nature of trade."[1] In most circumstances, the conduct of a business is readily identifiable by the nature of the activity: such activities as the manufacturing and processing of property for resale; mining, exploration, or drilling for natural resources; construction, logging, farming, or fishing; the selling of property as a retailer or wholesaler; transportation; and the offering of services in a trade or profession are all obvious business activities. As well, enterprises usually maintain identifiable evidence of their existence—a location, a business name, a special telephone listing, and so on.

It is important to note that the definition does not consider size to be a factor; nor does it require that the activity be ongoing, or that it provide evidence of its existence. This means that an individual who, from time to time, provides piano lessons for a fee is considered to be earning business income, even though that activity may be irregular, there is no formal evidence of a business enterprise, and the person may be gainfully employed in another occupation.

In some circumstances, an activity may constitute what is referred to as an "*adventure or concern in the nature of trade.*"[2] This occurs when a taxpayer (individual, corporation, or trust) acquires property for the purpose of reselling it at a profit, even though it is not the normal business of that person to conduct such an activity.[3] For example, consider the situation of an individual who discovers a used automobile for

---

1 ITA 248(1); IT-206R.
2 IT-459.
3 *MNR v. Taylor*, 57 DTC 1125.

sale at an apparent bargain price and acquires it with the intention of reselling it at a profit. This transaction is similar to those made by an automobile dealer, even though the person does not regularly carry on such an activity. The buying and selling of the automobile is, in this case, considered an adventure in the nature of trade. By definition, this constitutes a business, and the resulting profit or loss on sale is considered income or loss from business and is treated accordingly for tax purposes.

• **Business income versus capital**   A particular problem arises when a property is sold that, by its nature, had the ability to provide a long-term or enduring benefit to its owner. Depending on the reason for its acquisition and its subsequent use, the gain or loss on the sale of such property can be either a business activity or a capital transaction. The distinction is important, as capital transactions and business transactions are treated differently. While capital gains are not reviewed until Chapter 8, the reader has already learned that only one-half of capital gains are taxable, and that one-half of capital losses are available for deduction (though only against other capital gains). At the same time, business income is fully taxable, and business losses can be offset against all other sources of income. As demonstrated in Chapter 3, the impact on cash flow of a transaction being classified as one rather than the other can be substantial.

In making the distinction, one must recognize that the property in question has the *ability* to provide a long-term benefit to its owner but is not always acquired for that purpose. The *intended* use of a property on acquisition is the principal factor in deciding its tax treatment on a subsequent sale.[4] Capital treatment can be distinguished from business treatment by employing the following guidelines:

1. Property acquired for the purpose of providing the owner with a long-term or enduring benefit is *capital property* and its disposition results in a capital gain or loss.

2. Property acquired for the purpose of reselling it at a profit is *inventory* and its disposition results in business income or a business loss.

The following examples demonstrate how identical assets receive different tax treatment as a result of their intended use:

• A house constructed for use as a principal residence by its owner is capital property having a long-term benefit. A similar house constructed for resale by a property developer is inventory, as it was constructed with the intention of reselling at a profit.
• Land and buildings acquired by an investor for the purpose of generating a return on investment through rents is capital property, but land and buildings (even though rented out) acquired by a speculator for resale at a profit is inventory.
• Office equipment acquired by an enterprise to assist staff in carrying out their duties is capital property because it has a long-term benefit in that it contributes to the enterprise's earning process. The same equipment acquired for the purpose of resale by a retailer of office equipment constitutes inventory.
• Land acquired by a retail business as a parking area for customers is capital property because it provides a long-term benefit by contributing to the earning process of the owner. However, if the same retailer acquired land for speculative purposes as a side venture from its normal business, the particular land would be inventory. In this case, the entity holds two properties of a similar nature, but the tax treatment for each is entirely different.

---

4   *Regal Heights Ltd. v. MNR*, 60 DTC 1270; and *Irrigation Industries Limited v. MNR*, 62 DTC 1131.

- A used car acquired by an individual at a bargain price, if it is used for personal transportation, is capital property providing a long-term benefit. A used car acquired at a bargain price by the same individual for the purpose of resale at a profit is inventory, which means that business income or loss is created when it is resold.

It is sometimes difficult to assess the primary intention of a property acquisition; because of this, several guidelines have been developed in common law to provide an extended definition for determining capital as opposed to business treatment. These guidelines are discussed in Chapter 8, which reviews other aspects of capital transactions.

It is essential that the reader be familiar with the term "business" as it applies to the taxation of income. As previously mentioned, in most cases, the existence of a business activity is obvious. However, most individuals and business entities will, at one time or another, enter into transactions that are less obvious. Familiarity with the distinction between capital income and business income is important when it comes to assessing the risks of proposed financial transactions. The degree of risk involved in entering into a transaction is enhanced if the activity may result in a capital loss, rather than a business loss, because of the restrictions imposed on the deduction of capital losses against other sources of income.

II. General Rules for Determining Business Income

For income tax purposes, income derived from business activity is determined by computing an entity's net profit (or loss) for the taxation year, having taken into account six general limiting factors. These six general limitations constitute the general rules for determining business income for tax purposes for all entities. They are discussed later in this chapter.

A. Profit Defined

The *Income Tax Act* simply states that, subject to certain exceptions, "a taxpayer's income for a taxation year from a business is the profit therefrom for the year."[5] This very broad statement is the primary rule for business income determination. Interestingly, no attempt is made to define "profit," and as a result this task has been left to the courts.

The courts, in turn, have also failed to specifically define the term; instead, they have developed a set of general principles to be used in determining profit for income tax purposes.[6] The main principles are set out below:

1. The determination of profit is a question of law.

2. The profit of a business for a taxation year is determined by setting against the revenues from the business year the expenses incurred to earn that income.[7]

3. The goal in computing profit is to obtain an accurate picture of the taxpayer's profit for the year.

4. In ascertaining profit, the taxpayer is free to adopt any method provided that it is consistent with the provisions of the *Income Tax Act*, established case law principles or "rules of law," and *well-accepted business principles*.

---

5 ITA 9(1), (2).
6 *Canderel Limited v. Her Majesty the Queen*, 98 DTC 6100; *Toronto College Park Ltd. v. Her Majesty the Queen*, 98 DTC 6088.
7 *MNR v. Irwin*, supra; *Associated Investors*, supra.

Established case law deals with specific limited issues, and the *Income Tax Act* does not define *profit*. It follows that the above general principles must focus on well-accepted business principles as the fundamental starting point for determining profit. Because of the wide variety of commercial enterprises, it is impossible to identify a specific set of business principles. Most businesses determine profit in accordance with generally accepted accounting principles (GAAP). In fact, the courts have stated that well-accepted business principles include but are not limited to GAAP. They have also indicated that GAAP are not rules of law but, rather, significant interpretive aids for establishing well-accepted business principles. For many years, the courts have given considerable consideration to GAAP when dealing with conflicts between taxpayers and the CRA.[8] In 2011, Canada adopted International Financial Reporting Standards (IFRS) for publicly accountable enterprises. Entities that are not publicly accountable (private companies) have a choice of following IFRS and Accounting Standards for Private Enterprises (ASPE). These standards are part of GAAP and are considered as one element of well-accepted business principles for determining business profit. The International Accounting Standards Board and the [Canadian] Accounting Standards Board are independent standard-setting bodies that establish IFRS and ASPE respectively. These standards are laid out by the Canadian Institute of Chartered Accountants (CICA) in the *CICA Handbook*. GAAP constitute the most important interpretive aid in establishing profit. This profit is then modified according to the *Income Tax Act*, established case law, and well-established business principles.

Simply stated, business income for tax purposes is the *profit* determined in accordance with well-established business principles using GAAP as an interpretive aid; it *comprises the revenues earned in a taxation year less the expenses incurred for the purpose of earning such revenues.* While there are some limitations as to what expenses can be deducted for tax purposes, it is generally understood that all expenses incurred in an attempt to generate revenues are deductible for tax purposes.

B. Generally Accepted Accounting Principles

As related previously, GAAP are the primary interpretive aid for determining well-established business principles and profit. The guidance provided in the *CICA Handbook* is too extensive to review fully within the scope of this text. The standards cover a broad range of general accounting areas as well as issues relating to specific industries and business transactions. However, all of the guidelines are rooted in a short list of fundamental concepts that have guided the development of the specific accounting standards. This is generally referred to as the GAAP conceptual framework. A few of the major concepts are reviewed below to help the reader understand the meaning of the accounting concept of net profit or loss. As mentioned previously, net profit or loss consists of two basic parts.

Revenues	$XXX
minus	
Expenses	XXX
equals	
Net profit (loss)	$ XX

1. Revenue Recognition

Revenues are derived from the sales value of products sold or the fees charged for services rendered, before the deduction of expenses. For accounting purposes, and therefore, for tax purposes, revenues are recognized at the point in time when the earning process is substantially complete. Normally, the earning process is substantially

---

8   *The Queen v. Metropolitan Properties Co. Ltd.*, 85 DTC 5128.

complete when title to the property passes to the purchaser or, in the case of services, when the service contracted for has been provided.

The implication of this concept is that the recognition of revenue is not associated with the receipt of cash. When property is sold on credit, the full sales value is included in revenue, even though payment occurs at a later date. In some circumstances, cash is received in advance of delivery of the product or the rendering of the service, in which case the realization of revenue is delayed until the service is rendered or the goods are delivered.

2. Concept of Accrual

The accrual concept requires that expenses be recognized and recorded for accounting purposes when they are incurred, rather than when they are paid. Expenses, such as wages, utilities, interest, and so on, that are unpaid at the end of an accounting period must be recognized and deducted from revenues, even if the actual payment occurs in the following accounting period. In other words, the occurrence and recognition of expenses is not associated with the payment of cash. Similarly, revenues are recognized and recorded when earned as noted above.

3. Concept of Matching

The concept of matching requires that expenses incurred be deducted in the time period in which they contribute to the earning of revenue. This means that expenses incurred in one period that will have a benefit in future periods must be apportioned and allocated in some reasonable manner against those revenues to which they contribute.

Consider, for example, the treatment of inventory in a retail or wholesale business. Normally, an entity acquires and stores a supply of product for resale (inventory), which results in a cost at the time the goods are acquired. Even though an expenditure has occurred, the expense of each item held in inventory is recognized only when the product is sold—this way, the expense can be *matched* against the revenue associated with its sale. Often, there is a significant gap between the time a product is purchased and the time it is sold. This process is significantly more complex in manufacturing organizations because the cost of a finished product includes many types of expenses, including raw materials, direct labour costs, indirect labour costs for support staff, and a reasonable allocation of overhead expenses, such as depreciation on the manufacturing equipment and buildings that contribute to the creation of a new product. All of these costs must be accumulated, assigned to a particular product, and then held in abeyance until such time as the finished product is sold.

All costs of a capital nature that have a long-term or enduring benefit are treated in a manner similar to the one described above. Many items—buildings, equipment, vehicles, furniture, patents, franchises, licences, and so on—contribute to the revenue-earning process for a number of years. The matching principle requires that the cost of all these items be apportioned and deducted over those future years. For example, the cost of a $500,000 building with an expected life of 20 years may be expensed against the revenues of those years at $25,000 per year.

Consider the costs incurred in researching and developing a product and introducing it into the marketplace. These costs may contribute to revenues over a future number of years. Because there is a significant amount of uncertainty relating to whether research will actually result in future revenues, research costs are generally expensed when incurred. However, development costs are often capitalized (deferred) if certain criteria are met.

It can be seen that compliance with the matching principle requires considerable judgment on the part of those responsible for the allocations. In order to allocate the costs of *fixed* assets, such as buildings and equipment, or *intangible* assets, such as goodwill and the development costs of new products, one must estimate the extent of their useful life, their contribution to the revenue-earning process in future years, and their value (if any) at the end of their useful life. This process offers leeway for a wide range of opinions; as a consequence, businesses with similar financial results may present significantly different annual-profit determinations, even though in the long run of several years, the cumulative results will be the same.

4. Concept of Conservatism

This is a concept in transition. Historically, it has resulted in recognizing all losses when they are likely and measurable, rather than when they occur, while delaying the recognition of gains until they occur. In addition, when there is uncertainty as to measurement, the concept has generally supported choosing a measure that does not overstate assets nor income.

More recently, standard setters have adopted the view that financial statements should be unbiased and that conservatism, by definition, introduces a bias. The current view is that financial statement preparers should use their best efforts to deal with measuring uncertainty and to come up with a reasonable estimate that reflects the timing and uncertainty of cash flows. Although the conservatism concept has been removed from the IFRS conceptual framework, it is still embedded in many of the specific IFRS standards as well as GAAP for private enterprises.

This brief review of some of the fundamental concepts makes it clear that "profit" in accordance with the interpretive aid of accounting principles is by no means precisely determinable and that there is considerable room for unintended or intended misjudgment. The general limitations and specific exceptions detailed within the *Income Tax Act*, discussed below, are an attempt to provide a more uniform standard in the areas that are most flexible under the accounting guidelines.

C. General Limitations to Business Profit Determination

The determination of income from business for tax purposes is constrained by the imposition of six general limitations that apply to the deduction of expenses. In some cases, the limitations are in complete conflict with well-established business principles and generally accepted accounting principles; in such cases, the limitations imposed by the *Income Tax Act* take precedence. In order for any expense to be deductible in arriving at business income, the following conditions must be satisfied.

1. Income-Earning-Purpose Test

In order for an expense to be deductible for tax purposes, it must be incurred for the purpose of gaining, producing, or maintaining income from business.[9]

It is not necessary that an expense have a direct relationship to the generating of income; it must, however, have been inspired by and incurred as part of the process of carrying on a business activity with an expectation to profit. The fact that no income is generated from an incurred expense is irrelevant if the expense arose from an attempt to achieve, enhance, or maintain income.[10]

This test can be considered the primary test for the deductibility of expenses in arriving at business income, as it defines the concept of "allowable expense." At the same time, it broadly eliminates those expenses that have no real business value, such as extravagant expenditures that primarily benefit the person incurring them, rather than the income-earning process. This test is the CRA's main tool in its attempts to eliminate abusive deductions for tax purposes. The business sector is

---

9 ITA 18(1)(a); IT-104R3, -487; *Royal Trust Company v. MNR*, 57 DTC 1055; Proposed-ITA 3.1.
10 *Booth v. MNR*, 79 DTC 595; *Speck v. MNR*, 88 DTC 1518.

often accused of having an unfair advantage when it comes to the types of deductions permitted; however, the accusations usually focus on those deductions that are actually restricted by the income-earning-purpose test.

Sometimes, individuals carry on activities that create revenue but have no reasonable expectation of earning a profit. For example, raising pets as a hobby may incur a large amount of expenses but earn only small revenues to help offset the costs. If the nature of the enterprise suggests that there is no reasonable expectation of earning a profit, then the expenses are deductible only to the extent of the related revenue, and any loss is considered a personal loss and denied for income tax purposes.[11]

2. Capital Test

Even if an expenditure was incurred for the purpose of earning income, it must also pass the capital test in order to be directly deductible for tax purposes. The capital test dictates that no item is deductible in arriving at business income if it was incurred "on account of capital" or is an allowance in respect of "depreciation obsolescence or depletion" unless it is specifically permitted within the *Income Tax Act*.[12]

An expenditure on account of capital is one that results in a long-term or enduring benefit to the entity.[13] Such items as the cost of buildings, equipment, vehicles, land, patents, licences, and goodwill all contribute to revenues over a period of years and are therefore not deductible in accordance with the general limitation. In addition, the depreciation or amortization of these items is also not deductible.

The term "capital" must be liberally interpreted and applied to expenditures other than the obvious ones listed above. For example, the interest paid on a loan used to fund the acquisition of a capital asset is incurred on the account of capital and therefore falls within the general limitation. The major renovation of a delivery vehicle that extends its useful life beyond the original expectation is a capital outlay because its benefit is long term. Legal expenses to register the ownership of a building or to provide advice and execute the purchase documents on a business takeover have a long-term benefit and are not deductible. Such legal expenses are simply added to the cost of the building or of the business assets acquired, as the case may be.

The main reason for limiting expenditures of a capital nature is to remove from the calculation of accounting profit those items that are most flexible under accounting principles. The result of this limitation is that expense items, such as the depreciation and amortization of fixed assets and intangible assets, which can vary considerably with the owner's procedures for matching expense to revenues, are removed from the normal determination of profit. Instead, most of these items are dealt with specifically as exceptions to the general limitation, and a uniform system of allocation is utilized that applies to all business entities. These exceptions are reviewed later in this chapter.

3. Exempt-Income Test

Under this limitation, an expense is not deductible, even though it was incurred to earn income, if the income that is expected to be generated is itself not taxable revenue.[14] For example, the life insurance premiums paid by a business to insure its key executives are not deductible because any life insurance proceeds the business later received would not constitute taxable revenue. Similarly, as an extreme example, the purchase of a lottery ticket by a business is not deductible under this limitation because the possible lottery winnings are not subject to tax.

---

11 *Livergrant v. MNR*, 89 DTC; Proposed-ITA 3.1.
12 ITA 18(1)(b).
13 *British Insulated and Helsby Cables Ltd. v. Atherton* (United Kingdom—1926).
14 ITA 18(1)(c); IT-467R2.

4. Reserve Test

While the process of determining accounting profit permits the deduction of reserves in accordance with the principle of conservatism, the *Income Tax Act* on a general basis disallows as a deduction an amount transferred or credited to a reserve, contingent account, or sinking fund, except as expressly permitted.[15] Therefore, as a general test, *no reserves are deductible* for tax purposes. Again, it is important to note that exceptions are permitted and that some but not all reserves can be deducted within certain guidelines. (This will be reviewed later.)

5. Personal-Expense Test

Under this general limitation, no deductions are permitted for a taxpayer's personal or living expenses *except* for those travel expenses incurred away from home in the course of carrying on business.[16] Travel expenses include the amounts expended for meals and lodging. In effect, this limitation is an expansion of the income-earning-purpose test described earlier.

Personal or living expenses encompass the expenses of properties that are maintained by individuals for personal or family use and that are not maintained in connection with a business carried on for profit or with a reasonable expectation of profit. The cost of travel from home to work by a person carrying on a business, by virtue of this general limitation, is not deductible.

6. Reasonableness Test

The final general limitation that applies to the computation of business income—it also applies to deductions from all other sources of income—requires that an outlay or expense be deductible only to the extent that the outlay or expense is *reasonable in the circumstances*.[17] This means that even when the type of expense meets the other general criteria for deductibility, the amount that can be deducted is limited to a reasonable amount. For example, a salary paid to a spouse or child of the owner of a business is deductible if it is for the purpose of earning income, but the amount is limited to what would be reasonable considering the nature and extent of the work provided.

In many cases, reasonableness is difficult to establish, but the term implies that an amount would be unreasonable if it were significantly in excess of what other taxpayers in similar situations would incur.

This limitation is designed to combat the abuse of permitted business deductions and to confine business expenses to those that are legitimately incurred as part of the income-earning process.

Income from business is arrived at by first establishing the profit or loss in accordance with well-established business principles, taking into account GAAP. Each item of deduction must pass the six general limitation tests before it can be included in the calculation of profit. Notwithstanding these broad general principles, there are a number of specific exceptions that are designed primarily to create uniformity among taxpayers and to prevent abuse when the general rules described above are being applied.

III. Exceptions to the General Rules

The *Income Tax Act* responds to the general rules by listing specific exceptions. If a particular item is not listed as a specific exception, the general rules determine the outcome. The specific list of exceptions establishes the final parameters of the calculation and so completes the process of determining business income.

---

15 ITA 18(1)(e); IT-215R (archived).
16 ITA 18(1)(h), 248(1); *Cumming v. MNR*, 67 DTC 5312.
17 ITA 67; *Mulder Bros. Sand and Gravel Ltd. v. MNR*, 67 DTC 475.

The vast majority of exceptions to the general rules are listed in sections 12, 13, 14, 18, 19, and 20 of the *Income Tax Act*. Sections 12, 13, and 14 deal with items that increase income; sections 18, 19, and 20 outline the expense exceptions. The income tax system also permits inventory costing methods that may deviate from well-established business principles and GAAP.

A. Specific Income and Expense Exceptions

Sections 13 and 14 deal with income earned on the sale of depreciable property and other intangible assets, such as goodwill, patents, and licences. These items will be dealt with at length in the next chapter. Many of the items included in section 12 will also be discussed later, as most of them either relate to investment activities (see Chapter 6) or simply restate the treatment of business items provided by well-established business principles and GAAP.

However, three items in section 12 deserve special mention at this time—inducement payments, insurance proceeds, and payments based on production or use.

• **Inducement payments**   It is not uncommon for a business to receive an inducement from another party to carry out some activity. For example, a prospective tenant of a building may receive an inducement from a landlord as part of the lease agreement. Such an inducement may simply take the form of reduced future rents, in which case the tax impact to the tenant is recognized by a lower rent deduction for tax purposes. However, the inducement may be a cash grant or a cash reimbursement for all or a portion of the costs incurred by the tenant to improve the property (see leasehold improvements, Chapter 6). In such cases, the payments are treated as taxable business income and are included in income in the year of receipt.[18] As an alternative, the taxpayer can elect to apply the inducement payment as a reduction of the cost of the property acquired.[19] In other words, instead of including that payment in income, the tenant can use it to reduce the cost of the leasehold improvements for tax purposes. This means that future deductions for CCA (amortization) on those improvements will be lower as a result of the reduced cost base. In the event that an inducement payment has to be repaid, a deduction is permitted at that time.[20]

An inducement payment may be a grant, a subsidy, or a forgivable loan and may come from another business or from a government. The tax treatment for all of these is the same. In most cases, the taxpayer will choose to delay the recognition of income by electing to treat the payment as a reduction of the cost of the asset. However, this may not always be the case, especially when it is anticipated that tax rates will increase in the future or when the business is currently not taxable because of excessive losses.

• **Insurance proceeds**   When depreciable property is damaged or destroyed, insurance proceeds are likely to be received. When the property is destroyed (as opposed to damaged), the insurance proceeds are treated for tax purposes as proceeds from the disposition of the property. In other words, the insurance proceeds are the same as what the selling price would have been if the property had been sold. The amount of taxable income, if any, depends on the property's tax cost (see Chapter 6).

When the property is only damaged, the proceeds from an insurance policy are treated as taxable income, but only to the extent of the cost of the repairs made to the property.[21] For example, assume that the insurance proceeds are $12,000 but the subsequent actual repair costs amount to only $9,000. In this case $9,000 of the insurance proceeds must be included in income, which effectively offsets the repair expenses.

---

18 ITA 12(1)(x), 12(2.2).
19 ITA 13(7.4), 53(2)(s).
20 ITA 20(1)(hh).
21 ITA 12(1)(f).

The remaining insurance proceeds of $3,000 are treated as proceeds of a disposition of the depreciable property, much as if they were destroyed property (see Chapter 6).[22]

- **Payments based on production or use**   A payment received that is based on the production or use of property, even when it is an instalment payment from the sale of a property, is considered to be business or property income.[23] An example of such a payment is the receipt of a franchise royalty that has been calculated as a percentage of sales volume.

  The provisions may also apply when a property is sold and the selling price consists of both a fixed price and an additional amount that is based on the future income from that property. Consider a situation where the owner of an insurance business sells that business for a price equal to the value of the tangible assets (equipment and so on) *plus* a further amount that is equal to the sum of the commission revenue earned by the new owner for the next three years. The payments based upon the future commissions actually represent the capital value of the business (or the goodwill—see Chapter 6). However, because the variable amount is based upon future production, it may be considered business income to the vendor.[24] When part of the price of a property is based upon production or use, then only that variable portion is considered to be business income, and the fixed amount represents the normal proceeds from the disposition of property.[25]

Each of the above exceptions relates to items of income. There are also exceptions that deal with expenses. These can be divided into two basic categories:

- expenses denied
- expenses permitted

1. Expenses Denied

Sections 18 and 19 of the *Income Tax Act* list specific expenses that are not permitted as deductions, even though they would otherwise qualify under the general rules. The list is not extensive. Several of the expenses denied are reviewed here.

- **Use of recreational facilities and club dues**   Under this restriction, no business entity is permitted to deduct the expenses incurred for the use or maintenance of a yacht, a camp, a lodge, or a golf course unless such property is part of the entity's normal business (for example, the selling or leasing of yachts).[26] This restriction also denies the deduction of all expenses incurred as membership fees or dues in any club, the main purpose of which is to provide dining, recreational, or sporting facilities to its members.

  This restriction is designed to forestall the abuse of the general rule that permits the deduction of expenses if they are for the purpose of earning income. Facilities and clubs may provide a high degree of personal enjoyment and in that sense enhance a person's ability to generate revenue; still, they are simply denied altogether as a business expense in order to avoid the difficult task of sorting out the legitimate from the non-legitimate.

- **Political contributions**   No political contributions are deductible for tax purposes, even though they may have an income-earning purpose.[27] While such contributions

---

22 ITA 13(21), part (c) of *proceeds of disposition* definition.
23 ITA 12(1)(g).
24 *Gault v. MNR*, 65 DTC 5157.
25 IT-462, -426.
26 ITA 18(1)(l); IT-148R3.
27 ITA 18(1)(n).

are not deductible in arriving at net income, they do create a tax credit that permits the amount of tax payable to be reduced within certain limits (see Chapter 10).

- **Advertising expenses** In conflict with the general rules, the cost of advertising in a non-Canadian newspaper or broadcasting undertaking cannot be deducted *if* the advertisement is directed primarily at a Canadian market.[28] For example, advertising placed with an American-border television station to appeal to viewers in Canada is not deductible, but advertising on the same station to attract foreign customers is deductible. This exception is designed to provide assistance to Canadian media enterprises.

- **Allowance for an automobile** As discussed in Chapter 4, employees often receive a travel allowance from their employers. Such allowances are tax-free to the employee as long as they are reasonable in the circumstances. When the allowance relates to the use of an automobile, the employer who pays the allowance faces limits as to the amount that can be deducted for tax purposes.[29] The maximum allowance that can be deducted by an employer is 53¢ for each of the first 5,000 kilometres in a year, and 47¢ for each additional kilometre (an additional 4¢ is permitted in the Yukon, Nunavut, and the Northwest Territories).[30] These deductible rates are modified periodically. This limitation applies only if the allowance is tax-free to the employee. If the allowance is taxable to the employee, the employer can deduct the full amount, provided that it is reasonable.

- **Interest and property taxes on vacant land** Even though interest costs and property taxes are normally tax deductible (see below), a restriction applies when they relate to idle land. Land is considered to be idle if it is vacant and is not being used primarily to generate income or if it is being held primarily for resale or development.

  In such circumstances, the related interest costs and property taxes are deductible, but *only* to the extent that income is generated from that land.[31] For example, if vacant land generates temporary income of $8,000 (e.g., from rents) but incurs interest and property tax expenses of $11,000, the tax deduction is limited to $8,000. The unclaimed balance of $3,000 is added to the cost of the land. Therefore, the amount initially denied as a deduction ($3,000 in this case) can be deducted against the sale proceeds when the land is sold.[32] Keep in mind that the land may be classified as either inventory or capital property depending on the purpose of its acquisition. The above limitation may not apply if the entity's principal business is the leasing, rental, sale, or development of real property.[33]

- **Certain costs during construction period** While a building is being constructed or altered, certain costs during the construction period may be denied as deductions, even though they would normally qualify.[34] Such costs include legal and accounting fees, interest costs, mortgage costs, property taxes, and promotional expenses that relate to the construction project and ownership of the related land. These costs are instead considered part of the cost of the building and as such are eligible for a CCA deduction over a period of years (see Chapter 6).

---

28 ITA 19.
29 ITA 18(1)(r); Regulation 7306.
30 Regulation 7306 (effective September 1989).
31 ITA 18(2), (3).
32 ITA 53(1)(h), ITA 10(1.1).
33 ITA 18(2).
34 ITA 18(3.1) to (3.7).

- **Work space in a home** Individuals who operate a business may conduct all or part of that activity from a space in their home. The expenses applicable to that space are not permitted as a deduction for tax purposes unless one of the following conditions is met:[35]

- The space in the home is "the individual's principal place of business."
- The space is "used exclusively for the purpose of earning income from business and used on a regular or continuous basis for meeting clients, customers, or patients of the individual."

If either of these conditions is met, the permitted expenses include a proportionate amount of the home's common expenses (mortgage interest, property taxes, utilities, insurance, and so on), in addition to any expenses that relate specifically to the work space. However, the total expenses cannot exceed the business income for the year. If they do, the excess is considered to be an expense of the following year. Note that these expenses are more generous than those permitted to employees who use a home office (see Chapter 4).

- **Meals and entertainment** Although entertainment and out-of-town meal expenses are deductible if incurred for the purpose of earning income, the amount permitted as a deduction is limited to 50% of actual costs incurred. This limitation was established in response to significant taxpayer abuses; even so, it arbitrarily eliminates a portion (50%) of all legitimate expenditures incurred for this purpose. It should be pointed out that this rule is not found in sections 18 and 19 of the *Income Tax Act*, with the other denied expenses; rather, it is a general rule that affects all types of income.[36] One of the exceptions to this rule (which permits a 100% deduction) is the cost of food, beverage, and entertainment for events generally available to all employees. This exception is limited to six "occasional events" per year.

- **Costs of an automobile** As with meals and entertainment costs, arbitrary limitations are placed on certain costs relating to a passenger vehicle used to earn business income.[37] These include the following:

- Whatever the actual cost of an automobile, its cost for the purposes of claiming a deduction for CCA cannot exceed $30,000 (plus tax).[38]
- The interest cost on money borrowed to acquire a vehicle cannot exceed $300 per month.[39]
- The deduction for a leased automobile cannot exceed $800 (plus tax) per month.[40]

The dollar limitations described above change from time to time, and so the relevant sections should be examined in the applicable year.

- **Stock-based compensation** Corporations often reward employees by issuing shares as a bonus or granting stock options. The value of these benefits may be recorded for accounting purposes as an expense on the income statement. For tax purposes stock-based compensation is *not deductible*.[41] Where an amount has been deducted on the financial statements, it is merely added back in computing business income for tax purposes. Several types of stock-based compensation plans are reviewed in Chapter 4 (Part VIII, Section C3).

---

35 ITA 18(12); IT-514; *Marius Landry v. The Queen* (TCC); (Docket 1999–15[IT]I).
36 ITA 67.1; IT-518R.
37 IT-521R.
38 ITA 13(7)(g).
39 ITA 67.2; Regulation 7307(2).
40 ITA 67.3. A further limitation based on a formula tied to the suggested list price of the car and $30,000 may also apply. See IT-521R.
41 ITA 7(3)(b).

- **Unpaid remuneration** Employee remuneration, other than vacation pay, is not deductible in the year accrued unless it is paid by 180 days after the business year end.[42] See discussion in Part III, Section G of this chapter.

- **Unpaid amounts owing to related persons** An expense accrued that is owed to a person who is not at arm's length with the business must be paid by the end of the second year of the business after the year in which the expense was accrued. Otherwise, the accrued amount is added to the business income in the third year after the expense was accrued, unless a special election is made.[43]

2. Expenses Permitted

Section 20 of the *Income Tax Act* lists approximately 40 specific items that are permitted as deductions, even though according to the six general limitations, they do not normally qualify. Most of these exceptions modify either expenditures of a capital nature that have a long-term or enduring benefit or reserves put aside in recognition of certain anticipated expenses. Some but not all of these exceptions are identified and discussed below.

- **Capital cost allowance and amortization** The general rules prohibit the deduction of all depreciation and amortization of capital assets because their determination is subject to considerable variation by individual businesses and industries. However, the exception rules do permit the gradual expensing, in a controlled and uniform manner, of certain fixed assets and intangible capital property over a period of time.[44] The result is that all business entities are subject to the same application with respect to these items. This area is reviewed in detail in Chapter 6.

- **Interest** Interest incurred on loans used to acquire long-term assets is considered to be on the account of capital and is therefore denied by the general rules. However, section 20 permits interest of this nature to be deducted, provided that the long-term asset to which it relates is used to assist in the income process.[45]

  In addition, interest can, at the taxpayer's option, be deducted on a cash basis when paid, rather than by the accrual method required by GAAP.

  Two special options exist when money is borrowed to purchase depreciable property. Interest can be deducted as it is incurred; or it can be added to the cost of the depreciable property acquired, in which case it becomes eligible for a deduction over time in the form of CCA (see Chapter 6).[46]

- **Expenses of borrowing money or issuing shares** Expenses of this nature, even though they have a long-term benefit, are permitted as a deduction in equal proportions over five years (one-fifth per year).[47] Such items as the cost of registering a mortgage, appraisal fees for financing, selling commissions, and finder's fees are all deductible over five years. Life insurance premiums also may qualify as an expense of borrowing money. Normally, life insurance premiums are considered not deductible (where the company is the beneficiary) under the general rules because the income earned (life insurance) is not taxable revenue. However, if the insurance is required as loan collateral, it becomes a cost of borrowing money and an exception

---

42 ITA 78(4).
43 ITA 78(1)–(3).
44 ITA 20(1)(a), (b).
45 ITA 20(1)(c); IT-533.
46 ITA 21; IT-121R3 (archived).
47 ITA 20(1)(e); IT-341R4.

is permitted.[48] In addition, because the life insurance premium is an annual cost, it can be fully deducted each year when incurred, rather than amortized over five years.

• **Landscaping of grounds** Expenses incurred for the landscaping of property around a building or other structure that is used for the purpose of gaining or producing income are deductible when paid (not when incurred), even though such expenditure provides a long-term benefit through land enhancement.[49]

• **Reserves for doubtful debts and bad debt expense** Amounts receivable by a business entity, if it is anticipated that they will not be collected, are deductible as a reserve, provided that this reserve is reasonable and that the debt, when established, created income for the taxpayer.[50] Debts such as accounts receivable for the sale of inventory or the rendering of services are entitled to use this reserve. Entities whose business includes the loaning of money qualify for the reserve; this is the case even when such loans did not create income when first established.

Reserves that are based on an arbitrary percentage of total receivables are not considered reasonable and are, therefore, not deductible. For a reserve for doubtful debts to be considered reasonable in amount, it is necessary to identify the debts that are doubtful of collection and estimate the percentage of the doubtful debts that will probably not be collected. The CRA accepts a reserve calculated, as a percentage of the total doubtful debts or a series of percentages relating to an age-analysis of those debts, based on the taxpayer's past collection history.[51]

The above deals with the deduction of *anticipated* uncollectible trade accounts receivable. Ultimately, the debt will either be collected or determined to be uncollectible. If a deduction is made as a reserve in a particular year, that reserve must be added back to income in the flowing taxation year and then re-evaluated (see Section F—Treatment of Reserves). If it is still in doubt a new reserve can be deducted. However, if it is determined to be uncollectible, it is written off and *permanently deducted as bad debt*.[52] If the amount written off is subsequently collected, it must be added to income at that time.[53]

In some situations a business will sell all or a portion of its accounts receivable to a third party at a discount. An example is when a business *sells its trade accounts receivable to a factor.* The factor pays a discounted price for the receivables and makes a profit by collecting the face value of the debts. Factoring allows a business to speed up its cash inflows and is considered to be a form of financing. Any loss resulting from discounting is considered to be a deductible business expense (not a bad debt).[54]

• **Reserve for delayed payment revenues** A reserve may be deducted from income when inventory has been sold and all or part of the payment is not due until after two years from the date of sale.[55] This means that income from the sale of items that have a long-term payment schedule can be recognized for tax purposes over a period of time. However, such a reserve can be utilized for no more than three years, even though payments may extend beyond that time.

When the inventory sold is land, a reserve can be utilized to reduce profits in proportion to any deferred proceeds beyond the taxation year in which the sale was

---

48 ITA 20(1)(e.2); IT-309R2.
49 ITA 20(1)(aa); IT-296 (archived).
50 ITA 20(1)(l); IT-442R.
51 IT-442R
52 ITA 20(1)(p)
53 ITA 12(1)(i)
54 IT 188R, IT-442R
55 ITA 20(1)(n), 20(8)(b); IT-152R3, -154R.

made, for a maximum of three years. For example, assume that a profit of $40,000 is earned on land inventory that was sold for $100,000 in 20X1. The payment terms include $10,000 cash in 20X1 and the balance of $90,000 payable in 20X5. In 20X1, the profit of $40,000 can be reduced by a reserve of $36,000 ($90,000/$100,000 $\times$ $40,000), this being the portion of the sales proceeds that has been deferred. In 20X2 and 20X3, no income is realized because no further proceeds are received. The deferred profit of $36,000 must be recognized for tax purposes in 20X4 (the three-year reserve limit), even though the remaining proceeds are not received until 20X5. Further sample reserve calculations can be found in IT-154R, available from the CRA.

• **Expenses of representation** Sometimes, a business must make a representation to a government body, with long-term implications. For example, a business may present suggestions or concerns to a regulatory body relating to its industry. Or the business may be applying for a permit, franchise, patent, trademark, or broadcast licence. While such expenses are capital in nature, a full deduction is permitted in the year that they are paid.[56] As an alternative, the taxpayer can elect to deduct the amount at the rate of one-tenth per year over 10 years.[57]

• **Investigation of a site** A deduction is permitted for the cost of investigating a suitable site for a building to be used in a business. The deduction is allowed whether or not the site is actually acquired.[58]

• **Convention expenses** Usually, attending a convention or conference provides a long-term benefit for the taxpayer and therefore is a capital expenditure. Regardless, a deduction is permitted for the costs of attending up to two conventions in a year, provided that the location of the convention is within the territorial scope of the organization holding the convention.[59]

Convention expenses must be distinguished from expenses of training. Training costs are treated according to the common rules and are denied if they are capital in nature. For example, if an individual pays for a training program in order to *acquire* a new trade or profession, the cost is a capital item and cannot be deducted. However, a course taken to *maintain* or *upgrade* an existing skill is deductible. It should be noted that costs incurred by employers to train or retrain employees are usually considered to be fully deductible as they are incurred.[60]

• **Utilities service connection** A deduction is permitted for the cost of making a service connection to the taxpayer's place of business for the supply of electricity, gas, telephone service, and water or sewers, even though such costs are normally capital items.[61]

• **Private health services plans** Businesses often compensate employees with certain fringe benefits in addition to salaries. Private health services plan (PHSP) coverage is one such benefit. As was shown in Chapter 4, this benefit is deductible as an expense to the employer but is not taxable to the employee. An individual who is self-employed and is operating a business as a proprietor cannot employ himself or herself (as could be the case if the business was a corporation) and normally will not be able to deduct such premiums. A special rule covers this anomaly: Individuals can deduct the amounts paid for their PHSP coverage in computing business income, provided they are actively engaged

---

56 ITA 20(1)(cc).
57 ITA 20(9).
58 ITA 20(1)(dd); IT-350R.
59 ITA 20(10); IT-131R2.
60 IT-357R2.
61 ITA 20(1)(ee), IT-452 (archived).

alone or as a partner in a business, and either self-employment is their primary source of income in the year (more than 50%) *or* their income from other sources does not exceed $10,000. The deduction applies only if coverage is provided to all permanent full-time employees (other than employees who are related to the owner). Such coverage is deductible to a maximum of $1,500 each for the individual and spouse, and $750 per child. No limit applies to arm's-length employees.[62]

• **Expenses deductible on a cash basis** As previously described, expenses are normally deducted on an accrual basis when incurred, rather than when paid. However, certain expenses must actually be paid in order to obtain a deduction for tax purposes. These include *convention expenses, landscaping, representation fees, site investigation fees, utility service connections,* and *investment counsel fees* (see Chapter 7).

• **Contributions to the Canada Pension Plan (CPP)** These are legally required in Canada. The contribution cost is shared by the employer and the employee. The employer's share of such contributions is, of course, deductible in arriving at business income. See Chapter 9, Part II for a discussion of CPP contributions on self-employed earnings.

• **Registered Pension Plans (RPPs)** Registered Pension Plans were discussed in Chapter 4, Part VIII, Section C. Contribution limits for the two types of pension plans are reviewed below:

Money Purchase Plans—The contribution limit for the employer and employee, combined, is 18% of the employee's compensation for the year, limited to $23,820 (2012).

Defined Benefit Plans—The contributions made by an employer to a defined benefit RPP are deductible provided the payment is made pursuant to a recommendation by an actuary in whose opinion the contribution is required to be made so that the plan will have sufficient assets to pay pension benefits.[63]

The employer has until 120 days after the year end of the business to make the contribution to Money Purchase and Defined Benefit plans.[64]

• **Pooled Registered Pension Plans (PRPPs)** Many individuals do not have access to employer-sponsored pension plans that utilize professional pension advisors and obtain cost efficiencies. Instead, these individuals have had to develop their own pension plans through Registered Retirement Savings Plans (RRSPs—see Chapter 9). Recently introduced federal legislation proposes a new pension structure—Pooled Registered Pension Plans. The format allows financial institutions to organize large pools of funds that can be joined by individuals, thereby benefitting from lower investment management costs that result from participating in larger pooled pension plans. The PRPP will have attributes similar to money purchase RPPs with two basic differences—the annual contribution limit for the employer and individual for the PRPP and any RRSP cannot exceed the individual's RRSP limit ($22,970 in 2012) *and* the employer's contribution is optional. Employer contributions are fully deductible for the employer.[65] The employer has until 120 days after year end of the business to make the contribution. See Chapter 9 for a further discussion of PRPPs.

---

62 ITA 20.01.
63 ITA 20(1)(q), 147.2(2).
64 ITA 20(1)(q), 147.2(1).
65 ITA 20(1)(q);

• **Deferred Profit Sharing Plan (DPSP)**   Deferred Profit Sharing Plans were discussed in Chapter 4, Part VIII, Section C. The contribution limit for an employer is 18% of the employee's compensation for the year, limited to $11,910 (2012). The employer has until 120 days after the year end of the business to make the contribution.[66]

The above exceptions to the general rules do not constitute a complete list. It is extremely important that any entity conducting a business activity make the simple effort to obtain a full list from their tax advisor, with explanations of the 40 or so exceptions to the general rules, so that it can apply the general rules with certainty.

B. Treatment of Inventories

The cost of items sold in the business process normally constitutes a formidable expense in the calculation of profit. As previously explained, the process of recognizing this expense involves holding the costs of products acquired or manufactured in abeyance until they are sold, at which time the expense is matched to the sale. While the use of computer technology has simplified this task considerably, the process is still predicated on the accumulating, throughout the year, of all costs of products available for sale and on deducting from that total the cost of products unsold at the close of the fiscal period. The remainder, after deductions are made for the cost of unsold merchandise (inventory), is the cost of the product sold during the period. For example, the cost may be determined as follows:

Cost of products available to be sold:	
Inventory on hand at beginning of the year	$200,000
Product purchased or manufactured during the year	700,000
Total cost of goods available for sale	900,000
Cost of products unsold:	
Inventory on hand at the end of the year	(150,000)
Cost of products sold and matched to revenues	$750,000

It is obvious that the value assigned to the inventory at the end of the year has a major impact on the cost of goods sold and therefore on the profits.

The _Income Tax Act_ specifically permits the closing inventory to be valued using one of two methods:

1. Value _each_ item of inventory at the lower of its cost or market value.[67]

2. Value _all_ items of inventory at their market value.[68]

Each of these methods is likely to produce a different ending inventory value and, as a result, a different profit for tax purposes. Keep in mind that this variance is only temporary, since ultimately a business must expense its full costs.

The reader must understand the terms "cost" and "market" in order to appreciate the extent of the impact on profits of the above alternatives.[69] When possible, _cost_ refers to the actual cost of each specific item unsold at the end of the period (the specific identification method). Often, it is not practical or possible to identify the actual cost of each product because the cost of such items has varied throughout the year. In these circumstances, it is acceptable to cost each item of inventory at its most current cost, making the assumption that the inventory consists of the most recent purchases

---

66 ITA 147(5.1).
67 ITA 10(1).
68 Regulation 1801; IT-473R.
69 IT-473R.

and that the first goods purchased were the first goods sold (FIFO—first-in, first-out method). Alternatively, each item may be valued at the average of its costs during the year (average-cost method). It is not acceptable to assume that inventory consists of the older items and that new products acquired are the first sold (LIFO—last-in, first-out method), although this may be acceptable under GAAP.

The term *market* normally reflects the realization value of the inventory in that it is the expected selling price after the deduction of direct selling costs, such as sales commissions. In manufacturing concerns, inventory consists of finished goods ready for sale, unfinished goods (work in process), and raw materials. The selling price of finished goods can be reasonably estimated but is difficult to obtain for unfinished goods and raw materials. For these items, it is acceptable to use the replacement cost as a reasonable estimate of market.

Consider the following inventory, which consists of three automobiles held by a car dealer, and the impact on profits of the different valuation alternatives.

Car model	Cost	Market net realizable value	Lower of cost or market
A	$12,000	$14,000	$12,000
B	14,000	11,000	11,000
C	18,000	21,000	18,000
Total	$44,000	$46,000	$41,000

Each of the two permitted inventory valuation methods—all at market, and each item at the lower of cost or market—results in a different inventory value and therefore a different profit determination. When all inventory is finally sold, however, the accumulated profit over the time period is identical for each method.

In addition to the acceptable methods of inventory valuation, profit can also be altered as a result of errors—intended or unintended—during that part of the compilation process which involves the physical counting, the costing, and the determination of the market value of each item.

While there are several options available for valuing inventory, the ability to change from one method to the other is somewhat restricted. First of all, the opening inventory of a new period must be valued in the same manner as the closing inventory of the previous period. Also, a further restriction requires that the closing inventory of a business be valued using the same method as for the closing inventory for the previous taxation year unless a change is approved by the CRA.[70] This means that the choice of the initial valuation method for a new business is an important one, as it will have an impact on future years as well.

From a management perspective, the acceptable alternatives for valuing inventory must be viewed as tools to enhance cash flow by deferring the realization of income for tax purposes. This means that the information process must be capable of providing relevant information on a timely basis so that managers can take advantage of the flexibility the tax system provides. The function of inventory costing and control has to be expanded so that alternative inventory valuations for tax purposes can be examined and the best one chosen.

---

70 ITA 10(2), (2.1).

C. Taxation Year and the Individual Taxpayer

In Chapter 3, it was established that the taxation year for the corporation is the fiscal year and for the individual is the calendar year. This means that a corporation's taxation year can end on any day of the year, whereas an individual operating a proprietorship business must end his or her taxation year on December 31.

For certain businesses, having a year end on December 31 may create an administrative hardship; this is especially true for seasonal businesses that do high volumes of business during the months surrounding December. In recognition of this, individuals can elect to use an alternative fiscal period other than December 31.[71] If this election is made, a complex formula is applied to the fiscal period earnings to arbitrarily adjust the income for tax purposes to approximate the calendar-year income. Consider the following situation and analysis:

Situation:

An individual taxpayer starts a new business on March 1, 20X6. Normally, her first taxation year for the business would be December 31, 20X6, and would include the income earned from March 1 to December 31, 20X6. However, she wishes to close the first business cycle on February 28, 20X7, exactly 12 months from the opening date. Profits from the business for the first two years are as follows:

Year ended February 28, 20X7	$40,000
Year ended February 28, 20X8	$50,000

Analysis:

This woman must file a tax return for the 20X6 calendar year that includes income from all sources. However, her first business year end does not arrive until February 28, 20X7, and therefore no income from the business is included in her 20X6 calendar year tax return. Effectively, 10 months (March 1 to December 31, 20X6) of her first year's business profits have been deferred to 20X7. The deferred amount is estimated to be $33,333 ($40,000 × 10 months/12 months).[72] This is a prorated estimate based on time and does not consider that profits may vary each month.

For the 20X7 calendar year for which a tax return must be filed, this woman's income for tax purposes will include the business profit of $40,000 for the fiscal year end February 28, 20X7. In addition, a further amount is included that represents an arbitrary estimate of the profit earned from March 1 to December 31, 20X7.[73] The 20X7 and 20X8 incomes from business are as follows:

20X7	
Year ended February 28, 20X7	$ 40,000
Deduct portion included in 20X6	–0–
	40,000
Add estimated income from March 1 to December 31, 20X7	
$40,000 × 10 months/12 months	33,333
Total 20X7 income from business	$ 73,333
20X8	
Year ended February 28, 20X8	$ 50,000
Deduct portion included in 20X7 above	(33,333)
	16,667
Add estimated income from March 1 to December 31, 20X8	
$50,000 × 10 months/12 months	41,667
Total 20X8 income from business	$ 58,334

---

71 ITA 11(1), 249.1.
72 The actual proration is based on the number of days, rather than months.
73 ITA 34.1(1), (3).

Note that this election puts no business income in 20X6 but creates excessive income in 20X7, likely causing a higher tax rate. To avoid this outcome, this woman can make a further election to include the 10 months of 20X6 business income ($40,000 × 10/12 = $33,333) in her 20X6 income for tax purposes.[74] Doing this would create the following business incomes in 20X6, 20X7, and 20X8:

20X6

Elected amount above	$ 33,333

20X7

Year ended February 28, 20X7	$ 40,000
Less portion included in 20X6 above	(33,333)
	6,667
Add estimated income from March 1 to December 31, 20X7	
$40,000 × 10 months/12 months	33,333
Total 20X7 income from business	$ 40,000

20X8

Year ended February 28, 20X8	$ 50,000
Less portion included in 20X7 above	(33,333)
	16,667
Add estimated income from March 1 to December 31, 20X8	
$50,000 × 10 months/12 months	41,667
Total 20X8 income from business	$ 58,334

The above situation and analysis show that the arbitrary formula that attempts to convert fiscal-year earnings to calendar-year earnings is complex and may create undesirable results. It appears that if annual profits are constant, the calendar-year method and the alternative method should produce similar results for an ongoing business. When profits are rising, the calendar method offers the best timing, whereas when profits are declining, the alternative method is preferable. Note that the two methods produce only a timing difference; over time, the identical amount of profits will be recognized. Predicting future profits is difficult, and so most taxpayers choose the calendar-year format for simplicity.

The requirement to use a calendar year, rather than a fiscal year, also applies to partnerships that include individual partners, and to a special category of corporations called "professional corporations," which are used exclusively by six professions—medical doctors, dentists, accountants, lawyers, veterinarians, and chiropractors. There are also measures that limit the ability of a corporation to defer the taxation of income earned through a partnership (see Chapter 15, Part II, Section C).

D. Scientific Research and Experimental Development

Expenditures for scientific research and experimental development (SR&ED) are usually incurred to provide a long-term benefit to the entity. Consequently, the general rules would deny a deduction, on the basis that they are capital expenditures. However, SR&ED activity by the business community is important to the long-term strength and competitiveness of the Canadian economy, and so the federal government has put in place special tax provisions that apply to SR&ED outlays, with the goal of encouraging such activity.

---

74 ITA 34.1(2).

To the extent that SR&ED is carried on within Canada, the following special provisions apply:[75]

- Ongoing expenditures, even those that contribute to the long-term benefit of the project, can be deducted in full in the year incurred. These expenditures include salaries and wages, supplies, payments to approved universities or other business entities for research work, and so on.
- The cost of tangible assets, such as equipment, that are used all or substantially all of the time in the SR&ED process can be fully deducted in the year of acquisition. This eliminates the normal requirement that such costs be deducted over several years as CCA. Usually, this exception does not apply to buildings. Also, commencing January 1, 2014, capital expenditures will no longer be included in SR&ED expenditures.[76]
- The business can choose not to deduct any of the above items when incurred but instead carry them forward indefinitely as a deduction for any future year.

The above provisions improve cash flow because the SR&ED costs can be deducted immediately to create a tax saving. In addition, the indefinite carry-over period for unused deductions means that companies have a greater chance for such costs eventually resulting in tax savings.

These benefits are significantly reduced when the SR&ED activity is carried on *outside* Canada. In these circumstances, for example, the costs of tangible assets cannot be deducted in full in the year acquired, and unused deductions cannot be carried over indefinitely.[77]

For a taxpayer to take advantage of these special rules, the expenditures must qualify as an SR&ED activity. In general terms, this activity includes "experimental development of new products and processes in addition to applied research." Apparently, it is not intended to "include routine engineering or routine product development."[78] It is important to establish whether the proposed activities qualify as SR&ED before embarking on new projects.[79]

Some SR&ED expenditures may also qualify for an investment tax credit. This results in a direct reduction of tax payable and an immediate cash saving. In such cases, the SR&ED expense pool is reduced, in the following year, by the amount of the tax credit received.[80] (See Chapter 13, Part VII, Section H.)

E. Professionals

Individuals and corporations that provide professional services often perform these services over a long period of time before billing for the work. In most businesses, income is not recognized until the customer has an obligation to pay—that is, until the amount is billed and an account receivable is created. For professionals, work carried out before a bill is sent is referred to as "work in progress." Accounting principles require that the work in progress of professionals be included in income so that it can be matched with the related expenses in the year. As a general rule, this is also the case for tax purposes.[81]

An exception is made for accountants, lawyers, medical doctors, dentists, chiropractors, and veterinarians. These professionals can choose to exclude work in progress and recognize income only after an actual billing for services has been made.[82] However, once this election has been made, it must be continued in future years unless a change is approved by the CRA.

Choosing not to recognize work in progress delays the payment of tax until a future time period. This, of course, improves cash flow for the professional unless future tax rates will be significantly higher.

---

75 ITA 37(1); IT-151R5.
76 March 29, 2012 federal budget.
77 ITA 37(2).
78 *Tax Principles To Remember*, CICA, 2000, pp. 5–32.
79 IC 86-4R3.   80 ITA 37(1)(e).   81 ITA 12(1)(b).   82 ITA 34; IT-457R, IT-189R2.

F. Treatment of Reserves

As stated earlier in this chapter, an important general limitation in the determining of business income is that, with a few exceptions, no reserves are permitted as a deduction. For example, a reserve for anticipated warranty costs on products sold cannot be deducted for tax purposes, even though it is deducted for accounting purposes. However, the *actual* warranty costs incurred in the year can be deducted in the year that they occur.

Two important exceptions to this general limitation were discussed earlier: reserves for doubtful debts and reserves to delay the recognition of income when the sale agreement calls for extended payment terms. Whenever a reserve is allowed (including a capital gain reserve—see Chapter 8), the deduction must be added back to income in the year immediately following.[83] At that time, a new reserve can be deducted if it can still be justified.

It is important to note that a permitted reserve does not have to be claimed; rather, it is a discretionary reserve. Clearly, reserves are an important tool in that they enable the taxpayer to shift income from one period to another. Consider this situation.

Assume that a business deducted a reserve for doubtful debts of $75,000 in the previous year (20X0). Also assume that for the current year (20X1), the estimated uncollectible debts amount to $90,000 and that the business profit before the reserve is $110,000. If the taxpayer has chosen to claim the full available reserve in 20X1, income for tax purposes is $95,000, as follows:

20X1 income	$110,000
Add last year's reserve	75,000
	185,000
Deduct current year's reserve	(90,000)
20X1 income for tax purposes	$ 95,000

Alternatively, the business can choose not to claim any reserve in 20X1, in which case the income increases to $185,000. This means that no addition will have to be made to the following year's income (20X2) and that if a reserve is claimed in 20X2, that year's income will be significantly lower than it otherwise would have been. When the reserve is not claimed, the 20X1 income is higher and the 20X2 income is lower; in effect, income has been shifted from one period to another. As pointed out in Chapter 2, the shifting of income, even to an earlier year, is an important tax planning technique.

G. Unpaid Remuneration

Business income is determined on an accrual basis. This means that salaries are usually deductible by the employer when they are incurred, even if they have not been paid. However, employment income is included by the employee in income for tax purposes only when received (see Chapter 4).

In order to prevent the unwarranted delay of taxable remuneration payments, a special rule has been established limiting the employer's scope for deducting unpaid remuneration. This can be deducted by an employer for tax purposes only if it is paid within 180 days of its taxation year. If payment is delayed beyond that period, the employer can deduct the remuneration only in the subsequent year in which it is paid (see Chapter 9).[84]

H. Farming

Farming is a business and is subject to the normal rules for calculating income from business for tax purposes. One result is that, as a general rule, farming income is calculated on an accrual basis. However, taxpayers carrying on a farming business can, if they so elect, determine farming income using a cash basis of accounting.[85] In other

---

83 ITA 12(1)(d), (e), others.
84 ITA 78(4); IT-109R2.
85 ITA 28(1); IT-433R, -427R.

words, they can recognize income when it is received and deduct expenses when they are paid. This applies to all items except capital expenditures, which are subject to their normal treatment (CCA on depreciable property and so on).

When the cash basis is used, inventory costs are deducted at the time of payment and not when the inventory is sold. As a result, it is not unusual for farmers to experience extreme income fluctuations from year to year. Farmers can, at their option, choose to increase their income in a given year by an amount up to the inventory that would have been recorded if the accrual basis had been used. That increase is then deducted in a later year. This option permits them to "smooth" their income and escape the higher tax rates that might result from income surges. In fact, if a farming business incurs a loss in a year, an inventory adjustment to reduce the loss is mandatory. (This adjustment applies only to inventory that has been purchased.)

If a taxpayer's major occupation is not farming (that is, if operating a farm is a secondary activity to the taxpayer's main occupation),[86] the amount of loss that can be deducted against other sources of income in the year may be restricted.[87] In such cases, the farming loss deducted cannot exceed $8,750 in any year. It is further restricted to an amount equal to $2,500 plus one-half of the amount by which the actual loss exceeds $2,500. For example, an actual farming loss of $18,000 results in a maximum deduction for tax purposes of only $8,750, as follows:

$$\$2,500 + \tfrac{1}{2}\,(\$18,000 - \$2,500) = \$10,250$$

or

the limit of $8,750

The unused amount (in this case, $18,000 − $8,750 = $9,250) can be applied against farming income earned in the previous three years or the 20 subsequent years (10 years for restricted farm losses incurred before 2006). This carry-over forms part of the taxable income calculation after net income has been calculated for tax purposes (see Chapter 10).[88]

I. Partnerships

A partnership is not a taxable entity and bears no responsibility for tax on income generated within its sphere of operations. Rather, income earned or losses incurred by the partnership are allocated to the partners, in accordance with the agreed sharing ratio, for inclusion in each partner's income for tax purposes.[89] The income shared by the partners is allocated for tax purposes, regardless of whether such profits have actually been distributed to the partners. Thus, it is conceivable that a partner may bear the full tax liability on its share of income, even though the income remains in the partnership for reinvestment.

It is significant that losses incurred by a partnership are allocated to the partners as well and included in their separate determinations of taxable income.[90] This means that losses can be offset against the partners' other income, provided that other income exists.

All partnership income or loss allocated retains its source and characteristics when included in each partner's income. Business income of the partnership is business income to each partner and is treated accordingly for tax purposes. Capital gains and losses of the partnership become capital gains and losses of each partner. In this sense, the partnership is a conduit—it earns income like any other entity but then passes it on to the participants as if it had been earned directly by them. A detailed examination of partnerships is provided in Chapter 15.

---

86 *Moldowan v. The Queen*, 77 DTC 5213.
87 ITA 31; IT-322R.
88 ITA 111(1)(c); IT-232R3.
89 ITA 96(1).
90 ITA 96(1); IT-232R3.

J. Ceasing to Carry on Business

When a business is sold, the related transaction is not part of the normal operation of that business. As a result, the sale can be considered to be a capital transaction. This may be normal with regard to the sale of certain capital assets such as land and buildings. However two types of assets, accounts receivable and inventory, are a different matter. These two items are normally business transactions. There are special provisions designed to allow accounts receivable and inventories to receive normal business treatment when sold in bulk as part of the sale of the business rather than be treated as capital gains or losses. These provisions are discussed below.

• **Inventory**   Inventory that is sold as part of the disposition of a business is deemed to have been sold in the course of carrying on the business.[91] Therefore, any gain or loss from the sale is included as part of the business income (loss) calculation and cannot be considered to be a capital gain.

• **Accounts receivable**   When a taxpayer *ceases to carry* on business and the accounts receivable are sold, an unusual tax result occurs. Consider, for example, the situation where the vendor has accounts receivable of $50,000 from which the vendor has claimed a reserve for doubtful accounts of $10,000 in the previous year. If the receivables are sold for $40,000, no accounting gain or loss occurs. However, for tax purposes, the vendor first must add to income the reserve of $10,000 claimed in the previous year. This is normal (see Section F). The unusual part of the transaction is that the resulting $10,000 loss from the sale of the accounts receivable ($50,000 − $40,000) is treated as a capital loss rather than a business loss. Therefore, for tax purposes, only one-half of the $10,000 loss, or $5,000, is an allowable capital loss that can be deducted only against taxable capital gains.

The purchaser also has an unusual result. The acquired receivables (costing $40,000 in this case) are considered to be capital property. Therefore, if a lesser or greater amount is ultimately collected, the loss or gain is treated as a capital loss or a capital gain. The purchaser is also not permitted to claim a reserve for doubtful receivables because the receivables were not previously included in the purchaser's income (see page 144).

The unusual results described above can be avoided if the vendor and the purchaser file a joint election for the tax treatment of the receivables.[92] *When the election is filed, the vendor's loss on the sale of the receivables is deemed to be a business loss.* So, in the situation described above, the vendor first includes the previous year's reserve of $10,000 in income and then claims a business loss of $10,000 on the sale ($50,000 − $40,000). *The purchaser, who has paid $40,000 for the receivables, is deemed to have purchased them for a cost of $50,000 and to have deducted a reserve of $10,000* (*net $40,000*). So, in the future, the purchaser must add the reserve of $10,000 to income and claim a new reserve or deduct any actual bad debts as a business loss. The result of the election is that the vendor treats any loss as a business loss and the purchaser is permitted to deduct any loss as a business loss.

IV. Business Income and the GST/HST

It was indicated in Chapter 3 that most business entities are entitled to a full GST/HST rebate on all items purchased, provided that those purchases are for business purposes. This chapter has shown that a number of expenses cannot be deducted from business income for income tax purposes, in which case neither is

---

91 ITA 23; IT-287R2.
92 ITA 22; IT-188R.

a rebate allowed for the related GST on those expenses. There is a close relationship between the denial of an expense for income tax purposes and the denial of a GST/HST rebate.

Some of the expenses that are disallowed or are restricted for income tax purposes are listed here:

- The cost of leasing an automobile in excess of $800 per month.
- Personal and living expenses.
- Club memberships.
- 50% of all food, beverage, and entertainment costs.
- Expenses that are considered to be unreasonable in the circumstances.

In each of the above situations, the GST/HST on the good or service acquired is not eligible for a rebate (or input credit) against the GST/HST collected on goods or services sold.

A similar treatment applies to certain capital assets acquired (e.g., automobiles, which have a restricted cost of $30,000 for tax purposes). This treatment is discussed at greater length in subsequent chapters.

You may want to revisit Chapter 3, Part V, to review when a business must register for the GST/HST, what items are taxable, and when a GST/HST return must be filed.

Also, see Appendix A at the end of the text for a more in-depth review of the GST/HST.

V. Sample Calculation of Business Income

Outlined below is a simplified calculation of income from business for tax purposes. The format used applies the general rules to the accounting profit and then examines the specific list of exceptions. A financial statement for the company is shown on the next page.

Additional Information

1. Closing inventory, in addition to being valued at the lower of cost or market, has been reduced by a reserve of $6,000 for anticipated further declines in value.

2. Insurance expenses include a $2,000 premium for life insurance on the company president, the proceeds of which are payable to the company. The remaining insurance costs relate to insurance for property damage and public liability.

3. Amortization has been computed in accordance with reasonable estimates of each asset's useful life.

4. Legal expenses of $10,000 are made up of the following items:

Registration of a patent	$ 1,000
Collection of delinquent accounts receivable	5,000
Finder's fee for procuring mortgage funds	4,000

5. Research expenses of $15,000 relate to the apportionment of past and current research costs to several years, in accordance with their anticipated contribution to revenue. For the current year, actual research costs amount to $22,000, a substantial portion of which will be allocated to future years for accounting purposes.

6. Advertising and promotion includes television and newspaper advertising for products, as well as $4,000 for club memberships in sports-related facilities for the purpose of enhancing business contacts.

Condor Enterprises Ltd.
Statement of Income
Year ended June 30, 20X1

Revenue:		
Sales		$800,000
Service-contract fees		150,000
		950,000
Cost of goods sold:		
Inventory, beginning of year	$250,000	
Goods purchased during the year	550,000	
Goods available for sale	800,000	
Deduct inventory, end of year	200,000	600,000
Gross profit		350,000
Expenses:		
Selling commissions	22,000	
Insurance	8,000	
Amortization (depreciation) of building and equipment	15,000	
Amortization of goodwill	5,000	
Legal expenses	10,000	
Interest	5,000	
Research costs	15,000	
Advertising and promotion	30,000	
Salaries and wages	100,000	
Employee benefits	22,000	
Donations	5,000	
Repairs and maintenance	20,000	
Warranty costs	8,000	
Bad-debt expense	15,000	280,000
Income before income taxes		$ 70,000

---

7. Donations consist of $5,000 to registered charities.

8. Warranty costs are recorded annually, in the form of an estimated reserve, as 1% of the sales value of products sold (1% of $800,000 = $8,000). During the year, actual warranty costs paid on defective equipment amounted to $6,000, which was charged against the reserve account.

9. Bad-debt expense is also based on a reserve system, under which outstanding accounts receivable are reviewed and expected losses are forecast.

10. CCA for buildings and equipment (depreciable property), and a similar write-off for tax purposes for goodwill (CECA), have been calculated as $23,000.

Calculation of Income for Tax Purposes

The reported accounting profit of $70,000 is assumed to be consistent with accepted accounting principles and, therefore, is the starting point for calculating income for tax purposes. Each item is now examined to determine whether it contravenes one of the six general limitations. The specific exceptions to the general rules are then scrutinized. (References to the *Income Tax Act* are provided for each item.)

Income for Tax Purposes

Income for accounting purposes	$70,000
Analysis and adjustments (expenses disallowed are added back to increase income; additional expenses reduce accounting income):	
1. The reduction of inventory for anticipated future-value declines is a reserve disallowed by the general rules [18(1)(e)]. No specific exception is provided in the exception list.	6,000
2. The life insurance premium of $2,000 would earn income that is not taxable, and therefore the general rules negate this deduction [18(1)(c)].	2,000
3. Amortization on capital items is prohibited by the general rules [18(1)(b)]. (15,000 + 5,000)	20,000
CCA and CECA [20(1)(a) and (b)] is assumed to be:	(23,000)
4. Legal expenses for patent registration are on account of capital because they have a long-term benefit [18(1)(b)]. However, CCA for patents can be deducted and is part of the assumed deduction of $23,000 in item 3 above.	1,000
Collection of delinquent accounts is for the purpose of earning income and is acceptable.	—
A finder's fee for a mortgage has a long-term benefit and is disallowed by the general rules. However, a specific exception is provided for costs incurred to borrow money; one-fifth can be written off annually over five years [20(1)(e)]. Therefore, add back four-fifths of $4,000.	3,200
5. Research is on the account of capital and its write-off over a period of years is normally not permitted [18(1)(b)].	15,000
The exception list permits research costs to be written off when incurred or at the taxpayer's discretion [37(1)]. It is assumed the taxpayer chooses to deduct this year's actual cost, which is:	(22,000)
6. Promotion expenses in the form of club dues, while passing all of the general limitation tests, are specifically disallowed as an exception [18(1)(l)].	4,000
7. Donations to charities are not for the purpose of earning income and are disallowed under the general rules [18(1)(a)]. No exception for donations is made in calculating business income, although a deduction is permitted for corporations converting net income to taxable income (see Chapter 11). Individual taxpayers are permitted a tax credit for donations (see Chapter 10).	5,000
8. Warranty reserves for expected costs are eliminated by the general rule that no reserves are permitted [18(1)(e)]. A review of the specific exceptions provides no relief.	8,000
Actual warranty costs incurred for the year are deductible, in accordance with the general rules.	(6,000)
9. Bad debt reserves are disallowed by the general reserve limitation but are specifically permitted by the exception list [20(1)(l)].	—
Income from business for tax purposes	$83,200

(handwritten annotations: "exp. only can deduct 800"; "not deductible yet"; "already deducted in Y/S")

VI. Tax Planning Checklist ————————————————

The category of business income provides a number of tax planning opportunities. Some of these are listed below.

1. The sale of property may be treated as a business transaction or a capital transaction. When acquiring property, anticipate its tax treatment and plan for the best possible outcome in the event the property is sold.

2. Individuals starting a new business should choose its fiscal period carefully. Normally, it will be the calendar year. However, if a non-calendar fiscal period is desired for administrative purposes, the effects of the arbitrary alternative-method formula should be anticipated before a decision is made.

3. A business should regularly identify those items of expense and revenue over which it has some discretion as to when they are included in income for tax purposes. Some of those items are listed here:
   • Reserve for doubtful debts.
   • Reserve for sales whose payments extend over future years.
   • Capital cost allowance (CCA).
   • Expenses that qualify as scientific research and experimental development (SR&ED).
   • Interest on money borrowed to acquire depreciable property (which can be capitalized or not).

   These items must be considered when losses occur and cannot be offset against other sources of income. Because they are discretionary, their deduction can be delayed, resulting in a reduced loss for the current period. They can also be used as a means of shifting income to another period to take advantage of a preferential tax rate.

4. A business may be permitted to divide its income among family members. For example, when a salary is paid to a spouse or child, business income is reduced, and the salary to the family member may be taxed at a lower rate. However, such remuneration must be for genuine services, and the related salary must be reasonable. Opportunities for splitting income also exist when family members participate as partners (in an unincorporated business) or shareholders (in an incorporated business).

5. An incorporated business can employ its shareholder/manager. This means that the business can compensate the owner, in part, by providing all of the tax-free benefits permitted, such as private health insurance and disability insurance.

6. There are several accepted ways to value inventory—lower of cost or market, all at market, average cost, specific identification, and first-in, first-out (FIFO). Also, manufactured inventory can utilize either the absorption cost method (which allocates both fixed and variable overhead costs) or the direct cost method (which allocates only variable costs to inventory).[93] Every method recognizes the same amount of income but in a different time period. Because it may be difficult to switch to another option once a choice has been made, consider the alternatives carefully when organizing a new business.

7. Consider when SR&ED expenditures should be deducted. Since this must involve long-range forecasting of results, an element of uncertainty cannot be avoided.

————————————————
93 IT-473R.

8. Owing to the restrictions on passenger vehicles and to the related tax complexities when employees operate those vehicles for personal use, consider carefully whether to own or lease the vehicles and how to remunerate employees. While every business is different, an efficient outcome can be ensured by examining the special requirements of the business and its employees.

VII. Summary, Conclusion, and Management Perspective

A. Business Income—The Process

The determination of business income for tax purposes follows three basic steps.

1. As a general rule, business income for tax purposes is equivalent to accounting income determined in accordance with GAAP, which interpret well-accepted business principles.

2. Accounting income is modified by established case law and by the application of six general limitations found in the *Income Tax Act.* These limitations define the extent to which income for tax purposes can vary from accounting income.

3. Notwithstanding the general rule and general limitations, the amount of business income may be modified further by reference to two lists of specific exceptions; one of these denies the deduction of items otherwise permitted, while the other permits the deduction of items otherwise denied.

The process is fundamentally simple in that it starts with the broad definition of business income, establishes the general parameters of that definition, and provides a specific list of exceptions designed to deal with special problems, abuses, and political requirements.

It is vital to accept and utilize the three-step process described in this chapter, since it applies to every business transaction. The *Income Tax Act* does not attempt to deal with the multitude of various business activities; however, in the vast majority of cases, business income for tax purposes can be established by the general rules and limitations. Exhibit 5-1 diagrams the three-step process for dealing with business transactions.

B. Business Income versus Employment Income

It would now be useful to compare the two types of income for tax purposes that have been reviewed to this point. Both employment income and business income play a major part in the business decision processes of an enterprise.

One can simply compare the brief list of general rules presented opposite with those outlined in Chapter 4. This comparison indicates that there are three key differences between employment income and business income:

- method of accounting
- deductions permitted
- income excluded

• **Method of accounting** Employment income is accounted for on a cash basis, which means that income is recognized when received and expenses are deducted when paid. Business income, on the other hand, determines income *annually,* in accordance with accounting and business principles, and uses the accrual method, which requires that income be recognized when earned, rather than when received, and that expenses be deducted when incurred, rather than when paid.

Exhibit 5-1:

*The Decision Process
—Business Income*

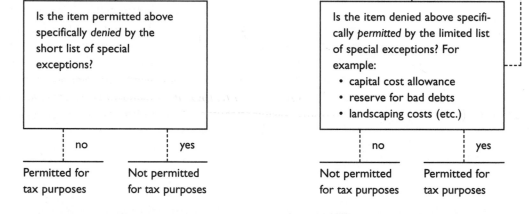

Is the item a revenue or expense in accordance with the determination of profit by *well-accepted business principles, generally accepted accounting principles,* and *established case law?*

no →

yes

If the item is an expense, is a deduction prohibited by the general limitations? i.e., is it
- not for the purpose of earning income
- on the account of capital
- for the purpose of earning income that is not taxable
- a reserve
- for personal or living expense
- unreasonable under the circumstances

no · · · · · · yes

Is the item permitted above specifically *denied* by the short list of special exceptions?

Is the item denied above specifically *permitted* by the limited list of special exceptions? For example:
- capital cost allowance
- reserve for bad debts
- landscaping costs (etc.)

no	yes		no	yes
Permitted for tax purposes	Not permitted for tax purposes		Not permitted for tax purposes	Permitted for tax purposes

- **Deductions permitted**   The employment income calculation permits no deductions, except those specifically allowed in the *Income Tax Act.* The business income calculation, however, permits the deduction of all expenses incurred for the purpose of generating income from business, *except those that are specifically denied or restricted.*

- **Income excluded**   Employees can earn, by virtue of their employment, a specified number of benefits that are not included in taxable income. The provisions for determining business income, on the other hand, contain no specific list of income that is tax-free.

The above fundamental differences are useful to remember when it comes to understanding the employer–employee relationship. For example, an employer determines the deductibility of all compensation costs in terms of whether or not they are incurred for the purpose of earning income from a business and uses the deduction to reduce business income when it is incurred. On the other hand, the employee who receives the benefit as employment income follows the employment income guidelines, regardless of how the employer must treat the benefit. The fact that a specific benefit may be tax-free to the employee is irrelevant when its deductibility to the employer is being determined.

C. Business Income and the Management Process

It is obvious that a business enterprise's primary source of taxable income is business activity, as opposed to property income and capital gains. Simple logic dictates that management must be familiar with the process of determining business income for tax purposes; this familiarity ensures that no more tax is paid than what is required and that the payment of tax occurs at the latest possible time. While external tax consultants can enhance this process, it is of little value if the business entity does not have an information system with the ability to highlight those items that are relevant to the tax process.

Familiarization with the general rules and with the specific exceptions that apply to the particular business is a strong catalyst that stimulates managers to recognize the need to expand their enterprise's information systems beyond the normal accounting function. Knowing, for example, that the tax provisions permit inventory to be valued all at market or at the lower of cost or market, for each item of inventory, is of no value unless information is generated that demonstrates how much difference the choice of one over the other would make.

In addition, familiarization with the business income rules permits managers to compare such income with other types of income and to use the resulting knowledge to their advantage. Often, by understanding the tax treatment to the other party in a transaction, managers have the opportunity to structure their activities to provide an advantage to that other party, which may, in turn, create cost efficiencies. For example, knowing how an investor is taxed on property income allows management to seek and review alternative methods of raising capital that provide the maximum tax advantage to that investor, which, in turn, enhances the value of the security offered.

The process of determining business income for tax purposes affects a very wide range of financial transactions but is not overly complex when viewed in terms of the three steps developed in this chapter. Any manager can understand and apply the process and, in so doing, systematically control the tax cost to the business enterprise.

Visit the Canadian Income Taxation Web site at **www.mcgrawhill.ca/olc/buckwold** to view any updated tax information.

Demonstration Questions

QUESTION ONE

TR Ltd. is a Canadian-controlled private corporation operating a franchised retail and mail order business in Vancouver. Denver Chan, the company's president, owns 100% of the corporation's share capital. The corporation was created on December 1, 20X7. For the year ended November 30, 20X8, TR earned a profit before income taxes of $126,000.

You have been retained to help prepare the company's first tax return and to advise on other tax-related matters. Financial information relating to the 20X8 taxation year is summarized below.

1. The following properties were purchased for the new business:

Franchise	$40,000
Land	30,000
Building	270,000
Delivery truck	40,000

The above items were recorded as assets on the balance sheet. The franchise, purchased on December 1, 20X7, permits the corporation to operate under the TR name for a period of 15 years.

The land cost of $30,000 consists of the purchase price of $20,000 plus $7,000 for permanent landscaping and $3,000 for water and sewer connections.

Depreciation and amortization expense of $28,000 has been deducted from income.

2. Legal fees include the following costs:

Preparing annual corporate minutes	$ 300
Incorporation costs for TR Ltd.	1,500
Negotiation of franchise agreement	2,000
Preparing and registering a mortgage loan	1,000

3. Repairs and maintenance expense includes the following items:

Paving the parking lot	$8,000
Cleaning and supplies	1,400
Replacing a broken window	1,000

4. Advertising expense includes a cost of $7,000 to acquire a permanent mailing list for the mail order business. The list has an expected life of six years. Other advertising items are listed below:

Cost of making a television commercial	$25,000
Travel costs for Chan to attend a franchiser convention Chan's spouse travelled with him and attended social functions (her expenses were $1,500).	3,000
Charitable donations	2,000
Meals and beverage costs for entertaining suppliers	1,800
Costs of leasing and maintaining a pleasure boat to entertain suppliers and employees	2,600
Television advertising:	
Vancouver station	11,000
Seattle station (directed at the Vancouver market)	6,000

5. A contingent reserve for possible defective products of $5,000 was recorded as a charge against cost of sales. During the year, $3,000 of products were returned.

6. On May 31, 20X8, TR invested $40,000 in a one-year bank certificate earning annual interest of 7%. TR intends to recognize the interest revenue upon receipt at its one-year anniversary date.

7. Interest expense includes $14,000 on the building mortgage and $700 from a temporary bank loan of $12,000. The bank loan funds were, in turn, loaned, without interest, to Y Ltd., a corporation owned by Chan's brother. Y Ltd. used all of its assets to operate an active business but in November 20X8 declared bankruptcy. The loss has been deducted from income as a bad debt.

8. Capital cost allowance for tax purposes has been correctly calculated to be $22,000.

9. Salary expense includes the following:

Wages to employees	$130,000
Year-end bonus to Chan—$5,000 was paid on November 30, 20X8, $4,000 is payable on January 31, 20X9, and $6,000 is payable on June 30, 20X9	15,000
Automobile allowance paid to an employee (10,000 kilometres × 51¢)	5,100

Required:

Determine TR Ltd.'s income from business for tax purposes for the 20X8 taxation year. In addition, identify any other types of income or loss that occurred in the year.

Solution:

Income per financial statement	$126,000
Landscaping cost is a capital item but is specifically allowed as a deduction—20(1)(aa)	(7,000)
Utility connection is a capital item but is specifically allowed as a deduction—20(1)(ee)	(3,000)
Depreciation and amortization is not deductible under the general rule—18(1)(b)	28,000
Legal fee for incorporation is a capital item—18(1)(b)—but it qualifies as an eligible capital expenditure to be deducted over a period of years (see Chapter 6)	1,500
Legal fee for negotiating franchise agreement is a capital item—18(1)(b)—but qualifies for capital cost allowance (CCA)	2,000
Legal fee for preparing mortgage is a capital item but is specifically allowed to be deducted over five years as an expense of borrowing money—20(1)(e), ⅘ × $1,000	800
Paving a parking lot is a capital item but qualifies for CCA	8,000
Mailing list is a capital item but qualifies as an eligible capital expenditure to be deducted over a period of years (see Chapter 6)	7,000
Cost of making a television commercial is a capital item but qualifies for CCA	25,000
Spouse travel is a personal item—18(1)(h)	1,500
Charitable donations are not for the purpose of earning income—18(1)(a)—but a deduction will be allowed when calculating taxable income for the corporation (see Chapter 11)	2,000
Meals and beverage expenses are limited to 50% of the actual cost—67.1—50% × $1,800	900
Boat lease and maintenance is specifically disallowed even though it is for the purpose of earning income—18(1)(l)	2,600
Television advertising on a foreign station and directed to the Canadian market is specifically disallowed—19	6,000
Contingent reserve for defective products is not allowed under the general rule that disallows reserves—18(1)(e)	5,000
Actual costs for replacing defective products are permitted	(3,000)
Interest expense on the bank loan used to make an interest-free loan is not for the purpose of earning income—18(1)(a)	700
The loss on the loan to Chan's brother cannot be claimed as a business bad debt because the loss is a capital loss (see Chapter 8 for tax treatment)	12,000
CCA is deductible—20(1)(a)	(22,000)
The bonus payable is unpaid remuneration and cannot be deducted on an accrual basis if it is not paid before 180 days of the taxation year. In this case, $6,000 is beyond the limit—78(4)	6,000
Automobile allowances are limited 53¢ on the first 5,000 km and 47¢ on the excess, assuming that the allowance is not taxable to the employee Adjustment is $5,100—(5,000 km × 53¢ + 5,000 km × 47¢) =	100
Income from business	**$200,100**

(handwritten annotation: "can't deduct, only 200 deductible")

Other sources of income and loss:

The interest income on the bank certificate is classified as property income (see Chapter 7). No income was recorded in the 20X8 taxation year; however, corporations are required to include interest income on an accrual basis, and therefore taxable property income of $1,800 ($40,000 × 7% × 6 months/12 months) must be included in the current taxation year.

The loss of the $12,000 loan to Chan's brother is a capital loss. Normally it would qualify as an allowable business investment loss because the loan was made to a small business corporation that used all of its assets in an active business. However, the capital loss is deemed to be nil because no interest was charged on the loan to Y Ltd.[94]

QUESTION TWO

In 20X7, HP Ltd. acquired two parcels of land. Parcel 1 was located adjacent to HP Ltd.'s retail store and was purchased for the purpose of providing additional parking for its customers.

Parcel 2 was located three blocks away from the retail store. It was acquired after the president of HP obtained information that a new bridge would be built nearby connecting two populated areas of the city. The president was certain that the property's value would rise and that it could be sold at a profit, giving the company increased funds to help retire a debt.

In 20X8, both properties were sold. Parcel 1 was sold when a public parking facility opened across the street, thereby removing the need for HP to expand its own lot. Parcel 2 was sold to a land developer. Details of the land transactions are as follows:

	Parcel 1	Parcel 2
Original cost	$70,000	$100,000
Selling price	60,000	250,000

Parcel 1 was sold for cash. Parcel 2 sold for $25,000 cash in 20X8 with the balance to be paid over the next five years at the rate of $45,000 per year plus an agreed interest rate. HP Ltd.'s only other income in 20X8 was the profit from the retail store of $100,000.

Required:
Determine the minimum net income for tax purposes for the 20X8 taxation year for HP Ltd. Ignore the tax implications of interest on the deferred proceeds from the land.

Solution:
First, it is necessary to determine the type of income earned from each of the land sales. Parcel 1 was acquired for the purpose of providing a long-term benefit to the retail business by improving the parking facilities. It was sold only after the need for parking was removed by the fortuitous construction of a public parking facility close by. The sale of parcel 1 is, therefore, a capital transaction, and the resulting loss on sale is a capital loss, of which one-half is allowable for tax purposes. HP Ltd. does not have any taxable capital gains in 20X8; therefore, the capital loss cannot be deducted in 20X8 in accordance with the formula for net income determination established in Chapter 3.

On the other hand, parcel 2 was purchased with the intention of reselling it at a profit. The land is considered to be inventory, and the resulting gain is business income. Because $225,000 of the proceeds ($250,000 − $25,000) is deferred to future years, a reserve can be deducted from the gain in 20X8. However, the full gain must be included in income by the end of the third taxation year following the taxation year in which the sale was made.

The net income for tax purposes in 20X8 is $115,000, calculated as follows:

---

94 ITA 40(2)(g)(ii).

Business income:		
Profit from retail store		$100,000
Sale of parcel 2		
Selling price	$250,000	
Cost	(100,000)	
	150,000	
Less reserve for deferred proceeds:		
$225,000/$250,000 × $150,000 =	(135,000)	15,000
Income from business		115,000
Taxable capital gains:	–0–	
Allowable capital loss:		
½ ($60,000 – $70,000)	(5,000)	–0–
Income for tax purposes		$115,000

QUESTION THREE

Sandra is a professional structural engineer and carries on a professional engineering practice as a sole proprietorship. For the year ended December 31, 20X4, she earned net income of $180,000.

You have been assigned to prepare Sandra's net income from business for tax purposes. The following additional information is provided:

1. Sales revenue was $430,000. This amount included accounts receivable at the end of the year of $35,000. On December 31, 20X4, Sandra had $70,000 worth of fees for services performed that were not billed. This amount was not included in revenues. At the end of the previous year, she had $62,000 of unbilled amounts for uncompleted jobs.

2. Sandra works from the basement suite of her home. The suite has a separate entrance. The space occupies approximately 20% of the home's entire space. Her total home costs for 20X4 consist of property tax—$4,000, mortgage interest—$11,000, utilities—$5,000, roof repairs—$2,000. These amounts have not been deducted in arriving at net income.

3. Sandra employs a secretary and a recent engineering graduate. In addition to their salaries she pays premiums to a private health insurance plan—$1,600 and to a group life insurance plan—$800. The engineer is required to use his own car to visit and inspect worksites. For this he received a travel allowance of $3,600 (being 60 cents for each of 6,000 kilometres).

4. Administrative expense includes the following items:

Legal fee to defend a lawsuit from a client	$2,700
Life insurance on Sandra as required collateral on a business loan	400
Increase in reserve for uncollectible unpaid fees	12,000
Reserve for potential loss from lawsuit	30,000
Appraisal fee on property used as collateral for business loan	1,000

5. Sandra uses her vehicle for business purposes. For the first three months of the year she used a leased vehicle and paid $2,600 (plus HST) in total for the three months. On April 1, 20X4 she purchased a new vehicle costing $60,000 (plus HST). For the remainder of the year she paid interest of $2,900 on a car loan. Operating costs for the entire year for both vehicles was $7,500. All vehicle costs were paid from the business. During the year, Sandra drove 24,000 kilometres of which 10,000 were for her business.

6. Sandra belongs to a golf club and paid annual dues of $4,000. She regularly entertains clients at the club's restaurant and bar and these costs amounted to $7,200. These amounts have been deducted in arriving at net income.

7. Other expenses include the following:

Amortization of tangible property	$18,000
Contributions to a political party	1,000
Donations to registered charities	3,000
Sponsorship of minor hockey team — business name on sweaters	4,200
Replacement cost of lost cell phone	600

8. The capital cost allowance for tax purposes is determined to be $22,000.

Required:

1. Determine Sandra's net income from business for tax purposes.

2. Compare Sandra's allowable deduction items for the home office to that of a person who is employed as a commission sales person and to a person who is employed and receives only a salary.

Solution:

1. *Net income from business for tax purposes:*

Net income per financial statement		$180,000
Increase in work-in-progress for the year		
$70,000 − $62,000—12(1)(b), IT-457R		8,000
Home office—20%($4,000 property tax + $11,000 mortgage interest		
+ $5,000 utilities + $2,000 repairs)—18(12), IT-514		(4,400)
Excess travel allowance—		
$3,600 − [(5000 km × 53¢) + (1000 km × 47¢)]		
—18(1)(r), regulation 7306		480
Reserve for potential loss from lawsuit—18(1)(e)		30,000
Property appraisal fee for loan—4/5 × $1,000—20(1)(e)		800
Non-eligible lease costs—$2,600 − ($800 × 3 months)—67.3		200
Non-eligible interest cost—$2,900 − ($300 × 9 months)—67.2		200
Personal portion of automobile costs:		
Eligible lease costs—$800 × 3 months	$2,400	
Eligible interest—$300 × 9 months	2,700	
Operating costs	7,500	
Capital cost allowance—(Chapter 6)		
—30%(1/2)($30,000)—13(7)(g)	4,500	
	$17,100	
Personal portion—14,000 km/24,000 km × $17,100 =		9,975
Golf club dues—18(1)(l), IT 148R3		4,000
Entertainment— 50% × $7,200—67.1, IT-518R		3,600
Amortization—18(1)(b)		18,000
Capital cost allowance (Chapter 6)		(22,000)
Political contribution—18(1)(n)		1,000
Charitable donation—18(1)(a)		3,000
Cell phone replacement—capital item— 18(1)(b)		600
Net income from business for tax purposes		$233,455

Comments:

Home office The home office expenses qualify for a deduction because the office is the individual's principal place of business. 18(12).

Employee insurance   Premiums for both the private health insurance and group term life insurance are deductible as employee compensation. From the employee's perspective, the private health insurance premiums are not a taxable benefit [6(1)(a)] but the life insurance premiums are.

Sandra's life insurance premium   Normally life insurance on the owner of the business is not deductible. However, because it is required as collateral for a business loan the premium is deductible on an annual basis. 20(1)(e.2), IT-309R.

Reserves   As a general rule, reserve are not deductible. 18(1)(e). However, an exception is made for a reserve for doubtful debts where a reasonable amount in respect of doubtful debts is computed. 20(1)(l).

General "carte blanche" debt reserves, provisions, etc., that are based on an arbitrary percentage of total receivables are not considered reasonable and are, therefore, not deductible. For a reserve for doubtful debts to be considered reasonable in amount, it is necessary to identify the debts that are doubtful of collection and estimate the percentage of the doubtful debts that will probably not be collected. CRA accepts a reserve calculated, as a percentage of the total doubtful debts or a series of percentages relating to an age-analysis of those debts, based on the taxpayer's past collection history. IT-442R.

Appraisal fee   Costs incurred to borrow money are capital items and normally would not be deductible. 18(1)(b). However, the costs can be deducted on a straight-line basis over 5 years. 20(1)(e), IT-341R4.

Cell phone   The cell phone is a capital item and not deductible. 18(1)(b). It is eligible for a deduction under the capital cost allowance rules (see Chapter 6).

Political contributions and charitable donations   Political contributions are specifically denied a deduction. 18(1)(n). Charitable donations are denied a deduction because they are not incurred to earn income. 18(1)(a). Individuals can obtain a tax credit for both political contributions and charitable donations (Chapter 10). Corporations are not allowed by law to make political contributions. Corporations are entitled to deduct charitable donations when calculating taxable income after net income for tax purposes has been determined (Chapter 11).

2. *Comparison of home office expenses*

Home Office Expenses	Salaried Employee	Commission Employee	Business/Self-Employed
Utilities	X	X	X
Property tax		X	X
Insurance		X	X
Maintenance	X	X	X
Mortgage interest			X

QUESTION FOUR

Make Inc., a Canadian-controlled private corporation, operates a manufacturing business in Nova Scotia. In 20X5, Make was awarded a provincial government grant of $100,000 to expand its manufacturing operations in the province. The grant agreement required that $60,000 of the funds be used to assist with the construction of a new building. The remaining $40,000 is to support wages for newly hired employees. Make began construction of the building on January 3, 20X6, and the building was completed on June 30, 20X6. The $100,000 grant was received in April 20X6. The following costs were incurred in connection with the expansion of the manufacturing business:

• Property taxes for 20X6 on the manufacturing property	$15,000
• Legal fee for agreement to obtain bridge financing on the building during the construction period	4,000
• Interest on the bridge financing loan	22,000
• Interest on the mortgage obtained upon completion of building	30,000
• Finder's fee to broker for obtaining bridge financing	8,000
• Utility connection cost to the building	10,000
• Investigation of site fee billed in 20X5 and paid in 20X6	5,000
• Architect's fee for building design	32,000
• Utility costs for the building during construction	9,000
• Landscaping of grounds	14,000

Required:

Briefly describe how each of the items mentioned above are treated for income tax purposes.

Solution:

Grant   The portion of the grant pertaining to wages ($40,000) must be included in income in the year received (20X6). The remaining amount can either be added to income in the year received or applied as a reduction of the building costs. If the latter is chosen the amount of the building cost eligible for capital cost allowance is reduced and the capital cost allowance deduction is lower for years in the future. Effectively, this method causes the grant to be taxable over a number of future years rather than in the year of receipt. 12(1)(x), 12(2.2).

Property taxes   Annual property taxes are normally deductible in the year incurred. However, to the extent the cost applies to the construction period of a building it is added to the cost of the building and becomes eligible for capital cost allowance. In this case, property taxes from the beginning of the year to June 30, 20X6, the date of completion, are considered capital costs. So, $7,500 is added to the cost of the building (half year) and the remaining $7,500 is deducted from income in 20X6. 18(3.1–3.7).

Legal fee for bridge financing and finder's fee to broker   Both of these items are considered to be costs incurred to borrow money. While they are actually capital items they can be deducted on a straight-line basis over 5 years. Therefore, the total cost of $12,000 ($4,000 + $8,000) can be deducted at $2,400 per year ($12,000/5). 20(1)(e), IT-341R4.

Interest on bridge financing   While interest is normally deductible [20(1)(c)], the $22,000 applicable to the construction period must be added to the cost of the building similar to the property taxes above. 18(1)(3.1–3.7).

Interest on mortgage   The interest on the mortgage applies to the post-construction period. Although it is a capital cost because it is incurred to acquire a long-term asset, the interest of $30,000 is deductible from income when incurred (in this case the accrual basis). 20(1)(c), IT-533.

Utility connection cost   This expenditure is on account of capital as it is part of the cost of developing the building. However, by exception, the $10,000 can be fully deducted in the year paid (cash basis). 20(1)(ee).

Investigation of site   This cost, similar to the utility service connection, is a capital item. However, it is fully deductible in the *year paid* (cash basis). So the $5,000 is deductible in 20X6 even though the amount was incurred and billed in 20X5. 20(1)(dd).

Architect's fee   The item has a long-term benefit to the taxpayer and so is not deductible from net income in the year. The $32,000 is added to the cost of the building and is deducted over a period of years under the capital cost allowance rules (Chapter 6). 18(1)(b).

Utility costs during construction   Utility costs are normally deductible in the year incurred. However, in this case, the utility costs of $9,000 must be added to the cost of the building (similar to a portion of property taxes and the bridge financing interest above) and is deducted over a period of years under the capital cost allowance rules. 18(1)(3.1–3.7).

Landscaping of grounds The landscaping costs are clearly a capital item because they provide a long-term benefit. However, by exception, the full cost of $14,000 can be deducted in the *year paid* (cash basis). 20(1)(aa).

Note that several items above must be recognized for tax purposes in the year that they are paid (cash basis) rather than when they occur (accrual basis). There are several of these items that are listed in the *Income Tax Act*. They include convention expenses, landscaping costs, representation fees, site investigation fees, utility service connection costs, and investment counsel fees (Chapter 7).

Review Questions

1. In order to earn business income, a taxpayer must be involved in an undertaking that constitutes a business. For tax purposes, briefly define "business."

2. Explain the term "adventure or concern in the nature of trade," and provide an example of such an activity.

3. Can an item of property (such as land) that has the potential to provide a long-term benefit to its owner create business income or a business loss when it is sold? Explain.

4. To what extent, if any, does the tax treatment of property that is classified as inventory, rather than as capital property, affect a taxpayer's financial risk in acquiring such property?

5. A taxpayer's income from business for tax purposes is defined simply as "the profit therefrom." Explain what is meant by this.

6. What impact do the accounting concepts of revenue recognition, accrual, and matching have on the determination of business income for tax purposes?

7. To what extent, if any, does the definition of business income for tax purposes deviate from the general definition of profit? (Note: this relates to the answer to question 5.)

8. Explain why the following expenditures are not deductible in arriving at business income for tax purposes, even though they may be consistent with the general definition of profit.
   (a) Small donations to a large number of charitable organizations.
   (b) A fee paid to a real estate consultant for finding an appropriate building for storing the inventory of a wholesale business.
   (c) A reserve for the anticipated cost of product guarantees relating to products sold in the current year.
   (d) The cost of entertaining business clients at the wedding of the daughter of the owner of the business.
   (e) Fees paid to an architect to draw a set of plans for the expansion of a company's head office building.
   (f) Office rent of $40,000 annually, when the building is valued at $100,000 and is owned by the spouse of the corporation's primary shareholder.

9. Explain why a business, in determining net income from business for tax purposes, can deduct a reserve for potentially uncollectible accounts receivable but cannot deduct a reserve for anticipated sales returns.

10. What is the significance of sections 18 and 20 of the *Income Tax Act*?

11. A business maintains a policy of providing memberships for senior employees at social clubs and clubs with sporting facilities. In some circumstances, such memberships are provided mainly to improve the business contacts of the employers; in others, they are provided solely as compensation. Explain the tax treatment of this kind of expense. In your answer, refer to the general rules for determining income from business.

12. What is the tax treatment when an item of inventory is sold in a particular year but the customer is required to pay for the item in equal annual instalments over four years?

13. At the end of its taxation year, a business has two unsold items of inventory. Item A has a cost of $10,000 and a market value of $15,000. Item B has a cost of $7,000 and a market value of $4,000. For tax purposes, what valuation methods can be used to determine ending inventory? Determine these amounts based on the information provided.

14. One often hears the comment "A business keeps two sets of records—one for the bank and one for tax purposes." While this comment has sinister connotations, to what extent is it not sinister? Explain how the failure to maintain separate records for tax purposes may reduce a company's rate of return on business activities.

15. Briefly compare and contrast the general treatment for tax purposes of employment income and business income.

Key Concept Questions

QUESTION ONE

Which one of the following transactions is most likely to be treated as business income for tax purposes? Which one will likely be treated as a capital gain? *Income tax reference: ITA 9(1); IT-218R.*

1. In Year 1, Bill purchased a parcel of land for $100,000 with the intention of building a rental property. In Year 5, Bill sold the rental property for $500,000.

2. In Year 1, Martha purchased a parcel of land for $100,000 with the intention of holding it until the land increased in value and could be sold at a gain. In Year 5, Martha sold the property for $500,000.

QUESTION TWO

Sharp Ltd. incurred the following expenses in the current year:

- $25,000 in legal and accounting fees with respect to the issue of a new class of preferred shares.

- $8,000 for landscaping around the office building.

- $1,200 in interest paid to the CRA for late income tax instalments.

- $2,700 in interest on funds borrowed to finance the purchase of new office equipment.

- $40,000 in scientific research and experimental development expenditures.

- $80,000 in stock-based compensation expense.

Comment on the deductibility for tax purposes of each of the expenses. *Income tax reference: ITA 18, 20(1), 37(1), (2).*

QUESTION THREE

Gary carries on an accounting business as a sole proprietor. The business is registered for HST purposes. In the current year he incurred the following expenses, among others:

- $12,312—Lease payment for his car (12 months). Eighty percent of the kilometres driven were for business purposes.

- $1,000—Donation to a registered charity.

- $5,000—Entertaining clients (meals and theatre tickets).

- $2.400—Golf club annual dues. Many of Gary's clients are members of the golf club.

Comment on the deductibility of these four expenses and the HST implications. *Income tax reference: ITA 18(1), 67.1, 67.3.*

QUESTION FOUR

In the current year SPL Ltd. paid tax-free automobile allowances of 50¢ per kilometre to two of its employees. Employee #1 drove 15,000 km and Employee #2 drove 6,000 km in carrying out their duties of employment. *Income tax reference: ITA 18(1)(r).*

Comment on the deductibility of the car allowance for SPL Ltd.

QUESTION FIVE

To improve the company's cash flow, Brick Inc. sold all its trade account receivables to a factoring company for a cash price of $430,000. At the time, the face value of the receivables was $500,000. The selling price of $430,000 was determined as follows:

Face value	$500,000
Deduct:	
Estimated uncollectible	40,000
Fee to factor company	30,000
Net cash price received	$430,000

Stone Inc. closed its business and sold all of its assets to a purchaser who continued to operate the business. The selling price allocated to the accounts receivable was $460,000 determined as follows:

Face value	$500,000
Less estimated uncollectible	40,000
Net cash price received	$460,000

Describe the tax treatment to Brick and Stone of the sale of the accounts receivable. *Income tax reference: ITA 22, 20(1)(l), (p).*

Problems

PROBLEM ONE

X, Y, and Z each purchased an identical piece of land at a cost of $4,000.

- X constructed a restaurant on her land and operated it profitably for several years.
- Y did nothing with her land. It simply remained unused for several years.
- Z rented out his land for a number of uses—car parking, summer carnivals, and so on. Reasonable returns were achieved.

Four years later, X, Y, and Z each sold their land for $12,000. X sold the land as part of the sale of the restaurant business. Y subdivided the land into three separate parcels and sold each for $4,000. Z had no intention of selling the land but received an offer that he felt he could not refuse.

Required:

Is the gain on sale of the land ($12,000 − $4,000 = $8,000) income from business for X, Y, and Z? Explain.

PROBLEM TWO

Carl Fenson of Winnipeg owned three taxicabs that operated for 24 hours a day (two shifts of 12 hours). Fenson worked one shift himself and hired drivers for the other shifts. At the time, in addition to the normal taxi licence, a special licence was required to deliver passengers to Winnipeg International Airport. This special licence was referred to as a "one-way" licence because it could be used to deliver passengers to the airport but not to pick up customers there. The licences were issued for 10-year renewable terms.

In 20X1, Fenson purchased three additional airport licences for $10,000 each, even though he did not have vehicles for their use. He immediately resold two of the licences for $18,000 each to a relative. Shortly thereafter, he purchased a minivan, assigned the third new licence to that vehicle, and rented the van with the licence to a third party.

In 20X3, Transport Canada converted all one-way licences to two-way licences. In response to an unsolicited offer, Fenson cancelled the van lease and sold the third licence for $45,000.

Required:

What type of income did Fenson earn from the licence sales? Explain.

PROBLEM THREE

Demo Ltd., a Canadian-controlled private corporation, sold two parcels of land during its 20X0 taxation year. Details of each transaction are as follows:

1. A one-hectare site in Winnipeg was sold for $200,000. The full price was received in cash. The land had been purchased five years before for $160,000. Demo had intended to construct a warehouse on the land for the purpose of storing inventory for its 12 retail stores. Subsequently, it was decided that the warehouse should be located in Saskatoon; for this reason, the Winnipeg site was sold.

2. A two-hectare site in Calgary was sold for $600,000. The land had been purchased two years previously for $320,000, with the intention that it would be sold after property values increased. Demo received a $90,000 down payment in 20X0. The full balance of the purchase price is due and payable in 20X4.

Required:

1. Determine the minimum increase to the 20X0 income for tax purposes of Demo Ltd. as a result of the two property sales (ignore interest considerations on any unpaid balance).

2. In what year will the entire taxable gain, if any, be recognized for the Calgary property?

PROBLEM FOUR

P.Q. Enterprises operates a wholesale business. Most of its sales are made on credit. Accounts receivable, therefore, make up a large portion of the company's balance sheet. At year end, the accounts receivable totalled $450,000. Of this amount, management estimates that $25,000 might not be collectible because no payments on account have been made for over 90 days.

In addition, the company loaned $15,000 to a former friend of the owner, charging 13% interest. This loan is also considered to be doubtful, as the friend refuses to acknowledge the existence of the debt.

Required:

1. What amount, if any, can be deducted from income in this particular year?

2. Assume that in the next year the doubtful accounts of $25,000 are re-analyzed, with the following results:

Still doubtful	$15,000
Considered good	4,000
Legally bankrupt	6,000
	$25,000

What is the tax impact in this second year?

PROBLEM FIVE

The controller of Mead Pipes Ltd. is completing the preparation of the corporation's 20X1 tax return but is uncertain about the tax treatment of the following eight expense items:

1. Finder's fee to obtain a mortgage on the company's buildings	$6,000
2. Property taxes on the company's new fishing lodge, which is used by employees	1,200
3. Interest for late payment of municipal property taxes for the warehouse	600
4. Brokers' fees for the purchase of publicly traded shares	1,400
5. Permanent landscaping of land around the head office buildings	4,800
6. Cost of investigating a site for a proposed warehouse, when the site was rejected	2,000
7. Hockey tickets to entertain customers	1,800
8. Reserve for the possible costs for guarantees of products sold in the year	8,000

Required:

Determine the amount by which the preceding items will reduce the net income for tax purposes of Mead Pipes Ltd. for 20X1. When an item has been totally excluded from your calculation, provide a brief reason why.

PROBLEM SIX

Central Products Ltd. is in the process of completing its 20X0 financial statements and tax return. A junior accountant has given you a list of items that he does not know how to treat for tax purposes. The list includes the following eight items:

1. Purchase price of a patent giving the company exclusive rights to manufacture a product — $120,000

2. Cost of annual dues to a golf club for three senior salespeople to entertain existing and potential customers — 8,000

3. The union contract expired four months before the year end and bargaining is still in process. A 3% wage increase is expected, and the company has recorded a reserve to cover the four-month period — 60,000

4. Legal fees paid for making a representation to a provincial government against a proposal to introduce a payroll tax — 15,000

5. Donations paid to a registered charity — 10,000

6. Advertising in a foreign trade newspaper that was distributed to Canadian customers — 4,000

7. Travel costs (airfare and lodging) for a senior executive to visit a foreign supplier to inspect and sign a purchase agreement for a new manufacturing machine. The machine was delivered and used in 20X0 — 3,000

8. Legal, accounting, and printing costs to prepare a prospectus offering common shares for sale to the public — 32,000

Required:

Describe how each of the above items will be treated for tax purposes for the 20X0 taxation year.

PROBLEM SEVEN

Simone Cherniak has just completed the second year of operating her veterinary clinic. You have been retained by Cherniak for tax assistance and advice. At a recent meeting, you gathered information on her practice, which is presented below.

For the year ended December 31, 20X2, the clinic showed a profit of $123,700, as follows:

Professional service	$321,000
Gross profit from surgical instrument sales	28,000
	349,000
Administration and other expenses	228,300
	120,700
Interest income	3,000
Net income	$123,700

Included in the above is depreciation/amortization expense of $23,000 on fixed assets and amortization of development costs of $4,400. Additional information is outlined below.

1. On February 28, 20X2, Cherniak purchased a competitor's business and merged it with her own. The following assets were acquired:

Truck	$ 18,000
Equipment	50,000

2. During the year, Cherniak designed and patented a new surgical instrument. On July 1, 20X2, a legal fee of $4,000 was paid for the patent (life of 20 years) registration; this amount is included in administration expenses. In October, $16,000 was spent on consultants to research metal alloys, and this cost is being amortized as development costs in the financial statement.

3. Professional services revenue includes the value of unbilled services compiled from a work-in-progress file. At December 31, 20X2, unbilled services amounted to $27,000, compared with $18,000 at the same time last year. In 20X1, Cherniak had made an election under section 34 of the *Income Tax Act* to exclude work in progress from income.

4. Some of the items included under administrative and other expenses are as follows:

Group life insurance for office staff	$1,100
Christmas gifts to staff (under $200 each)	1,400
Dues to golf club (for employee)	1,200
Meals and drinks for clients	400
Books (15-volume set on veterinary medicine)	3,000
Interest on car loan (six months)	2,100
Finder's fee for a loan to finance equipment	1,000

5. The income statement includes a cost of $3,150 for attending three conventions during the year. Convention #1 ($750) was in July 20X2. Conventions #2 ($1,350) and #3 ($1,050) were both in December 20X2. Each convention includes a cost of $100 for meals. For each of the December conventions, the airfare of $200 was included in accounts payable at the end of the year.

6. Vehicle costs include operating costs of $2,400 for the automobile (including $400 for car parking). The automobile was driven 24,000 km. Of this, 12,000 km was for customer travel, 2,000 km was for travel between her home and the clinic, and 10,000 km was for personal travel.

7. Cherniak expects that a number of the new manufactured surgical instruments will be returned for modification, which she will do at no extra cost to the customer. The income statement includes a $2,000 deduction based on her estimate of the returns. As of December 31, 20X2, $800 of costs were incurred for returned items.

8. Cherniak moved from rented premises to new rented premises on February 28, 20X2, with 20 months remaining on the old lease. The landlord accepted a payment of $8,000 in exchange for cancelling the lease. The accounting records have amortized this cost over the remainder of the lease term and accordingly have deducted $4,000 ($8,000 × 10 m/20 m) as rent expense.

9. Capital cost allowance (CCA) for tax purposes has been correctly calculated as $15,000.

Required:
Determine Cherniak's income from business for tax purposes for the 20X2 taxation year. Identify any other sources of income that are taxable in the year.

PROBLEM EIGHT

RR Inc. operates an active business. Financial statements for the year ended December 31, 201X report a net income before taxes of $300,000. The following additional information is provided:

1. RR's net income is summarized as follows:

Income from business operations	$280,000
Gain on sale of capital assets	15,000
Interest on a bond investment	5,000
	$300,000

2. During the year, RR completed construction of a new warehouse building and its cost of $600,000 was added to the balance sheet. The cost consists of the following:

Building construction	$500,000
Heating and cooling systems	80,000
Landscaping of grounds	20,000
	$600,000

3. The balance sheet of RR includes an amount for goodwill acquired from a previous business acquisition. During the year, a goodwill impairment loss of $30,000 was deducted from the income from business operations.

4. Legal expenses include $2,000 for drafting the mortgage document for the new warehouse, $1,000 to investigate a zoning limitation on the new warehouse site, and $5,000 for the audit fee.

5. A management bonus of $60,000 was announced and accrued in September 201X. The bonus was paid in two equal installments on January 31 and April 30 of the following year.

6. The income statement for the year ended December 31, 201X includes the following items:

Amortization	$41,000
Charitable donations	6,000
Volume rebates and discounts on purchases	13,000
Architect's fee for design of new warehouse building	25,000

7. Advertising and promotion includes $20,000 for airing a TV commercial, $30,000 for production of the TV commercial, $5,000 for club memberships in a sports-related facility to enhance business contacts and $12,000 for acquiring a permanent mailing list for seeking new customers.

8. Capital cost allowance and a cumulative eligible capital deduction for tax purposes has been correctly calculated as $58,000.

Required:

Determine RR's net income from business for tax purposes for the 201X taxation year.

PROBLEM NINE

The financial information shown in the following table was presented for Massive Enterprises Ltd. for the year ending May 31, 20X1.

Statement of Income

Sales		$1,700,000
Cost of sales		830,000
Gross profits		870,000
Expenses:		
Salaries and wages	$235,000	
Management bonuses	50,000	
Employee benefits	30,000	
Interest expenses	9,000	
Insurance	7,000	
Appraisal costs	8,000	
Legal and accounting	12,000	
Repairs and maintenance	22,000	
Travel	8,000	
Advertising and promotion	10,000	
Bad debts	36,000	
Provision for sales returns	17,000	
Depreciation/amortization	16,000	
Donations	4,000	
Loss on sale of marketable securities	6,000	470,000
		400,000
Other income:		
Interest on government bonds	$ 10,000	
Net gains on sales of land	40,000	50,000
Net income		$ 450,000

Additional Information:*

1. Cost of sales:

Opening inventory (at cost)	$ 280,000
Purchases	970,000
	1,250,000
Closing inventory (at lower of cost or market)	420,000
Cost of sales	$ 830,000

The closing inventory at the end of the previous year was valued at the lower of cost or market, which amounted to $270,000.

2. The salaries and wages of $235,000 included salaries of $95,000 to the president, $80,000 to the president's spouse (who worked as a full-time manager), and $15,000 to a full-time housekeeper, who looked after the children so that the president and the president's spouse could work full-time in the business.

3. Management bonuses:

Bonuses awarded and paid during the current year	$10,000
Bonuses awarded at the end of the current year, to be paid (with interest) at the end of the following fiscal year	30,000
Bonuses awarded at the end of the current year and paid on June 30, 20X1	10,000
	$50,000

* All relates to the statement of income.

4. Employee benefits:

Canada Pension Plan and Employment Insurance	$ 6,000
Contributions to the company's pension plan for three employees ($6,000 for each employee). The annual compensation for each of the employees is $60,000, $80,000, and $100,000 respectively.	18,000
Annual club dues to three golf clubs for senior managers	6,000
	$30,000

5. Interest expense included interest of $8,000 on a bank loan that was used to purchase new equipment during the previous year. In addition, $1,000 of interest arising from deficient income tax instalments was paid to the CRA.

6. Insurance expenses:

Public liability insurance for the current year	$ 2,000
Three-year fire and theft insurance premium beginning the first day of the current taxation year	3,000
Life insurance on the president of the company (required as collateral for a bank loan)	2,000
	$ 7,000

7. Appraisal costs:

To determine the replacement cost of business assets to establish the current year's fire and theft insurance requirements	$ 5,500
To value the assets of the business in order to establish the company's share value so that the shareholder could use the shares as collateral for a personal bank loan	2,500
	$ 8,000

8. Legal and accounting expenses:

Legal fees:	
To collect an account receivable	$ 400
Cost of amending the Articles of Incorporation	1,000
Costs of issuing a new class of preference shares and debentures	3,000
Accounting:	
Tax consultations for a submission to a federal government task force on sales tax reform	2,000
Annual audit fees	5,600
	$12,000

9. Repair and maintenance costs:

Office cleaning, snow removal, lawn care	$ 2,000
Cost of landscaping grounds	11,000
Repainting several offices	4,000
Engine replacement for one delivery truck	5,000
	$22,000

10. Travel costs (incurred for sales personnel):

Airfares	$ 5,000
Meals and beverages while travelling	3,000
	$ 8,000

11. Advertising and promotion costs:

Catalogues	$ 6,000
Meals and beverages for employees entertaining customers	3,000
Promotional pens	1,000
	$10,000

12. Bad debts expense of $36,000 represented an increase in the reserve for doubtful accounts receivable arising from the sale of merchandise.

13. As a result of past experience, the company began a new policy of providing a reserve of 1% of sales for expected future returns of defective merchandise sold. Although the year's provision was $17,000, only $12,000 of merchandise was returned.

14. The depreciation/amortization expense of $16,000 was based on the estimated useful life of depreciable property owned (equipment and vehicles). Capital cost allowance and amortization of eligible capital expenditures for tax purposes have been correctly calculated as $19,000 in total.

15. The loss on sale of securities resulted from the sale of shares in public corporations. These were acquired several years earlier using excess funds not needed for the business.

16. The net gain on the sale of land of $40,000 consisted of the following:

- *Property 1*, which was acquired three years earlier at a cost of $100,000 as a potential site for a new head office building. However, new leased space became available, thus eliminating the need for a new building. Because of this, the land has been sold at the market price of $160,000.

- *Property 2*, which was purchased four years earlier with excess corporate funds after it was learned that a new shopping centre was being planned for the area. The company believed that the new shopping centre would enhance property values and purchased the land at a cost of $90,000 in the hope that it could be sold at a substantial profit. But the shopping centre proposal was cancelled and the land was sold in the current year for $70,000.

Required:

1. For the year ended May 31, 20X1, determine the company's net income from business for tax purposes.

2. Also, determine the company's overall net income for tax purposes in accordance with the aggregating formula.

PROBLEM TEN

Shirley Jensen terminated her employment on May 31, 20X0, after earning taxable employment income of $20,000. On June 1, 20X0, she opened a proprietorship retail store. She has been informed that the taxation year for the business should be the calendar year. However, she is aware that an election can be made that permits her to use a non-calendar fiscal year. She has indicated that for administrative reasons, the desirable fiscal year end is May 31 of each year. Before she makes a decision, Jensen wants to know the tax implications of choosing one method over the other.

Her profits from the retail store for the next few years are estimated to be as follows:

	December 31	May 31
20X0—seven months	$50,000	–0–
20X1	85,000	85,000
20X2	90,000	90,000

Income tax rates for each year are assumed to be 26% on the first $41,000 of income, 34% on the next $42,000, 40% on the next $46,000, and 45% on income over $129,000. Jensen will have no other sources of income in each of the years, except the employment income of $20,000 in 20X0.

Required:

With the information provided, outline the tax consequences to Jensen for each alternative method of determining business income for each of the three taxation years. Which method will you recommend?

PROBLEM ELEVEN

Sharon Cloutier is semi-retired and sits on the board of directors of several Canadian public corporations. A summary of her 20X0 financial activity is presented below.

Interest on long-term bonds	$20,000
Gain on sale of farmland (Cloutier acquired the farmland three years ago with the intention of subdividing it into building lots for resale but sold it in 20X0 after losing a rezoning application.)	13,000
Director's fees from public corporations	22,000
Gain on sale of public corporations shares	16,000
Legal fees paid to collect a bonus on a former employment contract	2,000
Legal fees paid to dispute an income tax reassessment	1,500
Loss on sale of shares of a Canadian-controlled private corporation that qualifies as a small business corporation	8,000
Loss on sale of public corporation shares	20,000
Share of the operating loss from a partnership that operates a small grain farm with hired help	18,000
Qualified moving expenses	1,000

Required:

Determine Cloutier's income for tax purposes in accordance with section 3 of the *Income Tax Act.*

PROBLEM TWELVE

At a recent executive meeting of H Co., the president complained, "Our compensation program is unimaginative because we pay our employees by salary or commission only. Surely there are other forms of compensation which would make our company more attractive to employees."

Required:

As the personnel manager of H Co., prepare a list of compensation alternatives. For each, briefly describe the tax consequences to both the employee and the employer.

PROBLEM THIRTEEN

Carlson Electronics Ltd. is a Canadian-controlled private corporation that wholesales electronics equipment. The company also manufactures a small switching device and has begun a research program to improve the product.

The controller has just completed the first draft of the financial statements for the year ended December 31, 20X1. A profit of $100,000 is indicated. The company has recently secured some new major customers, and next year's profits are expected to be $570,000. The current year's income statement and next year's projected income statement are as in the table below.

As a Canadian-controlled private corporation, the company pays tax at an assumed rate of 15% on its first $500,000 of annual active business income and at 25% on income in excess of $500,000.

At a meeting with the company president, the controller provides the following additional information:

- As a result of improved administration and a revised credit policy, the amount of uncollectible receivables has declined. In fact, the 20X1 administrative expenses include a reserve for doubtful accounts of only $21,000; the previous year's reserve was $70,000.

	20X1 actual	20X2 projected
Sales	$1,280,000	$1,950,000
Cost of sales	810,000	1,008,000
Gross profit	470,000	942,000
Other expenses:		
Selling	146,000	162,000
Administrative	170,000	164,000
Research and development	62,000	54,000
	378,000	380,000
	92,000	562,000
Other income:		
Gain on sale of land	8,000	8,000
Net income	$ 100,000	$ 570,000

- The research and development expense of $62,000 in 20X1 includes direct costs (wages and materials) for designing and testing an improved switching device. Of these costs, 90% qualify as scientific research and experimental development costs for income tax purposes.
- In 20X1, the corporation sold a parcel of land for $216,000. The land, which is next to a proposed real estate development, was acquired the previous year for $200,000. Carlson had hoped to turn a quick profit by holding the land until a public announcement about the project was made. The selling price of $216,000 consisted of cash of $108,000, with the remaining amount of $108,000 payable (with interest) in 20X2. In accordance with the income tax provisions, the gain of $16,000 is being recognized as income over two years ($8,000 per year), and this is reflected in the financial statements.

Whenever possible, the company takes advantage of purchase discounts offered by its suppliers. Most suppliers offer a purchase discount of 2% of the merchandise cost if payment is made within 10 days; otherwise, the full purchase price is payable at the end of 30 days, with substantial interest charged thereafter. Owing to the anticipated sales volume increase for 20X2, the company's purchases will be heavy during the early part of the new year. Carlson has a line of credit at the local bank and usually pays interest at 8% on its loans. Currently, it has used up all of its approved line of credit.

Required:

1. Based on the financial statements provided, what amount of tax will the company be required to pay in 20X1 and in 20X2?

2. What actions can be taken to reduce the amount of tax payable over the two-year period? Calculate the tax savings, if any, that can be achieved by these actions.

3. Should the company take the actions suggested in question 2? Why, or why not?

CHAPTER 6

The Acquisition, Use, and Disposal of Depreciable Property

In many businesses, the most significant portion of capital is invested in long-term assets, such as machinery, equipment, buildings, and vehicles. Intuitively, it makes sense that because these assets contribute to the revenue-earning process over a long period of time, the cost should be allocated to and deducted from income for tax purposes gradually. The timing of such deductions is critical because they increase cash flow by reducing the amount of tax paid in the particular year. This enhancement of cash flow, in turn, makes it easier to fund the purchase of the asset by external financing.

The *Income Tax Act* departs dramatically from generally accepted accounting principles in the way it treats depreciable property. As a result, it is a source of confusion for decision makers whose task it is to acquire and dispose of a wide range of assets. It is also a source of confusion to those who examine financial statements, when they find that the amount of tax paid on business income may not conform to the known rates of tax because of the way that the deductions have been timed for accounting purposes (as opposed to tax purposes).

Although the tax method of dealing with depreciable property deviates from accounting methods, it is not overly complex. It is vital for any businessperson to understand this area of tax law, for it is not possible to contemplate the acquisition or disposal of individual assets—or an entire business—without considering it.

This chapter explains the fundamentals of the tax factors pertaining to the acquisition, use, disposition, and replacement of long-term assets by

(a) examining the rationale for a standardized format for dealing with depreciable property;

(b) outlining the general rules (and their exceptions) of the capital cost allowance system, and of the treatment of eligible capital property; and

(c) discussing the types of business decisions that may be affected.

I. A Standardized System for Depreciable Property

Business income was defined in the previous chapter as the profit determined in accordance with well-accepted business principles and generally accepted accounting principles, subject to certain general limitations. One of the general limitations denies the deduction of any expenditure of a capital nature and, as well, denies the deduction of depreciation and amortization.[1]

Depreciation or amortization is the process of allocating the cost of a productive asset over its useful life in order to match its cost against the income that it helps generate. (Recently, the Canadian accounting professions have dropped the term "depreciation" and now simply use the term *amortization* for all cost allocations.) The amortization/depreciation process is difficult because it requires that the owner estimate three things with regard to the asset:

- useful life
- salvage value at the end of the useful life
- contribution to the business in each year of the useful life

As this process requires judgment, similar businesses acquiring similar assets may reach different estimates of these things and, therefore, arrive at different incomes in each of the years that the asset is used. However, over time, the total cost deducted will be the same because the maximum deducted cannot exceed the original cost of the asset. As an example, following is the amortization expense on a $10,000 asset for business A and for business B, where A assumes a useful life of four years and an equal annual contribution

---

1 ITA 18(1)(b).

to revenues and B assumes a life of six years with a variable contribution to annual revenues. Both A and B assume no salvage value at the end of the asset's useful life.

	A Amortization	B Amortization
Year 1	$ 2,500	$ 1,000
2	2,500	2,000
3	2,500	3,000
4	2,500	2,000
5	–0–	1,000
6	–0–	1,000
	$10,000	$10,000

If A and B were permitted to use the above for tax purposes, the timing of the respective tax reductions would vary. Considering that a tax saving today is worth more than a tax saving tomorrow, the net after-tax cost of acquiring the asset would be different for each business. If we further assumed that both A and B paid tax at a rate of 40% and could invest their cash at an after-tax return of 15%, the tax savings and net after-tax cost of the asset to each business would be as shown in the table below.

	A Tax saving 40% of amortization	B Tax saving 40% of amortization
Year 1	$ 1,000	$ 400
2	1,000	800
3	1,000	1,200
4	1,000	800
5	–0–	400
6	–0–	400
Total cash saved	$ 4,000	$ 4,000
Net present value @ 15%	$ 2,855	$ 2,571
Cost of asset	$10,000	$10,000
Less net present value of tax savings	2,855	2,571
Net after-tax cost of asset	$ 7,145	$ 7,429

In this simple example, A is better off than B simply because it chose a faster amortization stream. For this reason, accounting amortization/depreciation is disallowed, and a uniform and arbitrary allocation of the asset's cost is imposed for tax purposes. The result is that all businesses have similar results relating to the purchase of similar assets.

The uniform system divides capital assets into two general categories. The first category is referred to as *depreciable capital property* and includes, primarily, tangible assets, such as equipment.[2] The allocation of the capital cost of the asset is given the term "capital cost allowance." The second category is referred to as *eligible capital property* and includes only intangible assets.[3] Examples of assets in the second category are purchased goodwill, incorporation costs, and unlimited life franchises and licences. Each of these categories is discussed separately below.

---

2   ITA 13(21), 20(1)(a).
3   ITA 14(5), 20(1)(b).

II. Depreciable Property and Capital Cost Allowance

In general, the calculation of capital cost allowance (CCA) consists of a few basic steps. One starts with the opening balance, then adds additional purchases and deducts any disposals. The appropriate CCA rate is then applied to obtain the deduction for tax purposes for the current year. However, in order to use this simple calculation, it is necessary to establish who qualifies for CCA, which assets qualify, which rates of CCA apply to particular assets, and when gains or losses on disposal of individual assets are recognized. As usual, there are some exceptions to the standard format.

A. Who Qualifies for CCA? and What Assets?

Both individuals and corporations qualify for CCA, provided that they acquire particular capital assets that are used for the purpose of producing income. The guidelines for determining whether or not an expenditure is of a capital nature were introduced briefly in the previous chapter and are discussed further in Chapter 8. Taxpayers who carry on a business or use assets to earn investment income can claim CCA on a number of different types of assets. Also, individuals who are employed are entitled to claim CCA on automobiles and aircraft they are required to use in the course of their employment duties.[4]

Business entities and investors can claim CCA on all tangible assets other than land. CCA can also be claimed on some but not all intangible assets (discussed below). To be eligible for CCA,

(a) the taxpayer must have legal title to the property or have all the incidents of title, such as possession, use, and risk;[5] and
(b) the asset must be available for use for the purpose of earning income from business or investments.[6]

This means that a building under construction or equipment not assembled does not qualify for CCA until construction or assembly is complete.

The total dollar amount available for allocation as CCA is referred to as the "capital cost" of the asset. The capital cost amount consists of the original purchase price plus all costs incurred to bring the asset to a state of working order.[7] Costs for delivery, taxes and duties, installation, and legal fees, as well as financing costs during a construction period and employee costs to bring the asset to a working state, are all part of the capital cost. GST or HST is not considered a cost when it is recoverable by the taxpayer. Subsequent major renovations to an asset that improve that asset beyond its original condition are of a capital nature and also become part of the capital cost.[8]

B. Rates of Capital Cost Allowance

The most difficult aspect of the CCA system involves how to determine what rate of CCA applies to a particular asset. The *Income Tax Act* assigns various types of assets to specific classes.[9] Each class has a specific rate attached to it.[10] For example, automotive equipment and movable equipment are included in class 10, which has been assigned a rate of 30%.

This rate signifies the *maximum* that can be applied in any year.[11] There is no requirement that the taxpayer claim this maximum—the taxpayer can choose to claim any amount it wishes to in any year up to the maximum. If the maximum is not claimed in a given year, the unclaimed portion is simply carried forward and is available in future years. Often, taxpayers who have incurred a loss will not claim CCA unless they are certain that other sources of income will be available for offset. The deduction of CCA is thus preserved for when it is needed in the future.

---

4 ITA 8(1)(j); IT-522R.
5 IT-285R2.
6 ITA 13(26), (27), (28), (29).
7 IT-285R2.
8 IT-128R.
9 Income Tax Regulations—Schedule II (classes 1–49).
10 Regulation 1100(1).
11 Regulation 1100(1)(a).

The system of classes ensures that different entities using similar assets will allocate the costs of those assets in a like manner. In some respects, this can be inequitable; for example, a business that uses its equipment 24 hours a day must claim the same rate of CCA as one that uses similar equipment for only eight hours a day.

Since currently there are over 40 separate classes of capital assets, it is often difficult to match a specific asset with its appropriate class. Several tax services publish alphabetical lists of assets, with corresponding classifications.[12] The most common classes are listed below, together with a description of some of the assets in each class.

Class 1 (4%)	Buildings or other structures, including component parts, such as plumbing, air-conditioning/heating equipment, and elevators, and escalators acquired after 1987.[13]
	An additional allowance of 6% (increasing the rate to 10%) is available on buildings acquired after March 18, 2007 provided that at least 90% of the building is used for manufacturing and processing purposes. To receive the additional allowance the building must be placed in a separate CCA class. The taxpayer can choose to place such a building in the standard class 1 pool and forgo the additional allowance. If a building acquired after March 18, 2007 does not meet the 90% manufacturing and processing requirement and is used for *non-residential* purposes, it will qualify for an additional allowance of 2% (increasing the rate to 6%). Again, to receive this additional allowance it must be placed in a separate CCA class. The taxpayer may forgo the additional allowance by placing it in the standard class 1 pool. *These enhanced rates (10% and 6%) do not apply to buildings that were used by any person or partnership prior to March 19, 2007.*[14]
Class 3 (5%)	Buildings, as above, acquired before 1988.
Class 8 (20%)	Equipment and machinery not included in another class, furniture, photocopiers, and facsimile machines.
Class 10 (30%)	Automotive equipment and movable equipment.
Class 10.1 (30%)	Passenger vehicle (automobile) that has a cost greater than the prescribed amount (currently $30,000). The prescribed amount is changed periodically.
Class 12 (100%)	Small tools and kitchen utensils costing less than $500, uniforms, tableware, linens, computer software other than systems software, and videotapes.[15]
Class 13	Improvements made to leased premises.[16]
Class 14	Franchises, concessions, and licences having a limited legal life.[17] Also, patents, if a choice is made to exclude them from class 44 below.
Class 17 (8%)	Parking area, including paving roads and sidewalks.
Class 29	Manufacturing and processing equipment, which would otherwise qualify as class 43, acquired between March 19, 2007 and December 31, 2013, can apply a straight-line CCA rate of 25% in the first year, 50% in the second year, and the remainder in the third year.
Class 43 (30%)	Property, such as machinery and equipment, used directly or indirectly in the manufacture or processing of goods for sale or lease.[18]
Class 44 (25%)	Patents and rights to use patents acquired after April 26, 1993.
Class 46 (30%)	Data network infrastructure equipment.

---

12 *Canadian Tax Reporter*, CCH Canadian, paragraph 5049.

13 IT-79R3.

14 Regulations 1100(1)(a.1) and (a.2), 1104(2), 1101(5b.1).

15 IT-283R2 (archived).

16 IT-464R.

17 IT-477.

18 IT-147R3.

Class 50 (55%)	Computer equipment and systems software for that equipment acquired between March 19, 2007 and January 27, 2009 and *after January 31, 2011*. Equipment acquired between March 23, 2004 and March 19, 2007 must apply a CCA rate of 45% and be placed in class 45. See class 52 for equipment acquired between January 27, 2009 and January 31, 2011.
Class 52 (100%)	Computer equipment and systems software for that equipment acquired after January 27, 2009 and before February 2011.[19]

Note that classes 13 and 14 do not have specific rates attached to them. Both these classes have rates that vary according to the nature of the particular asset. This will be discussed later in the chapter.

C. The Declining Balance Method

With a few exceptions, the capital cost allowance system uses the declining balance method of allocating capital cost over future years.[20] This method annually applies a constant percentage to the remaining undepreciated portion of the original capital cost. The percentage applied is the designated CCA rate for the class to which the asset is attached. For most classes, the amount of CCA that can be claimed in the first year of an asset's acquisition is restricted to one-half the normal rate.[21] Below is a simple demonstration of this method.

Situation: In 20X0 business A, which previously occupied leased premises, purchased a small warehouse building (in use prior to 2007) at a cost of $200,000.

Analysis: In accordance with the summary of classes shown on the previous page, the building qualifies as a class 1 asset and must use a CCA rate of no higher than 4% annually. The results are shown in the table below.

Class 1	
(20X0)	
Capital cost building #1	$200,000
CCA: 4% × $200,000 × ½*	4,000
Undepreciated capital cost	$196,000
(20X1)	
Undepreciated capital cost	$196,000
CCA: 4% × $196,000	7,840
Undepreciated capital cost	$188,160
(20X2)	
Undepreciated capital cost	$188,160
CCA: 4% × $188,160	7,526
Undepreciated capital cost	$180,634

* For declining business classes, one-half of the normal CCA rate applies to the excess of acquisitions over disposals in the year.

When the constant rate of 4% is applied to the reduced balance every year, the amount of CCA declines each subsequent year. Consequently, this method of allocation results in greater tax deductions in the earlier years of an asset's life, which, in turn, creates higher after-tax cash flow.

Note that this example did not provide the particular date in 20X0 when the building was acquired. This is because the date is not relevant, as the CCA rate is applied

---

19 Regulation 1100(1)(a)(xxxviii). To qualify for the 100% rate the equipment must be situated in Canada and owned by a business carried on in Canada.
20 Regulation 1100(1)(a); ITA 13(21).
21 Regulation 1100(2); IT-285R2.

to the balance at the end of the year. The rule that permits only one-half of the normal rate to be applied in the year of acquisition reflects the fact that an asset may be acquired at any time throughout the year.

It is important to note that the *one-half rule does not apply* to items in class 14 (discussed later in the chapter) or to certain specific items in class 12 (e.g., small tools, kitchen utensils, and linens).[22] Also, it does not apply to the temporary CCA rate of 100% on computer equipment (class 52). In addition, the amount of CCA that can be claimed may be further limited when the taxpayer has a taxation year that is less than 365 days (for example, the first taxation year of a new corporation or proprietorship). In such cases, the CCA that would otherwise apply (including the amount resulting from the application of the one-half rule) is prorated by the number of days in the taxation year divided by 365.[23]

For example, an individual starts a new business on September 1, 20X0, and purchases class 8 equipment costing $10,000. The first fiscal period ends on December 31, 20X0, and includes 122 days (September 1 to December 31). Capital cost allowance for the period is $334, calculated as follows:

$$\$10,000 \times 20\% \times \tfrac{1}{2} \times 122/365 = \$334$$

D. Pooling Assets of the Same Class

The above example dealt with the acquisition of a single asset. In most cases, a business will have many assets of the same class, such as a fleet of delivery vehicles or many items of furniture and equipment. The CCA system places all assets of the same class in a common pool, provided that those assets are all used in the same business.[24] As a result, each asset loses its individual identity as it gets added to the pool of its class.

The concept of pooling assets of a similar class is demonstrated in the situation/analysis at the bottom of this page, which incorporates the previous example.

In the same way that the purchase of a new asset will add that asset to the pool, the sale of a particular asset will remove that asset from the pool. For an example, see the situation/analysis at the top of the next page.

At this point, some further clarifications are needed. With respect to the *application of the one-half rule in the year of acquisition*, the examples provided in the situation/analysis are limited because they do not demonstrate what happens when *additions* and *disposals occur in the same year*. When this occurs, *the one-half rule for CCA applies only to the extent that the additions exceed the disposals*. For example, in the calculation for class 8 on the next page, the additions exceed the disposals by $10,000, and so the CCA rate of 20% is reduced by one-half only on that amount.

Situation:	In 20X3, business A acquired a second small warehouse building (also in use prior to 2007) at a cost of $250,000.

Analysis:	**Class 1 (4%)**

(20X3)	
Undepreciated capital cost (above)	$180,634
Purchase:	
Building #2	250,000
	430,634

---

22 Regulation 1100(2).
23 Regulation 1100(3) (does not apply to classes 14 and 15).
24 Regulation 1101(1); IT-206R.

CCA:

4% × $180,634	$7,225	
4% × $250,000 × ½	5,000	(12,225)
Undepreciated capital cost		$418,409

Situation: In 20X4, building #1 was sold for $150,000 and was not replaced.

Analysis:

Class 1

(20X4)

Undepreciated capital cost	$418,409
Purchases	–0–
Disposals:	
Sale of building #1	(150,000)
	268,409
Capital cost allowance:	
4% × $268,409	(10,736)
Undepreciated capital cost	$257,673

Class 8 (20%)

Undepreciated capital cost at beginning of year		$70,000
Purchases	$60,000	
Disposals	(50,000)	10,000
		80,000
Capital cost allowance:		
20% × $70,000	14,000	
20% × $10,000 × ½	1,000	(15,000)
Undepreciated capital cost		$65,000

If, in the above example, the disposals had exceeded the purchases, there would have been no requirement to apply the one-half rule.[25]

When assets are sold, the CCA pool is reduced only up to a maximum of the original capital cost of the asset disposed.[26] In the previous demonstration, building #1 was sold for $150,000 (the selling price) and the pool was reduced by that amount because it was less than the building's original cost of $200,000. If building #1 had been sold for $210,000, the class 1 pool would have been reduced by only $200,000. The excess of $10,000 would have constituted a capital gain on disposition (see Chapter 8).

E. Gains and Losses on Disposal of Depreciable Property— Recapture and Terminal Losses

It is easy to compute the gain or loss on the disposition of a single asset. Consider an asset that originally cost $10,000 and that, as a result of capital cost allowance, has an undepreciated capital cost of $4,000. If the asset is sold for $5,000, a gain of $1,000 is evident; if it is sold for $3,500, a loss of $500 occurs.

However, when multiple assets are pooled in a single class under the CCA system, no gain or loss is recognized on the sale of individual assets unless the sale price is greater

---

25 The one-half rule may not apply in certain circumstances when the purchaser does not deal at arm's-length with the vendor, Regulations 1100(2), (2.2), (2.3).
26 ITA 13(21)(d), (f)(iv); IT-220R2.

than the asset's original cost. When building #1 in the previous demonstration was sold for $150,000, the amount was actually less than its undepreciated balance, and therefore, a loss actually occurred. However, this loss simply remained in the pool, along with building #2, to be deducted as an expense at 4% per year over a period of time.

The pool concept recognizes that some assets in a given pool will be sold at less than their depreciated value and others at more. The result is that gains and losses are averaged over the life of the pool.

For tax purposes, gains and losses on depreciable property can occur at three particular points.

1. A loss has occurred if, at the end of a fiscal year, *all* assets in a class have been disposed of but a balance remains in the pool. This balance is written off in full against business or property income as a "terminal loss."[27] In effect, this loss reflects the net losses and gains accumulated over several years.

2. A gain has occurred if, at the end of any particular fiscal year, the balance of a class pool is negative, even if some assets still remain in the pool. This gain is fully taxable as business or property income and is referred to as a "recapture" or "recovery" of CCA.[28]

3. If, at any time, the selling price of a depreciable property exceeds the original cost of the specific property sold, the excess is recognized in the year as a capital gain (see Chapter 8).

Examples of these gains and losses are demonstrated below.

Situation: In 20X1, business X acquired two items of equipment. Item A cost $10,000, and item B cost $15,000. At the end of 20X2, the undepreciated capital cost of the class was $18,000. In 20X3, items A and B were sold for $6,000 and $7,000, respectively.

Analysis:

Class 8		
(20X3)		
Opening undepreciated capital cost		$18,000
Purchases:		–0–
Disposals:		
Item A	$(6,000)	
Item B	(7,000)	(13,000)
		5,000
Terminal loss		(5,000)
Undepreciated capital cost		–0–

As no assets were left in the pool at the end of the year, the full balance of $5,000 was deducted for tax purposes in 20X3.

Consider the tax impact if business X had purchased a $300 piece of equipment on the last day of the company's fiscal year. This very small acquisition would have eliminated its ability to claim a terminal loss because there would have been an asset left in the pool at the end of the year. If the $300 purchase had been made, the 20X3 deduction for tax purposes would have been only $1,060, as calculated at the top of the next page.

If the company had delayed the purchase of the $300 piece of equipment until the first day after the fiscal year end, the terminal loss of $5,000 would have been permitted in 20X3, and a new pool of $300 would have begun in 20X4.

---

27 ITA 39(1)(b)(i). A capital loss cannot occur on depreciable property (see Chapter 8).
28 ITA 13(1); IT-478R2.

Class 8		
Opening undepreciated capital cost		$18,000
Purchases		300
Disposals:		
Item A	$(6,000)	
Item B	(7,000)	(13,000)
		5,300
CCA: 20% × $5,300		(1,060)
Undepreciated capital cost		$ 4,240

next year beginning UCC

Situation: Business X has several pieces of equipment in its class 8 pool. The undepreciated capital cost of the pool at the end of 20X0 was $16,000. In 20X1, the company sold two large pieces of equipment for a total of $20,000. The equipment sold originally cost $22,000.

Analysis:

Class 8		
Opening undepreciated capital cost		$16,000
Purchases	–0–	
Disposals		(20,000)
		(4,000)
Recapture of CCA		4,000
Undepreciated capital cost		–0–

In the above situation, a recapture of CCA of $4,000 will be added to business income for tax purposes because the pool had a negative balance at year end. The gain is recognized, even though there are assets remaining in the pool. No further CCA is available on the remaining assets; when those are sold, a further recapture will occur.

Consider, also, the tax impact if the company had purchased additional equipment for $1,000 on the last day of the fiscal year. This would have reduced the amount of taxable income from the recapture from $4,000 to $3,000 as demonstrated below.

Class 8		
Opening undepreciated capital cost		$16,000
Purchases	$ 1,000	
Disposals	(20,000)	(19,000)
		(3,000)
Recapture of CCA		3,000
Undepreciated capital cost		–0–

In this situation, the company knew that a recapture of $4,000 was about to occur. By purchasing additional equipment before the year end, it reduced its taxable income by the full amount of the purchase. Effectively, the new equipment of $1,000 was fully written off in the year of purchase through the elimination of recaptured CCA. It is advantageous to acquire assets before year end when a recapture is expected.

Situation: Business X owns a building included in class 1. The undepreciated capital cost of the pool was $215,000 at the end of 20X0. The building, which originally cost $230,000, was sold in 20X1 for $235,000.

Analysis:

Class 1 (4%)	
Opening undepreciated capital cost	$215,000
Purchases	–0–
Disposals—reduction limited to original cost	(230,000)
	(15,000)
Recapture of CCA	15,000
Undepreciated capital cost	–0–
Capital gain calculation:	
Proceeds of disposition	$235,000
Cost	(230,000)
Capital gain	$ 5,000

Note that in this situation, the pool was reduced by $230,000, even though the building was sold for $235,000. This results from the rule that the pool cannot be reduced by an amount greater than the original cost of the asset sold. Therefore, in this situation, the sale of the building resulted in a recapture of CCA of $15,000, which is classified as business income, plus a $5,000 capital gain, of which, as will be explained in Chapter 8, only $2,500 (½ of $5,000) is taxable.

Capital gains and recapture of CCA do not always occur at the same time, as happened in this example. Recapture depends on the pool becoming negative, and this may not occur after every sale. A capital gain, on the other hand, occurs whenever the selling price of an asset exceeds its cost amount.

F. Special Treatment of Passenger Vehicles

As previously indicated, passenger vehicles that *cost more than $30,000* are considered class 10.1 assets, rather than class 10. Class 10.1 was established to limit the tax deduction for luxury cars. The treatment of these vehicles is summarized below.

- CCA can be claimed on only $30,000 plus tax, even though the vehicle may have cost more.[29] It is important to recognize GST and HST registrants do not add the GST/HST to the cost as the tax is fully recoverable. However, in provinces where PST is applicable, that tax is added to the $30,000 limit. So the cost amount for CCA purposes of an automobile costing $40,000 plus 5% PST (provincial sales tax) is limited to $31,500 ($30,000 + 5% of $30,000).
- Each car is placed in its own class, and CCA is calculated on each car separately. In other words, class 10.1 assets are not pooled.[30]
- When a vehicle is sold, neither a recapture of CCA nor a terminal loss is permitted.[31]
- CCA in the first year is limited to 15%. Also, CCA of 15% is allowed in the year of sale (i.e., the terminal year).[32] This unusual treatment is designed to provide relief from the fact that terminal losses are denied.

Note that vehicles which cost less than $30,000 qualify as regular class 10 assets and are subject to the normal treatment for depreciable property.

---

29 ITA 13(7)(g), Regulation 7307.
30 Regulation 1101(1af).
31 ITA 13(2), 20(16.1).
32 Regulation 1100(2.5).

G. Special Treatment of Faxes, Photocopiers, and Manufacturing Assets

Certain types of equipment have rapid obsolescence due to rapid advances in technology. These include photocopiers, facsimile machines, and telephone equipment, which are pooled in class 8. Normally, when the equipment is sold (usually for a nominal value) or junked, the undepreciated balance remains in the pool along with other assets of the class, to be depreciated at the specific rate for the class. To address this inequity, a special rule permits the taxpayer to elect to set up a separate class for *each* property costing more than $1,000.[33] This means that when the equipment is sold or junked, the loss will be fully recognized for tax purposes as a terminal loss of that separate class. This rule recognizes the fact that such equipment depreciates at rates that far exceed the permitted CCA rates. However, if the asset in the separate class has not been disposed of by the beginning of the fifth taxation year from the year it was acquired, the remaining amount is transferred to the general pool of class from which it came.

Similarly, taxpayers are permitted to elect to place eligible manufacturing assets costing more than $1,000 in a separate CCA class of class 43 property: a terminal loss will then occur on disposition.[34]

General-purpose electronic data-processing equipment cannot use this special treatment because it has a rapid CCA rate of 55% (page 187).

H. Exceptions to the Declining Balance Method

Several classes of assets, by their nature, do not lend themselves to the establishing of an average rate of CCA. For example, the life of improvements made to leased premises depends on the life of the particular lease contract. Similarly, the legal right to a franchise or licence is greatly affected by the agreement between the franchiser and the franchisee. These two exceptions are discussed below.

I. Leasehold Improvements

Contracts for leasing premises vary considerably. In many cases, the tenants are responsible for the cost of making the space suitable to their needs. It may be necessary to install internal walls, flooring, light fixtures, and wall coverings. These expenditures represent tangible improvements to the landlord's building and, at the end of the lease, cannot be removed. Costs of this nature qualify as depreciable property and are grouped in class 13.

Under class 13, the cost of improvements for each separate lease is allocated on a straight-line basis over a period equal to the life of that particular lease plus one renewable-option period.[35] However, a minimum allocation period of five years and a maximum allocation of 40 years is imposed.

Situation: A taxpayer in need of warehouse space enters a six-year lease agreement. The contract gives the tenant the option of renewing the lease for two additional four-year periods. If both options are exercised, the tenant will have use of the building for 14 years. In year 1, the tenant spends $30,000 on leasehold improvements. At the beginning of year 4, additional improvements of $7,000 are made.

Analysis: Under class 13, annual CCA, on a straight-line basis, is $3,000, calculated as follows:

$$\frac{\$30,000 \text{ (capital cost)}}{6 \text{ (lease term)} + 4 \text{ (1st option term)}} = \$3,000$$

In year 4, the additional capital improvements will increase CCA by $1,000 annually, calculated as follows:

$$\frac{\$7,000 \text{ (capital cost)}}{3 \text{ (remaining lease term)} + 4 \text{ (1st option term)}} = \$1,000$$

Class 13 has its own one-half rule so that in year 1, the deduction is reduced from $3,000 to $1,500, and in year 4, the deduction of $1,000 is reduced to $500.

33 Regulation 1101(5p).
34 Regulation 1101(5s).
35 Regulation 1100(1)(b); Regulations—Schedule III; IT-464R.

In the previous example, the taxpayer has the right to use the premises for a total of 14 years (6 + 4 + 4); however, the initial cost of improvements is allocated and deducted for tax purposes over a 10-year period (6 + 4). The initial lease period and first option period are critical in determining the speed of the deductions for tax purposes. For example, the premises could be tied up for the same 14 years by having an initial lease term of four years plus three option periods of one year, five years, and four years. While this still totals to 14 years, the initial improvements would be written off at $6,000 per year over five years, calculated as follows:

$$\frac{\$30,000 \text{ (capital cost)}}{4 \text{ (lease term)} + 1 \text{ (1st option term)}} = \$6,000$$

Under this arrangement, the net after-tax cost of the lease would be reduced, as cash flow from the deduction of CCA in the early years would be increased and available for further investment. Normally, the granting of option periods by the landlord also calls for an adjustment to the rent, and this possibility must be examined before lease terms are negotiated.

It may be necessary to make additional improvements some years after the original lease is signed. The CCA on the cost of those additional improvements is calculated separately from the CCA on the original improvements. The additional CCA is based on the number of years *remaining* in the lease plus one option period, and the one-half rule applies.

When a tenant enters into a short-term lease (less than five years), it is important to recognize the minimum write-off period of five years under the class 13 formula. For example, leasehold improvements costing $8,000 for a lease of four years (with no option to renew) result in annual capital cost allowance of $1,600, except in the first year, when the one-half rule is applied. This is calculated as follows:

Annual CCA = lesser of:

$$\frac{\$8,000}{4 \text{ (lease term)}} = \$2,000$$

$$\frac{\$8,000}{5 \text{ (minimum)}} = \$1,600$$

The undepreciated balance at the end of year 4 when the lease expires is deducted in full as a terminal loss, provided that there are no other leases in the class 13 pool.

In some situations, a landlord will persuade a prospective tenant to sign a lease by providing an inducement payment. The tenant can treat the inducement payment in one of two ways. The first is to include its full amount in business income in the year received. The second is to apply it as a reduction of the cost of the leasehold improvements in class 13 (see Chapter 5).[36] When the second option is chosen, the result is reduced CCA over the write-off period, which, in turn, creates higher taxable income (and tax) in those years. If tax rates in the future are likely to remain the same, this is usually the better option, as the income is then recognized over several future years consistent with the term of the lease.

However, if future tax rates are expected to increase, it may be better to take the first option—that is, to treat the inducement payment as income in the year of receipt. This requires an earlier payment of tax, but the overall amount of tax is likely to be lower. Consider that a significant increase in tax rates often occurs in a Canadian-controlled private corporation when its business income goes beyond an annual limit of $500,000 (see Chapters 11 and 13). In such situations, paying tax in an earlier year at a lower rate may be cheaper than paying the tax over several future years at a higher rate. To make an

---

36 ITA 12(1)(x), 13(7.4).

accurate assessment, one must determine the current value of the tax cost for both options. (See the discussion on capital expansion and cash flow later in this chapter.) The first option may also be wise when the taxpayer has losses and no tax will result.

2. Franchises, Concessions, and Licences

Another class that has special CCA treatment is class 14. In order to qualify under class 14, franchises, concessions, and licences must have a *limited legal life*. If the asset has an indefinite life, it does not constitute class 14 depreciable property. Instead, it is classified as eligible capital property, which is discussed later in this chapter.

CCA is determined separately for each item in this class, as is the case with class 13 items. The annual CCA for each asset is normally calculated on the straight-line basis by multiplying the original capital cost by the number of days the property was owned in the year divided by the total number of days in the life of the asset.[37] As an alternative to the straight-line method, the CRA will accept an apportionment of the cost of the asset over its useful life on *any reasonable basis* that reflects *economic value*.

Situation:	A company with a December 31 fiscal year end acquires a limited-life 10-year franchise on October 1, 20X0, at a cost of $50,000.

Analysis:

Class 14

(20X0)
   CCA:

$$\$50,000 \times \frac{92 \ (\# \text{ of days owned in 20X0})}{3,650 \ (\# \text{ of days in life of franchise})} = \$1,260$$

(20X1 and subsequent years)
   CCA:

$$\$50,000 \times \frac{365 \ (\# \text{ of days owned in 20X1})}{3,650 \ (\# \text{ of days in life of franchise})} = \$5,000$$

Note that in 20X0, the first year of ownership, the one-half rule was not applied. It is not necessary to apply this rule for class 14 items, as in the year of acquisition, any CCA is automatically prorated for the period in the year that it was owned. Similarly, CCA is not prorated when the taxation year is less than 365 days.

In some circumstances, *patents* may be classified as class 14 property. As shown earlier in this chapter, a patent is normally classified as a class 44 property with CCA at 25% (diminishing-balance method subject to the one-half rule). A taxpayer can elect to treat a new patent acquisition as a class 14 property using the straight-line method described above.[38] This election may be beneficial if the patent acquired has a short life, in which case the write-off time may be faster.

I. Involuntary and Voluntary Dispositions

The requirement that a negative balance in a CCA class result in the recapture of CCA is often a burden when assets are disposed of and there is not enough time available to replace them before year end. This is especially the case when the disposition is not voluntary. If assets are destroyed, lost, stolen, or expropriated, the receipt of insurance or compensation causes a disposition to occur.[39] When the disposition is

---

37 Regulation 1100(1)(c); IT-477.
38 Regulation 1103(2h).
39 ITA 13(21).

forced and a recapture occurs, the taxpayer is permitted to defer recognition of the recapture if a property with a similar use is acquired within 24 months of the year of forced disposition.[40] This 24-month replacement applies to all classes of depreciable property.

A similar opportunity applies to dispositions that are voluntary. However, voluntary dispositions are provided only a 12-month extension, and this extension applies only to property that is either a building or a leasehold interest in a building that is used for the purpose of earning business income.[41] The 12-month extension, for example, would not apply to the voluntary disposition of a building that was used to earn property (investment) income in the form of rents. The recapture of CCA is included in income in the year of disposition but is subsequently eliminated by filing an amended tax return in the year of replacement.

The concept for the deferral of recaptured CCA described above is readily understood. However, achieving the desired result is rather cumbersome. The technical process for a disposition and replacement is summarized as follows:

- Year of disposition—The proceeds of disposition (up to a maximum of the original cost of the disposed property) is credited to the relevant CCA pool. To the extent the pool balance is negative, a recapture of CCA is recognized as income for tax purposes.
- Year of replacement—An amended tax return is filed for the year of disposition that revises the original calculation above. The credit to the pool in the amended tax return is reduced by the lesser of the recapture previously recognized, or the cost of the replacement property. Normally, this eliminates the recapture for the year of disposition.
- The UCC of the replacement property acquired is then reduced by the amount of the deferred recapture from the year of disposition above.

These technical rules are demonstrated in the following situation and analysis.

Situation: In July 20X4, P Inc., which uses a December 31 fiscal year, had its class 43 equipment destroyed in a fire. At December 31, 20X3 the class 43 CCA pool had a UCC of $90,000. The original cost of the equipment in the class was $240,000. There were no equipment additions in 20X4. In September 20X4, P received insurance proceeds of $150,000 for the equipment. In December 20X5, P acquired replacement equipment costing $295,000.

Analysis: The loss of the equipment by fire results in a forced disposition with proceeds equal to the amount received from the insurance company. As a result, in 20X4 P must recognize a recapture of CCA of $60,000 in its business income for tax purposes as follows:

UCC at December 31, 20X3	$90,000
Additions in 20X4	0
Disposals in 20X4	(150,000)
	(60,000)
Recapture of CCA	60,000
Balance at December 31, 20X4	0

---

40 ITA 13(4); IT-271R (archived), -259R4.
41 ITA 13(4)(b); IT-259R4, -491.

When the equipment is replaced in 20X5, P must file an amended tax return to revise the 20X4 class 43 transaction as follows:

Balance December 31, 20X3			$90,000
Addition in 20X4			0
Disposal proceeds:			
Actual proceeds		$150,000	
Reduced by the *lesser of:*			
Replacement cost	$295,000		
Recapture of CCA (above)	60,000	(60,000)	(90,000)
Recapture of CCA and closing balance			0

The UCC of the replacement equipment in 20X5 is $235,000 determined as follows:

Balance at December 31, 20X4 as amended	$ 0
Addition in 20X5	295,000
Less deferred recapture of CCA above	(60,000)
Balance at December 31, 20X5	$235,000

In this situation the equipment was replaced within 24 months from the end of the taxation year that the original property was destroyed. While the replacement occurred in December, 20X5 it could have been delayed for another 12 months to the end of December 20X6. Note that the property in this situation is equipment. The same deferral opportunity would be available for other types of depreciable property such as a building under a forced disposition.

    If the disposition of the equipment had not been forced but had been voluntary, the option to defer the recapture would not have been available. A deferred recapture of CCA from a voluntary disposition is available only if the property is a building that had been used in a business. When this is the case, the deferral period is limited to 12 months compared to 24 months for a forced disposition.

J. Change in Use

Small enterprises will often use assets for business purposes that the owner had previously used for personal purposes. For example, a personal truck may be converted to business use for making deliveries, or a personal desk or business library may be converted to be used in a consulting business. A change from personal use to business use causes a deemed disposition for tax purposes.[42] In other words, the individual is deemed to have sold and bought the asset from himself or herself at a value equal to the asset's market value at that time. If the fair market value of the asset is lower than its original cost, then the fair market value becomes the cost for tax purposes, and CCA can be claimed on that amount. However, when the fair market value of the asset is *greater* than its original cost, then the amount on which CCA can be claimed is equal to the original cost plus the amount of the taxable capital gain included in income from the change in use deemed a disposition (one-half of the excess of deemed proceeds over the original cost). A similar rule applies when depreciable property is sold to a non–arm's-length party.

    Similarly, a change from business use to personal use causes a disposition at fair market value.[43] This may, depending on the value and whether or not there are other assets in the class, cause a recapture of CCA or a terminal loss.

---

42 ITA 13(7)(b).
43 ITA 13(7)(a).

K. Depreciable Property Acquired from Non–arm's-length Person

Special rules apply when a taxpayer acquires depreciable property from a non–arm's-length person and the purchase price is greater than the seller's capital cost.[44] The term "non–arm's-length" is defined in Chapter 9 (Part VII, Section D) but generally refers to related persons (including corporations). To the extent that the purchase price of the depreciable property is greater than the seller's cost, a capital gain is realized of which only one-half is taxable. Normally, the capital cost for CCA purposes is the purchase price. However, in this case the capital cost is arbitrarily reduced by the amount of the tax-free gain (one-half of the capital gain) of the seller. Future capital cost allowance for the purchaser is based on the reduced amount. Consider the following situation and analysis:

Situation: Individual A sells a building to her wholly owned corporation for $200,000. A originally purchased the building for $160,000. A does not deal at arm's-length with the corporation.

Analysis: The sale creates a capital gain of $40,000 for A of which only one-half ($20,000) is taxable. The corporation's cost of the building is $200,000 but the capital cost for tax purposes is deemed to be only $180,000. Technically this is calculated as being equal to the seller's capital cost ($160,000) plus one-half of the selling price in excess of the capital cost [$\frac{1}{2} \times$ ($200,000 – $160,000) = $20,000]. The corporation can claim CCA on only $180,000. For capital gains purposes, the corporation's cost remains the actual price of $200,000.

L. Terminal Loss Restriction on Sales to Affiliated Persons

A terminal loss that occurs on the sale of depreciable property to an affiliated person is deemed to be nil.[45] The amount of the denied terminal loss (referred to as a notional property) remains with the seller who can continue to claim CCA on the amount. The seller can recognize the terminal loss on the notional property (amount less CCA claimed) when the affiliated person disposes of the original depreciable property at a future time. An *affiliated person* means an individual and spouse and any corporation controlled by either of them. Two corporations are affiliated if they are controlled by affiliated persons.

M. Cost of a Business Website

Many businesses have Internet websites. Some are used for communication and promotion of the business' products or services. Others are more interactive and are used to actually sell products or services directly to customers or to allow customers to communicate with the business. The tax treatment for the cost of the design and development of a website is not completely clear. The question arises—is the website a capital item, which must be capitalized and deducted as capital cost allowance, or is it a current expenditure that can be deducted in the year incurred? The *Income Tax Act* does not provide specific mention for the development costs of a website. CRA has indicated that "although a website is not permanent and can be modified frequently and in some cases taken down and rebuilt, it is our opinion that some of the development costs are capital in nature."[46]

The cost of a website normally consists of design costs plus the cost of writing the computer code to insert the graphic designs and the functionality engine of the website. The graphics and functionality are integrated and form a package that can be considered to be an application software product. As such, the package can be classified as a class 12 depreciable property using a CCA rate of 100%.[47] Because of the one-half rule in the first year the tax write-off period is effectively two years on a straight-line basis.

---

44 ITA 13(7)(e).
45 ITA 13(21.2).
46 CRA document #2000-0004995(E)—tax treatment of website costs.
47 IT Regulations Schedule II, class (12)(o).

Some businesses acquire computers with special system software to host the website. The cost of the computer hardware and related system software would qualify as a class 50 property with a CCA rate of 55% on a declining balance basis. Most businesses use a third party to host their website and pay a monthly service fee. These costs are considered current expenditures.

Websites continually require modifications and improvements. Ongoing reprogramming costs for regular maintenance, tweaking, and improving the existing functionality normally can be considered a current expense and deducted for tax purposes in the year incurred. On the other hand, design and programming revisions that substantially alter or improve the website would be capital expenditures and the costs are added to class 12 depreciable property. For example a website that advertises current retail products that is altered to include a direct selling function allowing customers to purchase and pay for products online would constitute a capital improvement and a class 12 addition.

Some websites are very simple and consist of nothing more than a document or a series of documents that are converted to HTML. It can be argued that this simple conversion does not create software and perhaps a current full deduction is permitted.

III. The Treatment of Eligible Capital Property

Many capital expenditures do not fall within the definitions of the CCA classes. Normally, these items are intangible in nature and have no specific legal life. As a result it is extremely difficult to develop a logical method of allocating their cost over a time period that relates to the asset's usefulness.

Assets that fall into this category are referred to as "eligible capital property." For tax purposes, all of these various types of assets are grouped together in a single pool and allocated as a deduction from income over a common, arbitrary time period.

A. Eligible Capital Property Defined

Eligible capital property can generally be defined as a capital expenditure of an intangible nature for which there is no other provision of the act that permits or specifically denies its deduction from income.[48] In effect, it is a catch-all definition that has been arrived at by the process of elimination. Some of the common types of expenditures that qualify in this category are as follows:

- goodwill
- franchises, licences, and concessions that *do not have a specific legal limited life*
- trademarks
- customer lists
- incorporation costs

A patent with an unlimited life normally qualifies as a class 44 property with CCA at 25% (diminishing balance) but can, by election, be treated as eligible capital property.

Although the above capital expenditures have nothing in common with each other, they are, nevertheless, treated for tax purposes in a like manner. Such treatment may—as is the case with depreciable property—be significantly different from the accounting treatment under generally accepted accounting principles.

B. Goodwill Defined

The most common item of eligible capital property is goodwill. Though often encountered, its nature is often misunderstood, and so it is appropriate that the meaning of goodwill be discussed in this chapter.

Goodwill is the value that is attributed to a business in excess of the sum of the values of all other, more specific assets. Consider the following list of a business's specific identifiable assets:

---

48 ITA 14(5); IT-143R3, -386R; *The Queen v. Toronto Refiners and Smelters Limited*, [2003] 1 CTC 365.

	Fair market value
Cash	$ 20,000
Accounts receivable	120,000
Inventory	400,000
Equipment	300,000
Land	80,000
Building	430,000
Franchise	50,000
	$1,400,000

If each of the assets listed above were sold separately, a total value of $1,400,000 would be realized. However, for an established business that is secure in the marketplace and has a high degree of profitability, sound product lines, and good management, a buyer of the entire business may be willing to pay more than $1,400,000. If, for example, a buyer pays $1,800,000 to acquire the assets of this business in order to operate the business as a going concern, then the value attributed to the asset referred to as goodwill is as follows:

Value paid for the assets	$1,800,000
less	
Value attributed to specific assets	1,400,000
Goodwill	$ 400,000

The purchase price of $400,000 for goodwill would qualify, to the buyer, as an eligible capital expenditure for tax purposes. To qualify as eligible capital property, the goodwill must be purchased. It cannot be imputed.

C. Basic Rules for Eligible Capital Property

The deduction for eligible capital property is calculated, like CCA, using the declining-balance method. The amount available for deduction, however, is extremely low. The annual rate of write-off is 7%, and this rate is applied on a starting amount of only 75% of the original cost of the property. Individual gains and losses are not recognized at the time of sale but, rather, as with the CCA system, are averaged and recognized when the pool becomes negative or there are no assets left in the pool.[49]

There are some variations between the two systems, and for this reason, the eligible capital property system is summarized below.

1. Seventy-five percent of the cost of all eligible capital property is added to a common pool referred to as "cumulative eligible capital."[50]

2. Seventy-five percent of the selling price of any item, *even if that price is greater than the original cost*, is deducted from the common pool.[51]

3. If the pool is negative, the full amount is added to business income but only to the extent that it represents the recapture of amounts previously deducted.[52]

---

49 IT-123R4.
50 ITA 14(5).
51 ITA 14(5).
52 ITA 14(1).

4. If the pool is negative and exceeds the amount that represents the recapture of amounts previously deducted (item 3 above), two-thirds (⅔) of that excess is added to business income (reviewed later in this section).

5. If, at year end, the pool is positive and the business is continuing, the undepreciated balance is amortized at 7% using the declining-balance method.[53]

6. If the pool is positive at the end of the year but the business has discontinued, the full balance is deducted from income as a terminal loss.[54]

7. The one-half rule does not apply in the year of acquisition. However, if the taxation year has less than 365 days, the deduction is pro-rated by days.

Situation:

In 20X0, a corporation purchases an existing business and acquires, among other assets, a franchise (unlimited life) for $10,000 and goodwill for $50,000. In 20X2, the franchise is sold for $12,000, but the business continues.

Analysis:

Cumulative Eligible Capital

(20X0)	
Additions:	
Franchise (75% of $10,000)	$ 7,500
Goodwill (75% of $50,000)	37,500
	45,000
20X0 amortization (7% × $45,000)	3,150
Unamortized balance	41,850
(20X1)	
Additions and disposals	–0–
	41,850
20X1 amortization (7% × $41,850)	2,930
Unamortized balance	38,920
(20X2)	
Disposal:	
Sale of franchise (75% of $12,000)	(9,000)
	29,920
20X2 amortization (7% of $29,920)	(2,094)
Unamortized balance	$27,826

Note that although the franchise was sold for $12,000 and had a cost of $10,000 that was partly amortized, no gain on the sale was recognized. The actual gain simply reduced the pool, thereby diminishing the extent of amortization in future years.

An explanation is needed for the treatment of a negative balance to the cumulative deduction account. The treatment described previously is designed to first fully recapture the amounts previously deducted as annual write-offs of the cumulative deduction account. This is similar to the recapture of CCA. Adjusting any remaining negative amount by two-thirds is designed to treat that portion of the gain similar to the treatment of a capital gain. To demonstrate, consider a situation where a business purchases goodwill in year 1 for $10,000 and sells it in year 2 for $12,000. The cumulative eligible capital account and income for tax purposes is calculated as follows:

---

53 ITA 20(1)(b).
54 ITA 24.

Cumulative eligible capital account:	
Year 1	
Purchase of goodwill – ¾ × $10,000	$7,500
Deduction for the year – 7% × $7,500	(525)
	6,975
Year 2	
Sale of goodwill – 75% × $12,000	(9,000)
Negative balance end of year 2	($2,025)
Business income for tax purposes:	
Recapture of amounts previously deducted	$ 525
Taxable portion of excess – ⅔ × ($2,025 – $525)	1,000
Business income for tax purposes	$1,525

Note that the goodwill was sold for $2,000 more than its original cost and only one-half (½) or $1,000 of this amount was included in income. Although this is considered to be business income, the treatment is similar to that of a capital gain, which also includes one-half of the gain in income.

In some circumstances, when eligible capital property is sold, some or all of the price is paid over a period of years. Even though the proceeds of the sale are deferred, no reserve is permitted, and three-quarters of the full selling price must be credited to the cumulative eligible capital account in the year of sale.[55] However, if it is later established that some or all of the unpaid amount is uncollectible, a deduction is allowed for three-quarters of that amount (or two-thirds of three-quarters to the extent the income exceeded the recapture of amounts previously deducted).[56]

Sale to an affiliated person. It should also be noted that a loss resulting from the sale of eligible capital property to an affiliated person (defined previously—Part II, Section L) is denied when the seller is a corporation, partnership, or trust (not an individual). The denied loss remains with the seller and can be deducted at a time when the affiliated person eventually disposes of the original property.

IV. Accounting Rules versus Tax Rules

Now that the tax treatment of depreciable property has been examined, it is important to highlight how it differs from the *accounting* treatment of similar property.

• **Cost allocation**   Generally accepted accounting principles attempt to allocate the capital cost of an asset over its useful life in relation to its contribution to the revenue-earning process. The life expectancy of similar types of assets will vary considerably from taxpayer to taxpayer, depending on the manner in which the assets are used. Even within the same entity, similar assets may be used in different ways. For example, the useful life of automobiles used by travelling sales personnel may be three years, but the life of similar automobiles used for light messenger service within a city may be five years.

Despite this, the tax system arbitrarily sets the rate and the method of amortization/depreciation (CCA) for similar assets. Automobiles, for example, must use a rate of 30% applied to the declining balance whether the normal use of that automobile is

---

55 ITA 14(5).
56 ITA 20(4.2).

three years or five years. And a franchise cost must be allocated over its legal life, even if it has ceased contributing to income generation.

The arbitrary CCA rates imposed by the *Income Tax Act* usually are determined on the basis of the average normal use of particular types of assets, but in some cases, they are chosen to implement certain fiscal and economic policies. For example, for a period of time, the act permitted manufacturing equipment to be allocated over two years on a straight-line basis. The purpose of this fast write-off was to stimulate expansion of the manufacturing sector in order to create a broader base of permanent jobs.

• **Gains and losses**   Normal accounting rules recognize a gain or a loss on the sale of property in the year in which the sale is made. For tax purposes, as a result of averaging under the class pool concept, only capital gains (proceeds in excess of original cost) are recognized in the year of sale. Proceeds above or below the depreciated value remain in the pool and are recognized either when the pool becomes negative or when all assets have been disposed of.

In Chapter 5, a sample calculation of business income for tax purposes was demonstrated. This example was incomplete to the extent that it did not provide detailed information on the taxpayer's depreciable property. In order to complete the conversion of accounting income—as described in the financial statements—to income for tax purposes, these additional procedures are followed:

1. The amortization/depreciation expense relating to tangible fixed assets is removed from accounting income. In manufacturing concerns, a certain amount of amortization/depreciation will be allocated to product costs and inventory. These amounts must also be removed.

2. The amortization of intangible assets is removed from accounting income.

3. Any gain or loss realized for accounting purposes on the sale of depreciable property, and of eligible capital property, is eliminated.

4. CCA, the amortization of eligible capital property, and terminal losses, if any, are deducted.

5. Taxable capital gains and any recapture of CCA are added to income.

These procedures are shown in the demonstration questions and solutions at the end of this chapter.

V. Impact on Management Decisions

The tax treatment of depreciable capital property and eligible capital property has a significant impact on management decisions. First, the way that capital costs are allocated and gains and losses are treated influences the amount and timing of income tax, which, in turn, affects all decisions relating to capital expansion. Second, the tax method of dealing with depreciable property, however arbitrary it may be, still influences managers who must complete the difficult task of determining accounting amortization/depreciation. This, in turn, affects a wide range of business decisions relating to capital expansion.

A. Influence on Accounting Amortization/ Depreciation   Although the tax system of dealing with depreciable property is quite different from that of the accounting system, this question arises: Does the arbitrary tax formula for capital cost allowance and eligible capital property influence the depreciation policies of the business community? When one considers how much judgment is required to determine how much and for how long a specific capital asset will contribute to the generation of business revenue, it is easy to understand why a decision maker may attach undue influence to the published and recognized tax rates.

The fact is, the tax system does influence the rates and method of amortization/depreciation chosen by Canadian businesses. This influence is most dramatic in the small business sector, but big business is not immune. When in doubt, the normal human response is to rely as much as possible on hard data. The *Income Tax Act*'s list of CCA classes is one of the few available sources of independent hard data relating to the allocation of capital property costs.

To the extent that the tax system influences accounting amortization/depreciation and therefore profits, it will, in turn, affect a number of areas, such as pricing decisions, labour negotiations, and financing costs.

• **Pricing** While competition is the main influence on pricing decisions, perfect competition does not always exist. Prices also respond to costs. If inaccurate amortization/depreciation (i.e., too high or too low) forms part of the product cost, then the decision to respond to such costs by a pricing adjustment may weaken the entity's competitive position in the marketplace.

On a broader scale, this influence may have an impact on international expansion. Canadian tax rules are different from those of other countries. For example, the tax treatment of depreciable property in the United States is different from that in Canada. The American tax system influences American accounting-depreciation methods, which, in turn, have an impact on American companies' pricing policies. Canadian businesses must cope with this impact when pricing their products to compete in the American market.

• **Financing costs** A company's ability to sell an equity issue or a bond issue to finance its expansion plans depends not only on its existing financial structure but also on its earnings per share. Again, inaccurate amortization/depreciation—especially if it is too high in the early years—will alter the earnings-per-share balance and, as a result, raise the cost of arranging new sources of financing.

It is vital that a business enterprise develop a system that establishes amortization/depreciation policies that reflect the realities of its specific situation. Too often the tax rules are a dominating influence and are used as an excuse to maintain an unreliable system for allocating capital costs.

B. Capital Expansion and Cash Flow

It is important to understand that the criteria used to evaluate capital expansion decisions differ from those used to evaluate a company's performance. Company performance is evaluated by examining profits according to accepted accounting rules. Capital expansion, on the other hand, is evaluated by examining its impact on future cash flow. This analysis is referred to as "capital budgeting" and should be performed for all capital expansion decisions, including those that involve the acquisition of a complete business.

Cash flow will be influenced whenever a capital asset is purchased or sold. It will also be influenced by the resulting tax consequences with respect to the gain or loss on sale and the write-off rate of the new asset acquired. Capital budgeting is completely irrelevant unless the accounting consequences of the transaction are ignored and the tax rules, described in this chapter, are considered instead.

Cash-flow analysis is premised on the fact that it is more desirable to receive cash today than sometime in the future because that cash can be used now to generate more income or reduce the cost of debt. For example, the real cost of a piece of equipment is not its purchase price but, rather, the purchase price *less* the tax savings that can be achieved by claiming capital cost allowance in future years. As the tax savings will be received gradually over future years, their value is translated into a current value by discounting the future cash receipt at some accepted rate of return.

The present value of the tax savings arising from CCA based on the declining balance method can be determined by using this formula:

$$\frac{C \times T \times R}{R + I}$$

Where:

C = cost of the asset

T = tax rate

R = maximum rate of CCA

I = appropriate interest rate (usually expressed on an after-tax basis)

This formula does not take into account the one-half rule for the first year of an acquisition; however, the impact of that rule is normally not material and will seldom influence the decision.[57]

For example, assume that a business is contemplating the purchase of manufacturing equipment at a cost of $100,000. If the corporate tax rate is 25% and if the company usually can invest its funds in business activities to generate an after-tax return of 10%, the net cost of the acquisition, in terms of current value, is only $81,250, calculated as follows:

Current purchase price	$100,000
less	
Present value of future tax savings from CCA:	
$\dfrac{\$100{,}000 \times 0.25 \times 0.30 =}{0.30 + 0.10}$	18,750
Net after-tax cost	$ 81,250

Further assume that the new equipment will generate after-tax profits of $15,000 per year for 10 years as a result of reduced labour costs and greater capacity. The present value of $15,000 per year discounted at 10% is $92,168. The decision to acquire the equipment is favourable because the net present cost ($81,250) is less than the present value of its future benefits ($92,168), even after allowance for an after-tax return of 10%. If the one-half rule is incorporated into the formula, the net after-tax cost is $82,103, rather than $81,250. In this case, the difference does not materially affect the outcome.

Remember that the formula does not apply when CCA is calculated on a straight-line basis. In such cases, the tax saving is the same amount each year, and the net tax saving can be calculated as the present value of an annuity (except for the first year, if the one-half rule applies).

Examining capital acquisitions on an after-tax basis enables the decision maker to

(a) establish the real cash cost of the investment and its viability, as demonstrated above;

(b) determine the length of time required to recover the investment and thereby establish some sense of the risk attached to the acquisition; and

(c) present an accurate picture of the financing requirements and the ability to repay.

The previous example presented the simple acquisition of a single asset. There are many other decisions that must take into account the tax system for depreciable

---

57 The impact of the one-half rule can be included by using this formula:

$$\frac{C \times T \times R}{2(R + I)} \left(\frac{2 + I}{1 + I} \right)$$

property as well as capital-budgeting techniques. Decisions involving lease-or-buy, sale-and-leaseback, expansion of operations to new locations, and acquisitions of new businesses are but a few of these. While analyses for such decisions are more complex than the one in the example provided, the basic tax factors are applied in a similar manner. The tax implications of a complete business acquisition are examined in detail in Chapter 18.

It is important to recognize that the rate of CCA has a significant impact on the after-tax cost of asset acquisitions. Higher CCA rates provide faster deductions and thereby increase the present value of future tax savings.

Sometimes, a taxpayer acquires a group of assets for a single price. It is then necessary to allocate the total price among the individual assets. This must be done with care to ensure that the assets with the higher CCA rates are allocated the maximum portion that is reasonable in the circumstances. An unreasonable allocation may be revised by the CRA (see Chapter 9).[58]

VI. Tax Planning Checklist

The following tax planning items relate to the CCA system. Some of the items listed are discussed in more detail in later chapters.

1. Deductions for CCA are discretionary. This means that the taxpayer can shift income from one period to another. Consider delaying the CCA deduction when a loss occurs or accumulated losses from other years are at the risk of expiring (see Chapters 10 and 11).

2. The recapture of CCA and the recovery of eligible capital amounts must be included in income at the time of occurrence, even when the related proceeds from the sale are deferred for several years. In contrast, deferred proceeds that relate to capital gains (see Chapter 8) and inventory gains (see Chapter 5) can delay the recognition of that income and the payment of tax.

   Often, several assets are sold as a group. For example, the sale of real estate may include both land and buildings; or the sale of a business may include inventory, land, buildings, equipment, goodwill, and so on. In these situations, it may be prudent to write the sale agreement such that it allocates the deferred proceeds first to those assets that will have only a capital gain, with any remaining amount assigned to the other assets. In this way, the assets that can defer tax will be sold for deferred proceeds and little or no cash, with the other assets being sold for cash and little or no deferred proceeds. This will create the maximum tax deferral.

3. When acquiring depreciable property with borrowed funds, consider capitalizing the borrowing costs. These costs, which are added to the cost of the property, can then be deducted as CCA over a period of time. This may be beneficial if losses are at risk of being unused owing to insufficient income.

4. Be sure to properly consider the options when it comes to recognizing any inducement payments received while signing a lease (see Chapter 5). This will ensure that the maximum tax savings will occur.

5. When negotiating a lease, try to combine the initial lease period and the subsequent option periods in a manner that will speed up the deduction of CCA on any

---

58 ITA 68; IT-220R2.

leasehold improvements (see "Leasehold Improvements," page 193). However, take care not to compromise the associated rent costs.

6. Consider speeding up the purchase of new assets when a particular class of depreciable property is about to generate a recapture of CCA. Similarly, consider delaying the purchase of new assets until after the year end if a particular class is about to generate a terminal loss for tax purposes.

7. When purchasing a group of assets for a total price, carefully consider how to allocate that price among the various assets. Try to maximize (within reason) the amounts allocated to depreciable properties that have a high CCA rate. Remember, however, that the CRA has the right to revise unreasonable allocations.

8. Remember that the right to use an asset is what makes it valuable. Therefore, when acquiring an asset, be sure to consider leasing, rather than owning, comparing not just the cost but the amount and timing of any related tax savings (see Chapter 21).

9. Carefully analyze class 14 property in an attempt to justify a CCA rate that is faster than the traditional straight-line method. This may be difficult as it is often hard to determine economic value.

VII. Summary and Conclusion

This chapter has developed the fundamental tax rules that are applicable when the cost of capital property is allocated over a future period of time. This system can be summarized as follows:

1. Assets of a tangible nature as well as intangible assets that have a limited legal life are defined as depreciable property, and their capital cost is allocated over future years as capital cost allowance (CCA).

2. Various types of assets are grouped together in classes that define the maximum rate of CCA that may be claimed in each year. It is the taxpayer's right to claim any amount of CCA, in any year, up to the maximum permitted for the class.

3. All assets of a particular class are pooled together and averaged according to the following basic procedures:
   - All purchases are added to the undepreciated capital cost of the class.
   - When assets are sold, the class is reduced by the selling price up to a maximum of the original cost of the asset sold. Any proceeds in excess of the original cost are recognized as a capital gain.
   - If, at the end of the year, the balance of the class is positive and there is at least one asset remaining in the pool, the CCA rate is applied to that balance.
   - If, at the end of the year, the balance of the class is positive but there are no assets remaining, the full balance is deducted as a terminal loss.
   - The year-end closing balance, if negative, is taken into income as a recapture of CCA, even if assets remain in the pool.

4. Intangible assets that do not have a specific legal life are classified as eligible capital property. Seventy-five percent of the cost of all such assets is placed in a common pool referred to as cumulative eligible capital and amortized at 7% on a declining-balance basis.

Visit the Canadian Income Taxation Web site at **www.mcgrawhill.ca/ olc/buckwold** to view any updated tax information.

The above rules significantly influence all types of business decisions relating to the acquisition, use, disposition, and replacement of capital assets. Such decisions involve the examination of cash flow through the capital-budgeting process. This process can be applied only when the above tax rules are incorporated into the analysis.

Demonstration Questions

QUESTION ONE

Palay Ltd. is a Canadian-controlled private corporation located in Windsor, Ontario, and operating four retail electronics stores. You, Palay's treasurer, have just reported to the president that the pre-tax profit for the year ended June 30, 20X5, is $214,000.

As preparation for the upcoming management meeting, you are estimating this year's tax liability and preparing advice on certain tax-related matters. Your assistant has summarized the following information:

1. The reported profit of $214,000 consists of the following items:

Income from retail operations	$192,000
Net gain on sale of land, building, equipment, and goodwill	22,000
	$214,000

can't be

2. The previous year's income tax return shows the following account balances:

Depreciable property—undepreciated capital cost:	
Class 1	$420,000
Class 8	70,000
Class 10	40,000
Class 12	4,200
Cumulative eligible capital	28,000

Class 1 -4%, Class 8 -20%, Class 10 -30%, Class 12 -100%

3. The income from retail operations includes the following deductions:

Amortization/depreciation of tangible assets	$ 32,000
Salary and wages	380,000
Rent	26,000
Travel	11,000
Advertising	22,000
Amortization of goodwill	2,000

not deductible — *in Canada = deductible* — *not deductible*

4. On July 1, 20X4, store 2 was sold. A new store, in leased premises, was opened on the same date. Information on the sale of store 2 is given below.

	Selling price	Original cost
Assets sold:		
Land	$ 28,000	$ 4,000
Building	170,000	162,000
Fixtures and equipment	18,000	28,000
Goodwill	40,000	32,000

Intangibles class 8 ECE so use 162,

All of the assets were sold for cash.

5. The new store is located in leased premises. The purchase price included the following assets:

Franchise—unlimited life	$20,000
Fixtures and equipment	22,000
Leasehold improvements	36,000

CEC — class 13

The acquired lease had three years remaining in its term at the date of purchase. The lease contract provides for two renewable option periods of one year each.

6. "Other expense" includes the following items:

Site investigation for new store	$ 3,000
Attending two electronics conventions	4,200
Cost of new computer application software	2,000
Other	2,200
	$11,400

7. Advertising expense consists of the following items:

Radio and television commercials	$16,000
Promotion—meals and drinks for suppliers	1,000
Charitable donations	5,000
	$22,000

8. On June 30, 20X5, Palay sold its delivery truck for $43,000 and leased a new vehicle. The original cost of the truck was $49,000.

Required:

Determine the net income for tax purposes for Palay Ltd. for the 20X5 taxation year.

Solution:

Beginning with the net income from the financial statement of $214,000, adjustments are made for expenses that are not deductible, for the applicable CCA and cumulative eligible capital deductions, and for any taxable gains or losses on the sale of property. These are summarized below.

Net income per financial statement	$214,000
Accounting gain on sale of land, building, equipment, and goodwill	(22,000)
Amortization/depreciation of tangible assets	32,000
Amortization of goodwill	2,000
Promotion—meals—50% × $1,000	500
Charitable donations	5,000
Computer software—is a depreciable item (class 12)—note 1	2,000
Recapture of capital cost allowance—note 1	3,000
Capital cost allowance—note 1	(33,520)
Cumulative eligible capital deduction—note 2	(910)
Taxable capital gain on land— ½ ($28,000 − $4,000)	12,000
Taxable capital gain on building— ½ ($170,000 − $162,000)	4,000
Net income for tax purposes	$218,070

Note 1:

Class (rate)	1 (4%)	8 (20%)	10 (30%)	12 (100%)	13 (st. line)
Opening	$420,000	70,000	40,000	4,200	–0–
Additions		22,000		2,000	36,000
Disposals	(162,000)	(18,000)	(43,000)		
	258,000	74,000	(3,000)	6,200	36,000
Recapture			3,000		
CCA	*(10,320)	**(14,400)		***(5,200)	****(3,600)
Closing	$247,680	59,600	–0–	1,000	32,400

   * $258,000 $\times$ 4% = $10,320

  ** ($70,000 $\times$ 20% = $14,000) + ($22,000 – $18,000 = $4,000 $\times$ 20% $\times$ $1/2$ = $400) = $14,400

 *** ($4,200 $\times$ 100% = $4,200) + ($2,000 $\times$ 100% $\times$ $1/2$ = $1,000) = $5,200

**** Lesser of:
    $1/5$ $\times$ $36,000 $\times$ $1/2$ = $3,600; or
    $36,000 $\div$ (3 years + 1 year option) $\times$ $1/2$ = $4,500

Total CCA = $33,520

Note 2:

Cumulative eligible capital:	
Opening	$28,000
Addition—franchise (unlimited life)	
purchased—$3/4$ $\times$ $20,000	15,000
Disposal—goodwill sold—$3/4$ $\times$ $40,000	(30,000)
	13,000
Deduction—7% $\times$ $13,000	(910)
Closing	$12,090

QUESTION TWO

PX Industries Ltd. operates a wholesale business in Ontario. On October 1, 20X2, the company acquired the assets of a manufacturing business in order to produce some of its existing product lines. The net profit for the year ended December 31, 20X2, is $200,000, as follows:

	Income (loss)
Wholesale division	$335,000
Manufacturing division	(40,000)
Other	38,000
Provision for income taxes	(133,000)
Net income	$200,000

Information relating to the income statement above is summarized below.

1. Other income includes the following:

Gain on sale of furniture	$ 9,000
Interest	29,000
	$38,000

2. Included in the expenses are the following:

• Installation costs for a new computer system	$ 1,200
• Amortization/depreciation of tangible assets	58,000
• Reserve for bad debts	24,000
• Reserve on a potential loss from a lawsuit against the company by a customer for late product delivery	12,000
• Advertising and promotion includes the following:	
Memberships at recreational clubs	4,800
Newspaper advertisements	6,400
• Amortization of manufacturing licence	8,000
• Amortization of research and development costs	5,600
• Legal fees for revising manufacturing licence agreement (see #5)	2,000

3. After acquiring the manufacturing business, PX paid an engineering firm $22,000 to research and develop a new product. The cost is being amortized over several years.

4. At December 31, 20X1, the following properties had undepreciated capital cost:

Class 8	20%	$ 80,000
Class 10	30%	120,000
Class 12	100%	1,000

The balance in the cumulative eligible capital account was $23,000.

5. On October 1, 20X2, the manufacturing business was acquired, and the following assets were included:

Manufacturing equipment	$80,000
Goodwill	100,000
Licence	50,000

The licence permitted PX to produce a patented product in exchange for a royalty. The licence had 10 years remaining.

6. On December 31, 20X2, PX sold all of its office furniture to a leasing company for $70,000 under a sale/leaseback arrangement. The furniture originally cost $130,000. The CCA class to which the furniture belongs has no other assets in it.

7. On September 1, 20X2, PX purchased a computer and some accounting software. The price was $28,000, as follows:

Computer	$24,000
Accounting software	4,000
	$28,000

Required:

Determine PX's net income for tax purposes for the 20X2 taxation year.

Solution:

Regarding CCA issues, it is important to note that two items deducted as expenses should have been added to the cost of depreciable property. The installation costs of the new computer must be eliminated as a full deduction and added to the capital cost of the computer and included in class 45. Similarly, the legal fee for revising the licence agreement is a capital item and must be added to the acquisition cost of the licence and included in class 14.

The net income for tax purposes is calculated as follows:

Income per financial statement	$200,000
Provision for income taxes	133,000
Gain on sale of furniture	(9,000)
Installation cost of new computer	1,200
Legal fee for revising licence agreement	2,000
Amortization/depreciation of tangible assets	58,000
Reserve for potential loss from lawsuit	12,000
Club memberships	4,800
Amortization of licence	8,000
Amortization of research and development	5,600
Research and development costs—actual	(22,000)
Terminal loss from sale of office furniture—note 1	(10,000)
Capital cost allowance—note 1	(67,240)
Cumulative eligible capital deduction:	
7% × ($23,000 + ¾ [$100,000 goodwill])	(6,860)
Net income for tax purposes	$309,500

Note 1:

Class (rate)	8(20%)	10(30%)	12(100%)	14(st. line)	43(30%)/ 29(50%)	50(55%)
UCC 20X1	$80,000	120,000	1,000	–0–	–0–	–0–
Additions:						
Computer						24,000
Computer installation						1,200
Software			4,000			
Licence				50,000		
Legal for licence				2,000		
Manufacturing equipment					80,000	
Disposal:						
Furniture	(70,000)					
	10,000	120,000	5,000	52,000	80,000	25,200
Terminal loss	(10,000)					
CCA		(36,000)	(3,000)	(1,310)*	(20,000)	(6,930)
UCC 20X2	$ –0–	84,000	2,000	50,690	60,000	$18,270

Capital cost allowance calculations:

Class 10—$120,000 × 30% = $36,000

Class 12—($1,000 × 100%) + ($4,000 × 100% × ½) = $3,000

Class 14—92 days ÷ 3,650 days × $52,000 = $1,310 (Note: the one-half rule does not apply.)

Class 43—$80,000 × 30% × ½ = $12,000; or class 29—$80,000 × 25% (in first year) = $20,000 *if purchased after March 19, 2007 and no later than December 31, 2013.*

Class 50 (computer)—$25,200 × 55% × ½ = $6,930.

*Note: The class 14 CCA could have a different rate if it relates to the asset's economic value.

QUESTION THREE

Simple Inc., a Canadian-controlled private corporation, operates a small manufacturing business. The business began in 19X5. At that time, Simple acquired a small building to house the manufacturing operations. The building, which cost $400,000, was 35 years old. At December 31, 20X5 the undepreciated capital cost of its manufacturing assets was as follows:

Class 1	$220,000
Class 17	22,000
Class 43	180,000

In June 20X6, Simple decided to purchase another manufacturing building and some new manufacturing equipment. Two buildings were being considered. Building A was constructed in 20X3 and has been used by another company. Building B was recently constructed and completed in May 20X6. The cost of each building is $800,000. Approximately 93% of the floor space of the acquired building will be used for manufacturing. Both buildings have gravel parking facilities and Simple plans to pave either lot at a cost of $28,000. In 20X6, Simple sold used manufacturing equipment for $75,000 (the equipment originally cost $160,000) and will purchase new equipment for the new building at a cost of $400,000.

   The new building has extra space for expansion. In fact, it has enough space to absorb the entire operations of the existing building. However, the intention at this time is to preserve the extra space in the new building for anticipated business growth.

Required:
Describe the tax implications of the 20X6 transactions.

Solution:
If building A is purchased, the cost of $800,000 must be added to the existing class 1 pool because the building has been used by another party prior to March 19, 2007. CCA is available at 4% on a declining balance basis with the rate reduced by one-half in the first year for net additions in 20X6. The *CCA for 20X6 for class 1* would be $24,800 as follows:

UCC December 31, 20X5	$220,000
Addition	800,000
	1,020,000
CCA 20X6	
$(4\% \times \$220,000) + (4\% \times \$800,000 \times \frac{1}{2}) =$	(24,800)
UCC December 31, 20X6	$995,200

If Building B is purchased, Simple has the choice of including the cost of $800,000 in the existing class 1 pool (as above) or placing it in a separate class 1 pool that allows the CCA rate to increase to 10% on a declining balance basis. This is permitted because the building has not been used by another company and more than 90% of the floor space will be used for manufacturing and processing purposes. The *CCA for 20X6 for class 1* would be $48,800 as follow:

	Regular Class 1	New Class 1
UCC December 31, 20X5	$220,000	0
Addition in 20X6	0	800,000
	220,000	800,000
CCA—4% × $220,000	8,800	
CCA—10% × $800,000 × ½		40,000
UCC December 31, 20X6	$211,200	$760,000

The possible consequences of placing the new building in a separate class 1 pool must be considered. For example, if the anticipated business growth does not occur, it may be beneficial to sell the old building and move its operations into building B which is new and perhaps more efficient. In addition, such a sale would free up capital that could be used to buy new and more efficient equipment. If this were carried out, the sale of the old building would result in recaptured capital cost allowance and a major tax cost to Simple. If, on the other hand, Simple chooses to place the new building B in the same pool as the existing building, the annual CCA would be lower (same as demonstrated above for building A). If, on the other hand, the old building is sold, the recapture of CCA would be avoided as it would be blended with the UCC of the new building in one class 1 pool.

The $28,000 cost of paving the parking lot is not part of the building for CCA purposes. Instead, it qualifies as a class 17 property and must be added to the existing class 17 pool. The CCA rate is 8% using the declining balance method. The CCA for class 17 for 20X6 is $2,880 [(8% × $22,000) + (8% × $28,000 × 1/2)].

If the *manufacturing equipment* is acquired before 2014, it qualifies as a class 29 property with a 50% (straight line) CCA rate and becomes the only asset in that class. The CCA for the first year would be $100,000 (25% × $400,000). The sale of the used equipment reduces the class 43 pool by the selling price of $75,000. The class 43 pool has a CCA rate of 30% (declining balance) and the CCA for the year would be $31,500 (30% × ($180,000 − $75,000)). If the manufacturing equipment is acquired after 2013, it would be added to the class 43 CCA pool. The new equipment of $400,000 is combined with the existing class 43 pool. The sale price of $75,000 for the old equipment is deducted from this same pool. Remember, the class is reduced by the proceeds of disposition or the original cost of the equipment sold, whichever is the lesser amount. This ensures that the class will never be reduced by more than an asset's original cost. In 20X6, the CCA that can be claimed for the class 43 pool is $102,750 calculated as follows:

UCC December 31, 20X5		$180,000
Addition in 20X6	$400,000	
Disposal in 20X6	(75,000)	325,000
		505,000
CCA—(30% × $325,000 × 1/2) + (30% × $180,000)		(102,750)
UCC December 31, 20X6		$402,250

Note that the *one-half rule is applied to net additions* in the year of $325,000 and not to the gross additions of $400,000.

It should also be noted that a taxpayer has the option to place class 43 assets costing more than $1,000 in separate CCA pools provided that an election is made in writing and filed with the corporate tax return in the year of acquisition [Regulation 1101 (5q and 5s)] (see Part II, Section G of this chapter). So if the asset is scrapped or sold for a price below its UCC a terminal loss will result. If, after five years, the asset has not been scrapped or sold it must be transferred to the general class 43 pool. So, this option is beneficial for rapidly depreciating equipment.

QUESTION FOUR

GG Inc. operates a delivery business in Saskatoon having sales of approximately $600,000 annually. The company owns four delivery trucks, one passenger vehicle, and some office equipment. The UCC of its vehicle asset classes for tax purposes at the year ended May 31, 20X8 are as follows:

Class 10	$170,000
Class 10.1	10,000

In 20X9 GG purchased two new passenger vehicles. Vehicle A cost $38,000 including PST (5%) plus GST of $1,810. Vehicle B cost $29,000 including PST (5%) plus GST of $1,381. Also, GG sold a delivery truck for $17,000 (original cost $44,000) and a passenger vehicle for $12,000 (original cost $36,000).

Required:
Describe the tax implications of the 20X9 transactions.

Solution:
Vehicle A is a passenger vehicle costing more than $30,000 (or $30,000 plus PST). Therefore, it qualifies as a class 10.1 property with a 30% CCA rate (declining balance). The cost for CCA purposes is $31,500 ($30,000 limit plus 5% PST). The GST is not relevant because it is fully recoverable as a GST input credit. GG is a GST registrant as its sales are greater than $30,000. Each class 10.1 vehicle must be placed in a separate CCA class. So, the new passenger vehicle A has its own class 10.1 and the CCA in the first year is $4,725 (30% × $31,500 × ½).

The *passenger vehicle sold* for $12,000 is also a class 10.1 property because its original cost was greater than $30,000 plus PST. It is represented in the class 10.1 pool at the beginning of the year as shown above (opening UCC $10,000). The sale of a class 10.1 vehicle cannot result in a terminal loss or recapture regardless of its selling price. Instead, in the year of its disposal, CCA of one-half the normal rate can be claimed on the UCC. So, in this case, the CCA of the class 10.1 vehicle that was sold in the year is $1,500 (30% × $10,000 × ½). The selling price is not relevant and the asset is simply removed from the CCA records.

Vehicle B has a cost of $29,000 including the PST. The GST is not relevant because it is fully recoverable. Vehicle B is not a class 10.1 property because its cost is less than $30,000 plus PST. Instead vehicle B is a regular class 10 property and the cost of $29,000 is simply added to the class 10 pool. GG also sold a delivery truck for $17,000. This vehicle is a class 10 property and the sale price reduces that pool. The one-half rule applies to the class 10 *net additions* in 20X9 (see discussion in Question Three above). The CCA for class 10 for 20X9 is $52,800 as follows:

UCC December 31, 20X8		$170,000
Addition in 20X9	$ 29,000	
Disposal in 20X9	(17,000)	12,000
		182,000
CCA—(30% × $12,000 × ½) + (30% × $170,000)		(52,800)
UCC December 31, 20X9		$129,200

Review Questions

1. Under the income tax system, neither capital expenditures nor amortization/depreciation can be deducted when income for tax purposes is being calculated. The same system imposes an arbitrary and uniform method of cost allocation based on the type of asset used. Explain the reason for this significant departure from generally accepted accounting principles in arriving at income for tax purposes.

2. The cost allocation system divides capital assets into two general categories. Identify these categories, and briefly state, in general terms, what types of assets are included in each category.

3. Can an individual who earns employment income claim a deduction for CCA in arriving at income from employment? If the answer is yes, are any restrictions imposed?

4. A business acquires land for a customer parking lot and incurs the following costs:

Land	$50,000
Legal fees to complete purchase agreement	2,000
Legal fees in connection with obtaining a mortgage loan for the land	1,000
Small building for attendant	10,000
Exterior landscaping	2,000
	$65,000

Briefly explain the tax treatment of these costs.

5. A business can obtain the right to use property through ownership or leasing. Briefly compare the tax treatment of purchasing land and building with that of leasing land and building. Refer to both the amount and timing of the related deductions for tax purposes.

6. What is the meaning and significance of the term "capital cost" of an asset?

7. Explain why the deduction of capital cost allowance is a "discretionary" deduction.

8. Depreciable properties are divided into a number of different classes, and a specific allocation rate (CCA rate) is assigned to each class. Explain why this system is fair to some taxpayers, unfair to others, and more than fair to others.

9. Briefly explain what is meant by the "pool concept" in the CCA system.

10. "In all cases, the acquisition of a new asset in a particular class will result in the reduction of the normal maximum rate of CCA by one-half in the year of purchase." Is this statement true? Explain.

11. To what extent, if any, does the pooling concept inherent in the CCA system affect the tax treatment of any gains and losses that occur on the disposition of depreciable property? In general terms, explain when a gain or loss will occur.

12. Describe the possible ramifications of purchasing new depreciable property on the last day of the current taxation year as opposed to the first day of the next taxation year (that is, one day later).

13. What is a leasehold improvement, and how does its tax treatment vary from the normal CCA treatment?

14. Taxpayer A leases a building for 15 years. Taxpayer B secures the right to lease a building for 15 years by signing a three-year lease with two renewable option periods—one for two additional years and a second for 10 years. Both A and B incur leasehold improvement costs at the beginning of the lease. Explain the tax treatment of the leasehold improvements to both A and B. Which taxpayer has signed the better lease? Explain.

15. If the sale of an asset results in income from a recapture of CCA, is it necessary to acquire another asset in the same year in order to avoid the recapture? Explain.

16. Explain the tax consequences, if any, when an individual proprietor of a new business transfers personal-use office furniture for use in the business.

17. Describe two alternative tax treatments that may apply when a business purchases a franchise.

18. How does the treatment given eligible capital property differ from that given depreciable property?

19. Explain why a businessperson might view the cost of a $100,000 building as being significantly higher than the cost of a $100,000 delivery truck. Make a cost comparison, assuming the taxpayer is subject to a 45% tax rate and can invest funds to generate an after-tax cash return of 9%. Assume the building was used by the vendor before March 19, 2007.

Key Concept Questions

QUESTION ONE

In the current year, Eddie Enterprises purchased new office equipment costing $40,000. The vendor gave Eddie Enterprises $3,500 for the old office equipment which had been purchased three years ago for $6,000. At the beginning of the current year, the class 8 UCC balance was $10,000. *Income tax reference: ITA 13(21), 20(1)(a); Reg. 1100(1), (2).*

Calculate the maximum CCA deduction for class 8 for the current year.

QUESTION TWO

In the current year, Decrease Ltd. purchased class 8 equipment costing $20,000. Later in the year, Decrease Ltd. sold other class 8 equipment for $30,000. The equipment sold originally cost $108,000. At the beginning of the current year, the class 8 UCC balance was $42,000. *Income tax reference: ITA 13(21), 20(1)(a); Reg. 1100(1), (2).*

Calculate the maximum CCA deduction for class 8 for the current year.

QUESTION THREE

At the end of last year, the UCC balance for class 12 was $1,300. During the current year, a class 12 item with an original cost of $8,000 was disposed for $2,000. There were no other class 12 transactions in the current year. *Income tax reference: ITA 13(21).*

Calculate the effect of the disposal on business income for the current year.

QUESTION FOUR

A few years ago, Fast Ltd. purchased a new photocopier for $48,000 and elected to put the photocopier in a separate class 8. At the end of last year, the UCC balance for the separate class 8 was $33,000. During the current year, the photocopier was sold for $25,000. *Income tax reference: ITA 20(16).*

Calculate the effect of the disposal on business income for the current year.

QUESTION FIVE

On May 1, 20X6, Kayla purchased a Frosty Frozen Foods franchise and commenced carrying on business immediately as a sole proprietor. She paid $60,000 for the franchise. The franchise agreement has a 10-year term. The frozen foods business was so successful that Kayla quickly needed more space. On November 1, 20X6, Kayla purchased a small building for $200,000 (land $100,000 + building $100,000) and moved her business into it immediately. Assume the building had been constructed after March 18, 2007. *Income tax reference: ITA 20(1)(a.2); Reg. 1100(1)(a.2), (c), 1100(2), (3), 1101(5b.1).*

Calculate the maximum CCA deduction for these assets for 20X6 and 20X7.

QUESTION SIX

On October 1, 20X1, Neo Enterprises signed a lease for new office space. The contract gives Neo Enterprises the use of the space for four years with the option of renewing the lease for two additional three-year periods. In November, 20X1 Neo Enterprises spent $84,000 renovating the office space. In February, 20X2 an additional $30,000 was spent on leasehold improvements. Neo Enterprises has a December 31 year end.

Calculate the maximum class 13 CCA for years 20X1, 20X2 and 20X3. Assume the class 13 UCC balance at the end of year 20X0 is $0. *Income tax reference: ITA: 20(1)(a); Reg. 1100(1)(b).*

QUESTION SEVEN

X Ltd. is a GST registrant. At the end of last year, the class 10.1 UCC balance was $24,500. In the current year, X Ltd. disposed of the class 10.1 car for $28,000. The car had originally cost $33,000 plus GST and PST at 7%. At the same time, X Ltd. purchased a new car costing $38,000 plus GST and PST at 7%. *Income tax reference: ITA: 13(7)(g); 20(1)(a), 20(16.1); Reg. 1101(1af), 1100(2.5), 7307.*

Determine the income tax implications for X Ltd. for the current year. How would your answer change if X Ltd. was an HST registrant?

QUESTION EIGHT

Noluck Enterprises has a December 31 year end. On March 20, 20X6 the company's warehouse was destroyed by fire. The original cost of the warehouse was $120,000. At the time of the fire, the warehouse was valued at $300,000 and was insured. Class 1 had a UCC balance of $95,000 at December 31, 20X5. Noluck was forced to lease a warehouse until a new one could be acquired. On November 30, 20X8, Noluck purchased a new warehouse costing $325,000. Assume the new warehouse was constructed after March 18, 2007. *Income tax reference: ITA 13(1), (4).*

Calculate the minimum recapture of CCA on the disposal of the warehouse.

QUESTION NINE

In Year 1, Takeover Corp. purchased another business. The purchase price included $100,000 for goodwill. In Year 3, the acquired business was sold. The sale price included $140,000 for the goodwill. *Income tax reference: ITA: 14(1), (5), 20(1)(b).*

Calculate the amount to be included in Takeover Corp.'s business income in Year 3. Assume the CEC balance at the beginning of Year 1 is $0.

QUESTION TEN

In the current year, Tom sold a building that he owned personally to a corporation wholly owned by him and his wife. The corporation paid Tom $400,000 for the building. Tom purchased the building some years ago for $250,000. The UCC of the building at the beginning of the current year was $200,000. Tom does not deal at arm's length with the corporation.

Determine the tax consequences for Tom and the corporation. *Income tax reference: ITA 13(7)(e); Reg 1100(2.2).*

QUESTION ELEVEN

Karen sold equipment to her wholly owned corporation for it fair market value, $40,000. Karen initially purchased the equipment for $100,000 and at the beginning of the current year the UCC of the equipment was $65,000. The equipment was the last asset remaining in the Class. Karen does not deal at arm's length with the corporation.

Determine the tax consequences for Karen and the corporation. *Income tax reference: ITA 13(21.2), 13(7)(e)(iii), Reg 1100(2.2).*

QUESTION TWELVE

Kristin owns a rental property. She purchased the land for $200,000 and built the building at a time when construction costs were high. Her total cost for the building is $400,000. In the current year she sold the rental property for $450,000 (land $300,000; building $150,000). At the beginning of the year the UCC of the building was $320,000.

Determine the amount to be included in Kristin's income with respect to the sale of the rental property. *Income tax reference: ITA 13(21.1).*

Problems

PROBLEM ONE

State the class number for each of the following 13 items, and briefly describe the method and rate of cost allocation:

1. Furniture and fixtures
2. Tools (each costing less than $500)
3. Printing press used by a publisher of books (purchased after March 18, 2007 and before 2014)
4. Paving of a parking lot
5. Concession licence for a 10-year time period
6. Franchise for an unlimited life
7. Computer application software
8. Computer hardware
9. Customer list
10. Glasses and cutlery used in the operation of a restaurant
11. Sprinkler system in a building
12. Television commercial used to promote company products
13. Cost of reorganizing a corporation's share capital

PROBLEM TWO

A wholesale business with a December 31 year end purchased new equipment on November 25, 20X0, for $10,000. Before 20X0, the business owned no other equipment.

Required:

1. What are the tax consequences if in 20X2 the business sells the equipment for (a) $3,000? (b) $8,000? (c) $12,000?

2. How would your answer to (a) and (b) change if on December 31, 20X2, the business acquired new equipment costing $1,000? Would it be advisable to delay the purchase by one day (that is, until January 1, 20X3)?

PROBLEM THREE

Maple Enterprises Ltd. has always claimed maximum CCA. The following information relates to the corporation's capital transactions:

1. The undepreciated capital cost of certain CCA classes at the end of the previous taxation year was as follows:

Class 1	$200,000 (one building in class)
Class 8	190,000

2. In 20X1 (the current year), the company expanded into the manufacturing business by purchasing the following assets:

Equipment (manufacturing)	$30,000
Product licence for an indefinite period	10,000

3. The building was sold in 20X1 for $260,000 (original cost—$230,000).

4. During 20X1, the company purchased office furniture for $14,000.

Required:

1. Calculate the net increase or decrease in the corporation's net income for tax purposes for the 20X1 taxation year.

2. Given that the 20X1 taxation year has passed, can any action be taken in the 20X2 taxation year to reduce the net income for tax purposes of year 20X1? Explain.

PROBLEM FOUR

Wai Yeung is a self-employed insurance saleswoman. She started her business on July 1, 20X1, and ended her first taxation year on December 31, 20X1. On July 1, 20X1, she purchased a car for $32,000 plus HST. The car is financed with a bank loan. From July 1, 20X1, to December 31, 20X1, interest costs amounted to $1,960. Yeung incurred the following additional expenses relating to her automobile:

Repairs and maintenance	$ 300
Insurance	1,100
Gasoline	1,700
Parking while on business	420

During the period, Yeung drove 15,000 km, of which 12,000 were for business.

Required:

1. Determine the maximum amount that Yeung can deduct from her business income for tax purposes in 20X1.

2. Calculate the maximum CCA that Yeung can deduct in 20X2 and 20X3, assuming that business kilometres driven and total kilometres driven both remain constant and that Yeung's car is sold in 20X3 for $21,000 and replaced with a new car costing $34,000 plus HST.

3. Would your answers to 1 and 2 above change if Yeung were employed as an insurance saleswoman, rather than self-employed? Explain.

PROBLEM FIVE

Photo Tonight, a film-developing and camera-repair franchise, began business on January 1, 20X1. In the process of beginning operations, it incurred the following capital expenditures:

Developing equipment	$80,000
Furniture and fixtures	30,000
Small tools (under $500)	15,000
Franchise (expires in 20 years)	75,000
Incorporation costs	5,000
Pickup truck	12,000
Leasehold improvements (10-year lease)	30,000

The business was immediately successful and generated substantial profits for the years ended December 31, 20X1 and 20X2.

In 20X2, the truck was traded in for a larger unit costing $20,000. A value of $7,000 was assigned to the old truck when it was traded in.

In 20X3, the owner was forced to leave the business due to illness. As a result, the assets were valued and sold on December 31, 20X3, for the following values:

Developing equipment	$ 60,000
Furniture and fixtures	15,000
Small tools	10,000
Franchise	85,000
Incorporation costs	–0–
Pickup truck	15,000
Leasehold improvements	15,000
Goodwill	50,000
	$250,000

Required:
Determine the effect of all these transactions on net income for tax purposes for the 20X1, 20X2, and 20X3 taxation years.

PROBLEM SIX

Harley Krane purchased a side-by-side duplex in 20X0 for $120,000 (land $20,000, building $100,000). The units were designed and previously used for residential use but Krane used them for his business. Both units were used to conduct his law practice; one unit housed a small group of paralegals in his employ, who processed most of the real estate transactions for his clients.

In 20X2, Krane stopped practising real estate law in order to concentrate on family law and terminated the staff positions of all paralegals. Krane then occupied the freed-up duplex unit as his personal residence, which meant he no longer had to commute.

At the end of 20X1, the duplex building had an undepreciated capital cost of $94,000. Recently, a duplex of similar size across the street was sold for $150,000.

Required:
How will Krane's net income for tax purposes for 20X2 be affected by the above activity?

PROBLEM SEVEN

Window Shine Ltd. was incorporated on July 1, 20X1, and purchased an existing business on the same date. The purchase included the following assets:

Delivery truck	$40,000
Goodwill	12,000
Franchise	10,000

Immediately after incorporation, the company moved into leased premises, having signed a lease for three years with an option to renew for an additional three. Rental payments of $2,000 per month began in July 20X1. The premises required alterations, and in July 20X1, the company incurred costs of $15,000 for these.

The franchise that was purchased for $10,000 has a remaining legal life of five years. At the end of the five-year period, the franchise may be renewed at a nominal cost only if the franchiser is satisfied with the performance of the franchisee.

The company's fiscal year end is June 30, 20X2. A brief financial statement is presented below for this first year of operations.

Revenue		$120,000
Expenses:		
Wages	$26,000	
Office	4,000	
Building improvements	15,000	
Rent	24,000	
Delivery expense	3,000	
Amortization/depreciation (truck)	6,000	
Amortization of goodwill	2,000	
Amortization of franchise	2,000	
Other	12,000	94,000
Net income for the year		$ 26,000

Required:

Determine the corporation's net income from business for tax purposes for the 20X2 taxation year.

PROBLEM EIGHT

In late 20X0, Conrad Petry retired from his job of 30 years and began receiving a pension of $4,000 per month. Unable to cope with full retirement, he purchased a small retail business on January 1, 20X1. At that time, he moved into rented premises under a seven-year lease that included an option to renew for another three years. He immediately spent $12,000 to improve the premises. The business incurred a small loss in 20X1, but 20X2 was profitable. Information relating to the 20X2 business activity is provided below.

In addition, in 20X2, Petry disposed of an investment that he had owned for several years: shares of a small business corporation. He sold the shares, which originally had cost $20,000, for $12,000.

Additional information concerning retail business (20X2)

1. The financial statements indicate a profit of $9,500 for the year ended December 20X2.

2. During the year, Petry withdrew $1,000 each month from the business for personal use. However, in order to reflect the proper economic costs of the business, he insisted that the accountant deduct a fair salary for his own efforts in the business. Accordingly, salary expense was increased by $38,000, and Petry's equity was credited with an equal amount.

3. The profit includes a deduction for amortization/depreciation of $3,500.

4. On February 28, 20X2, additional improvements costing $18,000 were made to the leased premises. This amount appears on the balance sheet as a fixed asset.

5. On June 30, 20X2, Petry purchased the land beside the leased premises. This land is to provide extra parking space for customers but can also be used to build a company-owned store building when the current lease expires. The costs relating to the land totalled $58,200, determined as follows:

Land price	$40,000
Cost of paving parking area	12,000
Permanent landscaping costs paid	4,000
Legal fees to prepare purchase agreement	1,000
Legal and registration fees for first mortgage financing of the land	1,200
	$58,200

The land and the paving of the parking lot are recorded as fixed assets. The other costs have been deducted as 20X2 expenses.

6. In January 20X2, Petry purchased an automobile for $34,000 plus HST. All of the operating expenses (gas, oil, repairs, insurance, and so on) of $4,300 were paid by the business and included in travel costs. No amortization/depreciation was deducted. The car was used for the following purposes:

Travel to and from work	20%
Travel to Vancouver to see suppliers	25
Personal travel	55
	100%

7. Sales revenue has been reduced by $10,000 for a reserve for anticipated post-Christmas returns.

Required:
Determine Petry's net income from business and his overall net income for tax purposes for the 20X2 taxation year.

PROBLEM NINE

KC Restaurants Ltd., a Canadian-controlled private corporation, was incorporated on July 1, 20X0, and began operations immediately. By December 31, 20X0 (the corporation's first year end), three new restaurants had been opened, two of which were franchises.

During the first few months of operations, the following expenditures were made by KCR:

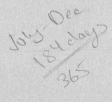

Legal fees for the cost of incorporation *eligible capital*	$ 4,000
Cooking equipment, including food processors, ovens, and hot plates *class 29*	320,000
Franchise #1 *class 14 = limited life*	40,000
Franchise #2 *ECE*	80,000
Cutlery, plates, glasses, and cups *class 12 – no half-year rule*	115,000
Computer programs for restaurant accounting *class 12 – half year*	3,000
Building (constructed after March 18, 2007) *class 1 – 6%*	220,000

Franchise #1 was purchased on October 1, 20X0, and will expire after 120 months.

Franchise #2, which was acquired on July 1, 20X0, has no expiry date and will continue indefinitely, provided that the terms of the franchise agreement are met. Other equipment, such as tables and chairs, was leased.

For the taxation year ending December 31, 20X0, KCR claimed a deduction for the maximum available CCA and cumulative eligible capital account. For tax purposes, after these deductions were made, the company lost $40,000 in 20X0.

The company became profitable in 20X1. A summary of the income statement prepared for accounting purposes for the year ended December 31, 20X1, with additional information, is provided below.

20X1 financial statement (summarized) and other information

Sales		$1,845,000
Cost of sales		1,011,000
Gross profit		834,000
Occupancy costs	$ 72,000	
Salaries and wages	275,000	
General overhead	301,000	
Advertising and other	96,000	744,000
		90,000
Gain on sale of goodwill		60,000
Net losses on sale of fixed assets		(22,000)
Net income		$ 128,000

The following additional information relates to the previous 20X1 financial statements:

1. On December 1, 20X1, KCR sold the non-franchised restaurant. The sale price included these proceeds:

	Proceeds	Original cost
Goodwill	$ 60,000	–0–
Land	15,000	12,000
Building	230,000	220,000
Cooking equipment	40,000	72,000
Cutlery, plates, glasses	26,000	37,000

2. Included in advertising expenses is $2,000 of donations made to a registered charity.

3. Salaries include an accrued bonus of $12,000 awarded on December 31, 20X1, to a manager. The bonus will be paid in three equal instalments of $4,000 on April 30, 20X2, August 31, 20X2, and December 31, 20X2.

4. Expenses include accounting amortization/depreciation of $102,000.

Required:

1. Calculate the undepreciated capital cost for tax purposes for each class of depreciable property at the end of the 20X0 taxation year after CCA claims for that year. Assume the 20X0 asset purchases were after March 18, 2007.

2. Calculate the balance in the cumulative eligible capital account at the end of the 20X0 taxation year after the deduction for that year.

3. For the taxation year ended December 31, 20X1, calculate KCR's net income for tax purposes. Begin your answer with net income per the financial statement, and add or subtract adjustments.

PROBLEM TEN

Samson Enterprises Ltd. achieved a profit in 20X1 of $120,000. The income statement is summarized below.

Sales	$1,300,000
Cost of sales	780,000
Gross profit	520,000
Administrative and selling expenses	451,000
	69,000
Other income (expenses)	51,000
Net income before tax	$ 120,000

Certain details of the summarized income statement are provided below.

1. Administrative and selling expenses include the following:

   (a) Donations to registered charities   3,000

   (b) Amortization/depreciation of tangible assets   12,000

   Note 1 At the end of the previous year, the undepreciated capital cost of certain asset classes was as follows:

Class 1	$80,000
Class 8	32,000
Class 10	50,000

   Note 2 During the current year, the company sold its land and building for $150,000 (land $40,000, building $110,000) and moved into leased premises. The original cost of the property was $130,000 (land $30,000, building $100,000). The building had an accounting book value of $70,000 at the time of sale.

   Note 3 The company owns several pieces of equipment. During the year, one unit that originally cost $10,000 and had a book value of $6,000 was sold for $8,000.

   (c) Legal fees:
   - Settling a dispute relating to the purchase of defective
     merchandise for sale   4,000
   - Reorganizing the corporation's share capital   8,000

   (d) Amortization   9,000

   Note: The current year's amortization expense applies to a number of intangible assets.
   - During the previous year (20X0), the company took over a competitor and purchased goodwill for $40,000 and a franchise (unlimited life) for $10,000.
   - During the current year, the franchise was sold for $8,000 when its book value for accounting purposes was $9,000. In addition, the company purchased an existing patent from a competitor for $20,000. The patent with a remaining legal life of 10 years was purchased on the first day of the current year.

2. Other income (expenses) includes the following:

Gain on sale of land	$10,000
Gain on sale of building	40,000
Gain on sale of equipment	2,000
Loss on sale of franchise	(1,000)
	$51,000

Required:

Determine the net income for tax purposes of Samson Enterprises for the 20X1 taxation year.

PROBLEM ELEVEN

East Side Products Ltd. (ESP) recently expanded its business by acquiring the operations of a competitor. As a result of the expansion, additional office space was needed. On the first day of the current fiscal year, ESP rented additional premises under a five-year lease agreement with two three-year renewal options. As an inducement to sign the lease, the landlord paid ESP $20,000 to cover part of the cost of improving the offices. Before occupying the premises, ESP spent $38,000 for necessary renovations.

Profits from business operations for the current year are expected to be $175,000. Because of the expansion, future years' profits are expected to exceed $550,000 annually.

For several years, ESP had invested its excess cash from annual profits in secure bonds. The proceeds from all of these bonds were used to acquire the competitor's business. For the next several years, the company will again invest excess cash in secure bonds; it expects to earn an average yield of 9%.

ESP is a Canadian-controlled private corporation. The first $500,000 of annual business profits are subject to a 15% tax rate. Annual business profits over $500,000 are taxed at 25%.

Required:

Describe the alternative tax treatments for the inducement payment. Which treatment should ESP use? Show a detailed calculation that compares the tax cost of each alternative.

Cases

CASE ONE   Patterson Traders Inc.

Patterson Traders Inc. has developed substantial cash reserves after several successive years of profitable operations. The company intends to use those reserves to diversify and has targeted two businesses for possible acquisition. Both target businesses are corporations. Patterson has stated that it wants to acquire only the individual assets of any business it acquires, rather than the shares of the corporation that owns the assets. In addition, Patterson has a strong cash position and so has no desire to incur debt.

Information relating to the two target businesses is as follows:

Assets	1	2
Land	$ 50,000	$ 40,000
Building	300,000	310,000
Equipment (manufacturing)	500,000	200,000
Goodwill	–0–	450,000
Licence	150,000	–0–
	$1,000,000	$1,000,000

Both target companies are manufacturers, though their products are different. Both are expected to generate annual profits of $400,000 before amortization/depreciation and income taxes.

One of the products of business 1 is manufactured under licence. The licence agreement extends for 15 years and stipulates payment of a royalty based on sales volume. The licensee has an option to renew the licence at the end of the 15-year period subject to a renegotiation of the royalty percentage.

Currently, the cash reserves are invested in secure bonds, which earn interest at 12% annually. These cash reserves are not sufficient to acquire both businesses, and so Patterson will acquire only one of them. The company intends to use the profits of the acquired business to again build up a cash reserve, which will be invested in secure bonds. The corporate tax rate is 25%.

Required:

Advise Patterson Traders whether it should purchase business 1 or business 2.

CASE TWO   Platt Enterprises Ltd.

Platt Enterprises started a wholesale business two years ago and has made a profit from the beginning. To date, the company has been storing merchandise inventory in a public warehouse, but the business has grown to a point where this policy is now cumbersome.

The company expects to enjoy unusually rapid growth for the next five years until it achieves a steady market share. Platt is seeking to acquire warehouse space for its exclusive use that will carry it through the growth period. After five years, it intends to obtain a more permanent space designed and built for its own specific needs.

A suitable site has been found that will meet Platt's needs for the next five years. The owner of the property has given Platt two options. Under the first of these, Platt would purchase the land and building for $200,000 ($50,000 for land, $150,000 for the building). Under the second, Platt would lease the land and building for five years at an annual rent equal to 11% of the property's current value ($200,000). The lease would be a net lease requiring Platt to pay for all operating costs associated with the property, including property taxes, insurance, utilities, and maintenance.

The company is having difficulty choosing between the two options. The rental rate of 11% of the property's value does not seem excessive, considering that the company can borrow funds at 10% (it currently has no major debt). In fact, there are sufficient cash resources to purchase the property with cash. The purchase option also appears attractive, even though the land and building will have to be sold at the end of five years. In particular, the company is aware that recent studies of the local real estate market predict that warehouse properties will increase in value at the rate of 5% annually for the next eight years.

Platt realizes that the same issue will have to be examined again in five years. A local real estate developer who is planning a long-term industrial real estate development is aware of Platt's five-year plan. The developer has indicated that it is prepared to design and construct a building for Platt that will be ready by the end of the five-year period. The developer has also indicated that a group of investors wants to own the proposed property and lease it to Platt under a long-term lease arrangement. Of course, Platt could also choose to own the future property. Platt Enterprises is subject to a 25% tax rate.

Required:

1. Prepare an analysis, and advise Platt Enterprises as to which option is most advantageous. You may assume that the future property needed after five years will be obtained through the lease arrangement suggested by the developer.

2. To what extent, if any, would your decision be affected if it were assumed that the future property needed after five years will be purchased by Platt, rather than leased?

Income from Property

Many individual and corporate taxpayers find themselves, at one time or another, in the enviable position of having excess cash flow available for investment. The marketplace abounds with investment opportunities in bonds, debentures, mortgages, bank certificates, shares of public and private corporations, life insurance, and real estate. The method by which the investment's income or loss is taxed will affect the ultimate returns that can be achieved on each type of investment.

This chapter will define and discuss the term "property income for tax purposes" and establish the basic rules that affect its determination. Specifically, this chapter covers the following areas:

1. It defines the term "property income" and gives the general scope of that definition.

2. It examines the basic rules for determining all types of property income.

3. It highlights the unique aspects of the primary types of investment income.

4. It reviews the impact that the taxation of property income has on investment and management decisions.

I. Income from Property Defined

As is the case with other significant terms, the *Income Tax Act* does not provide a specific definition of property income. However, a series of common-law court decisions has established that income from property can generally be defined as the return on invested capital where little or no time, labour, or attention has been expended by the investor in producing the return.[1] In this context, income from property includes the following:

1. The return of *dividend income* on the investment in capital shares of public and private corporations.

2. The return of *interest income* on investments in bank deposits, loans, mortgages, bonds, and debentures.

3. The return of *rental income* on the ownership of real estate or other tangible property.

4. The *royalty income* on the ownership of properties, such as patents and mineral rights.

In each case, property income is the annual or regular return received for allowing another party to use one's property. It does *not* include the gain or loss that may result from the sale of that property. The gain or loss on the sale of shares, for example, is normally classified as a capital gain or loss (see Chapter 8). Similarly, if rental real estate is sold, the sale may result in a gain in excess of the property's original cost as well as a recapture of capital cost allowance or a terminal loss. In this case, the gain in excess of the original cost is a capital gain, rather than property income. However, because capital cost allowance (CCA) was originally deducted to determine the property income earned from rents, any recapture of the CCA is property income, and any terminal loss is a property loss.

Further, it must be noted that the nature of the income does not, in itself, qualify the item as property income. To qualify as property income, interest must be earned in a relatively passive way, without the commitment of significant time, labour, and attention by the owner. Interest income earned by a small or large financial institution is not property income but *business* income because the taxpayer must expend significant effort in order to generate that income.

---

1   *Ginsberg v. MNR*, 53 DTC 445; IT-434R.

Having the income classified as business income, rather than property income, will not, in most cases, alter the method by which the income is calculated. However, there are a few circumstances in which a difference will occur; some of these *will* be referred to in this chapter.

II. General Rules for Determining Property Income

The general rules for establishing a taxpayer's property (investment) income are the same as those used for determining income from business. The *Income Tax Act* simply states that a taxpayer's income from property for the year is "the profit therefrom."[2] The term *property income* reflects the *net* property income; that is, it takes into account not only the revenues from such sources but also the related expenses incurred to earn those revenues.

Taxpayers generally understand what types of expenses are deductible from their business income; many are not so informed with respect to their investment income. The tax return that individuals must file does not directly indicate that property income is determined net of expenses. It does require that gross income from interest and dividends be included as a separate item; later in the return, certain undescribed deductions can be made. This unusual format, which is not used for business or rental income, confuses many individuals, who wonder how they can deduct expenses from property income.

In the chapter on business income, it was stated that profit is first determined in accordance with well-accepted business principles as interpreted by the courts and with generally accepted accounting principles (GAAP); this income is further modified by applying certain general limitations to the deduction of expenses; these, in turn, may be affected by two lists of specific exceptions. The same process is used to determine income from property. Using the guidelines established in Chapter 5, it can be said that, in general terms, expenses incurred to earn property income can be deducted for tax purposes provided that

(a) they are incurred for the purpose of earning income that is taxable;

(b) they are not an expenditure of a capital nature, an expenditure on the account of capital, or depreciation and amortization;

(c) they are not a reserve;

(d) they are not a personal or living expense; and

(e) they are reasonable under the circumstances.

Before continuing with this chapter, the reader may find it useful to review parts of Chapter 5 on business income—especially the area that describes the major exceptions to the above general rules—and apply them to the determination of property income. Also, it should be noted that certain interest and dividends from qualified investments held by an individual's TFSA (Tax-Free Savings Account) may be exempt from tax (see Chapter 9, Part VI).

Two further items require comment before the unique aspects of the various types of property income are examined.

A. Property Income and the Taxation Year

The taxation year for an individual is the calendar year; for a corporation, it is the fiscal year. All of an individual's property income must be determined annually on a taxation year coinciding with the calendar year. Corporations, of course, would use the fiscal period, as is generally required.

B. The Deduction of Interest Expense

Although interest expense incurred on a loan used to acquire an investment is on the account of capital, an exception to this general limitation permits the deduction of interest expense if the loan was incurred to acquire property that is used to generate

---

2   ITA 9(1).

property income.[3] This means that interest on loans used to purchase investments, such as bonds, bank certificates, shares of corporations, and real estate, is deductible against the interest, dividends, and rental income earned.

It is important that the taxpayer establish, through documentation, that a specific loan was used for the purpose of making an investment, since this ensures that interest can be deducted from income.[4] Consider, for example, a taxpayer, Mr. L, who intends to purchase a $10,000 personal automobile and, at the same time, invest $10,000 in shares. However, because Mr. L has only $13,000 of cash available, he must arrange a loan of $7,000 to fund the total cost. If the bank loan funds were added to the cash balance of $13,000 before the two purchases were made, it would be difficult to establish whether the loan was used entirely for the investment, entirely for the personal automobile, or for both. Obviously, in this situation Mr. L wants the loan to be used for the acquisition of shares; that way, the interest on it can be deducted from property income. However, unless he can prove that the loan was used for this purpose, the best that the tax authorities would accept would be that the loan was allocated to both purchases.

Establishing the purpose for which funds are used is best done by maintaining a separate bank account for investment activities. In the above example, if the loan is first deposited in an investment bank account and the only disbursements from that account are for investments, there is no question as to the use of the loan.

Individual taxpayers can borrow money for investments by increasing the mortgage on their personal residence. When this is done, the portion of the mortgage interest that was used to make the investment is deductible for tax purposes. Again, when using this source of financing, it must be shown that the mortgage funds were used to purchase the investment; also, again, a separate bank account is useful.

When individuals are in a position to acquire both personal assets and investment assets, they should apply the following principles with respect to loan financing in order to maximize their after-tax cash flow:

1. Personal assets should, to the extent possible, be acquired with excess cash. Such assets—cars, a house, a cottage, and the like—can then be used as collateral to obtain loans for investment purposes.

2. When individuals have both personal and investment loans, excess cash should first be used to repay the personal loans that are incurring non-deductible interest. It is important that separate loans be arranged for personal use and investment use.

It is not uncommon for an individual to have a personal loan outstanding while also owning clear-title investments yielding taxable income. Consider the situation where an individual has a personal loan outstanding of $10,000 (to acquire a cottage) but also owns bonds of $10,000. If both the loan and the investment bear interest at 10% and the rate of personal tax is 45%, the after-tax return to the individual is minus $450 annually, calculated as shown below.

This individual, by cashing in the bonds and paying off the loan, would at least be breaking even, as there would be no interest income and no interest expense.

---

3   ITA 20(1)(c); IT-533—Internet deductibility and related issues.
4   *The Queen v. Bronfman Trust*, 87 DTC 5097; *Singleton v. Canada*, 2001 DTC 5533 (S.C.C); *Ludco Enterprises Ltd. v. Canada*, 2001 DTC 5505 (S.C.C).

Cash in:	
Interest income on bond at 10%	$1,000
Less tax at 45%	(450)
Net income	550
Cash out:	
Interest paid on personal loan (not deductible)	(1,000)
Net cash cost	$ (450)

The above example demonstrates that it is worthwhile to use excess cash to reduce personal loans that are incurring non-deductible interest. It is important to realize that using excess cash in this manner does not prevent the taxpayer from making other investments when opportunities arise. A reduced personal debt makes for an expanded borrowing capacity, which, in turn, makes loans for investment purposes easier to obtain.

In summary, individuals who are in a position to acquire both personal-use and investment assets must take care to plan the related loans in a manner that will generate the greatest after-tax cash flow.

III. The Unique Features of Property Income

All of the major types of property income—interest, dividends, rentals—have distinguishing features, which are reviewed below.

A. Interest Income

"Interest income" is defined as the compensation received for the use of borrowed funds. In most circumstances, the amount of interest income earned on a debt obligation is readily identifiable from the stated interest rate attached to the obligation. However, in some situations, a loan is made without interest, or at a low rate of interest, but with the requirement that the debtor repay an amount greater than the original principal of the loan. To the extent that the additional payment of principal reflects the normal rate of interest that would have been charged on the particular transaction, that extra amount is treated as interest income. If, however, the extra principal amounts to more than normal interest, such amount is usually treated as a capital gain.[5]

- **Recognition of income** Different types of debt obligations require the payment of interest to the creditor at different times. Some debt obligations require that regular interest payments be made on a monthly, quarterly, semi-annual, or annual basis over the term of the loan. Others permit interest to be compounded and paid only at the end of the term of the loan. The timing of income recognition for tax purposes is important because it affects the net after-tax cash flow and, by extension, the yield on a particular investment.

All *corporations*, private and public, must recognize income according to the normal rules for profit determination and do so on an accrual basis.[6] This means that a corporation must include interest as income as it is earned on a daily basis, even though the interest may not have been received and may not be receivable until some future time.

---

5 IT-396R, paragraph 12; ITA 16(1).
6 ITA 12(1)(c), (3); IT-396R.

Situation: A corporation that has a December 31 taxation year end loans $10,000 on October 1, 20X1. The debtor is to repay the loan in two years. Interest is charged at the rate of 10% compounded annually and is payable in full at the end of the two-year period.

Analysis: Total interest on loan:

Year 1—10% × $10,000	$1,000
Year 2—10% × ($10,000 + $1,000)	1,100
	$2,100

Recognition of income by taxation year:

(20X1)   *Oct–Dec. 31*

$$\frac{92 \text{ days}}{365 \text{ days}} \times \$1,000 = \qquad \$\ 252$$

(20X2)   *Jan–Oct 1*

$$\frac{273}{365} \times \$1,000 = \qquad \$\ 748$$

plus   *Oct–Dec 31*

$$\frac{92}{365} \times \$1,100 = \qquad 277$$

$$\$1,025$$

(20X3)

$$\frac{273}{365} \times \$1,100 = \qquad \$\ 823$$

Total interest (20X1 + 20X2 + 20X3) $2,100

It can be onerous to pay tax in advance of the receipt of interest income when interest is compounded and payment is delayed over a long period of time.

Individuals, unlike corporations, have at their disposal, within a certain time limitation, the following three methods for recognizing interest income:[7]

- the receivable method
- the cash method
- the anniversary day accrual method

Individuals are entitled to use the receivable method or the cash method for a given investment, subject to the overriding rules of the anniversary day accrual method. Once the method is chosen it must then be used consistently for that investment. For example, one may choose to use the cash method for investment A and the annual accrual method for investment B.

Under the *receivable* method, interest is included in income only when the amount is legally due and payable. For example, a corporate bond may require interest to be paid semi-annually on June 15 and December 15 of each year. If at the end of the taxation year (December 31) the December 15 payment has not been received, it must still be included in that year's income because it is legally due and receivable.

Under the *cash* method, interest income is taken into income for tax purposes only if it has been received by the individual in the year.

When an investment requires that interest be paid after a long period of time (longer than one year), it appears that choosing the cash method or the receivable method would delay the payment of tax until the interest is received or becomes receivable. In fact, that is not the case. Even though the individual may choose either the cash or the receivable method, an overriding rule referred to as the *anniversary day accrual method* requires that interest income be recognized for every 12-month period from the date the investment was

---

7   ITA 12(1)(c), (4); IT-396R.

made.[8] This means that interest-income recognition can be deferred for only a limited period. Note that individuals cannot use the normal accrual method of accruing interest on a daily basis, as can corporations and partnerships. Consider the following situation:

Situation: An individual loans $100,000 on February 1, 20X1. The loan is to be repaid by the debtor in two years, on January 31, 20X3. Interest is charged at the rate of 12%, compounded annually, and is payable in full at the end of two years.

Analysis: Total interest earned on the loan is as follows:

Year 1: (12% × $100,000)	$12,000
Year 2: (12% × [$100,000 + $12,000])	13,440
	$25,440

Individuals determine income on a calendar-year basis. In this situation, the daily accrual method cannot be used, and no income is recognized in 20X1. The cash method and the receivable method would delay the recognition of interest income until the 20X3 taxation year. However, because of the anniversary day accrual method requirement, neither of these methods can be used. Under the special annual accrual method, interest must be recognized every 12 months from February 1, 20X1, until the end of the term of the loan. The income under this method is recognized as follows:

(20X1)	NIL
(20X2)	
February 1, 20X1, to January 31, 20X2	$12,000
(20X3)	
February 1, 20X2, to January 31, 20X3	$13,440
Total interest	$25,440

- **Foreign interest**   Interest earned on investments in a foreign country is recognized in terms of Canadian dollars under the same rules described above. In many cases, the foreign payer withholds an amount as payment of foreign tax. When foreign taxes are withheld from the payment, the full amount of interest, before the amount is withheld, must be included in property income. However, Canadian tax on this foreign income can be reduced through a foreign tax credit.[9]

  The foreign tax credit, which is described in a later chapter, reduces Canadian tax only to the extent that Canadian taxes are paid in the same year. This means that taxpayers who are forced to use the accrual method for recognizing foreign interest may pay Canadian taxes in the years before the interest is paid and the foreign tax is withheld. This would preclude the use of the foreign tax credit. In such circumstances, the taxpayer can, as an alternative, treat the foreign tax as an expense against property income. While this alleviates the problem somewhat, it does result in an element of double taxation. If foreign investments are contemplated, it is important that the payment of interest income coincide with its inclusion in income for tax purposes.

- **Life insurance policies**   Certain life insurance policies include both a savings component and a life insurance component (whole life insurance). Other policies are designed solely to provide life insurance protection (term life insurance). When a life insurance policy includes a savings element that accumulates interest returns, special rules govern the tax treatment of those returns. With respect to policies issued after

---

8   ITA 12(11), (4); IT-396R, paragraph 19.
9   ITA 126(1), (2).

1989, the tax treatment of earnings is similar to that for other investment vehicles—income must be reported annually.[10] However, certain policies are exempt from these rules. When the exemption applies, the combination of life insurance and savings can amount to a significant long-term tax deferral. The rules governing life insurance policies are complex and beyond the scope of this text. Before acquiring a new policy, a taxpayer should thoroughly investigate the tax treatment of its related investment returns.

• **Deductions from interest income**   Because property income is the "profit therefrom," interest income from property is calculated on a net basis—that is, as the revenue less the expenses incurred to earn the revenue. The types of expenses permitted can be determined by referring to the general rules and list of specific exceptions outlined in Chapter 5. For convenience, some of the typical expenses incurred to earn interest income are listed below.

- Interest expense on loans used to acquire interest-bearing investments.[11]
- Investment counselling fees.[12]
- Costs incurred to obtain a loan, such as legal fees, mortgage appraisal fees, and registration fees (amortized over five years at the rate of one-fifth per year).[13]
- Fees paid to managers of investment portfolios.
- Safe-custody costs, such as safety deposit box fees or fees paid to a financial institution for holding securities.
- Accounting fees for record-keeping and determination of income from property.
- Reserves or complete deductions for interest income that has been accrued but is not collectible because of the debtor's inability to pay.[14]

If the expenses incurred exceed the interest income, a loss from property occurs that can be offset against the taxpayer's other sources of income, in accordance with the general aggregating formula described in Chapter 3 and the "reasonable expectation of profit" test reviewed in Chapter 5.

B. Dividend Income

Dividends are the returns provided on the investment in shares of a corporation; they reflect the distribution of a portion of the corporation's profits to the shareholders. Ultimately, shareholders of corporations are individuals, but individuals can own shares in a corporation that, in turn, owns shares of other corporations. In other words, dividend income can be received by both individuals and corporations.

Exhibit 7-1 shows two basic structures of corporate ownership and dividend flows. Structure A consists of a single Corporation X, which is owned directly by an individual shareholder. In this situation, Corporation X earns income that is subject to tax.

Exhibit 7-1:

Simple Structure of Corporate Ownership

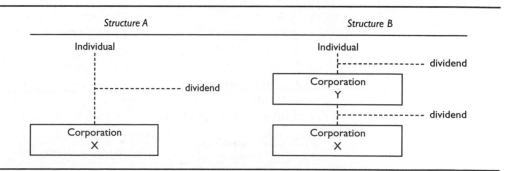

---

10 ITA 12.2(1); IT-87R2.
11 ITA 20(1)(c); *Stewart v. The Queen*, 2002 SCC 46.
12 ITA 20(1)(bb).
13 ITA 20(1)(e), (e.1).
14 ITA 20(1)(l).

The after-tax profits, which are referred to as retained earnings for accounting purposes, can be either retained by the corporation or distributed in whole or in part to the shareholder. If the earnings are retained, the value of the corporation, and therefore of its shares, will rise, increasing the potential for a capital gain when the shares are ultimately sold. Correspondingly, if the earnings are distributed as dividends, the share value will decline, eliminating the capital gain potential and substituting it with dividend income to the shareholder. In summary, corporate earnings are taxed in the hands of the shareholder, either as dividends (property income) or as capital gains, depending on whether or not the corporate profits are distributed.

Under structure A, the profits of Corporation X are subject to tax, and those after-tax profits are subject to a second level of tax when received as a dividend by the individual shareholder.

In comparison, structure B consists of Corporation X, whose shareholder is Corporation Y. The shareholder of Corporation Y is the individual. Under this structure, the after-tax profits earned by Corporation X are distributed and received as dividend income (property income) by Corporation Y. This increases the earnings of Corporation Y, which can either retain those earnings or distribute them as dividends to its shareholder (the individual). In this case, the after-tax profits of Corporation X are received as dividend income for tax purposes by both Corporation Y and the individual.

It would appear from the above discussion that the corporate profits in structure A are subject to double taxation and those in structure B to triple taxation. The methods by which dividends are included in income for individuals and corporations are designed to deal with the problem of multiple taxation. In some situations, multiple taxation of corporate profits is eliminated; in other situations, there remains some element of double taxation.

- **Dividends received by corporations**   Dividends paid by one corporation to another are included in the recipient's *net income for tax purposes* when they are received.[15] You will recall that the rate of corporate tax is applied to a base referred to as the corporation's *taxable income*. As described in Chapter 3, the taxable income of a corporation is determined by reducing net income for tax purposes by certain specific items, one of which is dividends received from other taxable Canadian corporations.[16] The result of this in-and-out calculation is that the dividends received by one Canadian corporation from another Canadian corporation are excluded from taxable income and are therefore not subject to normal tax. When Canadian dividends are excluded from taxable income, the possibility of multiple taxation from the flow of after-tax profits between corporations is eliminated. In Exhibit 7-1, for example, the dividends paid by Corporation X are not taxable to the shareholder, Corporation Y. (See Chapter 13 for certain exceptions.)

On the other hand, dividends received by a Canadian corporation from a *foreign* corporation are excluded from taxable income only if the foreign corporation qualifies as a foreign affiliate.[17] A foreign corporation qualifies as a foreign affiliate of a Canadian corporation if the owner's equity percentage in the *foreign* corporation is not less than 10%.

The subject of intercorporate dividends has important tax planning implications. A more detailed analysis of intercorporate dividends is carried out in Part Three of this text, which examines the complete corporate structure.

- **Dividends received by individuals**   Dividends earned by an individual on investments in taxable Canadian corporate shares are included in the individual's net income for tax purposes when received. The amount that must be included in the individual's income is not the actual amount received but rather an amount equal to

---

15 ITA 12(1)(j), (k), 82(1)(a); IT-67R3.
16 ITA 112(1).
17 ITA 113(1), 95(1).

either 125% *or* 138% of the dividend received.[18] All taxable dividends from *Canadian public corporations* (corporations whose shares are traded on a stock exchange) are grossed-up to include 138% of the dividend. Dividends received from *Canadian private corporations* are grossed-up to include 125% or 138% of the dividend depending on the source of the corporation's income. If the private corporation's income is investment income or business income that is entitled to a special low tax rate (small business deduction—see Chapters 11 and 13) then dividends from these sources are grossed-up to include 125% of the dividend. However, if the source is business income that is *not* entitled to the special low tax rate (no small-business deduction) the dividends from this source are grossed-up to include 138% of the dividend. For identification purposes dividends that require a 138% inclusion are referred to as *eligible dividends*. Those requiring a 125% inclusion are referred to as *non-eligible dividends*. A more detailed description of eligible and non-eligible dividends is provided in Chapter 10. While this gross-up of the dividend appears unfair, it must be viewed as part of an overall scheme to reduce the impact of double taxation when after-tax corporate profits are distributed and taxed a second time in the hands of individual shareholders. This scheme is summarized below.

1. Dividends received by individuals are grossed up to include 125% or 138% of the dividend when included in income. The gross-up supposedly reflects the corporate taxes already paid by the corporation on its income. In theory, the grossed-up dividend represents the pre-tax income earned by the corporation that has been distributed as a dividend.

2. The individual shareholders determine their tax on the same corporate earnings reflected in the grossed-up dividend by applying the individual tax rate to income. At this point, the corporate profits have been taxed twice.

3. The individual tax on the grossed-up dividend is then reduced by the amount of corporate tax that has already been paid on the same income. This is referred to as a "dividend tax credit." The dividend tax credit is more or less equal (depending on the provincial tax rate) to the gross-up because the gross-up, at least in theory, reflects the corporate taxes that have been paid.

Supposedly, this system eliminates double taxation by taxing the corporate income twice and then reducing personal taxes by the corporate taxes paid. However, the fixed inclusion rates of 125% and 138% make the assumption that corporate taxes are always 20% or 27.5% respectively. This, as has already been shown, is not always the case. The examples below demonstrate how the system works when the corporate tax rates are 20% or 27.5% and the individual tax rate is 45%.

Note that in these examples, the total tax paid by the corporation and the individual together is $45 on $100 of corporate profits. This is equal to the personal rate of tax of 45% and is what the individual would have paid if the corporation had not existed and the profits had been earned directly by the individual. The elimination of double taxation works in these examples only because the corporate tax rates are assumed to be 20% or 27.5%, which is consistent with the gross-up and dividend tax credit calculation. But when corporate taxes are greater, the dividend tax credit is not sufficient and some double taxation occurs. The theoretical system also breaks down when individual provinces do not apply a full dividend tax credit.

---

18 ITA 12(1)(j), 82(1)(b); IT-67R3.

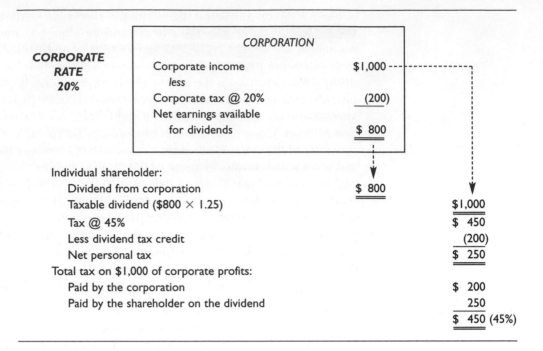

**CORPORATE
RATE
20%**

CORPORATION	
Corporate income	$1,000
less	
Corporate tax @ 20%	(200)
Net earnings available for dividends	$ 800

Individual shareholder:

Dividend from corporation	$ 800	
Taxable dividend ($800 × 1.25)		$1,000
Tax @ 45%		$ 450
Less dividend tax credit		(200)
Net personal tax		$ 250
Total tax on $1,000 of corporate profits:		
Paid by the corporation		$ 200
Paid by the shareholder on the dividend		250
		$ 450 (45%)

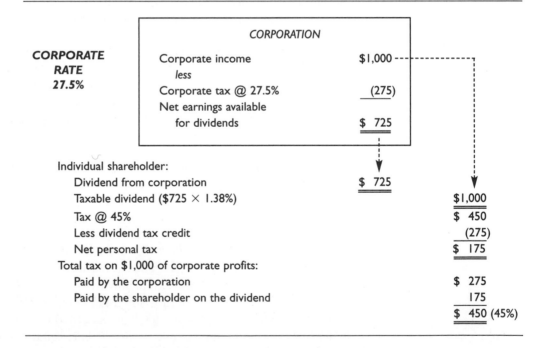

**CORPORATE
RATE
27.5%**

CORPORATION	
Corporate income	$1,000
less	
Corporate tax @ 27.5%	(275)
Net earnings available for dividends	$ 725

Individual shareholder:

Dividend from corporation	$ 725	
Taxable dividend ($725 × 1.38%)		$1,000
Tax @ 45%		$ 450
Less dividend tax credit		(275)
Net personal tax		$ 175
Total tax on $1,000 of corporate profits:		
Paid by the corporation		$ 275
Paid by the shareholder on the dividend		175
		$ 450 (45%)

Individuals receiving dividends from *foreign* corporations are not subject to the gross-up and dividend tax credit treatment described here. Instead, the actual amount of dividends from foreign corporations (before any withholding taxes) is included in income in the year received.[19] In effect, this tax treatment is identical to the treatment given to foreign-interest income described earlier in this chapter.

The tax treatment of dividends must also be examined in the context of its relationship to corporate finance and individual investment strategies. This is done in greater detail in several subsequent chapters.

---

19 ITA 12(1)(k), 90.

• **Stock dividends**   When a corporation issues additional shares in lieu of a cash dividend, the individual shareholders are considered to be receiving stock dividends. From the corporation's perspective, a stock dividend simply transfers a dollar amount from its retained earnings to its permanent capital account. From the shareholder's perspective, the amount transferred to the capital account is deemed to be a taxable dividend; if the shareholder is an individual, this amount is subject to the normal treatment, which includes a gross-up and dividend tax credit.[20]

In effect, a stock dividend is a forced reinvestment of dividend returns in the capital shares of the corporation, although no cash has traded hands. If shareholders wish to receive a cash return on the investment, they are free to sell all or a portion of the stock dividend shares. Because the value of the shares has already been included in income as a dividend, the stock dividend shares are considered to have been acquired at a cost equal to the increase in the paid-up capital of the shares of the issuing corporation (this is often equal to the trading value of shares at the issue date), and any gain or loss on their disposition is determined according to the normal capital gain treatment reviewed in Chapter 8.

C. Rental Income

Rental income is the compensation received for allowing another party to use one's tangible property. In most cases, rental income is derived from the ownership of real estate (land and buildings). It is not uncommon for taxpayers to derive rental income from other tangible assets, such as equipment, even though they are not in the leasing business. However, this chapter emphasizes the return of rental income from real estate.

• **Recognition of income**   Of the three general types of property income discussed in this chapter, rental income most conforms to the normal rules of profit determination. Accordingly, rental revenue is included in income for tax purposes on the accrual basis when earned, rather than when actually received. If rent payments are received in advance, revenue recognition can be delayed and included in the particular year to which the advance payment applies.

• **Deductions from rental income**   As with other types of property income, the permitted deductions from rental revenue are in accordance with the normal rules of profit determination for business that were outlined in Chapter 5. The following are some of the deductible expenses typically incurred to earn rental revenue:

- interest expenses incurred on loans used to acquire the rental property or to fund repairs and improvements
- costs incurred to obtain loan financing, such as mortgage fees, legal fees, and appraisal fees (amortized over five years at one-fifth of the cost per year)
- insurance expense
- property taxes
- repairs to the property of a non-capital nature
- maintenance costs, such as cleaning, lawn care, and snow and garbage removal
- utility costs (heat, power, and water)
- landscaping costs around a building, even though such costs may be of a capital nature
- capital cost allowance on the building as well as on other related tangible assets, such as furniture and equipment
- salaries and wages paid to employees who supervise and/or maintain the property

---

20 ITA 248(1); IT-88R2.

- property management fees paid to an independent property management organization
- accounting costs for record-keeping and income determination
- costs incurred to collect rents
- advertising

Whether or not an owner incurs such expenses depends on the nature of the property and also on the nature of the lease arrangements. Rental income is derived under two basic types of leases: the gross lease and the net lease. A gross rental agreement requires that the tenant pay only a specific rent; the owner (landlord) is responsible for all expenses associated with the property. A complete net lease, on the other hand, requires that the tenant pay a basic rent as well as all of the costs associated with the running of the property with the exception of financing costs. The gross lease and the complete net lease are the extremes; many lease arrangements fall somewhere between the two.

When the total expenses incurred by an owner exceed the annual rental revenue, a loss from property occurs. In accordance with the aggregating formula for determining a taxpayer's net income for tax purposes, the property loss from rentals can be offset against all other sources of income, such as employment income, business income, and capital gains (subject to the restriction discussed below).

- **Special rules for capital cost allowance** Capital cost allowance, terminal losses, and recapture of capital cost allowance all form part of the net income calculation for rental properties. There are two special rules that apply only to rental properties; together, they limit the treatment of capital cost allowance.

1. Capital cost allowance on rental properties can be deducted only to the extent that it does not create or increase a net loss from all rental properties combined.[21]

2. Each rental building having a cost of $50,000 or more must be held in a separate capital cost allowance class. This is contrary to the normal requirement that assets of a similar class be pooled.[22]

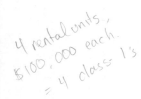
4 rental units, $100,000 each. = 4 class 1's

The above exceptions do not change the total capital cost allowance deductions or the income recognized over the full life of the rental property, but they can be a limiting factor on an annual basis, as demonstrated below.

Situation: A taxpayer owns two residential rental properties. The original cost of the buildings (exclusive of land) was $100,000 for building A and $200,000 for building B. In 20X1, these properties generated the following income or loss:

	Building A	Building B
Gross rental revenue	$ 20,000	$ 30,000
less		
Expenses, other than capital cost allowance	(12,000)	(32,000)
Income (loss) before capital cost allowance	$ 8,000	$ (2,000)

Analysis: Both buildings qualify as class 1 properties and have a maximum capital cost allowance rate of 4% annually. However, because each building cost more than $50,000, each falls into a separate pool. Assuming that buildings A and B have an undepreciated capital cost

---

21 Regulation 1100(11); IT-195R4.
22 Regulation 1101(1ac); IT-274R.

allowance balance of $90,000 and $170,000, respectively, the maximum capital cost allowance available for 20X1 is as follows:

	Class I A	Class I B	Total
Undepreciated capital	$90,000	$170,000	$260,000
Maximum capital cost allowance available (4%)	$ 3,600	$ 6,800	$ 10,400

Although a maximum of $10,400 of capital cost allowance is available, the actual capital cost allowance that can be claimed in 20X1 is $6,000, calculated as follows:

Net rental income (before capital cost allowance) on property A	$ 8,000
Net rental loss (before capital cost allowance) on property B	(2,000)
Combined rental income	6,000
Capital cost allowance allowed	6,000
Net rental income for tax purposes	NIL

In this example, the $6,000 of capital cost allowance can be claimed partly from the building A class and partly from the building B class, in any proportion up to the maximum available for each class. Alternatively, because the building B class has a $6,800 maximum available, the full $6,000 could be claimed from it.

If the calculation of rental income *before* capital cost allowance results in a combined loss, no capital cost allowance can be claimed in that year. The combined *loss before capital cost allowance* can be offset against other sources of income.

The requirement that each building costing $50,000 or more be placed in its own separate class has a significant impact when the property is sold. Because there is only one asset in each pool, any sale will always trigger the recognition of either a recapture of capital cost allowance or a terminal loss, depending on whether the selling price is greater than or less than the undepreciated balance of the building. In most cases, the selling price is greater than the undepreciated balance. This means that the sale of a rental building normally results in a recapture, even when a new building is acquired in the same year. This, of course, diminishes the amount of after-tax proceeds available for investment—a factor that must be considered in any capital budgeting analysis.

Often, certain furnishings, such as stoves, refrigerators, dishwashers, washers, and dryers, are part of the premises rented to a tenant. When this is the case, part of the rental income is for those furnishings. The amount of capital cost allowance that can be claimed on the furnishings cannot exceed the net rental income from the property.[23] However, assets of this nature are pooled together under the same class.

In some circumstances, an investor will acquire only part ownership in a building along with other owners under tenancy in common. If the cost of the shared building is less than $50,000, it can be pooled with other acquisitions in the same class. From a tax point of view, it is advantageous to acquire several partial ownerships under $50,000, rather than a lesser number of wholly owned buildings over $50,000, because sales and acquisitions can then be pooled to avoid recapture of capital cost

---

23 Regulation 1100(15).

allowance. Similarly, condominiums purchased in separate complexes can be pooled together if each costs less than $50,000. However, condominium units purchased in the same complex cannot be pooled together if their aggregate cost is over $50,000.[24]

The rules that limit the amount of capital cost allowance and create separate classifications for rental properties do not apply to a corporation or partnership of corporations "whose *principal business* [is] the leasing, rental, development or sale of real property owned by it."[25]

It should also be noted that the amount of capital cost allowance may be restricted on properties other than real estate. When other types of property (leasing property—equipment, vehicles, and so on) are leased, the amount of capital cost allowance in any year is limited to net rental income except for corporations whose principal business is the leasing or sale of such property.[26] This means that taxpayers who invest in leasing properties cannot create a loss by claiming capital cost allowance.

D. Royalty Income

Royalties are normally treated as property income from an investment when they are received for the use of owned property such as a trademark, copyright, patent, or other similar intangible properties when the taxpayer has acquired these properties by a purchase, gift, or inheritance. In other words, the royalties earned required little, if any, effort by the owner to achieve the revenue. For example, if you purchase a copyright, the royalties received from licensing the copyright to others is considered to be property income.

Royalty income may also be classified as business income. An author who writes a book or a musician who writes a music score and receives royalties for licensing the copyright is considered to have earned business income. In these situations, the royalties represent the revenue earned from the authors' businesses and considerable effort is made to earn that income.

IV. Impact on Investment Decisions

This chapter has examined the tax treatment of the basic types of investment returns—dividends, and rentals. It is readily apparent that the amount of tax on each of these basic types is different as is the timing of that tax. Consequently, the ultimate after-tax yields vary considerably. The tax treatment of the basic investments is summarized below. The discussion does not include investing in a TFSA (Tax-Free Savings Account) by an individual (see Chapter 9, Part VI).

A. Cash Flow and Return on Investment

• **Interest-bearing securities**   The return of interest is fully taxed when earned or, for individuals, at least every 12 months from the date the investment is made.

• **Investments in corporate shares**   In most cases, such investments present a combined annual yield in the form of both dividend payments and a growth in value of the shares. The dividend is taxed when received; however, for individuals, the dividend tax credit reduces the effective rate of tax. For example, as was previously demonstrated, an individual in a 45% tax bracket pays tax of $175, net of the dividend tax credit, on a cash dividend of $725 (grossed up to $1,000). Therefore, the effective tax rate on eligible dividends for this taxpayer is only 24% (175/725 = 24%).[27]

---

24 IT-274R.
25 Regulation 1100(12); IT-371.
26 Regulations 1100(15) to (20); IT-443.
27 Based on theoretical application of the 2012/2013 federal *and* provincial dividend tax credit. Actual rates should be consulted before relationships between dividends and capital gains are determined.

To the extent that common share investments grow in value, the resulting profit normally will be a capital gain for tax purposes. As described in the next chapter, only one-half of the capital gain is taxable, and the gain is taxed when the investment is sold, rather than when the growth in value occurs. Therefore, the effective rate of tax on capital growth for a person in a 45% tax bracket is 23% ($\frac{1}{2} \times 45\% = 22.5\%$; say, 23%), and tax is delayed until the gain is realized.

• **Real estate investments**   Investments in this type of property yield both rental income, which is fully taxable annually when earned, and capital growth, which is taxed as a capital gain only when the property is sold.

A distinguishing feature of this type of investment is that the cost of the building can be deducted as capital cost allowance against rental income over future years. This deduction is valuable because it is permitted, even though most rental buildings do not decline in value but rather appreciate in value. Of course, when the property is sold, the prior capital cost allowance may be recaptured and taxed at that time. The result is that rental income, due to the shelter of capital cost allowance, is not fully taxed until the property is sold. This delay enhances after-tax yields.

Further, to the extent that the property appreciates beyond the original cost, the gain is a capital gain and is not fully taxed until realized.

The dramatic impact of all this is demonstrated in the following situation:

Situation: An individual has the opportunity to invest $100,000 in one of three separate investments, each of which provides an annual pre-tax yield of 12%.

Investment 1
A bond paying annual interest of 12%.

Investment 2
Common shares of a public corporation that are expected to have an annual yield of 12%, broken down as follows:

Dividends	4%
Capital growth	8%
	12%

Investment 3
A residential rental property consisting of land ($10,000) and building ($90,000) yielding 12% as follows:

Net rents (before capital cost allowance)	7%
Capital growth	5%
	12%

The investment funds are available for only five years, at which time the investment will be sold and the funds used for other purposes. The individual is in a personal marginal tax bracket of 45%. All annual cash returns can be reinvested in an interest account yielding 12% annually.

Analysis: When analyzing the alternatives, it is first necessary to determine the after-tax yield for each type of return. The individual is in a 45% tax bracket. The tax rate and after-tax yield for each income type is as follows:

	(a) Tax rate	(b) After-tax amount 100% − (a)	(c) Pre-tax yield	(d) After-tax yield (b) × (c)
Interest	45%	55%	12%	6.60%
Rent	45%	55%	7%	3.85%
Dividends	24%	76%	4%	3.04%
Capital gain				
Shares	23%	77%	8%	6.16%
Real estate	23%	77%	5%	3.85%

Bond

At the end of five years the $100,000 bond investment will have grown to $137,653, calculated as follows:

Original investment	$100,000
Interest accumulated after tax:	
$100,000 × 6.6% (compounded) × 5 y	37,653
	$137,653

Common shares

The common share investment will grow in value to $153,481, calculated as shown in table A, below.

A. *Common Shares*

Original investment		$100,000
Dividends:		
Annual after-tax dividend is		
$100,000 × 3.04% = $3,040.		
At the end of each year, the after-tax dividend is deposited in an interest-bearing account yielding 6.6% after tax. After five years, this accumulates to:		17,343
Capital growth:		
As capital growth is taxed only when the asset is sold, the investment will compound at the pre-tax return of 8% annually.		
$100,000 × 8% (compounded) × 5 y =	46,933	
Less tax in year 5 @ 23%	(10.795)	36,138
		$153,481

Real estate

Over a period of five years the real estate investment will grow to a value of $144,113, calculated as shown in table B, next page.

B. *Real Estate*

Original investment $100,000

Rental returns:

Year	(a) Pre-tax rent	(b) Capital cost allowance	(c) Taxable income (a) – (b)	(d) Tax 45% (c)	(e) After-tax rent (a) – (d)
1	$ 7,000	(1,800)	5,200	2,340	$ 4,660
2	7,000	(3,528)	3,472	1,562	5,438
3	7,000	(3,387)	3,613	1,626	5,374
4	7,000	(3,251)	3,749	1,687	5,313
5	7,000	11,966*	18,966	8,535	(1,535)
	$35,000	–0–	35,000	15,750	19,250

* recapture

Returns of 6.6% on the deposit of annual rents to an interest-bearing account		3,589
Capital growth:		
Capital growth, taxed only when the property is sold, will compound at a pre-tax return of 5% annually.		
$100,000 × 5% (compounded) × 5 y	27,628	
Less tax @ 23%	(6,354)	21,274
		$144,113

In summary, the net after-tax returns of the above three investments indicate that there is a considerable difference in the percentage yields, compared as follows:

	Bond	Shares	Real estate
Original investment	$100,000	$100,000	$100,000
Value at the end of five years	$137,653	$153,481	$144,113
Effective after-tax yield to maturity	6.6%	9.0%	7.6%

The impact of the tax factor on these investments is better exhibited by comparing the differential yields over a longer term. For example, if the bond and share investments described above were extended over a 25-year period, the share investment would compound to a value of approximately $732,000, whereas the bond would grow to a value of only $494,000. The difference of $245,000 is due solely to the tax treatment applied to each investment. Certainly, in choosing between the two investments, the relative risks must be examined and compared in conjunction with the expected returns. But such a comparison is not relevant unless the risks are judged in the context of the *after-tax* yields, rather than the pre-tax yields.

B. Business Organization Structure

The special rules and definitions relating to property income can have an impact on corporate structures. For example, it is not uncommon for a business entity to separate the ownership of appreciating assets, such as real estate, from that of other business assets.

Exhibit 7-2:

Business Structure
Separating
Appreciating Asset

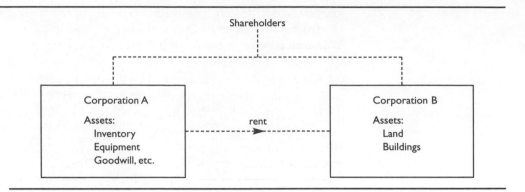

Consider Exhibit 7-2, where the shareholders of a business have placed the land and buildings used by the business in a separate corporation. Under this structure, Corporation A conducts the business operations and pays rent to Corporation B for the use of its land and buildings.

The purpose of this structure may be to shield the appreciating assets from the risk of business failure. Or the owner may want the employees to be able to share the profits from business operations but not the fortuitous gains that result from the appreciation of the real estate.

Because the land and buildings held in Corporation B earn rental income, they are classified for tax purposes as rental properties, not business properties. As a consequence, each building in Corporation B falls into a separate capital cost allowance pool; as a result of this, the normal business activity of disposing of a small warehouse building and acquiring a larger warehouse will cause the recapture of capital cost allowance. The resulting tax on the recapture will diminish the cash available to finance the new acquisition, thereby increasing financing costs. If the land and buildings were held in Corporation A along with the other business assets, the buildings would be pooled in a single class, and no recapture would occur on the disposal and new acquisition.

C. Corporate Financing

The tax treatment of property income has an impact on the cost of corporate financing. The managers of public corporations must have an intimate knowledge of how investment returns will be taxed in the hands of the investors who provide funds for business expansion.

Investors provide debt and equity capital and also lease equipment to businesses to assist in the funding of expansion opportunities. Clearly, the varying tax treatments of property income have an effect on the investor's after-tax rate of return. A corporation that issues securities should attempt to design them in a manner that takes into account the tax sensitivity of the investor who provides the funds. The tax aspects of property income and corporate financing are examined in detail in Chapter 21.

D. Splitting Property Income Among Family Members— Attribution Rules

Each member of a family may be subject to different tax rates due to the levels of their income. Regarding property income (interest, rents, and dividends), it may be desirable to have all or some of a family's investments held in the name of a lower tax rate member. For example, consider the situation where spouses both earn income but one spouse earns less than the other and is in a lower tax bracket. To the extent that the couple can save income and invest those savings, it would be beneficial, from a tax perspective, for the lower income spouse to save and invest the maximum from his or her income. That way, the future property income (return on investments) will be taxed at that spouse's lower tax rate.

The above maneuver seems trite. Why not simply invest a family's savings in the name of the family member with the lowest tax rate? This seems particularly reasonable for spouses whose savings after marriage become common property for family property purposes. However, for tax purposes, as a general principle, income from property is included in the income of the taxpayer who created the wealth to acquire the property. Where an attempt is made to shift property income to a spouse or child by means of a gift, a loan, or the creation of a trust, the future income on the related property may be attributed back to the person who transferred the property. This is the result of several anti-avoidance provisions of the *Income Tax Act* commonly referred to as "*Attribution Rules.*" The desire to split family income to relieve the tax burden is not limited to property income and can include capital gains, pensions, retirement saving plans, and other sources of income that are not reviewed until later chapters. Indeed, the *Income Tax Act* sanctions splitting certain types of income. Therefore, the attribution rules that limit the transfer of income to family members are *examined in detail in Chapter 9* (Part VII, Section F). Chapter 9 also reviews the types of income splitting that are sanctioned within the income tax system.

V. Tax Planning Checklist

Many of the tax planning activities relating to property income have been fully discussed in this chapter. Certain others will be reviewed in more detail in later chapters. Below is a brief list of the main tax planning items.

1. Property income is determined using the same rules as for business income. This means that most expenses incurred for the purpose of earning investment income are deductible. Since this is not made clear on the annual tax form, individuals must take special care to gather together all costs related to the investment process.

2. Interest costs often form a large part of investment expenses, and so one must be able to establish that borrowed funds were used for investment, rather than personal activities.

3. When possible, and as opposed to the reverse, individuals should pay cash for personal assets and then use those assets as collateral when borrowing to make investments.

4. In most cases, it is a good investment to use excess funds to repay personal loans that incur non-deductible interest.

5. Securities that compound and delay interest payments may provide higher returns; but they also require that income be recognized annually. This creates an annual tax cost. When possible, reserve such investments for tax-sheltered entities, such as RRSPs (see Chapter 9).

6. The rate of corporate tax on interest income is significantly higher than on Canadian dividend income. Therefore, corporations should always compare investment returns on an after-tax basis and then adjust those returns for risk variations (see Chapters 11 and 13).

7. Tax rates for individuals also vary according to whether the income is from interest or Canadian dividends (although not as dramatically as for corporations). In addition, the amount of the variance may differ with the individual's tax bracket (depending on surtaxes and special provincial taxes—see Chapter 10). While the pre-tax rate of return is usually lower from dividends than from interest, the after-tax amounts draw closer together and should be reviewed carefully.

8. The deduction of capital cost allowance on rental properties is restricted to the amount of net rental income. However, the tax deferral that can be achieved

from these investments is significant. Again, remember that it is the after-tax return and the difference in the timing of tax that is most relevant.

9. When making real estate investments, consider acquiring a group of partially owned building properties that cost less than $50,000 each because these can be pooled in the same class for capital cost allowance purposes. This way, recapture of capital cost allowance can be avoided to the maximum extent possible. However, it may be more difficult to sell a part-ownership than one that is 100% owned.

10. Entities that pay investment returns (interest, rents, and dividends) to various types of investors (individuals, corporations, pension funds, and so on) should try to understand the tax treatment that is applied to those investors so that they can design and market cost-efficient securities.

VI. Summary and Conclusion

Income from property is the passive return on investments and primarily includes interest, dividends, and rental income. Income from property for tax purposes is determined under the same rules used to determine income from business. The *Income Tax Act* defines property income as, simply, the profit therefrom; as such, the amount is determined by applying well-accepted business principles and generally accepted accounting principles to ascertain the revenues and subtracting the expenses incurred to earn those revenues. The accounting rules are modified by six general limitations and a specific list of exceptions, as outlined in Chapter 5.

The concepts of this chapter are not new. The key to understanding property income is to dwell on the unique treatment of interest, dividends, and rental income as highlighted by the exceptions, without losing sight of the general rules for profit determination.

The exceptions that give property income its unique features are summarized as follows:

1. Interest income
   - Corporations recognize interest income only on the accrual basis in accordance with accounting principles.
   - Individuals can recognize interest income when it is received, when it becomes receivable, or by the annual accrual method. The choice of method is the individual's, provided that the income from each investment is fully recognized at least every 12 months from the date the investment was made.

2. Dividend income
   - Individuals include in income the dividend received plus 25% or 38% of the amount received depending on the source of the dividend. The gross-up must be viewed in relation to the dividend tax credit, which reduces individual taxes payable in recognition of corporate taxes that have already been paid on the same income.
   - Corporations are generally not taxed on dividends from other Canadian corporations; the dividend income is first included in net income for tax purposes but is later deducted when arriving at taxable income.

3. Rental income
   - Both individuals and corporations determine rental income on the accrual basis, in accordance with accounting principles.
   - Capital cost allowance on rental property cannot be used to create a loss from rentals but can be deducted to reduce net rental income to nil.
   - Each rental building costing $50,000 or more is placed in a separate capital cost allowance class, which forces automatic recapture on the sale of each building.

The marketplace offers a wide range of investment opportunities in each category of property income. The terms and conditions imposed on the returns from interest-bearing securities, shares, and real estate can vary considerably. A thorough assessment of each investment and how it compares with others cannot be made unless the returns are expressed on an after-tax basis.

It is essential, especially in public corporations, that managers understand how the investment community is taxed on property income, in order that the corporation can achieve debt, equity, and leasing capital at the most efficient cost. Lease arrangements and public offerings of securities must reflect the realities of the tax system and attempt to take advantage of its unique aspects.

Visit the Canadian Income Taxation Web site at **www.mcgrawhill.ca/olc/buckwold** to view any updated tax information.

Demonstration Questions

QUESTION ONE

George Chan lives in Brandon, Manitoba. As an employee and minority shareholder of GG Ltd., a private corporation, his income has allowed him to accumulate a modest investment portfolio that includes rental properties.

In 20X4, he had several transactions relating to the residential rental properties and has requested your tax advice. These transactions and other information are provided below.

Information Relating to Rental Properties

1. Chan first acquired rental properties in 20X2, as follows:

	Land	Building	Total
Property A	$34,000	$220,000	$254,000
Property B	12,000	48,000	60,000
	$46,000	$268,000	$314,000

Subsequently, Chan realized that the properties were located in an undesirable area. He sold both of them in 20X4 for the following proceeds:

	Land	Building	Total
Property A	$36,000	$212,000	$248,000
Property B	16,000	44,000	60,000
	$52,000	$256,000	$308,000

2. In 20X4, Chan purchased rental property C for $70,000 (land $30,000; building $40,000). He also constructed rental property D, which was completed on October 31, 20X4, and included the following costs:

Land	$ 50,000
Building	300,000
Landscaping	6,000
Architect's fees	10,000
Paving (parking lot)	8,000
Heating system	12,000

3. The accounting statement for the year ended December 31, 20X4, for all properties showed a net loss of $40,400. The loss includes deductions for $3,200 of amortization/depreciation, as well as a $31,000 loss from the sale of rental properties.

4. At the end of 20X3, the undepreciated capital costs were $209,376 for property A and $45,696 for property B.

5. A review of the statement of loss includes the following:

- An amount of $800 was received in 20X4 from a tenant who failed to pay three months' rent in 20X3 and was evicted. The amount was credited to the rent receivable account. The former tenant still owes $400, which will not be collected. A reserve for unpaid rents of $1,200 had been deducted for tax purposes in 20X3. In June 20X4, Chan requested that new tenants pay the last month's rent of a 12-month lease at the time of signing. Included in rental income is $1,000 of these payments.

- Repairs and maintenance expense includes the following:

Painting interior suites	$2,300
Snow removal and lawn care	2,100
Installation of vinyl siding on the existing walls of building B before sale	5,200

- "Other expenses" includes land transfer taxes of $1,200 to acquire the new properties.

- Interest expense is made up of the following:

Mortgage interest paid (all properties)	$7,800
Bank interest on temporary loan to finance construction of property D.	10,000

- Legal fees include $1,500 to prepare the mortgage documents on property D and $500 to collect unpaid rents.

Other Financial Information

1. The year end of GG Ltd. is June 30. On May 1, 20X3, GG Ltd. loaned Chan $18,000 to assist him with the purchase of shares in GG Ltd. No interest was charged on the loan. On August 31, 20X4, GG Ltd. declared a dividend, of which Chan's share was $22,000. He received $4,000 in cash, and the remaining $18,000 cancelled his debt to the company. The CRA's prescribed interest rate for 20X4 was 4%. GG is a private corporation and all its income is business income subject to the small business deduction.

2. Chan received a salary from GG Ltd. of $90,000 in 20X4.

3. On July 1, 20X3, Chan purchased a four-year guaranteed investment certificate (GIC) for $40,000. The interest compounds at 8% the first year, 9% the second year, and 10% for the last two years. The entire interest will be paid on June 30, 20X7. Chan did not include any of the interest in his 20X3 income for tax purposes.

4. Chan's other receipts and disbursements in 20X4 included the following:

Receipts:	
Dividends from foreign corporations (after 10% withholding tax)	$9,000
Proceeds from the sale of public corporation shares:	
A Ltd. (original cost—$42,000)	50,000
B Ltd. (original cost—$30,000)	20,000

Disbursements:	
Investment counsel fees	500
Life insurance premium on policy required as collateral for a loan used to purchase shares in GG Ltd.	1,000
Interest paid on the mortgage on his home (The mortgage is $120,000, of which $80,000 was used to acquire the home and the balance was used to purchase public corporation shares.)	12,000
Donations to registered charity	4,000

Required:

1. Determine Chan's minimum net rental income for tax purposes for 20X4.

2. Determine Chan's overall net income for tax purposes for 20X4.

Solution:

Before we calculate the rental income, we explain certain items. Rental properties A and B acquired in 20X2 are both class 1 properties but are required to be put in separate classes because property A cost more than $50,000. The building of property B, which originally cost $48,000, can be pooled with the new building of property C, which has a cost of $40,000 in 20X4. The building of property D has a cost greater than $50,000 and therefore must be included in a separate class. The result of this is that the sale of property A will incur a recapture of capital cost allowance on its sale, whereas a recapture on the sale of property B is avoided because of the addition of property C to the class.

The construction of the building of property D must include in its cost all of the costs necessary to bring the building to a usable state, such as the architect's fees and interest during the construction period. Also, the cost of the heating system is part of the building cost.

The cost of paving the parking lot qualifies as class 17, which has a capital cost allowance rate of 8% (diminishing balance). The landscaping cost of $6,000 is fully deductible under section 20(1)(aa), even though it is a capital item. The cost of $5,200 for vinyl siding included as a repair expense is a capital item and must be added to the cost of building B before its sale.

Remember that capital cost allowance can be claimed only to the extent of the net rental income. The recapture of capital cost allowance resulting from the sale of property A is included as rental income and therefore increases the net rental income for the purposes of determining the maximum capital cost allowance that can be claimed.

Chan must include a deemed interest benefit on the loan from his employer. The amount is included in employment income. However, because the loan was used to acquire shares that can earn property income, the amount of the benefit can be considered as interest expenses and deducted in arriving at net income from property.

Calculation of rental income

Rental loss per financial statement	$(40,400)
Amortization/depreciation	3,200
Loss on sale of properties	31,000
Landscaping	(6,000)
20X3 reserve for uncollectible rents	1,200
Unpaid rent established to be a bad debt	(400)
Prepaid rent	(1,000)
Vinyl siding—capital item—add to cost of building B	5,200
Land transfer tax—capital item—add to cost of land	1,200
Interest during construction—add to cost of building D	10,000
Legal, financing cost (deductible at ⅕ per year)—⅘ × 1,500	1,200
	5,200

Recapture of capital cost allowance on property A	
($212,000 – $209,376)	2,624
Income before capital cost allowance	7,824
Capital cost allowance—limited to rental income	(7,824)
Net rental income	–0–

Capital cost allowance:

	Property A Class 1	Properties B, C Class 1	Property D Class 1	Class 17
UCC—20X3	$209,376	$45,696		
Dispositions (A and B)	(212,000)	(44,000)		
Additions:				
B—Vinyl siding		5,200		
C—Building		40,000		
D—Building			$300,000	
D—Paving				$8,000
D—Architect fees			10,000	
D—Heating system			12,000	
D—Interest (construction)			10,000	
	(2,624)	46,896	332,000	8,000
Recapture	2,624			
Available CCA		*1,852	**6,640	***320

Total CCA available—$8,812 ($1,852 + $6,640 + $320)

* (45,696 × 4%) + ([40,000 + 5,200 − 44,000] × 4% × ½) = $1,852
** 332,000 × 4% × ½ = $6,640
*** 8,000 × 8% × ½ = $320

Net income for tax purposes

Employment income:		
Salary		$90,000
Interest benefit—$18,000 × 4% × 8 months/12 months		480
		90,480
Property income:		
Rental income (above)	–0–	
Canadian dividend—$22,000 × 1.25	27,500	
Foreign dividend ($9,000 + $1,000)	10,000	
Interest, GIC—$40,000 × 8% – interest from		
July 1, 20X3 to June 30, 20X4 (annual accrual)	3,200	
	40,700	
Investment counsel fees	(500)	
Life insurance premium	(1,000)	
Deemed interest expense on employee loan (above)	(480)	
Interest on house mortgage—		
$12,000 × $40,000/$120,000	(4,000)	34,720
		125,200

Taxable capital gains:		
Land—properties A and B—½ ($52,000 − $46,000)	3,000	
Shares of A Ltd.—½ ($50,000 − $42,000)	4,000	
	7,000	
Allowable capital loss—½ ($30,000 − $20,000)	(5,000)	2,000
Net income for tax purposes		$127,200

QUESTION TWO

Kiranjit, in addition to her corporate business, has a personal investment portfolio. In February 20X6, she purchased a rental property for $750,000 (land $250,000; building $500,000). The property is financed with a mortgage from the vendor of $650,000. Her $100,000 equity contribution was borrowed from a local bank. As security, the bank obtained a first mortgage on her personal residence. Other information relating to her investments for 20X6 is outlined below:

1. Loss from the new rental property after deducting mortgage interest paid to the vendor and before CCA — $80,000

2. Legal fee and appraisal fee to obtain mortgage loan on home — 900

3. Interest on $100,000 mortgage loan on personal residence — 6,000

4. Fees paid to accountant to calculate investment income — 1,200

5. Purchased a GIC on September 30 for $50,000 with 6% interest payable annually; interest received — 0

6. Purchased a bond for a price that includes accrued interest of $250 — 28,650

7. Received bond interest to December 31 (7% average interest rate) — 3,700

8. Dividends received from a foreign public corporation net of a withholding tax of $400 — 3,600

9. Eligible dividends received from shares in Canadian public corporations — 8,000

10. Non-eligible dividends received from Kiranjit's corporation — 10,000

11. Shares in a Canadian public corporation received as a stock dividend valued at — 1,000

12. Interest (7%) paid on a loan used to acquire a summer cottage — 1,100

Required:
Determine Kiranjit's net income from property for tax purposes for the 20X6 taxation year. Recommend any tax planning actions that can be taken to improve Kiranjit's after-tax cash flow.

Solution:

Net income (loss) from property:	
Interest from bonds	$ 3,700
Less accrued interest purchased with bond acquisition	(250)
	3,450
Foreign dividends—before withholding tax ($3,600 + $400)	4,000
Eligible cash dividends—138% × $8,000	11,040
Non-eligible cash dividends—125% × $10,000	12,500
Stock dividend (eligible)—138% × $1,000	1,380
	32,370

Deduct:		
Loss from rental property	$80,000	
Legal and appraisal fee—$1/5 \times \$900$	180	
Interest on mortgage	6,000	
Total loss from rental property	86,180	
Accounting fees	1,200	(87,380)
Net loss from property		$(55,010)

This loss can be offset against any other source of income earned by Kiranjit in the taxation year. If there is not sufficient income in the year to absorb the loss, it can be carried forward or back to another taxation year (see Chapter 10).

The following explanations are added.

Bond interest   Bonds normally pay interest semi-annually. When an investor purchases a bond prior to the interest payment date the amount paid includes the purchase price of the bond plus accrued interest from the last interest date to the date of purchase. This means that the investor has paid the vendor for the vendor's share of the interest. The new investor then receives the interest for the entire six-month period. The new investor includes the interest received in income for tax purposes and deducts the accrued interest purchased from this amount leaving the investor with interest income from the date of purchase to the interest due date included in income. 12(1)(c), 20(14).

Foreign dividends   are included at the actual amount of the declared dividend before the deduction of foreign withholding tax. The amount included is the Canadian dollar equivalent of the foreign currency payment. Note that the foreign dividend is not grossed up like a dividend from a Canadian corporation, as there is no dividend tax credit available on foreign dividends. 12(1)(k).

Eligible cash dividends   Dividends from Canadian public corporations are normally classified as eligible dividends. The inclusion rate for eligible dividends is 138% of the actual dividend. 12(1)(j), 82(1).

Non-eligible dividends   The inclusion rate for non-eligible dividends is 125% of the actual dividend received. 12(1)(j), 82(1).

Stock dividend   The stock dividend from a public corporation is treated like a cash dividend and is normally an eligible dividend. Its inclusion rate is the same as a cash dividend. 12(1)(j), 82(1).

Loss from rental property   The loss from the rental property cannot be increased by a claim for CCA (capital cost allowance). The CCA deduction in computing rental income is limited to the taxpayer's net rental income before CCA (cumulative for all rental properties owned). In this case CCA cannot be claimed, as there is no net rental income for the year. Regulation 1100(11).

Legal and appraisal fees   Both of these expenses are considered to be costs incurred to borrow money. Consequently, they are considered to be capital costs. However, they can be deducted over a five-year period on a straight-line basis. 20(1)(e).

Interest on home mortgage   The loan of $100,000 was used directly to purchase the rental property and it is, therefore, an expense incurred to purchase a capital property that is, in turn, used to earn income. The interest is, therefore, deductible as part of the rental property expenses. 20(1)(c).

Accounting fees   These fees are deductible as they are incurred for the purpose of earning income. 18(1)(a).

GIC interest   The GIC interest was not received and is not receivable at the end of the taxation year. The interest will be included in the following taxation year when it is received, or on the one-year anniversary date of the investment. If the taxpayer were a corporation, the interest would have to be accrued from September 30 to the end of the taxation year if the year end was before the date the interest was received. 12(1)(c), 12(3),(4),(11).

Interest on cottage loan   This interest was not incurred for the purpose of earning income and is not deductible. 18(1)(a).

Planning opportunity   Kiranjit earns bond interest at an average rate of 7%. This income is taxable and its net return is the 7% minus the related tax. For example, if her marginal tax rate was 40%, the net after-tax return would be 4.2% (7% − 40% of 7%). At the same time, she pays 7% interest on a loan for her personal cottage. This interest cost is not deductible for tax purposes and, therefore, has an after-tax cost of 7%. It would be advantageous if Kiranjit sold some of her bonds and used the funds to repay the cottage loan. Effectively, that would save her 7% after-tax which is more than her current after tax return on the bonds.

Review Questions

1. Although the *Income Tax Act* specifically refers to property income as a separate type of income, it does not provide a specific definition of the term. Identify the source from which the definition of property income is derived, briefly explain the term's meaning, and provide examples of income from property.

2. Distinguish between income from property and the gains or losses that may occur from the sale of property.

3. Interest income earned on loans by a financial institution may, for tax purposes, be classified in a different way from interest income earned on loans by taxpayers who are investing their savings. Explain why.

4. Briefly explain how income from property is determined for tax purposes.

5. Compare and contrast the taxation year of an individual with that of a corporation with respect to the determination of business income and property income.

6. "An individual can deduct for tax purposes the interest expense incurred on the mortgage loan attached to his or her personal residence." Is this statement true? Explain.

7. A taxpayer has sold property (land) for $200,000 that was originally purchased for $70,000. The property was sold to an arm's-length party (not related). The terms of sale involve a cash payment of $100,000 on closing, with the balance to be paid at $20,000 per year for five years, with no interest charged on the unpaid balance. For tax purposes, what types of income may result for the vendor from this transaction?

8. An individual invests in a bank term deposit on July 1, 20X0. When does the individual recognize the interest income for tax purposes if the investment has a term of three years, with interest compounded annually but paid only at the end of the three-year term? Would your answer be different if the taxpayer were a corporation? Explain.

9. Can a taxpayer deduct a reserve for unpaid interest on a loan if the interest appears not to be collectible? Explain. How does the treatment of unpaid interest compare with the treatment of the loan principal when its repayment is in doubt?

10. Briefly explain why an individual who receives dividends from a Canadian corporation must include 125% or 138% of the dividend received in income for tax purposes, while a corporation receiving the same dividend includes only the actual amount of the dividend.

11. "If a loss occurs from the renting of real estate (that is, if annual expenses exceed rental income), the loss is not recognized in determining a taxpayer's overall net income for tax purposes." Is this statement true? Explain.

12. A building that costs $200,000 and is rental property will always create a terminal loss or a recapture of capital cost allowance when it is sold. The same result may not occur if the building is used directly in a business activity. Explain this.

13. An investor in real estate may achieve a higher rate of return by acquiring a small portion (part ownership) of several properties, rather than a lesser number of whole properties. Explain this.

14. Why is the purchase of rental real estate often referred to as a "tax-sheltered" investment?

15. Often, an enterprise conducting an active business will separate its business operations from its appreciating assets (such as real estate) by establishing a separate corporation for each. How may this type of structure impair future expansion activities?

Key Concept Questions

QUESTION ONE

Determine the amount of interest to be included in income in years 1, 2, and 3 for each of the following situations. *Income tax reference: ITA 12(1)(c), 12(3), (4), (11).*

- Percel Ltd. has a December 31 year end. In Year 1, Percel purchased a $10,000 bond on its issue date of November 1. The bond pays interest at 6% compounded annually. Percel will receive interest when the bond matures on October 31, year 3.
- Debra purchased a $10,000 bond on its issue date, November 1, Year 1. The bond pays interest at 6%, compounded annually. Debra will receive the interest when the bond matures on October 31, year 3.

QUESTION TWO

Anne received the following dividend income during the current year:

- $1,000 of eligible dividends from taxable Canadian corporations.
- $1,000 of non-eligible dividends from taxable Canadian corporations.
- $1,000 of foreign dividends. The foreign country withheld $150 in foreign tax and Anne received the net amount of $850.

Determine the amount of dividend income to be included in Anne's property income for the current year. *Income tax reference: ITA 12(1)(j), (k), 82(1).*

QUESTION THREE

A Ltd. received the following dividend income during the current year:

- $1,000 of eligible dividends from a taxable Canadian corporation.
- $1,000 of non-eligible dividends from a taxable Canadian corporation.

Determine the amount of dividend income to be included in A's property income for the current year. *Income tax reference: ITA 112(1).*

QUESTION FOUR

At the end of the current year, Fred owned two residential rental properties. Rental property #1 cost $125,000 (land $50,000; building $75,000) and at the close of last year had a UCC of $64,000. Rental property #2 was acquired in the current year for $210,000 (land $80,000; building $130,000). Revenue and expenses for the rental properties during the year were as follows:

	Property #1	Property #2	Total
Revenue	$13,200	$4,500	$17,700
Expenses:			
Mortgage interest	(0)	(3,000)	(3,000)
Repairs & maintenance	(5,000)	(0)	(5,000)
Property tax	(3,100)	(1,000)	(4,100)
Insurance	(500)	(200)	(700)
	(8,600)	(4,200)	(12,800)
Income	$ 4,600	$ 300	$ 4,900

Determine the maximum CCA deduction for the rental properties for the current year. *Income tax reference: Reg. 1100(11), 1101(1ac).*

Problems

PROBLEM ONE

On April 1, 20X0, a corporation with a December 31 taxation year purchased a three-year investment certificate for $20,000. The certificate pays interest only at the end of the three-year term but is compounded annually at the rate of 10%. Currently, the corporation's marginal tax rate is 28%. However, in 20X1, the marginal tax rate will decrease to 25%.

An individual makes the identical investment on April 1, 20X0. The individual's marginal tax rate in 20X0 is also 28% and is expected to drop to 25% in 20X1.

Required:

Calculate and compare the tax on the interest income for the three-year period for the individual and the corporation.

PROBLEM TWO

Ken Potman is the sole shareholder in Brickbase Enterprises Ltd., a Regina-based construction company. In addition, Potman is a 25% partner in a retail kitchenware store, although he does not actively participate in its management. The following information relates to Potman's financial affairs for the year 20X1:

1. Brickbase was organized three years ago. For its year ending May 31, 20X1, the company earned a profit of $88,000. Potman originally contributed $200,000 to the corporation, using $50,000 of his own savings and funding the balance with a bank loan. In return, the corporation issued Potman $1,000 worth of common shares and $199,000 of preferred shares. In 20X1, the company paid a dividend of $12,000 on the preferred shares. All of Brickbase's income is subject to the small business deduction.

2. During the year, Potman sold a warehouse property for $180,000 (land $15,000, building $165,000). The building was used by Brickbase to store construction equipment, and the company paid Potman a fair rental for use of the property. The property was originally purchased at a cost of $140,000 (land $10,000, building $130,000). At the end of 20X0 the building had an undepreciated capital cost of $110,000.

   Simultaneously with the sale, Potman purchased a larger warehouse property (constructed after March 18, 2007), which was also rented to Brickbase. The new property cost $400,000 (land $50,000, building $350,000). During the year, the company paid Potman net rents of $30,000 for both properties. The new property was financed with the proceeds from the sale of the old building as well as mortgage financing.

3. The retail store partnership earned $40,000 for its year ending December 31, 20X1. The profit consisted of a $32,000 profit from operations and $8,000 of interest income earned on excess undistributed cash deposits.

4. Potman's other cash receipts and disbursements for 20X1 are shown in the table below.

5. On July 1 of the previous year, Potman purchased a four-year guaranteed investment certificate for $30,000 that bears interest at 10%. The interest compounds annually but is not payable until the end of the four-year term. Potman did not include any amount of interest in his previous year's income.

6. During the year, one of the Canadian public corporations of which Potman is a shareholder issued him 100 additional shares as a stock dividend. The shares had a stated value of $40 per share. Potman placed the shares in his safety deposit box along with his other securities.

Receipts:	
Salary from Brickbase	$62,000
Dividends from Canadian public corporations	6,000
Dividends from foreign public corporations (net of 10% foreign withholding tax)	9,000
Winnings from provincial lottery	2,000
Interest on a loan to his daughter	1,000
Disbursements:	
Contribution to Brickbase employee pension plan	3,000
Investment counsel fees	1,000
Legal fees for registering mortgage on new warehouse	5,000
Life insurance premium on policy required as collateral for the bank loan used to purchase Brickbase shares	1,000
Interest on warehouse building mortgage	21,000
Interest paid on house mortgage (The house mortgage is $100,000, of which $70,000 was used to acquire the house. The balance was used to purchase public corporation shares.)	10,000
Interest on bank loan (re: Brickbase shares)	15,000
Donations to local charity	4,000
Safety deposit box fees	100

Required:

Determine separately, for the year 20X1, Potman's income for tax purposes from employment, business, and property.

PROBLEM THREE

Anne Osinski acquired a townhouse unit in 20X0 for $120,000 (land $10,000, building $110,000). She bought the unit in order to rent it. By the end of 20X2, the undepreciated capital cost of the building was $103,500. In August 20X3, Osinski decided to live in the unit herself. At that time, similar townhouses were selling for $136,000 (land $12,000, building $124,000). Prior to August, her 20X3 net rental income before capital cost allowance was $1,000.

In September 20X3, Osinski purchased, for rental purposes, a residential condominium unit for $145,000 (land $15,000, building $130,000). Between September and the end of the taxation year, the condo earned net rentals of $900 before capital cost allowance.

Required:

Determine the change to Osinski's 20X3 net income for tax purposes as a result of the above activity.

PROBLEM FOUR

After receiving an inheritance, Sandra Yaworski decided to invest her newly acquired funds in real estate. In 20X1, she purchased the following properties:

	Land	Building	Total
Property 1	$10,000	$ 40,000	$ 50,000
2	12,000	45,000	57,000
3	20,000	80,000	100,000
4	30,000	100,000	130,000

Each of the properties is a residential condominium unit, and each unit is part of a separate condominium high-rise project. Not all of the units were fully rented during the year of acquisition, and Yaworski determined that her net rental position (before capital cost allowance) for each of the properties was as follows for 20X1:

Property	1	2	3	4	Total
Rent revenue	$4,000	$5,000	$7,000	$12,000	$28,000
Expenses*	(6,000)	(3,000)	(6,000)	(9,000)	(24,000)
Income (loss)	($2,000)	$2,000	$1,000	$ 3,000	$ 4,000

* Property taxes, insurance, interest, maintenance.

In 20X2, one of Yaworski's close relatives ran into financial difficulty, and she was forced to sell two of the properties in order to provide financial assistance. She sold property 1 for $52,000 (land $12,000, building $40,000) and property 3 for $110,000 (land $24,000, building $86,000). In 20X2, the four properties (including the two sold properties to the date of sale) earned net rental income of $7,000.

Required:
Determine Yaworski's net income from property from the rental properties for 20X1 and 20X2.

PROBLEM FIVE

Toshiaki Minamiyama is a successful business executive. Over the years, he has allocated a portion of his large salary to the building of an investment portfolio. He currently has a net worth of $800,000 (exclusive of retirement plans), as follows:

Personal assets:	
Automobiles	$ 30,000
Sailboat	29,000
House	220,000
Investment assets:	
Corporate and government bonds (average interest return—10%)	200,000
Common shares of public corporations	306,000
Rental real estate	360,000
	1,145,000
Liabilities:	
First mortgage on house (interest at 9%)	(150,000)
Term financing on sailboat (12%)	(15,000)
First mortgage on rental real estate (10%)	(180,000)
Net worth	$ 800,000

Minamiyama seldom trades his investments, as his strategy is to hold various types of investments for a long time in order to delay any tax that may occur on their disposition. (He is in the 45% tax bracket.) In fact, he chose not to dispose of any investments when he needed money to purchase his house and sailboat.

Required:

From a tax planning perspective, what would you recommend he do in order to enhance his wealth accumulation? If possible, quantify how he would benefit from your recommendations, assuming a five-year time period.

PROBLEM SIX

Quantro Enterprises Ltd. and Baizley Holdings Ltd. (BHL) are both 100% owned by Harold Baizley. Both companies are Canadian-controlled private corporations. Quantro operates a wholesale business and pays rent to BHL for the use of a warehouse property.

BHL owns only one asset—the warehouse building and related land that is rented by Quantro for $36,000 per year. The property was originally owned by Quantro but was sold to BHL several years ago as a means to reduce the risk exposure of this appreciating asset.

On December 31, 20X1 (the year end of both companies), BHL sold the warehouse property to a third party for $370,000 (land $40,000, building $330,000). The property originally cost $320,000 (land $25,000, building $295,000). The undepreciated capital cost of the building at December 31, 20X0, was $254,000.

One month before selling the warehouse property, BHL purchased a newly constructed warehouse property for $480,000 (land $50,000, building $430,000).

Required:

Determine BHL's net income for tax purposes for 20X1.

PROBLEM SEVEN

Sally Corbet is the sole shareholder of Corbet Holdings Ltd. (CHL), a Canadian-controlled private corporation. The corporation holds investments in shares, bonds, and real estate. You have been retained to complete CHL's tax return for the year ended December 31, 20X2, and provide certain other tax advice.

It is now February 15, 20X3, and you have gathered the information outlined below.

1. The draft income statement for the year ended December 31, 20X2, is as follows:

Income		
Interest on bonds and certificates		$ 78,000
Dividends income		32,000
Net loss from real estate rentals		(19,000)
Gain on sale of land (Pelican Lake)		170,000
Share of profits of Pantry Products Ltd.		120,000
		381,000
Expenses		
Legal fees for general corporate affairs	$ 1,000	
Director's fees	21,000	
Donations—charitable	8,000	(30,000)
Income before income tax		$351,000

2. CHL owns a 40% interest in Delroy (a partnership), which has a June 30, 20X2, year end. The partnership's profit for the year was $200,000, which consisted of dividends from taxable Canadian corporations of $80,000 and royalties from mineral rights of $120,000.

On December 31, 20X2, CHL received $100,000 as its share of a partnership cash distribution. The partnership's results are not reflected in the above income statement.

3. On September 30, 20X2, CHL purchased a $100,000 guaranteed investment certificate bearing 9% interest. The company intends to record the interest of $9,000 on September 30, 20X3, its one-year anniversary date.

4. The dividend income of $32,000 consists of the following:

Canadian public corporations	$14,000
Turner Inc.—an American corporation—net of a 10% U.S. withholding tax	18,000

Not included in the above is a dividend received from Pantry Products Ltd. of $25,000. CHL owns 50% of its voting shares and records the investment using the equity method of accounting. Pantry earned business income of $240,000 in the current year.

5. During the year, CHL received 100 shares of Mustang Ltd. (a public corporation) as a stock dividend. Mustang increased its paid-up capital by $30 for each stock dividend share issued. CHL did not record the receipt of the stock dividend.

6. In January 20X2, CHL purchased three hectares of land at Pelican Lake for $130,000. The land was then rezoned and subdivided into six building lots. The entire subdivision was immediately sold to a building contractor for $300,000. The payment terms called for no cash down, but payments of $50,000 are required as the contractor completes construction on each lot. By December 31, 20X2, one payment of $50,000 had been received.

7. In 20X1, CHL had purchased two rental properties as follows:

	Land	Building	Total
Fourplex	$50,000	$150,000	$200,000
Townhouse 1	20,000	40,000	60,000
	$70,000	$190,000	$260,000

Maximum capital cost allowance was claimed in 20X1.
In 20X2, townhouse 1 was sold for $75,000 (land $25,000, building $50,000).
On December 1, 20X2, CHL purchased townhouse 2 for $50,000 (land $11,000, building $39,000). Also, in 20X2, CHL constructed a sixplex rental unit for $437,000, as follows:

Land	$ 80,000
Permanent landscaping	8,000
Labour and materials	300,000
Air-conditioning and heating equipment	49,000
	$437,000

All of the properties resulted in a net rental loss of $19,000 (as shown on the financial statement). The following items are included in the net loss calculation:

Cost of surveying land (new sixplex)	$ 2,400
Amortization/depreciation	28,000
Legal fees for mortgage (new sixplex)	2,000
Advertising for new tenants	4,000

Required:

Determine CHL's net income for tax purposes for the 20X2 taxation year. Also, prepare a breakdown of the net income for tax purposes showing the net income from property and any other sources of income. (Assume all rental properties are residential properties.)

PROBLEM EIGHT

Carol Wong is the president and major shareholder of CW Ltd., a Canadian-controlled private corporation that operates a construction business in Regina, Saskatchewan. CW earns only business income which is all subject to the small business deduction.

In 20X7, she had a number of financial transactions. She has asked you to help her prepare her 20X7 tax return and provide advice on other tax matters. The following additional financial information is provided:

1. Wong's 20X7 gross salary was $90,000, from which CW Ltd. deducted the following amounts:

Income tax	$30,000
CPP and EI premiums	3,147
Private health insurance premiums	600
Group sickness and accident insurance premiums	400

   In addition to her salary, CW Ltd. paid $2,000 to a deferred profit-sharing plan, $600 of private health insurance premiums, and $400 of group sickness and accident insurance premiums on Wong's behalf.

2. Wong is required to use her own automobile for company business. For this, CW Ltd. pays her an annual allowance of $3,600. In 20X7, Wong incurred automobile operating costs of $5,200. Also, in 20X7, she purchased a new automobile for $34,000 plus HST (13%), and received $18,000 as a trade on her old car. At the end of the previous year, the old car had an undepreciated capital cost allowance balance of $15,000 (class 10.1). Of the 20,000 kilometres driven in 20X7, 12,000 were for employment purposes.

3. For three months in 20X7, Wong was sick and could not attend work. She received $9,000 from the company's group sickness and accident insurance plan. Since the plan's inception, Wong had paid premiums totalling $2,000.

4. During 20X7, Wong purchased a warehouse property and leased it to CW Ltd. to store construction equipment. The property cost $250,000 (land 30,000, building 220,000). The building was originally constructed after March 17, 2007. The price for the land includes $2,000 of permanent landscaping completed just after acquisition. The 20X7 rental income is summarized below.

Rent received		$20,000
Expenses:		
Insurance	1,200	
Property taxes	4,000	
Interest	10,000	
Repairs:		
General maintenance	800	
Storage shed addition	3,000	(19,000)
Income		$1,000

5. Wong is a 30% partner in a computer software business but is not active in its management. The partnership financial statement shows a profit of $40,000 for the year ended December 31, 20X7. The profit consists of $32,000 from software sales and $8,000 from interest earned.

6. On July 1, 20X6, Wong purchased a three-year guaranteed investment certificate for $20,000 with interest at 10%. The interest compounds annually but is not payable until July 1, 20X9.

7. Wong received (made) the following additional receipts (disbursements) in 20X7:

Receipts:	
Dividends (eligible) from Canadian public corporations	$2,000
Dividends (non-eligible) from CW Ltd.	3,000
Dividends from foreign corporations (net of 10% foreign withholding tax)	900
Winnings from a provincial lottery	12,000
Disbursements:	
Contribution to RRSP (within allowable limits)	10,000
Dental expenses for children	3,500
Donation to a charity	2,000
Safety deposit box	100
Life insurance premium used as collateral for personal bank loan	800
Investment counsel fees	1,000

Required:

Determine Wong's minimum net income for tax purposes in accordance with the aggregating formula of section 3 of the *Income Tax Act*.

PROBLEM NINE

CB Ltd. is a Canadian-controlled private corporation owning a portfolio of investments including stocks, bonds, and rental properties. The financial statements for the year ended June 30, 20X1, show a profit of $104,300, summarized as follows:

Bond interest	$50,000
Taxable dividends from Canadian corporations	20,000
Gain on sale of assets	40,000
Rental loss	(5,700)
Income before income taxes	$104,300

Additional financial information is outlined below.

1. The previous year's corporation tax return includes the following tax account balances:

Undepreciated capital cost:	
Class 1—building A	$125,000
Class 1—building B	35,000
Class 1—building C	46,000

2. Taxable Canadian dividends totalling $20,000 include $8,000 from public corporations and $12,000 from X Ltd., a Canadian-controlled private corporation. CB Ltd. owns 30% of X Ltd.'s common shares.

3. The rental properties were purchased prior to March 18, 2007 as follows:

	A	B	C
Land cost	$ 20,000	$35,000	$21,000
Building cost	130,000	40,000	49,000
	$150,000	$75,000	$70,000

On February 28, 20X1, property A was sold for $170,000 (land 30,000, building 140,000) and property B was sold for $77,000 (land 40,000, building 37,000).

The combined rentals resulted in a loss of $5,700 after deducting amortization/depreciation of $3,000 for the year ended June 30, 20X1. The rental revenue includes a $1,000 rental deposit applying to the last two months' rent on a lease expiring December 31, 20X2.

For the year ended June 30, 20X0, CB Ltd. deducted a reserve for unpaid rents of $2,000. In January 20X1, $1,000 of the unpaid rents was received and credited to the reserve account. No reserve has been claimed at June 30, 20X1; however, $1,200 of the current year's rents remain unpaid.

Required:
Determine CB's minimum net income for tax purposes for the 20X1 taxation year.

Case

HELEN CHAPMAN

Helen Chapman is 56 years old and intends to retire in four years. Most of her investment funds are tied up in her employer's pension plan and in her personal registered retirement savings plan. In addition, she has managed to accumulate a personal investment fund of $100,000, which currently is invested in government treasury bills earning interest at 9%.

Immediately before retirement, Chapman intends to use her personal investments and her pension plans to acquire a life annuity that will provide her with a guaranteed monthly income. She is looking for an investment for the $100,000 currently invested in treasury bills that will maximize the value of the annuity. Her investment counsellor has proposed two secure investment options, as follows:

- *Option 1* is a corporate bond yielding annual interest of 13%. The counsellor has advised that Chapman could fund a purchase of $200,000 of the bonds with $100,000 of cash (from the treasury bills) and $100,000 of borrowed funds. Because her house is debt-free, her bank has offered to provide her with a term loan secured by a mortgage on the house. The loan interest rate would be 10%, and no principal payments would be required until the end of the term of the loan.

- *Option 2* is a real estate investment. A small, single-tenant commercial building is currently under construction and will be completed in six weeks. A prospective tenant has already agreed to a 12-year lease. The lease calls for rent payments of $40,000 annually for four years, at which time the annual rent will increase by 12% and then remain fixed for the remaining eight years of the lease. The tenant will be responsible for all costs associated with the property, including property taxes and insurance.

The developer is prepared to finance up to $300,000 of the project with a 10-year first mortgage that includes a requirement to pay only interest (no principal) at the rate of 9% per annum. The full principal balance is due at the end of 10 years. At the closing date, the property will be ready for tenant occupation, except that the landscaping will have to be arranged and paid for separately by Chapman. The total cost of the investment and the related funding is as follows:

Cost:	
Land	$ 40,000
Building	350,000
Landscaping	8,000
Legal fees to register first mortgage	2,000
	$400,000
Funding:	
Cash	$100,000
Mortgage (9%)	300,000
	$400,000

Whichever investment she chooses, Chapman intends to liquidate the investment at the end of four years and use the funds to acquire a life annuity for retirement. Her marginal tax rate is 45%.

Required:

Advise Chapman which investment will best meet her objectives.

CHAPTER 8

Gains and Losses on the Disposition of Capital Property—Capital Gains

Capital gains (or capital losses) refer to the gain (or loss) realized on the disposal of capital property. Capital property, by definition, is property that provides a long-term and enduring benefit to its owners; consequently, disposals of such property tend to occur irregularly and infrequently over a taxpayer's lifetime. Properties that are held for personal use and enjoyment, for investment purposes, or for the purpose of assisting in generating business activity, all have the potential for capital gains. Calculating a capital gain or loss for tax purposes is a very simple matter; however, it will become readily apparent that this calculation departs radically from the one used to determine other types of income with respect to the timing of income recognition, the amount of income subject to tax, and the utilization of losses when they occur. Some people regard the tax treatment of capital gains as preferential, and the treatment of capital losses as unfair. In either case, their tax treatment is a significant factor to consider when an investment in capital assets is being contemplated.

Of primary importance is the ability to recognize when a gain or loss on the sale of property is classified as a capital gain or loss as opposed to income or loss from business. Because the *Income Tax Act* does not provide specific guidelines, establishing whether a transaction is a capital one is the most complex aspect of the study of capital gains and losses.

This chapter develops a definition of capital gains for tax purposes, presents the basic rules for determining the amount and timing of gains and losses, and examines certain unique types of properties. In addition, the broad impact of the tax treatment of capital transactions on investment and business decisions is examined.

I. Capital Gain and Capital Loss Defined

A capital gain (or capital loss) is the gain (or loss) realized on the disposition of capital property. For a property to be classified as capital property, it must have been acquired and used for the purpose of providing the owner with a long-term or enduring benefit.

Note that the definition does not indicate that the property must be held for a long time or that it must provide a benefit; instead, it is enough that the *intended purpose* of the acquisition was to achieve benefits over a long period of time. Whether or not the property actually achieves its intended purpose is governed by future events that may or may not be controllable by the owner. The key to understanding the concept of capital gains (or losses) lies in focusing on the intended purpose of acquisition. Unfortunately, the ultimate results do not always provide proof of this intended purpose, and consequently, there are frequent disputes between the CRA and taxpayers as to what was, in fact, the original intention.

It is necessary to clarify the term "benefit." In the context of capital property, *benefit* refers to both direct and indirect benefits achieved from the use of the property. These benefits need not be financial in nature. The acquisition of a rental building will result in direct financial benefits in the form of rent receipts. The purchase of a warehouse building for use in a business will result in indirect financial benefits by creating the ability to store merchandise held for resale. The purchase of a summer cottage will result in a non-financial benefit in the form of personal enjoyment. Each of these items is capital property and is subject to capital gains treatment for tax purposes.

The general definition of capital gains and losses is subjective because it is based upon the intended purpose of the property acquisition, rather than on the actual results achieved. Because the circumstances surrounding each acquisition are different, each property must be assessed in the context of its unique position. Because the *Income Tax Act* does not provide definitive guidelines, it has been left to the common-law process to establish some general considerations. In order to fill out the overall definition of capital property subject to capital gains treatment, it is useful to do the following:

(a) compare the definitions of capital income and business income;
(b) review the principles established by common law for assessing intended purpose; and
(c) examine the categories of capital property established by the *Income Tax Act*.

A. Capital versus Business Income

The sale of property by any taxpayer can be classified as a business activity or as a capital transaction—it depends on the intended purpose of acquiring the property. The following points were made in Chapter 5:

1. Property acquired for the purpose of resale at a profit is classified as inventory. Its disposition results in business income or a business loss.

2. Property acquired for the purpose of providing the owner with a long-term or enduring benefit is classified as capital property. Its disposition results in a capital gain or loss.

Obviously, the above comparison does not mean that one cannot realize a profit on the sale of capital property. It does, however, hinge on the way in which that profit was generated. The profit on capital property (capital gain) arises from the mere enhancement of the capital value of an asset that was acquired for some other purpose.[1] The profit on other property (business income) results from a scheme of profit making that was the owner's intended purpose.

As stated in Chapter 5, the nature of the asset is not relevant. The same property may be capital property to one taxpayer but inventory to another. A truck that makes product deliveries provides a long-term benefit to the owner and is capital property, but a truck purchased by an automobile dealer for resale at a profit is inventory. Even within the same entity, similar assets may be classified differently. Land acquired to provide parking for customers is capital property. If that same business acquired other land for speculative purposes, it would be classified as inventory. The tax treatment on each land sale would be different.

It is recommended that the reader review the first few pages of Chapter 5, which provide a more detailed comparison of business income and capital gains on similar properties.

In some cases, the nature of the transaction is more complex, and the distinction between business income and capital gains is not so apparent. Consider the following example:

Situation: A Canadian corporation that was previously not active in business purchased a 40-year franchise permitting it to operate particular hardware stores across Canada. Subsequently, the corporation sold subfranchises (one for each province) to separate buyers in return for a cash amount and continued royalties based on sales. After seven years, the corporation sold the master national franchise at a substantial profit and ceased all operations in the hardware business. The purchaser of the national franchise obtained the rights to all future royalties from the subfranchises.

Analysis: The national franchise is capital property because it is an income source that brings an enduring benefit to the corporation in the form of continued royalties from the subfranchises. Because of its limited life of 40 years, the master franchise also qualifies as depreciable property under class 14 and can be amortized over 40 years against the royalty income (see Chapter 6).

---

1   *California Copper Syndicate Ltd. v. Harris* (1904), 5 DTC 159.

(handwritten margin notes)
Taxed
recapture -
assets
(-) pool balance

terminal loss -
no assets
(+) pool balance

> The sale of subfranchises constitutes business income. The right to subfranchise the master franchise is property that was acquired for the intended purpose of resale. It is therefore inventory, and the sale to 10 separate buyers constitutes income from business.
>
> The sale of the master national franchise is a sale of capital property that has appreciated in value. To the extent that the selling price is in excess of the original cost, a capital gain results. A recapture of capital cost allowance (business income) also occurs if capital cost allowance is claimed on the original cost.

The above example highlights the issue of "intended purpose" in a complex situation. The situation assumed that the taxpayer meant to obtain long-term benefits from the master franchise by selling royalty-based subfranchises. The corporation's original intention may have been to acquire the master franchise in order to sell it at a profit; if this had been the intention, the gain would have been classified as business income. But the facts were that the master franchise was held for seven years and that the corporation went through the process of selling subfranchises; neither fact is consistent with this intention.

B. Intention

Because the history of a transaction does not always reflect its original intention, numerous disputes between the CRA and taxpayers have been heard by the courts. These hearings attempt to determine the intended purpose by examining the manner in which the owner dealt with property.[2] While the facts surrounding each case are always different, the courts have consistently taken certain factors into account when establishing the original intention. These factors, which are outlined below, are not ranked, as the importance of each depends on the relative strength and weakness of the others in a particular case.

• **Period of ownership**   That a property is held for a long period of time substantiates the claim that it is capital property which was purchased to provide a long-term and enduring benefit. That a property is held for a short period of time speaks against such a claim, in that it is evidence that the property may have been purchased for resale. Obviously, property purchased for a long-term benefit may, owing to special factors, be sold after a brief ownership period, and property purchased for resale may be held for a long period of time; so, period of ownership by itself does not provide compelling evidence of intention. It is, however, a factor when examined in conjunction with the other factors discussed below.

• **Nature of the transaction**   The courts will examine the entity's course of conduct over the ownership of the property, dwelling on the point of acquisition, the use of the property during its ownership, and the reasons for and nature of its disposition.[3] The sale of raw land, even when it is held for a period of 15 years, may be regarded as business income if the owner cannot provide evidence of enduring benefit through rental or personal use and enjoyment. On the other hand, an individual who purchased vacation land with the intention of building a summer cottage but sold the raw land for a profit after a brief ownership period may be considered to have achieved a capital gain if the reason for the sale was that the original intention was frustrated by a sudden need for money, an inability to finance the cottage, a job transfer, or the like.

• **Number and frequency of transactions**   A historical pattern of frequent buying and selling supports the premise that the intended purpose of acquisition was to resell at a

---

2   *Regal Heights Ltd. v. MNR*, 60 DTC 1270; IT-459, IT-218R.
3   *MNR v. Taylor*, 56 DTC 1125.

profit.[4] This factor may be significant even though the property generated benefits during the ownership period. The frequent acquisition and sale of rental real estate properties may be considered as resulting in business income even though those properties were held for a respectable time period and reasonable rental profits were achieved. In some cases, the courts have decided that an individual has earned business income on the sale of his or her home when a historical pattern of acquisition, renovation, and sale has emerged, even though the home was used as a residence during the ownership period.

It should be pointed out that while a history of frequent transactions in similar property is strong evidence that the gains or losses are business income, the reverse is not true. The courts will consider but have not given significant weight to the argument that an isolated transaction suggests a capital transaction.

- **Relation of transaction to taxpayer's business** If the property sold is similar in nature to property normally dealt with as part of the owner's trade or occupation, it is difficult to establish that the ownership of such property was of a capital nature.[5] A person who makes his or her living by selling real estate is normally considered to have generated business income by selling a unit of rental real estate even when the property was held for a reasonable period of time and generated normal rental returns. Similarly, a lawyer whose practice consists extensively of real estate transactions will have a more difficult time proving that real estate was acquired for the purpose of providing a long-term and enduring benefit.

The above factors indicate that even when the reason for acquiring a property is clear to the purchaser, it may not be so clear to the tax assessor. It is important that taxpayers, when possible, document their course of conduct relating to the acquisition, period of use, and sale of property. Evidence, such as copies of correspondence, internal memos, and the like, is invaluable, especially when the original intention was thwarted by external factors.

It is important to remember that the above factors are only guidelines that assist in establishing the primary intention. Each factor by itself is not significant; it is when *all* are considered together that a course of conduct becomes evident. Each transaction must be judged on its own merits. Do not lose sight of the fact that the process of establishing that a transaction was of a capital nature begins with establishing the original purpose of acquisition—that is to obtain a long-term or enduring benefit from its use.

There are two areas with respect to intention that require special mention. First, sometimes the intended purpose of ownership changes so that the property is held for a period of time for one purpose and for a period of time for another purpose. Second, certain properties—marketable securities, in particular—are often acquired for the dual purpose of providing annual benefits *as well as* a profit on sale. Each of these situations has a special tax treatment, which is discussed shortly.

It is worth noting first that the issue of intention may be further confused when a taxpayer enters into a transaction with both primary and secondary intentions. In other words, the taxpayer has considered that if one objective fails, a fall-back plan is available and viable. In such circumstances, there must be evidence that the taxpayer had the secondary objective in mind when acquiring the property.[6]

1. Change in Purpose

Property that was acquired to provide a long-term benefit and has been used for that purpose may, at some point, be converted into inventory and held for the purpose of resale.

---

4 *Brown v. MNR*, 50 DTC 200.
5 *McDonough v. MNR*, 49 DTC 621.
6 *Racine v. MNR*, 65 DTC 5098.

For example, farmland that has been used to produce farm revenue or a parking lot used for customer parking may cease to be used for such purpose and be subdivided and held for property development and resale. Such a change of purpose does not constitute a disposition for tax purposes. Similarly, property that was acquired as inventory for resale, such as a piece of equipment, may, if not sold, be converted to capital property and used to produce income. In both situations, when the property is ultimately sold, this question arises: Is the gain a capital gain, a business gain, or a combination of the two?

While the *Income Tax Act* provides no rules for such situations, the CRA has developed a policy which requires that the gain or loss be allocated between capital and business income in accordance with the property's value at the time the purpose changed.[7] In the land example above, the capital gain would be set at the difference between the property's market value at the time of change and the original cost. Any further gain would be business income. Both gains are recognized only at the time of the actual sale. In such circumstances, it is important that the owner attempt to establish the property's value at the time of the change in use, in order to take maximum advantage of the allocation.

2. Canadian Securities

Investments in marketable securities almost always have a dual purpose: to generate annual returns and to realize a profit on resale. Historically, the CRA has applied the common-law principles described previously in a lenient manner; that is partly in recognition of the dual purpose but also a reflection of the government's desire to promote investment in equity securities. With respect to the investment in *Canadian* securities only, the *Income Tax Act* permits taxpayers (other than security dealers) to remove themselves from the common-law rules of intention and simply elect to have all sales of Canadian securities treated as capital transactions.[8] A Canadian security is considered to be (with some minor exceptions) a share of the capital stock of a resident Canadian corporation, a unit of a mutual fund, or a bond, debenture, bill, note, mortgage, or other similar obligation issued by a resident of Canada.

While making this election ensures capital treatment of all security transactions, it also locks the investor into using this method indefinitely. This may not always be desirable, especially considering the limitations on the use of capital losses when they occur. Many investors choose not to make the election and subject themselves to the lenient application of the common-law rules. This gives them the option of treating substantial trading losses as business losses (if the facts support that position), which can readily be offset against other sources of income.

C. Categories of Capital Property

In order to understand which properties are subject to capital gains treatment for tax purposes, it is useful to outline the categories of capital property. The *Income Tax Act*, directly or indirectly, defines three categories of capital property:

- personal-use property
- listed personal property
- financial property

Of the above, only personal-use property and listed personal property are specifically defined in the *Income Tax Act*. After these two specific definitions have been examined, the third definition—for financial property—will be clear.

- **Personal-use property** Personal-use property is property owned by the taxpayer that is used primarily for the personal use or enjoyment of the taxpayer, or persons related to the taxpayer, and that does not generate financial returns.[9] All personal

---

7   IT-102R2, IT-218R; *Armstrong v. The Queen*, 85 DTC 5396.
8   ITA 39(4) to (6); IT-479R.
9   ITA 54; IT-332R (archived).

property, such as a car, a boat, land, a house, a cottage, furniture, a piano, and so on, is personal-use property and subject to capital gains treatment.

- **Listed personal property**   Property in this category includes items that are for personal use but also have some element of investment value. This category is limited to several specific items, which are listed in the *Income Tax Act* as follows:[10]

  - a print, etching, drawing, painting, or sculpture, or other similar works of art
  - jewellery
  - a rare folio, rare manuscript, or rare book
  - a stamp
  - a coin

  Any property not listed above that is for personal use and enjoyment is personal-use property.

- **Financial property**   In this category is included all capital property that was acquired primarily to generate a benefit through a financial reward. It includes such items as shares, bonds, loans, land, buildings, equipment, patents, licences, franchises, and vehicles. Only a few capital properties are excluded from this category, the main one being property that qualifies as eligible capital property, as described in Chapter 6.

  Clearly, the capital gains provisions encompass a wide range of properties. When examining the disposition of a capital property, it is important to establish it in one of the above categories because, as will be described later in the chapter, certain aspects of transactions are treated differently in each category.

II. Determining Capital Gains and Losses—General Rules

Capital gains and losses were introduced in Chapter 3 as one of the five income categories. You will recall that the aggregating formula, which combines all the types of income to arrive at a taxpayer's net income for tax purposes, includes only the amount by which the total taxable capital gains for the year exceed the total allowable capital losses for the year.[11] Hence, the principle is established that capital losses can be offset only against capital gains and cannot be used to offset other sources of income earned by a taxpayer. (The same restriction is not placed on other sources of income; business losses and property losses can be offset against any other source of income for tax purposes.) The cash-flow implications of this special treatment were discussed in Chapter 3 and are reviewed again later in this chapter; this section restricts itself to establishing the format for calculating the capital gain or loss on each individual asset sold. However, it is important to relate the individual calculation to the aggregating formula in order to establish its effect on the amount of tax payable.

A. General Calculation

The capital gain or loss on the disposition of a given capital property is calculated by completing the following simple procedure:[12]

Proceeds of disposition		xxx
less		
Adjusted cost base (ACB)	xx	
Expenses of disposition	x	xx
Capital gain or capital loss		xx

10 ITA 54.
11 ITA 3(b).
12 ITA 40(1)(a)(i).

Only *one-half* of the above capital gain is included in net income for tax purposes; it is referred to as "taxable capital gain."[13] Similarly, only one-half of a capital loss is included in the calculation of net income for tax purposes; it is referred to as "allowable capital loss." At the end of each taxation year, the taxable capital gains and the allowable capital losses on all properties are totalled separately and included in the aggregating formula.

Note that the terminology used in the above calculation is different from the normal accounting terminology used in the disposal of long-term assets. The taxation terms "proceeds of disposition" and "adjusted cost base" are much broader than the accounting terms and require special examination.

B. Disposition and Proceeds of Disposition

Capital gains and losses are recognized for tax purposes only when a disposition of the property occurs.[14] If an investment in shares of a public corporation increases in value during the year, no capital gain is recognized. Similarly, if the investment declines in value, a capital loss does not occur. In comparison, when a bond compounds interest annually but pays nothing for 10 years, the investor who purchased it must recognize accrued interest annually.

Normally, a disposition of property occurs when[15]

(a) property is sold;
(b) property is involuntarily eliminated by theft, destruction, or expropriation;
(c) a share, bond, debenture, note, or similar property is cancelled, redeemed, or settled; or
(d) a share owned by a taxpayer is converted by amalgamation or merger (see Chapter 14).

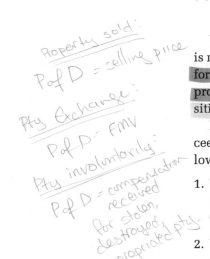

When property is sold, the proceeds of disposition is the selling price, whether it is received in cash or is payable at some future time. Property that is sold in exchange for other property has proceeds of disposition equal to the fair market value of the property received in exchange. The proceeds of disposition for an involuntary disposition is the compensation received for stolen, destroyed, or expropriated property.

In some circumstances, property is *deemed* to be disposed, even though no proceeds of disposition are received. A deemed disposition of property occurs in the following circumstances:

1. When property is transferred by way of a gift to another party, the taxpayer is deemed to have sold the property at its fair market value at that time (see Chapter 9).[16]

2. When the use of property changes from personal use to business or investment use, or when it is changed from business or investment use to personal use, the property is deemed to have been sold at its fair market value.[17]

3. Property is deemed to have been sold at fair market value when a taxpayer ceases to be a resident of Canada for tax purposes.[18] Certain properties, such as real estate situated in Canada, and inventory, eligible capital property, and capital property from a business in Canada are exempted. However, if adequate security is posted, the tax payment can be delayed until the property is sold. (See comment in Part C below on the adjusted cost base of property owned by a person who become a resident of Canada in a year.)

---

13 ITA 38.
14 ITA 39(1).
15 ITA 54, "disposition" and "proceeds of disposition."
16 ITA 69(1)(b).
17 ITA 45(1).
18 ITA 128.1; IT-451R.

4. On the death of an individual, all of that person's capital property is deemed to have been sold immediately prior to death (see Chapter 9).[19]

The definitions of *disposition* and *proceeds of disposition* are very broad when the concepts of actual disposition and deemed disposition are combined.

C. Adjusted Cost Base

Normally, the adjusted cost base of a property is the original purchase price plus other costs incurred to make the acquisition, such as brokerage fees, installation costs, and legal fees. Sometimes, the original cost is expanded, as described in Chapter 6, when the original cost of depreciable property is increased by the cost of substantial repairs and alterations. There are, however, a number of adjustments to cost for tax purposes that may or may not also be accepted for accounting purposes.[20]

The *Income Tax Act* lists, in section 53, a number of specific additions to and deductions from cost that can be made to arrive at the adjusted cost base of a property. For example, when a taxpayer receives a government grant or subsidy to acquire an asset, the purchase price of the asset is reduced by the amount of the grant to arrive at the adjusted cost base for tax purposes. If the asset is subsequently sold, the capital gain will be determined as the difference between the selling price and the lower cost base, rather than between the selling price and the original cost. The adjustment to the cost base ensures that the grant or subsidy will be taxable as a capital gain if and when it is recovered through an asset sale. The taxable benefits received when shares are purchased under an employee stock-option arrangement are added to the cost of the shares to ensure that the same income is not counted twice (see Chapter 4). These examples demonstrate that the adjustments to cost base are technical and specialized in nature. A detailed review is beyond the scope of this text.

In some cases, it is possible for the accumulated cost base reductions to be greater than the cost of the asset. When this occurs, the negative balance is considered a capital gain and is recognized in the year in which it occurs.[21] By exception, a negative adjusted cost base of an interest in a partnership normally does not create a capital gain (see Chapter 15).

Special provisions apply to the adjusted cost base of a property that was acquired before 1972 and is still owned by the taxpayer.[22] Before 1972, capital gains were not taxable; to reflect this, the adjusted cost base of property acquired before that year is tied to its fair market value at December 31, 1971.

In some circumstances, property may be acquired without a cost. A person who receives a gift of property has no actual cost. However, as described above, the person who made the gift is deemed to have sold the property at fair market value, and consequently, the recipient of the gift is deemed to have an adjusted cost base of the same amount.[23]

A taxpayer immigrating to Canada is deemed to acquire all assets immediately before immigrating. The acquisition amount is the asset's fair market value and this becomes the assets' adjusted cost base. Therefore, immigrants are taxable in Canada only on gains above the market value of property at the date of arrival.

D. Expenses of Disposition

Because of the nature of capital property, the owner often requires assistance to complete the sale transaction. All costs incurred to complete the disposition are deductible when arriving at the capital gain or loss; such costs include legal fees to complete the sale agreement, brokerage fees or commissions to agents, advertising, and mortgage discharge fees.[24]

---

19 ITA 70(5).
20 ITA 52, 53, 54.
21 ITA 40(3).
22 ITAR 26(3), 26(7), 20; IT-84, IT-139R (archived).
23 ITA 69(1)(c).
24 ITA 40(1).

E. Deferred Proceeds

Capital property, by its nature, often commands a relatively high selling price; this often means that the buyer must fund the purchase with a combination of cash reserves and debt financing. In order to facilitate a sale, a vendor may act as the financier for the purchaser by accepting payment in the form of an immediate down payment in cash, with the balance, with interest, to be paid over some future time period. When this occurs, the capital gain rules permit the vendor, subject to a time limitation, to recognize the taxable capital gain over a period of years in proportion to the receipt of the proceeds of disposition.[25] The deferred recognition of capital gains is restricted to a maximum of five years, and a minimum of 20% of the capital gain must be recognized, on a cumulative basis, for each of the five years. This method for recognizing capital gains is optional for each property sold.

It should be noted that the time limit of five years is extended to 10 years when the sale is made to a child of the taxpayer *and* the property sold is shares of a small business corporation, farm property, or an interest in a family farm partnership.[26]

If the taxpayer chooses to use this method, the capital gain calculation referred to previously must be modified, as demonstrated next.

Situation:

A taxpayer sold property in 20X0 for $200,000. The property had an adjusted cost base of $130,000, and selling costs of $20,000 were incurred. The selling price of $200,000 is to be paid to the vendor as follows:

Cash on sale (20X0)	$ 80,000
20X1	30,000
20X2	–0–
20X3	90,000
	$200,000

Analysis:

Capital gain:		
Proceeds of disposition		$200,000
less		
Adjusted cost base	$130,000	
Expenses of disposition	20,000	(150,000)
Capital gain		$ 50,000
Taxable capital gain ($1/2 \times \$50,000$)		$ 25,000

(20X0)	
Capital gain	$50,000
Less deferred portion—capital gains reserve—lesser of:	
(1) $\dfrac{\$120,000 \text{ (deferred proceeds)}}{\$200,000 \text{ (total proceeds)}} \times \$50,000 = \$30,000$	
(2) $4/5 \times \$50,000 = \$40,000$	(30,000)
Capital gain	$20,000
Taxable capital gain ($1/2 \times \$20,000$)	$10,000

Note that the deferred portion of the gain is in the proportion of the unpaid price to the total price. The *capital gain recognized in 20X0 of $20,000* is 40% of the total gain, as 40% of the total proceeds (40% of $200,000 = $80,000) was received in 20X0. Because 40% of the gain is recognized in 20X0, the requirement to recognize at least 20% per year has been satisfied for both 20X0 and 20X1.

---

25 ITA 40(1)(a)(iii); IT-236R4 (archived).
26 ITA 40(1.1).

(20X1)

Unrecognized gain (prior year's reserve)	$30,000
Less deferred portion—capital gains reserve—lesser of:	

$$(1)\ \frac{\$90,000\ (deferred\ proceeds)}{\$200,000\ (total\ proceeds)} \times \$50,000 = \$22,500$$

(2) $3/5 \times \$50,000 = \$30,000$ (unrecognized C.G.)es

	(22,500)
Capital gain	$ 7,500
Taxable capital gain ($1/2 \times \$7,500$)	$ 3,750

(20X2)

In 20X2, no additional payment is received. However, a portion of the gain must be recognized because the cumulative 20% minimum has not been met. By the end of 20X2, only 55% of the price has been received ($110,000/$200,000 = 55%), but a minimum of 60% (20% × 3 years) must be included in income. The capital gain recognized in 20X2 is 5% × $50,000 = $2,500.

Unrecognized gain (prior year's reserve)	$22,500
Less deferred portion—capital gains reserve—lesser of:	

$$(1)\ \frac{\$90,000\ (deferred\ proceeds)}{\$200,000\ (total\ proceeds)} \times \$50,000 = \$22,500$$

(2) $2/5 \times \$50,000 = \$20,000$ (unrecognized C.G.)

	(20,000)
Capital gain	$ 2,500
Taxable capital gain ($1/2 \times \$2,500$)	$ 1,250

(20X3)

In 20X3, the full balance of the proceeds is received, and therefore, the balance of the gain must be recognized.

Unrecognized gain (prior year's reserve)	$20,000
Less deferred portion—capital gains reserve—lesser of:	

$$(1)\ \frac{\$0\ (deferred\ proceeds)}{\$200,000\ (total\ proceeds)} \times \$50,000 = \$0$$

(2) $1/5 \times \$50,000 = \$10,000$

		(0)
Capital gain		$20,000
Taxable capital gain ($1/2 \times \$20,000$)		$10,000
Summarized as follows:		
Total capital gain (above)		$50,000
Less previously recognized:		
20X0	$20,000	
20X1	7,500	
20X2	2,500	(30,000)
Capital gain recognized in 20X3		$20,000
Taxable capital gain ($1/2 \times \$20,000$)		$10,000

Deferring the recognition of the capital gain to future years in proportion to the receipt of the proceeds is referred to as a reserve. The reserve is deducted from the capital gain in the year to arrive at the taxable amount. It is important to recognize that claiming the reserve is *discretionary* and that the taxpayer can choose not to defer the recognition of the gain. This may be desirable if the taxpayer has a capital loss in the year to offset the gain or if it is anticipated that tax rates will be higher in the future years. When the reserve is claimed, a formula exists to ensure that the reserve will not exceed the requirement that at least 20% of the gain be included in income on an accumulated basis. The formula states that the maximum reserve in any year is equal to the lesser of

(a) deferred proceeds/total proceeds × gain (as demonstrated above),

   or

(b) 80% of the gain in year 1, 60% in year 2, 40% in year 3, 20% in year 4, and zero in year 5.

An alternative formula for calculating the deferred portion of a capital gain is permitted when the property being sold is already encumbered with a debt and when the buyer assumes that debt as part of the purchase obligation.[27] In such cases, the taxpayer can recognize the gain in proportion to receipt of the equity in the property. For example, if capital property has a value of $100,000 but is encumbered by a first mortgage of $40,000, the owner's equity interest is $60,000. If that owner sold the property for $100,000 and the purchaser settled the price by assuming the first mortgage of $40,000, paying cash of $10,000 and owing the balance of $50,000, the deferred capital gain would be calculated as follows:

$$\frac{\$50,000 \text{ (deferred proceeds)}}{\$60,000 \text{ (equity in property)}} \times \text{gain}$$

This method permits a greater deferral than the method previously demonstrated, provided that the 20% rule does not limit its application. The obvious benefit of deferring the proceeds of disposition and thereby the related tax is that it permits the owner to reinvest a greater amount of the proceeds on a pre-tax basis by charging interest to the purchaser on the unpaid portion.

This section has developed the general rules for computing the capital gain or loss on the disposal of a single capital asset. With the exception of the rules relating to deferred proceeds, the principles are straightforward and easy to apply. Before examining how the taxation of capital property affects investment and management decisions, it is necessary to review some unique aspects of capital losses and the treatment of special types of property.

III. Unique Aspects of Capital Losses

In accordance with the general rules established in the previous section of the chapter, capital losses are recognized only when a disposition occurs; and as a result of the aggregating formula outlined in Chapter 3, they can be deducted for tax purposes only to the extent that capital gains were realized in the same year. Because of this restriction, a taxpayer who has incurred a capital loss should consider disposing of other capital property that has appreciated in value. Conversely, a taxpayer who is facing a capital gain should consider disposing of property that has declined in value in order to create an offsetting loss.

If a capital loss cannot be used in the current year, it can be carried forward indefinitely and used in the future when a capital gain occurs, or it can be carried *back* to the previous three years provided that capital gains were incurred in those years. This carry-forward and carry-back procedure is not part of the overall net income calculation; rather, it is applied when the net income for the year is reduced to taxable income. This topic will be discussed in detail in Chapter 10.

Normal rules do not apply to certain types of capital losses, some of which are discussed below.

---

27 IT-236R4 (archived), paragraph 8.

A. Allowable Business Investment Losses

An allowable business investment loss (ABIL) is the allowable capital loss (one-half of the actual loss) incurred on the disposition of a loan to a small business corporation, or on a sale of that corporation's shares (provided that sale is made to an arm's-length party).[28] In general terms, a small business corporation is a *private* corporation that is Canadian controlled and that uses all or substantially all of its assets (valued at fair market value) to conduct an active business.[29] The CRA holds the view that "substantially all" means at least 90% of the assets.

When such a loss occurs, the aggregating formula permits it to be offset against all other sources of income derived by the taxpayer, as an exception to the normal capital loss rules. In this way, the after-tax risk of investing in small business corporations is reduced relative to other capital investments because the tax savings on a loss, if one should occur, are readily usable.[30]

B. Deemed Disposition on Loans and Shares

The rule that a capital loss can be recognized only when the property is disposed of is a burden to taxpayers when a market is not available for the sale of the property. In particular, when an investment in shares of a corporation has declined in value because the corporation has suffered extreme financial problems or when an outstanding loan is uncollectible due to the debtor's inability to pay, the owner may be unable to sell the property and trigger the disposition. In recognition of this problem, property that is a loan or a share of capital stock of a corporation is subject to deemed-disposition rules that permit the loss to be recognized before an actual disposition occurs, as follows:[31]

1. An outstanding debt is deemed to be disposed of for a value of nil at the time it is established that it is a bad debt.

2. A share of the capital stock of a corporation is deemed to be disposed of for a value of nil at the time the corporation has become legally bankrupt. If the corporation is not legally bankrupt, a deemed disposition may still be permitted if, at the end of the year, the corporation is insolvent, it has ceased operating its business (with no intention to resume), the value of its shares is nil, and the corporation is expected to be dissolved.

It is clear from all this that it is easier to recognize a loss on a bad loan than on a share because in the case of a loan, it need only be established that the loan is uncollectible, whereas with a share, the owner must wait for legal bankruptcy or other specified conditions to occur. Also, the loss from the deemed disposition may be classified as an allowable business investment loss if the loan or the shares are from a small business corporation, as discussed previously.

C. Depreciable Property

Under no circumstances can a capital loss occur on the disposition of capital property that is also classified as depreciable property. As described in Chapter 6, the original cost of depreciable property is written off through the capital cost allowance system. Therefore, any actual loss arising when property is sold for a price less than its original cost is automatically reflected in the annual capital cost allowance calculation or the terminal loss or recapture, if any.

For example, suppose that all of the depreciable property of a class originally cost $10,000 and has an undepreciated capital cost of $8,000. If it is sold for $7,000, a terminal loss of $1,000 occurs at the time of sale. The selling price of $7,000 is $3,000 less than the original cost of $10,000; this loss is fully recognized for tax purposes as follows:

---

28 ITA 38(c), 39(1)(c), 251(1); IT-484R2.
29 ITA 248(1).
30 Also, when an ABIL is incurred, an individual is restricted from claiming the capital gain deduction (see Chapter 10) in future years until taxable capital gains of an equal amount have been included in income. Conversely, if a capital gain deduction has been claimed in a prior year, the ABIL may be restricted.
31 ITA 50(1), (2), 40(2)(g); IT-159R3.

Capital cost allowance in previous years	$2,000
Terminal loss on sale	1,000
	$3,000

D. Superficial Losses

When property has declined in value, a taxpayer who has no real intention of ridding himself or herself of the property may dispose of it in an attempt to trigger the recognition of a capital loss; subsequently or before the sale, that person may reacquire the same property. In such circumstances, when the reacquisition occurs within 30 days of the sale of the original property, the resulting loss is classified as a superficial loss and is deemed to be nil for tax purposes.[32] The actual loss is not permanently denied but, rather, is added to the adjusted cost base of the new identical property and will be recognized when the new property is sold.[33]

Situation:

On December 31, 20X0, a taxpayer sold 500 shares of Corporation X for $8,000 that originally cost $10,000. On January 5, 20X1, the taxpayer reacquired 500 shares of Corporation X for $7,500.

Analysis:

(20X0)	
Proceeds of disposition	$ 8,000
less	
Adjusted cost base	(10,000)
Actual capital loss	$ 2,000
Superficial loss deemed to be	NIL
(20X1)	
Cost of new shares:	
Actual cost of 500 shares	$ 7,500
plus	
Loss previously denied	2,000
Adjusted cost base of new shares	$ 9,500

When the new shares are ultimately sold, the original loss of $2,000 is deducted from the selling price as part of the cost of the new shares sold.

The same treatment applies when a taxpayer incurs a loss from the sale of property to a spouse, to his or her own controlled corporation, or to a corporation controlled by a spouse. In these circumstances, the loss is deemed to be zero.[34] A capital loss is also denied when it results from the transfer of property by an individual to an RRSP or TFSA.

As was stated, the superficial loss that is denied to the seller is simply added to the cost base of the newly acquired property and is recognized when that property is eventually sold. It should be noted that this treatment applies when the *seller* is an *individual*. Where the *seller* is a *corporation,* a slightly different result occurs. The selling corporation is denied the capital loss (similar to an individual), however, the denied loss is retained by the seller corporation and is not transferred to the cost base of the new property. Instead, the seller simply defers the recognition of the

---

32 ITA 54, 40(2)(g).
33 ITA 53(1)(f).
34 ITA 54. Technically, the superficial-loss rules apply where the property is repurchased by the taxpayer, his or her spouse, or an "affiliated" person, 30 days before or after the sale of property on which the loss has occurred.

capital loss[35] until the affiliated person sells the property (and it remains sold for 30 days) or the asset is deemed sold under the deemed disposition rules (discussed earlier—example on death). The loss can also be recognized if there is a change in control of the seller corporation or there is a taxable wind-up.

E. Personal-Use Property

As previously mentioned, personal-use property is capital property from which the owner derives a long-term benefit—that is, personal use and enjoyment.[36] For tax purposes, any loss suffered on the sale of personal-use property is deemed to be nil, even though gains on such property are taxable.[37] Presumably, this policy reflects the fact that the loss on sale is equivalent to the enjoyment received from the use of the property.

This restriction is applied to each item of personal property, which means that the capital loss on one item of personal-use property cannot be offset against a capital gain realized on the sale of another personal-use property.

Personal-use property is further distinguished from other capital property by having a deemed minimum cost for tax purposes of $1,000 and deemed minimum proceeds of $1,000.[38] Therefore, small items of personal-use property will be subject to capital gains treatment only to the extent that the proceeds of disposition exceed the minimum amount of $1,000.

F. Listed Personal Property

Listed personal property was defined previously as personal-use property that has personal value as well as investment value; it is restricted by definition to specific items, such as works of art, rare books, jewellery, stamps, and coins.[39]

Listed personal property is different from personal-use property in this way: a loss from the sale of listed personal property is recognized for tax purposes. However, capital losses from listed personal property can be offset only against capital gains from listed personal property; they cannot be offset against other capital gains or other forms of income.[40] To the extent that capital losses on listed personal property cannot be used in the current year (because there are not sufficient capital gains from listed personal property), the unused loss can be carried back three years or forward seven years and deducted against listed personal property gains, if any, in those years. These carry-overs form part of the calculation of annual net income for tax purposes (see Chapter 3, also Exhibit 10-1 in Chapter 10).

As is the case with personal-use property, each item of listed personal property that costs less than $1,000 is deemed to have a minimum cost for tax purposes of $1,000. Each property also has a deemed minimum proceeds of $1,000.

G. Assets Transferred to an RRSP or TFSA

Individuals sometimes transfer certain investments to an RRSP or a TFSA. If the asset transferred has a market value less than the investment's ACB, the resulting capital loss is deemed to be zero.[41] Therefore, one should not contemplate transferring such assets directly to an RRSP or TFSA. As an alternative, an individual could sell the investment, trigger the capital loss, and then transfer the cash to the RRSP or TFSA. This preserves the capital loss for offset against current or future capital gains. If it is desired to hold the same investment in the RRSP or TFSA, the individual should then wait for at least 30 days after selling the initial investment before re-acquiring an identical investment to avoid the application of the superficial loss rule described in Part D above. The individual and the RRSP or TFSA are considered to be affiliated persons.[42] Therefore,

---

35 ITA 40(3.4).
36 ITA 54; IT-332R (archived).
37 ITA 40(2)(g).
38 ITA 46(1) to (3).
39 ITA 54.
40 ITA 41(1), (2).
41 ITA 40(2)(g)(iv).
42 ITA 251.1.

a loss from a sale by the individual followed by a purchase by the affiliated person (RRSP or TFSA) within 30 days would cause the initial loss to be designated as a superficial loss and deemed to be zero.[43]

IV. Unique Aspects of Specific Capital Properties

Certain specific types of property require special mention either because the tax treatment deviates from the general principles of capital gains or because it is difficult to establish whether or not the property is capital property. Several of these items are discussed briefly in this section of the chapter.

A. Identical Properties

Often, several properties of an identical nature are acquired over a period of time and at different costs. For example, an investor may acquire shares of the same corporation over a period of years, with the per-share price different at each time of acquisition. It is difficult in this situation to distinguish one share from another; if some but not all of the shares are sold, this question arises: What is the adjusted base of the shares sold?

The adjusted cost base of each identical property acquired is the weighted average cost of all the identical properties acquired up to the point of sale.[44] This calculation is demonstrated below.

Situation:

An investor acquired shares of X Corporation as follows:

Year	No. of shares	Cost per share	Total cost
20X0	100	$ 6	$ 600
20X1	200	8	1,600
20X2	80	10	800
	380		$3,000

In 20X2, the investor sold 150 shares of Corporation X for $9 per share.

Analysis:

Proceeds of disposition (150 × $9)	$1,350
Adjusted cost base of one share: $3,000/380 = $7.89	
Cost base of all shares sold: 150 × $7.89	1,183
Capital gain	$ 167
Taxable capital gain (½ × 167)	$ 84

In the above example, if additional shares are subsequently purchased, they are added to the cost base of the 230 shares (380 − 150) remaining, which now have a total average cost of $1,815 (230 × $7.89).

B. Convertible Securities

Normally, the exchange of one property for another will result in a disposition for tax purposes. However, when securities, such as shares, bonds, and debentures, are issued and the owner has the right to convert or exchange them for shares of the same corporation, and the owner makes use of that right, a disposition is not considered to have occurred. Instead, the adjusted cost base of the old security becomes the cost base of the new security, and a gain or loss is recognized when the new security is eventually sold.[45]

---

43 ITA 40(2)(g).
44 ITA 47(1), (2); IT-387R2. (Also see proposed ITA 47(3).)
45 ITA 51(1), (2).

C. Options and Warrants

In order to secure the opportunity to acquire property at some future time, a taxpayer may pay an amount that grants him or her the right or option to purchase property at a specified price over some limited time period.

From the payer's perspective, this type of transaction has no tax consequences at the time of payment. If, at a subsequent time, the payer exercises the option and purchases the property, the cost of the option is added to the adjusted cost base of the property acquired. On the other hand, if the payer allows the option to expire and does not purchase the property, the full cost of the option is considered a capital loss in the year of expiry.[46]

The tax treatment to the taxpayer who granted the option and received the payment is somewhat different. In this case, the amount received for granting the option is considered a capital gain in the year in which it is received. If, in a subsequent year, the option is exercised, the original option amount received is included as part of the proceeds of disposition in that year, and the original option amount reported as a capital gain in the earlier year is reversed through the filing of an amended tax return.[47]

D. Commodities and Futures Transactions

Commodities and commodity futures cannot, by definition, be classified as capital property because no long-term or enduring benefit can result from their acquisition. Commodities are acquired solely for the purpose of obtaining a gain on resale and are therefore inventory of trade. But in spite of the obvious position of commodity transactions, the CRA has set a policy that allows taxpayers to choose between capital treatment and business-income treatment, provided that the chosen method is used consistently in future years.[48] However, this option is not permitted for taxpayers who are associated with the commodity business or who are taking commodity positions as part of their normal business or trade. For example, farmers who grow wheat must treat commodity transactions in wheat as part of their business income.

E. Goodwill and Eligible Capital Property

The tax treatment of eligible capital property was described in Chapter 6. Eligible capital property includes goodwill as well as other intangible assets, such as franchises and licences, that do not have a limited legal life. It is important to note that although such properties are capital in nature, they are not usually subject to capital gains treatment for tax purposes. Gains or losses on the sale of eligible capital property are determined as described in Chapter 6 and are treated as business income or business losses.

In comparison, depreciable properties of a limited legal life (class 14), such as buildings, equipment, and franchises, are both depreciable property *and* capital property and, therefore, may have a capital element as well as a business element (see Chapter 6).

F. Principal Residence

A principal residence (which is specifically defined in the *Income Tax Act*) can generally be regarded as a housing unit owned, either directly or through a cooperative, by the taxpayer and ordinarily inhabited for personal use.[49] A principal residence is personal-use property, as previously defined; as such, it may be subject to a capital gain on sale, but it cannot realize a capital loss.

The capital gain realized on the sale of a principal residence is reduced by the following formula:[50]

$$\frac{1 + \text{Number of years designated as principal residence}}{\text{Number of years owned}} \times \text{Gain}$$

If a taxpayer owns more than one personal residence—for example, a house as well as a summer cottage—only one can be designated for any particular year. Further, only one property can be designated for each family (husband and wife). It is clear from the above formula that if one residence is designated as the principal residence for each year of ownership, the reduction is equal to the full capital gain.

---

46 ITA 54 (disposition).
47 ITA 49(1) to (5).
48 IT-346R.
49 ITA 54; IT-120R6.
50 ITA 40(2)(b), 40(6).

The "+ 1" is included in the formula to cover the year in which two houses are owned as a result of the normal process of selling one house and acquiring a new one.

It is easy to make the principal residence calculation when the individual owns a single residence. However, when more than one residence is owned, the problem of designation is complex because of the nature of the formula. The decision to designate a particular property is made at the time of sale, not when the property is acquired. This is demonstrated below.

Situation: A taxpayer acquired a house in 20X1 for $100,000. In 20X3, the same taxpayer acquired a vacation home for $50,000. In 20X5, both properties were sold: the house for $150,000 and the vacation home for $95,000.

Analysis:

Vacation home:

Capital gain ($95,000 − $50,000)	$45,000
Exemption:	
$\dfrac{2 + 1}{3} \times \$45,000 =$	45,000
Net capital gain	–0–

House:

Capital gain ($150,000 − $100,000)	$50,000
Exemption:	
$\dfrac{3 + 1}{5} \times \$50,000 =$	40,000
Net capital gain	$10,000
Taxable capital gain (½ × $10,000)	$ 5,000

In this example, the house realized a capital gain of $50,000 over five years, or $10,000 for each year of ownership. The vacation home had a capital gain of $45,000 over three years, or $15,000 for each year of ownership.

Because the exemption formula is based on both the period of ownership and the amount of the gain, the summer home will receive an exemption of $15,000 for each year designated, whereas the house exemption will be only $10,000 per year. Therefore, even though the total gain on the house is greater, it is better to emphasize the vacation home. Because of the "+ 1" in the formula, one only needs to designate the vacation home for two years in order to receive the full exemption. This, in turn, permits the house to be designated for three years.

It was mentioned previously that a deemed disposition occurs (at fair market value) when property that has a personal use is altered so that it has a business or investment use. This rule also applies when a principal residence is converted into a rental property. However, an individual can elect to have this rule not apply to a former principal residence.[51] This is particularly valuable when that individual rents the home and later resumes using it as a principal residence. In order to qualify for this exception, the owner cannot claim capital cost allowance on the property while it is being rented out.[52] This election can continue until the property is sold or converted back to a principal residence. When the property is eventually sold, the vendor can choose to designate the property as a principal residence for up to four years of the election period. For example if the property is sold after nine years from the year in which the change in use election was made, any four of the nine years can be designated as principal residence years. This four-year period can be extended indefinitely in special circumstances such as when a person is required to move for employment purposes.[53] Conversely, when you change a

---

51 ITA 45(2), (3).
52 ITA 45(4).
53 ITA 54.1; IT-120R6.

rental property to a principal residence, an election can be made to delay the disposition until the property is eventually sold. At the time of sale you can designate as a principal residence up to four of the years prior to the time it is occupied as a principal residence.[54]

Transactions relating to a principal residence are very common and affect a large number of taxpayers. It is unfortunate that the tax rules relating to such transactions are exceedingly complex. This area has been reviewed in a very superficial manner; the more detailed rules are significantly more complex and should be consulted if more than one residence is owned.[55]

G. Voluntary and Involuntary Dispositions

Special treatment is provided for the recognition of capital gains on the disposition of real estate (land and buildings) that is used to conduct a business. In such cases, the recognition of the capital gain can be deferred, provided that replacement property is acquired in the same year the property is sold or before the end of the first taxation year that begins after the property was sold.[56] The replacement property must be used for a similar purpose as the original property. The capital gain that would normally have been recognized is used instead to reduce the adjusted cost base of the replacement property acquired; in this way, it is deferred until the replacement property is sold without being similarly replaced. Similar treatment is available for the recapture of capital cost allowance (see Chapter 6).

It should be noted that this exception does not apply to real estate that is used to earn property income from rentals. Nor does it apply to personal-use real estate.

A similar treatment applies to property that has been lost, stolen, destroyed, or expropriated and for which compensation has been received. In such cases, the capital gain can be deferred if replacement property is acquired before the end of the second taxation year that begins after the property was disposed. The opportunity to defer the recognition of the capital gain is not restricted to business real estate. It also applies to rental properties as well as machinery and equipment.

H. Mutual Funds

It is common for individuals to invest in mutual funds. When the investment is owned directly by the individual and not through an RRSP, there are a number of possible tax consequences. These are reviewed below.

An investor acquires units of a particular mutual fund at a specified cost. As the units are capital property, the purchase price represents the units' adjusted cost base for tax purposes. The money is pooled with that of other investors and is used to purchase a variety of publicly traded securities, such as shares, bonds, mortgages, treasury bills, and commercial paper. On a regular basis—usually quarterly—the mutual fund distributes its gains to the unit holders. For tax purposes, these distributions retain the source and characteristics of the income earned by the mutual fund—capital gains, dividends, interest, and ordinary income—and are included in each unit holder's income for tax purposes in the taxation year of the distribution. Often, investors choose to reinvest the distribution by acquiring additional units of the mutual fund. When they do, the distribution is still taxable to the unit holder as capital gains, dividends, interest, or ordinary income (as the case may be), and the total amount of the distribution is added to the adjusted cost base of the investment. For example, assume an individual previously acquired 1,000 units of a mutual fund for $20 per unit. The ACB is, therefore, $20,000 (1,000 × $20). In the subsequent year the fund makes a distribution to the owner of $1,000 and the amount is reinvested to acquire 40 additional units at $25 per unit (the current market value). The new ACB of the 1,040 units is $21,000 or $20.19 per unit (20,000 + 1,000/1,040 unit).

A disposition for tax purposes occurs whenever all or some of the units are redeemed for cash or transferred to another mutual fund. The disposition will result

---

54 ITA 45(3); IT-120R6.
55 IT-120R6.
56 ITA 44(1), (2); IT-259R4.

in a capital gain or loss to the extent that the redemption price or transfer value varies from the adjusted cost base of the units at the time.

I. Eligible Small Business Investments

To improve access to capital for small business corporations, *individuals* who dispose of a small business investment can *defer* the recognition of a limited amount of the related capital gain if the proceeds from the sale are used to make other small business investments.[57] There are a number of qualifications that must be met to be eligible for the deferral. An important qualification is that the new investment be in newly issued *treasury* common shares of a replacement entity. Purchasing shares from an existing shareholder does not qualify for the deferral. This means that the replacement entity is strengthened by the receipt of additional capital resources that can be used to support its growth. The eligible capital gain is deferred until the new investment is eventually sold or the proceeds of its sale are again reinvested in another qualified replacement investment. The concept of the deferral is demonstrated in the following situation:

Situation:

In 20X2, an individual sells her shares in Corporation X for $1,000,000. The shares are eligible small business investments having an adjusted cost base of $400,000. Within the qualifying time period, she reinvests $900,000 of the sale proceeds in Corporation Y treasury shares, which are new small business investments. In 20X5, she sells the shares of Corporation Y for $1,200,000.

$\mathrel{\llcorner}$ eligible to defer. C, G

Analysis:

The sale of the Corporation X shares in 20X2 results in a capital gain of $600,000 ($1,000,000 − $400,000). However, because 90% of the proceeds from the sale of Corporation X ($900,000/$1,000,000 = 90%) are reinvested in Corporation Y (a qualified small business investment), she can defer only 90% of the capital gain. Her capital gain recognized in 20X2 is $60,000, as follows:

Capital gain from sale of Corporation X	$600,000
Less amount deferred – 90% × $600,000	(540,000) *defer*
Capital gain in 20X2	$ 60,000

The deferred portion of the capital gain ($540,000) reduces the adjusted cost base of the new investment in Corporation Y shares from $900,000 to $360,000 ($900,000 − $540,000). Therefore, when the shares of Corporation Y are sold in 20X5, a capital gain of $840,000 is recognized, as follows:

Proceeds of disposition	$1,200,000
Adjusted cost base	
($900,000 − $540,000 deferred from 20X2)	(360,000)
Capital gain in 20X5	$ 840,000

Note that the 20X5 capital gain of $840,000 includes the deferred gain from 20X2 of $540,000 plus the actual gain of $300,000 from the sale of the corporation Y shares ($1,200,000 − $900,000).

Some further qualifications that must be met to be eligible for the deferral are outlined below.

- The deferral is available to individuals only.
- The deferral applies to the capital gains realized from the sale of shares in an eligible small business corporation. Normally, this refers to a Canadian-controlled

---

57 ITA 44.1.

private corporation with at least 90% of its assets used in active business carried on primarily in Canada. In addition, the corporation's total assets cannot be greater than $50 million immediately after the investment.[58] Corporations that do *not* qualify include professional corporations, specified financial institutions, corporations whose net real estate assets exceed 50% of their total asset value, and corporations whose principal business is the leasing, rental, development, or sale of real property.

- The replacement eligible investment must be purchased at any time during the year of sale of the former shares or 120 days after the end of the taxation year.

J. Gifts of Canadian Public Securities

A special rule regarding capital gains applies on the disposition of Canadian public securities when they are transferred directly to a public charity as a gift. When this occurs the unrealized gain on the security is deemed to be nil and no income tax cost results. At the same time, the taxpayer receives a charitable donation receipt for the full value of the security providing a substantial tax saving (usually equal to the taxpayer's marginal tax rate). Consider the situation where an individual owns a public security with a market value of $10,000 but originally cost only $2,000. Assuming the taxpayer's marginal tax bracket is 45%, the potential tax on the disposition of the security is $1,800 (45% × (1/2)($10,000 − $2,000)). If the security was first sold and the after-tax proceeds of $8,200 ($10,000 − $1,800 tax) gifted to a charity, the taxpayer would receive a donation receipt for $8,200 and obtain a tax saving of $3,690 (45% × $8,200—see Chapter 10 for charitable donation tax credits). However, if the security was given directly to the charity, the taxpayer would have no taxable capital gain, no tax on the transfer, and would receive a donation receipt for the full value of the security ($10,000). The resulting tax saving of $4,500 (45% × $10,000) is $810 greater than the former method ($4,500 − $3,690).

V. The Aggregating Formula Revisited

Because the aggregating formula (described in Chapter 3) for determining a taxpayer's net income from all sources imposes special restrictions on capital losses, it would be useful to examine how the various items reviewed in this chapter relate to that formula.

Situation: A taxpayer, in addition to earning business income of $50,000, property income of $18,000, and other sources of income of $4,000, had the following capital transactions in the year:

Property	Proceeds of disposition	Cost base and selling costs	Gain or (loss)
Shares of company X	$60,000	$40,000	$20,000
Shares of company P	17,000	41,000	(24,000)
Art	8,000	6,000	2,000
Boat	9,000	12,000	(3,000)
Grand piano	11,000	10,000	1,000
Stamp collection	18,000	21,000	(3,000)
Shares of small business corporation	8,000	20,000	(12,000)

---

58 Applies to transactions after October 17, 2000. A different limit applied to transactions between February 28, 2000 and October 18, 2000.

Analysis: This taxpayer sold property of all three general types—financial property, personal-use property, and listed personal property.

Loss: 2,000 – 3000 = 1000

• **Listed personal property** The art incurred a capital gain of $2,000 and the stamp collection a loss of $3,000. Because losses from listed personal property can be offset only against gains from listed personal property, the net gain from this type of property is zero.

• **Personal-use property** The loss on the boat is deemed to be zero. The piano had a gain of $1,000, of which $500 (½ of $1,000) is taxable.

• **Financial property** Shares of company X have a taxable capital gain of $10,000 (½ of $20,000).
  Shares of company P have an allowable capital loss of $12,000 (½ of $24,000).
  Shares of the small business corporation are a business investment loss, of which $6,000 (½ of $12,000) is allowable.

Aggregating formula:

(a) Business income		$50,000
Property income		18,000
Other income		4,000
		72,000
(b) Taxable capital gains:		
Listed personal property	$ –0–	
Piano	500	
Shares of company X	10,000	
	gain 10,500	
Allowable capital loss:		
Shares of company P	*loss* $(12,000)	–0–
		72,000
(c) Other deductions		–0–
		72,000
(d) Allowable business investment loss on shares of small business corporation		(6,000)
Net income for tax purposes		$66,000

Note that in part (b) of the formula the net effect of the capital gains and losses is zero, even though the capital losses exceed the capital gains. The excess net capital loss of $1,500 can be carried back three years and forward indefinitely when *taxable income* is computed, provided that sufficient capital gains are available (see Chapter 10). In addition, the unused listed personal property loss ($3,000 – $2,000 = $1,000 × ½ = $500) can be carried back three years and forward seven years and used in arriving at *net income*, provided that listed personal property gains are available.

Also, note that the allowable business investment loss on the shares of the small business corporation is included in part (d) of the formula and, as a result, is deducted from all other sources of income for the year.

As stated previously, it is important that when applying the normal rules for determining individual gains and losses on capital property, those rules be approached in the context of the aggregating formula. This way, that formula's effect on the tax payable for the particular year can be more readily understood.

VI. Impact on Investment and Management Decisions

The influence of the tax treatment of capital properties on investment and management decisions centres on the fact that *preferential* treatment is given to capital gains, regarding the amount taxable and the timing of income recognition; whereas *restricted* treatment is given to the utilization of capital losses. Managers must build these fundamental variables into the decision process when forecasting the returns on alternative investment opportunities and also when considering the downside risk if a particular investment is not successful and results in a loss.

A. Return on Investment

The fact that only one-half of a capital gain is taxable at the time of disposition substantially increases the after-tax yield over other forms of investment returns. For example, for a taxpayer in a 45% tax bracket, a $100,000, 20-year investment in a property that will increase in value by 12% annually will provide $411,000 more in after-tax returns over the life of the investment than would an investment of the same amount in property yielding 12% in annual interest.

Capital growth:	
Gross value at end of 20 y:	
$100,000 + (12% × 20 y)	$965,000
Less tax payable in year 20:	
45% × (½) ($965,000 − $100,000)	195,000
Future value after tax	$770,000
Annual interest return:	
The 12% return is taxed annually at 45%, resulting in an	
after-tax yield of 6.6%. Future value of investment, after tax:	
$100,000 + (6.6% × 20 y)	$359,000
Difference in after-tax yield	$411,000

In most cases, achieving a return by capital growth involves greater risk (example—shares) or greater effort (example—real estate) than is the case with interest-bearing securities. However, one cannot properly assess the importance of additional risk or effort without examining the after-tax yield potential. In the above example, the after-tax returns are so substantial that the concept of risk takes on a different meaning.

The above example compared the decision to invest in property that yields a capital gain with the decision to invest in a venture yielding property income. The impact of tax on capital gains is also relevant when a decision is being made whether to sell one capital property and replace it with another. Because tax must be paid on the sale of the first property, there will be less after-tax value to invest in the second property.

Assume that a taxpayer in a 45% tax bracket owns investment A, which originally cost $10,000 but is now worth $100,000. The taxpayer is contemplating the sale of investment A in order to acquire investment B. If investment A were sold, a tax of $20,250 (45% × ½ [$100,000 − $10,000]) would be payable, leaving only $79,750 for reinvestment in investment B. When a sale of property A to acquire property B is being considered, this question must be asked: Is an investment of $79,750 in property B equivalent in value to the investment of $100,000 in property A? In order to justify acquiring property B, that property would have to be significantly more attractive in terms of its future potential than property A.

The above examples again emphasize the need to examine investment and asset-replacement decisions on an after-tax cash flow basis.

B. Downside Risk

In addition to considering the tax impact of a given investment, it is important to consider the potential loss in the event that the investment must be sold at a loss. While it is difficult to assess the real risk of an investment, the investor should at least know the potential magnitude of the loss. The real loss is the after-tax loss; therefore, the amount of the loss and the timing of the loss utilization to reduce taxes payable are both vital considerations.

For example, an investment of $100,000 in a capital property by a taxpayer in a 45% tax bracket may incur a loss of only $77,500, calculated as follows:

Maximum loss	$100,000
Less tax saving on utilization of the loss:	
45% $\times$ ($\frac{1}{2}$) ($100,000)	(22,500)
Net loss after tax	$ 77,500

In this situation, an investment of $100,000 can result in a maximum cash loss of only $77,500; this knowledge may well alter the investor's attitude toward the risk. Unfortunately, in most cases, the ability to utilize capital losses is uncertain because such losses can be offset only against capital gains. This means that a taxpayer who is able to realize capital gains when capital losses occur is at less risk from an investment than an investor who cannot readily utilize the loss.

You will recall that the restrictions on the use of capital losses are relaxed for certain types of property. When this is the case, the downside risk of such an investment is reduced owing to the enhanced ability to generate tax savings through the utilization of losses if they occur. Consider a loan to, or an investment in shares of, a small business corporation. If a capital loss occurs on disposition, one-half of the loss is classified as an allowable business investment loss and can be offset against the investor's other sources of income such as business income, property income, and employment income. Note that a loss on a loan to the corporation is realized for tax purposes when it is established to be uncollectible, whereas a loss on the shares can be realized only when the corporation is legally bankrupt. Therefore, there is less downside risk if the investors in a small business corporation contribute capital to the company primarily by way of loans and less by way of share capital (see Chapter 12).

VII. Tax Planning Checklist

The following tax planning opportunities were discussed briefly in this chapter:

1. When contemplating an investment opportunity, anticipate the potential tax treatment (capital gain versus business income, capital loss versus business investment loss, and so on). This way, the ultimate after-tax position can be assessed in relation to the risks associated with that investment.

2. Remember that achieving a return via a capital gain delays tax until the property is sold, and even then, only one-half of the gain is taxable. So, be sure to carefully compare investments that have capital growth potential with other types of investments on an after-tax basis, rather than on a pre-tax basis.

3. Review capital properties regularly throughout the year. Consider selling those that will result in a loss in order to offset capital gains that have occurred. As well, consider selling properties that have appreciated in value to trigger a capital gain that can utilize an existing unused loss.

4. When selling one property to obtain funds to acquire a new, higher-yield property, bear in mind that the tax on the sale of the first property will reduce the amount available for reinvestment and that the actual overall return on investment may thus be lower than it was previously.

5. When investing in private corporations, attempt to minimize investments in share capital and maximize shareholder loans. This may speed up any loss recognition if the company should fail or run into severe financial difficulty.

6. Whenever possible, take advantage of the available reserve for deferred proceeds on capital properties in order to delay the recognition of taxable income. Keep in mind that it may sometimes be better not to use the reserve if a tax advantage can be gained by recognizing income earlier (e.g., if current tax rates are lower than those expected in future years or if the taxpayer has accumulated losses). However, before accepting an agreement to defer proceeds on a sale, be sure there is sufficient cash available to meet the tax obligations as they come due.

7. Capital gain reserves are optional, which means that the reserve provisions constitute an opportunity to shift income from one time period to another within specified limits.

8. When selling a security for a loss, remember to consider the superficial loss rules if contemplating a reinvestment in that property.

9. When investing in Canadian securities, consider electing capital gains treatment on those and future properties. However, keep in mind that capital losses can be offset only against capital gains. A similar decision must be made when investing in commodity futures.

10. When replacing properties in order to defer the related capital gain, be aware of the time limits—one year for business real estate after a voluntary disposition and two years for assets destroyed, stolen, or expropriated. Eligible small business share replacements also have time limits.

11. When investing in shares of a private corporation, regularly review its dividend policy. When a corporation does not declare a dividend, the value of its shares increases and so does the potential capital gain. The greater the dividend a corporation declares, the lower are the share value and potential capital gain.

VIII. Summary and Conclusion

Capital gains and losses occur when property that was acquired for the purpose of providing the owner with a long-term or enduring benefit is disposed of. It is the *intended purpose* of acquisition that establishes its capital nature, not the nature of the asset itself. The tax authorities, in an attempt to determine "purpose," examine the owner's course of conduct with the property over the period of ownership; this process may or may not substantiate the owner's claims regarding intended purpose. Owners should be aware of the subjective nature of the definition and look on this as part of the overall risk when making investment decisions.

In relation to the overall scheme of income determination for tax purposes, capital gains have preferential treatment because

(a) only one-half of the gain is taxable; and
(b) the gain is included in income only when a disposition of the property occurs.

Because capital gains are given preferential treatment, capital losses are treated in a restrictive manner compared with other types of losses.

A capital gain or loss on a property is calculated as the difference between the proceeds of disposition and the sum of its adjusted cost base and selling expenses. This formula is simple but also limited. Note that no deductions are available for the costs associated with maintaining the property or financing its acquisition. If the property is of a financial nature and provides long-term benefits from business revenues, interest, dividends, or rent, expenses associated with the property can be deducted against those sources of income. However, if the property is personal-use property, the related expenses are ignored for tax purposes.

The reader may be aware that individuals, but not corporations, are exempt from a certain amount of capital gains through the capital gain deduction. This deduction, which applies in limited situations for individuals, forms part of the calculation that converts net income for tax purposes to taxable income and will be discussed in Chapter 10.

The impact of capital gains and losses on decisions involving investment and—for businesses—capital expansion and replacement is tied to the special tax treatment afforded to capital property transactions. Investors and business managers faced with long-term investment decisions should recognize that these tax preferences are continually being debated in the political arena. There are those who argue that capital gains should not be taxable at all, especially if the proceeds of disposition are reinvested in capital expansion. (This concept already applies, in a limited manner, to real estate used to conduct an active business.) Others argue that it is unfair to tax only a portion of capital gains, which are earned by a small minority of taxpayers, when the great majority of low- and middle-income taxpayers, who are unable to invest in capital property, are fully taxable on their normal sources of income. Because investment in capital properties is a long-term process, decision makers must be cognizant of the debate and consider its possible outcome. Capital gains were not taxable at all before 1972. Beginning that year, 50% of capital gains were taxable. In 1990, this was increased to 75%. In 2000, the inclusion rate was reduced to 50%. What may it be in the future?

Visit the Canadian Income Taxation Web site at **www.mcgrawhill.ca/ olc/buckwold** to view any updated tax information.

Demonstration Questions

QUESTION ONE

Teresa Sereti, a resident of Halifax, Nova Scotia, has requested your tax advice regarding a number of financial transactions that occurred in 20X5. Information relating to these transactions is outlined below.

1. In 20X0, Sereti purchased shares of Pluto Inc., a Canadian-controlled private corporation, for $20,000. After several years of financial problems, the corporation recently ceased operations and is insolvent. When operations ceased, all of Pluto's assets were being used in an active business.

2. In 20X3, Sereti purchased, for $30,000, a three-hectare parcel of land in a rural area. In 20X5, two of the three hectares were sold separately for $20,000 per hectare. She used the proceeds to construct a greenhouse on the remaining land. She will use the greenhouse to grow and sell vegetables in her spare time. Sereti could have acquired a one-hectare site in 20X3 but opted for the larger property in the hope that she could sell part of the property at an increased value and raise funds to help pay for the cost of constructing the greenhouse. Sereti paid property taxes of $500 per year on the three-hectare site.

3. Sereti's previous employer, Seaco Ltd., a public corporation, provided her with options to acquire shares. Information relating to these options is outlined below.

	1st option	2nd option
# of shares	1,000	1,000
Date option granted	May 20X1	June 20X2
Option price	$12.00	$13.00
Value at date granted	$12.40	$13.20
Date acquired by Sereti	September 20X3	July 20X4
Value at date acquired	$13	$16

In December 20X5, Sereti sold 500 of the Seaco shares for $20 per share.

4. In 20X4, Sereti invented a board game and incurred $6,000 in legal fees to obtain a patent. She had intended to manufacture and market the game herself, but a feasibility study showed that she did not have the necessary financial resources or management expertise. As a result, she sold the patent and the distribution rights to a marketing company in 20X5 for $36,000 plus an annual royalty on sales. Her 20X5 royalty receipts totalled $12,000.

5. Sereti's mother had died several years ago and left her a house valued at $90,000 and a gold bracelet worth $600. Sereti's brother is using the house until it is sold.

In 20X5, a land developer paid Sereti $6,000 for an option to purchase the house. As of December 31, 20X5, the option had not been exercised. Also, in 20X5, Sereti sold the gold bracelet for $2,000. Sereti's 20X4 tax return shows an unused listed personal property loss of $400 carried forward from the previous year.

6. Sereti sold the following other properties in 20X5:

1937 classic automobile	$25,000
Camper trailer	7,000
Shares of Tex Inc., a public corporation	6,000

Sereti purchased the classic automobile, which she drove only on warm summer days, in 20X0 for $8,000; restoration costs for it were $6,000. She had acquired the camper trailer in 20X1 for $16,000, and the Tex Inc. shares that same year for $60,000.

7. In 20X5, Sereti earned a salary of $85,000. She contributed $2,000 to her employer's registered pension plan and also made an allowable contribution of $7,000 to her RRSP.

Required:
Determine Sereti's net income for tax purposes for the 20X5 taxation year.

Solution:
Each transaction is discussed below before net income is calculated for tax purposes.

The shares of Pluto Inc. are deemed to have been sold for nil because the corporation has ceased to carry on business and is insolvent. The result is a capital loss of $20,000. The shares are qualified small business corporation shares because the company was a Canadian-controlled private corporation that used all of its assets in an active business. Consequently, the capital loss is also classified as an allowable business investment loss.

Part of the farmland was purchased with the intention of selling it at a profit; therefore, the profit is considered to be income from business. The property taxes on the two hectares of vacant land that were sold cannot be deducted from annual income, except to the extent of any incidental income earned on the property. The property taxes are, however, added to the cost of the land (see Chapter 5—interest and property taxes on vacant land).

When Sereti acquired the shares of Seaco Ltd. under the stock-option agreement, she earned employment income equal to the difference between the value of the shares at the date of acquisition and the purchase price. The recognition of the stock option/employment benefit could not be deferred to the year when the shares were sold because the value of the shares was greater than the option price at the date the options were granted (see Chapter 4—stock options). The adjusted cost base (ACB) of the shares is increased by the amount of employment income, resulting in the ACB being equal to the shares' market value at the acquisition date. The two acquisitions in 20X3 and 20X4 are identical properties, and therefore the ACB is determined as the weighted average of the two purchases.

The patent on the board game is a capital property because it was developed with the intention of generating a long-term benefit. Its adjusted cost base is the cost of registering the patent.

The house is a capital property having an ACB of $90,000 (the market value at the time of her mother's death). It does not qualify as Sereti's principal residence because she does not occupy it. The receipt of the option results in a capital gain in the year of receipt. If the option is subsequently exercised, the capital gain will be the amount by which the selling price plus the option proceeds of $6,000 exceed the ACB of $90,000. The capital gain from the option received in 20X5 can then be eliminated by filing an amended tax return for that year. If the option expires, the capital gain of $6,000 in 20X5 stands.

The gold bracelet that Sereti received from her mother's estate is listed personal property (jewellery), or LPP. Its ACB would normally be $600, but as LPP, it has a deemed minimum ACB of $1,000. The unused LPP loss from her 20X4 tax return must have occurred because an LPP loss exceeded the LPP gain in a previous year. Unused LPP losses can be carried back three years and forward seven years, and can be deducted from LPP gains only. This carry-over is deducted in arriving at net income for tax purposes, unlike other types of losses (net capital losses and non-capital losses), which are deductible after net income for tax purposes in arriving at taxable income (see Chapter 10).

The classic automobile and the camper trailer are both personal-use properties. The ACB of the automobile is $14,000 (original cost of $8,000 plus the $6,000 for restoration). The camper trailer incurred a loss, but as personal-use property, the loss is deemed to be nil.

Net income for tax purposes:

(a) Employment income:

Salary		$ 85,000
Registered pension plan		(2,000)
		83,000
Business income:		
Sale of farm land—proceeds	$ 40,000	
Less—cost (2/3 × $30,000)	(20,000)	
—property taxes on vacant land		
2/3 ($500 × 3 y)	(1,000)	19,000
Property income—royalties		12,000
		114,000

(b) Taxable capital gains:

Seaco shares:

Proceeds—500 × $20			10,000
ACB	1,000 @ $13 = $13,000		
	1,000 @ $16 = 16,000		
	2,000 $29,000		

Average—$29,000 ÷ 2,000 = $14.50 × 500 shares	(7,250)
	2,750

Taxable—½ × $2,750	1,375
Patent—½ ($36,000 – $6,000)	15,000
Option—½ ($6,000)	3,000
Classic automobile—½ ($25,000 – [$8,000 + $6,000])	5,500
Camper trailer—loss deemed to be nil	–0–
Net gain on LPP:	
Bracelet—½ ($2,000 – deemed cost of $1,000) – loss	
carry-over of ½ ($400)	300
	25,175

Allowable capital loss:		
Tex Inc.—½ ($6,000 – $60,000) = $27,000		
Limited to taxable capital gains	(25,175)	–0–
		114,000

(c) Other deduction:		
RRSP contribution		(7,000)
		107,000

(d) Loss:		
Pluto shares—allowable business investment loss CCPC		
½ ($20,000)		(10,000)
Net income for tax purposes		$ 97,000

QUESTION TWO

In 20X3, in anticipation of retirement, Philip Portnoy sold several properties. Information relating to these transactions is outlined below.

1. In 20X1, Portnoy purchased a recreational parcel of land for $20,000 near a mountain resort, with the intention of building a cottage for personal use. The cottage was never built because of Portnoy's declining health. The land was sold in 20X3 for $21,000. A commission of 10% of the selling price was paid to a real estate broker.

2. On November 30, 20X3, he sold all of his 1,000 shares of TR Ltd. (original cost— $21,000) for $18,000. He also sold a bond for $62,000 (including accrued interest of $200) that he had purchased in January 20X3 for $64,000 (including $600 accrued interest). Prior to these sales, he had received bond interest of $2,800. On December 15, 20X3, on the advice of his broker, he purchased another 500 shares of TR Ltd. for $8,000.

3. In 20X0, Portnoy had sold shares of Hazel Ltd. (a Canadian-controlled private corporation) for $50,000, with the proceeds payable over several years. The original cost of the shares was $10,000. By the end of 20X3, $15,000 of the $50,000 selling price remained unpaid. Portnoy's 20X2 tax return shows that he claimed a capital gain reserve of $24,000.

4. On December 31, 20X3, Portnoy sold a rental property for $120,000 (land $50,000, building $70,000). He had acquired the property seven years earlier for $90,000 (land $10,000, building $80,000). At the end of the previous year, the building had an

undepreciated capital cost of $58,000. A net rental loss of $6,000 was incurred in 20X3 after a deduction of $2,000 for amortization/depreciation. Portnoy intends to purchase a new rental property in early 20X4 for $300,000.

5. Portnoy bought and sold commodity futures in 20X3 and made a profit of $15,000. He first traded commodities in 20X2, incurring a loss of $23,000, which he fully deducted against his employment earnings for that year.

6. During 20X3, Portnoy sold shares of PC Ltd., a Canadian-controlled private corporation operating a small manufacturing business, for $30,000. He had acquired the shares in 20X0 for $40,000. He paid legal fees of $1,000 to draw up the sale agreement. At the time of the sale, PC Ltd.'s balance sheet had total assets of $600,000 (equal to their fair market value) as follows:

Current assets	$220,000
Manufacturing equipment	215,000
Government of Canada bonds	165,000
	$600,000

7. Portnoy's only other income in 20X3 was his salary of $80,000.

Required:
Calculate Portnoy's net income for tax purposes for the 20X3 taxation year. Also, what are the tax implications if Portnoy purchases a new rental property in 20X4?

Solution:
Each transaction is discussed before the net income is calculated for tax purposes.

The cottage property results in a capital loss of $1,100 (proceeds of $21,000 less the adjusted cost base of $20,000 and the selling commission of $2,100 [10% × $21,000]). However, for tax purposes, the property is classified as personal-use property, and the loss is deemed to be nil.

   The sale of the TR Ltd. shares would normally result in a capital loss of $3,000 ($18,000 − $21,000). However, because 1,000 shares were sold on November 30, 20X3, and 500 shares were repurchased within 30 days on December 15, 20X3, a superficial loss results with respect to the 500 shares replaced. The allowable capital loss for 20X3 is, therefore, $750, calculated as follows:

Proceeds of disposition	$18,000
Adjusted cost base	(21,000)
	3,000
Deemed superficial loss:	
500 shares/1,000 shares × $3,000	(1,500)
Capital loss	$1,500
Allowable capital loss—½ ($1,500)	$ 750

   The superficial loss of $1,500 that was denied recognition in 20X3 is added to the adjusted cost base of the newly acquired shares, giving them a total adjusted cost base of $9,500 ($8,000 + $1,500). The loss will be recognized when the new shares are eventually sold.

   The bond proceeds include accrued interest of $200, which must be included in property income. Similarly, the purchase price of the bond includes accrued interest of $600, which must be deducted from property income. The allowable capital loss on the bond is $800 (½ × [($62,000 − $200) − [$64,000 − $600)]). Property income from the bond is

$2,400 ($2,800 plus the sale of accrued interest of $200 minus the purchase of accrued interest of $600).

The shares of Hazel Ltd. were sold in 20X0, resulting in a capital gain of $40,000 ($50,000 − $10,000). Because some of the proceeds are being paid over several years, Portnoy has been claiming a capital gain reserve and deferring the recognition of the gain. In 20X2, a reserve of $24,000 was claimed, and this amount must be included as a 20X3 gain, from which a new reserve can be deducted. As 20X3 is the fourth year from the date of sale, this year's reserve cannot exceed 20% of the gain (a minimum of 20% of the gain must be recognized each year, which means that 80% must be recognized by the end of 20X3). The taxable capital gain for 20X3 is $8,000, calculated as follows:

Inclusion of 20X2 reserve	$24,000
Less 20X3 reserve—lesser of:	
$\frac{1}{5}$(20%) × $40,000 = $8,000	
$15,000/$50,000 × $40,000 = $12,000	(8,000)
Capital gain	$16,000
Taxable capital gain ($\frac{1}{2}$ × $16,000)	$ 8,000

The rental property income of $8,000 is calculated as follows:

Net rental loss	$(6,000)
Amortization/depreciation not deductible	2,000
Recapture of capital cost allowance on the building ($70,000 − $58,000)	12,000
	$ 8,000

The disposition of land results in a taxable capital gain of $20,000 ($\frac{1}{2}$ × [$50,000 − $10,000]). Note that there is no capital loss on the building, even though it was sold for $70,000, which is less than its original cost of $80,000. This loss of $10,000 has been fully deducted as capital cost allowance in prior years. The undepreciated capital cost of the building at the end of 20X2 was $58,000, indicating that $22,000 of capital cost allowance had been deducted to that time. The sale for $70,000 resulted in income from the recapture of capital cost allowance of $12,000 ($70,000 − $58,000); this left a net deduction over the years of $10,000 ($22,000 − $12,000).

The gain of $15,000 from the trading of commodity futures appears to be business income. In the previous year, a loss of $23,000 was fully deducted against employment income, indicating that a choice was made not to treat the transaction as a capital item. Therefore, Portnoy's tax treatment for the 20X3 transaction must be treated in the same manner.

The sale of shares of PC Ltd. results in an allowable capital loss of $5,500 ($\frac{1}{2}$ × [$30,000 − $40,000 − 1,000]). The shares are not qualified small business corporation shares because all or substantially all of the corporation's assets at the time of the sale were not used in an active business. The corporation does carry on an active business, but 28% of its assets ($165,000/$600,000) are invested in bonds. Therefore, the loss cannot be classified as an allowable business investment loss. Here, it is of no consequence because there are sufficient taxable capital gains from which the capital loss can be deducted.

Net income for tax purposes:		
(a) Employment income—salary		$ 80,000
Business income—commodity trading		15,000
Property income:		
Net rentals	$8,000	
Interest on bond	2,400	10,400
		105,400

(b) Taxable capital gains:

Rental property land	20,000	
Shares of Hazel Ltd.	8,000	
	28,000	
Allowable capital losses:		
Shares of TR Ltd.	(750)	
Bond	(800)	
Shares of PC Ltd.	(5,500)	20,950
Net income for tax purposes		$126,350

The purchase of a new rental property in 20X4 will have no tax effect on Portnoy's 20X3 income. If the land and building sold in 20X3 had been used for business purposes, rather than to earn income from property, the capital gain and recapture of capital cost allowance realized in 20X3 could have been deferred if a replacement property had been acquired within one taxation year from the end of the 20X3 taxation year.

QUESTION THREE

In 20X8, Cameron had several capital transactions. Information regarding the transactions is outlined below.

In July, Cameron sold 500 shares of Pink Inc., a Canadian public corporation, for $30 a share. His records show the following Pink share transactions:

20X4—purchased 1,000 shares @ $10 = $10,000
20X5—purchased 2,000 shares @ $7.50 = $15,000
20X6—sold 1,200 shares @ $20 = $24,000
20X7—purchased 1,000 shares @ $22 = $22,000

Also, in February 20X8, Cameron received 100 shares of Pink as a stock dividend. The shares were valued at $26 per share.

In September, Cameron sold 800 shares of Quanto Inc., a Canadian-controlled private corporation for $500 a share. Cameron paid $100 a share in 20X2. For the past 6 years Quanto has operated an active business in Canada and throughout this period at least 95% of its assets have been used to operate the business. In February 20X9, Cameron invested in Blue Inc., a Canadian-controlled private corporation conducting an active business in Canada. Blue Inc. issued 5,000 new shares directly to Cameron for $30 a share. In addition, Cameron purchased another 3,000 shares of Blue for $30 a share from a former shareholder.

Cameron moved from the United States to Canada in 20X1 and became a Canadian resident. At the time, he owned several investments in U.S. public corporations. In 20X8, he sold 400 shares of BB Inc. (a U.S. public corporation) for $90 a share. The shares were purchased fifteen years previous at a cost of $20 a share. Upon arrival in Canada in 20X1, the shares of BB were trading at $40 a share on the New York Stock Exchange.

In 20X7, Cameron sold his share of a farm property for $100,000 that he had purchased as a capital investment in 20X2 for $40,000. He received 25% of the proceeds in 20X7. In 20X8, he received a further 10% of the proceeds.

During the year Cameron's home was broken into and a valuable painting was stolen. It was purchased for $4,000 in 20X3 and had a current value of $8,000. He received insurance proceeds of only $2,000 for the loss. In December 20X8, he sold a painting for $2,500 that originally cost $600 in 20X2.

Required:
Determine Cameron's net taxable capital gains for 20X8.

Solution:
Each of the above items is discussed separately, followed by a summary calculation.

Pink shares   The proceeds of disposition is $15,000 (500 shares x $30 = $15,000). The issue here is the adjusted cost base calculation. The ACB of each share on hand, before a sale, is equal to the weighted average of all the shares acquired. This is demonstrated below:

Date	# of shares	Price	Total	Average ACB
20X4 Purchase	1,000	$10.00	$10,000	$10 (10,000/1,000)
20X5 Purchase	2,000	7.50	15,000	
	3,000		25,000	**8.33** (25,000/3,000)
20X6 Sale	(1,200)	**8.33**	(10,000)	
Net	1,800		15,000	8.33 (15,000/1,800)
20X7	1,000	22.00	22,000	
Net	2,800		37,000	13.21 (37,000/2,800)
20X8 stock dividend	100	26.00	2,600	
	2,900		$39,600	**13.65** (39,600/2,900)

The ACB of the shares sold in 20X8 is $13.65 a share. Note that the pool of shares was reduced by the ACB of the shares sold in 20X6, leaving the remaining shares in the pool at the average cost to that date. The capital gain from the sale of the Pink shares is $8,175 [$15,000 − (500 × $13.65) = $8,175].

Quanto shares   The shares of Quanto qualify as *eligible small business corporation shares*. Therefore, a portion of the capital gain can be deferred if some, or all, of the proceeds from the sale are reinvested in a small business investment within the same year, or 120 days following the taxation year in which the sale occurred. A further requirement is that the shares purchased in the new corporation must be shares that are newly issued from the treasury of the corporation. In this case, the individual's taxation year is December 31, 20X8 and the reinvestment was made in February 20X9, which is within the 120-day limit. However, only some of the shares in Blue were acquired directly from the corporation. Of the 8,000 shares purchased by Cameron, only 5,000 were from the treasury. So, the available deferral is limited to the reinvestment in the 5,000 shares in Blue for a total cost of $150,000 (5000 x $30). Cameron's capital gain from the sale of Quanto shares is calculated as follows:

Proceeds—800 shares x $500	$400,000
ACB—800 shares x $100	80,000
Capital gain	$320,000
Deduct capital gain deferred:	
$150,000/$400,000 x $320,000	120,000
Capital gain	$200,000

The deferred capital gain is the proportion of the proceeds reinvested in an eligible investment multiplied by the capital gain. The deferred gain of $120,000 reduces the ACB of the new shares acquired in Blue. It should be noted that the opportunity to defer a capital gain on eligible small business corporation shares by reinvesting the proceeds from the sale is available only to individuals and not corporate taxpayers.

BB shares   Although Cameron's actual cost is $20 a share, the stock was trading at $40 at the time he entered Canada on a permanent basis. Therefore, the ACB of these shares is the Canadian currency equivalent of $40 at the date Cameron entered Canada (currency exchange assumed equal). The capital gain on the sale of BB shares is $20,000 [(400 × $90) − (400 × $40) = $20,000].

Farm land The farm land was sold in the previous taxation year (20X7). The capital gain was $60,000 ($100,000 − $40,000). All of the proceeds were not received in 20X7 and so Cameron had the option of deducting a reserve from the gain based on the proportion of proceeds that were due after 20X7. A taxpayer may not always choose to claim the reserve, especially if capital losses are available to offset the gain or the tax rate in future years will be substantially higher. Assuming Cameron claimed the reserve in 20X7 the capital gain would have been as follows:

Capital gain (above)	$60,000
Deduct reserve—lesser of:	
4/5($60,000) = $48,000 or	
$75,000 (deferred proceeds)/$100,000 × $60,000 = **$45,000**	45,000
20X7 capital gain (25% of total)	$15,000

In 20X8, the previous year's reserve of $45,000 must be added to capital gains (this is the untaxed portion of the capital gain) and Cameron has the option of claiming a new reserve based on proceeds not due until after 20X8. In 20X8, a further 10% of the $100,000 proceeds was received and so 65%, or $65,000 of the proceeds remains unpaid (100% − 25% in 20X7 and 10% in 20X8). Assuming he claims a new reserve the 20X8, the capital gain would be $9,000 calculated as follows:

20X7 reserve added	$45,000
Deduct reserve—lesser of:	
3/5($60,000) = **$36,000** or	
$65,000/$100,000 × $60,000 = $39,000	36,000
20X8 capital gain	$ 9,000

Note that 40% of the capital gain has been included in income after two years ($15,000 + $9,000 = $24,000/$60,000 = 40%) even though only 35% of the proceeds has been received. This is because the reserve calculation requires that at least 20% of the gain be included each year and the full gain must be included within five years.

Paintings The paintings are categorized as listed personal property. The proceeds of disposition for the stolen painting are $2,000 which results in a listed personal property loss of $2,000 ($2,000 − $4,000 cost). This loss can be offset only against gains from other listed personal property. The painting sold results in a listed personal property gain of $1,500 ($2,500 − $1,000 deemed cost). Note that the ACB of this painting is deemed to be $1,000 rather than its actual cost of $600. The ACB of listed personal property is deemed to be the greater of the actual cost or $1,000. Similarly, the selling price of listed personal property is deemed to be the greater of the actual proceeds or $1,000.

The net taxable capital gains for 20X8 is as follows:

Pink shares	$ 8,175
Quanto shares	200,000
BB shares	20,000
Farm land	9,000
	237,175
	× 1/2
	118,588

Net gains from listed personal property:	
Painting sold (gain)	$1,500
Painting stolen (loss)	(2,000)
	0
$1/2 \times 0 =$	0
Taxable capital gains	$118,588

Note that the listed personal property loss of $2,000 is deducted only to the extent of the capital gains from listed personal property. The unclaimed amount of $500 can be carried back to the three previous years or forward to the next seven years and deducted against any listed personal property gains in those years.

Review Questions

1. A capital gain or capital loss is the gain or loss realized from the disposition of capital property. What is meant by the term "capital property," and how is it different from other types of property?

2. Is it necessary for property to provide a long-term benefit to its owners in order for the gain or loss on sale to be considered a capital gain or capital loss?

3. When it is unclear whether a gain or loss on a sale of property is of a capital nature, what factors are considered when judging the transaction?

4. An investor acquired a residential high-rise apartment as an investment. The property has now been owned for 11 years and annually has provided reasonable net rental income. This net rental income has been reinvested in other types of properties as well as in improvements to the apartment building. The owner is considering either selling the property to another investor or dividing the property into separate condominium units that will be marketed to existing tenants and to the public. Explain how a gain on sale will be treated for tax purposes under each alternative.

5. Distinguish among financial property, personal-use property, and listed personal property. Which of these three categories is (are) subject to capital gains treatment?

6. Distinguish between a capital gain and a taxable capital gain and between a capital loss and an allowable capital loss.

7. Explain why the tax treatment of capital gains is often described as preferential, while the treatment of capital losses is often considered unfair.

8. "A capital gain or loss can be recognized for tax purposes only when capital property is sold." Is this statement true? Explain.

9. A corporation acquires a licence that permits it to manufacture a patented product for 10 years in exchange for the payment of a royalty. Describe the tax treatment that will occur if the taxpayer sells the licence for more than its cost or less than its cost to another party before the 10-year term expires. Would the tax treatment be the same if the licence had an unlimited life?

10. What advantage can a taxpayer achieve by incurring a capital gain on property and permitting the purchaser to pay for the property over a number of years?

11. Because of the tax treatment, an investment in shares of a small business corporation may present less risk than an investment in shares of a public corporation. Explain why.

12. What difference does it make when the sole shareholder of a corporation provides $10,000 of additional capital to the corporation as a loan (shareholder's loan), rather than in return for additional share capital?

13. "The sale of a warehouse building used by a taxpayer to operate a business can result in a capital gain but not a capital loss." Is this statement true? Explain.

14. Explain how the tax treatment of personal-use property deviates from the normal tax treatment of capital property.

15. When an investor buys some shares of a corporation at one price and later buys more shares of the same corporation at another price, how does the investor determine the cost for tax purposes when some, but not all, of the shares are eventually sold?

16. When an investor acquires a commodity or a contract to purchase a commodity in the future, what type of property does that investor own? Can a gain or loss on the sale of commodities or futures contracts result in a capital gain or loss?

17. An investment in capital property that appreciates in value at 10% per year is more valuable than an investment in capital property that provides an annual return, such as interest, of 10%. Explain why.

Key Concept Questions

QUESTION ONE

Colin sold capital property in 20X1 for $600,000 and incurred $24,000 in selling costs. The property had an adjusted cost base of $176,000. Colin received $150,000 at the time of the sale and a note for the balance. The note is to be repaid over nine years in equal instalments of $50,000, commencing in 20X2. *Income tax reference: ITA 40(1)(iii).*

Determine the minimum taxable capital gain to be reported by Colin in 20X1, 20X2, and 20X3.

QUESTION TWO

Which of the following corporations are *small business corporations* (SBC) as defined in section 248 of the *Income Tax Act?*

a) A Ltd. is a public corporation with 95% of the fair market value of its assets used in an active business carried on primarily in Canada.

b) B Ltd. is a Canadian-controlled private corporation with 60% of the fair market value of its assets used in an active business carried on in Canada. The remaining 40% is an investment in long-term bonds.

c) C Ltd. is a Canadian-controlled private corporation with 80% of the fair market value of its assets used primarily in an active business carried on in Canada. The remaining 20% is term deposits.

d) D Ltd. is a Canadian-controlled private corporation that owns one asset. The asset is a warehouse that is used by a related corporation in carrying on its active business in Canada.

QUESTION THREE

In 20X1 Ross loaned $10,000 to a small business corporation. The loan bears interest at 6% per annum and is due on demand. Ross did not receive his interest in 20X3 although he reported it on his 20X3 tax return. By December 31, 20X4, it was established that the loan was bad and that Ross would not be receiving the $10,000 principal and the interest for 20X3 nor 20X4. *Income tax reference: ITA 20(1)(p), 39(1)(c), 50(1).*

Determine the 20X4 tax consequences for Ross.

QUESTION FOUR

Determine the loss to be reported for tax purposes for each of the following dispositions. *Income tax reference: ITA 20(16), 39(1)(b)(i), 40(2)(g), 40(3.3), (3.4), 53(1)(f), 54.*

a) Anita sold a class 10 depreciable asset for $10,000. The asset cost $25,000 when it was purchased. The UCC of class 10 was $16,000 before the sale. After the sale, there are no assets left in class 10.

b) Bill sold his home for $180,000. The home cost $210,000 when it was purchased.

c) Cathy transferred shares of X Ltd. worth $18,000 to her RRSP. She paid $25,000 for the shares when she purchased them a few years ago.

d) Dan sold 100 shares of N Ltd. for $10,000 on December 15th, 20X7. The ACB of the 100 shares was $17,000. On January 5, 20X8, the value of N Ltd. declined further and Dan repurchased 40 shares of N Ltd. for $3,200.

e) On June 30, 20X0, Old Inc. sold its investment in shares of Blue Ltd. (1% of Blue's outstanding shares) to New Inc. for $30,000. The shares had been acquired 4 years previous for $40,000. Carla is the controlling shareholder of both Old Inc. and New Inc. In February, 20X1, New Inc. sold the shares of Blue Ltd. for $46,000. The taxation year end for New Inc. and Old Inc. is December 31.

QUESTION FIVE

In the current year, Valerie disposed of the following personal items:

	Proceeds	Cost
Car	$1,500	$6,000
Jewellery	200	1,200
Oil painting	2,000	800
Antique table	1,800	900

Valerie has an unclaimed capital loss on listed personal property of $3,000 that was incurred five years ago. *Income tax reference: ITA 3(b), 40(2)(g)(iii), 41(1), (2), 46(1), 54.*

Determine Valerie's net taxable capital gains to be reported for the current year.

QUESTION SIX

Mr. Market traded in shares of Blue Inc. during the current year. His transactions were as follows:

		No. of shares	Cost per share	Total
January 15	Purchased	200	$45	$9,000
March 7	Purchased	300	$22	$6,600
November 21	Sold	(100)	$45	$4,500

Determine the ACB of the shares sold. Mr. Market did not own any shares of Blue Inc. before January 15. *Income tax reference: ITA 47(1).*

QUESTION SEVEN

Early last year, Hazel purchased 100 units of Sky mutual fund for $12 per unit. She received a T3 from the fund for last year showing the following distributions from the fund, all of which were reinvested in her account resulting in the purchase of three additional units:

• Actual amount of eligible dividends	$30.00
• Taxable amount of eligible dividends	$41.40
• Capital gains	$10.00
• Interest	$ 8.00

On January 4th of the current year, Hazel sold 50 of her mutual fund units for $900. *Income tax reference: ITA 47(1).*

Determine the taxable capital gain to be reported by Hazel in the current year.

QUESTION EIGHT

Jane acquired a house in 20X1 for $300,000. In 20X3 she acquired a cottage for $150,000. She lived in the house in the winter and in the cottage in the summer. In 20X5 she sold both properties. She received $400,000 for the house and $250,000 for the cottage. *Income tax reference: ITA 40(2)(b).*

Determine the minimum taxable capital gain to be reported by Jane on the sale of the two properties.

QUESTION NINE

Richard is employed by a Canadian oil company. In year 3, he was transferred from Toronto to Calgary. He rented his home to a tenant while he was in Calgary (year 3 to year 9). In the middle of year 9 he moved back into his home in Toronto. In year 12 he sold his Toronto home. The value of the home at relevant dates was as follows:

Year 1 (purchase price)	$250,000
Year 3 commenced renting the home	$320,000
Year 9 moved back into the home	$450,000
Year 12 sold the home	$490,000

Determine the minimum taxable capital gain(s) to be recognized by Richard—(a) without a subsection 45(2) election, and (b) with a subsection 45(2) election. *Income tax reference: ITA 40(2)(b), 41(1), 45(2), 54, 54.1.*

QUESTION TEN

On March 20th of the current year, Stephen sold his common shares of Salt Ltd., an eligible small business corporation, for $800,000. His shares had an ACB of $100,000. On October 1st of the current year, Stephen purchased newly issued common shares of Pepper Ltd., also an eligible small business corporation. He paid $400,000 for the shares of Pepper Ltd. *Income tax reference: ITA 44.1.*

a) Determine the maximum amount of capital gain on the sale of the Salt Ltd. shares that can be deferred.

b) What will be the ACB of the Pepper Ltd. shares, assuming Stephen elects to defer the maximum capital gain possible, on the Salt Ltd. shares.

QUESTION ELEVEN

On March 20, 20X7, Growth Ltd. moved its head office into its newly acquired building in Toronto. The new building cost $800,000 (land $300,000; building $500,000). The former office building, in downtown Toronto, was sold in January, 20X6 for $650,000 (land $200,000; building $450,000). Growth Ltd. operated from leased space in the meantime. The former office building cost $400,000 (land $150,000; building $250,000). Class 1 had an UCC balance of $220,000 at the end of 20X5. Growth Ltd. has a December 31 year end. *Income tax reference: ITA 13(4), 44(1), (5).*

Describe the tax consequences of the move, including the capital cost and UCC for the new building, assuming Growth Ltd. wishes to minimize taxes.

QUESTION TWELVE

In the current year, James earned the following income:

• Employment income		$80,000
• Property income		2,000
• Gains:		
• Shares of Corporation X	$12,000	
• Personal-use property	7,000	
• Listed personal property	1,600	20,600
• Losses:		
• Shares of Corporation Y	(15,000)	
• Shares of small business corporation	(4,000)	
• Listed personal property	(300)	(19,300)
		$83,300

Determine net income in accordance with the aggregating formula in section 3 of the ITA.

Problems

PROBLEM ONE

Jennifer Farmer farmed for 36 years. She has recently sold her farm assets. Her primary crop was asparagus, and 20 of Jennifer's 25 hectares of land were devoted to growing this vegetable.

The land had cost her $10,000 in 1967. She has sold it for an all-inclusive price of $175,000 that includes an unharvested asparagus crop that is 70% mature.

Asparagus is a perennial plant consisting of a strong root stock which, when planted, remains in the soil for many years and requires little annual maintenance. Every year, the root stock provides two or three asparagus crops, which are harvested at little cost and sold directly to a food wholesaler.

The sale agreement for $175,000 included a cash down payment of $35,000 and a first mortgage of $140,000 held by Farmer. The mortgage is to be paid in seven annual instalments of $20,000. Interest of 12% will be charged on the unpaid balance.

Farmer has sought your advice concerning the tax implications of the sale.

Required:

1. Describe to Farmer how the preceding transaction will be treated for tax purposes.

2. What additional information will you require to determine the actual amount of income for tax purposes created by the transaction?

PROBLEM TWO

Murray George is a professional musician and composer. For 15 years, he has made a good living from this profession. He derives his income from concert appearances (for substantial fees) and from royalties on original musical compositions.

As of 20X0, George has been internationally famous in the classical music field. In 20X1, the Canadian National Music Library agreed to purchase a number of documents from him. These documents included

(a) 26 of George's original manuscripts, written in his own hand;

(b) a box containing 15 of his youthful works, including first drafts and final versions; and

(c) a copy of George's personal diary, to be exhibited to the public only after his death.

For these items, he received $50,000, to be paid in the amount of $30,000 in 20X1 and $20,000 in 20X2. Over the years, the compositions (other than his youthful works) had generated income from royalties, which George had declared as professional income for tax purposes.

The Canadian National Music Library is not a commercial enterprise. It is a registered charitable foundation.

Before filing his 20X1 tax return, George obtained the CRA's advice on how the receipt of $50,000 should be handled. Their response was that the $50,000 clearly represents business revenue and should be added to his professional earnings in 20X1.

Required:

State whether you agree or disagree with the CRA's advice, and provide reasons for and against your position.

PROBLEM THREE*

R.M. Inc. (RMI) manufactures earth-moving and excavation equipment. RMI is owned and managed by Ross Meister.

It is now February 15, 20X2. Meister has asked you to help the company deal with a tax problem. The CRA is questioning the capital gains treatment of a 20X1 sale of land by RMI; it believes that the full amount of the gain should have been included in income. Meister wants to know what arguments the CRA will likely present and how RMI can counter them. Also, he wants to know what the tax consequences will be if the CRA succeeds in making an adjustment. Details of the land transaction are offered below.

RMI purchased 50 hectares of vacant land in an industrial park on December 2, 20X0, for $1.35 million. The purchase was financed, in part, by a five-year first mortgage of $500,000 with interest at 12%. At first, Meister intended to move RMI from its current location to the new location just north of Toronto. He knew that even if he decided later not to move from his current premises, he had purchased the land at a bargain price and would be able to make a profit if he sold it.

On April 1, 20X1, RMI accepted an offer of $3.68 million for 40 hectares of the vacant land. RMI took back a $685,000 first mortgage, repayable at $30,000 per year, with the balance due in 20X6. In RMI's 20X1 corporate tax return, the land disposition was recorded as a capital gain. The remaining 10 hectares of land were retained by RMI. Meister decided to build RMI's new warehouse on the 10-hectare site. RMI will retain its current location as a garage for storing and servicing construction equipment.

RMI is subject to a 25% tax rate on all of its income.

Required:

Prepare a brief report that answers Meister's questions.

PROBLEM FOUR

In 20X0, Kiranjit Dhillon acquired 1,000 shares of Pluton Ltd. (a Canadian public corporation) at a cost of $21,000 plus a brokerage commission of $600. During 20X0, she received cash dividends of $1,200. In 20X1, Pluton failed to pay the cash dividend owing to a cash-flow shortage; instead, it issued a stock dividend, whereby Dhillon received an additional 100 shares. At the time of the stock dividend, the share value was $18 per share.

---

* Adapted, with permission, from the 1991 Uniform Final Examination ©1991 of the Canadian Institute of Chartered Accountants, Toronto, Canada. Any changes to the original material are the sole responsibility of W.J. Buckwold and have not been reviewed or endorsed by the CICA.

On December 15, 20X1, with the company's financial position continuing to decline, Dhillon sold all of her shares of Pluton for $15,000. She felt relieved when the share values declined further over the next two weeks. She incurred brokerage fees of $300 on the sale.

Early in the new year, Pluton apparently solved its financial crisis by selling an unprofitable subsidiary. Dhillon's broker recommended that she again invest in Pluton's shares. On January 11, 20X2, she purchased 1,000 shares at a cost of $12,000 plus brokerage fees of $200.

In June 20X2, she gifted all of her shares in Pluton to her son, who was about to attend university. At that time, the shares were valued at $20,000.

Required:

Calculate the amount by which Dhillon's net income for tax purposes will be affected by the above transactions for the years 20X1 and 20X2.

PROBLEM FIVE

For the year ended August 31, 20X0, Zefer Ltd., a Canadian-controlled private corporation, reported a net income before income taxes of $485,000. The statement of income is summarized as follows:

Income from operations	$380,000
Other income:	
Interest	5,000
Net gain on sale of assets	100,000
	$485,000

The net gain on the sale of assets consists of the following amounts:

• **Gain on sale of franchise—$40,000**   The franchise to operate a retail store was acquired seven years previously at a cost of $110,000. It was sold in 20X0 for $140,000. The sale proceeds included a cash down payment of $20,000, with the balance payable in seven annual instalments of $20,000 plus interest beginning in 20X1. The franchise, which qualified as a class 14 asset, had an undepreciated capital cost of $92,000 at the time of the sale and was the only asset in its class.

• **Gain on sale of warehouse property—$80,000**   In July 20X0, a warehouse property was sold for cash proceeds of $430,000 (land $180,000, building $250,000). The property had an original cost of $370,000 (land $60,000, building $310,000). The building, which was the only asset in class 1, had an undepreciated capital cost of $290,000. After the sale of the warehouse, temporary premises were leased until a new, larger warehouse was constructed. New land was purchased in January 20X1 for $200,000. Construction of the new warehouse would be completed by July 20X1.

• **Loss on sale of shares of subsidiary—$20,000**   Zefer sold shares of a subsidiary corporation for cash proceeds of $450,000. The shares were acquired five years ago for $470,000. Legal fees of $2,000 were paid to draw up the sale agreement and were charged to the legal expense account.

Required:

1. Calculate Zefer's net income for tax purposes for the 20X0 taxation year.

2. What are the tax implications relating to the construction of the new warehouse in 20X1?

PROBLEM SIX

Charles Bartello intends to leave Canada and start a new life in southern Florida. Before leaving, he intends to dispose of all his property so that he will have sufficient capital to acquire a business in the United States.

Bartello has provided the following information:

1. He currently owns 40% of the shares of a Canadian small business corporation, which are valued at $70,000. The shares were purchased four years ago for $100,000. Bartello is employed by the corporation and anticipates that his salary up to the date of departure will be $75,000.

2. At the beginning of the current year, he purchased a rental property as an investment. To date, the property has provided rental revenue of $14,000; however, Bartello has incurred cash expenses for property taxes, maintenance, interest, and insurance of $17,000. At the same time, the property has appreciated in value by $12,000. When he purchased the property, Bartello was not yet thinking of leaving Canada.

3. Three years ago, Bartello loaned $10,000 to a small business corporation owned by a friend. The business has suffered serious losses, and he has little hope of being repaid. In addition, no interest has been paid on the loan, although in the past two years Bartello has included interest in income for tax purposes on the anniversary dates. The total interest included is $2,000.

4. His home is worth $180,000 (original cost, $150,000.) He has owned the home for eight years and has lived in it all that time.

5. Bartello owns the following additional properties:

	Cost	Value
Motorboat	$ 14,000	$ 10,000
Furniture	21,000	6,000
Shares of public corporation X	10,000	14,000
Shares of public corporation Y	50,000	15,000
Corporate bond	100,000	102,000
Art collection	600	3,000
Stamp collection	20,000	16,000
Grand piano	10,000	14,000

Required:

Determine Bartello's net income for tax purposes for the year in which he leaves Canada. Would Bartello's net income change if he left Canada still owning all of the above assets?

PROBLEM SEVEN

The following financial information is provided for the 20X0 taxation year of Virginia Couture:

Interest income	$20,000
Net loss from retail store for the year ended December 31, 20X0	(7,000)
Gain on sale of public corporation shares	8,000
Loss on sale of shares of a CCPC qualified as a small business corporation	(10,000)
Dividends from foreign corporations, net of $300 withholding tax	2,700
Loss on sale of land that was originally purchased to build a rental property. The project was cancelled after a rezoning application was lost.	(38,000)
Gain on sale of an oil painting	4,000
Director's fees for attendance at corporate meetings	6,000
Loss on sale of personal jewellery	(5,000)

In 20X0, Couture gifted shares of a Canadian-controlled public corporation (CCPC) to her 16-year-old son. The shares, which originally cost $8,000, had a value of $10,000 at the time of the gift.

Also, in 20X0, Couture had a rental loss of $3,000 (before amortization/depreciation and capital cost allowance). The property was originally purchased for $70,000 (land $9,000, building $61,000). The class 1 building had an unamortized capital cost of $50,000 at the end of the previous year. On the last day of 20X0, Couture sold the property for $100,000 (land $12,000, building $88,000). She intends to purchase a new rental property in early 20X1 for $200,000 (land $20,000, building $180,000).

In the previous year, by agreement, Couture obtained the exclusive licence to distribute a certain product in Canada. In 20X0, she divided the country into six sales territories and sold 10-year sub-licences to individuals in each territory. Total proceeds were $24,000.

Required:

1. Calculate Couture's income for tax purposes for the 20X0 taxation year in accordance with the aggregating formula of section 3 of the *Income Tax Act*.

2. What are the tax implications if Couture acquires the new rental property in 20X1?

PROBLEM EIGHT

Cindy Tse retired in April 20X9 and moved from Thunder Bay to Vancouver Island. During her retirement she plans to accept the occasional small consulting contract. Her financial transactions for 20X9 are summarized below.

1. Tse sold her home in Thunder Bay for $240,000. She paid a real estate commission of $8,000 and legal fees of $2,000 to complete the sale. Tse had purchased the home in 20X3 for $110,000.

    In 20X6, she purchased a summer cottage for $74,000. She sold it in 20X9 for $175,000. She paid a legal fee of $1,000 to draw up the sale agreement. Tse had used the summer cottage regularly for summer vacations.

2. Tse's gross salary from January 1, 20X9, to her date of retirement was $30,000.

3. Three years ago, Tse purchased 20% of the shares of T Ltd. and 15% of the shares of Q Ltd. Both are Canadian-controlled private corporations. T's assets consist entirely of investment properties, including shares, bonds, and rental properties. All of Q's assets are used to operate an active business. Tse sold her shares in both corporations in 20X9. Details of the transactions are outlined below.

	T Ltd.	Q Ltd.
Cost	$30,000	$40,000
Selling price	63,000	28,000

    Tse received $9,000 in cash for the T Ltd. shares, with the balance payable at the rate of $9,000 annually for the next six years. The Q Ltd. shares were sold for cash.

4. A local farmer has been trying to purchase Tse's hobby farm land. Tse purchased the land in 20X2 for $69,000. In July 20X9, Tse received $2,000 from the farmer, for which she granted him an option to purchase the land. The option is open for two years and allows the farmer to purchase the land for $100,000.

5. In February 20X9, Tse paid an investment counsellor $300 for investment advice. The same month, she purchased 5,000 units of ABC mutual fund for $10 per unit. An additional 3,000 units were purchased in April 20X9, at $14 per unit. On October 31, 20X9, ABC fund distributed $1,500 of taxable Canadian dividends, which Tse

reinvested in the fund, thereby acquiring another 100 units. On December 3, 20X9, Tse sold 2,000 units of ABC at $16 per unit. At year end, the fund units were valued at $18.

6. To obtain the funds to complete the purchase of the ABC mutual fund units, Tse increased the mortgage on her house by $20,000. She incurred interest of $500 on this amount before paying off the mortgage when the house was sold.

7. In 20X8, Tse invested in a real estate project with her friend, a real estate agent and part-time developer. Together, they purchased a parcel of land and constructed four town homes at a cost of $500,000. In 20X9, the four town homes were sold for $580,000 to a single buyer, who planned to use them as rental properties. Tse's share of the gain was 40%. No cash was invested in the project, which had been funded entirely with bank financing.

8. Tse sold shares of X Ltd. (a public corporation) for $18,000 during the year. She had acquired the shares in 20X4 for $25,000.

9. Most of Tse's investments have been in blue-chip shares that pay dividends. Recently, she has decided to invest and trade in speculative Canadian mining shares and commodity futures. Before she does so, she wants to know the tax implications of gains and losses on such trading.

Required:

1. Calculate Tse's minimum net income for tax purposes for the 20X9 taxation year in accordance with the aggregating formula of section 3 of the *Income Tax Act*.

2. Explain to Tse the potential tax consequences of gains and losses realized on trading speculative Canadian mining shares and commodity futures.

3. What will be the tax consequences to Tse if the option on the farmland is exercised the following taxation year?

PROBLEM NINE

Sheila Ram is a professional engineer. In 20X7, she sold her consulting business and retired. Her financial information for the year 20X7 is outlined below.

1. On January 1, 20X7, Ram sold her engineering consulting business to a senior employee. The business had been operated as a franchised proprietorship with a December 31 fiscal year end. The following assets were sold:

	Original cost	Price
Goodwill	38,000	40,000
Franchise	40,000	50,000
Library	2,000	1,000
Office equipment	12,000	4,000

The sale agreement called for cash proceeds for all assets, except the franchise, which required a down payment of $20,000 at closing, with the balance payable on June 30, 20X8.

The accounts receivable of $90,000 were not sold but were retained by Ram for collection. During 20X7, Ram collected $82,000 of the receivables. The remainder is uncollectible.

On August 15, 20X7, Ram paid $4,000 to a former employee for a bonus awarded on December 31, 20X6.

A review of Ram's 20X6 income tax return showed the following:

Undepreciated capital cost:	
Class 8	$ 6,800
Class 14	24,000
Cumulative eligible capital	20,460
Reserve for bad debts	10,000
Unused listed personal property loss	800

2. In January 20X7, Ram sold her home for $230,000. She had acquired the house in 20X0 for $200,000. In May 20X7, she sold her Ontario vacation home, which she had acquired in 20X3 for $50,000, for $140,000. She also sold an oil painting for $1,400 that originally had cost $600.

3. Also, in 20X7, she received $30,000 from the sale of her 10% interest in Q Ltd., a Canadian-controlled private corporation. She had purchased the shares in 20X0 for $50,000. Q operates a small manufacturing business, and at the time of sale, its assets were appraised as follows:

Working capital	$200,000
Manufacturing assets	300,000
Goodwill	100,000
Government bonds (three-year term)	200,000

4. In 20X7, Ram withdrew $45,000 from her RRSP.

Required:

Determine Ram's net income for tax purposes for the 20X7 taxation year.

PROBLEM TEN

Simon Shansky is about to sell his shares in a private corporation for $100,000. He has owned the shares for many years, having originally acquired them at a cost of $20,000. Shansky intends to invest the proceeds from the sale in interest-bearing securities yielding 10%.

Two potential purchasers have made offers on the shares. One purchaser has offered to pay the full purchase price in cash. The other has offered to pay $40,000 at the date of sale and the balance of $60,000 in three annual instalments of $20,000, plus interest of 10% on the unpaid balance. The unpaid balance would be secured with adequate collateral. Shansky is subject to a 45% tax rate.

Required:

1. Which option should Shansky accept?

2. Calculate the amount of funds that Shansky will have after three years under each option.

3. What rate of return would have to be earned on the invested proceeds of sale under the full cash payment option to provide the same capital value as under the deferred payment option after three years?

4. Indicate, without providing detailed calculations, whether your answer to question 2 would be different if Shansky were selling a building for $100,000 that originally cost $80,000 and had an unamortized capital cost of $35,000.

PROBLEM ELEVEN

Jordana Lea has accumulated a substantial portfolio of investments in bonds and shares of public corporations. She selects shares that provide low dividends and maximum long-term growth but is risk averse and will purchase only shares of corporations in secure industries. Currently, all of her investments are achieving capital growth but her investment in shares of Cory Corporation is providing the lowest yield. This year, her share value in Cory increased to $50,000, a 10% increase (i.e., from $45,000) over the previous year. Cory has consistently maintained this growth rate. The shares were purchased several years ago at a cost of $20,000.

Lea's investment counsellor has recommended that she sell her shares in Cory and use the proceeds to purchase shares in J2 Industries Ltd. J2 is in the same industry as Cory but has recently achieved industry dominance. There is strong evidence that the shares of J2 will maintain a growth rate of 13% annually for the next five years.

Lea has high earnings from her annual salary, and her marginal tax rate is 45%.

Required:

1. Should Lea dispose of the Cory shares and use the proceeds to acquire the J2 shares?

2. What rate of return on the J2 shares is required to justify the exchange of securities?

PROBLEM TWELVE

Sharon Sutherland owned a home in Toronto, Ontario, a ski chalet in Whistler, BC, and a condominium in Florida, USA until June 15, 20X7 when she sold all three properties and moved into a seniors' residence. She provided the following information with respect to the properties:

Property	Year Acquired	Cost	Selling Price (net of commission and other selling costs)
Home	20X1	$400,000	$460,000
Condo	20X2	$200,000	$245,000
Chalet	20X4	$300,000	$336,000

For the years that Sharon owned each property, she ordinarily inhabited it at some time in the year. She tended to spend the winter in Florida, the summer in Toronto, and the fall in Whistler.

Required:

1. Determine the minimum taxable capital gain to be reported by Sharon on the sale of the three properties.

2. How would the answer change if Sharon had moved out of the Toronto home in 20X3 when it was worth $410,000 and earned rental income from the Toronto home from that date until she sold it in 20X7?

Cases

CASE ONE   The Concorde Theatre Ltd.

The Concorde Theatre Ltd., a local company owned by J. Bleet, operates a small neighbourhood cinema. The business is usually profitable, but this year, because of unusual events, a net loss has occurred. The income statement for the year ended December 31, 20X1, is summarized in the table below.

The company does not usually invest in real estate. The land and building that was sold for a gain of $70,000 was acquired seven months before its sale. An acquaintance of Bleet who ran into some serious financial difficulties required immediate cash to stop bankruptcy proceedings and asked Bleet to purchase his real estate. Bleet had no money to invest in real estate and was not in the market for such an investment. However, the acquaintance pleaded with Bleet to help him out and kept reducing the purchase price to provoke an immediate cash sale.

Bleet, watching the price drop to below what he felt was the fair market value, finally gave in. Concorde Theatre borrowed 100% of the purchase price and bought the property. The loan from the bank was payable on demand.

Sales	$ 600,000
Cost of sales	400,000
Gross profit	200,000
Operating expenses	170,000
Operating income	30,000
Other:	
Gain on sale of land and building	70,000
Loss on sale of land	(110,000)
Net loss	$ (10,000)

Four months later, the company received an offer from a local real estate investor to buy the property for $65,000 above the original purchase price. The same day, the original owner, who had improved his financial situation, asked if he could buy the property back. He was upset when Bleet agreed only if the price was $70,000 above the original price. Reluctantly, the acquaintance agreed to pay that much, provided that the closing date was delayed to three months hence.

The land, the sale of which resulted in a $110,000 loss, had been purchased three years earlier. The land was across the road from the theatre, and Bleet had intended to turn it into a parking lot for theatre patrons. However, because of the traffic patterns on the street, the city refused to grant vehicle access for the property. After a long battle, Bleet gave up and posted the land for sale. After six months without an offer, he finally accepted a reduced price to free up needed cash.

Bleet has just met with his accountant, who has informed him that the company will have to pay income tax of $25,000 for the year ended December 31, 20X1. Bleet knows that the corporate tax rate is 25% on income but cannot believe that a tax of $25,000 is payable on a net loss of $10,000.

Bleet asks his accountant to explain how such a result is possible and asks whether there is any possibility of a more logical result.

Required:
As the accountant, outline your response to Bleet.

CASE TWO   Pan Li Ltd.

Pan Li Ltd. is a Canadian private corporation owned 100% by David Benjamin. The corporation operates an active business. Its most recent statement of financial position is summarized in the table below.

PAN LI LTD.
Statement of Financial Position

Assets:		
Current assets		$ 100,000
Land		50,000
Building	400,000	
Equipment	700,000	
	1,100,000	
Accumulated depreciation	(400,000)	700,000
Goodwill, at cost		200,000
		$1,050,000

Liabilities and shareholders' equity:		
Liabilities		$ 600,000
Common shares	20,000	
Retained earnings	430,000	450,000
		$1,050,000

Benjamin purchased the shares of Pan Li seven years ago from the previous shareholders at a cost of $100,000. He is considering retirement and has let it be known that the business is for sale. Recently, he received an offer of $700,000 for the shares of the corporation.

A second potential group of buyers has indicated that it would like to buy the business but does not want to buy the shares of the corporation. Instead, it wants to purchase the individual assets (current assets, land, building, equipment, and goodwill). Benjamin knows that certain of the corporate assets are worth more than their stated value on the financial statement and has asked his advisor to provide an appraisal. If he sold to the asset-buying group, the buyers would assume the corporation's liabilities of $600,000 as part of the purchase price.

Both potential buyers have indicated that they have sufficient cash resources to pay only 70% of the purchase price and that the remaining 30% will have to be paid over three years, with appropriate interest.

Benjamin does not understand the tax implications of selling the shares, rather than the assets. Once the business is sold, he intends to use the funds to buy investments that will provide an annual return to supplement his retirement income.

Required:

1. Keeping in mind Benjamin's objectives, explain to him the general tax implications of selling the shares of Pan Li, rather than the company's individual assets.

2. What difference does it make to the purchasers whether they acquire the shares from Benjamin or the individual assets from Pan Li?

CHAPTER 9

Other Income, Other Deductions, and Special Rules for Completing Net Income for Tax Purposes

The previous chapters introduced and developed the primary sources of income in the Canadian income tax system—employment income, business income, property income, and capital gains. In order to complete the process of determining a taxpayer's overall net income for tax purposes, it is necessary to examine the treatment of transactions that do not fall into one of the four primary income sources. Transactions of this nature are grouped together and referred to as "other sources of income" and "other deductions." The items in this category have little in common with each other; consequently, there are no general rules that apply to this classification.

In terms of the aggregating formula described in Chapter 3, the total of other sources of income is separated from the total of other deductions and included at a different part of the formula.

Other sources of income and *other deductions* apply primarily to individuals. With the exception of retirement savings plans, they normally do not have a significant impact on investment strategies or business decisions. The *Income Tax Act* has a list of special rules relating to the computation of income from all sources. These rules cover unusual aspects of transactions and usually override the standard rules developed for each of the income categories described previously.

This chapter will finish explaining how to calculate net income for tax purposes for both individuals and corporations. By the end of this chapter, the full scope of income for tax purposes under the *Income Tax Act* will be apparent.

Specifically, this chapter will

(a) highlight the process for determining other sources of income and other deductions;

(b) examine the list of special rules for overall income determination and, where applicable, their impact on investment and management decisions; and

(c) revisit the aggregating formula outlined in Chapter 3 and provide a sample calculation of net income for tax purposes.

I. Other Sources of Income

"Other sources of income" is a catch-all category that captures taxable income which does not qualify as one of the primary sources. It is important to recognize that the items classified as other sources of income are *all* from a specific list found in sections 56 through 59.1 of the *Income Tax Act*. The scope of this category, therefore, is very limited. The major types of income that are taxable as other sources of income are as follows:[1]

- Benefits received from a *registered retirement savings plan,* either as a lump sum or over a period of time in the form of an annuity.
- Benefits received from a *registered retirement income fund* created from a registered retirement savings plan.
- *Pension benefits* received from an employer's pension plan either as a lump sum or by way of regular payments over a period of time.
- *Old Age Security* payments from the Government of Canada.
- Benefits from the *Canada and Quebec pensions plans.*
- Benefits received from an employer's *deferred profit-sharing plan.*
- Foreign pension benefits.
- *Retiring allowances* received from an employer in recognition of a period of service as an employee.
- Employment benefits received from the government's *Employment Insurance plan.*
- Income from a *registered education savings plan* (see Part V).
- Amounts received by a student as *scholarships, fellowships,* or *bursaries* are exempt from tax. This exemption applies only to amounts received by a

---

1 ITA 56(1)(a) to (c), (h), (i), (n), (o), (q), 146, 147.

student enrolled in a program entitling the student to claim the education tax credit (see Chapter 10) or elementary and secondary programs. Otherwise, such receipts, including prizes for achievement in a field of endeavour, are exempt only to the extent of $500 annually.

- **Research grants** received in excess of expenses incurred to conduct the related research activity.

- **Support payments** received from a former spouse, provided that they are received as periodic payments (not in a lump sum) and are pursuant to a court order or written agreement. Note that support payments are taxable only to the extent that they are for a former spouse. Payments received that are for the support of a child are not taxable.[2]

- Amounts received under the **Universal Child Care Benefit Program** (UCCB; $100 per month for each child under the age of 6) are taxable in the hands of the lower income spouse or common-law partner.[3] In the case of a single parent, the UCCB amount can be included in the taxable income of the child that is claimed for the *equivalent-to-spouse credit* (see Chapter 10) instead of the income of the single parent.

The above list is not complete and does not describe particular details that may apply to specific items.

Note that several of the above items relate to transactions that originally pertained to an employment activity. For example, in Chapter 4, it was determined that a contribution by an employer to a registered pension plan or deferred profit-sharing plan is *not* included in the employment income of the employee as a benefit received. When these contributions plus the related investment returns are paid from the plans to the employee, the income is not recognized as employment income but is included, as mentioned above, with other sources of income.

The total of a taxpayer's other items of income is included in the first part of the aggregating formula for overall net income determination, along with employment income, business income, and property income. This positioning is important in that other deductions and losses from employment, business, and property, and allowable business investment losses, are deducted subsequently. As a result, losses from, for example, business or investments can be offset against the taxpayer's other sources of income, such as pension income and alimony.

In reviewing other sources of income, it is important to be familiar with the items included, but it is equally important to think in terms of which items are *not* included. Doing so provides an answer to this question: What items are not subject to tax under the Canadian tax system? Consider, for example, the receipt of lottery winnings. To determine whether such a gain is taxable, one must first determine its nature. It is not employment income earned from providing services; it is not business income earned from trading property or providing services; it is not property income earned as a return on investment; and it is not a capital gain from the disposition of property acquired to provide a long-term or enduring benefit. The only remaining category is other sources of income, which may be a logical home for lottery winnings. However, lottery winnings are not specifically included in the list of other sources of income; therefore, they are not subject to income tax. Similarly, such items in the following list are *not taxable* because they are excluded from the list of other sources of income.

- The receipt of a gift.
- The receipt of an inheritance.

---

2 The exclusion of child support payments applies to agreements made or modified after April 30, 1997. IT-530R: Support Payments.

3 A single parent has the option of including the UCCB in the income of the child claimed for the Equivalent to Married tax credit or, if no such credit is claimed, the UCCB can be included in the income of any of the children.

- Life insurance proceeds on the death of an individual.
- Profits from betting or gambling, when conducted for pleasure or enjoyment (as opposed to a gambling business enterprise).
- Proceeds from accident, disability, sickness, or income maintenance insurance policies. However, if an employer has paid all or part of the premiums for such policies (see Chapter 4), a different treatment applies: The insurance proceeds received from a claim are taxable as employment income to the extent that they exceed any premiums paid in past years by the employee.[4]

II. Other Deductions

"Other deductions," like "other sources of income," is a catch-all category that permits the deduction of items that do not qualify under the four primary sources of income. Deductions in this category must come from a specific list of items found in sections 60 through 66.8 of the *Income Tax Act*. Some of the major items included in this list are as follows:

- Contributions to an individual's private **registered retirement savings** plan.[5]
- **Support payments to a former spouse,** provided that such payments are paid on a regular, periodic basis (not in a lump sum) and are pursuant to a written agreement or court order.[6] Payments are deductible only to the extent that they are for the support of a former spouse. **Support payments for a child** are not deductible.[7]
- Amounts paid by a taxpayer as fees or expenses to conduct an **objection** or **appeal** in relation to an assessment under the *Income Tax Act*.[8]
- **Moving expenses** incurred by an individual for relocation to commence a business or employment in another part of Canada or to attend a university or other post-secondary school, to the extent of income earned in the new location. Deductible moving expenses include travel costs (including meals and lodging and automobile expenses)[9] incurred while moving, transportation and storage of belongings, temporary board and lodging near the new or old residence (up to 15 days), costs of cancelling a lease for the old residence, selling costs of the old residence (commission, legal fees, and mortgage prepayment fees), and legal fees and land transfer taxes for the purchase of a new residence if an old residence is sold.[10] Also included is the cost of maintaining a vacant former residence up to a maximum of $5,000. Such maintenance costs include mortgage interest, property taxes, insurance, heat, and power. In addition, eligible moving expenses will include the cost of revising legal documents to reflect a change of address, replacing driver's licences, and obtaining utility connections and disconnections.

  Moving expenses are *eligible for a deduction* only if the *new residence location is at least 40 kilometres closer to the new work location* than the previous residence. Also, if a person is employed or self-employed, the deduction is limited to the amount of employment income or business income earned at the new location. If all or a portion of the expenses cannot be deducted in the year of the move because of insufficient income at the new location, the unclaimed portion can be carried forward and deducted in the following year. An example of a moving expense calculation is shown in the demonstration question at the end of this chapter.

[handwritten: 40 km closer to new work than old house.]

---

4 ITA 6(1)(f); IT-54.
5 ITA 60(i), 146; IT-124R6.
6 ITA 60(b); IT-530R: Support Payments.
7 Applies to agreements made or modified after April 30, 1997; IT-530R: Support Payments.
8 ITA 60(o).
9 For meals and automobile travel costs a taxpayer can use actual costs or a simplified flat rate formula of $17 per meal (daily maximum of $51) and a per kilometre rate for automobiles that varies by province. The 2012 rates will be available in 2013.
10 ITA 62; IT-178R3.

- *Child care expenses* (within certain limits), such as babysitting, day care, or lodging at a boarding school, for children 16 years of age or less, provided that the expenses were incurred so that the taxpayer could pursue employment, business, or research activities. The age limit does not apply if the child is dependant because of mental or physical infirmity. The actual child care expenses are deductible only to the extent that they do not exceed $4,000 per child ($7,000 if the child is under seven years of age at year end; $10,000 if the child has a serious physical or mental disability and is eligible for the disability tax credit [see Chapter 10]); or two-thirds of the taxpayer's "earned" income for the year. The term *earned income* means the total of the individual's employment income, business income, research grants, bursaries and scholarships, and a government disability pension. If more than one person supports a child, the deduction usually must be claimed by the person with the least amount of income for tax purposes.[11]

- *Canada Pension Plan contributions on self-employed earnings.* When an individual operates a business as a sole proprietor, he or she cannot be employed by himself or herself. Consequently, the individual is required to contribute both the employer's and the employee's share of the contributions. When this occurs, the individual can deduct the employer's share of the contribution in arriving at net income for tax purposes.[12] This is part of the "other deductions" portion of the net income for tax purposes calculation and not part of income from business. This deduction reduces tax at the individual's highest marginal tax bracket. The remaining employee's share of the contribution is claimed as a tax credit (see Chapter 10) and reduces tax at the individual's lowest tax-bracket rate.

- *Taxable retiring allowances* that are included in other sources of income can, within specified limits, be transferred to an RRSP or a RPP and deducted from income within specified limits. The eligible amount for transfer and deduction is equal to the sum of $2,000 for each year, or part year, of employment with the employer *prior to 1996*. The eligible amount is increased by an additional $1,500 for each year, or part year, of employment with the employer *prior to 1989* for which there were no vested employer contributions to an RPP or DPSP.[13]

The category of other deductions also houses extensive provisions relating to exploration and development in the specialized resource industries—oil and gas, mining, and timber. While exploration and development expenses are of a capital nature (because they may provide a long-term benefit), they are permitted a quick write-off in recognition of the high risk and cost of such activity.

In terms of the aggregating formula for determining net income for tax purposes, the total of other deductions is included *after* income from employment, business, property, and other sources, and capital gains, but *before* the deduction of losses from those sources. For example, alimony and maintenance expense, because of its position in the formula, can be deducted against all sources of income for that year; the deduction, however, must be claimed to reduce net income before a deduction is made for business losses or a loss from property.

The other-deductions category is important because it is the last test in the income tax scheme for determining the deductibility of an expenditure. If an expenditure cannot be deducted in accordance with the rules for determining employment income,

---

11 ITA 63; IT-495R3. Certain other limits are also available where the higher-income spouse makes a claim because the other spouse is disabled or pursuing full-time or part-time education.
12 ITA 60(e).
13 ITA 60(j.1).

business income, property income, or capital gains, the only remaining area for examination is other deductions. If the expenditure is not specifically listed in this category, it is simply not deductible when arriving at net income for tax purposes.

III. Registered Retirement Savings Plans

The other-deductions category permits individuals to deduct contributions to a registered retirement savings plan (RRSP). As such plans are used by many taxpayers, their general principles are reviewed in this section of the chapter.

An RRSP is a private, tax-sheltered retirement savings program initiated and controlled by the individual taxpayer for his or her exclusive use. It is different from a registered pension plan (RPP), which is initiated and controlled by the employer for the benefit of a number of employees. An RRSP can be an individual's primary retirement vehicle, or it can be used to supplement the retirement program provided by the employer.

A. Benefits of Investing in an RRSP

Investments made through an RRSP have a substantially higher return. This is because they permit the investment of pre-tax earnings (from employment, business, and certain other sources) to generate returns that are not taxed until they are required for personal use. Specifically, this is achieved as a result of the following:

1. Contributions to an RRSP are deductible from income, which reduces the amount of tax that would otherwise be payable. The tax reduction increases the amount of funds available for investment.

   Normally, to make an investment, an individual must first pay tax on earnings and then invest some portion of the after-tax amount. Consider an individual who, after paying tax and personal expenses, has $3,300 for investment purposes. An individual in a 45% tax bracket could afford to invest $6,000 through an RRSP as follows:

Contribution to the RRSP	$6,000
Tax savings generated:	
(45% × $6,000)	(2,700)
Net cost of investment	$3,300

   Obviously, if you have $3,300 available for an investment, it is better to acquire one that provides a return on $6,000, rather than on $3,300. Effectively, through an RRSP, taxpayers are permitted to delay the payment of tax and invest those funds for their own benefit.

2. Investment returns accumulated on funds contributed to the plan are not subject to annual taxation, which means that investments compound on a pre-tax basis, rather than on an after-tax basis. In the previous example, if the invested funds generate a 10% annual return, an investment in an RRSP will provide 10% on $6,000, compounded annually; an investment outside the plan would provide only 5.5% (10% − tax @ 45%) on $3,300, compounded annually.

3. Funds accumulated within the plan, from contributions and investment returns, are subject to tax only when removed from the plan. Usually, funds are removed from the plan on retirement in the form of a regular pension payment, although all or a portion of the funds can be removed if the investor wishes. Some funds can be withdrawn on a tax-free basis. Individuals are able to make tax-free RRSP withdrawals of up to $10,000 per year over a four-year period (provided that the total withdrawals do not exceed $20,000) to finance full-time education or training for the plan holder or his or her spouse. Amounts withdrawn must be

repaid (without interest) in equal instalments over a 10-year period. If the withdrawals are not repaid, they will be included in income. Also, first-time home buyers can withdraw funds up to $25,000 on a tax-free basis to purchase a home. Up to 15 years are allowed for repayment; otherwise, any unpaid portion will be taxable.

The significance of this tax deferral can be more easily seen by examining its impact over a long period of time. For example, if the individual in the situation above had after-tax cash flow of $3,300 available for investment every year for 30 years, the results would be as shown below.

The difference between $1,086,000 and $252,000 is dramatic, although it must be remembered that the $1,086,000 is fully taxable once removed from the plan. However, even the worst-case scenario, where the funds are withdrawn in a lump sum after 30 years and taxed at a rate of 45%, would still leave $597,000 in after-tax value. An individual who invested $3,300 annually without using an RRSP, in order to achieve an after-tax value of $597,000 after 30 years, would have to find an investment yielding 18% annually instead of 10%.

Investment through an RRSP	
Annual investments in RRSP	$ 6,000
Tax savings @ 45%	(2,700)
Net annual cost	$ 3,300
Total cost ($3,300 × 30 y)	$ 99,000
Future value of investment:	
$6,000 × 30 y × 10% (compounded)	$1,086,000
Investment outside an RRSP	
Total cost ($3,300 × 30 y)	$ 99,000
Future value of investment:	
$3,300 × 30 y × 5.5% (compounded)	$ 252,000

The impact of the tax factors on RRSP investments is so substantial that one cannot afford to exclude such plans from one's investment strategy.

B. Contribution Limits

The amount of the contribution to an RRSP that can be deducted for tax purposes is subject to an annual limit.[14]

If an individual *does not belong* to an employer's registered pension plan or deferred profit sharing plan, the annual RRSP contribution limit is equal to 18% of the individual's prior year's "earned income," up to a maximum of $22,970 in 2012[15] and increasing to $23,820 in 2013.

For example, the most an individual can contribute to an RRSP in 2011 is 18% of the 2010 earned income, to a maximum of $22,450. When an individual chooses not to contribute the maximum, the unused portion can be carried forward indefinitely and contributed as a deductible contribution in any future year.[16] While it is advantageous to make the contribution as early as possible, the carry-forward provides flexibility to individuals in terms of their particular cash-flow requirements.

When individuals also *belong* to an employer's pension plan, deferred profit-sharing plan, or the proposed pooled registered pension plan, the RRSP contribution limit is integrated with those plans. For example, an individual with earned income

---

14 ITA 60(i), 146; IT-124R6.
15 The contribution limit will be indexed to increases in the average industrial wage.
16 ITA 146(1)(l).

of $50,000 has a normal contribution limit of $9,000 (18% of $50,000). However, if the individual's employer contributes $3,000 to a deferred profit-sharing plan, the RRSP contribution limit is reduced to $6,000.

As a further example, consider a situation where, in 20X3, an employer has contributed $3,300 to the company's registered pension plan (RPP) and the employee has contributed an equal amount. Assume that the RPP is a money-purchase type of plan (i.e., that will acquire a pension with whatever funds the employee has available in the plan), rather than a defined benefit plan (i.e., that must provide a pension based on an established formula). Also, assume that the individual's earned income in 20X3 was $60,000. Based on these assumptions, the maximum contribution that the individual can make to an RRSP in 20X4 is $4,200, as follows:

Total limit—18% of $60,000	$10,800
RPP contributions —employer	(3,300)
—employee	(3,300)
	$ 4,200

In the above example, if the employee's salary was $130,000, the total limit for the year would be the maximum of $22,970 (using the 2012 limit), rather than 18% of the earned income (18% of $130,000 is $23,400 and is in excess of the absolute limit). The contribution limit for 20X4 would then be $16,370 ($22,970 − [$3,300 + $3,300]).

The value of the contributions to the RPP ($3,300 + $3,300 = $6,600) is technically referred to as the pension adjustment (PA). When the employer's RPP is a defined benefit plan, the value of this pension adjustment may be different from the actual pension contributions because it is based on a formula related to the defined pension benefit. As noted earlier, the pension adjustment also includes contributions by an employer to a deferred profit-sharing plan. Employees cannot contribute to an employer's deferred profit-sharing plan.

Keep in mind that the RRSP contribution limit, as calculated in the above example, is further increased by any unused contribution limits carried forward from previous years.

The calculation of the maximum deductible RRSP contribution for the current year can be summarized as follows:

Prescribed dollar limit (current year)	$22,970 (A)*
18% × earned income of the *previous year*	$ xx,xxx (B)
Lesser of A and B above	$ xx,xxx
Add:	
Accumulated unused RRSP contribution limit at the end of the *previous year*, if any	x,xxx
Deduct:	
Pension adjustment from the *previous year*,† if any	(x,xxx)
Maximum deduction for the *current year*	$ xx,xxx

* Using the 2012 limit.
† A further reduction may occur if the employer makes a past-service contribution to the pension plan.

It should also be noted that the contribution limit of 18% applies to "earned income," which is determined by a special calculation, the details of which are easily found in the tax guide accompanying the annual tax return. In general terms, earned income includes employment income (excluding the deduction for contributions to a registered pension plan), rental income, royalty income, alimony and maintenance income, and research grants net of related expenses.[17] This amount must be

---

17 ITA 146(1) earned income definition; IT-124R6.

reduced by negative amounts of a similar nature—business losses, rental losses, and deductible alimony payments. Note that the calculation of earned income excludes certain passive types of income, such as interest, dividends, and capital gains.

Usually, all contributions that exceed the annual limit are subject to a penalty tax of 1% per month on part of that excess until the overcontribution is removed.[18] However, an individual is permitted to overcontribute up to $2,000 during his or her lifetime without penalty. This overcontribution can be carried forward and deducted from income in a future year when sufficient earned income is available.

An example of an RRSP contribution limit calculation is provided in the demonstration question at the end of this chapter.

C. RRSP Investment Opportunities

RRSP funds are restricted to certain types of investments. The list of qualified investments includes most of the common securities, such as cash deposits in banks or other financial institutions, term deposits, government-insured or guaranteed bonds, bonds and debentures of public corporations, shares of public corporations, mutual funds, and mortgages on real estate (including one's own mortgage).

RRSP investments are normally managed by banks, trust companies, insurance companies, and other similar financial institutions. Alternatively, an individual can create a self-administered RRSP and manage his or her own investment portfolio.

Special attention should be given to the type of investment and to the amount of returns that can be achieved within the plan. Too often, the attractiveness of the tax savings from the deductible contribution overshadows, in the investor's mind, the importance of maximizing the return on investments. Because the return on the investment compounds on a pre-tax basis, a slight variation in the rate of return can significantly alter the wealth accumulation—and the ultimate retirement benefits.

Exhibit 9-1 demonstrates the ultimate value of investing $6,000 per year at various rates of return. Increasing the return from 8% to 10% will increase the ultimate value from $734,000 to $1,086,000, providing an extra $352,000 in retirement benefits. Note that because of the compounding factor, each successive yield increase of 2% affects the final total by a greater amount. For example, expanding the return from 10% to 12% will increase the ultimate value by $536,000 ($1,622,000 − $1,086,000), compared with an increase of only $352,000 when the return is increased from 8% to 10%. Also note that doubling the return from 8% to 16% increases the ultimate value fivefold, from $734,000 to $3,691,000.

Of course, with increased returns comes increased risk, and it is unwise to expose retirement funds to excessive risk. However, by regularly reviewing RRSP investments, maximum returns can be achieved within the acceptable boundaries of risk.

In addition to the amount of expected returns, consideration should be given to the *type* of investment return earned by the RRSP. Capital gains, for example, receive

Exhibit 9-1:

Value of $6,000 Invested Annually for 30 Years	Return on investment	Value after 30 years	Impact of 2% increase
	6%	$ 503,000	–0–
	8%	$ 734,000	231,000
	10	1,086,000	352,000
	12	1,622,000	536,000
	14	2,440,000	818,000
	16	3,691,000	1,251,000

18 ITA 146(8.2); IC 77-18.

preferential treatment, as only one-half of the gain is taxable. Capital gains that are realized in an RRSP are not taxable while they remain in the plan; however, they are *fully* taxable as pension income when paid out of the plan. This means that an individual who invests in common shares through an RRSP is converting otherwise tax-free gains into taxable pension income. This consequence is important for those individuals who hold a variety of investments both inside and outside an RRSP. It is prudent for those investors to hold investments yielding capital gains outside the plan, and interest-bearing securities (which do not have preferential tax treatment) within the plan.

D. Retirement Options

Funds accumulated in an RRSP can be paid out in a lump sum or gradually over a period of time in the form of a pension, depending on the individual's particular requirements. If those funds are paid out gradually in the form of a pension, the funds remaining in the plan continue to generate investment returns without tax consequences. In order to receive regular payments from an RRSP, the plan must be formally converted into a pension vehicle. Financial institutions offer these. Three general types of pension vehicles are available, each of which is described briefly below.

- **Life annuity** Under this option, the accumulated RRSP funds are used to purchase an annuity that provides a monthly payment for the life of the owner. The amount of the payment depends on the age of the individual and on the prevailing interest rates at the date of purchase. This option is considered to be a risk vehicle because if the annuitant dies before his or her normal life expectancy, the payments cease, and the remaining funds in the plan accrue to the benefit of the financial institution that issued the annuity. Because of this risk, life annuities usually provide the highest pension income. The risk of life annuities can be tempered by arranging a guaranteed payment term (e.g., a life annuity with payments guaranteed for 10 years, or a life annuity for the life of the annuitant and his or her spouse), but reducing the risk this way also reduces the regular pension payments. After age 65, an individual can arbitrarily transfer up to one-half of life annuity income from an RRSP to a spouse and achieve a tax benefit from income splitting.

- **Guaranteed fixed-term annuity** This option guarantees that the full RRSP funds will be paid out over a period of time to the owner or any designated beneficiaries. Regular payments are made over a term that begins with the date of purchase and ends when the annuitant or his or her spouse reaches the age of 90. For example, an annuity purchased at age 65 will be paid over 25 years (90 − 65) whether or not the annuitant lives to age 90. This type of annuity usually consists of fixed, equal payments; however, arrangements can be made to have regular payments tied to specific investment returns.

- **Registered retirement income fund (RRIF)** Under this option, the RRSP funds are invested and guaranteed to be fully paid out over the remaining lifetime of the holder (or the holder's spouse). However, the regular payment is fixed at a low minimum, with the annuitant having the right to withdraw any additional amount desired in any particular year. This option provides the greatest flexibility by permitting the owner to alter the payments in accordance with his or her needs. After age 65, an individual can arbitrarily transfer up to one-half of RRIF income to a spouse and achieve a tax benefit from income splitting.

When must an individual convert his or her RRSP to one of the above-mentioned retirement options? It is mandatory to convert all of the accumulated RRSP funds to a retirement income vehicle by December 31 of the year in which the individual reaches 71 years of age.[19] Retirement income can begin in the following calendar year.

---

19 ITA 146(2)(b.4).

It is not necessary to wait until age 71 to make the conversion; retirement income can begin earlier than age 71, if desired. It should be noted that failure to convert by age 71 will result in the automatic cancellation of the RRSP at the beginning of the following year, in which case the full amount of the plan will be taxable.

E. Spousal RRSP

An additional important tax planning opportunity is available to taxpayers who are married and contribute to an RRSP. Once an individual's total contribution limit has been established, that individual can contribute all or any part of that limit to the RRSP of a spouse. The person who makes the contribution is entitled to claim the related tax deduction. This does not affect the normal contribution limit of the spouse.[20] This type of contribution does not create any immediate tax advantage because the maximum deduction for the contributor remains the same. However, the long-term benefits may be substantial.

The point of designating contributions to a spouse's plan is that it allows the future payout—usually in the form of an annuity—to be included in the spouse's taxable income, rather than that of the contributor. If a couple can equalize their RRSP funds, future withdrawals can be divided between them upon retirement. This will usually result in lower annual taxes than would have been levied if all of the withdrawals had been included in one person's income. This form of income splitting between spouses, along with the life annuity and RRIF options described above, is specifically permitted; other types of income splitting between spouses are usually discouraged (as is discussed later in this chapter).

In order to prevent abuses of this program, there is an anti-avoidance rule stating that any contributions withdrawn from such a plan by the spouse within two taxation years of the contribution year must be included in the contributor's income. However, once the two-year period (for any contribution) passes, the amounts are taxable only to the spouse.

In conclusion, the RRSP is an important tool for maximizing wealth accumulation through the use of tax-sheltered funds.

IV. Pooled Registered Pension Plans

The federal government has proposed the creation of a new retirement savings vehicle— The Pooled Registered Pension Plan (PRPP).[21] Under the proposal, financial institutions will administer the plans in large pooled funds with low administration costs. The plans will operate similar to a Registered Pension Plan (RPP) but with greater flexibility for individuals and employers. An individual may join a plan without being employed or where an employer does not have a plan. An employer can choose to contribute to a plan or not contribute to the plan. Similarly, an employer can join a PRPP for its employees but the employee's contribution will be optional. The PRPP will be especially attractive to small business employers and to self-employed individuals who currently have access to only the RRSP vehicle.

Similar to an RPP, employer contributions will be deductible[22] but will not be immediately taxable to the employee. Contributions by the employee are *deemed to be RRSP contributions* and are deductible as such in arriving at net income for tax purposes.[23] The maximum annual contribution by the employer and the employee combined will be tied to the individual's annual RRSP limit including unused amounts from previous years. For example, if an individual has a RRSP limit of $20,000 in a

---

20 ITA 146(5.1), 146(8.3).
21 Department of Finance, December 14, 2011 draft legislative proposals.
22 ITA 20(1)q).
23 Draft ITA 147.5(11); ITA 60(1)(i); or 60(j.1), 60(l).

particular year and has contributed $5,000 to an RRSP, the maximum PRPP contribution available to an employer and individual combined will be $15,000 ($20,000 RRSP limit—$5,000 RRSP contribution). Similar to an RRSP, an individual will be able to make contributions to a PRPP up to 60 days after the calendar year. Individuals will be able to transfer retiring allowances into the plan and withdraw funds for the Home Buyer's Plan and the Lifelong Learning Plan within designated limits.

Investment returns earned by the plan will not be taxable. The withdrawal of funds by the individual will be taxable as pension income similar to RPP withdrawals and will qualify for income splitting with a spouse and for the pension tax credit. Upon retirement, payments can be made from the plan in the form of a lump sum, life annuity or a variable payout system similar to a RRIF.

V. Registered Education Savings Plans

A Registered Education Savings Plan (RESP) is a formal tax entity designed to assist families save funds for a child's post-secondary education. The tax treatment of an RESP is unique and creates both tax deferral and income splitting benefits. The basics of an RESP are described below.

A. Contributions to an RESP

An individual, normally a family member, can contribute funds to an RESP at any time before a child reaches 31 years of age. There is no annual contribution limit but there is a lifetime contribution limit of $50,000.[24] Money contributed is managed and invested by a financial institution. Annual earnings from investment returns such as interest, dividends, and capital gains are not taxed when earned within the plan but will be taxed (normally as income to the student) when funds are withdrawn. This permits returns to accumulate and compound on a tax-free basis similar to an RRSP. However, unlike an RRSP, contributions are not deductible from income for tax purposes.

In addition to allowing income to accumulate tax-free, the RESP can receive a federal government Canada Education Saving Grant (CESG) for children ages 17 or under. The maximum lifetime grant per child is $7,200 but is limited to an annual amount of 20% of the contribution to a maximum of $2,500. So, an annual contribution of $2,500 will receive a grant of $500 (20% × $2,500) and the RESP will have $3,000 to invest. The annual grant limit of $500 may be increased to up to $1,000 to make up for years when no contributions were made or the maximum grant was not received. The CESG can be marginally increased when a family's qualified income is below certain levels.[25] Other grants may also apply in certain provinces and federally if family income levels are below a prescribed minimum. If the child (or children in the case of a family plan) does not pursue post-secondary education the CESG is returned to the government.

B. Withdrawals from an RESP

The primary purpose of an RESP is to provide Educational Assistance Payments (EAPs) for a child to support the cost of studies at a post-secondary education institution. Students may receive EAPs from an RESP when enrolled full-time at a post-secondary institution such as a university, college, or certain other designated institution in or out of Canada. Part-time students may also qualify if they are at least 16 years old. Payments are limited to $5,000 for full-time students and $2,500 for part-time students for the first consecutive 13 weeks of study. Thereafter, there is *no limit to the amount of EAPs.*[26]

---

24 ITA 146.1.

25 An additional 10% of the first $500 of contributions if qualified family income is between $42,707 and $85,414; or 20% of the first $500 of contributions if qualified family income is below $42,707.

26 If a student is not enrolled for a consecutive 12-month period, the 13-week $5,000 limit may reapply upon subsequent enrollment.

EAPs received by students are partly taxable. To the extent payments received are from *income earned* or from *grants* received by the RESP, the amounts *are taxable* to the student in the year of receipt.[27] Payments from the plan that *originated from contributions* made by contributors are *not taxable.*

When funds are not used by a student but are returned to a contributor, they may consist of both original contributions and earned income. To the extent original contributions are returned to the contributor they are not subject to tax. However, the earned income portion is subject to two levels of tax. First, the income is included in the contributor's normal taxable income for that year and taxed accordingly. Second, the same income is subject to a special 20% federal tax. Presumably, this second tax eliminates any tax deferral benefits that may have arisen and also acts to prevent individuals from creating RESPs that were never intended for education purposes. Both levels of tax may be avoided if the contributor contributes the amount to an RRSP. To do this requires that the contributor has unused RRSP contribution room to make the deduction.

C. Benefits of an RESP

An RESP provides significant benefits when used for its intended purpose. First, although contributions are not deductible, investment returns within the plan accumulate and compound on a pre-tax basis similar to an RRSP. This pre-tax compounding allows for maximum investment growth. Second, the amount saved is enhanced by the federal grant of $7,200 plus the investment returns that the grant generates. Third, amounts accumulated from investment returns and distributed to children for education purposes are taxed as their income at lower rates than those of the contributor resulting in income splitting benefits.

Depending on the rates of return and when they are earned, the fund's growth from various contribution approaches vary. Some contributors may want and can afford to contribute the lifetime limit of $50,000 in the first year. This approach means that only $500 of a federal grant is received. Others may contribute $2,500 annually until the maximum grant of $7,200 is achieved followed by a lump sum contribution, or contribute equal amounts over time. Some of these approaches are demonstrated below assuming a 6% rate of return and a 25-year time frame.[28]

	Accumulated Value
• Contribute $50,000 in year 1 (total grant $500)	$217,000
• Contribute $2,500 annually for 14 years followed by one contribution of $15,000 (total grant $7,200)	$156,000
• Contribute $15,000 in year 1 followed by $2,500 annually for 14 years (total grant $7,200)	$186,000

The above demonstrates that, given steady returns, it is better to contribute more funds earlier in the RESP life. An RESP must terminate by its 35th anniversary date, which leaves significant time to accumulate savings and provide for many years of education.

VI. Tax-Free Savings Accounts

Canadian resident individuals can use an investment savings entity called a Tax-Free Savings Account (TFSA) to achieve preferential tax treatment on investment returns. While the annual permitted contributions to a TFSA are limited and not tax deductible, all qualified investment income such as interest, dividends, and capital gains are tax-

---

27 ITA 56(1)q).
28 Brian Ginsler, Northwood Stevens Private Council, *The Globe and Mail,* March 24, 2007.

free *when earned and when withdrawn from the account.* Essentially, the TFSA is a vehicle designed to earn permanent tax-free investment income rather than the deferred tax format of an RRSP. The basic tax treatment of a TFSA is outlined below.

- *Contributions*   Canadian resident individuals who are at least 18 years of age can contribute up to $5,000 annually to a TFSA. The contributions are *not tax deductible* and so must be made with after-tax income. The contribution limit is not dependent on a person's level of income. Any unused portion of the annual limit can be carried forward indefinitely and contributed in any future year.[29] The *annual limit is indexed* and will increase with inflation, but only in $500 increments. So the current inflation rate is not high enough to increase the $500 limit. An individual, age 18 or older in 2009, who has not contributed to a TFSA in prior years, can contribute $20,000 ($5,000 × 4 years) in 2012. Interest on money borrowed to invest in a TFSA is not deductible.[30]

- **Overcontribution**   If the TFSA has an overcontribution, a 1% per month penalty will apply on the amount of the excess.[31]

- *Investments*   Accumulated contributions to a TFSA can be invested in qualified investments similar to those permitted in an RRSP.[32] Generally these include publicly traded securities such as bonds, debentures, shares of public corporations, deposits in financial institutions, and so on.

- *Income*   Investment income, including capital gains, is not taxed when earned in the TFSA nor is it taxable when withdrawn (see below).[33] Similarly, losses are not deductible.

- *Withdrawals*   All funds, including original contributions and income earned in the TFSA, can be withdrawn in whole or in part at any time and are *not taxable* to the individual. In addition, the amount of any withdrawal is added to the accumulated contribution limit in the following year and can be recontributed at any time. Therefore, funds can be extracted when needed and replaced at a later time without consequence.

- *Attribution*   Individuals can contribute to their own and a spouse's TFSA without attribution consequences.[34] This means that spouses and common law partners have a combined annual contribution limit of $10,000 regardless of the source of the contributions.

- *Wind-up*   A TFSA has no age-based wind-up requirement. It can be wound up at any time or maintained until death. On wind-up the assets are deemed to be disposed of at fair market value and accrued gains are not taxable. A TFSA can continue on a tax-free basis after death if left to a spouse or common law partner.[35]

The TFSA is an important long-term savings tool for individuals. The ability to compound investment returns on a pre-tax basis is an extremely valuable wealth builder as demonstrated in Part III of this chapter. Unlike the RRSP, contributions are not tax deductible. However, the TFSA, when started, offers greater flexibility than an RRSP because the income is permanently tax-free, the account has no mandatory wind-up requirement, and the earned income can be used at any time by the individual as needed without tax consequence. Unlike an RRSP, a TFSA can be used as security for a loan, subject to certain conditions.[36]

---

29 ITA 207.01(1).
30 ITA 18(11)(j).
31 ITA 207.02.
32 ITA 207.01(1) Qualified investments exclude investments in entities that are not at arm's-length with the contributor or are entities of which the contributor is a specified shareholder (10% or more).
33 ITA 146.2 (6), 149(1)(u.2).
34 ITA 74.5 (12).
35 ITA 146.2 (8), (9).
36 ITA 146.2 (4).

Which plan is preferred is difficult to answer and depends on many factors. Certainly when an individual is in a high tax bracket, having a deductible contribution to an RRSP is valuable. A person in a 40% tax bracket can place $8,400 in an RRSP for investment at a cost of only $5,000 after tax ($8,400 − tax saving of $3,400). If a TFSA is used, that same person will have only $5,000 to invest. So, the RRSP should grow faster. On the other hand, the TFSA offers great personal flexibility for withdrawals and recontributions. Not knowing future personal tax rates and when funds may be needed makes the decision difficult. If one can afford it, both plans should be utilized. Also, when tax-free capital is received, such as from an inheritance, the TFSA may be a preferred option, especially if a large contribution room is available from unused annual limits.

Exhibit 9-2, below, compares the outcomes from investing in a TFSA and an RRSP or PRPP over a 20-year period when the individual's tax rate remains the same at 40% during the contribution years and the retirement years.[37] Under this scenario the outcomes are identical. However, it is clear that if tax rates after retirement are lower, the RRSP gives a better result.

Exhibit 9-2:

Value of $1,000 after 20 years

	TFSA	RRSP or PRPP
Pre-tax income	$1,000	$1,000
Tax (40%)	400	N/A
Net contribution	$ 600	$1,000
Value after 20 years (annual return 6%)	$1,924	$3,207
Tax on withdrawal (40%)	N/A	$1,283
Net withdrawal	$1,924	$1,924

VII. Special Rules for Net Income Determination

The parameters of net income for tax purposes have been established to include five sources of income. Each source, with the exception of "other income," is calculated in accordance with its own set of fundamental principles. Within each source of income, unusual transactions may occur, the treatment of which is not clearly answered by the established general principles. In addition, taxpayers may attempt to structure transactions in such a way as to avoid the application of the general principles. Consequently, the *Income Tax Act* includes a set of special rules for determining net income; these provide greater certainty when the established general rules are applied in unusual transactions and also forestall certain tax-avoidance schemes.

The special rules are grouped together in sections 67 through 81 of the *Income Tax Act*. In some cases, these rules are in conflict with the previously established principles; when they are, the special rules take precedence. Although the special rules are presented separately, they apply to all of the five sources of income. For example, when business income is being determined, the special rules must be viewed in terms of their application to business transactions. In other words, the special rules outlined in this section of the chapter should be thought of as an extension of the rules that have been established for each source of income.

The fundamental application of several of the special rules is described briefly below.

---

37 Federal Budget papers February 2008.

A. The Reasonableness Test

All items that are deductible from any source of income are deductible only to the extent that the expenditure is considered reasonable in the particular circumstances.[38] The question of what is "reasonable" is a difficult one; the answer depends on the nature of the transaction. For example, a portion of automobile expenses incurred to earn business income or employment income may be denied when the cost of the automobile is too high for the particular purpose. Similarly, overly extravagant entertainment expenses may be deemed unnecessary for the intended purpose.

The denial of a deduction for unreasonable salaries paid to related parties is extremely punitive. A small business owner may be denied the deduction of all or a portion of the salary paid to a spouse or child if the payment is excessive in relation to the services provided; but the actual salary paid to the spouse or child remains as taxable employment income in their hands. Effectively, this creates double taxation within the family unit.

The general reasonableness test was reviewed in several previous chapters, especially Chapter 5, which dealt with the determination of business income. It is important to recognize that the reasonableness test applies to deductions for *all* types of income. In addition to the general reasonableness test, there are several more specific reasonableness tests that apply to various categories of income. One of these limits the deduction for meals, beverages, and entertainment expenses to 50% of the actual costs (provided that those costs meet the general reasonableness test). Another places limits on the deduction of interest, lease costs, and the capital cost of a passenger vehicle (see Chapters 4, 5, and 6).[39]

B. Allocation of Purchase Price for Multiple Assets

In some cases, a number of different properties may be acquired or sold as a group. This is most common when the assets of an entire business are sold. The total price may include such items as inventory, land, buildings, equipment, and goodwill. Similarly, when real estate is sold, the price includes the land and the building(s). While the total price is obvious, it may be difficult to allocate that price among the various assets included in the transaction.

A conflict often arises between the purchaser and the vendor. It is in the buyer's interests to allocate a greater amount to assets that are permitted a faster write-off rate for tax purposes. For example, the buyer achieves greater tax benefits if, in a real estate purchase, a greater amount is allocated to the building and a lesser amount to the land. Similarly, when a complete business is purchased, it is to the buyer's advantage to increase the value of equipment and reduce the value of goodwill, which has a slower write-off rate. On the other hand, it is in the vendor's interest to reduce the amount of tax on the sale. A vendor will often try to enhance the value of properties yielding capital gains (land, for example) because only one-half of such gains is taxable and reduce the value of properties that create a recapture of capital cost allowance, which is fully taxable.

The special rules permit the CRA to allocate or re-allocate the total price for both parties, in accordance with the apparent fair market values of individual properties.[40] The CRA is permitted to do so, irrespective of the legal agreement of sale. It should be pointed out, however, that when the parties are dealing at arm's length (i.e., are not related), an agreed allocation in the legal agreement of sale carries considerable weight in the absence of evidence of a scam or scheme to reduce taxes.

It is important that decision makers, when they are about to acquire or sell a group of assets, give reasonable consideration to how the total price is allocated so that they can forecast both the related tax consequences and the impact on cash flow of the proposed transaction.

---

38 ITA 67; *No. 511 v. MNR*, 58 DTC 307.
39 ITA 67.2 to 67.4; IT-521R.
40 ITA 68; *Schellenberg v. MNR*, 86 DTC 1463.

C. Transactions with Inadequate Consideration

When taxpayers enter into a transaction with non–arm's-length (related) parties, special rules apply that prevent the elimination or reduction of tax by selling at a price other than fair market value. Taxpayers are considered *not* to be dealing at arm's length if they are related to each other. The term "related" has a specific limited definition within the *Income Tax Act* and can apply to both individuals and corporations, as discussed later in this section.

The following rules apply to taxpayers not dealing at arm's-length:[41]

1. Property sold at a legal price less than its fair market value is deemed to have been sold by the vendor at fair market value. No adjustment is made to the purchaser, for whom the cost of the property for tax purposes remains the actual price paid.

2. Property sold at a price higher than its fair market value is not adjusted to the vendor, and the selling price constitutes the proceeds of disposition. However, the cost to the purchaser is deemed to be equal to the fair market value, not the actual purchase price.

3. Property transferred by way of a gift is deemed to have been sold at fair market value by the person making the gift. The recipient of the gift is deemed, for tax purposes, to have purchased the property at a cost equal to its fair market value. This particular rule applies even when the gift is made to an arm's-length party.

Note that the first two of the above rules apply to only one party in the transaction. As a result, the application of those rules is extremely punitive, as demonstrated in the following situation:

Situation:

> Corporation X, a manufacturer, has inventory on hand that was produced at a cost of $10,000. The inventory if sold direct to retail stores is worth $18,000, and if sold on the wholesale market is worth $13,000. Corporation Y is a sister corporation of X, as it is owned by the same shareholders.
>
> Corporation Y is a wholesale enterprise that buys manufactured products for resale to retail stores. Corporation X sells the above inventory to its sister corporation for $10,000, which is its cost amount. Subsequently, Corporation Y sells the inventory to retail stores for the going price of $18,000.

Analysis:

> Corporation X and Corporation Y are related and do not deal at arm's length because they have common ownership.

Impact on Corporation X (seller):	
Deemed selling price at fair market value	$13,000
Cost	(10,000)
Business income for tax purposes	$ 3,000
Impact on Corporation Y (purchaser):	
Actual selling price to retail stores	$18,000
Actual cost paid to X	(10,000)
Business income for tax purposes	$ 8,000

In the above example, the combined taxable income of Corporation X and Corporation Y was $11,000 ($3,000 + $8,000) on the sale of inventory, even though a real profit of only $8,000 had been realized. The impact of these rules is severely punitive; managers *must* take great care in their transfer-pricing decisions in a related group of companies.

---

41 ITA 69(1)(a) to (c); IT-405 (archived).

The punitive provisions may apply even when the parties have intended to deal at fair market value but have erred while estimating that value. In such cases, the related parties can protect themselves with a covering written agreement which indicates that the established price is a reasonable estimate of fair market value and that if found to be in error, the price charged and paid will be altered accordingly.[42] Usually, the existence of such an agreement will cause the CRA to adjust both sides of the transaction, thereby eliminating the punitive result, which is double taxation.

Similar provisions also apply for the sale of property and services between a Canadian taxpayer and a non–arm's-length foreign entity. This means that transactions between a Canadian subsidiary and its foreign parent corporation cannot unduly shift the burden of tax from one jurisdiction to another by means of transactions at other than reasonable values (see Chapter 20).[43]

D. Non–Arm's-Length Defined

Normally, the values placed on financial transactions are determined by the free market forces of supply and demand. In such circumstances, the parties to the transaction are said to be dealing at *arm's length*. Sometimes, however, supply and demand are *not* the motivating factors, in which case the parties are considered not to be dealing at arm's length. For tax purposes, the *Income Tax Act* deems parties not to be dealing with each other at arm's length if they are *related*[44] and their transactions may be subject to scrutiny, as was shown in Section C above. Non–arm's-length transactions can occur between (related)

- an individual and another individual,
- an individual and a corporation, and
- a corporation and another corporation.

The rules that deem the above parties to be related are complex. Outlined below are some of the most *common* relationships.

• **Transactions between individuals**   For tax purposes, individuals are related to each other if they are direct-line descendants (grandparents, parents, children, grandchildren, and so on) or if they are brothers, sisters, spouses, or in-laws.[45] Excluded from the definition are cousins, aunts, uncles, nieces, and nephews.

• **Transactions between individuals and corporations**   An individual is related to a corporation if he or she controls the corporation, is a member of a related group that controls the corporation, or is related to an individual who controls the corporation. Control, in this context, usually means the ownership of a majority of the corporation's voting shares. Consider the following ownership structures:

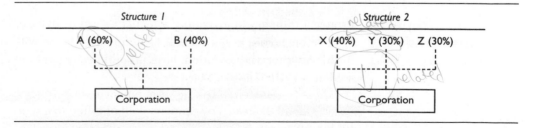

In structure 1, the corporation is controlled by individual A (60%), and therefore individual A and the corporation are related and do not deal at arm's length.

42 IT-405 (archived).
43 ITA 69(2), (3).
44 ITA 251(1)(a); IT-419R2.
45 ITA 251(2), 252(1), (2).

Individual B (40%) is not related to the corporation unless he or she is also related to individual A (e.g., is the sister, child, or parent of individual A). In structure 2, none of the individual shareholders is related to the corporation because none of them has control. However, if individual X (40%) and individual Y (30%) were themselves related, they would together control the corporation (70%), and each would be considered related to the corporation.

- **Transactions between corporations**   Two corporations are related if one corporation controls the other corporation, if both corporations are controlled by the same person, or if one corporation is controlled by one person who is related to the person who controls the other corporation. Consider the following ownership structures:

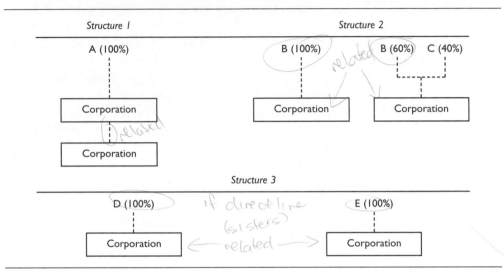

In structure 1, the two corporations are related because one controls the other. In structure 2, both corporations are controlled by individual B (100% and 60%), which means that the two corporations are related. In structure 3, the two corporations are not related because they are controlled by different shareholders. However, if shareholders D and E are related to each other, the two corporations will also be related because one corporation is controlled by a person who is related to a person who controls the other corporation.

Note that even when parties are *not related*, it is a question of fact whether they are dealing at arm's length for a particular transaction.[46] Where there is sufficient cause, the CRA can deem two unrelated parties not to be dealing at arm's length.

E. Property Transferred to a Spouse or Child

Property transferred to a child, whether by gift or by sale, is deemed for tax purposes to have been sold at fair market value in accordance with the rules described earlier in this chapter. By exception, farm property transferred to children is permitted to be sold at less than fair market value.[47]

Property transferred to a spouse, however, is not subject to the rules regarding fair market value. Instead, any property sold or gifted to a spouse is automatically deemed, for tax purposes, to have been sold and acquired at its cost amount.[48] As a result, capital property is deemed to have been sold at its adjusted cost base (see Chapter 8) and depreciable property at its undepreciated capital cost (see Chapter 6). The result is that no taxable income is created on the transfer of property between spouses.

---

46 ITA 251(1)(b).
47 ITA 73(3).
48 ITA 73(1), (2).

Alternatively, a taxpayer can choose to recognize a gain on a spousal transfer. This may be attractive when losses are available that can be offset against the resulting income.

F. The Attribution Rules—Income Splitting

The above section described the tax treatment resulting from the actual transfer of property to a spouse or child. Additional special rules govern the treatment of income that may be earned on the property after it has been transferred. For example, the property may generate interest, dividends, or rents, or may incur a gain or loss when it is subsequently resold.

Income from Property Transferred to a Spouse

Subsequent income received by the *spouse* on transferred property must be included in the net income for tax purposes of the original owner for as long as the couple remains married.[49] This rule prevents a taxpayer from transferring his or her income to a spouse, who may be in a lower tax bracket. The process of allocating subsequent income back to the original owner is referred to as "attribution." Similarly, if interest-free loans are made to a spouse, any income earned by the spouse on the loaned funds is attributed to the lender.

The attribution rules do not apply if property is transferred to a spouse in a manner equivalent to an arm's-length transfer.[50] This means that a loan to a spouse must have a reasonable interest rate and that property sold to a spouse must be paid for in normal commercial terms. In addition, the spouse who made the transfer must recognize the related gain on the transfer if the transfer value is greater than the cost amount (see discussion in Section C). As noted in Part VI of this chapter, the attribution rules do not apply when an individual transfers money to a TFSA owned by a spouse.

The following situation and analysis demonstrates some of the above rules.

Situation: In 20X7, a wife gifted shares of a public corporation to her spouse. The shares originally cost $12,000 and at the time of the gift had a market vale of $26,000. In 20X8, the spouse received dividends of $1,000 from the shares and then sold them for $30,000.

Analysis: At the time of the gift, the wife is deemed to have sold the shares to her spouse at an amount equal to their adjusted cost base (see Section F above) of $12,000. Therefore, the wife has no taxable gain resulting from the transfer of the shares. Similarly, the spouse receiving the gift is deemed to have acquired the shares at a cost of $12,000. In 20X8 the taxable dividend of $1,380 [$1,000 × 1.38] received by the spouse is attributed to the wife and included in her income for tax purposes. A taxable capital gain of $9,000 ($\frac{1}{2}$ × ($30,000 − $12,000)) is also attributed to the wife. To the extent that the spouse invests the dividend of $1,000 and capital gain of $18,000 ($30,000 − $12,000) the income on the investment will not be attributed back to the wife. Attribution could have been avoided if, in the year of the gift, the wife had elected to treat the transaction as sale at fair market value and accepted a market form of payment from the spouse such as cash or a note payable with a prescribed rate of interest. If that had been done, the wife would have had a taxable capital gain of $7,000 ($\frac{1}{2}$ × ($26,000 − $12,000)) in 20X7 and the spouse would have had a taxable capital gain of $2,000 ($\frac{1}{2}$ × ($30,000 − $26,000)) and taxable dividend of $1,380 in 20X8 minus any interest paid on a loan.

The following further demonstrates the attribution rules for spouses.

Situation: On January 1, 20X7, a husband lent $20,000 to a spouse who used the borrowed funds to purchase shares in a public corporation. The terms of the loan require an interest payment of 5% annually which was the CRA prescribed rate at the time. On December 31, 20X7, the spouse sold the shares for $24,000. During the year she received dividends of $800.

---

49 ITA 74.1, 74.2(1), (2).
50 ITA 74.5(1), (2).

Analysis: In this situation, the funds were transferred in a commercial manner and the attribution rules do not apply. In 20X7, the spouse will include in her income for tax purposes a taxable capital gain of $2,000 ($1/2 \times$ ($24,000 − $20,000)) and a taxable dividend of $1,104 ($800 $\times$ 1.38). She can also deduct $1,000 of interest paid to her husband (5% $\times$ $20,000) on the loan. If the loan had been made without interest or at less than the prescribed rate of interest, the entire taxable capital gain and taxable dividend would have been attributed to the husband.

Property Transferred to a Minor Child

Similarly, income on property transferred to a child under the age of 18 is attributed to the parent until the child's 18th birthday.[51] However, in the case of children, subsequent capital gains or losses are not subject to attribution. Usually, transfers of property occur between parents and children. However, these attribution rules are not restricted to children; they may also apply when property is transferred to other minors, such as a niece or nephew.

Situation: In 20X7, a parent purchased shares of a public corporation for the benefit of her 16-year-old child. During 20X7, the child received dividends of $1,000 and the shares were sold for an amount that was $8,000 greater than the cost.

Analysis: The shares were purchased as a gift for a minor child (under the age of 18). Consequently, the taxable dividend of $1,380 [$1,000 $\times$ 1.38] is attributed to the parent and included in her income for tax purposes in 20X7. However, the taxable capital gain of $4,000 ($1/2 \times$ $8,000) is not subject to attribution and is included in the income of the child for tax purposes. With respect to the capital gain, income splitting has been achieved. If the child invests the dividend of $1,000 and capital gain of $8,000 in another investment, the related income is not attributed to the parent. Attribution on income (except capital gains) from the original capital will continue to be attributed to the parent until the child reaches 18 years of age.

Tax on Split Income   In the past, tax planners have found creative ways to avoid the attribution rules for dividend distributions from private corporations to minor children. To counter this, an anti-avoidance rule is in force.[52] Dividends received by *minor children* (directly or through a trust) from a *private* Canadian or foreign corporation are not subject to the attribution rules described in the above paragraph. Instead, those specific dividends are subject to tax at the top marginal tax rate (less any applicable dividend tax credit). Because the dividends are taxed at the top rate, the benefit of splitting dividend income from private corporations is eliminated.

The anti-avoidance rule that charges the high tax rate on dividends from private corporations to minors (discussed above) normally does *not apply to capital gains from the sale of shares from private corporations*. However, when the *capital gain is derived from the sale of shares of private corporations to a non–arm's-length party* and any dividends on the shares would have been subject to the high tax rate, the capital gain will be *treated as dividends* subject to the high rate of tax and will not be eligible for the capital gain exemption.[53] A capital gain by a minor on the sale of private corporation shares to an arm's-length party is not treated as a dividend and is not subject to the attribution rules, but is taxed in the hands of the minor at whatever tax rate is applicable to that person in the year.

---

51 ITA 74.1(2).
52 ITA 120.4. The special tax may also apply to certain income derived from the sale of goods or services to a business carried on by a relative of the child.
53 ITA 120.4(4) e(5).

Transfers and Loans to Corporations

To create a structure that will pay dividends to children or spouses, a high tax rate family member may loan funds or transfer property to a corporation (or a trust) that has the spouse and or children as shareholders (or beneficiaries of the trust). To achieve splitting, the transferor usually does not receive interest on amounts owing as a result of the transfer. This allows the corporation to invest the funds and pass the income on to the shareholders. This type of transaction is not a problem if the corporation is a small business corporation. However, when the corporation is *not a small business corporation*, CRA may include a prescribed rate of interest in the transferor's income if the main purpose of the loan or transfer is to reduce the transferor's income in order to benefit a spouse or related person less than 18 years of age.[54] This result is punitive as the corporation is taxed on its investment income, the children or spouse is taxed on the dividends, and the transferor is also taxed. Dividend income from shares of public corporations continues to be subject to the attribution rules mentioned previously.

Loans to Adult Family Members

It was previously stated that transfers of property to adult family members other than a spouse are not subject to the attribution rules. However, when a taxpayer makes a *loan to a non–arm's-length person 18 years of age or older* with no interest, or charges an interest rate below a commercial rate, a specific anti-avoidance rule may apply. If one of the *main reasons* for the loan is to *reduce or avoid tax* on property income then the income earned on the property (or substituted property) acquired with the loaned funds will be attributed to the person making the loan.[55] The rule applies only to loans and not gifts to a non–arm's-length adult. The rule will also not apply if the borrower uses the loaned funds for personal expenses or to acquire non-income producing property.

Income Splitting Permitted by the Income Tax Act

In spite of the significant attempt to prevent families from splitting income to achieve lower taxes, the *Income Tax Act* specifically permits certain income to be shared by family members. These circumstances have been reviewed briefly in past chapters and some of them are summarized below:

- Canada Pension Plan income can be shared with a spouse to a maximum of 50% of that income. This is accomplished by application directly to the Canada Pension Plan, which will then direct the payments accordingly.
- Individuals can contribute to a spousal RRSP (see Part III of this chapter) that allows the higher income spouse to claim the contribution deduction but the future income on maturing of the plan goes to the lower income spouse.
- Individuals earning eligible pension income can annually allocate up to 50% of that income to a spouse for tax purposes.[56] This is achieved by simply designating the transfer while completing the annual tax returns of both spouses. For individuals aged 65 and over, eligible pension income includes lifetime annuity payments from a registered pension plan or pooled registered pension plan, an RRSP, a DPSP, and amounts withdrawn from a RRIF. Eligible income for taxpayers under age 65 is limited primarily to annuity payments from a registered pension plan.
- Amounts received from the Universal Child Care Benefit Program ($100 per child) can be invested on behalf of the child. Any future income earned from the investment is not attributed to the parent.

---

54 ITA 74.3, 74.4, 74.4(1).
55 ITA 56(4.1).
56 ITA 60(c), 60 .03(1), 118(7).

- Capital gains on property transferred to minors are not subject to attribution as demonstrated above.
- Income from property transferred to children over the age of 17 is not attributed to a parent. An interest free or no interest loan to a child (or other non–arm's-length person) over the age of 17 may result in attribution if the primary purpose is to shift income for tax purposes.
- Within specified limits, an individual can contribute funds into a spouse's Tax-Free Savings Account (TFSA). Income earned in the fund is tax-free and is not subject to attribution.

G. Unpaid Remuneration

In Chapter 5, it was established that business income is determined on an accrual basis. This means that salaries are normally deductible by the employer as are other forms of remuneration that have been incurred but not paid to an employee. However, employment income is included by the employee in income for tax purposes only when received (see Chapter 4). In order to prevent the undue delay of taxable remuneration payments, the special rules limit the deductibility of unpaid remuneration.[57] The employer can deduct unpaid remuneration for tax purposes only if it is paid within 180 days of its taxation year. If payment is delayed beyond that period, the employer can deduct the remuneration in a subsequent year when it is paid. Unpaid remuneration is also discussed in Chapter 5.

H. Mortgage Foreclosures and Default Sales

Property is often acquired with borrowed funds (e.g., through a mortgage on real estate) and then pledged as collateral security to the lender. A debtor who is faced with financial difficulty may decide to default on the loan payments, thereby allowing the creditor to take ownership of the secured property. The tax treatment of this unusual type of transaction is specifically provided for in the *Income Tax Act*.

From the debtor's perspective, a foreclosure means that a debt has been extinguished and that a property has been disposed of in satisfaction of the debt. For tax purposes, the taxpayer is deemed to have sold the property for a price equal to the principal amount of the debt owing. As a result, depending on the amount of the deemed proceeds, the transaction may result in a recapture of capital cost allowance and/or a capital gain.[58]

From the creditor's perspective, a foreclosure means that an amount receivable has been satisfied. For tax purposes, the creditor is deemed to have acquired the property at a cost equal to the principal amount of the debt outstanding, less any reserves that were previously claimed. The creditor may eventually recognize a gain or loss for tax purposes when the acquired property is eventually sold.

I. Gain on Settlement of Debt

An individual or a corporation may be in a position to settle an outstanding debt for less than the amount of principal owing. Often, this situation arises under conditions of extreme financial difficulty. It may also occur when the creditor offers a discount as an inducement for early payment and the debtor utilizes this inducement or when a debt is forgiven. In effect, the debtor achieves a gain from the transaction. The treatment of that gain for tax purposes is unusual.[59]

When this type of gain occurs, it is not directly included in taxable income. Instead, it is first applied to reduce any losses that have been carried over from other years, in the following order (see Chapter 10 for a discussion of these loss carry-overs):

---

57 ITA 78(4); IT-109R2.
58 ITA 79; IT-505.
59 ITA 80(1) to (18); Regulations 5400, 5401; IT-293R.

- non-capital losses (business and property losses, but excluding allowable business investment losses)
- farm losses
- restricted farm losses (when farming is not the chief source of income)
- allowable business investment losses
- net capital losses

When a taxpayer has such unused losses, a reduction in their amount results in an increase in future taxable income. In effect, the gain is taxed but in some future year. Any unapplied portion of the gain after the reduction of the losses can be applied to reduce the capital cost and undepreciated capital cost of depreciable property, the cumulative eligible capital balance of eligible capital property, and the adjusted cost base of capital assets, at the election of the taxpayer, through a series of designations. However, these reductions must be applied in order, and to the maximum extent possible.

When the cost of these assets is reduced, any subsequent sale results in either a greater gain or a lesser loss for tax purposes. This, in turn, means that the gain on debt settlement is delayed for tax purposes until the particular asset is sold. It should be pointed out that within each of the preceding asset categories, the taxpayer has the right to choose which asset's cost will be reduced, and so should make an attempt to reduce the cost of an asset that will not be sold in the near future.

If all of the forgiven debt is not consumed by applying it to the above items, one-half of the remaining amount will be included in the taxpayer's income in that year.

J. Death of a Taxpayer

Unfortunately, although life ceases, financial matters—including imposition of tax—continue. Below is a brief summary of the tax implications triggered by the death of an individual taxpayer.

1. Income from all sources is accrued up to the date of death. Some items require further mention.

   - *Reserves*—Reserves that are normally deductible from income are generally not deductible in the year of death. Therefore, a reserve for bad debts or a capital gain reserve for deferred proceeds from property dispositions must be included in the deceased taxpayer's income in the year of death. A legal representative of the deceased *may elect to* deduct the reserve if the related property is transferred to a spouse or common law partner.[60]

   - *Unmatured RRSP*[61]—Payments from an unmatured RRSP to a spouse or common law partner who is a named beneficiary are included in the taxable income of the beneficiary and not the deceased taxpayer. The surviving spouse may avoid tax on the receipt by transferring it to his or her own RRSP. Where the beneficiary is the estate of the deceased, the fair market value of the property in the RRSP is taxable to the deceased in the year of death. The taxable amount may be avoided if it is paid out of the RRSP to the spouse or to the estate of which the spouse is a beneficiary in which case the amount may be taxable to the estate or the surviving spouse.

   - *Matured RRSP*[62]—In the case of a matured RRSP where annuity payments have begun prior to the death of the annuitant, continued payments are included in the income of the surviving spouse when he or she is named as the beneficiary.

---

60 ITA 72(2); CRA form T2069.
61 ITA 60(l); 146(8.8) and (8.91); IT 500R.
62 ITA 60(l); 146(8.8) and (8.91); IT 500R.

If the estate is named as the beneficiary, an election can be made to have the surviving spouse become the annuitant. If the beneficiary of the RRSP or the estate is not a spouse, the fair market value of the property in the RRSP is taxable to the deceased taxpayer in the year of death. Similar rules apply to a RRIF.

2. All capital property that was owned by the deceased is deemed to have been sold.[63] Capital property, including depreciable property, is deemed to have been sold at a fair market value. Usually, this results in the recognition of capital gains and a recapture of capital cost allowance. However, if the above assets are left to a spouse or spouse trust, they are deemed to have been sold at their cost amount, and no taxable gains occur. The legal representative of the deceased taxpayer may elect to have the transfer of any property to a spouse result in a deemed disposition at the property's fair market value rather than its cost amount.[64] This permits income to be recognized where it is beneficial to do so, such as when the deceased has the ability to use the capital gains deduction or has unused losses or unused charitable donations.

3. The determination of taxable income and tax for a deceased taxpayer is discussed in Chapter 10 with special emphasis on the treatment of unused losses and the filing of optional tax returns.

4. Representatives of the deceased, referred to as "executors," are given control of the assets. After all the liabilities have been satisfied, the assets are either sold or transferred to the beneficiaries, or to trusts for the benefit of beneficiaries, in accordance with the terms of a will. During the period that assets are held by the executors, they may generate income; this income, for tax purposes, constitutes income of the executor's trust. Thereafter, income from the assets is included in the income of the beneficiaries, or of the trusts that have been established for the beneficiaries. When the trust disposes of property it may incur a capital loss or a terminal loss. Normally these losses are deducted against income of the trust. However, if the losses occur in the first year of the trust an executor may elect to claim such losses in the final return of the deceased taxpayer.[65] This may be advantageous if the deceased has a high tax rate in the year of death and the trust has insufficient income to use the losses or has a low tax rate.

Exhibit 9-3 diagrams the flow of income for tax purposes of the deceased taxpayer and the beneficiaries.

Exhibit 9-3:

Death of a Taxpayer

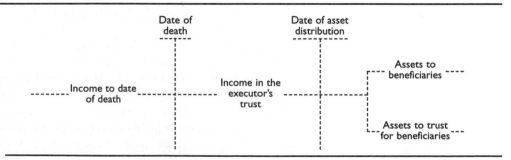

Tax on death can be significant. Individuals should consider acquiring life insurance so that properties do not have to be sold to pay the tax on the deemed disposition.

---

63 ITA 70(1) to (6).
64 ITA 70(6.2).
65 ITA 164(6); ITR 1000.

K. Amounts Not Included in Income

A number of items are given preferential treatment and excluded from income for tax purposes, even though they fall within the normal sources of income. These items are unusual in nature and are specifically listed in section 81 of the *Income Tax Act*. For example, allowances received from employers are taxable in accordance with the principles of employment income, but the special rules exempt allowances received by members of a provincial legislature, municipality, or school board. Similarly, pension income is taxable as other sources of income, but special pensions received by members of the RCMP (Royal Canadian Mounted Police) for injury or disability are exempt.

The special rules for determining net income for tax purposes described above are not all-inclusive and have been examined only briefly. Even so, it is important to recognize that they form an integral part of the overall process of determining income for tax purposes and that they are the source for determining the treatment of unusual transactions that may occur within one of the primary sources of income.

VIII. Review of Net Income for Tax Purposes

A. The Scope of Income Tax in Canada

The apparent complexity of the Canadian income tax system is significantly diminished when its parameters are understood. The preceding chapters have shown these parameters and developed a fundamental framework that can be used to apply the income tax to both personal and business financial activities.

This framework, which was outlined in Chapter 3, established that any individual, corporation, or trust resident in Canada is subject to tax on world income in each taxation year. In addition, it established that non-residents are taxed on certain income earned in Canada. Fundamental to the tax system is the process for determining the amount of the income to which the tax applies. This process is reviewed below.

1. Each of the primary entities is required to pay tax on its taxable income. Taxable income is the taxpayer's net income for tax purposes less special reductions. (These special reductions, which are few in number, will be reviewed in two subsequent chapters.)

2. Individuals and corporations determine their net income for tax purposes in the same manner. There are five potential sources of income: employment income, business income, property income, capital gains, and other sources of income and deductions. These sources are summarized below.

    A *Employment income*   Employment income, which takes the form of a wage, salary, or other benefits, is derived from the provision of personal services under a contract of employment. Such income is determined in accordance with the following basic rules:

    • Remuneration is included in income on a cash basis—that is, when received.
    • All benefits (subject to specific exceptions) received or enjoyed by virtue of employment are taxable.
    • All amounts received as allowances (subject to specific exemptions) are taxable.
    • No deductions are permitted from employment income, except those indicated in a specific, limited list.

    B *Business income*   Business income encompasses a wide range of activities but is generally considered to be income from an enterprise that sells goods or services with the intention to profit. Business income is determined as follows:

    • Business income is the profit therefrom and is determined in accordance with well-accepted business principles, which are normally interpreted through generally accepted accounting principles and case law.

- The accounting rules are modified by six general limitations specified in the *Income Tax Act*.
- The accounting income, subject to the six general limitations, may be further modified by two lists of specific exceptions. One of these lists denies the deduction of specific items, the other permits the deduction of items denied by the general rules.

C *Property income*   Income from property is the return on invested capital in the form of interest, dividends, rents, and the like. Property income is determined in accordance with the same basic rules as those that govern business income.

D *Capital gains*   Capital gains are the profits realized on the disposition of property that was acquired to provide a long-term or enduring benefit to the owner. Capital gains or losses are determined by the following basic rules:

- A gain or loss is recognized only when a disposition occurs or is deemed to occur.
- One-half of the gain or loss is applicable.
- The gain or loss is calculated as the proceeds of disposition less the sum of the adjusted cost base of the property and the expenses of disposition.
- The recognition of capital gains can be deferred (within limits) in relation to the receipt of the proceeds of disposition.

E *Other sources of income and deductions*   "Other sources of income" includes items of income that cannot otherwise be placed in one of the above four primary categories. Similarly, "other deductions" includes items that do not fall within the definition of the primary sources. Items in this category are limited to a specific short list—a list that constitutes the final parameter of income sources. There are no general rules for determining income in this category.

3. The normal income determination methods for each of the primary income sources may be modified by the special rules for income determination. These rules are grouped together in the *Income Tax Act* and deal with unusual transactions for each of the primary income sources.

4. The net income from each source is combined by means of an aggregating formula, which is used by both individuals and corporations. The formula establishes that losses from employment, business, and property and allowable business investment losses can be offset against any of the five types of income earned by the entity. Allowable capital losses, however, can be offset only against taxable capital gains. The total of the aggregating formula is referred to as the taxpayer's net income for tax purposes (see Exhibit 3-4 in Chapter 3 and Exhibit 10-1 in Chapter 10).

In order to understand the tax treatment of a particular transaction, managers must first assign that transaction to one of the five sources of income. Once this has been done, they can determine the amount and timing of the tax payment from the general principles of income determination for that specific source. They can then assess the impact of that tax treatment on cash flow. If a transaction does not fall within one of the five sources of income, it is outside the fundamental framework and not subject to income tax.

In the following section is a sample calculation of net income for tax purposes. The example uses as the taxpayer an individual who has income from several sources. The information that follows is presented randomly. Each income item is assigned a source; net income is then determined for each source. Finally, the aggregating formula is used to arrive at net income for tax purposes.

B. Sample Calculation of Net Income for Tax Purposes

Summary of Information

Carla Fenson is employed as a financial executive. In addition, she is a partner in a retail store and maintains a portfolio of investments. Information with respect to these activities for 20X5 is given below.

1. Carla's job as an executive provided a gross annual salary of $70,000. In addition, her employer contributed $3,000 to the company pension plan in her name. Carla made an equal contribution of $3,000 to the plan. In the summer of 20X5, Carla used the company's vacation home for a one-month personal holiday at no cost to her. When the vacation home is not used by employees, the company rents it out for $2,000 per month.

   Also, Carla received a bonus of $10,000 in 20X5, which was awarded for her special efforts in 20X4.

2. The retail store in which Carla is a partner suffered a loss of $40,000 for the fiscal period ending December 31, 20X5. Her share of the loss amounted to $10,000 and was calculated by an accountant in accordance with the required tax rules.

3. In 20X0, Carla had purchased three rental properties. Financial information on each property is as follows:

	Property 1	Property 2	Property 3
Land cost	$10,000	$ 4,000	$ 8,000
Building cost	60,000	40,000	45,000
Undepreciated capital cost (20X4)	52,000	37,000	40,000
20X5 net rental income (loss) before capital cost allowance	4,000	(5,000)	4,000

   In 20X5, Carla sold property 1 for $80,000 ($12,000 for the land, $68,000 for the building).

4. In 20X5, Carla gifted shares of a public corporation to her 16-year-old son. The shares had cost her $10,000 and were worth $13,000 at the time of the gift. After receiving the gift, the son received dividends of $1,000 on the shares. Also, in 20X5, Carla gifted shares of a public corporation to her husband. The shares, which had a value of $15,000 at the time of the gift, had originally cost $9,000. No dividends were received.

5. In 20X1, Carla had purchased some shares of a Canadian-controlled private corporation (a qualified small business corporation) that was set up to start a new business venture. She recently sold the shares, which cost $30,000, for $20,000.

6. Carla also sold the following assets in 20X5:

	Cost	Proceeds
Shares of public corporation X	$22,000	$27,000
Shares of public corporation Y	40,000	18,000
Grand piano	14,000	9,000

7. She also received the following additional items:

Dividends from public corporations	$4,000
Lottery winnings	6,000
Lump-sum payment from a former employer's registered pension plan	1,500

8. Carla paid out the following in 20X5:

Interest on a bank loan to purchase shares	$2,000
Interest on a loan to acquire a personal automobile	1,200
Contribution to a registered retirement savings plan	1,000
Donations to charitable organizations	3,000

Calculation of Net Income for Tax Purposes (20X5)

Employment income:

Gross salary		$ 70,000
20X4 bonus received in 20X5		10,000
Employment benefit—use of vacation home		2,000
		$ 82,000
Contribution to company pension plan		(3,000)
Net income from employment		$ 79,000

Business income (loss):

Share of loss from partnership	$(10,000)

Property income:

Dividends received ($4,000 × 1.38%)		$ 5,520
Dividends received by son, attributed to Carla ($1,000 × 1.38%)		1,380
		6,900
Interest on loan to acquire shares		(2,000)
Net dividend income		4,900
Real estate:		
Rental income before capital cost allowance:		
Property 1	4,000	
Property 2	(5,000)	
Property 3	4,000	
	3,000	
Recapture of capital cost allowance (below)	8,000	
	11,000	
Capital cost allowance (below)	(3,080)	7,920
Net income from property		$ 12,820

Capital cost allowance:

	Class 1 Property 1	Class 1 Property 2 & 3
Undepreciated capital cost	$52,000	$ 77,000*
Disposal (to maximum of cost)	(60,000)	–0–
	(8,000)	77,000
Recapture	8,000	
Capital cost allowance (4%)	–0–	(3,080)
Undepreciated capital cost	–0–	$ 73,920

* Note: Properties 2 and 3 are combined, as the original cost of each building was less than $50,000.

Capital gains:

	Proceeds	Cost	Gain
Property 1:			
Land	$12,000	$10,000	$ 2,000
Building	68,000	60,000	8,000
Gift to son	13,000	10,000	3,000
Shares of Corporation X	27,000	22,000	5,000
			$18,000
Taxable capital gains—$18,000 × ½			$ 9,000

Note: The gift of shares to spouse is deemed to have been sold at the adjusted cost base, and therefore no gain occurs.

Capital losses:

Shares of Corporation Y		
Proceeds	$ 18,000	
Adjusted cost base	(40,000)	
	$(22,000)	
Allowable capital loss: $22,000 × ½		$(11,000)

Note: The loss on the sale of the piano is deemed to be nil, as it is personal-use property.

Allowable business investment loss:

Shares of private small business corporation:		
Proceeds	$ 20,000	
Adjusted cost base	(30,000)	
	$(10,000)	
Allowable loss: $10,000 × ½		$(5,000)
Other sources of income:		
Receipt of pension income		$ 1,500
Other deductions:		
Contribution to RRSP		$(1,000)

Items excluded from calculation:

- The contribution of $3,000 by the employer to the registered pension plan is excluded as a taxable benefit.
- Lottery winnings do not conform to any of the five sources of income and therefore are not taxable.
- Interest paid on the loan for the personal automobile does not conform to the primary sources of income and is not specifically listed in other deductions; therefore, it is not deductible.
- Charitable donations are not specifically listed as other deductions and consequently are not deductible when arriving at net income for tax purposes.

The aggregating formula:	
(a) Employment income	$79,000
Business income	–0–
Property income	12,820
Other sources of income	1,500
	93,320

(b) Taxable capital gains	$ 9,000	
Allowable capital losses		
($11,000) to a maximum of	(9,000)	–0–
		93,320
(c) Other deductions		(1,000)
		92,320
(d) Business loss	(10,000)	
Allowable business investment loss	(5,000)	(15,000)
Net income for tax purposes		$77,320

IX. Tax Planning Checklist

The items discussed in this chapter affect a number of tax planning opportunities. As can be expected, many of them relate to investing in an RRSP. Some of the items are reviewed below.

1. When acquiring a group of assets for a single purchase price, carefully consider how to allocate the total price among the assets. Remember that the CRA has the power to revise the allocations. Within reason, allocate the price to properties that can be deducted quickly for tax purposes. Be prepared to justify the method used to the tax authorities.

2. When a taxpayer dies, assets that are left to beneficiaries, other than a spouse, usually are deemed to have been disposed of for tax purposes at fair market value. Knowing this, individuals can take steps to transfer assets during their lifetime to the intended beneficiaries. This allows future value increases to accrue to those beneficiaries and minimizes taxes on death. Often, such transfers can be achieved on a tax-deferred basis. This activity is referred to as an "estate freeze" (see Chapter 19).

3. Upon separation or divorce, carefully negotiate alimony or maintenance agreements to ensure the best possible tax treatment for both parties.

4. Taxpayers can split income with children who are 18 years of age or older by gifting them property that will earn investment income. This may take advantage of their lower tax rate while ensuring that they can use all available deductions and tax credits. Loans made to adult children may be subject to attribution if one of the main reasons for the loan is to reduce or avoid tax on property income unless a commercial rate of interest is applied. When commercial interest rates are very low, consideration should be given to using commercial interest-rate loans to split income with adult children if investment returns on the borrowed funds are anticipated to be higher. Loans to spouses should also be considered in these circumstances.

5. Attribution does not apply when property is transferred to children who are under 18 years of age when the income is a capital gain. Therefore, consider loaning funds to children and using those funds to obtain capital growth investments. Keep in mind that capital losses will also remain with the child.

6. In some families, the income of one spouse is higher than that of the other. When this is the case, family expenses should first be paid with income earned by the high-income spouse. The result will be that all or most of the family savings available for investment purposes will belong to the lower-income spouse and will be taxed at a lower rate.

7. Be certain to equalize the retirement funds of each spouse by utilizing spousal RRSP contributions. This will result in income splitting on retirement.

8. An RRSP or PRPP contribution can be made within 60 days after the year for which it will be deducted. However, taxpayers can and should contribute the funds as early as possible in the applicable year to increase the amount of income that will be sheltered from tax.

9. RRSP funds must be carefully monitored and managed. As previously shown, a small increase in the percentage return on investment can significantly increase the retirement balance in the long term. However, keep in mind that increased returns may involve an increased risk.

10. If funds are available, consider making the permitted $2,000 overcontribution to an RRSP. This will increase the amount of tax-sheltered earnings and in the long term compound to a substantial sum. The excess contribution can be deducted from income in a later year. This action should also be considered for a spouse and children who are not under the age of 19.

11. Remember that all amounts removed from an RRSP are fully taxable. This means that incomes which have preferential tax treatment, such as capital gains (one-half taxable or fully exempt) and dividends (dividend tax credit), become fully taxable when distributed from an RRSP. Some individuals have both an RRSP and a personal investment portfolio and invest in shares as well as interest-bearing securities. Except for investments within a TFSA, these individuals should place the interest-bearing securities in the RRSP and the investments that have preferential tax treatment in the personal portfolio.

12. Individuals who are employed by their own corporation should attempt to receive sufficient annual salary to meet the "earned income" requirements for maximum RRSP deductions. Dividends from the corporation do not qualify as "earned income."

13. Carefully consider the RRSP retirement options and attempt to choose a vehicle that will balance the payouts with the need for funds. A registered retirement income fund (RRIF) may provide more flexibility but may also require more fund management.

14. When possible, contribute the maximum to a TFSA as well as an RRSP or PRPP. When a choice between the two must be made, carefully consider which plan is most suitable. An RRSP seems more appropriate for individuals with incomes above the first tax bracket and who do not anticipate early withdrawals from the plan. This is so because of the tax deduction and long-term compounding of investment returns. However, income earned in an RRSP loses its character on payout. So capital gains in an RRSP are fully taxable when withdrawn. A TFSA is more flexible for income splitting and making withdrawals from time to time as needed. It may help to think of the RRSP as a pension that will not be used until retirement, whereas the TFSA is a savings plan to build wealth and to be used for personal needs when required.

X. Summary and Conclusion

This chapter has finished establishing the parameters that limit the types of income subject to Canadian income tax. "Other sources of income" and "other deductions" are catch-all categories in that they define the extent to which income items or deductions that fall outside the four primary categories are included in net income for tax purposes.

This chapter has also identified and discussed the list of special rules that deal with the treatment of unusual transactions within each of the main sources of income. These special rules should be included as an "appendix" to the principles previously established for each of the five sources of income.

The process of establishing net income for tax purposes for individuals and corporations is now complete. This process can be summarized as follows:

1. Define the nature of a transaction to determine which of the five income sources it relates to.

2. Apply the principles of income determination attached to that specific source of income.

3. Ascertain whether any of the special rules of income determination may override the established principles.

4. Relate the income to the aggregating formula.

The fundamental principles all taxpayers use to establish net income are not overly complex. Nor is the basic process. Even when transactions are extremely complicated, the general tax impact can usually be ascertained by analyzing them in terms of the basic principles developed in Chapters 3 through 9. Applying these principles enhances the effectiveness of financial decision making by allowing managers to locate the points along the cash-flow path where the tax factor is relevant.

The process for determining net income for tax purposes is now fully explained. The next step is to convert net income into taxable income and establish the method of calculating tax. At this point, the common ground between individual and corporate taxpayers disappears. The unique issues involved in determining taxable income and tax for each type of entity are examined in the next two chapters.

Visit the Canadian Income Taxation Web site at **www.mcgrawhill.ca/ olc/buckwold** to view any updated tax information.

Demonstration Questions

QUESTION ONE

In November 20X5, Walter Spink's employer transferred him from Winnipeg to Edmonton. His financial information for the 20X5 taxation year is provided below.

1. Spink received a salary in 20X5 of $80,000, of which $7,000 was earned at his new location in Edmonton. His employer contributed $3,000 to a money-purchase registered pension plan on Spink's behalf. Spink also contributed $3,000 to the plan. The employer also contributed $1,000 to a deferred profit-sharing plan. Spink is required to use his own automobile for employment purposes and, in 20X5, incurred allowable costs for tax purposes of $3,600.

2. On January 2, 20X5, Spink sold a residential rental property to his wife for $150,000 (land $20,000, building $130,000). Payment consisted of a non–interest-bearing demand loan of $150,000. The original cost of the property was $100,000 (land $10,000, building $90,000), and at the end of 20X4, the undepreciated capital cost of the building was $72,000. In 20X5, the rental property incurred a net loss of $4,000 before capital cost allowance.

3. On June 1, 20X5, Spink gifted cash of $30,000 to his 19-year-old son, who attends university. The son invested the funds and, in 20X5, earned interest income of $1,200, which was used to support his education. At the same time, Spink gifted shares of a public corporation to his 17-year-old daughter. The shares, which originally cost $10,000, were valued at $12,000 at the time of the gift. During the year, the daughter received a dividend of $600 and then sold the shares for $15,000.

4. The following costs were incurred to move Spink and his family to Edmonton:

Real estate commission on the sale of his former residence	$ 7,000
Interest, property taxes, and utility costs for maintaining former residences for two months prior to sale	6,000
Transportation of household effects	6,000
Automobile expenses—travelling to Edmonton	300
Hotel accommodation and meals for 20 days in Edmonton	4,000
Land transfer tax on purchase of new residence	2,000
Legal fees to sell former residence	800
Legal fees to purchase new residence	1,000
	$27,100

limit 5000 (handwritten)
limit 15 days (handwritten)
all deductible (handwritten)

5. In his spare time, Spink operates a small consulting business. He earned $6,000 in 20X5 prior to arriving in Edmonton.

6. During the year, Spink received interest income of $5,000 and dividends from taxable Canadian *public* corporations of $1,000. *Dividend 1,000 × 1.38* (handwritten)

7. In 20X5, Spink contributed $4,000 to his registered retirement savings plan, which was the maximum allowed for the year. At the same time, he withdraw $5000 from his TFSA Tax-Free Savings Account. *RRSP = deductible* (handwritten)

8. In 20X5, Spink's wife, Sally, earned a salary of $30,000, consulting income of $15,000, and interest income of $3,000. She paid child care expenses of $5,000 relating to their nine-year-old daughter.

Required:

1. Determine Spink's net income for tax purposes for the 20X5 taxation year.

2. What is the maximum allowable RRSP contribution that Spink can make in 20X6?

3. Determine the net income for tax purposes of Sally Spink for the 20X5 taxation year.

Solution:

Before we answer the above questions, we provide the following comments on several of the transactions:

• *Rental property sale*   The sale of the rental property to his wife is a non–arm's-length transaction that would normally be subject to the fair market value rules described in this chapter. However, because the transfer is to a spouse, Spink is deemed to have sold the land at its adjusted cost base and the building at its undepreciated capital cost. Therefore, no income is generated on the sale. The rental loss of $4,000 on the property, which occurred after the transfer, must be attributed to Spink and included in the calculation of his income for the year. If his spouse subsequently sells the property, any capital gain or recapture of capital cost allowance will also be attributed to Spink. The attribution rules could have been avoided if the transaction had been subject to normal commercial terms (a reasonable interest rate on the loan and specific repayment terms) and if Spink had elected to recognize the taxable gain and the recapture of capital cost allowance that would result if the property were sold at fair market value.

• *Cash gift to the son*   The gift of the cash has no tax effect. The future income earned on the investment made is taxable to the son. It is not attributed to Spink because the son is over 17.

• *Gift of shares to the daughter*   The gift results in a deemed disposition of the shares at fair market value, resulting in a taxable capital gain to Spink of $1,000 (½ × [$12,000 − $10,000]). The daughter is deemed to have acquired the shares at a cost of $12,000. The dividend of $600 must be attributed to Spink and included in his taxable income because the daughter is under 18. The sale of the shares by the daughter results in a taxable capital gain of $1,500 (½ × [$15,000 − $12,000]). This gain is taxable to the daughter and is not attributed to Spink. This treatment is different from a capital gain or loss that may occur on property that has been transferred to a spouse.

- **Moving expenses**   All of the various types of moving expenses are eligible for deduction. However, three restrictions apply. First, the cost of accommodation and meals in a hotel at the new location is limited to expenses for 15 days. Therefore, the eligible moving expenses must be reduced by $1,000 ($4,000 × 5 days/20 days), from $27,100 to $26,100. Second, the costs of maintaining the former residence are limited to a maximum of $5,000. Therefore, $1,000 of these costs do not qualify for a deduction, and the qualified moving expenses are further reduced to $25,100 ($26,100 − $1,000). Third, moving expenses in 20X5 can be deducted only to the extent of the earned income at the new location, which is $7,000. The unused expenses from 20X5 of $18,100 ($25,100 − $7,000) can be carried forward and deducted in 20X6. Travel expenses can be calculated under the simplified method without receipts. Since the move commenced in Manitoba, a flat rate of 49¢ km (2011; 2012 rate available in 2013) can be used for vehicle expenses.[66] Meals can be calculated using a flat rate of $17 a meal per person to a maximum of $51 per day (2010). In this case there are four people so the meal cost would be $51/day × 4 people.

- **Child care expenses**   Normally, child care expenses must be deducted from the spouse with the lower income. In this situation, the expense is deducted by Sally Spink. The deductible amount is limited to the least of these: the actual expense of $5,000; the prescribed limit of $4,000 for children who are seven years of age or older; and two-thirds of Sally Spink's earned income of $45,000 (this includes the salary of $30,000 and the consulting income of $15,000 but excludes interest income of $3,000). Thus, the deduction is limited to $4,000.

- **Withdrawal from TFSA**   Withdrawals from a TFSA are not taxable.

1. Net income for tax purposes—Spink

Employment income—salary		$80,000
Automobile expenses		(3,600)
Registered pension plan contribution		(3,000)
		73,400
Business income—consulting		6,000
Property income		
Daughter's dividend attributed—$600 × 1.38	828	
Other dividends—$1,000 × 1.38	1,380	
Interest income	5,000	7,208
		86,608
Taxable capital gain		
Gift of shares to daughter—½ ($12,000 − $10,000)		1,000
		87,608
Other deductions		
RRSP	4,000	
Moving expenses—above	7,000	(11,000)
		76,608
Loss—rental loss attributed from spouse		(4,000)
Net income for tax purposes		$72,608

2. Allowable RRSP deduction for 20X6

Calculation of earned income for 20X5	
Employment income—above	$73,400
Add back registered pension plan deduction	3,000
Adjusted employment income	76,400
Business income	6,000
Rental loss	(4,000)
Earned income for 20X5	$78,400

---

66 The flat rate to be used for each province under the simplified method can be found at www.cra.gc.ca/travelcosts.

Note that the earned income does not include the property income (other than rentals), the taxable capital gain, and the other deductions.

Allowable 20X6 deduction is the least of:		
18% of 20X5 earned income—18% × $78,400 = $14,112; *or*		
the prescribed limit for the year—$22,970 (2012 limit)		$14,112
Less the pension adjustment for 20X5:		
Employer's contribution to the registered pension plan	3,000	
Spink's contribution to the registered pension plan	3,000	
Employer's contribution to the deferred profit-sharing plan	1,000	(7,000)
20X6 allowable RRSP deduction		$7,112

3. Net income for tax purposes—Sally Spink

Employment income—salary	$30,000
Business income—consulting	15,000
Property income—interest	3,000
	48,000
Other deduction—child care (determined above)	(4,000)
Net income for tax purposes	$44,000

QUESTION TWO

Carl was divorced in 20X6 and now lives with his 16-year-old son in a rented house. Shortly after the divorce, he was injured in a car accident and terminated his employment. In 20X7, Carl enrolled in a doctoral program at a university. Outlined below is Carl's 20X7 financial information:

- Carl received a lump sum settlement of $100,000 from his former spouse. In addition, he received a total of $6,000 per month (for 12 months) as support payments—60% of the support payments were designated as support for him and 40% for the support of his son.

- Carl contributed $15,000 to a Tax Free Savings Account (TFSA) on December 15, 20X7. He had not made eligible contributions in the previous two years.

- In 20X5, Carl had borrowed $20,000 for a six-year term to acquire an investment. Due to a sudden rise in interest rates, the creditor offered to settle the debt for an immediate cash payment of $17,000. Carl agreed and made the payment on January 2, 20X7.

- Carl was a minority shareholder in a Canadian-controlled private corporation that was controlled by his former spouse. All of the corporation's assets were used in an active business. In 20X7, he sold the shares for $20,000. They had cost $25,000 in 20X2.

- The university awarded Carl a scholarship of $10,000 and a research grant of $8,000. During the year he spent $6,000 on tuition, $2,000 on books, and $9,000 for a research assistant and research supplies.

- For the previous five years, Carl was employed as a biologist with a large corporation. In 20X6, he published an article in a topical biology magazine. In 20X7, he was awarded $2,000 from the publisher as the "article of the year."

- Carl had no other income in 20X7. As of December 31, 20X7 his only assets consisted of his personal car and shares in his father's private corporation, which were given to him by his father in 20X7. At the time of the gift the shares were valued at $12,000.

Required:
Determine Carl's net income for tax purposes for the 20X7 taxation year. Explain the reasoning for each of the items listed.

Solution:

Divorce settlement and support payments The lump sum settlement of $100,000 is not taxable to Carl, nor is it deductible by his former spouse. However, support payments for Carl that are made on a periodic basis and are pursuant to a written agreement or court order are taxable to Carl and are deductible by his former spouse. Assuming the payments are pursuant to a written order, Carl must include his percentage of 60% of the monthly payments in his income. So, his taxable amount is $43,200 [60% × ($6,000 × 12 months)]. The monthly payments relating to child support are not taxable to Carl and not deductible by his former spouse. 56(1)(b), 56.1(4), 60(b).

TFSA contribution TFSA contributions are not deductible for tax purposes. Carl has not made eligible contributions for the previous two years and, therefore, can contribute the maximum $5,000 for each of those years plus an additional $5,000 for the current year. So the $15,000 contribution in 20X7 is an eligible contribution. Future income earned in the plan is not taxable nor is it taxable when withdrawn. 207.01(1), 146.2(6), 149(1)(u.2).

Debt settlement The $20,000 debt was settled for $17,000 resulting in a gain to Carl of $3,000. This gain is not immediately taxable, but will have tax consequences in the future. Carl is first required to apply the gain of $3,000 to reduce any loss carryovers from other years that are non-capital losses, farm losses, restricted farm losses, allowable business investment losses, and net capital losses, in that order. Carl does not have any of these. So, he may then apply the gain to reduce the capital cost and undepreciated capital cost of depreciable property, the cumulative eligible capital balance of eligible capital property, and the adjusted cost base of capital assets by electing to do so through a series of designations. However, these reductions must be applied in order, and to the maximum extent possible. Carl's only property is the shares in his father's corporation. Therefore, he may reduce the ACB of the shares by $3,000 from $12,000 to $9,000. When the shares are sold, his capital gain will be $3,000 higher than it would be otherwise. If the gain is not applied to reduce the ACB of the shares, then one-half of the gain would have to be taken into income in 20X7 (the year the debt was settled). 80(2)–(9).

Sale of shares The shares that were sold are small business corporation shares and the loss is an allowable business investment loss of $2,500 [1/2($20,000 − $25,000)]. The $2,500 can be deducted from any source of income earned in the year. 248(1), 38(c).

Scholarship and research grant and university costs Assuming that Carl's university program qualifies for the education tax credit, the scholarship of $10,000 would not be taxable. If he did not qualify for the education credit, the amount in excess of $500 (in this case $9,500) would be taxable. The $8,000 research grant is taxable to the extent that it exceeds the costs incurred to carry out the research. Of the $9,000 for a research assistant and research supplies, $8,000 can be deducted from the grant total of $8,000 resulting in a net amount of zero. The actual loss of $1,000 ($8,000 − $9,000) from the grant cannot be offset against other income. The tuition fee and book costs are not deductible expenses, but qualify for a tax credit when calculating tax payable (see Chapter 10). 56(1)(n),(o), 56(3).

Publisher's award The award of $2,000 is a prize of achievement in Carl's field of endeavour. It is taxable to the extent it exceeds $500. So, the taxable amount is $1,500. 56(1)(n), 56(3).

Net income for tax purposes for 20X7:

Support payments	$43,200
Prize of achievement	1,500
	44,700
Allowable business investment loss	(2,500)
Net income for tax purposes	$42,200

QUESTION THREE

Francois and Nadine, a married couple, are both 68 years of age and retired. They have the following incomes in 20X8:

	Francois	Nadine
CPP	$7,800	$4,800
OAS	6,000	6,000
Pension from former employer	68,200	0
RRIF	0	8,200
Total	$82,000	$19,000

The marginal tax rates are assumed to be 24% up to income of $42,000 and 32% on income between $42,000 and $85,000.

Required:

How can Francois and Nadine minimize their income tax cost in 20X8? What is the maximum tax that can be saved?

Solution:

The married couple can minimize income tax by electing to split their pension income and take advantage of the lowest possible tax rates available to each spouse. In this case, Francois pays tax on $42,000 of income at 24% and 32% on his income between $42,000 and $82,000. Nadine pays tax at the rate of 24% on all of her income. The pension and RRIF incomes are both eligible for splitting because both individuals are over 65. If they were under 65, only the pension income would be eligible for splitting. So, Francois can simply elect and designate that a portion of his pension income be allocated to Nadine and taxed at her marginal tax rate. Francois can allocate up to 50% of his pension income to Nadine. However, it is not necessary to transfer the maximum. 56(1)(a.2), 60(c), 60.03.

If Francois allocates $23,000 to Nadine, her income will increase from $19,000 to $42,000. Anything above this amount will put Nadine into the 32% marginal tax rate and that is the same as Francois' current top rate. So, a transfer of $23,000 will reduce the tax for Francois by $7,360 (32% × $23,000) and increase Nadine's tax by $5,520 (24% × $23,000); a net saving of $1,840 (32% − 24% = 8% × $23,000 = $1,840).

This allocation is achieved simply by completing form T1032 when filing the tax returns for each spouse. It is not a requirement that the actual pension cash flow be transferred. CPP income is also eligible for splitting (up to 50%), however, it is activated by direct application to the CPP benefits office and the actual CPP payments have to be paid according to the split. This is obviously more cumbersome and less flexible.

QUESTION FOUR

Which of the following situations has taxpayers that are related to each other and, therefore, not dealing at arm's-length? Provide a brief reason.

1. Individual A and her Uncle B.

2. Individual A owns 20% of the voting shares of X Inc. Individual B and individual C each own 40% of voting shares of X Inc. Individuals A and C are brothers.

3. Individual X and her great-granddaughter, individual Y.

4. The voting shares of Q Inc. are owned by Individuals A, B, and C. The voting shares of R Inc. are owned 70% by individual C and 30% by individual D. Individuals A, B, and C are sisters. D is the first cousin of A, B, and C.

Solution:

1. Individual A and B are not related for tax purposes. Individuals are related if they are direct-line descendants, brothers and sisters, spouses or in-laws. 251(6).

2. Individuals A and C are related because they are brothers. Together, they are a related group that controls corporation X and, therefore, are both related to X Inc. 251(2)(b).

3. Individual X and her great-granddaughter, Y, are related for tax purposes. 251(6).

4. Individuals A, B, and C are related because they are sisters. They are not related to their first cousin, individual D. A, B, and C are a related group controlling Q Inc. and are, therefore, each related to Q Inc. R Inc. is controlled by individual C. So C and R Inc. are related. R Inc. and Q Inc. are also related because one is controlled by C who is part of a related group that controls the other. 251(6), 251(2)(b)(i),(ii), 251(2)(c)(iii).

Review Questions

1. In addition to income from employment, business, property, and capital gains, taxpayers must include income from "other sources" when determining their income for tax purposes. How does the *Income Tax Act* limit the scope of "other sources of income"?

2. Explain why the receipt of property from an inheritance is not included in net income for tax purposes.

3. Can an individual deduct for tax purposes the amount of regular support payments to a former spouse? Would it matter if that individual's only source of income were from interest on bond investments? Explain.

4. Why is the category "other deductions" considered to be the last test for determining the deductibility of an expenditure?

5. Briefly explain why an RRSP is an attractive investment.

6. If you hold investments both inside and outside an RRSP and usually invest in both corporate bonds and corporate shares, which type of investment would you prefer to hold within the RRSP? Explain.

7. Briefly explain why a TFSA is an attractive investment. How does a TFSA differ from an RRSP?

8. Briefly explain the tax treatment of an RESP.

9. What is the significance of the special rules for net income determination, and how do they relate to the five categories of income that are taxable?

10. "When in doubt, it is always best to claim a deduction for an expenditure because the worst possible result is that the CRA will simply deny the deduction." Is this statement true? Explain.

11. If a group of business assets is being sold for a total agreed price, is it important that the vendor and the purchaser seriously consider how the total price will be allocated to the separate assets in the group? Explain.

12. What are the tax consequences if a parent sells property to a child at a price that is less than the actual value of the property? What difference would it make if the property were simply gifted to the child?

13. What are the tax consequences if an individual sells property to his or her spouse at a price that is less than the property's market value but more than its cost?

14. How are property income (losses) and capital gains (losses) treated for tax purposes if the funds used to acquire the property were provided by the taxpayer's spouse? How does the tax treatment differ if the funds are provided by the taxpayer's parent?

15. What is the implication to the employer and to the employee if the employer delays the payment of remuneration to the employee?

16. What difference does it make for tax purposes when an individual's last will and testament bequeaths property to a spouse, rather than to a child?

17. The scope of the income tax system is defined by five specific types of income—employment, business, property, capital gains, and other sources. This being so, why is it necessary for the *Income Tax Act* to specifically list a number of items that are not included in income?

18. Briefly outline the process that can be used to establish the tax treatment of a particular transaction.

Key Concept Questions

QUESTION ONE

Fred contributed $12,000 to his RRSP in November 20X7 and $10,000 to a spousal RRSP in February of 20X8. Fred had earned income of $80,000 in 20X6 and $100,000 in 20X7. Fred's notice of assessment showed unused RRSP deduction room at the end of 20X6 of $5,000. His T4 for 20X6 showed a pension adjustment (PA) of $3,000. *Income tax reference: ITA 60(i), 146(1), (5), (5.1).*

Determine Fred's maximum RRSP deduction for 20X7.

QUESTION TWO

Victoria had income for tax purposes for the current year as follows:

Salary	$65,000
Taxable benefits	5,000
Registered pension plan deduction	(3,000)
Employment income for tax purposes	67,000
Loss from a part-time business	(6,000)
Spousal support received	12,000
Interest income	1,000
Rental income	22,000
	$96,000

Determine Victoria's earned income for RRSP purposes for the current year. *Income tax reference: ITA 146(1) earned income definition.*

QUESTION THREE

Tom retired from X Corp. on June 30th of the current year after turning 65 in December of last year. He plans to travel with his wife who is 45 years of age. On retirement, Tom received a retiring allowance of $40,000 for his years of loyal service. Tom started his employment with X Corp. in 1990. *Income tax reference: ITA 56(1)(a), 60(j.1).*

Determine the income tax consequences of the retiring allowance for Tom.

QUESTION FOUR

In November of the current year, Beth withdrew $24,000 from her spousal RRSP. Her husband had contributed $2,500 to the spousal RRSP on February 1st of each of the last 20 years. She also withdrew $8,000 from her TFSA. All contributions to her TFSA were made by her husband. *Income tax reference: ITA 56(1)(h), 146.2, 146(8.3).*

Determine the tax implications, if any, of the RRSP and TFSA withdrawals.

QUESTION FIVE

Wendy received the following amounts in the current year:

• Support payments from her former spouse ($4,000 × 12)	$48,000
• Employment insurance benefits	4,100
• Inheritance	20,000
• Scholarship	5,000
• RRSP withdrawal (LLP)	10,000
• Canada child tax benefit	3,450
• Universal child care benefit ($100 × 12)	1,200
• Lottery winnings	300

The support payments are in accordance with Wendy's divorce agreement, which calls for monthly support payments of $1,500 for Wendy and $2,500 for her 4-year-old daughter. Wendy became frustrated during the year with not being able to find suitable employment and returned to school. She enrolled as a full-time student at the University of Toronto. She withdrew $10,000 from her RRSP to help finance her education. *Income tax reference: ITA 56(1)(a), (b), (n), (h), (h.2), 56(3), (6) 56.1(4), 60(b), 122.6, 146.02.*

Determine the amount to be included in Wendy's income for tax purposes for the current year.

QUESTION SIX

Norman moved from the Ottawa office of Safety Corp. to the head office in Toronto, in October of the current year. He incurred a loss of $35,000 on the sale of his Ottawa home after it had sat empty for five months while the real estate agent tried to sell it. The real estate commission of $20,000 and legal fees of $1,200 are included in the $35,000 loss. In addition, he incurred the following costs with respect to the move:

- Airline ticket ($1,000), hotel room for two nights stay ($400), and meals ($100) when Norman and his wife made a trip to Toronto to search for a new home—$1,500

- Purchase price of new home—$420,000

- Legal fees and land transfer tax on purchase of new home—$1,800

- Moving company to pack their belongings and move them to their new home in Toronto—$6,000

- Gasoline and other car expenses plus two meals for each of the five family members. Norman drove himself and his family from Ottawa to their new home in Toronto (450 km)—$210

- Cost of carrying Ottawa house for five months while vacant (mortgage interest, property tax, and utilities)—$7,200

- Cost of revising legal documents to reflect the new address—$25

Norman's T4 slip showed employment income for the year of $120,000 of which $30,000 was earned after his move to Toronto. *Income tax reference: ITA 62; IT-178R3.*

Determine Norman's maximum deduction for moving expenses for the current year.

QUESTION SEVEN

Dan and Janet have three children, ages 6, 9, and 17. While Janet was a full-time student at university, January through April (15 weeks), her mother looked after the children. Janet found full-time employment in July. Her 17-year-old son looked after the younger two children during July while Janet worked. In August, the two younger children spent four weeks at an overnight camp in northern Ontario. Janet hired a live-in nanny to look after the children from September through December. Dan paid all of the child care costs for the year, which totalled $17,600 (Janet's mother $6,000 + son $1,600 + camp $4,000 ($2,000 per child) + nanny $6,000). Dan is employed full time as a salesman. He received commission income of $125,000 during the current year. He was able to claim sales expenses of $25,000 on this tax return. Janet had the following sources of income in the current year—scholarships $3,000; spousal support from her former spouse $12,000; rental income $8,000, and salary plus taxable benefits $36,000. *Income tax reference: ITA 63.*

Determine the maximum tax deduction for child care available to Dan and Janet for the current year.

QUESTION EIGHT

Neil owns 100% of the issued shares of N Ltd. His wife, Susan, owns 60% of the issued share of S Ltd. Their son, Ron, owns 50% of the shares of R Ltd. The remainder of the shares of S Ltd. and the remainder of the shares of R Ltd. are owned by Susan's sister, Mary. *Income tax reference: ITA 251.*

Determine which of the corporations and individuals are related.

QUESTION NINE

Early in the current year, Alex gifted shares of a public corporation to his 16-year-old son. Alex had paid $1,000 for the shares. They were worth $15,000 at the time of the gift. After receiving the gift, his son received dividends of $800 on the shares. Also in the current year, Alex sold shares of a public corporation to his wife. The shares, which had a value of $10,000 at the time of the sale, originally cost $2,000. Alex sold them to his wife for $7,000. His wife received dividends of $500 on these shares. *Income tax reference: ITA 69(1), 73(1), 74.1, 74.2.*

Determine the tax consequences of these transactions.

QUESTION TEN

Brody has a lawn care business, which he incorporated in the current year. On incorporation, Brody and his 15-year-old son, who often works with him, each subscribed for 1 common share at $100 per share. Brody paid the $200 for both the shares. The corporation will pay dividends to Brody and his son, annually. *Income tax reference: ITA 120.4.*

Describe the tax treatment of the dividend income received by Brody's son.

QUESTION ELEVEN

X Ltd. is in financial difficulty. It has just learned that its major supplier is willing to forgive $100,000 of the debt owed by X Ltd. in order that X Ltd. will not be forced to declare bankruptcy. X Ltd. has built up non-capital losses of $80,000 over the last few years. It still owns the following assets: land (cost $70,000), building (cost $120,000; UCC $92,000), equipment (cost $40,000; UCC $32,000), intangibles (cost $5,000; CEC $4,700). *Income tax reference: ITA 80.*

Determine the tax implications of the debt forgiveness.

QUESTION TWELVE

Irene died in the current year. At the time of her death she owned the following assets:

- Antique furniture (FMV $30,000; cost $10,000)
- Rental property—land (FMV $100,000; cost $60,000); building (FMV $60,000; cost $50,000; UCC $45,000)
- RRSP (FMV $80,000)

In her will, Irene directed her executors to transfer the antique furniture to her husband and the rental property to her son. Her husband was the named beneficiary on her RRSP. *Income tax reference: ITA 60(l), 70(5), 70(6).*

Determine the tax implications for the above assets on Irene's death.

Problems

PROBLEM ONE

Harvey Caseman died on July 15, 20X1. At the time of his death, he owned the assets listed in the table below.

		Cost	Value
Rental Property—Land		$10,000	$15,000
—Building		40,000	60,000
Piano		5,000	8,000

Over the years, Caseman had claimed capital cost allowance on the building. Its undepreciated capital cost is $28,000.

In his last will and testament, Caseman directed his executors to transfer the rental property to his two children and the piano to his spouse.

Required:

1. Determine to what extent, if any, Caseman's net income for tax purposes for 20X1 will be affected by his death.

2. What are the tax implications to the spouse and children if they sell the property immediately after they receive ownership?

PROBLEM TWO

Blue Ltd. is a Canadian corporation owned 100% by Karen Samson. Blue manufactures hockey sticks that are marketed to retail sporting goods stores across Canada and Europe. Green Ltd. is a Canadian corporation also owned 100% by Samson. Green operates a retail sporting goods store. It purchases hockey sticks from Blue.

Blue charges $10 a stick to all of its customers in Canada, except Green, which pays only $8 a stick. Each stick costs Blue $4 to manufacture. Last week, Green purchased 1,000 sticks from Blue and sold them to retail customers for $14 each.

Required:

1. With respect to the 1,000 sticks, determine the income for tax purposes of both Blue and Green.

2. How would your answer to question 1 change if Blue charged Green $12 per stick?

PROBLEM THREE

For each of the following independent transactions, determine the amount of net income or loss for tax purposes and the taxpayer to which it applies.

1. A woman purchased a $10,000 bond for her 15-year-old daughter. During the year, the bond paid interest of $1,000. property income

2. A student who is 20 years old borrowed $20,000 from his parent and used the funds to purchase shares in a public corporation. After receiving a dividend of $1,000, the student sold the shares for $24,000. (How would your answer change if the student were 17 years old?) CG w/ child, dividend w/ parent

3. A woman gifted to her husband shares of a public corporation, for which she had paid $15,000. At the time of the gift, the shares had a value of $30,000. After receiving the gift, the husband received a dividend of $1,000 and then sold the shares for $26,000.

4. A man loaned money to his wife, who used the borrowed funds to purchase a rental property. During the year, the rental property earned net rentals of $7,000. The amount of the loan, which is interest-free, is $60,000. (How would your answer change

if the loan were subject to a reasonable interest rate of 6% and was secured by a mortgage on the rental property?) *— FMV consideration now.*

5. A man gifted common shares of a Canadian-controlled private corporation to his 16-year-old daughter. At the time of the gift, the shares were valued at $10,000. Their original cost was $6,000. During the year, the daughter received a dividend of $1,000 from the shares and then sold them for $15,000. All of the corporation's income was subject to the small business deduction. *— type of dividend paid → grossup!* *private.* *minor* *grossup of 25.*

6. A woman contributed $5,000 to her husband's TFSA. The funds were invested in bonds earning interest.

PROBLEM FOUR

Health Kicks Ltd. is a Canadian-controlled private corporation owned 100% by Wally Bose. The company's year end is December 31, and its 20X1 fiscal period has just come to a close.

Following is certain information in the accounting records of the company for the year ended December 31, 20X1:

- **Rent expense ($22,000)**   The company rents a warehouse building for $2,000 per month from Joe Holy, a schoolteacher. As of December 31, 20X1, the December rent had not been paid owing to an employee error. Holy had purchased the building as an investment several years ago for $180,000. During 20X1, he incurred operating expenses for the building (taxes, insurance, interest, and the like) totalling $20,000. The undepreciated capital cost (UCC) of the building is $120,000.

- **Repairs and maintenance expense ($70,000)**   This account includes snow removal and lawn-care costs, in addition to $62,000 for building improvements: the installation of an air-conditioning system and three additional loading docks (ramps and doors). The $62,000 was paid to a warehouse contractor that is an American corporation operating a branch office in Winnipeg.

- **Accounting and legal expense ($16,000)**   This amount was paid to a law firm for the following services:
  — Registering of a debenture against the company's assets on a loan from the bank ($4,000).
  — Drawing up of a legal agreement to purchase all of the common shares of Dash Ltd., which now operates as a wholly owned subsidiary ($9,000).
  — Preparing of articles of amendment to revise the company's articles of incorporation ($3,000).

- **Interest expense ($22,000)**   Several years ago, the company purchased a small warehouse in Winnipeg. The previous owner, a resident of England, permitted Health Kicks to pay a small amount down and the balance over eight years, with interest at 11%. Of the above interest, $7,000 represents interest paid on this obligation. The remaining interest of $15,000 was paid to a shareholder, Bose, on a loan he made to his own company.

- **Land cost ($19,000)**   This represents the cost of landscaping the grounds around the company's office building (trees, shrubs, and flower beds), and was added to the capital cost of the land. The $19,000 was paid to Wesley Perkins, a management student who operates a summer lawn service.

- **Salary and remuneration expense ($290,000)**   This account is made up of the following items:

Salaries	$238,000
Sales commissions accrued but not paid until 20X2	30,000
Retirement gift to the sales manager	1,000
Clothing allowance to senior executives so that they can acquire	
expensive wardrobes to maintain their image	21,000
	$290,000

- *Licence cost ($120,000)*   Health Kicks purchased a licence to manufacture a health product that was patent-protected by another company. The licence permitted Health Kicks to manufacture and sell the product for six years. The licence was acquired from Bobo Enterprises Ltd., which sold several licences for this product to other companies in certain geographic areas. Health Kicks can sell the product only in western Canada.

Required:

Discuss, in point form, the tax implications of the preceding transactions from the point of view of (a) Health Kicks, and (b) the other party to each transaction.

PROBLEM FIVE

The following information relates to Perry Somer's financial affairs in 20X1:

1. Somer is employed as a salesman and is remunerated by commissions. He must pay all of his own expenses. During 20X1, he earned commissions of $28,000. His expenses were as follows:

Automobile (operating costs)	$3,000
Entertainment	1,000
Convention (related to his employment)	500
Donations	500
Telephone long-distance charges (personal use was 80%)	1,000

The personal-use portion of his automobile expense is 20%. The UCC of his automobile at the end of the previous year was $5,000.

2. He made the following capital transactions:

	Gain (loss)
Shares of public corporation A	$10,000
Shares of public corporation B	(18,000)
Shares of Canadian-controlled private corporation C (a small business corporation)	(6,000)

3. In 20X0, Somer acquired two residential rental properties.

	Property X	Property Y
Land	$10,000	$15,000
Building	70,000	60,000
	$80,000	$75,000

Maximum capital cost allowance was claimed in 20X0.

In 20X1, the city expropriated property Y for $77,000 (land $17,000, building $60,000). Perry was pleased because property Y was vacant for part of the year after a tenant vacated unexpectedly.

In 20X1, net rental income from both properties (after all expenses but before capital cost allowance) was $1,000.

4. Somer's other income and expenses are as follows:

Income:	
Taxable dividends—Canadian public corporations	$2,000
Interest on foreign bonds (net of 15% withholding tax)	1,700

Expenses:	
Interest on a loan used to acquire the foreign bonds	1,300
Investment counsel fee	800

5. During the year, he made a contribution to a registered pension plan of $1,000, which was matched by his employer. In addition, Somer contributed $2,000 to his RRSP.

6. Somer currently lives in rented premises but is considering moving into rental property X and occupying one-half of the building sometime in 20X2.

Required:

1. Calculate Somer's minimum 20X1 net income in accordance with the aggregating formula for determining net income for tax purposes.

2. What would be the tax consequences, if any, if Somer occupied rental property X?

PROBLEM SIX

Peter Carletti is a professional architect employed by a Halifax-based architectural firm. He is 58 years old and married, and has a 22-year-old son. Peter's wife, Carla, recently returned to university and will complete a law degree in three or four years. Their son, who lives with them, also attends university and will continue to do so for at least three years.

Peter has asked you to review his family's financial position and tell him what tax planning opportunities are available. Also, he does not have a will and would like you to tell him what tax consequences may occur at the time of his death. He provides you with the following information:

1. The Carlettis' home in Halifax is owned by Carla. She had acquired the property five years ago for $200,000 with funds received from her father's estate. The home is now worth $230,000 and has no mortgage. She has no other assets.

2. Last year, Peter purchased a vacation home on the Atlantic coast. The property cost $150,000 and has already increased in value to $180,000. Upon purchase, Peter assumed the mortgage of $90,000, which has an interest rate of 8%.

3. Peter owns a term life insurance policy that will pay $400,000 upon his death.

4. Peter's annual salary is over $100,000. Carla currently has no income. Annually, Peter contributes to an RRSP, which is now worth $200,000. The plan invests primarily in secure common shares and earns capital gains and dividends.

5. Peter owns a rental property, for which he paid $240,000 (land $40,000, building $200,000) five years ago. It is debt-free and currently worth $300,000 (land $50,000, building $250,000). The UCC of the building is $166,000.

6. Peter owns the following other investments:
   - $50,000 of Nova Scotia Hydro Bonds, which earn interest of 10%.
   - Bank term deposits (one-year terms) of $170,000, which earn 9% interest.
   - Common shares of a Canadian public corporation that are valued at $90,000. He purchased the shares two years ago for $40,000. Peter has not sold any capital property in the past 10 years.

Required:
Prepare a brief report for Peter Carletti outlining the tax consequences that may occur on his death. The report should also suggest what he might do now to minimize annual taxes during his lifetime.

PROBLEM SEVEN

In 20X3, Carol Fortier was transferred by her employer to Vancouver from Toronto. She has made a number of financial transactions related to the move. Fortier has asked you for help in determining her 20X3 income for tax purposes. She has provided the following information:

1. Fortier is divorced and supports her two children Lise (age 17) and Randy (age 19). In the summer of 20X3, Randy earned net profits of $4,000 as a street vendor. Lise's only source of income was from an investment purchased for her by her mother. The investment, bonds of a Canadian public corporation, paid interest of $1,000 during the year.

2. Fortier began work in Vancouver in February 20X3, as a senior saleswoman for a clothing manufacturer. During 20X3, she received a gross salary of $110,000 as well as selling commissions of $5,000. In addition, on June 30, 20X3, her employer's year end, she was awarded a bonus of $12,000 payable in 12 monthly instalments of $1,000 beginning July 31, 20X3. During 20X3, she contributed $3,700 to the company's registered pension plan, and her employer contributed the same amount. She also paid $2,307 to the Canada Pension Plan and made Employment Insurance contributions of $840.

3. Fortier's employer has certified that she is required to pay some of her own expenses as part of her selling duties. In 20X3, she incurred the following costs:

Purchase of computer		$ 3,000
Advertising and promotion		1,800
Entertainment:		
Meals and drinks	2,000	
Golf club dues	2,400	4,400
Automobile—gas, repairs, and insurance		4,200
		$13,400

Fortier uses her own car for business activities. At the end of 20X2, the car had an unamortized capital cost of $20,000 (original cost in 20X2, $22,000). In 20X3, she drove the car 30,000 kilometres, of which approximately 12,000 was for personal use. In 20X3, she acquired a computer (see table), which she uses at home to maintain customer files and industry information. She estimates that 90% of her 20X3 computer time was employment related.

4. On January 15, 20X4, Fortier contributed $7,000 to an RRSP. On the same date she contributed $4,000 to a TFSA. For the 20X2 taxation year, her earned income was $63,889. In 20X2, the combined (employer and employee) contribution to her employer RPP was $6,400.

5. Fortier drove herself and two children from Toronto to Vancouver. The 4,400 km trip took 5 days and cost $400 for gasoline, $480 for accomodation (4 nights), and $500 for meals (5 days). As well, she incurred the following relocation costs:

Real estate commission on sale of former home	$19,000
Moving furniture	14,000
Legal fees to purchase new home	2,000
Legal fees on sale of former home	2,500
Temporary lodging and meals, in Toronto after the sale of the former home and in Vancouver before taking possession of the new home (30 days)	6,000
	$43,500

Her employer, in accordance with company policy, paid her the maximum $10,000 as a partial reimbursement for transporting furniture to Vancouver.

6. Fortier wrote an article on selling strategies in the fashion industry. It was published in a national trade journal. The article received wide acclaim. In September 20X3, she was awarded a $2,000 prize for the best article of the year.

7. In January 20X3, Fortier sold her home in Toronto for $300,000. She had acquired the home in 20X0 for $180,000 and had occupied it until the move to Vancouver.

8. Five years ago, Fortier purchased 5% of the common shares of Prentice Ltd. for $20,000. Prentice is a Canadian-controlled private corporation manufacturing specialized furniture. In June 20X0, when the company had cash-flow problems, Fortier lent Prentice $10,000. The loan was unsecured and payable on demand. Although Fortier has received no interest to date, in 20X1 and 20X2, she included in her taxable income interest of $1,500 ($750 × 2 y = $1,500) based on the agreed 7½% interest rate on each anniversary date. In 20X3, she demanded payment of the loan and accrued interest, but the company was unable to pay. The company's only assets, other than the leased manufacturing equipment, were inventory and receivables, which were pledged on a bank loan; these were insufficient to meet even that obligation. In March 20X4, Prentice closed operations and declared bankruptcy.

9. Fortier sold the following properties in 20X3:

	Original cost	Selling price net of disposal costs
4,000 shares of Teulon Ltd. (a public corporation)	$22,000	$114,000
Oil painting	800	4,000
Commodity futures contract	16,000	28,000

The sale of the commodity futures contract was Fortier's second commodity transaction. In 20X1, she purchased and sold a similar contract but lost $14,000. She deducted the full $14,000 in computing her 20X1 taxable income.

10. Fortier owns a residential rental property in Toronto. She acquired the property in 20X2 for $414,000 (land $54,000, building $360,000). She incurred a substantial loss in 20X2 as a result of an unexpected vacancy. She found a new tenant in 20X3. She received gross rents of $46,000 in 20X3. Expenses for utilities, taxes, insurance, interest, and maintenance were $47,100 that year. One of the tenants failed to pay its December 20X3 rent of $2,000. However, she received that payment on January 20, 20X4.

11. Fortier received the following additional amounts in 20X3:

Eligible dividends from taxable Canadian public corporations	$6,000
Interest on bank deposits	7,000
Winnings from a provincial lottery	800

12. Fortier hired an investment counsellor in 20X3. On his recommendation, she used $40,000 of the $200,000 mortgage loan on her new home to acquire Canadian public securities. Her mortgage interest payments in 20X3 totalled $22,000. She paid the investment counsellor $2,000 for his advice.

13. In 20X3, Fortier made donations to registered charities of $4,000.

14. During 20X3, Fortier's 20X1 tax return was reassessed. She hired a lawyer to prepare an appeal. The legal fee was $1,200. The appeal was not successful.

Required:

For the 20X3 taxation year, calculate Fortier's net income for tax purposes. Prepare the calculation in accordance with the net income formula, and organize the items of income by the categories described in that formula.

PROBLEM EIGHT

A Review of Net Income for Tax Purposes

Mr. Active holds a job, operates a small farm, and makes numerous investments. A description of his financial activities for 20X1 is given below.

1. Active is a lawyer and is employed in the legal department of a large public corporation. In 20X1, he received a gross salary of $72,000. In addition, the corporation provided the following items of remuneration:

   • A car allowance of $400 a month to cover costs of travel in the performance of his duties. During 20X1, Active used his own car to travel from his home to work and back. Rarely was the car used during working hours on company business.
   • A contribution of $3,000 to a deferred profit-sharing plan.
   • A group term life insurance policy for $100,000 (premium cost, $800).
   • A cash bonus of $3,000 that was awarded to him in the previous year and that he received in the current year.

2. Active's employer gives all senior executives the option to acquire a certain number of shares of the corporation at a price that is guaranteed for two years. In 20X0, the employer granted Active an option to purchase up to 5,000 of its shares for a price of $10 per share. At the time the option was granted, the shares were valued at $10.75 per share. During 20X1, Active purchased 500 shares at a cost of $10 per share. At the date of purchase, the corporation's shares were trading at $14 per share.

3. Active purchased a small parcel of land (20 hectares) in 20X1 and began raising goats. In 20X1, he lost $1,000 from this operation.

4. In 20X1, Active purchased 1,000 shares of Canadian public corporation X for $20 per share and received a stock dividend of 100 additional shares of the same class. During the year, he sold the 100 shares at $21 per share, for the same value as on their date of issue.

5. Three years ago, Active had purchased three residential rental properties and has provided you with the following information:

	Property 1	Property 2	Property 3
Land cost	$10,000	$ 4,000	$ 8,000
Building cost	60,000	40,000	45,000
Building UCC (31/12/20X0)	52,000	37,000	40,000
20X1 net rents (before CCA)	3,000	(5,000)	4,000

   In 20X1, Active sold property 1 for $80,000 (land $12,000, building $68,000), and property 2 for $50,000 (land $6,000, building $44,000). Also, in 20X1, he purchased property 4 for $90,000 (land $30,000, building $60,000). In 20X1, property 4 had net rentals before capital cost allowance of $1,000.

6. During the year, Active gifted 1,000 shares of Shell Canada Ltd. (a public corporation) to his daughter. The shares had cost him $10 each and had a value at the time of the gift of $12 each. In 20X1, his daughter (16 years old) received dividends of $1,000; she then sold the shares for $30 each.

7. In 20X1, Active gifted 2,000 shares of Exxon Ltd. (a public corporation) to his wife. The shares had a value of $40 each at the time of the gift. He had paid $30 per share several years before. His wife sold the shares in 20X1 for $28 per share during a market slump.

8. Active's mother died in 20X0 and left him her house. The house cost $40,000 at the time of purchase and had a value in 20X0 of $60,000. Active sold the house in 20X1 for $66,000.

9. Three years ago, Active purchased 15% of the shares of two private corporations. Each carried on an active business. He sold the shares of both corporations in 20X1. Information relating to the shares is as follows:

	PC 1	PC 2
Cost	$40,000	$35,000
Proceeds of sale	56,000	20,000
Terms of payment	$8,000/yr for 7 yrs	All cash

10. In 20X1, during a market slump, Active sold 500 shares of public corporation A for $30,000; the shares had cost him $40,000. Two weeks later, as the market began to strengthen, he purchased 500 shares of the same corporation for $29,000.

11. Active also sold the following assets in 20X1:

	Cost	Proceeds
Public corporation B shares	$10,000	$12,000
Public corporation C shares	47,500	20,000
Stamp collection	8,000	12,000
Jewellery	6,000	1,000
Boat	5,000	2,000
Stereo set	800	900

12. Active had the following additional receipts in 20X1:

Dividends from Canadian public companies	$4,000
Interest on bonds	1,000
Lottery winnings	6,000

13. Active paid out the following in 20X1:

To purchase a computer for use at home when working on his employer's business	$ 700
Interest on bank loan to purchase shares of public corporation	2,000
Interest on house mortgage (mortgage funds of $60,000 were used —$40,000 for the purchase of the house, $20,000 for the purchase of shares)	6,000
Lump-sum alimony settlement to ex-wife	9,000
Tuition fees for attending university	1,000
Donations	4,000
Gift to a registered federal political party	1,000
Contribution to an RRSP	2,800
Annual dues to the provincial law society	1,000

Required:

Calculate Active's net income for tax purposes for 20X1.

Case

TRANS-AM SUPPLIERS LTD.

Trans-Am Suppliers Ltd. is just completing negotiations to sell its manufacturing division to a competitor. The purchaser has agreed to purchase the inventory, manufacturing equipment, licence, and goodwill for $1,200,000.

The payment terms require that the purchaser pay $900,000 on the closing date, with the balance of $300,000 deferred for two years. The unpaid balance is subject to annual interest of 10%. Trans-Am intends to use the proceeds from the sale to expand its wholesale division, which is expected to generate returns of 24% annually before tax. The company's tax rate is 25%.

Although the total price and payment terms have been agreed to, a conflict has arisen between Trans-Am and the purchaser regarding the price of each asset sold. The sources of the dispute are as follows:

- **Inventory**   Trans-Am's accounting records indicate that the inventory amounts to $300,000, valued at the lower of cost or market. Traditionally, the company has been conservative in establishing the market value. The purchaser, after examining the merchandise, feels that the proper value is $340,000 and expects that it could all be sold within one year.

- **Equipment**   The manufacturing equipment, which originally cost $600,000, has a book value for accounting purposes of $300,000. The undepreciated capital cost is $320,000. Trans-Am has valued the equipment at $400,000, but the purchaser's appraiser is confident that the equipment has a value of $450,000 in the used-equipment market.

- **Licence**   One of Trans-Am's products is manufactured under licence from a company that holds the patent. The licence, which has a life of 10 years, was purchased only six months earlier for $100,000. Shortly after the purchase, the product gained wide recognition; the company that holds the patent rights now sells licences in other geographic areas at a price of $300,000. Both Trans-Am and the purchaser agree on this value.

- **Goodwill**   No discussion was held with respect to the goodwill, as both parties acknowledge that its value reflects the difference between the total purchase price of $1,200,000 and the combined values of the other specific assets.

The president of Trans-Am is concerned that the negotiation process will be stalled if the above issues are not settled. He is prepared to make some concessions but feels that before doing so, he must understand what the differences mean to Trans-Am. Also, the president thinks it would be useful to know the impact of his own stance on the purchaser, as this will suggest how rigid he should appear at the next round of discussions.

The president has asked you to report to him and provide the information requested. In addition, he has asked you to separately examine the tax implications of the deferred payment terms and determine whether the agreement should state the terms of payment for each asset as opposed to the total package.

Required:

Prepare an outline of the report, including any necessary calculations.

CHAPTER 10

Individuals: Determination of Taxable Income and Taxes Payable

So far in the text, the structure of the tax system has treated all taxable entities (individuals, corporations, and trusts) according to a common set of principles. It has been established that an individual who earns business income, property income, and capital gains determines his or her net income for tax purposes in exactly the same manner as a corporation that earns the same types of income.

A taxpayer's net income for tax purposes must be converted to taxable income before tax can be calculated. It is important to recognize that individuals determine their taxable income and tax payable by a different method from that for corporations. Even so, because the ultimate shareholder of a corporation is the individual, the different tax treatments of the two entities must, in the final analysis, be viewed together. The relationship between a corporation and its shareholders is reviewed briefly in Chapter 11 and more extensively in Part Three of the text, which deals exclusively with corporations.

For individuals, the process of converting net income for tax purposes to taxable income focuses largely on two areas: the utilization of losses and the lifetime capital gain deduction. The influence of this process on the individual's finances is, therefore, limited.

The calculation of tax for individuals follows a basic format. However, parts of the calculation are subject to frequent changes as the government alters its fiscal and social policies. While these areas of frequent change affect an individual's tax cost, they seldom have a major impact on decision making for investment and business purposes. In most cases, it is the basic format and the comparative marginal rates of tax that are relevant to the decision maker.

This chapter examines the two main areas that affect the determination of taxable income for individuals and highlights their importance to investment and business decision making. Also discussed is the framework for the calculation of tax.

I. Determination of Taxable Income

It was established earlier that a taxpayer's taxable income for a taxation year is determined by the following simple formula:

Taxable income = Net income − Special reductions

In this formula, net income consists of the aggregate of the five sources of income established in Chapters 4 through 9. The special reductions are grouped together in Division C of the *Income Tax Act*. Several of these reductions apply to individuals; the most important of these are the loss carry-over provisions and the lifetime capital gain deduction. A third important reduction relates to employment income derived from stock options; this was reviewed in Chapter 4 and will not be commented on in this chapter.

The above simple formula can be expanded to show how overall taxable income is calculated for an individual. This is done in Exhibit 10-1. The formula represents the complete framework for establishing the base to which tax is applied.

Note that in part 1 of this formula, (b) includes the item "net taxable gains from listed personal property." This item was excluded from the formula when it was first described in Chapter 3. It requires that only net *gains* be included in the formula.[1] Net taxable gains in this context are the taxable gains for the year in excess of the allowable losses. If the losses exceed the gains, the amount entered into the formula is zero. As described in Chapter 8, losses from listed personal property can be offset only

---

1   ITA 3(b)(i)(B).

Exhibit 10-1:

The Taxable Income Formula for an Individual

1. *Net income for tax purposes:*
   (a) The aggregate of:

Employment income	+
Business income	+
Property income	+
Other items of income	+
	+ or 0

   plus

   (b) The amount by which:

Taxable capital gains	+	
Net taxable gains from listed personal property	+	
	+ or 0	

   exceed

Allowable capital losses	–	+ or 0
		+ or 0

   less (to the maximum of above)

(c) Other items of deduction	–
	+ or 0

   less (to the maximum of above)

   (d) The aggregate of:

Employment losses	–	
Business losses	–	
Property losses	–	
Allowable business investment losses	–	– or 0
Net income for tax purposes		+ or 0

2. Special reductions:
(a) Stock option deduction[a]		
(b) Home relocation loan deduction[b] (see Chapter 4, Part III, Employee Loans)	–	
(c) Social assistance, workers' compensation, and amounts exempted by treaty[c]	–	
(d) Losses not utilized in other years[d]	–	
(e) Capital gain deduction[e]	–	– or 0
Taxable income		+ or 0

a ITA 110(1)(d), (d.1); IT-113R4; see Chapter 4 for stock option deduction details.
b ITA 110(1)(j); least of: benefit on home relocation loan (Ch. 4) or prescribed rate × $25,000.
c ITA 110(1)(f).
d ITA 111.
e ITA 110.6.

against gains from listed personal property. However, a loss that cannot be used in a given year can be carried back three years or forward seven years for use against a listed personal property gain in those years. This carry-over forms part of the net income calculation. In other words, the net taxable gain for the year is the amount by which the current year's taxable gains exceed the allowable losses from the current year *plus* those from a carry-over year, if any. This treatment differs from that for other carry-over losses, which are described later in the chapter.

The items in the formula must be included in the order in which they appear. The special reductions applied to arrive at taxable income should not be merged with the net income calculation, since in some cases the special reductions depend on the amount of net income otherwise determined. The net income portion of the formula is reserved exclusively (except for listed personal property loss carry-overs) for transactions of the current year. The special-reduction portion of the formula deals with transactions of other years or modifies the treatment of certain items in the net income portion.

II. Loss Carry-Overs

Losses incurred in a particular taxation year can be offset against other sources of income, provided they follow the restrictions of the aggregating formula for determining net income for tax purposes. Capital losses can be deducted only to the extent that capital gains were realized in the year. Losses from business, employment, and property, and allowable business investment losses, can be offset against all other sources of income; however, they too may be restricted if the losses are greater than the combined total of other income sources.

In previous chapters, it was indicated that losses incurred in a year, if they are restricted by the aggregating formula, are available for carry-over to other years. Such carry-overs have limited application, and because of this, their use is not certain. As indicated in Exhibit 10-1, loss carry-overs are deducted as special reductions after the taxpayer has determined net income for that particular year. This means that losses incurred in the particular year must be deducted first, as part of net income, before losses of other years can be applied.

The fundamental principles for applying loss carry-overs are different for capital losses from those for other types of losses.[2] This is discussed below.

A. Net Capital Losses

Allowable capital losses incurred in a current year, if they cannot be utilized in arriving at net income (because there are insufficient taxable capital gains), are reclassified as *net capital losses*. These can be carried back three years and forward indefinitely.[3] During this carry-over period, the net capital losses can be deducted only to the extent that the taxpayer has realized net capital gains (gains minus losses) for that year. In other words, capital losses carried back or forward continue to have restricted use in that they can be used only to offset capital gains. However, upon the *death* of an individual, the unused losses may be utilized as a deduction against any other type of income earned in the year of death or in the preceding year.[4]

B. Non-Capital Losses

Most other losses incurred in a year, if they cannot be used, are reclassified as *non-capital losses*. In effect, employment losses, business losses, and property losses, as well as allowable business investment losses, if they cannot be used because there is insufficient income in the year, discard their identity and become lumped together as non-capital losses.

Non-capital losses can be carried back three years and forward for 20 years. Such losses can be deducted in arriving at taxable income, regardless of the type of income earned in those other years.[5]

There is one *exception* to the 20-year carry-forward limit. A non-capital loss that was created by an *allowable business investment loss* can be carried forward for only 10 years. If the loss is unused after the 10-year carry-forward period, that unused loss is reclassified as a net capital loss and can be carried forward indefinitely to be used against future capital gains. This does not apply to non-capital losses that are derived from business, property, or employment losses.

---

2   IT-232R3.
3   ITA 111(1)(b).
4   ITA 111(2).
5   ITA 111(1)(a). The carry-forward period for non-capital losses incurred between March 23, 2004 and December 31, 2005 is 10 years. Prior to March 23, 2004, the carry-forward period was 7 years.

C. Farm Losses and Restricted Farm Losses

There are two further categories of loss carry-overs—farm losses and restricted farm losses. *Farm losses* concern taxpayers whose chief source of income is farming or fishing. These losses are actually business losses and are created in the same way as the non-capital losses described above. Farm losses can be carried back three years and forward 20 years.[6]

Restricted farm losses are losses from farming where farming is not the primary source of income of the taxpayer (see Chapter 5). The annual deductible loss in this situation can be no more than $2,500 plus one-half of the next $12,500 (i.e., $8,750 annually). To the extent that losses are limited by the formula, they are classified as restricted farm losses. These unused losses can be carried back three years and forward 20 years but can only be deducted to the extent that farming income was earned in those years.[7]

D. Sample Calculation of Loss Carry-Overs

A simple application of loss carry-overs for capital losses and other types of losses is demonstrated below.

Situation:

An individual taxpayer has the following sources of income and losses in 20X0 and 20X1:

	20X0	20X1
Employment income	$12,000	$18,000
Business income (enterprise A)	20,000	–0–
Business loss (enterprise B)	(50,000)	–0–
Other items of income	4,000	–0–
Taxable capital gains	8,000	4,000
Allowable capital losses	(13,000)	(1,000)
Allowable business investment losses	(6,000)	–0–
Other deductions	(2,000)	–0–

The individual had no income or losses in the preceding years.

Analysis:

(20X0)
Net income:

(a) Employment income		$12,000
Business income (enterprise A)		20,000
Other sources		4,000
		36,000
(b) Taxable capital gains	8,000	
Allowable capital losses	(13,000)	–0–
		36,000
(c) Other deductions		(2,000)
		34,000
(d) Business loss (enterprise B)	50,000	
Allowable business investment loss	6,000	(34,000)
Net income for tax purposes		–0–
Special reductions		–0–
Taxable income		–0–

---

6   ITA 111(1)(d). The carry-forward period is 10 years for farm losses incurred in years before 2006.
7   ITA 111(1)(c). The carry-forward period is 10 years for *restricted* farm losses incurred in years before 2006.

The unused losses available for carry-over are as follows:

Net capital losses:		
$13,000 − $8,000 =		$ 5,000
Non-capital losses:		
Business loss		$50,000
Allowable business investment loss		6,000
		56,000
Used in 20X0		(34,000)
Available for carry-over		$22,000
(20X1)		
Net income:		
(a) Employment income		$18,000
(b) Taxable capital gains	$ 4,000	
Allowable capital losses	(1,000)	3,000
		21,000
(c) Other deductions		–0–
(d) Losses in 20X1		–0–
Net income for tax purposes		21,000
Special reductions:		
Net capital losses forward	(3,000)	
Non-capital losses forward	(18,000)	(21,000)*
Taxable income		–0–
Net capital losses:		
Amount in 20X0		$ 5,000
Used in 20X1		(3,000)
Carried forward		$ 2,000
Non-capital losses:		
Amount in 20X0		$22,000
Used in 20X1		(18,000)
Carried forward		$ 4,000

* Because of a tax credit available to all individuals, there is no federal tax on approximately the first $10,822 (in 2012) of taxable income. Consequently, in this example, the taxpayer should reduce the loss carry-over claim by that amount.

In the preceding example, the remaining net capital losses can be carried forward indefinitely, but the non-capital losses remaining can be carried forward for 19 more years. A taxpayer who had income and taxes in the years before 20X0 could carry back the losses to those years and receive a tax refund.

The timing of the loss carry-overs is up to the taxpayer. Obviously, the faster they are utilized, the faster any after-tax cash flow will be increased. However, consideration must also be given to the rates of tax applicable in particular years. For example, in the above situation, the 20X1 income was relatively low ($21,000) and would have been subject to the lowest tax rate for individuals. Taxpayers who anticipate that their 20X2 income will be much higher and therefore subject to the higher rate of tax, may prefer to delay utilizing the non-capital loss until 20X2. However, the reduced 20X1 cash flow and the degree of certainty regarding the 20X2 income must also be considered. Also, taxpayers must remember that there is a limited time period available for using the loss carry-over.

A second alternative is available in the above example. The taxpayer could have chosen to claim the maximum non-capital loss of $21,000 to reduce the net income to zero, thereby leaving the entire net capital loss for future years. This may be prudent if there is a possibility that the non-capital loss will expire before it can be used. The net capital loss can then be carried forward indefinitely, awaiting a taxable capital gain.

It should be pointed out that the losses incurred in a given year *must* be used to the extent possible in that year when determining net income for tax purposes. Only the unused loss carry-over can be utilized in other years at the taxpayer's discretion.

III. Loss Utilization—Impact on Decision Making

The previous chapters have regularly demonstrated the extent to which increased returns on investments are created by delaying recognition of income for tax purposes. The reverse is true when it comes to recognizing losses: the sooner losses are utilized, the sooner cash flow will be increased as a result of reduced taxes. However, losses have this added dimension: the taxpayer must utilize them against sources of income within a specified time period. Consider the timing of the following incomes and losses of a business venture:

Year 1	$ 50,000 profit
2	100,000 profit
3	–0–
4	–0–
5	–0–
6	(150,000) loss (business operations cease)

In the above situation, the business earned total profits of $150,000 in years 1 and 2, broke even for the next three years, and then lost $150,000 in year 6 before ceasing operations. Over the six-year period the business has zero income ($150,000 of profits minus $150,000 of losses). However, it is subject to tax on $150,000 because the loss in year 6 can be carried back only three years and therefore is not available for offset against the profits of the first two years. If the taxpayer was in a 40% tax bracket in the first two years, the after-tax cost of breaking even on the venture is $60,000 ($150,000 profits – $150,000 loss – $60,000 tax). While the loss of $150,000 in year 6 can be carried forward for 20 years and used against other sources of income if they should arise, the time differential between the payment of tax in years 1 and 2 and the tax recovery from the loss is considerable.

Similarly, a taxpayer who realizes a capital gain of $200,000 in year 1, then suffers a capital loss of $200,000 in year 5, and has no further capital transactions will not be able to utilize the loss, as it can be carried back only three years.

Obviously, when investing in an active business or making a passive investment, the taxpayer must consider the method in which potential losses can be utilized, in order to assess the overall after-tax risk if the investment should result in a loss.

A. Forms of Business Organization

The organizational structure chosen to carry on an active business has an influence on loss utilization. Exhibit 10-2 outlines two basic structures that are being contemplated to conduct a business venture.

Under structure A, the individual carries on the business as a proprietorship. A proprietorship is not a taxable entity; instead, any profits it realizes or losses it incurs belong directly to the individual proprietor and are merged by the aggregating formula with all other sources of income generated by the taxpayer. This means that if losses occur in the proprietorship, they can be offset against the owner's other income sources in the year of loss or carried over to other years, also against all other sources of income.

Exhibit 10-2:

Two Basic Business Structures

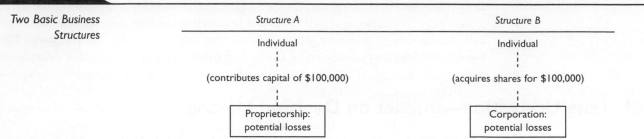

Under structure B, the business is operated as a corporation. For tax purposes, the individual and the corporation are two separate taxable entities. The individual's only tie with the corporation is the investment in share capital of $100,000, which may or may not generate dividend income. If the business suffers losses, the share value will decline, but such a loss can be recognized only by the shareholder when the shares are sold or if the corporation becomes legally bankrupt or is insolvent. The business losses of the corporation are separate from the shareholder and can be offset only against the corporation's own income. Therefore, a business loss in the corporation must be carried over to the years in which that corporation generates income. This is true, even though the individual shareholder may have substantial other sources of income.

In the above example, choosing the corporate structure diminishes the taxpayer's opportunity to use the losses as quickly as possible and, in so doing, reduces the annual cash flow and after-tax return on investment.

Consideration should also be given to the possibility of a complete business failure and the cessation of operations. Under structure B, the losses incurred from operations and the disposal of assets would remain in the corporation and would not be available for use by the shareholder. Thus, there is an increased risk that losses may expire owing to the restricted carry-over period. Indirectly, the individual shareholder would recognize the business losses when the shares were disposed of at a loss. However, this loss would be a capital loss, of which only one-half would be available for use against other capital gains. If the share loss qualified as an allowable business investment loss, one-half of the loss would be available for carry-over against other sources of income.

Exhibit 10-2 demonstrated the situation of a single individual considering an organization structure for a business activity. Although choosing a corporate structure increases the risk that any losses will be unusable, the individual who controls the company can at least take whatever steps are at his or her disposal to utilize the losses as quickly as possible and before they expire. This flexibility is reduced when an investment is made jointly with other parties.

An individual who is contemplating investing in a venture with other parties must weigh the risks of a partnership structure of several partners against those of a corporate structure of several shareholders. The partnership structure, like the proprietorship, is not a taxable entity, and therefore losses are allocated directly to the individual partners. Such business losses can be immediately offset against the individual's other sources of income or carried over to other years against all other income sources. On the other hand, if a corporate structure with several shareholders is used, the corporation's losses are locked into the corporation, and the individual shareholder's ability to utilize those losses is diminished. The risk of using a corporate structure is increased further when the shareholder making the investment does not control the actions of the corporation and is unable to take the necessary steps to utilize corporate losses. In addition, there is less flexibility in triggering a capital loss on the shares if the corporation is in serious financial difficulty. A detailed comparison of the partnership and corporate structures is made in Chapter 15.

In summary, when an individual chooses a corporate structure over a proprietorship or partnership, the risk of not being able to use a loss for tax purposes is increased. Creating two taxable entities, rather than one, effectively doubles the restrictions that apply to loss carry-overs. There may be other reasons for choosing a corporate structure. For example, when there is a risk of losses, the limited-liability features of a corporation may be more important than any loss utilization features. As well, the corporate structure is often chosen to take advantage of special tax rates on business income, without regard to the treatment of losses, should those occur (see Chapter 11). It should be pointed out that business structures are not permanent and that a proprietorship or partnership can later be converted into a corporation after losses have been incurred and the operations become profitable.

B. Preserving Tax Losses

The restrictions placed on the use of loss carry-overs may be onerous. The risk of loss expiration can be minimized by making decisions that create taxable income or reduce deductible expenses, thereby permitting a greater amount of the loss carry-over to be used. While this statement sounds trite, it does not mean that an individual should stimulate new income by entering new ventures or cut actual expenses that are necessary to earn income. Rather, it means that actual expenses should be deferred for tax purposes, when possible, and that accrued gains should be realized sooner than later.

• **Reducing expenses**   There are a number of expenses which can be claimed at a time that is at the discretion of the taxpayer. If the expenses are not claimed in a particular year, they can be deducted in a subsequent year. For example, a taxpayer can choose not to claim the full amount of capital cost allowance in a year, thereby increasing the amount of taxable income available to be offset against a loss carry-over that may expire. Or a business may choose not to claim capital cost allowance when it is regularly incurring losses; this would diminish the loss that is subject to the time restriction. By not claiming capital cost allowance, the undepreciated capital cost of the asset's class would remain at a higher amount; the capital cost allowance deduction would thus be preserved for future years.

Similarly, it is not necessary to claim a reserve for accounts receivable that may be uncollectible. If the receivables still remain doubtful in future years, they can be deducted at that time, after the loss carry-overs have been utilized.

• **Creating income**   There are a number of ways that taxable income can be created at the individual's discretion. Often, an individual owns business assets, investments, or personal-use assets that have appreciated in value. These gains can be realized for tax purposes by triggering a disposition. An individual who does not wish to actually dispose of a property can sell it to a spouse or to a corporation owned by the individual; in doing so, that individual retains the ownership in another form. The sale of such property can create capital gains and/or recapture of capital cost allowance, which can be used to offset the losses carried over. Because the property has been sold and reacquired, its cost base for tax purposes is increased by the gain. Effectively, this activity transfers the loss carry-over to the cost of the asset(s), preserving it for a deduction when the property is ultimately sold to a third party.

Similarly, a financially troubled business may want to dispose of appreciating assets but still retain their use through a sale-and-lease-back arrangement. This process creates much-needed cash and uses up losses before they expire and still keeps the assets(s) available for use.

**C. Future
Investment
Strategies**

The existence of loss carry-overs, especially of capital losses that can be offset only against future capital gains, can change investment strategies with respect to the redeployment of capital investments. In an example in Chapter 8 on capital gains, where the taxpayer was contemplating selling investment A and replacing it with investment B, the proceeds on the sale of investment A were reduced from $100,000 to $79,750 as a result of the tax on the capital gain realized. This meant that only $79,750 was available for investment B. It was indicated that in order to justify the disposal of a $100,000 investment in property A, property B would have to be significantly more attractive than property A in terms of future potential.

The availability of a capital loss carry-over would completely change the return-on-investment requirements in the above example. The disposal of property A would generate $100,000 of cash for investment in property B because there would be no tax on the sale. Therefore, this transaction could be justified if the potential return on property B were only marginally better than on property A.

Clearly, it is important to re-examine strategies relating to investment and business-asset replacement decisions when loss carry-overs are available.

IV. The Capital Gain Deduction

The final step in arriving at the taxable income of an individual is to apply the capital gain deduction. The deduction applies *only* to gains realized on three specific types of property—qualified small business corporation shares, qualified farm property, and qualified property used in a family fishing business. All individuals who are resident in Canada are permitted to reduce their taxable income by the net capital gains realized on these properties over their lifetime to a maximum of $750,000. As only one-half of capital gains are included for tax purposes, the maximum deduction is $375,000 of net taxable capital gains.[8]

A qualified small business corporation must be a small business corporation at the time the shares are sold. That means it is a Canadian-controlled private corporation that uses all or substantially all of its assets to conduct an active business in Canada (Chapter 8). There are two further requirements to be met. The shares must not have been owned by another non-related person in the past 24 months, and during that same period, more than 50% of the fair market value of the assets of the corporation must have been used in an active business.[9] Qualified farm and fishing property include real property, eligible capital property (such as quotas) used in the business of farming and fishing, a share of a family farm or fishing corporation, and an interest in a farm or fishing partnership.

The deduction is discretionary, and in some circumstances, it may be desirable to forgo its use until a later year. For example, some individuals may not want to claim the deduction in a year of low income if they are reasonably certain that further capital gains on the specified properties will be realized in future years, when their tax rate will be substantially higher.

The ability to claim the capital gain deduction is limited by two items—capital losses incurred (including allowable business investment losses), and accumulated investment losses, which are referred to as the cumulative net investment loss.[10] Each item is reviewed briefly below.

To demonstrate the first item, consider this situation. Assume that an individual has, in the current year, a taxable capital gain of $40,000 from the sale of qualified small business corporation shares, allowable capital losses of $10,000, and an allowable business investment loss of $4,000. In addition, she has unused net capital losses

---

8 ITA 110.6(4). $750,000 applies to transactions after March 19, 2007; previous limit was $500,000.
9 ITA 110.6(1).
10 ITA 110.6(1).

of $12,000 carried over from a previous year. Assuming that she has a capital gain deduction available (i.e., that has not been previously used), the maximum deduction she can claim in this particular year is $14,000, as follows:

Net income:	
Taxable capital gain	$40,000
Allowable capital losses	(10,000)
Net gain for the year	30,000
Allowable business investment loss	(4,000)
Increase to net income	26,000
Taxable income:	
Net capital losses of other years	(12,000)
Available for capital gain deduction	$14,000

If, in the above example, the taxpayer had chosen not to claim the $12,000 loss carry-over, the available capital gain deduction would have been $26,000. The purpose of this calculation is clear: It is to provide a deduction only to the extent that lifetime capital gains exceed capital losses. However, timing is an important factor. For example, if an individual with no previous capital losses (since 1984, when the capital gain deduction began) achieves a qualified capital gain of $750,000 ($375,000 taxable), a full capital gain deduction is available. If in a subsequent year a capital loss occurs, it will not affect the original deduction.

The second limiting item, the cumulative net investment loss (CNIL), is more difficult to understand. It is based on the premise that an investment in capital property normally results in two types of returns—the annual net income (loss) from rents, dividends, or interest (property income), *and* the change in the value of the investment itself (capital gain or loss). Consider the following extreme example:

An individual invests $20,000 in qualified small business corporation shares. After one year, interest expense of $5,000 is incurred on a loan used to buy the shares. The property is then sold for $25,000, resulting in a capital gain of $5,000. If the capital gain deduction were permitted for the $5,000 capital gain and the interest expense were deducted against other income, as is permitted, a tax saving would occur, even though no real profit had been achieved. The actual gain from the investment would be as follows:

Capital gain on sale	$5,000
Interest expense	(5,000)
Net gain to investor	–0–

Assuming a 45% tax rate, the investor's tax position would be this:

Tax on capital gain (if deduction is allowed)	–0–
Tax saving from interest expense (45% of $5,000)	2,250
Overall tax reduction	$2,250

Because of this apparent inequity, the CNIL was introduced in 1988. Under its provisions, a capital gain deduction cannot be claimed to the extent that the accumulated annual investment returns (from *all* types of property) from 1988 to the year in question are in a negative position. In other words, if property expenses exceed property incomes on a cumulative basis, the capital gain deduction is reduced by that amount. For example, assume that an individual has a taxable capital gain from qualified small business corporation shares of $20,000 in a particular year. In addition, she has a cumulative net investment loss of $14,000, as follows:

Investment income (interest, rents) from 1988 to the present	$ 39,000
Expenses incurred to earn the above income	(53,000)
Accumulated loss	$ (14,000)

Assuming that a capital gain deduction is available, the maximum deduction that can be claimed in that year is $6,000 ($20,000 – $14,000). It is important to note that the CNIL does not eliminate or reduce an individual's total available capital gain exemption; it simply delays its use until a later year.

An example of the capital gain deduction rules is presented in the following situation and analysis:

Situation: In 20X6, an individual sold all of her shares of ABC Ltd., a Canadian-controlled private corporation, realizing a gain of $280,000. ABC operates a retail business, and all of its assets are used to operate the active business. The individual owned the shares of ABC Ltd. for several years. Also, in 20X6, this individual sold shares of a public corporation— a move that resulted in a loss of $40,000—and had a rental loss of $4,000. In 20X5, the individual had claimed her first capital gain deduction of $135,000. At the end of 20X5, her cumulative net investment loss (CNIL) was $31,000. No net capital losses are being carried forward.

Analysis: The shares of ABC Ltd. are qualified small business corporation (QSBC) shares because, at the time of sale, the corporation is a small business corporation (it is a Canadian-controlled private corporation and all or substantially all of its assets are used to operate an active business, presumably in Canada), the shares were not owned by a non-related person in the 24 months before the sale, and during the same period, more than 50% of the fair market value of the corporation's assets were used in the active business. The unused capital gain deduction at the end of 20X6 is $240,000 (maximum allowable $375,000 – used in prior years $135,000). The accumulated property losses (CNIL) at the end of 20X6 are $35,000 (balance at 20X5 $31,000 + current-year loss of $4,000). The capital gain deduction for 20X6 is $85,000, calculated as follows:

Taxable capital gain—ABC Ltd.—$280,000 × ½	$140,000
Allowable capital loss—public corporation shares—$40,000 × ½	(20,000)
Net gain qualified for the deduction	$120,000
Deduct the cumulative net investment loss (CNIL) at the end of 20X6	(35,000)
Capital gain deduction for 20X6	$ 85,000

The unused capital gain deduction at the end of 20X6 is $155,000 ($240,000 – $85,000). Note that the qualified deduction in 20X6 of $140,000 was reduced by the allowable capital loss on the public corporation shares. If the individual had additional taxable capital gains in the year from other sources, the allowable capital loss would first reduce those gains before reducing the qualified gain from the qualified small business corporation shares.

The capital gain deduction of $85,000 above has been calculated using a conceptual approach. The actual calculation is more complex. For information purposes a more detailed calculation is presented below in a summarized format.

Unused capital gains deduction:	
Lifetime limit ($750,000 × 1/2)	$375,000
Claimed previously	(135,000)
Available for the current year	$240,000
Annual gains limit:	
Lesser of:	
(i) Net taxable capital gains (QSBC $120,000 + Other $0)	
$120,000	
(ii) Net taxable capital gain (QSBC) $120,000	$120,000
Deduct net capital losses (in excess of other net gains)	(0)
Deduct allowable business investment losses (ABIL)	(0)
	$120,000
Cumulative gains limit:	
Qualifying taxable capital gains (1985–2012)($135,000 + $120,000)	$255,000
Net capital losses in excess of other net gains (1985–2012)	(0)
ABILs deducted (1985–2012)	(0)
Capital gains deductions claimed (1985–2012)	(135,000)
CNIL at end of current year (2012)	(35,000)
Deduction for current year	$ 85,000

The capital gain deduction must be built into the overall decision process described in Chapter 8. The deduction was originally introduced to the tax system as a means to stimulate investment in capital property. Whether this objective was achieved is questionable. Most investors realize that the decision to invest carries an inherent risk and that diminished risk stimulates greater investment. From a tax perspective, the risk in capital investments is reduced if potential losses can easily be utilized to gain a tax recovery. The restrictions on the use of capital losses serve to increase the risk inherent in capital investments, whereas the capital gain deduction may have little, if any, impact. The capital gain deduction, like other preferences given to capital gains, is a continuing source of contention. The chances of its being removed are therefore high, and this should be considered with all the other factors when investment decisions are being made.

V. Calculation of Tax for Individuals

Income tax is imposed by the federal government and all 10 provinces.[11] Federal tax is expressed in terms of a tax rate applied to the individual's taxable income. In all provinces and territories, taxes for individuals are expressed as a *percentage of the taxpayer's taxable income*. Non-residents do not pay provincial tax but instead pay an additional tax (48%) that is a percentage of the federal basic tax.[12]

The rates of federal tax are reasonably stable. Provincial tax rates vary considerably from province to province and are subject to regular changes based on provincial budget demands. The federal and provincial governments attempt to implement certain social and economic policies by reducing the tax otherwise payable for certain individuals or types of transactions. These reductions are provided in the form of tax credits. There are many federal and provincial tax credits, which are subject to frequent changes in amount.

---

11 ITA 117(2).
12 ITA 120(1).

While the existence of numerous tax credits increases the complexity of the overall tax calculation, this is seldom relevant to the decision-making process for business and investment activities. From a business and investment perspective, decision makers want to know when and how much additional tax (federal and provincial) they will have to pay from potential income on contemplated transactions. Conversely, they wish to know when and how much tax they may save if they incur certain expenses or if proposed activities result in a loss instead of a profit. Therefore, what is relevant is the marginal tax rate that will apply to each additional dollar earned or lost in new activities.

This part of the chapter attempts to develop the relevant marginal rates of tax that apply to decision making. It is recognized that these particular rates may change from time to time as federal and provincial policies evolve. Even so, while the specific rates developed in the following examples may not be current, the process for determining them does not change. *It is important that the reader update the specific rates at the time they are needed for a particular decision.* Keep in mind that the rates in effect at the time the decision is being made may have changed by the time the income or loss from the transaction is realized. In an attempt to project rates of tax in the future, consideration must also be given to the government's fiscal position at the time.

While this chapter does describe the overall tax calculation for individuals, it should be recognized that this is done for the purpose of showing the overall process, rather than to provide a detailed tax calculation guide. Such information can be obtained from a number of other sources, including the personal tax return guide and forms.

A. Overall Tax Calculation

The overall calculation for determining federal and provincial tax for an individual is outlined in Exhibit 10-3.

Note that the federal tax is reduced by tax credits, which have been divided into two categories. Each of these categories will be discussed later. The first category of tax credits reduces the primary federal tax to an amount referred to as the "basic federal tax."

Each segment of the overall tax calculation outlined in Exhibit 10-3 is then examined. An accompanying sample tax calculation is also provided.

Exhibit 10-3:

Determination of Tax for an Individual

(a) Federal tax:			
Federal tax (rate × taxable income)			xx
Personal tax credits			(x)
Basic federal tax			xx
Other tax credits			(x)
Total federal tax			xx
(b) Provincial tax:			
Primary provincial tax*			
(graduated rates × taxable income)		xx	
Provincial surtax (some provinces)		x	
Specific provincial tax credits		(x)	xx
(c) Combined federal and provincial taxes			xx

* Non-residents do not pay provincial tax. Instead, non-residents pay an additional tax of 48% of the *basic federal tax*.

B. Federal Tax

The federal tax is determined by applying progressively higher tax rates to higher levels of annual income.[13] Exhibit 10-4 outlines the rates of tax applicable to each range of taxable income.

---

13 ITA 117(2), 117.1(1)(d).

Exhibit 10-4:		
Federal Tax Rates	*Taxable income range 2012**	*Rate*
	Up to $42,707	15%
	$42,708–$85,414	22%
	$85,415–$132,406	26%
	Over $132,406	29%

* The taxable income range is adjusted regularly by a cost-of-living factor.

Each rate of tax is applied separately to the portion of the individual's income that falls within the applicable range. For example, an individual who has taxable income of $90,000 would calculate primary federal tax as follows:

On the first $42,707 of income:	
15% × $42,707	$ 6,406
On income between $42,707 and $85,414:	
22% × $42,707	9,396
On income between $85,414 and $90,000:	
26% × $4,586	1,192
Total primary federal tax	$16,994

The overall effective rate of tax for this individual is 19% ($16,994/$90,000); however, each additional dollar earned by the taxpayer over $90,000 is subject to tax at the marginal rate of 26% until $132,406 of income is reached and then 29% on income over $132,406. It is these rates, combined with provincial taxes, that are most relevant to the decision-making process.

C. Personal Federal Tax Credits

Before reviewing the tax credits that fall within this category, it is worthwhile to explain the difference between a tax credit and a tax deduction.

A tax credit is a specific reduction of the tax otherwise payable and has a value equal to its stated amount. For example, a tax credit of $150 reduces the tax otherwise payable by $150, whatever the individual's tax bracket.

A tax deduction, on the other hand, reduces taxable income; the related amount of tax saving is based on the marginal tax bracket of the individual for that particular year. Thus, a tax deduction of $150 would reduce federal taxes by $44 for taxpayers in the 29% tax bracket, and by $23 for taxpayers in the 15% tax bracket. Tax credits benefit all individuals equally, whereas tax deductions provide a greater benefit to those in higher tax brackets.

The various tax credits outlined below must be claimed in a particular order, as it effects the ability to claim or transfer subsequent credits. While the dividend tax credit is the first credit reviewed below, *it is not the first credit required to be claimed*. The required ordering of the tax credits is shown in Exhibit 10-5 on page 385.

The personal tax credits available to individuals are described below. The amounts relate to the 2012 taxation year and are subject to change periodically. These credits *reduce the basic federal tax*. The credits are normally established as 15% (the lowest federal tax bracket rate) multiplied by a designated amount.

Basic All individuals receive a basic credit of $1,623, which is equivalent to $10,822 of taxable income (15% × $10,822).[14] This means that income below $10,822 is not subject to federal tax.

---

14 ITA 118(1)(c).

Spouse or equivalent to spouse Individuals supporting a spouse (including a common-law spouse) receive an additional credit of $1,623, which is equivalent to taxable income of $10,822 (15% × $10,822).[15] The credit is reduced by 15% of the spouse's *net income*. If, for example, a supported spouse has net income of $2,000, the credit to the supporting spouse is $1,323 (15% × [$10,822 − $2,000]). The spouse credit is not available when support payments are being made to a spouse who is separated and living apart.

In some cases, an individual is unmarried but supports another person who lives with him or her, such as a child or other relative. A credit, sometimes referred to as the "equivalent to spouse" credit, is available and is exactly the same as the spouse credit described earlier. This normally applies to a dependent child who is under the age of 18 at any time in the year or who is over the age of 18 and dependent by reason of physical or mental infirmity. The dependant could also be a parent or grandparent (regardless of age) or another related individual (subject to the same age restrictions as children). This credit is not available for a person making support payments as a consequence of marriage breakdown.[16]

Child A credit of $329 (15% × $2,191) for each child under age 18 at the end of the year can be claimed by either parent when the child resides with the parents throughout the year. Any unused credit can be transferred to the other parent. Where a child does not reside with both parents, the credit can be claimed by the parent eligible to use the wholly dependant person credit (equivalent to spouse credit above).[17]

Infirm dependants A credit of $960, which is equivalent to $6,402 of taxable income (15% × $6,402), is available for supporting a related person who is at least 18 years of age and is dependent by reason of physical or mental infirmity.[18] The credit is reduced by 15% of the dependant's net income in excess of $6,420. It is not necessary that the dependant be living with the supporting individual. However, dependants, other than children, must be resident in Canada.

Caregiver Individuals who provide in-home care for a parent or grandparent who is 65 years of age or over *or* for a dependent relative who is infirm are entitled to a $660 tax credit against federal tax (15% × $4,402). The credit is reduced by 15% of the dependant's net income in excess of $15,033. The credit is completely eliminated when the dependant's income exceeds $19,435.[19]

Family Caregiver The amounts on which the credits for family members are based are increased by $2,000 where the dependant is infirm.[20] The $2,000 is added to each of the following amounts:

- Spouse or equivalent spouse amount ($10,822 increased to $12,822).
- Child under 18 amount ($2,191 increased to $4,191).
- Caregiver amount ($4,402 increased to $6,402).

The tax credit is 15% of the increased amounts.

Age amount Individuals who are 65 years of age or older can claim an additional credit of $1,008, which is equivalent to taxable income of $6,720 (15% × $6,720).[21] The limit of $6,720 is reduced by 15% of the taxpayer's net income in excess of $33,884. The 15% credit is then applied to this reduced amount. This reduction is more complicated than the others because of the added 15% feature. For example, a taxpayer with net income of $40,000 is entitled to a credit of $870 (15% × ($6,720 − 15% [$40,000 −

---

15 ITA 118(1)(a), (b).
16 ITA 118(5).
17 ITA 118(1)(b.1).
18 ITA 118(1)(d), (e).
19 ITA 118(1)(c.1).
20 ITA 118(1)(a), (b), (b.1), (c.1).
21 ITA 118(2).

$33,884])). The credit is completely eliminated when net income reaches $78,684. If the age credit is unused it can be transferred to a spouse.

Pension   Individuals can claim a credit of 15% of the first $2,000 of qualified pension income received in a year.[22] If the taxpayer is 65 years of age or older, the credit applies to a wide range of retirement income, including annuity payments from a superannuation or pension fund, RRSP, RRIF, or DPSP. When the annuitant is under 65 years of age, annuities from an RRSP, RRIF, or DPSP do not qualify for the credit unless received because of the death of a spouse. Canada Pension Plan and Old Age Security payments do not qualify at any time. Couples who elect to split pension income can double-up on the credit. If the pension credit cannot be used due to insufficient income, all, or a portion, can be transferred to a spouse.

Employment credit   Individuals who are employed can claim a credit of 15% of $1,095 ($165) in 2012. This credit is designed to recognize certain expenses incurred by employees.[23]

Adoption expenses   A credit of 15% for eligible adoption expenses on completed adoption of an eligible child, up to a maximum of $11,440.[24]

Public transit pass   A credit of 15% of the cost of monthly public transit passes for unlimited travel on local buses, streetcars, subways, commuter trains or buses, and local ferries. The credit is available for transit passes for the taxpayer, a spouse and children under age 19 at the end of the year.[25]

Children's fitness credit   The credit is a maximum of $75 (15% of the fees paid in 2012 (maximum $500)) that relate to the cost of registering a child, under age 16 at the beginning of the year, in a program of physical activity. This includes hockey, baseball, dance, and so on.[26]

Children's arts tax credit   Similar to the children's fitness credit (above), the arts credit is a maximum of $75 (15% of the fees paid in 2012 (maximum $500)) that relate to the cost of registering a child, under the age of 16 at the beginning of the year, in an eligible program of artistic, cultural, recreational or development activities.[27]

First-time home buyer's credit   Individuals who acquire a qualifying home for the first time can claim a credit of 15% on up to $5,000 for a maximum credit of $750.[28] To claim the credit the individual and his or her spouse cannot have owned a home in the past four years. Most types of housing located in Canada qualify for the credit (existing and newly constructed) including mobile homes and a share in a housing cooperative.

Volunteer Firefighters   Volunteer firefighters who perform a minimum of 200 hours of volunteer hours of firefighting services to a fire department can claim a tax credit of $450 (15% of $3,000).[29] The taxpayer must obtain written certification from the fire chief, or designate, indicating the hours performed for eligible duties.

Charitable donations   Gifts to charities receive a credit of 15% on the first $200 of contributions and 29% on the remainder.[30] Annual donations cannot exceed 75% of the individual's net income for the year.[31] Donations in excess of the limit can be carried forward for five of the subsequent taxation years. Qualified donations include gifts to registered charities, to Canadian amateur athletic organizations, to Canadian

---

22 ITA 118(3).
23 ITA 118(10).
24 ITA 118.01.
25 ITA 118.02.
26 ITA 118.03.
27 ITA 118.031.
28 ITA 118.05.
29 ITA 118.06
30 ITA 118.1(3).
31 This limit is increased to 100% for the year of death and the preceding year.

universities (and certain foreign universities), to the United Nations, and to Canada and the provinces. Special rules may apply for gifts of property, gifts of cultural property, and gifts of ecologically sensitive land.

Medical expenses   The tax credit for medical expenses is 15% of the qualified medical expenses that exceed either 3% of the taxpayer's net income for the year, or $2,109, whichever is less.[32] For example, if a taxpayer has net income for tax purposes of $40,000, the 15% credit can be applied only on medical expenses above $1,200 (3% × $40,000). The $2,109 threshold occurs at net income of $70,300 (3% × $70,300). Taxpayers with net income above $70,300 can deduct all medical expenses above $2,109. The credit is available for medical expenses paid on behalf of the taxpayer, a spouse, or children under 18 at the end of the year. The tax credit for medical expenses paid for *other dependants* (example—children over 18) is 15% of the qualified medical expenses that exceed either 3% of the *dependant's* net income for the year, or $2,109, whichever is less. Medical expenses qualifying for the credit include amounts paid in *any 12-month period ending in the year.*[33]

Disability   An individual with a severe and prolonged mental or physical impairment can claim an additional credit of $1,132, which is equivalent to taxable income of $7,546 (15% × $7,546 = $1,132).[34] To the extent that the credit exceeds the tax payable of the disabled person, the unused amount can be transferred to a spouse, parent, or grandparent. An additional credit of $660 (15% × $4,402) is available for a person under the age of 18.

Education amount, tuition fees, and textbook amount   Individuals who attend a university, college, or other certified post-secondary institution can claim a credit of 15% of tuition fees paid.[35] Tuition fees include examination fees paid to obtain a professional status or be licensed to practise a profession or trade in Canada. In addition, when the student is in full-time attendance at the qualified institution, an additional credit is available equal to 15% of $465 ($400 for attendance and $65 for textbooks) for each month of full-time attendance.[36] This amounts to $70 per month (15% × $465). Also, a *part-time* education credit of 15% × $140 ($120 for attendance and $20 for textbooks) ($21) is available for each month of attendance. To qualify, the student has to be enrolled at an educational institution in Canada, in an eligible program involving a minimum of 12 hours of courses each month.[37]

The student may not have sufficient income to utilize the above credits. In this situation, the unused portion is transferable (within limits) to a spouse, parent, or grandparent. Alternatively, the student may keep the unused credit and carry it forward indefinitely until such time as he or she has sufficient income to use the credit.[38] The maximum credit that may be transferred to a spouse or parent is $750 annually (15% × $5,000) *less* any credit used to reduce the student's tax to zero. The unused credit is determined after deducting the carry-forward amount, plus personal tax credits, such as basic, employment, public transit pass, disability, and CPP/EI.[39]

A student has taxable income of $12,000, and CPP/EI contributions of $300, and has paid tuition fees of $6,000 to attend university for eight months. The unused tuition and education credit for the year is $1,326, as calculated below.

---

32 ITA 118.2(1).
33 The period is extended to 24 months in a year that includes the date of death.
34 ITA 118.3(1).
35 ITA 118.5; IT-516R2.
36 ITA 118.6(2).
37 ITA 118.6(2), (2.1).
38 ITA 118.9.
39 ITA 188.9 and 118.61.

Federal tax—15% × $12,000	$1,800
Basic credit	(1,623)
CPP/EI credit—15% × $300	(45)
Federal tax before education and tuition credit	132
Tuition credit—15% × $6,000	(900)
Education and textbooks credit—15% × $465 × 8 months	(558)
Unused credit	$(1,326)

The student can carry forward the $1,326 unused credit for use in the future or transfer to a supporting spouse, parent, or grandparent any amount up to $618, being the $750 maximum amount transferable reduced by the $132 required by the student to reduce his or her federal tax to nil.

Interest on student loans An individual is entitled to deduct 15% of the interest portion of *student loan payments*.[40] The credit applies to interest payments (not principal payments) on outstanding loans under the Canada Student Loan Program and provincial student loan programs. The credit may be claimed in the year it is earned (the year of interest payment) *or* in any of the following five years. The optional five-year carry-over provides a greater opportunity to use the full credit to reduce tax.

CPP and EI Individuals are required to make contributions to the Canada Pension Plan and the Employment Insurance plan. Taxpayers can claim a tax credit of 15% of their maximum allowable CPP and EI contributions in any year.[41]

D. Dividend Tax Credit

From a decision-making perspective, the most important tax credit is the *dividend tax credit*.[42] There are two dividend tax credit calculations. Determining which one to use depends on the type of dividend received by an individual. Dividends designated as *eligible* receive a dividend tax credit of 6/11 of the 38% gross-up, which is 15% (*actually 15.019%*) *of the taxable amount* (138% of the cash dividend—see Chapter 7). Eligible dividends refer to the following:

- Taxable dividends from Canadian public corporations.
- Taxable dividends from Canadian private corporations that are *not* Canadian controlled (see Chapter 13).
- Taxable dividends from Canadian-controlled private corporations whose income source is either business income taxed at the high corporate tax rate (no small business deduction) *or* dividends received by the corporation from another corporation that have been designated as eligible dividends (see Chapter 13).

Non-eligible dividends receive a dividend tax credit of 2/3 of the 25% gross-up, which is 13 1/3% of the taxable amount. The taxable amount of a *non-eligible* dividend is 125% of the actual dividend received (see Chapter 7). Non-eligible dividends refer to the following:

- Taxable dividends from Canadian-controlled private corporations whose income source is active business income taxed at the lower corporate tax rate (small business deduction).
- Taxable dividends from Canadian-controlled private corporations whose source is investment income (rents, interest, taxable capital gains) *or* non-eligible dividends received by the corporation from another corporation.

---

40 ITA 118.62
41 ITA 118.7.
42 ITA 121.

Having two categories of dividends with separate tax credits that apply to amounts greater than amounts actually received creates complexity to the taxation of corporate dividends. However, as explained in Chapter 7, these calculations are part of a scheme to diminish the impact of double taxation when after-tax corporate income is distributed as dividends.

The receipt of a $1,000 cash dividend reduces federal taxes by a tax credit amount of either $207 or $167, as shown below.

	Eligible	Non-eligible
Cash dividend received	$1,000	$1,000
Dividend included in taxable income and subject to primary federal tax: $1,000 × 1.38 or 1.25	$1,380	$1,250
Dividend tax credit:		
15% of $1,380 or 6/11 of the $380 gross-up	$207	
13⅓% × $1,250 or ⅔ of the $250 gross-up		$167

The tax credit of $207 or $167 is received whatever the individual's tax bracket; in other words, a taxpayer in the 15% bracket will receive the same $207 or $167 credit as a taxpayer in the 26% or 29% bracket.

E. Other Federal Tax Credits

The most important tax credit in this group of federal tax credits is the *foreign tax credit*. Individuals who earn income in a foreign country may be subject to tax on that income both in the foreign country and in Canada. To avoid the full impact of double taxation, Canadian taxpayers can reduce their Canadian taxes through the foreign tax credit.[43] Separate credits are provided for foreign investment income and foreign business income. In both cases, the foreign tax credit is based on the amount of foreign tax paid on income that is also taxable in Canada; this amount, however, cannot exceed the equivalent amount of Canadian tax on that income. The credit for foreign investment income is further limited to 15% of the foreign income earned; however, any unused amount can be used as a deduction from income, rather than a credit.[44] Unused foreign tax credits from foreign business income can be carried back three years and forward 10 years. A more detailed review of business foreign tax credits is made in a later chapter on international business expansion.

Other tax credits in the second category include the following:[45]

- political contributions
- investment tax credits for the purchase of certain equipment in designated regions of Canada
- labour-sponsored fund credit

The tax credit for *federal political contributions* is based on a graduated scale. The annual credit is 75% of the first $400, 50% of the next $350, and 33⅓% of contributions over $750. However, the total annual political contribution credit cannot exceed $650. This figure is reached when contributions total $1,275.

---

43 ITA 126; IT-270R2.
44 ITA 20(11).
45 ITA 127(1) to (26), 127.1 to .4, 127(3).

Exhibit 10-5:

Required Ordering of Tax Credits for Individuals[46]

Basic personal amount	Children's arts credit
Spouse or common-law credit	First-time home buyers' tax credit
Equivalent to spouse credit	Mental or physical impairment credit
Child tax credit	Unused tuition, education & textbook credits
Caregiver credit	Tuition credit
Infirm dependants age 18 and over	Education credit & textbook credit
Age credit	Tuition/Education/Textbook credits transferred
EI and CPP credit	Credits transferred from spouse or
Pension credit	common-law partner
Employment credit	Medical expense credit
Adoption expense credit	Donation credit
Public transit pass credit	Interest on student loans credit
Children's fitness credit	*Dividend tax credit*

The personal and other tax credits mentioned above can be used only to the extent of the taxes otherwise payable by the individual.

F. Provincial Taxes

All of the provinces and territories determine their primary tax by applying specified tax *rates* to the *federal taxable income*. The rates of tax and income brackets to which they apply vary widely from province to province. These provinces also specify their own tax credits similar in nature to the federal non-refundable tax credits described earlier in the chapter. For example, in 2012, British Columbia and Ontario applied the following tax rates to the federal taxable income:

British Columbia

Bracket	Rate
$0 – $37,013	5.06%
$37,014 – $74,028	7.7%
$74,029 – $84,993	10.5%
$84,994 – $103,205	12.29%
Over $103,205	14.7%

Ontario*

Bracket	Rate
$0 – $39,020	5.05%
$39,021 – $78,043	9.15%
$78,403 – $500,000	12.16%
Over $500,000	12.16%[†]

* Plus Ontario surtax of 20% of basic provincial tax in excess of $4,213 plus 36% of basic provincial tax in excess of $5,392.
[†] Beginning July 1, 2012, a surtax of 2% of taxable income over $500,000 will apply. (12.16% is prorated for 2012.)

Note that the above income ranges do not correspond with the federal income ranges for particular tax rates. They are also not the same as those of other provinces. As a further example, some of Ontario's and British Columbia's non-refundable tax credits are as follows:

	British Columbia	**Ontario**
Dividends—Eligible	10% grossed-up dividend	6.4% × grossed-up dividend
Non-eligible	3.4% × grossed-up dividend	4.5% × grossed-up dividend
Basic personal credit	5.06% × $11,354 = $575	5.05% × $9,405 = $475
Charitable donations	5.06% ($200); 14.7% over $200	5.05% ($200); 11.16% over $200

*Information on various provincial tax rates and credits can be obtained by accessing links on this text's Web site at **www.mcgrawhill.ca/olc/buckwold**.*

---

46 ITA 118.92.

Individuals are subject to tax in a particular provincial jurisdiction if they resided in that province on the last day of the calendar year—December 31. An exception to this rule requires that an individual who resides in a particular province but carries on business from permanent establishments in other provinces must allocate business income to those provinces.[47] This allocation is based on an arbitrary formula relating to sales and salaries and does not necessarily reflect the actual business profits in a particular province. The allocation procedure is demonstrated in the following situation:

Situation: An individual resides in Manitoba. In 20X0, she earned net income of $140,000 consisting of property income of $40,000 and net income of $100,000 from a business. The head office of the business is in Manitoba, but a branch location is maintained in Ontario that has staff and inventory. An analysis of the business operations provides the following information:

	Manitoba	Ontario	Total
Sales	$600,000 (75%)	$200,000 (25%)	$800,000 (100%)
Salaries	200,000 (80%)	50,000 (20%)	250,000 (100%)
Actual profits	$ 70,000	$ 30,000	$100,000

Analysis: The allocation of the business income to each province is based on the average of sales and salaries in each province, as follows:

Manitoba:		
Sales	75%	
Salaries	80%	
Average	(80% + 75%)/2 =	78%
Ontario		
Sales	25%	
Salaries	20%	
Average	(25% + 20%)/2 =	22%
		100%

Allocation of business income to Ontario is as follows:

22% × $100,000 =	$22,000

All remaining income is allocated to Manitoba.

Note that in the example situation, the amount of income allocated to Ontario was $22,000, even though the actual profits earned in that province were $30,000. The allocation formula, which is tied to sales and wages, arbitrarily shifted Ontario profits to Manitoba, which has a different provincial tax rate. If the mixture of sales and salaries had been different, the opposite might have occurred, resulting in a higher profit allocated to Ontario. It should also be pointed out that this formula applies only because a permanent establishment exists in Ontario. If sales had been made to Ontario directly from Manitoba, no allocation would have been made, and all business activity in Ontario would have been taxed in Manitoba.

---

47 ITA Regulations 2600 to 2607.

G. Sample Calculation of Tax

A sample calculation of taxable income and of the related federal and provincial income tax is performed below. The purpose of the demonstration is to highlight the *form* of the calculation, rather than its technical accuracy. The federal tax brackets, certain tax credits, and the rates of provincial tax may have changed since publication. *A more detailed tax calculation is shown in the demonstration question at the end of this chapter.*

Summary of Facts

An individual who resides in British Columbia has net employment income of $120,000 for a particular year. He maintains a small portfolio of investments that resulted in a taxable capital gain of $5,000 from the sale of qualified small business corporation shares (the lifetime capital gain deduction is available). The investments also generated eligible dividends of $5,000 and non-eligible dividends of $3,000 from Canadian corporations, and interest income of $2,000 from the a foreign country. From the $2,000 of foreign interest income, he paid $200 (10% of $2,000) on account of foreign taxes. During the year, this taxpayer made payments of $3,000 to charitable organizations. He is single. *This example will use **2012** as the demonstration year.*

Calculation of Tax

Before calculating tax for the year, one must determine the taxable income.

Net income:		
(a) Employment		$ 120,000
Property:		
Dividends—Eligible—($5,000 × 1.38)	$6,900	
Dividends—Non-eligible—($3,000 × 1.25)	3,750	
Foreign interest	2,000	12,650
		132,650
(b) Net taxable capital gains		5,000
Net income for tax purposes		$137,650
Special reductions:		
Capital gain deduction		(5,000)
Taxable income		$132,650

gross up

Tax can then be calculated on the basis of taxable income of $132,650, as shown on the next page.

H. Tax Calculation— Impact on Decision Making

As was mentioned at the beginning of this section, the impact of the tax calculation on investment and business decisions centres on how the marginal tax rates will be applied to cash flows generated from proposed financial activities. For every proposed transaction, it is necessary to project the following:

(a) the nature of the expected income or potential loss that may occur;
(b) when the particular income or loss will be recognized for tax purposes;
(c) the tax bracket that the income or loss will fall into, considering expected other sources of income; and
(d) the combined federal and provincial taxes that will apply.

In order to determine the marginal tax rate for each bracket of income, it is necessary to combine the federal and provincial tax calculations. This can be confusing because the tax rates and the income brackets to which those rates apply differ from province to province.

Federal tax:

Primary federal tax (2012)

15% on first	$ 42,707	$ 6,406
22% on next	42,707	9,396
26% on next	46,992	12,218
29% on balance	244	71
	$132,650	$28,091

Personal tax credits:

Individual tax credit (2012 rate)		(1,623)
Employment credit: 15% × $1,095		(165)
Donation tax credit:		
On first $200 of donations		
($200 × 15%)	30	
On donations over $200		
($2,800 × 29%)	812	(842)
Dividend tax credit—Eligible: 15% × $6,900		(1,035)
Dividend tax credit—Non-eligible: 13⅓% × $3,750		(500)
Basic federal tax		$23,926

Other tax credits:

Foreign tax credit	(200)
Total federal tax	$23,726

Provincial tax (British Columbia):

5.06% on first	$ 37,013	$ 1,873
7.70% on next	37,015	2,850
10.5% on next	10,965	1,151
12.29% on next	18,212	2,238
14.7% on balance over $103,205	29,445	4,328
	$132,650	12,440

Tax credits:

Dividend tax credit—Eligible: 10% × $6,900		(690)
Dividend tax credit—Non-eligible: 3.4% × $3,750		(128)
Basic individual credit (2012)		(575)
Donation tax credit:		
On first $200 of donations		
($200 × 5.06%)	10	
On donations over $200		
($2,800 × 14.70%)	412	(422)
Total provincial tax		$10,625
Total federal and provincial tax		$34,351

Handwritten marginalia:

ON
0 - 39,020   5.05
- 78,043   9.15
- 500,000   11.16
>500,000   12.16

Exhibit 10-6 calculates the combined federal and provincial tax rates for an *unspecified* province, using *arbitrary provincial tax rates* of 9%, 10%, 14%, and 16% that correspond to each of the four federal income brackets. The calculations for the actual provinces and territories would be similar, except that the particular provincial rates would have to be substituted.

Exhibit 10-6 indicates that any income on a proposed financial activity in this province would incur a tax cost of either 24%, 32%, 40%, or 45%, depending on the amount of income from other sources that would be earned in the applicable years. Similarly, any loss would generate tax savings of the same magnitudes. ***Most sample calculations throughout the text use tax rates based on Exhibit 10-6 for demonstration purposes.***

Exhibit 10-6:					

		INCOME RANGE (2012)			
Combined Federal and Provincial Marginal Tax Rates		*Up to $42,707*	*$42,708 to $85,414*	*$85,415 to $132,406*	*Over $132,406*
	Primary federal tax rate	15%	22	26	29
	Add provincial tax	9	10	14	16
	Combined tax rate	24%	32%	40%	45%

When applying the marginal rates of tax, remember that the actual amount of income or loss is not always the same as the amount that must be included for tax purposes. For example, an actual capital gain of $100 results in only $50 (½ of $100) of taxable income. In this case, the marginal tax rates that are applicable to an *actual* capital gain are as follows:

First bracket	24% × ½ = 12%
Second bracket	32% × ½ = 16%
Third bracket	40% × ½ = 20%
Fourth bracket	45% × ½ = 23% (rounded)

Similarly, an actual dividend of $100 requires that either $138 or $125 be included in taxable income. In this situation, the calculation of the marginal rate of tax is complicated by the dividend tax credit, which reduces federal tax by the same amount for each tax bracket. Also, most provinces have a separate fixed dividend tax credit. *To demonstrate, we assume provincial dividend tax credit rates of 9% for eligible dividends and 5% for non-eligible dividends for* an *unspecified* province. A cash dividend of $100 (for which either $138 or $125 is included in income) will generate combined federal and provincial dividend tax credits in this province of $34 or $23, calculated as follows:

	Eligible	*Non-eligible*
Actual dividend received	$100	$100
Federal dividend tax credit:		
15% × $138 (Eligible)	$ 21 (rounded)	
13⅓% × $125 (Non-eligible)		$ 17 (rounded)
Provincial dividend tax credit:		
9% × $138 (Eligible)	$ 13 (rounded)	
5% × $125 (Non-eligible)		$ 6 (rounded)
Total tax reduction	$ 34	$ 23

In other words, every $100 of *cash* dividends received will reduce federal and provincial taxes by approximately $34 (Eligible) or $23 (Non-eligible). With this information, the marginal rate of tax on dividends earned in the unspecified province can be calculated as follows:

Eligible Canadian Dividends

Normal combined tax rates	24%	32%	40%	45%
Cash dividend received	$100	$100	$100	$100
Taxable income ($100 × 1.38)	$138	$138	$138	$138
Tax (rate × $138)	$33	$44	$55	$62
Combined dividend tax credit	(34)	(34)	(34)	(34)
Net tax on a $100 dividend	$0	$10	$21	$28
Marginal rate of tax	0%	10%	21%	28%

Non-eligible Canadian Dividends

Normal combined tax rates	24%	32%	40%	45%
Cash dividend received	$100	$100	$100	$100
Taxable income ($100 × 1.25)	$125	$125	$125	$125
Tax (rate × $125)	$30	$40	$50	$56
Combined dividend tax credit	(23)	(23)	(23)	(23)
Net tax on a $100 dividend	$7	$17	$27	$ 33
Marginal rate of tax	7%	17%	27%	33%

In applying the rates of tax to investment and business decisions, it is important to relate the rate of tax to the amount of cash income or loss, rather than to the special amount that is included in income for tax purposes. The preceding calculations are summarized and presented in Exhibit 10-7, which highlights the marginal tax rates of various types of income. Keep in mind that these rates were calculated using provincial tax rates from a *fictitious province*. Note, for example, that for a person in the second bracket, the tax rate on eligible dividends is 6% lower than on capital gains (16% versus 10%). Since an investment in shares of a corporation may provide both dividends and capital growth, a person in this bracket may seek out shares that provide higher dividends and lower capital growth, rather than the reverse. However, capital gains are preferred in third and fourth brackets. On the other hand, when non-eligible dividends are involved, capital gains show preference at the third and fourth brackets. This analysis must be tempered by the fact that dividends are taxed when received, whereas capital gains are taxed only when a disposition occurs and, further, may be exempt under the lifetime capital gain deduction.

Exhibit 10-7:

Marginal Tax Rates by Type of Income (excluding provincial surtaxes)

Income range (2012)	Capital gains	Canadian dividends		Ordinary income
		Eligible	Non-eligible	
Up to $42,707	12%	0%	7%	24%
$42,708 – $85,414	16	10	17	32
$85,415 – $132,406	20	21	27	40
Over $132,406	23	28	33	45

The marginal rates shown in Exhibit 10-7 also permit decision makers to compare the after-tax yields on various types of investments. For example, a person in the highest tax bracket who earns interest income at 10% will receive an after-tax yield of 5.5% (10% − [45% of 10%] = 5.5%). The same after-tax yield can be earned on a share investment yielding eligible dividends of 7.6% (7.6% − [28% of 7.6%] = 5.5%) or on an investment yielding a capital gain of 7.1% (7.1% − [23% of 7.1%] = 5.5%). Although the timing of the related tax for each type of investment may vary, the comparative after-tax yields are relevant when the relative risk is examined for each type of investment.

The marginal tax rates developed in Exhibit 10-7 are fundamental to decision making; but the overall tax calculation should also be examined for unusual aspects that may affect certain business decisions. For example, the arbitrary formula for allocating business income to various provinces has an impact on business expansion decisions. Expansion to other provinces can be carried out by selling directly from the home province or by establishing a more formal structure, such as branch locations in the other provinces. Each of these basic alternatives involves certain costs and benefits from a marketing perspective. As well, each has a different effect on the amount of tax payable. The decision to establish a branch location has a big impact on the amount of provincial tax and so does the location of the branch. The effect of the arbitrary tax formula must be factored into the cost/benefit analysis of the expansion decision if the complete costs of each alternative are to be known (see Chapter 20).

- **Actual marginal tax rates**   As previously indicated, the marginal tax rates developed in Exhibit 10-7 were based on fictitious provincial rates. ***Throughout the text, the marginal rates in Exhibit 10-7 are used for demonstration purposes.*** Exhibit 10-8 shows the *actual* top marginal tax rates for each province and territory. These rates relate to the *2012* taxation year. *It is important that the reader update the rates at the time they are needed for a particular decision.* A complete set of marginal tax rates for all provinces and territories is available by accessing the Web links shown on this text's Web site at **www.mcgrawhill.ca/olc/buckwold**.

Exhibit 10-8:

Actual 2012 Marginal Tax Rates—Top Income Bracket Only	Top Income Bracket	Ordinary Income & Interest	Capital Gains	Canadian Dividends	
				Eligible	Non-eligible
	Alberta	39%	20%	19%	28%
	British Columbia	44%	22%	26%	34%
	Manitoba	46%	23%	32%	39%
	New Brunswick	43%	22%	22%	31%
	Newfoundland and Labrador	42%	21%	22%	30%
	Nova Scotia	50%	25%	36%	36%
	Ontario*	46%	23%	30%	33%
	Prince Edward Island	47%	24%	29%	41%
	Quebec	48%	24%	33%	36%
	Saskatchewan	44%	22%	25%	33%
	NWT	43%	22%	23%	30%
	Nunavut	41%	20%	28%	29%
	Yukon	42%	21%	19%	30%
	Non-resident	43%	21%	29%	29%

Note: All percentages are rounded. The rates assume the provinces and territories will also choose to use a 50% inclusion rate for capital gains. The rates are based on information available in May 2, 2012 and may be altered by provincial budgets occurring after the date of this publication. See **www.mcgrawhill.ca/olc/buckwold** for updated marginal tax rates.
* Excludes 2% surtax on taxable income in excess of $500,000 effective July 1, 2012.

VI. Special Adjustments to the Tax Calculation

In certain circumstances, special rules apply that increase the amount of tax payable beyond the normal amount. To a great extent, these rules are politically motivated and are a response to public and media pressures, which are often based on misconceptions. For example, the media often report how many individual and corporate taxpayers earn high incomes but do not pay income tax. For obvious reasons, such statements upset many taxpayers, most of whom are struggling along under the normal tax burden. The problem is that many of the statistics quoted in the media are misleading. For example, an individual who earns business income of $100,000 in 20X1 but who then reduces that income by applying a large loss carry-over from the previous year may well be reported as having income in 20X1 of $100,000 and no tax payable. Many CRA statistics report net income and the related tax figure, rather than *taxable* income and its related tax.

There are two basic areas where the normal tax calculation may be adjusted to a higher amount. These areas relate to what are sometimes called the "give and take-back rules." One is the alternative minimum tax; the other is the special tax on old-age security benefits. Both are discussed next.

A. The Alternative Minimum Tax

The alternative minimum tax (AMT) rules are designed to impose a minimum level of tax on individuals when the normal amount of tax has been reduced as a result of certain "tax preference" items being included in income.[48] It is important to establish at the outset that this additional tax is not a permanent tax. Any additional minimum tax that is paid in one year can be carried forward for up to seven years to reduce the normal tax of a future year to the extent that the minimum tax rules do not apply. For example, consider the following information:

	20X1 Income reduced by tax preference items	20X2 Normal income (no tax preference)	Total
Taxable income	$20,000	$100,000	$120,000
Normal tax	$ 4,000	$ 40,000	$ 44,000
Tax increase (decrease)			
due to minimum tax	7,000	(7,000)	–0–
Actual taxes paid	$11,000	$ 33,000	$ 44,000

For 20X1, the income was reduced by a number of tax preferences so that the actual tax increased from $4,000 to $11,000. However, there were no tax preference items in the 20X2 income, and so the tax for that year was reduced by the previous year's increase. Consequently, the total tax for the two years was the same ($44,000), but the years in which the tax was paid was adjusted.

When the AMT is calculated, taxable income is revised to exclude certain tax preference items to the extent that they exceed a base amount of $40,000. The entire income is then subject to a federal tax rate of 15%, rather than the graduated rates that normally apply (15%, 22%, 26%, and 29%). The dividend tax credit is also excluded (as a result of the elimination of the gross-up already described). If the revised federal tax is greater than the normal federal tax, the former applies. Provincial taxes are then calculated on the revised amount.

Some of the tax preference items referred to here are now listed. Taxable income is increased by the following:

• 30% of net capital gains earned.

---

48 ITA 127.5 to 127.55.

- Deductions claimed from certain specified tax-shelter investments, including Canadian exploration expenses, Canadian oil and gas property expenses, and capital cost allowance and finance changes on certified Canadian film investments, to the extent that any of these create losses.
- ⅗ of employee stock option deductions.
- Losses allocated from a limited partnership.
- The home relocation loan deduction.
- Investment losses required to be identified under the tax shelter identification rules.

And taxable income is reduced by the following:

- The gross-up on Canadian dividends (see Chapter 7).
- 60% of ABILs deducted.
- A basic exemption of $40,000.

It will be clear from the next sample calculation that the increases to taxable income are offset, to a large degree, by both the $40,000 exemption and the lower tax rate of 15%. Unless a taxpayer has major losses from a tax-shelter investment, the minimum tax will often not apply.

When calculating the minimum tax, the 15% rate is first applied to the adjusted taxable income for purposes of the AMT and then personal non-refundable tax credits are deducted. However, there are several non-refundable tax credits that are excluded from this calculation. These are the pension income credit, any tax credit that has been transferred from a spouse or dependant (example tuition, pension, and disability credits), pension credit, labour sponsored credit, and investment tax credits. In addition, the dividend tax credit and political contribution credits are excluded.

To demonstrate, consider a taxpayer who, in a particular year, received a salary of $140,000, and a capital gain of $400,000 (taxable – $200,000), of which $75,000 was eligible for the capital gain deduction on qualified small business corporation shares. She also received eligible Canadian dividends of $4,000 ($5,520 after the gross-up). This taxpayer is single.

The normal taxable income and the revised (AMT) taxable income are calculated and compared in the first table below. The normal tax payable for the year (assuming provincial taxes of a fictitious province as used in Exhibit 10-6) would be $102,413, calculated as shown in the second table.

The AMT does not apply unless its federal tax calculation is greater than the normal federal tax amount. In this case, the federal tax under the AMT calculation is $52,350 (15% of $349,000 = $52,350, less the personal tax credit of $1,623 = $50,727; note that the dividend tax credit was ignored). The normal federal tax is greater—$65,622. Therefore, in spite of the tax preferences, the AMT has no effect on this taxpayer.

It should be noted that the AMT applies only to individuals.

	Normal taxable income	Taxable income for AMT	Increase (decrease)
Business income	$140,000	$140,000	–0–
Dividends (Eligible)	$ 5,520	4,000	(1,520)
Capital gain	200,000	320,000	120,000
Net income	345,520	464,000	118,480
Capital gain deduction	(75,000)	(75,000)	–0–
AMT exemption	–0–	(40,000)	(40,000)
	$270,520	$349,000	$78,480

Federal tax (2012 rates):		
First	$ 42,707 @ 15%	$ 6,406
Next	$ 42,707 @ 22%	9,396
Next	$ 46,992 @ 26%	12,218
Remaining	$ 138,114 @ 29%	40,053
	$270,520	68,073
Personal credit (2012 rate)		(1,623)
Dividend tax credit [15% (2013) of $5,520]		(828)
Basic federal tax		65,622
Provincial tax		36,791
		$102,413

B. Special Tax on Old Age Security Benefits

The federal government provides monthly Old Age Security payments on a universal basis. These payments are taxable (see Chapter 9).

As a challenge to the concept of universal social services, the income tax system imposes a special tax on individuals who receive Old Age Security benefits and also earn more than $69,562 (in 2012) (indexed) in net income for tax purposes.[49] The special tax is equal to 15% of net income (i.e., not taxable income) in excess of $69,562, up to a maximum of the Old Age Security payments.[50] For example, an individual who earns $90,000 of property income plus $6,000 of Old Age Security (total income—$96,000) pays an additional tax of $3,966 (15% of [$96,000 − $69,562] = $3,966, slightly lower than the maximum of $6,000). The full Old Age Security benefit is eliminated when a pensioner's net income reaches $112,762.

As compensation for the fact that Old Age Security benefits have already been included in the income, the amount of the special tax can be deducted in arriving at net income for the year. Effectively, this removes the regular tax cost on that income in favour of a higher special tax. Because the tax on these benefits can equal 100% of the income, the special tax is referred to as a "clawback"—that is, what is given is fully returned. The only result is higher administration costs for both the government and each taxpayer to whom it applies. A similar clawback tax applies to employment insurance benefits, but with a different threshold amount.

VII. Final Returns of Deceased Taxpayers

It was shown in Chapter 9 (Part VII) that special rules apply to determine net income for tax purposes in the year a person dies. This segment reviews additional unique rules for calculating taxable income and tax for a deceased taxpayer.

A. Taxable Income and Net Capital Losses

Normally, when calculating taxable income, net capital losses are only deductible to the extent of any net taxable capital gains earned in that year. However, in the year of death, net capital losses that are unused can be *deducted from any source of income in the year of death or the previous year*.[51] It should be noted that the amount available for this application is the unused net capital losses at the date of death minus any capital gain deductions claimed in prior years (see Part IV of this chapter).

B. Tax Returns and the Use of Tax Credits

In the year of death, representatives of the deceased taxpayer must file a *final tax return* (see Chapter 3, Part IV) and include all income accrued to the date of death. When calculating federal tax on the final return, all non-refundable tax credits can be

---

49 This amount is indexed and adjusted periodically.
50 ITA 180.2(1) to (3).
51 ITA 111(2).

claimed in full regardless of the date of death. To alleviate the burden of tax in the year of death, the taxpayer's legal representative may file up to three additional optional tax returns depending on the types of income earned. The most important of these is the *Rights and Things* return[52] which is reviewed below.

The term "rights or things" refers to certain types of income that were not paid at the time of death but would otherwise have been included in income if they had been received. Some examples of typical rights and things include employment earnings that were owed at the date of death and relate to a pay period ending before death, uncashed matured bond coupons, unpaid bond interest due before the date of death, and unpaid dividends that were declared before the date of death. Some other unique business and farming items are also included.

Income that qualifies as a right or thing may be included in the final tax return of a deceased taxpayer or optionally included in a separate "rights and things" return. The benefit of using the additional optional return is that the income is taxed using a separate set of graduated personal tax rates as if it was a separate taxpayer. Additionally, the rights and things return can claim full personal tax credits in addition to those claimed on the regular final return (these include the basic personal amount and the age, spouse, eligible dependant, child, infirm dependant, and caregiver amounts). Other credits such as the employment credit, pension credit, tuition credits, donation credit, medical credit, and others may be split between the final return and the rights and things return, however the total of these credits cannot exceed the amount that would be claimed if no optional (right and things) return was filed.[53] Credits such as the employment credit and pension credit must be claimed on the tax return containing the related income.

The rights and things return is a useful tool to reduce the amount of tax on death. Unfortunately it applies to limited types of income.

VIII. Tax Planning Checklist

Below are the primary tax planning items relating to the major topics discussed in this chapter.

1. Always remember the definition of a qualified small business corporation, and plan for the opportunity to use the capital gain deduction of $750,000. Steps can be taken to ensure that the shares of the corporation qualify for the higher deduction.

2. Try to minimize the cumulative net investment loss (CNIL), whenever possible, in order to retain the option of utilizing the full capital gain deduction. For example, if funds are borrowed, try to use the loans for business purposes and any available cash for investment acquisitions. This shifts expenses to the business activities and reduces investment borrowing costs. Also, a taxpayer who owns shares of a private corporation can declare dividends to increase investment income and offset the CNIL.

3. Charitable donations in excess of $200 have a higher tax credit, and so a greater tax saving will occur if family donations are claimed by only one spouse.

4. A taxpayer who wishes to reduce taxable income and who can choose between a capital gain deduction and a net capital loss carry-over, should opt for the former because of the risk that it may be repealed.

5. The capital gain deduction does not apply to proprietorships. Consequently, consider incorporating the business so that it qualifies as a small business corporation.

---

52 ITA 70(2).
53 ITA 118.93.

6. Political donations should be divided among family members so that the highest-rate tax credit can be enjoyed as many times as possible.

7. The deduction of loss carry-overs is optional. Consider delaying this deduction if income in future years is likely to be taxed at a higher rate.

8. Non-capital losses have a limited carry-over period. Be sure to use the discretionary provisions of the *Income Tax Act* to delay expenses (or create income) when there is a risk those losses may expire.

9. Always consider alternative business structures (proprietorship, corporation, partnership, and so on) before consummating a new venture. While doing so, anticipate the tax treatment of possible losses and consider choosing the structure that will allow the greatest use of those losses at the earliest time possible. Remember that it is more difficult to use the losses when the entity is controlled by other parties (see Chapters 15 and 16).

10. If net capital losses are available for carry-over, future investment strategies should be reviewed. It may be possible to dispose of one investment without incurring tax on the gain (by using the loss carry-over) and to replace it with a higher-yield investment. Previously, this may not have been possible if the situation was such that the potential tax on sale of the first asset overcame the advantage of the higher yield on the proposed new investment.

11. Always apply the marginal tax rates of the various types of income when making investment decisions so that after-tax returns and the potential after-tax losses, if those should occur, can be compared.

IX. Summary and Conclusion

This chapter has completed the tax framework for individuals by examining the conversion of net income for tax purposes to taxable income and the structure for the calculation of tax. The reader is reminded that this chapter applies only to taxpayers who are individuals—previous chapters applied to *all* taxpayers.

An individual's taxable income is determined by reducing net income for tax purposes by a limited number of special reductions. The most important special reduction is the one that allows the deduction of losses from other years that could not be used in the year incurred because of a lack of income in those years. Loss carry-overs of a capital nature can be used only to the extent that capital gains were achieved; all other types of loss carry-overs can be utilized against any source of income. Because of the restrictions placed on the use of such losses, the taxpayer must give them special attention in order to ensure that they will be utilized so as to maximize after-tax cash flow.

To reduce the risk of loss expiration, an individual can delay the deduction of certain discretionary expenses, such as capital cost allowance, and can also trigger the realization of gains attached to assets that have appreciated in value. Before embarking on business activities, taxpayers should examine the possibility of future losses with an eye to considering which organization structures would speed up their utilization and reduce the risk of their expiring. In addition, unused losses must be factored into future investment strategies so that accurate after-tax returns can be projected.

The calculation of tax is affected by both provincial and federal tax jurisdictions. Federal tax has four specific rates, which apply to different levels of the individual's taxable income. All provinces and territories also have multiple rates that apply to various levels of income. Of primary importance to the decision-making process is the combined federal and provincial rate of tax that will apply to future returns on investment. The individual must not only understand the current marginal rates but also

Visit the Canadian Income Taxation Web site at **www.mcgrawhill.ca/ olc/buckwold** to view any updated tax information.

anticipate future marginal rates in light of economic trends. While the fundamental principles of income determination rarely change, the rates of tax applicable to income (especially provincial rates) are subject to frequent changes. It is the reader's responsibility to impose these rate changes on the framework developed in this chapter.

Demonstration Questions

QUESTION ONE

Carol Tse is employed as a marketing manager for TX Ltd., a Canadian-controlled private corporation. She is divorced and supports her two children. In September 20X5, Tse was transferred from Regina to TX Ltd.'s head office in Calgary, Alberta. Her 20X5 financial information is summarized on the following page.

1. Tse received a salary of $90,000. From this, TX deducted Canada Pension Plan (CPP) and Employment Insurance (EI) of $3,147 and income tax of $27,000. During 20X5, Tse sold shares of TX Ltd. for $30,000. She had acquired the shares in 20X1 under a stock option arrangement for $12,000. At the time of purchase, the shares were valued at $14,000. TX Ltd. has indicated that all of its assets are being used in an active business. In 20X5, Tse received non-eligible taxable dividends of $3,000 from TX Ltd.

2. Tse incurred moving expenses in 20X5 of $7,000, which qualified as allowable deductions for tax purposes.

3. In 20X3, Tse inherited a small farm acreage. The farm is operated by a neighbour, who assumes 25% of the farm's revenues and expenses. In 20X5, Tse's share of the profits was $6,000.

4. During the year, Tse sold a work of art for $3,000 that originally cost $2,000.

5. Tse's 19-year-old daughter attended university for eight months in 20X5 and paid tuition fees of $3,000. She earned a salary of $6,000, from which the employer deducted CPP/EI of $250. Tse's son is 14 years old and earned income of $1,000 from a bond inherited from his grandmother. During 20X5, Tse paid dental fees of $2,500 on behalf of the son.

6. In 20X5, Tse contributed $500 to a registered political party and $2,000 to registered charities.

7. A review of Tse's 20X4 tax return shows the following amounts carried forward to 20X5:

Net capital loss	$ 4,000
Listed personal property loss	2,000
Restricted farm loss	8,000
Unused capital gain deduction	210,000
Cumulative net investment loss (CNIL)	5,000

Required:

For the 20X5 taxation year, calculate Tse's *net income for tax purposes*, *taxable income*, and *federal income tax*.

Solution:

Before we complete the calculation, a few items require comment. Tse earned income in two provinces in 20X5. However, she will be subject to provincial tax in Alberta because it is the location of her residence on the last day of the taxation year (the Alberta tax is excluded from the calculations). The TX Ltd. shares sold in 20X5 are qualified small business corporation shares and therefore eligible for the capital gain deduction, provided that it has not been used to this point. Also, the shares were part of a stock option arrangement from 20X1. This means that the employment income from the exercise of the option in 20X1 is taxable in 20X5 (the year of sale), rather than in the year of acquisition, as might be the case if the shares were from a public corporation (see Chapter 4). There are some items in the calculation that can be claimed at the option of the taxpayer. These were claimed in 20X5 and are discussed in the solution.

Net income for tax purposes and taxable income:		
Employment income:		
Salary		$ 90,000
Stock option (TX shares)—$14,000 – $12,000		2,000
		92,000
Business income—farming		6,000
Property income—Non-eligible Canadian dividends		
$3,000 × 1.25		3,750
		101,750
Taxable capital gains:		
TX shares—½ ($30,000 – $14,000)	8,000	
Net gains from listed personal property:		
Work of art—½ ($3,000 – $2,000)	500	
Listed personal property loss		
carried forward from 20X4	(500) –0–	8,000
		109,750
Other deduction—moving expenses		(7,000)
Net income for tax purposes		102,750
Deduct:		
Stock option reduction—½ × $2,000		
(employment benefit)		(1,000)
Net capital loss forward		(4,000)
Restricted farm loss (to the limit of 20X5		
farming income)		(6,000)
Capital gain deduction (note below)		(2,750)
Taxable income		$ 89,000

Note:

As indicated, the gain on the TX shares of $8,000 is eligible for the capital gain deduction, and there is a sufficient amount of unused lifetime deduction available ($210,000). However, the eligible gain of $8,000 must be reduced by the net capital loss claimed in 20X5 and the CNIL at the end of the year. The capital gain deduction is therefore reduced to $2,750, as follows:

Qualified gain for the year		$8,000
Deduct:		
Net capital loss claimed		(4,000)
CNIL:		
Balance at end of 20X4	5,000	
20X5 property income—dividends	(3,750)	(1,250)
		$2,750

It is important to remember that the deduction of the net capital loss in the current year is optional. If it is not claimed in the current year, it can be carried forward indefinitely. This would increase the amount available for the capital gain deduction in the current year by $4,000. It may be prudent to do this, as there is always a possibility that the capital gain deduction will be cancelled in a future year.

Federal income tax:

Primary tax:

15% × $42,707		$ 6,406
22% × $42,707		9,396
26% × $ 3,586		932
$89,000		16,734

Deduct personal tax credits:

Basic	$10,822	
Equivalent to spouse (son has lowest income)—		
$10,822 – $1,000	9,822	
Child—son, under 18	2,191	
Employment	1,095	
Total tax credit amounts	$23,930	
Tax credit—15% × $23,930	$3,590	
Charitable donations—(15% × $200) + (29% × $1,800)	552	
Medical expenses—15% × ($2,500 – $2,109)	59	
Tuition and education transferred from daughter (below)	750	
CPP/EI—15% × $3,147	472	5,423
Deduct dividend tax credit—(Non-eligible) 13⅓% × $3,750		(500)
Basic federal tax		10,807
Deduct other tax credit:		
Political contributions—(75% × $400) + (50% × $100)	—	(350)
Total federal tax		$10,457

Note:

Transfer of education and tuition credits from daughter:

Daughter's taxable income	$ 6,000
Federal tax—15% × $6,000	$ 900
Deduct:	
Basic credit	(1,623)
Employment credit—15% × $1,095	(165)
CPP/EI credit—15% × $250	(38)
Tax before education and tuition credit	–0–
Tuition credit—15% × $3,000	(450)
Education and textbooks credit—	
15% × ($400 + $65) × 8 months	(558)
Unused credit	$ 1,008
Maximum available for transfer ($5,000 × 15%)	$ 750

Remember, the transfer of the unused education and tuition credits is optional. The daughter can choose to retain the credits and carry them forward (indefinitely), to be used by her in a future year when she earns sufficient income.

QUESTION TWO

Olga is 71 years of age, married, and retired. In 20X6, she received income from the following sources:

Canada Pension Plan (CPP)	$ 7,800
Old Age Security (OAS)	6,500
RRIF receipts	42,000
Employer's pension fund	21,000
Canadian eligible dividends	4,000

Throughout the year Olga helped support her infirm sister (age 78) who lived with her and her husband. She estimated that $4,700 was spent for this support. In 20X6, her sister had net income for tax purposes of $17,000.

Due to her failing eyesight, Olga sold her automobile and began using public transit and taxis for transportation. Her ophthalmologist certified that she has a permanent physical impairment and retains only 20% of her eyesight. In 20X6, she paid $300 for an annual bus pass and $900 for taxis.

Olga's husband earned investment income of $40,000 in 20X6.

Required:

Calculate Olga's 20X6 federal income tax. Use 2012 as the applicable taxation year.

Solution:

Before calculating the overall federal tax it is necessary to first determine if Olga is required to pay the special 15% tax on Old Age Security benefits. This tax will apply in 2012 if her overall net income for tax purposes exceeds $69,562. The reason this tax must be determined in advance is that any tax payable can then be deducted from net income for tax purposes before calculating the regular income tax.

Olga's net income for tax purposes before the Old Age Security tax is $82,820 as follows:

CPP	$ 7,800
OAS	6,500
RRIF	42,000
Pension	21,000
Eligible dividends—$4,000 × 1.38	5,520
Net income before tax on OAS	$82,820

The net income for tax purposes is greater than $69,562 (in 2012) and so a tax must be paid on OAS. The tax is $1,989 [15% × ($82,820 − $69,562)]. Note that the net income for tax purposes in this calculation includes the grossed-up dividends received and not the cash amount received.

The OAS tax of $1,989 is now deducted from net income for tax purposes. The revised net income for tax purposes is $80,831 ($82,820 − $1,989). There are no reductions to arrive at taxable income, so net income for tax purposes is equal to taxable income in this case. The federal tax is calculated below:

Federal tax:			
15% × $42,707			$6,406
22% × 38,124			8,387
$80,831			14,793
Deduct personal tax credits:			
Basic	$10,822		
Caregiver—($4,402 + $2,000) − ($17,000 − $15,033)	4,435		
Age—$6,720 − ($80,831 − $33,884)	0		
Pension	2,000		
Disability (for Olga)	7,546		
Disability (for infirm sister)	7,546		
Total tax credit amounts	$32,349		
Credit—15% × $32,349	$4,852		
Public transit— 15% × $300 (actual amount paid)	45		(4,897)
Deduct Dividend tax credit—15% × $5,520			(828)
Federal tax on taxable income			9,068
Plus tax on Old Age security			1,989
			$11,057

Note that Olga claimed the Caregiver credit for support of her sister rather than the Infirm Dependant credit because her sister lives with her in the same home. She is entitled to claim either the Caregiver credit or the Infirm Dependant credit, but not both. The tax credit amount for both credits is the same ($960). However, the Caregiver credit has a higher income threshold for the supported person ($15,033 compared to $6,420). Also note that the Caregiver credit is based on a fixed amount and is not related to the actual expenses incurred for the support. 118(1)(c.1).

Olga's sister is infirm but she does not have sufficient taxable income to use the disability credit. The federal tax on her $17,000 of income is reduced to nil by her other tax credits (basic personal amount $10,822 + age credit amount $6,720 = $17,542). In cases such as this, the disability credit may be transferred to a supporting person. 118.3, 118.3(2).

QUESTION THREE

Individuals A, B, and C each invested $100,000 in Canadian securities. All three are in the top marginal tax bracket. In the current year, individual A earned $5,000 of interest, individual B earned $4,000 of eligible dividends, and individual C earned $4,000 from a capital gain. A boasted that she has achieved the highest rate of return on the investment.

Required:

Is A correct that she has the highest rate of return? Explain. Calculate the rate of return for the dividend and capital gain that is equal to a rate of return on interest for an individual who is in the top marginal tax bracket.

Solution:

Based on the marginal tax rates shown in Exhibit 10-7, the after-tax returns for each of the investors is as follows:

	A—Interest	B—Dividend	C—Capital gain
Actual pre-tax rate of return	5%	4%	4%
Pre-tax dollar return	$5,000	$4,000	$4,000
Marginal tax rate	45%	28%	23%
After-tax return	$2,750*	$2,880**	$3,080***

* $5,000 − (45% × $5,000) = $2,750
** $4,000 − (28% × $4,000) = $2,880
*** $4,000 − (23% × $4,000) = $3,080

Clearly, B and C have earned higher after-tax amounts than A. A's after-tax return from interest of $5,000 is $2,750. If B and C were taxed on their returns in the same manner as A (at 45%), the pre-tax amounts would be $5,236 for B (× − 45%× = $2,880) and $5,600 for C (× − 45%× = $3,080). So, B's dividend return of $4,000 is equivalent to $5,236 of interest return or 5.24% ($5,236/$100,000). C's capital gain return of $4,000 is equivalent to $5,600 of interest return or 5.6% ($5,600/$100,000). So, A would have to earn 5.24% of interest to have the same after-tax amount as B's 4% dividend, and 5.6% of interest to have the same after-tax amount as C's 4% capital gain.

Using the marginal tax rate in Exhibit 10-7 the after-tax amounts from the three types of investment returns are as follows:

Income	After-tax return
Interest (return − 45% tax =)	55%
Dividend (return − 28% tax =)	72%
Capital gain (return − 23% tax =)	77%

Therefore, based on the tax rates in Exhibit 10-7, it can be said that:
An eligible dividend return is equal to 1.31 times an interest return (55% × 1.31 = 72%). A capital gain return is equal to 1.4 times an interest return (55% × 1.4 = 77%). Note that

the tax rates for eligible dividends in Exhibit 10-7 are based on the dividend gross-up of 1.38% and a federal dividend tax credit of 15%.

Review Questions

1. Briefly explain the difference, for individuals, between net income for tax purposes and taxable income.

2. Explain the difference between an allowable capital loss and a net capital loss.

3. Describe the tax treatment of net capital losses.

4. Explain how a non-capital loss is created and how it is treated for tax purposes.

5. Is it always worthwhile to utilize a net capital loss or a non-capital loss as soon as the opportunity arises? Explain.

6. Is it possible for taxpayers to pay tax on more income than they actually earned over a period of years? Explain.

7. How does the risk of not being able to utilize a business loss for tax purposes vary for each of the following individuals?

   - *Individual A* operates the business as a proprietorship.
   - *Individual B* is the sole shareholder of a corporation that owns the business.
   - *Individual C* is a 30% shareholder of a corporation that operates the business.
   - *Individual D* is a 30% partner in a business partnership.

8. What can a taxpayer do to reduce the risk of not being able to utilize a net capital loss or a non-capital loss?

9. Two separate taxpayers are considering investing in shares of the same public corporation. How is it possible that the risk associated with that investment may be greater for one taxpayer than for the other?

10. If an individual has a net taxable capital gain in a year that qualifies for a capital gain deduction, is there any advantage to not claiming the applicable portion of the deduction in that year? Explain.

11. If an individual is considering selling his business to a daughter, does it make any difference to him whether that business is a proprietorship or is housed within a corporation?

12. What is the difference between the basic federal tax and the total federal tax?

13. What is the difference between a tax deduction and a tax credit?

14. An individual usually has taxable income in a year of $130,000 and pays federal and provincial taxes totalling $43,000. Would this information be relevant when the implications of investing in a partnership that operates a small retail business are considered?

15. Does an individual who lives in Alberta and receives a $100 dividend obtain the same tax reduction from the dividend tax credit as an individual who resides in New Brunswick? Explain.

16. In what circumstances may an individual be subject to provincial tax in more than one province in a particular year?

17. An individual resides in Manitoba and operates a business that has no profit from its Alberta operations. Is it possible for that person to have a tax liability in Alberta in a particular year?

Key Concept Questions

QUESTION ONE

In the current year, Beth has a taxable capital gain of $20,000 from disposing of shares of various public companies. She has a net capital loss of $7,500 from 1998 when the capital gains inclusion rate was $3/4$. *Income tax reference: ITA 111(1)(b), 111(1.1).*

Determine the maximum net capital loss deduction for the current year.

QUESTION TWO

Kendra disposed of shares of A Ltd., a qualified small business corporation (QSBC), in the current year realizing a taxable capital gain of $350,000. She has net capital losses from last year of $10,000 which she wants to claim in the current year. Her cumulative net investment loss (CNIL) account at the end of the year is $3,000. Kendra claimed an allowable business investment loss (ABIL) of $12,000 on her previous year's tax return. She incurred a taxable capital gain of $75,000 on QSBC shares four years ago and claimed an equivalent capital gains deduction. *Income tax reference: ITA 110.6(1), (2), (2.1).*

Determine the capital gains deduction claimable by Kendra in the current year.

QUESTION THREE

At the end of last year, Ryan had a balance in his cumulative net investment loss (CNIL) account of $14,500. In the current year, Ryan earned net rental income of $5,000 and received eligible dividends from Canadian corporations of $1,000. He incurred interest expense of $3,000 relating to his stock portfolio. *Income tax reference: ITA 110.6(1).*

Determine Ryan's CNIL balance at the end of the current year.

QUESTION FOUR

X Ltd. is a Canadian-controlled private corporation carrying on business in Canada. The net fair market value of X Ltd. is estimated to be $80,000, calculated as follows:

Cash	$ 1,000
Marketable securities	16,000
Accounts receivable	11,000
Furniture and equipment	32,000
Goodwill	40,000
	100,000
Bank loan	(20,000)
	$ 80,000

The shares of X Ltd. have been owned by Alexander for the last two years and throughout that time, the relative values of the assets and liabilities have remained constant. *Income tax reference: ITA 110.6(1).*

Determine if X Ltd. is a qualified small business corporation.

QUESTION FIVE

In 20X1 Jack loaned $10,000 to a small business corporation. By the end of the current year, it was established that the loan was bad and that Jack would not be receiving the $10,000 principal. Jack has sheltered $4,000 of capital gains with the capital gains exemption in prior years. *Income tax reference: ITA 39(1)(c), 39(9), 50(1).*

Determine the tax consequences for Jack for the current year.

QUESTION SIX

Angelina has taxable income of $130,000 for the current year, including $120,000 of employment income. She is not married and lives alone. Angelina's employer withheld CPP and EI premiums of $3,147 as well as income tax. *Income tax reference: ITA 117(2), 117.1(1), 118(1)(c), 118(10), 118.7.*

Determine Angelina's federal tax payable for the current year.

QUESTION SEVEN

Mr. Senior turned 65 in the current year and received pension income from the following sources:

• Old-age security pension	$ 5,800
• Canada Pension Plan	7,300
• Pension income from former employer	32,000
	$45,100

Mr. Senior had no other income for the year. His wife, age 66, had net income of $6,000 (OAS and interest income) in the current year. *Income tax reference: ITA 56(1)(a.2), 60(c), 60.03, 117(2), 117.1(1), 118(1)(a), 118(2),(3), 118.8.*

Determine Mr. Senior's federal tax payable for the current year assuming

(i) He does not elect to split his pension income.

(ii) He elects to split his pension income.

QUESTION EIGHT

Brent is unmarried and lives alone. During the current year he earned employment income of $120,000. His employer withheld CPP and EI premiums of $3,147, as well as income tax. He has a portfolio of investments that generated eligible dividends from Canadian corporations of $10,000. He donated public company shares worth $1,000 to the Canadian Cancer Society. The adjusted cost base (ACB) of the shares donated was $400. *Income tax reference: ITA 38(a.1), 117(2), 117.1(1), 118(1)(c), 18.01(5), 118.1(3), 118.7, 121.*

Determine Brent's federal tax payable for the current year.

QUESTION NINE

Michelle attended a Canadian university on a full-time basis for eight months during the current year. Her only income for the year was $4,500 of employment income earned during the summer. She paid tuition fees of $7,000 for the current year. *Income tax reference: ITA 118.5, 118.6, 118.61, 118.81, 118.9.*

Determine the amount of tuition, education, and textbook credit available to Michelle. What options are available with respect to the unused education credits?

QUESTION TEN

Glen and Kelly have two children, Ben, age 14, and Cody, age 20. The medical expenses and net income for each member of the family for the current year is as follows:

	Medicals	Net income
Glen	$ 2,000	$100,000
Kelly	3,000	40,000
Ben	600	500
Cody	12,000	9,000

All of the medical expenses were paid by Glen in the 12-month period ending December 31. *Income tax reference: ITA 118.2(1).*

Determine the maximum medical expense credit for the current year.

QUESTION ELEVEN

Carol registered her daughter, Kristin, in an eligible physical activity program and paid the registration fee of $650 on January 5 of the current year. The program started on February 1, and continued, one night a week for thirteen weeks. *Income tax reference: ITA 118.03.*

Determine the children's fitness tax credit claimable for the current year.

QUESTION TWELVE

Ellen received old-age security (OAS) payments during the current year totalling $6,200. Her net income for the current year is $85,000. No amount was withheld from the OAS payments as her income was lower in previous years. *Income tax reference: ITA 60(w), 180.2.*

Determine Ellen's OAS repayment (Part I.2 tax) for the current year.

QUESTION THIRTEEN

In 20X0 Jonathan, who is single, earned employment income of $10,000, capital gains of $100,000, and Canadian non-eligible dividends of $20,000. He is exempt from CPP and EI. In addition, Jonathan is a limited partner in a Canadian Limited partnership from which he was allocated a business loss of $34,000. *ITA 127.5 to 127.55.*

Does Jonathan have to pay any alternative minimum federal tax in the year and if so, how much? Also, briefly explain how any federal minimum tax in excess of the normal federal tax will be dealt with in future years.

Problems

PROBLEM ONE

The financial results of an individual are outlined below for three years.

	20X1	20X2	20X3
Employment income	$22,000	$27,000	$40,000
Capital gains:			
Listed personal property	–0–	–0–	5,000
Other capital property	40,000	–0–	12,000
Capital losses:			
Listed personal property	–0–	(9,000)	–0–
Shares of a small business corporation	–0–	(40,000)	–0–
Other capital property	–0–	(48,000)	–0–

Share of a business partnership's income (loss)	7,000	(57,000)	–0–
Actual dividends from Canadian corporations—Non-eligible	12,000	4,000	–0–
RRSP contributions	4,000	–0–	–0–

Required:

1. Determine the individual's net capital losses, non-capital losses, and unused listed personal property losses for 20X2.

2. Determine the individual's minimum taxable income for 20X1 and 20X3.

PROBLEM TWO

Barbara Legault operates a full-time law practice in southwestern Ontario. In her spare time, she maintains a small rural acreage for the purpose of growing and selling Christmas trees. In addition, she derives income from various investments and is an art collector.

Below are her financial results for 20X1.

Net income from law practice	$ 97,000
Loss on tree farm operation	(12,500)
Gross rents received on rental property	28,000
Operating expenses on rental property before capital cost allowance	37,000
Gain on sale of shares of public corporations	80,000
Loss on sale of summer cottage	4,000
Gain on sale of oil painting	8,000
Gain on sale of shares of a small business corporation	20,000
Lump-sum payment to ex-husband as part of divorce settlement	40,000
Loss on sale of shares of a public corporation	14,000

At the end of 20X0, the following tax accounts existed:

Net listed personal property losses forward from 20X0 (represents the actual loss)	$ 4,000
Undepreciated capital cost allowance on rental property	160,000
Net capital losses	7,000
Cumulative net investment loss	14,000

Legault had not previously used any of her lifetime capital gain deduction.

Required:

What is Legault's taxable income for 20X1?

PROBLEM THREE

In 20X1, Gary Kwok, who is single, earned the following income and incurred the following losses: employment income, $16,000; business loss, $4,000; taxable capital gains, $7,000; property income (interest), $18,000; allowable capital loss from the sale of shares of public corporations, $9,000; allowable capital loss from the sale of shares of a Canadian-controlled private corporation that qualifies as a small business corporation, $2,000.

At the end of 20X0, Kwok had unused net capital losses of $16,000 and unused non-capital losses of $37,000. Kwok does not want to pay any federal tax in 20X1. For 20X1, Kwok is entitled to a basic personal tax credit, the Canada Employment credit, and a CPP/EI credit of $900.

Required:

Assuming Kwok's wishes are met, what is the maximum amount of non-capital losses remaining for carry-forward after 20X1?

PROBLEM FOUR

Abra Swan is 30 years old and single. She is employed as a middle-level manager with a national Canadian company. After living and working for five years in Regina, Saskatchewan, she was transferred to her employer's office in Winnipeg on December 15, 20X1.

Her financial transactions for the 20X1 taxation year are shown below.

1. Swan received an annual salary of $50,000, but her take-home pay for the year was only $34,853 (see below).

Gross salary	$50,000
Amounts withheld by employer:	
Income tax	(10,000)
Company pension contribution	(2,000)
Canada Pension Plan	(2,307)
Employment Insurance	(840)
	$34,853

2. During the current year, Swan purchased 1,000 shares of her employer's company (a public corporation) under a stock-option program. The shares cost $10 each and at the time of purchase had a market value of $14 per share. When the stock option was granted two years ago, the share price was $11. To fund the purchase, she borrowed $10,000 from her bank. During the year, she paid interest of $800 on the loan.

3. The previous year, Swan had unwisely invested in commodity futures and lost a large portion of her savings. She considered this loss to be a business loss but was unable to use the full amount for tax purposes because her other income was not sufficient. Of the total loss, $6,000 was unused.

4. As well, Swan had the following receipts for 20X1:

Dividends from taxable Canadian corporations (Eligible)	$ 4,000
Dividends of $2,000 from a foreign corporation,	
less foreign taxes of $200	1,800
Cash received from RRSP withdrawal	2,000
Proceeds from the sale of public corporation shares	
(originally purchased for $20,000)	26,000

5. In 20X1, she made the following disbursements:

Winnipeg home down payment (first home)	$60,000
Mortgage payments on her new home	1,000
Life insurance	400
Charitable donations	800
Contribution to a federal political party	800
Tuition fees to a university (one-day course)	300

Required:

For the 20X1 taxation year, determine Swan's

(a) net income for tax purposes;

(b) taxable income; and

(c) federal tax liability.

To which province will Swan pay provincial tax?

PROBLEM FIVE

Carl Kay is the vice-president of KM Ltd., a Canadian-controlled private corporation located in Halifax, Nova Scotia. KM operates a real estate development business constructing and selling commercial buildings and residential apartments. Kay's 20X3 financial transactions include the following:

- Kay received a salary of $95,000 from KM. From this amount, KM deducted CPP and EI of $3,147 and income tax of $30,000. The company provided him with a car that cost $40,000 and that has an undepreciated capital cost of $18,000. The operating costs of $3,000 were paid by KM. In 20X3, Kay drove the car 20,000 km, of which 8,000 km was for employment purposes. KM contributed $4,000 on Kay's behalf to a deferred profit-sharing plan. Although KM does not have a group life insurance plan, it paid Kay's personal life insurance premium of $1,000 (coverage – $75,000).

- During the year, Kay sold 1,000 shares of KM Ltd. for $10 per share. He had acquired the shares three years earlier for $6 per share as part of a company stock-option plan. At the time of purchase, the shares were valued at $7 per share.

- In 20X2, Kay constructed a 10-suite apartment block. He sold the property in 20X3 for $800,000, which was $150,000 more than the original land and building cost. He received $80,000 of the proceeds in cash, with the balance due in five annual instalments beginning in 20X4. The property incurred a net rental loss of $7,000 (before amortization).

- Kay sold his summer cottage for $90,000 after it was announced that a waste disposal site would be developed in the area. He had purchased the cottage six years earlier for $120,000.

- In 20X0, Kay loaned $16,000 to Alloy Ltd., a Canadian-controlled private corporation. All of the company's assets are used in an active business. The 20X2 interest of $1,400, which Kay included in income, has not been received. The company is in severe financial difficulty and may not survive beyond next year.

- Kay sold shares of a public corporation, purchased in 20X1 for $12,000, for $20,000.

- In November, Kay received a legal bill for $2,000 relating to a dispute over a tax reassessment. Kay paid $1,200 in December 20X3 and the balance in January 20X4.

- Kay received eligible dividends of $2,000 and non-eligible dividends of $1,000 from Canadian corporations and $1,800 from a foreign corporation. The foreign corporation remitted a 10% withholding tax to its government.

- Kay celebrated his 65th birthday in December 20X3. He supports his spouse, who is retired. She had investment income of $4,000 in 20X3. During the year, Kay made gifts of $3,000 to a local charity. He paid tuition fees of $900 to attend a three-month evening course at a university.

- Kay has used his entire capital gain deduction. At the end of 20X2, he had unused net capital losses of $12,000 and non-capital losses of $7,000.

Required:
Calculate Kay's minimum 20X3 net income for tax purposes, taxable income, and federal income tax.

PROBLEM SIX (comprehensive)

Sandra Dumont is a lawyer. For five years, until June 30, 20X5, she had been employed by Calco Ltd., a national restaurant company. On July 1, 20X5, she began to practise law as a sole proprietor from an office in her home.

Dumont has asked you to prepare her 20X5 income tax return. At a recent meeting, you gathered the information provided in Exhibits I and II.

Required:

1. Determine Dumont's *minimum income for tax purposes* in accordance with the aggregating formula of section 3 of the *Income Tax Act* and her *minimum taxable income* for the 20X5 taxation year.

2. Based on your answer to question 1, calculate Dumont's *federal income tax* for the 20X5 taxation year.

3. Why did the CRA deny the deduction of Dumont's 20X3 convention expenses? Can she obtain a deduction for the proposed 20X6 convention? If so, why?

Exhibit 1:

Sandra Dumont
Information Regarding
Work at Calco and
Law Practice

1. Dumont's salary to June 30, 20X5, was $51,200. From this, Calco deducted CPP and EI of $3,147, income tax of $16,000, and $300 for Dumont's portion of the private group medical insurance premium. An additional premium of $300 was paid by Calco. Also, Calco paid the $200 premium for Dumont's group term life insurance coverage of $50,000.

2. On June 30, 20X5, Dumont returned the company car that Calco had provided her. The car had a cost of $32,000, and Calco's undepreciated balance was $18,000. Calco also had paid the operating costs for the car, which amounted to $2,100. Dumont had driven her car 16,000 km, of which 12,000 km were for business use.

3. Dumont travelled by air when working for Calco. Dumont used her personal credit card and accumulated frequent flyer points. She was reimbursed by Calco for travel costs. In March 20X5, she and her husband used some of her accumulated frequent-flyer points to obtain free airline tickets for a vacation. As a result, they each saved the $800 airfare.

4. In 20X3, Dumont borrowed $20,000 from Calco. She has paid interest at 5% on the loan. Dumont used the borrowed funds for the down payment to purchase a rental property. The CRA's prescribed interest rate was 9% in 20X5. Dumont repaid the loan on June 30, 20X5.

5. On June 30, 20X5, Dumont sold 500 shares of Calco Ltd. for $20 per share to the company's controlling shareholder. Calco had issued the shares to Dumont at $10 in 20X2. At that time, the shares were appraised at $12. Calco Ltd. is a Canadian-controlled private corporation. At the time of the share sale, all of Calco's assets were being used in an active business.

6. Dumont began practising law from her home office on July 1, 20X5, and registered for HST. She purchased the client list and files of a retiring lawyer for $50,000. She also purchased a computer for $4,000 and a legal library for $5,600.

7. On July 4, 20X5, Dumont purchased an automobile for $34,000 plus HST. She used the car 60% of the time for her law practice.

8. For the six months ended December 31, 20X5, the financial statements of Dumont's law practice showed a profit of $41,000. The gross revenue of $88,000 consisted of the following:

Fees billed and received	$47,000
Fees billed but unpaid at the year end	24,000
Work in progress—not billed	17,000
	$88,000

Dumont indicated that she wanted to elect under section 34 of the *Income Tax Act*.

9. Operating expenses for the law practice included the following:

Liability insurance	$ 2,200
Depreciation and amortization	9,100
Reserve for bad debts	1,200
Golf club dues—while attending the club, clients are entertained approximately 30% of the time	1,600
Charitable donations	800
Promotion—client lunches	400
Secretarial services	12,000
Computer software—word processing and billing program	900

10. Dumont uses 12 square metres of her house exclusively as an office for her law practice. Expenses for the entire 80-square-metre home for all of 20X5 consist of the following:

Insurance	$ 700
Mortgage interest	9,000
Property taxes	2,300
Utilities	3,000
	$15,000

The financial statements do not include the home-office costs.

Exhibit II:

Sandra Dumont Other Financial Information

1. Dumont owns a residential rental property, which she had purchased in 20X3. Details of the rent and expenses in 20X5 are as follows:

Rental		$6,000
Repairs and maintenance	1,200	
Property tax	900	
Interest on first mortgage	3,300	(5,400)
		$ 600

As of December 31, 20X5, there were no unpaid rents from the tenant.

2. In 20X3, while employed at Calco, Dumont attended a national law convention. She deducted her expenses of $2,300 on her 20X3 tax return. Her employer willingly gave her the time off from work to attend the convention, even though it was not directly related to her work. In 20X5, Dumont received a reassessment notice from the CRA disallowing the entire convention expense deduction. Now that Dumont is practising law, she will attend the 20X6 convention to upgrade her skills.

3. In 20X5, Dumont contributed $11,000 to her RRSP and another $1,000 to a spousal RRSP. She has contributed the same amount to the spousal plan for the past four years. On December 20, 20X5, her husband withdrew $4,000 from this spousal account.

4. The following additional receipts and disbursements occurred during 20X5:

Paid dental fees	$2,900
Paid contributions to a registered federal political party	1,400
Paid interest on late payment of 20X4 income tax	240
Received cash dividends (Non-eligible) on Calco shares	1,000
Received proceeds from the sale of a silver tea set (original cost—$1,600)	1,100

5. In 20X5, Dumont received 100 shares of Parla Ltd., a public corporation. The shares were a stock dividend (Eligible) on the 2,000 shares she had purchased in 20X1 at $4 per share. At the time of the stock dividend, the shares were at $8. She sold the 100 stock dividend shares in December 20X5, at $7.

6. Dumont's husband earned $110,000 in 20X5.

7. A review of Dumont's 20X4 tax return showed the following:

Maximum RRSP deduction available in 20X5	$10,500
Capital gain deductions claimed in past years	75,000
Net income from real estate rentals (after deducting a reserve for uncollectible rents of $500)	860
Undepreciated capital cost—class 1 (rental property)	52,000
Reserve for unpaid rents	500

PROBLEM SEVEN

Victor is 63 years old and retired from his employment with Meter Ltd., a Canadian public corporation, on September 30, 20X8.

Victor has asked you to help him prepare his 20X8, tax return and to advise him on certain other tax matters. Information regarding his financial activities for 20X8 is summarized below.

1. Victor's gross salary to September 30, 20X8, was $85,000. From this amount, Meter deducted income tax of $22,000 and CPP and EI of $3,147. In addition to salary, Meter paid $9,000 directly into Victor's RRSP at a local bank. Victor paid the annual RRSP administration fee of $100.

    During the year, until September 30, 20X8, Victor had the use of the employer's automobile. Meter paid the *monthly* lease cost of $400 plus monthly operating expenses of $200. Victor drove the car a total of 16,000 km, of which 4,000 km was for personal use.

2. Victor suffered an illness in 20X8 and was off work for six weeks. During this period, the employer's group sickness and accident insurance policy paid Victor $4,000 for lost salary. The entire premium of $500 was paid by Meter in 20X8. Due to his illness, Victor incurred and paid medical expenses of $3,000 in 20X8.

3. In 20X5, Meter granted Victor an option to acquire up to 5,000 of its shares at $8 per share. At that time, the shares were trading at the same price. In January 20X8, he purchased 2,000 shares when they were trading at $10 per share. He purchased an additional 1,000 shares in July 20X8, when they were trading at $15 per share. In November 20X8, Victor sold 2,000 shares at $20 per share after receiving a cash dividend (Eligible) of $800.

4. In 20X7, as a sideline, Victor began carving wood bowls for sale. He hoped to generate a small profit and keep himself occupied during his retirement. He made his first sales in 20X8, which resulted in a loss of $8,850. This excludes amortization but includes a deduction of $4,000 for the full cost of woodworking equipment purchased in 20X8.

5. On January 2, 20X8, Victor gifted his stamp collection to his grandson. He had acquired the collection over the past 15 years at a cost of $7,000. The collection has recently been appraised at $12,000. At the same time, he gifted a convertible bond valued at $20,000 to his wife. The bond had been purchased in 20X3 for $16,000.

6. On November 15, 20X8, Victor received $1,000 from an acquaintance in exchange for an option to purchase a small piece of land he had acquired four years earlier with the intention of constructing a rental property. For financial reasons, the construction plan had been terminated.

7. Victor is married and lives with his wife. She retired in 20X7 and will begin receiving her pension in 20X9. During 20X8, she earned interest income of $5,000, which includes $900 from the convertible bond she received from her husband.

8. Victor's tax return from the previous year showed the following balances:

Listed personal property losses forwarded to 20X8	$ 1,000
Maximum RRSP deduction available in 20X8	11,000

Required:

1. Determine Victor's *minimum net income for tax purposes* in accordance with the format of section 3 of the *Income Tax Act* for the 20X8 taxation year.

2. Based on your answer to question 1, calculate Victor's *minimum federal income tax liability* for the 20X8 taxation year.

3. Now that Victor is retired, can he make a contribution to his RRSP in 20X9? If so, estimate the maximum deduction available.

PROBLEM EIGHT

Harvey and Walter Bachynski operate a welding supply business as a partnership in Sackville, New Brunswick. Over the years, their sales territory has expanded steadily, as they maintain an efficient, customer-oriented business.

However, their success has created problems. More and more customers are demanding their services, and the time required to reach those customers has increased. The brothers feel that because of this, service to distant areas is suffering from a lack of efficiency. In response, during the current year, they opened their first service depot in Amherst, Nova Scotia, 50 km away, just across the provincial boundary. The new depot is in rented premises. It maintains a supply of inventory and is staffed by two new employees.

Because of the start-up costs, the new depot operation has suffered a loss of $20,000 in the current year. However, the brothers are convinced that they have made the right decision.

A summary of the partnership income statement for the year is provided in the following table:

Sales		$400,000
Cost of sales		100,000
Gross profit		300,000
Expenses:		
Salaries and wages	100,000	
Travel and delivery	20,000	
Rent	12,000	
Advertising and promotion	4,000	
Office and supplies	2,000	
Insurance	4,000	
Utilities	6,000	148,000
		152,000
Net loss from new depot operation		(20,000)
Net income before taxes		$132,000

The brothers are pleased with the profit, although a large portion of it is a result of their own efforts. As the business is a partnership of two individuals, the brothers do not pay themselves salaries. Instead, they simply draw out some of their profits for personal living expenses.

The net loss of $20,000 from the new depot is calculated in the following table:

Sales		$ 70,000
Cost of sales		30,000
Gross profit		40,000
Expenses:		
Rent	7,000	
Salaries	40,000	
Advertising	10,000	
Supplies	2,000	
Insurance	1,000	60,000
Net loss		$ (20,000)

Each brother has other sources of income that generate approximately $30,000 annually.

Required:

For each brother, determine the amount of taxable income that will be subject to provincial income tax in New Brunswick and Nova Scotia for 20X1.

PROBLEM NINE

Sam Collins had been investing for several years. Most of his investments were in the stock market. For several years, he made substantial capital gains. As his success grew, he began to invest in riskier shares.

Last year, after a serious market downturn, Collins suffered significant losses that left him with cash resources of only $50,000. He was unable to use all of the capital losses for tax purposes and was left with unused net capital losses of $70,000.

The substantial losses have shattered his confidence in the stock market. He has requested that his broker find him a secure bond in which to invest his remaining $50,000. Collins is not destitute, as he has a substantial annual salary of $130,000.

His broker has suggested a five-year corporate bond that will provide an interest return of 13%, and at the same time, he has tried to convince Collins to remain in the stock market but to acquire only high-level blue-chip shares. In this vein, he has suggested, as a possible alternative to the bond, a common-share investment in a utility company that historically provides an annual dividend return (Eligible) of 5% as well as capital growth of 6%.

In addition, the broker has indicated that any annual cash returns can be invested in treasury bills earning 13% annually.

Required:

1. Which investment will best help Collins recover his lost capital? (Use a five-year period for your analysis.)

2. What rate of return must the bond offer in order for it to yield the same return as the share investment?

PROBLEM TEN

Jennifer Jones has decided to open a small business that will be supervised by a hired manager. With her current cash resources, she will be able to acquire the necessary assets for the business and provide basic working capital. However, any losses that occur will have to be funded by an infusion of additional capital.

Jones and the new manager have just finished drawing up a business plan. It projects the following operating results over the next five years:

Year 1	loss	$(20,000)
2	loss	(10,000)
3	break even	–0–
4	profit	10,000
5	profit	20,000
Profit after 5 years		–0–

Although Jones has substantial wealth, all of her capital will be tied up for several years. In addition, all of her after-tax annual income is committed to personal living expenses. Her pre-tax annual income is over $130,000.

Jones has made an arrangement with her bank, which will provide an annual loan to cover any losses from the business. The bank will charge 10% interest. As cash flow is generated from the business, the loan will be repaid. She has yet to decide whether the business will be operated as a proprietorship or a separate corporation owned by her.

Required:

Determine the amount of the outstanding loan at the end of year 5 under both the corporate structure and the proprietorship structure. Assume that any bank loans will be obtained or repaid at the end of each year. Assume Jennifer lives in a province with a combined federal and provincial personal income tax rate of 45% in the top tax bracket.

Corporations—An Introduction

The concept of imposing an income tax on corporations is subject to two extreme points of view. At one extreme, it is argued that a corporation is simply an extension of the individual shareholders and that any income generated should be allocated to the shareholders for tax purposes. At the other extreme is the argument that corporations control economic power and that they, rather than the individual shareholders, should be subject to full taxation. Canadian tax policy adheres to neither of these extremes and taxes both the corporation and the individual shareholder on the basis that each is a distinct entity.

To understand the full impact of corporate taxation, one must accept two things: first, that the corporation is separate from its owners and, second, that there exists a relationship between the two in which income flows first to the corporation and then to the shareholders. This two-level approach enables decision makers to identify when tax occurs along the cash-flow path and to determine whether, and when, double taxation results.

In isolation, the tax framework for corporations is completed in much the same way as it is for individuals. First, net income for tax purposes is converted to taxable income by the applying of special reductions. The most important special reductions are loss carry-overs and dividends from other corporations. Next comes the calculation of corporate tax, which follows a simple format; however, certain corporations and certain types of income are provided tax preferences.

This chapter completes the basic framework of the Canadian tax system by providing an overview of corporate taxation and establishing the fundamental relationship between the corporation and its shareholders. It also serves as an introduction to Part Three of the text, which examines the corporate structure in greater detail.

I. Relationship between the Corporation and Its Shareholders

When a company is incorporated, an artificial person that is separate from its owner or owners is created.[1] This artificial person is recognized by law as an entity that has the power to act in its own right and to enter into enforceable legal agreements with individuals or other corporations.

A. Corporation Defined

As a separate entity, the corporation can own property. Property owned by a corporation is not considered to be owned by the shareholders. While the shareholders who control the actions of the corporation may have the right to decide on how the corporate property is used and may ultimately receive the benefits from its use, they are not the legal owners of the property.

This separation between the corporation and its owners also extends to the liability for outstanding debts and losses. Shareholders are liable for the debts of the corporation only to the extent of their contributions to the corporation in the form of share capital. In some cases, however, the net of limited liability is opened when shareholders agree to guarantee the payment of certain debts of the corporation.

In accordance with the above definition, a corporation, separate from its owners, can buy, own, sell, and lease property and can borrow funds for its own use as well as loan funds to others.

Exhibit 11-1 illustrates which parties can form relationships with a corporation. Shareholders provide equity capital, creditors provide borrowed capital, suppliers provide property and services, customers acquire goods and services, employees provide human resources, and lessors rent property to the corporation.

---

1 IT-343R.

The Corporation and Its Fundamental Relationships

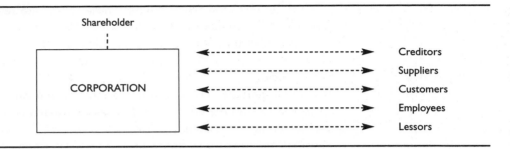

It is important to recognize that a shareholder may have more than one relationship with the corporation. The shareholder, in addition to providing equity capital to the corporation, can also act as the following:

(a) a creditor who loans funds to the corporation;

(b) a supplier who sells to the corporation such property as land, buildings, equipment, goodwill, franchises, and the like;

(c) a customer who buys property or services from the corporation;

(d) an employee who is paid for services provided to the corporation; and

(e) a lessor who rents property to the corporation.

Each of these relationships has different legal obligations and different financial results. Consequently, the tax status of income generated from each relationship may vary. In order to understand the tax impact on the shareholder and the corporation, it is necessary to compartmentalize the types of transactions that the shareholder and the corporation enter into.

B. Tax Impact of Shareholder/ Corporate Relationships

The legal separation of the corporation from its shareholders creates a two-tier system of taxation. The corporation, as a separate entity, is subject to tax on its income, which is calculated in accordance with the principles established in previous chapters. The shareholder is also a separate entity and is subject to a second level of tax on income derived from the corporation. While the shareholders of a corporation may be other corporations, all corporate income ultimately flows to individuals. Discussions in this section of the chapter relate to the fundamental structure of a corporation owned by a shareholder who is an individual.

The corporation's primary relationship is, of course, with the shareholder as the provider of equity capital to the corporation. The tax consequences of this relationship differ radically from those of the secondary relationships—those in which the shareholder also acts as a creditor, supplier, customer, employee, or lessor to the corporation. The tax consequences of both the primary and the secondary relationships are reviewed separately below.

1. The Primary Relationship

Under the primary relationship the shareholder provides equity capital to the corporation by contributing cash or other property to the corporation in exchange for shares. Shares issued can have various rights attached to them. Most commonly, shares entitle the owner to part of the accumulated earnings of the corporation on a pro rata basis. Some of the earnings may be distributed to the shareholder as dividends; this is at the discretion of the corporation's directors. The undistributed earnings remain in the corporation and will ultimately be distributed to the shareholder upon dissolution of the corporation. Such shares are referred to as "participating shares" or "common shares," and increase in value as corporate earnings are accumulated. Other shares do not participate fully in corporate earnings but, rather, pay a fixed dividend; any corporate profits in excess of such a dividend accrue to the benefit of the common shareholders. These shares are referred to as "non-participating shares" and usually do not increase in value.

Shareholders who provide share capital to a corporation can realize a return on investment through dividends or through a capital gain when they sell their shares at a profit.

It is important to recognize that dividends and capital gains (or losses) from corporate shares are interconnected. Increased dividends reduce the potential for capital gains; reduced dividends (for earnings retention) increase the potential for capital gains. Exhibit 11-2 diagrams the basic relationship among corporate earnings, dividends, and capital gains.

Exhibit 11-2 can be analyzed as follows:

- Profits earned by the corporation are subject to corporate tax, which is the first level of taxation on corporate income.
- The after-tax profits of the corporation can be either retained for corporate investment or distributed in whole or in part to the shareholders.
- If the corporate profits are retained, no further immediate tax occurs. However, because the undistributed profits belong to the participating shareholders, the value of the shares increases to reflect the undistributed profits. A shareholder has the right to dispose of the shares to a new shareholder, at which point he or she recognizes a capital gain for tax purposes and a second level of tax occurs. Because the capital gain is tied to corporate profits, the second level of tax means that, indirectly, the corporate profits have been taxed a second time.
- If corporate profits are distributed as dividends, the value of the shares declines, and accordingly, the potential for a capital gain also declines. The dividend is included by the individual shareholders in their income for tax purposes. Because the dividend represents the distribution of after-tax corporate profits, the corporate income is taxed a second time, indirectly.

The overall impact of the two levels of tax is diminished somewhat by the dividend tax credit and by the preferential treatment given to capital gains, only one-half of which are taxable. In the previous chapter, it was shown that for individuals, the marginal rates of tax on capital gains are different from those for dividends and that the degree of difference varies in each of the four federal tax brackets.

In summary, corporate profits are taxed a second time at the shareholder level, as either dividends or capital gains. The extent to which double taxation occurs depends on the rate of corporate tax and the extent of the dividend tax credit. This will be reviewed later in the chapter. The relationship between dividends and capital gains is demonstrated in the following example:

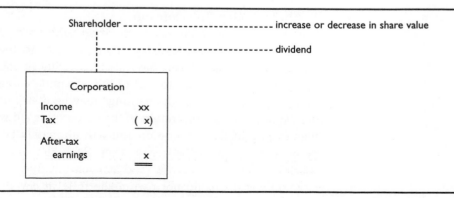

Relationship of Corporate Income, Dividends, and Capital Gains

Situation: Individual A established a new corporation by contributing $1,000 as initial share capital in exchange for common shares. The corporation is a Canadian-controlled private corporation and its dividends are designated as non-eligible. In the first year, the corporation earned profits of $10,600 and paid corporate tax of $1,600, leaving $9,000 in after-tax retained earnings. The financial position of the corporation at the end of its first year is as follows:

Assets		Shareholders' equity	
Cash	$10,000	Share capital	$ 1,000
		Retained earnings	9,000
	$10,000		$10,000

At the end of the first year, the shareholder decided to discontinue the business and to convert his share investment into cash.

Analysis: Assuming individual A is in the highest personal tax bracket, the marginal rate of tax is 33% for non-eligible dividends and 23% for capital gains (see Chapter 10, Exhibit 10-7).[2]

As the controlling shareholder of the corporation, individual A has two basic options available for converting the share investment into cash: he can sell the shares, which are assumed to have a value of $10,000, to individual B; or he can wind up the corporation and pay out its earnings and share capital to himself. The tax impact for each of these alternatives is as follows:

A sells shares to B	
Proceeds of disposition	$10,000
Adjusted cost base of shares	(1,000)
Capital gain	$ 9,000
Tax @ 23%	$ 2,070
A winds up corporation	
Dividend income	$ 9,000
Tax @ 33%	$ 2,970
Return of share capital:	
Proceeds of disposition	$ 1,000
Adjusted cost base of shares	(1,000)
Capital gain	–0–

In the above situation, individual A earned profits from the business venture of $10,600 and paid tax on those profits at two levels at different times. Note that the amount of tax payable varies with the method by which the corporate income is realized by the shareholder. The after-tax effects of the two options are compared in the following table.

	Dividend option	Capital gain option
Corporate profits	$10,600	$10,600
Corporate tax	(1,600)	(1,600)
Shareholder tax	(2,970)	(2,070)
After-tax income	$ 6,030	$ 6,930

---

2   As indicated in Chapter 10, these rates may vary from province to province.

The primary relationship can be further demonstrated by extending the previous situation one step further.

Situation: Assume that individual A in the above situation chose to sell the shares of the corporation to individual B for $10,000. Immediately after acquiring the shares, B decided that the purchase was a mistake; she now wants to convert the investment in shares into cash for investment in another venture. Individual B is subject to the same rates of marginal tax. The financial position of the corporation immediately after her acquisition is unchanged from the previous situation.

Analysis: Individual B, like individual A, also has two options available for converting the share investment into cash: she can either sell the shares to new shareholder C (for $10,000) or wind up the corporation and distribute the assets. The results are given below.

B sells shares to C	
Proceeds of disposition	$10,000
Adjusted cost base of shares	(10,000)
Capital gain	–0–
Tax	–0–
B winds up corporation	
Dividend income	$ 9,000
Tax @ 33%	$ 2,970
Return of share capital:	
Proceeds of disposition	$ 1,000
Adjusted cost base	(10,000)
Capital loss	$ (9,000)
Tax *savings* if capital loss can be utilized:	
$9,000 @ 23%	$ (2,070)

Keep in mind that although the shares have changed ownership at a price of $10,000, the corporation remains unchanged, with $1,000 of share capital and $9,000 of retained earnings.

Note that in the above situation, the investment in shares by B at a cost of $10,000 was not paid to the corporation but, rather, to the previous shareholder, A. The $10,000 cost is represented in the company by $1,000 (initial share capital) plus $9,000 (retained earnings). Therefore, the wind-up of the corporation that returned B's investment of $10,000 was made up of dividend income of $9,000 and a capital loss of $9,000. While the dividend and capital loss balance out to zero in absolute terms, the capital loss will create tax savings at a different rate than the dividend income will create a tax cost. This greatly affects B's tax treatment. In addition, the capital loss can be offset only against capital gains unless it qualifies as an allowable business investment loss.

2. The Secondary Relationships

Where the shareholder has a secondary relationship with the corporation as a creditor, supplier, employee, customer, or lessor, the resulting tax consequences and cash flows between the parties are significantly different from those in the primary relationship. For example, because the corporation is a separate legal entity, the shareholder can be employed by the corporation and receive salary or other benefits as compensation. The compensation paid can be deducted by the corporation from its pre-tax income and is fully taxable when received by the employee/shareholder. The result of this treatment is that corporate income paid as compensation to the employee/shareholder is converted from corporate income into employment income and taxed only once within the overall system.

Similarly, when a shareholder loans money to a corporation and receives interest or leases property to a corporation and receives rents, corporate income is shifted to the individual shareholder and taxed only once.

Consider also the situation where the shareholder acts as a supplier and sells property to the corporation. The sale of property at fair market value may result in taxable gains to the shareholder, but the cost of the asset to the corporation is established by the selling price; this reduces corporate income for tax purposes. The timing of the deduction from corporate income will depend on the nature of the property acquired (that is, whether it is inventory, depreciable property, or something else).

The fundamental difference between the primary relationship and the secondary relationships centres on the tax treatment given to income flows between the corporation and its shareholders. In the primary relationship, *dividends paid* by the corporation are *not deductible* by the corporation for tax purposes but are taxable to the recipient shareholder. In secondary relationships, such payments as salaries, interest, and rents *are* deductible by the corporation and taxable to the recipient. This difference is particularly important in closely held corporations, which are controlled by a single shareholder or by a relatively small group of shareholders. Decisions by such corporations—whether the corporation should be capitalized with shareholder debt, rather than equity; whether the owners should take salaries, rather than dividends; and whether property should be owned by the corporation, rather than leased from the shareholders—all relate back to how the corporation and its shareholders are taxed in primary and secondary relationships. In widely held corporations, such as public corporations, secondary relationships usually do not exist; however, the two-tier system of tax in the primary relationship affects such corporations' decisions concerning whether to raise capital by debt or by equity. This question is examined in subsequent chapters.

In order to understand the tax impact of the two-tier system of tax for corporations on cash flow, it is first necessary to establish the taxable income and the rates of tax for corporations.

II. Determination of Taxable Income

A corporation's taxable income, like an individual's, is determined by reducing net income for tax purposes by a short list of special reductions.

Exhibit 11-3 outlines the basic framework for converting net income for tax purposes to taxable income. Note how this framework differs from the one for individuals. The corporation does not have a capital gain deduction. Also, it treats charitable donations as a reduction of taxable income, whereas the individual treats such donations as a tax credit. Of particular importance is the special reduction for dividends received from other Canadian corporations and from foreign affiliate corporations. This reduction and the loss carry-over reductions are reviewed briefly following Exhibit 11-3.

Exhibit 11-3:			
Taxable Incomes of a Corporation	Net income for tax purposes		xxx
	Special reductions:		
	Donations to charitable organizations*	x	
	Net capital losses	x	
	Non-capital losses	x	
	Dividends from taxable Canadian corporations	x	
	Dividends from foreign affiliates	x	(xx)
	Taxable income		xx

* ITA 110.1(1)(a).

A. Loss Carry-Overs

The loss carry-over provisions for corporations are the same, structurally, as they are for individuals.[3] Net capital losses incurred can be carried back three years and forward indefinitely to the extent of taxable capital gains realized in those years. Non-capital losses (business losses and property losses) incurred in a year can be carried back three years and forward 20 years as a special reduction against any other source of income. Non-capital losses arising from allowable business investment loss can be carried back three years and forward 10 years against any source of income. As the calculation for these items—and its application to investment and business decisions—was examined in Chapter 10 for individuals, it is not repeated in this chapter. However, because of the nature of the corporate structure, there are certain aspects of loss carry-overs that apply to corporations only. These are reviewed below.

• **Change in control**   Although a corporation is a separate legal entity, beneficial ownership of the corporation can change when shares are transferred from one shareholder or group of shareholders to another. This means that the carry-forward of unabsorbed losses may be attractive to acquiring shareholders if they can use those losses against income they can generate in the corporation. Whenever a new shareholder or group of shareholders acquires control of a corporation, the unabsorbed losses being carried forward may be restricted as to use or entirely eliminated.[4] In general terms, a change in control will affect the unabsorbed loss carry-over as follows:

1. The net capital losses that exist in the corporation at the time of change in control are deemed to have expired. This is the case even though the corporation may hold assets that have appreciated in value and that will create capital gains in the future when a disposition occurs.

2. Non-capital losses that resulted from a business operation continue to be carried forward but can be utilized only against income generated from the business that incurred the loss and against income of a business that is similar to the business that incurred the loss. This is a significant departure from the normal carry-forward rules, which permit non-capital losses to be offset against any other source of income. Further, the business that incurred the loss must be carried on at a profit or with a reasonable expectation of profit throughout the taxation year in which the losses are deducted. Any losses incurred by the corporation after the change in control can be carried forward in the normal manner against any other source of income.

The purpose of the above restrictions is to prevent the transfer of unabsorbed corporate losses to other parties through a change in share ownership. However, the fact that business loss carry-overs can be utilized against income from a similar business opens up a narrow opportunity with respect to business sales and acquisitions. For example, the shareholders of a corporation that has significant unabsorbed business losses may achieve a higher price on their shares by selling them to a party that operates a similar business and can take steps to combine some of its profitable operations with those of the corporation it is acquiring (see Chapter 14). When conducting a search for a possible buyer, it is important to target potential buyers who are in the same or a similar line of business. Similarly, profitable businesses that are considering an expansion should seek out corporations in a similar line of business that have substantial unabsorbed business losses which can be merged with their profitable operations. In this context, the term "similar business" is subjective. However, it does include vertical-integration acquisitions, where, for example, a chain of retail stores acquires a manufacturing operation to produce products sold to the retail operation.[5]

---

3 ITA 110.1(1)(a).
4 ITA 111(4), (5), (5.4); IT-302R3.
5 IT-206R, IT-259R4.

These restrictions relate to the treatment of losses that have already occurred but have not been absorbed by later, profitable operations. When a change in share ownership occurs, the acquired corporation may own certain assets that have declined in value. In such cases, after the ownership change, additional losses will occur if those assets are sold. For example, a corporation may own depreciable property that has an undepreciated capital cost for tax purposes of $500,000 but is actually worth only $400,000. After a change in control, the new owners can sell the asset and create a terminal loss of $100,000; this loss would not fall under the restrictions reviewed earlier.

To ensure that unrealized losses do not escape the restrictions, the corporation's year end is deemed, for tax purposes, to end immediately before the control change.[6] This adds any operating losses since the previous year end to the non-capital losses, which makes them subject to the restrictions. After the acquisition of control, the corporation can select a new year end for tax purposes. Also, depreciable property, eligible capital property, and other capital property are all deemed to have been sold at their market value *if* that value is below the tax cost.[7] This means that in the above example, the depreciable property would be deemed to have been sold for $400,000, the result being a realized terminal loss of $100,000 that is also subject to the restrictions. These further adjustments to the control rules are indicative of the Department of Finance's commitment to placing limits on loss transfers. *A more detailed description of the acquisition of control rules are provided below.*

It is important to recognize that these restrictions do not apply when control is acquired by a related party (see Chapter 14).[8]

Acquisition of Control—summary of rules—An acquisition of control occurs when control over the voting rights of a corporation (greater than 50% of the voting shares) is acquired by an unrelated person or group of persons.[9] The tax implications resulting from an acquisition of control are summarized below followed by a brief sample calculation.

- *Year end*   A taxation year end is deemed to occur immediately prior to the date of the acquisition of control.[10] The corporation is required to file a tax return for that period. If the period is less than 365 days any tax rules relating to short taxation years will apply such as the prorating of CCA. The corporation is free to choose a new taxation year (fiscal year end).[11]

- *Inventory*   At the deemed year end, inventory is valued at the lower of cost or market and any resulting loss is recognized for tax purposes.[12]

- *Accounts receivable*   The normal reserve for bad debts is not permitted. Instead, the corporation must examine each account receivable and claim any uncollectible amount as a bad debt.[13] Amounts written off that are subsequently received will be added to income.[14]

- *Depreciable property*   To the extent that the fair market value of property in each class is less than the UCC of the class at the end of the deemed year (after the CCA deduction for that year, if any), the difference is deemed to be a deduction of CCA of that class for the year reducing the UCC accordingly. For capital gains purposes the original ACB is retained.[15]

- *Cumulative eligible property (CEC)*   To the extent that three-quarters of the fair market value the eligible capital property is less than the balance of the

---

6 ITA 249(4).
7 ITA 111(5.1), (5.2); IT-302R3 (paragraphs 14–15).
8 ITA 256(7).
9 ITA 256(7); IT-302R3.
10 ITA 249(4)(a).
11 ITA 249(4)(d).
12 ITA 10(1).
13 ITA 111(5.3), 20(1)(p), 20(1)(l); IT-442(R).
14 ITA 12(1)(i).
15 ITA 111(5.1), 20(1)(a).

CEC account (after the CECA deduction for the deemed year, if any) the balance is written down by that difference.[16]

- *Non-depreciable capital property*   To the extent that the fair market value of each non-depreciable capital property is less than the adjusted cost base of that property, the difference is deemed to be a capital loss for the period and a reduction to the adjusted cost base.[17] The loss can be offset against any capital gains in the period or carried back to a previous year. However, it cannot be carried forward. To alleviate the possibility that such a loss may be eliminated forever, the corporation can elect to recognize accrued gains (if they exist) on any non-depreciable or depreciable property creating a capital gain and/or recapture that can offset the capital loss created in the deemed year or any unused capital loss carryovers from a previous year. It should be noted that if recapture occurs it can only be offset by current non-capital losses or non-capital loss carryovers. However, the use of the losses to offset recapture, may not be the best use of the losses if the non-capital losses can be carried forward (albeit with restrictions discussed above) to future years to reduce taxable income. Therefore, the election is used most often on non-depreciable capital properties. The corporation can choose an elected amount between the adjusted cost base and the fair market value of the chosen property to create the desired gain. The elected amount then becomes the new adjusted cost base of the property.[18]

- *Loss carry-overs*   While the rules in this section were reviewed previously they are briefly reiterated here. On acquisition of control *net capital losses and allowable business investment losses expire* and cannot be used after the deemed year end.[19] Also, any unused donations cannot be carried forward.[20] Non-capital losses can be carried forward provided that the business that incurred the loss is carried on with a reasonable expectation of profit throughout the year that the loss carryover will be deducted. If this condition is met, such non-capital losses are deductible to the extent there is income from the business that generated the loss and/or income from a business selling similar products or providing similar services.[21]

To demonstrate the application of the above rules consider the following situation and analysis.

Situation:

Buy Inc. acquired all of the voting shares of Sold Inc. on June 1, 20X9. Sold's normal taxation year ends on December 31. At the date of acquisition, Sold owned the following properties:

	Cost	UCC/CEC	FMV
Inventory	$400,000		$380,000
Accounts receivable	210,000		170,000
Furniture & equipment—class 8	80,000	48,000	30,000
Manufacturing equipment—class 29	250,000	80,000	150,000
Eligible capital property	120.000	75,000	80,000
Marketable securities	100,000		90,000

---

16 ITA 111(5.2), 20(1)(b).
17 ITA 111(4)(c), (d).
18 ITA 111(4)(e).
19 ITA 111(4)(a), 111(5).
20 ITA 110(1.2).
21 ITA 111(5)(a)(ii)

On December 31, 20X8 Sold Inc. had net capital losses of $40,000. No capital gains were earned in 2009. The UCC of the class 8 and 29 properties shown above is the amount after deducting the CCA for the 5-month period from January 1, 20X9 to May 31, 20X9. Remember, the normal CCA was prorated for the number of days in the short taxation year (151 days) over the number of days in the year (365).

Analysis: The acquisition of control of Sold Inc. on June 1, 20X9 results in a deemed taxation year end on May 31, 20X9. As Sold's previous year end was December 31, 20X8 it will have a short 5-month taxation year for which it must determine its taxable income and file a tax return. If, in the future, Sold wants to retain its December 31 year end it will have to incur another short taxation year from June 1, 20X9 to December 31, 20X9. Alternatively, Sold can choose a new taxation year end provided it is no longer than twelve months from May 31, 20X9.

The fair market value of inventory is $20,000 less than its cost and, therefore, Sold will recognize a loss of $20,000 for tax purposes and the new cost of the inventory becomes $380,000, its fair market value. Similarly, the accounts receivable will recognize a bad debt expense of $40,000 ($210,000 − $170,000).

The class 8 property (furniture and fixtures) has already claimed its CCA for the short deemed taxation year. As the fair market value of the class 8 property is $18,000 less than its UCC, Sold is deemed to claim a further CCA amount of $18,000 ($48000 − $30,000). Accordingly, the UCC is reduced to $30,000 from $48,000. The class 8 property will retain its original cost for purposes of calculating any possible future recapture or capital gains.

The fair market value of the class 29 property is greater than its UCC and, therefore, no adjustment is required.

With respect to the cumulative eligible capital, the CEC must be written down by $15,000. While the fair market value of the property is greater than the CEC amount, it is necessary to compare three-quarters of the fair market value to the CEC balance. So 3/4 × $80,000 is $60,000, which is $15,000 less the balance CEC amount of $75,000.

Finally, the non-depreciable capital property (marketable securities) must recognize a capital loss of $10,000 because the fair market value ($90, 000) is less than the adjusted cost base ($100,000). The new adjusted cost base of the property becomes $90,000. The capital loss cannot be used in the taxation year as Sold had no capital gains in the period. So, the loss of $10,000 increases the net capital loss from $40,000 to $50,000. However, the acquisition of control causes the entire $50,000 net capital loss to expire and so it cannot be used in future years. If Sold owned capital property that had a fair market value greater than its adjusted cost base, an election could be made to recognize some or all of the accrued capital gain. This would allow the net capital loss to be offset against the deemed gain and eliminate the expiration. However, in this situation Sold does not have any accrued capital gains and the election is not possible.

• **Loss utilization in corporate groups**   Often, a shareholder or group of shareholders will control a number of corporations that conduct various separate business activities. Although each corporation in the group is controlled by the same shareholders, each corporation is, nevertheless, a separate entity for tax purposes and determines its income or losses separately. This structure can be onerous when some companies in the group are profitable and subject to tax, while others have unabsorbed losses.

Consider Exhibit 11-4, in which the same shareholder(s) directly or indirectly control three separate corporations, of which two are profitable and one has substantial losses. The combined financial results are as shown in the table that follows.

Exhibit 11-4:

Corporate Groups and Loss Utilization

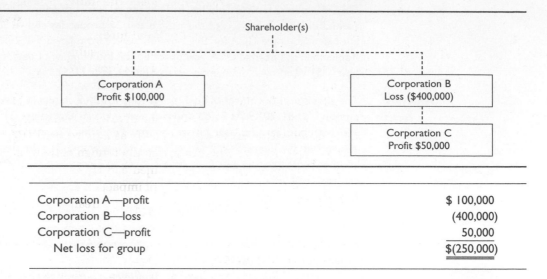

Corporation A—profit	$ 100,000
Corporation B—loss	(400,000)
Corporation C—profit	50,000
Net loss for group	$(250,000)

Even though the group as a whole has lost $250,000, both Corporation A and Corporation C will pay tax on their profits of $100,000 and $50,000 respectively, and the loss in Corporation B will remain unused. While Corporation B may be able to absorb its losses in future years, the immediate cash flow of the group is diminished, with the result that it must forgo investment opportunities or, if it is in financial difficulty, face the increasing risk of a business failure.

In this type of situation the profits and losses of the various corporations can be combined *if* the operations of each corporation are formally merged and housed in a single corporate entity. For example, the operations of Corporations B and C can be merged with those of Corporation A. While this will not alter the past year's results, it *will* permit B's losses to be absorbed by the future profits of the other operations. (A number of methods can be used to reorganize corporations. They are examined in Chapter 14.)

The difficulty of combining losses with profits in a corporate group should be remembered when making expansion decisions. For example, a corporation that is contemplating an expansion into new activities can either house the expansion operation as a branch within the existing corporation or establish a subsidiary corporation. If the new venture is going to incur losses in the initial years, a branch structure would permit the losses to be used immediately against the profits of other operations; the subsidiary structure, on the other hand, would separate the profits of the existing operations from the losses incurred by the expansion activity. The increased cash flow from the immediate tax savings under the branch structure can be used to fund the losses of the expansion operation and thus reduce the risk of its failure. It should be remembered, however, that the subsidiary structure provides some protection in the form of limited liability as well as the opportunity to merge the operations at a later time when it is clear the new operation will succeed (see Chapter 20).

B. Dividends from Other Canadian Corporations

It will be recalled that a corporation includes dividends received from other corporations as property income when determining net income for tax purposes. In order to avoid multiple taxation on the distribution of corporate after-tax income, a corporation's taxable income is reduced by the amount of dividends received from other taxable Canadian corporations.[22] The dividend is first included in net income and then removed in calculating taxable income. This means that dividends can flow tax-free between Canadian corporations and are not subject to a second level of tax until they

22 ITA 89(1)(i), 112(1), 248.

are received by the ultimate shareholder—the individual. In simpler terms, it can be said that corporate profits, once taxed by the initial corporation, can be shifted to other corporations via dividends without further taxation.

In certain cases, private corporations may be subject to a temporary tax (Part IV tax) on dividends received from other corporations (see Chapter 13). However, for most *business* structures, Canadian intercorporate dividends flow tax-free.

In addition, Canadian corporations that receive dividends from a foreign affiliate corporation are also not taxable on such dividends as a result of the special reduction in arriving at taxable income.[23] To qualify as a foreign affiliate, the Canadian corporation must have an equity percentage in the foreign corporation that is at least 10%.

This ability to move after-tax retained earnings freely from one corporation to its corporate shareholder has an important impact on the relationship between dividends and capital gains. Consider the alternative tax treatments in the following situation:

Situation: An individual owns all of the shares of Corporation A. Corporation A has used its funds to acquire, at a cost of $100,000, all of the shares of Corporation B, which operates an active business. Corporation B has been profitable and has accumulated after-tax retained earnings of $400,000. Corporation A is contemplating disposing of its investment in Corporation B. The shares of Corporation B have recently been valued at $700,000, and a willing buyer is available.

Analysis: The organization structure in this situation is as follows:

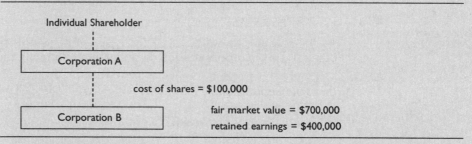

Individual Shareholder

Corporation A

cost of shares = $100,000

Corporation B

fair market value = $700,000
retained earnings = $400,000

The value of Corporation B's shares is $700,000, even though its retained earnings are only $400,000. This difference in value results from the fact that the corporation has assets, such as land, buildings, and goodwill, that have appreciated in value but have not been sold.

Corporation A can realize its investment in Corporation B by selling the shares for $700,000 or by selling the shares for a reduced value after declaring a dividend from Corporation B to Corporation A. Keep in mind that the payment of the dividend will reduce the value of the shares by an equivalent amount. The tax treatment of these two alternatives is as follows:

Sale of shares for $700,000	
Proceeds of disposition	$ 700,000
Adjusted cost base	(100,000)
Capital gain	$ 600,000
Combination dividend and sale of shares	
Dividend (equal to retained earnings)	$ 400,000
Amount of dividend taxable	NIL
Sale of shares:	
Proceeds ($700,000 − $400,000)	$ 300,000
Adjusted cost base	(100,000)
Capital gain	$ 200,000

23 ITA 113, 95(1).

In the above situation, both alternatives provide the owner with total proceeds of $700,000. However, in the second alternative, the payment of a tax-free dividend of $400,000 to Corporation A reduces the value of Corporation B's shares by $400,000. In turn, the amount of the capital gain on the sale of the shares is reduced from $600,000 to $200,000. By arranging for a dividend, rather than a capital gain, Corporation A now has a greater amount of after-tax proceeds for reinvestment in another venture. Of course, utilizing the dividend option in this structure results in a tax deferral and not a tax saving because ultimately a second level of tax will be incurred when dividends flow to the individual who owns Corporation A.

The concept of tax-free intercorporate dividends is fundamental to the relationship between corporations and their shareholders. An investor can interpose a holding corporation between himself or herself and the active corporation, transfer after-tax retained earnings into it, and reinvest those earnings on a tax-deferred basis. This use of holding companies is discussed in greater detail in Chapter 14.

III. Calculation of Corporate Tax

Corporations are divided into three basic categories for tax purposes.

1. *Public corporations,* which are companies that are resident of Canada and whose shares are traded on a stock exchange.[24]

2. *Private corporations,* which are corporations resident in Canada and which are not public corporations or controlled by public corporations.[25]

3. *Canadian-controlled private corporations* (*CCPCs*), which are corporations that are resident in Canada, do not qualify as public corporations, and are not controlled by non-residents of Canada.[26]

The two main corporate structures in the Canadian tax system are public corporations and Canadian-controlled private corporations, although all three types are subject to federal and provincial taxes.[27] The overall format for calculating corporate income tax for all types of corporations is outlined in Exhibit 11-5. Note that provincial taxes are expressed as a percentage of *taxable income*, and as a result, it is easy to determine the basic marginal tax rates.

A. Federal Tax The primary federal tax is calculated by applying a flat-rate tax of 38% to the corporation's taxable income. In order to provide room for the provinces to impose a tax, the federal rate of 38% is reduced by 10% as a federal abatement for provincial taxes. So, the basic rate of federal tax is actually 28% (38% − 10%) for all corporations.[28]

The federal rate of tax may be increased or reduced further on specific types of income earned by certain corporations. These are reviewed on the following page.

---

24 ITA 89(1).
25 ITA 89(1).
26 ITA 89(1), 125(7)(b); IT-458R2.
27 ITA 89(1)(f).
28 ITA 123(1), 124(1).

Exhibit 11-5:			

Determination of	(a) Federal tax: 36 %		
Tax for Corporations	Primary federal tax (rate × taxable income)		xx
	Abatement for provincial tax 10%		(x)
			x
	Refundable tax on investment income		x
			xx
	less		
	General rate reduction	x	
	Small business deduction	x	
	Manufacturing and processing deduction	x	
	Federal tax credits	x	x
	Federal tax-Part I of the *Income Tax Act*		*xx
	(b) Provincial tax:		
	Primary provincial tax (*rate × taxable income*)	x	
	Specific provincial tax credits	(x)	x
	(c) Combined federal and provincial taxes (a + b)		xx

* An additional tax under Part IV of the ITA is applicable on certain dividends received by a private corporation. This tax is reviewed in Chapter 13. Also, the refundable tax on investment income and the small business deduction do not apply to public corporations.

• **General tax reduction**   A general tax reduction applies to particular types of income earned by corporations.[29] These are listed below.

Public corporations—Federal tax is reduced by 13% of the corporation's taxable income other than its income from manufacturing and processing activities (M&P), which has a separate reduction described below.

Canadian-controlled private corporations—Federal tax is reduced by 13% on active business income (other than income qualifying for the M&P reduction described below) that is above the annual limit to which the small business deduction applies (see below). This reduction does *not* apply to the tax on its *investment* income or personal service business income (see Chapter 13).

• **Refundable tax on investment income**   This special tax is applied only to the investment income (not active business income) of Canadian-controlled private corporations. The rate of tax is 6⅔% of the corporation's investment income and is *fully refundable* to the corporation when dividends are paid to its shareholder(s).[30] This tax, which has a special purpose, is reviewed in Chapter 13.

• **Small business deduction**   The small business deduction is available only to Canadian-controlled private corporations. This deduction permits the normal federal tax rate to be reduced by 17% so that the net federal tax is 11% (28% − 17%); this applies only to the first $500,000 of annual active business income of the corporation or to its taxable income, whichever is lower.[31] Two or more corporations owned by similar shareholders may have to share this $500,000 limit (see Chapter 13).

Consider this example: A Canadian-controlled private corporation has active business income of $125,000 and taxable income of $110,000 (after deducting a loss carry-over of

---

29 ITA 123.4
30 ITA 123.3.
31 ITA 125(1); IT-73R6; May 2006 federal budget.

$10,000 and charitable donations of $5,000). Its small business deduction for the year is $18,700, calculated as follows:

17% × the least of:	
Active business income	$125,000
Taxable income	110,000
Annual limit	500,000
17% × $110,000 = $18,700	

The small business deduction effectively creates a progressive rate structure for Canadian-controlled private corporations. *The tax treatment of Canadian-controlled private corporations is examined in greater detail in Chapter 13.*

• **Manufacturing and processing deduction** Profits that result from manufacturing and processing activities are subject to a rate reduction of 13% for all public corporations.[32] Canadian-controlled private corporations are entitled to the same manufacturing reduction, but only on annual manufacturing profits in excess of the $500,000 small business deduction limit described previously. Therefore, the net federal rate of tax on manufacturing activities (except those eligible for the small business deduction) is 15% (28% − 13%). Note that the general tax reduction (described above) applicable to other types of income is also 13%. Therefore, most corporate income will be subject to a net federal tax rate of 15%. Four provincial/territorial jurisdictions have special rates for manufacturing and processing income (on which the federal manufacturing and processing deduction is claimed—*Saskatchewan, Ontario, Newfoundland,* and *Yukon*), and so the following discussion remains relevant.

The following arbitrary formula is used to determine the manufacturing profits subject to the rate reduction. The result of this formula may be higher or lower than the actual manufacturing profits. The details of this rather complex formula can be obtained from the federal tax return.[33] Its fundamentals are presented below, for use in a later discussion on how it affects business structure and organization.

$$\frac{MC + ML}{TC + TL} \times \text{Total business profits} = \text{Manufacturing profits}$$

Where:

MC = manufacturing capital, determined as the annualized cost of all *depreciable* property used directly in qualified manufacturing activities[34]

TC = total capital, determined as the annualized cost of all depreciable property of the corporation

ML = manufacturing labour, determined as the total wages paid for qualified manufacturing activities[35]

TL = total labour, determined as the total wages and salaries paid by the corporation

Note that the above formula arbitrarily determines manufacturing profits as a function of the labour and capital employed in such activities. Consider the impact this may have on the corporate structure of an enterprise that carries on both manufacturing

---

32 ITA 125.1(1).
33 IT-145R.
34 The annualized cost is calculated as 10% of the original cost of owned property plus the annual rent for leased property. This sum is grossed up by an arbitrary amount of 100/85. Total capital is calculated in a similar manner, except that the gross-up is not applied.
35 Manufacturing labour is the actual amount grossed up by an arbitrary amount of 100/75. Total labour is not grossed up.

and non-manufacturing activities. Exhibit 11-6 diagrams alternative structures for conducting a combined retail/manufacturing operation.

Exhibit 11-6:

Alternative Structures for Manufacturing and Other Activities

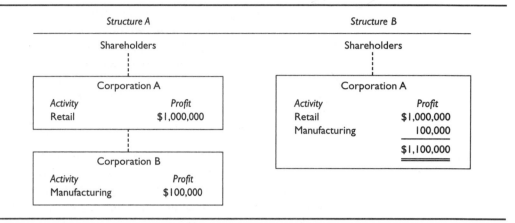

Under structure A, the activities are divided between two corporations. Because manufacturing is carried on only in Corporation B, the maximum profit eligible for the 13% federal and some provincial manufacturing reductions is $100,000.

However, under structure B, the manufacturing and retail operations are combined in one corporation that has a total profit of $1,100,000. The portion of this total profit that is considered to be manufacturing profit is based on the arbitrary formula and is governed by the capital and wages employed in each operation. If, for example, this relationship amounted to 30%, the manufacturing profits eligible for the 13% rate reduction and *certain provincial rate reductions* would be $330,000, as follows:

$$\frac{MC + ML}{TC + TL} = 30\% \times \$1,100,000 = \$330,000$$

In structure B, the overall tax may be lower, simply because the operations are combined, rather than separated. This, of course, is not always the result; the reverse could happen if the relationships were altered. The organization structure of a business is influenced by a number of factors, one of which is the tax factor.

• **Full-rate taxable income and GRIP**   Taxable income that does not benefit from the small business deduction, and is not investment income earned by a Canadian-controlled private corporation, is referred to as full-rate taxable income. When full-rate taxable income, less the related income tax, is paid to shareholders as a dividend, the dividend qualifies as an *eligible dividend* that is subject to a higher gross-up and dividend tax credit. The paying corporation must designate a dividend to be an eligible dividend at the time the dividend is paid and the shareholder must be informed of the dividend's status.[36]

Canadian-controlled private corporations keep track of this type of after-tax income by maintaining a General Rate Income Pool (GRIP). A corporation's GRIP is increased annually by 72% of its full-rate taxable income.[37] The 72% represents the approximate

---

36 ITA 89(14).
37 ITA 89(1).

after-tax amount. Eligible dividends are then paid from the corporation's GRIP. A *further discussion of the GRIP rules is provided in Chapter 13.*

Normally, all of the income of public corporations (also private corporations that are not Canadian-controlled) is classified as full-rate taxable income and it is not necessary for them to maintain a GRIP calculation. However, public corporations (also private corporations that are not Canadian-controlled) may receive non-eligible dividends from a Canadian-controlled private corporation. These dividends cannot be classified as full-rate taxable income. Instead, they are tracked in a tax account called the Low Rate Income Pool (LRIP)[38] which, when paid as a dividend, maintains its non-eligible status. Public corporations (also private corporations that are not Canadian-controlled) are subject to a penalty if they have a LRIP balance at the time eligible dividends are paid.[39] To avoid the penalty, public corporations must pay dividends first from the LRIP before designating other dividends as eligible dividends.

B. Provincial Tax

As previously mentioned, provincial corporate tax rates are expressed as a percentage of corporate taxable income. Each province and territory imposes a primary flat rate of tax on all corporate income. These rates vary from province to province. Exhibit 11-7 outlines the primary provincial tax rates applicable for 2012. They are subject to frequent changes and are presented here merely to show the range of provincial rates. The reader should update these rates to conform to the particular period in question. Information on provincial tax rates can be obtained by accessing this text's Web site at **www.mcgrawhill.ca/olc/buckwold.**

In addition, certain provinces apply a reduced rate of tax to the first $500,000 (or more) of active business profits of Canadian-controlled private corporations, and some reduce the rate for manufacturing profits. For example, in Ontario, the primary rate of 11% is reduced to 4.5% for active business profits that qualify for the federal small business deduction and to 10% (2012) for manufacturing income.

A corporation incorporated or based in a particular province will be taxed entirely in that province *unless* it carries on business in another province through a permanent establishment, such as an office, branch, warehouse, or factory. If such a permanent establishment exists, the profits attributable to that location are based on the ratio of *sales* in

Exhibit 11-7:

Primary Provincial Tax Rates—2012

	Regular income	Income eligible for small business deduction		Regular income	Income eligible for small business deduction
Alberta	10%	3%	Nova Scotia	16%	4%*
British Columbia	10	2.5	Nunavut	12	4
Manitoba	12	0	Ontario	11.5	4.5
New Brunswick	10	4.5	P.E.I.	16	1
Newfoundland and			Quebec	11.9	8
Labrador	14	4	Saskatchewan	12	2
Northwest Territories	11.5	4	Yukon	15	4

As applicable in March 2012 and subject to change.

Note: Special rates also apply to manufacturing income—Newfoundland 5%, Ontario 10%, Saskatchewan 10%, and Yukon 2.5%.

*Rate reduced to 3.5% in 2013.

---

38 ITA 89(1) LRIP definition.
39 ITA 89(1) excessive eligible dividend designation.

the province to total sales, and the ratio of *wages* paid in the province to total wages, multiplied by the total business profits of the whole corporation.[40] For example:

(a)
$$\frac{\text{Wages paid in Alberta}}{\text{Total wages paid by corp.}} = 33\%$$

(b)
$$\frac{\text{Sales in Alberta}}{\text{Total sales of corp.}} = 45\%$$

Average of (a) and (b):
$$\frac{33 + 45}{2} = 39\%$$

Therefore, 39% of the total business profits of the corporation are taxed at Alberta rates, even though the real profits in Alberta may be higher or lower.

No provincial allocations are made when corporations carry on business in other provinces by way of direct sales from the home province. The use of alternative business-expansion strategies, such as direct sales, branch operations, and separate corporations, significantly alters the rates of corporate tax (see Chapter 20).

C. Combined Federal and Provincial Taxes

It would be useful to review federal and provincial taxes by establishing the marginal rates of tax for each type of corporation. Exhibit 11-8 combines the federal tax rates with those of a province to demonstrate how the calculation is made. The exhibit combines the federal rates for 2012 with those of *a province having a 10% rate on normal income, and a 4% rate on income subject to the small business deduction.*

Note the significantly lower tax rate (15%) for the first $500,000 of annual active business income in the Canadian-controlled private corporation. Not only is the rate lower than other rates of corporate tax, but it is also lower than the personal rates of tax described in Chapter 10. (The benefits of incorporating a small business are reviewed in Chapter 13.) Actual marginal rates for this type of income range from 11% to 19% in 2012.

Included in Exhibit 11-8 is the special rate of tax on *investment income* earned by Canadian-controlled private corporations. This income is subject to an additional refundable tax of $6\frac{2}{3}\%$ and is reviewed in Chapter 13.

Exhibit 11-8:

Combined Federal and Provincial Taxes 2012

	Public corporations	Canadian-controlled private corporations		
	Income	1st $500,000 of business income	Other business income	Investment income
Primary federal tax	38%	38%	38%	38%
Federal abatement	(10)	(10)	(10)	(10)
General tax reduction	(13)		(13)	
Refundable tax on investment income				$6\frac{2}{3}$
Small business deduction		(17)		
Federal tax	15	11	15	$34\frac{2}{3}$
Provincial tax	10	4	10	10
Combined rate	25%	15%	25%	$44\frac{2}{3}\%$

For demonstration purposes, these assumed rates will be used throughout the text. Combined federal and provincial tax rates for all provinces and territories are calculated in Appendix B at the end of the text.

---

40 ITA 124(4)(a); Regulations 400–415; IT-177R2.

Actual combined federal and provincial corporate tax rates may vary from province to province. These actual tax rates can be obtained by accessing links on this text's Web site at **www.mcgrawhill.ca/olc/buckwold**.

IV. The Integration of Corporate and Individual Taxation

At the beginning of this chapter, a review of the primary relationship between a corporation and its shareholder(s) established that corporations, as separate legal entities, are taxed on their profits separate from the shareholders. The review further established that although after-tax corporate profits can be shifted freely to corporate shareholders, the ultimate shareholder of a corporation is the individual, who is taxed a second time when after-tax corporate profits are distributed as dividends. This two-tier system creates the possibility of some double taxation. In order to fully understand the impact of corporate taxation on financial decisions, it is necessary to establish the degree to which double taxation, if any, results from the two-tiered structure.

The effect of double taxation is modified by the dividend tax credit, which the individual can apply to reduce the personal tax on dividends received from Canadian corporations. This reduction represents a credit for all or a portion of the corporate taxes paid on the income represented by the dividend. In Chapter 7, it was established that the dividend tax credit attempts to reduce double taxation by reducing personal taxes and assumes that the corporate tax rate is approximately either 27.5% or 20%. Exhibit 11-8 indicates that the corporate tax rate is not, in fact, always 27.5% or 20%.

By applying the corporate rates in Exhibit 11-8 and the individual tax rates on dividends in Exhibit 10-7 (see Chapter 10), the extent of double taxation on the flow of corporate income to shareholders can be determined. Remember, there are two categories of dividends—eligible and non-eligible—each having a different dividend tax credit. The table below illustrates what happens when a *public corporation* pays its after-tax profits to an individual shareholder who is in the top marginal tax bracket. The same table also demonstrates that business income earned by a public corporation and then transferred to its shareholder will incur a combined tax rate of 46%; whereas if the same business income were earned directly by the individual, a tax rate of only 45% would apply.

	PUBLIC CORPORATION	
Business income	$1,000	
Corporate tax (25%)	(250)	
Retained earnings	$ 750	

Individual shareholder:	
Dividend income—Eligible	$750
Tax @ 28% (net of dividend tax credit)	(210)
Net cash, after tax, to shareholder	$540

Total tax on $1,000 of corporate income:	
Tax paid by corporation	$250
Tax paid by individual shareholder	210
	$460

Effective rate of tax (rounded)	46%*

Amount of double taxation:	
Combined corporate and shareholder tax	46%
Maximum personal tax rate on business income (Exhibit 10-7)	45%
Double taxation	1%

---

* This rate varies by province.

The same calculation can be applied to a Canadian-controlled private corporation that earns business income subject to the small business deduction (see table below). In this example, because the corporate tax rate is only 15%, the dividend tax credit more than eliminates the element of double taxation. However, it should be noted that annual business income in excess of $500,000 is subject to a higher rate of corporate tax; consequently, that income is subject to double taxation, much like income from public corporations.

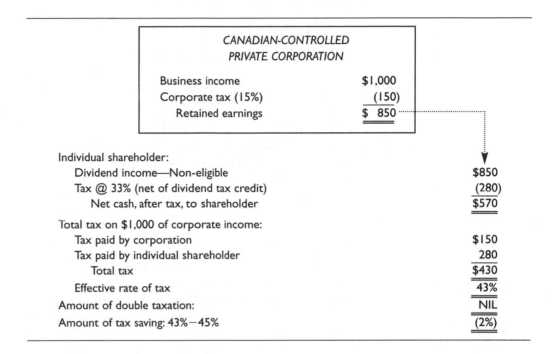

CANADIAN-CONTROLLED PRIVATE CORPORATION	
Business income	$1,000
Corporate tax (15%)	(150)
Retained earnings	$ 850
Individual shareholder:	
Dividend income—Non-eligible	$850
Tax @ 33% (net of dividend tax credit)	(280)
Net cash, after tax, to shareholder	$570
Total tax on $1,000 of corporate income:	
Tax paid by corporation	$150
Tax paid by individual shareholder	280
Total tax	$430
Effective rate of tax	43%
Amount of double taxation:	NIL
Amount of tax saving: 43%−45%	(2%)

The amount of double taxation is an important component in the calculation of the long-term return on investment in corporations. So is the timing of that taxation. In a public corporation, double taxation on returns to the owner is automatic; in a Canadian-controlled private corporation, it may or may not occur depending on the nature of the income (see Chapter 13). In either case, the combination of corporate tax and tax on distributions to shareholders has an impact on dividend policy, capital (debt/equity) structures, and the form of business organization (see Chapters 12 and 13).

Consider, for example, the impact of double taxation on a public corporation that must choose between two alternatives for raising capital: the acquiring of additional debt or the issuing of preferred shares bearing a fixed dividend rate. If the going interest rate for corporate debt were 10%, an individual investor in the top tax bracket would receive a net return of 5.5% after tax (10% − tax @ 45%). In order to receive an after-tax return of 5.5% on a dividend, the dividend rate would have to be 7.6% (7.6% − tax @ 28% = 5.5%). To provide the same after-tax return to an investor, the corporation can issue debt that bears interest at 10% or preferred shares with a dividend rate of 7.6%. Because the interest is deductible from corporate income, the corporation could invest the borrowed funds at 10% in order to generate enough income to pay out 10% interest. However, for the preferred shares, the dividend is not deductible and an element of double taxation occurs. Therefore, given that the corporate tax rate is 25%, the corporation would have to generate a return of about 10.1% with the equity capital in order to have sufficient funds to pay a dividend of 7.6% (10.1% − tax @ 25% = approximately 7.6%).

The above example demonstrates the effect that double taxation has on the cost of equity capital and compares it with the cost of debt in public corporations. (A more detailed review of corporate financing is made in Chapter 21.) Similar analyses can be applied to Canadian-controlled private corporations. It must be noted that in private corporations, the corporation/shareholder relationship is much stronger because there are only a few shareholders. In such circumstances, the shareholder can reduce the impact of double taxation by also acting as creditor and provide debt capital to the corporation in return for interest or lease assets to the corporation in return for rents. In such circumstances, double taxation is avoided because interest and rents are deducted from corporate income (see Chapter 12).

The above sample integration calculations have applied tax rates using a fictitious provincial tax rate. When actual provincial tax rates are used, the element of double tax for public corporations (and business income of Canadian-controlled private corporations with no small business deduction) vary widely by province. Similarly, business income eligible for the small business deduction often result in overintegration providing overall tax savings when income is passed through a corporation. The following table outlines the integration rates by province for 2012.

Business income *not eligible* for the *small business deduction*:[41]

	Double Taxation %		Double Taxation %
Alberta	.5	P.E.I.	3.4
British Columbia	.6	Quebec	2.7
Manitoba	4.15	Saskatchewan	1.1
New Brunswick	(1.5)	NWT	.2
Newfoundland	2.7	Nunavut	6.6
Nova Scotia	5.9	Yukon	(1.2)
Ontario	1.8		

Business income *eligible* for the *small business deduction*:[42]

	Tax Saving %		Tax Saving %
Alberta	1.2	P.E.I.	(.9)
British Columbia	1.0	Quebec	(.2)
Manitoba	.6	Saskatchewan	2.0
New Brunswick	1.8	NWT	2.9
Newfoundland	1.8	Nunavut	.9
Nova Scotia	4.2	Yukon	1.6
Ontario	3.4		

Detailed integration calculations for 2012 are shown in Appendix B at the end of the text.

V. Tax Planning Checklist

As this chapter presents only an *overview* of corporate taxation, an extensive list of tax planning items cannot be drawn from it. The next three chapters examine a number of corporate tax planning issues in more depth. The main tax planning items relating to this chapter are listed below.

1. Shareholders of a closely held corporation should consider maintaining some secondary relationships. By acting as creditors, lessors, and/or employees, they may be able to alter the amount and timing of tax payable so that it is less than would have resulted on a dividend distribution.

---

[41] Tax News Network, Pricewaterhouse Coopers, as of April 1, 2012. Individual rate assumed at top marginal bracket. Percentages are rounded.

[42] Tax News Network, Pricewaterhouse Coopers, as of April 1, 2012. Individual rate assumed at top marginal bracket. Percentages are rounded.

2. An increase in the value of shares arising from accumulated corporate profits can be realized in the form of a dividend or a capital gain. A shareholder who controls a corporation should regularly review these two methods and take advantage of the option that results in the minimum amount of tax.

3. When a change in the controlling shareholder(s) is being considered, the treatment of loss carry-overs should be reviewed. Non-capital losses from business operations have restricted use after a control change. These restrictions are less onerous when control is acquired by an entity in the same or a similar line of business. A vendor may do well to target this type of buyer.

4. Some businesses divide their operations among several corporations. In such structures, it is important for the taxpayer to monitor the potential for losses in each corporation to ensure that steps can be taken to utilize those losses against profits in other operations as soon as possible after they occur.

5. When contemplating expansion activities, the structure (i.e., separate corporations versus branch of the existing corporation) should be chosen carefully from the perspective of loss utilization as well as liability exposure.

6. Dividends usually flow tax-free from one corporation to another (see Chapter 13 for exceptions). In such circumstances, it is worthwhile to realize returns on intercorporate investments by way of dividends, rather than capital gains. As well, dividend policies should be reviewed regularly, especially when a disposal of share investments is being contemplated.

7. Corporations that engage in both manufacturing and non-manufacturing activities should examine how the corporate structure affects the arbitrary formula which determines the amount of the manufacturing tax reduction. Depending on the capital and labour input of the two activities, tax savings may be achieved by either separating or combining those activities.

8. When attempting to extend operations into new provinces, the taxpayer is strongly advised to consider the effect of alternative expansion structures on provincial taxes. Different expansion methods, such as direct sales, an out-of-province branch location, or a separate corporation will result in different provincial tax costs.

VI. Summary and Conclusion

This chapter has completed the framework of corporate taxation by showing how net income for tax purposes is converted into taxable income and by outlining the structure for calculating corporate tax.

Corporate taxable income is determined by reducing net income by a small number of special reductions. As is the case with individuals, the utilization of loss carry-overs has an important effect on cash flow and return on investment. A unique aspect of corporate loss carry-overs is that further restrictions are imposed when shareholder control of the corporation changes. When this occurs, net capital losses cease to exist, and unabsorbed business losses at the time of the change in control can be used in future years only against profits from the business that incurred the losses, or against the profits of a similar business. In addition, the calculation of corporate taxable income permits the deduction of certain intercorporate dividends, which means that corporate after-tax retained earnings can be shifted from one corporation to another without additional tax being incurred.

Corporate tax is determined at both the federal and provincial levels; in each case, the tax payable is expressed as a percentage of taxable income. Public corporations and private corporations are subject to similar rates of tax, although both federal and provincial taxes are reduced for manufacturing profits and for a portion of the business income earned by Canadian-controlled private corporations.

A significant portion of this chapter was devoted to establishing the relationship between the corporation and its shareholder(s). There is a two-tiered system in which income is taxed first in the corporation and then a second time when distributed as a dividend to shareholders. The second level of tax can be avoided when the corporation does not declare dividends, but this increases the share value, which ultimately may be recognized as a capital gain on disposition.

In conclusion, the corporation, although treated as a separate entity within the tax system, cannot be viewed in isolation from the shareholders when the tax impact of investment and management decisions is being considered. What affects the corporation will, at a different time perhaps, also affect the shareholders because of the fundamental relationship between the two.

Visit the Canadian Income Taxation Web site at **www.mcgrawhill.ca/ olc/buckwold** to view any updated tax information.

VII. Conclusion to Part Two

This chapter brings to a conclusion Part Two of the text, which was designed to provide an overview of the fundamentals of income determination and tax for the two primary entities—individuals and corporations. Chapters 3 through 11 have developed the framework of the Canadian income tax system by establishing who is subject to tax, what income is taxable, and how tax is calculated. This framework can be summarized as follows:

1. Individuals and corporations are the two primary entities subject to tax in Canada. A third entity, trusts, is examined in Chapter 17.

2. Individuals and corporations that are resident in Canada are taxable on their world income. Non-resident individuals and corporations are taxable only on certain income derived in Canada.

3. Taxable income for the primary entities is the net income for tax purposes less limited special reductions.

4. Net income for tax purposes consists of five specifically defined types of income:
   • employment income
   • business income
   • property income
   • capital gains
   • other specific sources of income

Each of the above income sources is clearly identifiable and is determined in accordance with its own set of fundamental principles.

The overall system, while sometimes complex, has an innate logic and direction. Of primary importance is the statutory scheme, or aggregating formula, which is the foundation of income determination. The tax treatment of most financial transactions can be understood if such transactions are first related to the aggregating formula. The dividend tax credit and the treatment of intercorporate dividends are the ties that bind together the corporation and its shareholders.

As stated in the introductory chapter, one need not be a tax specialist to apply taxation questions to business and investment decisions. In most cases, the after-tax cash flows of alternative business opportunities and strategies can be projected by applying the fundamentals of the tax system. Chapters 3 to 11 have attempted to relate the basic principles to business and investment decisions through a number of specific examples. These examples were designed primarily to stimulate the reader to develop an "after-tax" approach to business and investment decisions. Taxation of income cannot be placed in a vacuum but, rather, must be included, in a formal way, in all financial decision making.

Demonstration Questions

QUESTION ONE

Tap Inc., a Canadian-controlled private corporation, was incorporated on January 1, 20X1, and was profitable in its first fiscal period ending December 31, 20X1. Substantial losses were incurred in 20X2, but in 20X3, modest gains were achieved. Tap Inc. sells farm implements. As a sideline, the company operates a small grain farm. The farm is a minor part of the corporation's business activity.

Tap Inc. has asked you to examine the effect of the 20X2 loss on the company's tax position. From the financial statements, you have summarized the following information:

	20X1	20X2	20X3
Business income (loss)	$76,000	$(120,000)	$30,000
Canadian taxable dividends	—	—	10,000
Capital gains	4,000	4,000	8,000
Capital losses	—	(28,000)	—
Farm income (loss)	4,000	—	(15,000)
Charitable donations	(28,000)	—	(2,000)
Income (loss)—financial statements	$56,000	$(144,000)	$31,000

You have noted that the 20X2 capital losses of $28,000 include a loss of $8,000 from the sale of shares of a qualified small business corporation.

Required:

1. Assuming that Tap Inc. wants to use the maximum losses as soon as possible, determine its net income and taxable income for 20X1, 20X2, and 20X3.

2. For each type of unused deduction, determine the carry-forward balance, if any, and briefly explain the time period remaining before it expires.

3. In what circumstances, if any, may it be beneficial for Tap Inc. to delay the use of a loss carry-over beyond a year in which it could be used?

Solution:

1. Calculation of losses available for carry-over.

20X2
Net capital loss
  Taxable capital gains—½ ($4,000) $ 2,000
  Allowable capital losses—½ ($28,000 – $8,000 ABIL)   (10,000)
                                                                   $ 8,000

Non-capital loss
  Business loss $120,000
  ABIL—½ ($8,000)   4,000
                                                                   $124,000

20X3
Restricted farm loss
  Actual loss $ 15,000
  Allowed in 20X3—$2,500 + ½ ($15,000 – $2,500)   8,750
                                                                   $ 6,250

20X1 net income and taxable income
  Business income $ 76,000
  Farm income   4,000
  Taxable capital gains—½ ($4,000)   2,000
    Net income   82,000

Donations (actual—$28,000)—lower than limit of 75% of net income	(28,000)
Net capital loss—from 20X2 (limit to taxable capital gains)	(2,000)
Restricted farm loss—from 20X3 (limit to farm income)	(4,000)
Non-capital loss—from 20X2 (balance)	(48,000)
Taxable income	–0–
20X2 net income and taxable income	–0–
20X3 net income and taxable income	
Business income	$ 30,000
Dividends	10,000
Taxable capital gains—½ ($8,000)	4,000
Farm loss—limit (see above)	(8,750)
Net income	35,250
Donations (actual in 20X3—$2,000)	(2,000)
Dividends	(10,000)
Net capital loss—from 20X2 (limit to taxable capital gains)	(4,000)
Non-capital loss—from 20X2 (balance)	(19,250)
Taxable income	–0–

2. Carry-forwards after 20X3

Net capital loss—$8,000 – ($2,000 + $4,000)	$ 2,000
Carried forward indefinitely against future capital gains.	
Non-capital loss—$124,000 – ($48,000 + $19,250)	$ 56,750
Carried forward for next 19 years (20 years after 20X2).	
Restricted farm loss—$6,250 – $4,000	$ 2,250
Carried forward for 20 years.	

3. It may be beneficial to delay the use of a non-capital loss when a higher tax rate is anticipated in a future year. For example, a corporation could decline the use of a loss carry-forward when all of its income in the particular year is subject to the small business deduction and use it in a year when there is income not subject to the small business deduction (i.e., ABI over $500,000).

QUESTION TWO

Salco Ltd. is a Canadian *public* corporation. The company operates a chain of retail stores in Ontario. The financial statement for the year ended December 1, 20X6, is summarized below.

Income from retail operation	$740,000
Interest income	40,000
Taxable dividends from Canadian corporations	10,000
Net income before income tax	$790,000

Required:

1. Calculate Salco's *net income for tax purposes, taxable income*, and *federal and provincial income taxes* for the 20X5 taxation year.

2. If Salco Ltd. were a *Canadian-controlled private corporation*, how would its federal and provincial income taxes change?

Solution:

1. As there is no detailed information about the revenues and expenses for the year, it can be assumed that the net income for tax purposes is equal to the net income reported on the financial statement.

Net income for tax purposes	$790,000
Deduct:	
Taxable Canadian dividends	(10,000)
Taxable income	$780,000
Federal tax:	
Primary federal tax—38% × $780,000	$296,400
Less abatement—10% × $780,000	(78,000)
	218,400
General tax reduction—13% × $780,000	(101,400)
Total federal tax	$117,000
Provincial tax:	
Ontario—11% × $780,000	$ 85,800

2. If it is assumed that Salco Ltd. is a Canadian-controlled private corporation, several changes to the tax calculation arise. First, the small business deduction is applicable. For this purpose, the active business income is the retail profits of $740,000. Second, the special refundable tax of 6⅔% applies to the investment income. Here, the investment income is the interest income of $40,000. Third, the general tax reduction changes as shown below. The dividend income is excluded because it is deducted in arriving at taxable income. In Chapter 13, it will be shown that taxable capital gains are also subject to the special refundable tax. Finally, the provincial income tax will change, as Ontario has a lower rate (4.5%) on the first $500,000 of active business income.

Federal tax:	
Primary federal tax—38% × $780,000	$296,400
less abatement—10% × $780,000	(78,000)
	218,400
Refundable tax on CCPC investment income	
6⅔% × $40,000	2,667
Small business deduction—17% × least of:	
Active business income—$740,000	
Taxable income—$780,000	
Annual limit—$500,000	
17% × $500,000	(85,000)
General tax reduction (calculated below)	(31,200)
Total federal tax	$104,867
Provincial tax:	
Ontario	
4.5% × $500,000 (amount eligible for the small	
business deduction)	$22,500
11% × ($780,000 − $500,000)	30,800
Total provincial tax	$ 53,300

0.0666667 (handwritten annotation)

The above calculation does not include the possible tax on dividends received by a private corporation (referred to as a Part IV tax). This tax, which is fully refundable when dividends are paid to the shareholder(s), is not discussed until Chapter 13.

The general rate tax reduction of 13% applies to income in excess of income eligible for the small business deduction, income eligible for the M&P reduction, and investment income and is calculated below.

Taxable income	$780,000
Deduct:	
Investment income	(40,000)
Income eligible for the small business deduction	(500,000)
Income eligible for the M&P reduction	0
Income eligible for the 13% general tax reduction	$240,000
General tax reduction—13% × 240,000	$ 31,200

QUESTION THREE

XT Inc. is a CCPC operating a retail business. Its fiscal year end is December 31. On October 1, 20X8, the controlling shareholder sold all of her XT shares to YY Inc. YY is not related to XT. As of September 30, 20X8, XT had net income from business of $400,000. A review of XT's balance sheet revealed the following:

	Cost	Undepreciated capital cost	Market value
Inventory	$600,000		$550,000
Investment in shares of CCPC	100,000		20,000
Land	100,000		400,000
Building	600,000	420,000	700,000

At the end of the previous year, XT had a net capital loss for tax purposes of $30,000 incurred in 20X7.

Required:
Review the tax implications for XT from the change in share ownership.

Solution:
A arm's-length party has acquired control of XT. As a result, XT has a deemed year end on September 30, 20X8 (the date immediately before the control change). XT must calculate its taxable income to that date. It will be necessary to pro-rate the CCA based on the number of days in the short taxation year in relation to 365 days.

Inventory is valued at the lower of cost ($600,000) or market ($550,000). The resulting $50,000 loss reduces the business income for the deemed year end. Generally, where the tax value of an asset exceeds its market value, the tax value must be reduced.

Where the UCC of a class of depreciable property exceeds the fair market value of the assets in the class, the UCC must be reduced to the fair market value. The only depreciable asset in this case is the building, and the UCC of Class 1 does not exceed the fair market value of the building. Therefore, no adjustment is required.

Where the ACB of a non-depreciable asset exceeds its fair market value, the ACB must be reduced to the fair market value and the reduction is deemed to be a capital loss for the tax year ended September 30, 20X8. The ACB of the investment ($100,000) exceeds its market value ($20,000) by $80,000. The ACB of the investment is reduced to $20,000 and the $80,000 reduction is deemed to be a capital loss for the tax year ended September 30, 20X8 (allowable capital loss of $40,000). The market value of the land is higher than its tax value, so no adjustment is required for the land.

The net capital loss of $30,000 carried forward from 20X7, and the allowable capital loss of $40,000 from the deemed disposition of the investment will expire on September 30, 20X8 as there are no taxable capital gains earned in the taxation year to which they can be offset. However, XT can elect to recognize an accrued gain on any non-depreciable or depreciable capital property. In this case, the land has a market value that is $300,000 higher than its ACB (market value $400,000 – cost $100,000) and XT should recognize a portion of this accrued gain in order to offset the allowable capital losses that are about to expire. XT needs to create a taxable capital gain of $70,000 ($30,000 + $40,000) for this purpose. So, XT should elect a deemed disposition price of $240,000 for the land. This would result in a taxable capital gain of $70,000 [$1/2 \times$ ($240,000 − $100,000 ACB). The land will have an ACB of $240,000 going forward into the future. The increased ACB is the benefit obtained by making the election.

It would not be prudent to elect a gain on the depreciable property (building), as it would create a significant recapture of capital cost allowance before the capital gain could be recognized. This would increase taxable income.

Net income and taxable income for XT Inc. for the deemed year ended September 30, 20X8 is $337,435 as follows:

Business income		$400,000
Less Inventory write-down		(50,000)
Less CCA ($420,000 $\times$ 4% $\times$ 273/365 days)		(12,565)
		337,435
Taxable capital gain (elected)	$70,000	
Allowable capital loss	(40,000)	30,000
Net income		367,435
Net capital loss		(30,000)
Taxable income		$337,435

QUESTION FOUR

Sheila is the sole shareholder of Bender Inc, a CCPC. Bender has a policy of paying an annual dividend equal to 60% of the company's after-tax income. In 20X8, Bender earned $100,000 of active business income. Bender has never earned more than $100,000 in past years. In 20X9, Sheila will sell all of her shares in Bender. Sheila is in the top marginal tax bracket and has used her entire capital gains deduction in previous years.

Required:
Should Bender maintain its dividend policy in 20X8?

Solution:
It is first necessary to establish the applicable tax rates. Based on the personal tax rates developed in Exhibit 10-7 (Chapter 10), and the corporate tax rates developed in Exhibit 11-8, the relevant rates are as follows:

Corporate tax rate—active business income	15%
Individual:	
Ordinary income	45%
Eligible dividends	28%
Non-eligible dividends	33%
Capital gains	23%

Bender's after-tax income in 20X8 is $85,000 [$100,000 − 15% $\times$ $100,000)]. Based on this income, the historical dividend policy requires a 20X8 dividend of $51,000 (60% $\times$ $85,000). As Bender has regularly earned only active business income that is eligible for the small business deduction, the dividend is classified as a non-eligible dividend. The tax on a non-eligible dividend of $51,000 is $16,830 ($51,000 $\times$ 33%).

The declaration of a $51,000 dividend in 20X8 reduces the value of the company and, therefore, its share value by the same amount. If Bender does not pay the dividend in 20X8, the value of the shares will be $51,000 higher when they are sold in 20X9. As a result, the capital gain on the share sale will be $51,000 higher. The tax on the higher capital gain will be $11,730 ($51,000 $\times$ 23%). However, because the dividend was not paid, Sheila will not incur the tax on the dividend of $16,830.

So, if the dividend is not declared in 20X8, Sheila's overall tax cost will be reduced by $5,100 ($16,830 − 11,730). Sheila should not declare the dividend in 20X8.

Review Questions

1. "A corporation is an artificial person separate and distinct from its owners." Briefly explain this statement.

2. Identify the types of relationships that can exist between a corporation and its shareholders.

3. What factors may influence the value of a corporation's common share capital?

4. Identify two ways in which a shareholder can realize a return on a share investment. Describe the relationship between them.

5. "Given the choice, individual shareholders of a corporation prefer to receive their return on investment by way of dividends, rather than from the sale of shares at a profit." Is this statement true? Explain.

6. "A shareholder may have a primary relationship as well as secondary relationships with the corporation. The difference between the two relationships relates to the tax treatment of income flows between the corporation and the shareholder." Explain.

7. Corporations and individuals determine their taxable income in different ways. What are the differences?

8. How are the net capital losses and non-capital losses of a corporation affected when voting control of the corporation shifts from one shareholder to another?

9. If the shares of a corporation that has non-capital losses are about to be sold and if those losses arise from business operations, why is it important for the vendor to consider the nature of the purchaser?

10. An existing corporation that operates a profitable retail business is considering expanding its activities to include manufacturing. The expansion business can be organized in either of two basic ways. Describe them. Also, what factors must be considered when a choice is being made between the two structures?

11. How does the tax treatment of intercorporate dividends affect the relationship between dividends and capital gains when one corporation invests in shares of another corporation? (Assume that both entities are taxable Canadian corporations.)

12. Explain why the federal tax reduction of 13% or a provincial tax reduction on manufacturing and processing activities may apply to an amount that is greater than or less than the corporation's actual income from manufacturing. Is it possible for a corporation that earns $500,000 from retail activities and suffers a loss of $50,000 from manufacturing activities to be eligible for the 13% manufacturing reduction?

13. What is the marginal tax rate for a public corporation in Ontario on income derived from a chain of restaurants? Show calculations.

14. Because income earned by a corporation is first subject to corporate tax and then taxed a second time when after-tax profits are distributed to individual shareholders, shareholders are entitled to claim a dividend tax credit. Does the dividend tax credit eliminate the double taxation of corporate profits? Explain.

15. The following statement appeared in the media: "There are 60,000 Canadian corporations that earned a profit for the year but incurred no income tax liability." Is it possible that this statement is true? If it is, explain the principal reasons why, and state your opinion as to whether changes to the tax system are warranted.

Key Concept Questions

QUESTION ONE

A Canadian corporation with a December year end has incurred the following losses:

	Amount	Year Incurred
Non-capital loss	$10,000	2009
Non-capital loss	$12,000	2005
Non-capital loss	$14,000	2002
Net capital loss	$16,000	2000

Determine the expiry date for each of the above losses. *Income tax reference: ITA 111(1)(a), (b).*

QUESTION TWO

Moon Corp., a Canadian public corporation, has correctly computed its income (loss) for the 20X7 taxation year.

Income from property including dividends of $12,000 received from taxable Canadian corporations		$ 50,000
Taxable capital gains	$18,000	
Allowable capital losses	(8,000)	10,000
Loss from business		(100,000)
		$ (40,000)

Moon Corp. contributed $5,000 to various charities in the current year. Moon Corp. has net capital losses of $15,000 available. These losses were incurred in 20X6. *Income tax reference: ITA 110.1(1), 111(8), 112(1).*

Determine Moon Corp.'s maximum non-capital loss for the 20X7 taxation year.

QUESTION THREE

Nelson Ltd. has net income for tax purposes of $300,000 for the 20X7 taxation year. Included in this amount are dividends of $20,000 received from taxable Canadian corporations and taxable capital gains of $15,000. During the year, Nelson Ltd. donated $40,000 to the Canadian Cancer Society. Nelson Ltd. has non-capital losses of $10,000 (incurred in 20X5) and net capital losses of $18,000 (incurred in 2000) available. *Income tax reference: ITA 110.1(1), 111(1)(a), (b), 112(1).*

Determine Nelson's taxable income for the 20X7 taxation year.

QUESTION FOUR

Loser Ltd. has non-capital losses of $60,000 from business operations and net capital losses of $40,000 (both incurred two years ago). On October 1 of the current year, the shares of Loser Ltd. were acquired by an arm's-length person. *Income tax reference: ITA 111(4), (5), 249(4).*

Determine the tax implications for Loser Ltd.

QUESTION FIVE

On November 1st of the current year, X Ltd. purchased 80% of the shares of Y Ltd. from an unrelated person. Details of the assets owned by Y Ltd. at that time are summarized below:

	Class 1	Class 8	Class 12	CEC
Fair market value	$400,000	$20,000	$ 5,000	$ 4,000
Cost	300,000	30,000	25,000	10,000
UCC/CEC	275,000	27,000	0	3,500

Determine the adjustments required to the tax values of the assets owned by Y Ltd. and the effect on Y's business income for its taxation year ended October 31. *Income tax reference: ITA 111(5.1), (5.2), 249(4).*

QUESTION SIX

On April 1st of the current year, Carl purchased 60% of the shares of P Ltd. from an unrelated person. Details of the inventory and other assets owned by P Ltd. at that time are summarized below.

	FMV	Cost
Investment in A Ltd.	$ 10,000	$24,000
Inventory	50,000	30,000
Land	100,000	80,000
Building (UCC $75,000)	120,000	90,000

Determine the tax implications for P Ltd. *Income tax reference: ITA 111(5.1), (5.2), 249(4).*

QUESTION SEVEN

Free Corp. is a Canadian public corporation that operates a retail store in Ontario. Free Corp.'s taxable income for the current year is $100,000. *Income tax reference: ITA 111(4), 123(1), 124(1), 123.4(2).*

Determine the federal tax payable for the current year.

QUESTION EIGHT

Easy Corp., a Canadian public corporation, carries on business in Canada and in the United States. The revenue and salaries allocated to the permanent establishment in each location are as follows for the current year:

	Revenue	Salaries
Canada	$ 8,000,000	$ 600,000
United States	2,000,000	400,000
Total	$10,000,000	$1,000,000

Easy Corp. has taxable income of $600,000 for the current year. *Income tax reference: ITA 123(1), 124(1), 123.4(2); Reg. 402.*

Determine the federal tax payable for Easy Corp. for the current year.

QUESTION NINE

Manu Corp. is a Canadian public corporation that carries on manufacturing and distribution operations in British Columbia. Manu Corp.'s taxable income for the current year is $900,000. The balance sheet shows that the cost of all depreciable property owned by Manu Corp. at the end of the year is $1,100,000. Of this amount, $800,000 is used in the manufacturing business. The income statement shows income from the manufacturing operations of $300,000, income from the wholesaling operations of $500,000, and investment income of $100,000. The total payroll for the year is $2,200,000, of which $1,000,000 is paid to employees directly involved in manufacturing activities. *Income tax reference: ITA 125.1; Regs. 5200, 5201, 5202.*

Determine the federal manufacturing and processing deduction for the current year.

QUESTION TEN

Gold Corp., a Canadian public corporation, carries on business in Canada. For the current year, Gold Corp. has manufacturing and processing profits (M&P) of $300,000, calculated in accordance with prescribed rules. Gold Corp. has total taxable income of $1,000,000. *Income tax reference: ITA 123(1), 124(1), 123.4(2), 125.1.*

Determine the federal tax payable for the current year.

Problems

PROBLEM ONE

U.P.I. Industries Ltd., a Canadian corporation, has recently been designated a public corporation. Its shares are traded on the TSX Venture Exchange.

Over the past year, the company has pursued an aggressive expansion policy. Sales personnel based at head office have travelled to North Dakota and Minnesota and have achieved moderate success in developing new customers in the United States. In addition, the company has opened a branch location in Alberta by establishing an office and manufacturing plant staffed by new Alberta personnel. The Alberta manufacturing plant is the company's first venture into manufacturing.

Selected financial information for the company's current fiscal period is presented below.

1.

	Head office	Alberta branch
Canadian sales	$7,000,000	$1,300,000
Foreign sales	700,000	–0–
Cost of sales	4,620,000	910,000
Salaries and wages	1,200,000	200,000
Profit from operations	1,200,000	10,000
Dividend income	80,000	–0–
Taxable capital gains	70,000	–0–

2. At the end of the previous year, the company had net capital losses of $90,000 and non-capital losses of $120,000 that were available for carry-forward.

3. The Alberta branch location includes a building and equipment. The company's accountant is in the process of determining the corporation's tax liability and indicates that the annualized cost of manufacturing capital employed in the Alberta branch is $200,000 and that the corporation's total annualized cost of tangible property used amounts to $800,000. The accountant also indicates that the manufacturing labour in the Alberta branch amounts to $120,000. This amount has been calculated in accordance with the income tax rules for determining manufacturing labour.

4. The *assumed* provincial corporate income tax rate is 12% in Manitoba and 10% in Alberta.

When organizing the Alberta expansion, management had considered establishing a separate corporation. They decided instead on the branch structure because of anticipated losses in the first year of expansion. As it turned out, the branch generated a small profit of $10,000. Management is now considering converting the branch into a separate subsidiary corporation. U.P.I. already owns two separate subsidiaries in Manitoba that account for the dividend income described earlier.

Required:

1. For the current year, determine U.P.I.'s
   (a) net income for tax purposes;
   (b) taxable income; and
   (c) federal and provincial tax liabilities.

2. How would the overall federal and provincial tax liabilities be different if the Alberta branch had been incorporated from the outset? Show calculations.

PROBLEM TWO

During the 20X1 taxation year, K2 Ltd., a Canadian-controlled private corporation located in Nova Scotia earned $160,000 of active business income. In addition, the company made the following capital transactions:

Gain on sale of shares of a public corporation	$ 48,000
Loss on shares of a public corporation	(20,000)
Gain from settling a long-term debt of $300,000 for a reduced amount of $240,000	60,000

At the end of the previous taxation year, the following unused losses were available for carry-forward:

Net capital losses	$29,000
Non-capital losses	42,000

Required:

For the 20X1 taxation year of K2 Ltd., calculate
(a) net income for income tax purposes;
(b) taxable income; and
(c) total federal income tax.

PROBLEM THREE

Patrice Dupuis is the sole shareholder of Dupuis Distributors Ltd., a successful Canadian-controlled private corporation that wholesales automobile parts. The corporation's profits are in excess of $550,000.

Inventory for the corporation's business is stored in a warehouse owned by Dupuis. He acquired the building five years ago and began charging his corporation an annual rent of $20,000. At the time the building was acquired, the annual rent of $20,000 was considered realistic in terms of the real estate market at the time.

The lease is renewed annually on an informal basis, but the rental amount has never been adjusted, even though rental rates for similar properties have increased substantially. Dupuis has never considered a rental adjustment important because "it would just be transferring money from one pocket to the other."

Both Dupuis and the corporation are located in Winnipeg, where there is little available warehouse space. A leasing agent recently informed Dupuis that the building could be rented to a third party under a five-year lease for $38,000 per year.

Required:

Should Dupuis enter into a five-year lease with Dupuis Distributors, charging an annual rent of $38,000? What tax savings could Dupuis and the company achieve as a result of this adjustment?

PROBLEM FOUR

MX Wholesale Ltd. is a Canadian-controlled private corporation located in Ontario. The company regularly earns pre-tax profits of $600,000.

The common shares of MX are owned 50/50 by Mr. and Mrs. Waldman. Only Mrs. Waldman works for the business, and she is paid a substantial salary for her efforts. Mr. Waldman is a lawyer and earns a large income from his law firm. In addition, the Waldmans receive annual dividends from MX. The company has consistently maintained a policy of distributing half its after-tax profits to the shareholders.

The Waldmans are dismayed at the amount of tax both they and the corporation must pay when corporate profits are distributed. They have asked you to explain to them the tax effect of distributing the corporate profits. In addition, they intend to sell the shares of the company in the next two or three years and want you to explain what the effect would be if they stopped paying dividends from MX.

The assumed provincial income tax rate in Ontario is 11% for corporations. However, the corporate rate is reduced to 4.5% on income eligible for the small business deduction. Both Waldmans have already used up their capital gain exemption. The marginal tax rate the Waldmans personally pay is 46% on regular income, 30% on eligible dividends, and 33% on non-eligible dividends.

Required:

1. What rate of tax are the Waldmans paying on the profits of MX that are distributed to them annually (corporate and personal tax combined)? Show calculations.

2. Should the Waldmans stop paying dividends? Your answer should indicate how their overall tax rate would be affected.

PROBLEM FIVE

Hope Enterprises Ltd. is a Canadian-controlled private corporation that operates a jewellery retailing business in southwestern Ontario. The company was profitable for a number of years until a new competitive environment put the company in financial difficulty.

For the past eight years, Hope Enterprises has suffered serious losses. Currently, it has unused non-capital losses of $650,000. Jean Talouse, the president and sole shareholder, has called a meeting of his senior staff to review the company's operations for the year and to plan a survival strategy. The meeting begins with the accountant presenting the current year's financial statements and a projection of operating results for the next three years. Part of this information is outlined in the tables on the next page.

The accountant reports the following additional information:

1. The company realized a gross profit of 20% on sales of $4,000,000, which is considerably lower than normal. However, all of the bad inventory has been cleaned out, and the current inventory can be sold to realize a 25% gross profit.

2. The accounts receivable represents a true evaluation of what can be collected. A reasonable reserve has been taken into account, and the credit policy has been adjusted to reduce the losses on future sales.

3. Both the bank loan and the loan from the shareholders are payable on demand and require interest payments of 9%. The bank is not uncomfortable with the current level of debt and has adequate security in the receivables and inventory.

4. To ensure that only a minor loss will result this year, expenses have been cut to the bone. The projections are that over the next three years, if conditions remain basically the same, the company will suffer minor losses or perhaps break even.

5. The $650,000 loss carry-forward for tax purposes is a cause for concern. Some of this loss was incurred 18 years ago, and so there is a possibility that the company will not generate profits in time to meet the time limit for carry-forwards.

The president is pleased that the company has got the losses under control. He instructs the accountant to determine whether any action can be taken to minimize the risk of the losses expiring.

Although he did not say so at the meeting, the president has decided to investigate the possibility of selling the company, as he feels that things may get worse in spite of the accountant's projections.

Required:

1. What steps can be taken to ensure that the loss carry-forward of $650,000 will not expire before profits are generated? Be specific, and indicate the amount of losses that will be preserved by your actions.

2. What can the president do to maximize the value of the shares in the event that he actively solicits a buyer for the company?

Balance Sheet		
Assets:		
Cash		$ 20,000
Accounts receivable	1,250,000	
Allowance for doubtful accounts	(310,000)	940,000
Inventory, at lower of cost or market		750,000
Equipment, at cost	400,000	
Accumulated amortization	(250,000)	150,000
		$1,860,000
Liabilities:		
Accounts payable		699,000
Bank loan		500,000
Due to shareholder		400,000
		1,599,000
Shareholder's equity:		
Share capital	1,000	
Retained earnings	260,000	261,000
		$1,860,000

Statement of Income (Loss)		
Sales		$4,000,000
Cost of sales		3,200,000
Gross profit		800,000
Expenses		
Selling and administrative salaries	300,000	
Shareholder's salary	60,000	
Delivery	50,000	
Rent	79,000	
Utilities	12,000	
Amortization (equal to CCA)	40,000	
Insurance	9,000	
Legal and accounting	12,000	
Interest	108,000	
Other expenses (including bad debts, office, repairs)	160,000	830,000
Net loss for the year		$ (30,000)

PROBLEM SIX

Norex Distributors Inc. is a small Canadian public corporation that derives all of its business income from the wholesale distribution of floor coverings.

Currently, Norex does not manufacture any of its products and purchases all of its inventory from manufacturers in eastern Canada.

Norex has decided to acquire a small manufacturing plant in Saskatchewan. The following assets will be acquired:

Assets	Cost
Land	$ 80,000
Building	300,000
Manufacturing equipment	600,000
Goodwill	50,000
	$1,030,000

The planned acquisition date is July 1, 20X1, the day after the year end of Norex. The company's vice-president realizes that the manufacturing business can be purchased and operated through a newly created subsidiary corporation and that the subsidiary's manufacturing profit of $240,000 (see below) can result in a federal manufacturing and processing deduction of $31,200 at the most. The province of Saskatchewan offers a 2% rate reduction on manufacturing income.

As an alternative, Norex can purchase the assets and operate the manufacturing business as a division. The vice-president has asked you to determine, from a tax perspective, whether this alternative is preferable to the other. Norex has provided you with estimated results for the first year of operations *after the acquisition* (i.e., year ended June 30, 20X2). These results are summarized below.

Information relating to new manufacturing plant

1. Manufacturing activities take up 80% of the building's space. The remaining space is used for storing finished products and for administrative offices.

2. Estimated net income for tax purposes is $240,000, after appropriate deductions for capital cost allowance, eligible capital property, and the following:

Direct labour	$ 320,000
Utilities	14,000
Property taxes	4,000
Raw materials	610,000
Administrative and office salaries allocated from Norex (see below)	80,000
	$1,028,000

Information relating to Norex (excluding new manufacturing plant)

1. Estimated net income for tax purposes is $4,730,000, including:

Interest income on long-term bonds		$130,000
Administrative salaries	630,000	
Warehouse and sales salaries	340,000	
	970,000	
Salaries allocated to new plant	(80,000)	890,000
Rent for fleet of delivery trucks		80,000

2. In estimating the net income of $4,730,000, an appropriate deduction for CCA was made on the following properties:

	Original cost of assets in class	Undepreciated CC (after CCA)
Class 1	$1,340,000	$ 965,000
Class 8	190,000	75,000
Class 10	360,000	190,000
	$1,890,000	$1,230,000

Required:

Should Norex operate the proposed new manufacturing operation as a separate subsidiary corporation or as a division? Provide calculations to support your answer.

PROBLEM SEVEN

Global Inc., an international cosmetics wholesaler, has a history of substantial profits. It is now October 1, 20X6. For its current year ending December 31, 20X6, it projects pre-tax profit of $7,000,000.

Frost Foods Inc. is a distributor of frozen Canadian beef. Frost Foods Inc. was profitable until 20X0. Large losses were incurred in years 20X0 through 20X3. Since then, it has managed to break even. At the beginning of its current taxation year, Frost Foods Inc. had the following unused losses:

	Non-capital	Net capital
Incurred in its year ended Dec. 31, 20X3	$300,000	$75,000
Incurred in its year ended Dec. 31, 20X4	$500,000	

Global Inc. plans to purchase all of the issued shares of Frost Foods Inc. on November 1, 20X6 and immediately amalgamate Frost Foods Inc. and Global Inc. into one corporation. The plan is to reduce Global Inc.'s taxable income for 20X6 by $875,000 by deducting the losses incurred by Frost Foods Inc.

Global Inc. and Frost Foods Inc. are unrelated Canadian corporations.

Required:
Comment on Global Inc.'s ability to utilize the Frost Foods Inc. losses.

PROBLEM EIGHT

On September 1, 20X6, Perfect Ltd., a steel recycling company, purchased 90% of the issued voting shares of Loser Ltd., a distributor of sportswear, from an arm's-length person. Loser Ltd. had incurred the following losses in prior years:

	Year ended	
	Dec 31/X4	Dec 31/X5
Non-capital losses (business)	$40,000	$60,000
Net capital losses	15,000	5,000

Loser Ltd. incurred an additional loss of $75,000 in carrying on the sportswear distribution business for the period January 1, 20X6 through August 31, 20X6. No further capital losses were incurred.

On September 1, 20X6, Loser Ltd.'s assets had the following values:

	Cost	UCC	Fair Market Value
Marketable securities*	$50,000	N/A	$300,000
Inventory	33,000	N/A	45,000
Land	90,000	N/A	200,000
Building	120,000	$83,000	180,000
Equipment	85,000	34,000	20,000

* Perfect Ltd. planned to sell the marketable securities as soon as possible after purchasing Loser Ltd.

The amalgamation of Loser Ltd. and Perfect Ltd. took place on September 1, 20X6. The corporation, formed on amalgamation, chose December 31 as its year end. Income for 20X6 and 20X7 was as follows:

	Income from Steel recycling	Income from Sportswear distribution	Total
20X6	$500,000	$30,000*	$530,000
20X7	400,000	60,000	460,000

* Income for the period September 1 through December 31, 20X6

Required:

1. Using the assumption that Loser Ltd. does NOT use any elections to minimize the unused net capital loss balance, calculate the amount of non-capital and net capital losses that would remain after the acquisition of the shares by Perfect Ltd. on September 1, 20X6.

2. If Loser Ltd. makes the election(s) necessary to utilize those losses which would expire at the acquisition of control, indicate the asset(s) on which the election should be made and the amount that should be elected.

3. Indicate the September 1, 20X6 adjusted cost base (ACB) and undepreciated capital cost (UCC), where applicable, for each of the assets listed, assuming the election(s) in part 2 above is made.

4. What conditions must be met in order to deduct the non-capital loss balance at September 1, 20X6 in a future taxation year? Are these conditions met? Indicate the maximum amount of non-capital loss carry-forward that can be used at December 31, 20X6 and December 31, 20X7 respectively. Give a brief explanation for your answer.

5. Assume the management of Perfect Ltd. decided that the sportswear distribution business would not be continued after September 1, 20X6. Discuss the tax implications for Loser Ltd.

PROBLEM NINE

Michael purchased 100 % of the issued shares of Sentry Inc., a Canadian-controlled private corporation that owns and operates an assisted-living retirement home in Ontario. Sentry has a December 31 fiscal year end. The transaction closed on October 1, 20X4. At that time, the values of certain assets owned by Sentry were as follows:

	Cost	UCC/CEC	FMV
Land	$120,000	N/A	$300,000
Building	240,000	$90,000	290,000
Furniture and fixtures	100,000	65,000	50,000
Computer equipment	12,000	6,000	8,000
Inventory	55,000	N/A	52,000
Marketable securities	24,000	N/A	10,000
Incorporation/organization costs	10,000	1,000	500

Michael selected December 31, 20X4 as the first fiscal year end for Sentry after the acquisition. The following is a schedule of Sentry's income and unused losses for the period January 1, 20X3 through December 31, 20X5:

	Business income (loss)	Taxable capital gain	Net capital loss
January 1, 20X3–December 31, 20X3	($100,000)	$ Nil	($22,000)
January 1, 20X4–September 30, 20X4	(200,000)	Nil	Nil
October 1, 20X4–December 31, 20X4	(70,000)	Nil	Nil
January 1, 20X5–December 31, 20X5	40,000	10,000	Nil

Required:

1. Assuming Sentry does not make an election to recognize accrued gains or recapture under paragraph 111(4)(e) of the *Income Tax Act*,

   (a) Calculate the business loss for tax purposes for the period January 1, 20X4 through September 30, 20X4.

   (b) State the tax value (e.g. ACB, UCC, or CEC) for each of the assets at October 1, 20X4.

   (c) What conditions must be met in order for the non-capital losses incurred in the period January 1, 20X3 through December 31, 20X4 to be deductible by Sentry in 20X5 and future taxation years?

   (d) What is the maximum amount of non-capital losses that can be deducted for the year ended December 31, 20X5? Explain.

   (e) What are the maximum net capital losses that can be claimed for the year ended December 31, 20X5? Explain.

2. Assume Michael expects to be able to use Sentry's losses by amalgamating Senty with another corporation he owns. Should Sentry make an election (ITA 114(4)(e)) to recognize capital gains and recapture at September 30, 20X4? Explain, including the benefit, if any, to Sentry of making such an election. Show all calculations.

3. Michael is the sole shareholder of two other corporations—M Ltd., which operates a food distribution business (annual profits $600,000) and R Ltd., which operates a retirement home (annual profits $200,000). Both corporations are located in Ontario. Which one of these two corporations should be amalgamated with Sentry in order to save income tax? Explain.

Case

NATIONAL INDUSTRIES LTD.

National Industries Ltd. is a Canadian venture corporation that holds investments in several industries. The company owns shares in a number of active business corporations in both Canada and the United States. Its income consists of dividends and management fees from the subsidiaries.

Charles Prokopchuk is a vice-president of National and is responsible for acquiring companies in the transportation industry. Currently, National owns three subsidiary corporations in this industry. Prokopchuk monitors their progress and provides head office management services.

Three months ago, Prokopchuk sought a buyer for and negotiated the sale of Tri-Lon Transport Ltd. The shares of Tri-Lon were sold for $14,000,000. He is extremely pleased with the sale because he was instrumental in acquiring the shares of Tri-Lon seven years earlier for a price of $2,000,000. At that time, Tri-Lon was in its early growth stages; Prokopchuk is happy that he recognized the company's potential so early on. After acquiring Tri-Lon, Prokopchuk had hired new managers, streamlined the operations, and focused expansion in the areas where the company was strong. Profits grew rapidly, so that by the time the shares were sold, Tri-Lon had retained earnings of $8,000,000.

The president of National Industries congratulates Prokopchuk for a job well done and indicates that the cash generated from the sale of Tri-Lon shares was vital, as the company is facing the termination date of one of its major bond issues. However, even after receiving the additional cash from the Tri-Lon sale, National will still have to restructure its debt and obtain new long-term financing. The president has indicated that it is critical for the company to get a high rating on its bonds in order to secure the lowest possible interest costs. He informs Prokopchuk:

"Your success with Tri-Lon will make a big impact on our bottom line and earnings per share for the current year. Stock prices should improve and our proposed new bond issue will be better accepted in the market. You have carried out your responsibilities perfectly."

Historically, the shares of National Industries have traded on the Toronto Stock Exchange at a price equivalent to 12 times after-tax earnings. The company has 8,000,000 shares outstanding, and the president is certain that the share price will be $60 after the current year's earnings have been released.

Required:

Do you agree with the president's assessment of Prokopchuk's success? Explain

PART 3

The Corporate Structure

Business, more than any other occupation, is a continual calculation, an instinctive exercise in foresight.

HENRY LUCE

CHAPTER 12

Organization, Capital Structures, and Income Distributions of Corporations

The basic framework for the taxation of corporations was introduced in Chapter 11. This part of the text expands that framework by examining, in three separate chapters, the organization of corporations, the implications of carrying on business within a Canadian-controlled private corporation, and complex corporate structures and their reorganization.

While the subject matter of each chapter relates to complex provisions of the *Income Tax Act* and other corporate statutes, the information is presented in a simplified and abbreviated form that emphasizes the fundamental concepts that have an impact on business decision making. Having read these chapters, the reader will understand the implications of alternative corporate structures and be able to compare those structures with other forms of business organization, which are discussed in Part Four of the text.

Chapter 12 explains how corporations are formed. It also discusses alternative capital structures and the entry and departure of shareholders. Specifically, this chapter covers three basic areas:

1. The implications of capitalizing a corporation with shareholder debt as opposed to equity.

2. Alternative methods of transferring assets to a corporation.

3. Income distributions to shareholders.

I. Corporate Capitalization—Debt or Equity

It was indicated in previous chapters that a corporation is a separate legal entity distinct from its owners, the shareholders. As such, both private and public corporations are subject to tax on their income, and their shareholders are subject to a second level of tax at the time corporate profits are distributed.

The process of creating a corporation requires that, at a minimum, share capital be issued to the shareholder in return for some consideration. This means that a corporation can be created by issuing some shares to an owner in exchange for a nominal asset, such as a cash contribution of $1. In addition to this initial contribution, the corporation, in order to function, must have a capital base for the purposes of acquiring assets and conducting business. This capital base is also contributed by the shareholder(s) and can be in the form of debt or equity. Capital contributed by a shareholder in the form of debt is referred to as a "shareholder loan." Capital contributed in the form of equity consists of additional share capital, which can relate to fixed value shares that do not participate in corporate profits, or to shares that participate in profits and fluctuate in value, depending on the extent of corporate earnings.

It should be pointed out that a corporation can obtain capital by borrowing funds from parties that are not shareholders. However, discussion in this chapter relates to capitalization by debt or equity by the shareholder(s).

From the shareholder's perspective, both debt (loans receivable from the corporation) and equity (shares owned in the corporation) constitute capital property for tax purposes and yield a return on investment in the form of interest or dividends. As capital property, both debt and equity are subject to capital-gains treatment if and when disposed of at a value different from the initial cost.

The value of a shareholder loan may decrease if the assets within the corporation decline in value and are insufficient to satisfy the obligation or increase in value if the debt bears a long-term interest rate that is high in relation to current economic conditions. The value of shares may change as a result of the following factors:

1. Profits earned or losses incurred by the corporation.

2. Increases or decreases in the value of assets owned by the corporation, such as land, buildings, equipment, goodwill, and other intangibles.

3. The distribution of profits by corporate dividends.

The capitalizing of a corporation by a combination of share capital and shareholder debt is most often found in closely held private corporations in which the affairs of the corporation and the shareholders are closely linked. In widely held corporations, such as public corporations, this method is not common. However, this alternative may be used by public corporations to capitalize either a subsidiary corporation or a corporation whose shares are closely held by a small group of public corporations.

Each of these two alternatives—capitalization by share equity and capitalization by a combination of share equity and shareholder debt—has advantages and disadvantages that are a function of the tax treatment resulting from

(a) the return on the invested capital—interest versus dividends;
(b) any losses that occur when the shares or loans are disposed of; and
(c) the return of all or a portion of the original capital to the investor.

Both debt and equity capitalization are examined below in terms of the above three elements.

A. Corporate Capitalization by Shareholder Debt

Shareholder debt can take several different forms. The terms attached to the debt instrument can provide security to the lender (shareholder) by attaching specific assets of the corporation, or they can provide no security; they can provide specific repayment terms or call for payment on demand; and they can provide for interest at normal rates or no interest at all.

Shareholder debt, by definition, is arranged in conjunction with the ownership of share capital, and the ratio of debt to equity can vary. Exhibit 12-1 shows the initial capitalization of a corporation using a minimum of share capital and a maximum of shareholder debt. The initial capital base provided by the shareholders is $200,000, consisting of a shareholder's loan of $199,999 and share capital of $1.

If the corporation in Exhibit 12-1 wishes to obtain additional credit or loans from outside sources, it may find it necessary to subordinate the shareholder loan of $199,999. For example, a lending institution may advance funds to the corporation only on the condition that its loan takes precedence over the shareholder's loan and, further, that any repayments of the shareholder's loan be made only with the concurrence of the lending institution. Under these conditions, the lending institution views the shareholder's loan as part of the equity capital of the corporation, even though in legal terms it constitutes a debt obligation.

The reasons for regarding the shareholder loan as part of the shareholder's equity in Exhibit 12-1 should be readily apparent—they have to do with the extreme ratio of debt to equity. Usually, a corporation capitalized with $1 of equity would have great difficulty acquiring debt funding of $199,999 from an outside source. Therefore, the shareholder's willingness to provide the loan reflects a need for additional equity. If the shareholders provided $200,000 to the corporation by way of $150,000 of share capital and a $50,000 shareholder loan, it would be difficult to establish whether or not the loan constituted a true debt, rather than part of the equity base. Normally, the marketplace, which provides outside debt financing, will establish the real nature of shareholder debt.

Exhibit 12-1:

Capitalization—
Maximum Debt and
Minimum Equity

		Corporation		
Assets	$200,000		Shareholder loan	$199,999
			Share capital	1
	$200,000			$200,000

For tax purposes, a shareholder loan qualifies as debt, regardless of how it may be viewed by the marketplace. However, it is important to recognize that the decision to use shareholder debt for tax reasons may have an impact on other, non–tax-related issues. For example, independent credit reports may indicate unfavourable debt/equity ratios when shareholder capital is included as debt, rather than equity. As well, to properly value the equity of a business for acquisitions and divestitures, it is necessary to establish the true nature of the shareholder's capital (see Chapter 20).

• **Return on investment**   As previously mentioned, shareholder loans may bear some rate of interest or be interest-free.

Interest paid by the corporation is deductible for tax purposes; this reduces corporate taxable income and increases the shareholder's taxable income by an equivalent amount. Effectively, the payment of interest converts corporate business income into property income of the shareholder and funnels a certain amount of corporate income directly to the shareholder. This reduces the amount of corporate income that is subject to two levels of taxation.

If the shareholder loan does not bear interest, corporate taxable income will be higher, the result being increased corporate taxes and a further tax when corporate retained earnings are distributed as a dividend.

In the following situation, a shareholder loan that bears interest is compared with one that does not.

Situation: X Corporation is subject to a corporate tax rate of 25% and earns business income of $1,000 before the payment of interest. A shareholder loan of $10,000 to the corporation can bear interest of 10% or be interest-free. The shareholder's personal income is subject to a tax rate of 45%.

Analysis: If the shareholder debt is subject to a 10% interest rate (10% × $10,000 = $1,000), the combined tax to the shareholder and the corporation amounts to $450, calculated as follows:

Corporation:	
Business income	$1,000
Interest paid	(1,000)
Income for tax purposes	–0–
Corporate tax	–0–
Shareholder (individual):	
Interest income	$1,000
Personal tax @ 45%	$ 450
Combined tax ($0 + $450)	$ 450

If the shareholder's debt is interest-free, the combined corporate and shareholder tax will ultimately be $460, calculated as follows:

Corporation:	
Business income	$1,000
Interest paid	–0–
Income for tax purposes	$1,000
Corporate tax @ 25%	$ 250
Shareholder (individual):	
Potential dividend ($1,000 − $250)	$ 750
Tax (net of dividend tax credit)*	$ 210
Combined tax ($250 + $210)	$ 460

* 28% of $750 = $210; eligible dividend, see Exhibit 10-7 in Chapter 10.

In the above example, the payment of interest eliminated the corporate tax of 25% and shifted the income to the shareholder, who was taxed on it at 45%. While the amount of immediate tax (45% versus 25%) is higher, the payment of deductible interest eliminates the potential for double taxation that occurs when no interest is paid. This result stems from the fact that when a corporation is subject to a high tax rate, some double taxation will occur when the after-tax corporate profits are distributed to the shareholder as dividends at some future time. (See varying provincial double tax rates in Chapter 11.) If the rate of corporate tax were lower—for example, if the corporation were subject to the small business rate of approximately 15%—the tax results of paying or not paying interest would be different.

Assuming the same facts as in the above situation, except that the corporate rate of tax is reduced to 15% from 25%, the following results would occur.

If the shareholder debt is subject to 10% interest, the combined corporate and shareholder tax remains the same, as follows:

Corporation:	
Corporate income after interest	–0–
Corporate tax	–0–
Shareholder (individual):	
Tax @ 45% on $1,000 of interest income	$450
Combined tax	$450

If the shareholder debt is interest-free, the combined corporate and shareholder tax is ultimately about $430, as calculated below.

Corporation:	
Business income	$1,000
Interest paid	–0–
Income for tax purposes	$1,000
Corporate tax @ 15%	$ 150
Shareholder (individual):	
Potential dividend ($1,000 − $150)	$ 850
Tax (net of dividend tax credit)*	$ 280
Combined tax ($150 + $280)	$ 430

* 33% of $850 = $280 (non-eligible dividend).

Note that in the previous example, the interest-free method results in a combined tax saving of 2%. Also, if no interest is paid, the *immediate* tax to the corporation is only $150, as opposed to $450 paid by the shareholder under the interest-paying option. It is important to note that the second level of tax on corporate distributions may occur at some time in the future and that it is necessary to consider not only the ultimate amount of tax payable but also when that payment must be made.

The results of the previous two analyses are compared in Exhibit 12-2. The exhibit indicates that when corporate taxes are 15%, an interest-free loan is preferable because the immediate tax is substantially lower at $150 *and* the overall combined tax is lower. However, when the corporate tax rate is 25% the preference is less clear. An interest-bearing loan results in higher immediate tax (45% versus 25%) but the ultimate total tax is lower due to double taxation being avoided.

Exhibit 12-2:				
Interest versus No Interest on Shareholder Debt		*Immediate tax*	*Future tax on dividend distribution*	*Total*
	Corporate tax rate (15%):			
	Interest	$450	–0–	$450
	No interest	150	280	430
	Corporate tax rate (25%):			
	Interest	$450	–0–	$450
	No interest	250	210	460

In each of the previous examples, the tax impact was calculated on the assumption that the corporation earned income in the particular year. However, when the corporation is incurring losses, paying interest on a shareholder loan has a negative impact. In such cases, the interest paid out increases the corporate loss, which remains unused until future corporate profits are achieved; the related interest income to the shareholder is fully taxable, however. In effect, although the economic entity has suffered a loss, taxation still occurs in that year. This diminished cash flow reduces the shareholder's ability to provide further contributions to the corporation if those are required to fund the losses and restore the original capital base. This factor is particularly important when the corporation is a new venture that is suffering losses during its start-up years and requires maximum shareholder support.

• **Loss of investment**   When providing capital to a corporation, the investor must consider the possibility of ultimately losing all or a portion of the investment if the corporation should encounter financial difficulty. In particular, the investor must determine when and to what extent such a loss can be used for tax purposes to generate additional funds through the reduction of tax otherwise payable.

As the shareholder debt is capital property to the shareholder, a loss incurred on it is a capital loss, of which only one-half is available for tax purposes. If the loan is to a small business corporation (see Chapter 8), the capital loss becomes a business investment loss, and one-half of the loss can be offset against all other sources of income; otherwise, it can be offset only against other capital gains. While the amount of loss that can be used for tax purposes is the same for share capital and shareholder debt, the timing for recognizing those losses in order to create cash flow by reducing taxes is different.

As indicated in Chapter 8, a loss on a loan is recognized for tax purposes in the year in which it is *established* to be uncollectible, whereas a loss on share capital is recognized only when the shares are actually sold, the corporation is insolvent and has ceased operations, or the corporation has become legally bankrupt.[1] Therefore, a loss on shareholder loans can normally be recognized for tax purposes before a loss on share capital. This treatment provides an advantage to the shareholder for two reasons:

1. Recognizing the loss earlier, rather than later, diminishes the real loss—in cash-flow terms—on the initial investment.

2. The shareholder loss can be recognized when a corporation is in extreme financial difficulty but is not yet bankrupt and still has a chance of survival. The cash flow created for the shareholder from the early loss recognition can be used to strengthen the corporation and increase its chances for survival.

For example, a shareholder loan of $200,000 that is established to be a bad debt may generate tax savings to the shareholder in a 45% tax bracket of $45,000 (45% × ½ of $200,000). The shareholder can choose to keep the $45,000 to reduce the investment loss from $200,000 to $155,000 ($200,000 – $45,000), or can contribute the $45,000 to the corporation to strengthen its capital base. Either way, the tax treatment has diminished the downside risk of the investment.

- **Return of capital**   The capital base contributed to a corporation by its shareholder(s) is not permanent. A corporation may require additional capital for expansion, or its financial strength may be in excess of its capital requirements so that a return of all or a portion of the shareholder's initial capital is appropriate.

Shareholder capital contributed in the form of debt can be returned with relative ease and without tax consequences. Consider the capital structure described in Exhibit 12-3. The structure is based on the initial capital structure outlined in Exhibit 12-1, in which the shareholder contributed $200,000 to the corporation by way of share capital of $1 and a loan of $199,999. Suppose that the corporation subsequently generated and retained after-tax profits of $200,000, increasing its total equity to $400,000. If the company is able to operate with a capital base of only $200,000, it can return $200,000 to the shareholder.

The $200,000 can be returned to the shareholder in two ways:

1. The company can declare a dividend from its retained earnings.

2. The company can repay the loan of $199,999 to the shareholder.

Exhibit 12-3:				
Capital Structure—		Corporation (before)		
before and after				
Return of Capital	Assets	$400,000	Shareholder loan	$199,999
			Share capital	1
			Retained earnings	200,000
		$400,000		$400,000
		Corporation (after)		
	Assets	$200,001	Share capital	$ 1
			Retained earnings	200,000
		$200,001		$200,001

---

1   ITA 50(1), (2); IT-159R3, IT-239R2 (archived).

[handwritten margin note: repayment (shareholder's view) – dividend taxable – loan not taxable]

The dividend payment is taxable to the shareholder; the loan repayment constitutes a return of capital and is not taxable. Obviously, the shareholder would prefer that the debt be repaid because this would delay the tax on a dividend distribution until some future time.

This tax treatment results because the retained earnings are attached to the share capital, rather than to the loan. The share capital, which had an original value of $1, has increased in value to $200,001 and, in certain circumstances, may be taxable if returned to the shareholders, as described in Section B.

B. Corporate Capitalization by Share Capital

A corporation can be capitalized with share capital in several ways. It can issue several different classes of shares under a wide range of terms and conditions. Corporate law does not normally assign labels to the various classes of shares; however, the *Income Tax Act* does make reference to common shares and preferred shares.

For tax purposes, a *common* share is a share that entitles the owner to share in corporate assets and earnings beyond the initial share price plus a fixed premium or dividend rate.[2] A *preferred* share is a share that entitles the owner to participate in corporate assets and earnings *only* up to an amount equal to the initial share price plus a fixed dividend rate, regardless of the extent of corporate earnings.[3] Consequently, common shares increase or decrease in value in relation to the accumulation of corporate earnings or losses; preferred shares seldom increase in value because the potential return is predetermined and fixed but can decline in value if corporate assets are depleted. It should be noted that certain preferred shares pay dividends that fluctuate in relation to changes in interest rates at particular times. Therefore, the value of those shares will fluctuate accordingly.

[handwritten margin note: C.S value ↑ or ↓ w/ corp. earn/loss   P.S value ↑(rarely) ↓ w/ corp. asset depleted]

The initial shareholders can provide base capital to the corporation either by common shares alone or by a combination of common shares and various types of preferred shares.

- **Return on investment**   Share capital provides a return to its owners in the form of dividends. Dividends are not deductible by the corporation and are taxable to the individual shareholder. This treatment imposes the two-tier system of taxation that was described in Chapter 11. The corporation must earn income, pay tax, and use its after-tax earnings to pay dividends. In comparison, a corporation issuing debt can pay interest from pre-tax profits.

As previously mentioned, to the extent that corporate profits are taxed at the high rate of 25%, the combination of corporate tax and the subsequent tax on dividend distributions results in some double taxation. Corporate profits taxed at the lower rate, however, are not subject to double taxation. When a corporation is subject to the higher corporate rate of tax, it is in the shareholder's interest to provide capital to the corporation with a maximum amount of shareholder loans in order to increase the return in the form of interest and reduce the impact of double taxation. This occurs when the shareholder requires an annual cash return on investments. Consider the following situation:

Situation: A corporation that is earning $1,000 of business income and is subject to tax at a rate of 25% requires $10,000 of shareholder capital. The shareholder can provide a loan of $10,000 bearing interest at 10% (10% × $10,000 = $1,000) or provide share capital of $10,000 that provides a dividend equal to the corporation's after-tax profits. The shareholder, an individual, is in a 45% tax bracket.

Analysis: The calculation for this analysis is identical to the previous analysis that compared a shareholder loan paying 10% interest with one that paid no interest. The results are summarized in the following table.

---

2   ITA 248.
3   ITA 248.

Shareholder debt with interest:	
Corporate tax (owing to deductible interest)	–0–
Shareholder tax on interest	450
Total tax	$450
Share capital with dividends:	
Corporate tax	$250
Shareholder tax on dividend	210
Total tax	$460

If the shareholder does not require an annual cash return on the investment the decision is more difficult. One must choose between a lower immediate tax on share capital (25% versus 45%) with potential for a small percentage of double tax in the future or avoid double taxation with shareholder debt and higher immediate tax.

If, in the above situation, the corporate tax rate had been 15%, the combined tax would have been lower and the share capital option would have been preferred because in such cases, the shareholder can also choose to delay the payment of dividends so that the immediate tax is only 15%.

• **Loss of investment**   A loss incurred on a share capital investment is normally a capital loss, of which one-half is recognized for tax purposes. However, unlike losses on shareholder loans, a share capital loss is recognized only in the year in which the shares are disposed of, the corporation becomes legally bankrupt, or the corporation is insolvent and has ceased operations. From the perspective of downside risk, share capital is inferior to shareholder debt, which usually can be recognized for tax purposes at an earlier time.

• **Return of capital**   Before reviewing how share capital is returned to the corporate shareholder, it would be useful to examine the methods available for acquiring shares in a corporation.

Corporate shares can be acquired in two ways:

1. The prospective shareholder can purchase all or a portion of previously issued shares from other shareholders.

2. The prospective shareholder can purchase, directly from the corporation, new shares issued from the corporate treasury.

Each of these alternatives has different tax and price implications to the parties involved in the transaction.

1. Acquisition of Shares Directly from the Corporation

Under this alternative, the new shareholder contributes cash or other assets directly to the corporation in exchange for shares of an equivalent value.

The receipt of assets in exchange for shares in the corporation has no tax consequences to the corporation. In effect, the corporation has acquired property (cash or other assets) and paid for it by issuing new share capital. The stated value of the shares to the corporation is equal to the value of the property exchanged. When the corporation receives equipment valued at $10,000 in exchange for five common shares, the stated value of each share is $2,000 ($2,000 × 5 shares = $10,000). For tax purposes, the stated value of the shares is referred to as "paid-up capital."[4]

---

4   ITA 89(1)(c); IT-463R2.

From the shareholder's perspective, the receipt of shares represents the acquisition of capital property having an adjusted cost base for tax purposes equal to the value of the property exchanged. In the previous example, the adjusted cost base of the five shares received is $10,000 ($2,000 per share), being the value of the equipment given up in exchange.[5]

When a corporation with existing shareholders admits a new shareholder by issuing additional shares, referred to as "treasury shares," there are no tax consequences to the existing shareholders. Exhibit 12-4 diagrams a change in the share structure of an existing corporation. The "before" diagram indicates that the corporation was originally owned by a single shareholder and had a total value of $100,000. In the "after" diagram a new shareholder has acquired a 50% ownership of the corporation by acquiring shares directly from the corporation. It is important to recognize that the original shareholder did not dispose of any shares, even though his/her ownership interest diminished from 100% to 50%. In such cases, there are no tax consequences to the original shareholder.

Exhibit 12-4:

Admitting New Shareholders by Issuing Treasury Shares

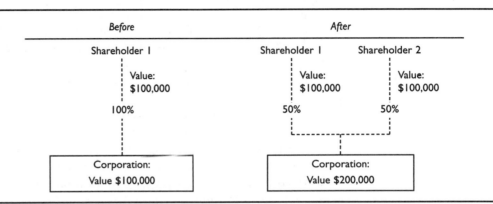

Also, note that in order to acquire a 50% ownership of the corporation, which had an original value of $100,000, the new shareholder contributed $100,000 to the company and not $50,000 (half of $100,000). The result of this transaction is that the value of the company has increased from $100,000 to $200,000. The additional resources are available for business expansion or debt retirement. The original shareholder now has a diluted ownership percentage but still holds shares worth $100,000.

2. Acquisition of Shares from Other Shareholders

Under this alternative, the new shareholder buys the shares directly from the other shareholders, and no funds are contributed to the corporation. The original shareholders will have a capital gain or loss on the sale of whatever shares they have sold, whether this involves all their shares or only a fraction of them.

From the buyer's perspective, the shares acquired will have an adjusted cost base for tax purposes equal to the purchase price. However, it should be noted that the paid-up capital value of the shares in the corporation remains unchanged, even if the purchaser has acquired the previously issued shares at a price different from the original issued value.

Consider the situation in Exhibit 12-5, in which a corporation with a value of $100,000 is owned 100% by a single shareholder. A new shareholder acquires 50% of the shares by purchasing half the original shareholder's shares. In this situation, the purchase price for 50% of a $100,000 company is only $50,000, compared with $100,000 when shares are purchased from the corporation.

---

5   ITA 53(1).

Exhibit 12-5:

New Shareholder Acquires Shares from Other Shareholders

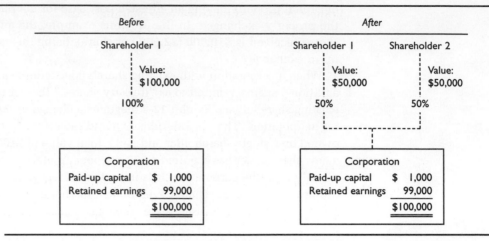

Also, note that the resources of the company remain the same after the new shareholder arrives—they consist of share capital of $1,000 plus retained earnings of $99,000 for a total value of $100,000. The new shareholder owns shares that, for tax purposes, have an adjusted cost base of $50,000 but a paid-up capital value on the corporate balance sheet of only $500 (half of $1,000). The difference ($49,500) has implications if and when share capital is returned to the shareholders.

Corporate share capital is divided into a number of units represented by the number of shares held. For example, an owner can contribute $100,000 to a corporation in return for one share or a number of shares. Capital can be returned to the shareholder when that shareholder disposes of all or a portion of the shares. (There is a second method for returning capital—see point 5.) Common shares, which participate in earnings, change in value over time, and as a result, the disposition of shares to provide a return of capital may have tax consequences.

A shareholder can dispose of shares in two ways:

1. The shares can be sold to other shareholders.

2. The shares can be bought back by the corporation for cancellation.

Each alternative has its own tax implications, which are reviewed below.

3. Sale of Shares to Other Shareholders

Under this alternative, the sale of shares creates a capital gain or a capital loss depending on whether the shares have increased or decreased in value. This alternative allows the shareholder to realize a return on the original investment as well as any share appreciation resulting from corporate earnings. It should also be noted that when shares are sold to other shareholders, the vendor's percentage ownership in the corporation is diminished.

Since transactions of this nature are between the shareholders, the corporation's resources and capital base remain unchanged.

4. Sale of Shares Back to the Corporation

This type of transaction is referred to as a "share redemption" or "buy-back." It involves the distribution of corporate assets (normally cash) to the shareholders and a cancellation of all or some of their shares. This alternative automatically diminishes the value and resources of the corporation because it involves the direct return of share equity to the shareholders.

This type of transaction is useful when a corporation wishes to return some of its equity on a proportionate basis to all existing shareholders without changing the ownership ratio. It can also be used to buy the shares of one or a few of the shareholders, thereby automatically expanding the ownership percentage of the remaining shareholders.

Consider the situation in Exhibit 12-6. A corporation with two equal shareholders has a value of $100,000 consisting of $10,000 of common share capital and $90,000 of retained earnings. Shareholder 2 departs by selling shares back to the corporation for $50,000. Note that after the transaction, the corporate resources have diminished from $100,000 to $50,000 as a result of the cancellation of half the entity's shares and a distribution of half its retained earnings. After the share redemption, shareholder 1 is the sole shareholder. The interesting aspect of this transaction is that shareholder 1 has acquired control not by purchasing any additional shares but by removing the other shareholder, thereby depleting the corporation's resources.

The redemption value of corporate shares is the sum of two separate values—the original capital value of the shares and the change in value resulting from corporate earnings accumulated and attached to those shares. The *tax consequences* to the shareholder when a *redemption* occurs are summarized as follows:

- To the extent that the redemption price exceeds the paid-up capital (original issue price) of the shares, a *dividend* is deemed to have been distributed.[6]
- In addition, the shareholder is deemed to have sold the shares, for the purpose of determining the capital gain or capital loss, at an amount equal to the paid-up capital of the shares.[7]

In other words, a share redemption involves both a dividend payment and a sale of shares.

The tax consequences of this are demonstrated using the share redemption example in Exhibit 12-6. In order to complete the calculation, an assumption must be made with respect to the adjusted cost base of the shares owned by shareholder 2. If shareholder 2 were an original shareholder who had acquired shares directly from the corporate treasury, the adjusted cost base of the shares would be $5,000, which is equal to the paid-up capital. However, if those same shares were purchased from a previous shareholder, they would have a cost for tax purposes that would not be the same as the paid-up capital. Assuming that shareholder 2 acquired the shares as an original shareholder, the result of the redemption is as follows:

Deemed dividend:	
Redemption price	$50,000
Paid-up capital	(5,000)
Dividend to shareholder 2	$45,000
Capital transaction:	
Deemed proceeds of disposition (selling price of $50,000 minus dividend)	$ 5,000
Adjusted cost base	(5,000)
Capital gain	–0–

The above indicates that shareholder 2 received the return of original capital without tax consequences. However, any additional value was treated as a dividend and *not* as a capital gain, which would have occurred had the shares been sold to a new shareholder. It is important to recognize that when redeeming corporate shares, the company cannot simply repay the original share capital but also must distribute the attached retained earnings as a dividend.

---

6 ITA 84(3).
7 ITA 54 definition "proceeds of disposition" (redemption value less deemed dividend).

Exhibit 12-6:

Corporate Redemption
of Shares

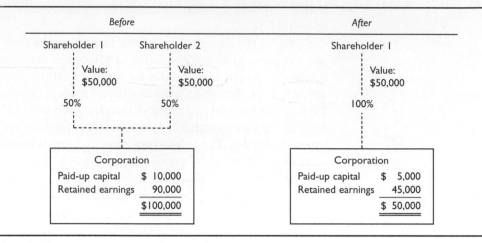

5. Reduction of Paid-up Capital

As an alternative, a corporation can return only its paid-up capital to the shareholders without redeeming any of its shares. The tax treatment of this option varies, depending on whether the corporation is private or public. If the proper legal steps are taken, a *private* corporation can make a payment to its shareholders that constitutes a return of capital. There are no tax consequences for this transaction, provided the payment reduces and does not exceed the paid-up capital value.[8]

Consider the three capital structures shown in Exhibit 12-7. Each includes $100,000 of capital. If each entity is a private corporation, in each case, the company can return the original capital to the shareholders without triggering a simultaneous distribution of taxable dividends.

In contrast, a public corporation that executes the same transaction and reduces paid-up capital *of any class of shares* is normally considered to have paid a taxable dividend for the entire payment.[9]

Exhibit 12-7:

Alternative Capital
Structures

	A	B	C
Shareholder loans	$ 99,000	–0–	–0–
Preferred shares	–0–	99,000	–0–
Common shares	1,000	1,000	100,000
	100,000	100,000	100,000
Retained earnings	50,000	50,000	50,000
	$150,000	$150,000	$150,000

While the amount of capital a corporation requires in order to function may be clear, the manner in which that capital is provided by the shareholder is not. The opportunity exists for a wide variety of capital formats, including shareholder debt, preferred shares, and common shares. Each format will have a different effect on the amount and timing of future tax costs, and on the resulting cash flows.

Shareholders must determine which capital structure is most appropriate by examining the tax implications of the following: regular returns provided on the capital; the possible loss of the investment; and the return of the original capital.

---

8   ITA 84(4); IT-67R3.
9   ITA 84(4.1), 53(2)(a).

II. Transferring Assets to a Corporation

It was mentioned earlier that a shareholder may capitalize a corporation by providing assets in exchange for share capital or debt. The assets exchanged can consist of either cash or other assets, such as land, buildings, equipment, franchises, and the like. The transfer of assets to the corporation constitutes a sale and disposition for the shareholder. To the extent that those assets appreciated in value before the transfer, there will be tax implications.

A corporation need not acquire assets in order to use them, as the right of use can be achieved by leasing the asset from the shareholder. However, this section of the chapter restricts itself to a discussion of asset transfers.

For tax purposes, an existing or proposed shareholder (individual, corporation, or trust) can transfer an asset to a corporation either at the fair market value or at an elected value, which is normally equal to the asset's cost for tax purposes. Each alternative has different tax implications to the shareholder and to the corporation.

A. Transfer of Assets at Fair Market Value

When assets are transferred at fair market value, any gains on the sale are recognized by the shareholder. Depending on the nature of the asset transferred, the resulting income may be a capital gain, a recapture of capital cost allowance, or normal business income.

The recognition of taxable income is not necessarily a negative consequence. For example, the shareholder can use the income from an asset sale to offset accumulated losses that could not otherwise have been used.

The corporation that acquires the asset at fair market value has an increased cost for tax purposes that may, in turn, reduce the taxes payable by the corporation. Consider the following situation:

Situation: A shareholder who owns equipment that originally cost $100,000 and that has an undepreciated cost of $60,000 sells the equipment to a corporation at the fair market value price of $90,000 in exchange for a combination of shares and debt. The shareholder's tax rate is 45%, and the corporation's tax rate is 25%.

Analysis: The sale of the equipment creates taxable income to the shareholder of $30,000 ($90,000 − $60,000 = $30,000).

The cost of the equipment to the corporation that is available for capital cost allowance is $90,000. Since the pre-transfer undepreciated capital cost of the equipment was $60,000, the corporation will have additional capital cost allowance deductions, over a period of time, of $30,000.

While most taxpayers automatically shy away from paying tax up front in return for future reductions in tax, the circumstances should always be considered in real cash-flow terms. For example, a taxpayer in the 45% income bracket may well feel overwhelmed at the prospect of incurring taxable income of $30,000. However, the real cost of transferring the asset at fair market value in the preceding situation is $8,500 (assuming the discount factor for the time value of money is 10%), calculated as follows:

Immediate tax cost on transfer:	
$30,000 × 45%	$13,500
less	
Present value of tax savings from additional capital cost allowance	
in the corporation (using the formula described in Chapter 6):	
$\dfrac{\$30,000 \times 0.25 \times 0.20}{0.20 + 0.10} =$	(5,000)
Net cost in cash-flow terms	$ 8,500

Although the result is still negative, the impact is softened when measured in real cash-flow terms. It should also be pointed out that the tax cost (above) might have been lower if the particular asset had had a higher capital cost allowance rate or if the personal rate of tax had been lower than the corporate rate of tax.

B. Election to Transfer Assets at Tax Values

The *Income Tax Act* permits assets to be transferred to a Canadian corporation at their tax cost, provided that certain formal procedures are adhered to. This option is permitted even though the transfer price for legal purposes may be at fair market value. For example, using the facts in the previous situation, the shareholder could legally sell the equipment to the corporation for $90,000 and receive full consideration in exchange but, for tax purposes, elect that the equipment's sale price was $60,000 (its undepreciated capital cost). The result of such an election would be that the shareholder had no taxable income from the transfer and that the corporation would incur any taxable income in the event that it ultimately sold the equipment to a third party.

Such an election is often called a "roll-over" because the shareholder's potential taxable income is rolled over to the corporation but not eliminated.

- **Election limitations** The tax provisions that apply to the procedure for electing a transfer price other than fair market value are complex. Even so, from a decision-making perspective, the reader must be aware of when the election applies and of the resulting tax consequences in terms of cash flow to the shareholder and the corporation. The fundamental limitations of the election procedure are presented below.[10] *Additional technical information is provided in a supplement to this chapter.*

The corporation acquiring the asset can pay the shareholder in the form of either share consideration or non-share consideration. Share consideration can consist of various types of common or preferred shares. Non-share consideration can consist of cash, a debt owing to the shareholder, the assumption by the corporation of shareholder liabilities, or the exchange of some other corporate asset. For example, a shareholder building valued at $100,000 but encumbered by a $60,000 mortgage can be purchased by the corporation by assuming the $60,000 mortgage liability and issuing additional preferred shares for $40,000.

The primary limitations of the election procedure relate to the nature of the consideration paid for the asset. In order for the transfer to avoid tax, the consideration must include some shares, although there is no specified amount; as well, the non-share consideration (cash or debts owing to the shareholder) cannot be greater than the elected value of the asset transferred. (The elected value is normally the asset's tax cost.)

The above limitations are demonstrated in the following situation:

Situation: A shareholder owning a building that originally cost $100,000 and that has an undepreciated capital cost of $90,000 and a fair market value of $130,000 transfers the property to a corporation and wishes to avoid tax on the transfer.

Analysis: Notwithstanding that the legal selling price would be $130,000, taxable income can be avoided if the shareholder and the corporation agree that the transfer price for tax purposes is $90,000, which is the building's undepreciated capital cost. In accordance with the preceding limitations, payment must include some shares, but the non-share payment cannot be higher than $90,000. Therefore, the legal form of the transfer can be as follows:

---

10 ITA 85(1); IT-291R3.

Legal selling price	$130,000
Payment consideration:	
Debt owing to shareholder	$ 90,000
Preferred shares	40,000
	$130,000

• **Tax implications to the shareholder and the corporation** In this situation, choosing the elective option avoids tax to the shareholder at the time of the transfer. However, there will be future tax implications, and these should be anticipated before the decision to use the election is made in order that the real impact on cash flow can be understood. The above situation will have the following implications:

1. The legal purchase price of the building was $130,000, and the corporate accounting balance sheet may reflect this amount. However, the cost of the building to the corporation *for tax purposes* is dramatically different. Because the elected tax value was $90,000, the corporation is deemed to have an undepreciated capital cost of $90,000 and an original cost of $100,000 for the building.

   As a result, if the corporation were to subsequently sell the building for, say, $130,000, no accounting gain would occur, but taxable income would be created as follows:

Recapture ($100,000 − $90,000)	$10,000
Taxable capital gains:	
($130,000 − $100,000 = $30,000) × ½	15,000
	$25,000

   Note that this is the same amount of taxable income that the shareholder would have incurred upon selling the building for tax purposes at fair market value.

   The after-tax corporate income from the asset sale may ultimately be distributed as a dividend to the shareholder, causing a second level of tax, at which time, if the corporation is subject to the high rate of tax on business income, some double taxation will occur. This means that delaying taxation by using the election may create greater taxation in the long run.

2. After the transfer, the shareholder will own a note receivable from the corporation of $90,000 and preferred shares of $40,000, both of which are capital property. Because the transfer price was $90,000 for tax purposes, this amount represents to the shareholder the cost base of debt and the shares, with the amount being allocated first to the debt. Thus, the cost base of the loan is $90,000, and the cost base of the shares is zero.

   In addition, the preferred shares are deemed to have a nominal paid-up capital.[11] If those shares are subsequently redeemed, a deemed dividend occurs for the full redemption amount. However, if the loan of $90,000 is paid out to the shareholder, no tax consequences occur. In this way, the elective option permits the shareholder to recover, free of tax, an amount up to the elected tax transfer price.

The elective option is designed to provide flexibility when assets are incorporated. However, in exchange for this flexibility, there may be other long-term implications that diminish the attractiveness of satisfying immediate tax concerns. While it is usually advantageous to defer tax to a later period, this is not always the case. Therefore, it is vital that decision makers anticipate future events when deciding whether to use the election.

---

11 ITA 85(2.1).

C. Applying the Election Option

A wide range of assets can be transferred to a corporation at the tax cost, rather than at fair market value. The following types of assets are eligible for such election:[12]

1. Capital property, both depreciable and non-depreciable, such as land, buildings, equipment, and depreciable intangibles, including patents, franchises, and licences of a limited legal life.

2. Inventory.

3. Eligible capital property (see Chapter 6), such as goodwill, patents, franchises, and licences with an undefined legal life.

4. Resource property.

The above list includes virtually all types of assets. A few exceptions exist; for example, real estate that is being held for resale (in other words, that is not capital property but inventory) and real estate owned by a non-resident (unless used in a business) are not permitted the roll-over election.

The elective option is available to various types of transactions. Its use is most often associated with transactions involving the creation or altering of corporate structures by related parties for business and estate planning; however, there is no requirement that its use be restricted to parties that are not at arm's-length. The following transactions often make use of the election:

1. The incorporation of a proprietorship where the proprietor becomes the shareholder of the new corporation.

2. The transferring of assets from a parent corporation to a new or existing subsidiary corporation. For example, if a corporation wants to operate one of its divisions as a separate company, the assets of the division can be transferred at tax values to a newly created subsidiary corporation.

3. Shareholders often own several "sister" corporations. The elective option is useful in transferring assets from one sister corporation to another within the corporate group.

4. A corporation or an individual can sell assets to an unrelated third party and defer tax by using the election. For example, Corporation X may want to dispose of its business by selling assets to Corporation Y. The parties can defer tax by opting for transfer at the tax cost, provided that Corporation X (the seller) becomes a shareholder in Corporation Y (the buyer).

Several of the above transactions are examined in greater detail in Chapter 14.

D. Sale of Accounts Receivable

The tax implications for accounts receivable when a business ceases to exist was reviewed in detail in Part III (J) of Chapter 5. The transfer of a business from an individual to a corporation, or from one corporation to another, results in a cessation of business for the transferor and an unusual tax treatment of accounts receivable. Recall that, automatically, a loss on the transfer of accounts receivable upon the cessation of a business results in a capital loss to the vendor. Normally only one-half of the loss can be deducted against taxable capital gains. However, if the sale is to an affiliated person (a corporation that is controlled by you or your spouse or common-law partner) the capital loss is deemed to be nil.[13] Additionally, the purchaser is deemed to have acquired a capital property and any subsequent gain or loss is treated

---

12 ITA 85(1.1).
13 ITA 54, superficial loss.

[handwritten margin note: joint election, vendor loss = business loss.]

as a capital gain or loss. As indicated in Chapter 5, this unusual result can be avoided if the vendor and purchaser file a joint election to treat the sale of the accounts receivable as a business transaction for both parties.[14] Therefore, when transferring a business to a corporation, even as part of a re-organization, it is important to remember to file the necessary joint election.

III. Corporate Distributions to Shareholders

Corporate distributions to shareholders consist of either accumulated profits or the return of capital. As indicated previously, any distribution of property from a corporation that relates to share capital is automatically considered to be, first, a distribution of earnings and therefore a dividend, and second, a return of capital. This holds true not only when dividends are declared in the normal fashion but also when a corporation redeems or buys back its own shares.

This section of the chapter briefly examines certain unique forms of corporate distributions as well as the general tax treatment resulting from the wind-up and elimination of a corporation.

A. Stock Dividends

A stock dividend involves the issuing of additional shares in lieu of a cash distribution. From the corporation's perspective, there are no tax or cash implications, as the transaction simply involves making an accounting entry that reduces retained earnings and increases the share capital.

The shareholder who receives additional shares as a result of a stock dividend is deemed, for tax purposes, to have received a normal taxable dividend. The amount of the dividend is equal to the amount the corporation transfers from retained earnings to paid-up capital on the corporate balance sheet.[15] If the shareholder is an individual, the dividend must be grossed-up by the appropriate amount. As indicated in Chapter 7, this treatment forces the shareholder to reinvest the dividend in additional share capital of the corporation. In the event that the share is later sold, its cost base for tax purposes is equal to the deemed dividend previously included in income.

B. Special Distributions of Canadian-Controlled Private Corporations

The possibility of double taxation is applied fully for public corporations. However, it applies to Canadian-controlled private corporations only to the extent that their earnings represent business income in excess of $500,000 annually. For example, it was demonstrated previously that business income taxed at the low corporate rate does not result in double taxation when distributed because the dividend tax credit provides sufficient relief. However, the low rate of tax applies only to business income and not to property income or to the taxable portion of capital gains.

A Canadian-controlled private corporation is taxed on property income (interest, rents, and so on) at a high corporate rate (36% to 44% depending on the province or territory) plus a special refundable tax of $6\frac{2}{3}\%$. In order to avoid double taxation, a portion of this tax is refunded to the corporation when dividends are distributed from this source (see Chapter 13). Any dividend declared is considered to have come first from this source of income, to the extent that it exists.

In addition, certain income earned by corporations is *tax-free*—for example, *life insurance proceeds* and *one-half of capital gains*. In order to eliminate double taxation, these amounts, net of any losses from similar sources, are permitted to be distributed by private corporations as a tax-free dividend referred to as a **"capital dividend."** Dividends from this source are not automatic and require a special election.[16]

Both of the above items are examined more closely in Chapter 13.

---

14 ITA 22.
15 ITA 248, 89(1)(c); IT-88R2.
16 ITA 83(2), 89(1)(b); IT-66R6.

C. Distributions Other than Cash

While corporate distributions are normally made in the form of cash, a corporation can pay a dividend by transferring ownership of corporate assets to the shareholder. This is referred to as a "dividend in kind."

If the asset distributed has a value greater than the corporation's tax cost, the corporation is deemed to have disposed of the asset at fair market value, which results in taxable income to the corporation. Similarly, the taxable dividend received by the shareholder is equal to the fair market value of the asset received.[17] For example, consider the situation where a corporation transfers land that is capital property, having a fair market value of $100,000 and a cost base of $70,000, to a shareholder as a dividend distribution. The corporation will incur a taxable capital gain of $15,000 ($100,000 − $70,000 = $30,000 × ½), and the shareholder will receive a dividend of $100,000. The adjusted cost base of the land received from the dividend will be $100,000 for the shareholder, and any gain or loss from a subsequent sale will be measured against that base.

D. Wind-up of a Corporation

A corporation can end its existence by disposing of all its assets, meeting its debt obligations, and distributing all its earnings and capital to the shareholders.

On wind-up, the corporate assets can be converted to cash through a sale on the open market, or the assets can be distributed to the shareholders as part of the distribution of capital and earnings. If assets are first sold on the open market, taxable income will occur to the extent that the proceeds of disposition exceed the tax cost of the various assets. This additional income will, after the tax liability has been satisfied, form part of the earnings distribution on the wind-up.

Similarly, if corporate assets are distributed as part of the wind-up proceedings, the corporation is deemed to have sold them at fair market value, which provides the same tax result as if they had been sold on the open market.[18] It is important to recognize that, except when a 90%-owned subsidiary is being wound up into its parent corporation, there is no opportunity to defer tax through election options when assets are being transferred to the shareholder on wind-up. This, of course, is in complete contrast to the situation where a corporation is being created; at such a time, a shareholder can choose to defer tax on assets transferred into the company. In short, the process of getting into a corporation provides significant flexibility, but the process of getting out of a corporation is very restrictive.

The comments in this section were brief and were designed to provide an overview of the general treatment of corporate wind-ups. A more detailed examination of wind-ups and their implications is made in Chapter 18. In addition, a review of the procedures for winding up a subsidiary into its parent corporation is made in Chapter 14.

IV. Summary and Conclusion

This chapter has examined the tax factors and implications on cash flow relating to the start-up, maintenance, and wind-up of corporations.

At the outset, shareholders organizing a corporation must decide how to capitalize that corporation—that is, how to use share capital and shareholder debt. Each possible alternative affects the amount and timing of tax with respect to returns received on the capital invested, the treatment resulting from the possible loss of the capital

---

17 ITA 52(2).
18 ITA 84(2); IT-149R4.

invested, and the repatriation of capital for reinvestment by the shareholders. These areas are compared below.

• **Return on investment**   Capitalization by shareholder debt permits the shareholders to receive part of their return in the form of interest, which is deductible from corporate income. By shifting corporate income to the shareholder, the two-tier system of corporate tax and shareholder tax is circumvented. To the extent that the corporation is subject to the high rate of tax, interest payments eliminate double taxation.

Capitalization by share capital imposes a return by dividends. This dooms the structure to double taxation unless the corporation is subject to the low rate of corporate tax that is applicable on a portion of a Canadian-controlled private corporation's income.

• **Loss of capital**   To the extent that a shareholder's capital investment is lost, shareholder debt holds a distinct advantage over share capital. A loss on a shareholder debt can be recognized for tax purposes—which may create tax savings—in the year in which it is established to be bad, whereas a loss on share capital can be recognized only when the shares are sold or the corporation becomes legally bankrupt or insolvent and ceases operations. Speeding up the loss recognition enhances cash flow, which, in turn, reduces the overall risk factor.

• **Repatriation of capital**   Capitalization by shareholder debt permits the repayment of the initial capital to the shareholder at any time without tax consequences and leaves accumulated corporate profits to be distributed at a later time. On the other hand, share capital, unless it consists of preferred shares, can only return the initial capital without tax consequences if the entity is a private corporation.

Visit the Canadian Income Taxation Web site at **www.mcgrawhill.ca/ olc/buckwold** to view any updated tax information.

Where assets are transferred from a shareholder to a corporation, or from a corporation to a shareholder, the transaction automatically is deemed to occur at fair market value. As an alternative, an election that transfers assets into a corporation at an agreed value is permitted for tax purposes; this can delay the tax until the asset is ultimately disposed of by the corporation. No such opportunity exists when assets are transferred from the corporation to the shareholders, except during the wind-up of a subsidiary into its parent corporation.

This chapter has demonstrated the need to anticipate the long-term implications of investing in and utilizing the corporate structure. It is important to consider the tax treatment of corporate income (see Chapter 11) and, as well, to recognize that the tax treatment accorded to the different methods of getting into and out of a corporation has a significant impact on the ultimate cash return from the investment.

Supplement: Technical Information on Transferring Assets to a Corporation

The following information contains detailed rules for Section 85 elections. It expands on the general rules discussed earlier in the chapter. If the general rules are sufficient for your purposes, this section can be omitted.

Detailed Rules for the Transfer of Assets using an Elected Transfer Price under Section 85 of the *Income Tax Act*

A Section 85 election involves the shareholder (existing or proposed) and the corporation agreeing on a price to be used for tax purposes for the transfer of an asset to the corporation. This is accomplished by entering the agreed amount on a prescribed form (T2057 for transfers from an individual, trust, or corporation; T2058 for transfers from a partnership) signed by both the shareholder and the corporation. The election form is due the same day the shareholder's income tax return is due for the year the transfer takes place, or earlier if the corporation is required to file an income tax return for the year earlier than the shareholder.[19]

The elected transfer price (elected amount) becomes the three following values for tax purposes:

1. Sales proceeds for the shareholder.[20]

2. Cost of the asset acquired by the corporation.[21]

3. Cost of the property received by the shareholder from the corporation as consideration for the asset transferred.[22]

The elected amount is allocated to the property received by the shareholder (as payment for the assets sold) in the following order:

1. Non-share consideration (limited to fair market value).[23]

2. Preferred shares (limited to fair market value).[24]

3. Common shares (remainder).[25]

The transfer price for legal purposes must be at fair market value if adverse tax consequences are to be avoided. Thus, the fair market value of the consideration received must equal the fair market value of the asset transferred. Earlier in the chapter it was stated that in order to avoid tax on the transfer, the consideration must include shares and that the non-share consideration cannot exceed the elected amount[26] (the elected amount being the asset's tax cost in this case). There are circumstances where the shareholder may wish to recognize a specific amount of taxable income (for example to use up a loss carry-over). This can be accomplished by electing a transfer price that is higher than the tax value.

The following looks at the range of elected amounts possible for non-depreciable property, depreciable property, and eligible capital property and the resulting implications for the shareholder and the corporation. Regardless of the type of property, there is one overriding rule—the elected amount can never exceed the fair market value of the asset transferred.[27] Therefore, the top of the range is always the fair market value. The bottom of the range is the tax value, which is different for each type of property. The tax value is the cost or adjusted cost base for non-depreciable assets,[28] the UCC for depreciable assets,[29] and 4/3 of the CEC for eligible capital property.[30]

A. Non-depreciable Property

Situation:

The shareholder owning land (non-depreciable capital property), which originally cost $20,000 and is now worth $100,000, transfers the property to a corporation receiving as payment debt of $20,000 and preferred shares with a value of $80,000.

---

19 ITA 85(6).
20 ITA 85(1)(a).
21 ITA 85(1)(a).
22 ITA 85(1)(f), (g), (h).
23 ITA 85(1)(f).
24 ITA 85(1)(g).
25 ITA 85(1)(h).
26 ITA 85(1)(b).
27 ITA 85(1)(c).
28 ITA 85(1)(c.1).
29 ITA 85(1)(e).
30 ITA 85(1)(d).

Analysis: Notwithstanding that the legal selling price would be $100,000, the shareholder and the corporation can file a Section 85 election, choosing to use a different transfer price for tax purposes. The range for the elected amount is from the FMV ($100,000) down to the ACB ($20,000).

In order for the shareholder to avoid recognizing a capital gain at the time of the transfer, the elected amount must be $20,000, the ACB of the asset. Since the non-share consideration does not exceed $20,000 it is possible to elect a transfer price of $20,000. The elected amount ($20,000) becomes the proceeds for the shareholder, the cost of the asset for the corporation and the cost of the consideration received.

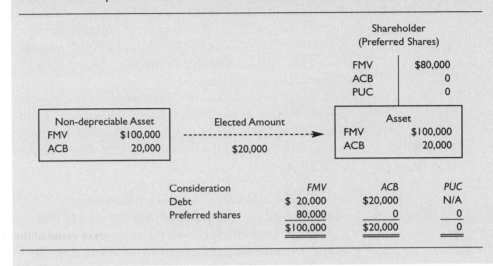

The tax implications of electing a transfer price of $20,000 are as follows:

1. The shareholder avoids paying tax at the time of the transfer. The capital gain is nil (Proceeds $20,000 − ACB $20,000).

2. Although the corporation's legal purchase price for the asset is $100,000, its cost for tax purposes is $20,000 (elected amount). As a result, if the corporation subsequently sells the asset for $100,000 no accounting gain will occur, but there will be a capital gain of $80,000 (Proceeds $100,000 − ACB $20,000). Note that this is the same amount of capital gain that the shareholder would have incurred upon selling the asset for tax purposes at fair market value.

3. After the transfer, the shareholder will own a note receivable from the corporation of $20,000 and preferred shares worth $80,000, both of which are capital property. The elected amount of $20,000 becomes the cost of the debt and the shares, with the amount being allocated first to the debt, up to its fair market value ($20,000), leaving nothing to be allocated to the shares. Thus, the cost base of the debt is $20,000 and the cost base of the shares is zero. If the shareholder subsequently sells the shares for $80,000 there will be a capital gain of $80,000 (Proceeds $80 − ACB $0). Note that this is the same amount of capital gain that the shareholder would have incurred upon selling the asset for tax purposes at fair market value.

4. The paid-up capital (PUC) of the preferred shares received by the shareholder in this case is nil. If those shares are subsequently redeemed, a deemed dividend occurs for the full redemption amount ($80,000).

5. The note of $20,000 can be paid out to the shareholder, tax-free. In this way the shareholder recovers, free of tax, an amount up to the elected transfer price.

Determining the paid-up capital (PUC) of the shares received is important as it represents the amount that can be returned tax-free to the shareholder on a redemption of the shares in the future. Generally, the PUC is equal to the legal stated capital on the financial statement which in turn reflects the fair market value of the property or service received by the corporation in return for the issued shares, in this case $80,000.

When assets are transferred to a corporation at their tax value using Section 85, it is anticipated that the tax deferred on the transfer will be paid in the future by the shareholder on the sale or redemption of the shares or by the corporation on the sale of the asset. If the legal stated capital, $80,000 in this case, is the value used for the PUC of the issued shares, this amount could be withdrawn from the corporation on a tax-free basis and the capital gain deferred on the transfer would permanently escape taxation. To ensure that this is not so, a PUC reduction occurs where a Section 85 election is made.[31] Generally, the PUC is reduced from the fair market value of the shares to nil. However, when the Section 85 elected amount exceeds the non-share consideration, the excess will be allocated to the PUC. This results in the PUC and the ACB of the shares being the same amount.

If more than one class of shares are taken as consideration on the transfer, the ACB and the PUC must be allocated among the classes. The ACB is allocated on a sequential basis as described earlier. The PUC is allocated on a pro rata basis based on the relative fair market values of the classes. The following situation demonstrates the allocation of ACB and PUC.

Shareholder takes less non-share consideration: If the shareholder, in the situation above, had received as payment debt of only $15,000, preferred shares with a value of $34,000, and common shares with a value of $51,000, the range for the elected amount would remain the same, from the FMV ($100,000) down to the ACB ($20,000). Assuming the shareholder still wishes to defer paying tax on the transfer, $20,000 would remain as the elected amount and would be the cost of the consideration package, in total. The cost would be allocated on a sequential basis; first to the debt up to its fair market value ($15,000), next to the preferred shares up to their fair market value ($5,000) leaving nothing to be allocated to the common shares.

The PUC of both classes of shares combined is reduced from its legal stated capital of $85,000 (preferred $34,000 + common $51,000) to $5,000 being the excess of the elected amount ($20,000) over the non-share consideration ($15,000). The PUC of $5,000 is allocated between the preferred and common shares based on their relative fair market values. $2,000 ($34,000/$85,000 × $5,000) is allocated to the preferred shares and $3,000 ($51,000/$85,000 × $5,000) is allocated to the common shares.

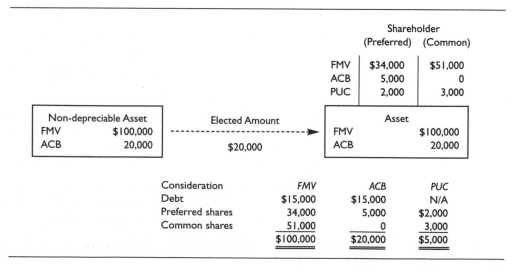

		Shareholder	
		(Preferred)	(Common)
	FMV	$34,000	$51,000
	ACB	5,000	0
	PUC	2,000	3,000

Non-depreciable Asset		Elected Amount	Asset	
FMV	$100,000	------→	FMV	$100,000
ACB	20,000	$20,000	ACB	20,000

Consideration	FMV	ACB	PUC
Debt	$15,000	$15,000	N/A
Preferred shares	34,000	5,000	$2,000
Common shares	51,000	0	3,000
	$100,000	$20,000	$5,000

---

31 ITA 85(2.1).

The tax implications to the shareholder of taking less debt is that the shareholder holds a note of $15,000 that can be paid out to the shareholder, with no tax consequences, and shares with a PUC of $5,000 that can be recovered tax-free in the future on a redemption of the shares. Otherwise, all other tax implications for the shareholder and the corporation remain unchanged. Normally, the shareholder will prefer to receive the maximum amount of debt possible while still deferring the tax on the transfer of the property. Therefore, the shareholder will normally prefer to receive debt of $20,000.

Shareholder takes more non-share consideration: If the shareholder in the initial situation had received as payment debt of $70,000 and preferred shares with a value of $30,000, the range for the elected amount would be from $100,000 (FMV) down to $70,000 (non-share consideration). Remember that the elected amount cannot be less than the non-share consideration received. The elected amount ($70,000) becomes the proceeds for the shareholder, the cost of the asset for the corporation and the cost of the consideration received.

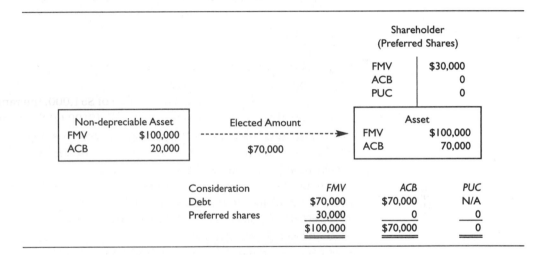

The tax implications of taking debt in excess of the tax value of the asset are as follows:

1. The shareholder recognizes a capital gain at the time of the transfer. The capital gain is $50,000 (Proceeds $70,000 − ACB $20,000).

2. The corporation's cost of the asset for tax purposes is $70,000 (elected amount). As a result, if the corporation subsequently sells the asset for $100,000 a capital gain of $30,000 (Proceeds $100,000 − ACB $70,000) will occur.

3. After the transfer, the shareholder will own a note receivable from the corporation of $70,000 and preferred shares worth $30,000. The elected amount of $70,000 is allocated first to the debt, up to its fair market value ($70,000) leaving nothing to be allocated to the shares. If the shareholder subsequently sells the shares for $30,000 there will be a capital gain of $30,000 (Proceeds $30,000 − ACB $0).

4. The paid-up capital (PUC) of the preferred shares received by the shareholder in this case is nil. If those shares are subsequently redeemed, a deemed dividend occurs for the full redemption amount ($30,000).

5. The note of $70,000 can be paid out to the shareholder tax-free.

Before the transfer of the property, the shareholder owned an asset with an accrued gain of $80,000. The shareholder recognized a capital gain of $50,000 on the transfer, deferring a gain of $30,000. After the transfer, the shareholder owns shares with an accrued gain of $30,000 (FMV $30,000 − ACB $0) and the corporation owns the asset with an accrued gain of $30,000 (FMV $100,000 − ACB $70,000).

Normally, the shareholder will prefer to avoid paying tax on the transfer and therefore will limit the non-share consideration to the tax value of the asset transferred. However, there are situations when triggering a capital gain at the time of the transfer might be desirable, that is, when the shareholder has net capital losses.

B. Depreciable Property

Situation:

A shareholder owning a building that originally cost $40,000, and has an undepreciated capital cost (UCC) of $30,000 and a fair market value (FMV) of $100,000, transfers the property to a corporation receiving as payment debt of $30,000 and preferred shares with a value of $70,000. The building is the only asset in the class.

Analysis:

The range for the elected amount is from the FMV ($100,000) down to the UCC ($30,000).

For depreciable assets the lower limit for the elected amount is the least of the UCC for the class, the fair market value of each property in the class, and the cost of each property in the class.[32] Where more than one asset belonging to the same class is being transferred, the assets are treated as if they were transferred one at a time and the taxpayer can choose the order.[33] With each sequential disposition the UCC of the class changes. In this case, the building is the only asset in the class.

Where the elected proceeds are less than the original cost of the depreciable asset, the original cost becomes the corporation's capital cost for the asset.[34] However, the UCC remains at the elected amount. This rule prevents the shareholder from permanently avoiding recapture by transferring the asset to a corporation.

In order for the shareholder to avoid recognizing a capital gain at the time of the transfer the elected amount cannot be higher than $40,000, the ACB of the asset. In order to avoid recognizing recapture, the elected amount cannot be higher than $30,000, the UCC of the asset. Since the non-share consideration does not exceed $30,000 it is possible to elect a transfer price of $30,000, which is what the shareholder would generally want to do.

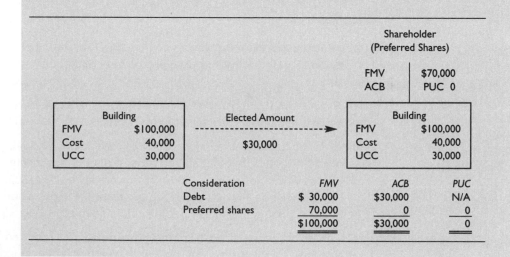

		Shareholder (Preferred Shares)		
		FMV	$70,000	
		ACB	PUC 0	

Building		Elected Amount	Building	
FMV	$100,000	- - - - - - -→	FMV	$100,000
Cost	40,000	$30,000	Cost	40,000
UCC	30,000		UCC	30,000

Consideration	*FMV*	*ACB*	*PUC*
Debt	$ 30,000	$30,000	N/A
Preferred shares	70,000	0	0
	$100,000	$30,000	0

---

32 ITA 85(1)(e).
33 ITA 85(1)(e.1).
34 ITA 85(5).

This is similar to the situation discussed earlier in the chapter. The tax implications of electing a transfer price of $30,000 are as follows:

1. The shareholder avoids paying tax at the time of the transfer. There is no capital gain and no recapture (UCC $30,000 − Proceeds $30,000).

2. Although the corporation's legal purchase price of the building is $100,000 the corporation is deemed to have a UCC of $30,000 (elected amount) and a capital cost of $40,000.[35] Note that all three values (FMV, cost, and UCC) to the corporation are identical to those before the transfer. As a result, if the corporation subsequently sells the asset for $100,000, there will be a capital gain of $60,000 (Proceeds $100,000 − ACB $40,000) and recapture of $10,000 (UCC $30,000 − cost $40,000).

3. After the transfer, the shareholder will own a note receivable from the corporation of $30,000 and preferred shares worth $70,000. The elected amount of $30,000 is allocated first to the debt, up to its fair market value ($30,000) leaving nothing to be allocated to the shares. If the shareholder subsequently sells the shares for $70,000 there will be a capital gain of $70,000 (Proceeds $70,000 − ACB $0). Note that this equals the total of the capital gain and recapture that the shareholder would have incurred upon selling the building for tax purposes at fair market value (capital gain $60,000 + recapture $10,000).

4. The paid-up capital (PUC) of the preferred shares received by the shareholder in this case is nil. If those shares are subsequently redeemed, a deemed dividend occurs for the full redemption amount ($70,000).

5. The note of $30,000 can be paid out to the shareholder tax-free.

This is the most common manner in which a depreciable asset would be transferred to a corporation. However there are some cases where the shareholder would prefer to recognize the recapture and a portion of the capital gain.

Shareholder recognizes recapture and a portion of the capital gain: Assume that the shareholder and the corporation elect a transfer price of $50,000 for tax purposes in the above situation, and that the shareholder and the corporation are related.

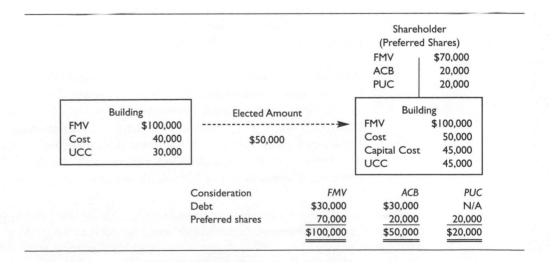

35 ITA 85(5).

The tax implications of electing a transfer price of $50,000 are as follows:

1. The shareholder will have recapture of $10,000 (UCC $30,000 − Cost $40,000) and a capital gain of $10,000 (Proceeds $50,000 − ACB $40,000). Only one-half of the capital gain is taxable ($5,000). Thus, the shareholder has taxable income of $15,000.

2. The $50,000 elected amount becomes the ACB of the building for the corporation. However, where the shareholder and the corporation are related and the elected proceeds are higher than the original cost of the asset, the corporation's capital cost and UCC of the building for CCA purposes are limited to the shareholder's UCC for the building plus the taxable income recognized by the shareholder on the transfer (see Chapter 6).[36] Thus, in this case, the corporation's capital cost and UCC are limited to $45,000 ($30,000 + $15,000). The half-year rule will not apply in the year the corporation acquires the asset provided that the asset was owned by the shareholder for at least 364 days before the year end of the corporation.[37] These rules apply to all depreciable assets acquired from related persons and were discussed earlier in Chapter 6. As a result, if the corporation subsequently sells the building for $100,000, there will be a capital gain of $50,000 (Proceeds $100,000 − ACB $50,000) plus recapture.

3. After the transfer, the shareholder will own a note receivable from the corporation of $30,000 and preferred shares worth $70,000. The elected amount of $50,000 is allocated first to the debt, up to its fair market value ($30,000) leaving $20,000 to be allocated to the shares. If the shareholder subsequently sells the shares for $70,000 there will be a capital gain of $50,000 (Proceeds $70,000 − ACB $20,000). Note that before the transfer the shareholder owned an asset with an accrued gain of $60,000. A capital gain of $10,000 was recognized on the transfer, while deferring a gain of $50,000. After the transfer of the asset, the shareholder owns shares with an accrued gain equal to the deferred gain $50,000 (FMV $70,000 − ACB $20,000) and the corporation owns the building with an accrued gain of $50,000 (FMV $100,000 − ACB $50,000).

4. The paid-up capital (PUC) of the preferred shares received by the shareholder in this case is $20,000. If those shares are subsequently redeemed, a deemed dividend of $50,000 occurs (redemption amount ($70,000 − PUC $20,000)).

5. The note of $30,000 can be paid out to the shareholder tax-free.

The shareholder could have taken an additional $20,000 of debt in this case without paying additional tax at the time of the transfer.

Asset value below the UCC: In some cases the FMV of the depreciable asset is less than the UCC. In this case, the upper and lower limits of the range for the elected amount are both the same. Remember that the elected amount can never be greater than the FMV.[38] If the Section 85 elected amount is equal to the FMV of the asset transferred, then there is no benefit to making a Section 85 election. If the shareholder and the corporation are affiliated persons and the asset being transferred has an unrealized terminal loss, a Section 85 election cannot be made.[39]

Situation: A shareholder owning a class 12 asset that originally cost $40,000, and has an undepreciated capital cost (UCC) of $30,000 and a fair market value (FMV) of $5,000, transfers the property to an affiliated corporation receiving as payment preferred shares with a value of $5,000. The asset transferred is the only asset in the class.

36 ITA 13(7)(e).
37 Reg. 1100(2.2).
38 ITA 85(1)(c).
39 ITA 13(21.2)(d).

Analysis: A Section 85 election cannot be made.

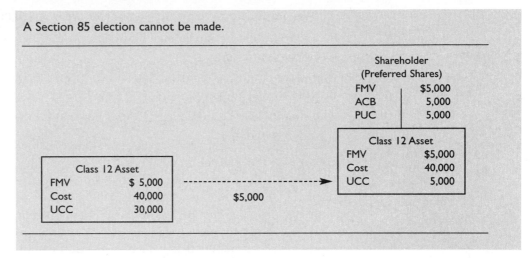

The tax implications of transferring *to an affiliated corporation* at a price of $5,000 are as follows:

1. The terminal loss of $25,000 (UCC $30,000 − FMV $5,000) is denied.[40] The $25,000 balance remains in class 12 and the shareholder may continue to claim CCA on this amount. Any portion of the denied loss not claimed as CCA may be recognized as a terminal loss, if there are no other assets in the class, at the time that the asset is no longer owned by an affiliated person for a 30-day period. The denial of terminal losses on transferring assets to affiliated persons was discussed in Chapter 6.

2. The corporation has a cost of $40,000 and UCC of $5,000 for the asset.

3. The shareholder has a cost and PUC of $5,000 for the preferred shares.

Note that if the shareholder and the corporation were not affiliated, the tax implications of the transfer would be the same, other than that the shareholder would be permitted the $25,000 deduction for the terminal loss.

C. Eligible Capital Property

Situation: A shareholder owning eligible capital property that originally cost $40,000, and has a cumulative eligible capital (CEC) balance of $18,000 and a fair market value (FMV) of $100,000, transfers the property to a corporation receiving as payment preferred shares with a value of $100,000.

Analysis: The range for the elected amount is from the FMV ($100,000) down to $24,000, being the CEC ($18,000) × 4/3. Since the non-share consideration does not exceed $24,000, the shareholder can elect at $24,000 and would normally do so in order for the transfer to be tax-free.

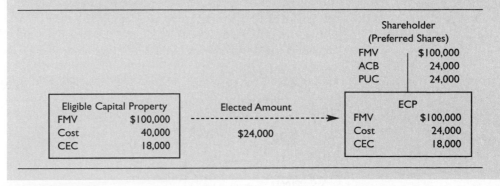

---

40 ITA 13(21.2)(e).

The tax implications of electing a transfer price of $24,000 are as follows:

1. The shareholder has no income for tax purposes (CEC $18,000 − $^3/_4$ × Proceeds $24,000).

2. The corporation has a cost of $24,000 and CEC $18,000 ($24,000 × $^3/_4$) for the eligible capital property.

3. The shareholder has a cost and PUC of $24,000 for the preferred shares.

The shareholder could have taken non-share consideration up to $24,000 without paying tax on the transfer. In most cases the shareholder would prefer to do so.

Goodwill is the most common eligible capital property transferred. An individual transferring a business to a corporation generally does not have a balance in the CEC account because the goodwill has not been purchased but has built up over time. Only purchased goodwill is included in the CEC. While the lower limit of CEC × 4/3 would suggest an elected amount of nil, such an election would not be valid. To have a valid election the minimum elected transfer price must be a nominal amount (example $1.00). This $1 election results in the shareholder recognizing business income of $0.50 ((CEC $0 − $1 × $^3/_4$) × $^2/_3$). On a purchase of eligible property for $1, the corporation would add $0.50 (i.e., $^3/_4$ × $1 − $^1/_2$ × $0.50 (the shareholder's income)) to its CEC account.[41]

Consideration received not equal to the fair market value of the transferred property: It is important that the shareholder receive consideration from the corporation equal to the fair market value of the asset transferred to the corporation.

If the consideration received is below the value of the asset transferred and other members of the shareholder's family are also shareholders of the corporation adverse tax consequences will result. The difference will be considered as a gift made by the shareholder for the benefit of related shareholders and the elected transfer price will be increased by the amount of the gift without any increase in the adjusted cost base of the shares received.[42]

If the consideration received by the shareholder is higher than the value of the asset transferred, the shareholder will be taxable on a deemed dividend for the increase in PUC in excess of the increase in net assets[43] as well as a shareholder benefit.[44]

Situation: A person owning non-depreciable capital property, which originally cost $20,000 and is now worth $100,000, transfers the property to a corporation in which the person's spouse owns the common shares; receiving as payment debt of $20,000 and preferred shares with a value of $50,000.

Analysis: In this case, the Section 85 elected amount would normally be $20,000 in an attempt to avoid tax on the transfer. However, since the FMV of the property transferred ($100,000) exceeds the FMV of the consideration received ($70,000), and the spouse owns shares of the corporation, the $30,000 excess will be considered a gift made by the person for the benefit of his spouse. Consequently, the elected transfer price will be increased by the amount of the gift *without any increase in the adjusted cost base of the shares received.*[45]

---

41 ITA 14(5).
42 ITA 85(1)(e.2).
43 ITA 84(1).
44 ITA 15(1).
45 ITA 85(1)(e.2).

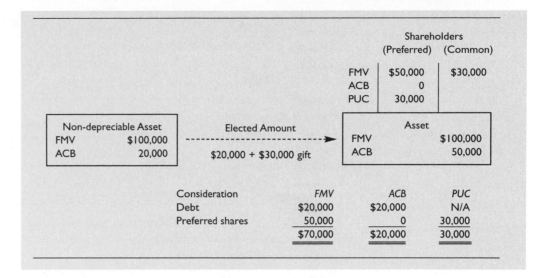

The tax implications are as follows:

1. The shareholder's proceeds are $50,000 ($20,000 + gift $30,000) resulting in a capital gain of $30,000.

2. The corporation has a cost of $50,000 for the property acquired.

3. The elected amount of $20,000 is the cost of the consideration received by the shareholder and is allocated first to the debt ($20,000) leaving nothing to be allocated to the shares.

4. The preferred shares have a PUC of $30,000 being the excess of the increased elected amount over the non-share consideration.

5. The value of the shares of the corporation owned by the shareholder's spouse has increased by $30,000 with no increase in the ACB. Thus, when the spouse sells these shares, the spouse will pay tax on this $30,000 gain.

To avoid having the $30,000 capital gain subject to tax twice (shareholder and shareholder's spouse) the value of the consideration received should always equal the fair market value of the property transferred to the corporation.

Demonstration Questions

QUESTION ONE

Carol Chomsky owns 20% of the common shares of Tindell Ltd., a Canadian-controlled private corporation. She had acquired the shares from a former shareholder in 20X2 for $40,000. The corporation's balance sheet indicates that the paid-up capital of her shares is $2,000. In 20X8, Chomsky decided to sell her shares for $100,000. The controlling shareholder has offered to purchase the shares. Alternatively, she can sell the shares back to Tindell Ltd. for cancellation.

Chomsky's personal marginal tax rates are 45% on regular income and 33% on non-eligible taxable Canadian dividends. In past years, Chomsky had used her entire capital gain deduction. The shares of Tindell Ltd. are qualified small business corporation shares. All of Tindell's income is business income and subject to the low corporate tax rate. Its dividends are designated as non-eligible.

Required:

Describe the tax treatment to Chomsky if she sells the shares to the controlling shareholder and if she sells the shares to Tindell Ltd.

Solution:

Sale of shares to controlling shareholder:

Under this option, Chomsky has a taxable capital gain of $30,000 and tax of $13,500, calculated as follows:

Proceeds of disposition	$100,000
Adjusted cost base	(40,000)
Capital gain	$ 60,000
Taxable capital gain—½ × $60,000	$ 30,000
Tax—45% × $30,000	$ 13,500

If Chomsky had not used her entire capital gain deduction in past years, the taxable capital gain would have been eligible for the capital gain deduction and all or a portion of the tax would have been eliminated.

Sale of shares to Tindell Ltd.:

Under this option, Chomsky has a taxable dividend of $98,000 and an allowable capital loss of $19,000. These amounts and the resulting tax are calculated as shown below.

Dividend portion:	
Selling price	$100,000
Less paid-up capital of the shares	(2,000)
Deemed dividend	$ 98,000
Tax on non-eligible dividend—33% × $98,000	$ 32,340
Capital portion:	
Proceeds of disposition	$100,000
Less deemed dividend (above)	(98,000)
Adjusted proceeds (equal to paid-up capital of shares)	2,000
Adjusted cost base	(40,000)
Capital *loss*	$ 38,000
Allowable capital *loss*—½ × $38,000	$ 19,000

Normally, the capital loss of $19,000 is classified as an allowable business investment loss (ABIL), which can be offset against any source of Chomsky's income and saving tax at the rate of 45%. However, because Chomsky has, in the past, used her full capital gain deduction, the ABIL status is denied, and the loss is treated as a regular allowable capital loss. This means that the allowable capital loss of $19,000 can be deducted only to the extent that Chomsky has net taxable capital gains in the year. If we assume Chomsky has sufficient taxable capital gains from other sources, a tax saving of $8,550 occurs (45% × $19,000). The net tax under this option is calculated as follows:

Tax on deemed dividend	$32,340
Tax saving from allowable capital loss	(8,550)
Net tax	$23,790

If Chomsky had no taxable capital gains in the year, the tax on the deemed dividend would have been $32,340 and the allowable capital loss would be carried back three years and forward indefinitely until capital gains were obtained.

Clearly, in this situation, the sale of shares to the controlling shareholder is preferred, even if Chomsky can deduct the allowable capital loss on the sale of shares to the corporation. This result may not always occur, especially in tax brackets where capital gains and dividends are taxed at similar marginal rates.

QUESTION TWO

Monica has operated her business as a proprietorship and plans to incorporate. The tax costs (ACB, UCC, CEC) and fair market values (FMV) for the assets of the business are as follows:

	FMV	Tax Value
Cash	$ 5,000	$ 5,000
Marketable securities	24,000	10,000
Accounts receivable	25,000	29,000
Inventory	50,000	40,000
Land	80,000	60,000
Building (capital cost $70,000)	100,000	65,000
Equipment (capital cost $20,000)	12,000	15,000
Goodwill	40,000	0
Total assets	$336,000	$224,000

Monica wants to avoid tax on the transfer of the assets to the corporation. The business has liabilities of $30,000 that will be assumed by the newly incorporated company, M Ltd. As consideration for transferring the business to M Ltd., Monica wants to receive the maximum possible debt and the balance as preferred shares of M Ltd.

Required:

Determine the appropriate transfer price under Section 85 for each asset that can and should be transferred to the corporation. Determine the amount of debt and share consideration that Monica can accept without any adverse tax consequences. Determine the ACB and PUC for the preferred shares received as consideration.

Solution:

The first step is to determine what assets, if any, should not be transferred to M Ltd. In this case the marketable securities should not be transferred to M Ltd. They are not used in the business and transferring them to M Ltd. could jeopardize M Ltd. qualifying as a small business corporation.

The second step is to determine if there are assets that are not qualifying assets for purposes of a Section 85 election or for which a Section 85 election is not recommended or not necessary.

- Cash is not a capital asset and therefore is not eligible for a Section 85 election.[46] Transferring the cash to the corporation in exchange for a $5,000 promissory note will not result in taxable income for Monica.

  Since the equipment is in a terminal loss position and Monica and M Ltd. are affiliated persons, Section 85 is not applicable[47] and the terminal loss is denied (see Chapter 6).[48] The equipment should be sold to M Ltd. for $12,000 (FMV) in exchange for a note of the same amount. M Ltd. will have a UCC for the equipment of $12,000. The capital cost will be $20,000 since it it is acquired from a related person.[49]

- If the accounts receivable are sold to M Ltd. with no election there is a $4,000 capital loss. If a Section 85 election is made the elected amount can only be $25,000 and that also results in a $4,000 capital loss. In both cases, since Monica and M Ltd. are affiliated persons, the capital loss is a superficial loss and is denied (see Chapter 8).[50] The $4,000 denied loss is added to the ACB of the receivables in M Ltd. raising the ACB to $29,000.[51]

46 ITA 85(1.1).
47 ITA 13(21.2)(d).
48 ITA 13(21.2)(e).
49 ITA 13(7)(e)(iii).
50 ITA 54 and 40(20(g).
51 ITA 53(1)(h).

- To avoid the above result and allow Monica to treat the loss as a business loss a joint election can be made under Section 22 of the *Income Tax Act* by Monica and M Ltd. The election allows the $4,000 loss to be treated as a fully deductible business loss (bad debt) by Monica. With this election M Ltd. is assumed to have acquired the receivables in the ordinary course of business. Therefore, it must add $4,000 to its income and then deduct an equal reserve for bad debts. Effectively, M Ltd. will have receivables costing $29,000 from which a reserve of $4,000 has been deducted (net $25,000). Monica should receive a $25,000 note from M Ltd. as consideration for the accounts receivable.

The third step is to set up a chart for the assets on which a Section 85 election will be made outlining their market values, tax values, elected amounts, and types of consideration.

Asset	FMV	Tax value	Elected amount	Non-share	Share	Total
				— Consideration Received —		
Inventory	$ 50,000	$ 40,000	$ 40,000	$ 40,000	$ 10,000	50,000
Land	80,000	60,000	60,000	60,000	20,000	80,000
Building	100,000	65,000	65,000	65,000	35,000	100,000
Goodwill	40,000	0	1	0	40,000	40,000
Total	$270,000	$165,000	$165,001	$165,000	$105,000	$270,000

Note that while the tax value of the goodwill is nil, the elected amount is $1. To have a valid election, an amount must be elected. Since nil is not considered to be an amount, it is impossible to elect at an amount less than $1. The above is summarized in the following diagram.

Monica
(Preferred Shares)

	FMV	$105,000
	ACB	$1
M Ltd.	PUC	$1

	Inventory	Land	Building	Goodwill
FMV	$50,000	$80,000	$100,000	$40,000
Cost	$40,000	$60,000	$ 70,000	N/A
UCC/CEC	N/A	N/A	$ 65,000	0.50*

Monica's Consideration

	FMV	ACB	PUC
Liabilities assumed	$ 30,000	$ 30,000	N/A
Debt	135,000	135,000	N/A
	165,000	165,000	
Preferred shares	105,000	1	$1
	$270,000	$165,001	$1

*On a purchase of eligible capital property for $1, M Ltd. would add $0.50 ($^3/_4 - {}^1/_2 \times$ $0.50, Monica's income) to its CEC account.

The appropriate elected amount for each asset is included in the above chart. Monica can take non-share consideration of $165,000 without adverse tax consequences. Since the liabilities of $30,000 are to be assumed by M Ltd., the new debt issued should be limited to $135,000. Preferred shares valued at $105,000 should be issued to Monica. The ACB and PUC of the preferred shares is $1.

Review Questions

1. "To function, a corporation must have some capital contributed by its shareholders. When capitalizing a corporation, the shareholder must provide only share capital." Is this statement true? Explain.

2. Why is it that a corporate debt owed to a shareholder may be considered as part of the shareholder's equity of the corporation? How is a shareholder's loan treated for tax purposes?

3. "When a corporation is partly capitalized with shareholder debt, the amount of corporate income that may be subject to double taxation is reduced." Explain. Does it matter whether the shareholder debt pays interest or not?

4. If a corporation that is in financial difficulty has been capitalized with shareholder debt and a small amount of share capital as opposed to the reverse, the shareholder may be at less financial risk and the corporation may have a better chance of surviving. Why is this so?

5. A corporation owned solely by shareholder A has a value of $100,000. Individual B intends to acquire a 50% equity interest in the corporation. The cost to that individual of acquiring 50% of the corporation's shares may be either $100,000 or $50,000. Explain.

6. What is a buy-back of corporate shares?

7. Describe the tax treatment to the shareholder when a corporation buys back its own shares. Is the tax treatment to the shareholder different if that shareholder sells the shares to another party, rather than back to the corporation that issued them?

8. "If a corporation no longer requires the initial common share capital provided by the shareholders, all or a portion of it can be returned to the shareholders without any tax consequences to the shareholders." Is this statement true? Explain.

9. Would your answer to Question 8 be different if the share capital consisted of non-participating preferred shares or if the initial capital had been provided by the shareholders as a shareholder loan?

10. Identify and briefly explain two alternative tax treatments that can apply when assets are transferred to a corporation by a shareholder or a proposed shareholder.

11. When a shareholder sells property to his or her corporation at fair market value for tax purposes, what impact may the sale have on the shareholder and on the corporation?

12. If a shareholder sells property to a corporation at fair market value for legal purposes but elects an alternative price for tax purposes, what are the tax implications to the shareholder and to the corporation acquiring the asset? Why is this election option referred to as a "roll-over"?

13. When a shareholder sells property to a corporation, that property has a value greater than its cost amount, and the shareholder chooses to use the elective option for tax purposes, what is the maximum amount of non-share consideration that the shareholder can receive from the corporation as payment?

14. A corporation purchases an asset from a shareholder for the market value price of $20,000 and pays the shareholder by issuing preferred shares of $8,000 and a note payable to the shareholder for $12,000. Both the shareholder and the corporation elect that the transfer price for tax purposes is $12,000. What are the tax consequences for the shareholder if the corporation pays the debt and buys back the

shareholder's preferred shares? What would the tax consequences be if the shareholder sold the acquired preferred shares to another party?

15. What types of property, if any, are not eligible for the elective option when they are transferred to a corporation?

16. Can the elective option be used when one corporation transfers property to another corporation?

17. What are the tax consequences to a corporation and its shareholder when that corporation declares a dividend but, instead of paying cash, distributes to the shareholder property that has a value greater than the cost amount to the corporation?

Key Concept Questions

QUESTION ONE

On incorporation of X Ltd., 1,000 common shares were issued to Anne for $1,000. At the beginning of Year 2, 800 common shares of X Ltd. were issued to Bill for $8,000, the fair market value of the shares on that date. At the end of Year 3, 500 Class A preferred shares of X Ltd. were issued to Carl for $7,000, the fair market value of the preference shares on that date. *Income tax reference: ITA 89(1) (definition of paid-up capital), 54 (definition of adjusted cost base).*

At the end of Year 3, determine the following:

a) The paid-up capital (PUC) of the common shares and the preference shares of X Ltd.

b) The PUC and adjusted cost base of the shares of X Ltd. owned by each of Anne, Bill and Carl.

QUESTION TWO

William owns 100% of the issued common shares of W Ltd., which have an adjusted cost base (ACB) and paid-up capital (PUC) of $100 and are currently worth $200,000. William wants Victor to acquire a 50% interest in W Ltd. Victor can acquire his 50% interest by purchasing shares from William or by purchasing previously unissued shares from W Ltd. *Income tax reference: ITA 89(1).*

For both alternatives, determine the purchase price for Victor, the ACB and PUC of the shares acquired by Victor, and the tax implications for William.

QUESTION THREE

Veronica owns shares of a Canadian private corporation that are worth $100,000 and have an adjusted cost base (ACB) and paid-up capital (PUC) of $60,000. *Income tax reference: ITA 54 (definition of proceeds), 84(3).*

Determine the tax implications for Veronica if the shares are

a) Sold to an arm's-length party for $100,000; or

b) Redeemed by the corporation for $100,000.

QUESTION FOUR

Eric owns a building that originally cost $100,000 and has an undepreciated capital cost of $70,000. Eric sells the building to a corporation at the fair market value price of $140,000 in exchange for debt of $80,000 and preferred shares with a value of $60,000. Eric and the corporation will make a Section 85 election with respect to the sale. *Income tax reference: ITA 85(1).*

Determine the minimum elected transfer price under Section 85.

QUESTION FIVE

Pat owns a non-depreciable capital asset that originally cost $20,000 and is now worth $80,000. Pat transfers the asset to a corporation, receiving as payment debt of $60,000 and preferred shares with a value of $20,000. Pat and the corporation will elect under Section 85 to avoid paying tax on the transfer. *Income tax reference: ITA 85(1), (2.1).*

Determine the appropriate transfer price under Section 85. Determine the cost of the asset for the corporation, and the ACB and PUC for the preferred shares received as consideration.

QUESTION SIX

Cathy owns equipment that originally cost $40,000 and that has an undepreciated capital cost of $25,000. She sells the equipment to a corporation at the fair market value price of $30,000 in exchange for a combination of preferred shares and debt. Cathy and the corporation will make a Section 85 election in order that Cathy can avoid paying tax on the sale. *Income tax reference: ITA 85(1), (2.1).*

Determine the appropriate transfer price under Section 85. Determine the amount of debt and share consideration that Cathy can accept without any adverse tax consequences. Determine the corporation's ACB and UCC for the equipment acquired. Determine the ACB and PUC of the preferred shares received as consideration.

QUESTION SEVEN

Susan owns a non-depreciable capital asset that originally cost $40,000 and is now worth $160,000. She transfers the asset to a corporation receiving as payment debt of $10,000, preferred shares of $20,000, and common shares of $130,000. Susan and the corporation will elect under Section 85 to avoid paying tax on the transfer. *Income tax reference: ITA 85(1), (2.1).*

Determine the appropriate transfer price under Section 85. Determine the ACB and PUC for the preferred shares and common shares received as consideration.

Problems

PROBLEM ONE

Shelter Tent Ltd. is a Canadian-controlled private corporation owned 50/50 by two individual shareholders. The corporation has consistently achieved annual profits of between $500,000 and $600,000.

Recently, the company has experienced a cash shortage as the result of an expansion to the tent and awning business. The bank offered some relief, but the shareholders will have to contribute additional capital to the corporation. Although both shareholders have alternative uses for their personal capital, they are prepared to provide the funds necessary to alleviate the cash squeeze.

The shareholders have approached you for advice on how they should contribute their capital to the corporation. Under its articles of incorporation, the company is permitted to issue both common shares and preferred shares. The preferred shares have a fixed non-cumulative dividend rate of 8%.

Required:

1. Identify three methods by which the shareholders can provide additional capital to the corporation.

2. Outline the tax factors that should be considered in evaluating the three alternatives.

[Handwritten annotations in left margin:]

390

① proceeds   60,000
   PUC   (1,000)
   non-eligible 59,000   DD ×33⅓
   ~~proceeds   60,000~~   =19,470
   ~~DD   59,000~~   Tax

② proceeds   60,000
   DD   (59,000)
   P of D   1,000
   ACB   (20,000)
   C.L   (19,000) × ½ × 45%
   only against C.G. = (4,275)

   net funds (60,000 − 19,470)
              = 40,530

   P of D − FMV = 60,000
        + CB = (20,000)
        C.G   40,000
        TCG   20,000
        → Taxes   45%
              $9,000
   net funds   51,000

PROBLEM TWO

Cynthia Yeung owns 10% of the common shares of Bantam Brokers Ltd. She had acquired the shares, which have a stated paid-up capital amount of $1,000, from a previous shareholder in 20X0 at a cost of $20,000. Since 20X0, Yeung has worked for the company as a senior broker earning a salary and commissions. The remaining 90% of Bantam's shares are owned by three other senior executives of the company.

Yeung has decided to leave the company and has agreed to dispose of her Bantam shares, which have a current fair market value of $60,000. A shareholders' agreement stipulates that she must sell her shares either to the other shareholders or back to the corporation for cancellation, with payment terms to be negotiated.

Currently, Bantam does not have substantial cash resources, nor does it have non-business properties that it could sell and convert into cash. Consequently, if the company is going to buy back its shares from Yeung for $60,000, deferred payment terms will have to be established.

Similarly, none of the other shareholders have any cash reserves. Although each earns a high salary, all have committed their income to personal expenditures. In addition, none of them holds any other investments, and each looks to the company as his/her sole source of cash.

After a negotiation, these options are presented to Yeung:

1. Bantam will buy back her shares immediately for $60,000. Payment would involve $20,000 cash, with the balance of $40,000 paid in two annual instalments of $20,000, with interest at 8%.

2. The other shareholders will immediately purchase her shares for $60,000 under terms identical to those in option 1.

The other shareholders realize that if Yeung accepts option 2, they will have to either borrow the money from a bank to make the payments or distribute funds to themselves from the company. Even if they borrow the money, they will have to look to the company for help in repaying the principal.

Bantam is a Canadian-controlled private corporation and has annual profits of approximately $100,000. Its dividends are normally classified as non-eligible. Yeung, like the other shareholders, usually pays personal tax at the rate of 45%.

Required:

1. Which option should Yeung accept? In your answer, include a comparative analysis of the options listed, and state any assumptions you feel are necessary. Yeung has already used her capital gain deduction. *Take option 2. ↑ net funds.*

2. If you were one of the other shareholders, which option would you prefer? Explain. *redemption. less S.H / Other S.H need to come up w/ 60k af/tax*

PROBLEM THREE

Ms. Kline, a resident of Canada, is the sole shareholder of KI Inc. She plans to transfer four assets, which she owns, to KI Inc. in exchange for cash and preferred shares of KI Inc. She wishes to receive the maximum amount in cash that she can receive and still defer the recognition of income for tax purposes on the transfer of the assets. Ms. Kline and KI Inc. will jointly make a Section 85 election for each of the assets. The following are the details of the assets:

	FMV	ACB	UCC/CEC
Land	$200,000	$ 40,000	N/A
Building	100,000	70,000	$50,000
Equipment	8,000	30,000	8,000
Goodwill	40,000	0	0
	$348,000	$140,000	$58,000

Required:

1. For each of the four assets individually, state the amount that should be elected as proceeds under Section 85 of the *Income Tax Act*.

2. For each of the four assets individually, state the amount of cash and the value of the preferred shares that Ms. Kline should accept as payment for the assets.

PROBLEM FOUR

In each of the following independent situations, Mary transfers an asset to a taxable Canadian corporation owned by her and makes an election under Section 85 of the *Income Tax Act* with respect to the transfer.

	ONE	TWO	THREE	FOUR
Asset transferred		Depreciable		Marketable
	Land	Asset	Goodwill	Securities
ACB & capital cost	$5,000	$100	Nil	$17,000
FMV	$8,000	$ 80	$10,000	$11,000
UCC/CEC	N/A	$ 50	Nil	N/A
Sale price	$8,000	$ 80	$10,000	$11,000
Payment received—Cash	$6,000	$ 30	Nil	$ 2,000
Shares (FMV)	$2,000	$ 50	$10,000	$ 9,000

Required:

For each of the four situations, determine the following:

a) The minimum elected amount under Section 85 of the *Income Tax Act*.

b) The income or loss for tax purposes to be recognized by Mary.

c) The corporation's ACB, capital cost and UCC/CEC for the assets purchased.

d) The ACB of the shares of the corporation received by Mary.

e) The PUC of the shares of the corporation received by Mary.

PROBLEM FIVE

Using Section 85 of the *Income Tax Act*, Jason Goorwah transfers non-depreciable property to a corporation at an elected value of $6,000. The property has an adjusted cost base of $6,000 and a fair market value of $17,000. As consideration he receives a note for $1,000, preferred shares with a fair market value of $2,000, and common shares with a fair market value of $14,000.

Required:

Determine the adjusted cost base (ACB) and paid-up capital (PUC) of the preferred shares and the common shares received by Jason.

PROBLEM SIX

Harvey Malon has decided to incorporate his proprietorship. Certain properties of the business have a current value that is greater than their cost amount for tax purposes. These assets are as follows:

	Fair market value
Land	$ 40,000
Building	180,000
Goodwill	70,000
	$290,000

The original cost of the land and building was $175,000 (land, $25,000; building, $150,000). The building currently has an undepreciated capital cost of $120,000.

The goodwill was purchased from the previous owner for $50,000, and the balance in the cumulative eligible capital account is $30,000.

In addition, the business has some current assets (primarily inventory), which have not appreciated in value and have a cost of $90,000. The proprietorship's only liabilities are amounts payable to trade creditors totalling $70,000.

Malon is aware that a shareholder can transfer assets to a corporation and defer tax on the transfer by using a special election of the *Income Tax Act*. He finds this option attractive, as his personal tax rate is very high and he needs all the cash flow he can get.

Within the next year or two, Malon intends to sell the land and building and acquire larger premises for the business. At this point, he is uncertain whether he will buy or lease the proposed new premises.

Required:

1. Assuming that Malon will sell the assets to the corporation using the elective option for tax purposes, determine the elected amounts required for tax purposes to avoid recognition of taxable income.

2. Suppose that the corporation will assume Malon's liabilities and issue debt and preferred shares to him in exchange for the properties, determine (a) the maximum amount of debt, and (b) the amount of preferred shares that would be issued.

3. What would be the tax consequences to Malon if the corporation later repaid the debt and bought back the preferred shares? Would the result be different if he sold the preferred shares to a third party?

4. Prepare a brief balance sheet for the corporation after the assets are acquired, showing the accounting value for each item. How do the values of the real estate and goodwill for accounting purposes compare with their tax values to the corporation?

5. Since Malon may sell the land and building to a third party within two years, he could choose to retain ownership for two years and lease it to the corporation, rather than transfer it to the corporation and then sell it to the third party. Briefly outline the tax factors to consider when making this decision.

PROBLEM SEVEN

Not long ago, Colson and Harmantz formed a corporation to carry on a construction business. Each owned 50% of the common shares, which were issued at a nominal cost. In addition, each shareholder sold certain of his own property to the corporation.

Colson sold construction equipment to the corporation for $60,000 (its fair market value). He originally purchased the equipment for $75,000. At the time of the sale, it had an undepreciated capital cost of $40,000. For tax purposes, the corporation and Colson elected that the transfer price was $40,000. Consideration for the sale consisted of the following:

Note payable to Colson	$40,000
Preferred shares	20,000
	$60,000

Two months after the incorporation, Harmantz and Colson had a dispute that they could not resolve. Colson now has decided to leave the company. The departure agreement includes the following terms:

- Colson will buy back his old equipment from the corporation at the current fair market price of $60,000, paying in cash.

- Immediately after the equipment sale, the corporation will use its new cash of $60,000 to pay off its debt of $40,000 to Colson and buy back his preferred shares for $20,000. In addition, the corporation will buy back Colson's common shares for a nominal cost.

Although the corporation has not begun any construction, it expects to earn a large profit in its first year if the contract bid is accepted. Some of the expected profits will be subject to a corporate tax rate of 25%. Colson has significant personal income and is subject to a 45% tax rate.

Required:

1. What are the tax consequences to both the corporation and Colson as a result of the above transactions?

2. Will double taxation occur? If it will, calculate the amount.

3. If you were Harmantz, would you have agreed to have the corporation pay Colson $60,000 for the debt and the preferred shares? Explain.

4. Assume that Colson was the sole shareholder of the corporation and had sold the equipment to the corporation in the same manner as described previously. Assume further that shortly after incorporation, the company sold the equipment to a third party for cash and discontinued its existence by paying off its debt and cancelling its shares. What amount would Colson have received? Calculate the amount of double taxation, if any. Would your calculation be different if the corporate tax rate were 15%?

PROBLEM EIGHT

Dan Dash has decided to incorporate his retailing business. On July 1st he plans to transfer the assets of the business to Dash Inc., a corporation owned wholly by him, in exchange for a note of $535,000, being the fair market value of the assets.

The assets of the retailing business are as follows:

	FMV	COST	UCC/CEC
Accounts receivable	$ 5,000	$ 8,000	
Inventory	200,000	120,000	
Land	60,000	20,000	
Building	180,000	160,000	$100,000
Class 8 Equipment	50,000	100,000	70,000
Goodwill	40,000	0	0
Total	$535,000	$408,000	$170,000

Dan also plans to transfer his shares of Grape Expectations, a publicly traded company, to Dash Inc. He purchased the shares of Grape Expectations two years ago for $60,000. He plans to transfer them to Dash Inc. for $50,000, the estimated fair market value.

Required:

Prepare a memo for Dan outlining the tax implications of his plans and provide detailed recommendations as to how he can accomplish his goals in a more tax-effective manner.

The Canadian-Controlled Private Corporation

The Canadian-controlled private corporation (CCPC) is a widely used organization structure in Canadian enterprise. This type of entity is used to house both small and large business operations as well as investment portfolios in bonds, shares, and real estate.

Canadian-controlled private corporations and their shareholders are provided with certain tax incentives and other unique opportunities that distinguish them from other types of corporations. Because the incentives are designed to apply only within certain guidelines, the related tax rules appear to be more complex. This chapter will examine the unique aspects of the taxation system for Canadian-controlled private corporations and discuss their implications on cash flow and return on investment. In particular, this chapter will

(a) provide a definition of the Canadian-controlled private corporation and state the fundamental principles underlying that definition;
(b) show how various types of corporate income are taxed;
(c) examine the benefits of incorporating business income and investment income;
(d) develop a policy for distributing corporate earnings to the shareholders; and
(e) develop a complete, detailed tax calculation for the Canadian-controlled private corporation.

I. Definition and Basic Principles

at least
50% controlled
by Canadian

A Canadian-controlled private corporation is a private corporation that is not controlled by a public corporation or a non-resident of Canada.[1] Note that the definition does *not* say that certain parties have control[2] but, rather, indicates that in order to qualify, certain parties *cannot* control. For example, a private corporation whose shares are owned 50% by Canadian residents and 50% by non-residents is considered to be Canadian controlled because the 50% ownership does not provide control to the non-residents.

Corporations that qualify as Canadian-controlled private corporations are distinguished from other corporations in three basic areas: rates of tax, double taxation, and secondary relationships.

• **Rates of tax**   The same rates of tax do not apply to all types of income earned by the corporation. In particular, the first $500,000 of annual active business income is subject to a reduced rate of tax (see Chapter 11, Exhibit 11-8). Not only is this reduced rate of tax substantially lower than other corporate rates, but it is also lower than the majority of personal rates of tax that would be applicable if the business income were earned directly by an individual from a proprietorship or partnership.

• **Double taxation**   Except for business income over $500,000 annually, the income generated by Canadian-controlled private corporations is not subject to double taxation. In other words, the combined tax—corporate income tax plus the tax on subsequent dividend distributions to the shareholders—is no greater than what the tax would have been if the income had been earned directly by the individual without the use of a corporation. Therefore, to the extent that double taxation does not occur, there are no long-term adverse consequences arising from utilization of the corporate form of organization. However, because some income is subject to double taxation and some is not, there is more complexity with respect to corporate distributions.

---

1 ITA 125(7)(b), 89(1)(f); IT-458R.
2 ITA 256(5.1).

- **Secondary relationships**   In Chapter 11, it was established that shareholders can have both primary and secondary relationships with the corporation. A secondary relationship exists when a shareholder also acts in another capacity, for example, as a creditor loaning money to the corporation, a lessor renting property to the corporation, or an employee providing services to the corporation. Because the shares of a Canadian-controlled private corporation are not traded on a public stock exchange, the number of shareholders is relatively few. Such a corporation is referred to as a "closely held corporation." Often, in closely held corporations, the affairs of the corporation and the shareholders are closely associated, and as a result, shareholders have the opportunity to form secondary relationships with the corporation.

For example, in an owner-managed corporation, the shareholder is also an employee hired to manage the affairs of the corporation. In such situations, that individual can receive a return from the company through a combination of dividends and salary, the ratio of which he or she has a right to establish. This right to establish secondary relationships increases the corporation's flexibility when it comes to transferring corporate income to the individual. By paying its employee–shareholder interest on debt, rent on leases, and salaries for services performed, the corporation can reduce the amount of its income that is subject to double taxation.

The above three principles constitute the base upon which tax planning activities for Canadian-controlled private corporations are built. Together, they form a unique framework that puts this type of entity in a class of its own.

II. Taxation of Income Earned by a Canadian-Controlled Private Corporation

In Chapter 11, it was indicated that corporate tax is determined by applying the corporate rate of tax to taxable income. Taxable income has been defined as net income for tax purposes less special reductions. Net income is determined in accordance with the aggregating formula described in Chapter 3 and consists of five basic types of income. Of the five basic types of income, corporations are capable of earning only three—business income, property income, and capital gains. Notwithstanding that corporate tax is based on normal taxable income, its calculation for Canadian-controlled private corporations makes special adjustments relating to certain categories of income. Before those special tax adjustments can be applied, the corporation's net income for tax purposes must be slotted into five separate areas:

- active business income
- specified investment business income
- capital gains
- personal services business income
- dividends

Each of the above categories may receive special tax treatment. This is discussed on the following pages.

A. Active Business Income

An active business carried on by a corporation is technically defined as *any business* carried on by the corporation *other than* a specified investment business or a personal services business.[3] Therefore, one must review these two other definitions before one can appreciate the full scope of the term. Effectively, almost all business activity results in active business income, including manufacturing, farming, construction,

---

3   ITA 125(7)(a), 129(6); IT-73R6.

transportation, fishing, logging, mining, the selling of property as a retailer or wholesaler, and the selling of services in a trade or profession.

Note that the above definition excluded income from a personal services business. This exclusion should not be interpreted to mean that income derived from personal services is not active business income. As will be explained later, the term "personal services business" has an extremely narrow definition and seldom has application. It can be stated here that a corporation that derives income from selling services—for example, a consulting business or a plumbing service business—normally has active business income.

In some circumstances, a business may earn property income that is closely related or incidental to its business activities. For example, interest income earned on overdue accounts receivable from product sales is actually property income but is treated as part of active business income when the special tax adjustments are calculated.[4]

The actual calculation of active business income starts with the corporation's *net income for tax purposes* (not taxable income). This amount is *reduced* by specified business investment income, including net taxable capital gains, taxable Canadian dividends, and personal services business income. The calculation is reviewed in Part VI at the end of this chapter.

• **Tax treatment of active business income**   A Canadian-controlled private corporation that realizes active business income is entitled to reduce its federal taxes otherwise payable by 17% for the first $500,000[5] of active business income earned in each taxation year. In addition, most provinces apply a reduced provincial rate of tax on the same income.

This reduction of tax is referred to as the "small business deduction," and applies to the first $500,000 of annual profits. This annual limit of $500,000 may be reduced or eliminated when the corporation exceeds a certain size (a point that is reviewed later in this chapter). The combined federal and provincial rate on the first $500,000 of active business income is approximately 15% (assuming there is a particular provincial tax rate—see Exhibit 11-8). This is significantly lower than the normal rate of 25%. The reader is reminded that the normal tax rates vary from province to province, may change from year to year, and so may require updating. For example, in 2012, combined federal/provincial small business rates (including provincial surtaxes) are as follows:

Manitoba	11%
Prince Edward Island	12%
Saskatchewan	13%
British Columbia	13.5%
Alberta	14%
Nova Scotia, Newfoundland, NWT, Nunavut, and Yukon	15%
Ontario and New Brunswick	15.5%
Quebec	19%

Combined federal and provincial/territorial tax calculations are presented in Appendix B at the end of the text.

It is important to recognize that the $500,000 small business deduction limit is an annual amount. If the full amount is not used in a given year, the unused portion will not be available for carry-over to other years. Consider the situation in Exhibit 13-1. Both Corporation A and Corporation B earned a total of $1,000,000 over a two-year period. However, Corporation A earned $400,000 in year 1 and $600,000 in year 2,

---

4   ITA 125(7)(c).
5   ITA 125(1), (2); 17% applies to net Canadian active business income up to the maximum annual limit or taxable income—whichever is least.

Exhibit 13-1:

*The Annual
Small Business
Deduction Limit*

	Corporation A	Corporation B
Active business income:		
Year 1	$ 400,000	$ 500,000
Year 2	600,000	500,000
Total over two years	$1,000,000	$1,000,000
Tax payable:		
Year 1	$ 60,000	$ 75,000
Year 2	100,000	75,000
Total over two years	$ 160,000	$ 150,000

whereas Corporation B earned $500,000 in each of the two years. While both corporations earned the same total income, Corporation A has a tax liability of $160,000 compared with $150,000 for Corporation B. This is only because each corporation earned its income in different years.

Corporation A's tax is calculated as follows:

Year 1:		
15% on $400,000		$ 60,000
under 500,000. limit		
Year 2:		
15% on first $500,000	$ 75,000	
25% on remaining $100,000	25,000	100,000
Total tax		$160,000

anything over limit taxed at 25%.

Because Corporation A earned only $400,000 in year 1, it lost a portion of its small business deduction. Corporation B fully utilized the small business deduction in both years, incurring tax on all of its income at 15% (15% × $500,000 = $75,000 for each year).

When possible, a corporation should take steps to maximize its use of the small business deduction. For example, in the previous situation, Corporation A could have increased its year 1 income by choosing not to deduct a reserve for doubtful accounts receivable in year 1 and delaying it until year 2 (see Chapter 5). This would have increased income in year 1 and decreased it in year 2. To the extent that the timing of income or expense recognition is discretionary, the taxpayer can shift income from one year to another; this is an important tool that can be used to take the fullest advantage of the small business deduction.

• **Tax treatment of income distributions** Canadian-controlled private corporations are taxed on active business income at both the low rate and the high rate, which creates a two-tier effect on corporate distributions to shareholders. The tax implications of corporate distributions were reviewed in Chapter 12 and personal tax rates on dividends were reviewed in Chapter 10. Exhibit 13-2 summarizes the tax treatment of a corporation earning active business income and of a shareholder receiving a distribution from that corporation. The example assumes that the shareholder is in the highest individual tax bracket.

Exhibit 13-2 indicates that *active business income subject to the small business deduction does not result in double taxation upon distribution.* The combination of corporate tax at 15% and shareholder tax on the dividend totalled only 43%, which left the shareholder with 57% of the active business income earned. If the owner had

Exhibit 13-2:			1st $500,000 of active business income	Income in excess of $500,000
Combined Corporate and Shareholder Tax on Active Business Income				
	Corporate tax rate[a]		15%	25%[c]
	Corporate income		$1,000	$1,000
	Tax		(150)	(250)
	Income available for dividends		$ 850	$ 750
	Shareholder income (dividend)		$ 850	$ 750
	Tax (net of dividend tax credit)[b]		(280)	(210)
			$ 570	$ 540
	Total tax:			
	Corporation		$ 150	$ 250
	Shareholder		280	210
			$ 430	$ 460
	Combined tax rate		43%	46%

a Chapter 11, Exhibit 11-8.
b Eligible, 28% of dividend; non-eligible, 33% of dividend—Chapter 10, Exhibit 10-7.
c The same rate applies to eligible manufacturing income.

earned the active business income directly as a proprietor, the tax cost would be approximately 45%, leaving 55% for the owners. It should be pointed out that the timing of the dividend distribution is discretionary; that is, the corporation could have chosen not to pay a dividend, with the result that the immediate tax would have been only 15%, and 75% of the income would have been retained in the corporation for business expansion.

In the same example, income in excess of $500,000 was subject to an immediate tax of 25% plus an additional tax on distribution that brought the total to 46%. This is greater than the 45% rate that would have been incurred if the owner had earned the business income directly without the use of a corporation. Clearly, the impact of double taxation can be reduced or eliminated if corporate active business income in excess of $500,000 can be shifted from the corporation to the shareholder without being flowed through the corporation as a dividend. This is possible only if the shareholder also has secondary relationships with the corporation. Payments of interest on shareholder debt, rent on assets leased from the shareholder, and salaries or bonuses to shareholder/employees all reduce corporate taxable income by shifting that income directly to the shareholder to be taxed only once. This is discussed in more detail later in this chapter.

B. Specified Investment Business Income

A specified investment business of a Canadian-controlled private corporation is defined as a business whose principal purpose is to derive income from property.[6] As described in Chapter 7, property income consists of the return on invested capital and includes interest, rents, dividends, and royalties. It was indicated in Chapter 11 that dividends received from other Canadian corporations and from foreign affiliates are not taxable to the recipient corporation. Therefore, the property income referred to in this definition includes only interest, rents, royalties, and dividends from non-affiliated foreign corporations.

6 ITA 125(7)(e); IT-73R6.

Because these items are classified as specified investment business income, they are automatically disqualified as active business income and are not entitled to the 17% small business deduction or the 13% general rate reduction when corporate tax is calculated.

It was also indicated in Chapter 7 that property income has been earned when the return on investment was achieved with little attention or labour on the part of the owner—if this were not so, such income as interest, rents, and royalties could be considered business income. The decision as to whether a given item constitutes property income is very subjective and, for the purposes of the small business deduction, is made on an arbitrary basis. One result is that two arbitrary exceptions are made to the definition of specified investment business income:

1. Rental income that is derived from the leasing of movable property—for example, vehicles and equipment (but not real estate)—is deemed to require sufficient attention and labour to be automatically considered active business income; as such, it is eligible for the low rate of corporate tax.

2. Other property income, such as interest, royalties, and rents from real property, is considered to be active business income only if the corporation employs more than five full-time employees to generate that income.[7]

In many cases, the above arbitrary rules appear unfair. For example, a corporation that employs four employees to administer a portfolio of loans earning interest is not eligible for the low rate of tax on that income, but a corporation with six employees is.

• **Tax treatment of specified investment business income** As indicated above, property income from interest, rents, and royalties, if it is not deemed to be active business income by the two exceptions, is not eligible for the small business deduction. It is also not eligible for the general rate reduction (13%) described in Chapter 11. Therefore, the total standard *federal* tax rate for specified business investment income amounts to 28% (38% − abatement 10% = 28%). Using the same provincial rate of 10% used in Chapter 11, the total standard tax rate is 38%. Provincial tax rates vary; some are below 10%, and others are above 10%. *For discussion and demonstration purposes* in this and other chapters, we have chosen to use a provincial rate of 10%, which results in a combined standard tax rate of 38% (28% + 10%) *for specified business investment income.*

In addition to the standard corporate tax rate of 38%, income in this category is subject to a special *refundable tax* of 6⅔% called refundable tax on CCPC's investment income.[8] This means that the combined federal and provincial tax rate is 44⅔% (38% + 6⅔%). The special refundable tax is added because the top corporate tax rate (38%) is lower than the top tax rate on similar income earned by individuals (in all provinces). The purpose of the special refundable tax is to eliminate the tax advantage that occurs when an individual opts to hold investments in a private corporation. Remember that the 6⅔% tax is fully refundable to the corporation when the income to which it applies is distributed to the shareholder(s) as a dividend.

Combined federal and provincial/territorial tax calculations are presented in Appendix B at the end of the text.

• **Tax treatment of income distributions** Dividend distributions of property income from a Canadian-controlled private corporation to its shareholders are not subject to double taxation. The fact that the property income is subject to the high rate

---

7   ITA 125(7).
8   ITA 123.3.

of tax implies that double taxation will occur on distribution; however, a portion of the tax paid is refundable to the corporation if and when the corporation decides to distribute the after-tax income as a dividend.

All property income that is subject to the high rate of corporate tax is entitled to a tax refund of 26⅔% when it is distributed to the shareholders.[9] In a province where the corporate tax rate is 44⅔% (38% + 6⅔%), the refund reduces the effective tax rate to 18% (38% + 6⅔% − 26⅔%). The impact of this is demonstrated in Exhibit 13-3.

Note that the calculation in Exhibit 13-3 indicates three separate points of tax activity. First, the corporation pays tax at 44⅔%, leaving 55⅓% of the income in the corporation for reinvestment. Second, at some future time, when it is decided to distribute corporate earnings, 26⅔% of the property income is refunded to the corporation.[10] Third, the individual shareholder is taxed on receipt of the dividend. Thus, assuming that the individual shareholder is in the top personal tax bracket, the combined corporate tax and shareholder tax amounts to 45%. This is the same as what would have been paid (45%) if the individual had earned the property income directly, rather than passing it through a corporation.

Exhibit 13-3:

Combined Corporate and Shareholder Tax on Property Income

Corporate income (from interest, rents, royalties)	$1,000
Corporate tax @ 38%	(380)
Special refundable tax @ 6⅔% *CCPC inv. inc. refund*	(67)
Net available for the corporation	553
Potential refund when dividends are paid	
(26⅔% of $1,000)	267
Available for dividend	$ 820
Shareholder income (dividend)	$ 820
Tax (net of dividend tax credit)*	(271)
	$ 549
Total tax:	
Corporation ($380 + 67 − 267)	$ 180
Shareholder	271
	$ 451
Combined tax rate	45%

---

* Non-eligible dividend 33% of $820 = $271—see Chapter 10.

In the above example, almost perfect integration has occurred. In some provinces, the combined tax rate is higher than the personal tax rate or slightly less.

Integration calculations for each province and territory are presented in Appendix B at the end of the text.

The concept of applying a high rate of tax to investment income, followed by a refund, for the purpose of avoiding double taxation is easy to understand. The actual mechanism to achieve this is more complex. In order to keep track of the amount of tax eligible for a refund as a result of paying dividends, the corporation maintains a running balance referred to as the *refundable dividend tax on hand account (RDTOH)*.

---

9 ITA 129(3). Referred to as "refundable dividend tax on hand" and usually calculated as 26⅔% of the *least* of aggregate investment income or the taxable income less the income subject to the small business deduction.

10 ITA 129(1); IT-243R4. Usually, the dividend refund is equal to one-third of the dividend paid or the balance in the refundable dividend tax on hand account.

When dividends are distributed, the refund is equal to 33⅓% of the dividend paid or the balance in the RDTOH account, whichever is the least. This mechanism is reviewed later in the chapter.

C. Capital Gains

The tax treatment of capital gains earned by a Canadian-controlled private corporation is *identical* to the tax treatment given specified investment business income (property income). The taxable capital gain (one-half of the capital gain) in excess of the allowable capital loss for a year is taxed at the high corporate rate of 38% plus a refundable tax on CCPC's investment income of 6⅔%; however, 26⅔% of the taxable gain is refunded in the event that the income is distributed to the shareholder. In this way, double taxation is avoided. Therefore, the calculations shown in Exhibit 13-3 are also applicable to the taxable portion of capital gains.

In order to fully avoid double taxation on capital gains, a mechanism must be available to distribute the tax-free portion of the gain (one-half of the capital gain) to the shareholders. The non-taxable portion of the capital gain can be distributed by means of a special dividend referred to as a "capital dividend."[11] Capital dividends received by the shareholder are fully exempt from tax. Consequently, capital gains earned by a corporation and flowed through to the shareholder are taxable as if they had been earned by the shareholder directly, without the use of a corporation.

The amount of tax-free capital dividends available for distribution is accumulated in a corporate tax account referred to as the ***capital dividend account***. The capital dividend account is a running balance that includes the non-taxable portion of capital gains (one-half of capital gains) less the non-allowable portion of capital losses (one-half of capital losses). The account also includes the non-taxable portion of gains on eligible capital property (see Chapter 6) and the receipt of non-taxable life insurance proceeds. The capital dividend account is discussed in Part IV, Section C of this chapter.

D. Personal Services Business Income

A personal services business can generally be defined as a business that provides services, when the person providing those services is a *specified shareholder*[12] of the corporation, and the relationship between the person providing the services and the entity receiving the services is of an employment nature.[13] For example, consider the situation of an employed executive who resigns her position and returns immediately to offer the same services to the employer in the form of a service contract with a newly created corporation owned by the executive. In such cases, the fees earned by the corporation may be classified as personal services business income if the real relationship between the parties remains unchanged and an indirect employer/employee relationship continues to exist.

A Canadian-controlled private corporation earning this type of income is not eligible for the small business deduction on that income and faces significant restrictions regarding the types of expenses that can be deducted from income. In addition to losing the small business deduction, a CCPC earning personal service business income is not entitled to the 13% general rate reduction.[14] So, the federal tax rate for a personal service corporation is 28% rather than standard 15% allowed other corporations earning full rate taxable income. When a provincial tax rate is added to the federal rate of 28%, the combined rate varies from 38% to 44% depending on the province or territory. The loss of the small business deduction and the general rate reduction combined is very punitive and effectively rules out any planning opportunities using a corporation to earn personal service business income. This category exists to prevent the abuse of the small business deduction; because of the inherent restrictions, most corporations avoid carrying on activities of this nature.

---

11   ITA 83(2), 89(1)(b); IT-66R6.
12   ITA 248 (definition of specified shareholder), ownership by the taxpayer or a related person of 10% or more of the issued shares of any class.
13   ITA 125(7), definition of personal services business; IT-73R6.
14   Department of Finance draft legislation, October 31, 2011; ITA 123.4(1).

It is important to recognize that this category does not include income from any type of service where an employee/employer relationship does *not* exist. This means that most corporations which provide services on a fee-for-service basis, even if that work is done by a shareholder, are considered to be earning active business income that is eligible for the low rate of tax. Also excluded from personal services business income is income received from an associated corporation and income earned by a corporation that employs more than five full-time employees in the business throughout the year.

E. Dividends

It was established in Chapter 11 that dividends received by one corporation from another Canadian corporation are not taxable because although they are included in net income for tax purposes, they are deducted in arriving at taxable income. The purpose of this exemption is to eliminate multiple taxation on the same income as it flows from one corporation to another via dividends.

Taxable Canadian dividends received by a Canadian-controlled private corporation are subject to special tax treatment. This special treatment depends on the degree of ownership that the corporation has in the corporation paying the dividend. When a Canadian-controlled private corporation owns *more than 10%* of the voting shares and more than 10% of the fair market value of all the classes of issued shares of another corporation, the two corporations are said to be *connected*.[15] The actual definition of a connected corporation is more technical (see footnote below); but in most situations, owning more than 10% of another corporation's voting shares will cause the two corporations to be connected. On the other hand, if a Canadian-controlled private corporation owns *10% or less* of the voting shares of another corporation, the two are considered to be *non-connected*. For example, a Canadian-controlled private corporation investing in a small number of shares of a public corporation would be non-connected. Similarly, a Canadian-controlled private corporation owning 8% of the voting shares of another Canadian-controlled private corporation would be non-connected with that corporation. The special tax treatment of dividends received from non-connected and connected corporations is reviewed below.

1. Dividends Received from Non-connected Corporations

It would appear that given the above exemption, an individual who owns a portfolio of public corporation shares paying dividends should find it possible to transfer these shares to his or her own corporation, thereby ensuring that any dividends received can be reinvested on a tax-free basis. In fact, the *Income Tax Act* has rules in place to forestall such transactions—private corporations are subject to a special refundable tax on the receipt of dividends from other non-connected Canadian companies. This special tax is referred to as a "Part IV tax" because it is administered under Part IV of the *Income Tax Act*.[16] The rate of tax is 33⅓% of the actual dividend received; this tax, however, is *fully refundable* to the corporation if and when the dividend is distributed to the shareholder.[17] Exhibit 13-4 demonstrates the tax treatment of non-connected dividends received by a Canadian-controlled private corporation. *In this case the dividends are from a public corporation and are classified as eligible.*

The calculation assumes that the individual shareholder is in a tax bracket of 45% and therefore would incur a tax on dividends, net of the dividend tax credit, of 28% on eligible dividends (see Chapter 10, Exhibit 10-7).

---

15 ITA 186(4). Technically, two corporations are connected if one controls the other (together with related persons owns more than 50% of the voting shares) *or* if one corporation owns more than 10% of the voting shares and more than 10% of the fair market value of all shares of the other corporation.

16 ITA 186(1); IT-269R4.

17 ITA 129(3), 129(1); IT-243R4.

Refundable Tax on Dividends from Non-connected Corporations

Corporation income:	
Dividends from portfolio shares	$1,000
Normal income tax	NIL
Special Part IV tax @ 33⅓%	(333)
Available for reinvestment	$ 667
Refund of Part IV tax on distribution	333
Dividend to shareholder	$1,000
Shareholder income:	
Dividend from corporation	$1,000
Tax (net of dividend tax credit—28% for eligible dividend)	(280)
Net to shareholder	$ 720
Total tax:	
Corporation ($333 − $333)	$ –0–
Shareholder	280
	$ 280

Upon receipt of the dividend, the corporation pays a special Part IV tax of 33⅓% that leaves 66⅔% of the dividend available for reinvestment by the corporation. If the corporation decides to distribute these earnings to the shareholder at some future time, the 33⅓% tax is fully refunded to the corporation, effectively eliminating the corporate tax. *In addition, dividends received will retain their source and characteristic as they pass through the CCPC. So a CCPC that receives an eligible dividend of $1,000 can in turn pay out an eligible dividend of $1,000.* In this way, the dividend paid by the company is equal to the original dividend received from the non-connected corporation. As a consequence, the tax payable by the shareholder is the same as what would have been paid if the portfolio dividends had been received directly, rather than via the holding corporation.

It is important to note that in this example, the corporate tax rate is 33⅓%, whereas the individual's tax rate on dividends is 28%. This means that it would not be worthwhile to leave the dividend in the corporation for reinvestment. If it were passed on to the shareholder, the corporation would receive a refund of the 33⅓% tax and the individual would pay a 28% tax, leaving a greater amount for reinvestment. This is not always the case. If the dividends are classified as non-eligible the personal rates of tax are much higher. A review of Exhibit 10-8 in Chapter 10 shows that after provincial surtaxes are considered, the tax rate on non-eligible dividends for individuals in the top tax bracket ranges from 28% to 41%. This means that in some situations, the Part IV tax rate of 33⅓% is slightly more attractive than the individual rate. Note also that in the lower tax brackets, the tax rate on both eligible and non-eligible dividends is much lower than the Part IV rate for corporations.

2. Dividends Received from Connected Corporations

Dividends received by a private corporation from a *connected* corporation are normally *not* subject to the standard Part IV tax of 33⅓%.[18] There is one exception: If the connected corporation that pays the dividend obtains a refund of tax (from its RDTOH account), the corporation that receives the dividend must pay a Part IV tax equal to its proportionate share (share percentage) of the paying corporation's refund. Consider the following situation and analysis:

---

18 ITA 186(1); IT-269R3.

Situation:	A Ltd., a Canadian-controlled private corporation, owns 20% of the voting shares of B Ltd., also a Canadian-controlled private corporation. B earns active business income that is subject to the small business deduction, and also investment income that is taxed at the high corporate rate, of which a portion is refundable on payment of dividends. At its year end, B paid a dividend of $20,000. The dividend payment triggered a refund of $3,000 to B.
Analysis:	A's share of the dividend is $4,000 (20% × $20,000). A and B are connected corporations because A owns more than 10% of B's voting shares. Consequently, the standard Part IV tax of 33⅓% is not applicable. However, because B received a tax refund of $3,000 from the payment of the dividend (referred to as a dividend refund), A must pay a Part IV tax of $600, which is 20% (A's percentage ownership of B) of $3,000 (B's refund). The Part IV tax of $600 is fully refundable to A when it declares a dividend to its shareholder(s).

The above shows that the Part IV tax on dividends received from a connected corporation is applicable only when the dividend triggers a refund to the payer. As explained earlier, such refunds occur only when the payer corporation earns investment income or taxable capital gains, or itself pays Part IV tax on dividends received. To the extent that the payer corporation earns active business income and passes that on as a dividend to the connected shareholder, no Part IV tax is applicable and the dividend flows completely tax-free. Therefore, when investing in a Canadian-controlled private corporation that operates an active business, it may be wise to hold that investment through a holding corporation. This structure would permit dividends from the active business corporation to be received tax-free for reinvestment. The benefits of using a corporation to hold investments in other business corporations are reviewed in detail in Chapter 14.

F. Summary

The tax treatment for Canadian-controlled private corporations presented in this chapter introduces significant complexities to the two-tier system of corporate taxation. The complexities are a result of government policies that provide tax incentives to Canadian small business operations while also providing Canadians with the opportunity to hold their investments within private corporations without long-term adverse consequences.

The tax treatment of the various types of income is summarized for comparison in Exhibit 13-5. Except in the case of business income over $500,000, income earned is not subject to double taxation. Note that this is achieved in different ways. Active business income is subject to an initial rate of tax that is low enough to provide an immediate tax incentive and eliminate future double taxation. Property income and capital gains are initially taxed at a high rate that provides no incentive; for these types of income, double taxation is avoided by means of a subsequent reduction in corporate taxes.

It is important to remember that the above tax treatments apply only to Canadian-controlled private corporations and not to public corporations.[19]

III. Benefits of Incorporation

The process of deciding whether to operate a business or hold investments within a private corporation involves consideration of both tax and non-tax issues. While non-tax issues, such as limited liability, are important, this section restricts its discussion to the tax implications of incorporating business or investment income, concentrating on the major tax factors affecting cash flow for the immediate owner. It does not attempt to examine matters involving ownership transfer or estate planning.

---

[19] Part IV tax and capital dividends apply to all private corporations as well as Canadian-controlled private corporations.

Exhibit 13-5:

	Tax treatment to the corporation	Double taxation on distribution
Business income:		
First $500,000 of income	15%	No
Income in excess of $500,000	25%	Yes
Property income:		
Interest, rents, royalties	44⅔% (38% + 6⅔%) Reduced by 26⅔% on distribution	No
Canadian (non-connected) dividends	33⅓% Fully refunded on distribution	No
Canadian (connected) dividends	–0–	No
Taxable capital gains	44⅔% (38% + 6⅔%) Reduced by 26⅔% on distribution	No

While business income incorporation is discussed separately from investment income incorporation, the reader should keep in mind that a single corporation can earn more than one type of income.

A. Benefits of Incorporating a Business

1. Tax Deferral—The Small Business Deduction

The major benefits associated with incorporating a business enterprise are given below.

The primary advantage of incorporating a business as a Canadian-controlled private corporation is this: It permits the achievement of significantly lower tax rates as a result of the small business deduction on the first $500,000 of active business profits. As described in Chapters 10 and 11, an individual in the top tax bracket paying tax on business income at a rate of 45% would pay only 15% after incorporating the business, thereby deferring 30% (45% − 15% = 30%) of the income tax.

This benefit is a tax d*eferral*, rather than a tax *saving*, because the lower tax of 15% will ultimately be followed by a second level of tax to the shareholder when after-tax corporate profits are distributed as dividends or when the shares are sold. It should be pointed out that no tax benefit will be achieved by incorporating business income if the individual shareholder intends to withdraw all of the corporate profits from the corporation for personal use. When the shareholder does this, the combined corporate and personal tax is slightly less (2% − depending on the province) than the tax on a proprietorship.

Deferring tax on business income has two basic advantages:

1. The increased cash flow produced by the reduced tax rate can be reinvested in business expansion or in passive investments that result in greater ultimate returns on investment. By making certain assumptions, this benefit can be quantified.

2. Increased cash flow at the early stages of a business reduces the risk of failure. Such an increase also provides additional resources that can be used to respond to changes in the marketplace requiring asset retooling or new business development. Increased cash flow also makes for greater borrowing capacity in that it increases an entity's ability to repay debt obligations. This type of benefit is more subjective and hence more difficult to quantify.

The long-term benefits derived from the small business deduction remain significant, provided that the tax deferral is reinvested to generate returns of income that are either subject to the low rate of tax or are in the form of property income, which is not double-taxed on distribution. However, when the increased cash flow is reinvested to generate business income over the $500,000 limit, double taxation will occur that over time may significantly reduce the benefits of the small business deduction. This is demonstrated in the two separate scenarios that follow:

Situation: A corporation earning $10,000 of business income annually for 20 years reinvests the after-tax profits to generate an additional *business return* on investment of 20% before tax. After 20 years, all accumulated profits are distributed to the shareholder, who is subject to tax at the rate of 45% (therefore 33% on non-eligible dividends after the dividend tax credit).

Analysis: The $10,000 of business income generates $8,500 after tax ($10,000 − 15% tax = $8,500), which is reinvested to earn an after-tax return from business expansion of 17% (20% − 15% tax = 17%). If the income were earned by an individual proprietorship, it would generate $5,500 after tax ($10,000 − 45% tax = $5,500), which would be re-invested at an after-tax return of only 11% (20% − 45% tax = 11%). These alternatives would produce results after 20 years.

As a corporation:	
$8,500 annually × 20 y × 17%	$1,293,000*
Tax on non-eligible dividend distribution ($1,293,000 × 33%)	(427,000)
Net to owner	$ 866,000
As a proprietorship:	
$5,500 annually × 20 y × 11%	$ 392,000
Benefit of incorporation	$ 474,000

* Calculation assumes annuity-due formula. Future value of regular deposits.

In the above situation, the small business deduction more than doubled the owner's ultimate return on investment. The after-tax return increased by 121% ($474,000 ÷ $392,000) as a result of incorporation. This is because the increased cash flow was invested to create higher after-tax returns that were not double taxed when paid out to the shareholder.

Dramatically different results occur when the return on the investment of after-tax profits is in the form of business income subject to the highest rate of corporate tax.

Situation: A corporation earning $600,000 of business income annually for 20 years reinvests the after-tax profits in business expansion providing 20% returns.

Analysis: As the annual profits of $600,000 use up the full limit of the small business deduction ($500,000), all future returns from business expansion are taxed at 25% and so are ultimately subject to double taxation. Looking *only* at the annual $500,000 of profit subject to the small business deduction, the after-tax corporate profits on this $500,000 of business income is $425,000 ($500,000 − 15% tax = $425,000). This $425,000 generates after-tax returns of 15% (20% − 25% tax = 15%) compared with 17% in the previous example. If the business were operated as a proprietorship, the after-tax profits from the first $500,000 of business income available for reinvestment would be $275,000 ($500,000 − 45% tax), providing an after-tax return of 11%. Remember, income taxed at the low rate is distributed as a non-eligible dividend and other business income is distributed as an eligible dividend.

As a corporation:

$425,000 annually × 20 y × 15%		$50,069,000*
Tax on dividend distribution of $50,069,000:		
Income taxed at low rate—non-eligible dividend		
$425,000 × 20 y = $8,500,000 × 33%	$ 2,805,000	
Income taxed at high rate—eligible dividend		
$50,069,000 − $8,500,000 =		
$41,569,000 × 28%	$11,639,000	$14,444,000
Net to owner		$35,625,000
As a proprietorship:		
$275,000 annually × 20 y × 11%		$19,598,000
Advantage from incorporation		$16,027,000

*Future value of regular deposits.

In the above situation, the benefit achieved from increased cash flow due to the small business deduction is lower than in the previous example because the resulting returns on the cash reinvestment were subject to high corporate tax rates and a small amount of double taxation on distribution. In this particular example, the after-tax return increased by 82% ($16,027,000 ÷ $19,598,000) as a result of incorporation compared with 128% in the previous example. However, the results could have varied depending on the time frame used.

It should also be pointed out that the above example did not consider the importance of the corporation achieving increased cash flow on an annual basis. That extra cash flow, although ultimately lost on distribution, might have been vital to the success of the business.

Finally, consider a situation where corporate profits are invested to provide a return in the form of property income.

Situation: A corporation earning business income of $500,000 for 20 years reinvests the after-tax profits of $425,000 ($500,000 − 15% tax = $425,000) in bonds, yielding interest of 8% before tax and 4.4% after tax (8% − 38% − 6⅔% tax = 4.4%). After 20 years, all accumulated profits are distributed to the shareholder.

Analysis: In this situation, the future returns result from property income, not business expansion. Although those returns are taxed at 44⅔% (38% + 6⅔% refundable tax), the refund on future distributions will eliminate double taxation. The net comparative results are as follows:

As a corporation:

$425,000 annually × 20 y × 4.4%	$13,775,000*
Potential refund of tax on distribution (next page)	2,543,000
Available for distribution	$16,318,000
Tax on non-eligible dividend distribution ($16,318,000 × 33%)	(5,385,000)
Net to owner	$10,933,000
As a proprietorship:	
$275,000 annually × 20 y × 4.4%†	$ 8,913,000
Benefit of incorporation	$ 2,020,000

*Future value of regular deposits.
†8%−45% tax = 4.4%.

The refund is calculated as follows:

Total income accumulated	$13,775,000
Less earned from business:	
$425,000 × 20 y	8,500,000
After-tax investment income	$ 5,275,000
Pre-tax investment income:	
$5,275,000 ÷ .5533 (1 − 44²/₃% tax rate)	$ 9,534,000
Refund: 26²/₃% of $9,534,000	$ 2,543,000

The preceding three situations demonstrate that the small business deduction normally results in an increased rate of return over a long period of time. In order to maximize the cash returns of a business operation, it is important to consider not only the immediate tax but also the future tax relating to the distribution of profits to the shareholders.

2. Employment Benefits

In most small business corporations, the shareholder also participates in the management of corporate affairs and is entitled to receive compensation as an employee. The corporation can provide the owner/manager with various types of employment benefits. As described in Chapter 4, a number of these benefits are fully deductible from the employer's income but are not taxable to the employee.[20] For example, the corporation can provide disability insurance as an employee benefit, which is not taxable to the employee/shareholder.

When a business is operated as a proprietorship, the owner cannot be an employee because the business is not distinct from the owner. Consequently, to acquire the above-mentioned insurance policies the owner must first pay tax on business profits and then acquire the policies with after-tax funds.

While these items do not constitute a significant annual dollar amount, over a period of time, their value can be substantial.

A corporation can also provide a registered pension plan that is available to the owner/employee. Under a proprietorship structure, the owner cannot participate in such a plan.

3. Flexibility in Family Ownership

Many businesses are family run. The corporate structure allows for the issuing of share capital, which provides flexibility when it comes to bringing family members into ownership positions or changing the percentage ownership of family members.

Also, people who own shares of a qualified small business corporation may be entitled to a $750,000 capital gains deduction when those shares are transferred to their children (see Chapter 8). No such deduction exists when all or part of a proprietorship business is transferred to children. The same $750,000 capital gains deduction may apply when shares of a qualified small business corporation are sold to third parties.

4. Stabilization of Annual Income

The corporate structure, which imposes a two-tier system of taxation, gives the shareholder the right to choose when the second level of tax (on dividend distributions) will occur. While this may, in part, be governed by the shareholder's need for funds, the payment of dividends can be delayed until such time as they will receive the most

---

20 ITA 6(1)(a); IT-470R.

favourable tax treatment. For example, in a year in which the shareholder's other sources of income are very low, a dividend distribution can be made that results in a lower rate of tax on that dividend than would normally apply. Similarly, a shareholder may delay the payment of dividends from a private corporation until after retirement, when other sources of income are reduced. This flexibility permits the owner to fully utilize the progressive tax rates imposed on individuals.

5. Primary Disadvantages

The major disadvantage to incorporating a business as a Canadian-controlled private corporation relates to the utilization of losses. As pointed out in previous chapters, losses within a corporation cannot be offset against income earned by the shareholder. This restricts the opportunity to use losses to generate cash flow through reduced taxes on other income.

From a tax perspective, the benefits of incorporation all relate to periods of profitability. Even so, new businesses are often incorporated in the anticipation of profits, without regard to the possibility of losses in the start-up period. Limited liability, while an obvious consideration, must be viewed in the context of after-tax costs before a realistic decision can be made on which entity structure to use (see Chapter 20).

B. Benefits of Incorporating Investments

The incorporation of investment income (interest, rents, and royalties) and capital gains does not result in substantial tax advantages for the individual. Since property income and capital gains are taxed at the high corporate rate (plus the special refundable tax of $6\frac{2}{3}\%$), no substantial tax deferral occurs, as the corporate rate is higher than the highest personal tax rate in all provinces.

Dividends from non-connected Canadian corporations that are received by a Canadian-controlled private corporation are subject to a special (Part IV) refundable tax of $33\frac{1}{3}\%$, and this removes any substantial tax-deferral opportunities. Exhibit 10-8 in Chapter 10 showed that the tax rate for individuals on non-eligible dividend income can be as high as 40%; when it is that high, a small deferral of tax can be achieved through incorporation. Incorporating investment in shares of a *connected* corporation that earns active business income would eliminate the Part IV tax of $33\frac{1}{3}\%$ on dividends received. This provides a major tax deferral. However, the incorporation of an investment in the shares of a connected active business corporation may have a future disadvantage: If the shares are subsequently sold, any capital gain would not be eligible for the $750,000 capital gain deduction, as the deduction is available only to an individual who sells such shares. The benefits of using a holding corporation to invest in shares of other corporations are examined fully in Chapter 14.

IV. Dividend Policy

Because of the varying tax treatments applied to income earned by Canadian-controlled private corporations and to the shareholders receiving dividends from such corporations, it is difficult to establish a single policy to govern the method and timing of distributions to owners. Distributions to owners can be in the form of dividends or in the form of compensation for secondary relationships (salaries, interest, rents, and the like). These distributions can be made either sooner or later, depending on the shareholder's need for funds and the ultimate tax cost of distribution.

This section of the chapter develops some general guidelines relating to the decision to distribute corporate profits derived from an *active business*.

A. Ordering of CCPC Dividend Distributions

A CCPC can distribute three categories of taxable dividends—*capital, eligible,* and *non-eligible.* The tax consequence to a shareholder who is an individual is significantly different for each category of dividend. Capital dividends are tax free. Eligible dividends have a larger dividend tax credit than non-eligible dividends and, therefore, a much lower rate of tax for the shareholder.

When a CCPC declares and pays a dividend it must formally designate the dividend as capital, eligible, or non-eligible. A capital dividend is limited to the balance in the capital dividend account (discussed earlier in this chapter). An eligible dividend can be paid only to the extent the CCPC has a positive balance in its *General Rate Income Pool* (GRIP) at the end of the taxation year. Typically, this pool includes a CCPC's after-tax business income that did *not* receive the benefit of the small business deduction (see Chapter 10, Part V, Section D). For purposes of the calculation, the tax is assumed to be 28%, and so 72% (100% − 28% = 72%) of the business income not subject to the small business deduction is added to the account annually. The pool also includes eligible dividends received from other corporations and dividends from foreign affiliate corporations. A more detailed GRIP calculation is provided later in this chapter (see Part VII, Section G).

Both eligible and non-eligible dividends trigger a refund of refundable tax when there is a balance in the RDTOH account. It is intuitive that when a CCPC has a GRIP balance it would always designate the maximum eligible dividend to provide the lowest tax rate for the shareholder. Therefore, the following dividend ordering should be considered:

1. Capital dividends.

2. Eligible dividends.

3. Non-eligible dividends.

B. Distributions— Dividends versus Salary

A Canadian-controlled private corporation that is also managed by its shareholder(s) can distribute corporate income by salary payments or by dividends. Salaries reduce the corporate income that accrues to the shareholders but do not disturb the relationship between shareholders if paid out in proportion to the ownership ratio. For example, a corporation owned 60% by one manager/shareholder and 40% by another could pay additional salaries of $60,000 and $40,000, respectively, to each shareholder without disturbing the normal share of profits.

As indicated in Chapter 5, salaries paid are deductible from taxable income only if they are reasonable in the circumstances.[21] This means that the salary option cannot be used to distribute corporate income to shareholders who do not perform services for the company. Even when shareholders do participate in management, the salaries or bonuses paid are subject to a reasonableness test. In most cases, the CRA is extremely liberal in applying the reasonableness test on salaries paid to shareholders who are fully active in the management of the corporation.[22]

Currently, business income earned by a Canadian-controlled private corporation is taxed at two rates, depending on the amount of annual income. These are as follows:

Income subject to the small business deduction ($500,000)	15%
Income over $500,000	25%

Consider situations where a corporation is taxed at the above rates on its active business income. The sole shareholder is also the manager, who is in a 45% tax bracket as

---

21 ITA 67.
22 IC 88-2 (paragraph 18); "CRA," Report of Proceedings of the 55th Tax Conference, 2003, Canadian Tax Foundation, 8A: 12–14.

a result of his base salary from the corporation and other sources of income. In these situations, the dividend/salary policy of the corporation could be analyzed as follows:

1. *On income over $500,000*   In any particular year, the shareholder may or may not need additional funds for personal use. If the shareholder needs them, the corporation should pay an increased salary, as this would reduce corporate income (and save 25% tax) and increase the shareholder's personal income (and tax, at the 45% rate and lower in some provinces). If the payment were in the form of a dividend, the combined corporate tax and tax to the shareholder on the dividend would amount to approximately 46%, as shown in previous examples.

    If the shareholder does *not* need additional funds, the decision is complicated. Here, in situations where the shareholder does not need immediate funds, a decision to leave the funds in the corporation to gain a 20% tax deferral (45% − 25%) must be weighed against the impact of the double taxation that will occur when funds are distributed to the shareholder in the future. Keep in mind that the element of double taxation is only about 1% (46% versus 45%) and therefore the consequence of double taxation is reduced as the time of the tax deferral increases. The rate of double taxation varies by province and is often greater than 1% (see Chapter 11, Part IV, and the integration tables in Appendix B at the end of the text).

2. *On the first $500,000 of income*   In this situation, if the shareholder needs additional funds, the decision whether to pay salary or dividends is also important. Paying additional salary would shift corporate income to the shareholder, who would be taxed only once, at the rate of 45%. Under the dividend option, corporate income would first be taxed at 15%; a second tax would follow on the dividend, resulting in a combined tax that is close to 43%.[23] In most provinces/territories, the combined corporate tax and the personal tax on the dividend is less than the tax on a salary in which case a dividend is preferred (see Chapter 11, Part IV, and Appendix B at the end of the text for tax savings on dividends by province.)

    If the shareholder does *not* require additional funds, no payment in either form should be made. Instead, the corporate income should be retained to be taxed at the low rate of 15% and then used for reinvestment in the knowledge that any further distribution is not subject to double taxation.

The above analysis applied to a structure involving a single shareholder whose rate of tax was specifically defined. Similar analyses can be applied to structures that involve both multiple shareholders and varying tax rates.

C. Capital Dividend Account and Capital Dividends

In order to avoid double taxation, non-taxable gains earned by a private corporation are accumulated in the Capital Dividend Account. Non-taxable gains include the net non-taxable portion of capital gains, eligible capital property gains and life insurance proceeds. At any time, the corporation can elect to pay a capital dividend to its shareholders to the extent of the balance in the capital dividend account. The capital dividend paid is not taxable to the shareholder. Therefore, the non-taxable gains earned in a corporation can flow through the corporation to the shareholder without further tax. This concept has been discussed earlier in this chapter, and will be looked at further in Chapter 12, in explaining the tax treatment of capital gains earned by a private corporation and the concept of integration.

The Capital Dividend Account balance is a cumulative amount that is carried forward and adjusted regularly as relevant transactions occur. When a capital dividend distribution is contemplated, it is the balance of the Capital Dividend Account at that time (immediately before the dividend is paid) that is relevant, not the balance at the end of the previous year. To declare a capital dividend, the corporation must file a formal election with CRA.[24]

---

23. See Chapter 11, Part IV, the integration of corporation and individual taxation.
24. ITA 83(2); T2055–Election for a Capital Dividend.

The calculation of the Capital Dividend Account[25] at a particular date includes the relevant transactions from the later of the date of incorporation or the first day of the taxation year after 1971. Additions and deductions during the current year to immediately before the dividend declaration are summarized as follows:

- Add one-half of capital gains;
- Deduct one-half of capital losses;
- Add one-half the proceeds of disposition from eligible capital property minus one-half the cost of eligible capital property;
- Add proceeds from a life insurance policy minus the adjusted cost base of the policy;
- Add capital dividends received from other corporations;
- Deduct capital dividends paid out.

It should be noted that the non-taxable portion of capital gains was not always one-half of the gain. In various years, the non-taxable portion was one-third and one-quarter.

V. Loans to Shareholders

In certain circumstances, a shareholder may be able to secure temporary use of corporate funds without declaring a taxable dividend or paying a taxable salary.

In particular, a corporation is permitted to advance or loan funds to a shareholder, provided that the shareholder is also an employee and that the loan is advanced due to the employment relationship, as follows:[26]

1. To assist the employee/shareholder or his or her spouse in acquiring a personal residence.

2. To permit the employee/shareholder to acquire treasury shares in the corporation.

3. To assist the employee/shareholder in acquiring an automobile to be used in performing employment duties.

4. For any purpose to a shareholder who is not a specified employee. A specified employee is an employee who (alone or together with related persons) owns 10% or more of any class of the corporation's shares or does not deal at arm's-length with the corporation.[27] So, loans are permitted to an employee who is a shareholder, but owns less than 10% of the outstanding shares of the corporation and deals at arm's-length with the corporation.

Loans for the above purposes are not included as income to the shareholder, provided that the repayment terms are reasonable and documented at the time the loan is made. For example, a loan to acquire a house could be repaid over 25 years, as this is reasonable for a house loan. There is no requirement that the loan bear interest; however, to the extent that no interest is charged or interest is less than a prescribed rate, a taxable benefit will occur (see Chapter 4).[28] Keep in mind that the tax treatment of the loan principal is different from the tax treatment of interest.

It is important to recognize that for the loan principal to be exempt from tax, the loan to the shareholder must be made because of his/her employment relationship. In an owner-managed business this may be difficult to establish. One test that can be used is whether a loan given to a shareholder manager is also available to other non-shareholder employees with similar responsibilities. For example, it is unlikely that an owner-managed

---

25 ITA 89(1)(b); IT66R6–Capital Dividends.
26 ITA 15(2), (2.2), (2.3), (2.4); IT-119R4. A corporation can also loan funds to a shareholder if the lending of money is part of the corporation's ordinary course of business.
27 ITA 248(1).
28 ITA 80.4; IT-421R2.

business would provide large housing loans to several non-shareholder employees. In some cases, there are no other employees in a corporation other than the shareholders. This makes the employment test more difficult. While CRA has indicated that it will consider the loan policies of other Canadian-controlled private corporations to help establish that a loan is based on the employment relationship, it is extremely difficult to obtain that information. So, unless a housing loan is for a relatively small amount and is available to other non-shareholder employees, the current practice of Canadian-controlled private corporations is to avoid making housing loans to shareholders.

A corporation is not precluded from loaning funds to shareholders for reasons other than those mentioned above. However, in such cases, the loan must be repaid within one year after the end of the corporation's taxation year in which the advance was made;[29] otherwise, the full amount of the loan will be taxable to the shareholder as property income. If these loans are later repaid, a deduction from income is permitted in the year of repayment.[30]

Consider this situation. In February 20X6, a corporation with a May 31 year end loans $50,000 to a shareholder to fund a personal investment. The loan is repaid in August 20X7. In this situation, the loan remains unpaid at the corporation's year end of May 31, 20X7, which is one year following the year the loan was made (20X6). Consequently, the shareholder must include $50,000 in his or her 20X6 income for tax purposes and pay the related income tax. In 20X7, which is the year the loan is repaid, the shareholder can deduct $50,000 from his or her income for tax purposes. Note the timing in this situation: The shareholder has taxable income in the year the loan is received and obtains a deduction only in the year the loan is repaid.

Note also that one-year shareholder loan rules will not apply if the shareholder attempts to "extend" the loan by repaying it just prior to the one-year limit and then re-borrowing it immediately after the corporation's year end. This is referred to as a series of loans and repayments. The original loan will be included in the shareholder's income in the year the loan was made, and no deduction will be permitted if and when the loan is repaid.

VI. Limitation of the Small Business Deduction

A. Associated Corporations

As shown earlier, a Canadian-controlled private corporation is normally permitted to claim the small business deduction (resulting in the low tax rate of 15%) on the first $500,000 of annual active business income.

The fact that the small business deduction is limited to $500,000 of annual business profits may entice a corporation's shareholders into utilizing a number of corporations to conduct their business activities. The claiming of multiple small business deductions in this manner is, however, greatly limited by what are referred to as the "associated corporations" rules.

If two or more corporations are found to be *associated*, a single $500,000 income limit on the use of the small business deduction will apply to all of the associated corporations combined. However, the owners can apportion this limit among those corporations on an annual basis in any proportion desired.[31]

Whether or not two or more corporations are associated is governed by definition sections in the *Income Tax Act* that are complex.[32] In addition, the CRA can, at its discretion, deem corporations to be associated when it may reasonably be considered that one of the main reasons for the separate existence of those corporations is to

---

29 Except when the corporation's business includes lending money.
30 ITA 20(1)(j).
31 ITA 125(3), (4); IT-64R4.
32 ITA 256(1) to (9); IT-64R4.

reduce taxes.[33] Notwithstanding the limitations, expansion of the small business deduction can be achieved, and this fact plays a vital role in business-expansion decisions (see Chapter 20).

The most important factor when deciding if corporations are associated is the issue of *control*. While control normally means having a majority of the voting shares, in this context, it also means having indirect control when a shareholder (or group) that does not have a majority of votes can exercise significant influence over other shareholders.[34]

As stated above, the definition for associated corporations is complex. Presented below are five basic associated corporation rules with diagrams and brief explanations.

(a) One Corporation Controlling Another

Two corporations are associated if one of the corporations controlled, in any manner whatever, the other corporation.[35]

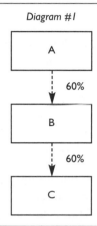

Diagram #1

Clearly, in Diagram #1, A and B are associated and B and C are associated because A controls B and B controls C. However, looking at A and C, A has a beneficial ownership interest of only 36% of C (A owns 60% of B who owns 60% of C). Regardless, A and C are also associated because A indirectly controls C through its control of B.

(b) Control by the Same Person or Group of Persons

Two corporations are associated if they are both controlled by the same person or group of persons.[36]

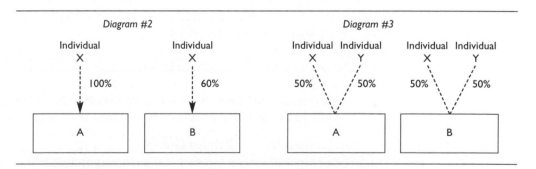

Diagram #2   *Diagram #3*

---

33 ITA 256(2.1).
34 ITA 256(5.1).
35 ITA 256(1)(a).
36 ITA 256(1)(b); where shares are owned by a child under the age of 18, the shares will normally be deemed to be owned by the parent, ITA 256(1.3).

In Diagram #2 both corporations are controlled by X and are associated. In Diagram #3, both corporations are controlled by the same group consisting of X and Y and so corporations A and B are associated. A shareholder need own only one share to be included in the group.

(c) Related Person Control

Two corporations are associated if each of the corporations was controlled by a person *and* that person was related to the person who controlled the other corporation provided that either person owned at least (not less than) 25% of any class of shares of both corporations.[37] See Chapter 9, Part VI (D) for a discussion of **related persons**.

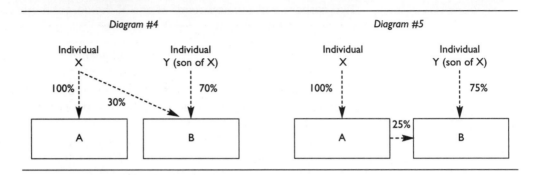

In Diagram #4, A and B are associated because individual X (who controls A) is related to individual Y (X's son who controls B) and X owns at least (not less than) 25% of the shares of B. In Diagram #5, individual X indirectly owns at least (not less than) 25% of B and so A and B are associated.[38]

(d) Control by One Person and a Group of Persons

Two corporations are associated if one of the corporations was controlled by one person who was related to *each* member of a group that controlled the other corporation if that person owned at least (not less than) 25% of any class of shares of the corporation controlled by the group.[39]

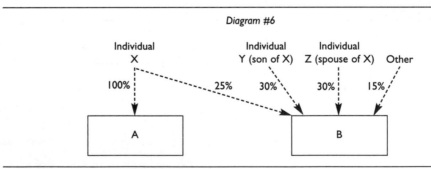

In Diagram #6, A and B are associated because X controls A, the group consisting of Y (30%) and Z (30%) controls B, and X owns at least (not less than) 25% of B's shares.

(e) Control by Two Related Groups

Two corporations are associated if *each* corporation was controlled by a related group and each of the persons from one group was related to each member of the other

37 ITA 256(1)(c); Reference hereafter to "any class of shares" excludes shares of a specified class as defined in ITA 256(1.1).
38 ITA 256(1.2)(d).
39 ITA 256(l)(d).

group; and, one or more persons who were members of both groups owned at least (not less than) 25% of any class of shares of both corporations.

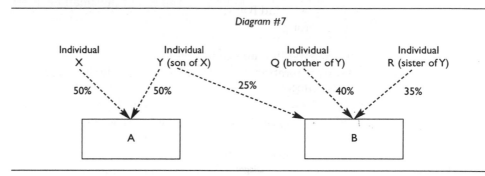

Diagram #7

In Diagram #7, A and B are associated because X and Y (who are a related group) control A, and Q and R (a separate related group) control B. As well, each member of each related group is related to each member of the other related group and individual Y owns at least (not less than) 25% of the shares of both corporations.[40]

It should be noted that where Corporation A is not otherwise associated with Corporation B, but both A and B are associated with Corporation C, then A and B are deemed to be associated because they are both associated with the same corporation. In such a case, corporation C can elect not to be associated with either A or B, in which case C cannot claim any small business deduction, but A and B can each claim the full amount.[41]

In spite of these strong association rules, businesses are often able to gain the benefit of multiple small business deduction limits with careful planning.

Consider the business-expansion structures in Exhibit 13-6. In both situations, Corporation A, which is owned entirely by shareholder Y, has decided to expand a segment of its business by creating a new Corporation B that includes a new participating shareholder X.

Exhibit 13-6:

Associated and Non-Associated Structures

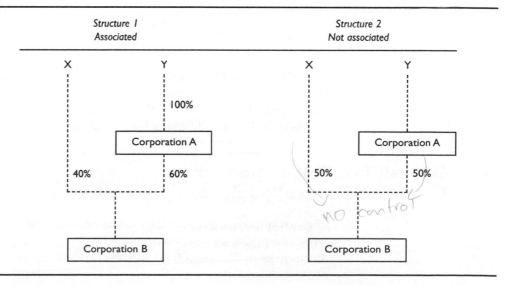

40 ITA 256(l)(e).
41 ITA 256(2).

Under structure 1, Corporation A controls Corporation B because it holds 60% of the voting shares. Thus, Corporation A and Corporation B are associated and must share the $500,000 limit on the use of the small business deduction. On the assumption that Corporation A will use the full $500,000 for its income, Corporation B will have all of its income taxed at the high corporate rate.

In structure 2, neither shareholder controls Corporation B. This means that A and B are not associated, so *each* can apply the low rate of tax to its first $500,000 of business income. Corporation A has thus indirectly expanded its small business deduction: It can apply the full $500,000 limit to itself; at the same time, its 50% ownership of Corporation B entitles it to a half-share of that new corporation's $500,000 limit. Note that structure 2 has enhanced the after-tax cash flow of B, thereby increasing that entity's chances of success.

Various possible methods of increasing the small business deduction by means of business expansion are discussed in more detail in Chapter 20.

B. Large Corporations

True to its name, the small business deduction applies only to Canadian-controlled private corporations (CCPC) that are of a certain size. Beyond that size, the annual small business deduction limit of $500,000 on active business income is gradually reduced until it is eliminated. For this purpose, the size of a CCPC is measured not by the amount of annual income but, rather, by the amount of the capital (referred to as taxable capital) it uses in Canada to conduct its operations. Corporations with taxable capital in excess of $10 million are considered to be large corporations. For each $1 million of taxable capital in excess of $10 million, the small business deduction limit of $500,000 is reduced by $100,000.[42] The entire annual limit is eliminated when the taxable capital of the corporation and its associated corporations (discussed earlier) reaches $15 million, as follows:

Taxable capital	Annual limit
$10 million	$500,000
$11 million	$400,000
$12 million	$300,000
$13 million	$200,000
$14 million	$100,000
$15 million	0

The rules for establishing the corporation's taxable capital are complex, and explaining them is beyond the scope of this text. In general terms, taxable capital consists of the corporation's shareholders' equity (share capital and retained earning), plus corporate debt, less an allowance for cost of investments in other corporations.

VII. Overall Tax Calculation for a Canadian-Controlled Private Corporation

The actual tax calculation for a Canadian-controlled private corporation (CCPC) is more complex than was demonstrated earlier in this chapter and in Chapter 11. The discussions to this point have focused on the basic tax treatment of the various types of income earned by a CCPC and on how this treatment affects shareholders when

---

42 ITA 125(5.1). Actual formula—Annual business limit is *reduced by* [$500,000 (or less if shared with associated corporation) X .225% (taxable capital − $10 million)]/$11,250.

after-tax profits are distributed as dividends. This section summarizes the detailed tax calculation and then reviews each of its major parts. A complete tax calculation is provided in a demonstration question at the end of the chapter.

Summary Tax Calculation

Part I tax[43]

Federal basic tax—38% × taxable income	xxx
Less abatement—10% × taxable income	(x)
	xx

Plus refundable tax on investment income—6⅔% of the least of:
- Aggregate investment income
- Taxable income less amount subject to the small business deduction (below) → x

Less *small business deduction*—17% of the least of:
- Active business income (ABI)
- Taxable income (TI) less (10/3 × foreign tax credit for non-business income and 4 × foreign tax credit for business income)
- Annual business limit ($500,000 less amounts allocated to associated corporations and the large-corporation reduction, if applicable) → (x)

Less *manufacturing and processing (M&P) deduction*—13% of the least of:
- M&P profits less amount subject to the small business deduction (above)
- Taxable income less:
    —amount subject to the small business deduction, plus
    —aggregate investment income → (x)

Less *general rate reduction*—13% of the amount by which the taxable income (TI) *exceeds* the *total* of
- Income subject to the 13% M&P deduction, *plus*
- Income subject to the 17% small business deduction, *plus*
- Aggregate investment income → (x)

Less *foreign tax credit*	(x)
Federal Part I tax	xx
Provincial tax—Provincial rate × taxable income	x
Total federal and provincial Part I tax	xx

Part IV tax (federal)[44]

On dividends received from non-connected corporations	
33⅓% of taxable Canadian dividends	xx
On dividends received from connected corporations	

$$\text{Dividend refund of the connected corporation} \times \frac{\text{Taxable Canadian dividends received from the connected corporation}}{\text{Total taxable dividends paid by the connected corporation in the year}}$$

	xx
Total Part IV tax	xx

Dividend refund (federal)[45]

Lesser of:
- ⅓ (or 33⅓%) × dividends paid in the year
- Balance in the RDTOH before refund → (xx)

---

43 ITA 123(1), 123.3, 123.4, 124(1), 125(1), 125.1(1).
44 ITA 186.
45 ITA 129(1),(3).

RDTOH (federal)

Balance at beginning of year	xx
Less dividend refund for preceding year	(x)
Add:	
• Part IV tax	x
• Refundable portion of Part I tax – the least of:	
—26⅔% × aggregate investment income	
—26⅔% × (taxable income – amount subject to the small business deduction)	
—Part I federal tax	x
RDTOH at end of year	xx

General rate income pool (GRIP)[46]

Balance at the end of the previous year	xx
Add:	
(a) 72% × the following net amount:	
Taxable income before applying loss carry backs	
Less:	
Income subject to the small business deduction	
Aggregate investment income	
(b) Eligible dividends received from other corporations	
(c) Dividends from foreign affiliates	
Deduct:	
(a) Eligible dividends paid in the previous year	
(b) 72% of the losses carried back to the 3 previous years reducing full-rate taxable income	x(x)
GRIP at the end of the year (positive or negative)	xx

Note: Regarding the general rate reduction, certain limitations relating to resource allowances, credit unions, and specified partnerships have been ignored.

The main parts of the above calculation will now be reviewed. For demonstration purposes, a situation with a common set of facts is used. These facts are as follows:

- X Ltd. is a Canadian-controlled private corporation operating a wholesale business and a manufacturing business. Also, X owns 60% of the voting common shares of S Ltd.

- For the year ended December 31, 20X8, X has taxable income of $540,000, as follows:

Net income for tax purposes	$570,000
Less	
Net capital loss	(10,000)
Charitable donations	(5,000)
Taxable Canadian dividends from shares of public corporations	(15,000)
Taxable income	$540,000

The net income for tax purposes includes $18,000 of net taxable capital gains and $12,000 of interest income from bonds. It also includes $15,000 of dividends from public corporations (these were deducted in arriving at taxable income above). Manufacturing and processing (M&P) profits qualifying for the M&P deduction are $400,000.

- X's RDTOH at the end of 20X7 was $9,000. The dividend refund for 20X7 was $3,000.

- X's GRIP balance at the end of the previous year was $18,000.

---

46 ITA 189(1).

- During the year, X paid a dividend of $30,000 to its shareholders. No dividends were paid in the previous year.
- S Ltd. and X Ltd. are associated for tax purposes. For the year ended December 31, 20X8, S claimed the small business deduction on $110,000 of its active business income. S did not pay any dividends in 20X8.

A. Small Business Deduction[47]

Before calculating the small business deduction, we must determine the corporation's active business income and its annual business limit. As shown earlier, the *active business income* is determined by reducing *net income for tax purposes* by the corporation's property income (interest, dividends, rents, and royalties) and net taxable capital gains (gains − losses). In the above situation, the active business income is $525,000, calculated as follows:

Net income for tax purposes	$570,000
Less	
Interest income from bonds	(12,000)
Dividends from taxable Canadian corporations	(15,000)
Net taxable capital gains	(18,000)
Active business income	$525,000

Normally, the active business income eligible for the small business deduction is $500,000 (the annual business limit). However, S, an associated corporation, used $110,000 of this limit. Therefore, the business limit for X is $390,000, as follows:

Total business limit	$500,000
Less amount claimed by associated corporation S	(110,000)
Business limit available to X	$390,000

The small business deduction for X in 20X8 is $66,300, calculated as follows:

17% of the least of:
- Active business income — $525,000
- Taxable income — $540,000
- Annual limit ($500,000 − $110,000 allocated to associated corporation) — $390,000

$$17\% \times \$390,000 = \$66,300$$

B. Refundable Tax on CCPC's Investment Income[48]

As shown in the summary tax calculation, the refundable tax is $6\frac{2}{3}\%$ of the least of these: aggregate investment income, *or* taxable income minus the amount on which the small business deduction is applied. The latter of these may apply when substantial loss carry-overs or charitable donations are deducted in arriving at taxable income. However, in most situations, the $6\frac{2}{3}\%$ rate is simply applied to aggregate investment income. For this purpose, and other parts of the tax calculation, the term *investment income* has a special meaning.[49] It includes Canadian and foreign net property income (interest, rents, and royalties, less related expenses) as well as net taxable capital gains (gains minus losses) for the current year less any net capital losses from other years claimed in the current year. Note that dividends from taxable Canadian corporations are excluded from the definition. This is because such dividends were deducted in arriving at taxable income and are not subject to tax under Part I of the *Income Tax Act*.

---

47 ITA 125(1).
48 ITA 123.3.
49 ITA 129(4).

In the above situation, the aggregate investment income is $20,000 (net taxable capital gains of $18,000 + interest income of $12,000 − net capital losses of $10,000). The refundable tax is $1,333, as follows:

$6\frac{2}{3}$% of the least of:

• aggregate Investment income	$ 20,000
• Taxable income ($540,000) minus income subject to the small business deduction ($390,000)	$150,000

$6\frac{2}{3}$% × $20,000 = $1,333

C. Manufacturing and Processing Deduction[50]

If X Ltd. earns its manufacturing income in a province with a reduced provincial corporate rate for income subject to the federal manufacturing and processing deduction, then the federal manufacturing and processing deduction (13%) will be claimed. If this is not the case, the manufacturing and processing deduction will not be claimed and instead the manufacturing income will be subject to the general rate reduction (13%).

Normally, the 13% manufacturing and processing deduction applies only to the M&P profits that are not subject to the small business deduction. This usually means that the deduction applies to profits over the $500,000 small business deduction limit. In the above situation, X Ltd. earned M&P profits of $400,000. However, the small business deduction applied to only $390,000 because an associated corporation used $110,000 of the $500,000 limit. Consequently, the M&P deduction for X Ltd. is $1,300, calculated as follows:

13% of the least of:

• M&P profits ($400,000) − Income subject to the small business deduction ($390,000)	$ 10,000
• Taxable income ($540,000) − (Income subject to the small business deduction [$390,000] + aggregate Investment income, calculated earlier [$20,000])	$130,000

13% × $10,000 = $1,300

Note the wide spread between the two "least of" items in the calculation. In most situations, the 13% M&P deduction will apply to the M&P profits in excess of the income that is subject to the small business deduction. The latter part of the calculation may apply when the corporation deducts significant loss carry-overs or charitable donations in arriving at taxable income.

D. General Rate Reduction[51]

The general rate reduction of 13% applies to the corporations' *taxable income other than* income eligible for the M&P and small business deductions, resource income, and aggregate investment income. As a result, the amount of income eligible for the general rate reduction is $120,000, and the tax reduction is $15,600, calculated as follows:

Taxable income	$540,000
Less	
Income eligible for the M&P deduction	(10,000)
Income eligible for the small business deduction	(390,000)
Aggregate investment income	(20,000)
Income eligible for the general rate reduction	$120,000
General rate reduction—13% × $120,000	$ 15,600

---

50 ITA 125.1(1).
51 ITA 123.4.

E. Refundable Dividend Tax on Hand[52]

The refundable dividend tax on hand (RDTOH) is designed to accumulate the eligible tax refund that occurs when dividends are paid to shareholders. In general terms, the potential refund consists of all Part IV taxes paid by the corporation (these are fully refundable) *plus* 26⅔% of all investment income earned. As shown earlier, the investment income for this purpose includes net Canadian and foreign-property income (excluding taxable Canadian dividends) *plus* net taxable capital gains.

In the above situation, X Ltd. pays Part IV tax of $5,000 on the dividends from public corporations (33⅓% of $15,000 = $5,000). The RDTOH at the end of its 20X8 taxation year (before the current refund) is $16,333, calculated as follows:

RDTOH at end of previous year		$ 9,000
Less dividend refund for preceding year		3,000
		6,000
Add		
Part IV tax paid in the current year		5,000
Refundable portion of Part I tax – the least of:		
• 26⅔% × aggregate investment income ($20,000)	$ 5,333	
• 26⅔% × (taxable income [$540,000] – income subject to the small business deduction [$390,000])	$40,005	
Part I tax	not calculated	
Least of is		5,333
RDTOH end of year		$16,333

The last part of the above calculation limits the potential refund to the amount of Part I tax paid in the current year. It normally does not apply unless significant loss carry-overs are deducted in arriving at taxable income. It was not calculated in the above demonstration because it is obvious that the total Part I tax is much greater than the lowest amount, which is $5,333.

F. Dividend Refund[53]

As shown earlier in the chapter, a corporation that has taxes eligible for a refund receives that refund when dividends are distributed to its shareholder(s). The tax refund (referred to as the "dividend refund") is equal to 33⅓% of the dividend paid, but it cannot exceed the balance in the RDTOH. In the situation at hand, X Ltd. paid a dividend of $30,000, and its dividend refund is $10,000, calculated as follows:

Least of:	
• ⅓ of the dividend paid ($30,000)	$10,000
• Balance in the RDTOH	$16,333
Least of is $10,000	

The refund reduces the RDTOH to $6,333 ($16,333 − $10,000) at the end of 20X8, and this amount is carried over to the 20X9 taxation year.

G. General Rate Income Pool (GRIP)[54]

The General Rate Income Pool is designed to accumulate the amount of after-tax earnings that can be paid as an eligible dividend. Generally, it reflects the *after-tax business income* earned that is *not eligible for the small business deduction,* and is therefore taxed at a higher rate. The result is that dividends paid out of this pool

---

52 ITA 129(3).
53 ITA 129(1).
54 ITA 89(1).

receive a higher dividend tax credit when included in the income of a shareholder who is an individual. This significantly reduces the amount of double tax that would otherwise occur and is an important part of the integration process. The pool recognizes that the corporation may receive dividends from other corporations that were paid from their General Rate Income Pool by including those dividends in the recipient's pool.

The balance in the GRIP account at the end of the 20X8 taxation year for X Ltd. is $126,600 calculated as follows:

Balance at the end of the previous year		$ 18,000
Add:		
– 72% of:		
Taxable income	$540,000	
Less:		
Income subject to the small business deduction	(390,000)	
Aggregate investment income	(20,000)	
	$130,000	
72% × $130,000		93,600
– Eligible dividends received from other corporations		15,000
		126,600
Deduct:		
– Eligible dividends paid in the previous year		0
Balance at the end of the current year		$126,600

The taxable income less the income subject to the small business deduction and the investment income reflects the *business income taxed at the high general rate*. The calculation assumes a notional tax rate of 28% on this income and therefore, the after-tax amount is 72% (100% − 28% = 72%). The actual tax rate may be higher or lower.

In 20X8 the corporation paid a dividend of $30,000, all of which can be designated as an eligible dividend. Additionally, this eligible dividend triggered a dividend refund from the RDTOH account (see Section F above). The refund would also occur if the dividend is elected to be treated as a non-eligible dividend (see planning discussion in Part IV, Section A).

The above calculations are complex. The "least of" calculations tend to confuse the fundamental tax treatment applied to the various types of income earned by Canadian-controlled private corporations. Remember the following fundamentals:

1. The first $500,000 of active business income is taxed at the low rate of 15% (depending on the province) as a result of applying the small business deduction.

2. M&P profits and other active business income in excess of the $500,000 small business deduction limit are subject to a 13% federal tax reduction.

3. Property income (other than taxable Canadian dividends) is subject to the high rate of tax of 44⅔% (standard rate of 38% + refundable tax of 6⅔%). The tax rate on this income is reduced by 26⅔% when dividends are paid to shareholders.

4. Certain dividend income is subject to a Part IV tax of 33⅓%, which is fully refundable when dividends are paid to shareholders.

H. Investment Tax Credit (SR&ED)

A business has significant flexibility when deducting Scientific Research and Experimental Development (SR&ED) costs. Expenditures qualifying for the SR&ED classification and the alternative deduction methods available were discussed in Chapter 5 (Part III, Section D). In addition to reducing net income for tax purposes, qualified SR&ED expenditures may also be eligible to receive an investment tax credit (ITC) to reduce the income tax payable and/or create a cash refund. Generally the ITC for

Canadian corporations is equal to 20% of qualified expenditures[55] and will be reduced to 15% on January 1, 2014.[56] However, this rate is enhanced to 35% for Canadian-controlled private corporations (CCPC) and will remain at 35% after January 1, 2014.

The basic ITC rules on SR&ED expenditures for a CCPC are briefly outlined below:

- The enhanced ITC rate of 35% applies to the first *$3 million* of *annual* SR&ED expenditures.[57] The standard rate of 20% applies on expenditures above $3 million.
- When a current year's income tax is lower than the investment tax credit available for that year, the unused ITC can be carried back 3 years and forward 20 years to reduce taxes in those years.[58] Alternatively the corporation can claim and receive a cash refund for the excess ITC.[59] The amount of the refund available varies depending on the nature of the SR&ED expenditures. The 35% ITC on *current expenditures* is 100% refundable. However, only 40% of the ITC that was created from *expenditures of a capital nature* is refundable.
- The availability of the enhanced ITC rate of 35% is restricted further based on a CCPC's annual taxable income and its taxable capital employed in Canada. The 35% rate is gradually reduced to the standard 20% rate when the corporation's taxable income of the previous taxation year is between $500,000 and $800,000 (together with associated corporations) and when taxable capital employed in Canada is between $10 million and $50 million.[60]
- When an ITC is claimed as a tax reduction or cash refund the amount is deducted from the pool of unused SR&ED expenditures (see Chapter 5, Part III, Section D) in the following year. If the pool in the following year is insufficient the remainder is added to income.[61]

The combination of the flexible treatment of SR&ED expenditures and the use of the ITC provide a significant incentive for a CCPC and enhances it competitive strength in the global market place.

VIII. Tax Planning Checklist

Much of this chapter was devoted to describing the tax benefits of operating a business or holding investments in a corporation. These benefits, and some additional tax planning considerations, are summarized below.

1. Consider incorporating a business whenever the annual business profits consistently exceed the funds required for personal use. The low rate of corporate tax on those profits will increase the cash available for use in the business.

2. At the time of incorporation, consider including family members as shareholders to achieve income splitting on future profits. (See Chapter 9 for special rules on dividends paid to minors from private corporations.)

3. If the corporation will be providing services, be sure that the activity does not qualify as a personal services business, as neither the 13% general rate reduction nor the 17% small business deduction are permitted for any income generated by such a business.

---

55 ITA 127(5).
56 Federal budget, March 29, 2012.
57 ITA 127(10.1).
58 ITA 127(9)–definition of "investment tax credit."
59 ITA 127.1.
60 ITA 127(10.2); The $3 million limit for the 35% rate is reduced by about $10 for each $1 of income in excess of $500,000 up to $800,000. It is further reduced by $0.075 for every $1 of capital over $10 million.
61 ITA 12(1)(t).

4. Before incorporating, consider the problems that might arise if the corporation were to incur losses and how those losses might be used to reduce future taxes.

5. As a shareholder/manager, be certain to utilize the employment provisions in the *Income Tax Act* that allow employees to receive tax-free benefits. Also, make sure that the owner's salary is sufficient to allow him or her to make the maximum permitted RRSP contributions every year.

6. Consider paying bonuses or increased salaries to shareholders who are active in the business, thus reducing or eliminating double taxation for corporate business income that is in excess of the $500,000 annual small business deduction limit.

7. Remember that the small business deduction limit of $500,000 is an *annual* amount and that any unused portion cannot be carried forward to another year. When the current year's business profit is below the limit but the following year's profit is expected to exceed the limit, consider increasing the current profit by not claiming certain discretionary deductions, such as a reserve for bad debts. This shifts income from the following year, which would have been taxed at the high corporate rate, to the current year, where it will be taxed at the low corporate rate.

8. When possible, time the corporation's dividend distributions to obtain a tax deferral and the lowest possible tax rate. For example, wait until a year in which the shareholder has unusually low income. Also, when the corporation has an RDTOH balance, consider paying a dividend sufficient to recover the RDTOH.

9. A shareholder/employee who will need funds from the corporation should consider making use of shareholder loans and/or deferred bonuses. This would delay the payment of tax for the longest possible time.

10. When acquiring or creating new corporations that will be owned with other shareholders, be sure to seek advice on the rules governing associated corporations, with the goal of establishing a separate $500,000 small business deduction limit.

11. A minority shareholder should be aware that the controlling shareholder has the power to allocate the annual small business deduction limit of $500,000 to another corporation that he or she controls, leaving the minority shareholder with a higher tax rate. The minority shareholder can avoid this problem by making sure that the deduction's allocation is set out in the shareholders' agreement.

XI. Summary and Conclusion

The Canadian-controlled private corporation is a commonly used structure designed to house a wide range of business activities and investments. The tax treatment of its income and subsequent distributions to shareholders deviates from the standard principles of corporate taxation. These deviations are designed to provide temporary tax incentives to incorporated small businesses; at the same time, they provide neither advantages nor disadvantages to the incorporation of investment income. Because of the different tax treatments accorded to various types of corporate income, additional complexities arise that tend to cloud the decision-making process by making it difficult to estimate the resulting cash-flow impact.

Active business income earned by the corporation receives a significant tax preference through the application of the small business deduction on the first $500,000 of annual business income. This deduction, combined with similar provincial incentives, reduces corporate tax on such income to approximately 15%. As this rate is significantly lower than the top marginal personal tax rate, incorporation provides increased after-tax cash flow, which enhances returns on investment as well as the chances of business success. Although additional taxes are payable when the business income is distributed to the shareholders, double taxation does not occur because the dividend tax credit is designed to offset the corporate taxes of 20% and the current small business income tax rate is only 15% in many provinces.

Active business income in excess of $500,000 is subject to higher rates of corporate tax, the result being some double taxation in the future. In some circumstances, double taxation can be avoided by maintaining a salary/dividend policy that shifts income in this category directly to the shareholder.

An entity earning investment income and capital gains derives no substantial tax benefit from incorporation. However, double taxation is avoided through a refund mechanism when investment income or a capital gain is distributed as a dividend to the shareholders.

It is essential that decision makers anticipate the effect that corporate decisions will ultimately have on the shareholders.

Visit the Canadian Income Taxation Web site at **www.mcgrawhill.ca/ olc/buckwold** to view any updated tax information.

Demonstration Questions

QUESTION ONE

TL Ltd. is a Canadian-controlled private corporation operating a retail mail-order business and a small manufacturing operation. At December 31, 20X5, the company's year end, all of the outstanding shares were owned by Jason Tallon.

On November 30, 20X5, Tallon informed you, the treasurer, that he wants to declare a dividend of $80,000 on December 31, 20X5. He has asked you for advice on how to minimize tax on the dividend. He also wants to know if there will be sufficient cash to pay the dividend. With this in mind, you have prepared a projected income statement for the year ended December 31, 20X5, and intend to estimate the corporate tax liability.

Information regarding the company's financial transactions is provided below.

TL Ltd.
20X5 Financial Information

1. The projected profit for the year ended December 31, 20X5, is $273,000, as summarized below.

Mail-order profit	$221,000
Loss from the manufacturing operation	(32,000)
Dividends from taxable Canadian corporations	19,000
Interest income on bonds	5,000
Gain on sale of asset	60,000
	$273,000

2. The mail-order profit includes the following expense items:

Advertising	$37,800
Amortization	66,400
Charitable donations	3,000
Legal —Collection of accounts receivable	1,500
—Drafting debenture agreement for bank financing	4,000
Rent	72,600

3. On February 1, 20X5, TL began a policy of providing a warranty on its manufactured products. The manufacturing loss includes the deduction of $8,000 as a reserve for anticipated product returns. In 20X5, the actual returns were $6,000.

4. Dividends from taxable Canadian corporations include $9,000 from public corporations and $10,000 (non-eligible) from Q Ltd. (a Canadian-controlled private corporation). TL owns 20% of Q's voting common shares. Q's total dividend paid was $50,000 (TL's share – $10,000). As a result of the dividend, Q received a dividend refund of $6,000.

5. TL's 20X4 tax return shows the following information:

Refundable dividend tax on hand	$ 3,000
General rate income pool	12,000
Eligible dividends paid in 20X4	40,000
Capital dividend account	–0–
Cumulative eligible capital (see comment in next paragraph)	–0–
Undepreciated capital costs:	
Class 8	72,000
Class 43	144,000
Class 14	13,000

During 20X5, TL Ltd. purchased welding equipment costing $36,000 for use in the manufacturing operation. In 20X3, the company acquired a licence for $15,000 to manufacture a patented product. The licence has a legal life of 10 years. No deductions have ever been made from the cumulative eligible capital account.

6. A segment of the mail-order business was sold on October 1, 20X5. The proceeds included $70,000 for inventory and $40,000 for a permanent customer list. TL developed the customer list over the past 10 years. Also, TL sold shares of a public corporation, resulting in a gain of $20,000.

7. The treasurer's assistant analyzed the accounting records and provided the following tax-related information:

Manufacturing capital (MC)	$212,000
Manufacturing labour (ML)	196,000
Total capital (TC)	460,000
Total labour (TL)	323,000

8. Jason Tallon purchased all of his brother's shares in TL Ltd. in January 20X5 for $120,000. His brother had acquired the shares in 20X0 for $150,000. A summary of the assets of TL Ltd. and their fair market values at the time of the sale is provided below.

Current assets—business	$ 700,000
Mail-order assets	340,000
Manufacturing assets	516,000
Investment in shares of public corporations	150,000
	$1,706,000

Excluding the sale of shares, the brother's taxable income in 20X5 was $12,000. His marginal tax rate in 20X4 was 45%.

9. In addition to owning all of the TL Ltd. shares, Jason Tallon owns 60% of the voting shares of PY Ltd., a Canadian-controlled private corporation. PY Ltd. earned active business income of $470,000 for its taxation year ending December 31, 20X5. It claimed the small business deduction on all of this income.

Required:

1. Under Part I of the *Income Tax Act*, determine the *minimum income for tax purposes* and the *minimum taxable income* for TL Ltd. for the 20X5 taxation year.

2. Based on your answer to part 1, calculate the Part I and Part IV federal income tax for the 20X5 taxation year, before the dividend refund, if any.

3. What is the maximum capital dividend that can be paid in 20X5? Determine the dividend refund for the 20X5 taxation year based on the planned dividend payment?

4. What amount of any taxable dividend can be designated as an eligible dividend?

5. Briefly describe the tax implications for Tallon's brother from his sale of the TL Ltd. shares.

Solution:

Before the solution is completed, two items are explained. First, TL Ltd. and PY Ltd. are associated for tax purposes because both are controlled by Jason Tallon (TL 100%; PY 60%). Therefore, TL and PY must share the small business limit of $500,000. As PY has already used $470,000 of this limit, TL's business limit for 20X5 is reduced to $30,000 ($500,000 − $470,000). Second, TL Ltd. and Q Ltd. are connected corporations because TL owns more than 10% of Q's voting shares. Therefore, standard Part IV taxes are not applicable on the dividend received by TL from Q. Instead, TL pays a Part IV tax equal to its proportionate share of any dividend refund that Q received as a result of the dividend. This can be calculated as follows:

$$\frac{\text{Dividend received by TL—\$10,000}}{\text{Total dividend paid by Q—\$50,000}} \times \text{Q's dividend refund (\$6,000)} = \$1,200$$

Effectively, TL's Part IV tax is 20% (percentage share ownership) of Q's refund of $6,000 (20% × $6,000 = $1,200). The dividends received from the public corporation (which is not connected) are subject to the full Part IV tax.

1. Income for tax purposes and taxable income

Projected income		$273,000
Gain on sale of assets		(60,000)
Amortization		66,400
Charitable donations		3,000
Legal fees for debenture—⁴/₅($4,000)		3,200
Warranty reserve		8,000
Actual warranty costs		(6,000)
CCA —Class 8—$72,000 × 20%		(14,400)
—Class 43—$144,000 × 30%		(43,200)
—Class 14—$15,000 ÷ 10 y		(1,500)
—Class 29—$36,000 × 25%		(9,000)
Taxable capital gain—public corporation shares—½ ($20,000)		10,000
Gain on sale of eligible capital property, customer list—½ ($40,000)		20,000
Income for tax purposes		249,500
Deduct		
Donations	3,000	
Dividends	19,000	(22,000)
Taxable income		$227,500

2. PART I FEDERAL TAX

Federal—38% × $227,500	$ 86,450
Abatement—10% × $227,500	(22,750)
	63,700

Refundable tax on CCPC's investment income—6⅔% × least of:

- Aggregate Investment income—interest $5,000 + taxable capital gain $10,000 = $15,000

- Taxable income—$227,500 – $30,000 (amount subject
  to small business deduction below) = $197,500

  $6\frac{2}{3}\% \times \$15,000$ 1,001

Small business deduction—17% × least of:

- Active business income—$215,500 (see below)
- Taxable income—$227,500
- Annual limit—$30,000 ($500,000 – $470,000 used by PY Ltd.)

  17% × $30,000   (5,100)

       59,601

Active business income:

Net income for tax purposes	$249,500
Less	
Taxable Canadian dividends	(19,000)
Interest from bonds	(5,000)
Taxable capital gain	(10,000)
	$215,500

M&P deduction:

$$\frac{\$212,000\ (MC) + \$196,000\ (ML)}{\$460,000\ (TC) + \$323,000\ (TL)} \times \$215,500\ (ABI) = \$112,291$$

M&P profit		$112,291	
Less amount subject to small business deduction		(30,000)	
Deduction—	13% ×	82,291	(10,698)
General rate reduction (see next paragraph)			(13,027)
			$ 35,876

Note that the M&P profit determined by the formula is $112,291, even though the manufacturing operation actually lost $32,000. This is so because the formula applies to the total active business income, including the retail income. The income eligible for the general rate reduction of 13% is $100,209 (taxable income of $227,500 minus [income eligible for the M&P deduction – $82,291; income eligible for the small business deduction – $30,000; aggregate investment income – $15,000]). The reduction is $13,027 (13% × $100,209).

PART IV TAX

Dividends from non-connected public corporation—33⅓% × $9,000	$3,000
Dividends from connected corporation, Q Ltd.—20% × $6,000	1,200
	$4,200

3. *Capital dividend account*

Opening	$ –0–
Add the non-taxable portions of:	
Eligible capital property gain—½ ($40,000)	20,000
Capital gain—½ ($20,000)	10,000
	$30,000

The balance in the capital dividend account can be distributed as a tax-free capital dividend if appropriate forms are filed. TL intends to declare a dividend of $80,000 and wants to minimize tax to the shareholder. Therefore, it should pay a capital dividend of $30,000 and the balance of $50,000 ($80,000 – $30,000) as a taxable dividend.

RDTOH

Opening	$ 3,000
Part IV tax	4,200
Refundable portion of Part I tax—the least of:	
26⅔% × $15,000 (aggregate investment income, above) = $4,000	
26⅔% × $197,500 (taxable income $227,500, minus $30,000	
of income subject to the small business deduction) = $52,667	
Part I tax = $35,876	
Least of	4,000
RDTOH end of year	$11,200

Dividend refund:

Least of:	
RDTOH, above—$11,200	
⅓ or 33⅓% × taxable dividend paid ($50,000) = $16,650	
Least of	$11,200

4. The General Rate Income Pool at the end of the current year is $112,400 calculated below. The intended taxable dividend for the current year is $50,000 so this amount can be designated as an eligible dividend to minimize the tax for the shareholder.

GRIP:

Balance at the end of the previous year		$ 12,000
Add:		
– 72% of:		
Taxable income	$227,500	
Less:		
Income subject to the small business deduction	(30,000)	
Aggregate investment income	(15,000)	
	$182,500	
72% × $182,500		131,400
– Eligible dividends received from public corporations		9,000
		152,400
Deduct:		
– Eligible dividends paid in the previous year		40,000
Balance at the end of the current year		$112,400

5. The sale of shares by Tallon's brother results in an *allowable business investment loss* of $15,000 (½ [$120,000 – $150,000]). This is so because over 90% of the company's assets are used in an active business, making the corporation qualify as a *small business corporation*. As the brother's income in 20X5 is $12,000, the loss of $15,000 creates a non-capital loss in 20X5 of $3,000 ($15,000 – $12,000). This loss can be carried back to 20X4 and recover taxes of $1,350 (45% × $3,000).

QUESTION TWO

Karen Toor owns and operates a retail store as a proprietorship. For the past several years, the store has earned annual profits of approximately $80,000. Toor is planning an expansion of the store. The expansion cost will be financed with a bank loan. Financial projections for the expanded store show that annual profits will increase to $140,000 annually.

Toor also has substantial income from bond investments. Consequently, her marginal tax rate (federal and provincial) is 45% on regular income and 33% on non-eligible taxable Canadian dividends.

In past years, most of the store profits had been used by Toor for personal spending. She estimates that in the future she will have to withdraw $50,000, after tax, from the business to meet her personal spending requirements.

Because of the anticipated increase in profits from the store expansion, Toor is considering incorporating the business. She wants to increase the after-tax profits so that the expansion bank loan can be paid down as quickly as possible. Toor has heard that incorporation can result in lower income taxes but is aware that double taxation may occur because of dividend payments to shareholders.

Required:

Will incorporation of the retail store increase the business's after-tax cash flow? If so, by how much? If the store is incorporated, will double taxation occur if dividends are paid to Toor in the future? Explain.

Solution:

If the retail store remains as a proprietorship, the annual after-tax cash flow available for reinvestment in the business (and to pay down the bank loan) will be $27,000, calculated as follows:

Projected business income	$140,000
Income tax @ 45%	(63,000)
Income after tax	77,000
Required by Toor for personal expenses	(50,000)
Available for business reinvestment	$ 27,000

If the business is transferred to a corporation owned by Toor, the first $500,000 of active business income will be taxed at 15% (depending on the provincial tax rate). After incorporation, Toor will have to extract funds from the company to meet her personal spending needs of $50,000 after tax. To achieve this, she can have the corporation pay her a salary of $91,000, which, after personal taxes at 45%, will leave her with approximately $50,000. The salary will reduce corporate profits to $49,000. The annual after-tax cash flow available to the corporation for reinvestment will be $41,650, as follows:

Projected income	$140,000
Less salary to owner	(91,000)
Net income	49,000
Corporate tax @ 15%	(7,350)
Available for business reinvestment	$ 41,650

Thus, incorporating the business will increase after-tax cash flow by $14,650 ($41,650 − $27,000).

If and when dividends are paid by the corporation, double-tax will not occur because the corporation's income is subject to the low corporate tax rate (15%). To demonstrate, assume that all of the after-tax corporate profits above are paid to the shareholder as a dividend. Her total tax on the $140,000 of business income earned is calculated below.

Tax paid by corporation on $49,000 of business income	$ 7,350
Tax paid by Toor on salary of $91,000	41,000
Tax paid by Toor on non-eligible dividend—33% × $41,650	13,745
Total tax	$62,095

As a proprietorship, Toor's tax on $140,000 is $63,000 (45% × $140,000), which is slightly higher than the $62,095 of total taxes paid under the corporate option.

QUESTION THREE

The following are three independent situations regarding loans by a Canadian-controlled private corporation to its shareholder.

1. X Inc. has a policy offering housing loans of up to $30,000 to its senior executives. Senior management consists of the president and three vice-presidents. The president is the sole shareholder of the corporation. To date, two vice-presidents have taken advantage of this policy. In the current year, X loaned $30,000 to the spouse of the president to assist with the down payment on a new home. The loan is repayable over 10 years with regular monthly installments but without interest.

2. Saul owns 8% of the common shares of P Inc. and is employed as the company's general manager. He is not related to any of the other shareholders. P offers loans to its senior employees of up to $10,000 with interest payable at the prescribed rate designated by CRA. Recently, Saul borrowed $10,000 and used the funds for a family holiday trip celebrating his 25th wedding anniversary. The loan is repayable over the following three years in equal quarterly installments.

3. Sonya operates an independent commercial insurance business. The business is incorporated and employs Sonya as the president and one other employee as Sonya's assistant. The corporation has a March 31 year end. In January 20X1, Sonya borrowed $200,000 from the corporation to purchase a summer cottage. The loan is repayable over 25 years with interest at a commercial rate.

Required:

For each of the above, discuss the tax implications of the loans by the corporations to the shareholders.

Solution:

1. Based on corporation's policy that all employees at a certain level are entitled to obtain a loan and the fact that non-shareholder employees have actually borrowed funds, it can be determined that the loans are based on an employee relationship rather than on a shareholder relationship. Therefore, the loan to the spouse of the president/shareholder meets one test for an extended shareholder loan. The second test—at the time the loan was made *bona fide* arrangements were made for repayment of the loan within a reasonable time—is also met as the loan is payable over a 10-year period in regular installments.[62]

   The lack of interest does not disqualify the principal from the benefit of the shareholder loan provisions that permit a loan to be made to acquire a home. However, the president will have to include an employee benefit for an interest-free loan, calculated using a prescribed rate of interest, in employment income for tax purposes each year.[63]

   If the two tests were not met, the $30,000 loan would be included in the spouse's property income for tax purposes since it was the spouse that received the loan.[64] If the loan is included in income, there is no shareholder or employee benefit for an interest-free loan.[65]

2. Although Saul is a shareholder/employee of the corporation, he is not a *specified employee* because he owns less than 10% of the common shares and apparently deals at arm's length with the corporation. Therefore, he is entitled to receive a loan from the corporation for any purpose provided that he received the loan because of his employment relationship and not because of his shareholder relationship, which appears to be the case. Also there are *bona fide* terms for repayment within a reasonable time in place at the time the loan is made. The loan has regular repayment requirements and the three-year term appears reasonable. Therefore, the $10,000 loan is not included in Saul's income for tax purposes.[66]

---

62 ITA 15(2.4)(b),(e),(f).
63 ITA 80.4(1).
64 ITA 15(2).
65 ITA 80.4(3)(b).
66 ITA 15(2.4)(a),(e),(f).

CRA will normally accept their prescribed rate of interest as reasonable and so no taxable benefit (shareholder or employee benefit for low-interest loans) will occur here.[67]

3. In Sonya's case, the terms of the shareholder loan appear to provide *bona fide* arrangements for repayment of the loan within a reasonable time, and the purpose of the loan qualifies for the shareholder extended loan provisions of the *Income Tax Act*.[68] However, it would be difficult for Sonya to argue that the loan is due to her employment position. As a sole shareholder in a company with only one other lower-level employee, it seems apparent that the loan is the result of her shareholder relationship. To have this loan accepted over a long term it would be necessary to establish that other Canadian-controlled private corporations provide loans of this magnitude to employees who are not shareholders. This would be very difficult. Therefore, Sonya must repay the loan by the end of the following taxation year of the corporation (March 31, 20X2) or the loan will be added to her income as property income in the calendar year the loan was made (20X1).[69] If this occurs she can, at a subsequent time, repay the loan and obtain a deduction from income in the year the loan is repaid.[70] If she wants to retain the loan funds on a permanent basis, Sonya should repay the loan within the one-year time limit and then pay the amount out again to herself as a dividend, getting the advantage of the dividend tax credit.

QUESTION FOUR

Q Inc. is a Canadian-controlled private corporation. In 20X9, Q received taxable Canadian dividends of $40,000 from the following:

PP Inc. – a public corporation	$ 5,000
TT Inc. – a CCPC	20,000
AB Inc. – a CCPC	15,000
	$40,000

Q owns 40% of the voting share capital of TT. In its 20X9 taxation year, TT paid a total dividend of $50,000. TT's refundable dividend tax on hand account at the time was $6,000.

Q owns 5% of the voting share capital of AB. In its 20X9 taxation year, AB paid a total dividend of $300,000. AB's refundable dividend tax on hand account at the time was $200,000.

Required:

Explain the tax treatment on the dividend income earned by Q in 20X9.

Solution:

The total dividend income of $40,000 is included in Q's net income for tax purposes. However, the entire amount is deducted from net income for tax purposes to arrive at taxable income.[71] Therefore, there is no tax under Part I of the *Income Tax Act*. However, Q, being a private corporation, is subject to Part IV tax on the dividends.

All of the dividends from PP (public corporations) are subject to the refundable Part IV tax. The tax is $1,667 (33 1/3% × $5,000).[72]

TT is connected with Q because Q owns more than 10% of the voting shares of TT.[73] As a connected corporation, the basic rule is that dividends received are not subject to a Part IV tax. However, if the connected corporation receives a refund from its refundable dividend tax on hand account (RDTOH) as a result of the dividend paid, the corporation receiving the dividend must pay a Part IV tax equal to its percentage share of that refund.[74] In this case,

---

67 ITA 80.4(1),(2),(3).
68 ITA 15(2.4)(b).
69 ITA 15(2.6).
70 ITA 20(1)(j).
71 ITA 112(1).
72 ITA 186(1)(a).
73 ITA 186(4).
74 ITA 186(1)(b).

TT received a refund of $6,000 [the lesser of the balance in the RDTOH account ($6,000) or 1/3 of the dividend paid (1/3 × $50,000 = $16,667)].[75] So Q must pay a part IV tax of $2,400 being 40% (Q's ownership percentage) of TT's total refund of $6,000.

AB is not connected with Q because Q owns only 5% of AB's voting shares. Therefore, Q must pay a Part IV tax on the total dividend received from AB − 1/3 × $15,000 = $5,000.[76] The amount of AB's refund from RDTOH account is not relevant here.

Review Questions

1. Explain why a Canadian corporation whose voting share capital is owned 50% by Canadian residents and 50% by non-residents is classified as a Canadian-controlled private corporation.

2. Canadian-controlled private corporations differ from public corporations in the rate of tax, the extent of double taxation, and the degree of secondary relationships with shareholders. Briefly describe these differences.

3. "A business that derives its income from selling personal services (plumbing repairs, for example) cannot be viewed as earning active business income." Is this statement true? Explain. How is a personal services business different from an active business?

4. Why may a Canadian-controlled private corporation that earns business income of $100,000 in year 1 and $500,000 in year 2 (total: $600,000) pay less tax than a corporation earning $50,000 in year 1 and $550,000 in year 2 (total: $600,000)?

5. In question 4, what might the latter corporation be able to do to ensure that it pays the same amount of tax as the first corporation? If these options are, in fact, available, what other factors must be considered before a decision is made to take such actions?

6. "The use of the small business deduction by a Canadian-controlled private corporation does not result in a tax saving; rather, it creates a tax deferral." Explain.

7. Interest income and/or rental income earned by one Canadian-controlled private corporation may be treated as specified investment business income. At the same time, income from the same source(s) earned by another Canadian-controlled private corporation may be treated as active business income. Why is this? And to what extent will the rate of tax applied to that income be different for the two corporations?

8. Identify and briefly explain the mechanism that is used to reduce the incidence of double taxation when specified investment business income is distributed by a Canadian-controlled private corporation to its shareholders.

9. Does double taxation occur when a Canadian-controlled private corporation earns capital gains and distributes those gains as dividends to individual shareholders? Explain.

10. "An investor can achieve a tax deferral on portfolio dividends received from public corporation shares if those shares are owned by his or her private corporation." Is this statement true? Explain.

11. There are several advantages to deferring tax by utilizing the small business deduction. Briefly state two of them.

12. A Canadian-controlled private corporation can obtain a tax deferral from the small business deduction. Will the corporation's owner always benefit from investing the extra cash flow that results, regardless of the type of return that may be received from the investment? Explain.

---

75 ITA 129(1).
76 ITA 186(1)(a).

13. Briefly state the advantages and disadvantages of earning investment income in a Canadian-controlled private corporation.

14. Why may it be worthwhile for a corporation to pay an additional salary or bonus to its shareholder/manager, even though he or she does not require additional funds?

15. Is it possible for a shareholder to obtain personal use of corporate funds without first declaring a dividend or salary? Explain.

16. Individual A is about to acquire 30% of the shares of a new corporation (a Canadian-controlled private corporation) that will carry on an active business. The remaining 70% of the shares will be owned by X Corporation, a company that also owns an active business. What concern should individual A have regarding the tax treatment of the new corporation's income?

Key Concept Questions

QUESTION ONE

Determine the type of business income being earned by each of the following Canadian-controlled private corporations. *Income tax reference: ITA 125(7), 129(6).*

a) Corporation A earns interest and dividends from numerous Canadian corporations. Corporation A employs three full-time employees.

b) Corporation B earns rental income from leasing automobiles.

c) Corporation C carries on a wholesaling business. In the current year Corporation C earned interest income on overdue accounts receivable in addition to income from the wholesaling business.

d) Corporation D earns interest income from numerous sources. Corporation D employs 10 full-time employees.

e) Corporation E earns consulting income from services provided to X Ltd. Eddy is the sole shareholder and the only employee of E Ltd. Eddy was previously employed by X Ltd. as VP operations.

f) Corporation F provides consulting services to several clients. Fred is the sole shareholder and only employee of Corporation F.

g) Corporation G earns interest income on a loan to an associated corporation. The interest was deducted in computing the active business income of the associated corporation that carries on an active business.

QUESTION TWO

Can Corp., a Canadian-controlled private corporation, has net income and taxable income of $100,000 for the current year. The income is specified investment income. *Income tax reference: ITA 123(1), 124(1), 123.3.*

Determine the federal Part I tax payable.

QUESTION THREE

A Canadian private corporation incurred the following transactions in previous years:

- In 1997, sold a capital asset that resulted in a capital gain of $12,000.

- In 2004, sold a capital asset that resulted in a capital loss of $4,000.

- In 2005, paid a capital dividend of $1,000.

- In 2007, eligible capital property was purchased for $20,000. A CECA deduction of $1,050 was claimed on the corporate tax return.

- In 2008, the eligible capital property was sold for $28,000.
- In 2009, received life insurance proceeds of $50,000. The policy had an adjusted cost base of $10,000.

In the current year, a capital dividend of $15,000 was received. *Income tax reference: ITA 89(1).*

Determine the current balance in the capital dividend account based on the above information.

QUESTION FOUR

Black Ltd., a Canadian private corporation, owns 40% of the voting shares of White Ltd. In the current year, White paid a dividend of $60,000, which triggered a dividend refund of $20,000 to White. Black also received dividends of $40,000 from its wholly-owned subsidiary, Red Ltd., and dividends of $30,000 from sundry Canadian public corporations in which Black owns less than 1% of the issued shares. Red carries on an active business and, thus, did not receive a dividend refund. *Income tax reference: ITA 186(1), (2), (4).*

Determine the refundable Part IV tax payable by Black Ltd. for the current year.

QUESTION FIVE

On March 1, 20X7, Martin received an interest-free loan from his employer, X Ltd., a private corporation, owned by his wife. Martin used the loan to purchase the condominium in which he lives. A loan agreement was signed by Martin agreeing to repay the loan in full after three years. Such a loan is not available to other employees. X Ltd. has a June 30 year end. *Income tax reference: ITA 15(2), (2.1), (2.4), (2.6), 20(1)(j), 80.4(3).*

Determine the tax implications of the loan for Martin.

QUESTION SIX

Howard owns 2% of the shares of Y Ltd. He is also employed by Y in a middle management position. On August 1, 20X7, Howard received a loan from Y that he used to repay personal debts. Howard signed a loan agreement, agreeing to pay interest on the loan at the bank prime rate in effect on August 1, 20X7 and to repay the loan over three years by monthly payroll deductions. Similar loans have been made in the past to mid-level management employees. Y has a December 31 year end. *Income tax reference: ITA 15(2), (2.4), (2.6), 80.4(3).*

Determine the tax implications of the loan for Howard.

QUESTION SEVEN

Consider each of the following unrelated situations.

1) Sally owns 80% of the issued share of Salt Ltd. and 20% of the issued shares of Pepper Ltd. Her friend owns the remaining 20% of Salt Ltd. and 80% of Pepper Ltd.

2) Bob owns 70% of the issued shares of B Ltd. that in turn owns 40% of the shares of X Ltd. Bob's father owns the remaining 60% of the shares of X Ltd.

3) Glen and his brother each own 50% of the shares of A Ltd. Glen's son owns 50% of the shares of B Ltd. The remaining shares of B Ltd. are owned equally by Glen and his father.

4) Wayne owns 100% of the share of W Ltd. His son, Stephen, owns 100% of the common shares of S Ltd. Wayne owns 100% of the preference shares of S Ltd. The preferred shares are non-voting, have a fixed dividend rate (4%), have an issue price of $1,000 per share and are redeemable at $1,000 per share. The prescribed rate was 5% when the shares were issued.

For each situation, determine whether the two corporations are associated and if so, state the paragraph in S.256(1) which makes them associated. Income tax reference: *ITA 256(1), (1.1), (1.2)*.

QUESTION EIGHT

TV Ltd. is a Canadian-controlled private corporation. The taxable income for its current year has been correctly calculated below.

Business income profits	$440,000
Taxable capital gains	100,000
Taxable dividends from Canadian public corporations	24,000
Interest on five-year bonds	10,000
Net income for tax purposes	574,000
Dividends	(24,000)
Net capital losses	(30,000)
Non-capital losses	(20,000)
Taxable income	$500,000

TV Ltd and Nano Ltd. are associated corporations. For the current year, Nano Ltd. claimed the small business deduction on $120,000 of its active business income. The taxable capital of the two corporations, combined, is below $10,000,000. *Income tax reference: ITA 125(1), (2), (3)*.

Determine the small business deduction for TV Ltd.

QUESTION NINE

Using the information provided in Question Eight, determine TV Ltd.'s refundable tax on investment income. *Income tax reference: ITA 123.3, 129(4)*.

QUESTION TEN

Using the information provided in Question Eight, determine TV Ltd.'s general rate reduction. *Income tax reference: ITA 123.4(1)*.

QUESTION ELEVEN

TV Ltd. has Part I tax payable for the current year of $68,133. TV Ltd. had a balance in its refundable dividend tax on hand (RDTOH) account at the end of the previous year of $27,000. TV Ltd. calculated a dividend refund of $6,000 for the previous year, based on dividends paid in the previous year. Using the information provided in Question Eight, determine TV Ltd.'s RDTOH balance at the end of the current year. *Income tax reference: ITA 129(3), 186(1)*.

QUESTION TWELVE

Assume TV Ltd. has a RDTOH balance of $50,333 at the end of the current year, and that taxable dividends of $90,000 and tax-free capital dividends of $30,000 were paid in the current year. *Income tax reference: ITA 129(3)*.

Determine the dividend refund for the current year.

QUESTION THIRTEEN

EX Ltd. is a Canadian-controlled private corporation operating a retail business in Canada. For the current year EX Ltd. has net income of $662,000 and taxable income of $600,000. Included in net income are taxable capital gains of $46,000 and interest from Canadian sources of $30,000 as well as $42,000 of dividends from Canadian public companies. Net capital losses of $20,000 were deducted in computing taxable income. EX Ltd. is claiming a small business deduction of $85,000 ($500,000 × 17%), which reduces the Part I tax payable to $204,433. The RDTOH balance at the end of the previous year was $12,000. During the current year taxable dividends of $27,000 were paid. Dividends were not paid in the previous year. *Income tax reference: ITA 129(1), (3), (4), 186(1).*

Determine the dividend refund for EX Ltd. for the current year.

QUESTION FOURTEEN

Ready Ltd. is a Canadian-controlled private corporation operating a business. Ready Ltd. is not associated with any other corporation and its taxable capital is under $10,000,000. For its current year ended, its records showed the following amounts:

Income from retail business	$600,000
Interest income	10,000
Eligible dividend received from a Canadian company	40,000
Net income	650,000
Dividend	(40,000)
Taxable income	$610,000

Ready Ltd. has not paid dividends in the last few years and had a general rate income pool (GRIP) account balance of $50,000 at the end of the previous year. *Income tax reference: ITA 89(1)—definition of GRIP.*

Determine the GRIP account balance at the end of the current year.

QUESTION FIFTEEN

Hitech Ltd., a Canadian-controlled private corporation, spent $1,000,000 in current expenditures for scientific research and experimental development (SR&ED), as well as $500,000 in capital expenditures for SR&ED in the current year. Hitech Ltd. is not associated with any other corporation. Its taxable income for the previous year was $120,000, which resulted in federal tax payable of $13,200. There was no tax payable for the two years before that. The taxable capital is below $10,000,000. Taxable income for the current year is $100,000.

Determine the following:

(a) The investment tax credit earned by Hitech Ltd.

(b) The cash refund available due to the investment tax credit.

(c) The investment tax credit available for carry over.

Problems

PROBLEM ONE

John Basler is employed in the transportation industry and earns a substantial salary. His personal marginal tax rate is 45% (federal and provincial).

He also owns 100% of the shares of Truck Ltd. The corporation is a 20% partner in a small trucking business. In 20X1, the partnership earned a net profit of $80,000.

Basler intends to do some consulting work starting in 20X2 while continuing in his present employment. A small trucking company has requested that he provide advice on how to set up a proper accounting system. He would be paid on a fee-for-service basis. The contract, if he accepts it, would likely last for two years and earn him $20,000 per year. It would also use up his entire available consulting time. In the future, he may accept two or three smaller contracts a year.

Basler has requested advice on whether he should incorporate his proposed consulting activities. He has indicated that he will not require the income for personal use and intends to invest the after-tax profits.

Required:

1. What are the tax benefits, if any, to Basler if he incorporates his consulting activities? Provide any appropriate calculations.

2. Would your answer change if Basler required all of the income for personal use? Show calculations.

3. Should Basler incorporate a separate company or simply use his existing company?

PROBLEM TWO

Ruth Delaney owns all of the common shares of Delaney Fast Food Services Ltd. In addition, she has several investments that generate reasonable annual cash returns, as follows:

	Income
Corporate bonds	$ 5,000
Land and building	10,000
Shares of public corporations	8,000

The property has the following relevant values:

	Cost	UCC	Fair market value
Land	$30,000	$ –0–	$ 50,000
Building	70,000	50,000	95,000
Shares	75,000	–0–	105,000
Corporate bonds	40,000	–0–	42,000

Delaney has expressed an interest in using a corporation to hold her investments and has sought your advice. She has suggested that the investments could be transferred to Delaney Fast Food Services, which operates three restaurants.

Delaney's marginal tax rate is 45% (federal and provincial) on regular income, 28% on eligible dividends and 33% on non-eligible dividends. The provincial corporate tax rate in her province is 10%. To date, she has not used any of her lifetime capital gain deduction.

Required:

1. Advise Delaney on the benefits, if any, of incorporating her investment income. Show sample calculations. Your answer should be specific with respect to (a) interest and rents, (b) capital gains, and (c) dividends.

2. Discuss the implications of Delaney's suggestion regarding transferring the investments to her active business corporation.

3. Assuming that she decides to incorporate the investments, outline a plan that will enable the investments to be transferred to the corporation without tax consequences.

PROBLEM THREE

Investco Ltd., a private corporation, received dividend income from taxable Canadian corporations during its year ended December 31, 20X6, as follows:

Portfolio dividends from public corporations	$60,000
Dividends from Subsidiary	30,000
	$90,000

Investco Ltd. owns 80% of the issued shares of Subsidiary. Subsidiary's dividend refund for its year ended December 31, 20X6 was $4,000.

Required:
Calculate the Part IV tax payable by Investco Ltd. for its year ended December 31, 20X6.

PROBLEM FOUR

Canco Ltd. is a Canadian-controlled private corporation. For its fiscal year ended December 31, 20X6, Canco Ltd. had income of $100,000, comprised as follows:

• Interest income	$20,000
• Taxable capital gains	30,000
• Taxable dividends received from	
• A Ltd.	40,000
• B Ltd.	10,000

During the same year Canco Ltd. paid taxable dividends of $16,000 and capital dividends of $4,000.

Canco Ltd. owns 40% of the issued shares of A Ltd. and 5% of the issued shares of B Ltd. A Ltd. received a dividend refund of $20,000 and B Ltd. received a dividend refund of $8,000 as a result of paying dividends during their respective taxation years ended December 31, 20X6.

Required:
Determine the dividend refund for Canco Ltd. for its 20X6 taxation year. Assume the balance in its RDTOH account at January 1, 20X6 was nil.

PROBLEM FIVE

Wrap Ltd. is a Canadian-controlled private corporation. At the end of 20X5, Wrap had the following tax account balances:

• Non-capital losses	$ 8,000
• Net capital losses (incurred in 20X3)	2,000
• RDTOH	7,000
• Dividend refund	1,000
• CDA	12,000

For the current year, 20X6, net income for tax purposes is $261,000. Included in this amount is the following:

• Income from an active business carried on in Canada	$200,000
• Taxable capital gain	6,000
• Dividends from Canadian public companies	15,000
• Canadian bond interest	30,000
• Foreign bond interest	10,000

The following is a summary of other information for Wrap Ltd. for the 20X6 year:

• Taxable income	$236,000
• Capital dividend paid	12,000
• Taxable dividend paid	75,000
• Small business deduction	34,000
• Foreign tax credit—non-business income	1,000
• Total Federal Part I tax payable	33,480

Required:
Determine the dividend refund for 20X6. Would the dividend refund change if Wrap Ltd. was not a CCPC but instead was a private corporation or a public corporation?

PROBLEM SIX

Quality Quo is a Canadian-controlled private corporation, (CCPC), carrying on business in Canada. For its year ended December 31, 20X6 Quality Quo earned income from the following sources:

> Active business income
> Gain on sale of asset used in the active business
> Dividends from taxable Canadian corporations

Quality Quo is associated with one corporation, Pear Inc. Pear Inc. was allocated a Business Limit of $160,000 for 20X6. The taxable capital of the two corporations, Quality Quo and Pear Inc., combined is less than $10,000,000.

Required:
Describe in detail how each source of income is taxed federally.

PROBLEM SEVEN

Pembroke Realtors Ltd. is a closely held Canadian-controlled private corporation. At the end of 20X2, during which it earned an unusually high profit, the corporation paid additional salaries of $200,000 to its officers, who are also the shareholders. The salaries were paid in proportion to each shareholder's holdings in the corporation.

After reviewing the transaction, the CRA proposed to disallow $60,000 of the $200,000 salaries as an expense for tax purposes.

Required:

1. On what basis may the CRA justify such a proposal?

2. If the $60,000 is properly disallowed, what impact will it have on the shareholders who received the salary? Explain.

PROBLEM EIGHT

Joe Crum is a restaurant consultant and also owns two restaurants. His corporate structure and activities are outlined below.

Crum Restaurants Ltd.
- Owned 100% by Crum.
- Owns and operates Crum Slow Foods.
- Provides consulting services to a large number of small restaurants.
- Provides managerial and administrative services to Hamburger Joint Ltd., a company owned 15% by Joe Crum.
- 20X1 income is as follows:

Consulting services	$ 10,000
Managerial services (Hamburger Ltd.)	35,000
Crum Slow Foods	60,000
	$105,000

Pecky's Restaurant Ltd.
- Owned 100% by Crum Restaurants Ltd.
- Owns and operates Pecky's Coffee Shop.
- 20X1 income is $440,000.

Real Co. Ltd.
- Owned 51% by Crum and 49% by his wife.
- Owns several commercial and residential real estate properties, including the building occupied by Pecky's.
- 20X1 income is as follows:

Rents:	
Outside parties	$40,000
Pecky's Coffee Shop	10,000
	$50,000

Required:

1. Diagram the organization structure of Crum's financial activities.

2. Describe the type of income each entity earns, and explain the related tax treatment.

3. Identify any problems that the existing structure may present, and suggest changes that you feel would be appropriate. If you are suggesting structural changes, briefly explain how they would be accomplished.

PROBLEM NINE

CKG Ltd. is a Canadian-controlled private corporation owned equally by Mr. and Mrs. Ducharme. The company has been profitable for several years, largely because of the efforts of the Ducharmes, who both participate actively in the management of the business.

The current year's business profit, before taxes, is expected to be $540,000. This is a record high for the company and is $50,000 higher than in the previous year. Over the past two years, the company has built up substantial cash reserves. The Ducharmes are considering using the funds as follows:

- A competitor wants to sell out and has offered to sell its shares to CKG for $500,000. The following summary of the competitor's most recent operating results was provided to the Ducharmes:

Sales	$850,000
Cost of sales	378,000
Gross profit	472,000
Operating expenses	370,000
Income	102,000
Income taxes	(15,300)
Net income	$ 86,700

- The Ducharmes recently agreed to purchase a large new personal residence, which they will take possession of in two months. They have not yet sold their existing home, but when they do, they will need an additional $100,000 to complete the purchase.

The Ducharmes feel that CKG has sufficient resources to fund both of the above transactions. They are particularly interested in purchasing the competitor's business and feel that the purchase price of $500,000 is reasonable, as it will provide an after-tax return on investment of 17% ($86,700 ÷ $500,000).

Both Ducharmes are paid an annual salary of $130,000.

Required:

1. Comment on the purchase of the competitor's business by CKG.

2. What methods should CKG use to provide funds to the Ducharmes so that they can meet their cash needs in acquiring their new home? Explain.

PROBLEM TEN

Carol Stoller is the president and sole shareholder of Modern Floors Ltd., a Canadian-controlled private corporation based in your province. It is one month before the company's year end, and Stoller is reviewing the company's financial information. The operating results, to date, are good, and her accountant has projected the following results to the end of the fiscal year:

Sales		$1,400,000
Cost of sales		740,000
Gross profit		660,000
Expenses:		
Salaries and wages	100,000	
Rent and utilities	19,000	
Amortization	8,000	
Travel and delivery	17,000	
Insurance	3,000	
Reserve for doubtful debts	22,000	
Advertising	15,000	
Charitable donations	5,000	
Other	6,000	195,000
Operating income		465,000
Other income:		
Interest on bonds	15,000	
Dividends from taxable Canadian public corporations	8,000	
Capital gain on the sale of securities	40,000	63,000
Net income before tax		$ 528,000

In preparing the year-end projection, the accountant determined the ending inventory based on an estimated value at the lower of cost or market (which is $20,000 lower than the estimate of the inventories cost). Amortization is equal to CCA for tax purposes.

Stoller has noticed that the financial statement does not provide an estimate of the company's tax liability and has asked her accountant to provide this. Also, the following two developments have taken place that may affect the company's tax position as well as Stoller's personal tax position:

- Modern Floors has signed a long-term contract to supply products to a large national chain organization. The contract will begin early in the new year. Operating profits for next year will increase by approximately $180,000.

- Stoller has decided to sell 30% of her common shares in the company to a senior manager for $400,000. She originally purchased the entire share capital of the company seven years ago for $100,000.

While Stoller is pleased with these developments, she is also concerned about their tax consequences. She understands that corporate tax rates increase when a certain level of income is reached. Stoller has never sold any capital property before but is aware that a friend of hers recently sold the shares of his corporation and was entitled to claim a capital gain deduction of $750,000. Stoller now asks you to address these issues and explain what steps, if any, she can take to minimize the overall tax impact on the company and on herself.

Stoller's personal marginal tax rate is 45%. Assume a provincial corporate general rate of 10% and a small business income rate of 4%.

Required:

1. For the current taxation year, determine the following for Modern Floors: (a) net income for tax purposes; (b) taxable income; and (c) federal and provincial tax payable.

2. Explain to Stoller the tax impact of the projected higher corporate profits for next year.

3. Identify any actions which the corporation can take this year or next year that will be advantageous for the corporation and/or Stoller.

4. Describe the tax consequences to Stoller arising from the proposed sale of shares. What steps, if any, can she take to minimize any potential tax on the sale?

PROBLEM ELEVEN

Cinder Inc. is a Canadian-controlled private corporation based in your province. The company operates a wholesale business. The following information is provided for its year ended May 31, 20X5:

1. Net income for tax purposes is $212,000. Included in this amount is the following:

• Interest income from bonds	$10,000
• Interest income on overdue trade accounts receivable	1,000
• Taxable capital gain on sale of land	14,000
• Dividends from Canadian public corporations	12,000
• Dividends from PQ Ltd. (see item 2 below)	6,000

2. PQ Ltd. is a Canadian-controlled private corporation. Cinder owns 60% of its common voting shares. In 20X5, PQ claimed the small business deduction on $320,000 of its active business income. PQ paid a dividend of $10,000, of which Cinder's share is $6,000 (60%). As a result of the dividend, PQ received a dividend refund of $1,000.

3. Cinder made contributions of $4,000 to registered charities. This amount has been correctly adjusted for in computing net income for tax purposes.

4. At the end of 20X4, Cinder had the following tax account balances:

• Non-capital losses	$5,000
• Refundable dividend tax on hand	2,000

5. On May 31, 20X5, Cinder paid a dividend of $20,000 to its shareholders.

Required:
Determine Cinder's federal income tax for the 20X5 taxation year.

PROBLEM TWELVE

TR Ltd. is a Canadian-controlled private corporation operating a franchised retail and mail-order business in Vancouver. Denver Chan, the company's president, owns 100% of the corporation's share capital. The corporation was created on December 1, 20X5. For the year ended November 30, 20X6, TR Ltd.'s financial statement reported income before income taxes of $126,000.

You have been retained to help prepare the company's first tax return and to advise on other tax-related matters. Financial information relating to the 20X6 taxation year and to the corporation's financial statement is summarized below.

TR Ltd.
Selected Financial Information

1. The following properties were purchased for the new business:

Franchise	$ 40,000
Land	30,000
Building	270,000
Delivery truck	40,000

The franchise, purchased on December 1, 20X5, permits the corporation to operate under the TR name for a period of 15 years. A renewable period of another 15 years is available, subject to satisfactory performance.

The land cost of $30,000 consists of the purchase price of $20,000, $7,000 for permanent landscaping, and $3,000 for water and sewer connections. The building was constructed after March 18, 2007.

On October, 15, 20X6, the truck was involved in an accident. The damage was not repairable, and TR immediately signed an agreement with the insurance company to settle the claim for $31,000. The cash was received on December 10, 20X6. Another truck was obtained under a lease arrangement.

Amortization expense of $28,000 has been deducted from income.

2. Legal expense includes the following costs:

Preparing annual corporate minutes	$ 300
Incorporation costs for TR Ltd.	1,500
Negotiation of franchise agreement	2,000

3. Repairs and maintenance expense includes the following items:

Paving the parking lot	$8,000
Cleaning and supplies	1,400
Replacing a broken window	1,000
Small tools costing less than $500	1,200

4. Advertising expense includes a cost of $7,000 to acquire a permanent mailing list for the mail-order business. The list has an expected life of six years. Other advertising items are listed below.

Cost of making a television commercial	$25,000
Travel costs for Chan to attend a franchiser convention. Chan's spouse travelled with him and attended a social function (her expenses were $1,500)	3,000
Charitable donations	2,000
Meals and beverage costs for entertaining suppliers	1,800
Costs of leasing and maintaining a pleasure boat to entertain suppliers and employees	2,600
Television advertising	
Vancouver station	11,000
Seattle station directed at the Vancouver market	6,000

5. A contingent reserve for possible defective products of $5,000 was recorded as a charge against cost of sales. During the year, $3,000 of products were returned.

6. On May 31, 20X6, TR invested $40,000 in a one-year bank certificate earning annual interest of 7%. TR intends to recognize the interest revenue upon receipt at its one-year anniversary date.

7. Interest expense includes $14,000 on the building mortgage and $700 from a temporary bank loan of $12,000. The bank loan funds were, in turn, loaned, without interest, to Y Ltd., a corporation owned by Chan's brother. Y Ltd. used all of its assets to operate an active business but declared bankruptcy in November 20X6.

8. TR is planning to sell a new product in 20X7—a bracelet with a charm depicting a popular cartoon character. The bracelet and charm will be ordered from separate suppliers, and TR's staff will assemble the two pieces and package them in a specially designed box.

9. Shortly after incorporation, TR acquired 46% of the voting common shares of Q Ltd., a Canadian-controlled private corporation that supplies certain products to TR and other retailers. On October 31, 20X6, TR received a dividend of $15,000 from Q Ltd. At the time, Q Ltd. had an RDTOH account of $2,000.

    An opportunity exists for TR to purchase an additional 5% of the voting common shares of Q Ltd. early in 20X7. A decision will be made in January 20X7.

10. On November 30, 20X6, TR declared and paid a taxable dividend of $40,000.

Required:

1. Under Part I of the *Income Tax Act*, determine the *minimum income for tax purposes* and *taxable income* for TR Ltd. for the 20X6 taxation year.

2. Based on your answer to 1, calculate TR's *minimum Part I and Part IV federal income tax* for the 20X6 taxation year.

3. Briefly describe the tax consequences, if any, if TR Ltd. purchases the additional 5% of the shares of Q Ltd. in January 20X7.

4. Advise TR Ltd. on the tax implications, if any, of selling its new charm bracelet in the 20X7 taxation year.

PROBLEM THIRTEEN

Dave owns 100% of the issued shares of D Ltd. His wife, Mary, owns 100% of the issued shares of M Ltd.

D Ltd. owns 48% of the shares of X Ltd. while M Ltd. own only 5% of the shares of X Ltd. The remaining 47% of the shares are owned by strangers.

Dave and Mary have a 32-year-old son, Sam. He owns 100% of the issued shares of S Ltd. Sam's cousin, Ben, and S Ltd. each own 50% of the issued shares of Y Ltd.

All of the corporations are Canadian-controlled private corporations and all of the issued shares are common shares.

Required:

1. Which of the individuals and/or corporations are related persons, as defined in the *Income Tax Act*?

2. Which of the corporations are associated corporations, as defined in the *Income Tax Act*?

3. Which of the corporations are connected corporations, as defined in the *Income Tax Act*?

4. Which of the individuals and/or corporations are affiliated persons, as defined in the *Income Tax Act*?

PROBLEM FOURTEEN

Each of the following cases is independent.

1. Edward and Kris are unrelated individuals. Edward owns 80% of the issued shares of E Ltd. and 25% of the issued shares of Pro Ltd. Kris owns 20% of the issued shares of E Ltd. and 75% of the issued shares of Pro Ltd.

2. Jeremy owns 100% of the issued shares of J Ltd. which in turn owns 55% of the issued shares of K Ltd.

3. Al and Kevin are brothers. Al owns 100% of the issued shares of A Ltd. and 25% of the issued shares of K Ltd. The remaining shares of K Ltd. are owned by Kevin.

4. Robert and Raymond are brothers. They each own 50% of the issued shares of Barone Ltd. Raymond and his wife, Debra, each own 50% of the issued shares of Tee Ltd.

5. Kim and Kristin are cousins. They each own 35% of the issued shares of K Ltd. Their grandmother, Anna owns 100% of the issued shares of A Ltd. and the remaining 30% of the issued shares of K Ltd.

6. Clarence owns 100% of the issued shares of C Ltd. His two sons, Robert and Raymond, each own 50% of the issued common shares of R Ltd. Clarence helped finance R Ltd. by purchasing preference shares of R Ltd. The preference shares were issued to Clarence for $100,000 and are redeemable for the same amount. The preference shares are non-voting and have a non-cumulative dividend fixed at 3%, the prescribed rate in effect at the time the shares were issued. Clarence is the only owner of preference shares.

Required:

Determine which of the above corporations are associated. Support your answer with a reference from section 256 of the *Income Tax Act*.

PROBLEM FIFTEEN

Each of the following six situations is independent. Assume all individuals are over the age of 18 unless otherwise noted.

1. Susan owns 100% of her holding company, Susan Inc., which owns 43% of the issued common shares of Sumi Inc. Mike owns 8% of Sumi, and Agnes, an unrelated individual, owns the remaining 49% of Sumi. Susan and Mike are siblings.

2. Vicki owns 75% of the common shares of Vicki Inc. with the other 25% being owned by an unrelated individual. Marc owns 55% of Marc Inc. with the other 45% of the common shares owned by Vicki Inc. Vicki is Marc's mother.

3. Matt, Bill, and Marg are brothers and sister. Each owns $1/3$ of the shares of Sibling Inc. Carol and Matt are married to each other and each owns 50% of the shares of Spouses Inc.

4. Connie owns 100% of the common shares of Connie Inc. Aileen owns 100% of the common shares of Aileen Inc. with a current value of $350,000. Connie, who is Aileen's husband's grandmother, lent $190,000 to Aileen Inc. in June, 1998. The loan bears interest at the current bank rate plus $1/2$% and is due on demand.

5. Andrew and Cheryl are first cousins and each owns 50% of the common shares of Breton Inc. The value of a 50% shareholding of Breton Inc. is $45,000. Arch owns 100% of the common shares of Arch Inc. Arch is Andrew and Cheryl's grandfather and owns the one and only non-voting redeemable preference share in Breton Inc. which was issued for $50,000 in March 1995. The preferred share is redeemable at $100,000. (The preference share is not a share of a specified class as defined in S.256(1.1)). At all relevant times during the company's taxation year the value of the preference share was $100,000 and the value of all the Breton Inc. common shares was $90,000.

6. Jeff and Valerie are spouses who each own 100% of their respective companies, Jeff Inc. and Valerie Inc. Chelsea Inc. is 100% owned by Chelsea. Chelsea is Jeff's and Valerie's 16-year-old daughter.

Required:

In each of situations outline the reasons why any of the corporations are associated. Support your answer with references from the *Income Tax Act*. Assume that there is no indirect influence which, if exercised, could result in *de facto* control except in situation 4. Also, assume the anti-avoidance provision ITA 256(2.1) would not apply to otherwise deem the companies to be associated.

PROBLEM SIXTEEN

Each of the following three situations is independent.

1. Len is an employee and the sole shareholder of Laser Ltd. On July 1, 20X6 Len entered into a loan agreement with Laser Ltd. wherein Laser Ltd. agreed to loan $30,000 at 3% interest to Len to enable him to purchase a car to be used in carrying out his duties of employment. The loan is to be repaid in full at the end of three years. The interest is to be paid annually. Although Laser Ltd. has 65 employees, Laser Ltd. has never made a car loan to any other employee. Laser Ltd. has a June 30 year end.

2. Karen is a shareholder and key employee of X Ltd., a CCPC with a November 30, fiscal year end. Karen's daughter, age 19, a full-time student at the University of Toronto, received an interest-free loan of $10,000 from X Ltd. on December 31, 20X6 to pay her tuition. The loan is repayable in full in 20X9, one year after she graduates.

3. Wayne Fry is a 60% shareholder and president of Attack Ltd., a Canadian-controlled private corporation with a November 30th year end. On March 1, 20X6, Wayne received a $300,000 loan from Attack Ltd. to assist him with the purchase of a new home, located 10 km from his previous home. The loan is repayable over five years in equal instalments of principal payable on the anniversary date. The loan has an interest rate of 1% per annum. The interest is payable monthly.

Required:

What are the tax implications for the individuals receiving the loans? Assume the prescribed rates of interest were as follows:

	20X6	20X7
Jan – Mar	3%	5%
Apr – June	3%	5%
July – Sept	4%	5%
Oct – Nov	4%	5%

Cases

CASE ONE   Hockey Facilities

Don Cameron operates Hockey Facilities as a sole proprietorship. The operations consist of two retail outlets that sell all types of hockey equipment, as well as a separate manufacturing facility that manufactures the famous Slap Shot hockey stick.

Financial information for the most recent 12-month period is outlined in Exhibits I and II on the following pages.

In addition to the income derived from Hockey Facilities, Cameron has substantial investments that generate high returns. The investment income by itself has put Cameron in the top marginal tax bracket of 45%. That income consists of dividends from shares of public corporations and interest on bonds.

As the proprietor, Cameron draws funds from Hockey Facilities to pay his personal expenses and income taxes. He usually requires $40,000 annually for living expenses exclusive of any income taxes.

You have recently met with Cameron to discuss the possibility of incorporating Hockey Facilities' business operations. At the meeting, Cameron provided you with the following additional information:

1. Expected profits from Hockey Facilities are as follows:

20X2	$475,000
20X3	520,000
20X4	570,000

2. The assets described in the attached balance sheet have the following current fair market values:

Current assets	$300,000
Land	150,000
Buildings	400,000
Equipment	100,000
Licence	120,000
Goodwill	200,000

3. The undepreciated capital cost of depreciable property at December 31, 20X1, after current capital cost allowance, is as follows:

Buildings	$240,000
Equipment	90,000
Licence	70,000

4. The cumulative eligible capital account at December 31, 20X1, amounted to $22,000 after the 20X1 deduction.

5. The financial statements include amortization at an amount equal to the available capital cost allowance.

6. Cameron does not have a detailed breakdown of manufacturing profits and retail profits, although he estimates the retail profits to be $100,000.

Cameron is confused about how a corporate structure would be worthwhile and is concerned that, according to what he had heard, double taxation might result in certain circumstances.

Cameron's son Eric is 23 years old and is actively involved in the business, earning a salary of $40,000 annually. Eric has spent most of his time at the manufacturing plant but intends to become involved in the retail operations as well. Cameron looks at the manufacturing activity as a separate business from the retail operation.

The meeting ended with you agreeing to provide a report to Cameron on the issues discussed.

Required:

Prepare the report, together with any supporting calculations and analyses you feel are necessary.

Exhibit 1

HOCKEY FACILITIES
Balance Sheet
31 December 20X1

Assets

Current assets		$300,000
Fixed assets (at cost):		
Land	100,000	
Buildings	300,000	
Equipment	200,000	
	600,000	
Accumulated amortization	(220,000)	380,000
Slap Shot manufacturer's licence (at cost)		80,000
Goodwill, at cost		60,000
		$820,000

Liabilities and Equity

Liabilities	$600,000
Proprietor's equity	220,000
	$820,000

Exhibit II

HOCKEY FACILITIES
Statement of Income
Year Ended December 31, 20X1

Sales (retail and manufacturing)		$1,600,000
Cost of sales:		
Opening inventory	$ 300,000	
Purchases and manufacturing costs	800,000	
	1,100,000	
Closing inventory	200,000	900,000
Gross profit		700,000
General administrative and selling expenses		250,000
Net income		$ 450,000

CASE TWO   Eastern Smallwares Ltd. and Byron Ltd.

Sheila Stekylo is the sole shareholder of Eastern Smallwares Ltd., a Canadian-controlled private corporation based in southwestern Ontario. The company wholesales smallwares to retail variety stores in eastern Canada. Two years ago, ESL purchased 40% of the common shares of Byron Products Ltd., a company in a similar line of business but operating in western Canada. The remaining 60% of BPL's shares are owned by Ranjit Dhillon. Dhillon is actively involved in managing BPL's operations.

It is two months before ESL's year end and Stekylo has completed a review of the company's financial information. ESL's operating results, to date, are good. The company's internal accountant has prepared projections to the end of the year (see Exhibit I). Stekylo notices that the projections do not include an estimate of the current year's taxes and tells her internal accountant the following:

"We need an estimate of the current year's tax cost for ESL so we can properly plan our cash flows. Also, there are a lot of planned activities that you and I have discussed that are going to have tax consequences and may require some planning... Also, some changes are happening at BPL. For example, BPL has taken out a $200,000 life insurance policy on both me and Dhillon as part of the buy/sell agreement, and I have no idea what the tax implications are if BPL collects on that insurance. And Dhillon is talking about acquiring a separate business in his own name. Prepare as much information as you can, and send it over to our accountants at Carlson and Kominsky (C&K). Have them estimate this year's tax cost for ESL, and then have them explain to us the tax implications of the various planned events and make any planning suggestions."

As a member of C&K, you have been assigned to report to Stekylo. You intend to prepare a preliminary draft report for review based on the information provided in Exhibits I, II, and III. Your report will include an estimate of ESL's net income for tax purposes, taxable income, and tax cost for the current year.

Required:

Prepare the preliminary draft report for Stekylo.

Exhibit 1

EASTERN SMALLWARES LTD.
Projected Year-End Statement of Income
with Supplementary Notes

Sales		$1,333,000
Cost of sales		690,000
Gross profit		643,000
Expenses:		
Salaries and wages	320,000	
Rent and utilities	24,000	
Repairs and maintenance	23,000	
Amortization	8,000	
Travel and delivery	17,000	
Interest	26,000	
Insurance	7,000	
Reserve for doubtful debts	37,000	
Advertising	11,000	
Charitable donations	5,000	
Legal and accounting	20,000	
Other	15,000	513,000
Income from operations		130,000
Other income:		
Interest on bonds	35,000	
Dividends from taxable Canadian public corporations	8,000	
Gain on sale of marketable securities	40,000	
Net gain on land sales	15,000	98,000
Net income before tax		$ 228,000

Supplementary Notes:

1. The insurance expense of $7,000 consists of three separate premiums: fire and theft ($2,500), public liability ($1,500), and term life insurance on Stekylo that has been pledged to the bank as required collateral for a loan ($3,000).

2. Legal fees include $2,700 for the collection of delinquent accounts receivable, $7,000 for preparing a debenture agreement to obtain an expanded line of credit with the bank, and $8,000 for amending the company's articles of association. The remaining costs relate to annual audit fees.

3. Repairs and maintenance include the following:

Office cleaning, snow removal, lawn care	$ 4,500
Engine replacements on two delivery trucks	18,000
Other	500
	$23,000

4. This year, the company began a new policy of establishing a reserve of 1% of sales for future returns of defective merchandise. This reserve, along with several other minor items, is included as a deduction under "other" expenses. During the year, only $9,000 of defective merchandise was returned.

5. On the first day of the current taxation year, the company rented additional premises under a six-year lease agreement. The agreement includes two three-year renewal options. Improvements costing $28,000 were made to the premises. As an inducement to sign the lease, the landlord paid ESL $10,000 to cover some of these improvements. This amount was credited to contributed surplus on the balance sheet.

6. The undepreciated capital cost of certain assets at the end of the previous year was as follows:

Class 8	$27,000
Class 10	31,000

There were no acquisitions or sales of equipment during the current year.

7. At the end of the previous year, the following additional tax accounts existed:

Refundable dividend tax on hand	$ 2,000
Capital dividend account	9,000
Cumulative eligible capital	12,000

8. The net gain on land sales ($15,000) resulted from two transactions. One property was acquired five years ago as a possible site for a warehouse. However, when new leased space became available, ESL sold the land for $40,000 more than it cost. The other property was sold for a loss of $25,000 after being held by ESL for only six months. It had been acquired in the expectation that its value would rise rapidly after a new shopping centre was developed nearby. However, the shopping centre project was cancelled, and land values in the area declined.

9. Not reflected in the projected income statement is an anticipated dividend from BPL. Dhillon has informed Stekylo that BPL intends to declare a dividend of $200,000. The dividend will be received before the current year end.

10. Included in the amount for salaries and wages are estimated bonuses of $30,000 for senior staff. These will be accrued at year end. The bonuses will be paid in three instalments of $10,000 over the next taxation year. The first instalment will be paid four months after year end, the remaining two at 8 and 12 months, respectively.

Exhibit II

EASTERN SMALLWARES LTD.
Anticipated Developments

1. ESL has just signed a long-term contract to supply products to a large national chain organization. The contract will begin early in the new year. Operating profits for next year will increase by approximately $380,000.

2. Stekylo has agreed to sell 33⅓% of her common shares in the company to a senior manager for $400,000. She had purchased the entire share capital of the company seven years before, for $570,000.

    She intends to use all of the proceeds to pay off what she still owes the previous owner of ESL. Stekylo's personal marginal tax rate is 45% on normal income except dividends, which are subject to a 28% marginal tax rate on eligible dividends and 33% marginal rate on non-eligible dividends.

3. Early in the new year, Stekylo will need $300,000 in cash to finish paying for the construction of her new personal residence. Except for her salary of $80,000 per year from ESL, she has no personal cash. She plans to extract $300,000 from ESL and wants

to keep her tax bill to a minimum. The following summary of the ESL balance sheet indicates that there are sufficient assets to fund the distribution:

Cash, receivables, inventory	$ 640,000
Equipment and leaseholds	108,000
Goodwill, at cost	100,000
Investment in bonds	320,000
	$1,168,000
Current and long-term liabilities	$ 366,000
Shareholders' equity	802,000
	$1,168,000

Exhibit III

Information Pertaining to Byron Products Ltd.

1. BPL has consistently earned from operations pre-tax profits of between $150,000 and $200,000. It does not earn any investment income. In the taxation year just passed, BPL earned profits from its business operations of $180,000 and paid taxes of $36,000 on that income.

2. Dhillon and Stekylo have recently signed an agreement which states that if one dies, the survivor must purchase the interest of the deceased. The agreement does not specify how the buy-out is to be structured. In conjunction with the agreement, BPL has purchased a $200,000 term life insurance policy on both individuals, with BPL as the beneficiary. The entire shares of BPL were recently valued at $600,000. At the most recent year end, BPL had retained earnings of $480,000. ESL had purchased its 40% interest for $100,000. The paid-up capital of the BPL shares owned by ESL is $1,000.

3. BPL will soon declare a dividend of $200,000 (see Exhibit I). Dhillon has initiated the dividend in order to free up cash so that he can purchase another business. Dhillon has informed Stekylo that he is about to buy 100% of the shares of a highly profitable manufacturing corporation.

CHAPTER 14

Multiple Corporations and Their Reorganization

Up to this point in the text, the corporate structure has been examined in its simplest form—that of a single corporation owned by shareholders who are individuals. While simple structures are commonplace, far more complex structures are found in the financial community.

Often, the business affairs of a group of shareholders are spread among a number of different corporations; those corporations may, in turn, own subsidiary corporations. While each corporation in the group may be controlled directly or indirectly by the same shareholder(s) and those corporations may together form a single economic resource, each nevertheless constitutes a separate entity for tax purposes. Over time, the need for placing business activities in one corporation, rather than another, may disappear, at which time a reorganization of some or all of the activities of the group will be desirable.

This chapter will describe the basic techniques for combining or separating financial activities within an economic group, and the related tax implications. While these techniques are used primarily in reorganization activities, they are also applicable to business acquisitions and divestitures (see Chapter 19 for a full discussion including share for share exchanges). This chapter will also examine the use of holding corporations, and the resulting implications to after-tax cash flow.

I. Corporate Reorganizations

Relocating business activities from one corporation to another involves the transfer of assets. For example, if a corporation decides to close its business it may sell its assets, such as land, buildings, and equipment, to an arm's-length purchaser. To the extent that the assets' fair market value exceeds their cost, the selling corporation incurs taxable income. In effect, the corporation has changed the substance of its activities by converting business assets into cash or notes receivable. However, when the transfer of the assets is to another corporation owned by the same shareholders, a change in form has occurred but not a change in substance. In other words, the same owners continue to conduct the same business, but from within a different entity. This type of transaction is referred to as a reorganization.

Similarly, two independent corporations owned by different shareholders may decide to combine their operations into a single economic force. For example, a corporation operating a chain of retail stores in eastern Canada may join with a corporation operating a similar chain of stores in western Canada and do so in such a way that shareholders of both corporations will participate in the larger combined entity. This type of transaction may also be considered a reorganization because both parties have a continuing interest in the combined activity. It is different from a sale, which requires that one party give up its interest by removing itself from the activity in exchange for cash, notes receivable, or other assets that do not include shares in the continuing activity.

All of this means that corporate reorganizations can occur within a related group of companies having similar shareholders or among independent business entities in the form of combinations and divestitures.

Current tax policy provides that when a reorganization occurs, the parties, if they so desire, may elect a form of transaction that does not result in the fair market value disposition of assets for tax purposes and, thereby, the creation of taxable income is deferred. The types of transactions that can be used to execute a reorganization are outlined below. The discussions deal primarily with reorganizations within a related corporate group, but they are also applicable to reorganizations of independent entities.

The reorganizations discussed in this chapter involve the techniques for transferring assets from one entity to another one and share capital reorganizations. Chapter 19 discusses the application of the reorganization provisions as they apply to business acquisitions and divestitures.

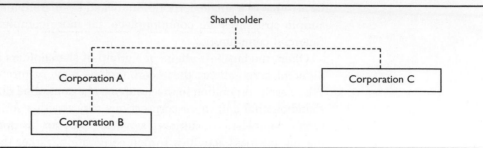

Exhibit 14-1:

Multiple Corporate Structure

A. Basic Reorganization Techniques

Before examining the reasons for, and the tax impact of, various reorganization transactions, it would be useful to have a mental picture of the change in structure that results from the reorganization.

Consider the multiple corporate structure presented in Exhibit 14-1. A single shareholder directly owns both Corporation A and Corporation C and indirectly owns Corporation B, which is a subsidiary of Corporation A.

It is assumed that each corporation owns business assets used to conduct a separate business. If the shareholder wishes to combine some or all of the business activities, two basic formats are available:

1. Assets can be transferred directly from one corporation to another.

2. The corporate structure can be altered by combining two or more of the corporations into one corporation.

For example, the activities of Corporations A and C could be combined by having A sell its business assets to C or vice versa. Another alternative is for A and C to combine to form a single legal entity, thereby creating Corporation AC. While both of these basic methods have the same result—combining of the business activities—the longer-term tax implications may differ. Much depends on the reasons for carrying out the reorganization.

Each of the basic reorganization techniques is reviewed below; following this, a simple case study is analyzed that shows the impact of choosing one technique over the others.

B. Asset Transfers

The transferring of assets from one entity to another is the simplest form of reorganization because it does not involve the restructuring of the corporations themselves. This method provides considerable flexibility in that it permits a corporation to transfer either all of its activities or only a specified part of its activities. For example, a corporation that operates several divisions within its business could transfer the assets of one of the divisions to a separate corporation, leaving the other divisions in the original corporation.

Asset transfers involve an actual sale of property by one corporation to another; for this reason, for legal purposes, there must be an established selling price and an equivalent amount of payment. Notwithstanding the established legal selling price, the transfer price for tax purposes can be determined in one of two basic ways:

1. The transfer price of assets can automatically be deemed equal to the fair market value.[1]

2. If the corporations so elect, an agreed transfer price can be chosen that is usually equal to the cost for tax purposes (see Chapter 12).[2]

↳ undepreciated asset cost.

The above alternatives are available for each asset transferred, which means that when a group of assets is transferred together, some of the assets may be transferred at fair market value and others at an agreed lower value.

---

1   ITA 69(1); IT-405 (archived).
2   ITA 85(1); IT-291R3.

Exhibit 14-2:

A Vertical Transfer of Assets

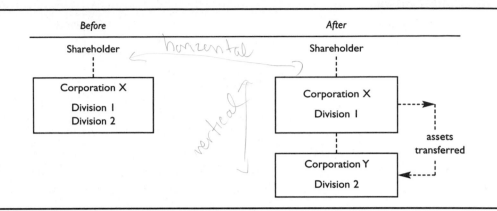

The choice of methods depends on the circumstances of the parties and the reasons for the transfer. For example, if the selling corporation has accumulated losses that are about to expire, it may want the transfer price to be at fair market value in order to create taxable income against which those losses can be offset. The corporation acquiring the assets would have a higher cost base for tax purposes, which may create future tax savings from capital cost allowance deductions.

Alternatively, the selling corporation may choose not to create taxable income on the transfer, by electing a transfer price equal to the tax cost. For example, a depreciable asset may be sold with an elected price for tax purposes equal to its undepreciated capital cost. When this is done, the selling corporation has no taxable gain on the transfer. The acquiring corporation will use the asset to generate income from business or property and can claim capital cost allowance based on the lower transfer price. If the asset is subsequently sold to a third party at fair market value, the acquiring corporation will incur all of the taxable income associated with that asset, even though part of the value increase occurred when the asset was owned by the original corporation. In effect, the tax status of the asset has been transferred from the original corporation to the acquiring corporation.

It should be pointed out that choosing the elected-price method involves certain formalities and restrictions. These were discussed in Chapter 12.

Within a corporate group, assets can be transferred vertically or horizontally. The terms "vertical" and "horizontal" refer to the corporate group's organization chart. A vertical transaction occurs between a parent and its subsidiaries, whereas a horizontal transaction occurs between two corporations that are owned by the same shareholders.

A vertical transfer of assets is diagrammed in Exhibit 14-2, in which Corporation X, consisting of two separate business divisions, transfers the assets of division 2 to a new Corporation Y (the subsidiary). The assets of division 2, which may consist of land, buildings, equipment, inventory, goodwill, and patents, can be transferred to the subsidiary at fair market value or at tax values. The result of the reorganization is that all future business income of division 2 is now taxed separately in Corporation Y. The after-tax profits of Corporation Y can be transferred back up to the parent corporation by way of a dividend distribution, which is not taxable to the parent.

This same reorganization could also have been achieved by a horizontal transfer of assets, as diagrammed in Exhibit 14-3. Under this alternative, Corporation X sells the assets of division 2 to Corporation Y. The transfer price can be at fair market value or at tax values. As explained in Chapter 12, in order to use an elected price at tax values, the seller must take back some shares of the buyer as part of the payment. Therefore, in this case, Corporation Y would be owned by both Corporation X and the regular shareholder.

In both of the above examples, the business operations of division 2 could have been transferred to Corporation Y without necessarily transferring all of the assets associated with the division. For example, while it may have been necessary to transfer the inventory and goodwill, Corporation X could have retained ownership of the land, buildings,

Exhibit 14-3:

A Horizontal Transfer of Assets

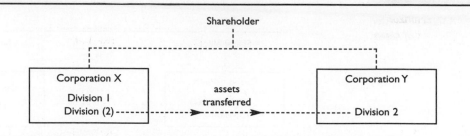

equipment, and patents and leased them to Corporation Y in return for rents and royalties. This would have avoided any complications associated with the asset transfers; it would also have changed the amount of income being shifted to Corporation Y. This point is made to stress the concept that there is a difference between the right to operate a business and the assets used to maintain those operations. The opportunity of leasing adds another dimension to the reorganization process.

In summary, asset transfers as part of a reorganization can involve some or all of the assets, can be transferred horizontally or vertically, and can be transferred at fair market value or at tax values. This provides a wide range of options and significant flexibility.

C. Amalgamations

An amalgamation involves the complete merging of the assets, liabilities, and shareholdings of two or more corporations.[3] By law, all of the former corporations cease to exist, and a new corporation is born.[4] In effect, all of the corporations amalgamated have disposed of their assets to a new corporation, and all of the shareholders have disposed of their shares in the former corporations in exchange for shares of the new corporation. The number and value of shares distributed by the new corporation to the former shareholders depend on the proportionate values of the corporations entering into the merger. This form of reorganization is used to restructure corporations within a related group and is also used extensively in arm's-length business acquisitions and mergers.

Corporate amalgamations, like asset transfers, can be vertical or horizontal. Consider the vertical amalgamation in Exhibit 14-4: an amalgamation of parent Corporation A and subsidiary Corporation B completely eliminates the former corporations; in their place is a single new corporation, AB, which now houses the combined operations.

Exhibit 14-4 uses a wholly owned subsidiary as an example. However, Corporation A need not own all of the shares of Corporation B in order to enter into an amalgamation. For example, if Corporation A owned only 60% of Corporation B, with the balance of shares owned by a non-related party, an amalgamation would still result in the creation of Corporation AB. However, the other shareholders of the former Corporation B would now be shareholders in the combined operations.

Exhibit 14-4:

Vertical Amalgamation

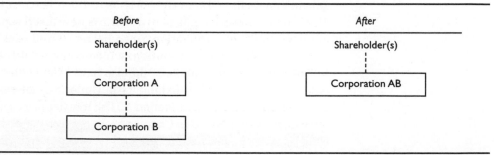

---

3 ITA 87(1).
4 ITA 87(2)(a). The taxation year of the new corporation commences at the date of amalgamation. As with any new corporation, a fiscal year end can be chosen. The former corporations have a deemed year end immediately before the amalgamation.

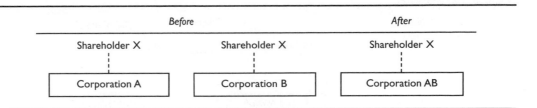

Exhibit 14-5:

Horizontal Amalgamation

Before		After
Shareholder X	Shareholder X	Shareholder X
Corporation A	Corporation B	Corporation AB

Exhibit 14-5 demonstrates a horizontal amalgamation of two sister corporations owned by the same shareholder. Upon amalgamation, both Corporation A and Corporation B cease to exist, and Corporation AB is created.

- **Tax treatment**   Provided that certain criteria are met, the amalgamation of two or more corporations results in a tax-free merger of the entities. The predecessor corporations are deemed to have sold their assets to the new corporation at their tax values.[5] Similarly, the shareholders are deemed to have sold their former shares at a value equal to their cost base in exchange for shares of the new corporation that have the same cost base.[6] In other words, all former tax positions are preserved in the combined entity.[7] It should be noted that a particular tax benefit may occur under a *vertical amalgamation* if the parent owns 100% of the subsidiary's shares. The benefit results in an increase in the tax value of certain assets, referred to as *a "step-up" or "bump,"* when the parent's adjusted cost base (ACB) of the subsidiary's shares is greater than the sum of the tax values of the subsidiary's net assets.[8] This is explained in more detail in Section D of this chapter (Wind-up of a Subsidiary) as the applicable calculation is identical.

The taxation year of the predecessor corporations is deemed to end immediately before the amalgamation and the first taxation year of the new corporation begins on the day of the amalgamation.[9] The new corporation may then select any date within 53 weeks after the amalgamation for its year end.

Of major importance is the treatment of any tax losses being carried forward by the predecessor corporations. In most circumstances, all losses being carried forward by the former corporations become, upon amalgamation, losses that can be carried forward by the new, combined corporation.[10] Any restrictions that were previously attached, such as limits to the time period for loss carry-forward or to the types of income that losses can be offset against, simply continue as restrictions in the combined corporation.

The tax treatment of corporate losses was examined in Chapter 11. Recall that business loss carry-overs may become restricted and capital loss carry-overs are eliminated when a change in control occurs. The amalgamation of corporations within a related corporate group does not result in a change of control for this purpose, and so an amalgamation does not normally alter the usual treatment of losses. Indeed, one of the major purposes of amalgamations is to combine the losses of one entity with the profits of another.[11]

Losses may be affected on amalgamation when an unrelated party achieves control of the amalgamated entity. For example, in Exhibit 14-6, Corporation A has losses carried forward and is controlled by shareholder 1. Corporation B is profitable and is controlled by shareholder 2, who is unrelated to shareholder 1. Upon amalgamation, shareholder 1, who previously controlled the loss company, does not control the new corporation. This constitutes a change in control. As a consequence, any net capital

---

5 ITA 87(2)(b) to (j.2); IT-474R.
6 ITA 87(4).
7 Including the capital dividend account—ITA 87(2)(z.1), and the refundable dividend tax on hand account—ITA 87(2)(aa).
8 ITA 87(11), 88(1)(d).
9 ITA 87(2)(a).
10 ITA 87(2.1); IT-302R3.
11 ITA 256(7).

Exhibit 14-6:

Change in Control on Amalgamation

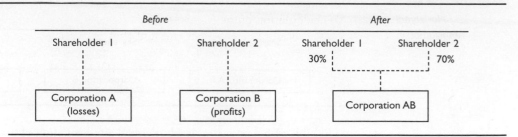

Before		After	
Shareholder 1	Shareholder 2	Shareholder 1 30%	Shareholder 2 70%
Corporation A (losses)	Corporation B (profits)	Corporation AB	

loss carry-overs are eliminated. Business loss carry-overs (non-capital losses) can be offset only against the income from the business that incurred the loss or from a similar business; thus, if Corporations A and B are in a similar line of business, the business loss carry-overs are unaffected.[12]

In order for an amalgamation to result in a tax-free combination, the following conditions must be met:[13]

1. All of the corporations must be Canadian corporations.

2. All assets and liabilities of the old corporations must become assets and liabilities of the new corporation.

3. All of the shareholders of the old corporations must become shareholders of the new corporation.

These conditions follow the basic principle of a reorganization—that owners must maintain a continuing interest in the venture.

D. Wind-up of a Subsidiary

The wind-up of a subsidiary corporation involves the transfer of all of the assets of the subsidiary to its parent corporation, followed by the termination of the subsidiary's existence. Subsidiary wind-ups differ from amalgamations in that they result in the elimination of the subsidiary *only*—the parent corporation continues its normal existence.

The tax treatment of a wind-up is similar to that of an amalgamation. In most cases, no tax occurs on the transfer of assets from the subsidiary to the parent, as the transfer price is considered to be equal to the tax values of the assets transferred. In addition, any tax accounts of the subsidiary become available to the parent.[14] For example, accumulated unused losses of the subsidiary are transferred to the parent and continue to be carried forward under the same restrictions, if any, that were imposed on the subsidiary.[15]

The parent is prohibited from claiming the losses of the subsidiary until the taxation year following the taxation year in which the wind-up occurred.[16]

In order to utilize the tax-free wind-up provisions, the parent company must own at least 90% of each class of the subsidiary's shares. If the parent owns less than that 90%, it must resort to the amalgamation procedure in order to achieve the desired tax relief.

When a wind-up occurs, it is possible that the tax values of certain assets will be increased providing tax relief in the future. This increase is referred to as a *"step-up"* or *"bump" of the tax values*. A step-up or bump can occur *upon wind-up* if the parent corporation has previously acquired the shares of the subsidiary at a price that is greater than the tax values of the net assets of the subsidiary at the time they are transferred to

[handwritten margin notes: 2001 wind-up   2002 con claim losses from wind-up]

---

12 ITA 111(4), (5), (5,4).
13 ITA 87(1).
14 ITA 88(1); IT-488R2 (archived).
15 ITA 88(1.1), (1.2); IT-302R3.
16 ITA 88(1.1).

the parent on wind-up. The step-up or bump *applies only to non-depreciable assets.* The calculation of the increase is as follows:

Available increase—The amount that is available for the bump is the amount by which the adjusted cost base (ACB) of the subsidiary's shares (normally the parent's purchase price) exceeds the tax values (UCC, ACB, CEC, etc.) of the net assets of the subsidiary (at the wind-up date) and any dividends (regular or capital dividends) paid to the parent. The term "net assets" refers to the tax values of the assets plus the cash minus the liabilities and certain reserves.

Actual increase—The available increase (above) is then allocated to particular assets. The allocation applies only to non-depreciable assets and cannot exceed the fair market value (FMV) of those assets at the time the parent acquired the subsidiary.[17]

Consider the following situation:

Situation

Parent acquired 90% of the shares of Subsidiary on December 31, 20X4 for $700,000. At the acquisition date the fair market value of the depreciable property (equipment) was $400,000 and the fair market value of the non-depreciable property (land) was $150,000.

On December 31, 20X8, Subsidiary was wound-up into Parent. The tax value balance sheet is as follows:

Cash	$50,000	Liabilities	$30,000
Land, at cost	115,000	Shareholders' Equity	435,000
Equipment, at UCC	300,000		
	$465,000		$465,000

The fair market value of the land at December 31, 20X8 was $180,000. Since acquisition, Parent has received dividends of $45,000 from Subsidiary.

Analysis

On wind-up the assets of the subsidiary are deemed to be sold to the parent at their tax values (land at $115,000 and equipment at $300,000). However, the parent will receive a tax value increase (bump) to the land (non-depreciable property) of $35,000 raising its adjusted cost base to $150,000. This is calculated as follows:

Available increase:		
ACB of subsidiary shares (acquisition price)		$700,000
Deduct tax values of net assets of subsidiary:		
Land	$115,000	
Equipment	300,000	
Cash minus liabilities ($50,000 − $30,000)	20,000	
Dividends paid to parent	45,000	(480,000)
Available increase		$220,000
Actual increase:		
FMV of land at date parent acquired Subsidiary − 20X4		$150,000
Deduct ACB of land at wind-up date − 20X8		(115,000)
Increase allocated to land is limited to		$ 35,000

So the revised ACB of the land in the combined entity after wind-up is $150,000 ($115,000 + $35,000). Note that the remainder of the available increase is lost as it cannot be applied to the depreciable property. Also, if the available increase was only $10,000 rather than $220,000, the amount of the bump to the land would be $10,000 as it does not exceed the limit of $35,000.

17 ITA 88(1)(d)(ii).

As noted previously, this step-up or bump in the tax value of certain assets is also available when a subsidiary has a vertical amalgamation with the parent. However, under the amalgamation method the step-up or bump is available only when the parent owns 100% of the subsidiary's shares compared to the wind-up method which requires only 90% ownership.[18]

E. Reorganization of Share Capital

Each of the previous reorganization methods involved the transfer of assets from one entity to another. In some circumstances, the shareholders may wish to alter the *nature* of their interest in the corporation without changing the *amount* of dollar capital that they have invested in that corporation. For example, shareholders may convert some of their common shares to preferred shares; this will alter the way future profits are apportioned, even though the amount of capital invested is the same. When there is a reorganization of share capital that maintains a continued interest of all parties, the shareholders are permitted to exchange all shares of a particular class for shares of another class on a tax-deferred basis.[19]

Consider the change in ownership structure diagrammed in Exhibit 14-7. Before the reorganization, shareholders 1 and 2 each own 50% of the common shares of a corporation valued at $100,000. A change in this ownership ratio can be achieved by completing the following steps:

1. Both shareholder 1 and shareholder 2 convert their common shares, worth $50,000, into fixed-value preferred shares that have a value of $50,000 and bear a fixed dividend rate. At this point, the full value of the company is attached to the preferred shares, which will achieve no further growth in value.

2. Because the full value of the company is now tied up in the preferred shares, new common shares can be issued at a nominal value. The corporation therefore issues 10 new common shares at $1 each. Shareholder 1 purchases eight of these shares and shareholder 2 the remaining two.

The result of all this is not only that the existing full value of the company ($100,000) is frozen in the form of preferred shares in the former ratio of $50,000 for each shareholder but also that any future change in the corporation's value will accrue at 80% to shareholder 1 and 20% to shareholder 2.

This transaction permitted a change in ownership ratio without immediate tax consequences. In normal circumstances, a change in ownership ratio would require that one shareholder purchase shares of the other or that the company buy back some of its shares; both these alternatives would have tax consequences to the shareholder.

Exhibit 14-7:

Change in Ownership Ratio by Share Reorganization

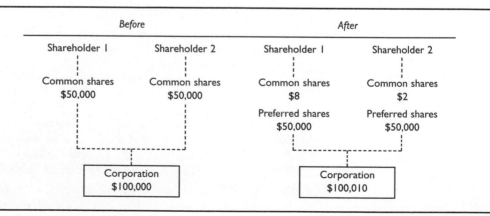

18 ITA 87(11), 88(1)(d).
19 ITA 86.

Exhibit 14-8:

New Shareholders and
Share Reorganization

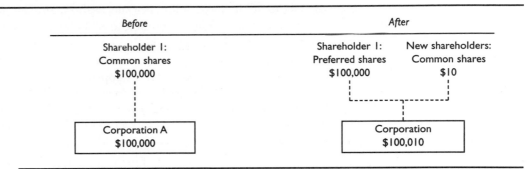

The previous example demonstrated how share capital can be reorganized among existing shareholders; the technique is also useful as a means of admitting *new* shareholders without the requirement of a substantial cash contribution. For example, consider the situation where the sole shareholder of a corporation valued at $100,000 wants to transfer ownership to a group of employees who are capable of managing the company but have no capital with which to make the purchase. Exhibit 14-8 diagrams a share reorganization plan that achieves this goal. Before the reorganization, shareholder 1 owned 100% of the common shares having a value of $100,000. Shareholder 1 exchanges all of the common shares for preferred shares valued at $100,000. The company then issues 10 new common shares for $10 to the new employee/shareholders.

Note that after the reorganization, the company is still worth $100,010; however, almost all of the value belongs to shareholder 1 in the form of preferred shares. Over a period of time, the company can buy back the preferred shares from shareholder 1, at which time that shareholder will incur taxable income.

Changing the ownership of a business using the share reorganization method is reviewed in more detail in Chapter 19 (Business Acquisition and Divestitures— Tax Deferred Sales). In particular, Chapter 19 demonstrates a case example that transfers a family business to adult children on a tax-deferred basis by reorganizing the share capital. The chapter also includes several key Concept Questions on the topic.

F. Reorganization Procedures and Case Analysis

Each of the reorganization methods has the same objective, which is to combine or separate business activities within a group of corporations. However, the choice of method in a particular set of circumstances is not obvious. In addition, to accomplish a particular end, it may be necessary to use two or more of the techniques in a sequence. In most cases, the methods used to reorganize a corporation are determined by trial and error, by performing the following procedures:

1. Define the problem in the existing structure and the objective to be satisfied by changing that structure.

2. Choose and test one of the reorganization techniques. This involves determining the immediate and future tax implications of the method chosen.

3. Determine whether the immediate and future tax implications satisfy all or a portion of the problem and also whether any new problems are created by the proposed new structure. This means anticipating possible future activities and considering how they will be treated under the proposed structure.

4. If all of the problems are not solved and/or if new difficulties are created from the proposed structure, choose another method and perform the analysis again.

In the simple corporate reorganization examined below, the above procedures are used to establish the most appropriate method of completing a corporate reorganization.

Summary of Facts

Blue Ltd., a Canadian corporation, is a successful manufacturer of men's clothing. The current year's pre-tax profits amounted to $700,000, and similar profits are expected in the future. Blue Ltd. has two wholly owned subsidiaries, A Ltd. and B Ltd.

A Ltd. was acquired five years ago and manufactures a line of men's winter clothing. A Ltd. generates a modest profit of approximately $50,000 annually.

Blue Ltd. acquired the shares of B Ltd. two years ago. At the time of acquisition, B Ltd. had unused business losses carried forward of $200,000. Since the acquisition, B Ltd. has incurred additional losses of $150,000; it is expected to lose an additional $80,000 in each of the next three years. B Ltd. operates a small retail chain of clothing stores. Although B Ltd. rents most of its locations, it *does* own the land and buildings that house two of its stores. This property has appreciated in value.

The organization structure of the group is as follows:

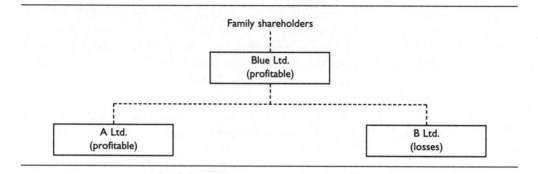

Analysis

The major problem with the existing structure is that Blue Ltd. and A Ltd. are profitable and taxable on their operations, while B Ltd. has accumulated unused losses. For example, next year, the group will have a combined profit as follows:

Blue Ltd.	$700,000
A Ltd.	50,000
B Ltd. (loss)	(80,000)
	$670,000

However, it will be taxable on $750,000 (profits of Blue Ltd. and A Ltd.).

The accumulated losses of B Ltd. have two limitations that must be dealt with. First of all, the losses that existed at the time of acquisition are restricted and can be offset only against income from that business or a similar business (see Chapter 11). As all three corporations appear to be in a similar line of business, this restriction is not a major problem. Second, all of the losses are subject to a time limitation (each year's loss can be carried forward twenty years), and so it must be determined when the losses will expire.

Some, but not all, of the reorganization alternatives are discussed briefly below.

• **B Ltd. sells assets to A Ltd.** This option involves the loss company selling its assets to a company that has continued, though modest, profits. Within this option, there are several sub-alternatives: the assets may be sold at fair market value or at tax values; further, all of the assets or only some of the assets may be sold.

One possibility is to sell, at fair market value, only the assets that have appreciated in value. B Ltd. has land and buildings which, if sold, would create taxable income to B Ltd. and use up some or all of the existing losses carried forward. However, this alternative would leave the business operations in B Ltd., which would continue to generate losses over the next few years that would remain unused until the retail stores become profitable.

A second possibility is for B Ltd. to sell not just the land and buildings but the entire business operations to A Ltd. This procedure has two potential advantages: The taxable income on the sale of land and buildings might use up the accumulated losses in B Ltd., thereby preventing their expiration; also, all future losses ($80,000 annually) will occur in A Ltd., where they can be offset against A Ltd.'s profits ($50,000 annually). While this method addresses the concerns regarding both accumulated and future losses, it nevertheless has two shortcomings:

- The future profits of A Ltd. are less than the future losses from the retail stores. For this reason, the issue of future losses is not totally satisfied.
- While the sale of assets at fair market value prevents B's losses from expiring, no immediate tax reductions are achieved. Effectively, the accumulated losses are preserved in the form of a higher cost base of the assets now owned by A Ltd. Therefore, future taxes will be reduced as A Ltd. claims capital cost allowance on the higher building value or when the land is finally sold. Even though the losses are preserved, cash flow is increased later, rather than sooner.

- **A Ltd. sells assets to B Ltd.**   This option requires the transfer of A Ltd.'s business operations to B Ltd. In order to avoid tax on the sale, the assets would have to be transferred at tax values in exchange for notes and shares of B Ltd. After the transfer, B Ltd. would operate both a manufacturing business (men's winter clothing) and a chain of retail stores. The future profits from the manufacturing business ($50,000) would first be offset against the future losses of the retail stores ($80,000).

While this option eliminates the taxes on the $50,000 manufacturing profit, it leaves approximately $30,000 annually of new losses as well as all of the accumulated unused losses in B Ltd.

- **Amalgamation of A Ltd. and B Ltd.**   This method eliminates both corporations and creates a new corporation, AB Ltd., that combines the operations of A and B. The result would be similar to that from the previous alternative and would not resolve the matter of how to use the annual future losses and the accumulated past losses.

- **Wind-up of B Ltd. into Blue Ltd.**   With this option, all of the assets of the loss company are transferred at tax values to the parent company. B Ltd. would cease to exist; the parent company would operate its clothing manufacturing business as well as the chain of retail stores. In addition, the accumulated losses of B Ltd. would be transferred to the parent company and would be available for use in future years.

As the parent company's profits are $700,000 annually, there would be sufficient income in the first year after the wind-up to absorb all of the accumulated losses of B Ltd. ($200,000 + $150,000 = $350,000) as well as the annual loss of $80,000. This alternative is extremely attractive because the accumulated losses would be used rapidly and the method of utilization (deduction against taxable income) would generate immediate tax savings. This enhanced cash flow could be used for business expansion or to fund the losses from the retail chain.

This result could also have been achieved by amalgamating Blue Ltd. and B Ltd.

The combining of the retail operations with the manufacturing operations may have other tax consequences, which should be anticipated before the decision is made. For example, the amount of profit eligible for the manufacturing and processing tax reduction is determined by an arbitrary formula based on the amount of capital and labour employed in manufacturing activities. Combining the retail and manufacturing operations will alter this calculation and may either expand the manufacturing base or diminish it, depending on the ratio of retail labour and capital to manufacturing labour and capital (see Chapter 11).

It is important to recognize that the above analysis is not complete and that there are other alternatives which could have been explored. In addition, while winding up B Ltd. into Blue Ltd. appears to provide the most favourable outcome in this particular set of circumstances, this may not be the case if the assumed facts are altered. The most satisfactory outcome can only be determined by exploring the consequences of several alternatives and evaluating their immediate tax impact as well as their impact on anticipated future activities.

II. Holding Corporations and Intercorporate Investments

An individual who owns shares in one or more business corporations can choose to interpose a corporation between himself/herself and the operating corporations. The interposed corporation is referred to as a "holding corporation," as its primary purpose is to own shares of other corporations.

A holding corporation can be a private company that owns shares in other private or public corporations or a public corporation created for the purpose of investing in other public corporations. The benefits derived from the use of such a structure are tied to the tax treatment given to intercorporate dividends paid by the operating companies to the holding corporation. The tax treatment of intercorporate dividends is examined below. So is the resulting impact on certain business decisions.

A. Tax Treatment of Intercorporate Dividends

It was established in previous chapters that dividends received by a corporation from another Canadian corporation are not included in taxable income.[20] However, it was also indicated that certain dividends received by a private corporation are subject to a special 33⅓% refundable tax (see Chapter 13).

Chapter 13 dealt with the situation where a private corporation receives dividends from another Canadian private corporation. When this occurs, the dividends received may, in limited circumstances, be subject to a special refundable tax. These limited circumstances are as follows:

1. When the dividend received is from a corporation that is not substantially owned by the receiving corporation, a special refundable tax of 33⅓% is applicable to the recipient.[21] One corporation does not have substantial ownership of another if it owns 10% or less of the other corporation.[22] In Chapter 13, it was said that such corporations are non-connected.

2. Notwithstanding the degree of ownership, a special refundable tax is also payable whenever the paying corporation receives a refund as a result of the dividend payment.[23] As explained in Chapter 13, this occurs when a private corporation distributes any investment income that it has earned.

The application of the special refundable tax has been described here in general terms. The specific provisions of the *Income Tax Act* are more detailed and complex and *were discussed in detail in Chapter 13*. For the purposes of this text and for the discussion of holding corporations in general, the following generalizations can be made with respect to intercorporate dividends:

1. All Canadian dividends received by a public corporation are tax-free.

2. Dividends from one private corporation to another flow tax-free, provided that the dividends are paid from the paying corporation's business income and the recipient owns more than 10% of the paying corporation's shares.

---

20 ITA 112(1).
21 ITA 186(1)(a); IT-269R3.
22 ITA 186(2), (4). The recipient usually does not pay Part IV tax when the dividend is paid from a "connected" corporation. A corporation is connected if the receiving corporation owns more than 10% of the payer's voting shares and more than 10% of the fair market value of all shares issued.
23 ITA 186(1)(b); IT-269R4.

Exhibit 14-9:

*Business Structure and
Holding Corporations*

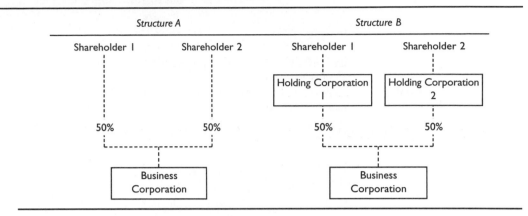

With these generalizations in mind, the benefits of using a holding corporation are reviewed below from the perspective of both public corporations and private corporations that hold a substantial interest in another business corporation.

B. Dividend Reinvestment

The primary benefit of establishing a holding corporation is that it permits the shareholder to receive dividends from the operating company, free of tax, for reinvestment.

Consider the two corporate structures outlined in Exhibit 14-9. Under structure A, both shareholder 1 and shareholder 2 are individuals and own directly 50% of the shares of a private corporation carrying on a business. If the business corporation pays a dividend with its excess funds, both individual shareholders will pay tax on the dividend, leaving the after-tax amount available for investment in another venture.

Under structure B, both shareholders own 100% of their own separate holding corporations. Each corporation in turn owns 50% of the shares of the active business corporation. In this case, any dividends paid by the business corporation flow tax-free to the holding corporations, which can reinvest the full amount of the dividends. In effect, the tax on the dividends is deferred until either shareholder decides to make a distribution for personal use.

The use of holding corporations under structure B permits maximum flexibility when the operating company has excess cash that is not needed for business expansion. For example, shareholders 1 and 2 may want to be business partners but not investment partners, as the types of investments that each prefers are different. When a holding company is used, the operating company can distribute all of its excess funds on a regular basis without further tax; the shareholders can then invest in ventures of their choice. Similarly, shareholder 1 may want funds for personal use while shareholder 2 does not. If dividends are paid first to the holding companies, shareholder 1 can pass the dividend on to himself or herself for personal use and pay the required tax; shareholder 2 can leave the funds in the holding corporation and continue to defer the tax.

A structure that permits the operating company to maintain a policy of distributing all of its excess cash to the shareholders also has the effect of keeping the operating company at its minimum value. In the long run, this makes it easier for the shareholders to sell the shares of the operating company to an independent buyer or to each other.

In summary, holding corporations give shareholders access to corporate profits in such a way that they do not immediately have to pay a second level of tax. This second level of tax should have to be paid only when the shareholder requires the funds for personal use.

C. Holding Companies and Corporate Acquisitions

A holding corporation can also be extremely useful as a vehicle for acquiring shares in an active business corporation, especially when the purchaser uses borrowed funds to make the purchase.

Consider the cash-flow requirements for purchasing a corporation in the following situation:

Situation: Ms. X intends to acquire all of the shares of Opco for $400,000. She intends to borrow the full $400,000 to fund the purchase. Opco is a Canadian-controlled private corporation that will earn $100,000 annually. The corporation pays tax at a rate of 15%. Ms. X is in a 45% marginal tax bracket. She intends to use the future profits of Opco to retire the debt of $400,000 as quickly as possible.

Analysis: To make the purchase, Ms. X can borrow the funds and purchase the shares in her own name or, create a holding corporation that would borrow the funds and purchase the shares in the corporation's name. In both cases, the cash flow generated from future profits will be used to repay the loan. Both alternatives are reviewed below.

• **Shares purchased by Ms. X** To obtain funds to make payments on the loan, Ms. X will have to extract funds from the corporation by dividend distributions or increased salaries, both of which are taxable. Interest incurred on the loan is deductible from her income, which will reduce the taxes payable on the salary or dividend payments. However, payments on the loan principal are not deductible and must therefore be paid after all taxes have been paid by the corporation and Ms. X.

The after-tax annual profits available for principal repayment are as follows:

Corporate income (Opco)		$100,000
Corporate tax	15,000	
Shareholder tax on non-eligible dividend	28,000	(43,000)
After-tax annual funds		$ 57,000
Pay-back period:		
$\dfrac{\text{Loan (\$400,000)}}{\text{Annual cash (\$57,000)}} =$		7 years*

* Interest on the debt has been excluded from the calculation. A complete cash-flow analysis must consider the after-tax cost of interest to establish a realistic pay-back period.

As a result, even though the company is entitled to the small-business deduction, the shareholder must pay the second level of tax to obtain the personal funds to repay the debt principal.

• **Shares purchased by holding corporation** Under this option, Ms. X creates a new holding corporation capitalized with a nominal amount of share capital. The corporation borrows $400,000 and purchases the shares of Opco as an intercorporate investment.

To repay the loan's principal, Opco can pay dividends to the holding corporation, which are tax-free. The after-tax funds available for debt repayment are as follows:

Corporate income (Opco)		$100,000
Corporate tax	15,000	
Tax on dividend	–0–	(15,000)
After-tax annual funds		$ 85,000
Pay-back period:		
$\dfrac{\text{Loan (\$400,000)}}{\text{Annual cash (\$85,000)}} =$		5 years

In the above example, the use of a holding corporation permitted the loan principal to be repaid in five years, rather than seven, because the second level of tax was avoided. While the holding corporation method described above appears preferable, it may also create a problem: The holding corporation will also incur the annual interest cost, which is, of course, deductible from income. However, if the holding company's only source of income is dividends from Opco—which are tax-free—the interest will remain unused in the holding company as losses carried forward.

When the holding corporation has no other sources of taxable income, the problem of unused losses from interest can be solved by applying the reorganization techniques described earlier in this chapter. For example, immediately after the holding corporation acquired the shares of Opco, the two companies could be amalgamated. As a result, Ms. X would own a single corporation that combines the affairs of both original corporations. The new corporation would operate the business and earn $100,000 annually but would also have the loan of $400,000 as its obligation. The interest would be deductible against the business profits, and the remaining after-tax income (taxed at only 15%) would be available to repay the loan principal.

The above situation and analysis provide an example of a "leveraged buy-out" whereby the purchaser funds a large portion of the price with borrowed funds and looks to the acquired corporation to provide the cash flow to repay the debt. In effect, the corporation is paying for itself by committing some of its resources not to business expansion but to distributions to the purchaser for the purpose of funding the take-over. In this form of buy-out, it is vital to minimize the amount of tax on the distribution of corporate funds. This is achieved by the use of a holding corporation.

In a corporate buy-out, while the expected future profits are a primary source of funding, the purchaser may also use the corporate assets as an immediate source of cash to fund a portion of the purchase price. For example, consider the following balance sheet of a company that is targeted for a purchase of its shares:

Assets		Liabilities and equity	
Working capital	$300,000	Liabilities	$400,000
Equipment	50,000	Share capital and	
Business real estate	200,000	retained earnings	250,000
Marketable securities	100,000		
	$650,000		$650,000

Upon acquiring the shares of the above company, the new owner could cash in the marketable securities of $100,000, which are not needed for the business, and distribute the cash to himself/herself to help fund the share purchase. If the shares were purchased with a holding corporation, the distribution would be tax-free. Similarly, the business real estate may have appreciated in value, in which case it could either be sold and leased back or re-mortgaged to create additional cash resources for distribution to the new owner's holding company.

D. Holding Companies and Corporate Divestitures

A holding company is also useful as a means to minimize tax on the sale of shares of a corporation.

Consider the corporate structure shown in Exhibit 14-10. A holding corporation owned by an individual shareholder is contemplating the sale of shares that it owns in an operating company. The value of the shares to be sold will depend on the strength of the operating company—that is, on the amount of its retained earnings and the value of its assets, such as land, buildings, equipment, goodwill, and so on. To the extent that the value of the shares exceeds the shares' original cost, the holding corporation will recognize a taxable capital gain on disposition that will diminish the amount of after-tax proceeds available for reinvestment. However, if before the sale For Sale Corporation distributed all of its retained earnings as a tax-free dividend to the holding corporation, the value of the shares would diminish to the extent of the dividend paid. The shares

Exhibit 14-10:

Holding Corporation and Corporate Divestitures

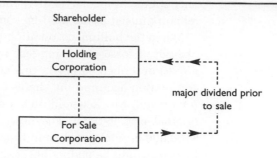

could then be sold for a lesser amount, resulting in less tax on the disposition and increased after-tax proceeds (from the dividend and share sale) available for reinvestment in another venture. A more detailed example of this procedure was made in Chapter 11. As indicated in that chapter, to the extent that share values are represented by accumulated retained earnings, the potential capital gain from that value can always be delayed by transferring the retained earnings value to a holding corporation before a sale. Special anti-avoidance rules exist that prevent tax-free distributions greater than the retained earnings when those distributions are in anticipation of a share sale.[24]

Situation: Holding Corporation (a CCPC) acquired all of the shares of Target Corporation for a cost of $200,000. Several years later Holding decides to sell its investment in Target. The shares of Target are currently valued at $1,200,000 and the company has accumulated retained earnings of $600,000. Before the sale, Target plans to pay a dividend of $1,000,000 to Holding, thereby reducing the fair market value of the Target shares to $200,000. Holding will then sell the shares for $200,000. This price is equal to the adjusted cost base of the shares.

Analysis: The dividend flows tax-free from Target to Holding. Holding and Target are connected and Holding will only pay a Part IV tax to the extent that Target has a RDTOH balance.

However, the $1,000,000 dividend is $400,000 greater than the $600,000 retained earnings of Target. Consequently the anti-avoidance rule may apply.

The anti-avoidance rule in subsection 55(2) is applicable where:

- A corporation has received dividends that are not taxable as part of a series of transactions, involving a disposition of shares;
- One of the purposes of the dividend was to effect a significant reduction in a capital gain which, in the absence of the dividend, would have been realized on the disposition of shares; and
- The disposition is to an arm's-length person.

The result is that $400,000 of the $1,000,000 dividend is recharacterized as proceeds and added to the actual proceeds of $200,000 resulting in a capital gain of $400,000. The remaining $600,000 is a tax-free dividend. The calculation is as follows:

Actual proceeds of disposition		$200,000
Add: Deemed proceeds—		
Dividend received	$1,000,000	
Retained earnings	(600,000)	$400,000
Proceeds		600,000
ACB		(200,000)
Capital gain		$400,000

---

24 ITA 55(1) to (5).

> If the shares had been sold for $1,200,000 without the dividend, a capital gain of $1,000,000 would have occurred ($1,200,000 − $200,000). By having a tax-free dividend equal to the retained earnings of $600,000 the capital gain is reduced to $400,000. This demonstrates that a potential capital gain can be reduced by a pre-sale tax-free dividend distribution only to the extent of the retained earnings of the company being sold.

All of the above examples demonstrate the significant impact that holding corporations have on cash flow generated from investment returns. It should also be pointed out that a holding corporation does not always have to be in existence from the outset in order for its benefits to be utilized. For example, if, in Exhibit 14-10, the individual shareholder directly owned the shares of For Sale Corporation, a holding corporation could be interposed just before the contemplated sale of shares. This could be achieved using one of the reorganization methods described in the first section of the chapter. Specifically, the individual could sell the shares of For Sale Corporation to a newly created holding company and elect that the transfer price occur at tax values. The proper organization structure would then be in place to pay intercorporate dividends; this would be followed by a sale of shares by the holding corporation.

III. Summary and Conclusion

Businesses often divide their operations among several separate corporations in order to satisfy various business objectives and to facilitate changes in ownership participation. The income tax system recognizes that these complex organizations often require restructuring and provides a number of means by which businesses can adapt to the changing business environment. Specifically, the following basic reorganization methods are available:

1. Transfer of assets from one corporation to another.

2. The reorganization of share capital and ownership rights of the corporation.

3. The amalgamation of two or more corporations into a single, combined corporation.

4. The wind-up of a subsidiary corporation into its parent corporation.

With each of the above methods, the reorganization can occur without triggering taxable income, even though assets have been transferred from one entity to another. While no tax occurs on the reorganization, this does not mean that tax has been permanently avoided. The tax positions that existed before the reorganization remain preserved in the new structure and will ultimately be triggered when assets are sold to third parties.

This concept of tax deferral is based on the premise that a reorganization constitutes a change in *form*, rather than a change in *substance*, in that all parties to the transaction continue to have an interest in the restructured entity. It is for this reason that independent parties are permitted to use these same reorganization alternatives to combine their operations. As long as the parties have not converted their interest into cash or some other hard asset and maintain some form of share ownership, the reorganization can occur on a tax-deferred basis.

The details of the tax provisions for completing a reorganization are extremely complex. Even so, managers must strive to understand the nature of reorganization activities—specifically, how those activities are best performed and their impact on immediate and future cash flows. While corporate restructuring is motivated primarily by certain business objectives, the related tax treatment and cash-flow implications must be anticipated so that the related business decision can be fully assessed.

When deciding on the method of business reorganization, managers must be able to envision the consequences of the available options. With this in mind, this chapter has stressed the methods available, when to use them, and their general tax impact, rather than the specifics of how to carry out those methods.

This chapter has also demonstrated the important role of holding companies as a means of transferring accumulated earnings from one corporation to another via tax-free dividends. The shifting of after-tax corporate profits from one corporation to another also constitutes a change in form, rather than substance, and is therefore an important part of corporate reorganization activities. Holding companies have a dramatic impact on after-tax investment returns; they also affect specific decisions relating to business acquisitions and divestitures.

This chapter concludes Part Three of the text, which was devoted solely to corporate structures. While some of the concepts appear complex, they all relate to the corporation/shareholder relationship in a two-tiered tax system that taxes corporate income separately from distributions to the shareholder(s).

Part Four of the text will examine business organizations that are alternatives to the corporation.

Visit the Canadian Income Taxation Web site at **www.mcgrawhill.ca/ olc/buckwold** to view any updated tax information.

Review Questions

1. "A corporate reorganization usually involves a change in form, rather than a change in substance." Explain this statement.

2. What unique tax treatment does a corporate reorganization provide? What is the logic for permitting this to occur?

3. Is it possible for unrelated corporations to combine their business activities through a reorganization? If it is, what must occur in order to ensure that the transaction will not be treated as an outright sale of property at fair market value?

4. Identify four basic reorganization techniques.

5. Briefly describe two alternative tax treatments when the business assets of one corporation are transferred to another corporation. Are these two alternatives available only if the corporation acquiring the assets is owned by the corporation selling the assets? Explain.

6. If Corporation A wishes to transfer its business operations to Corporation B by way of an asset transfer, must all of the assets relating to that business be transferred? Explain. How will the future income of each corporation be different if some but not all of the business assets are transferred?

7. Describe what takes place when two or more corporations amalgamate.

8. Distinguish between a wind-up of a wholly owned subsidiary corporation and an amalgamation of the parent and subsidiary.

9. What is the tax treatment of a corporation's unused net capital losses and/or non-capital losses after that corporation has been amalgamated with another corporation or has been wound up into its parent corporation?

10. What form of reorganization permits the current common shareholders to retain their existing value in the corporation and, at the same time, alters the ratio relating to the sharing of future growth beyond the existing value? Explain how this reorganization can be accomplished without any immediate tax consequences to the shareholders.

11. What is a holding corporation?

12. Dividends received by a corporation from another taxable Canadian corporation are excluded from taxable income and therefore are not usually subject to tax. However, in certain circumstances, a Canadian-controlled private corporation may be subject to a special refundable tax on the receipt of Canadian dividends. In what circumstances will this special tax apply, what is the rate of tax, and why is it referred to as a "refundable tax"?

13. What is the primary benefit of using a holding corporation to hold investments in the shares of other corporations, rather than holding those investments personally?

14. Briefly explain why a holding company may be useful when the shares of an active business corporation are being acquired.

15. Briefly explain how using a holding company to own the shares of an active business corporation may be beneficial when the shares of the active business corporation are about to be sold. In what circumstances may using a holding company be disadvantageous when the shares of the active business corporation are being sold? Explain.

Key Concept Questions

QUESTION ONE

[handwritten: Taxation yr. ended Mar. 31.]
[handwritten: - new corporation Born.]

Hazel owns all of the shares of H Ltd. Kristin, owns all of the shares of K Ltd. The owners plan to combine their businesses by amalgamating the two corporations on April 1st of the current year. The shares of H have an ACB of $100 and are currently worth $40,000. The shares of K have an ACB of $200 and are currently worth $60,000. H and K are both Canadian corporations. *Income tax reference: ITA 87(1), (2), (4).*

Describe the tax implications of the amalgamation of H Ltd. and K Ltd. *[handwritten: deemed to sold assets at tax values (ACB, UCC, CEC)]*

QUESTION TWO

[handwritten: tax free > 90%.]

M Ltd., a Canadian corporation, owns 100% of the shares of P Ltd. The P shares have an ACB of $40,000 and are now worth $100,000. P's only asset is land having a cost of $25,000 and a current value of $100,000. The land was worth $40,000 when M purchased P's shares. Both corporations have December 31 year ends. *Income tax reference: ITA 88(1), (1.1), (1.2).*

Determine the tax implications for M Ltd. and P Ltd. from winding up P Ltd. into M Ltd. on April 1, 20X8.

QUESTION THREE

[handwritten: <90% not taxfree windup]

Profit Ltd., a Canadian public corporation, owns 85% of the shares of Loss Ltd. Profit Ltd. has a December 31 year end while Loss Ltd. has a July 31 year end. The fair market value and tax value of the non-depreciable assets owned by Loss Ltd. total $8,000,000 and $3,000,000, respectively. The values have increased substantially from their $5,000,000 value at the time Profit Ltd. acquired Loss Ltd. The shares of Loss Ltd. are currently worth $10,000,000 and have an ACB of $4,000,000. Profit Ltd. wants to use the losses of Loss Ltd. to reduce its taxable income. Profit Ltd. and Loss Ltd. will be combined on August 1st of the current year. *Income tax reference: ITA 87, 88.*

Should a wind-up of Loss Ltd. into Profit Ltd. or an amalgamation of Profit Ltd. and Loss Ltd. be used to combine the two corporations? Explain why.

QUESTION FOUR

Mr. Senior owns all of the issued shares of X Ltd. These common shares have an ACB and PUC of $100 and are worth $1,200,000. Senior would like to freeze his interest in the company at today's value so that future increases in value accrue to his son, Mark. To accomplish this, Senior exchanged his common shares for preferred shares of X in the course of a reorganization of share capital. The preferred shares are redeemable for $1,200,000. Mark then acquired newly issued common shares of X for $100. *Income tax reference: ITA 84(3), 86(1), (2.1).*

Determine the tax implications for Mr. Senior.

QUESTION FIVE

Valerie owns all of the common shares of V Ltd. The shares have an ACB and PUC of $10,000 and are worth $800,000. In the course of a reorganization of capital, Valerie exchanges all of her common shares for $700,000 of redeemable preferred shares of V and $100,000 of debt. *Income tax reference: ITA 84(3), 86(1), (2.1).*

Determine the tax implications for Valerie.

QUESTION SIX

X Ltd. owns all of the shares of Y Ltd. The shares of Y have an adjusted cost base of $40,000 and a fair market value of $940,000. Y has retained earnings of $100,000 (earned after 1971) and an RDTOH balance of nil. Y plans to pay a dividend of $900,000 to X. Subsequently, X will sell the shares of Y Ltd. to an arm's-length person for $40,000. *Income tax reference: ITA 55(2).*

Determine the tax consequences to X Ltd. of these transactions.

Problems

PROBLEM ONE

Concrete Ltd. is a Canadian-controlled private corporation that manufactures concrete blocks in its Regina plant and also operates a general contracting business.

In 20X1, Concrete acquired 100% of the shares of Little Ltd., which owns a concrete plant in Saskatoon. At the time of acquisition, Little had non-capital losses carried forward in the amount of $175,000 and net capital losses carried forward of $10,000. These losses related to the 20X0 fiscal period.

Both Concrete and Little have a December 31 year end.

The common shares of Concrete are owned 60% by A Ltd., 35% by B Ltd., and 5% by C Ltd. A Ltd., B Ltd., and C Ltd. are owned by Mr. A, Mr. B, and Mr. C, respectively. They are all employed by Concrete and are not related to each other.

The three shareholders intend to meet to review the current year's financial results (20X2) and to discuss several other matters. The financial results and other issues that will be discussed are outlined below.

1. After it was acquired, Little continued to lose money. For the year ended December 31, 20X2, it suffered a loss of $60,000. At the time of acquisition, the owners planned to make major changes to Little's operations, but they have not been able to complete these on schedule.

2. Concrete had a pre-tax profit of $190,000 for 20X2. Of this amount, $120,000 related to the general contracting business. The contracting business subcontracted all of its work and maintained only a small staff of estimators and administrators.

3. Concrete has accumulated cash reserves that will not be needed for business expansion. The owners are considering paying a $100,000 dividend out of Concrete to the three corporate shareholders. Each holding company will use its share of the dividend for investment purposes.

4. During the year, an agreement was made among A Ltd., B Ltd., and C. Ltd. stating that in the event of the death of A, B, or C, Concrete must buy back the shares owned by the deceased's holding corporation. At the time of the agreement, Concrete purchased a life insurance policy on each individual that would provide it with funds to buy back the shares.

5. Several months earlier, A had suggested that Concrete acquire a profitable swimming pool installation business. B and C had vetoed the idea. A intends to inform B and C that he will make the acquisition on his own and intends to acquire the business through A Ltd.

Required:

1. Diagram the financial structure of the shareholders and the corporations described above.

2. What tax advice would you provide with respect to the operations of the subsidiary, Little, considering its poor financial results?

3. Discuss the implications of declaring a dividend of $100,000 from Concrete.

4. If one of the individuals died, what tax implications would arise from the realization of life insurance proceeds?

5. How might the proposed business acquisition by A Ltd. affect B and C? What addition to the shareholder's agreement should B and C propose?

PROBLEM TWO

Jimmy Divine owns five of the 100 issued common shares of Poultry Products Ltd. The remaining shares are owned by six other individuals, some of whom are employed by the corporation. The others are passive investors.

Divine has informed the shareholders that he wants to dispose of his shares for their market value, which is $60,000. The shares have a paid-up capital of $50, but Divine had purchased the shares a number of years ago from one of the other shareholders for $10,000. None of the other shareholders has funds to purchase Divine's shares. Unfortunately, the corporation is also temporarily short of cash.

The other shareholders have agreed that the corporation will buy back Divine's five shares at the rate of one share per year over the next five years but that the total price will remain at $60,000. Divine realizes that the value of the unredeemed shares will grow in the next five years as the company continues to earn profits. He is prepared to forgo these profits, provided that the company pays him a fixed dividend on the unredeemed shares of 8% per annum. The company normally pays non-eligible dividends. In addition, he does not want to pay tax on the share sales until he actually receives the cash for them.

Required:

1. What can the company do to buy back Divine's shares at the rate of one share per year so that any unredeemed shares will not change in value before they are redeemed?

2. What amount of net income for tax purposes will Divine earn from the share buy-back in each of the five years?

PROBLEM THREE

Betty Borsboom and Walter Good each own 50% of the shares of KM Supplies Ltd. The company has enjoyed steady growth since it began, and all corporate profits have been reinvested in business expansion. The shareholders do not expect this growth to continue, as their market share has reached its peak. In fact, this year, for the first time, the company has generated excess cash flow that is not needed for expansion. Borsboom and Good plan to meet to discuss what they should do with this excess.

Borsboom is 32 years old and Good is 58, and their personal investment strategies are quite different. Borsboom anticipates that as Good reaches retirement age she will have to buy his 50% interest in the company—unless, of course, they decide to sell the entire company to some other party.

The company has invested the excess funds in treasury bills as a temporary measure while the owners are deciding on a course of action. Good has suggested that the company simply find a more permanent investment; Borsboom has concerns about the future implications of this strategy and may suggest that the company establish a policy of paying a dividend with any excess funds generated.

Required:

1. Identify the problems that may arise if these funds, as well as future funds, are left in the company and used to acquire a permanent investment.

2. What impact would a policy of regular dividend distributions have on the wealth accumulation of Borsboom and Good?

3. Could their problems be solved if each organized a separate holding corporation, which would, in turn, acquire their shares in KM Supplies? Explain.

PROBLEM FOUR

Judy Whyte owns all of the common shares of Danube Manufacturing Ltd. Whyte purchased the shares 10 years ago directly from the corporate treasury at a cost of $50,000. The company regularly earns a pre-tax profit from an active business of $180,000.

Whyte has decided to sell the shares of the company to Peter Blue for $700,000. Blue has only $400,000 cash available, but a local bank has agreed to provide a loan of $300,000 for the balance of the purchase price.

Information relating to the company as of the last fiscal year end is as follows:

Paid-up capital of the common shares	$ 50,000
Retained earnings	500,000

Both Whyte and Blue have other sources of income and are in a 45% marginal tax bracket on regular income, 28% on eligible dividends and 33% on non-eligible dividends.

Whyte has asked for your advice with respect to the sale of the company. She has mentioned that a friend recently sold his company after transferring his shares to a holding company and that in so doing he gained some deferral benefits.

You are also the accountant for Blue, and he has also sought your advice.

Required:

1. Compare the tax consequences, to Whyte, of the following alternatives:
   - Whyte sells shares directly to Blue.
   - The corporation buys back all the common shares from Whyte and issues new shares to Blue. This alternative should examine both eligible and non-eligible dividends.

2. Outline to Whyte the advantages, if any, of first transferring the shares to a holding corporation. Show calculations for each of the alternatives mentioned in 1, and inform Whyte of the short-term and long-term implications.

3. How could Whyte transfer her shares of Danube to a new holding corporation without any immediate tax consequences?

4. Assuming that Whyte will sell her shares directly to Blue for $700,000, answer the following questions with respect to Blue:
   (a) How will the interest payments on the bank loan be treated for tax purposes?
   (b) If Blue must obtain money from Danube to repay the principal of the bank loan, what is the fastest possible time period that the loan can be repaid? (You may assume that interest can be paid from personal funds.)
   (c) If Blue establishes a holding corporation to borrow money ($300,000) to buy the shares, how fast will he be able to repay the loan principal? (Exclude interest considerations.)
   (d) If the holding corporation makes the acquisition, what problem does the interest cost present? How can a later corporate reorganization overcome this problem, and when should this occur?
   (e) If Blue uses a holding corporation, he will contribute $400,000 of his own cash to the company to assist with the purchase. Should he loan the $400,000 to the corporation or acquire $400,000 of its common shares? Explain.

PROBLEM FIVE

Jaime owns 100% of the issued shares of Big Ltd. which in turn owns 100% of the issued shares of Small Ltd. Big paid $1,000,000 for the shares of Small in 20X3. Small carries on an electronics repair business and has incurred non-capital losses in its years ended December 31, 20X4 and December 31, 20X5 of $20,000 and $30,000 respectively. Jaime plans to merge the two companies by a wind-up on August 31, 20X6 or an amalgamation on September 1, 20X6. Jaime wants a March 31 year end for the business going forward. Big Ltd. currently has a March 31 year end.

The table below contains the anticipated balance sheet of Small at August 31, 20X6 with the fair market value of the assets both at August 31, 20X6 and at the time Big acquired Small in 20X3.

	Cost	FMV Aug. 31, 20X6	FMV in 20X3
Shares of public companies	$ 10,000	$ 60,000	$ 40,000
Accounts receivable	80,000	75,000	
Allowance for doubtful accounts	(5,000)		
Goodwill	0	200,000	200,000
Land	120,000	445,000	300,000
Building	250,000*	400,000	350,000
Total assets	$455,000		
Bank loan	$100,000		
Common shares	5,000		
Retained earning	350,000		
Total liabilities	$455,000		

* UCC of building

Small paid dividends of $12,000 to Big in both 20X4 and 20X5.

Required:

Explain the tax consequences for Big Ltd. and Small Ltd. if the merger is accomplished by:

1) a wind-up, or

2) an amalgamation.

PROBLEM SIX

Holding Ltd., a Canadian-controlled private corporation, acquired 100% of the shares of Operating Ltd. on incorporation in 20X0 for $100,000. The shares of Operating Ltd. have appreciated in value since then. A large part of the share appreciation is attributed to land Operating Ltd owns which has doubled in value. The retained earnings of Operating Ltd. are currently $500,000.

An arm's-length company, Acquisition Corporation, has offered to purchase 100% of the shares of Operating Ltd. for $900,000.

In the course of the acquisition discussions, Holding Ltd. causes Operating Ltd. to pay a dividend of $800,000.

Acquisition Ltd. then buys 100% of the Operating Ltd. shares for $100,000.

Required:

Explain the tax implications for Holding Ltd. on the sale of the shares of Operating Ltd.

Cases

CASE ONE The Mavis Group

Mavis Corporation, a Canadian company, is a major wholesaler of women's shoes. The company has a history of substantial profits. In 20X7, its net income before tax amounted to $700,000.

Mavis Corporation owns (100%) three subsidiary corporations. The corporate structure is outlined below.

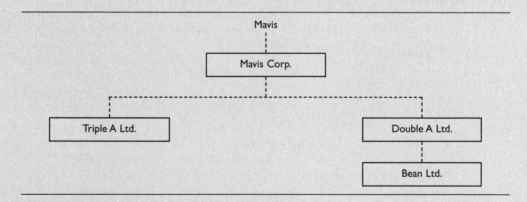

Information relating to the subsidiaries is provided below.

• **Triple A Ltd.**   This corporation was acquired five years ago, in 20X2. The company retails women's casual summer shoes and usually earns an annual pre-tax profit of $100,000.

• **Double A Ltd.**   Double A was acquired in 20X3 and retails women's high-fashion shoes. The company was profitable for two years after acquisition but has since suffered regular losses. At the end of the current year (20X7) it has unused business losses (non-capital losses) of $400,000. Losses of $50,000 are expected for each of the next three years. The company's assets include land and buildings that have risen in value.

• **Bean Ltd.**   This subsidiary operates a canning business, and its main customer is a large chain of retail food stores. The company was acquired in 20X6, and at the time of acquisition had unused business losses of $150,000 and an unused capital loss of $40,000. In 20X7, Bean suffered a further operating loss of $250,000. Management is concerned about the amount of this loss and is considering whether to close the factory or perhaps sell it.

Bean does not have any significant assets, as it rents its land and building under a short-term lease. It does own the manufacturing equipment, but this has little value.

Required:

Review the existing financial structure of the Mavis Group of companies and discuss what steps might be taken to enhance the company's growth potential.

CASE TWO   Charles Bert

Charles Bert is a successful Canadian businessman. For the past 15 years, he has been president of Bert-Ram Electronics Ltd., a company he started with Peter Ramper. Ramper, who is not employed by the company, obtained shares in the company in exchange for patent rights on one of his inventions.

For many years, Bert-Ram suffered the typical growing pains of a new business, including cash-flow shortages. In the past few years, however, the company has generated substantial profits as well as cash flow in excess of expansion requirements.

Bert is not a "high liver," and his annual salary is sufficient to meet his personal needs.

Realco Corporation owns two rental properties and generates rental income of $130,000 annually. Bert owns 25% of the common shares of Realco; the remaining shares are owned 25% by each of three other investors.

Bert currently has a net worth of $1,500,000, as follows:

Personal assets	$ 300,000
Common shares of Bert-Ram (75% of the common shares)	800,000
Bonds	200,000
Common shares of Realco	200,000
	$1,500,000

In 20X1, Bert-Ram earned an after-tax profit from business of $500,000, of which only $100,000 was required for business expansion. The company currently has $250,000 of cash invested in bank term deposits. Bert and Ramper recently argued about how to invest this cash—Ramper is keen on the stock market, while Bert prefers real estate investments.

Bert's personal income for 20X1 consists of the following:

Salary (Bert-Ram)	$100,000
Interest	15,000
Dividends:	
Bert-Ram	50,000
Realco	15,000
	$180,000

Recently, Bert was given the opportunity to purchase 100% of the common shares of LOBD Software Ltd., a Canadian software wholesaler. The company generates profits of $100,000 after tax and has a strong management team that could run the business without a significant time commitment from Bert. The asking price for the shares is $600,000 cash. The most recent balance sheet of LOBD is shown below.

Bert has decided to purchase the LOBD shares, and his bank has agreed to finance the full $600,000 purchase price. Bert will use his bonds and shares of Bert-Ram as collateral for the loan. The bank requires that at least $80,000 of the loan principal be repaid each year in addition to interest.

Required:

Review Bert's financial structure and outline what steps he can take to maximize his net worth in the future.

LOBD SOFTWARE LTD.
Balance Sheet
May 31, 20X1

Assets:		
Current assets (cash, receivables, and inventory)		$565,000
Fixed assets (at cost):		
Vehicles	60,000	
Equipment	110,000	
	170,000	
Accumulated amortization	(65,000)	105,000
Investment in long-term bonds		100,000
		$770,000
Liabilities:		
Accounts payable		$350,000
Income taxes payable		20,000
		370,000
Shareholder's equity:		
Share capital	10,000	
Retained earnings	390,000	400,000
		$770,000

PART 4

Other Forms of Business Organization

*If you can run a business well,
you can run any business well.*

RICHARD BRANSON

CHAPTER 15

Partnerships

To this point in the text, discussions of business structures involving single or multiple owners have been restricted to the two primary taxable entities—individuals and corporations. There are four other forms that a business organization can take: standard partnership, joint venture, limited partnership, and trust.

The first three can be referred to as the "secondary" or "non-taxable" entities. *Non-taxable* does not mean that the entity's earned income is not subject to tax but, rather, that the entity itself is not directly liable for tax on its earned income. The last entity (trusts) is a *hybrid* entity because it has some discretion with how its income is taxed. A trust normally can choose if some, or all, of its income will be taxed as trust income or allocated to beneficiaries and taxed as part of their income. Those beneficiaries may be individuals, corporations, or other trusts such as pension plans and RRSPs.

Each of the four entities is different from the others, but all are structured on similar principles. It is important to recognize that each of the secondary entities can be useful to, and form part of, any business structure, whether that structure involves individuals or corporations and whether it involves a giant conglomerate or a small business enterprise. The standard partnership form of organization is often considered to be useful only to individuals who practise together in a profession or a small business. Actually, the standard partnership often forms part of the business structure of large public and private corporations.

Partnerships, limited partnerships, and joint ventures are available as alternative structures whenever a proposed business activity is to be carried out with other parties. The fact that a venture includes other parties complicates the management of cash flows and the related tax variable. The commitment of funds to such ventures requires that a structure be developed which permits the easy return of the original capital invested as well as the return to the investor of any profits for further investment in other ventures.

Cash flow from investments in activities with other parties will be affected by the way in which the profits from the separate venture are taxed and the losses, if any, can be utilized. Cash flow will also be affected by the tax treatment in the event that the original capital is lost and the venture fails, as well as by the tax consequences of repatriating the original capital and accumulated profits. The commitment of funds to any investment activity must take the long view and consider not only the project at hand but also its impact on the investor's ability to participate in other immediate and future activities. This concern is of greater significance when other parties are participating in a venture.

This chapter is devoted solely to the standard partnership form of organization and covers three general areas:

1. The definition and general format of the partnership entity.

2. The taxation of partnership profits and its impact on cash flows.

3. The advantages and disadvantages, in terms of cash flow, of establishing a partnership, rather than a corporation.

I. The Standard Partnership—Definition and Format

A. Definition

The *Income Tax Act* does not define "partnership"; it merely outlines the tax treatment of income generated by one. A broad, generally accepted definition is that a partnership is the relationship that exists between entities carrying on a business in common with a view to profit.[1] The entity is created when two or more entities jointly conduct an ongoing business enterprise whose scope is defined by mutual agreement. It is characterized by the partners sharing in the final net results of the enterprise in an agreed ratio, rather than by the mere division of gross receipts.

---

1 IT-90.

Partnerships are often confused with joint ventures or "co-ownership." A joint venture is similar to a partnership in that it involves two or more entities conducting a business activity together but is different in that it is usually formed for a single purpose or a single transaction (see Chapter 16).[2] A co-ownership usually involves the joint ownership of an investment property, rather than an operating business. When several individuals or corporations own a block of rental apartments, that is an example of co-ownership.

This text will not define the legal principles that distinguish these forms of organization from each other; rather, it will demonstrate how these forms can be utilized and their impact on the decision process. Even so, the reader should appreciate that creating such entities raises complex legal issues that often vary within Canadian and foreign jurisdictions.

B. Partnership Agreement

A partnership venture consists of the *partnership entity*, which conducts its affairs as a separate organization, and a particular number of *partners*. The partners are usually one of the two primary entities (individuals or corporations), although other kinds of entities, such as trusts or other partnerships, may also be participating partners. Exhibit 15-1 demonstrates three simple partnership structures; each consists of the minimum of two partners, with one holding a 60% interest and the other a 40% interest.

The three structures are distinguished by the nature of the participating partners. In structure A, both partners are individuals. In structure B, one partner is an individual and the other is a corporation. In structure C, both partners are corporations. Although individual X and individual Y are directly or indirectly involved in each structure, it is important to recognize that they are not the partners in each of the three partnership ventures; the direct influence of the standard partnership extends from

Exhibit 15-1:

Basic Business Structures Involving Partnerships

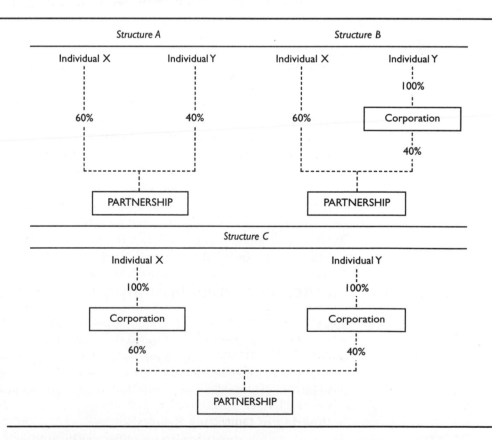

2 *Woodlin Developments Ltd. v. MNR,* (TCC), 86 DTC 116.

the partnership entity itself to the actual partners and not beyond. In each structure, neither partner, whether individual or corporate, is precluded from conducting other activities. In structure C, for example, one or both of the corporate partners may carry on other, unrelated business or investment activities; their involvement in the partnership venture may constitute only a minor part of their separate operations.

A partnership is created by the execution of a *partnership agreement* among the various partners. This agreement becomes the working framework of the entity. Within certain limits, partnership agreements can be tailored to suit the specific needs of the partners. Because of this, the standard partnership is more flexible than the corporation in terms of the procedures for administering the venture's affairs.

The general nature and unique aspects of a particular partnership are developed in the partnership agreement, which gives special attention to three fundamental areas:

1. Each partner's required contributions to the entity.

2. The format and rules for decision making and the management of the partnership's business affairs.

3. How profits or losses are to be shared by the participating partners.

1. Partner's Contribution

A partner can participate in a partnership venture by contributing capital, effort, or a combination of the two. It is not always necessary that each partner commit a proportionate amount of financial resources to the venture. When financial resources are required as a contribution, they are usually provided in the form of cash; however, specific assets, such as land, buildings, equipment, patents, franchises, and the like, can also be contributed. The cash or the value of specific assets contributed constitutes the partnership's equity base; if further resources are required, the partnership can incur debt. In summary, a partnership is a self-contained entity holding assets, liabilities, and partner's equity.

2. Management

Usually, all partners participate in the management of the enterprise, although by agreement specific partners may be excluded from this process, in which case they are entitled only to share in the operating results.

A special aspect of standard partnerships is that the procedures for decision making can be tailored to the wishes of the participating partners. It is not required that the partner or partners holding a majority financial interest have the final say on all decisions. For example, the agreement may entitle all partners to one vote each, whatever the amount of their financial interest, so that a simple majority of votes will settle minor day-to-day decisions; at the same time, the same organization may require a unanimous vote for important policy decisions.

Management decision making within a partnership is completely flexible and can be as democratic or as autocratic as the partners wish. This can be contrasted with the corporate form of organization, in which decisions are made by a board of directors, elected by shareholders, whose voting power is determined by the number of voting shares owned. Some flexibility can be achieved in a corporation but not nearly as much as in a partnership. A minority shareholder of a corporation is often powerless, whereas a minority partner in a partnership can be provided with a great deal of influence if the partners so choose. This flexibility makes a partnership attractive, as its structure can be designed to mirror the specific objectives of the participants.

3. Sharing of Operating Results

The partnership structure also provides significant flexibility in the way profits or losses from operations are shared by the partners. Profits or losses are usually shared as a function of capital contributions, the degree of effort or participation in the business process, or both. As a partner, an entity may participate in profit sharing on the basis of special expertise or a comparatively greater degree of management effort, even though its financial contribution is non-existent or substantially less than that of other partners. The sharing of profits and losses is a function of the partnership agreement, which can be tailored to the economic realities of the specific situation.

Referring again to Exhibit 15-1, it can be seen that the existence of a 60/40 partnership interest does not adequately describe the relationship between the two participating partners in any of the three structures, as it is not known if the ratio applies to profit sharing, capital contributions, or decision-making powers. Each of these items may involve a different relationship. This, more than anything else, is what makes standard partnerships unique.

C. Partner Liability

The standard partnership is a separate functioning entity for management purposes. However, it is not a protected *legal* entity that is separate from the affairs of the partners. This means that all obligations and debts incurred by the partnership or by partners acting in the course of partnership business, and all negligent activities performed by them, are the *full responsibility* of *each partner* participating in the venture. Each partner is jointly and severally liable for all partnership activities, which means that every partner's liability exposure not only goes beyond the amount of capital invested in the venture but also goes beyond the proportionate share of partnership involvement. A creditor may seek full satisfaction from any or all of the partners; and it is usual for the partner with the greatest financial strength to be targeted for full satisfaction, even though that partner may hold a smaller partnership interest.

In limited circumstances, risk insurance that limits the partners' exposure may be obtained by the partnership. However, the most common method used to avoid liability exposure involves each intended partner interposing a limited-value holding corporation as the actual partner. Consider the two business structures outlined in Exhibit 15-2. The high-risk structure involves two independent business corporations entering into a 50/50 partnership requiring $1,000,000 of capital. While both corporate partners have contributed $500,000 of capital, their liability exposure is considerably different. Corporation A has a net worth of $1,000,000, whereas Corporation B has a net worth of $8,000,000. Since both partners are jointly and severally liable for the partnership obligation, B bears a greater burden of exposure because of its much higher net worth. For A, which has a net worth of only $1,000,000, the potential consequences of being exposed to the full obligations of the partnership may be catastrophic.

Both partners can limit their risk by developing the low-risk structure outlined in Exhibit 15-2. In this structure, A and B each capitalize a holding corporation with $500,000, that amount being the required contribution to the partnership. Each holding corporation then contributes the $500,000 to the partnership. The partners in this structure are the two holding corporations, not the two business corporations. While each holding company is exposed to the full obligations of the partnership, the liability of each is limited to its net worth of only $500,000. As well, any partnership profits distributed to the partners can, in turn, be passed on as tax-free intercorporate dividends to the two parent corporations for reinvestment. Usually, it is not a good idea to hold the accumulated profits in the holding corporation, since this increases that corporation's net worth and therefore its risk exposure.

Exhibit 15-2:

Partner Liability and Business Structure

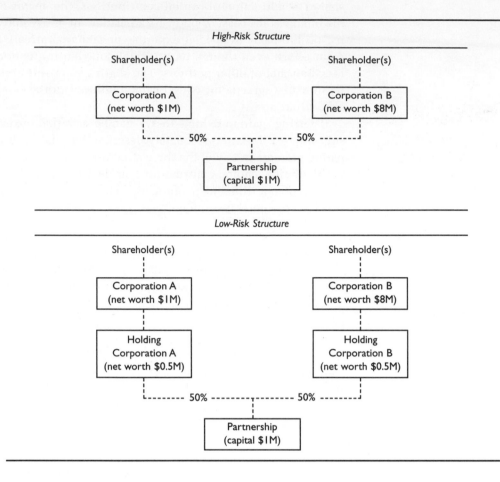

II. Taxation of Partnership Operations

A. Partnership Income and Losses

A partnership is not a taxable entity and bears no responsibility for tax on income generated within its sphere of operations. Instead, income earned or losses incurred by the partnership are allocated to the partners, in accordance with the agreed sharing ratio, for inclusion in each partner's income for tax purposes.[3] The income shared by the partners is allocated for tax purposes, regardless of whether such profits have actually been distributed to the partners. Thus, it is conceivable that a partner may bear the full tax liability on its share of income, even though the income remains within the partnership for reinvestment.

It is very significant that losses incurred by a partnership are also allocated to the partners and are included in their separate determinations of taxable income.[4] This means that losses can be offset immediately against the partners' other income, provided that other income exists. This is especially advantageous during the start-up period of a new venture, when losses are common. By utilizing losses immediately, the partner can reduce its tax bill and use the extra cash to strengthen the new venture.

The amount of income earned or losses incurred by the partnership is determined for allocation as if the partnership were a separate taxable entity. The partnership can earn business income, property income, and capital gains; all of these are determined according to the normal rules for arriving at income for tax purposes. Capital cost allowance and the amortization of goodwill and other eligible capital property are determined and applied at the partnership level before allocation.[5]

---

3 ITA 96(1).
4 ITA 96(1); IT-232R3.
5 ITA 96(1)(a) to (c).

All partnership income allocated retains its *source and characteristics* when included in the partner's income (see Exhibit 15-3).[6] A dividend to the partnership is a dividend to the partner and is treated accordingly for tax purposes. Capital gains and losses of the partnership become capital gains and losses of the partner. In this sense, the partnership is a *conduit* or *funnel*—it earns income like any other entity but passes it on to the participants as if it had been earned directly by them.

Exhibit 15-3:

Example of Partnership Allocation by Source

Type of activity	Partnership	Allocated	
		60% Partner A	40% Partner B
Business:			
Retail income	$500,000	300,000	200,000
Manufacturing loss	(100,000)	(60,000)	(40,000)
Property:			
Interest income	10,000	6,000	4,000
Eligible dividend income	40,000	24,000	16,000
Rental income	100,000	60,000	40,000
Capital gains	50,000	30,000	20,000
Capital losses	(30,000)	(18,000)	(12,000)
	$570,000		

Profits retained in the partnership form part of each partner's capital or equity and are available for distribution whenever the partners so decide. When accumulated profits are distributed to the partner, this constitutes a return of capital, which is not subject to further taxation. Put another way, the repatriation of profits has no tax implications for the members of a partnership; this is not the case for corporate entities, which must distribute their after-tax profits as taxable dividends.

The amount of tax paid on partnership profits depends on the nature of the given partner, rather than on the nature of the partnership itself. As a result, the operating results of a particular partnership are subject to various tax implications depending on

(a) whether the separate partners are individuals or corporations;
(b) the rates of tax applicable to the various partners; and
(c) the other sources of income of each partner.

For example, a partnership loss may be readily offset against the other income of one partner, while sitting idle for another partner who has a minimal amount of income from non-partnership activities. This can result in conflict between the partners. For example, the rate of capital cost allowance is determined by the partnership and, once determined, applies to each partner accordingly. The partner who has other sources of income may want to claim the maximum capital cost allowance, while the other partner, who has only losses and no other income, may prefer to claim the minimum in order to reduce the possibility of losses expiring.

When contemplating forming a partnership, the prospective partners must assess the amount and the timing of future tax costs in terms of their own individual tax status, rather than that of the partnership. In effect, the partnership is a component of each partner's own separate organization for tax purposes. Any income earned or loss incurred is simply intermingled with the partner's other sources of income. The profits are not subject to further tax when repatriated to the partners.

---

6 Political contributions and charitable donations are also allocated to the partners for use in the appropriate manner.

In order to ensure that income of a ***corporate partner*** is subject to tax on a timely basis, *special rules apply to corporate partners (other than professional corporations) when the partnership has a fiscal period different from the corporation's taxation year.* In computing a corporation's income for a taxation year, in respect of a fiscal period of the partnership that begins in the taxation year and ends in a subsequent year, the corporation will be required to accrue income from the partnership for the portion of the partnership's fiscal period that falls within the corporation's taxation year.[7] For these rules to apply, the corporate partner, together with affiliated and related parties, must be entitled to more than 10% of the partnership's income at the end of the last fiscal period of the partnership that ended in the taxation year.[8] The rules apply only to corporate income—losses are not accrued.

As mentioned above, a corporation that is affected by these rules must accrue income from the partnership year end for a period that falls within the corporate partners' year end. This is referred to as the stub period. The accrual is based on a formula that prorates the actual partnership income allocation for the partnership's taxation year for the number of days remaining in the corporation's taxation year. This inclusion is then deducted from the corporation's income in the subsequent taxation year. This is demonstrated below.

Situation:	Woodbar is a partnership with a June 30 fiscal year end. All of the partners are corporations. X Ltd. owns a 20% partnership interest in Woodbar. X's fiscal year end is September 30. For the year ended June 30, 20X5, Woodbar allocated $30,000 to X representing X's 20% share of the partnership income for tax purposes. In its previous taxation year, X accrued $5,000 of partnership income.
Analysis:	For the taxation year ending September 30, 20X5, X must include $32,561 as its share of the partnership profits calculated as follows:

Partnership profit for the year ending June 30, 20X5	$30,000
Add accrual for the year − $30,000 × 92 days/365 days	7,561
Deduct amount accrued in the previous year	(5,000)
Net partnership income for tax purposes	$32,561

Note that this is a notional accrual based on the actual profits allocated by the partnership. The accrual period is simply the number of days from the partnership year end of June 30 to the corporation's year end of September 30 (92 days). This period is technically referred to as "the adjusted stub period accrual." If the corporation has knowledge of the actual income in the stub period, the formula amount can be reduced. However if an error is made, an adjustment is made in the following taxation year.

It should be noted that if any member of the partnership is an individual, the taxation year of the partnership must be a calendar year (December 31) unless an alternative election is made (see Chapter 5).

B. The Partnership Interest

The participation of an entity as a partner in a partnership venture is recognized through the ownership of a "partnership interest." A partner is considered to own a partnership interest whenever that partner has rights and obligations created by being party to a partnership agreement. The partnership interest is a tradeable asset that can be bought and sold, much like a share of a corporation's capital stock. This makes it possible to change the participating partners without disturbing the partnership

---

7   ITA 34.2(2).
8   ITA 34.2(1).

enterprise itself. In most circumstances, a partnership interest is treated as capital property for tax purposes; as such, its disposition results in a capital gain or loss.

Usually, a partnership is created when the participants contribute capital in the form of cash or assets in return for a partnership interest, whose rights and obligations are defined in the partnership agreement. Thereafter, an unrelated entity can become a partner by

(a) purchasing a departing partner's interest, or acquiring a portion of the interest of each remaining partner; or

(b) contributing cash or specific other assets directly to the partnership in return for a new partnership interest (thereby diluting the earlier partner ratio of participation).

Conversely, existing partners can depart or diminish their percentage of participation by

(a) selling all or a portion of their partnership interest to a new partner or existing partner(s); or

(b) withdrawing their capital directly from the partnership treasury (thereby enhancing the ownership percentage of the remaining partners).

Note that in both situations, the alternatives involve either a transaction between the partners, which has no effect on the partnership entity, or a transaction between the partnership and a specific partner, which *does* affect the partnership entity. The financial and tax considerations are different for each alternative, as demonstrated in the following example.

Assume that an existing partnership consists of two partners, A and B, who share profits equally. A and B intend to admit a third partner, C, and thereafter share profits on the basis of one-third each. The existing partnership has a net worth of $100,000, of which $50,000 belongs to A and $50,000 to B. New partner C can enter the partnership in one of two ways, as diagrammed in Exhibit 15-4. The transaction under alternative 1 is between new partner C and the partnership. As the existing partnership has a net worth of $100,000, C must contribute $50,000 to achieve a one-third interest. The contribution of $50,000 to the treasury increases the partnership's net worth by $50,000 to a total of $150,000. Partners A and B each retain a $50,000 interest in the entity; however, their interests have been diluted to one-third each as a result of the enhanced financial strength of the partnership arising from C's contribution. Since neither A nor B has directly disposed of any existing partnership interest, this alternative has no tax consequences to the parties.

A new partner can also enter the partnership under alternative 2; however, in this case, the financial and tax consequences are different. Under this alternative, new partner C obtains a one-third interest in the partnership by purchasing some of the

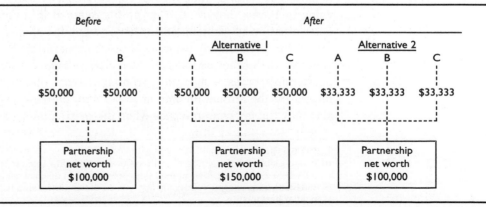

Exhibit 15-4:

Partnership Structure of A and B before and after Admitting C

partnership interest of both A and B. The transaction is among the partners, rather than between a partner and the partnership entity. The cost of a one-third interest is $33,333, which is one-third of the entity's net worth of $100,000. One-half of this amount is paid to A, the other half to B. As a result, A and B receive financial consideration but the partnership retains its former financial strength. Both A and B have disposed of a portion of their partnership interest; this may result in a capital gain or a capital loss, depending on the cost of the partnership interest.

The distinguishing features of the two alternatives relate to the financial strength of the enterprise and to how its partners are taxed. In the above example, alternative 1 enhanced the financial strength of the business; alternative 2 did not change the financial strength of the business but only the original partners' positions in it. In the same way, the departure of a partner will diminish the resources of an enterprise if that partner leaves with his capital; but if the remaining partners use their separate resources to purchase the departing partner's interest, the partnership's resources will be unchanged.

Disposing of a partnership interest, as pointed out previously, will normally result in a capital gain or loss depending on whether that interest's value has increased or diminished in relation to its cost. This, of course, has tax implications. A partnership interest, like a share of a corporation, will increase or decrease in value as a result of

(a) the accumulation, within the entity, of undistributed profits or the occurrence of operating losses; and

(b) the increase or decrease in the value of assets owned by the partnership, such as land, buildings, equipment, goodwill, and so on.

An important feature of partnerships is that any change in value of the partnership interest resulting from *profits retained* or *losses incurred* does not create a capital gain or capital loss when the partnership interest is disposed of. Capital gains or losses on the sale of a partnership interest occur only to the extent that the individual assets owned by the partnership have changed in value. This results from an arbitrary adjustment to the cost base, for tax purposes, of the partnership interest.[9] The actual cost base of a partnership interest (being the contribution amount by the partner to the partnership or the cost of acquiring another partner's interest) is automatically increased or decreased for tax purposes whenever profits or losses are allocated to the partners and whenever accumulated profits are withdrawn.[10] For example, if a partner is allocated $20,000 of profits for inclusion in income, the value of the partnership interest is increased by $20,000 if such profits are not withdrawn. The cost base of the partnership interest is arbitrarily increased by $20,000, and therefore, both value and cost increase by the same amount. Later, if the partnership interest is sold, the increase in value from the retained profits of $20,000 is offset by the exact increase in cost of $20,000, and no capital gain occurs.

Partnership profits or losses are funnelled directly to the separate partners for inclusion in income determination and are not taxed again when the partnership interest is disposed of. This treatment must be compared with that given to corporations. Share value increases that result from profits retained in a corporation are included in the determination of capital gains or losses when the shares are disposed of, even though the profits have already been taxed in the corporation. Entities that enter into business ventures with other parties can often choose between organizing the new venture as a partnership or as a separate corporation with shareholders. Not only will the tax impact on the annual income or losses vary between these two basic options, but so also may the tax consequences when the participants' equity is ultimately sold.

---

9 ITA 53(1)(e), 53(2)(c).

10 It is possible for the adjusted cost base of a partnership interest to be a negative value. By exception (ITA 40(3.1)), this negative amount does not result in a deemed capital gain (until all partners' rights are satisfied). This exception does not apply to a limited partnership (Chapter 16) or to passive partners in a regular partnership.

C. Transactions with Partners and Reorganizations

A partnership, although a non-taxable entity in terms of income, is considered to be a separate entity for purposes of holding assets. This means that if partners buy property from the partnership or sell it to the partnership, those transactions are automatically considered to have taken place at fair market value. If, for example, a partner transfers a property that has increased in value to the partnership, that partner is considered to have disposed of the property at fair market value, which may result in taxable income and therefore a tax cost to that partner.[11] The partnership that has acquired the property is considered to have incurred a cost equal to that property's fair market value and consequently may receive certain tax benefits. If, for example, the acquired property is depreciable, capital cost allowance can be claimed by the partnership based on this new cost, thereby reducing the taxable income earned by the partnership and allocated to the partners. In other words, what is lost by the partner may be regained by the partnership, although over a different time period.

As an alternative, a partner can choose to transfer property into a partnership at a value equal to the partner's cost for tax purposes.[12] This eliminates the creation of taxable income to the partner; but the partnership will also have a lower cost for tax purposes, and capital cost allowance will only be claimable on the lower amount.

Similarly, when an existing partnership transfers its assets to a partner, those assets are considered to have been sold at fair market value.[13] This may also create income to the partnership, which, of course, is allocated to the various partners for inclusion in their taxable income. In limited circumstances, partnership assets can be transferred to the partners without tax consequences; however, such circumstances rarely arise in the normal business process.[14]

The areas of tax law affecting transactions between partners and partnerships are complex and normally require professional advice; even so, the reader should be aware that the movement of assets into and out of a partnership has some flexibility and that the related tax consequences can vary.

It should also be recognized that the choice of a partnership form of organization is not binding on the participants. An existing partnership can be converted into a corporation in which the former partners are shareholders. While the transfer of partnership assets to a new corporation is subject to fair market value rules similar to those discussed above, a partnership can, if it so elects, convert itself into a corporation without immediate tax consequences.[15] In summary, it is not difficult for partners to change a partnership's structure whenever it is in their interest to do so.

D. Small Business Deduction and Private Corporate Partners

As outlined in Chapters 11 and 13, a Canadian-controlled private corporation is entitled to a lower corporate tax rate (15% in some provinces). This is a result of the small business deduction (SBD) that applies to the first $500,000 of annual active business income.

If a Canadian-controlled private corporation is a partner in a partnership activity, it is entitled to use the small business deduction on the active business income earned by the partnership and allocated to it. However, the active business income earned by the partnership that is eligible for the small business deduction is limited to $500,000 annually. In effect, the partnership has a separate annual limit which determines the amount of partnership income that is eligible and that can be applied to the partners' separate limits.[16]

Exhibit 15-5 shows a business partnership. The partners are two Canadian-controlled private corporations that share the partnership's profits equally. Each corporate partner has an annual small business deduction limit of $500,000. The partnership also has a

---

11 ITA 97(1).
12 ITA 97(2); IT-413R, -471R.
13 ITA 98(2).
14 ITA 98(3) to (6).
15 ITA 85(2), (3); IT-378R.
16 ITA 125(1)(a), 125(7); IT-73R6 (paragraphs 20–21).

Exhibit 15-5:

*Small Business
Deduction on
Partnership Profits*

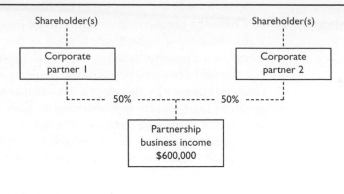

Partnership income:	Partnership		Allocated to	
			Partner 1	Partner 2
Eligible for SBD				
if partner qualifies	$500,000		$250,000	$250,000
Not eligible for SBD	100,000		50,000	50,000
	$600,000		$300,000	$300,000

limit of $500,000. The example assumes that the partnership has earned active business income of $600,000.

Only $500,000 of the partnership income is entitled to the lower corporate tax rate; the remaining $100,000 is not. Therefore, each corporate partner must include $300,000 (50% of the total partnership profits) in its income, and of that amount, only $250,000 (50% of the partnership's $500,000 limit) is eligible for the small business deduction. The balance of $50,000 is subject to normal rates of tax. Keep in mind that each corporate partner has a small business limit of $500,000 and that the eligible income from the partnership of $250,000 applies against this total. Each partner can earn active business income from other sources that is eligible for the small business deduction until the $500,000 limit is reached. The $500,000 annual limit of corporate partner 1 is as shown in the table below.

	Available for SBD	Not available for SBD
Partnership income allocated ($300,000)	$250,000	$50,000
Potential business income from sources other than partnership	250,000	unlimited
	$500,000	

If a corporate partner has active business income from non-partnership sources in excess of $500,000, its small business limit is already fully utilized and none of the income allocated to it from the partnership qualifies for the low rate of tax. In such circumstances, this is a drawback to the partnership form of organization and one that a corporation must keep in mind when deciding which kind of organization to use as a vehicle to carry on an enterprise with other parties. This is demonstrated in the next two segments of this chapter.

E. Partnership Information Return

Although partnerships do not file income tax returns, they are required to file information returns (T5013 Return) reporting the income or loss of the partnership for the year and the share earned by each of the partners.[17] The information return is due

---

17 ITA 233(1), Reg. 229(1).

within five months after the end of the fiscal period where all partners are corporations; otherwise by March 31 of the following year.[18]

III. Partnership Structure—Impact on Decision Making _____

When a choice of business structure is being made, the standard partnership entity cannot be analyzed in isolation; instead, it must be considered in relation to other possible structures. The main alternative to the partnership is the separate corporation, the shares of which are held by the participating entities. Each of the structures has different tax and non-tax implications that must be considered. From a tax perspective, the decision maker should attempt to develop a vehicle that will minimize the cash needed to start up the venture and maximize the return of cash back to the investor for reinvestment. Whenever an entity is considering participating in a venture with other parties, it must consider these four fundamental tax issues:

1. What will be the tax cost on the annual operating profits generated from the new venture? The objective, of course, is to minimize tax on an ongoing basis, but it is especially important to do so during the initial years, in order to improve cash flows and thereby increase the venture's chances of success.

2. If operating losses are expected during the start-up phase, how and when can such losses be utilized against other sources of income of the venture itself or of the participating parties? Even if start-up losses are not anticipated, the investors should consider the implications of unexpected losses. The utilization of losses is as vital to cash flow as the minimizing of tax on profits.

3. What will the tax implications be if the venture fails and is either terminated or sold off at a loss? The loss of all or a portion of an investor's capital will affect that investor's tax position; the resulting tax benefits will reduce the burden of the loss. The participating entities must assess their downside risk by identifying the after-tax cash loss that will occur if the venture fails.

4. How will the capital invested and the accumulated profits be returned to the investor? The investor will want this done in a way that minimizes the amount of tax. The repatriation of capital and profits takes on greater importance when other parties are involved, as their intention is usually to join forces for a specific venture, and surplus funds that are not needed for that specific venture will be distributed.

The tax implications as they relate to each of the above issues will vary with the type of entity—corporation or standard partnership—that is chosen. The amount and timing of the tax cost or benefit must therefore be identified for each alternative so that true cash flows can be determined and a decision made within the normal capital budgeting procedure. Such an analysis is performed in the following case study.

IV. Case Study—A New Venture Organization Structure _____

Summary of Assumed Facts

1. Krisco Ltd. is a Canadian-controlled private corporation owned by two wealthy Ontario business families. The company has a net worth of $6,000,000 and generates after-tax profits from its clothing import and wholesale business of approximately $1,200,000 annually.

_____

18 Reg. 229(5).

2. Brandi Ltd. is also a Canadian-controlled private corporation. It is owned by a group of Manitoba investors and manufactures denim jeans. The company has suffered losses in the past few years, but a turnaround is imminent, and its survival is not in question. Business losses of $2,000,000 have accumulated and are being carried forward for tax purposes over seven years. In spite of the losses, the corporation has a net worth of $3,000,000.

3. Krisco and Brandi intend to jointly develop a new enterprise that will manufacture a special line of clothing for East European countries. Krisco has imported foreign products in the past and, in so doing, has developed a network of prominent international contacts that it will contribute to the venture. Brandi will contribute its manufacturing and design experience. Each corporation will commit $1,000,000 to the new venture, which, however, will also require substantial bank financing so that it can acquire the manufacturing assets and fund its operations. Each corporation will own 50% of the new venture.

4. The parties have developed what they consider to be accurate projections of the operating results. While losses are expected in the first three years, the venture should become profitable in the fourth year. By the sixth year, profits should level off at about $700,000 annually before tax. The projected operating results are as follows:

	Profit (loss)
Year 1	$(400,000)
Year 2	(200,000)
Year 3	(200,000)
Year 4	300,000
Year 5	500,000
Year 6	700,000 (and thereafter)

Basic Structures Available

The new venture can utilize one of two basic structures.

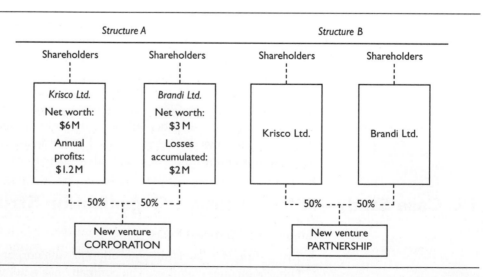

Structure A involves a separate corporation to house the new venture, with Krisco and Brandi each owning 50% of the share capital. Such a structure would require a shareholders' agreement outlining the course of conduct in the event that the shareholders, which have equal voting rights, are stalemated on significant issues.

Structure B is a partnership; the partners are the two corporations Krisco Ltd. and Brandi Ltd. The decision-making process would be established by the partnership agreement.

Analysis

The following analysis is viewed from the perspective of Krisco Ltd. and is presented in terms of the four fundamental considerations outlined previously.

• **Taxation of operating profits**   Although profits are not anticipated until year 4, their impact should be considered before a commitment is made to a particular structure. Under structure A, the new venture is a separate corporation and as such will be directly taxed on its annual profits. The new corporation is a Canadian-controlled private corporation. Because the ownership ratio is 50/50 (neither share-holder controls), it is not associated with Krisco or Brandi. The new corporation is therefore eligible for the small business deduction on the first $500,000 of annual profits. The tax rates on the new venture's profits (see Exhibit 11-8 in Chapter 11) are as follows:

	Manufacturing	Non-manufacturing
First $500,000 of annual income	15%	15%
Income in excess of $500,000	24%*	25%

* Due to provincial incentives.

This represents an expansion of the small business deduction for Krisco, which is also entitled to an annual small business deduction of $500,000 on its own profits. As a result, Krisco's overall activities are entitled to a low rate of tax on $750,000 of annual income, as follows:

Available directly to Krisco	$500,000
Available indirectly through the new venture (50% of $500,000)	250,000
	$750,000

The availability of the small business deduction will improve the new venture's cash flow by reducing taxes by up to $50,000 (25% − 15% = 10% × $500,000) annually; this will improve its competitive position and increase its chances of success.

On the other hand, if the new venture is operated as a partnership (structure B), all profits will be allocated directly to the partners. Profits allocated to Krisco will be added to its total income from other operations. As Krisco has already fully utilized its annual small business deduction, all partnership profits from the new venture will be taxed at the high rates of 24% for eligible[19] manufacturing profits and 25% for non-manufacturing profits.

The impact of the higher tax rates may be softened a little by the formula for determining manufacturing profits. Under the partnership format, Krisco, when determining its manufacturing profits, can include in the calculation its share of the partnership's manufacturing capital and labour (see Chapter 11). This may enhance the arbitrary percentage of manufacturing profits and capture some of Krisco's profits from non-manufacturing activities. This saving, if any, should be viewed as a reduction of tax on the partnership profits.

In terms of profits, Krisco would favour the corporate structure over the partnership.

---

19 Manufacturing profits in excess of $300,000 annually.

- **Utilization of operating losses**   The new venture expects to incur losses in the first three years of operations that total $800,000. Under structure A, the new-venture corporation will have to retain those losses for its own use; they are not immediately available to the participants. The losses will sit within the corporation until profits are generated; according to the projections, they will be fully utilized by the end of year 5. If the full losses ($800,000) from the first three years are applied to the profits of years 4 and 5 (which also total $800,000), they will eliminate tax in each of those years. However, since the tax on the first $500,000 of each year's income is at the low rate, it may be more desirable to use the losses in each year to reduce income to the $500,000 level, thereby eliminating taxes at the high rate. This would, of course, delay utilization of the entire loss into the sixth year.

Under the partnership format, the losses incurred in the first three years are allocated directly to the partners for their own use. From Krisco's point of view this is attractive, as the allocation of $400,000 of losses (one-half of $800,000) will create tax savings to Krisco of about $100,000 over the first three years. The losses from the new venture will be used immediately and the cash-flow benefits will be received in the first three years instead of years 4, 5, and 6.

In terms of loss utilization, Krisco prefers the partnership form of organization. This contrasts with its preference for the corporate form when the venture is profitable.

- **Downside risk**   While both parties assume the venture will be a success, the possibility of failure exists, and so the tax implications of the loss of the total investment must be considered. Under the corporate structure, overpowering losses from the operations would be locked into the corporation. Each shareholder, as a separate entity, would recognize its loss through the decline in value of the shares acquired in, or the loans made to, the new-venture corporation. In this particular case, the loss of the $1,000,000 of share or loan equity by each party would qualify as an allowable business investment loss, one-half of which could be offset against other sources of income. The downside risk of the investment following its total loss is $875,000, as follows:

Cash invested and lost	$1,000,000
Tax saving on loss utilization	
[25% × ½ ($1,000,000)]	(125,000)
Net cash exposure	$ 875,000

In some cases, shareholders may guarantee certain debts within the corporation, and that must be considered as a separate risk factor (see Chapter 20). Losses on the shares or loans to a corporation can be used for tax purposes only when the shares or loans are disposed of. In the case of a loan, a deemed disposition occurs when the owner reasonably considers it to be uncollectible, and therefore an actual disposition is not required. A loss from the decline in value of shares can be recognized only when those shares are sold, when the corporation is formally bankrupt, or when the corporation is insolvent and has ceased operations. In this case, it would be advisable for both parties to invest their $1,000,000 in the corporation by way of a substantial amount of debt and a small amount of share capital. This may, at some time in the future, speed up the loss recognition if the business should begin to falter.

The losses from operations that are locked into the corporation are simply eliminated unless steps can be taken by the shareholders to utilize them. With a 50/50 ownership ratio, this would be difficult to accomplish (see Chapter 14).

When a partnership structure is used, the downside risk has different implications. As the partnership's operating losses are allocated directly to each of the partners, the loss of the investment is effectively recognized as a full business loss. If, for example, the partnership had lost $2,000,000 from operations and then simply dissolved, each partner would have lost the $1,000,000 of capital invested. The allocation of an operating loss reduces the cost base of a partnership interest simultaneously with its decline in value; as a result, a capital loss is not incurred. The downside risk to Krisco on the total loss of the $1,000,000 investment in the partnership is therefore $750,000, calculated as follows:

Cash invested and lost	$1,000,000
Tax savings on operating losses allocated	
(25% × $1,000,000)	250,000
Net cash exposure	$ 750,000

Unfortunately, the tax benefits resulting from the loss of the partnership investment may be tempered by the fact that the partners are not limited in liability and that losses beyond the capital contributions fall to the partners. In this case, Krisco has a net worth of $6,000,000 compared with Brandi's $3,000,000. Krisco may ultimately be responsible for the full loss of the venture if Brandi is unable to meet its obligations. Krisco and Brandi may consider establishing holding companies to act as the partners; each holding company would be capitalized with the required $1,000,000 contribution.

This structure (diagrammed below) would limit the liability of each partner to $1,000,000. Unfortunately, the use of holding companies is not without consequences. The losses incurred by the partnership would be allocated to the holding companies and would sit idle, with no other income for offset except that which was generated by the partnership itself. At the same time, although the losses would be locked into the two holding corporations, those corporations would be owned 100% by Krisco and Brandi, respectively, and as such belong fully to each party. As a result, each party would have greater flexibility with respect to the use of those losses (see Chapter 13).

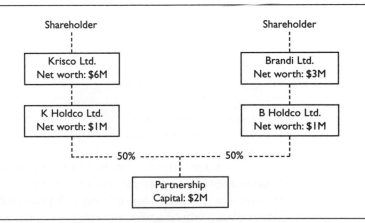

• **Repatriation of capital and profits** Under a corporate structure, accumulated profits are returned to the shareholders as dividends, which are received by each shareholder corporation free of tax. Consequently, with this structure, 85% of the new-venture profits that are subject to the small business deduction ($500,000 annually) would be available to Krisco Ltd. and Brandi Ltd. for reinvestment in other ventures. This is calculated as follows:

Profit to the new venture	100%
Tax to new-venture corporation	15%
Net retained in new-venture corporation	85%
Tax on receipt of dividend	NIL
Net available for reinvestment	85%

Income in a new-venture corporation that is not subject to the small business deduction also can be distributed without any further tax; in this case, the net profits repatriated to Krisco and Brandi would thus be 76% and 75%, calculated as follows:

	Manufacturing	Non-manufacturing
Profits to the new venture	100%	100%
Tax to new-venture corporation	24	25
Net retained in new-venture corporation	76%	75%
Tax on receipt of dividend	NIL	NIL
Net available for reinvestment	76%	75%

Under the partnership structure, there are no tax consequences when profits are distributed to the partners, since all profits have been fully taxed in the hands of the corporate partners (Krisco and Brandi). However, in the case of Krisco Ltd. all partnership profits would be subject to the high rates of tax, as that company's small business deduction had been used up from other sources, and so a lesser amount of repatriated profits would be available for reinvestment purposes.

From Krisco's perspective, the percentage of new-venture profits available for reinvestment after repatriation is as shown next.

	Partnership	Corporation
First $500,000 of annual profits:		
Manufacturing	76%	85%
Non-manufacturing	75%	85%
Profits in excess of $500,000 annually:		
Manufacturing	76%	76%
Non-manufacturing	75%	75%

With respect to the return of the original capital invested, both structures have similar results in this particular situation.

Intuitively, without projecting cash flows over the next several years, it would appear that Krisco would prefer a partnership form of organization during the initial years in order to ensure immediate loss utilization but would prefer the corporate form once the venture becomes profitable in order to gain an enhanced small business deduction. If limited liability were not an issue, the conflicting preferences could be overcome by using the partnership in the early years and then incorporating when the venture becomes profitable. However, this would expose Krisco to full liability in the start-up years, when the risk perhaps is at its greatest. At the same time, the full utilization of losses results in a tax advantage that reduces that risk. This risk can be roughly quantified and compared with that of the corporate structure. For example, if Krisco invested $1,000,000 in the corporate structure and it failed, the after-tax cost of that loss would be $875,000, as previously calculated. If, on the other hand, Krisco chose the partnership and exposed itself to greater liability, it could lose approximately $1,167,000 and still be no worse off than if it had invested $1,000,000 in the corporate structure. This comparison is shown in the following table:

	Partnership	Corporation
Actual loss incurred	$1,167,000	$1,000,000
Related tax savings	(292,000)	(125,000)
Net after-tax cash loss	$ 875,000	$ 875,000

It is also worth noting that the tax savings for the partnership would be achieved annually as they occur, whereas the $125,000 tax saving on the corporate investment would be realized much later, when the venture is completely terminated. This analysis throws a completely different light on the liability issue and is very much worth remembering when assessing the overall risk of any venture. All in all, the partnership form of organization is worthy of serious consideration in spite of the liability issue.

To complete the analysis, each party should map the flow of funds into and out of the venture for each alternative and consider the *timing differences* by measuring the cash-flow impact in net *present value terms*. The profit returns for each investor will, of course, vary with the venture's need for funds for expansion and debt repayment.

To this point, the position of Brandi Ltd. has not been considered in detail. The available alternatives would not affect its cash flow in the same way they did that of Krisco Ltd. This is primarily owing to Brandi's extensive current-loss position, which effectively makes it a non-taxable entity for several years. The partnership allocation of losses simply adds to Brandi's loss position; as a result, that entity achieves no real benefit in the early years from the partnership format, except that such a format gives it direct ownership of the losses for possible future use.

With respect to the profitable years, Brandi would benefit from the partnership structure, as the allocated profits could be used to offset the major losses that are being carried forward, thereby minimizing tax on the new venture's operations and reducing the risk of the losses expiring. This, of course, is in direct conflict with what Krisco wants, which is to incorporate the profit years in order to gain access to the small business deduction. In addition, the fact that Brandi's financial strength is significantly less than Krisco's increases the former's concern about unlimited liability, which is a characteristic of the partnership format. Brandi would favour a partnership format that includes a holding company as the direct partner. In the early years, the losses locked into the holding company would be of little consequence, in view of Brandi's existing non-taxable position. As the new venture became profitable and the risk of failure was reduced, Brandi and the holding company could easily be amalgamated, which would permit the future allocated profits to be offset directly against Brandi's losses.

In the case study presented here, the participants were private corporations; however, the alternatives considered in the analysis are not restricted to the private corporate sector. Public companies can also give serious consideration to the standard partnership form of organization for ventures involving other participants. In such circumstances, the same four basic points of consideration are also relevant; the analysis would be similar to that for Krisco and Brandi, except that the small business deduction would be omitted as a factor.

V. Summary and Conclusion

The partnership structure is an alternative to the corporate structure for ventures involving multiple owners. Both structures have the same objectives but receive dramatically different tax treatment. The tax treatment of a partnership can be summarized as follows:

1. A partnership is not a separate entity for tax purposes and is not directly subject to tax on income.

2. Income earned by a partnership is allocated for tax purposes and included as income of the partners. Income is deemed to have been allocated to the partners on the last day of the partnership's fiscal year, whether or not those profits were distributed.

3. The profits allocated to partners retain the source and characteristics of the income earned by the partnership.

4. Losses incurred by the partnership are also allocated to the partners and included in each partner's determination of income.

5. The actual distribution of profits to the partners is not taxable income.

6. Although the partnership is not a taxable entity, the partnership *interest* is considered capital property, and its disposition by the owner can result in a capital gain or loss.

The above tax treatment is significantly different from the one given to corporations, whose profits are taxed first as corporate income and a second time in the hands of the individual shareholders after distribution. Consequently, both the amount of tax and the timing of the payment of tax are different for each of the two structures.

When contemplating an investment with other partners, the advantages and disadvantages of a partnership should be compared with those of a corporation on the basis of four fundamental issues:

1. What is the annual tax cost on profits earned by the new venture?

2. How and when can operating losses of the new venture be used for tax purposes?

3. What is the maximum after-tax loss to the investor (partner or shareholder) if the investment is a complete failure?

4. What is the tax cost, if any, of repatriating profits of the new venture?

The partnership, as opposed to the corporation, is a dynamic alternative that can be viable for all business entities, regardless of their size.

Visit the Canadian Income Taxation Web site at **www.mcgrawhill.ca/ olc/buckwold** to view any updated tax information.

Review Questions

1. Identify three "non-taxable entities." Does "non-taxable" mean that the income earned by these entities is not subject to tax? Explain.

2. What is a standard partnership, and how is it different from a joint venture and from a co-ownership?

3. What types of entities can be partners in a standard partnership? Does each partner in a partnership have to be the same type of entity? Explain.

4. Must each partner in a partnership contribute an amount of capital that is proportionate to its profit-sharing ratio? Explain.

5. To what extent is each partner liable for the obligations of the partnership? Compare this with the obligations of shareholders in a corporation.

6. How can a partner that has a substantial net worth organize its investment in a partnership so that its liability exposure is limited?

7. "The amount of tax paid on partnership profits depends on the nature of the separate partners and not on the nature of the partnership itself." Explain.

8. "Profits of a partnership are included in the income of the partners only when those profits are distributed to them." Is this statement true? Explain.

9. A partnership may be preferable to a corporation when the business venture is new and expects to incur losses in its early years. Explain why.

10. When net income from business for tax purposes is being determined, the timing of certain expense deductions is discretionary. For example, a taxpayer may claim all of, some of, or none of the available capital cost allowance. Similarly, the deduction of certain reserves is discretionary. In a partnership structure, is the deduction of discretionary items decided by the partnership as a whole, or can each partner make a separate decision on its proportionate share? What conflict can arise as a result?

11. "Partnership profits or losses allocated to the partners retain their source and characteristics." What does this mean? How does this compare with the manner in which a corporation's profits or losses affect its shareholders?

12. On distribution, for tax purposes, accumulated partnership profits to partners are treated differently from accumulated corporate profits to shareholders. How?

13. What is a partnership interest? What type of property is it considered to be for tax purposes?

14. The value of the shares of a corporation changes when corporate profits or losses are accumulated and when corporate assets change in value. The value of a partnership interest changes in exactly the same manner. Explain how the tax treatment applied to the sale of a partnership interest differs radically from that applied to the sale of corporate shares.

15. Explain the general tax implications, both to the partner and to the partnership, when a partner transfers property to the partnership that has appreciated in value beyond its cost amount. Is there an alternative treatment? Explain.

16. "A Canadian-controlled private corporation that earns $100,000 from its own active business plus an additional $400,000 from its 50% interest in a business partnership is entitled to apply the small business deduction to its combined income of $500,000." Is this statement correct? Explain.

17. Identify four factors that managers must consider when deciding whether a new business venture with other parties will be organized as a partnership or as a corporation.

18. An investor may be able to afford to lose more money from a failed business venture if it is organized as a partnership, rather than a corporation. Explain why.

Key Concept Questions

QUESTION ONE

Jennifer Black and Pete White carry on a security service business through a partnership. Jennifer and Pete are both active in the business and share profits equally. In the current year they each received a salary of $40,000 from the partnership.

Black & White Partnership
Income Statement
For the year ended December 31, 20X8

Income:	
Security service fees	$200,000
Gain on sale of public company shares	12,000
Eligible dividends	10,000
Interest income	3,000
	225,000
Expenses:	
Office rent	15,000
Capital cost allowance	8,000
Salaries paid to staff	30,000
Salaries paid to partners	80,000
Donations to registered charities	2,000
	135,000
Net income	$ 90,000

Compute net income for tax purposes for the partnership. *Income Tax Act reference: ITA 96(1)(a), (b), (c).*

QUESTION TWO

Jennifer Black is not married. She lives alone. Her sole source of income is from the Black & White Partnership (Question One).

Compute Jennifer's net income, taxable income, and federal tax payable for the current year. *Income Tax Act reference: ITA 96(1)(f), 117, 118(1)(c), 118.1(3), (8), 121.*

QUESTION THREE

A Ltd. and B Ltd. are partners in the Triple M partnership. A Ltd. and B Ltd. share equally in the income or loss of the partnership annually. The partnership earned business income of $100,000 and $300,000, respectively, for its years ended June 30, 20X8 and June 30, 20X9.

Income from the Triple M Ltd. partnership was A Ltd.'s only source of income for its year ended December 31, 20X8. In 20X7, A Ltd. accrued, and included in income, $20,000 of stub period partnership income. Determine the amount of business income to be reported for tax purposes by A Ltd. for its year ended December 31, 20X8. *Income Tax Act reference: ITA 34.2(2), 96(1)(f).*

QUESTION FOUR

Tom, Mary, and Chris are partners in the TMC Partnership. Tom is the only partner who is involved in the daily activities of the partnership and, thus, the partnership agreement stipulates that 70% of the partnership business income and losses will be allocated to Tom; the remaining 30% will be shared equally by Mary and Chris. The three partners share equally in all other sources of partnership income. For the current year the TMC Partnership had the following sources of income (losses):

Business income	$400,000
Rental loss	(30,000)
Interest income	9,000
Taxable capital gains	21,000
Allowable capital losses	(15,000)
	$385,000

The partnership did not distribute any of the current year profits to the partners. Prepare a chart showing the allocation of the income (losses) to the partners for tax purposes. *Income Tax Act reference: ITA 96(1)(f), (g).*

QUESTION FIVE

Canadian partnerships are required to file an annual information return (T5013) containing the following information:

a) Income or loss of the partnership.

b) Name, address, and social insurance number (if applicable) of each partner.

c) Share of the income or loss for each partner.

d) Share of each deduction, credit, or other amount for each partner.

e) Share of scientific research and experimental development (SR&ED) for each partner.

f) Other information as may be required by the prescribed form.

When is the information return (T5013) due? *Income Tax Act reference: ITA 233(1); Regs. 229(1), (5).*

QUESTION SIX

In March of Year 1, Sally and Peter began to carry on business in partnership. Each contributed cash of $75,000 and agreed to share income and losses equally. The following information was provided for the first fiscal year of the partnership.

a) The partnership net income of $328,000 consisted of the following sources of income:

Business income	$300,000
Eligible dividends	20,000
Taxable capital gains	10,000
Allowable capital losses	(2,000)
	$328,000

b) In addition, the partnership received a tax-free capital dividend of $12,000 and donated $3,000 to registered charities.

c) Each partner took draws totalling $60,000.

Determine the adjusted cost base for the partnership interest of each of the partners at January 1, Year 2. *Income Tax Act reference: ITA 53(1)(e), 53(2)(c).*

QUESTION SEVEN

Lindsay Shaw is a partner in a Canadian partnership. On April 30th of the current year she transferred title of a piece of land that she held as a capital asset to the partnership in exchange for cash of $40,000. The land was valued at $100,000 at the time of the transfer. Lindsay had paid $40,000 for the land when she purchased it several years ago.

Determine the tax consequences resulting from the transfer of title to the land to the partnership. *Income Tax Act reference: ITA 97(1).*

QUESTION EIGHT

Reconsider the scenario in Question Seven. Assume that Lindsay and her partners made a joint tax election choosing to transfer the land to the partnership at its tax value ($40,000).

Determine the tax consequences resulting from the transfer of the title to the land to the partnership under this assumption. *Income Tax Act reference: ITA 97(2).*

Problems

PROBLEM ONE

Pierre X owns 100% of the shares of Corporation X. Corporation X owns 50% of the shares of Corporation XY, which holds several investments. The investments in Corporation XY consist of bonds, rental real estate, and a 40% interest in a partnership that operates a chain of retail stores. The remaining 50% of the shares of Corporation XY are owned by Corporation Y. Corporation Y is wholly owned by John Y.

The partnership and all three corporations account for their income on an annual basis at the following fiscal year ends:

Partnership	February 28
Corporation XY	February 28
Corporation X	January 31
Corporation Y	December 31

The partnership and all three corporations distribute their profits to the owners on the last day of the fiscal year.

In April 20X0, the partnership earned an unusually high monthly profit.

Required:

1. Prepare a diagram of the financial structure of these entities from the information provided above.
2. Which entities within the structure are subject to income tax?
3. Based on the activities described, which types of income for tax purposes will be earned by each entity?
4. Based on each entity's distribution policy, what is the last date on which Pierre X can report the unusually high profits earned by the partnership in April 20X0? Provide a brief analysis tracing the April profits through the organizational structure.

PROBLEM TWO

George Gingero is a one-third partner in Sweet Tooth, a restaurant that specializes in desserts. Gingero maintains a full-time job and earns a salary of $140,000. In the evenings and on weekends, he works at the restaurant, as do the other partners.

The partnership year end is December 31. The financial results for 20X1 and other information are provided below.

1. The amortization expense relates to the restaurant's equipment. At the end of the previous year, the undepreciated capital cost of the class 8 equipment was $30,000, and of the class 43 equipment was $20,000.

2. During the year, Gingero received cash distributions of $10,000 from the partnership. In addition, the donations paid by the partnership were designated one-third to each partner.

3. One of the other partners recently offered to buy Gingero's partnership interest for $100,000. Gingero refused the offer, as he plans to continue working in the restaurant. At the end of 20X0, the partnership's accountant had informed him that the adjusted cost base of his partnership interest was $40,000.

Sales	$600,000
Cost of sales	210,000
Gross profit	390,000

Expenses:		
Salaries	150,000	
Rent	50,000	
Maintenance	8,000	
Amortization	12,000	
Donations	3,000	
Supplies	10,000	
Other	17,000	250,000
		140,000
Other income:		
Capital gain on sale of previous franchise		60,000
Dividends (non-eligible) from Canadian corporation		9,000
Net income		$209,000

Required:

1. Calculate Gingero's net income for tax purposes for the 20X1 taxation year.

2. If Gingero had sold his partnership interest at the end of the current year for $300,000, how would his net income for tax purposes have changed?

3. Would it be worthwhile for Gingero to set up a corporation to be the partner in the restaurant? Explain.

4. If Gingero sells his partnership interest in Sweet Tooth to his own corporation, how will this affect his tax position?

PROBLEM THREE

Conquest Enterprises is a partnership that operates a smallwares wholesale firm. The partners are Cameron Traders Ltd. and Kando Construction Ltd. They share profits equally.

The partnership business has improved this year, and it is anticipated that by year end, profits before capital cost allowance will amount to $620,000 (compared with $290,000 the previous year). During the year, the partnership acquired two additional delivery vehicles for $80,000. At the end of the previous year, the partnership held the following property:

Class	Undepreciated capital cost
1	$800,000
8	100,000
10	100,000

Cameron Traders is a Canadian-controlled private corporation owned by George Cameron. The company operates an import/export business and earns trading commissions from a wide range of customers. For years, it has earned a modest profit ($30,000 last year, after a reasonable salary to Cameron). However, his years of hard work establishing international contacts have finally paid off, and he expects this year's profits to be $300,000 and future years' profits to continue at least at this level.

Kando Construction is owned by Sheila Hampton. Kando has suffered major losses over the past years even after earnings have been allocated from the partnership. Currently, the company has unused non-capital losses of $600,000, of which $300,000 will expire in two years. The company appears to have its losses under control and is not in serious financial difficulty, although cash flow has been tight.

The partnership has been seeking to acquire a new warehouse building. Coincidentally, Hampton personally owns a warehouse property, which will be vacated by its tenant in six months. The property has appreciated in value and is worth $80,000 more than its original cost. Hampton has claimed capital cost allowance of $30,000 over the years. She is willing to sell the property to the partnership, as she could use the cash to strengthen Kando. However, she needs all the cash she can get and is not anxious to pay tax on the sale.

The partnership and the two partners have December 31 fiscal year ends.

Required:

1. Determine the minimum and maximum business income for tax purposes that might be earned by the partnership (Conquest Enterprises) for the current year and allocated to the partners.

2. Which amount of income from the partnership would Cameron Traders and Kando prefer? Explain.

3. Estimate the tax liability of Cameron Traders for the current year.

4. If you owned Cameron Traders, would you recommend that Conquest Enterprises be incorporated? Explain.

5. How would the incorporation of the partnership affect Kando?

6. What can Hampton do to avoid tax on the sale of the warehouse property to the partnership and generate the maximum amount of cash to help Kando?

PROBLEM FOUR

Samborski Enterprises Ltd. is a successful Canadian-controlled private corporation operating a plumbing contracting business. The company consistently earns pre-tax profits in excess of $600,000. The profits are typically used to expand the company's own business or to buy out smaller businesses in the same industry. Usually, these acquisitions have been successful; they have provided after-tax returns on investment of between 14% and 20%.

Three years ago, the company invested $300,000 in common shares of TQ Ltd. This represented a 30% interest in that company. The other shares were acquired by two other investors. Samborski and the other shareholders created TQ to manufacture a new type of pipe that was expected to revolutionize the plumbing industry. The venture was not successful, and the shareholders decided to shut down the operations. After the assets were sold and the liabilities were paid, there was nothing left for the shareholders. Over the three years, the company had lost $1,000,000, as follows:

Year 1	$ 500,000
Year 2	300,000
Year 3 (including the sale of assets)	200,000
	$1,000,000

The shareholders were relieved to close the business before further losses were incurred, as they would have had to either contribute additional capital or declare bankruptcy. They have instructed their lawyer to wind up the corporation.

At the time the venture was organized, the investors had considered structuring the venture as a partnership. But after only a brief discussion, the idea was rejected because of the potential risk associated with the venture; as well, none of the parties had wanted exposure beyond their initial investment.

Required:

1. Considering that Samborski Enterprises invested $300,000 in share capital three years ago, what after-tax cash loss has it suffered from this investment? Determine the loss on a net present value basis.

2. How much would Samborski Enterprises have lost if it had chosen a partnership structure for TQ, rather than a corporate structure?

3. "If the partnership structure had been used, the new venture could have lost even more money and Samborski Enterprises would have been no worse off than if it had used the corporate structure and lost $1,000,000." Is this statement true? If it is, what would have been the amount of this extra loss?

4. Assume the following scenario: TQ was organized as a partnership, but to ensure limited liability, Samborski Enterprises organized a subsidiary corporation, to which it contributed capital of $300,000; the subsidiary corporation then invested the $300,000 as a partner of TQ. Explain how Samborski Enterprises might have utilized its $300,000 loss, and calculate the amount of its after-tax cash loss in a manner similar to that used in 1 and 2 above.

Case

DART AND SILVER

Heather Dart owns 100% of the shares of Dart Ltd., a Canadian-controlled private corporation. The company operates a successful printing business that produces advertising flyers and catalogues. Dart Ltd. has retained earnings of $1.5 million and earned profits of $600,000 in the previous year.

David Silver is the editor of a local newspaper and earns a substantial salary. For years, he has envisioned publishing a high-quality magazine that would capture the interests of western Canadians. Silver has had many discussions with Heather Dart, and they have decided to develop and publish *People West*. Silver will quit his job and work full time on the new venture, for which he will be paid a good salary. Heather Dart will not work for the venture but will provide production advice, especially in the start-up phase.

The new venture will require owners' capital of $600,000. As the venture will be shared on a 50/50 basis, both parties must provide $300,000 at the outset. This is not a problem for Heather Dart, as she has decided that Dart Ltd. will provide her share of the capital and will be the owner of her portion. But obtaining the $300,000 is not so easy for Silver: he has personal savings of only $280,000 and will have to obtain a second mortgage on his house for the balance.

The venture will require, in addition to the owners' capital, financing of $400,000, which a local bank has agreed to advance.

A financial advisor has developed financial projections after discussions with David Silver. These are summarized in the following table:

Year	Income (loss)
1	$(200,000)
2	(120,000)
3	80,000
4	250,000
5	$ 500,000

In addition, Heather Dart has asked that the financial advisor prepare a report outlining alternative organization structures for the venture.

Required:
As the financial advisor, prepare the report.

Limited Partnerships and Joint Ventures

While the standard partnership is the primary alternative to the corporation, both limited partnerships and joint ventures are also viable alternatives in certain circumstances. In particular, limited partnerships are becoming more common now that the limited partnership statutes have been revised in most provinces.

The tax treatment of limited partnerships and joint ventures is very similar to that of standard partnerships, which was described in detail in Chapter 15. However, both structures have special attributes that distinguish them from standard partnerships. It is these unique aspects that make the limited partnership and the joint venture attractive alternatives in certain types of ventures that involve a group of investors.

This chapter defines the limited partnership and joint venture entities, describes the unique aspects of their tax treatment, and discusses their appropriate use and their impact on cash-flow decision making.

I. The Limited Partnership

A. Definition of Limited Partnership

The limited partnership is a formal entity created, as are corporations, by legal statute. In general terms, a limited partnership has all the attributes of a standard partnership, except that certain partners are entitled, by law, to enjoy limited liability.

To qualify as a limited partnership, the entity must have two separate classes of partners—*general* partners and *limited* partners.[1]

The general partner is fully liable for the obligations of the partnership and is responsible for managing its business affairs. In effect, the general partner is treated in the same fashion as a partner in a standard partnership.

The limited partners, on the other hand, are responsible for the obligations of the limited partnership only to the extent of their investment in the partnership.[2] Therefore, a limited partner who has contributed $10,000 of capital to the partnership can lose no more than $10,000 in the venture, whatever the financial condition of the partnership.

In order to qualify as a limited partner, that partner must not take part in the management and control of the business carried on by the partnership. By definition, the limited partner is a passive investor; the general partner is an active participant.

A basic limited-partnership structure is diagrammed in Exhibit 16-1. Each partner, whether general or limited, can be either an individual or a corporation. Note that the limited partnership has been capitalized with $40,000 of partner contributions, of which $30,000 came from the limited partners and $10,000 from a single general partner. Although the general partner has invested only $10,000, it is, nevertheless, responsible for the full obligations of the limited partnership's business in the event of financial failure. As this imposes a substantial risk to the general partner, it is common for that partner to arrange its affairs so as to limit that risk. It usually does this by establishing a separate corporation with a limited amount of capital to act as the general partner.

Exhibit 16-1:

Limited-Partnership Structure

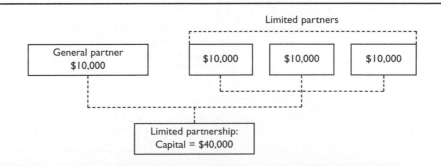

Limited partners

| General partner $10,000 | | $10,000 | $10,000 | $10,000 |

Limited partnership:
Capital = $40,000

---

1 McQuillan and Thomas, *Understanding the Taxation of Partnerships*, CCH Canadian, 1991.
2 ITA 96(2.4); IT-232R3.

For example, consider the structure in Exhibit 16-2. Corporation 1, which has a net worth of $500,000, has entered into a limited partnership as a general partner by creating a subsidiary corporation to act as that general partner. The subsidiary, Corporation 2, is capitalized with only $10,000 of share capital and uses those funds to purchase a standard partnership interest. Although Corporation 2, as the general partner, is fully liable for the debts of the partnership, it can only lose $10,000 because it is itself a limited liability corporation.

In effect, the limited partnership described in Exhibit 16-2 is a complete limited-liability entity similar to a corporation in that both the limited partners and the general partner are fully protected. In substance, a limited partnership is a partnership with limited liability for its partners.

B. Tax Treatment of Partnership Income and Losses

A limited partnership, like a standard partnership, is not a taxable entity. Instead, the net income or loss of the limited partnership is allocated for tax purposes directly to the partners, in accordance with their profit-sharing ratio.[3] The limited partnership simply acts as a conduit.

Income or loss is allocated to the partners at the end of each fiscal year (normally December 31 if one or more of the partners is an individual) and included in their income whether or not an actual cash distribution has been made. If, at some later time, the accumulated profits are distributed to the partners, those profits are not taxed again. The limited partnership's income is, therefore, taxed only once—at the partner level—unlike a corporation's income, on which two levels of tax are imposed.

Income allocated by the limited partnership retains its source and characteristics. Accordingly, active business income earned in the partnership is allocated as active business income to the partners. This is so even though the limited partners are, by definition, passive partners that are not active in the management of the limited partnership's business.[4] The tax treatment of a limited partnership's income and losses therefore depends on the tax position of each separate partner. If the partner is a corporation, the active business income is eligible for the small business deduction, subject to the limitations described in Chapter 15. If the partner has losses accumulated from other sources, the partnership profits allocated to that partner can be offset against those losses.

A special restriction applies to the use of losses allocated under the limited-partnership structure. Notwithstanding the amount of losses allocated to them, limited

---

Exhibit 16-2:

Limiting the General Partner's Liability

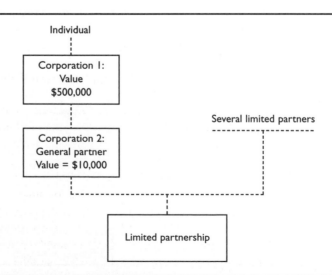

---

3   ITA 96(1).
4   ITA 125(7)(f); IT-73R6.

partners are entitled to claim those losses *only* to the extent of their investment in the partnership.[5] For example, a limited partner who has invested $30,000 in the limited partnership is entitled to claim losses for tax purposes only up to a maximum of $30,000, which is the amount that he or she is at risk for. This restriction is not imposed on the general partners because they do not have limited risk.

C. Impact on Decision Making

The limited partnership, like the standard partnership, cannot be analyzed in isolation when a business structure is being chosen for a new venture involving several parties. Instead, it must be compared with the possible alternatives—a separate corporation owned by a group of shareholders or a standard partnership as described in Chapter 15.

As was the case in previous discussions, the decision maker's goal is to develop a structure that will minimize the cash requirements to start up the venture and maximize the return of cash back to the investor for reinvestment. The following considerations are appropriate:

1. What is the annual tax cost on profits earned by the new venture?

2. How and when can operating losses of the new venture be used for tax purposes?

3. What is the maximum after-tax cash loss to the investor if the new venture should fail?

4. What is the tax cost, if any, of repatriating profits of the new venture?

Each of these considerations was reviewed in detail in the previous chapter, and so they will not be re-examined in this chapter except to the extent that they have a bearing on the unique aspects of the limited partnership. Below, the limited partnership is compared with both the standard partnership and the corporation.

1. Limited Partnership versus Standard Partnership

The limited partnership is different from the standard partnership in three ways:

1. Some of the partners in a limited partnership have limited liability; all of the partners in a standard partnership are fully exposed to the partnership's obligations.

2. A limited partnership must have some partners (the limited partners) who are passive investors and do not participate in management. The standard partnership does not face this restriction.

3. In a limited partnership, the use of tax losses allocated to the passive limited partners is restricted to a maximum of the "at risk" amount, whereas all partners in a standard partnership can use the full amount of losses allocated.

The above differences have a significant impact on a new entity's ability to attract investment capital. Because of the unlimited-liability feature of the standard partnership, that structure tends to attract partners who want to participate actively in management in order to protect their investment and gain full utilization of the partnership losses if those should occur. While standard partnerships can and do attract passive investors in spite of the risk, such investors tend to be few in number and of the type who can afford the related risk owing to their substantial wealth. It is rare that a standard partnership can gather capital from a large number of small investors, each of whom invests a small amount for a minor partnership interest, because the risk of unlimited liability is too great.

In comparison, the limited partnership provides broader access to sources of capital. Since limited partners are passive investors with limited liability, the partnership base can be divided into a larger number of smaller-sized units. Since small investors can participate in the entity with limited risk, the venture can tap a whole new source of capital.

---

5   ITA 96(2.1) to (2.7).

2. Limited Partnership versus Separate Corporation

The tax impact on cash flow from establishing a corporation, rather than a limited partnership, is similar to the impact discussed in Chapter 15 in relation to standard partnerships. However, this issue is briefly re-examined below in the context of limited partnerships, in particular as it pertains to the limited partners, who receive special treatment.

• **Loss utilization**   New ventures often suffer start-up losses as part of their development. In order to fund such losses, the venture must have a sufficient capital base. For example, assume a new venture requires $10,000 of capital from a passive investor, of which $6,000 will be used to acquire new-venture assets and provide working capital and $4,000 will be used to fund the anticipated start-up losses. Whether a corporation or a limited partnership is used, the new entity must receive $10,000 in absolute-dollar contributions.

However, the amount of cash required by the passive investor to make the $10,000 contribution is different under each structure. If the investor (assumed to be an individual) makes the $10,000 contribution to a limited partnership, the new venture will have its $10,000, but the cash cost to the investor may be only $8,200, calculated as follows:

Cash contributed	$10,000
Tax savings in year 1 from allocation of $4,000 loss	
(45% × $4,000)	(1,800)
Net cash required in year 1	$ 8,200

The flow-through of the venture's start-up loss to the passive investor permits an immediate use of the loss; the resulting tax savings are enjoyed by the investor, rather than by the new venture itself. If a corporation had been utilized instead, the investor's cash requirements would have been the $10,000, as the loss incurred would have been locked into the company and unusable until the venture became profitable.

This makes limited partnerships extremely attractive to small passive investors in that less cash is required to join in the venture, which makes it easier to participate. This, along with the limited-liability feature and the option to utilize losses immediately, makes it easier for a new venture to raise capital to get the project started. (Immediate loss utilization is itself a source of capital.)

• **Distribution of profits**   A corporation's profit distributions are taxed in a different manner than those of a limited partnership. This is particularly significant when the recipients consist of a large number of passive investors. In most cases, many of those investors will be individuals who are subject to high marginal tax rates. Under the corporate structure, the corporation and the shareholders are automatically subject to two levels of tax when profits are distributed. When the corporation is a public company or a Canadian-controlled private corporation earning business income not subject to the small business deduction, some double taxation will occur as described in previous chapters. As indicated in Chapter 13, a Canadian-controlled private corporation can overcome this problem by paying the shareholder in the form of a deductible salary or bonus. However, this option is not available when the shareholder is a passive investor and has no basis for receiving this form of payment.

Under the limited-partnership structure, no double taxation can occur when profits are allocated to individual passive investors. They are simply taxed once at the partner level. While this structure avoids double taxation automatically, it may present cash-flow problems to the limited partner if profits are allocated but no cash distribution is made. However, most limited-partnership agreements require that some portion of profits be distributed whenever taxable income is allocated.

Limited partnerships are known primarily for their ability to flow losses through to the passive investors; the benefit that double taxation is avoided when the venture becomes profitable is often overlooked. Obviously, the elimination of double taxation will, in the long run, enhance the investors' returns.

• **Capital structures** One of the major features of a corporation is that it can raise equity capital or debt capital from the general public. It can raise debt capital by issuing bonds, debentures, or mortgages or share capital by issuing a wide variety of classes of shares—common or preferred, voting or non-voting, and so on. This feature, along with the feature of limited liability, is the reason the corporation is the primary business entity. This is so even though investing in a corporation may result in double taxation and investors may find it difficult to utilize any losses.

The limited partnership also provides considerable flexibility when it comes to raising funds from the public. Limited partnership units offer limited liability to equity investors. In addition, those units can be divided into a number of different classes, each of which has different rights relating to the sharing of profits and losses. In effect, limited-partnership units can be designed with the same flexibility as corporate shares, with some unit holders having preference over others. Similarly, the limited partnership can also issue debt securities, such as debentures and mortgages.

A major distinction between the corporation and the limited partnership exists with respect to the feature of limited liability for the equity investors. Limited liability in a corporation is automatic, whereas in a limited partnership, it is granted only if certain conditions exist as specified by the limited-partnership statutes of the province in question. One result is that there is a risk that the limited-liability feature may be lost if the partnership later stops complying with those conditions. This has restricted the use of limited partnerships as an alternative to the corporation.

D. Uses of the Limited Partnership

The limited partnership has a wide range of business applications. In general terms, it can be used in any venture that requires a significant amount of equity capital from outside passive investors. It is especially valuable where the venture anticipates losses, as such losses can be flowed through to the passive investors to create immediate tax savings that minimize the risk of their investment.

1. High-Risk Ventures

The limited partnership is extremely valuable as a means of raising capital for a high-risk venture. Ventures, such as oil and gas exploration and drilling, mining exploration, and scientific research and development, all have the following common elements:

• A high risk of failure.
• A need for a significant amount of initial capital.
• A likelihood of substantial losses in the early years.
• If ultimately successful, a long wait before profits are realized.
• Special incentives with respect to the timing of deductions for tax purposes.

It is difficult for the initiator of a high-risk project to raise capital by debt financing. A limited partnership enables the venture to raise equity capital from a large number of investors, who are provided with the security of limited liability and who can quickly recover a large portion of their investment by immediately using the venture's tax losses.

In addition, the initiator can set up a separate limited partnership for each separate project. In this type of structure, different investors can participate in either some of the projects or all of them. The initiator would participate in and manage each limited partnership as the general partner.

2. Medium-Risk Ventures

While medium-risk ventures have greater access to borrowed funds, this access may be restricted until a reasonable track record is established. The accessibility of borrowed funds may be further diminished if the initiator does not have sufficient capital or collateral and the venture anticipates losses in its first few years of operation.

Consider, for example, a situation where the initiator wants to expand a chain of hotels rapidly but cannot provide all of the necessary capital. Each new hotel will probably incur start-up losses and, as well, will have a high capital cost allowance base in the building and hotel furniture and equipment. The available capital cost allowance (see Chapter 6) will remain unused unless it can be passed on to the investors. In situations like this one, a limited partnership is especially attractive to the passive investor, and as a result, there is a greater potential for raising funds.

3. Low-Risk Ventures

Low-risk ventures have substantial access to borrowed funds and therefore require less equity capital. In addition, they often do not suffer any substantial initial losses. Consequently, the flow-through of losses is not an important issue. Because of all this, limited partnerships are not often used in low-risk ventures. However, one should consider that the limited partnership does not lead to double taxation. Therefore, highly profitable low-risk ventures that require outside equity capital should give serious consideration to the limited-partnership structure, since it increases the after-tax returns to the investor, who, for this reason, may be willing to pay a higher price for the security.

For example, consider the situation in which a corporation must raise additional equity capital to fund an expansion. The anticipated corporate profits are $1,000,000 annually, but to achieve them, the existing owners must give up 40% of the share equity to new investors. Assume that the corporation's tax rate is 25% and the individual investor's tax rate is 45%. The ultimate after-tax return to the new investor under the corporate structure can be compared with the return under a limited-partnership structure, as follows:

	Corporation	Limited partnership
Investors' share of profits	$400,000	$400,000
Tax to the business entity	$100,000	NIL
Tax to the investor (on eligible dividends)	84,000	180,000
	$184,000	$180,000
After-tax return	$216,000	$220,000
Combined tax rate	46%	45%

Under the corporate structure, the company pays 25% tax on its earnings and the shareholder incurs additional tax either when dividends are distributed or when the shares are sold at a capital gain that reflects the undistributed profits. Under the limited-partnership structure, only the investor is subject to tax on the venture's profits, with no further tax when profits are distributed. If the limited partner sold the partnership interest before profits were distributed, no additional capital gain would result on the value increase pertaining to the undistributed profits (see Chapter 15). Keep in mind that because the limited partnership pays no tax but shifts this burden to the investors, a policy would need to be established that distributes a portion of the venture's profits to provide cash to investors to meet their personal tax liability.

The difference in results in the above example is important. If the investors are willing to accept an after-tax return of $216,000 under the corporate structure (being 40% of the venture's profits), they may also be willing to accept the same after-tax return from a limited partnership, as the risk factor has not changed. To receive a $216,000 after-tax return from the limited partnership, they need share in only $393,000 of the venture's profits ($393,000 − 45% tax = $216,000). Therefore, under the limited-partnership structure, the existing owners would be required to give up 39.3% of their equity compared with 40% under the corporate structure. This benefit grows in provinces that have a corporate tax rate greater than 25%.

E. Example of a Business Expansion Using a Limited Partnership

The following case situation is presented to demonstrate the significant impact of the tax variable when capital is raised by means of a limited partnership. The facts have been simplified in order to stress the importance of the organizational structure and its effect on return on investment.

The Problem

Diamond Ltd. is a Canadian-controlled private corporation that owns and operates two successful Toronto restaurants. The company is wholly owned by one individual, who provides general management services to both restaurants. The owner wants to develop several new restaurants in Toronto. However, Diamond Ltd. has limited resources that will not permit rapid expansion to several new locations simultaneously. A decision has been made to expand as quickly as possible by raising additional equity from passive investors.

Projected financial information for each new location is summarized in the following table:

Land, buildings, and equipment:	
Cost	$800,000
Mortgage financing	(600,000)
Net cash requirement	$200,000
Permanent working capital	$ 50,000
Initial opening costs:	
Cutlery, tableware, glasses, menus, staff training,	
testing, and opening advertising	$200,000
Operating projections:	
Opening year (loss)	($100,000)
2nd year (loss)	($ 50,000)
3rd year (break even)	–0–
4th year (profit)	$ 30,000
5th year (profit)	$100,000

Based on the number of locations available, Diamond Ltd. can afford to contribute only $50,000 to each location. It is anticipated that each restaurant will eventually produce annual profits of $100,000.

The Organization Structure Used

The capital requirements for starting up each new location total $600,000, as follows:

Equity in building and equipment	$200,000
Working capital	50,000
Initial opening costs	200,000
Cash losses in first two years	150,000
	$600,000

In order to further reduce this requirement, a decision was made at the outset to lease the land, buildings, and equipment. An arrangement has since been made with a local developer, who will acquire the land and construct and equip the building to specifications. The developer will then sell the building with a long-term lease to a group of real estate investors. The cash requirement for each location is thereby reduced to $400,000, which will be obtained as follows:

From Diamond Ltd.	$ 50,000
From outside investors	350,000
	$400,000

Initially, Diamond Ltd. attempted to attract one or two wealthy investors to provide the outside equity. This proved to be unacceptable because in return for making a large investment, these investors demanded a high percentage of the ownership; as well, they wanted control over major operating decisions. While Diamond Ltd. is prepared to give up some equity, it is not prepared to give up decision-making control. Diamond Ltd. has decided to seek out a larger number of small investors in order to spread the risk and maintain control. After considering both a corporate structure and a limited-partnership structure, it has decided to organize a separate limited partnership for each new location. The details of each limited partnership are outlined here:

1. Contributions to the partnership are divided as follows:

General partner	$ 50,000	13%
Limited partners	350,000	87
	$400,000	100%

2. The general partner is a subsidiary corporation of Diamond Ltd. and is capitalized with $50,000. The general partner will manage the restaurant and receive a fee of 4% of gross sales. In addition, the general partner will receive a 30% share of the operating profits.

3. The limited partners constitute 35 separate units of $10,000 each ($10,000 × 35 = $350,000). An investor may purchase more than one unit if it wishes. The limited partners are entitled to share in 70% of the profits and will be allocated 70% of the losses.

4. The limited partnership must distribute at least 50% of its annual profits to the partners, although it is a stated objective that all profits will be distributed.
    A diagram of the above structure is shown in Exhibit 16-3.

Analysis

Under the limited-partnership structure described above, Diamond Ltd. will achieve its objective—immediate expansion—without giving up management control and without giving up too much of its equity. As a general partner, Diamond retains full control of management decisions. Note that it contributes only 13% of the total capital ($50,000) but receives 30% of future profits. As future profits are anticipated to be $100,000 annually, Diamond's share is $30,000, which represents a pre-tax return on investment of 60% ($30,000/$50,000).

Exhibit 16-3:

*Limited Partnership
Structure for
Restaurant Expansion*

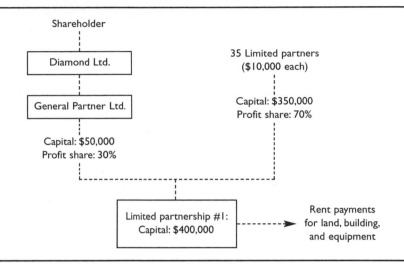

On the assumption that Diamond Ltd. has substantial profits from its existing two restaurants, the profits allocated to the general-partner corporation will be taxed at the high corporate rate of 25%, as the small business deduction limit will have been used up (see Chapter 13). If the new entity had been a corporation, rather than a limited partnership, a new small business deduction could have been created provided that Diamond Ltd. did not control the new corporation. Remember, however, that the initiator considered it important to retain control, and so a small business deduction base would not have been achieved under either structure.

By establishing a separate subsidiary corporation, capitalized with only $50,000, to act as the general partner, Diamond Ltd. limits its risk exposure in the new venture. Consequently, in the first two years of operations, the general partner will have no other income that can be used to offset the anticipated losses. However, after the risk of failure has lessened, the general-partner corporation can be wound up into Diamond Ltd. (see Chapter 14); this will transfer the losses to Diamond Ltd. for use against income from its operations.

From the outside investors' perspective, the limited-partnership structure is also attractive, even though they contribute 87% of the capital ($350,000) but share in only 70% of the profits. This is because they can use the allocated losses in the first two years of operations to create tax savings.

The amount of the loss allocated for tax purposes in the first year is magnified because of the initial opening costs. Recall that each venture will spend $200,000 for glasses, tableware, cutlery, advertising, and staff training. Even though these items are capital in nature (because they have a long-term benefit), they are nevertheless fully deductible for tax purposes in the first year. For example, the glasses, tableware, and cutlery are all class 12 assets that have a capital cost allowance rate of 100% (the one-half rule is not applicable—see Chapter 6). Therefore, the partnership's tax losses in years 1 and 2 will total $350,000, as follows:

Year 1:	
Opening costs	$200,000
Operating loss	100,000
	300,000
Year 2:	
Operating loss	50,000
	$350,000

Assuming that the limited partners are in a 45% tax bracket, the cash cost of their investment and subsequent cash returns will be as follows:

	Total	Per investor
Cash invested	$350,000	$10,000
Early tax savings:		
$350,000 × 70% × 45%	(110,000)	(3,150)
Net cash invested	$240,000	$ 6,850
Expected future profits:		
70% of $100,000	$ 70,000	$ 2,000
Pre-tax return on cash invested		29%
After-tax return on cash investment:		
29% − 45% tax		16%

In this way, the limited-partnership structure permits the new venture to raise $350,000 from outside investors at a cash cost to those investors of only $240,000. If a corporate structure were used, the losses would not be available to the investors, and their cash requirements for acquiring the shares would be $350,000, or $10,000 per investor.

The limited partners receive a relatively high after-tax return partly because double taxation has been eliminated. Profits attributed to the passive investors are taxed only once, at their personal marginal tax rates. Under the corporate structure, some double taxation would occur if Diamond Ltd. chose to maintain voting control over the new venture. For example, Diamond Ltd. might still own 30% of the equity shares (leaving 70% to the passive investors) but might issue itself a special class of shares having full voting authority over the passive investors. Consequently, Diamond Ltd. and the new corporation would be associated (see Chapter 13) and would have to share the small business deduction. If the new venture were not entitled to a small business deduction, the venture's profits would be first taxed at 25%, or higher in some provinces, and then taxed again on distribution to the passive shareholders. The after-tax return to the passive investors would therefore be lower than under the limited partnership structure.

A final point: The limited partnership structure provides the lowest downside risk to the passive investor. In the event of a complete business failure resulting from excessive operating losses, each limited partner stands to lose no more than $5,500 after tax ($10,000 less 45% tax savings = $5,500) because all operating losses up to $10,000 per investor are allocated as they occur. Under the corporate structure, the passive shareholder would recognize a loss from business failure as a capital loss when the shares were sold or the corporation became insolvent. As only one-half of a capital loss is recognized for tax purposes as an allowable business investment loss (see Chapter 8), each investor would stand to lose a maximum of $7,750 ($10,000 less 45% tax savings on ½ of $10,000 = $7,750).

In summary, the limited-partnership structure in the above example has the following benefits:

1. It permits the project initiator to raise capital by spreading the risk of the investment among a large number of small investors.

2. It permits the venture to raise $10,000 per unit holder at a real cost of only $6,850 to each investor because of the way that start-up costs are allocated.

3. It provides limited liability to the passive investors, who face a downside risk of only $5,500 for each $10,000 invested.

4. It permits the initiator to give up a minimum of equity (70% of profits for 87% of the capital) because the elimination of a small amount of double taxation combined with the lower cash cost of entry ($6,850, rather than $10,000) gives the passive investors an acceptably high after-tax return.

5. It permits the initiator to retain absolute management control of the venture as the general partner, who by law must have full responsibility for management decisions.

The limited partnership is a viable and appealing business structure. While it is more complicated to establish and maintain than a corporation, it also significantly improves after-tax cash flow and must be seriously considered for all business expansions that require capital from outside passive investors.

It should be pointed out that the preceding case was given only a superficial analysis. It was presented primarily to show the results of choosing the limited partnership structure. A proper review would involve comparing the after-tax cash flows under a proposed corporate structure with those under a limited-partnership structure, taking into account the timing of both loss utilization and the anticipated distributions to the investors.

II. Joint Ventures

The term "joint venture" is commonly and loosely used in the financial community in situations where partners join together to conduct a common business or investment activity. The term is often used even when the entity is actually a partnership or separate corporation. For tax purposes, the term must be confined to its narrow legal meaning.

A. Definition of Joint Venture

There is no legal statute governing joint ventures, nor does the *Income Tax Act* define the term or describe its specific tax treatment. Even so, joint ventures do exist and are recognized in Canada as a distinct type of entity.

A joint venture is not the same thing as a corporation or partnership. Generally, it can be described as "an association of two or more entities for a given limited purpose without the usual powers and responsibilities of a partnership."[6] What distinguishes a joint venture from a partnership is the concept of "limited purpose." A partnership usually represents an ongoing business relationship, whereas a joint venture is formed for the purpose of a single transaction or an activity of limited duration.

Joint ventures are commonly found in the construction industry, when two or more construction companies, each having special expertise, join together to bid on and complete a single construction project. Joint ventures are also widely used in the resource industry for conducting exploration activities, as well as in research and development projects, and in the entertainment industry for financing concerts, plays, and movies.

In some cases, limited-purpose or limited-duration projects are referred to as "syndicates." This term reflects the fact that there are many participants in the specific project. In this sense, a syndicate is usually a joint venture having a relatively large number of participants.

A joint venture is represented by a joint-venture agreement that describes the nature of each participant's role in the project and the extent to which each is entitled to the project's revenues and responsible for the project's expenses.

B. Tax Treatment of Joint Ventures

A joint venture, like a partnership, is not itself subject to tax. Instead, each member of the joint venture includes its share of the venture's revenues and expenses as part

---

6 *Encyclopedic Dictionary of Business Finance*, Englewood Cliffs, New Jersey: Prentice-Hall, 1960; IT-90; McQuillan and Thomas, *Understanding the Taxation of Partnerships*, CCH Canadian, 1991.

of its own taxable income or loss. The joint venture simply funnels its profits or losses directly to its separate members.

While the tax treatment of joint ventures is very similar to the tax treatment of partnerships, there are some distinguishing features.

One major difference relates to the method of calculating the income or loss that is allocated for tax purposes. A partnership, even though it is not a taxable entity, is considered to be a separate entity for the purposes of determining the income or loss that is allocated; the partnership itself determines the extent to which discretionary items are used, and each partner must then follow that approach. For example, the amount of capital cost allowance to be claimed is discretionary. Under the partnership structure, the partnership decides on the amount of capital cost allowance claimed in a particular year; each partner is subject to that decision whether it is in its interests or not (see Chapter 15). A joint venture, however, does *not* constitute a separate entity for determining income; because of this, each member of the joint venture is free to choose the amount of capital cost allowance on joint-venture property in accordance with its own particular needs. Also, because a joint venture is not a separate entity it *cannot have a fiscal period*. So, the joint ventures must calculate the income for each joint venture participant separately. This is a simple matter if all of the participants have the same fiscal year end because a single determination will apply to all. However, if the joint venture participants use different fiscal periods, an income determination is required at several points in a year to correspond with each participant's fiscal year end.[7] Some joint ventures and syndicates have many participants and the accounting process is burdensome.

The process for determining business income for tax purposes (see Chapter 5) permits a number of discretionary deductions aside from the one for capital cost allowance. These include reserves for doubtful debts, other types of reserves, and the amortization of eligible capital property. Up to a point, the taxpayer can also choose its preferred method of valuing inventory. Under a joint venture, which is an informal entity, each member can control the timing and use of these items.

Joint ventures are also distinguished by the way property is transferred into and out of the venture. A partnership is a formal, separate entity, and any transfer of assets into or out of it must result in a deemed disposition at fair market value, which may create taxable income. While certain elective provisions are available, they are not without complications and may not apply in certain situations. The joint venture, as an informal structure, has no such fair market value rules. Therefore, a joint venture can easily be created and dismantled without significant tax problems relating to the transferring of assets between the joint venture and its members.

Finally, the joint venture and the partnership differ in the way the small business deduction is applied to the active business income allocated to the members. The amount of active business income earned by a partnership that is available for the low rate of corporate tax when allocated to corporate partners is restricted to $500,000 and divided among the partners according to their profit-sharing ratio (see Chapter 15). This means that a corporate partner owning a 50% interest in a partnership earning $900,000 is entitled to use the low rate of tax on only $250,000 of its share of the profits, even though its actual share of the profits is $450,000. Under a joint-venture structure, this limitation does not apply; the joint venturist corporation is entitled to use the full $500,000 small business limit, provided it has not been used for other sources of business income. Of course, this special tax treatment applies to smaller joint-venture activities only when the joint-venture member is a Canadian-controlled private corporation.

---

7   CRA announced administrative policy—November 29, 2011 applicable to taxation years ending after March 22, 2011. Previous policy permitted a joint venture to use a year end separate from the joint venture participants.

It is important to recognize that the joint-venture structure has limited use and a relatively narrow application. It does, however, create greater flexibility than a partnership and should be considered as an alternative when the nature of the project indicates that a joint venture may be permitted. In some cases, it is unclear whether the specific venture qualifies as a joint venture or a partnership. In these circumstances, the parties should be aware of the tax consequences in the event that the CRA rules that an intended joint venture is, in fact, a partnership.

III. Summary and Conclusion

This chapter has introduced two additional non-taxable business entities. The limited partnership and the joint venture, like the standard partnership, are not directly taxable on their income; rather, they funnel their operating results directly to the participants.

The limited partnership, like the corporation, is a formal organization having statute recognition. In general terms, it has all of the attributes of a standard partnership, except that certain partners have limited liability.

The limited partners are passive investors and do not participate in the management of the partnership's business. In turn, their liability is limited to the extent of their investment in the partnership. The general partners are fully liable for the debts of the partnership and have full responsibility for managing the partnership's business.

A limited partnership restricts the investors' liability and allows them to utilize the partnership's operating losses against their other sources of income. As a consequence, this type of entity is particularly attractive to an initiator who must raise capital from a large number of passive investors for a high-risk venture or for a venture that is expected to incur losses in its start-up years. Because a limited partnership flows losses through to the passive investors, those investors can immediately reduce their taxes and increase their cash flow. This substantially diminishes the amount of risk attached to the investment, which makes it easier for the project's initiator to raise capital from the marketplace.

Visit the Canadian Income Taxation Web site at **www.mcgrawhill.ca/ olc/buckwold** to view any updated tax information.

Joint ventures have a restricted purpose. In effect, a joint venture is a partnership formed to complete a particular transaction or to carry on a limited activity for a specific period of time. It is often difficult to distinguish between a joint venture and a partnership. If it can be shown that an entity is, in fact, a joint venture, the partners in that entity will have greater flexibility when it comes to determining their taxable income and creating or demolishing the entity.

Review Questions

1. A limited partnership consists of two general classes of partners. Identify these classes, and describe the rights and obligations of each.

2. What can be done by a general partner to limit the extent of its obligations to the limited partnership?

3. "The tax treatment of limited partnership income and losses depends on the tax position of each partner." Explain.

4. What key factors distinguish the limited partnership from the standard partnership?

5. "A limited partnership provides broader access to sources of capital." Is this statement true? Explain.

6. Why is there less risk for the passive investor when a business venture is organized as a limited partnership, rather than a corporation?

7. Why is it that the passive investor in a profitable business venture may receive a higher rate of return if the venture is organized as a limited partnership, rather than a corporation?

8. What is a joint venture, and how is it different from a partnership?

9. With respect to the following, how does the tax treatment applied to a joint venture differ from that for a partnership?
   (a) Determination of capital cost allowance.
   (b) Active business income eligible for the small business deduction.

Key Concept Questions

QUESTION ONE

On March 1 of the current year, Mathew acquired a one percent interest in a partnership that carries on a nursing home business in several provinces in Canada. Mathew paid $10,000 for the partnership interest. The partnership reported a loss for the current year. Mathew was allocated a business loss of $16,000 from the partnership. *Income Tax Act reference: ITA 96(2.1), 111(1)(e).*

Describe the tax implications of the loss for Mathew under the following two assumptions:

1) Mathew has a limited partnership interest, and

2) Mathew has a general partnership interest.

QUESTION TWO

Bill owns a 5% interest in a limited partnership. The adjusted cost base of his partnership interest at the beginning of the current year was $40,000. For the current year Bill was allocated $8,000 of capital gains and $22,000 of business income from the partnership. At the end of the current year Bill had a loan from the partnership in the amount of $12,000. Determine Bill's at-risk amount at the end of the current year. *Income Tax Act reference: ITA 96(2.2).*

Problems

PROBLEM ONE

Georgio Enterprises is a limited partnership that operates a chain of family restaurants. The partnership was profitable from its inception and is now generating consistent annual pre-tax profits of $1,000,000.

The partnership includes 20 limited partners, each of whom contributed $60,000 when the venture began. The limited partners, as a group, share 40% of Georgio's annual profits. As the partnership has not expanded for several years, most of the annual profits are distributed to the partners within six months of the year end.

Most of the limited partners are individuals who are subject to a marginal personal tax rate of 45%.

Required:

1. What is the annual after-tax return on investment for each limited partner?

2. If Georgio Enterprises had been organized as a corporation, how would the rate of return to the investors differ? Show calculations.

3. Assume that Georgio Enterprises (as a limited partnership) made an annual cash distribution sufficient only to cover each limited partner's tax liability, and retained the balance for expansion. How would the investors' after-tax returns be affected by this, considering that in order to realize their investment they may have to sell their partnership interest for an increased value? Would the return on investment be different if Georgio were a corporation and paid no dividends?

PROBLEM TWO

A new business venture requires $600,000 of equity capital from passive investors in addition to the $400,000 of capital that is being provided by the initiator of the project. The $600,000 will be raised by selling 30 units for $20,000 each. The 30 unit holders will participate in 60% of the venture's profits.

It is anticipated that business operations will begin on October 1, 20X1. The entity will use a December 31 year end. Investors must contribute their funds on October 1, 20X1.

The equity capital of $1,000,000 will be used as shown below.

Working capital	$ 200,000
Equipment	300,000
Start-up costs, staff training, and opening advertising	200,000
Operating losses:	
20X1 (for the three-month period)	250,000
20X2	50,000
	$1,000,000

The initiator is uncertain how to organize the new venture and is trying to decide between a separate corporation that will issue shares, and a limited partnership.

Required:

Which type of entity will make it easier for the initiator to raise the $600,000 of equity capital from passive investors? Explain, using a single investor as an example.

Cases

CASE ONE   Contesso Travel Inns Ltd.

Contesso Travel Inns Ltd. is a successful Canadian-controlled private corporation that owns and operates a small chain of eight hotels in western Canada. The hotels offer high-quality lodging at economy rates and provide only limited services to their guests.

Contesso has succeeded because of its unique approach to the lodging industry and its strong hotel management expertise. The company has designed and constructed all of its existing units—in fact, a sister corporation owned by the same shareholders (Contesso Developments Ltd.) maintains a small staff whose sole function is to develop new hotels. Contesso Developments has made a profit on each of the eight hotels it has developed over the past five years.

Contesso's success has been noticed in the hotel industry, and a number of similar hotels have sprung up across the country. The executives of Contesso realize that a race is on and that a number of other companies will be competing for the most suitable sites for expansion. They estimate that within eight years, the number of remaining quality sites will decline considerably as more hotels are developed across the country.

Contesso seriously considered going public and raising a large amount of capital to embark on a major expansion program. However, it rejected this proposal because it would have had to give up a significant percentage of its equity and because it could not project a realistic expansion plan in view of the increasing competition. At the same time, the company cannot expand rapidly while still owning each new hotel, as each unit requires more than $2,000,000 in equity capital as well as mortgage financing.

Contesso, therefore, has decided to concentrate on its two strengths—hotel management and hotel development—and to permit outside investors to own each unit.

The expansion plan is as follows:

- Contesso will identify and secure the right to acquire suitable sites.

- The equity requirement for each new hotel is approximately $2,000,000. This will be obtained for each project by the issuing of 200 ownership units to private investors. Each investor may acquire any number of the 200 units. Contesso will receive a fee for organizing the investors and issuing the ownership units.

- Contesso Developments will develop the hotels and assist with the acquisition of all equipment. In addition, the company will arrange mortgage financing for a fee.

- Each hotel will be managed by Contesso under a long-term contract (12 years) in exchange for a fee of 5% of the hotel's gross revenue.

Contesso's executives are satisfied that this plan will result in rapid expansion and, as well, provide their company with significant income from management fees and development profits. Also, after the expansion program is complete, the company will be in a solid position to acquire ownership of the hotels if the outside investors wish to sell.

Each new hotel will be sold to a different investor group in a different city, and the company executives are uncertain about which organization structure to choose. Each new hotel could be organized as a separate corporation, in which case 200 common shares would be issued; or each could be organized as a limited partnership, in which case 200 limited partnership units would be issued.

Financial information relating to each expansion unit is provided in Exhibits I and II.

Required:
Prepare an analysis of the financial information and advise Contesso which organization structure will be most attractive to prospective investors for each of the hotel units.

CONTESSO TRAVEL INNS
Financial Requirements and Cost Allocations

Exhibit I

1. Project cost and financing

Cost:	
Land, building, equipment, and start-up costs	$4,500,000
Financing:	
1st mortgage (35-year amortization), interest at 12%	$2,500,000
Investors' contributions:	
200 × $10,000	2,000,000
	$4,500,000

2. Cost allocations

Land	$ 400,000
Building	2,600,000
Furniture and equipment	500,000
Landscaping	50,000
Linens and supplies	90,000
Costs of arranging mortgage	70,000
Opening advertising and staff training	290,000
Agent's fees for selling equity units	350,000
Expense of issuing units (prospectus, legal, etc.)	150,000
	$4,500,000

Exhibit II

CONTESSO TRAVEL INNS
Anticipated Operating Information

Year	I*	2	3	4
Average room rate	40	42	44	46
Occupancy percentage	60%	63%	66%	70%
Gross revenue	$400,000*	$900,000	$1,100,000	$1,200,000
Operating profit before debt service and depreciation	200,000	400,000	480,000	520,000

* Note: The entity's year end will be December 31. Information for year 1 represents a half-year operation period. Also, the operating profits exclude any of the start-up cost allocations of $4,500,000.

CASE TWO   Realco*

Realco, a real estate developer, is proposing to obtain land and build a small mall that will house five stores. The five stores that lease the property will be responsible for all operating costs (maintenance, property taxes, utilities and repairs, and so on). The project will be constructed in 20X1 on behalf of a group of investors and will cost $700,000, as follows:

Building	$430,000
Land	120,000
Parking lot	40,000
Interest during construction period	30,000
Landscaping	20,000
Mortgage finder's fee	6,000
Legal fees:	
Land purchase	4,000
Mortgage documents	2,000
Investor offering	6,000
Appraisal fee for mortgage	4,000
Broker's fee for finding investors	38,000
	$700,000

The maximum mortgage available on the proposed property is $450,000. The annual interest rate will be 11%. The only security required for the mortgage is the property itself.

Realco has found 10 individuals who are each prepared to borrow $25,000 personally to invest. Its role in the project is now simply to develop the property on behalf of the investors. The ownership structure has yet to be determined. It is expected that the property will be rented beginning in January 20X2 for 10 years at $75,000 per year and that the property will be sold to the tenants at the end of the lease. The sale price will be based on the fair market value at that time. After the property is sold, the ownership structure will be liquidated, with all proceeds going to the investors.

Realco has asked you to prepare a report that analyzes alternative structures for holding the property and recommends the best from a tax perspective. The investors are interested in paying the minimum amount of tax over the life of the investment. Indicate in your report what the maximum tax write-off would be in 20X1 and 20X2, as well as the possible ramifications if one of the investors decides to dispose of his or her interest before the end of 10 years.

Required:
Prepare the report.

---

* Adapted, with permission, from the 1989 Uniform Final Examination© 1989 of the Canadian Institute of Chartered Accountants, Toronto, Canada. Any changes in the original material are the sole responsibility of W.J. Buckwold and have not been reviewed or endorsed by the CICA.

Trusts

I. The Trust Entity

A. Definition of a Trust

The *Income Tax Act* does not define "trust," it merely outlines the tax treatment of income generated by one. A broad generally accepted definition is that a trust, under common law, is "a legal arrangement whereby a person (the "settlor") transfers property to another person ("the trustee") to hold for the benefit of one or more persons ("the beneficiaries").[1] The trust does not have the status of a legal person like a corporation. Rather its format is closer to a partnership in that its existence is created by the writing of a trust document or deed spelling out the obligations of the trust. A trust constitutes a relationship between the *settlor* who places property under the management of a trustee for the enjoyment of designated *beneficiaries*. Beneficiaries may be entitled to enjoy the income or the capital of the trust, or both.

Trusts have certain unique features. The most important relates to income. Income earned by a trust can be taxed in the trust itself as a separate taxpayer *or* all or some of its income can be allocated to beneficiaries and taxed as part of their income. Any income allocated to beneficiaries is deducted from the trust's income and therefore trust income is only taxed once—either as trust income or as beneficiary income. In some circumstances the trust document specifically states what income is to be allocated; in other circumstances it is left to the discretion of the trustee to determine if, when and what amount is to be allocated. After income is taxed in the trust it forms part of the trust's capital and is not subject to further tax when it is eventually distributed.

So, a trust is like a partnership in the sense that income can be allocated to participants and taxed only once. However, in a partnership the allocation is mandatory and all income must be allocated, whereas in a trust the allocation is discretionary. It is important to note that the use of trusts and partnerships result in only one level of tax on income unlike a corporation whose income is subject to tax at the corporate level and at the shareholder level. Other unique features of trusts vary depending on the type of trust created. The various types of trusts are described below.

B. Types of Trusts

The two primary types of trusts are:

Inter vivos trust

Testamentary trust

An *inter vivos trust* is one that is created by the settlor during his or her lifetime. For example, while alive, an individual may establish a trust to hold certain investment properties for the benefit of children or other family members. A *testamentary trust* is established upon the death of an individual as dictated by her/his last will and testament.[2] For example, an individual's will may direct an executor to establish a trust or trusts for surviving children that holds and invests certain property until they reach a desired age. When inter vivos or testamentary trusts are created for the benefit of a spouse they are categorized as spousal trusts.[3]

The above trust characterizations can be further divided into two broader categories—*personal trusts* and *commercial trusts*. A *personal trust* includes inter vivos and testamentary trusts whose *beneficiaries did not purchase their trust interests*. Effectively they receive their trust interest from the goodwill of others who are typically a parent or a spouse.[4] Generally personal trusts are used for estate and tax planning purposes. A *commercial trust* generally refers to trusts whose *beneficiaries purchase their trust interests* or units. Examples of commercial trusts include

---

1   Chan and Morin, "Distributions by Canadian Testamentary Trusts," *Canadian Tax Journal*, 2005, Vol. 53, No. 4, p. 1091.

2   ITA 108(1).

3   IT-305R4.

4   ITA 284(1).

mutual funds, real estate investment trusts (REITs), business or investment income trusts, and royalty trusts. Typically, commercial trusts are traded on stock exchanges and, except for mutual fund and real estate investment trusts, have limited appeal as an alternative to the historical use of corporations as a primary business structure.

Each of the above trust categories present unique tax treatments that separate them from each other, and from the taxation of individuals and corporations. These unique features are reviewed further in this chapter along with an explanation of how trusts are used in business and personal estate and tax planning.

II. Tax Treatment of Trusts

For tax purposes a trust is considered to be an *individual*.[5] Therefore the trust, whether inter vivos or testamentary, represents a separate entity as if it were a separate individual taxpayer. The taxation of individuals has been reviewed in Chapters 3 through 10 and so this segment of the chapter highlights the specific rules and exceptions to the normal taxation of individuals.

A trust is taxable in Canada if it is resident in Canada at any time during the year. For tax purposes the trust is represented by the trustee(s) who manages and controls the trust[6] property. The residence of a trust is determined by the jurisdiction where the central management and control of the trust resides, regardless of the residence of the trustees.[7] In most cases all of the trustees are Canadian residents, so the question of where the central control and management resides is not an issue. Where some or all of the trustees reside in a foreign country, the central control and management determination is important. This test is similar to the test for determining the residency of a corporation (see Chapter 3). Even when all the trustees reside in Canada it may be necessary to apply the central management and control test to establish which provincial jurisdiction is relevant.

A. Determination of Taxable Income and Tax

Net income for tax purposes of a trust is determined using the net income formula established in Chapter 3 and again in Chapter 9. Net income for tax purposes is then converted to taxable income by applying the rules established in Chapter 10 of which the non-capital loss and net capital loss carry-overs are most important. There are several major exceptions that apply to determining trust income. They involve amounts allocated to beneficiaries. The exceptions are reviewed below.

When arriving at net income for tax purposes an inter vivos trust and a testamentary trust *deduct* from its income *any income that is payable to a beneficiary*.[8] Income is considered payable if it was paid in the year or the beneficiary was entitled to enforce payment in the year. Any amount that is not allocated is subject to tax in the trust, at which point it becomes part of the trust's residual capital and can subsequently be distributed tax-free. A trust can choose to designate an amount that is actually payable to a beneficiary, not to have been payable. The designated amount is then taxed in the trust rather than as part of the beneficiary's income.[9] This may be desirable if the trust's rate of tax is lower than the beneficiary's in a particular year. It should be pointed out that if losses of a trust exceed income during a year, they remain with the trust as either non-capital losses or capital losses and may be carried back or forward in accordance with the normal loss carry-over

---

5 ITA 104(2).
6 ITA 104(1).
7 Garron Family Trust v. the Queen, 2009 TCC 450; St. Michael Trust Corp v. Her Majesty the Queen, 2010 FCA 309, 2012 SCC 14
8 ITA 104(6); IT-286R2.
9 ITA 104(13.1), (13.2).

rules. This treatment of losses is different than the treatment by partnerships. Recall that losses incurred by a partnership are automatically allocated to the partners at year end.

In some circumstances a trust may allocate income and deduct that amount from its income for tax purposes even though it is not payable to the beneficiary. This may occur when trusts are created for minor children and income is accumulated on their behalf until they are 21 years of age or older.[10] This option permits income splitting by allocating trust income to minor children who may not be taxable because of low amounts of income.

Before reviewing the rates of tax for trusts it is necessary to define the *taxation year of a trust*. As a trust is considered to be an individual, its taxation year is automatically the calendar year (December 31).[11] However, a testamentary trust may choose to accept the calendar year *or* choose a taxation year that ends within 12 months of the trust's inception.[12] By choosing an initial period with a short taxation year, lower tax rates may be achieved or income deferred to the next period. While this may present some benefits there are also advantages to choosing a December 31 taxation year end. Tax returns, other tax forms, and tax rates normally apply to the calendar year. As well, beneficiaries use the calendar year. So, for ease of administration, trustees of testamentary trusts often accept the calendar year as the taxation year. It should be noted that the taxation year for an inter vivos trust is always the calendar year.

Testamentary and inter vivos trusts have dramatically *different tax computations*. The *inter vivos trust* must apply the highest federal personal tax rate (29%) to all of its income.[13] Provincial tax is also calculated at the applicable province's top tax rate. Using the marginal tax rates for a certain province developed in Chapter 10 (Exhibit 10-7), the tax rates for an inter vivos trust are as follows:

Ordinary income	45%
Eligible taxable dividends	28%
Non-eligible taxable dividends	33%
Capital gains ($1/2$ of ordinary income)	23%

In contrast, the *testamentary trust* can apply the full range of rates in the individual's graduated tax scale. Therefore, all of the rates and tax brackets developed in Chapter 10, Exhibit 10-7 apply to income earned in a testamentary trust. The rates in Exhibit 10-7 are as follows:

Marginal Tax Rates by Type of Income
(excluding provincial surtaxes)

Income range (2012)	Capital Gains	Canadian Dividends		Ordinary Income
		Eligible	Non-eligible	
Up to $42,707	12%	0%	7%	24%
$42,708 – $85,414	16	10	17	32
$85,415 – $132,406	20	21	27	40
Over $132,406	23	28	33	45

---

10 ITA 104(18).
11 ITA 249(1).
12 ITA 104(23).
13 ITA 122(1); IT-406R2.

This graduated rate scale provides a separate tax base for all or a part of a trust's income. For example, a trust having two equal income beneficiaries with nominal other income may divide its $60,000 of trust income through appropriate allocations as follows:

Trust income	$60,000
Less allocated	(40,000)
Taxable trust income	$20,000
Taxable income of	
Beneficiary A	$20,000
Beneficiary B	$20,000
Total income	$60,000

As three separate taxpayers, each having access to a separate tax base, the entire $60,000 is taxed at the lowest possible rates. Therefore, the testamentary trust allows for valuable income splitting.

When calculating tax for inter vivos and testamentary trusts the federal tax can be reduced by the dividend tax credit, donations and gifts tax credits, foreign tax credit, political contribution tax credit, and various investment tax credits. *Neither type of trust can deduct any of the personal tax credits.*

B. Income Allocations and Beneficiaries

Trusts earn a variety of types of income of which some, such as capital gains and Canadian dividends, have preferential tax treatment. As indicated earlier, the trust can allocate income to beneficiaries thereby reducing the trust income. In making the allocation, the trust may designate the source and characteristic of certain types of income as being transferred to the beneficiary. The most important of these pertain to capital gains and taxable Canadian dividends. For capital transactions, the trust may designate its *net taxable capital gains* for allocation to the beneficiaries.[14] The allocation can include capital gains eligible for the capital gain deduction. Net taxable capital gains refer to taxable capital gains minus the allowable capital losses to the extent the amount is positive. As indicated previously, net capital losses are retained by the trust for deduction against capital gains of other years. As a result, beneficiaries are taxed on only one-half of the net capital gains. Taxable Canadian dividends allocated to beneficiaries will be classified as eligible or non-eligible, and grossed up for the beneficiaries tax purposes to 138% or 125% of the actual dividend with appropriate dividend tax credits available.[15] The trustee may decide to allocate income types to beneficiaries in different proportions provided that each of the beneficiaries receives the desired benefit and is treated equitably. For example, the trustee may allocate more capital gains to a beneficiary who has unused loss carry-overs from past years. Other beneficiaries may then receive a greater proportion of other types of income provided that they are not economically disadvantaged.

A trust may also designate other types of income to be allocated such as tax-free capital dividends,[16] foreign business and non-business income (including foreign tax credits), certain pension incomes, and others.

C. The 21-Year Rule

Although a trust is considered to be an individual it may have an unlimited lifespan. Individuals, on the other hand, have a limited life and upon death have a deemed disposition of certain property at market values. So, in order to prevent a trust from

---

14 ITA 104(21), 104(21.2) and (21.3); IT-381R3.
15 IT-524.
16 ITA 104(20).

escaping tax on property that it holds for an extended time period, inter vivos and testamentary trusts are deemed to have sold certain properties at market value on its 21st anniversary date and every 21 years thereafter.[17] The properties include:

- capital properties (non-depreciable)
- depreciable properties
- land that is inventory
- resource property

An exception to this rule is property owned by a spousal trust, which is discussed on the next page.

In many cases the trust can successfully avoid the deemed disposition at fair market by transferring the particular properties to the beneficiary prior to the 21-year anniversary date. Such transfers are normally deemed to be a disposition at the property's cost amount.[18] Therefore, the beneficiary simply takes over the tax position of the property received from the trust. Once the property is in the hands of the beneficiary, it will be taxed when sold by the beneficiary or upon his/her death.

When a trust holds property beyond 21 years and triggers a deemed disposition, for tax purposes it will recognize the related gains or losses on the relevant properties as if they were sold. The trust then is deemed to reacquire the properties at fair market value, which becomes the new cost amount of the property for the trust. Consider the following properties:

	Original Cost	UCC	Market Value
Land	$ 50,000	N/A	$ 70,000
Building #1	$200,000	$160,000	$210,000
Building #2	$100,000	$ 80,000	$ 95,000

On the day of the trust's 21-year anniversary, the properties are deemed sold at market value resulting in the following gains:

	Taxable Capital Gain	Recapture of CCA
Land – ¹/₂ (70,000 – 50,000)	$10,000	–
Building #1 – ¹/₂ (210,000 – 200,000)	5,000	–
– 200,000 – 160,000	–	$40,000
Building #2 – 95,000 – 80,000	–	15,000
	$15,000	$55,000

After recognizing a capital gain of $15,000 and recapture of CCA of $55,000, the trust cost amounts for the land and Building #1 are $70,000 and $210,000 respectively. However for Building #2 the market value ($95,000) was lower than the original cost ($100,000) of the building and so the trust is deemed to have acquired Building #2 for a cost of $100,000 (equal to original cost) but has a deemed undepreciated capital cost of $95,000. Future CCA is based on $95,000. However, if in the future Building #2 is sold for more than the $95,000 current value, a recapture of CCA may occur up to $100,000 and a capital gain realized for proceeds over $100,000.

---

17 ITA 104(4), (5).
18 ITA 107(2).

D. Transactions with Settlors and Beneficiaries

This segment reviews the tax implications of the transfer of property from a settlor to the trust and the transfer of trust property to beneficiaries. The comments in this segment apply to personal trusts (inter vivos and testamentary), but exclude those classified as spousal trusts. Part E below deals with the unique features of spousal trusts.

As previously noted, a trust is a separate taxpayer and when property is transferred to the trust (usually by the settlor) a disposition of property occurs (subject to minor exceptions).[19] This disposition normally occurs at market value. Consequently the market value of the asset transferred becomes its cost base in the trust.

From time to time, and certainly at the time a trust is terminated, property of the trust is transferred to beneficiaries. The tax treatment on the transfer depends on the type of beneficiary receiving the property—they may be an income beneficiary, a capital beneficiary, or both. A beneficiary who is entitled to receive income from the trust is considered to have an "income interest" in the trust, and is an income beneficiary. If the beneficiary is entitled to receive capital, they have a "capital interest."[20] In many cases a beneficiary has both a capital and an income interest.

When trust property is transferred to a beneficiary who has only an income interest, the trust is deemed to have disposed of the property at market value that may realize taxable income.[21] The opposite occurs when trust property is transferred to a capital beneficiary or a person who is both a capital and income beneficiary. Here the disposition is deemed to be at the property's cost amount.[22] It is less common for a trust to distribute property to a beneficiary who is only an income beneficiary. So, as a *general rule* one can say that property transferred from a trust to a beneficiary is deemed to be sold by the trust at its cost amount and the beneficiaries assume the tax position formerly held by the trust. The cost amount of property refers to:

> Capital property—ACB
> Depreciable property—UCC
> Cumulative eligible capital—4/3 of the CEC

When depreciable property is transferred, the beneficiary assumes the capital cost of the property *and* its undepreciated capital cost. Therefore, on a subsequent sale a potential recapture of CCA can occur.

E. Spousal Trusts

Special rules apply for personal trusts that qualify as a spousal trust. In general terms, a trust is a spousal trust if the spouse of the settlor is entitled to receive *all of the income* of the trust and no person other than that spouse can use or receive the capital of the trust before the death of the spouse.[23] The most common use of a spousal trust is one that holds assets of a deceased person under terms that allow the income generated from the assets to be distributed to the spouse but preserves the assets for future distribution to children. The distribution to children occurs on the death of the spouse. In this way capital is preserved for the next generation but can be used by the surviving spouse to generate income during his/her lifetime.

There are three unique features of a spousal trust. These are:

1. When property is transferred into the trust, the settlor is deemed to have sold the property at its cost amount. Therefore, the tax status of the property prior to its transfer is assumed by the trust.

---

19 ITA 248(1) (disposition defined).
20 ITA 108(1).
21 ITA 106(3).
22 ITA 107(2).
23 ITA 70(61), 104(4).

2. The 21-year deemed disposition requirement is waived for the first 21-year anniversary. Therefore, in most situations, the property remains without tax until the death of the beneficiary spouse.

3. Upon the death of the spouse who is the beneficiary, the spousal trust property is deemed to be sold at market value and taxable income may then be created.[24]

The above features are the opposite of the tax treatment for non-spousal personal trusts.

F. Estates

Following the death of an individual, an executor or administrator takes control of property owned by the deceased. The executor discharges all debts and obligations and distributes property to beneficiaries. So, an estate is actually an administrative period that exists until debts are settled and assets distributed to beneficiaries. Beneficiaries of an estate can be:

- Individuals, or
- Testamentary trusts such as spousal trusts or trusts for children until they reach a certain age or satisfy other conditions.

Therefore, an estate life is limited and lasts until the executor's duties are completed. Exhibit 17-1 demonstrates the estate period.

For tax purposes the estate period is considered to be a separate trust.[25] When assets are transferred to testamentary trusts as shown in Exhibit 17-1 new trusts begin as separate taxpayers from the estate. Income earned during the estate period is taxed in the estate trust and may include property income, capital gains and other sources of income resulting from the disposition of certain assets. Remember, that upon death, an individual is deemed to have sold assets at fair market value unless they are bequeathed to a spouse or spouse trust. So except for assets going to a spouse or spouse trust, the estate assumes the assets at a cost equal to the market value of the asset at the time of death. If the estate subsequently sells such an asset any gain or loss is calculated by comparing the selling price to the asset's market value at the time of death.

The estate trust is automatically terminated when all assets are transferred to the beneficiaries.

Exhibit 17-1:

Estate Period

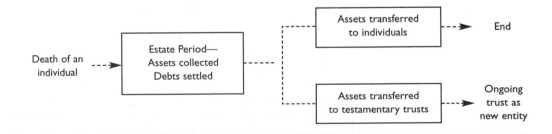

G. Other Trusts

There are certain other types of trusts that are widely used and deserve brief mention. These include tax deferred income plan trusts, unit investment trusts, and bare trusts.

Trusts governed by deferred income plans include, Registered Pension Plans (RPP), Registered Retirement Savings Plans (RRSP), Deferred Profit Sharing Plans (DPSP), Registered Retirement Income Funds (RRIF), and Registered Educations Savings Plans (RESP).[26] These plans are not taxable and hold income for distribution to beneficiaries

---

24 ITA 104(4).
25 ITA 104(1).
26 ITA 146, 147, 146.3, 149(1).

at a later time. Therefore, tax is deferred on income until distributions are made from the trusts at which time the beneficiary is subject to tax.

Bare trusts are entities whose sole purpose is to hold property on behalf of others. It is a structure used for convenience. For example a corporation may act as the trustee to hold a real estate investment on behalf of a number of individual owners. This permits the real estate to be registered to one party rather than to many separate investor owners. As a bare trust it is not taxable in any form.

The *unit investment trust* has wide application in the Canadian securities and investment community. This category includes mutual funds, real estate investment trusts (REIT), income trusts, and royalty trusts. All of these vehicles have one important tax status in common—income earned can be allocated to unit holders and taxed in their hands. This avoids the double taxation impact that may occur when a corporate structure is used. Ownership of these trusts is widely distributed through units and these are typically traded on stock exchanges. In addition, most unit trusts qualify for ownership in retirement vehicles such as RRSPs, RPPs, and so on. The commercial use of income trusts is examined in Part IV of this chapter.

III. The Use of Personal Trusts

Personal trusts have a number of non-tax as well as tax uses. Some, but not all, of these are reviewed below. Remember, personal trusts include both inter vivos and testamentary trusts.

The estate freeze

The concept of an estate freeze was reviewed in previous chapters (see Chapter 14 under "Reorganization of Share Capital" and Chapter 19 under "Sale to Family Members"). Typically, the estate freeze involves a family business or an investment corporation whose shares are growing in value and are subject to capital gains tax on the death of the owner. The estate freeze is designed to reduce the impact of this tax and often involves the parent exchanging common shares in the company for non-participating fixed value preferred shares. At that point, new common shares, which continue to grow in value, are issued to family members who are typically children. The parent now owns only fixed value preferred shares and the potential capital gain will not increase. An inter vivos trust can be used to hold the growth shares on behalf of children, especially if they are minors. In this way increases in share values accrue to the children and avoid the related tax on the death of the parent.

Income splitting

There are significant anti-avoidance rules that prevent the splitting of income amongst family, especially for inter vivos trusts. There are, however, some income splitting opportunities that remain with the use of inter vivos trusts. In particular, capital gains on property previously transferred by a parent or grandparent to minor children are not attributable to the transferor. Where possible, parents or grandparents can transfer capital growth properties to inter vivos trusts with children as beneficiaries. Future capital gains can then flow through the trust and be taxed as part of the children's income presumably at a lower rate.[27] This allocation is very useful where a beneficiary is entitled to claim the capital gain deduction on eligible capital gains (for example, a gain on shares of a small business corporation).[28] Testamentary trusts can also achieve some income splitting benefits. After death, there is no attribution and therefore testamentary trusts can be used for surviving

---

27 ITA 104(21).
28 ITA 104(21.2).

minor children to take advantage of lower tax rates or allocate income to be taxed as part of the children's income.

Also, income earned as a result of reinvesting past income is not subject to the normal attribution rules. For example, if a parent transfers property to a trust for minor children and the property earns interest and dividends from public corporations, that income is normally attributed to the parent for tax purposes. However, when that income is reinvested, the returns on the reinvestment belong to the trust. As an inter vivos trust the tax to the trust would be at the top personal rate. It would therefore be desirable and possible to allocate this income to the beneficiaries to be taxed in as part of their income.

Administrative benefits

While tax advantages are often associated with the use of trusts, their fundamental benefits are from non-tax related estate planning. Some of these are summarized below:[29]

- A trust may provide a vehicle to manage property for persons who cannot manage their own affairs.
- A trust may provide direction on how to use property after a person's death and may span several generations.
- A trust may be used to preserve property and reduce the risk of wasting an asset. For example, parents may settle property for their children to be used for specific needs of those children such as education.
- A trust may be used to hold property for persons not yet born such as future grandchildren.

The trust is a unique and flexible structure that has a broad range of uses in family estate planning.

IV. The Use of Commercial Trusts

Commercially, inter vivos trusts are used as a vehicle for *mutual funds* and *income trust funds*. Typically, mutual funds simply hold a variety of investments in publicly traded securities such as stocks and bonds. Their purpose is to allow smaller investors to participate in a wide variety of investments, spread risk, and gain access to professional investment management. In contrast, an income trust is a structure to operate a business. Its primary purpose was to achieve a tax efficient alternative to the corporate structure by avoiding a two-tier tax format and possible double taxation. However, recent tax changes have rendered the income trust to a marginal structure. This segment of the chapter deals with the changes to income trusts and briefly examines their types and basic tax and organizational structure.

The primary incentives for using income trusts as an alternative to the corporate structure were twofold:

1. The trust income was not taxable because its income could be allocated to the unit holders (beneficiaries) and taxed as part of their income; and

2. The allocation to unit holders retained its source and characteristic for tax preferred income like capital gains and dividends.

There are three types of income trusts: investment trusts, royalty trusts, and real estate investment trusts (REIT). The above incentives were eliminated for investment trusts and royalty trusts (not real estate investment trusts) that are created after

---

29 Kandev and Purkey, "Practical Application of Trusts," Report of Proceedings of the Fifty-Sixth Tax Conference (2004), Canadian Tax Foundation, p. 40.6.

October 31, 2006 and replaced with a tax system that essentially treats their income similar to a public corporation. As noted above, real estate investment trusts (REITs) will continue to receive the above trust incentives. The tax treatment of investment and royalty trusts are described below separate from real estate investment trusts.

A. Investment and Royalty Trusts Created *after* October 31, 2006

An investment trust is used to operate an active business. A royalty trust is used in the resource industry with oil and gas resources playing a dominant role. Typically, both investment and royalty trusts distribute all, or substantially all, of their income to the trust beneficiaries or unit holders. These trusts are now technically referred to as "specified investment flow-throughs" (SIFTs).[30] Normally a trust reduces its income for tax purposes by deducting distributions to beneficiaries. However, a SIFT entity is not allowed to deduct most distributions[31] and instead must pay a special tax on the amount of the distributions.[32] The rate of tax is a combination of a federal rate plus an additional rate in lieu of provincial tax. The combined tax rate is 25% (15% federal + 10%[33] addition). Note that this rate is similar to the combined federal and provincial general tax rate for corporations. The trust tax relating to the distributions means that beneficiaries receive only the after-tax amount of the available distribution.

From the beneficiary's perspective, the distribution does not retain the characteristics of its source in the trust. Instead, for tax purposes *the trust distribution is deemed to be an eligible dividend* with the related dividend tax credit benefits.[34]

The income earned and distributed by a SIFT entity to an individual beneficiary in a 45% personal marginal tax bracket is shown below.

The Trust:	
Trust income earned and available for distribution	$1,000
Distribution tax—25% (in 2012)	(250)
Net amount to beneficiary	$750
The Beneficiary:	
Received from trust	$750
Tax, as eligible dividend—28%	(210)
Net to beneficiary	$540
Total Tax:	
Trust	$250
Beneficiary	210
	$460
	46%

Note that the overall tax result is the same as a distribution from a public corporation. There is a minor amount of double taxation—1% (46% − 45%). All of this demonstrates that *there is little, if any, benefit to structuring a business as an investment trust or a royalty trust. The same rules apply to publicly traded limited partnership entities.*

---

30 ITA 248.
31 ITA 104(6)(b)(iv).
32 ITA 122(1)(b), 122(1.01).
33 The provincial component varies by and applies to each province where a SIFT has a permanent establishment.
34 ITA 104(16), 89(1).

B. Investment and Royalty Trusts Created *before* October 31, 2006

Investment and royalty trusts that fall into this category retained their normal trust status until the end of their 2010 taxation year.[35] During that period the trusts could deduct distributions from trust income, thereby eliminating tax at the trust level.

In 2011, trusts in this category lost their attractiveness as they are now subject to the distribution tax described previously. This leaves only one form of income trust that will retain the benefit of income flowing directly to investors without first being taxed. That trust is the real estate investment trust (REIT), which is reviewed below.

C. Real Estate Investment Trust (REIT)

The real estate investment trust is not considered to be a SIFT entity.[36] Therefore, it continues to be treated for tax purposes as a normal inter vivos trust with all the related benefits described previously in Part II of this chapter.

The real estate investment trust is used as a vehicle to own real estate and earn rental income. A feature of this type of trust is that it normally owns the income-producing property directly. The net rental income is then flowed to the unit holders creating a deduction in the trust and eliminating its tax. The real estate owned by the trust creates a tax shelter by claiming capital cost allowance, which is a non-cash expense. Therefore, the amount of income allocated (after claiming CCA) is usually lower than the net cash flow from the rentals. This permits the trust to have a distribution amount greater than the taxable amount. This excess is considered a return of capital and is not taxable upon receipt. It does, however, reduce the cost base of the investor's units and increase the potential for a future capital gain.

Some real estate investment trusts are created simply to support the real estate needs of an operating business such as a hotel chain. The trust owns the real estate and collects rents from the operating company that manages the hotel. The trust normally owns equity in the operating corporation. Other real estate investment trusts simply invest in a number of real estate properties and earn rental income from third partners who have no association with the trust.

V. Summary and Conclusion

The trust entity is used to achieve certain estate and tax planning objectives for individuals and as an alternative to the corporate structure for large businesses with a widely held ownership structure. The tax treatment of trusts can be summarized as follows:

1. A trust is a separate taxable entity. For tax purposes it is considered to be an individual.

2. An inter vivos trust is taxed at the highest rate of tax for an individual. A testamentary trust applies the full graduated rate scale for individuals. Neither trust can deduct personal tax credits.

3. All trusts can reduce taxable income by amounts allocated to the beneficiaries. Income not allocated to beneficiaries is taxable to the trust, but thereafter can be distributed to beneficiaries tax-free.

4. Income allocated from a trust to its beneficiaries can retain the source and characteristics of taxable Canadian dividends, tax-free dividends, capital gains, and foreign income.

5. As a general rule, assets transferred to a trust are considered to be disposed of by the transferor at fair market value. The market value is therefore the trust's cost for tax purposes. The exception to this rule pertains to assets transferred to spousal trusts in which case the transferor has a deemed disposition at the asset's cost amount for tax purposes.

---

35 ITA 104(6).
36 ITA 122.1.

6. As a general rule, assets transferred from the trust to beneficiaries who have a capital interest in the trust are deemed to be disposed of by the trust at the asset's cost amount for tax purposes. This rule does not apply to testamentary spousal trusts whose assets are deemed to have been sold at fair market value when they pass to children.

7. Assets held by a trust are deemed to be disposed of at fair market value every 21 years. This rule does not apply to the spousal trusts (which has a disposition on the death of the spouse) or to commercial trusts such as REITs and investment and royalty trusts.

The above tax treatment demonstrates that the trust entity is a *hybrid* in that it is a taxable entity, but it normally can avoid tax by allocating taxable income to beneficiaries. Income earned by a trust is taxable only once—either in the trust or as part of the beneficiaries' income. The standard trust rules do not apply to certain commercial trusts.

This chapter concludes Part Four of the text, which examines the secondary business structures that flow their income directly to the participants. In Chapter 1, it was indicated that while only individuals, corporations, and trusts are taxable entities, there are nevertheless six basic business structures—proprietorships, corporations, partnerships, limited partnerships, joint ventures, and trusts. We have now examined and compared all six in terms of their individual characteristics. All six differ dramatically with regard to the amount and timing of the related tax. Consequently, choosing one structure over another will alter the related cash flows and have an impact on the ultimate return on investment.

The choice of business structure is a vital component in investment decisions. Before choosing the form of business organization, one must examine each option and anticipate its impact on future cash flows. A venture receives capital and invests it with a view to generating a profit and ultimately must realize a cash return to the investor. By anticipating and following this path of activity, an informed analysis can be made of any proposed business structure, and structures can be created that best suit the particular situation.

All forms of organization, except the proprietorship, are applicable to both large and small business ventures. Ventures may differ in size, but all conform to similar tax concepts and require the same basic method of analysis.

The remaining chapters of this text examine specific types of business decisions. Very few new tax concepts will be introduced in these chapters, which apply the basic principles developed in Chapters 3 to 17 to the specific decisions under consideration.

Visit the Canadian Income Taxation Web site at **www.mcgrawhill.ca/ olc/buckwold** to view any updated tax information.

Review Questions

1. What is a trust, and how does it differ from a partnership and corporation?

2. Briefly explain the basic unique features of a trust?

3. What are the definitions of a testamentary trust and an inter vivos trust?

4. What are the differences between a personal trust and a commercial trust?

5. Explain when a trust is liable for tax in Canada.

6. What are the unique features for determining the taxable income of a trust?

7. "A trust is considered to be an individual for tax purposes and therefore its taxation year is the calendar year." Is this statement true? Explain.

8. Compare the methods for calculating tax payable for testamentary trusts and inter vivos trusts.

9. A trust can deduct from taxable income amounts allocated to a beneficiary. Identify the unique features of this process and how the allocation may differ from allocation made by a partnership.

10. "Capital assets held by a trust are only subject to tax on a disposition that results from a sale or when they are distributed to beneficiaries." Is this statement correct? Explain.

11. How does a spousal testamentary trust differ from a non-spousal testamentary trust?

12. What is an income trust? Briefly explain why they are used.

Key Concept Questions

QUESTION ONE

In each of the following cases, an individual has established a trust.

1) Anita established a family trust to hold investments in shares of public corporations for the benefit of her children.

2) Bob established a trust for the benefit of his wife. His wife is entitled to receive all of the income from the trust and no one, other than his wife, can have the use or enjoyment of the assets held by the trust until after her death.

3) Carol's will directed that on her death a trust be established to hold assets for her children until the youngest reaches age 25.

4) Dan died in the current year leaving substantial assets under the control of the executor of his estate.

Determine the type of trust that has been established in each case. *Income Tax Act reference: ITA 108(1).*

QUESTION TWO

During the current year an inter vivos trust received the following income:

Interest	$30,000
Eligible dividends	20,000
Capital gains	12,000

One half of the income was paid to a beneficiary of the trust, Gail, a 22-year-old student, with no other source of income. The remainder of the income was retained by the trust. The trust designated the source of the income paid to the beneficiary as follows: interest $15,000, eligible dividends $10,000, and capital gains $6,000.

Determine the net income, taxable income, and federal tax payable for both Gail and the trust. *Income Tax Act reference: ITA 104(2), (6), (19), (21), 122(1), (1.1).*

QUESTION THREE

During the current year a testamentary trust earned interest income of $45,000, all of which was paid to Bill, the sole beneficiary of the trust. Bill has other sources of income which total $300,000.

What can be done to reduce the overall tax liability? *Income Tax Act reference: ITA 104(13.1).*

QUESTION FOUR

During the current year, a trust had the following income (losses):

Capital gains	$ 20,000
Capital losses	(50,000)
Business loss	(40,000)
	$(70,000)

Beverley, the sole beneficiary of the trust, has income from other sources that puts her in the top tax bracket. Determine the appropriate allocation of income from the trust. *Income Tax Act reference: ITA 104(21).*

QUESTION FIVE

A trust had the following results for the current year:

Capital gains	$100,000
Capital losses	20,000

The trust has net capital losses of $35,000 incurred in 2006 available. Determine the maximum amount that can be allocated to a beneficiary. *Income Tax Act reference: ITA 104(21), (21.3).*

QUESTION SIX

Susan, age 14, is the sole beneficiary of a trust. The trust document indicates that the income earned by the trust is to be retained by the trust until Susan turns 18.

Does this mean that the income must be subject to tax in the trust until Susan turns 18? *Income Tax Act reference: ITA 104(18).*

Problems

PROBLEM ONE

Rhonda is divorced and lives with her 12-year-old daughter. Rhonda plans to settle a trust for her daughter and transfer $200,000 in cash to it, which will be invested for the benefit of her daughter. The terms of the trust are as follows:

1. The trust will invest the funds in Canadian marketable securities.

2. Income will accrue annually to the benefit of the daughter. However, no income will be distributed until the daughter reaches 21 years of age.

3. When the daughter reaches the age of 35 all of the trust's capital will be distributed and the trust will cease.

The trustee has developed a financial plan that includes certain mutual fund investments. The anticipated annual return on the investment is 12%. Returns that are distributed by the mutual funds will be reinvested in the funds. It is expected that the 12% annual return will consist of the following:

Interest	1%
Dividends	3%
Capital gains	4%
Total mutual fund allocations	8%
Capital growth	4%
Total annual return	12%

Required:

Explain the overall tax treatment of the trust during its existence and recommend any tax planning opportunities that are available to the trustee.

PROBLEM TWO

Harvey's last will and testament provides for bequests to his spouse, daughter, and grandson. Upon his death, his wife is to receive $200,000 in cash. In addition, $800,000 of specific assets are to be held in trust on her behalf. This trust is required to pay his wife, during her lifetime, all of the annual income generated by the trust. Upon the death of his wife, the trust's assets will be distributed equally to his daughter and grandson. The remaining assets in Harvey's estate are to be divided into separate trusts for each of his daughter and grandson. Harvey has indicated that a particular real estate investment be shared—50% for his wife's trust and 25% for each of the other trusts.

The trust for his daughter will require all income to be distributed annually until she reaches the age of 40 at which time the assets will be distributed to her. The trust for the grandchild will hold all of its income in trust until he reaches the age of 25. Thereafter, the grandson will receive the annual income and upon reaching the age of 40 will receive all of the assets owned by the trust.

Harvey died in 20X9 when his daughter was 35 years old and his grandson was 15. The following assets are transferred to the trusts.

Property (Market Value)	Wife	Daughter	Grandson
Land	$100,000	$ 50,000	$ 50,000
Building	400,000	200,000	200,000
Bonds	100,000	300,000	300,000
Stocks (public corporations)	200,000	200,000	200,000
	$800,000	$750,000	$750,000

The land and building represents a single rental property that generates net cash rental income of $300,000. The property was purchased in 20X1 for $800,000 (land $150,000; building $650,000). The UCC of the building at the time of death was $500,000. Future rental income will be shared 50% by the trust for Harvey's wife and 25% for each of the other two trusts. The bonds earn interest at the rate of 6% and the stocks generate dividends of 3%. The stock portfolio has a cost base of $600,000. Harvey's spouse will have earned income of $30,000 from sources other than the trust. His daughter earns an annual salary of $100,000 and his grandson has no income.

Required:

1. What are the tax consequences to Harvey at the time of death relating to the assets described above?

2. What are the cost amounts for tax purposes of the assets received by each of the trusts?

3. Develop a plan for each trust for managing the trust income that will minimize the overall tax for the beneficiaries and the trusts. Show calculations where appropriate.

4. What are the tax consequences that will result when the trust assets are distributed to the beneficiaries? Assume the trust will own the same assets throughout.

PROBLEM THREE

K Inc. is a Canadian corporation whose shares are traded on a stock exchange. K operates three divisions within its corporate structure. Two of the divisions are in the technology field and are in the early stages of their growth cycles. They are both profitable with strong research and development capabilities. The third division is older and very mature. Its products are widely accepted and profitable. Its income and cash flow are very stable and predictable. K's management feels that its share value is not fully exploited because the divisions have diverse characteristics. Consequently raising capital for new development in younger divisions is costly.

To alleviate this problem K is considering selling off the third division as a separate entity. They feel this can be achieved by setting up a separate corporation to house the division. The separate corporation would issue shares to the public and the funds used to acquire the division from K Inc. Management has also been looking at the use of an income trust as an alternative to the corporate format.

K has requested your advice on this matter.

Required:

1. Explain to K how each of the structures work with respect to profits, tax, and distribution to investors. Demonstrate with calculations where possible.

2. Is an income trust appropriate in this situation? Explain.

3. Would your answer to 2 (above) be different if the third division was a group of real estate rental properties?

PART 5

Selected Topics

The promises of yesterday are the taxes of today.

MACKENZIE KING

CHAPTER 18

Business Acquisitions and Divestitures— Assets versus Shares

The decision to sell or acquire an existing business is subject to a number of different influences. Obviously, price is a key factor in that the vendor wants to achieve the maximum realization and the purchaser wants to obtain the highest possible return on investment.

The price paid for a business, although established primarily by market conditions, is influenced by tax considerations. The vendor's real proceeds from a sale are the selling price less the related tax costs resulting from the sale. A vendor that can reduce or defer the amount of tax otherwise payable may be willing to accept a lesser purchase price provided that the after-tax value is the same as or greater than what would normally be expected. The purchaser is actually acquiring a stream of future profits that will be subject to tax. A purchaser that can reduce the amount of tax otherwise payable on that income may be prepared to pay a higher price. The amounts of taxes payable by the vendor as a result of the sale and by the purchaser on future earnings may be influenced by the form of the transaction.

While business acquisitions and divestitures can take many forms, there are only two fundamental options—the sale of specific business assets or the sale of the corporation that owns those specific assets. The tax implications of these two alternatives have a significant effect on both the purchaser and the vendor and, in turn, on the price of a business.

This chapter examines both alternatives—the asset sale and the share sale—and their impact on the selling price of a business. Specifically, it examines the tax implications to both the purchaser and the seller, presents the method of analysis for equating the two, and reviews part of the decision process for the purchaser. The chapter concludes with a brief examination of the principles of business valuations.

I. Assets versus Shares

Before examining the specific tax implications of asset sales and share sales, it is important to establish the nature of each type of transaction.

Consider the diagram in Exhibit 18-1. Shareholder X owns 100% of the shares of For Sale Corporation, which operates an active business. For Sale Corporation owns a number of assets, which may include inventory, land, buildings, equipment, goodwill, patents, and franchises. In addition, it has liabilities. Shareholder Y owns 100% of Buyer Corporation, which also operates an active business. Buyer Corporation wants to buy the business operated by For Sale Corporation.

There are two basic possible ways to transfer For Sale's business to Buyer Corporation. The first possibility is for shareholder X to sell the shares of For Sale Corporation to Buyer Corporation. In this case, payment of the purchase price will flow directly to shareholder X. Buyer Corporation will own For Sale Corporation as a wholly owned subsidiary that will continue to operate its business with the same assets and related liabilities. It is important to recognize that nothing has changed within For Sale Corporation—the balance sheet and the tax values of its assets remain the same. Only the shareholder has changed.

Exhibit 18-1:

Alternative Methods of Selling a Business

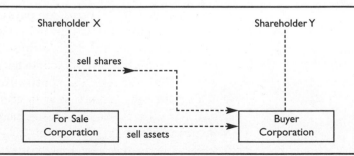

The second possibility is for For Sale Corporation to sell each individual business asset directly to Buyer Corporation. In other words, For Sale Corporation would sell its inventory, land, buildings, equipment, goodwill, and franchises for a specific price for each asset. In this case, payment of the purchase price flows directly to For Sale Corporation, which continues to be owned by shareholder X. In purchasing each specific asset, Buyer Corporation may or may not be assuming the related liabilities of the business. It is not uncommon for specific assets to be purchased and paid for by a combination of cash, an amount owing, and the assumption of the attached liabilities.

Both alternatives result in a tax liability to the vendor when the selling price is greater than the cost for tax purposes of the property sold. Referring again to Exhibit 18-1, a sale of shares at a price in excess of their original cost would result in a taxable gain to shareholder X, leaving the after-tax proceeds available for investment. However, after a sale of specific assets, For Sale Corporation would incur a tax liability. While this would leave after-tax proceeds in the corporation for possible investment, those proceeds would ultimately have to flow to shareholder X, at which time a second level of tax would occur. Clearly, the amount and timing of tax to the vendor is different under each alternative.

The question arises whether this difference in tax treatment also leads to a difference in sale price. If the price established for an asset sale is the same as for a share sale, it follows that considering that the tax implications are different, the vendor would prefer the method that provides the greatest after-tax proceeds for reinvestment. Similarly, in order for the vendor to receive the same after-tax proceeds from each method, it will be necessary to establish one price for an asset sale and another for a share sale. In this case, the purchaser would prefer the price that provided the greatest after-tax return on investment.

In order to establish the relationship between an asset price and a share price, one must first examine in greater detail the tax implications to the vendor and the purchaser for each of the basic alternatives.

II. Implications for the Vendor

A. Sale of Assets

As mentioned previously, the sale of specific assets by a vendor corporation will usually result in two levels of tax. It is, therefore, important to establish the following:

1. The amount of tax payable by the corporation and the timing of the payment of tax.

2. The amount of tax payable by the shareholder and when that tax may occur.

The types of income or loss generated from the sale of specific assets may vary with the nature of the assets sold; consequently, the resulting tax treatment may also vary.

The sale of capital property may result in a capital gain, of which one-half is taxable (see Chapter 8). The sale of depreciable property may result in recapture of capital cost allowance as well as a capital gain (see Chapter 6). On a sale of business assets, the recapture of capital cost allowance constitutes business income. The sale of intangibles, such as goodwill or patents, franchises, and licences having an unlimited life, may result in eligible capital property income (see Chapter 6), which is classified as business income.

The amount of tax payable on the above types of income depends on the nature of the corporation. A public corporation pays a high rate of tax on all types of income. On the other hand, if the selling company is a Canadian-controlled private corporation, the tax payable on profits classified as business income may be eligible for the lower small business rate if other sources of income have not already used up the annual $500,000 limit. Often, a Canadian-controlled private corporation will choose to sell its assets on the first day of a new taxation year in order to achieve an additional small business deduction base. Taxable capital gains earned by a Canadian-controlled private corporation are subject to a high rate of tax but eligible for a partial refund when the gains are distributed to the shareholders as a dividend (see Chapter 13).

In most cases, a corporation must recognize any income from asset sales in the year of disposition. However, income derived from capital gains may be realized over future years if the related proceeds from the sale are deferred over future years. As was indicated in Chapter 8, the option to realize taxable capital gains over a period of years is subject to certain limitations.

The amount and timing of the tax to the corporation can be determined with relative certainty; the amount of the second level of tax on corporate distributions is more difficult to determine precisely. When assets are sold, the corporation that previously housed the business continues to exist unless the shareholder chooses to wind it up. Immediately after the sale, the corporation will continue to own assets in the form of cash or amounts due from the purchaser. If the after-tax proceeds from the sale are retained in the corporation for investment purposes, the second level of tax to the shareholders can be delayed until some future time. When possible, shareholders often delay the second level of tax to gain maximum tax deferral, even though the rate of tax that may apply in the future is uncertain. As will be seen later, this complicates the comparative analysis of asset and share sales.

B. Sale of Shares

In contrast to the sale of assets, the sale of the shares of the entire corporation is relatively simple because it involves the sale of only one type of asset and usually results in only one level of tax.

The shares of the vendor corporation constitute capital property to the shareholder. Consequently, any gain realized from a sale is a capital gain, only one-half of which is taxable to the vendor. In addition, an individual shareholder may be eligible to shelter $750,000 of the gain from tax by using the capital gains deduction if the vendor's shares are qualified small business corporation shares. A qualified small business corporation must be a *small business corporation* at the time the shares are sold. As well, throughout the 24 months preceding the sale three tests must be met:

1. The corporation must be a Canadian-controlled private corporation.

2. The vendor's shares must not be owned by a person not related to the vendor.

3. More than 50% of the fair market value of the assets of the corporation must be assets used in an active business and/or an investment in shares of a *connected* corporation meeting the 50% asset test. When shares of a *connected* corporation meeting the 50% test are included, the 50% is increased to at least 90% for the corporation being sold, unless the connected corporation has at least 90% of the fair market value of its assets used in an active business.

The calculation of the capital gains deduction was discussed in Chapter 10, Part IV.

When the shareholder of the vendor corporation is an individual, the after-tax proceeds from the sale of shares are not subject to any further taxation and are fully available for reinvestment or for personal use.

As the sale of shares results in the complete sale of the corporation, no tax consequences result to the corporation itself. Even though the price of the shares reflects the fact that certain assets within the corporation have increased in value, such increase is not recognized in the corporation.

III. Implications for the Purchaser

The purchaser's return on investment from a business acquisition results from the future stream of annual profits generated by the acquired business. The amount of pre-tax cash flow that will be generated will be identical whether the purchaser acquires the specific assets of the business or the shares of the corporation which houses that business. However, the purchaser's return on investment is determined not from pre-tax but from after-tax profits. In most situations, the after-tax profits arising from an asset purchase will differ considerably from those arising from a share purchase.

A. Purchase of Assets

The most important feature of an asset purchase is that the purchaser can deduct from future income all or a portion of the purchase price by claiming capital cost allowance on depreciable property and amortization of eligible capital property, such as goodwill. Because the purchaser is acquiring each individual asset of the business and not the corporation itself, the cost base of each asset for tax purposes is equal to the price paid.

Consider the specific list of assets being acquired under an asset purchase in Exhibit 18-2. Note that each of the assets has a fair market value in excess of the vendor's tax cost. On sale, each asset would create taxable income for the vendor corporation in the form of capital gains and the recapture of capital cost allowance. From the purchaser's perspective, the cost amount of each asset acquired is the fair market value price paid, and therefore the cost of the building ($900,000) can be deducted from future income at a rate of 4% annually (or it may meet the qualification for a new manufacturing building and a CCA rate of 10% or a new non-manufacturing business building and a CCA rate of 6%). The manufacturing equipment ($500,000) is a class 43 asset available for a 30% write-off rate (or class 29 and a 50% rate if purchased within a specified time frame). The limited life franchise ($150,000) is a class 14 asset, the full cost of which can be deducted at 10% annually on a straight-line basis or faster if justified economically. Note that no annual deduction is available for the land because it is not depreciable property. However, if the purchaser sells the land at some future time, its cost for tax purposes will be the purchase price of $75,000.

Exhibit 18-2:				
Assets Acquired in an Asset Purchase	Asset	Vendor's tax value	Fair market value	Write-off rate
	Land	$ 50,000	$ 75,000	—
	Building	600,000	900,000	4% (declining balance)*
	Manufacturing equipment	300,000	500,000	30% (declining balance)†
	Franchise (life 10 y)	100,000	150,000	10% (straight line)
		$1,050,000	$1,625,000	

* or 10% or 6% as described above
† or 50% (straight line) as described above

The amount of capital cost allowance available to the purchaser is significantly higher than was available to the vendor prior to the sale. For example, the vendor corporation could claim capital cost allowance on the manufacturing equipment based on its undepreciated capital cost of $300,000, whereas the purchaser will be able to claim capital cost allowance on $500,000. Therefore, while pre-tax profits were the same for the vendor as they are now for the purchaser, the after-tax profits are considerably different. As discussed below, the same variance would not occur if the purchaser acquired the shares of the vendor corporation, rather than the specific assets.

In an asset sale of a business, the purchaser and seller may find it easy to agree on a total purchase price but may have difficulty agreeing on how to allocate that total price among the individual assets. When the vendor wishes to minimize tax on the sale and the purchaser wishes to maximize future capital cost allowance, a conflict occurs. For example, referring to Exhibit 18-2, it is in the purchaser's interest to allocate more of the total price to the manufacturing equipment, rather than to the land or building, because the manufacturing equipment can be written off at 30% (or 50%), whereas the write-off on the building is only 4% (or 10% or 6%) and no deduction is available on the land. The vendor, however, will want to allocate more of the total price to assets that will result in a capital gain, rather than to those that will create more recapture of capital cost allowance, because only one-half of capital gains are taxable.

In many cases, purchase and sale agreements avoid the allocation problem by simply listing the assets as a group and providing a total purchase price for that group. Each party can then determine its own allocation. However, decision makers should be aware that the CRA can reallocate the total purchase price in accordance with the reasonable fair market values of each separate asset.[1] When making an acquisition, the purchaser is advised to make a reasonable attempt at establishing a fair allocation; this will provide an accurate picture of cash-flow savings from capital cost allowance.

As the amount of capital cost allowance available to the purchaser is an important factor, consideration should also be given to the capital cost classifications of the various assets being purchased. The capital cost allowance classes reviewed in Chapter 6 often change over time. For example, manufacturing equipment has been moved from class 8 (20%) to class 29 (50%) to class 39 (25%) to class 43 (30%), and back to class 29 when purchased before 2014. This means that the classification for the vendor corporation may not be the same as for the purchaser.

B. Purchase of Shares

Purchasing a business by acquiring the shares of the vendor corporation disturbs neither the asset base nor the activity within the vendor corporation. As only the shares have changed ownership, the vendor corporation continues, without interruption, in the same manner as it did before the change in ownership.[2] Consequently, the following tax treatment occurs:

1. The assets within the corporation remain at their tax values, even though their fair market values are higher, as indicated in the price of the shares.

2. Capital cost allowance after the acquisition continues from the same tax base as existed before the acquisition.

As a result, the after-tax cash profits of the acquired business following a share purchase will usually be lower than the after-tax cash profits following an asset purchase. When the reader refers again to Exhibit 18-2, the magnitude of this difference becomes obvious. If the shares of the vendor corporation are purchased, the amount of future deductions from income from capital cost allowance is $1,000,000 (building $600,000 + equipment $300,000 + franchise $100,000). If the specific assets are purchased, the total deductions from future income amount to $1,550,000 (building $900,000 + equipment $500,000 + franchise $150,000). Even though these deductions occur over a number of years, this difference has a dramatic impact on after-tax cash flow.

In effect, under the share purchase method, the purchaser simply takes over the tax position of the vendor corporation. This means that in addition to having lower capital cost allowance, the purchaser may be liable for tax in the event that the acquired vendor corporation should subsequently sell some of its assets. For example, after acquisition, if the new owner decided to sell the franchise at its fair market value of $150,000, the corporation would have taxable income because its tax value was inherited at $100,000.

Because the share purchase method results in lower after-tax cash flow *and* because the purchaser inherits a potential tax liability if it later sells some of the corporation's assets, the purchaser will attempt to establish a price for the shares that is lower than would have been paid for the assets. The amount of this discount is not

---

1   ITA 68; IT-220R2 (paragraphs 4–7); *The Queen v. Waldorf Hotel (1958) Ltd. et al.*, 75 DTC 5109 (FCTD).
2   Except when the acquired corporation has loss carry-overs (see Chapter 11—change in control).

always easy to establish and is subject to negotiation with the vendor. The relationship between the asset price of a business and its share price is examined in Parts IV and V of this chapter.

When the shares are acquired by a person who is not related to the vendor, the tax implications of an acquisition of control, discussed in Chapter 11, must be taken into consideration. The acquired corporation's current taxation year will be deemed to end, the tax values of assets in the acquired corporation are required to be reduced to their fair market value if the fair market value is lower, net capital losses expire, and the ability to use any non-capital losses in the acquired corporation is restricted.

C. Structure after Acquisition

It is important to recognize that the form of the purchase—assets or shares—does not dictate the nature of the organization structure after the purchase has been made. For example, consider a share purchase similar to the one diagrammed in Exhibit 18-1. Immediately after the purchase, For Sale Corporation becomes a wholly owned subsidiary of Buyer Corporation. If the purchaser wishes, this structure can continue, with the business operations of the parent and subsidiary in two separate taxable entities. Or the purchaser can, by means of a wind-up or amalgamation, combine the two entities and operate them within one taxable entity (see Chapter 14). Similarly, if a business is acquired by an asset purchase, the new business can be operated as part of the purchaser's business, or it can be turned into a subsidiary corporation.

The post-acquisition structure may have an impact on the tax cost of future activities. For example, when a manufacturing business purchases a non-manufacturing business, the amount of income available for the lower manufacturing rate of corporate tax (in some provinces) will vary, depending on whether the entities were combined or kept separate. This is because manufacturing income for tax purposes is determined arbitrarily in accordance with the ratio of manufacturing capital and labour to the entity's total capital and labour (see Chapter 11). Therefore, combining or separating the two entities may have a positive or negative impact on the rate of tax payable.

IV. The Relationship between Asset Price and Share Price

As described above, for both the seller and the purchaser, the tax impact of an asset sale is different from that of a share sale, with regard to both the amount of tax payable and the timing of the tax payment. Both parties must recognize that the price attached to the sale of a business will vary with the form of the transaction.

The degree to which the price varies cannot be measured with certainty. A vendor can accurately anticipate the tax liability to the corporation if the assets are sold but cannot be as certain with respect to the amount and timing of the subsequent level of tax when the corporation distributes its earnings to the shareholder. Similarly, a purchaser can accurately anticipate the capital cost allowance available after acquisition under either method, but with the share purchase method will find it difficult to determine the tax liability in the event that the acquired corporation disposes of some of its assets. Any negotiated purchase and sale of a business has some risk with respect to the tax impact. However, this risk can be diminished if both parties understand the tax consequences that would result from an assumed worst-case scenario.

From the vendor's perspective the worst-case scenario is most likely an asset sale whereby the vendor corporation pays tax on the sale of its assets and then immediately winds up the corporation by distributing all of its earnings. The worst-case scenario for the purchaser would involve a purchase of the shares of the vendor corporation and soon thereafter a sale of all of the assets of the newly acquired corporation. Both scenarios would result in full tax liability for the respective parties. Once the worst-case scenarios are known, both parties can assess the likelihood of their occurrence in view of the particular circumstances and build that factor into the negotiation process.

A. Establishing the Worst-Case Scenario

Once a business has been targeted for acquisition, it is important to establish the worst-case scenario for the vendor. Both the vendor and the purchaser are interested in this analysis. For example, if the worst-case scenario for a vendor is an asset sale and the net after-tax proceeds from this form of sale are known, the vendor can establish the share price that would provide the same after-tax proceeds. This information is critical to vendors because it permits them to establish a minimum share price that corresponds, on an after-tax basis, to an asset price. Presumably a vendor would not accept a share price that is below this minimum.

At the same time, a purchaser who knows the tax position of the vendor and also knows the share price that corresponds to the asset price in the worst-case scenario has a starting point from which to begin negotiations.

The process of establishing the worst-case scenario for the vendor will vary, depending on whether the vendor corporation is a small company or a large company and whether it is a public corporation or a private corporation. Consider the two vendor structures outlined in Exhibit 18-3.

Structure A shows a closely held private corporation. Because the corporation and the shareholder are so closely tied, the worst-case scenario involves

(a) sale of assets at fair market value;
(b) payment of corporate taxes on taxable gains from the sale of assets; and
(c) distribution of all cash to the shareholder, who incurs an immediate second level of tax.

Structure B is quite different. Under structure B, a large number of shareholders own a large public corporation that intends to continue operations indefinitely. The corporation for sale is a subsidiary of the public corporation. If the subsidiary corporation sold its assets, it would incur tax on the sale; however, no second level of tax would occur, even if dividends were paid to the parent public corporation, as intercorporate dividends flow tax-free. One could compute the tax effect if dividends were flowed straight through to the large number of individual shareholders, but this would be unrealistic, as the public corporation is not likely to alter its normal dividend policy. Therefore, the worst-case scenario under structure B is different from that under structure A.

It is important that the decision maker involved in a business acquisition or sale establish a realistic worst-case scenario in order to ascertain which investor will be directly affected by the transaction. In structure A, it is the individual shareholder; in structure B, it is the public corporation, which will reinvest the funds for an indefinite time period.

Exhibit 18-3:

Worst-Case Scenario under Alternative Structures

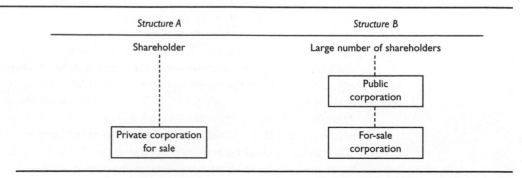

B. Equating the Asset Price with the Share Price

The calculations for determining the tax impact of the worst-case scenario for a vendor corporation and for determining an equivalent share price are presented and analyzed below. *The facts in the situation are greatly simplified in order to stress the method of analysis, rather than the details that may be required for the computations.*

Summary of Facts

For Sale Corporation is a Canadian-controlled private corporation that operates a small wholesale business. The company is owned directly by two individual shareholders, neither of whom participates in the management of the business. A recent balance sheet of the corporation, presented below, indicates the tax values of the assets, together with their fair market values.

For Sale Corporation: Current Position

	Tax value	Fair market value
Assets:		
Current assets	$400,000	$ 400,000
Equipment:		
Cost	600,000	
Capital cost allowance	(400,000)	
Undepreciated capital cost	200,000	500,000
Goodwill	–0–	200,000
	$600,000	$1,100,000
Liabilities	$200,000	
Shareholders' equity:		
Share capital	50,000	
Retained earnings	350,000	
	$600,000	

The following additional information is provided:

1. If a sale of assets occurs, the transaction date will be one month before the corporation's year end. Normal operating profits, to that date, will equal the small business deduction limit of $500,000. The rate of tax on additional business income is 25%.

2. Both shareholders are subject to a personal tax rate of 45% and to a dividend tax of 28% on eligible dividends and 33% on non-eligible dividends, net of the dividend tax credit.

3. The two shareholders, who are the original shareholders of the corporation, acquired their shares from the corporate treasury at a cost of $25,000 each for a total of $50,000, which is the same amount as the share capital on the corporation's balance sheet. After the sale of the business, the shareholders do not intend to continue investing together.

4. The sale would be made in cash. If assets are sold, the purchaser will assume the liabilities of the corporation.

Analysis

In the above situation, the worst-case scenario for the vendor would be a sale of assets at fair market value followed by a wind-up of the corporation so that the after-tax proceeds from the sale were distributed to the shareholders. It is now necessary to anticipate the tax liability to the corporation and to the shareholders. On a sale of assets followed by a wind-up of the corporation, the shareholders would receive a total of $602,000 after the payment of all taxes, as shown here.

Value of assets sold:	
Current assets	$ 400,000
Equipment	500,000
Goodwill	200,000
Total asset price	1,100,000
Liabilities (assumed by purchaser)	(200,000)
Net cash received from purchaser	900,000
Corporate tax on asset sales (below)	(100,000)
Net cash available for wind-up	$ 800,000
Cash received by shareholders	$ 800,000
Tax on dividend distributions (below)	(198,000)
Net after-tax cash to shareholders	$ 602,000

The amount of corporate tax and shareholder tax noted above requires an explanation. The sale of assets created the following income and tax for the corporation:

Current assets	–0–
Equipment:	
Recapture of capital cost allowance	
($500,000 – $200,000)	300,000
Goodwill:	
Eligible capital property gain (½ of $200,000)	100,000
Total income	$400,000
Corporate tax (25% × $400,000)	$100,000

The above corporate tax calculations are summarized in the table below:

Asset	Proceeds	Business Income	Taxable capital gains	Capital Dividend Account
Current assets	$ 400,000	$ 0	$0	$ 0
Equipment	500,000	300,000	0	0
Goodwill	200,000	100,000	0	100,000
	1,100,000	$400,000	$0	$100,000
Liabilities	(200,000)			
Income tax (25% × $400,000)	(100,000)			
Available for distribution	$800,000			

In order to compute the personal tax to the shareholders, one must first determine the nature of the cash distribution on wind-up. The $800,000 available for distribution consists of $50,000 of share capital and retained earnings of $750,000. It is not necessary to reconcile the pre-sale and post-sale retained earnings in order to arrive at the $750,000 because any amount available for distribution other than the share capital can only be retained earnings. However, the following reconciliation is presented for further clarity:

Retained earnings before the sale	$350,000
Gain on sale of equipment ($500,000 – $200,000)	300,000
Gain on sale of goodwill ($200,000 – 0)	200,000
	850,000
Tax on sale	(100,000)
Retained earnings after the sale	$750,000

Note that the actual gain on the sale of goodwill is $200,000 although only one-half, or $100,000, is taxable (see Chapter 6). The $100,000 tax-free portion of the goodwill gain can be distributed as a special tax-free capital dividend to the shareholders, as described in Chapter 12. As $50,000 of the distribution represents share capital and a further $100,000 represents a tax-free dividend, the remaining portion of the $800,000 is a taxable dividend to the shareholders.[3] A summary of the distribution and related tax follows.

Distribution:		
Share capital		$ 50,000
Retained earnings:		
Tax-free dividend (capital dividend)	$100,000	
Taxable dividend	650,000	$750,000
		$800,000
Tax to shareholders*		
Eligible dividend—$320,000 × 28%		$ 90,000
Non-eligible dividend—$330,000 × 33% (rounded)		108,000
	$650,000	$198,000

* The $650,000 taxable dividend is assumed to be divided as eligible—$320,000 and non-eligible—$330,000.

It should also be pointed out that the return of share capital for $50,000 results in a disposition of the shares to the shareholders. In this case, no capital gain or loss occurs because the cancellation price of $50,000 is equal to the cost of the shares to the shareholders.[4]

So, under the worst-case scenario, the shareholders will achieve net after-tax proceeds of $602,000. A share price can now be computed that yields the same $602,000 after the tax on the sale of the shares.

The sale of shares will result in a capital gain, one-half of which is taxable at a rate of 45%. As the gain is the difference between the selling price and the cost of the shares (which is $25,000 for each shareholder for a total of $50,000), the selling price necessary to yield net proceeds of $602,000 can be determined by making the following calculations:

(a) Selling price – tax = $602,000
(b) Selling price – 45% ($\frac{1}{2}$) (selling price – $50,000) = $602,000
(c) Selling price = $762,000

3 ITA 88(2); IT-149R4.
4 ITA 54.

The above analysis indicates that under the worst-case scenario, the vendor could accept a price of $762,000 for the shares or $900,000 for the net assets of the corporation (value of assets sold [$1,100,000] − liabilities assumed [$200,000] = $900,000) and receive the same after-tax proceeds of $602,000. Having established these values, the vendor could be sure that a corporation with assets valued at $1,100,000 would not sell all of its shares for less than $762,000.

At the same time, the vendors can argue that the equivalent share price should be higher than $762,000 because after selling the assets, they would not immediately wind up the corporation; rather, they would hold off doing so in order to delay the second level of tax until some future time. This scenario is possible, even though the two shareholders have indicated that after the sale they will not continue to invest together. For example, after a sale of assets but before the distribution to the shareholders, both shareholders could transfer their shares to their own separate holding corporations (see Chapter 14). They could then wind up For Sale Corporation by distributing its $800,000 of after-tax proceeds to those holding companies, which would receive the dividends tax-free. Both shareholders would thus have their share of the $800,000 in their own holding corporations available for reinvestment. The second level of tax would thus be delayed until they transferred the funds from their own holding companies to themselves for personal use.

The purchaser, on the other hand, would argue that avoidance of the second level of tax is not permanent, that the tax will ultimately be incurred, and that any adjustment to the share price should reflect only the value of the delay. And so the negotiations would proceed, until an acceptable share price was established.

It is important to recognize that the above result is specific only to the circumstances provided and that in other roughly similar situations, the tax impact of a worst-case scenario may be different. For example, the income from the sale of assets may be subject to the lower rate of corporate tax if the small business deduction is available. Further, when a private corporation is subject to high rates of tax, an element of double taxation may be avoided on wind-up if additional salaries or bonuses are paid to those shareholders who also manage the business (see Chapter 13). Each particular business must be examined with an eye to identifying its unique attributes so that the tax consequences resulting from its sale can be anticipated.

This part of the chapter stressed the implications to the vendor; the following part compares the impact of an asset purchase with that of a share purchase from the purchaser's perspective.

V. The Decision to Purchase

The impact of taxation on future cash flow and return on investment is a vital factor in the decision to acquire a business. The concept of business valuations is not discussed until a later chapter; however, it is generally understood that the value of a business to a purchaser is directly related to the after-tax profits that the acquired business will generate.

There are three major tax issues that the purchaser must examine when contemplating a business acquisition in the form of an asset or share purchase. The purchaser must

(a) anticipate the rate of tax that will apply, after the acquisition, on expected future profits;

(b) determine how much extra cash flow will be generated as a result of deducting capital cost allowance and amortizing eligible capital property; and

(c) when the purchase is by way of a share acquisition, assess the likelihood of incurring additional tax liabilities if the acquired corporation should later dispose of any of its assets.

Each of these three major considerations is examined below.

A. Future Rates of Tax

The rate of tax on business income after acquisition can differ considerably from the rate that was applicable before the acquisition. For example, a business that was entitled to the low corporate tax rate on its first $500,000 of annual business income may be subject to the high rate of corporate tax after the acquisition, if the purchaser is a public corporation or another private corporation that has substantial other sources of business income.[5] The reverse may apply when a corporation that cannot use the small business deduction (because of its association with other companies) becomes eligible for the lower rate of tax after acquisition. In addition, tax rates may be altered as a result of a combining of the purchased business with the business operations of the purchaser. For example, in certain provinces, the combining of manufacturing and non-manufacturing activities will alter the amount eligible for the special manufacturing rate of tax, as was discussed previously in this chapter and Chapter 11. Similarly, combining operations in different provincial jurisdictions will alter the results of the arbitrary formula that establishes provincial tax rates.

When after-tax profits are factored in, the value of a business to the vendor may well be different from its value to the purchaser. This is because different tax rates may apply to each party. As well, the rates of tax and therefore the value of the business may vary among potential purchasers. If the post-acquisition tax rates are particularly favourable to a purchaser, that purchaser may have a competitive advantage, since it can afford to pay a higher price than other potential buyers.

It is important for the purchaser to anticipate the post-acquisition tax rates as part of its acquisition strategy; it is equally important for the vendor to attempt to anticipate the purchaser's position. Targeting a purchaser that will receive a special tax benefit from the acquisition may result in a higher sale price.

B. Asset Price or Share Price— Impact on Cash Flow

After examining the potential future profits and the anticipated rates of tax, the purchaser must make the following two decisions:

1. Should the target business be purchased or not?

2. If the purchase is made, what form should it take—assets or shares?

While many factors influence the decision to purchase, it is a key requirement that the acquisition provide an acceptable rate of return in relation to the purchase price. One method of determining whether this requirement will be met is to compare the anticipated future after-tax cash flows on a net present value basis with the required purchase price. The future cash flows are discounted at the acceptable return rate; if their present value is greater than the purchase price, the acquisition is justifiable, at least in monetary terms. Because the price for an asset purchase will be different from that for a share purchase, the analysis should be completed for both methods to determine which provides the highest result.

The most difficult aspect of this analysis has to do with estimating the amount of pre-tax profit that will be generated. In the example that follows, this process is highly simplified—by assuming a constant profit for an indefinite time period—in order to

---

5 ITA 125(3).

stress the tax aspects and method of analysis. The example uses the *same information* given in the situation described in Part IV of this chapter, which calculated an asset price and a share price in a specific situation.

Summary of Facts

The situation in Part IV of this chapter concluded that under the worst-case scenario for the vendor, a net asset price of $900,000 (fair market value of assets less assumed liabilities) would provide the same after-tax return to the vendor as a share price of $762,000. However, as the vendors can avoid the worst-case scenario by delaying the payment of the second level of tax, they have decided that they will only accept a share price of $850,000. The following additional information is provided:

1. The business is expected to generate pre-tax cash profits of $225,000 annually for an indefinite period of time. Pre-tax cash profits consist of profits before any capital cost allowance or amortization of eligible capital property.

2. The purchaser will make the acquisition only if it can achieve a return on investment in excess of 20% before tax. The purchaser's tax rate is assumed to be 25% and so the after-tax minimum acceptable rate of return is 15%.

Analysis

Having analyzed its own tax structure and having proceeded with negotiations, the vendor presents the purchaser with two clear options:

1. Purchase the individual assets for the following values and payment terms:

Current assets	$ 400,000
Equipment	500,000
Goodwill	200,000
	1,100,000
Liabilities assumed	(200,000)
Cash required	$ 900,000

2.   Purchase the shares of For Sale Corporation at a price of $850,000.

   Both options will provide pre-tax cash profits of $225,000 annually for an indefinite period of time. To calculate the net present value of this stream of cash flow, an arbitrary time period of 20 years will be used here (see the following table). A longer time period would diminish the degree of certainty and would not change the results significantly.

Present value of future profits:	
Annual profit	$225,000
Tax @ 25%	(56,000)
After-tax profit	$169,000
Present value of $169,000 annually for 20 y, discounted at 15%	$1,058,000

Note that both the annual profit and the discount rate are on an after-tax basis to reflect real cash flows. The calculation of tax has ignored capital cost allowance and the amortization of goodwill, even though both will enhance cash flow by reducing taxes. As these items will affect cash flow for a share purchase differently than for an asset purchase, they are examined separately below.

The present value of the cash flow generated from capital cost allowance and amortization of eligible capital property can be determined using the formula introduced in Chapter 6.

$$\frac{C \times T \times R}{R + I}$$

Where:

C = Cost of the asset acquired.
T = Rate of corporate tax.
R = Rate of capital cost allowance or eligible capital property amortization.
I = After-tax discount rate or acceptable rate of return.

If the purchaser acquires the individual assets, the tax base that is eligible for future tax deductions is $500,000 for the equipment and $150,000 for the goodwill. (Only three-quarters of the goodwill's $200,000 cost is eligible for amortization, as explained in Chapter 6.) As the equipment is not used for manufacturing, it falls within class 8 and has a 20% capital cost allowance rate (diminishing balance). The $150,000 tax base of the goodwill is eligible capital property, which has an amortization rate of 7% (diminishing balance). Therefore, the present value of future tax savings from these two items under an asset purchase is approximately $83,000, calculated as follows:

Equipment: $\dfrac{\$500,000 \times 0.25 \times 0.20}{0.20 + 0.15} =$ $71,000*

Goodwill: $\dfrac{\$150,000 \times 0.25 \times 0.07}{0.07 + 0.15} =$ $\underline{12,000}$

$\underline{\underline{\$83,000}}$

* The formula does not include the effect of the one-half rule for new acquisitions of depreciable property (in this case, equipment). To include this the formula would be:

$$\frac{C \times T \times R}{2(R + I)} \left(\frac{2 + I}{1 + I} \right)$$

On the other hand, the purchase of *shares* does not increase the cost base of the assets held within the corporation. Although the value of the equipment and goodwill is reflected in the price of the shares, the cost of the shares to the purchaser is not eligible for a tax deduction until the shares are sold. Therefore, the equipment within the corporation will continue to have an undepreciated capital cost of only $200,000 (see page 655). As the goodwill had no cost within For Sale Corporation, no tax deductions will be available after the acquisition. Because the purchaser, under a share purchase, inherits the tax values of the vendor's assets, the present value of future tax savings is only $29,000, calculated as follows:

Equipment: $\dfrac{\$200,000 \times 0.25 \times 0.20}{0.20 + 0.15} =$ $29,000*

Goodwill: $\underline{-0-}$

$\underline{\underline{\$29,000}}$

* The one-half rule does not apply because the corporation has owned the equipment for several years.

The relative positions of an asset purchase and a share purchase can now be summarized and compared on a net present value basis as follows:

	Purchase of assets	Purchase of shares
Cash inflow:		
Future profits	$1,058,000	$1,058,000
Tax savings from:		
Equipment	71,000	29,000
Goodwill	12,000	–0–
Total cash inflows	$1,141,000	$1,087,000
Cash outflow:		
Purchase price	(900,000)	(850,000)
Excess cash inflow	$ 241,000	$ 237,000

The above summary indicates that both the asset purchase and the share purchase provide a return on investment significantly greater than the required minimum return of 15% after tax. It also indicates that a marginally greater return will be achieved if assets are purchased, even though an asset purchase requires an $50,000 higher purchase price. More than compensating for this higher purchase price are the tax benefits resulting from the higher levels of capital cost allowance and goodwill amortization.

It is clear that the tax treatment relating to business acquisitions has a major impact on the return on investment. It is therefore important that the purchaser thoroughly analyze the tax treatment of the specific assets involved in an acquisition.

C. Potential Tax Liability after Share Acquisition

A share acquisition results in the buyer assuming the tax position of the vendor corporation. In such cases, there is always a possibility that after acquisition, the acquired corporation will dispose of all or some of its assets, thereby incurring taxable income. For example, in the previous situation the purchaser, by acquiring the shares of For Sale Corporation for the lower price of $850,000, inherited a potential tax liability of $100,000, calculated as follows:

	Tax value of assets in For Sale Corporation	Fair market value	Potential taxable income
Equipment	$200,000	$500,000	$300,000
Goodwill	–0–	200,000	100,000
			$400,000
Potential tax liability ($400,000 × 25%)			$100,000

An extreme worst-case scenario for the purchaser is one in which immediately after buying the shares for $850,000, it is forced to sell the acquired corporation's assets at fair market value. The acquired corporation would be left with $800,000, as calculated in the table below.

Fair value of assets sold:	
Current assets, equipment, goodwill	$1,100,000
Liabilities	(200,000)
Net cash received	$ 900,000
Tax on sale of assets	(100,000)
Cash remaining in corporation	$ 800,000

So, a purchase price of $850,000 for shares bears a risk of a $50,000 loss ($850,000 − $800,000 = $50,000). It should be noted that if the shareholder is an individual, a further tax may result if the corporation is wound up.

The extent of this type of risk varies with the particular circumstances. In the preceding situation, the business would not likely sell the equipment and goodwill shortly after acquiring it. In addition, the purchaser has the option of selling the shares in the same fashion as they were purchased. However, in some cases, the potential tax liability is of greater concern. For example, a purchaser may make a share acquisition of a company that has extensive real estate holdings and then later have to sell some of that property to raise funds for business expansion or to meet financial obligations. Similarly, certain property may face a strong possibility of being expropriated. Whenever a purchase of shares is contemplated, in the course of establishing an acceptable price, the purchaser must try to anticipate possible future events relating to the assets that are held within the acquired corporation and decide whether or not the risk requires a further discounting of the share price.

VI. Basic Principles and Methods of Business Valuations _____

The very essence of a business operation is that it consists of a number of assets, both physical and intangible, that work together for the purpose of generating a long-term stream of profits. The value of a business as a going concern is tied to and dependent on its income-earning potential.

It should be pointed out that a business does not have to be sold as a going concern. Presumably, a vendor will take whatever steps are necessary to obtain the highest price from the disposition of the business. The sale of a business can, therefore, involve the cessation of business operations followed by the sale of the individual assets that were used in the business. In such cases, the value of the business is tied not to its income-earning potential but, rather, to the value of each of its separate individual assets.

This means that there are two fundamental approaches available to business valuations—the earnings approach and the asset approach.

A. Earnings Approach

A purchaser usually acquires a business for the sole purpose of operating it as a going concern. In essence, it is paying a price for a group of assets that will generate a future stream of profits. While the real value of the future profits will eventually be known, the process of valuing those future profits before the actual purchase is extremely speculative.

Assuming that future profits can be anticipated, the value of the business is determined by capitalizing those anticipated earnings based on a rate of return that reflects the nature and relative risk of the particular business. For example, if anticipated profits are $100,000 annually, and if the purchaser considers that a 25% rate of return is normal for that business or industry, the value of the business is $400,000 ($100,000/0.25 = $400,000). In other words, a price of $400,000 would yield a 25% return on investment, or $100,000 annually.

This value of the business does not reflect any particular asset of the business but, rather, represents the total value of all assets working together. The total value may, in fact, be higher than the sum of the values of the individual identifiable assets; in such cases, it is clear that an intangible asset referred to as "goodwill" is present (see Chapter 6).

The earnings approach to business valuations is based on the principle that assets in use have a different value from that of assets being held for liquidation or sale. For example, a delivery truck can be purchased for $25,000, but its in-use value—that is, its value when used to produce delivery revenues—may be substantially higher because of the returns that it generates.

B. Asset Approach

The asset approach to valuations involves the separate valuation of each individual asset within an entity, rather than the valuation of a group of assets together as a productive economic force. This method is often referred to as the "adjusted book value method" because it simply takes each asset on the entity's balance sheet and adjusts its recorded book value to an appraised market value in anticipation of liquidation.

The asset approach has limited application. Usually, it is used to value investment companies, or a business entity that will not be sold as a going concern because it is not profitable enough.

- An investment company may own several assets, each of which produces income on its own but does not act in concert with other assets in a specific economic operation. The value of such a company will be equal to the sum of the values the individual assets would realize if disposed of separately.
- A business that consists of a number of assets and that has a poor profit potential may find that the sale of its individual assets to different buyers will result in a higher sale price than if those assets were sold as a going concern. In such cases, a simple appraisal of each separate asset would provide a liquidation value for the entity.

C. Earnings Approach and Asset Approach Combined

It is important to recognize that there may be a difference between the value of the business operations and the value of the entity that houses those operations. For example, a single corporation may operate more than one distinct business as well as maintain a portfolio of passive investments. In this situation, the value of each business might be determined using the earnings approach based on its own separate profit potential, but the investment portfolio would be valued using an asset approach. The value of the total entity would consist of the combined values of the separate sub-entities; this would reflect the unique structure of the entity's operations and the diversity of its asset composition.

Even when valuing the business operations based on potential earnings, a separate asset valuation may have to be performed. Consider the situation in which a business operation will be sold by means of an asset sale, rather than a sale of the shares of the entire corporation. The total value of the business operations will be based on profit potential, but once that price is agreed on, the total value will have to be distributed among the various assets to determine the price of each separate asset in order that the related tax implications to the vendor as well as to the purchaser can be determined.

D. Other Valuation Methods

A number of other specific valuation methods exist. Some industries and professions often use rule-of-thumb formulas to establish business value. Insurance brokers, certain types of bars and restaurants, grocery stores, retail jewellery stores, professional businesses, such as legal, accounting, and medical firms, real estate brokers, and so on, often base business value on a multiple of annual gross revenues earned. For example, an accounting firm may be valued at 125% of gross annual fees plus the appraised value of specific tangible assets.

In some industries, a rule-of-thumb multiple is applied not to gross sales or net profits but, rather, to annual cash flow, which can be defined as profits before depreciation and debt service. Hotels and motels are often valued in this manner;

this reflects the fact that the major asset in the business operation is real estate, which normally appreciates in value and is capable of servicing a wide range of debt capacity.

Rule-of-thumb formulas must be considered as having limited usefulness in valuing a specific business because they do not take into account the changing economic variables that constantly affect the profitability of a particular business within any industry. The rule-of-thumb methods are, however, a valuable starting point in the valuation process, as long as it is kept in mind that adjustments must be made to reflect the unique character of the specific business operation being valued.

It is clear that these other methods of valuation are still based on the fundamental principle that the value of a business is mainly a function of its profit potential. The primary method of valuing a business is examined in greater detail on the next page.

* An extensive appendix on business valuations is presented on the Online Learning Centre at www.mcgrawhill.ca/olc/buckwold.

VII. Summary and Conclusion

The tax implications relating to the purchase and sale of a business are numerous and play an important role in maximizing return on investment. Chapter 14 examined the important role of the holding company for both the purchaser and vendor in structuring acquisitions and divestitures. This chapter has examined the two fundamental methods of completing a sale and purchase of a corporate business—the sale of assets by the corporation and the sale of shares of the corporation that houses the business.

The tax treatment relating to each method varies for both the vendor and the purchaser; this results in a different price structure for each method. The effects on the seller and on the purchaser for the two basic methods can be summarized as follows:

Sale of Assets

Effects on the vendor:

1. The sale of assets at fair market value creates taxable income or losses to the vendor corporation.

2. Although the after-tax proceeds from the sale of assets can be retained by the corporation for reinvestment, they ultimately must be distributed to the shareholders, at which time a second level of tax may be incurred.

Effects on the purchaser:

1. Having purchased specific assets at fair market value, the purchaser obtains a cost base for the assets acquired that is equal to the price paid.

2. The new cost base of the assets purchased provides future tax savings from the deduction of capital cost allowance and amortization of eligible capital property. Consequently, the after-tax profits for the purchaser will be higher than they were for the vendor corporation.

Sale of Shares

Effects on the vendor:

1. The vendor disposes of the entire corporation and therefore sells a single asset.

2. The sale of shares results in a capital gain or loss to the vendor, leaving the after-tax proceeds available for reinvestment.

Effects on the purchaser:

1. The purchaser, by acquiring the entire vendor corporation, assumes the tax status of the assets within the corporation; there is no increase in the cost base of these assets, even though the asset values are reflected in the price of the shares.

2. Future tax savings from capital cost allowance and amortization of eligible capital property are the same as they were before the acquisition.

Because of these differences in tax treatment, a vendor will normally accept a lower price for shares than for assets. Similarly, a purchaser is normally prepared to pay a higher price for assets, knowing that additional tax benefits will occur. One often hears the generalization that the purchaser prefers an asset acquisition, whereas the vendor prefers a share sale. The analysis presented in this chapter indicates that this generalization is invalid. The preference depends on the particular circumstances as they relate to the corporate structure, the nature of the assets, and the tax status of both vendor and purchaser. While a reduced share price may seem attractive to the purchaser, it is worth considering only if the future after-tax return on investment is greater than it would be for an asset purchase.

The vendor must understand the relationship between the share price and the asset price before realistic negotiations can begin. It is equally important for the vendor to determine, to the extent possible, the tax treatment to the purchaser after the acquisition so that a maximum price can be achieved. Similarly, the purchaser must anticipate the future tax impact of each method on the vendor and on itself in order to establish the parameters of the price negotiation.

Although the examples presented in this chapter have been simplified, the basic concepts developed in them apply equally to all business acquisitions and divestitures, whatever their complexity or size.

Visit the Canadian Income Taxation Web site at **www.mcgrawhill.ca/ olc/buckwold** to view any updated tax information.

Review Questions

1. "The sale of business assets by a vendor corporation normally results in two levels of tax, rather than a single level of tax, as is the case when the shares of the business corporation are sold." Explain this statement.

2. In general terms, what types of gains or losses may occur for tax purposes when specific business assets are sold?

3. If a business is to be sold on terms that require deferred payments, why may the timing of the related tax cost to the vendor be different if the specific business assets, rather than the shares of the business corporation, are sold?

4. If a group of business assets is sold with specific values attached to each item, what difference, if any, does it make whether the terms of payment (that is, the amount of cash and deferred payments) are expressed separately for each asset sold or as a total for the group of assets sold?

5. When a corporation sells its business by disposing of its business assets, the amount of tax to the corporation resulting from the sale can be determined with relative certainty. Does the same degree of certainty exist with respect to determining the second level of tax when the proceeds of the asset sale are distributed to the shareholder? Explain.

6. The after-tax cash flow from the earnings of the acquired business may be different for the purchasers if they acquire the shares of the vendor corporation, rather than its specific assets. Explain why.

7. Why is it important for the purchaser to establish an accurate value for each individual asset acquired when a group of business assets is being purchased for an agreed-upon total price?

8. "When a purchaser acquires the shares of a vendor corporation, it may be assuming a potential tax liability of the vendor corporation." What is meant by this statement? To the extent that such a potential liability exists, what impact may this have on the purchase price, and how can it be measured?

9. To what extent, if any, should the vendor to be concerned about the tax status of the purchaser when contemplating the sale of a business?

10. Why is it important for the purchaser of a business to anticipate the post-acquisition organization structure before making the acquisition?

11. When a business can be sold under either an asset sale or a share sale, why is it important that both the vendor and the purchaser attempt to determine the vendor's tax cost from the sale under a worst-case scenario?

12. What is the worst-case scenario when an individual who owns the shares of a business corporation is considering the sale of that business? How is that individual's tax position affected if the business for sale is held within a corporation that is a subsidiary of a large public corporation?

13. What are the three major tax issues that a purchaser must examine when deciding whether to acquire the assets or the shares of a business?

Key Concept Questions

QUESTION ONE

Stewart, a Canadian resident, is considering selling his shares of AA Ltd., which operates a printing business in Canada. He hopes that he will be able to use the capital gains deduction to shelter the gain from tax. Stewart purchased his shares of AA Ltd. four years ago for $1,000,000 and he estimates that they are now worth $2,000,000. Stewart owns 100% of the company. The latest balance sheet for AA Ltd. is below.

AA Ltd.

Balance Sheet

Assets		Liabilities & Shareholder's Equity	
Cash	$ 100,000	Liabilities	$ 900,000
Inventory	20,000	Share capital	1,000
Due from shareholder	800,000	Retained earnings	899,000
Equipment	180,000		$1,800,000
Land and building	700,000		
	$1,800,000		

The value of the current assets approximates their fair market value. The business premises (land and building) are estimated to be worth $1,600,000. The equipment is valued at $80,000. The goodwill is estimated to be worth $500,000. The relative values of the assets have remained consistent throughout the last two years.

Determine if AA Ltd. is currently a qualified small business corporation. *Income tax reference: ITA 110.6(1) qualified small business corporation definition.*

QUESTION TWO

A sale of the assets of B Ltd. took place on January 2, 20X2. The assets and liabilities of B Ltd. at that time were as follows:

	Fair Market Value
Inventory (cost $200,000)	$300,000
Accounts receivable (face value $600,000)	450,000
Equipment (cost $100,000; UCC $70,000)	30,000
Land (cost $400,000)	700,000
Building (cost $300,000; UCC $230,000)	500,000
Goodwill (cost $0; CEC $0)	100,000
Liabilities	6,000

B Ltd. and the purchaser made a joint election under section 22 of the *Income Tax Act* with respect to the Accounts receivable.

An examination of the corporate tax return for the year ended December 31, 20X1 showed the following:

- B Ltd. is a Canadian-controlled private corporation.

- An allowance for doubtful accounts of $100,000 was claimed at the December 31, 20X1 year end.

- The paid-up capital of the corporation is $10,000.

- The General Rate Income Pool (GRIP) balance was nil.

- The corporation has a Capital Dividend Account balance of $20,000 and a balance in its refundable dividend tax on hand (RDTOH) account of $9,000.

Determine the amount available for distribution to the shareholders after the sale of the assets.

QUESTION THREE

Based on the information in Question Two, if the winding up of B Ltd. takes place immediately after the assets are sold, determine the components of the distribution to the shareholders. *Income tax reference: ITA 88(1), 83(2).*

Problems

PROBLEM ONE

Carl owns 100% of the common shares of Extra Ltd., a Canadian-controlled private corporation operating a wholesale business in eastern Canada. Extra's fiscal year end is May 31, 20X8. It is now April 15, 20X8, and Carl has just signed a letter of intent to sell the wholesale business to Q Ltd.

The initial discussions involved the sale of specific assets of Extra, but a sale of the shares of the company may also be considered. Carl has requested your assistance in estimating the tax liability to Extra *if the business assets are sold*. Information relating to the sale and to the current year's operating income is provided below.

1. The balance sheet of Extra at May 31, 20X8, is estimated as follows:

Accounts receivable	$ 120,000
Inventory, at cost	400,000
Land, at cost	30,000
Building, at book value	280,000
Equipment, at book value	170,000
Licence, at book value	40,000
	$1,040,000
Liabilities	$600,000
Share capital	1,000
Retained earnings	439,000
	$1,040,000

2. Net income before income tax and net gains from the sale of assets for the year ended May 31, 20X8, is estimated as follows:

Income from wholesale operations	$490,000
Dividend income	1,000
Net income before tax	$491,000

The following additional information relates to the net income:

- The dividend income is from a Canadian public corporation, the shares of which were sold during the year for proceeds equal to their original cost.

- Expenses deducted from revenues included the following items:

Legal fees for collection of bad debts	$ 2,000
Donations to registered charities	3,000
Meals and beverages to entertain customers	4,000
Dividend paid to Carl on March 31, 20X8	20,000
Replacing a broken window in the building	2,400

3. The 20X7 income tax return indicates the following tax account balances:

RDTOH	NIL
Capital dividend account	NIL
Cumulative eligible capital	NIL
GRIP	NIL
Undepreciated capital cost	
Class 1	290,000
Class 8	140,000
Class 14	42,000

4. The letter of intent regarding the sale of the business indicates that the closing date will be May 31, 20X8. The letter included the following list of assets to be sold, together with each asset's estimated market value. For information, the original cost of each asset is provided.

	Market value	Cost
Accounts receivable	$120,000	$120,000
Inventory	410,000	400,000
Land	40,000	30,000
Building	400,000	320,000
Equipment	90,000	200,000
Licence	45,000	50,000
Goodwill	100,000	
	$1,205,000	$1,120,000

Payment for the above assets would consist of cash plus the assumption of Extra's liabilities.

5. You have suggested to Carl that he consider selling the common shares of Extra, rather than the specific assets. You have estimated the market value of the shares to be $600,000. The shares were acquired in 20X1 for a cost of $100,000. In previous years, Carl had used the capital gain deduction to exempt from tax $120,000 of gains. His cumulative net investment loss (CNIL) at the end of 20X8 is estimated to be $40,000.

Required:

1. Under Part I of the *Income Tax Act*, determine the *minimum income for tax purposes* and the *minimum taxable income* for Extra for the 20X8 taxation year, assuming that all assets are sold.

2. Based on your answer to Requirement 1, calculate the *minimum Part I and Part IV federal income tax* (ignore surtaxes) for the 20X8 taxation year. Your answer should include a calculation of the RDTOH and dividend refund, if any.

3. If an agreement is made to sell the assets of Extra, would you recommend the planned closing date of May 31, 20X8, or a delay of one day to June 1, 20X8? Explain.

4. Briefly outline what the purchaser should consider when choosing between the purchase of assets and the purchase of shares.

5. If Carl decides to sell the shares of Extra, what amount will be added to his net income for tax purposes in his 20X8 taxation year?

PROBLEM TWO

Subpump Limited is an active business corporation owned 50% by Simpson and 50% by Clowes. The owners have been attempting to sell the company for several years and have recently received an offer from a serious buyer.

As of December 31, 20X1, the company's financial position was as follows:

Assets		
Accounts receivable		$200,000
Inventory (at cost)		70,000
Land		100,000
Building (at cost)	150,000	
Accumulated capital cost allowance	(60,000)	90,000
Equipment (at undepreciated capital cost)		40,000
Goodwill (at cost)		30,000
		$530,000

	Liabilities and Shareholders' Equity		
Current liabilities			$250,000
Shareholders' equity:			
Common shares		1,000	
Retained earnings		279,000	280,000
			$530,000

Additional information

1. Relevant asset values are as follows:

	Fair market value	UCC	Cumulative eligible capital
Inventory	$ 75,000	–0–	–0–
Land	120,000	–0–	–0–
Building	170,000	90,000	–0–
Equipment	35,000	40,000	–0–
Goodwill	50,000	–0–	4,000

2. On December 31, 20X1, the company had a balance of $9,000 in its capital dividend account. The balances in the RDTOH and GRIP accounts were NIL.

3. Each owner acquired his shares of Subpump 10 years ago for $50,000.

4. Clowes once owned shares of another small business corporation. He sold them last year and realized a capital gain of $800,000. He claimed the maximum capital gain deduction at that time.

5. The purchaser has stated two alternatives in his purchase offer:
   - A purchase of all assets at fair market value and an assumption of all liabilities. The balance will be paid in cash immediately.
   - A purchase of the shares for $340,000 in cash.

6. Both shareholders want to go their separate ways after the sale. Because of this, Clowes thinks the sale of shares is the best alternative, as it avoids additional tax costs.

7. Both shareholders are in a 45% marginal tax bracket. Both expect to remain in that bracket in the future. The combined (federal and provincial) marginal tax rate for both shareholders is 28% on eligible dividends and 33% on non-eligible dividends received (net of the dividend tax credit) and 45% on other income. Subpump's tax rate is 25% on business income not subject to the small business deduction and 15% on earnings subject to the small business deduction. Investment income is subject to a 38% tax rate plus a 6⅔% refundable tax.

Required:

1. Which offer should the shareholders accept? Show all calculations.

2. If the assets are sold, is there any way that the two shareholders can divide the cash remaining in the company without paying personal tax? If so, what is it?

PROBLEM THREE

Cole and Barker each own 50% of the shares of NRS Ltd., a Canadian-controlled private corporation. NRS had conducted a small active business, which was closed down two years ago, in late 20X0. The corporation sold its assets at that time and used the resulting cash to purchase several commercial real estate properties. At present, the corporation owns three parcels of real estate (all purchased before March 19, 2007), as follows:

	Cost	Current fair market value
Parcel 1 (acquired 20X0):		
Land	$10,000	$16,000
Building	40,000	60,000
Parcel 2 (acquired 20X0):		
Land	30,000	40,000
Building	70,000	80,000
Parcel 3 (acquired 20X1):		
Land	15,000	23,000
Building	30,000	42,000

Barker has recently informed Cole that he intends to withdraw as a shareholder of the company and wants to convert his shares to cash. In addition, he wants to own outright all of the real estate known as parcel 3. The shareholders' agreement calls for a wind-up of the corporation when one shareholder wishes to leave; however, Cole wants to keep NRS for himself. The shareholders have therefore agreed to the following:

1. Barker will dispose of his shares for cash at fair market value (transaction date: January 1, 20X3).

2. Immediately thereafter, Barker will purchase from NRS, for cash, the parcel 3 real estate (transaction date: January 2, 20X3).

At December 31, 20X2, the year end of NRS, the corporate balance sheet is as follows:

Assets

Cash		$ 10,000
Land (parcels 1, 2, 3) at cost		55,000
Buildings (parcels 1, 2, 3) at cost	140,000	
Accounting depreciation	(25,000)	115,000
		$180,000

Liabilities and Shareholders' Equity

Mortgage payable		$ 40,000
Shareholders' equity:		
Common shares (paid-up capital)	2,000	
Retained earnings	138,000	140,000
		$180,000

Barker had acquired his shares for $5,000. The paid-up capital of his shares is $1,000, as indicated on the balance sheet (½ of $2,000).

The corporation's retained earnings of $138,000 consist of a number of items from past years, as follows:

	Income before tax	Tax	Income after tax
Previous business operations	$98,570	$15,770 (16%)	$ 82,800
Net rentals on real estate			
(after capital cost allowance)	4,204	2,004 (41% + 6⅔%)	2,200
Taxable capital gain	63,061	30,061 (41% + 6⅔%)	33,000
Non-taxable portion of capital gain	20,000	–0–	20,000
	$185,835	$47,835	$138,000

Barker's personal marginal tax rate is 28% on eligible dividends and 33% on non-eligible dividends received (net of the dividend tax credit) and 45% on other taxable income. He has already used up his capital gain deduction.

Required:

1. In view of the shareholders' agreement, determine the value of the common shares owned by Barker.

2. What action should NRS take before Barker disposes of his shares? What effect will this have on the value of those shares and on the related tax when the shares are sold?

3. Describe the two basic ways in which Barker can dispose of his NRS shares, and recommend the best alternative. Show calculations to support your recommendation.

4. What are the tax consequences to NRS in 20X3 as a result of the sale of the parcel 3 real estate?

PROBLEM FOUR

For several years, Conrad Stone had wanted to acquire the Pineview Motel. The motel had a prime location and was thriving. Part of its property was adjacent to a scenic river, which was used as a picnic area for guests.

Stone felt that if he acquired the property, he could continue to operate the motel business but could also piece off its excess land along the river and develop a condominium project. Although the river frontage was not zoned for that purpose, Stone felt that with some effort, this could be changed.

The motel and the land were owned by Henson Enterprises Ltd., a corporation owned by Sheila Henson. She had refused two previous offers from Stone for the land, building, and equipment of the motel, partly because her corporation would have been heavily taxed on the sale.

After further pressure from Stone, Henson agreed to sell, provided that Stone purchased her shares of Henson Enterprises. In this manner, she would be able to claim the maximum capital gain deduction on the sale.

The most recent balance sheet of Henson Enterprises is shown on the next page.

The retained earnings of the corporation are relatively low because Henson has withdrawn most of the earnings through regular dividend distributions.

Over the years, Henson has claimed accounting amortization at a rate equal to the capital cost allowance rate permitted for tax purposes. At the end of the most recent year, the undepreciated capital cost was $350,000 for the building and $30,000 for the equipment.

To determine the share price, Henson first obtained an independent appraisal of the land, building, and equipment. She then suggested a price of $530,000, calculated as follows:

Asset values:		
Current assets		$ 15,000
Land (appraised)		150,000
Building (appraised)		850,000
Equipment (appraised)		30,000
		1,045,000
Liabilities:		
Current liabilities	15,000	
Mortgage payable	500,000	515,000
Share price		$ 530,000

Stone realized that buying the shares at that price would be a problem because the corporation would retain a potential tax liability in the event that its property were ever sold. After negotiations, Henson dropped the price to $450,000 and Stone purchased the shares for that amount of cash. Stone was not overly concerned about the corporation's tax liability, as the reduced price would provide some relief and he had no intention of selling the property. He would continue to operate the motel and begin to develop the condominium project.

Balance Sheet

Assets

Current Assets		$ 15,000
Land (at cost)		100,000
Building (at cost)	700,000	
Equipment (at cost)	100,000	
	800,000	
Accumulated amortization	(370,000)	430,000
		$545,000

Liabilities and Shareholder's Equity

Current liabilities		$ 15,000
Mortgage payable		500,000
		515,000
Shareholder's equity:		
Common shares	1,000	
Retained earnings	29,000	30,000
		$545,000

To purchase the shares, Stone used $50,000 of his savings and borrowed $400,000 from his bank, using his personal residence and the acquired shares as collateral. The bank loan is payable on demand.

Two months after Stone purchased the shares, the city announced that it intended to expropriate all of the motel's property to develop a riverbank park. The city had the property appraised and told Henson Enterprises that it would pay the appraised amount for the land, building, and equipment. The appraisal values arrived at by the city were the same as those obtained by Henson two months earlier.

Henson Enterprises has a tax rate of 15% on income subject to the small business deduction, 25% on other business income, and $44^2/3$% on investment income. Stone has a marginal tax rate of 28% on eligible dividends and 33% on non-eligible dividends received (net of the dividend tax credit) and 45% on other income. Prior to the expropriation, all business income earned by Henson Enterprises had been eligible for the small business deduction.

Required:

1. Determine the tax liability of Henson Enterprises as a result of the expropriation.

2. Determine what Stone's financial position will be after he repays his bank loan.

3. Would the result in 2 have been different if Stone had organized a holding corporation to borrow from the bank and purchase the shares? Explain, providing the calculations.

PROBLEM FIVE

Kronin Enterprises Ltd. is a public corporation operating a successful retail business that generates profits in excess of $700,000 annually. The company is about to acquire a wholesale business operated by KTL Ltd. A recent balance sheet for KTL is presented below.

Assets

Current assets		$ 100,000
Land (at cost)		50,000
Building (at cost)	400,000	
Equipment (at cost)	700,000	
	1,100,000	
Accumulated amortization	(400,000)	700,000
Goodwill (at cost)		200,000
		$1,050,000

Liabilities and Shareholders' Equity

Liabilities		$ 600,000
Shareholders' equity:		
Common shares	20,000	
Retained earnings	430,000	450,000
		$1,050,000

For tax purposes, the building (class 1) has an undepreciated capital cost of $300,000, and the equipment (class 8) has an undepreciated capital cost of $350,000. With respect to the goodwill, the amount of cumulative eligible capital is $100,000.

KTL has offered to sell the assets to Kronin for the following values and payment terms:

Values:	
Current assets	$ 100,000
Land	75,000
Building	550,000
Equipment	600,000
Goodwill	400,000
	$1,725,000
Terms of payment:	
Assumption of KTL liabilities	$ 600,000
Cash	1,125,000
	$1,725,000

Last year, KTL earned a pre-tax accounting profit of $220,000 after deducting $30,000 of amortization. Kronin is confident that it can achieve at least the same level of profits after acquisition.

Kronin has virtually decided to purchase the assets of KTL, provided that the investment will generate a minimum acceptable return on investment of 12% after tax.

At a recent meeting, the KTL executives stated that they may want to sell the shares, rather than the assets, and do so at a price different from the asset price. They will present an offer to Kronin shortly. Kronin thinks it would be useful to learn what share price would provide the same rate of return as would be achieved after a purchase of assets. The company could then make a quick assessment of the forthcoming share price.

Kronin is subject to a 25% corporate tax rate.

Required:

1. Assuming that an acquisition would be in the form of an asset purchase, should the purchase be made, considering Kronin's minimum return-on-investment requirement?

2. What share price would provide Kronin with the same rate of return as on a purchase of assets? Show calculations.

PROBLEM SIX

When selling a business it is important to know if the corporation that owns the "for sale" business qualifies as a small business corporation. If so, the shareholder(s) may qualify for all or some of the $750,000 capital gains exemption if the shares are sold. This question examines this qualification.

The following four situations, A through D, are independent.

	CCPC A	CCPC B	CCPC C	CCPC D
Assets at FMV:				
Term deposits	$ 0	$ 0	$15,000	$ 0
Land	50,000	0	0	40,000
Building	35,000	0	0	60,000
Equipment	0	80,000	0	0
Shares of X Ltd.	0	20,000	0	0
Shares of Y Ltd.	15,000	0	15,000	0
	100,000	100,000	30,000	100,000
Liabilities:				
Accounts payable	10,000	2,000	0	0
Bank loan	10,000	0	0	0
	20,000	2,000	0	0
Assets net of liabilities	$ 80,000	$ 98,000	$30,000	$100,000

Additional information:

- In each of the above situations, the land, building and equipment are used by the owner in an active business carried on in Canada, with the exception of D. In the case of D, the land and building are leased to Spousecorp, a CCPC, and are used by Spousecorp in its active business, which it carries on in Canada. D is owned by the spouse of the sole shareholder of Spousecorp.

- X Ltd. is a public company.

- Y Ltd. is a small business corporation, owned 50% by each of A and C.

Required:
Determine which of the above CCPCs are small business corporations and state the reason for your conclusion.

PROBLEM SEVEN

When selling a business it is important to know if the corporation that owns the "for sale" business is a qualified small business corporation. If so, the shareholder(s) may qualify for all or some of the $750,000 capital gains exemption if the shares are sold. This question examines this qualification.

The following four situations, (a) through (d), are independent.

	Assets used in an active business*	Investment in Subco	Other Assets	Total
(a) Holdco	$60,000	$25,000	$15,000	$100,000
Subco	20,000	0	80,000	100,000
(b) Holdco	$30,000	$50,000	20,000	$100,000
Subco	95,000	0	5,000	100,000
(c) Holdco	$45,000	$15,000	40,000	$100,000
Subco	70,000	0	30,000	100,000
(d) Holdco	$0	$75,000	$25,000	$100,000
Subco	92,000	0	8,000	100,000

* In each case, the active business is carried on in Canada and Holdco owns 100% of Subco.

The shares of Holdco and Subco have not changed hands since their incorporation five years ago. The assets of Holdco and Subco are stated at their fair market values in the chart, above. The assets and their values have remained constant for the past three years.

Required:
For each of (a), (b), (c), and (d), determine whether the shares of Holdco will be Qualified Small Business Corporation (QSBC) shares at the close of business tomorrow. Assume that all steps necessary to make Holdco a small business corporation at the close of business tomorrow will be taken.

Case

BAYLY CORPORATION

Bayly Corporation owns and operates a successful chain of retail pipe and tobacco stores. Bayly is a private corporation owned 100% by a large venture capital corporation.

During 20X1, Bayly earned a net profit *before* tax of $2,000,000, and its most recent balance sheet (see Exhibit 1, next page) shows its financial strength.

Bayly has accumulated large cash reserves for the purpose of acquiring a pipe-manufacturing business. Initially, Bayly was going to construct its own manufacturing plant, but recently it has targeted TOTO Pipes Ltd., a manufacturer of bluestem pipes, as a possible acquisition.

Donna Rose has been given the assignment of reporting to the VP Finance on the feasibility of acquiring TOTO.

Rose attends a meeting with the shareholders of TOTO Pipes and the vice-president of Bayly Corporation. The meeting is short, as its purpose is to get acquainted and gather preliminary information. Rose is able to gather the following information:

1. The common shares of TOTO are owned equally by John Drabinsky and Walter Scully. They started the corporation 15 years ago, when pipe smoking was again becoming popular.

2. In addition to providing the initial share capital, Scully had provided a substantial shareholder loan to TOTO Pipes that enabled the company to survive during its critical start-up years. This loan was paid off two years ago. Scully is a director of TOTO Pipes but is only partly active in its management. He also owns another business, with his son and daughter, where he spends most of his time. Walter Drabinsky is the president and senior manager.

3. Both Drabinsky and Scully are 62 years of age.

4. Drabinsky indicates that he and Scully are prepared to sell all of the assets of TOTO Pipes for the values indicated under "Additional Information" in Exhibit II. If, however, Bayly wants to acquire the shares, they are willing to consider a price of $2,600,000.

5. Certain financial information is provided by Drabinsky (see Exhibit II on the next page).

After the meeting, Bayly's vice-president instructs Rose to prepare a preliminary report on the proposed acquisition.

"First of all, we want to know if the prices indicated make sense, considering that Bayly's parent company insisted on a 13% after-tax return before approving any major capital acquisitions. I'm a little concerned about the life expectancy of the business because the patent on their major product has a life of only 10 years. They seem to be willing to accept a lower price for the shares than for the assets, and I wonder if they may be willing to accept an even lower share price. It would be useful to have this information before we enter into serious negotiations. In addition, provide any other analysis that might help us make a decision."

Rose begins her assignment by gathering certain tax information and determines that the maximum personal tax rates are 45% on most types of income. Dividends, however, are subject to 28% tax rate on eligible dividends and a 33% rate on non-eligible dividends (net of the dividend tax credit). Rose was unable to determine what dividends from TOTO would be eligible or non-eligible and would have to make an assumption. The corporate rates of tax are 15% for income subject to the small business deduction, 25% for non-manufacturing income not subject to the small business deduction, and 23% for manufacturing income. The tax rate on investment income is $44^2/3\%$, which includes the $6^2/3\%$ refundable tax.

Required:

Prepare the preliminary report.

Exhibit I

BAYLY CORPORATION
Balance Sheet
December 31, 20X1

Assets

Current assets:		
Cash		$ 200,000
Bank term deposits		3,000,000
Accounts receivable		400,000
Inventory		2,400,000
Fixed assets:		
Land		400,000
Buildings and equipment (at cost)	1,600,000	
Accumulated amortization	(700,000)	900,000
		$7,300,000

Liabilities and Shareholders' Equity

Current liabilities:		
Accounts payable		$ 700,000
Bank loan		600,000
		1,300,000
Mortgage payable		2,000,000
Shareholders' equity:		
Common shares	100,000	
Retained earnings	3,900,000	4,000,000
		$7,300,000

Additional information

1. The building and equipment are all used to house the retail outlets and management staff.

2. Total wages paid in 20X1 amounted to $500,000.

Exhibit II

TOTO PIPES LTD.
Balance Sheet
December 31, 20X1

Assets

Current assets:		
Cash and receivables		$ 600,000
Inventory		700,000
Fixed assets:		
Land		100,000
Building (at cost)	400,000	
Equipment (at cost)	800,000	
	1,200,000	
Accumulated amortization	(500,000)	700,000
Patents (on bluestem pipes, at cost)		–0–
Goodwill (at cost)		100,000
		$2,200,000

Liabilities and Shareholders' Equity

Liabilities:		
Accounts payable		$ 500,000
Bank loan (seven-year term)		300,000
		800,000
Shareholders' equity:		
Capital shares	100,000	
Retained earnings	1,300,000	1,400,000
		$2,200,000

Additional information

1. Over the past three years, the company profits have averaged $750,000 before depreciation, amortization, and income taxes. This average is expected to continue in future years.

2. The company operates solely in Saskatchewan.

3. Total salaries paid in 20X1 amounted to $400,000, of which $300,000 related directly to manufacturing and $100,000 was for management.

4. All fixed assets were used for manufacturing purposes.

5. The patent on a special pipe filter has 10 years of legal life remaining.

6. Inventory shows a cost of $700,000. However, the company has indicated that the actual cost was $800,000, as the company intentionally lowered its inventory to reduce taxes.

7. The fair market values of other assets are as follows:

Land	$200,000
Building	700,000
Equipment	600,000
Patent	300,000
Goodwill	400,000

8. The UCC of the depreciable assets is as follows:

Class 3	$150,000
Class 43	300,000
Class 44	–0–

The balance in the cumulative eligible capital account is $40,000.

9. The general rate income pool (GRIP) balance is nil.

CHAPTER 19

Business Acquisitions and Divestitures— Tax-Deferred Sales

Most business acquisitions and divestitures are completed on a fully taxable basis by one of the two methods described in the previous chapter. Fully taxable divestitures in the form of share sales or asset sales are characterized by the complete separation of the vendor from the business being sold; in other words, the vendor maintains no continued interest in the ongoing operations of the transferred business.

However, sometimes, the vendor chooses or is forced to maintain an ongoing equity interest in the business that is sold. In these cases, it is possible to structure the transaction so that the vendor's tax liability is deferred until that continued interest ceases.

This chapter examines the methods available for achieving a tax-deferred sale of a business, the circumstances in which they are relevant, and the resulting general tax treatment to both the vendor and the purchaser. The tax-deferred methods are then examined in two contexts: the sale of a closely held corporation to a third-party purchaser and the sale of a similar entity to family members.

I. Tax-Deferred Sales and Acquisitions

A. The Nature of and Reasons for a Tax-Deferred Sale

In order for the vendor to achieve a continued tax deferral on the sale of a business, it must be prepared to maintain a continuing equity interest in the purchaser's corporation or the vendor corporation. This equity interest can be in the form of common shares or preferred shares. A vendor who receives common shares as part of the sale transaction incurs continued risk but also the opportunity for continued growth in value. A vendor who receives preferred shares with a fixed dividend rate incurs a lesser risk but also no potential for future growth.

A tax-deferred sale is distinguished from a taxable sale by the nature of the payment received for the property. A *taxable* sale involves the payment of cash or a deferred payment of cash secured by notes bearing interest. A *tax-deferred* sale involves payment in the form of shares issued by the purchasing corporation.

There are three basic reasons that a vendor may be prepared to accept a greater risk by receiving shares, rather than cash or other secure assets:

1. The vendor wants to participate in the continued growth of the business. In such a case, the sale actually constitutes a business combination or merger (see Chapter 14). Increased profits can result from enhanced sales opportunities and from reduced expenses owing to improved economies of scale.

2. The vendor simply wants to enhance its after-tax return on investment. For example, by accepting the full purchase price in the form of preferred shares of the purchaser corporation together with a reasonable fixed dividend rate, the vendor will receive an annual return on the full selling price. If the payment were in the form of cash or notes, the vendor would be able to reinvest only the after-tax proceeds, which would provide a lower annual return.

3. The purchaser may not have sufficient cash to make the acquisition, or perhaps no other acceptable buyers are present. When the vendor accepts preferred shares in the buyer corporation, the purchaser can pay for the business over a period of time by gradually redeeming the preferred shares as future profits and cash flow are generated. This type of situation is common when a business is sold to employees or to family members.

When arranging a tax-deferred sale of a corporate business, one must utilize the special provisions of the *Income Tax Act* that are designed to provide tax relief when corporations are reorganized. Corporate reorganizations were reviewed extensively in Chapter 14 in the context of the combining or separating of business activities within a related group of companies. These same methods apply equally to the sale of a business to an independent third party. When arranging the tax-deferred sale of a business, the following alternative courses of action are available:

1. A sale of assets by one corporation to another at an elected transfer price for tax purposes equal to the assets' tax values.

2. A sale of the corporation's shares to a corporate purchaser at an elected transfer price equal to the tax value of the shares.

3. An amalgamation of two or more corporations.

4. A reorganization of share capital.

Each of these methods is re-examined below in the context of a sale to arm's-length purchasers. The following situation, which is both common and simple, is used as the basis for examining and comparing each method.

Buyer Corporation, which is owned entirely by shareholder X, intends to acquire the business operated by Seller Corporation. Seller Corporation is 100% owned by shareholder Y. The corporate structure prior to the acquisition is diagrammed below.

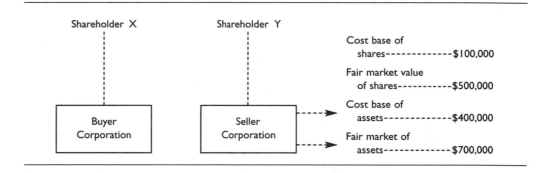

Note that the cost base to Y of the shares of Seller Corporation is $100,000 and that the fair market value is $500,000. Therefore, a sale of shares would usually result in a capital gain on disposition. Also, note that the assets in Seller Corporation have a fair market value in excess of their tax values; this would usually create taxable income to the corporation if the individual business assets were sold.

B. Sale of Assets

A tax-deferred sale can be achieved by arranging for the vendor corporation to sell individual assets to the buyer corporation at a price for tax purposes equal to the assets' cost amount.[1] This can be done even though the actual selling price for legal purposes is equal to the assets' fair market value. In the sample situation, the assets of Seller Corporation have a tax cost of $400,000 and a fair market value of $700,000. In this scenario, the assets are sold for $700,000 for legal purposes but only $400,000 for tax purposes. In accordance with the elective rules described in Chapter 12, Seller Corporation can be paid in the form of cash or notes to a maximum of $400,000 (the elected amount), with the balance in the form of shares of Buyer Corporation. The sale and payment terms are summarized on the next page.

---

1   ITA 85(1); IT-291R3.

Sale price of assets	$700,000
Payment consideration:	
Cash or notes	$400,000
Shares of Buyer Corporation	300,000
	$700,000

The shares received from Buyer Corporation can be common shares or preferred shares, depending on whether the vendor intends to participate in the future growth of Buyer Corporation. This transaction is diagrammed below.

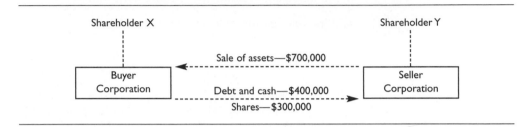

Note that by electing $400,000 as the tax transfer price, Seller Corporation avoids tax on the asset values in excess of their tax cost ($700,000 − $400,000 = $300,000). Consequently, the shares received as consideration are deemed to have a tax cost of zero, even though their fair market value is $300,000.[2] At some future time, when Seller Corporation disposes of the shares, taxable income may be created, although the nature of that income may be different from what would have been created from a normal sale of assets at fair market values.

The tax deferral permits the vendor to fully invest the pre-tax proceeds of the sale to provide a return on investment. In this example, the vendor will receive a return on investment from the $400,000 of cash and notes as well as from the $300,000 of shares received; this is more than it would have received if it had sold the assets at normal fair market values thereby incurring immediate taxable income. The vendor achieves a tax deferral and the potential for increased returns but also assumes an additional risk by accepting shares of the purchaser corporation as payment. The ability to recover a value from these shares depends on the future success of Buyer Corporation.

This form of purchase has both advantages and disadvantages to the purchaser. The major advantage is that the purchase can be achieved with a minimum of cash and debt because of the requirement that shares be issued as part of the payment terms. As a result, a greater amount of future cash flow is available to ensure the success of continued business operations. In addition, the company's ability to borrow operating funds, should those be required, is not significantly disturbed. How much of an advantage this is depends on the terms attached to the shares issued to the vendor. For example, the issuing of non-participating preferred shares to the vendor may carry with it an obligatory redemption program or may provide the vendor with the option of having the preferred shares redeemed in certain portions after a specified time period.

A major disadvantage to the purchaser is that the cost base of the assets acquired is deemed to be equal to the transfer price elected for tax purposes, rather than to the assets' fair market value. As a result, future capital cost allowance on depreciable property will be less than would have been available if the assets had been purchased

---

2   ITA 85(1)(f) to (h); IT-291R3. The paid-up capital is also reduced to a nominal amount—ITA 85(2.1); IT-463R2.

in the normal fashion (see Chapter 18). In addition, the lower cost base of the assets creates a potential tax liability for the purchaser if, after acquisition, all or some of the assets are disposed of at fair market value. Also, funding the purchase by issuing preferred shares usually requires a fixed obligatory dividend payment that is not deductible from the purchaser's income. Although the dividend rate will be less than the rate of interest on a debt, it may still result in an after-tax cost to the purchaser that is greater than the after-tax cost of interest (see Chapter 21). The purchaser must, therefore, weigh the impact of reduced funding requirements against the impact of reduced capital cost allowance and dividend requirements.

The above disadvantages are of less concern to the purchaser when the acquisition of assets on a tax-deferred basis is actually a business combination as opposed to a buy-out. For example, in the preceding situation, if Buyer Corporation had purchased the assets by issuing $700,000 of common shares to Seller Corporation, with the intention that Seller Corporation continue as a participating shareholder of the larger entity for an indefinite time, the transaction would have signified a business combination, rather than a complete take-over. As no cash or debt was exchanged, both parties would have continued to bear a proportionate share of the risk, and the negative aspects described above would have been of little consequence.

C. Sale of Shares

A vendor that wishes to sell a business by selling the shares of the vendor corporation, rather than assets, can obtain a tax deferral by using the same elective provisions as for an asset sale. Referring again to the sample situation, note that shareholder Y holds shares of Seller Corporation that have a cost base of $100,000 and a fair market value of $500,000. If Y sells the shares to Buyer Corporation in the normal manner, a capital gain of $400,000 will result, one-half of which will be taxable. This realization of a capital gain can be deferred by electing that the sale price for tax purposes is $100,000 (equal to the cost base), provided that at least $400,000 of the $500,000 purchase price is paid in the form of shares of Buyer Corporation.

After this transaction, the corporate structure would be as follows:

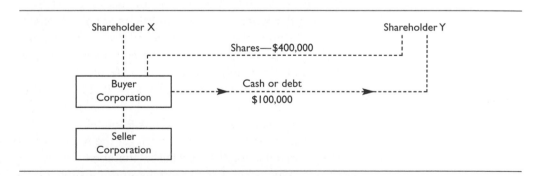

If the elective option is used, the shares of Buyer Corporation that are owned by the vendor, shareholder Y, will have a fair market value of $400,000 but a cost amount for tax purposes of zero. However, when shareholder Y disposes of those shares at some future time, a tax liability will occur.

As with the sale of assets, the vendor can receive either common shares or preferred shares or a combination of the two, depending on the nature of the take-over. In this particular situation, note that the ratio of cash and debt to share consideration for the asset sale was different from that for the share sale, assuming that each transaction involved the maximum permitted cash and debt. This difference is shown on the next page.

	Asset sale	Share sale
Total price	$700,000	$500,000
Consideration:		
Cash and debt	$400,000	$100,000
Shares	300,000	400,000
	$700,000	$500,000
Percentage as shares	43%	80%

The above result occurs because the relationship between asset cost and fair market value is usually not the same as the relationship between share cost and fair market value. The vendor's risk is increased when a greater portion of the payment is in the form of the buyer's shares. The vendor should consider this when deciding whether to accept a share sale, rather than an asset sale, under the elective provisions.

For both the vendor and the purchaser, the advantages and disadvantages of a tax-deferred sale of shares are similar to those for a tax-deferred sale of assets, and no further comment is necessary. However, it should be noted that one problem arises from the sale of shares; it has to do with the formal process involved in making the election to transfer shares at their tax values. To utilize this election, both the purchaser and the vendor must formalize their intentions by signing a tax agreement. While this is not a problem when there are few shareholders, it may be difficult when there are many shareholders, and virtually impossible when the corporation being sold is a public corporation. The parties can overcome this problem by using a less formal tax-deferred method of selling shares, referred to as a *share-for-share exchange*.

A ***share-for-share exchange*** has been made when a purchasing corporation acquires the shares of another corporation and the payments consist entirely of shares issued by the purchaser. In these circumstances, provided that certain other conditions are met, each separate vendor is entitled to declare that its shares have been sold at their cost amount, thereby deferring tax on the sale.[3] This decision is made solely by the vendor when all other conditions are met. Consider the previous sample situation: a share-for-share exchange would occur if shareholder Y sold all of the shares of Seller Corporation to Buyer Corporation for $500,000 worth of shares of Buyer Corporation. Shareholder Y can choose to recognize all or part of the $400,000 capital gain, or none of it, in the year of sale. If shareholder Y chooses to recognize none of the gain, the $500,000 of shares in Buyer Corporation received in exchange are deemed to have a tax cost of $100,000 (equal to the cost of shares sold); any subsequent sales of those shares would trigger the recognition of the capital gain.

Unfortunately, for the purchaser, the share-for-share exchange method is not so attractive. This is because the purchaser's adjusted cost base of the shares acquired in a share-for-share exchange is equal to the lesser of the shares' paid-up capital or their fair market value. As the acquired shares' paid-up capital is normally lower than fair market value, the result is that the purchaser's cost for tax purposes is lower than the market value of the shares. This may result in additional taxes if the shares are subsequently sold. Therefore, when private corporations are involved, they usually prefer to use the elective option described earlier, rather than the share-for-share exchange option. However, the share-for-share exchange format may be useful when public corporations are involved.

---

3   ITA 85.1(1) to (3); IT-450R.

D. Amalgamation

As described in Chapter 14, an amalgamation involves the combining of two or more corporations into a single entity housing the business activities of the former corporations. As part of the amalgamation, the shareholders of the separate corporations must become shareholders of the amalgamated corporation and maintain a continued interest in the combined operations.

The amalgamation process combines a share sale with an asset sale in that the shareholders of the former corporations exchange their shares for shares of the new corporation, and all of the former corporations transfer their assets to the new corporation. This type of business combination automatically results in a tax-deferred exchange of shares and assets.[4]

Although, by definition, an amalgamation of two business corporations is a business combination, it is often referred to as a "take-over," which is an acquisition that results in one company significantly dominating the other. For example, assume that Buyer Corporation has a net worth of $2,000,000. The amalgamation of Buyer Corporation ($2,000,000) and Seller Corporation ($500,000) would result in the following structure:

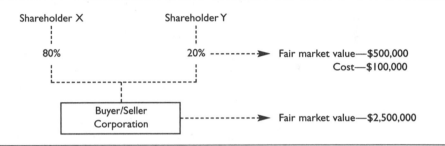

Although the two companies have joined their economic resources in a business combination, shareholder X, with its 80% holdings, clearly dominates shareholder Y, which has become a minority shareholder in the combined entity. In effect, the amalgamation amounts to a take-over by Buyer Corporation and its shareholders.

Business acquisitions using the amalgamation method are most common among public corporations because the former shareholders of the acquired company can dispose of the publicly traded shares of the new entity on the open market and in so doing realize their investment under the most favourable conditions.

E. Share Reorganization

A tax-deferred sale of a business can also be achieved by a reorganization of share capital as described in Chapter 14.[5] In this scenario, shareholder Y, before the acquisition, would convert the common shares, which have a value of $500,000 and a cost of $100,000, into fixed-value preferred shares of the same value. The purchaser would then acquire newly issued common shares for a nominal value. The corporate structure immediately after the acquisition would be as shown on the next page.

This method involves considerable risk for shareholder Y, as the opportunity to realize the value of the preferred shares depends entirely on the continued success of the vendor corporation. This method is quite different from the previous ones, all of which provided the vendor with shares of the purchaser corporation and thereby enhanced the vendor's security.

---

4   ITA 87(1) to (4); IT-474R.
5   ITA 86(1) to (3).

The share reorganization method is appropriate when the vendor has significant confidence in the purchaser's ability to manage the acquired business.

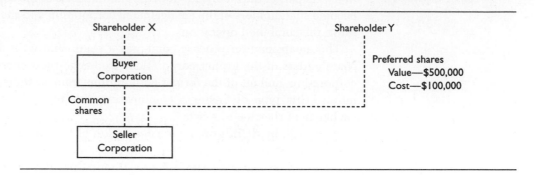

F. Conclusion   The above review indicates that several alternative methods are available to achieve a tax-deferred business sale and acquisition. It is clear that each method follows one of the two basic alternatives, which are the asset sale and the share sale. All tax-deferred acquisitions involving a share sale, an asset sale, an amalgamation, or a share reorganization have similar results for both vendor and purchaser. The vendor defers tax on the sale by accepting payment, in whole or in part, in the form of the purchaser's shares; in doing so, that vendor incurs greater risk. The purchaser assumes the disadvantage of a lower cost base for the assets acquired but is also able to issue shares as payment for the acquisition, which reduces the related cash and debt requirements.

The tax-deferred methods are almost always used when the transaction is a business combination in which two or more entities are joining forces and both or all will be participating in future operations. When the transaction is actually a take-over, the decision to use the tax-deferred method, rather than the taxable method, is based on the existing circumstances. The tax-deferred method is especially attractive when the vendor has confidence in the purchaser's management abilities. For example, a vendor may be more than willing to sell the business to its managers or employees, in the knowledge that the purchasers will continue to run the business successfully. However, in such a sale, the purchaser must usually look to the vendor for financing. The tax-deferred methods of payment by shares suit this type of transaction.

Similarly, the sale of a family business to children is usually highly leveraged; that is, the vendor provides the purchasers with the necessary financing in exchange for a long-term pay-out. In such cases, the tax-deferred methods are an appropriate way to match the tax liability with the receipt of payments. By maintaining a continued share interest, the parent can defer tax until the business generates sufficient funds that the purchasers can buy out the shares.

Because so many options exist, both tax-deferred and fully taxable (see Chapter 18), there is considerable flexibility in structuring a business divestiture and acquisition. The choice of method will depend on the needs of the vendor and the purchaser in the given circumstances. Every potential purchase or sale has its obstacles. The wide range of options makes it easier to overcome these and complete a successful sale transaction.

Because the best form of transaction for a particular situation is not always obvious, the decision-making process must involve examining each of the alternatives in terms of both its immediate and its long-term impact. On the next page, this process is reviewed in the context of the sale of a closely held corporate business.

II. Sale of a Closely Held Corporation

A. Distinguishing Features

A closely held corporation has either a single shareholder or a relatively small number of shareholders so that the relationship between the shareholders and the corporation is very close. This type of corporation often develops a financial structure that mixes the affairs of its primary business with those of its shareholders. Consequently, special circumstances may exist that affect the manner in which the business is ultimately sold, whether the sale is to independent third parties or to related family members.

Often, but not always, a closely held corporation will have the following features, which will affect any later sale of the business:

1. The corporation that houses the business has, in addition to the business assets, a number of investment assets that are not related to the operation of the business. The existence of investment assets is a result of the corporation's dividend policy, which normally involves distributing to the shareholder only the amounts he or she needs, with any remaining amount being held in the corporation to delay the incidence of tax.

   In addition, the corporation may also own certain business assets, such as land, buildings, and equipment, although the ownership of these assets may not be essential to the business, as their use could be secured by way of lease arrangements.

2. The owner of the business is usually under greater pressure to sell the business to immediate family members of the next generation or to senior managers or other employees who have given long service to the business. Typically, such employees and family members do not have the cash necessary to make the acquisition.

3. The business of a closely held corporation is often sold in response to the owner's wish to retire. Usually, this means that the vendor has a strong need to maximize future income from investment of the proceeds of sale. Obviously, taxation of the proceeds from a sale of assets or shares will diminish the after-tax funds available for reinvestment and any subsequent income.

So, the sale of a closely held corporation must be structured in such a way that the vendor's security is assured and the purchaser can make the acquisition. One such sale is demonstrated below. It is reviewed first as a third-party sale and then as a sale to family members.

B. Sale to Third Parties

The sale of a business to third parties may involve negotiations with a number of potential buyers, each of which faces a different financial situation and each of which has a different reason for making the acquisition. The following analysis examines only one particular negotiation and shows how the form of a sale can be structured to deal with all parties' particular circumstances.

Summary of Facts

Mr. X is the sole shareholder of For Sale Corporation, a Canadian-controlled private corporation that operates a medium-size business. He acquired the shares at a nominal cost when the company was incorporated, and the shares have increased in value substantially. Mr. X has decided to sell the business and retire. While a number of potential buyers are available, he has decided to sell the business to a small group of its senior managers provided that a workable arrangement can be made.

The managers can raise a limited amount of funds from their personal savings and from loans that would be secured by their personal assets.

The assets of For Sale Corporation are listed below. Except for the current assets and the bonds, the values of the assets exceed their cost amounts. The company does not have a substantial debt load and is heavily financed by retained earnings that have not been distributed to the shareholder.

Assets Related to the Business

Current assets:
    Accounts receivable
    Inventory
Fixed assets:
    Land
    Buildings
    Equipment
Other assets:
    Goodwill

Assets Not Related to the Business

Bonds
Real estate investments

Analysis

When this situation is examined, a number of things immediately become clear.

From the point of view of the vendor, a normal taxable sale of the entire corporation, by way of either an asset sale or a share sale, will create a tax liability that will reduce the after-tax proceeds that are available for generating a retirement income. It is also clear that a sale to the managers is going to require some funding by the vendor and that Mr. X must be concerned about the degree of security attached to the deferred payments.

The purchasers have limited resources, which means that a flexible, long-term payout must be arranged so that the purchase can be funded from future profits. The purchaser might obtain additional funding from venture capitalists; however, this would mean giving up a portion of the ownership and result in reduced repayment flexibility. Therefore, this is considered an alternative of last resort.

It is also clear that the purchasers do not need all of the assets within For Sale Corporation in order to operate the business they are acquiring. This presents two possibilities. The new owners could acquire the shares of For Sale Corporation, dispose of some or all of the redundant assets, and use the proceeds to fund part of the purchase price (see Chapter 14 on the use of holding companies). Alternatively, those owners could keep all the assets in the corporation and borrow against the redundant assets. For example, For Sale Corporation has a low debt load, and the new owners may be able to pledge the real estate or bonds as collateral in return for favourable long-term financing.

A second possibility is for the purchaser to reduce the overall purchase price by acquiring only the specific assets essential to operate the business. This would leave the remaining assets in the hands of the former owner. In this case, there would be no need to purchase the bonds and investment real estate, and therefore the price could be lowered so that it was more in line with the purchaser's resources. In addition, the land, buildings, and equipment needed for the business could be leased by the business, rather than purchased.

It is extremely critical that the purchasers examine the nature of the asset base of the entity they are acquiring. This is especially true when the entity is a closely held corporation and the shareholder is more flexible in terms of alternative buy-out arrangements.

The Sale and Acquisition Structure Chosen

In this situation, the purchaser and the vendor met their needs by means of a tax-deferred asset sale of only those assets required to operate the business. Specifically, the transaction involved the following:

1. The new managers created a new corporation (referred to as Purchase Corporation), to which they contributed their available funds in exchange for common share capital.

2. Purchase Corporation then acquired the following assets from For Sale Corporation:

> Current assets:
> Accounts receivable
> Inventory
> Other assets:
> Goodwill

Payment for these assets consisted of a limited amount of cash, the assumption of current liabilities, and a note payable (with interest) to For Sale Corporation, as well as the issuance of preferred shares to For Sale Corporation.

3. Both parties elected that for tax purposes, the transfer price of the goodwill was equal to an amount that would create no taxable income to the vendor. In accordance with the election provisions, the value of the preferred shares represented the difference between the fair value of the goodwill and the elected price for tax purposes.

4. The preferred shares paid a fixed dividend that was acceptable to both parties. While the purchaser could redeem the preferred shares at any time, those shares had to be fully redeemed by the end of 10 years. In addition, the preferred shares provided limited voting rights so that although the vendor did not control the new company, he could exercise a significant influence. In addition, the vendor had the option of calling for the immediate redemption of his shares in the event that Purchase Corporation failed to pay an annual dividend.

5. Purchase Corporation did not purchase the land, buildings, and equipment used to operate the business. Instead, it signed long-term leases that provided For Sale Corporation with net rents equal to 12% of the property's fair market value at the time. Purchase Corporation was granted an option to acquire the property at the end of the lease for a price equal to the fair market value of the assets at that future time. The above sale and purchase structure is shown on the next page.

Completing the sale in the preceding format met the needs of both the vendor and the purchaser in this specific situation. The vendor has maximized his future income, in part by deferring the tax that would have resulted from an asset sale. By retaining the land, buildings, and equipment, he has deferred recapture of capital cost allowance and (perhaps) capital gains. The lease arrangement provides a rental return based on the assets' fair market values; this return is much higher than it would have been if the assets had been sold and the resulting after-tax proceeds invested. Also, the goodwill that was sold on a tax-deferred basis provides a dividend return based on its fair market value, rather than its after-tax value.

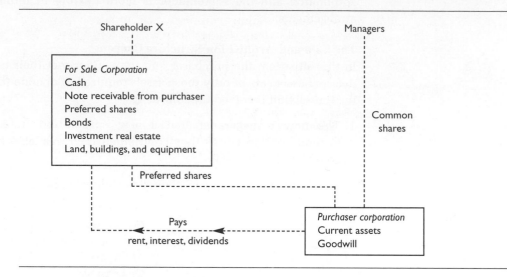

As well, the vendor has achieved significant security for the following reasons:

1. Retaining the land, buildings, and equipment under a lease arrangement fully protects that property from any risk associated with a possible failure of the business after it is taken over by the managers. In particular, the land and buildings will likely continue to increase in value and can be sold at any time.

2. Although part of the sale price is reflected in preferred shares, the nature of those shares provides For Sale Corporation with significant power, which can be exercised if the purchasers fail to meet their commitments.

3. The business is being sold to managers who have a keen knowledge of the business; their management skills are a known quantity.

4. The purchasers have shown a commitment to the purchase by investing a large portion of their own assets in the new corporation in the form of common shares, which are subordinated to the preferred shares.

The purchasers also achieved their objective, which was to acquire the business with limited capital resources. They have purchased only those assets that are absolutely necessary to run the business and have arranged favourable terms with the vendor, and so their chances of success are high. In this case, what is good for the vendor is also good for the purchaser—which is important to any successful sale and acquisition.

It is important to recognize that the consideration of tax factors played a major role in the successful sale negotiation. Both the vendor and the purchasers reviewed all the basic alternatives—asset sale, share sale, and tax-deferred sale—and found a satisfactory solution.

C. Sale to Family Members

The sale and purchase of a business within a family unit has all of the fundamental aspects of a sale to third parties. It can be an asset sale or a share sale as a fully taxable transaction, or it can use the various tax-deferred methods discussed earlier. However, unlike a sale to third parties, a family transaction is influenced by the dynamics of family relationships.

In some cases, the nature of the family relationship is such that a sale of a business by a parent to a child is treated as if it were a sale to a third party, in which case the discussion in the previous section is relevant. In most cases, however, the vendor in a family transaction is prepared to give preferential terms that will ensure a successful acquisition by the purchaser.

The sale of a family business to children may appear unnecessary considering that on the death of the parent, the business will likely pass to the children as a succession gift. There are two reasons that a parent may want to sell a family business to children well before an estate transfer:

1. An early transfer may minimize the tax liability that would otherwise occur on the death of the original owner.

2. The early transfer of a family business from one generation to another provides an orderly succession and a continuity of management responsibility.

Obviously, the sale of a business to family members is often motivated by personal factors, which, in turn, influence the form of the transaction. A sale to a third party must result in the best possible security for the vendor so that he or she can ultimately realize the full value of the business. The vendor will therefore use one of the tax-deferred methods (which require a continued share interest) only if the security of the transaction is more than adequate. In a sale to children, however, the vendor is less concerned about security, as the value of the business will likely pass to the children in any event through the vendor's estate. This means that the deferral and minimization of tax may be the primary concern when the method of transaction is being chosen.

Consider, for example, the same situation described previously involving the sale of a business to third parties, with this change: shareholder X's objectives are to transfer ownership of the business to an only child who is active in the business and to minimize taxes that may occur on death.

Both of shareholder X's objectives can be satisfied by utilizing the tax-deferred method of share reorganization. Under this method, shareholder X exchanges all common shares owned for fixed value preferred shares having a value equal to the common shares exchanged. As the full value of For Sale Corporation is locked up in the preferred shares, X's child can acquire the new common shares at a nominal cost. This form of transaction has the following results:

1. The parent, shareholder X, has fully financed the change in ownership by accepting fixed-value preferred shares in exchange for the former common shares.

2. The parent has received full value for the company in accepting preferred shares as payment; however, no immediate tax liability results. The parent will be subject to tax if he or she redeems the preferred shares or should die holding the shares.

3. The parent will have a continued source of income from the predetermined dividend attached to the preferred shares.

4. Although the preferred shares will eventually be subject to tax, their value will not grow beyond the value at the date of issuance; this means that the parent's potential tax liability is "frozen" at the date of the sale transaction. Consequently, the parent's ultimate tax liability is considerably less than it would have been if he or she had continued to hold the common shares, allowed them to grow in value, and left them to the child.

5. All growth in the value of For Sale Corporation beyond its value at the transaction date will accrue to the benefit of the child as the new common shareholder.

Another way to accomplish Shareholder X's objective on a tax-deferred basis is to use a holding company. The steps under this method are as follows:

- A new corporation (Holdco) is created and the child acquires the common shares for a nominal cost.

- Shareholder X then sells the common shares of For Sale Corporation (which houses the business) to Holdco. The shares are sold at fair market value, but for tax purposes an elected amount (Section 85) equal to their ACB is chosen. In exchange, Holdco issues to X debt (up to the elected amount) and preferred shares for the remainder.

- Alternatively, if For Sale is a qualified small business corporation and X is free to use the full $750,000 capital gain deduction, the transaction can be structured differently. In this situation, X can elect a transfer price equal to the ACB of the For Sale shares *plus* $750,000. A tax-free capital gain for X is the result. Therefore, the debt and preferred shares received by X as consideration will have an ACB equal to the $750,000 plus the ACB of the For Sale shares transferred. A subsequent sale of these properties to an arm's-length party would recognize this ACB. It should be noted that when the capital gain deduction is claimed as part of this type of transaction, X (the transferor) cannot extract that amount from Holdco without a tax cost due to an anti-avoidance rule.[6]

  Assume, in the above situation, that the For Sale shares have a fair market value of $1,000,000 and an ACB and paid-up capital amount of $50,000. When X sells the shares to Holdco for $1,000,000 the elected amount for tax purposes will be $800,000 ($50,000 ACB plus $750,000). In exchange, Holdco will issue to X debt of $50,000 and preferred shares of $950,000. The ACB of the debt is $50,000 and the ACB of the preferred shares is $750,000. However, the paid-up capital of the preferred shares is reduced to nil under an anti-avoidance rule (where an individual transfers shares to a related corporation and the two corporations are connected after the transfer).[7] So if X sells the preferred shares to an arm's-length person, no capital gain occurs. However, if Holdco redeems any of the preferred shares, X will have a deemed dividend. If, at the outset, the transaction attempts to issue debt greater than the ACB of the transferred shares (in this example $50,000), an immediate deemed dividend equal to the excess will occur.[8] For example, if Holdco issues debt of $800,000, an immediate deemed dividend of $750,000 would result. If the shares are subsequently sold, the proceeds are reduced by this deemed dividend to prevent double taxing.[9] So, to avoid the immediate deemed dividend and still get the capital gain deduction, the seller must accept share consideration for the amount of capital gain deduction claimed.

Note that in these forms of buy-out, the child gained entitlement to all property owned by For Sale Corporation—the business assets as well as the investment assets. This may not always be desirable when there are several children in a family and some of those children will not be involved in the business activity. In such cases, an alternative form of transaction could be utilized. For example, the business could be transferred to one child by having For Sale Corporation sell only its business assets, on a tax-deferred basis, to a new corporation created by the child. (This is similar to what was done in the sale to employees that was described earlier.)

As with third-party sales, it is important that in a family sale, the vendor and the purchaser investigate a number of alternative sale-transaction methods to determine which one best satisfies the needs of all parties concerned while maintaining the integrity of the transaction.

---

6   ITA 84.1. Actually, the debt consideration should not exceed the greater of the ACB or the paid-up capital of the For Sale shares transferred to Holdco.

7   ITA 84.1(1)(a).

8   ITA 84.1(1)(b). A dividend is deemed to be received by the shareholder to the extent that the non-share consideration (debt or cash) exceeds the greater of the PUC and the ACB of the exchanged shares.

9   ITA 54.

III. Summary and Conclusion

A business sale and acquisition can take a number of different forms. In addition to the normal taxable methods that involve selling shares or assets, there are tax-deferred methods.

The tax-deferred methods examined in this chapter are not new; they were also examined in Chapter 14 in the context of corporate reorganizations within a related group of companies. These methods apply equally well to arm's-length acquisitions and divestitures. It is important to recognize that the tax-deferred methods involve particular trade-offs. From the vendor's perspective, the attractiveness of delaying tax on the sale is lessened somewhat by the increased financial risk, which results from the requirement that all or some of the payment be in the form of a continued equity interest in the business. From the purchaser's perspective, the attractiveness of a lesser cash or debt requirement to complete the acquisition is moderated by the reduced deductions available from capital cost allowance on assets purchased and by the requirement that share capital be issued (as opposed to debt), which must be serviced by non-deductible dividends (as opposed to deductible interest).

Notwithstanding these trade-offs, the tax-deferred methods are viable and often-used alternatives. In the proper circumstances, they can be applied to the acquisition and divestiture of large businesses as well as small businesses and to public corporations as well as private corporations. It is vitally important that the decision maker who is responsible for making an acquisition or sale investigate all of the available transaction forms. Every purchase and sale has unique characteristics; among the array of alternatives, a method can usually be found that meets the particular needs of both the vendor and the purchaser.

The discussion in this chapter confined itself to the purchase and sale of a business involving both a corporate vendor and a corporate purchaser. Similar tax-deferred methods are also available when a business is sold by a corporation to a partnership, by one partnership to another, or by a partnership to a corporation.

Visit the Canadian Income Taxation Web site at **www.mcgrawhill.ca/ olc/buckwold** to view any updated tax information.

Review Questions

1. While vendors may gain a tax advantage by selling a business using a tax-deferred method, they may be subjecting themselves to more risk in terms of ultimately realizing the proceeds from the sale. How is a tax-deferred sale of a business distinguished from a taxable sale? Why does a tax-deferred sale involve greater risk?

2. Give three basic reasons that a vendor may be prepared to accept a greater risk in exchange for a tax deferral on the sale of a business.

3. What four basic methods can be used to achieve a tax-deferred sale?

4. What advantages and disadvantages may arise for the purchaser when the specific business assets are acquired from a vendor corporation and the parties elect transfer prices for tax purposes at amounts that will defer tax to the vendor?

5. What is a share-for-share exchange? How does it differ from a sale of shares in which the vendor and the purchaser elect a specific price for tax purposes?

6. Why is a business acquisition using the share-for-share technique attractive to both the purchaser and the vendor?

7. A tax-deferred sale of a business by a reorganization of share capital may present more risk to the vendor than a sale of its shares to a corporate purchaser and an election of a transfer price for tax purposes. Explain why.

8. When a business owned by a closely held corporation is being sold, the vendor is often persuaded to use tax-deferred methods to structure the sale. What is a

closely held corporation? What features may such a corporation have that make a tax-deferred sale attractive?

9. Why may the owner of a business want to transfer a business to children during his or her lifetime, rather than by way of an estate transfer upon death?

10. What feature is often found when a business is being transferred to a family member? How is the tax-deferred method of sale consistent with this feature?

11. How may the sale of a corporation's specific business assets to a purchaser with limited resources provide greater flexibility than the sale of shares of the corporation?

Key Concept Questions

QUESTION ONE

Eric owns common shares of CNR, a Canadian public company. His shares have the following attributes:

Fair market value	$12,000
Adjusted cost base	4,000
Paid-up capital	1

CPC, a widely held Canadian public company, has acquired all of the shares of CNR. In exchange for his shares of CNR, Eric received common shares of CPC worth $12,000. *Income tax reference: ITA 85.1, 85(1).*

Determine the tax consequences for Eric.

QUESTION TWO

Zoe owns all the shares of Z Ltd., a Canadian-controlled private corporation, carrying on a shoe importing business. Zoe is ready to retire and would like to sell her shares of Z Ltd. to a group of long-term, trusted employees. The employees do not have the funds or the borrowing power to purchase the shares of Z Ltd. for their current value, $2,000,000. Zoe has been told that she may be able to complete the sale to the employees by reorganizing the share capital of Z Ltd. *Income tax reference: ITA 86.*

Provide Zoe with an explanation of how a reorganization of the share capital of Z Ltd. can help her make the sale.

QUESTION THREE

Gary owns all the shares of G Ltd., a Canadian-controlled private corporation in the import/export business. He would like for his daughter, Lilly, who has been active in the business for the past five years to share, equally with him, in the future growth of the business. Unfortunately, Lilly has no savings and Gary would not like to see her borrow more than $200,000. The shares of G Ltd. are currently worth $1,000,000 and have a PUC and ACB of $1,000. Gary has no capital gains deduction available. *Income tax reference: ITA 86.*

Explain to Gary how his goals can be accomplished by either reorganizing the share capital of G Ltd. or by using a holding company.

QUESTION FOUR

Jane owns all of the shares of J Ltd., a Canadian-controlled private corporation with investments in numerous Canadian public companies. Her husband, Mike, owns all of the shares of M Ltd., a Canadian-controlled private corporation, with excess cash. They have decided to have M Ltd. purchase the shares of J Ltd. to provide Jane with the cash required to take advantage of another investment opportunity. The shares of J Ltd. are currently worth $900,000 and have a PUC and ACB of $100,000. The plan is for M Ltd. to pay Jane $900,000 in cash for the J Ltd. shares. *Income tax reference: ITA 84.1.*

Determine the tax consequences for Jane.

QUESTION FIVE

Nancy owns all of the shares of N Ltd., a Canadian-controlled private corporation with investments in numerous Canadian public companies. Her husband, Richard, owns all of the shares of R Ltd., a Canadian-controlled private corporation. They have decided to have R Ltd. purchase the shares of N Ltd. The shares of N Ltd. are currently worth $600,000 and have a PUC and ACB of $50,000. The plan is for R Ltd. to pay Nancy $50,000 in cash and preferred shares of R Ltd. worth $550,000. Nancy and Richard have agreed to make a joint election under section 85 of the *Income Tax Act* in order to defer tax on the transaction. *Income tax reference: ITA 84.1, 85(1).*

Determine the tax consequences for Nancy.

QUESTION SIX

Bill owns all of the shares of B Ltd., a Canadian-controlled private corporation carrying on a home design business. The shares of B Ltd. are currently worth $1,000,000 and have a PUC and ACB of $200,000. In order to crystallize his entitlement to the capital gains deduction, Bill has decided to set up a new corporation, H Ltd., and transfer his shares of B Ltd. to H Ltd. Bill and H Ltd. will file a joint election under section 85 of the *Income Tax Act*, electing proceeds of $950,000. As consideration for the transfer, Bill will receive a note for $950,000 and preferred shares of H Ltd. worth $50,000. *Income tax reference: ITA 84.1, 85(1).*

Determine the tax consequences for Bill.

Problems

PROBLEM ONE

For the past 30 years, Janice Kalinsky has been the president and owner of JK Wholesale Ltd. In contemplation of retirement, she has entered into negotiations to sell the shares of JK to Kaplan Brothers Ltd., a company that has been her major competitor. Although Kalinsky's planned retirement date is still five years away, she is prepared to sell now so that she can have a defined amount of capital available to provide a retirement income.

Kaplan Brothers has offered to purchase her shares in JK for $700,000. The shares have a cost base of $200,000. Kalinsky intends to invest the proceeds from the sale in interest-bearing securities that yield a 10% return for five years. The accumulated funds will provide her with a retirement income at the end of five years. In the meantime, she will be employed as the executive director of a national trade association.

Kalinsky is concerned about the amount of tax payable on the sale and has had discussions with Kaplan Brothers about using the elective provisions of the *Income Tax Act* to defer her tax on the sale of shares. Kaplan Brothers has agreed to this and has presented her with two options:

1. Purchase of her shares for $700,000, payable immediately in cash.

2. Purchase of her shares for $700,000, using the elective provisions of the *Income Tax Act* to defer her tax liability. Payment would consist of debt with 10% interest and preferred shares with an annual cumulative dividend rate of 8%. Kaplan Brothers would repay the full amount of the debt and redeem the preferred shares at the end of five years.

Kalinsky's personal marginal tax rate is 28% on eligible dividends and 33% on non-eligible dividends (net of the dividend tax credit) and 45% on other income. She used up her full capital gain deduction several years ago while selling a related business corporation.

JK Wholesale Ltd. has never claimed the small business deduction because the annual business limit is always allocated to an associated corporation.

Kaplan Brothers has earned profits of $500,000 before tax for the past two years.

Required:

1. Determine the amount of capital that Kalinsky will have for retirement purposes at the end of five years under each of the alternative buy-out methods.

2. What other factors must Kalinsky consider before she decides which option to accept?

3. What are the benefits and costs of option 2 for Kaplan Brothers?

PROBLEM TWO

Shane Plastics Ltd. is a Canadian-controlled private corporation. All of its outstanding common shares are owned by KS Holdings Ltd., a company owned by Karl Shane. KS Holdings also owns several real estate investments. Shane wants to sell the plastics business to four senior employees, one of whom is his son. Shane realizes that none of the employees has substantial financial resources and that they may be able to contribute only 25% of the purchase price. Even to obtain this amount, the four employees would likely have to take out personal loans.

A financial institution is prepared to finance the balance of the purchase price provided that Shane agrees to be the guarantor of the loan. Shane may be prepared to do this, even though it would leave the business with a severe debt load and no flexibility should the business have temporary problems.

The employees have asked Shane to finance the purchase by permitting a flexible, eight-year payment schedule. Shane is not averse to this offer, provided that he can continue to have some say in the major decisions of the business until most of the payments have been made.

The most recent balance sheet of Shane Plastics is summarized in the following table:

Current assets (cash, receivables, inventory)		$ 500,000
Land		50,000
Building	600,000	
Equipment	350,000	
	950,000	
Accumulated amortization	(400,000)	550,000
Marketable securities (bonds)		100,000
		$1,200,000
Current liabilities		$ 300,000
Mortgage on land and building		400,000
Shareholders' equity:		
Share capital	10,000	
Retained earnings	490,000	500,000
		$1,200,000

The following additional information is available:

1. The undepreciated capital cost of the depreciable property is as follows:

Building	$490,000
Equipment	100,000

2. The asset values are as follows:

Current assets	$500,000
Land	100,000
Building	720,000
Equipment	300,000
Marketable securities	100,000

In addition, the value of goodwill has been estimated at $400,000.

3. KS Holdings acquired the shares of Shane Plastics a number of years ago at a cost of $200,000. Recently, a competitor had offered to purchase the shares of Shane Plastics for $1,200,000; Shane had refused the offer because he wanted to sell to the employees.

Shane is prepared to accept the deferred payment schedule suggested by the employees but has concerns about the immediate tax liability associated with the sale. Shane is 50 years old and intends to maintain KS Holdings to hold his investment portfolio. He will also continue to be employed by Shane Plastics after the business has been acquired by the employees.

Required:

1. Assuming that either an asset sale by Shane Plastics or a share sale by KS Holdings will be made at fair market values, with deferred payments over eight years, which method should Shane prefer? You may assume a corporate tax rate of 25% on business income.

2. Suggest and briefly discuss several alternative methods that will defer the tax liabilities on the sale and also assist the purchasers in making the acquisition, considering their limited resources. Be as specific as possible, given the information provided.

PROBLEM THREE

Andy Marcus is the sole shareholder of Marcus Ltd., a Canadian-controlled private corporation. The common shares of Marcus Ltd. have a fair market value of $300,000, an ACB of $50,000, and a PUC of $1000. Through an amendment to the Articles of Marcus Ltd. all of the common shares are converted to preferred shares redeemable for $300,000 in the course of a reorganization of share capital.

Required:
Indicate the tax consequences of the transaction for Andy.

PROBLEM FOUR

Marie Hobbins owns all of the issued shares of H Ltd. She acquired the shares for $100,000 from a stranger in 20X0. The shares of H Ltd. have a PUC of $100. A widely held Canadian public company, P Corp., is interested in acquiring H Ltd. Marie is considering a proposal to sell her shares to P Corp. in exchange for common shares of P Corp. of the same value, $900,000.

Required:

1. Describe the tax consequences for Marie and P Corp. if the transaction takes place as described above.

2. Marie is certain that the shares of H Ltd. are QSBC shares. She would like to use the capital gains deduction to shelter her gain on the sale of her H Ltd. shares. Is this possible?

PROBLEM FIVE

Robert Blackwell owns 100% of the outstanding shares of Black Inc., a qualified small business corporation. The shares have a paid-up capital (PUC) and an adjusted cost base of $50,000 and a fair market value of $1,000,000. In order to make full use of his lifetime capital gains deduction, Robert uses section 85 of the *Income Tax Act* to transfer these shares to Holdings Ltd. at an elected value of $800,000. As consideration he receives a note for $700,000 and preferred shares with a fair market value and a legal stated capital of $300,000. Robert owns all of the shares of Holdings Ltd.

Required:
What are the tax consequences of this transaction for Robert?

Cases

CASE ONE   Delwin Corporation Ltd.

Carla Delwin has requested that you review her current financial position and her proposed plans and provide her with tax advice. In response to her request, you have gathered together the following information:

Delwin Corporation Ltd. is a Canadian-controlled private corporation that owns several retail clothing stores. Its common shares are owned 80% by Delwin and 20% by one of her senior managers. Information relating to the shares is as follows:

	Delwin	Manager
Number of shares	800	200
Paid-up capital	$8,000	$ 2,000
Cost	8,000	25,000

In the current year, DCL earned taxable income of $540,000 from the retail operations. It is expected that this level of profit will be maintained next year.

DCL is planning to expand into the manufacturing business and is currently negotiating for the purchase of equipment that will be used to manufacture winter ski jackets. Because the ski jackets have a ready market in her retail stores, profits are expected to be at least $40,000 in the first year.

The expansion will be funded by cash generated from the sale of a building. The building was sold last year and resulted in a capital gain of $200,000 to DCL. The funds are currently invested in short-term bank certificates.

After a major dispute with the senior manager, it was agreed that early in the new year, the manager would sell his shares for $120,000, leaving Delwin with 100% of the company. The parties have not discussed how to structure the transaction. However, Delwin has indicated to the manager that the full price will be paid in cash.

Delwin personally owns a commercial building that has generated rental revenue for several years. The current lease will end in the near future, and she has decided that rather than renew the lease, she will use the building to open a new retail location. The property was acquired a number of years ago for $100,000 ($80,000 for the building, $20,000 for the land). To date, she has claimed capital cost allowance totalling $30,000. A recent appraisal indicates that the land is worth $30,000 and the building $90,000. Delwin wishes to transfer the land and building to DCL.

In addition, Delwin personally owns several investments that generate Canadian dividends and interest income. She has been wondering if there would be any tax advantage to incorporating these investments.

Delwin contributes the maximum to retirement plans, and her RRSP currently has a value of $200,000, consisting solely of common share investments.

Delwin's son Eric, who had managed one of the retail stores, has recently been promoted to take on greater management responsibilities. Delwin has promised Eric that after a two-year period, he can become a 50% shareholder in DCL. She wants to know how this can be achieved, considering that Eric will have no money to make the acquisition. Also, Delwin is not anxious to pay tax when she restructures the ownership within the family.

Required:

Prepare a report to Delwin providing the tax advice she has requested. Include the tax implications to the manager on the proposed sale of shares.

CASE TWO*   Mattjon Limited

Matthew and Jonathan have owned a manufacturing company, Mattjon Limited, for 20 years. Matthew, who is 55 years old, retired from the business on December 31, 20X0. He and his wife plan to travel throughout Canada during his retirement.

It is now January 5, 20X1. Jonathan would like to purchase Matthew's 50% share of Mattjon. A recent appraisal put the value of the company at $2.0 million. Jonathan does not have the cash resources to complete the purchase and is concerned about his ability to meet the debt service costs if he has to borrow money to purchase Matthew's shares. As the two men are friends, Jonathan would like to structure the purchase so that it provides the greatest possible tax deferral to Matthew.

Jonathan has heard that holding companies are sometimes used in these situations, but he does not know what such an arrangement would involve. He has also heard about the capital gains deduction and wonders whether it could be applied to this transaction. Neither Jonathan nor Matthew has disposed of any capital property in the past. Extracts from the balance sheet of Mattjon are provided in Exhibit I on the next page.

The owners of Mattjon have asked you to prepare a memo suggesting how this transaction might be structured.

Required:

Prepare the memo.

Exhibit I

MATTJON LIMITED
Extracts from Balance Sheet
As at December 31, 20X0
(unaudited)

Assets (Note 1)		
Current:		
Cash	25,000	
Accounts receivable	150,000	
Inventory	300,000	$ 475,000
Fixed:		
Land (note 1)	50,000	
Building (net of accumulated amortization)	100,000	
Machinery and equipment (net of accumulated amortization)	75,000	225,000
Long term:		
Government bonds		300,000
		$1,000,000

---

* Adapted, with permission, from the 1990 Uniform Final Examination ©1990 of the Canadian Institute of Chartered Accountants, Toronto, Canada. Any changes to the original material are the sole responsibility of W.J. Buckwold and have not been reviewed or endorsed by the CICA.

Liabilities		
Accounts payable	70,000	
Income and other taxes payable	30,000	$100,000
Shareholders' Equity		
Capital stock (Note 2):		
2 common shares	200	
600 class A preferred shares	60,000	
600 class B preferred shares	60,000	
Retained earnings (Note 3)	779,800	900,000
		$1,000,000

Note 1: Mattjon is considering relocating its facilities to cheaper industrial land, as a recent appraisal valued the company's land at $550,000. The market value of all other assets approximates book value. Mattjon uses capital cost allowance rates for purposes of financial statement amortization.

Note 2: For tax purposes, all shares have paid-up capital and an adjusted cost base equal to $100 per share. Matthew owns the class A preferred shares and Jonathan the class B preferred shares. Both classes of preferred shares are non-voting, non-participating, and redeemable at their paid-up capital of $100 per share.

Note 3: All of the retained earnings are represented by past profits that have qualified for the small business deduction.

CHAPTER 20

Domestic and International Business Expansion

A business enterprise grows throughout its life. It does so by expanding existing product lines or services into new domestic markets, developing new products or services, and reaching into international markets. While an entity's expansion strategy is a function of its ability to exploit opportunities in accordance with its relative strengths and weaknesses, tax factors play a vital role in the decision-making process.

Every entity, in everything it does, tries to minimize risk and maximize after-tax returns on investment. After-tax cash flows are significantly influenced by the structure utilized to conduct the expansion. In Chapter 18, the influence of taxation on business expansion through *the acquisition of an existing business* was demonstrated. This chapter will review the tax implications of expansion through *internal growth and development.* Specifically, this chapter will

(a) briefly examine domestic expansion by consolidating a number of issues discussed in previous chapters; and

(b) develop the fundamental interrelationships between foreign taxation and Canadian taxation, as they relate to international business expansion activities.

I. Domestic Business Expansion

The process of expanding existing business operations usually involves committing capital and human resources. As with any investment decision, the decision maker must attempt to create an expansion structure that will minimize the start-up cash requirements and maximize the return of cash to the business for reinvestment. As indicated in previous chapters, the following fundamental tax considerations are relevant:

1. What will be the annual tax cost on new profits generated from the expansion?

2. How and when can operating losses during the start-up period be offset against other taxable income to generate cash flow?

3. What are the tax implications if the expansion fails and is discontinued?

4. How can the original capital invested, as well as accumulated profits, be returned from the expansion with a minimum amount of tax?

The choice of structure depends on whether the expansion is to be funded completely with internal equity and borrowing power or by a combination of internal equity and new outside equity. When an expansion opportunity exists but the entity's resources are limited, that entity must either limit the expansion or grasp the opportunity more fully by raising additional equity capital from new participants. Many of the alternative structures and their related tax implications have already been examined in this text; this section of the chapter simply summarizes and consolidates those discussions in the context of expansion decisions.

A. Expansion with Existing Resources

Expansion in Canada may be limited to the home province or involve activity in other provincial jurisdictions, each of which imposes a different rate of tax. In either case, two fundamental structural alternatives are available: the expansion activity can be operated as a division of the existing corporation or within a separate corporation that is a subsidiary of the parent corporation.

• **Loss utilization** A major difference between the divisional structure and the corporate structure relates to the ability to use any losses in the start-up years. As a division is housed within the existing structure, all losses incurred can immediately be offset against income from other, profitable divisions within the corporation. Consequently, immediate additional cash flow is generated from tax savings, which can be used to fund the expansion. However, utilizing the division structure also means forgoing limited liability so that the obligations of the new division become the obligations of the enterprise that established it. Using a separate corporation may limit liability, but it also limits the utilization of the start-up losses, since those can be used only by the separate corporation that was created to house the expansion. Therefore, when the expansion activity will involve start-up losses, the cash funding requirements for a corporation are greater than for a corporate division.

- **Expansion failure** If the expansion activity fails and is discontinued, either the losses and related obligations will be funded by the initial capital invested or the losses will require further funding to meet the obligations.

If the potential losses are limited to the capital invested, both the division structure and the separate corporation structure permit the eventual use of the incurred losses for offset against other income. Under the division structure, the losses would generate tax savings as they occur. Under the corporation structure, the losses would accumulate but could be used after a corporate reorganization that amalgamates the parent with the expansion corporation (see Chapter 14). The difference is timing.

However, when potential losses may exceed the capital invested, the impact of limited liability must be weighed against the after-tax cost of absorbing the losses. If a corporation structure were used and losses exceeded the capital invested such that bankruptcy was imposed, the owner would forgo the opportunity of amalgamating the loss company with a profitable company and, instead, recognize the loss as a capital loss of the initial capital provided to the expansion corporation. Only one-half of the initial capital loss could be offset against other capital gains, unless the expansion corporation was a small business corporation, in which case one-half of the loss could be offset against other income (see Chapter 8). An example of the impact of this on cash flow is demonstrated in the following situation:

Situation: An existing business invests $100,000 in an expansion project. The project loses $30,000 each year for five years (total losses $150,000) and is then discontinued. The existing entity is subject to a tax rate of 25%. If the company uses a division structure, an additional cash contribution of $50,000 is made at the end of year 4 to fund the excess losses. If a corporation structure is used, no additional contribution is made and bankruptcy of the separate corporation occurs.

Analysis: Under the division structure, the existing corporation pays out cash of $100,000 initially plus $50,000 at the end of year 4, which creates cash tax savings of $7,500 annually for each of the five years ($30,000 × 25% = $7,500). Under the corporation structure, the existing corporation pays out only $100,000 initially and incurs a capital loss on the investment of $100,000 in year 5, which creates a cash tax saving of $12,500 (½ of $100,000 = $50,000 × 25% = $12,500), assuming the capital loss can be utilized.

The cash flows from each alternative, together with the net present values, are summarized in the table on the next page.

This analysis indicated that although the division structure was exposed to greater losses in absolute terms ($150,000 compared with $100,000 for the corporate structure), the net after-tax consequences for that structure were significantly reduced in net present value terms. This is because the losses available for use receive preferential treatment under the division structure regarding both *timing* and *amount*. In summary,

	Division structure	Corporation structure
Initial investment	$100,000	$100,000
Year 1—tax saving	(7,500)	–0–
2—tax saving	(7,500)	–0–
3—tax saving	(7,500)	–0–
4—tax saving	(7,500)	–0–
—additional investment	50,000	–0–
5—tax saving	(7,500)	(12,500)
Net cash outflow	$112,500	$ 87,500
Net present value of cash outflows discounted at 12%	$104,800	$ 92,900

the apparent benefit of limited liability must be weighed against a realistic estimate of potential cash flows and the related tax effect when it is being decided which structure to use for expansion activities.

• **Taxation of expansion profits**   The amount of tax paid on profits from the expansion activity can vary, depending on whether a division or a separate corporation is established, if the expansion activity crosses provincial boundaries, and/or the nature of the expansion profits differs from existing profits. As explained in Chapter 11, the rates of provincial corporate tax vary from province to province. In addition, manufacturing profits may be subject to a lower rate of provincial tax. It was also indicated in Chapter 11 that when income is determined by the province for tax purposes, an arbitrary formula that provides different results under the division structure and the separate corporation structure is applied. The same is true when manufacturing income is separated from non-manufacturing income for tax purposes.

For example, consider the following situation, which concerns an expansion into another province:

Situation: Sask Ltd. is a Saskatchewan-based corporation that operates a wholesale distribution business. The company is contemplating an expansion into Alberta and projects the following results:

	Saskatchewan operations	New Alberta operations		Total
Sales	$1,000,000	$300,000	(23%)	$1,300,000
Salaries	300,000	70,000	(19%)	370,000
Profits	200,000	20,000	(9%)	220,000

Provincial tax rates at the time of expansion are 12% of taxable income in Saskatchewan and 10% in Alberta.

Analysis: If the above expansion uses a division structure, there are two basic possibilities:

1. A direct sales approach from the Saskatchewan head office, with customers in Alberta serviced by Saskatchewan-based personnel.

2. A permanent place of business in Alberta (i.e., a sales office and/or warehouse) staffed by Alberta-based personnel.

If the expansion involves a separate corporation, an Alberta-based corporation can be established to provide a permanent location and staff.

Assuming operating results as projected above, the amount of provincial tax under each method is as follows:

Direct Sales

Expansion profits are earned by the Saskatchewan corporation and are subject to Saskatchewan tax rates unless a permanent establishment exists in another province.

Tax: 12% × $20,000	**$2,400**

Branch Location

Branch profits also belong to the Saskatchewan corporation. However, the Alberta tax rate applies because the expansion operations are carried out from a permanent establishment there. Alberta profits are determined for tax purposes by an arbitrary formula based on sales and salaries (see Chapter 11), as follows:

Profits attributed to branch:		
Branch sales	23%	
Branch salaries	19	
Average: (23% + 19%)/2	21%	
Total profits	$220,000	
Allocated to Alberta branch		
(21% × $220,000)		$46,200
Tax from expansion:		
Alberta tax ($46,200 × 10%)		$ 4,620
Less tax saved on profits shifted to		
Alberta from arbitrary formula:		
Alberta allocation	$ 46,200	
Actual Alberta profits	(20,000)	
	$ 26,200	
Tax saved ($26,200 × 12%)		(3,144)
Incremental tax from expansion		$ 1,476

The reduced tax amount under the branch approach is a result of two things: the lower rate of Alberta tax and the fact that the income allocation formula arbitrarily allocated more profits to Alberta than were actually earned there ($46,200, rather than $20,000).

Separate Corporation

If a separate Alberta corporation is used, all actual profits in Alberta belong to the Alberta corporation, which is a separate entity, and so only the Alberta rate of tax applies on the actual expansion profits.

Tax: 10% × $20,000	**$2,000**

This situation demonstrates how the amount of tax varies significantly according to the expansion method employed. The three methods can be summarized as follows:

	Expansion profit	Tax	Effective rate
Direct sales	$20,000	$2,400	12%
Branch location	20,000	1,476	7%
Separate corporation	20,000	2,000	10%

Similar variances may occur when the expansion process involves manufacturing income. Expanding a non-manufacturing business by adding on a manufacturing component, or vice versa, may involve an arbitrary allocation of manufacturing and non-manufacturing income that may well affect the tax reduction available for manufacturing and processing profits. The impact of utilizing a division structure, rather than a separate corporation structure, in a situation involving manufacturing activities was shown in Chapter 11.

• **Repatriation of capital and accumulated profits**   The process of repatriating the original capital invested as well as the accumulated expansion profits is similar under both structures—division and separate corporation—for domestic expansion that does not involve new equity participants. As the division structure combines the expansion activity with existing activities within the same entity, repatriation is not an issue. However, when the expansion is housed in a separate, wholly owned subsidiary corporation, any dividends normally flow tax-free between the corporations, with the result that no tax implications arise on repatriation (see Chapters 11, 13, and 14).

B. Expansion with New Equity Participants

It is common for an existing business enterprise to encounter expansion opportunities when existing financial resources are inadequate. In such situations, the decision maker must choose between two strategies: limited expansion and slow growth, or rapid expansion through the raising of additional equity from new participants. Choosing the latter course raises a number of questions:

1. Will the new equity members share in the existing operations as well as the expansion activity or just in the expansion activity?

2. Will the new participants be active in the business or be passive investors?

3. Will the new participants consist of a small number of large investors or a greater number of smaller investors?

4. Can the expansion be divided into several separate operations with different participants for each?

5. How much equity must be given up to achieve the desired level of expansion?

Clearly, once a company decides to involve additional equity participants in a business expansion, it must then choose between alternative business strategies and then choose between alternative business structures. The choices it makes will be influenced greatly by the nature of the expansion business and the financial circumstances of the existing business. Regarding structure, the decision maker has three alternatives available, each of which was discussed in previous chapters:

- separate corporation
- standard partnership
- limited partnership

Because each of these three structures has different tax implications that lead to different cash flows, it is important to match the alternative structure with the range of alternative strategies for including new equity participants. In most cases, the strategy will influence the structure, but in some cases, the structure will influence the strategy. The process of determining potential cash flows is basically the same whether one is expanding an enterprise with new equity or with internal resources; in either case, the process centres on determining how future profits will be taxed, how operating losses will be used, how losses will be treated if the expansion fails, and how capital and accumulated profits will be repatriated for reinvestment. However, when new equity participants are included, the analysis is more complex because it includes the new participants as well as the initiator.

The tax implications of the alternative structures were examined in detail in two separate case studies in Chapters 15 and 16. In Chapter 15, a corporation that operated a clothing wholesale business expanded into clothing manufacturing with a new equity participant, who provided both capital and manufacturing expertise. In this particular case, the expansion strategy was predetermined—it required a single active participant with specific expertise. As a result, the alternative structures for the expansion were limited to either a separate corporation or a separate partnership, and the cash-flow implications were different for each participant.

The example of an expansion provided in Chapter 16 was quite different. The initiator wanted to expand his chain of restaurants and could do so by seeking out a small number of large, passive investors or a larger number of smaller passive investors. Also, it was possible to recruit different investors for each new location. In this case, the different attributes of the available structures significantly influenced the strategy chosen—the limited partnership, which provides a minimum of risk to passive investors along with preferential treatment of tax losses. Choosing this structure meant seeking out a larger number of smaller, passive investors for each location. By choosing this structure, the initiator as well as the investors achieved an enhanced return on investment. Also, by leasing the required real estate and equipment, the initiator—who had limited financial resources—was able to grasp the opportunities at hand and maintain control of the organization while giving up a minimum of equity.

- **Expansion of the small business deduction**   In some expansion situations, it may be desirable to give up more equity, rather than less, in order to achieve higher after-tax returns. This is especially desirable in private corporations if the expansion structure can increase the amount of income subject to the lower rate of corporate tax. Consider the following situation:

Situation: Roller Ltd. operates a number of amusement centres, each of which includes a roller rink and an indoor miniature golf facility. The existing operations generate profits in excess of $500,000 annually. Three new location opportunities exist, each of which has an annual profit potential of $150,000 and requires a capital investment of $500,000. It is important to expand rapidly; otherwise, the locations may be lost to competitors. Roller Ltd. has the financial strength to raise $1,000,000, which is two-thirds of what is required to expand to three new locations. Roller Ltd. also needs strong managers to run the locations. This introduces the possibility of raising equity capital from people who will also be active in the business. For demonstration purposes, Roller's top tax rate is assumed to be 25%.

Analysis:

One obvious possibility is to obtain three separate active participants (one for each location). Each participant would contribute one-third of the $500,000 required for a given location. Each location would be owned 67% by Roller Ltd. and 33% by the manager-participant and could be organized as either a separate partnership or a corporation. By following this course of action, Roller Ltd. would achieve the following return on investment:

Profits ($150,000 × 3)	$450,000
Tax @ 25%	(112,500)
After-tax profit	$337,500
Roller's share (⅔ of $337,500)	$225,000
Return on investment:	
$\dfrac{\$225,000}{\$1,000,000} =$	22.5%

This return would be the same whether a given location was run as a partnership or a corporation. If partnerships were used, profits would be allocated to Roller Ltd. and taxed at the high corporate rate. If separate corporations were used, each new corporation would be associated with Roller Ltd. because it controls each corporation, and therefore no additional small business deduction would be achieved (see Chapter 13).

The small business deduction base could be expanded by varying the ownership ratios and using a separate corporation structure. This would provide greater after-tax returns to all parties. For example, if Roller Ltd. relinquished 50% ownership of each separate location and used separate corporations, none of the corporations would be associated (see Chapter 13) and each would be entitled to the lower corporate tax rate of approximately 15% (for demonstration purposes). This structure (see the top of next page) would provide a greater after-tax profit to Roller Ltd. and require a reduced capital investment of $750,000 ($250,000 × 3).

This structure would provide a 25.5% return to Roller Ltd., as shown below.

Profit from each location	$150,000
Tax @ 15%	(22,500)
After-tax profit	$127,500
After-tax profit of three locations	
($127,500 × 3)	$382,500
Roller's share (50%)	$191,250
Return on investment:	
$\dfrac{\$191,250}{\$750,000} =$	25.5%

By giving up one-half, rather than one-third, of the equity, Roller Ltd. has reduced its share of after-tax profits by only $33,750 ($225,000 − $191,250), increased the after-tax return on investment from 22.5% to 25.5%, and saved $250,000 of cash resources, which can be used for other expansion opportunities.

The above discussion and examples show that cash returns on domestic expansion activities, whether funded with internal resources or additional equity, can be significantly affected by the structure chosen to implement the activities. In many cases, the optimum structure is not obvious, and the decision maker must explore and test a number of alternatives before determining which is best in terms of cash flow, tax treatment, and other non–tax-related factors.

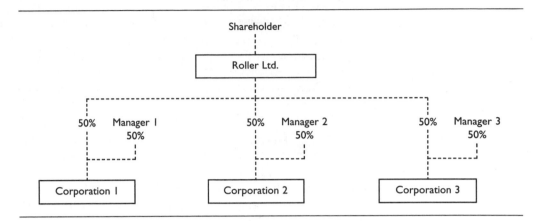

II. International Business Expansion

The expansion of a Canadian business enterprise into foreign markets is complicated because tax is imposed in the foreign jurisdiction as well as in Canada. Ultimately, cash will flow from the foreign operations back to Canada for reinvestment. It is vital to determine the amount and timing of tax when projecting future returns from such expansion. A Canadian business entity can utilize a number of alternative organization structures when expanding into a foreign jurisdiction. This part of the chapter briefly identifies and examines the fundamental tax implications of foreign business structures.

A. Basic Issues

There are two fundamental approaches to conducting foreign business operations. The foreign activity can be conducted from the home base in the form of direct export sales to consumers or distributors, or the foreign activity can be conducted by developing a formal foreign structure that involves a physical presence in the foreign jurisdiction. Formal structures can include the following:

1. A simple branch location.

2. A separate foreign corporation as a subsidiary of the Canadian parent corporation.

3. A separate foreign joint venture, partnership, or limited partnership.

4. An advanced, broadly based foreign structure that includes foreign holding corporations, finance companies, and sales and manufacturing entities.

The primary business structures for foreign expansion activities are diagrammed in Exhibit 20-1. These basic structures were reviewed briefly in Chapter 3 and are discussed in more detail later in this chapter. Each has different business, legal, and tax consequences. From a tax perspective, the main issues are these:

1. To what extent is tax imposed by the foreign jurisdiction on foreign business operations?

2. How does Canadian tax apply on the foreign business profits? And how can losses on foreign operations be utilized, should they occur?

Exhibit 20-1:

Basic Structures for Foreign Expansion

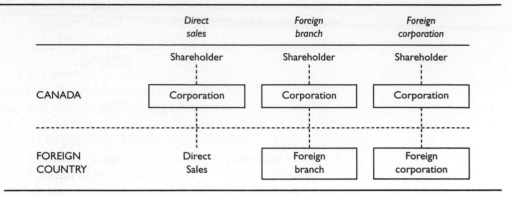

3. What tax treatment is applied to transactions between the foreign operation and the Canadian owner? The following types of transactions may occur:

- Intercompany sales of products and services between the Canadian entity and the foreign entity (intercompany pricing).
- The transfer of tangible and intangible assets from the Canadian entity to the foreign entity.
- The payment of rents or royalties on property leased by the Canadian entity to the foreign entity.
- The receipt of dividends from the repatriation of profits of a foreign subsidiary corporation.
- The payment of interest by the foreign entity to the Canadian entity on loans advanced to finance the foreign operations.
- Inter-entity management fees.
- The allocation of costs incurred by the home entity on behalf of the foreign entity.
- The reorganization of foreign structures; for example, the converting of a branch operation into a foreign subsidiary.

These issues are discussed below in terms of the three primary structures outlined in Exhibit 20-1. The discussions identify only the general tax principles relating to foreign operations, as the specific tax treatment will vary from country to country. As described in Chapter 3, Canada has entered into bilateral tax agreements with many countries, and each agreement identifies which jurisdiction has authority to impose tax on cross-border activities.

B. Foreign Currencies

Foreign exchange gains or losses will occur when transactions are completed in a foreign currency because exchange rates fluctuate constantly. For example, goods or services may be sold, accounts receivable collected, inventory purchased, accounts payable settled, capital assets purchased and sold, and long-term loans made, all in a foreign currency. Two questions must be answered when foreign exchange gains or losses occur on these types of transactions.

1. Is the gain or loss a capital transaction resulting in a capital gain or loss or, is it an income transaction resulting in business income or loss?

2. Should the foreign exchange gain or loss be recognized for tax purposes on an accrual basis or only when the transaction is ultimately settled?

The *Income Tax Act* is silent on these issues and so the tax treatment of foreign exchange gains or losses is determined by examining the underlying transaction that created it. For example, *transactions relating to the trading operations* of a business such as the sales, accounts receivable, accounts payable, inventory and short-term operating loans are treated as income transactions and result in *business gains or losses*. Balance sheet items will be settled at some time after they are created (inventory sold, accounts receivable collected, accounts payable and operating loans repaid). For example, an account receivable may be recorded at the time of a sale at one exchange rate but will be collected at a different rate. At the balance sheet date, the uncollected accounts receivable must be recorded at the current exchange rate and any gain or loss in relation to the original exchange rate is recognized for tax purposes. This means that *exchange gains or losses on income items from trading operations must be accrued* and recognized for tax purposes before they are settled[1]. On the other hand, foreign exchange gains or losses relating to the acquisition and sale of *capital assets* (equipment, land and buildings, investments in subsidiaries, patents, franchises, and so on) or long-term loans used to fund the acquisition of capital assets are considered to be *capital gains or losses*. However, the accrual method is not used for these gains. Foreign exchange gains that are capital in nature are only recognized for tax purposes when they are settled—when assets are sold, notes receivable are collected, or when capital loans are repaid.[2]

C. Direct Export Sales

From a tax perspective, direct sales by a Canadian company to a foreign market are treated quite simply. Recall from Chapter 3 that Canadian taxpayers are subject to Canadian tax on their world income. This means that direct sales by a Canadian business corporation to a foreign market are treated as if they were domestic sales and are fully taxable in Canada as business income.

For foreign tax purposes, most foreign countries tax only those non-residents who carry on business in the foreign country. At issue is what constitutes "carrying on a business." The tax treaty between Canada and the particular country will define the term more specifically. Usually, the term applies to business activity implemented from a permanent establishment in the foreign country. For example, the Canada–U.S. tax convention defines "permanent establishment" as a fixed place of business through which the foreign business operation is carried on; it includes a place of management, a branch, an office, and a factory.[3] However, a fixed place of business used solely for the storage, display, or delivery of merchandise is deemed not to be a permanent establishment. It should be noted that an enterprise providing extensive *services* to the other country without a fixed place of business may be *deemed to have a permanent establishment* in certain circumstances. This will occur when services are provided for an aggregate of 183 days in a 12-month period and relate to the same or connected projects. It will also occur when the services are performed by an individual who is present in the other country for periods of 183 days or more in a 12-month period and 50% of the active gross revenues of the enterprise are from services performed by the individual in the other country. Using these definitions as a yardstick, expansion activities into foreign markets by direct export sales usually are not subject to tax in the foreign country.

It is important to recognize that the definition of a "permanent establishment" may vary from treaty to treaty. Because of this, the specific definition used by the particular country targeted for expansion should be examined before export activities are undertaken.

D. Foreign Branch Location

A Canadian business corporation, rather than penetrating foreign markets by direct export sales, may decide to establish a physical presence in the foreign country in the form of a branch location (see Exhibit 20-1). A Canadian corporation can establish a foreign branch

---

1 IT-95R.
2 IT-95R.
3 Article V, Canada–U.S. Tax Convention (2008—Fifth Protocol).

simply by renting office space to house foreign personnel, who then perform sales, service, and administrative functions relating to the development of the foreign operations.

It is important to recognize that the foreign branch location is part of the Canadian corporation and does not constitute a separate legal entity. The tax treatment of profits earned by the foreign branch location is as follows:

1. Because the branch constitutes a permanent establishment in the foreign country, branch profits will be subject to the income taxes applicable in the foreign jurisdiction.

2. The foreign branch profits form part of the world income of the Canadian corporation (see Chapter 3) and are therefore also taxable in Canada as normal business income.

3. Canadian taxes payable on the business profits of the foreign branch can be reduced by the foreign tax credit (federal and provincial), which, within limits, provides for a Canadian tax reduction by the amount of foreign taxes paid.[4] The foreign tax credit calculation is discussed later in this chapter.

The impact of this tax treatment is demonstrated in the following example:

Situation: Canadian Ltd. maintains a branch business operation in a foreign country, from which it earns business income in a particular year. The foreign country imposes two rates of tax on corporate income—20% on the first $100,000 of income and 40% on income in excess of $100,000. The Canadian corporation is subject to a 25% tax rate (assumed), and its shareholders pay tax at the highest personal rate.

Analysis: The profits earned by the foreign branch are subject to three levels of taxation. First, the foreign profits are taxed in the foreign country. Second, the foreign profits are taxed within the Canadian corporation. And third, the Canadian shareholders are taxed when the profits are distributed as Canadian dividends from the Canadian corporation. The three levels of tax are calculated, as shown below, using the two foreign tax rates of 20% and 40% and assuming $1,000 of business profits in each category.

Foreign Branch	1st $100,000 of profits 20%	Profits over $100,000 40%
Foreign tax:		
Foreign income	$1,000	$1,000
Foreign tax	(200)	(400)
	800	600
Canadian corporate tax:		
Federal and provincial tax @ 25% of $1,000	(250)	(250)
Foreign tax credit	200	(250)
Net corporate tax	(50)	–0–
After-tax profit to Canadian corporation	750	600
Shareholder tax:		
Tax on dividend to shareholder net of dividend		
tax credit (28% of eligible dividend)*	(210)	(168)
Net cash to shareholder	$ 540	$ 432

---

4   ITA 126(2); IT-270R3.

Note that in this calculation, the tax on branch profits that were subject to a 20% foreign tax rate was fully credited against the Canadian tax rate of 25% by the foreign tax credit. The Canadian corporate tax simply represents the difference between the Canadian tax rate of 25% and the foreign tax rate of 20% (25% − 20% = 5%). However, on foreign profits taxed at the foreign rate of 40%, the Canadian foreign tax credit was limited to the amount of Canadian taxes paid on the foreign income (25%) and so the higher foreign tax rate of 40% prevailed. As a result of the limitation applied to the foreign tax credit in Canada, foreign branch profits are always taxed at the higher rate, whether foreign or Canadian.

The total of the taxes paid in the above example on $1,000 of foreign-branch income is calculated in the following table:

Foreign tax rate	20%	40%
Foreign tax	$200	$400
Canadian corporate tax	50	–0–
Canadian shareholder tax	210	168
Total foreign and Canadian taxes	$460	$568
Effective rate of tax	46%	57%

* Assumed to be eligible dividend subject to the higher dividend tax credit.

It is interesting to note that the foreign income earned by the branch ultimately is translated into a Canadian dividend when it is distributed to the Canadian shareholders. Consequently, the Canadian shareholder is entitled to a dividend tax credit for corporate taxes paid, even though all or at least some of the corporate taxes were paid to a foreign jurisdiction.

This example indicates that the foreign branch structure does not provide any tax benefits when the entity is operating in a country that imposes lower tax rates than Canada. A lower foreign tax rate of 20% simply means that a portion of the normal Canadian tax of 25% (assumed) is paid to the foreign jurisdiction.

However, the branch structure does provide one major advantage over the foreign corporation structure: Losses incurred by the foreign branch can immediately be used to offset profits made in Canada, thereby reducing Canadian taxes otherwise payable. This resulting increased cash flow can be retained in Canada or reinvested in the branch to enhance the opportunity for long-term success.

Future profits accumulated in the foreign branch operation usually can be repatriated to the Canadian corporate owner without further tax consequences. As the branch is part of the Canadian company, profit distributions do not constitute a dividend payment and therefore do not attract any foreign withholding taxes, as they would if a foreign subsidiary corporation had been established. (This is discussed below.) However, some foreign countries *do* impose a special additional *branch tax* equivalent to the tax imposed on the payment of dividends; decision makers should investigate this before choosing the branch structure.[5] Normally, the foreign branch tax is eliminated by the Canadian foreign tax credit.

E. Foreign Subsidiary Corporation

A company that expands into foreign markets by establishing a foreign corporation as a subsidiary of the Canadian corporation faces entirely different tax consequences than does a company that chooses the branch structure. Business profits earned by a foreign subsidiary corporation are subject to the following tax treatment:

---

5   The concept of a branch tax is described in IT-137R3; see also ITA 219.

1. The subsidiary corporation, being incorporated in the foreign jurisdiction, is subject to the prevailing income taxes of the foreign country.

2. As the foreign corporation is not a resident of Canada, it is not subject to Canadian tax on business profits earned within the corporation.

3. After-tax profits accumulated within the foreign corporation can be distributed to the Canadian parent corporation as a dividend. As described in Chapter 11, dividends received from a foreign affiliate are excluded from corporate taxable income and are therefore not subject to Canadian corporate tax.

4. Most countries impose a special tax on dividends paid to a foreign shareholder. The tax is withheld and remitted to the foreign jurisdiction by the payer. For example, the United States imposes a 5% withholding tax on dividends paid to Canadian shareholders.[6] Rates in other countries range from 5% to 25%. As the dividend is not subject to Canadian corporate tax, no foreign tax credit can be claimed to offset the foreign withholding tax on the dividend.

The impact of this tax treatment is demonstrated in the following example:

Situation: Canadian Ltd. carries on business operations in a foreign country through a wholly owned foreign subsidiary corporation. The foreign country imposes a tax rate of 20% on the first $100,000 of business profits, and of 40% on profits in excess of $100,000, as well as a 5% withholding tax on dividends paid to Canada. In Canada, both the Canadian corporation and its shareholders are taxed at the high rates of tax, which is assumed to be 25% for corporations and 45% for individuals.

Analysis: The business profits of the foreign corporation are subject to three levels of tax—foreign corporate tax, foreign tax on dividend distributions to the Canadian corporation, and Canadian tax on dividend distributions from the Canadian company to the Canadian shareholders. The three levels of tax are calculated in the following table, using the two foreign tax rates of 20% and 40% and assuming $1,000 of business profits in each category.

Foreign Subsidiary	1st $100,000 of profits 20%	Profits over $100,000 40%
Foreign tax:		
Foreign income	$1,000	$1,000
Foreign tax	(200)	(400)
After-tax income to foreign corporation	800	600
Foreign withholding tax:		
When dividends are paid (5%)	(40)	(30)
Net received by Canadian corporation	760	570
Canadian corporate tax:		
Corporate tax on foreign dividend	–0–	–0–
Funds available to Canadian corporation	760	570
Canadian shareholder tax:		
Tax on dividends to shareholders net of dividend tax credit (28% of eligible dividend)	(213)	(160)
Net cash to shareholders	$ 547	$ 410

---

6   Article X, Canada–U.S. Tax Convention; IC 76-12R4. The 5% rate applies when the recipient of the dividend is a company owning 10% or more of the voting shares; otherwise, the rate is 15%.

Summary of taxes paid:		
Foreign tax:		
On business income	$ 200	$ 400
On repatriation of dividends	40	30
Canadian corporate tax	–0–	–0–
Canadian shareholder tax	213	160
	$ 453	$ 590
Effective tax rate	45%	59%

This analysis indicates that the types of tax payable, the amounts of tax payable, and the timing of the tax payments are dramatically different when foreign expansion is implemented through a foreign corporation. Exhibit 20-2 compares the branch structure with the corporation structure under two rates of applicable foreign tax by summarizing the two examples given previously.

- **Foreign profits subject to 20% foreign tax**   The assumed 20% foreign tax rate is substantially lower than the assumed Canadian tax rate of 25%. In this situation, the corporation structure provides the lowest tax cost and therefore the highest after-tax cash flow. Because utilizing the corporation structure involves separating the expansion profits from the Canadian corporation, the expansion profits are subject only to the foreign tax rate of 20%; this leaves 80% of the profits available for further foreign expansion activity. In comparison, the branch structure imposes the Canadian rate of tax of 25%; this leaves only 75% of foreign profits for further foreign expansion.

Similarly, the amount of after-tax profits available for repatriation to the Canadian corporation is higher under the corporation structure when the foreign tax rate is substantially lower than the Canadian tax rate. The total tax after repatriation under the corporation structure is 24%; 76% of the foreign profits are thereby available for reinvestment in Canada. When the branch structure is used, however, total taxes are 25% after repatriation; in this case, only 75% of foreign earnings are available for Canadian reinvestment.

Exhibit 20-2:

Tax Treatment of
Foreign Branch versus
Foreign Corporation

	Foreign tax 20%		Foreign tax 40%	
	Branch	Corporation	Branch	Corporation
1. Tax paid when foreign profits are earned	$250	$200	$400	$400
2. Tax paid when foreign profits are repatriated*	–0–	40	–0–	30
	250	240	400	430
3. Tax paid when distributed to Canadian shareholders	210	213	168	160
Total	$460	$453	$568	$590
4. Effective tax rate	46%	45%	57%	59%

*Ignores possible foreign branch tax that is normally eliminated by the Canadian foreign tax credit.

And finally, the corporation structure increases the ultimate returns available to the shareholders of the Canadian corporation when dividends are declared in that it increases their overall yield by 1% as a result of Canadian reduced taxes (46% − 45% = 1%).

• **Foreign profits subject to 40% foreign tax**   As indicated in Exhibit 20-2, the reverse results occur when foreign tax rates are higher than the Canadian rates—the branch structure creates *greater* cash-flow returns. When foreign tax rates are 40%, both the branch structure and the corporation structure create immediate tax on foreign profits earned at a rate of 40%; this leaves the same after-tax funds available for further foreign expansion. However, when profits are being repatriated, the foreign corporation is subject to a withholding tax whereas the branch is not. Therefore, under the corporation structure, the Canadian parent incurs total taxes of $430, or 43%, upon repatriation, leaving only 57% of the foreign profits available for reinvestment or for distribution to the Canadian shareholders. Note, as well, that the foreign corporation structure results in overall taxes of 59% after distribution to the Canadian shareholders because of the high foreign taxes paid on expansion profits.

Although the choice of foreign structure may be influenced by a number of non–tax-related issues—business and legal considerations and so on—it is important to examine how tax treatment affects expansion cash flows under the basic alternatives, keeping in mind the anticipated cash requirements for further foreign expansion, the repatriation requirements, and the effect on distributions to Canadian shareholders. A number of other tax issues aside from this one arise when a foreign structure is being developed. These are discussed briefly below.

F. Alternative Cash Flows from a Foreign Subsidiary

The establishing of a foreign entity often requires significant support by the home-based entity. For example, the Canadian corporation may provide such assets as equipment, capital, rights to use patents and licences, and management services to the foreign operation. If a branch structure is used, these types of support usually have no tax implications, as the foreign branch is simply a part of the Canadian corporation. However, establishing a subsidiary corporation as a separate legal entity results in a different relationship. Consider the structure outlined in Exhibit 20-3.

The structure indicates that the Canadian parent corporation provides equity capital and also supplies the foreign corporation with the following: capital funds (through intercorporate loans), equipment for use in the foreign operations, production technology, and certain management services. Consequently, the foreign entity, as a separate corporation, may be required to pay for the use of those assets and services. This payment may take the form of interest, rents, royalties, and management fees.

Such payments are deductible from the foreign corporation's income and result in reduced profits to the foreign corporation and increased profits to the Canadian parent corporation. In effect, foreign income is shifted to Canada before foreign income tax is applied. Because of this, foreign countries impose a special withholding tax on such payments to nonresidents. The amount of withholding tax varies from country to country and is often modified by the applicable international tax treaty.[7] For example, the following tax rates apply to payments from an American subsidiary to its Canadian parent:

---

7   IC 76-12R6 (summary of withholding tax rates for treaty countries).

Exhibit 20-3:

Cash Flows between Foreign Subsidiary and Canadian Parent

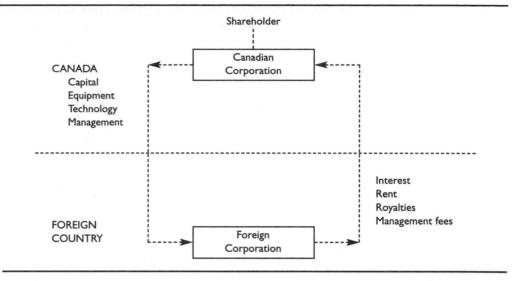

Interest	0%
Rent	25
Royalties	10[†]
Management fees	–0–

† Royalties for copyright for literary, dramatic musical, or other artistic work and/or royalties for computer software, a patent concerning industrial, commercial, or scientific experience have a 0% rate.

Any interest, rent, royalty, or management fee received by the Canadian corporation from its foreign subsidiary is fully taxable in Canada as property income or business income. The combination of Canadian tax and foreign withholding tax usually does not result in double taxation because the amount of Canadian tax is reduced by the foreign tax credit. For example, the payment of $10,000 of royalty from the foreign subsidiary to the Canadian parent would normally be taxed as shown in the following table:

Foreign tax:		
Royalty paid	$10,000	
Withholding tax @ 10%		$1,000
Canadian tax:		
Income	$10,000	
Corporate tax @ 25% (assumed)	$ 2,500	
Foreign tax credit	(1,000)	$1,500
Total foreign and Canadian tax		$2,500

Note that the total tax of $2,500 corresponds to the Canadian tax rate of 25%. The imposition of the withholding tax merely results in an allocation of the Canadian rate of tax between Canada and the foreign jurisdiction. Also, note that the treatment of interest, rents, royalties, and management fees is different from the treatment of dividends. As explained previously, the dividends are not taxable to the Canadian corporation, and so the foreign withholding tax on dividends is not available for a Canadian foreign tax credit.

All of this indicates that the manner in which a Canadian parent corporation provides support for its foreign subsidiary corporation can affect the ultimate cash returns on investment. For example, when the foreign subsidiary corporation is subject to a much lower tax rate than the Canadian parent, it may be advisable to provide additional capital to the subsidiary in the form of share capital bearing dividends as opposed to loans bearing interest. The payment of loan interest reduces foreign profits and shifts income to Canada, where it is taxed at the higher rate; whereas the provision of additional share capital leaves greater profits in the foreign subsidiary, which takes advantage of the lower corporate tax rate. The cash-flow analysis is the same as the one that was used to compare the corporation structure with the branch structure earlier in this chapter. Conversely, when foreign tax rates are much higher, funding by debt shifts income from the foreign entity to the Canadian corporation in the form of interest payments, the result being lower overall tax rates.

In order to avoid excessive shifting of profits from one country to another, most foreign countries have special tax provisions that limit the deductibility of expenses paid to non-resident parent corporations when such expenses are unreasonably high. In other words, fair pricing rules generally prevail. However, within limits, support for foreign operations can be designed in such a way that the amount of foreign and Canadian tax payable is minimized and the timing of that tax is optimized.

G. Foreign Tax Credit

Both the taxation of foreign branch income and the payments from a corporate subsidiary of dividends, interest, rent, royalties, and management fees are significantly affected by the application of this country's foreign tax credit. As indicated previously, the foreign tax credit is designed to limit the total tax to an amount that is no greater than the one imposed by the country with the higher rate of tax. (The actual formula can be obtained by examining the appropriate interpretation bulletins and is not discussed in this chapter.)[8]

While the concept appears simple, the actual calculation of the foreign tax credit is rather complex. As well, it is important to recognize that the calculation does not always provide the intended result. The Canadian foreign tax credit can only be applied to the foreign taxes on foreign income as determined by Canadian tax law. Income, however, may be determined differently in other countries in accordance with their procedures for calculating income and recognizing expenses. For example, a foreign branch operation that holds depreciable property may be subject to one rate of capital cost allowance in the foreign country and a considerably different rate in Canada. In such cases, the annual branch profits from which foreign tax is calculated may be different from those from which Canadian tax is calculated. This difference may result in a combined foreign and Canadian tax that is greater than the conceptual maximum of the highest tax rate of either country.

Canadian tax law deals with this problem by permitting companies with unused tax credits on foreign business income to carry those credits back three years and forward 10 years.[9] While this reduces the risk of losing foreign tax credits, it also alters the normal timing for the tax payments, which, in turn, affects cash flow and return on investment.

The carry-over provisions do not apply to unused foreign tax credits on non-business income. As a result, rents, interest, and royalties paid by a foreign subsidiary, when those items constitute property income to the Canadian parent, cannot be carried back or forward if they cannot be used in the current year. However, foreign taxes on non-business income that are not offset by a foreign tax credit can be deducted as a normal business expense.[10] This provides partial, though not total, relief from double taxation.

---

8 ITA 126(1), (2); IT-183, IT-270R3.
9 ITA 126(2); IT-520.
10 ITA 20(11), (12); IT-506.

In summary, decision makers who are contemplating a foreign expansion must consider not only the type of structure but also the nature of the transactions between Canada and the foreign entity when studying the resulting cash-flow implications.

H. Intercompany Transfer Pricing

An important aspect of international expansion involves the treatment applied to sales of products from the Canadian parent to its foreign subsidiary corporation. Consider the following three simple examples:

1. A Canadian manufacturing company sells finished products to its foreign subsidiary for distribution in the foreign market.

2. A Canadian company manufactures component parts in Canada and sells them to a foreign subsidiary for assembly and foreign-market distribution.

3. A Canadian company sells raw materials to a foreign subsidiary for processing, manufacturing, and foreign-market distribution.

In each of these examples, some of the business process is begun in one country and completed in another country. The question arises as to how much profit belongs to each country. Whenever there is a difference in tax rates between the Canadian parent corporation and the foreign subsidiary corporation, there is a desire to shift profits to the country with the lowest tax rate. The Canadian parent may attempt to either "underprice" or "overprice" such transactions—in other words, to manipulate the prices. Profits can also be shifted by means of service charges, commissions, interest charges, rents, and royalties.

Canadian tax law has adopted a reasonableness test with respect to the pricing of goods sold to foreign subsidiary corporations. As a result, products sold to a foreign subsidiary, whatever their stage of completion, are deemed to have been sold at a price that would reasonably have been expected in similar circumstances had the parties been dealing at arm's length.[11] It is often difficult to determine what constitutes "reasonable." Canada and many other countries have endorsed the pricing methods recommended by the Organization for Economic Cooperation and Development for establishing reasonable transfer prices.[12]

The most common method is to base the transfer price for non–arm's-length transactions on comparable arm's-length selling prices. In effect, a company is deemed to have sold the goods to its subsidiary at the same price at which it sells the goods to outside parties. When appropriate comparables are not available, two other specific methods are endorsed. One is the "cost plus" method, which is based on a reasonable mark-up over the vendor's actual cost for the product sold. The other is the "resale price" method, which starts with the foreign subsidiary's ultimate customer selling price and works backward by deducting an appropriate profit margin.

It is important to recognize that in order to avoid double taxation on international transfers, a pricing policy must be established that is based on normal commercial considerations, rather than on tax considerations. While some flexibility exists in the system, the consequences of extreme variations are significant and undesirable.

I. Converting a Foreign Branch to a Foreign Subsidiary

Foreign business expansion often involves a progression from one structure to another. For example, when expansion requires a physical presence in a foreign country, the branch structure may initially be used because of its simplicity and low cost and because branch losses in the start-up years can be offset against the

---

11 ITA 69; IT-468R.
12 IC 87-2R; ITA 247.

Exhibit 20-4:

Incorporation of a Foreign Branch

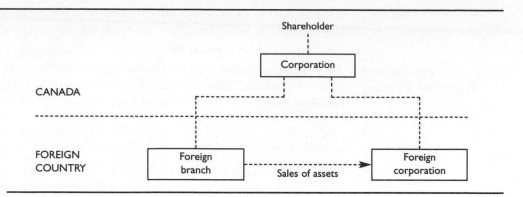

Canadian corporation's other taxable income. However, at some point, it may be necessary to convert the foreign branch into a foreign subsidiary corporation. As diagrammed in Exhibit 20-4, this procedure involves the transfer of assets, such as inventory, equipment, and goodwill, from the branch to the foreign corporation. As the branch is part of the Canadian corporation, the transfer of assets is actually between the Canadian corporation and the newly established foreign subsidiary corporation.

In Chapter 12, it was established that assets can be transferred from one corporation to another at tax values, rather than at fair market values. However, this option, under Canadian tax law, is available only when the assets are being transferred to another Canadian corporation. Usually, foreign-branch assets can be transferred to a foreign corporation only at fair market values; this results in Canadian tax if the values of those assets exceed their tax costs.

If the branch assets will result in a significant tax liability on incorporation, the Canadian corporation can choose to retain ownership of certain assets. For example, the Canadian corporation can retain ownership of physical assets, such as buildings and equipment, and lease them to the foreign corporation. The same corporation can also retain intangible assets, such as patents and goodwill, in which case the foreign corporation will pay royalties for their use. Such payment of rents and royalties amounts to a shifting of profits from the foreign company to Canada, and the Canadian corporation will be subject to a foreign withholding tax as previously described. This may or may not be advantageous—it depends on the income tax rates applicable on foreign income.

The process of deciding which form of business structure to utilize for foreign expansion must include consideration of the potential tax implications should it become necessary to alter the structure at some future time. International reorganizations do not have the same flexibility as domestic reorganizations.

The preceding discussions have provided a general perspective on the taxation issues relating to the expansion of a business to foreign jurisdictions. Clearly, the decision to embark on international business activities has cash-flow implications, and a significant amount of advance consideration is required when it comes to choosing the most appropriate organizational structure.

III. Summary and Conclusion

This chapter has examined the tax implications relating to the expansion of a business enterprise. An expansion can be conducted using any of a number of alternative business structures, each of which affects in a different manner how and when expansion profits are taxed, how operating losses may be used to generate tax savings, how tax savings are created if the expansion is discontinued, and how accumulated profits are taxed on repatriation.

Expansion can be domestic or foreign. A domestic expansion using internal resources can be structured utilizing either a division of the existing corporation or a separate operating corporation. Each of these structures has its own tax consequences relating to the timing and nature of tax savings resulting from expansion losses. As well, each affects, in a different manner, the application of provincial taxes and the taxes on manufacturing and processing activities.

When domestic expansion cannot be funded with internal resources, it may be necessary to include additional new equity participants. Such expansion activities can utilize a separate corporation, a standard partnership, or a limited partnership. These structures can be matched to alternative strategies that determine whether the new participants will be active or passive investors; whether there will be a small number of large investors or a greater number of smaller investors; and whether those investors will participate in all or only parts of the expansion program. In some cases, it may be preferable to give up more equity than is necessary, in order to achieve tax savings from an expanded small business deduction base and thereby greater after-tax returns on investment.

Expansion across international boundaries is even more complex because of the imposition of foreign income taxes and the need to integrate those taxes with the Canadian tax system. The three basic methods of achieving a foreign expansion are direct export sales, the establishment of a foreign branch location, and the formation of a separate foreign subsidiary corporation. Direct export sales are taxed only in Canada. Foreign profits earned by a foreign branch are subject to both foreign and Canadian income tax; but the Canadian foreign tax credit can be applied to ensure that the combined rate of tax is no more than that of the country with the higher tax rate. In addition, foreign branch losses can be offset against Canadian profits. Income earned by a foreign subsidiary corporation is at first taxed only in the foreign country, and after-tax profits are available for further foreign expansion. However, profits distributed by a foreign corporation as dividends are subject to a further foreign withholding tax.

While the decision to expand a business enterprise is based primarily on business and economic considerations, the methods chosen to implement that expansion can significantly affect the eventual cash returns. The expansion process therefore must involve examining alternative business structures and anticipating possible future results and scenarios; only in this way can the potential economic benefits be properly assessed.

Visit the Canadian Income Taxation Web site at **www.mcgrawhill.ca/ olc/buckwold** to view any updated tax information.

Review Questions

1. Domestic and international expansion decisions, like any investment decisions, should attempt to utilize a structure that will minimize the start-up cash requirements and maximize the cash returns to the initiator. Briefly outline the fundamental tax considerations that are relevant to the expansion process.

2. What are the two basic organization structures that can be used for domestic expansion activities without the participation of new equity investors? What is the major difference between these structures regarding tax?

3. The rates of applicable provincial tax and tax on manufacturing profits may be different solely as a result of the expansion structure chosen for new activities. Explain why.

4. What are the basic organization structures that can be used for domestic expansion activities requiring additional capital from new equity participants?

5. When new equity participants are required in order to complete an expansion, what decisions must be made before an analysis of the organizational structure is performed?

6. Is it possible to increase the after-tax rate of return by choosing to give up more equity, rather than less, when new equity participants are required for expansion? Explain.

7. What are the primary business structures used to conduct foreign expansion activities?

8. In most cases, what must be true before a Canadian entity will be subject to foreign taxes on foreign business activities?

9. When the tax rates in a foreign country are lower than Canadian tax rates, will the use of a foreign branch structure to conduct the Canadian entity's foreign activities be advantageous? Explain.

10. In what circumstances is a foreign branch structure preferable to a foreign corporation structure?

11. Assume that a Canadian individual owns a substantial portion of a foreign corporation's shares and receives a dividend from them. Would the tax treatment applied to that dividend be different if it were first paid to a Canadian corporation owned by that individual?

12. "If foreign tax rates are the same as Canadian tax rates, a Canadian corporation conducting profitable foreign activities will not care whether a foreign branch or a foreign corporation is used to house the foreign operations." Is this statement true? Explain.

13. A Canadian business corporation may, in addition to providing equity capital, support its foreign operations by providing loan capital, management services, technology, and equipment. What general implications does the foreign organization structure (branch versus corporation) have on these additional support activities?

14. Why may a Canadian business entity attempt to underprice or overprice products sold to its foreign subsidiary corporation? How do Canadian tax laws treat such transactions?

15. What tax consequences may result when the business operations of a foreign branch are transferred to a newly created foreign subsidiary corporation? How does this compare with the tax treatment resulting from the transfer of a Canadian branch operation to a Canadian subsidiary corporation?

Problems

PROBLEM ONE

Sanford Pipe Ltd. is a Canadian corporation operating a profitable business in eastern Canada. Four years ago, the company attempted to expand its operations to northern Mexico. At that time, Sanford invested $700,000 in a newly created Mexican subsidiary corporation. That corporation used those funds to acquire special equipment and as working capital for the new venture.

From the beginning, the foreign operations were plagued by a number of unexpected setbacks, including labour and production problems. As these setbacks occurred, Sanford contributed additional cash to keep the operations afloat. Sanford finally recognized that the Mexican subsidiary had no future and decided to close it. After the equipment was sold and all liabilities were paid, the Mexican corporation was wound up, and Sanford received $200,000.

The financial results of the Mexican venture are summarized below.

Year	Losses incurred	Cash provided by Sanford
20X1	$300,000	$ 700,000
20X2	200,000	100,000
20X3	200,000	200,000
20X4	100,000	–0–
	$800,000	$1,000,000

The president of Sanford regretted the decision to undertake the foreign expansion. Not only did it result in a substantial loss, but the cash requirements also resulted in the company forgoing a number of other opportunities that could have yielded 15% after tax. Assume Sanford is subject to a 25% corporate tax rate.

Required:

1. Determine the after-tax loss in cash flow terms to Sanford as a result of the foreign venture.

2. If the foreign venture had been organized as a foreign branch of Sanford, how much would it have lost?

PROBLEM TWO

Kronston Ltd. is a Canadian-controlled private corporation that imports irrigation equipment from Taiwan for distribution in southwestern Ontario. Last year, the company achieved a profit of $600,000 after tax.

Kronston is interested in expanding its operations to the Okanagan region of British Columbia. It recognizes that to be successful, it will require a committed manager who is familiar with the area and understands the special problems of irrigation in that region.

The Okanagan region is capable of generating profits of $250,000 annually. Sonia Harapiuk lives in Vernon, B.C., and has been active in the irrigation business for many years. She is interested in managing the Okanagan expansion, provided that she can have an equity interest in the venture. Kronston is not averse to this, as Harapiuk has proven expertise in the industry and her equity participation would ensure a long-term commitment. She has requested 50% equity in the venture and has sufficient funds to provide her share of the capital required to start the venture.

Kronston had been thinking of allowing Harapiuk to purchase a 25% interest in the Okanagan activity. The company feels that her participation is important but also sees other alternatives. Before making a decision, the president of Kronston has asked his financial manager to determine the financial cost of allowing Harapiuk to own 50% instead of 25% of the new venture. The project will require a total capital investment by the owners of $800,000. Kronston has other opportunities for investing its funds, and these opportunities can yield pre-tax returns of 25% annually.

Required:

What would be the financial cost to Kronston of permitting Harapiuk to have the equity interest in the new venture that she has requested? Assume corporate tax rates are 15% on income subject to the small business deduction and 25% on other business income.

PROBLEM THREE

Jean Dumenil is a senior executive for Dentex Ltd., a Canadian company operating a national chain of retail stores. His colleague and friend, George Watson, recently gave up his job as marketing manager with Dentex and has moved to the United States to start his own chain of retail stores.

Watson is trying to raise equity capital by selling shares of his new American corporation. He has approached Dumenil and offered him a 25% interest in that corporation in exchange for a $250,000 cash investment. Dumenil has confidence in Watson's abilities and has agreed to the investment. Watson has assured Dumenil that the American corporation will pay regular dividends of $20,000 annually to Dumenil as soon as adequate cash flows permit.

Dumenil is subject to a personal marginal tax rate of 45% on income, except on Canadian dividends, which are taxed at a rate of 28% on eligible dividends and 33% on non-eligible dividends. Watson has informed Dumenil that the American corporation will pay tax at a rate of 40% on its business income. American withholding tax on dividends is 15% if paid to an individual and 5% if paid to a Canadian corporation owning more than 10% of the shares.

Required:

1. Determine the amount of tax that Dumenil will be required to pay if annual dividends of $20,000 are paid.

2. What is the combined rate of foreign tax and Canadian tax that will be paid on Dumenil's share of the American business profits after they are distributed to him as dividends?

3. Would you advise Dumenil to create a Canadian holding corporation to own the shares of the American corporation? Explain, and provide supporting calculations.

4. If Dumenil uses a holding corporation but is going to require the annual dividends of $20,000 for personal use, how should he capitalize the holding corporation with his $250,000? Explain.

Cases

CASE ONE   Klondike Carpets Ltd.

Klondike Carpets Ltd. is a large Winnipeg retailer of home and office flooring. The company is a success because it keeps abreast of market changes and provides personalized service to its customers.

The company is owned by three brothers, each of whom plays a major role in the business operations. George, a CA, handles financing. Walter heads the buying department and travels extensively. Ken is the primary marketing person, the one who instills the concept of "personal service" in the sales organization.

Klondike's profits for the last fiscal year amounted to $550,000 after reasonable salaries to the three managing shareholders. The company has accumulated large cash reserves.

Recently, the brothers have been discussing what to do next in their successful business. They have listened to offers to sell the company that, if accepted, would give them sufficient net capital to live a comfortable life. But they have also considered just staying the way they are (that is, a successful local business) and letting their wealth accumulate. This sounds attractive, but they are all young enough to seriously entertain expansion possibilities.

Recently, Ken completed a tour of Canada and targeted 10 cities that he thought could support a successful operation like the one in Winnipeg.

The Winnipeg operation has two locations—the main store on Portage Avenue and a branch in Polo Park. The branch is managed by Shirley Friesen, who is exceptional in that she runs the business as if she owns it. In the previous year, she was rewarded with a bonus of 10% of profits.

Walter has expressed concern that Shirley, with her expertise and personality, may soon open her own store in competition. Although she does not currently have any substantial amount of capital, Walter is aware that she saves her entire bonus as well as a portion of her regular salary.

The brothers plan to meet to discuss these current issues. In preparation, George has assembled the following information:

Winnipeg branch store

Current profits	$120,000
Major assets:	
Working capital and inventory	300,000
Fixtures and leaseholds	nominal

Expansion stores

- New stores would be in rented premises.

- Possible good locations: 10.

- Capital required per store:

Working capital	$300,000
Leasehold improvements and fixtures	250,000
Start-up costs (opening advertising,	
giveaways, etc.)	50,000
	600,000
Available bank financing on new store	200,000
Net capital required	$400,000

- Profits are expected to be 30% of capital invested, or $120,000 per store (after amortization and so on).

- Klondike can raise about $2,000,000 for expansion by combining its cash reserves with a small amount of bank financing. The required bank financing is separate from the bank financing for each new store described above.

- Corporate tax rates are 15% on income subject to the small business deduction, 25% on other business income, and $44\frac{2}{3}\%$ of investment income.

Required:

Recommend a course of action for

(a) the Polo Park branch operations; and

(b) a possible expansion to the target cities.

CASE TWO   Cargill Transport Ltd.

Cargill Transport operates a Canada-wide trucking operation hauling commercial freight. In the past several years, a number of Canadian customers have had requirements involving shipments to their American operations.

Cargill does not have operating facilities or licences to operate in the United States and so, until now, has basically ignored this potential market.

Cargill's Winnipeg operation, however, has had so many requests for foreign hauling that it has set up an arrangement with a Minneapolis-based hauler. The arrangement is that Cargill hauls Canadian freight to the American border and leaves the trailer at the border to be picked up by the American hauler. Likewise, the American hauler brings American freight to the Canadian border and leaves the trailer to be picked up by a Cargill truck.

The arrangement is cumbersome for two reasons:

1. It is difficult to coordinate freight loads to match delivery deadlines, and often, the trucks are returned from the border without a trailer.

2. It is difficult to accurately allocate the fee between the two carriers, as the distance travelled by each is different and operating costs also vary.

Cargill wants to expand its operations into the entire United States. This will have to be done gradually, as Cargill's resources for expansion are limited.

Cargill is owned 50% by a British corporation and 50% by Turnbull Holdings Ltd., a Canadian investment corporation. Turnbull is entirely owned by the Pickle family of Toronto.

Cargill's executives in Toronto have recently decided to begin expanding into the United States. Winnipeg has been chosen to spearhead the expansion because it is the only location that has any foreign activity and connections.

Obtaining a licence to operate in the United States is rather complicated, especially in the highly regulated transportation industry. It is necessary to obtain both state and federal licences. One option, of course, is to acquire a major existing American company that is already licensed throughout the United States, but this is not practical because of Cargill's financial limitations.

Charles Wheeler, the vice-president (finance), is given the task of developing the American expansion. He wants to establish a base in Minneapolis and obtain a licence permitting hauls from there to Winnipeg.

The Winnipeg division of Cargill has 12 vehicles and trailers that are not being fully utilized, and Wheeler decides to relocate these to the United States to establish the company's presence there. The American base will require a small freight depot as well as parking and repair facilities; however, all major administration, such as accounting and payroll, will still be carried out at the administration office in Winnipeg. An American bank account will be established to collect American fees and pay American expenses.

Wheeler does not know how long it will take for the operations to become profitable, although he is reasonably certain that the route will eventually be lucrative. Wheeler is certain that as the operation grows and experience is gained, more American personnel will be hired to assist in the expansion program. In the meantime, market studies are to be carried out to determine where the next thrust should be.

Before investigating the expansion, Wheeler gathers together what limited information the company has on international taxation and on business organizations in foreign countries (see below).

CARGILL TRANSPORT LTD.

1. Canadian tax rate for Cargill (assumed)	25%
2. American tax rates for American corporation*	
First $40,000 profit	20
Next $60,000 profit	35
Profit over $100,000	43
3. American withholding tax on dividends	5
4. Canadian withholding tax on dividends to the United Kingdom	10

* The American tax rates are not actual American rates. They have been arbitrarily chosen to demonstrate various levels of foreign tax that may occur.

Required:

How should Wheeler proceed with the expansion so as to maximize the profits and returns for the entire organization?

COMPREHENSIVE CASES   (Chapters 12–20)

The following Comprehensive Cases are presented in the Online Learning Centre at **http://www.mcgrawhill.ca/olc/buckwold**.

- Seacourt Restaurants Ltd.
- Cambell Enterprises Ltd.

Tax Aspects of Corporate Financing

Corporations, in particular public corporations, can obtain capital funding in a great number of ways. The basic capital funding alternatives are these: debt, equity, and leasing. Within each of these basic categories, there are numerous sub-alternatives, including bonds, debentures, common shares, various types of preferred shares, and lease arrangements with varying terms and conditions.

Each of the basic financing methods has different tax implications, to both the corporation and the investor who provides the capital. These varying tax treatments affect the after-tax cost of obtaining corporate capital. The corporation's goal is always to develop a cost-efficient financial structure. While the financing treatment chosen may be influenced mainly by the existing financial structure and by market conditions, tax is also an important consideration.

An efficient capital structure is one that minimizes the after-tax cost of financing to the corporation and, at the same time, maximizes the after-tax returns to the investor. It is therefore critical that the decision maker examine financing options on a global basis by integrating corporate and investor tax considerations.

This chapter will examine the tax consequences of the basic financing alternatives. Specifically, this chapter will examine

(a) the tax implications of choosing debt, rather than equity, from the perspective of both the corporation and the investor;

(b) the tax treatment of financing charges relating to the issuing of debt and equity securities; and

(c) the tax implications of leasing assets, rather than purchasing them.

I. Debt versus Equity

As already mentioned, the cost of financing is influenced by the tax treatment to both the corporate issuer of securities and the investor who purchases those securities. The potential investors in corporate securities include individuals, private corporations, other public corporations, and an array of pension and other investment funds; each of these entities is subject to a different tax treatment. A particular type of security that will enhance the tax position of a particular type of investor may be in greater demand so that a corporation can issue it at a higher price, the result being lower financing costs. For example, investors with capital losses may prefer securities that pay nominal dividends but offer greater capital growth because this maximizes capital gains, which can then be offset against capital losses.

In order to take advantage of a tax-sensitive marketplace, the corporation must be familiar with investor tax concerns and, whenever possible, attempt to satisfy those concerns. A corporation must consider its finance costs in the context of investor needs.

A. Cost of Corporate Debt and Equity

The real cost of financing is the after-tax cost. Debt is serviced by the payment of interest, which is fully deductible by the corporation in arriving at its taxable income.[1] On the other hand, equity capital is serviced by the payment of dividends, which are not deductible and must be paid from after-tax corporate income. From the investor's perspective, interest income on debt is fully taxable, whereas dividend income receives special treatment.

The implications of this are shown in the simplified situation shown on the next page.

---

1 ITA 20(1)(c).

Situation: A corporation that is subject to a tax rate of 25% intends to raise $100,000 of capital for expansion purposes. Current market conditions indicate that debt funding would require an interest rate of 8%. As an alternative, the company could raise the capital by issuing preferred shares having a fixed dividend rate of 7%.

Analysis: While the dividend rate of 7% on the preferred shares is less than the interest rate of 8% on debt, this is not reflected in the resulting tax consequences to the corporation. When comparing the two alternatives, it is useful to determine the amount of corporate income required to service the dividends and the interest, respectively.

If debt is issued, the corporation can service the interest payments with $8,000 of corporate income as follows:

Corporate income required	$8,000
Interest paid (8% of $100,000)	(8,000)
Net income to corporation	$ –0–
Tax to corporation	$ –0–

However, if preferred shares are issued, the corporation must pay $7,000 of dividends from after-tax corporate profits. This means that the corporation must earn $9,333 to service $7,000 of dividends, calculated as follows:

Corporate income required	$9,333
Corporate tax: $9,333 @ 25%	(2,333)
Net after-tax income	$7,000
Dividends paid	(7,000)
Net cash to corporation	$ –0–

In order to fund debt interest of 8%, the corporation must invest the borrowed funds to return at least 8%. In comparison, to fund a dividend of 7%, the corporation must invest the funds obtained to return at least 9% (9.33%). In other words, the cost of a 8% debt is 8% but the cost of an 7% dividend is actually 9% (rounded).

This analysis indicates that debt financing has an advantage over equity financing. This advantage stems from the fact that by choosing to pay interest, and thereby shifting income directly to the investor, the corporation avoids double taxation. Note that in this example, if the corporate tax rate had been 15 to 17%, the cost of equity capital would have been more in line with the cost of debt capital. In Chapter 11, it was shown that the high corporate tax rate on business income is 25%.

The above comparison of debt and equity was examined in the context of equity in the form of preferred shares, which bear a stated dividend rate but do not otherwise participate in corporate profits. In this context, except for the fact that the tax treatment is different, preferred share financing and debt financing are similar from the perspective of the holder of common shares. Because common share equity participates in corporate profits, it is difficult to compare the cost of debt with the cost of common share financing.

In comparing the cost of debt with the cost of preferred share financing, the difference between the required interest rate and the required dividend rate is obviously important. In the previous example, the cost comparison was made by arbitrarily choosing an 8% interest rate as an alternative to a 6% dividend rate. The required dividend and interest rates are influenced not only by the financial strength of the company and by market conditions but also by how the investor is taxed on the different types of returns received. This variable in financing costs is discussed below.

B. Tax Treatment to Investors

Capital markets that provide financing to corporations are sensitive to how investment returns are taxed. Interest, dividends, and capital gains are all taxed in a different manner when received by the investor. Also, the tax treatment of each type of return may vary depending on the nature of the investor. Investors can be taxable entities, such as individuals, private corporations, and public corporations; or they can be non-taxable entities, such as pension funds, retirement savings funds, and charitable organizations.

The marginal tax rates for the different types of investment returns were developed in previous chapters and are summarized in Exhibit 21-1. It is important to remember that these rates are based on assumed federal and provincial rates of tax applicable in the particular year and should be updated by the reader for current decision making.

Exhibit 21-1:

Tax on Investment Returns by Type of Entity*

	Interest	Dividend		Capital gain
		Eligible	Non-eligible	
Individuals:				
Low bracket	24%	0%	7%	12%
Second bracket	32	10	17	16
Third bracket	40	21	27	20
Top bracket	45	28	33	23
Canadian-controlled private corporations	44⅔	33⅓	33⅓	22†
Public corporations	25	0	0	13

* These rates include an assumed provincial tax rate (see Chapters 10 and 13).
† ½ (44⅔%).

Exhibit 21-1 indicates that interest income is taxed at the normal rates applicable to individuals and corporations. The tax rate on capital gains is simply one-half of the tax rate on interest, reflecting the fact that only one-half of capital gains are taxable (subject to the lifetime capital gain deduction for individuals). The tax rate on dividend income for individuals is the normal rate of tax less the dividend tax credit (see Chapter 10). Portfolio dividends received by private corporations are subject to a special refundable tax of 33⅓% (see Chapter 13), whereas dividends received by public corporations are not taxable at all (see Chapter 11).

By applying the varying tax rates given in Exhibit 21-1, both the investor and the corporation issuing securities can determine which investment yields provide equivalent after-tax returns. For example, an individual in the top tax bracket can receive a 10% interest return, 7.6% eligible dividend, a 8.2% non-eligible dividend, or a 7.1% capital gain and achieve the same after-tax rate of return, calculated as follows:

	Interest	Dividend		Capital gain
		Eligible	Non-eligible	
Tax rate	45%	28%	33%	23%
Income	$100	$76	$82	$71
Tax	(45)	(21)	(27)	(16)
After-tax return	$ 55	$55	$55	$55
Rate of return	5.5%	5.5%	5.5%	5.5%

Therefore, ignoring at this time the relative risk of each investment, individual investors in the highest tax bracket would be indifferent to whether they receive 10%

interest, a 7.6% eligible dividend, a 8.2% non-eligible dividend, or a 7.1% capital gain, as each alternative provides an after-tax return of 5.5%.

The equivalent yields for a different type of investor may be quite different. For example, if the investor is a public corporation, a 10% interest return will result in the same after-tax income as a 7.5% dividend or a 8.6% capital gain, calculated as follows:

	Interest	Dividend	Capital gain
Tax rate	25%	NIL	13%
Income	$100	$75	$86
Tax	(25)	–0–	(11)
After-tax return	$ 75	$ 75	$75

Note that because intercorporate dividends received by a public corporation are not taxable, a 7.5% dividend received by such an entity provides the same after-tax return as 10% interest; whereas an individual would have to receive a 7.6% eligible dividend or a 8.2% non-eligible dividend to achieve what is equivalent to a 10% interest return.

A profile of *equivalent yields* is presented in Exhibit 21-2. *It is based on the assumed tax rates provided in Exhibit 21-1.* This exhibit shows the pre-tax returns required to yield equivalent after-tax returns on interest, dividends, and capital gains for each type of investor. A 10% interest rate is used as the base rate of comparison. Similar comparisons can be made using different rates of interest.

The type of information provided in Exhibit 21-2 is essential to corporations that are examining various financing alternatives, as it indicates how potential investors will view the security being considered for issue. For example, if current interest rates are 10% and the corporation is considering issuing preferred shares with a fixed eligible dividend rate of 7%, it will be wise to note that those shares will be less attractive than an interest-bearing security for all potential investors.

Similarly, when contemplating different types of equity issues, the issuing corporation should recognize that dividends and capital gains receive different tax treatment. Equity issues of common shares or of preferred shares that are convertible into common shares can provide the investor with both dividends and capital gains because they participate in corporate earnings. However, when the investor is an individual, the tax rate on dividends can be higher or lower than on capital gains, depending on the particular tax bracket. Because of this, some investors prefer greater dividend returns, even though capital growth will be lower, whereas other investors prefer capital growth despite the

Exhibit 21-2:

Equivalent Pre-Tax Yields

	Interest	Dividend		Capital gain
		Eligible	Non-eligible	
Individuals:				
Low bracket	10%	7.6%	8.2%	8.6%
Second bracket	10	7.6	8.2	8.1
Third bracket	10	7.6	8.2	7.5
Top bracket	10	7.6	8.2	7.1
Canadian-controlled private corporations	10	8.3	8.3*	7.1
Public corporations	10	7.5	7.5	8.6

* Assume received from non-converted corporation.

resulting reduced dividends. A corporation that issues both common shares with low dividends and higher growth potential and convertible preferred shares with a high dividend rate and a lower growth potential can attract a larger group of investors. This, in turn, results in a tax-efficient capital structure, which ultimately reduces the overall costs of financing.

The tax relationship between interest, dividends, and capital gains often changes when tax laws are revised. The amount of the dividend tax credit, for example, has been changed several times in the past few years. Similarly, the treatment of capital gains has undergone numerous changes. When such changes occur, corporations must re-evaluate their financial structures and develop alternative methods of obtaining capital that are consistent with the new tax regime.

C. Preferred Share Financing

The offering of preferred shares as an alternative to debt financing is severely constrained owing to the non-deductibility of dividend payments. With corporate tax rates being in the range of 25 to 31% (2012), corporations must earn a substantially higher dividend rate in order to meet their commitments on preferred share dividends.

Also, preferred share financing may be subject to a further tax burden, the nature of which was not discussed in previous chapters. Under Part VI.1 of the *Income Tax Act*, all Canadian corporations are subject to a special tax on preferred share dividends in excess of $500,000 annually.[2] This tax is payable by the payer of the dividend, rather than the recipient. The rate of tax varies, depending on the nature of the preferred shares; however, in most cases, the tax is 40% of dividends paid in excess of $500,000. While this tax appears excessive, it is fully recoverable against the normal income tax to which the company is subject. For example, if the corporation is usually subject to 25% tax on income, the special tax on preferred shares reduces the normal income taxes by an equivalent amount, thus completely eliminating the tax on the preferred share dividend. Provided that the corporation is subject to normal rates of tax, the preferred share dividend tax is effectively eliminated. The special tax is not eliminated if the corporation has no taxable income, but even in this case, through a carry-forward mechanism, it can be recovered in future years when taxable income is earned.

The purpose of the special tax on preferred share dividends is to prevent corporations that are not taxable from paying dividends to other public corporations that receive the dividends on a tax-free basis. In such circumstances, if it were not for the special tax, neither the payer nor the recipient would be subject to tax.

The special preferred share dividend tax prevents a narrow form of tax abuse; at the same time, however, it creates a risk for all large corporations issuing preferred shares. Although the tax is non-existent if the payer is normally taxable, the payer cannot be certain that future circumstances will be the same. Consider, for example, a company that has issued preferred shares but, at some future time, incurs losses that cause the company to be temporarily non-taxable. When dividends are paid on the preferred shares, the special tax applies, although it may be recoverable through the carry-over mechanism. Of course, the tax could be avoided by not paying the dividend in those particular years, but that, in turn, would lessen the attractiveness of the security to the investor.

There is no doubt that current tax laws make preferred share financing difficult for corporations. In spite of this burden, corporations still consider preferred share financing viable when debt loads reach their maximum. From the common shareholder's perspective, preferred share issues are always viable if expected returns are greater than the related high financing costs.

In particular, "perpetual" preferred shares, which have no fixed redemption requirements, increase the equity base of the corporation; this adds to its financial

---

2   ITA 191.

strength, which, in turn, permits it to obtain additional debt financing at a lower cost. In other words, the disadvantages of preferred share equity must be weighed against the benefits, which are increased borrowing power and lower debt-financing costs.

Perpetual preferred shares with no fixed redemption date may be less attractive to investors if the shares have a fixed dividend rate, as such shares are subject to value changes if market interest rates fluctuate significantly. In recent years, this problem has been overcome with the emergence of "floating rate preferred shares," which have a dividend rate that fluctuates in relation to the prime rate of interest. This built-in mechanism stabilizes the value of the shares, which are thus more attractive to the investor.

In summary, in spite of the tax burden to the corporate issuer, preferred share financing is a viable alternative to debt financing, especially if the share issue is so designed that it enhances the after-tax returns of potential investors.

II. Tax Treatment of Financing Charges

In addition to the normal costs of interest (on debt) and dividends (on equity issues), the process of obtaining capital funding may incur other types of costs. For both debt and equity securities, the corporation may incur certain costs in the process of implementing and selling the securities on the open market. Also, it may be necessary to issue the securities at a price other than the stated price of the security, the result being a discount or premium on sale. The tax treatment of these items is discussed briefly below.

A. Expenses Incurred to Issue Shares or Borrow Money

The corporation may incur certain costs in the process of developing securities and issuing them to investors. Such costs include the following:

1. Legal fees for the preparation of a prospectus.

2. Accounting and auditing fees to certify the financial statements and prepare other financial information.

3. Costs of printing the security certificates and the related prospectus.

4. Fees paid to a registrar or transfer agent.

5. Costs of filing information with any regulatory body.

6. Commissions and fees for the services of salespeople, agents, or dealers in securities.

7. Mortgage registration, processing, and appraisal fees.

8. Premiums on life insurance policies assigned as a collateral requirement of a debt obligation.

These and other similar costs are of a capital nature because they provide a long-term benefit over the life of the securities. As capital expenditures, these costs would not usually be permitted as a current deduction for tax purposes. However, by specific exception (see Chapter 5), expenses other than life insurance premiums, if incurred in the process of issuing shares or borrowing money, can be deducted in arriving at net income for tax purposes over a five-year period at the rate of one-fifth of the total cost per year.[3] Premiums on life insurance policies used as collateral for a debt are fully deductible when incurred, provided that the premium is an annual amount.

---

3 ITA 20(1)(e), (e.2); IT-341R4.

The after-tax cost of financing is therefore affected by the tax treatment of the associated costs. While the cost of interest or dividends is spread out over the life of the security, the implementation costs are arbitrarily subjected to a five-year allocation, even though the costs are incurred at the outset. When making business expansion decisions that involve financing by new capital, the decision maker must determine the after-tax cost of financing; this means considering the tax treatment of both the implementation costs and the ongoing service costs of interest or dividends.

B. Securities Issued at a Discount or Premium

In some circumstances, a corporation issuing a debt or equity security may receive a price less than or greater than the stated value of the security. This discount or premium affects the issuing corporation's financing costs. The related tax treatment of the discount or premium is an important factor in establishing those costs.

Debt and equity securities can be issued at amounts greater than or less than their stated amount. This normally occurs as a result of a change in economic conditions between the time the security is developed and the time it is put on the market. For example, a $100 bond bearing a 7% interest rate may end up selling for only $98 if interest rates have increased between the time the bonds were developed and the date of their issue. A price variance may also result if the investors' perception of the security's attractiveness is different from what was anticipated by the issuing company.

A premium or discount on equity issues for common and preferred shares has no tax impact on the issuing corporation. As the cost of equity financing through dividends is not tax deductible, the related discount or premium is similarly treated. Therefore, when a $100 preferred share bearing a 4% dividend is issued at $98, it simply means that the dividend rate is actually 4.08% ($4/$98) and must be financed from after-tax profits. However, in the case of debt securities, such as bonds and debentures, since the interest cost is deductible, the tax treatment of a premium or discount affects the after-tax cost of such securities. Because of all this, the comments that follow apply only to debt securities, and we examine discounts and premiums separately.

I. Issuing Debt Securities at a Discount

When a debt security is issued at a discount, the borrowing corporation receives an amount that is less than what it is obliged to repay at the end of the debt. The issuing company is also obliged to pay interest at the stated rate times the face value of the security. The issuing company therefore has two costs—the cost of interest, which is paid annually, and the cost of the discount, which is paid at the end of the debt term.

The tax treatment of the discount depends on the amount of the discount.[4] For tax purposes, debt issued with a discount of 3% or less is referred to as a "shallow" discount, while a discount of more than 3% is referred to as a "deep" discount. The full amount of a shallow discount is deductible as a business expense when it is repaid (which is usually at the end of the term of debt). However, only one-half of a deep discount can be deducted as a business expense. In effect, a deep discount is treated as if it were a capital loss, except that it is deductible from business income.

In this way, the issue of debt at a discount changes the timing of the tax deduction; in the case of deep discounts, it also changes the amount of the tax deduction. Consequently, the after-tax cost of financing debt issued at a discount is different from the after-tax cost of financing debt issued at face value, even though the pre-tax cost may be the same. Consider the following situation:

---

4   ITA 18(1)(f), 20(1)(f).

Situation: A corporation issues a $100,000, ten-year bond paying interest annually. Market conditions dictate that investors require an interest return of 9.25%. The after-tax cost of financing the debt is analyzed below. It is assumed that the corporation issued the bonds bearing an interest rate of 9.25%, 9%, or 8.5%. Assume a corporate tax rate of 25%.

Analysis: If the bonds are issued with an interest rate of 9.25%, which is the same as the market demands, they maintain their face value of $100,000 and incur annual interest costs of $9,250 before tax.

If the bonds are issued with a 9% interest rate, they are discounted to $98,000 in order to yield 9.25% to the investor, and the company pays $9,000 interest annually (9% × $100,000) for 10 years. While the company pays lower annual interest costs ($9,000, rather than $9,250) it has an additional up-front cost of $2,000 from the discount ($100,000 − $98,000 = $2,000). The discount of $2,000 constitutes a shallow discount, which is fully deductible for tax purposes *at the end of year 10*.

If the bonds are issued with an interest rate of 8.5%, they are discounted to $95,000 in order to yield the investor 9.25%. Annual interest costs decline to $8,500 (8.5% × $100,000). However, because the discount amount of $5,000 is greater than 3% ($5,000/$100,000 = 5%), this constitutes a deep discount, of which only one-half (½ of $5,000 = $2,500) is deductible for tax purposes at the end of year 10.

In each case, the company incurs a pre-tax cost of financing of 9.25%. However, each alternative results in a different rate of cash flow and a different tax result and therefore a different after-tax cost in cash-flow terms. This is summarized in the following table:

Interest rate	9.25%	9.00%	8.50%
Face value of bond	$100,000	$100,000	$100,000
Issue price	$100,000	$ 98,000	$ 95,000
Financing costs:			
Interest (years 1–10)	$ 9,250	$ 9,000	$ 8,500
Tax saving (25%)	(2,310)	(2,250)	(2,130)
Annual cost	$ 6,940	$ 6,750	$ 6,370
Discount (year 1)	$ –0–	$ 2,000	$ 5,000
Tax saving (in year 10)	–0–	(500)	(630)
	$ –0–	$ 1,500	$ 4,370
Pre-tax cost	9.25%	9.25%	9.25%
After-tax cost, considering timing			
of cash flows	6.94%	7.05%	7.16%

This analysis shows the impact of financing costs on after-tax cash flow. A discount tends to increase the cost of financing, and this must be considered when a debt issue is contemplated. The tax treatment outlined above is applied to most interest-bearing debt securities. In some cases, corporations will issue debt securities with no stated interest rate, which allows those securities to be substantially discounted in accordance with prevailing interest rates. In such cases, the discount is considered to be interest and is allocated over the term of the security based on a simple compound-interest approach.

2. Issuing Debt Securities at a Premium

When a debt security is issued at a premium, the borrowing corporation receives a price greater than the security's stated amount. For example, a $100,000 bond bearing 8% interest may be issued at $102,000 if the market interest rate at the time of issue is less than 8%. The issuing corporation will pay a higher rate of interest in exchange for a premium gain because it is required to repay only the stated value of the security ($100,000 in the above example).

The tax treatment of a premium to the corporation issuing the security is extremely favourable. Unless the issuing corporation is in the business of lending money, the premium is not taxable. Therefore, issuing debt securities at a premium will usually reduce the after-tax cost of financing; this is the opposite of what happens when securities are issued at a discount. For example, consider the issue of a $100,000, ten-year corporate bond bearing interest at 10% at a time when market interest rates are only 9.5%. To yield 9.5%, the bond could be issued for $103,000; this would provide the issuer with a $3,000 tax-free gain. The combination of a tax-free $3,000 gain and annual interest costs of $10,000 ($7,500 after tax, assuming a 25% tax rate) would result in a net after-tax financing cost of 7.3%. If the security had been issued at its par value of $100,000, with interest at the market rate of 10%, the after-tax cost of financing would have been 7.5% (10% − tax savings of 25% = 7.5%).

Both discounts and premiums are designed to compensate for interest rate fluctuations. However, since they are subject to special tax treatment, they must be considered a distinct item of financing costs; this means that their impact must be anticipated before any type of debt security is developed and issued. Premiums and discounts may also have tax consequences for the investor who purchases the securities.

3. Tax Treatment of Discounts and Premiums to the Investor

An investor who purchases a debt security at a discount will receive a lower-than-normal rate of interest but will also receive a gain when the security is repaid at its face amount. The reverse is true when the security is purchased at a premium. From the investor's perspective, as from the issuing corporation's, the discount or premium represents an adjustment of the interest rate and is subject to varying tax treatments.

When the lender (investor) is in a position to negotiate the terms of the loan, the premium or discount is treated as income and is fully taxable when the debt is repaid. When the security is a public issue (for example, a corporate bond or a debenture), the investor cannot usually dictate terms but can only react to the market situation. If this is the case, the tax treatment to the investor varies with the nature of the investor. When the purchasing of bonds and debentures is part of the investor's business, the gain or loss on a discount or premium is fully taxable at the time the debt is repaid. When the investor is not in the business of acquiring securities but, rather, is simply investing savings and when the investment in such securities is infrequent and forms a minor part of that investor's income-earning activity, the gain or loss is considered to be a capital gain or loss, only one-half of which is taxable.

An investor may generate more after-tax income by purchasing a bond at a discount (and thus achieving a capital gain) than by purchasing a bond at face value with a higher interest rate. The yield on a given corporate debt security varies with the tax position of the investor who purchases the security. While issuing bonds at a discount may be more costly to the issuer (as demonstrated above), it may also attract those investors who will receive favourable tax treatment as a result of purchasing that security and increase the likelihood that the debt issue will be successful.

Both the corporate issuer and the investor are sensitive to the tax treatment of discounts and premiums. Any decision to raise debt capital must include an analysis of the impact of discounts and premiums on both the company and the potential investors.

III. Leasing—An Alternative to Debt Financing

The value of an asset to a business arises from its use in the income-earning process. The right to use an asset can be obtained through ownership or through a lease arrangement. When a business secures the right to use an asset for a desired period of time in exchange for rental payments, it relieves itself of the financing costs required for ownership. In this way, leasing is an alternative to debt financing.

When a business is choosing between owning and leasing, it must consider a number of factors, of which a primary one is the effect on cash flows. Accordingly, the method of payment and the related tax treatment are both vital components in the decision process. This section of the chapter compares the after-tax cost of leasing with the after-tax cost of owning in the context of financing *equipment*. The analysis that follows can also be applied to real estate; however, such analysis is complicated by the fact that real estate is usually an appreciating asset.

A. Types of Leases

The right to use equipment can be obtained through an operating lease or a financial lease. A *financial lease* provides the business (the lessee) with the right to use the asset for a long period of time—usually for most of its useful life. In most cases, the lessee will be the only user of the equipment. The lease term and the rental payments under a financial lease are structured so that the leasing company can recover the full cost of the asset and, in addition, achieve a normal return on its investment; in this way, financial lease payments are similar to amortized loan payments. Most financial leases also provide the user with the option to purchase the asset either at the end of the lease term or during the term or to release the equipment after the initial term for a substantially reduced rental. This is possible because the leasing company has recovered the full cost of the asset and earned a normal return over the initial time period. Because a financial lease provides a right of long-term use and because the rental rates are tied to the cost of the equipment and normal interest rates, it is considered to be a direct alternative to purchasing assets with debt financing.

Operating leases are usually short-term and are used to obtain the use of short-lived, lower-cost assets, such as office furniture, equipment, and automobiles. Because such assets have a short life span, it makes little difference, in taxation terms, whether they are owned or leased. In such cases, the advantages of leasing have to do with the simplified administration of frequently changed assets.

B. Tax Treatment of Financial Leases

The tax treatment of leasing costs is not complex. Annual rental payments are fully deductible in arriving at net income for tax purposes. Therefore, provided that the business has taxable income, the rental payments will directly reduce taxable income by the amount of the lease payments. In other words, cash payments and tax savings occur simultaneously.

In comparison, if assets are purchased, the tax deductions may not occur at the same time the debt payments are made. Cash payments must be made for both the principal and the interest on the loan. At the same time, tax deductions for owned assets are determined by the applicable rate of capital cost allowance and the payment of interest. Payments relating to loan principal are not deductible.

When a business can choose between leasing and owning, it must compare the after-tax cash flows of each alternative. This analysis is demonstrated in the situation described below.

Situation:

A company requires new equipment that has a cost of $100,000. If the asset is purchased, the company must borrow the full $100,000; this will require principal repayments of $20,000 annually for five years as well as interest payments at 8%. The equipment is a class 8 asset for tax purposes and so has a capital cost allowance rate of 20% (see

Chapter 6). It is estimated that the equipment has a useful life of 10 years and no apparent salvage value.

Alternatively, the company can enter into a financial lease that requires an annual rent (payable in monthly instalments) of $25,000 over a five-year lease term. The company can renew the lease for a further five years at a substantially reduced annual cost of $2,100. The payment of $25,000 per year in the first five years reflects the fact that the leasing company will recover its full cost of $100,000 and, in addition, earn 10% before tax.

For demonstration purposes, the company pays tax at an assumed rate of 25%.

Analysis: If the company purchases the equipment with a $100,000 loan bearing 8% interest, it will be required to make the following pre-tax payments in the first five years:

Year	Principal	Interest	Total
1	$ 20,000	$8,000	$ 28,000
2	20,000	6,400	26,400
3	20,000	4,800	24,800
4	20,000	3,200	23,200
5	20,000	1,600	21,600
	$100,000	$24,000	$124,000

However, the above annual cash costs are reduced by tax savings at 25% of the interest component and by the capital cost allowance. The 20% capital cost allowance is applied on a diminishing-balance basis (see Chapter 6), and only one-half of the normal rate is applied in the first year. In addition, the capital cost allowance will continue beyond five years, creating continued tax savings after the loan is fully paid off.

Under the lease arrangement, pre-tax cash costs in the first five years total $125,000 ($25,000 × 5 y). As well, if the equipment is used for a further five years, additional lease costs of $10,500 ($2,100 × 5 y) will be incurred. As the lease costs are fully deductible, tax savings in each year amount to 25% of the annual lease payments.

The after-tax cash cost, together with a net present value analysis, is summarized below for each alternative.

Year	Net Cash Out		Leasing advantage
	Purchase	Lease	(disadvantage)
1	$23,500	$18,750	$ 4,750
2	20,300	18,750	1,550
3	20,000	18,750	1,250
4	19,520	18,750	770
5	18,900	18,750	150
	102,220	93,750	8,470
6–10	(9,220)	7,880	(17,100)
	$93,000	$101,630	$ (8,630)
Net present value cost	$77,470	$79,140	$(1,670)

This analysis indicates that an asset purchase will result in after-tax costs in the first five years of $102,220, but will result in cash *savings* in the second five years (from capital cost allowance) of $9,220; thus, the total after-tax cost of this arrangement is $93,000. In comparison, the lease alternative results in higher total after-tax costs of $101,630. However, it is important to recognize that the timing of these costs is different for each alternative. In the first five years, leasing costs are lower by $8,470, whereas in the latter five years they are higher by $8,630. When these timing differences are analyzed on a net present value basis (discount at the borrowing cost of 8%), it can be seen that purchasing holds a marginal advantage over leasing ($77,470 as opposed to $79,140).

In the above example, purchasing presents only a marginal advantage over leasing; however, the cash-flow situation in the early years is important. Note that in the first year, leasing provides $4,750 of additional cash flow to the business; over the first five years, it provides a total of $8,470 of additional cash flow. Every business expansion involves risk, and that risk is usually higher in the early years. In this particular case, the leasing option reduces the risk of expansion failure by creating more cash flow in the early years when it may be most needed. This advantage is difficult to quantify but is an important consideration when a choice is being made between the two alternatives.

There is no general rule that can be used to decide between leasing and owning. Each particular situation has its own unique circumstances. The terms attached to financial leases are negotiable, just as the terms of debt financing are negotiable. The decision-making process involves analyzing the after-tax cost of each alternative on a net present value basis.

Recent changes in the tax rules offer a second option relating to the tax treatment for leased equipment.[5] Under certain conditions, the lessee can treat a lease contract for tax purposes as if it were a purchase—in effect, the lessee can forgo rent payment deductions and claim capital cost allowance and an imputed interest deduction. This treatment requires agreement with the lessor; even so, it provides added flexibility to the financial lease alternative.

IV. Summary and Conclusion

This chapter has examined the impact of taxation on the cost of corporate financing through debt, equity, and leasing. All of these methods raise corporate capital by providing a return to an investor. These returns can take the form of interest, dividends, or rents. Each of these forms has a different tax treatment to the corporate issuer and so results in a different after-tax cost. Similarly, the tax treatment of the returns for the investor that provided the financing also varies.

Raising capital by issuing debt requires the payment of interest, which is fully deductible against the corporation's income for tax purposes. Therefore, debt can be serviced without profits being affected as long as the borrowed funds can be used by the corporation to earn a return equal to the interest rate on the debt.

In comparison, raising capital by issuing new equity in the form of preferred shares requires the payment of dividends, which are not deductible in arriving at net income for tax purposes. This means that in order to service equity, the corporation must use the funds to earn a substantially higher amount of income because it must fund the dividend payment with after-tax dollars. As a result, the cost of equity is usually higher than the cost of debt.

From the investor's perspective, interest received on debt is fully taxable; whereas dividends are tax-free to other public corporations, subject to a special refundable tax of 33⅓% to other private corporations, and taxable at a reduced rate (net of the dividend tax credit) when received by individuals. All of this means that the relationship between interest and dividends depends on the nature of the investor, and so there are different market demands for different securities.

In addition to the cost of interest and dividends, the issuing corporation may incur costs for developing and issuing the securities. Even though these costs are incurred

---

5   ITA 16.1; Regulations 8200 and 1100(1.13).

in the year of issue, most of them are deductible for tax purposes in equal amounts over a five-year period.

In some cases, corporate debt is issued at a price less than or greater than the face value of the security. Such premiums or discounts arise when the stated interest rate is different from the market interest rate. When debt is issued at a discount, the issuer receives less money up front but pays a lower rate of interest. However, because the cost of the discount is deductible only when the security is paid off, there is a significant gap between the time the cost is incurred and the time it can be deducted for tax purposes. Also, if discounts are greater than a defined limit, the future deduction is limited to one-half of the discount cost. This increases the overall costs of debt financing. When debt securities are issued at a premium, the reverse is true: the issuer receives more money up front, but the interest costs are higher. The premium received is usually not taxable, and so the after-tax cost of debt issued at a premium is reduced.

The right to use an asset can also be obtained through a financial lease. Because a financial lease bases the required rental payment on the full repayment of the asset's cost plus a reasonable return to the lessor, it is comparable with purchasing an asset with borrowed funds. However, the after-tax cost of leasing is different from the after-tax cost of owning because of the timing of the related tax deduction. Lease payments in the form of rentals are deductible when incurred; when an asset is purchased, only interest and capital cost allowance can be deducted.

Since different financing schemes receive different tax treatments, the decision maker must examine the related costs on an after-tax basis, taking timing differences into account. The decision maker must also anticipate the tax positions of the various types of investors in the marketplace, since they also calculate their rates of return on an after-tax basis. This global approach will assist in developing an efficient financial structure that minimizes financing costs to the issuer and maximizes returns to the investor.

Visit the Canadian Income Taxation Web site at **www.mcgrawhill.ca/olc/buckwold** to view any updated tax information.

Review Questions

1. Why is it important to examine the corporate cost of financing alternatives in conjunction with the tax position of the potential investors?

2. If a corporation is subject to a 25% tax rate, why may it be advantageous for it to issue debt as opposed to preferred shares?

3. If the corporate tax rate is 15%, what difference does it make whether the corporation issues debt bearing 8% interest or preferred shares with a 6¾% dividend rate?

4. A corporation issues 7% bonds as well as preferred shares with an annual 5.5% dividend rate. Excluding the risk factor, what type of investor would prefer the bond and what type would prefer the shares? Explain.

5. An investor who is an individual could earn a 10% return either from shares that pay a low dividend and have high growth or from shares that pay a high dividend and have low growth. Assuming that the risk related to each is the same, which investment would the individual prefer?

6. If the cost of preferred share financing is greater than debt, why are such securities issued by public corporations?

7. Briefly describe the tax treatment applied to expenses incurred to issue shares or borrow money (the cost of a prospectus, commissions to brokerage firms, and the like). What impact does this tax treatment have on the after-tax cost of financing?

8. If a corporation issues a bond at a price less than the face value of the security, the discount is amortized, for accounting purposes, over the life of the bond. How does this treatment of the discount compare with the treatment for tax purposes?

9. If a corporation issues a bond at a discount, will the after-tax cost of financing to the issuing corporation be higher or lower than if it had issued the bond at its face value? Explain.

10. Is the after-tax return to a casual investor who purchases a bond at a discount greater than or less than the after-tax return on a bond purchased at its face value? Explain.

11. How does the issuing of a bond at a premium affect the after-tax cost of financing to the corporate issuer?

12. Explain the difference between a financial lease and an operating lease.

13. What is the difference, in tax terms, between leasing and owning?

Problems

PROBLEM ONE

The Canadian Queen's Bank of Industry Ltd. is a large national Canadian bank. It has significant expansion opportunities. However, its ability to raise additional debt capital from bonds or debentures is restricted because of the debt/equity regulations of Canada's *Bank Act.*

The bank has decided to issue preferred shares. The financial highlights of the prospectus are as follows:

Proposed issue   4,000,000 floating rate, class A preferred shares (cumulative, redeemable, and without par value).

Price $100 per share.

Dividends   Dividends will be payable monthly. The dividend rate will float in relation to changes in the prime interest rate as set by the bank. The initial annual dividend rate will be equal to $2/3$ prime plus $1/2$% per annum. As dividends will accrue and be payable monthly, the normal dividend payment will be $1/12$ of the annual rate.

Redemption   The shares will be redeemable at the option of the bank in whole or in part from time to time.

At the time the prospectus was issued, the bank published the following interest rates for its customers:

Prime lending rate	7.5%
Savings account (interest monthly)	3.0
One-year term deposits	6.0
30-day term deposits	4.0

The bank is subject to an income tax rate of 25%.

Required:

1. Assume that the bank will issue all of the preferred shares proposed in the prospectus. What amount of additional income must the bank earn in order to service the preferred shares without diminishing the amount of earnings currently available to the common shareholders?

2. How would your answer to 1 be different if the bank could issue bonds with an interest rate equal to 1.5% less than the prime rate?

3. Are the preferred shares attractive to investors? Explain.

PROBLEM TWO

Orpin Industries Ltd. is about to make its first bond issue in the public market. Orpin is a small but growing company, and its shares are starting to be recognized. For the past two years, they have consistently traded at a price equal to 12 times the after-tax earnings per share.

The proposed bond issue will raise $20,000,000, which will be used to expand the corporation's retail operations into western Canada. The expanded operations should provide a minimum return on investment of 22%.

After receiving financial advice, the company decides to issue the bonds in units of $1,000 with an annual interest rate of 10% (interest payable annually). The financial advisor indicates that at this interest rate, the bonds can be sold (with a 10-year term) at their par value.

Just before the issue date, long-term interest rates in the market increase by half a percent. Orpin realizes that it will have to issue its bonds at a discount in order to obtain the full $20,000,000. Alternatively, the company could delay the issue for a short time, revise the prospectus, and print new bonds to reflect the higher interest rate. This would, of course, create additional costs. Before making the decision, Orpin wants to know if there would be any benefit to revising the interest rates.

Orpin is subject to a 25% tax rate.

Required:

1. If Orpin issues the bonds as originally proposed (that is, with an interest rate of 10%), how much will it have to discount them? Ignore any tax implications to the potential investors.

2. Based on your answer to 1, determine the after-tax cost of financing the bond issue under both the discount option and the revised interest rate option.

3. Assuming that the interest rate on the bond is revised, how may this affect the trading value of Orpin's common shares?

4. If the company chooses to issue the bonds at a discount, could the amount of the discount be affected by the tax treatment to the potential investor? Explain.

PROBLEM THREE

Anderson Enterprises Ltd. is a Canadian corporation wholesaling auto parts in eastern Canada. The company has decided to begin manufacturing a product that it currently wholesales.

The expansion will require manufacturing equipment costing $80,000. Anderson's bank has agreed to provide a term loan to finance the entire purchase. The terms of the loan call for monthly payments of $1,235 for eight years. Due to high risk, the payment includes interest at $10\frac{1}{2}$%. The bank provides the company with a payment schedule, which is roughly summarized on an annual basis in the table below.

Year	Principal	Interest	Total
1	$7,000	$7,820	$14,820
2	7,500	7,320	14,820
3	8,500	6,320	14,820
4	9,000	5,820	14,820
5	10,000	4,820	14,820
6	11,000	3,820	14,820
7	13,000	1,820	14,820
8	14,000	820	14,820

It is estimated that the equipment will have a useful life of 10 years and will be scrapped at the end of that time.

Anderson has also obtained some quotes for leasing the equipment. The quote with the most favourable terms involves a six-year lease with monthly payments of $1,565 and an option to renew on an annual basis for a mere $2,000 per year. Anderson likes this alternative because his company would not have to renew after six years if it wanted to acquire more modern equipment.

However, at this point, the company anticipates that it will use the equipment for its useful life of 10 years, at which time it will acquire replacement equipment.

Assume the company is subject to a 25% tax rate. It has expansion opportunities that can yield a minimum before-tax return of 22%.

Required:

1. Determine the financial cost to Anderson of leasing rather than owning the manufacturing equipment. Assume that at the end of 10 years, the company will scrap the equipment and purchase new equipment.

2. How would your answer to 1 change if, after 10 years, Anderson Ltd. leased, rather than purchased, the equipment?

3. What other factors, if any, should the company consider when making the decision?

PROBLEM FOUR

Brandi Manufacturing Ltd. has decided to expand. To raise additional capital, the company is considering selling $300,000 of its present manufacturing equipment to an insurance company and leasing it back for eight years, which is the estimated useful life of the equipment. The equipment will have no residual value after eight years. The annual rent on the lease-back would be $54,000.

The equipment to be sold under the sale-and-lease-back arrangement is not all of the equipment owned by the company. The undepreciated capital cost of all of the company's manufacturing equipment (class 43) was $800,000 at the end of the previous year. Of this $800,000, approximately $100,000 relates to the equipment that the company is thinking of selling.

The equipment that would be sold is used to manufacture a single specialized product. The equipment generates annual pre-tax revenues of $60,000 and is expected to continue to do so in the future.

Brandi is interested in the sale-and-lease-back arrangement because it will enable the company to obtain $300,000 of immediate funds with a related annual payment of $54,000, which appears to be equivalent to a low rate of interest. Assume the company is subject to a corporate tax rate of 25%. The company considers 12% to be a reasonable after-tax rate of return.

Required:

1. If Anderson does not sell the equipment, how much cash flow will be generated, in net present value terms, from the ownership and operation of that equipment?

2. What rate of interest is reflected in the lease arrangement?

3. What net present value cash flow would be obtained as a result of the sale-and-lease-back arrangement?

GST/HST Information Supplement

.

The concept of the GST/HST was described in Chapter 3 and does not need repeating here. Also, the basics of the GST/HST and how it relates to employment income and business income was briefly described in the latter part of Chapters 4 and 5. This appendix expands on GST/HST issues relevant to various aspects of the text and in particular to Chapters 4 and 5. It is not comprehensive, but is designed to enhance the reader's knowledge of the subject and demonstrate the connectivity between the *Income Tax Act* and the *Excise Tax Act* that contains the GST/HST law.

The reader should keep in mind that the HST or Harmonized Sales Tax has been adopted by a number of provinces that have eliminated their provincial sales tax (Ontario, Newfoundland, Nova Scotia, New Brunswick, and British Columbia[1]). While the HST places a burden on the consumer by taxing a number of items that were not subject to the PST, it presents a positive outlook for business because the HST paid by a business registrant is fully recoverable as an input tax credit. This was not always possible with the PST. Therefore, the cost of doing business should go down and consumers should ultimately benefit from lower prices of goods and services.

I. Employees and Employment Income

Salaries, commissions, and other forms of remuneration paid to an employee are not subject to GST. However, certain employee benefits and expense reimbursements may have GST/HST implications. Also, employees may be entitled to apply for a GST/HST rebate on certain expenses incurred by them for employment purposes—especially employees who incur a variety of expenses to earn commission income. The discussion below reviews the basic GST/HST issues relating to benefits and employee expenses.

A. Employee Benefits

Chapter 4 discussed the income tax treatment to the employee of benefits provided by the employer. Normally, to the extent that the benefits are taxable to the employee, GST/HST must be included in the value of the benefits and included as employment income. In provinces that do not use the HST, the taxable benefit must also include an amount equal to the PST if applicable. The employer includes the value of the benefit plus the GST/HST as a taxable item on the employee's T4 form at the end of the taxation year. The relevant provincial rate to be applied is from the province where the employee worked and received the benefit. It is not based on the employee's residence.

There are exceptions to the normal rule that taxable benefits are subject to the GST/HST. For example, taxable benefits from items provided by the employer that are zero-related (see Chapter 4), are not increased by a GST/HST amount. Zero-rated items include basic groceries, prescription drugs, and certain travel services to name a few. Also, benefits from items provided by employers that are GST/HST exempt are not subject to the normal rule. Exempt items include health care, educational, and financial services.

The Employer's Guide to Taxable Benefits (T4130) published by the Canada Revenue Agency includes a detailed discussion of the GST/HST application on a wide range of employee benefits. It also includes a chart summarizing which benefits must add the GST/HST amount to the taxable value for income tax purposes. Some of these are listed below.

	GST/HST applies
Automobile allowance	no
Automobile standby charge	yes
Automobile operating expense benefit	yes
Cellular phone service	yes
Child care expenses	yes

---

[1]   British Columbia will abandon the HST on April 1, 2013 and revert to the GST plus provincial sales tax model.

	GST/HST applies
Discounts on merchandise	yes
Educational allowance for children	no
Gifts, awards, and social events—in cash	no
Gifts, awards, and social events—no-cash	yes
Group term life insurance premiums	no
Interest-free and low-interest loans	no
Internet services (at home)—in cash	yes
Moving expenses and relocation benefits	yes
Overtime meal allowances	no
Parking	yes
Premiums for provincial health programs	no
Recreational facilities and club dues	yes
RRSP premiums	no
Scholarships and bursaries	no
Spouse travel expenses—cash allowance	no
Spouse travel expenses—non-cash	yes
Tuition fees	no*

*Certain fees are subject to GST/HST.

B. Employment Expenses— GST/HST Rebate

Some employees are required by their employer to pay certain expenses for employment purposes. Chapter 4 described when an employee may deduct expenses in calculating net income from employment for tax purposes. Some of the deductible expenses may include GST/HST. Where this is the case, the employee can apply for a rebate of the GST/HST that is included in the deductible expenses.[2] The rebate is added to the employee's income as a taxable item in the year the rebate is received—normally in the year following the year when the expenses were deducted.[3] While most employees apply for the rebate immediately, they have up to four years from the year end of the taxation year in which the expenses were deducted to apply for the rebate by filing form GST370 with CRA.

Some employees are entitled to claim a deduction for capital cost allowance (CCA) on an automobile owned by them and used for employment purposes. The CCA does not directly include GST/HST. However, the original cost of the automobile on which the CCA is based did include GST/HST. Therefore, an employee can claim a rebate on the portion of the CCA that is deducted from employment income. This rebate reduces the capital cost and UCC of the automobile in the year the rebate is received.

The rebate is calculated by applying a pre-determined ratio to the employment expenses. The ratio depends on the HST rate of a participating province or the general GST rate for provinces and territories that do not participate in the harmonized sales tax system. The rebate ratios for the provinces and territories are as follows:

British Columbia	12/112[4]
Ontario, New Brunswick, and Newfoundland	13/113
Nova Scotia	15/115
Quebec, Saskatchewan, Manitoba, Prince Edward Island, Nunavut, NWT, and Yukon	5/105

---

2   ETA 253(1).
3   ITA 6(8)(c).
4   Changes to 5/105 on April 1, 2013.

The following situation and analysis demonstrates the GST/HST rebate system for employees.

Situation

Carla lives in Ontario and is employed as a salesperson earning a salary and commissions. She is required to pay her own employment expenses. In 20X5, she paid and deducted the following items on her income tax return:

Automobile operating costs—gas, oil, and repairs	$ 4,800
Automobile insurance	1,000
Interest on automobile loan	2,000
Promotion—food, beverages, and entertainment	1,200
Supplies—postage, stationery, etc.	600
Parking	400
Capital cost allowance	3,000
Total	$13,000

The above items are the *net amounts after deducting any personal portions that are applicable.*

Analysis

In 20X5, Carla deducted the total of $13,000 from her employment salary and commissions. As a resident of Ontario, all of the expenses except the insurance, interest, and CCA would include an HST component of 13%. However, the CCA is deemed to include an HST component as it was paid when the automobile was originally purchased.

The deductible expenses with an HST component total $10,000 as follows:

Automobile operation costs	$ 4,800
Promotion	1,200
Supplies	600
Parking	400
	7,000
CCA	3,000
	$10,000

In 20X6, Carla can apply for an HST rebate when preparing her 20X5 income tax return based upon the deducted employment expenses. The rebate is $1,150 calculated as follows:

13/113 × $10,000 = $1,150

Assuming that this rebate is received by Carla in 20X6 (the year of application), Carla must increase her employment income and decrease the UCC of her automobile in 20X6 as follows:

Increase her employment income:	
$\dfrac{\$7,000 \text{ (above)}}{\$10,000} \times \$1,150 =$	$805
Decrease in UCC:	
$\dfrac{\$3,000 \text{ (above)}}{\$10,000} \times \$1,150 =$	$345
Total adjustment	$1,150

II. Carrying on a Business

Chapter 5 showed that all GST/HST registrants are required to collect and remit the GST/HST on all sales of goods and services other than zero-rated and exempt items. In addition, registrants can obtain an input credit for goods and services acquired. An entity engaged in a commercial activity must register, unless the entity is a "small supplier" (see Chapter 5) or the only commercial activity of the entity is the sale of real property other than in the course of business. The term "commercial activity" relates strongly to the definition of "business," which is defined in a slightly different manner for GST/HST purposes than for income tax purposes (see Chapter 5).[5] A detailed definition is not provided here.

This segment reviews certain key elements pertaining to the business activity of a GST/HST registrant.

A. Timing of Tax and Input Credits

The GST/HST is due on the sale of taxable goods and services and, therefore, eligible for remittance on the earliest of:[6]

1. The date of the invoice or the day the invoice is first issued.

2. The day the invoice would normally have been issued but for an undue delay.

3. The day on which the payment became due pursuant to a written agreement.

Notwithstanding the above, GST/HST on leased property is payable on the day the lease payments are required under the terms of the lease. Also, GST/HST is payable on the sale of real property on the day that the ownership or possession is transferred, whichever comes first.[7]

Input credits do not have to be claimed in the period they occur. Instead, they can be claimed anytime within four years from the date the GST/HST was paid. Most registrants claim the input credits in the reporting period when they occur for obvious cash flow reasons.

B. Bad Debts

Normally, when an amount owing from the sale of taxable goods or services becomes uncollectible and is established to be a bad debt, the GST/HST that has been remitted on the sale may be recovered.[8] The amount owing includes the GST/HST and, therefore, the recoverable amount is 5/105 of the amount owing for the GST and the appropriate ratio for the HST (for example, 13/113 in Ontario and 12/112 in B.C.[9]). The criteria for establishing when an amount owing becomes a bad debt is similar to the criteria used for income tax purposes.

C. Reasonableness

An input credit cannot be claimed to the extent that the GST/HST on the underlying cost or that portion of the cost of the good or service acquired is unreasonable in the circumstances.[10] This is similar to the reasonableness test on expenses that is applicable in the *Income Tax Act*.

D. Benefits and Allowances (other than for automobiles)

When an employer provides taxable benefits to an employee, GST/HST is added to the value of the benefit and included in the employee's income for tax purposes. This was discussed previously in this appendix. The employer who provides the benefit is considered to have charged and collected the GST/HST that is added to the benefit and, therefore, that imputed amount must be remitted as if it were collected. This GST/HST is considered to be collected from the employee on the last day of February following the year the benefit was provided (this is the deadline for filing a T4 form for the employee).

The amount of the GST/HST that is payable by the employer is not simply the rate of the GST (5%) or the applicable HST rate of a participating province. Rather, it is based on a specific ratio that is slightly lower that the actual rate. The ratio is applied to the taxable benefit values reported on employees' T4 forms (these values include

---

5   ETA 123(1).
6   ETA 152(1), 168(1), 168(2), and Wisner, Sheila, *A Practical Guide to the GST/HST*, CCH, 2010.
7   ETA 152(2).
8   ETA 231(1), 231(3).
9   B.C. changes to 5/105 on April 1, 2013.
10 ETA 170(2).

the GST/HST). Separate rules apply to automobile benefits and are discussed later. The following ratios are used to determine the GST/HST *required to be remitted by the employer on non-auto benefits*:

British Columbia (HST)	11.5/111.5*
Ontario, New Brunswick, and Newfoundland (HST)	12/112
Nova Scotia (HST)	14/114
Quebec, Saskatchewan, Manitoba, Prince Edward Island, Nunavut, NWT, and Yukon (GST)	4/104

*B.C. changes to 4/105 on April 1, 2013.

Note that these ratios are lower than the actual GST/HST rates for the applicable provinces. For example, Ontario's HST is 13%, but the ratio for the amount to be remitted for the benefits is 12/112.

E. Automobile Benefits

Two issues alter the standard treatment of benefits for the employer. One issue is the fact that the CCA deduction for a passenger vehicle is based on a cost that is limited to $30,000 although the actual cost may be higher. However, the employee's taxable benefit (standby charge) for the use of the automobile is based on the actual cost of the automobile including the GST/HST and PST if applicable. The other issue is that the operating cost benefit is based on a fixed amount of 26¢ (in 2012) per km driven for personal use.

The GST/HST to be remitted by the employer on the standby charge is calculated using the ratios shown above for non-automobile benefits. However, the GST/HST on the operating cost benefit for remittance purposes uses a different and arbitrary calculation as listed below:

British Columbia (HST)	5%†
Ontario, New Brunswick, and Newfoundland (HST)	9
Nova Scotia (HST)	11
Quebec, Saskatchewan, Manitoba, Prince Edward Island, Nunavut, NWT, and Yukon (GST)	3

†B.C. changes to 3.5% in 2013 and 3% for taxation years thereafter.

The GST/HST implications on automobile benefits for the employee and the employer are demonstrated below:[11]

Situation

An employer in Ontario purchased an automobile on January 1, 20X5 for $40,000. The automobile is used by an employee for employment and personal purposes. In 20X5, the employee drove 8,000 km for personal use (about 25% of the total kms driven). The total cost of the automobile was $45,200 ($40,000 plus 13% HST of $5,200).

Analysis

1. The employer's input tax credit on the automobile is based on the maximum deduction allowed for income tax purposes (2011):

$30,000 × 13% (HST)	$3,900

2. The employee's taxable benefit is:

Standby charge—$45,200 × 2% × 12 months	$10,848
Operating benefit—8,000 km × 24¢	1,920
	$12,768

3. Employer's HST liability:

On the standby charge—$10,848 × 12/112	1,162
On the operating cost benefit—$1,920 × 9%	173
Total to be remitted	$1,335

11 Adapted from example in Wisner, Sheila, *A Practical Guide to the GST/HST,* page 185, CCH, 2010.

A unique rule applies when an employer pays an allowance to an employee for the use of an automobile and that allowance is not taxable to the employee because it is considered to be a reasonable allowance. When this occurs, the employer is entitled to claim an input credit on the amount of the allowance paid.[12]

F. Food, Beverages, and Entertainment

An employer can claim the GST/HST input credit on the full amount of the cost of food, beverages, and entertainment throughout the year. However, consistent with the income rules, the total GST/HST input credits claimed at the end of the year must be adjusted to 50% of the total.[13]

III. Real Estate

Real estate transactions usually involve a high dollar value and often involve some structural complexity in the agreements. The unique features of the GST/HST on a multitude of real estate transactions are beyond the scope of this appendix. Some of the basic features are listed below.

- Newly constructed residential homes including the cost of the land are subject to GST/HST.

- New homes valued under $450,000 may be eligible for a partial GST rebate. Participating provinces using the HST also offer rebates based on various price limits. For example, Ontario rebates apply to new homes priced up to $400,000 and British Columbia has a rebate on homes priced up to $825,000 in 2012.

- The sale of previously occupied homes are generally not subject to GST/HST.

- Rental income from leasing residential properties (leases of at least one month) is not subject to GST/HST.

- Rental income from leasing commercial properties is subject to GST/HST unless the landlord is a small supplier and has not elected to be a registrant.

- The sale of a commercial property (new and previously occupied) is subject to GST/HST.

IV. Sale of a Business as a Going Concern

When a business is sold as a going concern, the vendor and the purchaser can jointly elect to have no GST/HST payable on the transaction provided that the purchaser acquires "ownership or use of at least 90% of the property that can reasonably be regarded as being necessary for the purchaser to be capable of carrying on a business."[14] An election may also be available when only a part of the business is being sold.

A joint election can only be filed by a "registrant when selling to another registrant; or a non-registrant when selling to a registrant or non-registrant."[15]

This appendix is a brief overview of certain aspects of the GST/HST that apply to particular items in the chapters in the text. More detailed information is available in the CRA publication—General Information for GST/HST Registrants (RC 4022). We also recommend the book—*A Practical Guide to the GST* by Sheila Wisner, CA published by CCH. Much of the information in this appendix was derived from these two publications.

---

12 ETA 174.
13 ETA 236(1.1).
14 CRA, General Information for GST/HST Registrants (RC 4022), page 68.
15 CRA, General Information for GST/HST Registrants (RC 4022), page 68.

Integration 2012

Integration (2012)
High-rate Business Income

	AB	BC	MB	NB	NL	NWT	NS	NUN	ON	PEI	QC	SK	YK
Corporation													
Business income	$100.00	$100.00	$100.00	$100.00	$100.00	$100.00	$100.00	$100.00	$100.00	$100.00	$100.00	$100.00	$100.00
Corporate tax	$25.00	$25.00	$27.00	$25.00	$29.00	$26.50	$31.00	$27.00	$26.50	$31.00	$26.90	$27.00	$30.00
Available for distribution	$75.00	$75.00	$73.00	$75.00	$71.00	$73.50	$69.00	$73.00	$73.50	$69.00	$73.10	$73.00	$70.00
Individual shareholder													
Tax on Eligible dividend	$14.47	$19.34	$23.55	$16.85	$15.95	$16.77	$24.88	$20.12	$21.71	$19.81	$23.98	$18.11	$11.15
Total tax (corporation + shareholder)	$39.47	$44.34	$50.55	$41.85	$44.95	$43.27	$55.88	$47.12	$48.21	$50.81	$50.88	$45.11	$41.15
Personal tax if unincorporated	$39.00	$43.70	$46.40	$43.30	$42.30	$43.05	$50.00	$40.50	$46.41	$47.37	$48.22	$44.00	$42.40
Tax savings (cost)	$(0.47)	$(0.63)	$(4.15)	$1.45	$(2.65)	$(0.22)	$(5.88)	$(6.62)	$(1.80)	$(3.44)	$(2.66)	$(1.11)	$1.25
Tax deferral (corporate tax – personal tax)	$14.00	$18.70	$19.40	$18.30	$13.30	$16.55	$19.00	$13.50	$19.91	$16.37	$21.32	$17.00	$12.40

Low-rate Business Income

	AB	BC	MB	NB	NL	NWT	NS	NUN	ON	PEI	QC	SK	YK
Corporation													
Business income	$100.00	$100.00	$100.00	$100.00	$100.00	$100.00	$100.00	$100.00	$100.00	$100.00	$100.00	$100.00	$100.00
Corporate tax	$14.00	$13.50	$11.00	$15.50	$15.00	$15.00	$15.00	$15.00	$15.50	$12.00	$19.00	$13.00	$15.00
Available for distribution	$86.00	$86.50	$89.00	$84.50	$85.00	$85.00	$85.00	$85.00	$84.50	$88.00	$81.00	$87.00	$85.00
Individual shareholder													
Tax on Non-Eligible dividend	$23.83	$29.16	$34.84	$26.05	$25.47	$25.20	$30.78	$24.61	$27.52	$36.23	$29.45	$29.00	$25.85
Total tax (corporation + shareholder)	$37.83	$42.66	$45.84	$41.55	$40.47	$40.20	$45.78	$39.61	$43.02	$48.23	$48.45	$42.00	$40.85
Personal tax if unincorporated	$39.00	$43.70	$46.40	$43.30	$42.30	$43.05	$50.00	$40.50	$46.41	$47.37	$48.22	$44.00	$42.40
Tax savings (cost)	$1.17	$1.04	$0.56	$1.75	$1.83	$2.85	$4.22	$0.89	$3.39	$(0.86)	$(0.23)	$2.00	$1.55
Tax deferral (corporate tax – personal tax)	$25.00	$30.20	$35.40	$27.80	$27.30	$28.05	$35.00	$25.50	$30.91	$35.37	$29.22	$31.00	$27.40

CCPC Investment Income

	AB	BC	MB	NB	NL	NWT	NS	NUN	ON	PEI	QC	SK	YK
Corporation													
Interest income	$100.00	$100.00	$100.00	$100.00	$100.00	$100.00	$100.00	$100.00	$100.00	$100.00	$100.00	$100.00	$100.00
Corporate tax	$44.67	$44.67	$46.67	$44.67	$48.67	$46.17	$50.67	$46.67	$46.17	$50.67	$46.57	$46.67	$49.67
Dividend refund	$(26.67)	$(26.67)	$(26.67)	$(26.67)	$(26.67)	$(26.67)	$(26.67)	$(26.67)	$(26.67)	$(26.67)	$(26.67)	$(26.67)	$(26.67)
Net corporate tax	$18.00	$18.00	$20.00	$18.00	$22.00	$19.50	$24.00	$20.00	$19.50	$24.00	$19.90	$20.00	$23.00
Distribution (3 × dividend refund)	$80.00	$80.00	$80.00	$80.00	$80.00	$80.00	$80.00	$80.00	$80.00	$80.00	$80.00	$80.00	$80.00
Individual shareholder													
Tax on Non-Eligible dividend	$22.17	$26.97	$31.32	$24.67	$23.97	$23.72	$28.97	$23.16	$26.06	$32.94	$29.08	$26.67	$24.33
Total tax (corporation + shareholder)	$40.17	$44.97	$51.32	$42.67	$45.97	$43.22	$52.97	$43.16	$45.56	$56.94	$48.98	$46.67	$47.33
Personal tax if unincorporated	$39.00	$43.70	$46.40	$43.30	$42.30	$43.05	$50.00	$40.50	$46.41	$47.37	$48.22	$44.00	$42.40
Tax savings (cost)	$(1.17)	$(1.27)	$(4.92)	$0.63	$(3.67)	$(0.17)	$(2.97)	$(2.66)	$0.85	$(9.57)	$(0.76)	$(2.67)	$(4.93)
Tax deferral (prepayment) if no dividends paid													
Personal tax	$39.00	$43.70	$46.40	$43.30	$42.30	$43.05	$50.00	$40.50	$46.41	$47.37	$48.22	$44.00	$42.40
Corporate tax before dividend refund	$44.67	$44.67	$46.67	$44.67	$48.67	$46.17	$50.67	$46.67	$46.17	$50.67	$46.57	$46.67	$49.67
Deferral (prepayment) of tax	$(5.67)	$(0.97)	$(0.27)	$(1.37)	$(6.37)	$(3.12)	$(0.67)	$(6.17)	$0.24	$(3.30)	$1.65	$(2.67)	$(7.27)
Tax deferral by delaying dividend payment													
Dividend refund	$(26.67)	$(26.67)	$(26.67)	$(26.67)	$(26.67)	$(26.67)	$(26.67)	$(26.67)	$(26.67)	$(26.67)	$(26.67)	$(26.67)	$(26.67)
Personal tax on dividend	$22.17	$26.97	$31.32	$24.67	$23.97	$23.72	$28.97	$23.16	$26.06	$32.94	$29.08	$26.67	$24.33
Tax deferred (prepaid)	$(4.50)	$0.30	$4.65	$(2.00)	$(2.70)	$(2.95)	$2.30	$(3.51)	$(0.61)	$6.27	$2.41	$(0.00)	$(2.34)

Corporate Tax Rates (2012)

	AB	BC	MB	NB	NL	NWT	NS	NUN	ON	PEI	QC	SK	YK
General Rate													
Federal	15%	15%	15%	15%	15%	15%	15%	15%	15%	15%	15%	15%	15%
Provincial	10%	10%	12%	10%	14%	11.5%	16%	12%	11.5%	16%	11.9%	12%	15%
Combined	25%	25%	27%	25%	29%	26.5%	31%	27%	26.5%	31%	26.9%	27%	30%
CCPC Small Business Income													
Federal	11%	11%	11%	11%	11%	11%	11%	11%	11%	11%	11%	11%	11%
Provincial	3%	2.5%	0%	4.5%	4%	4%	4%	4%	4.5%	1%	8%	2%	4%
Combined	14%	13.5%	11%	15.5%	15%	15%	15%	15%	15.5%	12%	19%	13%	15%
CCPC Investment Income													
Federal	34.67%	34.67%	34.67%	34.67%	34.67%	34.67%	34.67%	34.67%	34.67%	34.67%	34.67%	34.67%	34.67%
Provincial	10.00%	10.00%	12.00%	10.00%	14.00%	11.50%	16.00%	12.00%	11.50%	16.00%	11.90%	12.00%	15.00%
Combined	44.67%	44.67%	46.67%	44.67%	48.67%	46.17%	50.67%	46.67%	46.17%	50.67%	46.57%	46.67%	49.67%
M&P Provincial Rate Reduction	0	0	0	0	9%	0	0	0	1.5%	0	0	2%	12.5%

Top Combined (Federal + Provincial) Marginal Tax Rate on Dividends Received by Individuals (2012)

	AB	BC	MB	NB	NL	NWT	NS	NUN	ON*	PEI	QC	SK	YK
Type of Dividend													
Eligible	19.29%	25.78%	32.26%	22.47%	22.47%	22.81%	36.06%	27.56%	29.54%	28.70%	32.81%	24.81%	15.93%
Non-eligible	27.71%	33.71%	39.15%	30.83%	29.96%	29.65%	36.21%	28.95%	32.57%	41.17%	36.35%	33.33%	30.41%

Top Combined (Federal + Provincial) Marginal Tax Rate on Business Income Earned by Individuals (2012)

	AB	BC	MB	NB	NL	NWT	NS	NUN	ON*	PEI	QC	SK	YK
	39.00%	43.70%	46.40%	43.30%	42.30%	43.05%	50.00%	40.50%	46.41%	47.37%	48.22%	44.00%	42.40%

Future Provincial tax rate changes announced (updated to April 6, 2012):

The British Columbia general corporate tax rate increases to 11% effective April 1, 2014.

The Nova Scotia small business tax rate decreases to 3.5% effective January 1, 2013.

Ontario's general corporate tax rate was scheduled to decrease to 11% on July 1, 2012 and to 10% on July 1, 2013. These tax rate reductions have been delayed until Ontario's budget is balanced which is expected in 2017–18.

*Excludes 2% surtax on taxable income in excess of $500,000 effective July 12, 2012.

Index